ST/ESA/STAT/SER.S/32

**Department of Economic
and Social Affairs**
Statistics Division

**Département des affaires
économiques et sociales**
Division de statistique

Statistical Yearbook 2011
Fifty-sixth issue

Annuaire statistique 2011
Cinquante-sixième édition

United Nations | Nations Unies
New York, 2013

Department of Economic and Social Affairs

The Department of Economic and Social Affairs of the United Nations Secretariat is a vital interface between global policies in the economic, social and environment spheres and national action. The Department works in three main inter-linked areas: (i) it complies, generates and analyses a wide range of economic, social and environmental data and infomration on which States Members of the United Nations draw to review common problems and to take stock of policy options; (ii) it facilitates the negotiations of Member States in many intergovernmental bodies on joint courses of action to address ongoing or emerging global challenges; and (iii) it advises interested Governments on the ways and means of translating policy frameworks developed in United Nations conferences and summits into programmes at the country level and, through technical assistance, helps build national capacities.

Note

The designations employed and the presentation of the material in this publication do not imply the expression of any opinion whatsoever on the part of the Secretariat of the United Nations concerning the legal status of any country, city or area, or of its authorities, or concerning the delimitation of its frontiers or boundaries.

In general, statistics contained in the present publication are those available to the United Nations Secretariat up to December 2012 and refer to 2011 or earlier. They therefore reflect the country nomenclature currently in use.

The term "country" as used in the text of this publication also refers, as appropriate, to territories or areas.

The designations "developed" and "developing" which appear in some tables are intended for statistical convenience and do not necessarily express a judgement about the stage reached by a particular country or area in the development process.

Symbols of the United Nations documents are composed of capital letters combined with figures.

ST/ESA/STAT/SER.S/32

UNITED NATIONS PUBLICATION
Sales No. B.13.XVII.1.H

ISBN 978-92-1-061333-0
e-ISBN 978-92-1-056024-5
ISSN 0082-8459

Département des affaires économiques et sociales

Le Département des affaires économiques et sociales du Secrétariat de l'Organisation des Nations Unies assure le lien essentiel entre les politiques adoptées au plan international dans les domaines économique, social et écologique et les mesures prises au plan national. Il mène ses activités dans trois grands domaines interdépendants : i) il compile, produit et analyse une grand variété de données et d'informations économiques, sociales et écologiques dont les États Membres de l'ONU tirent parti pour examiner les problèmes communs et faire le point sur les possibilités d'action; (ii) il facilite les négociations que les États Membres mènent dans un grand nombre d'organes intergouvernementaux sur les moyens d'action à employer conjointement pour faire face aux problèmes mondiaux existants ou naissants; et (iii) il aide les gouvernements intéressés à traduire les orientations politiques établies lors des conférences et sommets de l'ONU en programmes nationaux et contribue à renforcer les capacités des pays en leur apportant une assistance technique.

Note

Les appellations employées dans la présente publication et la présentation de données qui y figurent n'impliquent, de la part du Secrétariat de l'Organisation des Nations Unies, aucune prise de position quant au statut juridique des pays, territoires, villes ou zones, ou de leurs autorités, ni quant au tracé de leurs frontières ou limites.

En règle générale, les statistiques contenues dans la présente publication sont celles dont disposait le Secrétariat de l'Organisation des Nations Unies jusqu'à décembre 2012 et portent su la période finissant en 2011. Elles reflètent donc la nomenclature de pays en vigueur à l'époque.

Le terme « pays », tel qu'il est utilisé dans la présente publication peut également désigner des territoires ou des zones.

Les appellations « développées » et « en développement » qui figurent dans certains tableaux sont employées à des fins exclusivement statistiques et n'expriment pas nécessairement un jugement quant au niveau de développement atteint par tel pays ou telle région.

Les cotes des documents de l'Organisation des Nations Unies se composent de lettres majuscules et de chiffres.

ST/ESA/STAT/SER.S/32

PUBLICATION DES NATIONS UNIES
Numéro de vente : B.13.XVII.1.H

ISBN 978-92-1-061333-0
e-ISBN 978-92-1-056024-5
ISSN 0082-8459

Preface

The 2011 United Nations *Statistical Yearbook* is the fifty-sixth issue of the publication, prepared by the Statistics Division of the Department of Economic and Social Affairs. Ever since the compilation of data for the *Statistical Yearbook* series was initiated in 1948, it has consistently provided a wide range of internationally available statistics on social and economic conditions and activities at the national, regional and world levels.

The tables include series covering from one to ten years, depending upon data availability and space constraints. The ten-year tables generally cover the period up to 2010 or 2011.

The *Yearbook* tables are based on data which have been compiled by the Statistics Division mainly from official national and international sources as these are more authoritative and comprehensive, more generally available as time series and more comparable among countries than other sources. These sources include the United Nations Statistics Division in the fields of national accounts, industry, energy and international trade, the United Nations Statistics Division and Population Division in the field of demographic statistics, and over 20 offices of the United Nations system and international organizations in other specialized fields. In some cases, official sources have been supplemented by other sources and estimates, where these have been subjected to professional scrutiny and debate and are consistent with other independent sources.

The United Nations agencies and other international, national and specialized organizations which furnished data are listed under "Statistical sources and references" at the end of the *Yearbook*. Acknowledgement is gratefully made for their generous and valuable cooperation in continually providing data.

The 64 tables of the *Yearbook* are organized in four parts. The first part presents key world and regional aggregates and totals. In the other three parts, the subject matter is generally presented by countries or areas, with world and regional aggregates shown in some cases only. Parts two, three and four cover, respectively, population and social topics, national economic activity and international economic relations. Following the last chapter are brief technical notes on statistical sources and methods for all tables of the *Yearbook*.

The three annexes contain information on country and area nomenclature and the conversion coefficients and factors used in the various tables, and list those tables which were added to or omitted from the last issue of the *Yearbook*.

The *Statistical Yearbook* is prepared by the Statistical Dissemination Section, Statistical Services Branch of the Statistics Division, Department of Economic and Social Affairs of the United Nations Secretariat. The programme manager is Mary Jane Holupka and the chief editor is Jacob Assa. They are assisted by David Carter, Anuradha Chimata and Aida Diawara. Bogdan Dragovic developed the software.

Comments on the present *Yearbook* and its future evolution are welcome. They may be sent via e-mail to statistics@un.org or to the United Nations Statistics Division, Statistical Dissemination Section, New York, NY 10017, USA.

Préface

L'Annuaire statistique des Nations Unies 2011 est la cinquante-sixième édition de cette publication, préparée par la Division de statistique du Département des affaires économiques et sociales. Depuis son instauration en 1948 comme outil de compilation des données statistiques internationales, l'*Annuaire statistique* s'efforce de constamment diffuser un large éventail de statistiques disponibles sur les activités et conditions économiques et sociales, aux niveaux national, régional et mondial.

Les tableaux présentent des séries qui couvrent d'un à dix ans, en fonction de la disponibilité des données et des contraintes d'espace. Les tableaux décennaux couvrent généralement la période jusqu'à 2010 ou 2011.

Les tableaux de l'*Annuaire* sont construits essentiellement à partir des données compilées par la Division de statistique et provenant de sources officielles, nationales et internationales; c'est en effet la meilleure source si l'on veut des données fiables, complètes et comparables, et si l'on a besoin de séries chronologiques. Ces sources sont: la Division de statistique du Secrétariat de l'Organisation des Nations Unies pour ce qui concerne la comptabilité nationale, l'industrie, l'énergie et le commerce extérieur, la Division de statistique et la Division de la population du Secrétariat de l'Organisation des Nations Unies pour les statistiques démographiques; et plus de 20 bureaux du système des Nations Unies et d'organisations internationales pour les autres domaines spécialisés. Dans quelques cas, les données officielles sont complétées par des informations et des estimations provenant d'autres sources qui ont été examinées par des spécialistes et confirmées par des sources indépendantes.

Les institutions spécialisées des Nations Unies et les autres organisations internationales, nationales et spécialisées qui ont fourni des données sont énumérées dans la section "Sources statistiques et références" figurant à la fin de l'ouvrage. Les auteurs de l'*Annuaire statistique* les remercient de leur précieuse et généreuse collaboration.

Les 64 tableaux de l'*Annuaire* sont regroupés en quatre parties. La première partie présente les principaux agrégats et totaux aux niveaux mondial et régional. Dans les trios parties suivantes, les thèmes sont généralement présentés par pays ou régions. Les agrégats mondiaux ou régionaux ne sont indiqués que dans certains cas seulement. Les trois parties autres sont consacrées à la population et aux questions sociales (deuxième partie), à l'activité économique nationale (troisième partie) et aux relations économiques internationales (quatrième partie). Le dernier chapitre est suivi par de brèves notes techniques sur les sources et les méthodes statistiques utilisées pour chaque tableau de l'*Annuaire*.

Les trois annexes donnent des renseignements sur la nomenclature des pays et des zones, ainsi que sur les coefficients et facteurs de conversion employés dans les différents tableaux. Une liste des tableaux ajoutés et supprimés depuis la dernière édition de l'*Annuaire* y est également disponible.

L'Annuaire statistique est préparé par la Section de la diffusion statistique, Service des statistiques de services de la Division de statistique, Département des affaires économiques et sociales du Secrétariat de l'Organisation des Nations Unies. La responsable du programme est Mary Jane Holupka, et le rédacteur en chef est Jacob Assa. Ils sont secondés par David Carter, Anuradha Chimata et Aida Diawara. Bogdan Dragovic est chargé des logiciels.

Les observations sur la présente édition de l'*Annuaire* et les suggestions de modification pour l'avenir seront reçues avec intérêt. Elles peuvent être envoyées par message électronique à statistics@un.org, ou adressées à la Division de statistique des Nations Unies, Section de la diffusion statistique, New York, NY 10017 (États-Unis d'Amérique).

Explanatory notes

Units of measurement

The metric system of weights and measures has been employed throughout the *Statistical Yearbook*. For conversion coefficients and factors, see annex II.

Country notes and nomenclature

As a general rule, the data presented in the *Yearbook* relate to a given country or area within its present de facto boundaries. A complete list of countries and territories is presented in Annex I. It should also be noted that unless otherwise indicated, for statistical purposes, the data for China exclude those for Hong Kong Special Administrative Region of China, Macao Special Administrative Region of China and Taiwan province of China.

Symbols and conventions used in the tables

.	A point is used to indicate decimals.
-	A hyphen between years, for example, 2008-2009, indicates the full period involved, including the beginning and end years.
/	A slash indicates a financial year, school year or crop year, for example 2008/09.
...	Data not available or not applicable.
*	Provisional or estimated figure.
#	Marked break in series.
^0	Not zero but less than half of the unit used.

A space is used as a thousands separator, for example 1 000 is one thousand. Details and percentages in the tables do not necessarily add to totals because of rounding.

Notes explicatives

Unités de mesure

Le système métrique de poids et mesures a été utilisé dans tout l'*Annuaire statistique*. On trouvera à l'annexe II les coefficients et facteurs de conversion.

Notes sur les pays et nomenclature

En règle générale, les données renvoient au pays ou zone en question dans ses frontières actuelles effectives. Une liste complète des pays et territoires figure à l'annexe I. Il convient de noter aussi que sauf indication contraire, les données statistiques relatives à la China ne comprennent pas celles qui concernent la région administrative spéciale de Hong Kong, la région administrative spéciale de Macao et la province chinoise de Taiwan.

Signes et conventions employés dans les tableaux

.	Les décimales sont précédées d'un point.
-	Un tiret entre des années, par exemple "2008-2009", indique que la période est embrassée dans sa totalité, y compris la première et la dernière année.
/	Une barre oblique renvoie à un exercice financier, à une année scolaire ou à une campagne agricole, par exemple "2008/09".
...	Données non disponibles ou non applicables.
*	Chiffre provisoire ou estimatif.
#	Discontinuité notable dans la série.
^0	Non nul mais inférieur à la moitié de l'unité employée.

Le séparateur utilisé pour les milliers est l'espace : par exemple, 1 000 correspond à un millier. Les chiffres étant arrondis, les totaux ne correspondent pas toujours à la somme exacte des éléments ou pourcentages figurant dans les tableaux.

Contents

**   Asterisks preceding table names identify tables that were presented in previous issues of the *Statistical Yearbook* which are not contained in the present issue. These tables will be updated in future issues of the *Yearbook* when new data become available.

Table des matières

** Ce symbole indique les tableaux publiés dans les éditions précédentes de l'*Annuaire statistique* mais qui n'ont pas été repris
    dans la présente édition. Ces tableaux seront actualisés dans les futures livraisons de l'*Annuaire* à mesure que des données
    nouvelles deviendront disponibles.

Introduction

The 2011 United Nations *Statistical Yearbook* is the fifty-sixth issue of this publication, prepared by the Statistics Division, Department of Economic and Social Affairs, of the United Nations Secretariat. The tables include series covering from one to ten years, depending upon data availability (as of 30 April 2013) and space constraints. The ten-year tables generally cover the period up to 2010 or 2011.

Objective and content of the Statistical Yearbook

The main purpose of the *Statistical Yearbook* is to provide in a single volume a comprehensive compilation of internationally available statistics on social and economic conditions and activities, at world, regional and national levels, covering a ten-year period to the extent possible.

Most of the statistics presented in the *Yearbook* are extracted from more detailed, specialized databases prepared by the Statistics Division and by many other international statistical services. Thus, while the specialized databases concentrate on monitoring topics and trends in particular social and economic fields, the *Statistical Yearbook* tables aim to provide data for a more comprehensive, overall description of social and economic structures, conditions, changes and activities. The objective has been to collect, systematize, coordinate and present in a consistent way the most essential components of comparable statistical information which can give a broad picture of social and economic processes.

The content of the *Statistical Yearbook* is planned to serve a general readership. The *Yearbook* endeavours to provide information for various bodies of the United Nations system as well as for other international organizations, governments and non-governmental organizations, national statistical, economic and social policy bodies, scientific and educational institutions, libraries and the public. Data published in the *Statistical Yearbook* may also be of interest to companies and enterprises and to agencies engaged in market research. The *Statistical Yearbook* thus provides information on a wide range of social and economic issues which are of concern in the United Nations system and among the governments and peoples of the world. A particular value of the *Yearbook* is that it facilitates meaningful analysis of issues by systematizing and coordinating the data across many fields and shedding light on such interrelated issues as:

- General economic growth and related economic conditions;
- Progress towards the Millennium Development Goals;
- Population by sex and rate of increase, surface area and density;
- Unemployment, inflation and prices;
- Energy production and consumption and the development of new energy sources;
- Expansion of trade;
- The financial situation of countries;
- Education, training and eradication of illiteracy;
- Improvement in general living conditions;
- Pollution and protection of the environment;
- Assistance provided to developing countries for social and economic development purposes.

Organization of the Yearbook

The 64 tables of the *Yearbook* are grouped into four broad parts:

- Part One: World and Region Summary (chapter I: tables 1-6);
- Part Two: Population and Social Statistics (chapters II-VI: tables 7-18);
- Part Three: Economic Activity (chapters VII-XV: tables 19-53);
- Part Four: International Economic Relations (chapters XVI-XIX: tables 54-64).

The more aggregated information shown in part one provides an overall picture of development at the world and region levels. More specific and detailed information for analysis concerning individual countries or areas is presented in the other three parts. Each of these parts is divided into chapters, by topic, and each chapter has corresponding "Technical notes" (following the last chapter), which provide brief descriptions of major statistical concepts, definitions and classifications required for interpretation and analysis of the data.

Part One, World and Region Summary, comprises six tables highlighting the principal trends in the world as well as in each of the regions and in the major economic and social sectors. It contains global totals of important aggregate statistics needed for the analysis of economic growth, the structure of the world economy, major changes in world population and expansion of external merchandise trade. The global totals are, as a rule, subdivided into major geographical areas.

Part Two, Population and Social Statistics, comprises 12 tables which contain more detailed statistical series on population, gender, education, nutrition and communication.

Of the 35 tables in Part Three, Economic Activity, 16 provide data on national accounts, interest rates, labour force, prices, energy, environment and science and technology; 17 tables provide data on production in the major branches of the economy (using, in general, the International Standard Industrial Classification, ISIC), namely agriculture, hunting, forestry and fishing, and manufacturing. Consumption data are combined with the production data in tables on specific commodities, where feasible.

Part Four, International Economic Relations, comprises 11 tables on international merchandise trade, international tourism and transport, international finance and development assistance.

Annexes and regional groupings of countries or areas

The annexes to the *Statistical Yearbook*, and the section "Explanatory notes" preceding the Introduction, provide additional essential information on the *Yearbook*'s contents and presentation of data.

Annex I provides information on countries or areas covered in the *Yearbook* tables and on their arrangement in geographical regions and economic or other groupings. The geographical groupings shown in the *Yearbook* are generally based on continental regions unless otherwise indicated. However, strict consistency in this regard is impossible. A wide range of classifications is used for different purposes in the various international agencies and other sources of statistics for the *Yearbook*. These classifications vary in response to administrative and analytical requirements.

Similarly, there is no common agreement in the United Nations system concerning the terms "developed" and "developing" when referring to the stage of development reached by any given country or area, and its corresponding classification in one or the other grouping. The *Yearbook* thus refers more generally to "developed" or "developing" regions on the basis of conventional practice. Following this practice, "developed" regions or areas comprise Canada and the United States in Northern America, Japan in Asia, Australia and New Zealand in Oceania, and Europe, while all of Africa and the remainder of the Americas, Asia and Oceania comprise the "developing regions". These designations are intended for statistical convenience and do not necessarily express a judgement about the stage reached by a particular country or area in the development process.

Annex II provides detailed information on conversion coefficients and factors used in various tables, and annex III provides a list of tables added and omitted in the present edition of the *Yearbook*. Tables for which a sufficient amount of new data is not available are not being published in this *Yearbook*. Their titles nevertheless are still listed in the table of contents since it is planned that they will be published in a later issue as new data are compiled by the collecting agency.

Data comparability, quality and relevance

The major challenge continuously facing the *Statistical Yearbook* is to present series which are as nearly comparable across countries as the available statistics permit. Considerable efforts have already been made among the international suppliers of data and by the staff of the *Statistical Yearbook* to ensure the compatibility of various series by coordinating time periods, base years, prices chosen for valuation, and so on. This is indispensable in relating various bodies of data to each other and in facilitating analysis across different sectors. Thus, for example, relating data on short-term interest rates to those on prices makes it possible to arrive at a general understanding about the inflation environment, and relating a country's data on tourism expenditure in other countries to those on its per capita GDP provides a gauge on that country's wealth status. In general, the data presented reflect the methodological recommendations of the United Nations Statistical Commission issued in various United Nations publications, and of other international bodies concerned with statistics. Publications containing these recommendations and guidelines are listed in the section "Statistical sources and references" at the end of the *Yearbook*. The use of international recommendations not only promotes international comparability of the data but also ensures a degree of compatibility regarding the underlying concepts, definitions and classifications relating to different series. However, much work remains to be done in this area and, for this reason, some tables can serve only as a first source of data, which require further adjustment before being used for more in-depth analytical studies. While on the whole, a significant degree of comparability has been achieved in international statistics, there will remain some limitations, for a variety of reasons.

One common cause of non-comparability of economic data is different valuations of statistical aggregates such as national income, wages and salaries, output of industries and so forth. Conversion of these and similar series originally expressed in national prices into a common currency, for example into United States dollars, through the use of exchange rates, is not always satisfactory owing to frequent wide fluctuations in market rates and differences between official rates and rates which would be indicated by unofficial markets or purchasing power parities. The use of different kinds of sources for obtaining data is another cause of incomparability. This is true, for example, in the case of employment and unemployment, where data are obtained from different sources, namely household and labour force sample surveys, establishment censuses or surveys, official estimates, social insurance statistics and employment office statistics, which are not fully comparable in many cases. Non-comparability of data may also result from differences in the institutional patterns of countries. Certain variations in social and economic organization and institutions may have an impact on the comparability of the data even if the underlying concepts and definitions are identical. These and other causes of non-comparability of the data are briefly explained in the technical notes to each chapter.

A further set of challenges relate to timeliness, quality and relevance of the data contained in the *Yearbook*. Users generally demand the most up-to-date statistics. However, due to the different development stages of statistical capacity in different countries, data for the most recent years may only be available for a small number of countries. For a global print publication, therefore, a balance has to be struck between presenting the most updated information and satisfactory country coverage. Of course the United Nations Statistics Division's website offers greater flexibility in presenting continuously updated information and is therefore a useful complement to the annual print publication. Furthermore, as most of the information presented in this *Yearbook* is collected through specialized United Nations agencies and partners, the timeliness is continuously enhanced by improving the communication and data flow between countries and the specialized agencies on the one hand, and between the United Nations Statistics Division and the specialized agencies on the other. The development of new XML-based data transfer protocols will address this issue and is expected to make international data flows more efficient in the future.

Data quality at the international level is a function of the data quality at the national level. The United Nations Statistics Division in close cooperation with its partners among the UN agencies and the international statistical system continues to support countries' efforts to improve both the coverage and the quality of their data. Metadata, as for example reflected in the footnotes and technical notes of this publication, are an important service to the user to allow an informed assessment of the quality of the data. Given the wide variety of sources for the *Yearbook*, there is of course an equally wide variety of data formats and accompanying metadata. An important challenge for the United Nations Statistics Division and its partners for the future is to work further towards the standardization, or at least harmonization, of metadata.

The final challenge relates to maintaining the relevance of the series included in the *Yearbook*. As new policy concerns enter the developmental debate, the United Nations Statistics Division will need to introduce new series that describe concerns that have gained prominence as well as to prune data as they become outdated and continue to update the recurrent *Yearbook* series that still address those issues which are most pertinent. Often choosing the appropriate moment when the statistical information on new topics has matured sufficiently so as to be able to disseminate meaningful global data can be challenging. Furthermore, a balance has to continuously be found between the ever-increasing amount of information available for dissemination and the space limitations of the print version of the *Statistical Yearbook*. International comparability, data availability and data quality will remain the key criteria to guide the United Nations Statistics Division in its selection.

Needless to say, more can always be done to improve the *Statistical Yearbook*'s scope, coverage, design, metadata and timeliness. The *Yearbook* team continually strives to improve upon each of these aspects and to make its publication as responsive as possible to its users' needs and expectations, while at the same time focusing on a manageable body of data and metadata. Since data disseminated in digital form have clear advantages over those in print, as much of the *Yearbook* information as possible will continue to be included in the Statistics Division's online databases. Still, the *Statistical Yearbook* will continue to claim its rightful place among the products of the Statistics Division as a useful resource for a general understanding of the global social and economic situation.

Introduction

L'Annuaire statistique des Nations Unies 2011 est la cinquante-cinquième édition de cette publication, établi par la Division de statistique du Département des affaires économiques et sociales du Secrétariat de l'Organisation des Nations Unies. Les tableaux présentent des séries qui couvrent d'un à dix ans, en fonction de la disponibilité des données (à la date du 30 avril 2013) et des contraintes d'espace. Les tableaux décennaux couvrent généralement la période jusqu'à 2010 ou 2011.

Objectif et contenu de l'Annuaire statistique

Le principal objectif de *l'Annuaire statistique* est de fournir en un seul volume un inventaire complet de statistiques internationales concernant la situation et les activités sociales et économiques aux niveaux mondial, régional et national, sur une période s'étalant, dans la mesure du possible, sur dix ans.

La plupart des données qui figurent dans l'*Annuaire statistique* proviennent de bases de données spécialisées davantage détaillées, préparées par la Division de statistique et par bien d'autres services statistiques internationaux. Tandis que les bases de données spécialisées se concentrent sur le suivi de domaines socioéconomiques particuliers, les données de l'*Annuaire* sont présentées de telle sorte qu'elles fournissent une description globale et exhaustive des structures, conditions, transformations et activités socioéconomiques. On a cherché à recueillir, systématiser, coordonner et présenter de manière cohérente les principales informations statistiques comparables, de manière à dresser un tableau général des processus socioéconomiques.

Le contenu de l'*Annuaire statistique* a été élaboré en vue d'un lectorat large. Les renseignements fournis devraient ainsi pouvoir être utilisés par les divers organismes du système des Nations Unies, mais aussi par d'autres organisations internationales, les gouvernements et les organisations non gouvernementales, les organismes nationaux de statistique et de politique économique et sociale, les institutions scientifiques et les établissements d'enseignement, les bibliothèques et les particuliers. Les données publiées dans l'*Annuaire* peuvent également intéresser les sociétés et entreprises, et les organismes spécialisés dans les études de marché. L'*Annuaire* présente des informations sur un large éventail de questions socioéconomiques liées aux préoccupations actuelles du système des Nations Unies, des gouvernements et des peuples du monde entier. Une qualité particulière de l'*Annuaire* est de faciliter une analyse approfondie de ces questions en systématisant et en articulant les données d'un domaine/secteur à l'autre, et en apportant un éclairage sur des sujets interdépendants, tels que :

- La croissance économique générale, et les conditions économiques qui lui sont liées;
- Les progrès accomplis dans la réalisation des Objectifs du Millénaire pour le Développement;
- La population selon le sexe, taux d'accroissement, superficie et densité;
- Le chômage, l'inflation et les prix;
- La production et la consommation d'énergie et le développement de nouvelles sources d'énergie;
- L'expansion des échanges;
- La situation financière des pays;
- L'éducation, la formation et l'élimination de l'analphabétisme;
- L'amélioration des conditions de vie;
- La pollution et la protection de l'environnement;
- L'assistance aux pays en développement à des fins socioéconomiques.

Présentation de l'Annuaire

Les 64 tableaux de l'*Annuaire* sont groupés en quatre parties:

- La première partie : Aperçu mondial et régional (chapitre I : tableaux 1 à 6);
- La deuxième partie : Statistiques démographiques et sociales (chapitres II à VI : tableaux 7 à 18);
- La troisième partie : Activité économique (chapitres VII à XV : tableaux 19 à 53);
- La quatrième partie : Relations économiques internationales (chapitres XVI à XIX : tableaux 54 à 64).

Les valeurs les plus agrégées qui figurent dans la première partie donnent un tableau global du développement à l'échelon mondial et régional, tandis que les trois autres parties contiennent des renseignements plus précis et détaillés qui se prêtent mieux à une analyse par pays ou par zones. Chacune de ces trois parties est divisée en chapitres portant sur des sujets donnés. Après le dernier tableau, les notes techniques de chaque chapitre apportent une brève description des principales notions, définitions et classifications statistiques nécessaires pour interpréter et analyser les données.

La première partie, intitulée "Aperçu mondial et régional", comprend six tableaux présentant les principales tendances dans le monde et dans les régions ainsi que dans les principaux secteurs économiques et sociaux. Elle fournit des chiffres mondiaux pour les principaux agrégats statistiques nécessaires pour analyser la croissance économique, la structure de l'économie mondiale, les principaux changements dans la population mondiale et l'expansion du commerce extérieur de marchandises. En règle générale, les chiffres mondiaux sont répartis par grandes régions géographiques.

La deuxième partie, intitulée "Population et statistiques sociales", comporte 12 tableaux où figurent des séries plus détaillées concernant la population, la situation des femmes, l'éducation et la communication.

La troisième partie, intitulée "Activité économique", comporte 35 tableaux, 16 qui présentent des statistiques concernant les comptes nationaux, les taux d'intérêt, la population active, les prix, l'énergie, l'environnement, et la science et technologie; et 17 qui présentent des données sur la production des principales branches d'activité économique (en utilisant en général la Classification internationale type, par industrie, de toutes les branches d'activité économique): agriculture, chasse, sylviculture et pêche, et industries manufacturières. Les tableaux traitant de certains produits de base associent autant que possible les données relatives à la consommation aux valeurs concernant la production.

La quatrième partie, intitulée "Relations économiques internationales", comprend 11 tableaux relatifs au commerce international de marchandises, au tourisme et transport internationaux, aux finances internationales, et à l'aide au développement.

Annexes et groupements régionaux des pays et zones

Les annexes à l'*Annuaire statistique*, et la section intitulée "Notes explicatives" qui précède l'introduction, offrent d'importantes informations complémentaires quant à la teneur et à la présentation des données figurant dans le présent ouvrage.

L'annexe I donne des renseignements sur les pays ou zones couverts par les tableaux de l'*Annuaire* et sur leur regroupement en régions géographiques et groupements économiques ou autres. Sauf indication contraire, les groupements géographiques figurant dans l'*Annuaire* sont généralement fondés sur les régions continentales, mais une présentation absolument systématique est impossible à cet égard car les diverses institutions internationales et autres sources de statistiques employées pour la confection de l'*Annuaire* emploient, selon l'objet de l'exercice, des classifications fort différentes en réponse à diverses exigences d'ordre administratif ou analytique.

Il n'existe pas non plus dans le système des Nations Unies de définition commune des termes "développé" et "en développement" pour décrire le niveau atteint en la matière par un pays ou une zone donnés ni pour les classifier dans l'un ou l'autre de ces groupes. Ainsi, dans l'*Annuaire*, on s'en remet à l'usage pour qualifier les régions de "développées" ou "en développement". Selon cet usage, les régions ou zones développées sont le Canada et les Etats-Unis dans l'Amérique septentrionale, le Japon dans l'Asie, l'Australie et la Nouvelle-Zélande dans l'Océanie, et l'Europe, alors que toute l'Afrique et le reste des Amériques, l'Asie et l'Océanie constituent les régions en développement. Ces appellations sont utilisées pour plus de commodité dans la présentation des statistiques et n'impliquent pas nécessairement un jugement quant au stade de développement auquel est parvenu tel pays ou telle zone.

L'annexe II fournit des renseignements sur les coefficients et facteurs de conversion employés dans les différents tableaux, et l'annexe III contient la liste de tableaux qui ont été ajoutés ou omis dans la présente édition de l'*Annuaire*. Les tableaux pour lesquels on ne dispose pas d'une quantité suffisante des données nouvelles, n'ont pas été publiés dans cet *Annuaire*. Comme ils seront repris dans une prochaine édition à mesure que des données nouvelles seront dépouillées par l'office statistique d'origine, ses titres figurent toujours dans la table des matières.

Comparabilité, qualité et pertinence des statistiques

Le défi majeur auquel l'*Annuaire Statistique* fait continuellement face est de présenter des séries aussi comparables entre les pays que la disponibilité des statistiques le permettent. Les sources internationales de données et les auteurs de l'*Annuaire* ont réalisé des efforts considérables pour faire en sorte que diverses séries soient compatibles, en harmonisant les périodes de référence, les années de base, les prix utilisés pour les évaluations, etc. Cette démarche est indispensable si l'on veut rapprocher divers ensembles de données, et faciliter l'analyse intersectorielle de l'économie. Ainsi, lier les données concernant les taux d'intérêt à court terme à celles des prix permet d'arriver à une compréhension globale de l'environnement de l'inflation; lier les données de dépenses touristiques d'un pays dans d'autres pays à celles de son PIB par tête fournit un indicateur de la richesse de ce pays. De façon générale, les données sont présentées selon les recommandations méthodologiques formulées par la Commission de statistique des Nations Unies, et par les autres entités internationales impliquées dans les statistiques. Les titres des publications contenant ces recommandations et leurs lignes directrices figurent à la fin de l'*Annuaire*, dans la section "Sources et références statistiques". Le respect des recommandations internationales tend non seulement à promouvoir la comparabilité internationale des données, mais elle assure également une certaine comparabilité entre les concepts, les définitions et classifications utilisés. Mais comme il reste encore beaucoup à faire dans ce domaine, les données présentées dans certains tableaux n'ont qu'une valeur indicative, et nécessiteront des ajustements plus poussés avant de pouvoir servir à des analyses approfondies. Bien que l'on soit parvenu, dans l'ensemble, à un degré de comparabilité appréciable en matière de statistiques internationales, diverses raisons expliquent que subsistent encore de nombreuses limitations.

Une cause commune de non comparabilité des données économiques réside dans la diversité des méthodes d'évaluation employées pour comptabiliser des agrégats tels que le revenu national, les salaires et traitements, la production des différentes branches d'activité industrielle, etc. Il n'est pas toujours satisfaisant de ramener la valeur des séries de ce type—exprimée à l'origine en prix nationaux—à une monnaie commune (par exemple le dollar des États-Unis) car les taux de change du marché connaissent fréquemment de fortes fluctuations, et parce que les taux officiels ne coïncident pas avec ceux des marchés officieux ni avec les parités réelles de pouvoir d'achat. Le recours à des sources diverses pour la collecte des données est un autre facteur qui limite la comparabilité. C'est le cas, par exemple, des données d'emploi et de chômage, obtenues par des moyens aussi peu comparables que les sondages, le dépouillement des registres d'assurances sociales et les enquêtes auprès des entreprises. Dans certains cas, les données ne sont pas comparables en raison de différences entre les structures institutionnelles des pays. Des changements dans l'organisation et les institutions économiques et sociales peuvent affecter la comparabilité des données, même si les concepts et définitions sont fondamentalement identiques. Ces causes, et d'autres, de non comparabilité des données sont brièvement expliquées dans les notes techniques de chaque chapitre.

Un autre ensemble de défis à relever concerne la fraîcheur, la qualité et la pertinence des données présentées dans l'*Annuaire*. Les utilisateurs exigent généralement des données les plus récentes possibles. Toutefois, selon le niveau de développement de la capacité statistique des pays, les données pour les dernières années peuvent n'être disponibles que pour un nombre limité de pays. Dans le cadre d'une publication mondiale, un équilibre doit être trouvé entre la présentation de l'information la plus récente et une couverture géographique satisfaisante. Bien entendu, le site Internet de la Division de statistique des Nations Unies offre une plus grande flexibilité, puisqu'il propose une information actualisée au fil de l'eau, et constitue ainsi un complément utile à la publication papier annuelle. Par ailleurs, étant donné que la plupart des informations présentées dans cet *Annuaire* sont collectées parmi les agences spécialisées des Nations Unies et autres partenaires, la fraîcheur des données est continuellement améliorée, grâce à une meilleure communication et un meilleur échange de données entre les pays et les agences spécialisées d'une part, et entre la Division de statistique des Nations Unies et les agences spécialisées d'autre part. Le développement de nouveaux protocoles de transfert de données basés sur le langage XML devrait contribuer à rendre, à l'avenir, les échanges de données internationales encore plus efficaces.

La qualité des données au niveau international est fonction de la qualité des données au niveau national. La Division de statistique des Nations Unies, en étroite collaboration avec ses partenaires dans les agences de l'ONU et dans le système statistique international, continue de soutenir les efforts des pays pour améliorer à la fois la couverture et la qualité de leurs données. Des métadonnées, comme l'illustrent les notes de bas de page et les notes techniques de cette publication, constituent un important service fourni à l'utilisateur pour lui permettre d'évaluer de manière avisée la qualité des données. Etant donné la grande variété des sources de l'*Annuaire*, il y a bien entendu une non moins grande variété de formats de données et de métadonnées associées. Un important défi que la Division de statistique des Nations Unies et ses partenaires doivent relever dans le futur est d'aboutir à la standardisation, ou au moins l'harmonisation, des métadonnées.

Le dernier défi concerne la constance de la pertinence des séries présentées dans l'*Annuaire*. Au fur et à mesure que de nouvelles préoccupations politiques pénètrent le débat lié au développement, la Division de statistique des Nations Unies doit introduire dans l'*Annuaire* de nouvelles séries qui leur sont liées, et, ce faisant, effectuer une coupe sombre parmi les données qui lui semblent dépassées, tout en s'assurant de continuer à actualiser les séries récurrentes de qui paraissent encore pertinentes. Souvent, choisir le moment idoine auquel les données statistiques sur de nouveaux thèmes sont suffisamment matures pour qu'elles puissent, au niveau mondial, être diffusées sans hésitation, est un défi en soi. Par ailleurs, un équilibre doit continuellement être trouvé entre le volume toujours croissant d'informations disponibles à la diffusion, et les contraintes d'espace de la version papier de l'*Annuaire* statistique. La comparabilité internationale, la disponibilité des données et leur qualité devront rester le principal critère à considérer par la Division de statistique des Nations Unies dans sa sélection.

Inutile de dire qu'il est toujours possible d'améliorer l'*Annuaire* statistique en ce qui concerne son champ, sa couverture, sa conception générale, ses métadonnées et sa mise à jour. L'équipe en charge de l'*Annuaire* s'évertue en permanence à améliorer chacun de ces aspects, et de faire en sorte que cette publication réponde au plus près aux besoins et aux attentes de ses utilisateurs, sans toutefois oublier de mettre l'accent sur un corpus gérable de données et de métadonnées. Puisqu'il est avéré que les données diffusées de manière digitale ont des avantages comparés à celles diffusées sur papier, autant d'informations de l'*Annuaire* que possible continueront d'être inclues dans les bases de données électroniques de la Division de statistique. L'*Annuaire* statistique garde toujours une place de choix parmi les produits de la Division de statistique comme une ressource utile pour une compréhension général de la situation sociale et économique globale.

Part One

World and region summary

Chapter I   World and region summary (tables 1-6)

This part of the *Statistical Yearbook* presents selected aggregate series on principal economic and social topics for the world as a whole and for the major regions. The topics include population and surface area, agricultural and industrial production, external trade, government financial reserves, and energy production and consumption. More detailed data on individual countries and areas are provided in the subsequent parts of the present *Yearbook*. These comprise Part Two: Population and Social Statistics; Part Three: Economic Activity; and Part Four: International Economic Relations.

Regional totals between series may be incomparable owing to differences in definitions of regions and lack of data for particular regional components. General information on regional groupings is provided in annex I of the *Yearbook*. Supplementary information on regional groupings used in specific series is provided, as necessary, in table footnotes and in the technical notes at the end of chapter I.

Première partie

Aperçu mondial et régional

Chapitre I   Aperçu mondial et régional (tableaux 1 à 6)

Cette partie de l'Annuaire statistique présente, pour le monde entier et ses principales subdivisions, un choix d'agrégats ayant trait à des questions économiques et sociales essentielles: population et superficie, production agricole et industrielle, commerce extérieur, réserves financières publiques, et la production et la consommation d'énergie. Des statistiques plus détaillées pour divers pays ou zones figurent dans les parties ultérieures de l'Annuaire, c'est-à-dire dans les deuxième, troisième et quatrième parties intitulées respectivement: population et statistiques sociales, activités économiques et relations économiques internationales.

Les totaux régionaux peuvent être incomparables entre les séries en raison de différences dans la définition des régions et de l'absence de données sur tel ou tel élément régional. A l'annexe I de l'Annuaire, on trouvera des renseignements généraux sur les groupements régionaux. Des informations complémentaires sur les groupements régionaux pour certaines séries bien précises sont fournies, lorsqu'il y a lieu, dans les notes figurant au bas des tableaux et dans les notes techniques à la fin du chapitre I.

1

World statistics: selected series
Population, production, external trade and finance

Statistiques mondiales : séries principales
Population, production, commerce extérieur et finances

Series Séries	Unit or base Unité ou base	2002	2003	2004	2005	2006	2007	2008	2009	2010
Population • Population										
World population [1] Population mondial [1]	million	6 277	6 353	6 429	6 506	6 584	6 662	6 740	6 818	6 896
Output / production • Production										
Gross domestic product • Produit intérieur brut										
GDP at current prices PIB aux prix courants	billion US $ milliard $ E.-U.	33 429	37 545	42 275	45 745	49 603	55 886	61 233	57 960	63 064
GDP per capita PIB par habitant	US $ $ E.-U.	5 346	5 932	6 600	7 057	7 562	8 420	9 119	8 533	9 178
GDP real rates of growth Taux de l'accroissement réels	%	2.1	2.8	4.1	3.5	4.1	4.0	1.4	-2.3	4.0
Agriculture, forestry and fishing production • Production agricole, forestière et de la pêche										
Index numbers - Indices										
All commodities [2] Tous produits [2]	2004-06 = 100	91	94	98	100	102	105	109	110	111
Food [2] Produits alimentaires [2]	2004-06 = 100	91	94	98	100	102	105	109	110	111
Quantities - Quantités										
Cereals [2] Céréales [2]	million t.	2 033	2 092	2 281	2 269	2 237	2 355	2 525	2 494	2 458
Meat [2] Viande [2]	million t.	228	233	238	245	251	257	263	268	275
Roundwood [2] Bois rond [2]	million m^3	3 395	3 449	3 506	3 571	3 530	3 553	3 436	3 289	3 401
Fish production Production halieutique	million t.	128	127	135	137	137	140	143	145	148
Industrial production • Production industrielle										
Quantities - Quantités										
Coal [2] Houille [2]	million t.	3 504	3 930	4 329	4 660	4 922	5 157	5 343	5484	...
Lignite and brown coal [2] Lignite et charbon brun [2]	million t.	1 350	1 371	1 381	1 395	1 443	1 470	1 488	1 429	...
Crude petroleum [2] Pétrole brut [2]	million t.	3 340	3 493	3 585	3 608	3 617	3 604	3 624	3 553	...
Natural gas [2] Gaz naturel [2]	petajoules pétajoules	100 114	103 572	107 008	110 009	113 702	116 353	120 923	116 966	...
Electricity [2, 3] Électricité [2, 3]	billion kWh milliard kWh	16 180	16 777	17 573	18 365	19 081	19 926	20 282	20 183	...
Sugar, raw Sucre, brut	million t.	137	141	147	148	153	157	163	161	165
Woodpulp [2] Pâte de bois [2]	million t.	167	170	175	174	176	181	178	161	171
Sawnwood [2] Sciages [2]	million m^3	393	400	426	438	447	443	399	364	390

Series / Séries	Unit or base / Unité ou base	2002	2003	2004	2005	2006	2007	2008	2009	2010
External trade • Commerce extérieur										
Value – Valeur										
Imports, c.i.f. / Importations c.a.f.	billion US $ / milliard $ E.-U.	6 526	7 610	9 292	10 581	12 159	14 033	16 224	12 472	15 085
Exports, f.o.b. / Exportations f.o.b.	billion US $ / milliard $ E.-U.	6 402	7 453	9 074	10 352	11 976	13 822	15 970	12 367	15 060
Volume: index of exports - Volume: indice des exportations										
All commodities / Tous produits	2000 = 100	103	109	122	133	148	157	165	142	165
Manufactures / Manufacturés	2000 = 100	103	111	128	139	153	145	146	126	144
Unit value: index of exports[4] - Valeur unitaure: indice des exportations[4]										
All commodities / Tous produits	2000 = 100	97	107	116	121	126	136	148	135	141
Manufactures / Produits manufactures	2000 = 100	98	104	110	111	114	125	131	121	124
Finance • Finances										
International reserves minus gold[5] - Réserves internationales moins l'or[5]										
All countries[2] / Tous les pays[2]	billion SDR / milliard DTS	1 857.1	2 122.0	2 489.6	3 071.3	3 527.9	4 275.1	4 813.5	5 447.2	6 263.3
Position in IMF[2] / Disponibilité au FMI[2]	billion US $ / milliard $ E.-U.	89.8	98.8	86.6	40.8	26.3	21.7	38.7	60.6	75.2
Foreign exchange[2] / Devises[2]	billion US $ / milliard $ E.-U.	2 407.8	2 954.7	3 642.2	4 188.9	5 123.9	6 585.4	7 196.4	7 950.6	9 023.7
SDR (special drawing rights)[2] / DTS (droits de triage spéc.)[2]	billion US $ / milliard $ E.-U.	29.3	32.0	33.3	30.7	32.3	33.9	33.0	319.8	314.6

Source:
Databases of the Food and Agriculture Organization of the United Nations (FAO), Rome; the International Monetary Fund (IMF), Washington, D.C.; and the United Nations Statistics Division, New York.

Source:
Les bases de données de l'Organisation des Nations Unies pour l'alimentation et l'agriculture (FAO), Rome; du Fonds Monétaire International (FMI), Washington, D.C. ; et de la Division de statistique de l'Organisation de Nations Unies, New York.

1   Mid-year estimates.
2   As of November 2012.
3   Electricity generated by establishments for public or private use.

4   Indices computed in US dollars.
5   End of period.

1   Les estimations au milieu de l'année.
2   De novembre 2012.
3   L'électricité produite par des entreprises d'utilisation publique ou privée.

4   Indice calculé en dollars des Etats-Unis.
5   Fin de la période.

2

Population, rate of increase, birth and death rates, surface area and density

Population, taux d'accroissement, taux de natalité, taux de mortalité, superficie et densité

Major areas and regions Grandes régions	Mid-year population estimates (millions) Estimations de population au milieu de l'année (millions)							Annual rate of increase Taux d'accrois-sement annuel %	Crude birth rate Taux bruts de natalité (p.1 000)	Crude death rate Taux bruts de mortalité (p.1 000)	Surface area Superficie (000 km²)	Density[1] Densité[1]
	1960	1970	1980	1990	2000	2010	2011	2010 - 2015			2011	2011
World **Monde**	3 038	3 696	4 453	5 306	6 123	6 896	6 974	1.1	19	8	136 127	51
Africa **Afrique**	287	368	483	635	811	1 022	1 046	2.3	34	11	30 312	35
Eastern Africa Afrique orientale	82	108	144	193	252	324	333	2.6	37	10	6 361	52
Middle Africa Afrique centrale	32	41	53	72	96	127	130	2.5	40	15	6 613	20
Northern Africa Afrique du Nord	68	87	113	146	176	210	213	1.6	23	6	8 525	25
Southern Africa Afrique australe	20	26	33	42	51	58	58	0.6	21	14	2 675	22
Western Africa Afrique occidentale	86	107	140	183	236	304	312	2.6	38	12	6 138	51
Northern America[2] **Amérique septentrionale**[2]	204	231	255	281	313	345	348	0.9	13	8	21 776	16
Latin America and the Caribbean **Amérique latine et Caraïbes**	220	286	362	443	521	590	597	1.1	18	6	20 546	29
Caribbean Caraïbes	21	25	30	34	38	42	42	0.7	17	7	234	179
Central America Amérique centrale	52	70	92	113	136	156	158	1.3	20	5	2 480	64
South America Amérique du Sud	148	192	241	296	347	393	397	1.0	17	6	17 832	22
Asia[3] **Asie**[3]	1 708	2 135	2 638	3 200	3 719	4 164	4 207	1.0	17	7	31 880	132
Eastern Asia Asie orientale	802	984	1 179	1 359	1 495	1 574	1 581	0.4	12	8	11 763	134
South-central Asia Asie centrale et du Sud	620	779	986	1 246	1 516	1 765	1 790	1.4	22	8	10 791	166
South-eastern Asia Asie du Sud-est	219	285	359	445	524	593	600	1.1	18	6	4 495	133
Western Asia[3] Asie occidentale[3]	67	87	114	149	184	232	237	1.9	23	5	4 831	49
Europe[3] **Europe**[3]	604	656	693	721	727	738	739	0.1	11	11	23 049	32
Eastern Europe Europe orientale	253	276	295	311	304	295	294	-0.2	11	14	18 814	16
Northern Europe Europe septentrionale	82	87	90	92	94	99	100	0.5	12	10	1 810	55
Southern Europe Europe méridionale	117	127	138	142	145	155	156	0.3	10	10	1 317	118
Western Europe Europe occidentale	152	166	170	175	183	189	189	0.2	10	10	1 108	171

2 Population, rate of increase, birth and death rates, surface area and density *(continued)*
Population, taux d'accroissement, taux de natalité, taux de mortalité, superficie et densité *(suite)*

Major areas and regions Grandes régions	Mid-year population estimates (millions) Estimations de population au milieu de l'année (millions)							Annual rate of increase Taux d'accrois-sement annuel %	Crude birth rate Taux bruts de natalité (p.1 000)	Crude death rate Taux bruts de mortalité (p.1 000)	Surface area Superficie (000 km²)	Density[1] Densité[1]
	1960	1970	1980	1990	2000	2010	2011	2010 - 2015			2011	2011
Oceania[2] Océanie[2]	15.8	19.5	23.0	27.0	31.1	36.6	37.2	1.5	17	7	8 564	4
Australia and New Zealand Australie et Nouvelle-Zélande	12.7	15.5	17.9	20.5	23.0	26.6	27.0	1.3	14	7	8 012	3
Melanesia Mélanésie	2.6	3.3	4.3	5.5	7.0	8.7	8.9	2.0	28	7	541	17
Micronesia Micronésie	0.2	0.2	0.3	0.4	0.5	0.5	0.5	1.2	20	5	3	181
Polynesia Polynésie	0.3	0.4	0.5	0.5	0.6	0.7	0.7	0.8	21	6	8	85

Source:
United Nations Statistics Division, New York, *Demographic Yearbook 2011*.

Source:
Organisation des Nations Unies, Division de statistique, New York, *Annuaire démographique 2011*.

1 Population per square kilometre of surface area. Figures are merely the quotients of population divided by surface area and are not to be considered either as reflecting density in the urban sense or as indicating the supporting power of a territory's land and resources.

2 Hawaii, a state of the United States of America, is included in Northern America rather than Oceania.

3 The European portion of Turkey is included in Western Asia rather than Europe.

1 Nombre d'habitants au kilomètre carré. Il s'agit simplement du quotient du chiffre de la population divisé par celui de la superficie, il ne faut pas y voir d'indication de la densité au sens urbain du terme ni de l'effectif de population que les terres et les ressources du territoire sont capables de nourrir.

2 Hawaii, un Etat des Etats-Unis d'Amérique, est compris en Amérique septentrionale plutôt qu'en Océanie.

3 La partie européenne de la Turquie est comprise en Asie Occidentale plutôt qu'en Europe.

3 Index numbers of total agricultural and food production
2004 – 2006 = 100

Indices de la production agricole totale et de la production alimentaire
2004 - 2006 = 100

Region, country or area	2001	2002	2003	2004	2005	2006	2007	2008	2009	2010
World Monde										
Agricultural - Agricole	**90**	**91**	**94**	**98**	**100**	**102**	**105**	**109**	**109**	**110**
Food - Alimentaire	**90**	**91**	**94**	**98**	**100**	**102**	**105**	**109**	**110**	**111**
Africa Afrique										
Agricultural - Agricole	85	88	93	96	100	104	103	109	110	112
Food - Alimentaire	84	88	93	96	100	105	103	110	111	113
Americas Amériques										
Agricultural - Agricole	90	90	94	99	100	101	106	107	106	109
Food - Alimentaire	90	91	95	99	100	101	107	108	107	110
Asia Asie										
Agricultural - Agricole	88	89	93	96	100	104	108	112	114	115
Food - Alimentaire	88	90	93	96	100	103	108	112	114	115
Europe Europe										
Agricultural - Agricole	98	98	96	103	99	98	97	102	102	98
Food - Alimentaire	98	98	96	103	99	98	97	102	102	98
Oceania Océanie										
Agricultural - Agricole	104	94	102	99	105	96	98	102	101	101
Food - Alimentaire	102	93	102	100	105	95	99	104	102	102

Source:
Food and Agriculture Organization of the United Nations (FAO), Rome, FAOSTAT data, last accessed March 2012.

Source:
Organisation des Nations Unies pour l'alimentation et l'agriculture (FAO), Rome, données FAOSTAT, dernier accès mars 2012.

4 Index numbers of per capita agricultural and food production
2004 – 2006 = 100

Indices de la production agricole totale et de la production alimentaire par habitant
2004 – 2006 = 100

Region, country or area	2001	2002	2003	2004	2005	2006	2007	2008	2009	2010
World Monde										
Agricultural – Agricole	**95**	**95**	**96**	**99**	**100**	**101**	**103**	**105**	**104**	**104**
Food - Alimentaire	**95**	**95**	**96**	**99**	**100**	**101**	**103**	**105**	**105**	**104**
Africa Afrique										
Agricultural - Agricole	93	95	97	98	100	102	99	102	101	100
Food - Alimentaire	93	94	97	98	100	102	99	103	101	101
Americas Amériques										
Agricultural - Agricole	94	94	96	100	100	100	104	104	102	104
Food - Alimentaire	94	94	97	100	100	100	104	104	102	104
Asia Asie										
Agricultural - Agricole	92	93	95	97	100	102	105	108	109	109
Food - Alimentaire	92	93	95	97	100	102	105	109	109	109
Europe Europe										
Agricultural - Agricole	99	99	96	103	99	98	97	102	101	97
Food - Alimentaire	99	99	96	103	99	98	97	102	101	97
Oceania Océanie										
Agricultural - Agricole	110	99	105	101	105	94	94	96	94	92
Food - Alimentaire	109	97	106	102	105	93	95	98	95	94

Source:
Food and Agriculture Organization of the United Nations (FAO), Rome, FAOSTAT data, last accessed March 2012.

Source:
Organisation des Nations Unies pour l'alimentation et l'agriculture (FAO), Rome, données FAOSTAT, dernier accès mars 2012.

5

Production, trade and consumption of commercial energy
Thousand metric tons of oil equivalent and kilograms per capita

Production, commerce et consommation d'énergie commerciale
Milliers de tonnes d'équivalent pétrole et kilogrammes par habitant

Region	Year Année	Primary energy production – Production d'énergie primaire					Changes in stocks Variations des stocks	Imports Importations	Exports Exportations
		Total Totale	Solids Solides	Liquids Liquides	Gas Gaz	Electricity Electricité			
World	2003	9 528 048	2 714 344	3 867 795	2 474 550	471 358	7 051	4 038 484	4 038 699
	2004	9 899 542	2 853 035	3 993 371	2 556 651	496 486	16 847	4 318 815	4 292 530
	2005	10 217 424	3 038 880	4 040 602	2 626 230	511 711	22 792	4 408 089	4 456 824
	2006	10 500 330	3 203 342	4 060 016	2 711 542	525 430	74 077	4 546 815	4 553 038
	2007	10 700 943	3 331 386	4 068 467	2 775 019	526 072	14 940	4 643 201	4 622 953
	2008	10 963 513	3 436 332	4 102 320	2 883 462	541 399	96 555	4 679 056	4 684 622
	2009	10 869 925	3 484 282	4 046 270	2 790 566	548 807	89 696	4 548 749	4 558 355
Africa	2003	713 399	129 466	439 729	135 640	8 565	1 455	90 621	480 562
	2004	764 795	131 541	479 660	144 562	9 031	-1 516	93 839	526 803
	2005	817 188	132 861	502 351	172 988	8 988	559	93 296	567 263
	2006	846 566	132 604	513 446	191 234	9 282	2 087	99 507	590 164
	2007	852 432	133 875	520 940	188 056	9 561	-3 305	114 443	596 877
	2008	862 888	135 058	527 202	190 920	9 708	3 021	106 245	587 340
	2009	833 836	134 673	507 517	181 597	10 049	-3 368	115 159	560 282
America, North	2003	2 112 197	562 365	692 591	720 490	136 752	-10 555	911 948	460 084
	2004	2 131 812	591 262	690 600	709 043	140 908	-1 780	969 660	476 010
	2005	2 119 583	602 726	670 688	702 444	143 725	-6 862	1 000 576	477 433
	2006	2 159 115	615 425	673 501	723 438	146 751	34 135	1 002 931	490 179
	2007	2 174 399	608 654	672 744	746 673	146 328	-17 145	1 012 384	509 064
	2008	2 190 461	619 037	653 293	767 782	150 350	4 188	982 662	529 473
	2009	2 156 588	566 528	667 310	772 269	150 480	29 686	898 214	512 786
America, South	2003	519 925	39 800	340 857	90 218	49 050	3 935	89 857	240 605
	2004	538 151	42 197	346 046	99 332	50 576	-688	104 749	262 553
	2005	563 801	46 520	362 153	101 801	53 327	-7 153	93 819	273 154
	2006	568 661	50 806	357 320	104 500	56 034	-950	99 296	266 919
	2007	563 033	53 686	348 683	103 035	57 628	5 813	108 139	252 899
	2008	575 120	55 462	353 949	107 735	57 976	1 311	108 275	250 823
	2009	605 377	56 350	385 836	103 301	59 890	6 884	101 555	275 087
Asia	2003	3 720 813	1 380 694	1 621 405	616 688	102 025	3 300	1 381 686	1 508 935
	2004	3 956 866	1 481 706	1 688 295	672 642	114 224	10 155	1 528 974	1 599 837
	2005	4 205 468	1 634 193	1 731 132	717 076	123 067	20 155	1 552 591	1 681 248
	2006	4 419 785	1 781 196	1 750 865	757 600	130 124	10 189	1 641 711	1 749 298
	2007	4 598 606	1 902 632	1 749 890	815 756	130 328	24 149	1 730 514	1 788 937
	2008	4 807 485	1 994 128	1 805 451	869 867	138 038	39 465	1 756 064	1 841 049
	2009	4 860 373	2 117 401	1 728 837	869 169	144 965	39 992	1 825 682	1 761 318
Europe	2003	2 187 254	404 018	739 886	872 306	171 044	8 954	1 526 302	1 168 360
	2004	2 228 173	400 311	758 774	891 557	177 531	10 617	1 583 122	1 242 491
	2005	2 220 368	405 542	747 416	888 721	178 690	15 428	1 626 221	1 264 641
	2006	2 212 781	405 075	738 623	889 903	179 180	27 873	1 659 391	1 262 001
	2007	2 202 055	402 329	747 676	873 906	178 144	-2 493	1 630 636	1 271 247
	2008	2 214 412	399 357	734 285	899 317	181 453	46 694	1 675 135	1 262 958
	2009	2 090 808	370 056	727 269	814 275	179 209	14 871	1 557 480	1 228 062
Oceania	2003	274 459	198 001	33 328	39 208	3 922	-38	38 070	180 153
	2004	279 745	206 018	29 995	39 516	4 217	59	38 470	184 836
	2005	291 015	217 037	26 863	43 200	3 914	664	41 586	193 086
	2006	293 422	218 236	26 260	44 866	4 059	744	43 978	194 477
	2007	310 419	230 212	28 533	47 593	4 082	7 920	47 086	203 928
	2008	313 146	233 290	28 141	47 842	3 874	1 877	50 676	212 979
	2009	322 944	239 275	29 501	49 955	4 213	1 630	50 659	220 820

Source:
United Nations Statistics Division, New York, the energy statistics database, last accessed June 2012.

5

Production, trade and consumption of commercial energy
Thousand metric tons of oil equivalent and kilograms per capita

Production, commerce et consommation d'énergie commerciale
Milliers de tonnes d'équivalent pétrole et kilogrammes par habitant

Air Avion	Sea Maritime	Unallocated Non distribué	Per capita Par habitant	Total Totale	Solids Solides	Liquids Liquides	Gas Gaz	Electricity Electricité	Year Année	Région
Bunkers - Soutes				**Consumption - Consommation**						
114 809	146 997	480 766	1 381	8 778 210	2 739 860	3 090 843	2 475 889	471 618	2003	Monde
122 799	162 152	509 920	1 417	9 114 108	2 877 442	3 188 382	2 551 536	496 748	2004	
130 705	162 029	497 049	1 438	9 356 112	3 001 056	3 222 779	2 620 351	511 926	2005	
135 265	173 266	501 257	1 460	9 610 242	3 165 759	3 248 766	2 669 916	525 801	2006	
143 786	182 416	500 754	1 483	9 879 297	3 284 918	3 271 392	2 796 295	526 691	2007	
142 321	180 374	475 364	1 493	10 063 334	3 362 319	3 288 746	2 870 051	542 217	2008	
134 938	178 745	468 001	1 465	9 988 939	3 373 678	3 256 113	2 808 590	550 559	2009	
5 352	7 191	21 985	330	287 476	96 647	113 944	68 101	8 784	2003	Afrique
4 495	6 191	22 109	337	300 551	103 380	115 370	72 572	9 228	2004	
4 893	5 993	14 508	348	317 268	102 013	117 852	88 228	9 175	2005	
4 821	5 458	21 712	345	321 831	103 557	120 943	87 681	9 650	2006	
9 407	5 590	21 529	353	336 776	106 108	131 044	89 430	10 194	2007	
5 713	2 754	22 827	356	347 479	108 471	136 058	92 472	10 478	2008	
5 777	2 683	31 162	353	352 459	112 002	137 446	92 136	10 875	2009	
24 593	23 924	70 953	4 871	2 455 147	574 386	1 024 786	719 315	136 661	2003	Amérique du Nord
25 500	29 402	73 533	4 906	2 498 809	590 274	1 056 122	711 529	140 884	2004	
27 314	30 426	64 961	4 909	2 526 887	598 389	1 072 929	711 850	143 719	2005	
27 639	32 518	64 630	4 830	2 512 945	590 488	1 062 457	713 356	146 645	2006	
28 297	35 148	59 890	4 892	2 571 528	592 337	1 068 494	764 422	146 275	2007	
28 340	30 808	28 563	4 804	2 551 752	583 677	1 046 574	771 114	150 387	2008	
25 666	28 770	18 280	4 546	2 439 614	518 913	1 006 093	764 144	150 463	2009	
3 303	6 024	37 982	878	317 933	20 293	158 583	90 155	48 902	2003	Amérique du Sud
4 236	6 378	22 836	947	347 585	20 438	175 969	100 634	50 543	2004	
4 157	7 096	28 979	946	351 387	21 169	174 560	102 208	53 450	2005	
4 174	7 146	26 060	970	364 609	21 362	180 964	106 064	56 219	2006	
3 878	8 072	25 194	987	375 315	22 480	191 686	103 317	57 832	2007	
4 687	9 617	21 572	1 029	395 386	24 167	204 306	108 755	58 159	2008	
4 794	8 703	21 445	1 004	390 018	20 606	203 811	105 458	60 144	2009	
34 558	60 654	273 425	835	3 221 626	1 488 667	1 018 896	611 984	102 078	2003	Asie
38 538	67 680	311 814	886	3 457 816	1 610 484	1 070 927	662 150	114 256	2004	
41 335	63 902	307 898	924	3 643 521	1 735 763	1 088 112	696 567	123 079	2005	
43 680	70 508	314 066	971	3 873 755	1 889 312	1 103 069	751 021	130 353	2006	
45 748	75 674	309 404	1 013	4 085 209	2 006 241	1 126 765	821 915	130 289	2007	
45 823	79 466	308 819	1 042	4 248 926	2 102 738	1 136 643	871 321	138 225	2008	
44 668	86 199	317 829	1 077	4 436 048	2 245 090	1 163 523	881 693	145 742	2009	
43 723	48 061	78 118	3 248	2 366 341	506 784	730 991	957 295	171 272	2003	Europe
46 936	51 299	82 354	3 259	2 377 597	498 507	726 052	975 419	177 620	2004	
49 367	53 311	82 577	3 259	2 381 266	486 939	723 681	992 058	178 588	2005	
51 238	56 217	74 642	3 278	2 400 203	503 149	736 359	981 819	178 876	2006	
52 402	56 671	84 338	3 231	2 370 524	500 799	708 575	983 131	178 019	2007	
53 767	56 326	94 178	3 231	2 375 624	485 904	717 135	991 491	181 094	2008	
50 069	51 139	80 465	3 018	2 223 681	419 257	695 669	929 632	179 122	2009	
3 280	1 145	-1 697	4 013	129 686	53 082	43 643	29 039	3 922	2003	Océanie
3 095	1 201	-2 726	4 015	131 751	54 359	43 943	29 232	4 217	2004	
3 640	1 302	-1 874	4 071	135 783	56 783	45 645	29 441	3 914	2005	
3 712	1 419	149	4 034	136 899	57 892	44 974	29 975	4 059	2006	
4 053	1 261	399	4 051	139 943	56 954	44 829	34 079	4 082	2007	
3 992	1 403	-594	4 098	144 166	57 363	48 031	34 898	3 874	2008	
3 964	1 251	-1 180	4 108	147 118	57 810	49 569	35 526	4 213	2009	

Source:

Organisation des Nations Unies, Division de statistique, New York, la base de données pour les statistiques énergétiques, dernier accès juin 2012.

6

Total imports and exports: index numbers
Volume and unit value indices and terms of trade (2000 = 100)

Importations et exportations totales : indices
Indices du volume et de la valeur unitaire et termes de l'échange (2000 = 100)

Region	2004	2005	2006	2007	2008	2009	2010	2011	Région
Total									**Total**
Imports : Volume [1]	**124**	**134**	**145**	**152**	**155**	**133**	**157**	**163**	**Imp. : Volume** [1]
Imports : Unit value indices US $ [2]	**114**	**120**	**127**	**138**	**157**	**141**	**145**	**165**	**Imp.: Indices de la val. unit. en $ E.-U.** [2]
Exports : Volume [1]	**122**	**133**	**148**	**158**	**165**	**142**	**166**	**180**	**Exp. : Volume** [1]
Exports : Unit value indices US $ [2]	**116**	**121**	**126**	**136**	**148**	**135**	**140**	**153**	**Exp.: Indices de la val. unit. en $ E.-U.** [2]
Developed economies [3]									**Economies développées** [3]
Imports : Volume [1]	118	126	136	140	139	120	134	138	Imp.: Volume [1]
Imports : Unit value indices US $ [2]	116	122	128	140	157	137	144	162	Imp.: Indices de la val. unit. en $ E.-U. [2]
Exports : Volume [1]	113	118	129	135	137	116	131	138	Exp.: Volume [1]
Exports : Unit value indices US $ [2]	121	126	131	143	157	143	147	163	Exp.: Indices de la val. unit. en $ E.-U. [2]
Terms of trade [4]	104	104	102	102	100	105	103	101	Termes de l'échange [4]
North America									**Amérique du Nord**
Imports : Volume [1]	117	124	130	132	128	107	123	128	Imp.: Volume [1]
Imports : Unit value indices US $ [2]	103	111	116	121	135	120	128	142	Imp.: Indices de la val. unit. en $ E.-U. [2]
Exports : Volume [1]	99	106	115	121	126	106	121	130	Exp.: Volume [1]
Exports : Unit value indices US $ [2]	107	113	117	124	132	122	130	141	Exp.: Indices de la val. unit. en $ E.-U. [2]
Terms of trade [4]	104	102	101	102	98	101	101	99	Termes de l'échange [4]
Europe									**Europe**
Imports : Volume [1]	118	126	139	145	146	128	141	145	Imp.: Volume [1]
Imports : Unit value indices US $ [2]	127	130	137	152	169	146	150	169	Imp.: Indices de la val. unit. en $ E.-U. [2]
Exports : Volume [1]	118	124	136	142	143	124	138	146	Exp.: Volume [1]
Exports : Unit value indices US $ [2]	130	134	138	154	170	152	152	169	Exp.: Indices de la val. unit. en $ E.-U. [2]
Terms of trade [4]	102	103	101	102	101	104	102	100	Termes de l'échange [4]
Asia and the Pacific									**Asie et le Pacifique**
Imports : Volume [1]	122	127	134	132	133	116	127	129	Imp.: Volume [1]
Imports : Unit value indices US $ [2]	104	113	120	133	162	137	157	189	Imp.: Indices de la val. unit. en $ E.-U. [2]
Exports : Volume [1]	112	113	121	127	126	97	116	112	Exp.: Volume [1]
Exports : Unit value indices US $ [2]	108	115	117	124	143	141	157	182	Exp.: Indices de la val. unit. en $ E.-U. [2]
Terms of trade [4]	104	101	98	93	88	103	100	96	Termes de l'échange [4]
Africa									**Afrique**
Imports : Volume [1]	123	143	...	...	...	...	...	...	Imp.: Volume [1]
Imports : Unit value indices US $ [2]	131	137	...	...	...	...	...	...	Imp.: Indices de la val. unit. en $ E.-U. [2]
Exports : Volume [1]	132	177	206	237	327	228	273	345	Exp.: Volume [1]
Exports : Unit value indices US $ [2]	122	123	123	127	122	119	127	128	Exp.: Indices de la val. unit. en $ E.-U. [2]
Terms of trade [4]	93	90	...	...	...	...	...	...	Termes de l'échange [4]
Northern Africa									**Afrique du Nord**
Imports : Volume [1]	166	180	182	206	285	282	319	340	Imp.: Volume [1]
Imports : Unit value indices US $ [2]	87	95	101	117	123	111	108	116	Imp.: Indices de la val. unit. en $ E.-U. [2]
Exports : Volume [1]	160	220	257	280	360	236	295	349	Exp.: Volume [1]
Exports : Unit value indices US $ [2]	99	100	102	110	116	114	112	116	Exp.: Indices de la val. unit. en $ E.-U. [2]
Terms of trade [4]	114	105	101	94	94	103	104	100	Termes de l'échange [4]
Sub-Saharan Africa									**Afrique subsaharienne**
Exports : Volume [1]	114	147	168	204	303	221	252	332	Exp.: Volume [1]
Exports : Unit value indices US $ [2]	141	149	148	146	128	124	140	140	Exp.: Indices de la val. unit. en $ E.-U. [2]
Latin America and the Caribbean									**Amérique latine et Caraïbes**
Imports : Volume [1]	114	113	122	132	130	103	126	142	Imp.: Volume [1]
Imports : Unit value indices US $ [2]	101	121	134	148	184	175	184	193	Imp.: Indices de la val. unit. en $ E.-U. [2]
Exports : Volume [1]	119	135	149	161	168	143	171	210	Exp.: Volume [1]
Exports : Unit value indices US $ [2]	110	118	127	134	149	134	144	142	Exp.: Indices de la val. unit. en $ E.-U. [2]
Terms of trade [4]	108	97	95	90	81	77	78	74	Termes de l'échange [4]
Latin America									**Amérique latine**
Exports : Volume [1]	119	134	148	159	166	143	171	209	Exp.: Volume [1]
Exports : Unit value indices US $ [2]	110	118	127	134	150	135	144	143	Exp.: Indices de la val. unit. en $ E.-U. [2]
Western Asia									**Asie occidentale**
Imports : Volume [1]	135	151	163	188	196	191	205	214	Imp.: Volume [1]
Imports : Unit value indices US $ [2,5]	123	133	144	158	187	154	167	193	Imp.: Indices de la val. unit. en $ E.-U. [2,5]
Exports : Volume [1]	137	168	192	202	228	185	225	270	Exp.: Volume [1]
Exports : Unit value indices US $ [2,5]	117	126	131	145	170	148	154	169	Exp.: Indices de la val. unit. en $ E.-U. [2,5]
Terms of trade [4]	95	95	91	92	91	96	92	87	Termes de l'échange [4]

6

Total imports and exports: index numbers *(continued)*
Volume and unit value indices and terms of trade (2000 = 100)

Importations et exportations totales : indices *(suite)*
Indices du volume et de la valeur unitaire et termes de l'échange (2000 = 100)

Region	2004	2005	2006	2007	2008	2009	2010	2011	Région
Other Asia									**Autre Asie**
Imports : Volume [1]	150	167	185	200	...	...	237	241	Imp.: Volume [1]
Imports : Unit value indices US $ [2]	105	110	116	124	...	...	138	165	Imp.: Indices de la val. unit. en $ E.-U. [2]
Exports : Volume [1]	156	181	208	235	254	231	274	295	Exp.: Volume [1]
Exports : Unit value indices US $ [2]	99	101	105	109	116	106	116	128	Exp.: Indices de la val. unit. en $ E.-U. [2]
Terms of trade [4]	94	92	90	88	...	...	84	78	Termes de l'échange [4]
Eastern Asia									**Asie orientale**
Imports : Volume [1]	160	173	192	214	218	213	262	280	Imp.: Volume [1]
Imports : Unit value indices US $ [2]	104	109	115	120	136	117	129	147	Imp.: Indices de la val. unit. en $ E.-U. [2]
Exports : Volume [1]	170	198	234	272	292	275	329	357	Exp.: Volume [1]
Exports : Unit value indices US $ [2]	98	100	101	103	109	97	106	115	Exp.: Indices de la val. unit. en $ E.-U. [2]
Terms of trade [4]	94	91	87	86	80	83	82	78	Termes de l'échange [4]
Southern Asia									**Asie australe**
Imports : Volume [1]	140	175	216	205	277	259	310	241	Imp.: Volume [1]
Imports : Unit value indices US $ [2]	132	142	137	177	177	155	170	285	Imp.: Indices de la val. unit. en $ E.-U. [2]
Exports : Volume [1]	135	163	182	199	259	202	220	242	Exp.: Volume [1]
Exports : Unit value indices US $ [2]	119	126	141	153	149	154	185	223	Exp.: Indices de la val. unit. en $ E.-U. [2]
Terms of trade [4]	90	88	103	87	84	100	108	78	Termes de l'échange [4]
South-eastern Asia									**Asie du Sud-est**
Imports : Volume [1]	130	143	151	164	181	151	184	199	Imp.: Volume [1]
Imports : Unit value indices US $ [2]	101	110	120	125	138	127	137	153	Imp.: Indices de la val. unit. en $ E.-U. [2]
Exports : Volume [1]	137	153	170	182	193	170	203	221	Exp.: Volume [1]
Exports : Unit value indices US $ [2]	96	99	105	110	120	111	120	130	Exp.: Indices de la val. unit. en $ E.-U. [2]
Terms of trade [4]	95	89	88	88	87	87	88	85	Termes de l'échange [4]

Source:
United Nations Statistics Division, New York, trade statistics database, last accessed October 2012.

Source:
Organisation des Nations Unies, Division de statistique, New York, la base de données pour les statistiques du commerce extérieur, dernier accès octobre 2012.

1 Volume indices are derived from value data and unit value indices. They are base-period weighted.

2 Regional aggregates are current-period weighted.

3 This classification is intended for statistical convenience and does not, necessarily, express a judgement about the stage reached by a particular country in the development process.

4 Unit value index of exports divided by unit value index of imports.

5 Index does not include data for the major oil producing countries.

1 Les indices du volume sont calculés à partir des chiffres de la valeur et des indices de valeur unitaire. Ils sont à coefficients de pondération correspondant à la période en base.

2 Les totaux régionaux sont à coefficients de pondération correspondant à la période en cours.

3 Cette classification est utilisée pour plus de commodité dans la présentation des statistiques et n'implique pas nécessairement un jugement quant au stade de développement auquel est parvenu un pays donné.

4 Indice de la valeur unitaire des exportations divisé par l'indice de la valeur unitaire des importations.

5 L'index n'inclut pas de données des pays producteurs de pétrole importants.

Part Two

Population and social statistics

Part Two of the *Yearbook* presents statistical series on a wide range of population and social topics for all countries or areas of the world for which data have been made available. The topics include population and population growth, surface area and density; gender; education; food supply and undernourished population; cellular mobile phones, internet subscriptions and cinema infrastructure.

Deuxième partie

Population et statistiques sociales

La deuxième partie de l'*Annuaire* présente, pour tous les pays ou zones du monde pour lesquels des données sont disponibles, des séries statistiques concernant une large gamme de questions démographiques et sociales : population et croissance démographique, superficie et densité ; éducation ; disponibilités alimentaires et population n'atteignant pas le niveau minimal d'apport calorique; abonnés au téléphone mobile, abonnements à l'internet et exploitation cinématographique.

7

Population by sex, rate of population increase, surface area and density

Population selon le sexe, taux d'accroissement de la population, superficie et densité

Country or area[+] Pays ou zone[+]	Date	Latest census Dernier recensement Both sexes Les deux sexes	Men Hommes	Women Femmes	Mid-year estimates Estimations au milieu de l'année ('000) 2005	2011	Annual rate of increase Taux d'accroiss- ement annuel % 2005-11	Surface area Superficie (Km[2]) 2011	Density[&] Densité[&] 2011
Africa · Afrique									
Algeria Algérie	16 IV 2008	*34 452 759[1]	17 428 500[1]	*17 024 259[1]	32 906[1]	*36 717[1]	1.8	2 381 741	15
Angola Angola	15 XII 1970	5 646 166	2 943 974	2 702 192	...	...	...	1 246 700	...
Benin Bénin	11 II 2002	6 769 914[1]	3 284 119[1]	3 485 795[1]	7 447[2]	9 067[2]	3.3	114 763	79
Botswana Botswana	17 VIII 2001	1 680 863	813 625	867 238	1 708[1]	1 850[1]	1.3	582 000	3
Burkina Faso Burkina Faso	9 XII 2006	14 196 259	6 842 560	7 353 699	13 374[1]	...	...	272 967	...
Burundi Burundi	16 VIII 2008	7 877 728	3 838 045	4 039 683	...	...	...	27 834	...
Cameroon Cameroun	11 XI 2005	17 052 134	8 408 495	8 643 639	...	19 865[1,3]	...	475 650	42
Cape Verde Cap-Vert	16 VI 2010	*491 575[1]	*243 315[1]	*248 260[1]	475	527	1.7	4 033	131
Central African Rep. Rép. centrafricaine	8 XIII 2003	3 151 072	1 569 446	1 581 626	...	...	...	622 984	...
Chad Tchad	8 IV 1993	6 158 992	2 950 415	3 208 577	...	...	...	1 284 000	...
Comoros Comores	1 IX 2003	575 660[4]	...	...	...	...	...	2 235	...
Congo Congo	28 IV 2007	3 697 490	1 821 357	1 876 133	3 488[2]	...	...	342 000	...
Côte d'Ivoire Côte d'Ivoire	21 XI 1998	15 366 672	7 844 621	7 522 050	*19 097	...	...	322 463	...
Dem. Rep. of the Congo Rép. dém. du Congo	1 VII 1984	29 916 800	14 543 800	15 373 000	...	...	...	2 344 858	...
Djibouti Djibouti	29 V 2009	*818 159	...	...	...	...	...	23 200	...
Egypt Egypte	21 XI 2006	72 798 031	37 219 056	35 578 975	70 653	80 410	2.2	1 002 000	80
Equatorial Guinea Guinée équatoriale	1 II 2002	1 014 999	501 387	513 612	...	...	...	28 051	...
Eritrea Erythrée	9 V 1984	2 748 304	1 374 452	1 373 852	...	...	...	117 600	...
Ethiopia Ethiopie	29 V 2007	73 750 932	37 217 130	36 533 802	73 044[5]	...	...	1 104 300	...
Gabon Gabon	1 XII 2003	*1 269 000	...	...	1 313[6]	...	...	267 668	...
Gambia Gambie	15 IV 2003	1 360 681	...	...	1 436	...	...	11 295	...
Ghana Ghana	26 IX 2010	*24 223 431	*11 801 661	*12 421 770	21 367	...	...	238 533	...
Guinea Guinée	1 XII 1996	7 156 406	3 497 979	3 658 427	...	...	...	245 857	...

Population by sex, rate of population increase, surface area and density *(continued)*
Population selon le sexe, taux d'accroissement de la population, superficie et densité *(suite)*

| Country or area[+]
Pays ou zone[+] | Date | Latest census
Dernier recensement | | | Mid-year estimates
Estimations au milieu
de l'année
('000) | | Annual rate
of increase
Taux
d'accroiss-
ement
annuel
% | Surface
area
Superficie
(Km[2]) | Density[&]
Densité[&] |
		Both sexes Les deux sexes	Men Hommes	Women Femmes	2005	2011	2005-11	2011	2011
Guinea-Bissau Guinée-Bissau	15 III 2009	1 520 830	737 634	783 196	1 326[2]	...	...	36 125	...
Kenya Kenya	24 VIII 2009	38 610 097	19 192 458	19 417 639	35 267[7]	*41 745	2.8	581 313	72
Lesotho Lesotho	13 IV 2006	1 741 406	818 379	923 027	...	1 897[2]	...	30 355	62
Liberia Libéria	21 III 2008	3 476 608	1 739 945	1 736 663	...	...	...	111 369	...
Libyan Arab Jamah. Jam. arabe libyenne	15 IV 2006	*5 657 692	*2 934 452	*2 723 240	...	...	...	1 759 540	...
Madagascar Madagascar	1 VIII 1993	12 238 914	6 088 116	6 150 798	17 550	20 696	2.7	587 295	35
Malawi Malawi	8 VI 2008	13 077 160	6 358 933	6 718 227	12 341[2]	15 034[2]	3.3	118 484	127
Mali Mali	1 IV 2009	*14 517 176[1]	*7 202 744[1]	*7 314 432[1]	11 732[8]	...	...	1 240 192	...
Mauritania Mauritanie	1 XI 2000	2 508 159	1 241 712	1 266 447	2 906[2]	3 297[2]	2.1	1 030 700	3
Mauritius[9] Maurice[9]	2 VII 2000	1 178 848[1]	583 756[1]	595 092[1]	1 243[1]	1 286[1]	0.6	1 969	653
Mayotte[1] Mayotte[1]	31 VII 2007	186 387	91 405	94 982	...	...	...	...	...
Morocco Maroc	1 IX 2004	29 680 069	14 640 662	15 039 407	30 172[10]	32 245[10]	1.1	446 550	72
Mozambique Mozambique	1 VIII 2007	20 252 223	9 746 690	10 505 533	19 420[2]	...	...	801 590	...
Namibia Namibie	27 VIII 2001	1 830 330	887 721[11]	942 572[11]	1 957[2]	...	...	824 268	...
Niger Niger	20 V 2001	11 060 291[1]	5 516 588[1]	5 543 703[1]	12 628[1,2]	15 731[1,2]	3.7	1 267 000	12
Nigeria Nigéria	21 III 2006	140 431 790	71 345 488	69 086 302	133 767[2]	...	...	923 768	...
Réunion Réunion	1 I 2006	781 962[1]	379 176[1]	402 786[1]	777[1]	*839[1,8]	1.3	2 513	334
Rwanda Rwanda	16 VIII 2002	8 128 553[1]	3 879 448[1]	4 249 105[1]	9 225[2]	10 718[2]	2.5	26 340[12]	407
Saint Helena ex. dep. S.-Hélène sans dép.	10 II 2008	4 257	2 165	2 092	...	...	...	122	...
Ascension Ascension	8 III 1998	712[1]	458[1]	254[1]	...	...	...	88	...
Tristan da Cunha Tristan da Cunha	31 XII 1988	296	139	157	...	...	...	98	...
Sao Tome and Principe Sao Tomé-et-Principe	25 VIII 2001	136 554	67 422	69 132	149	...	...	964	...
Senegal Sénégal	8 XII 2002	9 555 346	4 672 015	4 883 331	10 901[1,13]	12 842[1,13]	2.7	196 712[14]	65
Seychelles Seychelles	26 VIII 2002	81 755[1,15]	40 751[1,15]	41 004[1,15]	83	87	0.9	452	194
Sierra Leone Sierra Leone	4 XII 2004	4 976 871	2 420 218	2 556 653	5 095	5 890	2.4	72 300	81

Population by sex, rate of population increase, surface area and density *(continued)*
Population selon le sexe, taux d'accroissement de la population, superficie et densité *(suite)*

Country or area[+] Pays ou zone[+]	Date	Latest census Dernier recensement Both sexes Les deux sexes	Men Hommes	Women Femmes	Mid-year estimates Estimations au milieu de l'année ('000) 2005	2011	Annual rate of increase Taux d'accroiss- ement annuel % 2005-11	Surface area Superficie (Km[2]) 2011	Density[&] Densité[&] 2011
Somalia Somalie	15 II 1987	7 114 431	3 741 664	3 372 767	...	...	...	637 657	...
South Africa Afrique du Sud	10 X 2001	44 819 778	21 434 041	23 385 737	47 177[16]	50 587[16]	1.2	1 221 037	41
Swaziland Swaziland	11 III 2007	844 223	405 868	438 355	1 126	1 068	-0.9	17 363	61
Togo Togo	6 XI 2010	6 191 155[1]	3 009 095[1]	3 182 060[1]	5 212	...	...	56 785	...
Tunisia Tunisie	28 IV 2004	9 910 872	4 965 435	4 945 437	10 029	10 674	1.0	163 610	65
Uganda Ouganda	12 IX 2002	24 442 084	11 929 803	12 512 281	26 741	32 940	3.5	241 550	136
U. Rep. of Tanzania R.-Unie de Tanzanie	24 VIII 2002	*34 443 603	*16 829 861	*17 613 742	37 379	...	...	945 087	...
Western Sahara [17] Sahara occidental [17]	31 XII 1970	76 425	43 981	32 444	...	...	...	266 000	...
Zambia Zambie	16 X 2010	*13 046 508	*6 394 455	*6 652 053	11 441[2]	...	...	752 612	...
Zimbabwe Zimbabwe	17 VIII 2002	11 631 657	5 634 180	5 997 477	11 830[18]	...	...	390 757	...
America, North · Amérique du Nord									
Anguilla Anguilla	9 V 2001	11 430[19]	5 628[19]	5 802[19]	14	17	3.4	91	184
Antigua and Barbuda Antigua-et-Barbuda	28 V 2001	76 886	36 107	40 779	83	...	...	442	...
Aruba Aruba	29 IX 2010	101 484[1]	48 241[1]	53 243[1]	101[1]	103[1]	0.3	180	571
Bahamas Bahamas	3 V 2010	*353 658	*170 926	*182 732	325[2]	351[2]	1.3	13 943	25
Barbados Barbade	1 V 2000	250 010	119 926	130 084	273	...	...	430	...
Belize Belize	12 V 2010	*312 698	*157 935	*154 763	292	...	...	22 966	...
Bermuda Bermudes	20 V 2000	62 059[1,20]	29 802[1,20]	32 257[1,20]	64[1]	65[1]	0.3	53	1 221
British Virgin Islands Iles Vierges brit.	21 V 2001	20 647	10 627	10 020	...	...	...	151	...
Canada Canada	16 V 2006	31 612 895[1,21]	15 475 970[1,21]	16 136 930[1,21]	32 245[1,22]	*34 483[1]	1.1	9 984 670	3
Cayman Islands Iles Caïmanes	10 X 2010	55 036[1,20]	27 218[1,20]	27 818[1,20]	48[1]	*55[1]	2.2	264	209
Costa Rica Costa Rica	30 V 2011	*4 301 712[1]	*2 106 063[1]	*2 195 649[1]	4 266[1]	4 616[1,2]	1.3	51 100	90
Cuba Cuba	7 IX 2002	11 177 743[1]	5 597 233[1]	5 580 510[1]	11 243[1]	11 245[1]	^0.0	109 884	102
Dominica Dominique	14 V 2011	*71 293	*36 411	*34 882	71	69	-0.4	751	92
Dominican Republic Rép. dominicaine	1 XII 2010	*9 445 281[1]	*4 739 038[1]	*4 706 243[1]	9 226[2]	10 011[2]	1.4	48 671	206

Population by sex, rate of population increase, surface area and density *(continued)*
Population selon le sexe, taux d'accroissement de la population, superficie et densité *(suite)*

Country or area[+] Pays ou zone[+]	Date	Latest census Dernier recensement			Mid-year estimates Estimations au milieu de l'année ('000)		Annual rate of increase Taux d'accroiss- ement annuel %	Surface area Superficie (Km²)	Density[&] Densité[&]
		Both sexes Les deux sexes	Men Hommes	Women Femmes	2005	2011	2005-11	2011	2011
El Salvador El Salvador	12 V 2007	5 744 113[1]	2 719 371[1]	3 024 742[1]	6 049[23]	...	...	21 041[24]	...
Greenland Groenland	1 I 2008	56 462[1,25]	29 885[1,25]	26 577[1,25]	57[1,25]	57[1,25]	-0.1	2 166 086	^0
Grenada Grenade	25 V 2001	102 632	50 481	52 151	...	...	...	344	...
Guadeloupe Guadeloupe	1 I 2006	400 736[1,26]	188 720[1,26]	212 016[1,26]	446[1]	*402[1]	-1.7	1 705	236
Guatemala Guatemala	24 XI 2002	11 237 196[1]	5 496 839[1]	5 740 357[1]	12 701[1,27]	...	...	108 889	...
Haiti Haïti	11 I 2003	8 373 750[1]	4 039 272[1]	4 334 478[1]	9 292[1,28]	10 248[1,28]	1.6	27 750	369
Honduras Honduras	28 VII 2001	6 071 200	3 000 530	3 070 670	7 197[29]	8 215[29]	2.2	112 492	73
Jamaica Jamaïque	10 IX 2001	2 607 632[1,30]	1 283 548[1,30]	1 324 084[1,30]	2 650[1]	*2 706[1]	0.3	10 991	246
Martinique Martinique	1 I 2006	397 732[1]	185 604[1]	212 128[1]	396[1,8]	*396[1]	0.0	1 128	351
Mexico Mexique	12 VI 2010	112 336 538[31]	54 855 231[31]	57 481 307[31]	103 947[1,2]	...	...	1 964 375	...
Montserrat Montserrat	12 V 2001	4 491	2 418	2 073	5	...	...	102	...
Nicaragua Nicaragua	4 VI 2005	5 142 098[1]	2 534 491[1]	2 607 607[1]	5 450[1]	5 889[1]	1.3	130 373	45
Panama Panama	16 V 2010	3 405 813	1 712 584	1 693 229	3 228[32]	3 643[33]	2.0	75 417	48
Puerto Rico Porto Rico	1 IV 2010	*3 725 789[1,34]	*1 785 171[1,34]	*1 940 618[1,34]	3 912[1,34]	3 707[1,35]	-0.9	8 870	418
Saint Kitts and Nevis Saint-Kitts-et-Nevis	14 V 2001	45 841	22 784	23 057	*49	...	...	261	...
Saint Lucia Sainte-Lucie	10 V 2010	*173 720	*86 595	*87 125	164	...	...	539[36]	...
St. Pierre and Miquelon St.-Pierre-et-Miquelon	19 I 2006	6 125	3 034	3 091	...	...	...	242	...
St. Vincent-Grenadines Saint Vincent-Gren.	14 V 2001	109 022[37]	55 456[37]	53 566[37]	104	...	...	389	...
Trinidad and Tobago Trinité-et-Tobago	9 I 2011	*1 324 699	*665 119	*659 580	1 294[38]	...	...	5 130	...
Turks and Caicos Is. Iles Turq. et Caïques	10 IX 2001	19 886	9 897	9 989	31	...	...	948[39]	...
United States Etats-Unis	1 IV 2010	308 745 538[1,40]	151 781 326[1,40]	156 964 212[1,40]	295 753[1,40]	*311 592[1,40]	0.9	9 629 091	32
United States Virgin Is. Iles Vierges améric.	1 IV 2000	108 612[1,34]	51 864[1,34]	56 748[1,34]	110[1,34]	...	...	347	...
America, South · Amérique du Sud									
Argentina Argentine	27 X 2010	40 117 096	19 523 766	20 593 330	38 592[41]	40 900[41]	1.0	2 780 400	15
Bolivia (Plurin. State of) Bolivie (État plur. de)	5 IX 2001	8 274 325	4 123 850	4 150 475	9 427	10 624	2.0	1 098 581[42]	10

Population by sex, rate of population increase, surface area and density *(continued)*
Population selon le sexe, taux d'accroissement de la population, superficie et densité *(suite)*

Country or area[+] Pays ou zone[+]	Date	Latest census Dernier recensement Both sexes Les deux sexes	Men Hommes	Women Femmes	Mid-year estimates Estimations au milieu de l'année ('000) 2005	2011	Annual rate of increase Taux d'accroiss- ement annuel % 2005-11	Surface area Superficie (Km^2) 2011	Density[&] Densité[&] 2011
Brazil Brésil	1 VIII 2010	*190 755 799[1,43]	*93 406 990[1,43]	*97 348 809[1,43]	183 383[1,43]	192 376[1,43]	0.8	8 514 877	23
Chile Chili	24 IV 2002	15 116 435	7 447 695	7 668 740	16 267	17 248	1.0	756 102	23
Colombia Colombie	22 V 2005	41 468 384	20 336 117	21 132 267	42 889[44]	46 044[44]	1.2	1 141 748	40
Ecuador Equateur	28 XI 2010	*14 483 499	*7 177 683	*7 305 816	13 215[45]	15 248[45]	2.4	256 369	59
Falkland Is. (Malvinas)[46] Iles Falk. (Malvinas)[46]	8 X 2006	2 955	1 569	1 386	...	...	...	12 173	...
French Guiana Guyane française	1 I 2006	205 954[1]	101 930[1]	104 023[1]	199[1,8]	...	...	83 534	...
Guyana Guyana	15 IX 2002	751 223	376 034	375 189	758	...	...	214 969	...
Paraguay Paraguay	28 VIII 2002	5 163 198	2 603 242	2 559 956	5 899[18]	...	...	406 752	...
Peru Pérou	21 X 2007	27 412 157	13 622 640	13 789 517	27 811	29 798	1.2	1 285 216	23
Suriname Suriname	2 VIII 2004	492 829[1]	248 046[1]	244 783[1]	499[1]	540[1]	1.3	163 820	3
Uruguay Uruguay	1 VI 2004	3 241 003[47]	1 565 533[47]	1 675 470[47]	3 306[2]	*3 369	0.3	176 215	19
Venezuela (Bol. Rep. of) Venezuela (R. Bol. du)	30 X 2001	23 054 210[48]	11 402 869[48]	11 651 341[48]	26 577[49]	29 278[49]	1.6	912 050	32
Asia · Asie									
Afghanistan Afghanistan	23 VI 1979	13 051 358[50]	6 712 377[50]	6 338 981[50]	22 098[51]	...	...	652 864	...
Armenia Arménie	10 X 2001	3 002 594[52]	1 407 220[52]	1 595 374[52]	3 218[1]	3 268[1]	0.3	29 743	110
Azerbaijan Azerbaïdjan	13 IV 2009	8 922 447[1]	4 414 398[1]	4 508 049[1]	8 500[53]	9 059	1.1	86 600	105
Bahrain Bahreïn	27 IV 2010	1 234 571[1]	768 414[1]	466 157[1]	889	...	...	758	...
Bangladesh Bangladesh	15 III 2011	*149 772 364	*74 980 386	*74 791 978	138 600	...	...	147 570	...
Bhutan Bhoutan	30 V 2005	634 982	333 595	301 387	...	708[54]	...	38 394	18
Brunei Darussalam Brunéi Darussalam	21 VIII 2001	*332 844	*168 974	*163 870	370	...	...	5 765	...
Cambodia Cambodge	3 III 2008	13 395 682[55]	6 516 054[55]	6 879 628[55]	13 807[56]	14 521[57]	0.8	181 035	80
China Chine	1 XI 2010	*1 339 724 852[1,58]	*686 852 572[1,58]	*652 872 280[1,58]	1 307 560[1,59]	1 344 100[1,60]	0.5	9 596 961	140
China, Hong Kong SAR Chine, H. Kong RAS	14 VII 2006	6 752 674	...	...	6 813[1]	*7 072[1]	0.6	1 104	6 405
China, Macao SAR Chine, Macao RAS	19 VIII 2006	502 113[1]	245 167[1]	256 946[1]	473[1]	558[1]	2.7	30	18 603
Cyprus Chypre	1 X 2001	689 565[1,61]	338 497[1,61]	351 068[1,61]	758[1,62]	*851[1,63]	1.9	9 251	92

7

Population by sex, rate of population increase, surface area and density *(continued)*
Population selon le sexe, taux d'accroissement de la population, superficie et densité *(suite)*

Country or area[+] Pays ou zone[+]	Date	Latest census Dernier recensement			Mid-year estimates Estimations au milieu de l'année ('000)		Annual rate of increase Taux d'accroiss- ement annuel %	Surface area Superficie (Km²)	Density[&] Densité[&]
		Both sexes Les deux sexes	Men Hommes	Women Femmes	2005	2011	2005-11	2011	2011
Dem. P. R. Korea R. p. dém. de Corée	1 X 2008	24 052 231[1]	11 721 838[1]	12 330 393[1]	...	...	...	120 538	...
Georgia Géorgie	17 I 2002	4 355 673	2 049 786	2 305 887	4 361	4 469[8]	0.4	69 700	64
India Inde	9 II 2011	*1 210 193 422[64]	*623 724 248[64]	*586 469 174[64]	1 101 318[65]	*1 192 503[65]	1.3	3 287 263	363
Indonesia Indonésie	1 V 2010	237 641 326[1]	119 630 913[1]	118 010 413[1]	220 926[1,66]	236 954[1,66]	1.2	1 910 931	124
Iran (Islamic Rep. of) Iran (Rép. Islam. d')	28 X 2006	70 495 782[1]	35 866 362[1]	34 629 420[1]	69 390[1,67]	75 591[1,67]	1.4	1 628 750[68]	46
Iraq Iraq	16 X 1997	19 184 543[69]	9 536 570[69]	9 647 973[69]	27 963	33 402	3.0	435 244	77
Israel Israël	27 XII 2008	7 412 180[70]	3 663 910[70]	3 748 270[70]	6 930[1,71]	*7 759[1]	1.9	22 072	352
Japan Japon	1 X 2010	128 057 352[1,72]	62 327 737[1,72]	65 729 615[1,72]	127 773[1,72]	127 817[1,73]	^0.0	377 930[74]	338
Jordan Jordanie	1 X 2004	5 103 639[75]	2 626 287[75]	2 477 352[75]	5 473[76]	6 249[76]	2.2	89 328	70
Kazakhstan Kazakhstan	25 II 2009	*16 009 600	*7 712 200	*8 297 400	15 147	...	...	2 724 900	...
Kuwait Koweït	20 IV 2005	2 193 651	1 300 347	893 304	2 245	...	...	17 818	...
Kyrgyzstan Kirghizistan	24 III 2009	*5 107 700	*2 489 200	*2 618 500	5 007[77]	5 260[77]	0.8	199 951	26
Lao People's Dem. Rep. Rép. dém. pop. lao	1 III 2005	5 621 982[1]	2 800 551[1]	2 821 431[1]	5 679[78]	6 385[78]	2.0	236 800	27
Lebanon Liban	3 III 2007	3 759 134[79]	1 857 659[79]	1 901 475[79]	...	...	...	10 452	...
Malaysia Malaisie	6 VII 2010	28 334 135[1,80]	14 562 638[1,80]	13 771 497[1,80]	26 477[1,81]	28 553[1,81]	1.3	330 803	86
Maldives Maldives	21 III 2006	298 968[82]	151 459[82]	147 509[82]	294	325	1.7	300	1 084
Mongolia Mongolie	11 XI 2010	2 647 199	1 314 246	1 332 953	2 548	...	...	1 564 116	...
Myanmar Myanmar	31 III 1983	35 307 913	17 518 255	17 789 658	55 396	60 384	1.4	676 578	89
Nepal Népal	22 VI 2011	*26 620 809[1]	*12 927 431[1]	*13 693 378[1]	25 343[1]	28 585[1]	2.0	147 181	194
Occupied Palest. Terr. Terr. Palest. occupé	1 XII 2007	*3 761 646[83]	*1 908 432[83]	*1 853 214[83]	3 508	4 169	2.9	6 020	693
Oman Oman	12 XII 2010	*2 773 479	*1 612 408	*1 161 071	2 509	...	...	309 500	...
Pakistan Pakistan	2 III 1998	130 579 571[84]	67 840 137[84]	62 739 434[84]	144 367[1,85]	...	...	796 095	...
Philippines Philippines	1 VIII 2007	88 548 366[1]	...	...	85 261[1,86]	...	...	300 000	...
Qatar Qatar	21 IV 2010	1 699 435	1 284 739	414 696	906	1 625	9.7	11 607	140
Republic of Korea République de Corée	1 XI 2010	48 580 293[1,87]	24 167 098[1,87]	24 413 195[1,87]	48 138[1]	50 111[1]	0.7	100 033	501

Country or area[+] Pays ou zone[+]	Date	Latest census Dernier recensement Both sexes Les deux sexes	Men Hommes	Women Femmes	Mid-year estimates Estimations au milieu de l'année ('000) 2005	2011	Annual rate of increase Taux d'accroiss- ement annuel % 2005-11	Surface area Superficie (Km²) 2011	Density[&] Densité[&] 2011
Saudi Arabia Arabie saoudite	28 IV 2010	*27 136 977	*15 460 147	*11 676 830	23 330[88]	*28 376[88]	3.3	2 149 690	13
Singapore Singapour	30 VI 2010	3 771 721[1,89]	1 861 133[1,89]	1 910 588[1,89]	4 266[90]	5 184[90]	3.2	714	7 257
Sri Lanka Sri Lanka	17 VII 2001	16 929 689[91]	8 425 607[91]	8 504 082[91]	19 644	...	...	65 610	...
Syrian Arab Republic Rép. arabe syrienne	22 IX 2004	*17 921 000[92]	*9 161 000[92]	*8 760 000[92]	18 138[92]	21 124[92]	2.5	185 180	114
Tajikistan Tadjikistan	20 I 2000	6 127 493	3 069 100	3 058 393	6 850	...	...	143 100	...
Thailand Thaïlande	1 IV 2000	60 916 441[1,93]	30 015 233[1,93]	30 901 208[1,93]	64 839[1,2]	67 597[1,2]	0.7	513 120	132
Timor-Leste Timor-Leste	11 VII 2010	*1 066 582	*541 147	*525 435	983[2]	...	...	14 919	...
Turkey Turquie	31 XII 2008	71 517 100[1,94]	35 901 154[1,94]	35 615 946[1,94]	72 065	74 224	0.5	783 562	95
Turkmenistan Turkménistan	10 I 1995	4 483 251	2 225 331	2 257 920	...	...	...	488 100	...
United Arab Emirates Emirats arabes unis	5 XII 2005	4 106 427[95]	2 806 141[95]	1 300 286[95]	4 041[95]	...	...	83 600	...
Uzbekistan Ouzbékistan	12 I 1989	19 810 077[1]	9 784 156[1]	10 025 921[1]	*26 021	*29 123	1.9	447 400	65
Viet Nam Viet Nam	1 IV 2009	85 846 997[1]	42 413 143[1]	43 433 854[1]	82 394[96]	87 840	1.1	330 957	265
Yemen Yémen	16 XII 2004	19 685 161	10 036 953	9 648 208	20 283[97]	23 833[2]	...	527 968	45
Europe · Europe									
Åland Islands Îles d'Åland	31 XII 2000	25 776[1,25]	12 700[1,25]	13 076[1,25]	27[1,25]	28[1,25]	0.9	1 580	18
Albania Albanie	1 X 2011	*2 831 741	*1 421 810	*1 409 931	3 142	...	...	28 748	...
Andorra Andorre	31 XII 2000	65 844[1,25]	34 268[1,25]	31 576[1,25]	79[1,25]	79[1,98]	0.1	468	169
Austria Autriche	15 V 2001	8 032 926[1]	3 889 189[1]	4 143 737[1]	8 225[1]	8 423[1]	0.4	83 871	100
Belarus Bélarus	14 X 2009	9 503 807[1]	4 420 039[1]	5 083 768[1]	9 775	9 473	-0.5	207 600	46
Belgium Belgique	1 X 2001	10 296 350[1]	5 035 446[1]	5 260 904[1]	10 473[1]	10 996[1]	0.8	30 528	360
Bosnia and Herzegovina Bosnie-Herzégovine	31 III 1991	4 377 033[1]	2 183 795[1]	2 193 238[1]	3 843	*3 843[8]	^0.0	51 209	75
Bulgaria Bulgarie	1 III 2001	7 928 901[1]	3 862 465[1]	4 066 436[1]	7 740[1]	7 348[1]	-0.9	110 879	66
Croatia Croatie	31 III 2001	4 437 460[1]	2 135 900[1]	2 301 560[1]	4 442[1]	4 412[1,8]	-0.1	56 594	78
Czech Republic République tchèque	1 III 2001	10 230 060[1]	4 982 071[1]	5 247 989[1]	10 234[1]	*10 495[1]	0.4	78 865	133
Denmark[99] Danemark[99]	1 I 2001	5 349 212[1,25]	2 644 319[1,25]	2 704 893[1,25]	5 416[1,25]	5 567[1,25]	0.5	43 094	129

Country or area[+] Pays ou zone[+]	Date	Latest census Dernier recensement Both sexes Les deux sexes	Men Hommes	Women Femmes	Mid-year estimates Estimations au milieu de l'année ('000) 2005	2011	Annual rate of increase Taux d'accroiss- ement annuel % 2005-11	Surface area Superficie (Km²) 2011	Density[&] Densité[&] 2011
Estonia Estonie	31 III 2000	1 370 052[1]	631 851[1]	738 201[1]	1 346[1]	1 340[1]	-0.1	45 227	30
Faeroe Islands Iles Féroé	1 I 2008	48 433[1,25]	25 174[1,25]	23 259[1,25]	48[1]	48[1]	0.1	1 393	35
Finland Finlande	31 XII 2010	5 375 276[1]	2 638 416[1]	2 736 860[1]	5 246[1,25]	5 388[1,25]	0.4	336 851[100]	16
France France	1 I 2006	61 399 541[1,101]	29 714 539[1,101]	31 685 002[1,101]	61 181[1,101]	*63 294[1,101]	0.6	551 500	115
Germany Allemagne	28 III 2004	82 491 000[102]	40 330 000[102]	42 161 000[102]	82 464[1]	*81 798[1]	-0.1	357 121	229
Gibraltar Gibraltar	12 XI 2001	27 495[103]	13 644[103]	13 851[103]	29[104]	...	...	6	...
Greece Grèce	18 III 2001	10 964 020[105]	5 427 682[105]	5 536 338[105]	11 104[106]	11 326[107]	0.3	131 957	86
Guernsey Guernesey	29 IV 2001	59 807[1]	29 138[1]	30 669[1]	...	...	...	78	...
Holy See [108] Saint-Siège [108]	26 II 2010	*460[1]	...	...	...	...	...	^0[109]	...
Hungary Hongrie	1 II 2001	10 198 315	4 850 650	5 347 665	10 087	*9 974	-0.2	93 027	107
Iceland Islande	1 VII 2000	281 154[1,25]	140 718[1,25]	140 436[1,25]	296[1,25]	318[1,25]	1.2	103 000	3
Ireland Irlande	10 IV 2011	*4 581 269[1]	*2 268 698[1]	*2 312 571[1]	4 160[1]	4 484[1,110]	1.3	69 825	64
Isle of Man Ile de Man	27 III 2011	*84 497[1]	*41 971[1]	*42 526[1]	79[1,111]	...	...	572	...
Italy Italie	21 X 2001	57 110 144	27 617 335	29 492 809	58 607[1]	60 739[1]	0.6	301 336	202
Jersey Jersey	11 III 2001	87 186[1]	42 484[1]	44 702[1]	91[1]	98[1]	1.2	116	841
Latvia Lettonie	31 III 2000	2 377 383[1]	1 094 964[1]	1 282 419[1]	2 301[1]	*2 066[1]	-1.8	64 562	32
Liechtenstein Liechtenstein	5 XII 2000	33 307	16 420	16 887	35[1]	*36[1]	0.7	160	227
Lithuania Lituanie	6 IV 2001	3 483 972[1]	1 629 148[1]	1 854 824[1]	3 414[1]	3 222[1]	-1.0	65 300	49
Luxembourg Luxembourg	15 II 2001	439 539[1]	216 541[1]	222 998[1]	465[1]	512[1,8]	1.6	2 586	198
Malta Malte	27 XI 2005	404 962[1]	200 819[1]	204 143[1]	404[1,112]	418[1,113]	0.6	316	1 322
Monaco Monaco	9 VI 2008	31 109[1]	15 076[1,114]	15 914[1,114]	...	36[1]	...	2	18 063
Montenegro Monténégro	31 X 2003	620 145[1]	305 225[1]	314 920[1]	623[1]	618[1,8]	-0.1	13 812	45
Netherlands Pays-Bas	1 I 2002	16 105 285[1,115]	7 971 967[1,115]	8 133 318[1,115]	16 320[1]	16 693[1]	0.4	37 354	447
Norway [116] Norvège [116]	3 XI 2001	4 520 947[1,117]	2 240 281[1,117]	2 280 666[1,117]	4 623[1,118]	4 953[1,118]	1.1	323 787	15
Poland Pologne	20 V 2002	38 230 080[1,119]	18 516 403[1,119]	19 713 677[1,119]	38 161[1,119]	*38 204[1]	^0.0	311 888	122

| Country or area[+]
Pays ou zone[+] | Latest census
Dernier recensement | | | Mid-year estimates
Estimations au milieu
de l'année
('000) | | Annual rate
of increase
Taux
d'accroiss-
ement
annuel
% | Surface
area
Superficie
(Km^2) | Density[&]
Densité[&] |
	Date	Both sexes Les deux sexes	Men Hommes	Women Femmes	2005	2011	2005-11	2011	2011
Portugal Portugal	21 III 2011	*10 561 614	*5 047 387	*5 514 227	10 549[1]	...	...	92 212	...
Republic of Moldova Rép. de Moldova	5 X 2004	3 386 673[120]	1 629 689[120]	1 756 984[120]	3 595[1,120]	3 560[1,120]	-0.2	33 846	105
Romania Roumanie	18 III 2002	21 680 974[1]	10 568 741[1]	11 112 233[1]	21 624[1]	*21 385[1]	-0.2	238 391	90
Russian Federation Fédération de Russie	14 X 2010	143 436 145	...	...	143 114[1]	142 961[1]	^0.0	17 098 242	8
San Marino Saint-Marin	1 VII 2000	26 941[25]	13 185[25]	13 756[25]	30[25]	33[121]	1.9	61	547
Serbia Serbie	31 III 2002	7 498 001[1,122]	3 645 930[1,122]	3 852 071[1,122]	7 441[1,122]	7 276[1,123]	-0.4	88 361	82
Slovakia Slovaquie	21 V 2011	5 397 036[1]	2 627 772[1]	2 769 264[1]	5 387[1]	5 398[1]	^0.0	49 036[124]	110
Slovenia Slovénie	1 I 2011	2 058 051	1 019 826	1 038 225	2 001[1]	2 053[1]	0.4	20 273	101
Spain Espagne	1 XI 2001	40 847 371[125]	20 012 882[125]	20 834 489[125]	43 398[1]	46 125[1]	1.0	505 992	91
Sval. and Jan Mayen Is. Sv. et îles Jan Mayen	1 XI 1960	3 431[126]	2 545[126]	886[126]	2[127]	...	...	62 422	...
Sweden Suède	31 XII 2003	8 975 670[1,25]	4 446 656[1,25]	4 529 014[1,25]	9 030[1,25]	9 449[1,25]	0.8	450 295	21
Switzerland Suisse	5 XII 2000	7 288 010	3 567 567	3 720 443	7 437[1]	*7 911[1]	1.0	41 285	192
TFYR of Macedonia L'ex-R.Y. Macédoine	31 X 2002	2 022 547[1]	1 015 377[1]	1 007 170[1]	2 037[1]	*2 059[1]	0.2	25 713	80
Ukraine Ukraine	5 XII 2001	48 240 902	22 316 317	25 924 585	47 105	45 779[8]	-0.5	603 500	76
United Kingdom Royaume-Uni	29 IV 2001	58 789 187[128]	28 579 867[128]	30 209 320[128]	60 235	*62 436[8]	0.6	242 495	257
Oceania · Océanie									
American Samoa Samoa américaines	1 IV 2000	57 291[1,34]	29 264[1,34]	28 027[1,34]	66[1,34]	...	...	199	...
Australia Australie	8 VIII 2006	20 061 646[129]	9 896 500[129]	10 165 146[129]	20 395[1,130]	*22 621[1,130]	1.7	7 692 024	3
Cook Islands [131] Iles Cook [131]	1 XII 2006	19 342	9 816	9 526	22	*21	-0.6	236	88
Fiji Fidji	16 IX 2007	837 271	427 176	410 095	825	...	...	18 272	...
French Polynesia Polynésie française	20 VIII 2007	259 706[1]	133 109[1]	126 597[1]	253	...	...	4 000	...
Guam Guam	1 IV 2010	159 358[1]	...	...	169[1,132]	*160[1,133]	-0.9	549	291
Kiribati Kiribati	7 XII 2005	92 533	45 612	46 921	...	...	...	726[134]	...
Marshall Islands Iles Marshall	1 VI 1999	50 848	26 034	24 814	...	...	...	181	...
Micronesia (Fed. St. of) Micronésie (E. féd. de)	1 IV 2000	107 008[1]	54 191[1]	52 817[1]	108[1,2]	...	...	702	...

Population by sex, rate of population increase, surface area and density *(continued)*
Population selon le sexe, taux d'accroissement de la population, superficie et densité *(suite)*

Country or area[+] Pays ou zone[+]	Latest census Dernier recensement				Mid-year estimates Estimations au milieu de l'année ('000)		Annual rate of increase Taux d'accroiss- ement annuel %	Surface area Superficie (Km²)	Density[&] Densité[&]
	Date	Both sexes Les deux sexes	Men Hommes	Women Femmes	2005	2011	2005-11	2011	2011
Nauru Nauru	23 IX 2002	10 065	5 136	4 929	...	...	...	21	...
New Caledonia Nouvelle-Calédonie	27 VII 2009	245 580	124 524	121 056	234	252[8]	1.2	18 575	14
New Zealand Nouvelle-Zélande	7 III 2006	4 143 282[135]	2 021 277[135]	2 122 005[135]	4 134[1,136]	4 405[1,137]	1.1	270 467	16
Niue Nioué	9 IX 2006	1 625	802	823	2[1]	...	...	260	...
Norfolk Island Ile Norfolk	8 VIII 2006	2 523	1 218	1 305	2	...	...	36	...
Northern Mariana Is. Iles Marian. du Nord	1 IV 2010	53 883	...	...	71	46	-7.1	457	101
Palau Palaos	1 IV 2005	19 907[1]	10 699[1]	9 208[1]	...	...	...	459	...
Papua New Guinea Papouasie-Nvl-Guinée	9 VII 2000	5 190 786	2 691 744	2 499 042	...	...	...	462 840	...
Pitcairn Pitcairn	10 VIII 2012	48	...	...	...	...	...	5	...
Samoa Samoa	5 XI 2006	180 741	93 677	87 064	183	185	0.1	2 842	65
Solomon Islands Iles Salomon	21 XI 1999	409 042	211 381	197 661	471[2]	542[2]	2.3	28 896	19
Tokelau Tokélaou	19 X 2006	1 151	583	568	...	...	...	12	...
Tonga Tonga	30 XI 2011	*103 036[1]	*52 001[1]	*51 035[1]	102[138]	...	...	747	...
Tuvalu Tuvalu	1 XI 2002	9 561	4 729	4 832	10	...	...	26	...
Vanuatu Vanuatu	16 XI 2009	234 023[1]	119 091[1]	114 932[1]	...	...	...	12 189	...
Wallis and Futuna Isl. Iles Wallis et Futuna	21 VII 2008	13 445	6 669	6 776	...	...	...	142	...

Source:
United Nations Statistics Division, New York, *Demographic Yearbook 2011* and the demographic statistics database.

Source:
Organisation des Nations Unies, Division de statistique, New York, *Annuaire démographique 2011* et la base de données pour les statistiques démographiques.

[+] Unless otherwise indicated, figures refer to de facto (present-in-area) population for the present territory.

[&] Population per square kilometer of surface area in 2011. Figures are merely the quotients of population divided by surface area and are not to be considered either as reflecting density in the urban sense or as indicating the supporting power of a territory's land and resources.

[+] Sauf indication contraire, les chiffres se rapportent à la population effectivement présente sur le territoire (population de fait), tel qu'il est actuellement défini.

[&] Nombre d'habitants au kilomètre carré en 2011. Il s'agit simplement du quotient du chiffre de la population divisé par celui de la superficie: il ne faut pas y voir d'indication de la densité au sens urbain du terme ni de l'effectif de population que les terres et les ressources du territoire sont capables de nourrir.

1 De jure population.
2 Data refer to national projections.
3 Data refer to national projections. Data refer to 1 January.

4 Excluding Mayotte.

1 Population de droit.
2 Les données se réfèrent aux projections nationales.
3 Les données se réfèrent aux projections nationales. Données se rapportent au 1 janvier.

4 Non compris Mayotte.

7

Population by sex, rate of population increase, surface area and density *(continued)*
Population selon le sexe, taux d'accroissement de la population, superficie et densité *(suite)*

5	Projections based on the 1994 population census.	5	Projections fondées sur le recensement de la population de 1994.
6	Based on the results of the Gabonese Survey for the Evaluation and Tracking of Poverty.	6	Sur base des résultats de l'enquête gabonaise sur l'évaluation et le suivi de la pauvreté.
7	Post-censal estimates based on 1999 Population Census.	7	Les estimations post-censitaires fondées sur le recensement de la population de 1999.
8	Data refer to 1 January.	8	Les données se réfèrent au 1er janvier.
9	Excludes the islands of St. Brandon and Agalega.	9	Non compris les îles St. Brandon et Agalega.
10	Based on the results of the 2004 Population Census.	10	D'après des résultats du recensement de la population de 2004.
11	The number of males and/or females excludes persons whose sex is not stated (18 urban, 19 rural).	11	Il n'est pas tenu compte dans le nombre d'hommes et de femmes des personnes dont le sexe n'est pas indiqué (18 en zone urbaine et 19 en zone rurale).
12	Data produced by the Ministry of Natural Resources.	12	Les données sont produites par le ministère des ressources naturelles.
13	Data are based on projections from the 2002 Census. Data refer to 31 December.	13	Données fondées sur des projections tirées du recensement de 2002. Données se rapportent au 31 décembre.
14	Surface area is based on 2002 population and housing census.	14	La superficie est fondée sur les données provenant du recensement de la population et du logement de 2002.
15	Data have not been adjusted for under enumeration, estimated at 2.4 per cent.	15	Les données n'ont pas été ajustées pour compenser les lacunes du dénombrement, estimées à 2,4 p. 100
16	Mid-year estimates have been adjusted for under enumeration at latest census.	16	Les estimations au milieu de l'année tiennent compte d'un ajustement destiné à compenser les lacunes du dénombrement lors du dernier recensement.
17	Comprising the Northern Region (former Saguia el-Hamra) and Southern Region (former Rio de Oro).	17	Comprend la région septentrionale (ancien Saguia el-Hamra) et la région méridionale (ancien Rio de Oro).
18	Data are based on projections from 2002 Census.	18	Données fondées sur des projections tirées du recensement de 2002.
19	Excluding persons who were not contacted at the time of the census.	19	La population non comprend pas les personnes qui n'ont pas été contactées à l'heure du recensement.
20	Excluding the institutional population.	20	Non compris la population dans les institutions.
21	Because of rounding, totals are not in all cases the sum of the respective components.	21	Les chiffres étant arrondis, les totaux ne correspondent pas toujours rigoureusement à la somme des composants respectifs.
22	Final inter-censal estimates. Estimates adjusted for census net undercoverage (including adjustment for incompletely enumerated Indian reserves).	22	Estimations intercensitaires définitives. Ajusté pour la sous-estimation du recensement (y compris les réserves amérindiennes incomplètement énumérées)
23	Estimates based on 2007 Population Census.	23	Estimations fondées sur le recensement de la population de 2007.
24	The total surface is 21 040.79 square kilometres, without taking into account the last ruling of The Hague.	24	La superficie totale est égale à 21 040.79 km2, sans tenir compte de la dernière décision de la Haye.
25	Population statistics are compiled from registers.	25	Les statistiques de la population sont compilées à partir des registres.
26	Excluding data for Saint Barthélémy and Saint Martin.	26	Non compris les données pour Saint Barthélémy et Saint Martin.
27	Projections based on 2002 population census.	27	Projections fondées sur le recensement de la population de 2002.
28	Projections produced by l'Institut Haïtien de Statistique et d'Informatique (IHSI) and the Latin American and Caribbean Demographic Centre (CELADE) - Population Division of ECLAC.	28	Les données sont projections produits par l'Institut Haïtien de Statistique et d'Informatique (IHSI) et le centre démographique de l'Amérique latine et les Caraïbes - Division de la population de la CEPALC.
29	Data are based on projections of the 2001 Population and Housing Census data.	29	Les données sont basées sur les projections du recensement de 2001 de la population et de l'habitat.
30	Total represents population in private dwellings, the non-institutional population and persons found on the streets between the hours of 5 a.m. and 7 a.m. on September 26, 2001; the figures represent the census counts adjusted for under-coverage.	30	Le total représente la population vivant dans des logements privés et les personnes trouvées dans la rue entre 5 et 7 heures du matin le 26 septembre 2001, mais ne tient pas compte des personnes vivant dans des établissements; les chiffres sont ceux du recensement corrigés pour tenir compte du sous-dénombrement.
31	Including an estimation of 1 334 585 persons corresponding to 448 195 housing units without information of the occupants.	31	Y compris une estimation de 1 334 585 personnes correspondant aux 448 195 unités d'habitation sans information sur les occupants.
32	Data refer to projections based on the 2000 population census.	32	Les données se réfèrent aux projections basées sur le recensement de la population 2000.
33	Data refer to projections based on the 2010 Population Census.	33	Les données se réfèrent aux projections basées sur le recensement de la population de 2010.
34	Including armed forces stationed in the area.	34	Y compris les militaires en garnison sur le territoire.
35	Including armed forces stationed in the area. Data based on the 2010 Population Census results.	35	Y compris les militaires en garnison sur le territoire. D'après les résultats du recensement de la population de 2010.
36	Refers to habitable area. Excludes St. Lucia's Forest Reserve.	36	S'applique à la zone habitable. Exclut la réserve forestière de Sainte-Lucie.
37	Excluding residents of institutions.	37	À l'exclusion de personnes en établissements de soins.
38	Based on the results of the 2000 population census.	38	Basé sur les résultats du recensement de la population de 2000.
39	Including low water level for all islands (area to shoreline).	39	Incluent le niveau de basses eaux pour toutes les iles.
40	Excluding armed forces overseas and civilian citizens absent from country for an extended period of time.	40	Non compris les militaires à l'étranger, et les civils hors du pays pendant une période prolongée.
41	Data refer to projections based on the 2001 Population Census.	41	Les données se réfèrent aux projections basées sur le recensement de la population de 2001.
42	Data updated according to "Superintendencia Agraria". Interior	42	Données actualisées d'après la « Superintendencia Agraria ». Les eaux

waters correspond to natural or artificial bodies of water or snow.

43 Data include persons in remote areas, military personnel outside the country, merchant seamen at sea, civilian seasonal workers outside the country, and other civilians outside the country, and exclude nomads, foreign military, civilian aliens temporarily in the country, transients on ships and Indian jungle population.

44 Data based on the Population Census of 2005.

45 Data refer to national projections. Excluding nomadic Indian tribes.

46 A dispute exists between the governments of Argentina and the United Kingdom of Great Britain and Northern Ireland concerning sovereignty over the Falkland Islands (Malvinas).

47 Data refer to resident population in Uruguay according to Census Phase 1, carried out between the months of June and July 2004.

48 Excluding Indian jungle population.

49 Projections based on the 2001 Population Census.

50 Excluding nomad population.

51 Data refer to the settled population based on the 1979 Population Census and the latest household prelisting. The refugees of Afghanistan in Iran, Pakistan, and an estimated 1.5 million nomads, are not included.

52 The methodology used for calculating the number of the de facto and de jure population in the 2001 census data differs as follows from the methodology used in previous censuses: the duration that defines a person as being "temporarily present" or "temporarily absent" is now under one year; the previously applied definition was for 6 months.

53 Intercensal estimates.

54 Data refer to projections based on the 2005 population census.

55 Excluding foreign diplomatic personnel and their dependants.

56 Excluding foreign diplomatic personnel and their dependants. Data for estimates based on 1998 census result.

57 Excluding foreign diplomatic personnel and their dependants. Based on the 2008 Population and Housing Census.

58 For statistical purposes, the data for China do not include those for the Hong Kong Special Administrative Region (Hong Kong SAR), Macao Special Administrative Region (Macao SAR) and Taiwan Province of China.

59 For statistical purposes, the data for China do not include those for the Hong Kong Special Administrative Region (Hong Kong SAR), Macao Special Administrative Region (Macao SAR) and Taiwan province of China. Data have been estimated on the basis of the annual National Sample Surveys on Population Changes.

60 For statistical purposes, the data for China do not include those for the Hong Kong Special Administrative Region (Hong Kong SAR), Macao Special Administrative Region (Macao SAR) and Taiwan province of China. Data have been adjusted on the basis of the Population Census of 2010.

61 Data refer to government controlled areas. Including all persons irrespective of citizenship, who at the time of the census resided in the country or intended to reside for a period of at least one year. It does not distinguish between those present or absent at the time of census.

62 Data refer to government controlled areas.

63 Data refer to government controlled areas. Data have been adjusted on the basis of the Population Census of 2011.

64 Including data for the Indian-held part of Jammu and Kashmir, the final status of which has not yet been determined.

65 Data refer to national projections. Including data for the Indian-held part of Jammu and Kashmir, the final status of which has not yet been

intérieures correspondent aux étendues d'eau naturelles ou artificielles et aux étendues neigeuses.

43 Y compris les personnes dans des régions éloignées, le personnel militaire en dehors du pays, les marins marchands, les ouvriers saisonniers civils de couture en dehors du pays, et autres civils en dehors du pays, et non compris les nomades, les militaires étrangers, les étrangers civils temporairement dans le pays, les transitéés sur des bateaux et les Indiens de la jungle.

44 Données fondées sur le recensement de la population de 2005.

45 Les données se réfèrent aux projections nationales. Non compris les tribus d'Indiens nomades.

46 La souveraineté sur les îles Falkland (Malvinas) fait l'objet d'un différend entre le Gouvernement argentin et le Gouvernement du Royaume-Uni de Grande-Bretagne et d'Irlande du Nord.

47 Les données se rapportent à la population résidente en Uruguay d'après la phase 1 du recensement, qui a eu lieu entre juin et juillet 2004.

48 Non compris les Indiens de la jungle.

49 Projections fondées sur le recensement de la population de 2001.

50 Non compris les nomades.

51 Les données se rapportent à la population stationnaire sur la base du recensement de 1979 et du recensement préliminaire des logements le plus récent. Sont exclus les réfugiés d'Afghanistan en Iran et au Pakistan et les nomades estimés à 1,5 million.

52 La méthode utilisée pour dénombrer la population présente et la population légale dans le contexte du recensement de 2001 diffère de celle qui a été appliquée lors des recensements antérieurs en ce que la durée considérée pour définir la "présence temporaire" ou "l'absence temporaire" était dorénavant fixée à "moins d'un an" alors qu'elle était de 6 mois auparavant.

53 Estimations intercensitaires.

54 Les données se réfèrent aux projections basées sur le recensement de la population de 2005.

55 Non compris le personnel diplomatique étranger et les membres de leur famille les accompagnants.

56 Non compris le personnel diplomatique étranger et les membres de leur famille les accompagnants. Les estimations se réfèrent aux des résultats 1998 de recensement.

57 Non compris le personnel diplomatique étranger et les membres de leur famille les accompagnants. Basée sur le recensement de la population et de l'habitat de 2008.

58 Pour la présentation des statistiques, les données pour la Chine ne comprennent pas la Région Administrative Spéciale de Hong Kong (Hong Kong RAS), la Région Administrative Spéciale de Macao (Macao RAS) et la province de Taiwan.

59 Pour la présentation des statistiques, les données pour la Chine ne comprennent pas la Région Administrative Spéciale de Hong Kong (Hong Kong RAS), la Région Administrative Spéciale de Macao (Macao RAS) et Taïwan province de Chine. Les données on été estimées sur la base de l'enquête annuelle "National Sample Survey on Population Changes".

60 Pour la présentation des statistiques, les données pour la Chine ne comprennent pas la Région Administrative Spéciale de Hong Kong (Hong Kong RAS), la Région Administrative Spéciale de Macao (Macao RAS) et Taïwan province de Chine. Les données ont été ajustées à partir des résultats du recensement de la population de 2010.

61 Les données se rapportent aux zones contrôlées par le Gouvernement. Les chiffres comprennent toute la population, quelle que soit la nationalité, qui à l'époque de recensement avait résidé dans le pays, ou avait l'intention de résider, pendant une période d'au moins un an. Il n'y a pas de distinction entre les personnes présentes ou absentes au moment du recensement.

62 Les données se rapportent aux zones contrôlées par le Gouvernement.

63 Les données se rapportent aux zones contrôlées par le Gouvernement. Les données ont été calculées sur la base du recensement de population de 2011.

64 Y compris les données pour la partie du Jammu et du Cachemire occupée part l'Inde dont le statut définitif n'a pas encore été déterminé.

65 Les données se réfèrent aux projections nationales. Y compris les données pour la partie du Jammu et du Cachemire occupée par l'Inde dont le statut définitif n'a

	determined.		pas encore été déterminé.
66	Final intercensal estimates.	66	Estimations inter censitaires définitives.
67	Data refer to the Iranian Year which begins on 21 March and ends on 20 March of the following year.	67	Les données concernent l'année iranienne, qui commence le 21 mars et se termine le 20 mars de l'année suivante.
68	Land area only.	68	La superficie des terres seulement.
69	Excluding the population in three autonomous provinces in the north of the country.	69	La population des trois provinces autonomes dans le nord du pays est exclue.
70	Including data for East Jerusalem and Israeli residents in certain other territories under occupation by Israeli military forces since June 1967. Data are rounded for confidentiality reasons.	70	Y compris les données pour Jérusalem-Est et les résidents israéliens dans certains autres territoires occupés depuis 1967par les forces armées israéliennes. Chiffres arrondis pour des raisons de confidentialité.
71	Including data for East Jerusalem and Israeli residents in certain other territories under occupation by Israeli military forces since June 1967.	71	Y compris les données pour Jérusalem-Est et les résidents israéliens dans certains autres territoires occupés depuis 1967 par les forces armées israéliennes.
72	Excluding diplomatic personnel outside the country and foreign military and civilian personnel and their dependants stationed in the area.	72	Non compris le personnel diplomatique hors du pays ni les militaires et agents civils étrangers en poste sur le territoire et les membres de leur famille les accompagnants.
73	Excluding diplomatic personnel outside the country and foreign military and civilian personnel and their dependants stationed in the area. Estimates based on the complete counts of the 2010 Population Census.	73	Non compris le personnel diplomatique hors du pays ni les militaires et gents civils étrangers en poste sur le territoire et les membres de leur famille les accompagnants. Estimations basées sur le dénombrement complet du recensement de la population de 2010.
74	Data refer to 1 October 2007.	74	Les données se réfèrent au 1er octobre 2007.
75	Excluding data for Jordanian territory under occupation since June 1967 by Israeli military forces. Excluding foreigners, including registered Palestinian refugees.	75	Non compris les données pour le territoire jordanien occupé depuis juin 1967 par les forces armées israéliennes. Y compris les réfugiés palestiniens enregistrés et les Jordaniens à l'étranger.
76	Data refer to 31 December. Excluding data for Jordanian territory under occupation since June 1967 by Israeli military forces. Excluding foreigners, including registered Palestinian refugees.	76	Données se rapportent au 31 décembre. Non compris les données pour le territoire jordanien occupé depuis juin 1967 par les forces armées israéliennes. Non compris les étrangers, mais y compris les réfugiés de Palestine enregistrés.
77	Data are calculated from results of Population and Housing Census of 2009.	77	Les données sont calculées à partir des résultats de recensement de la population et de l'habitat de 2009.
78	Based on the results of the 2005 Population and Housing Census.	78	Données fondées sur les résultats du recensement de la population et de l'habitat de 2005.
79	Based on the results of a household survey.	79	D'après les résultats d'une enquête de ménages.
80	Data have been adjusted for under enumeration, at latest census.	80	Les données ont été ajustées pour compenser les lacunes du dénombrement lors du dernier recensement.
81	Data refer to 30 June. Data refer to projections based on the 2000 Population Census.	81	Données se rapportent au 30 juin. Les données se réfèrent aux projections basées sur le recensement de la population de 2000.
82	Total Population is taken as de facto and de jure together.	82	Population totale considérée comme de fait et de droit.
83	Data have been adjusted for under enumeration, estimated at 2.70 per cent.	83	Les données ont été ajustées pour compenser les lacunes du dénombrement, estimées à 2,70 p. 100.
84	Excluding data for the Pakistan-held part of Jammu and Kashmir, the final status of which has not yet been determined.	84	Non compris les données pour le Jammu et Cachemire occupée par le Pakistan dont le statut définitif n'a pas encore été déterminé.
85	Excluding data for the Pakistan-held part of Jammu and Kashmir, the final status of which has not yet been determined. Based on the results of the Pakistan Demographic Survey (PDS 2005). These estimates do not reflect completely accurately the actual population and vital events of the country.	85	Non compris les données concernant la partie du Jammu et Cachemire occupée par le Pakistan dont le statut définitif n'a pas été déterminé. D'après les résultats de l'enquête démographique effectuée par le Pakistan en 2005. Ces estimations ne dénotent pas d'une manière complètement ponctuelle la population actuelle et les statistiques de l'état civil du pays.
86	Data are based on projections of the 2000 Population and Housing Census data.	86	Les données sont basées sur les projections du recensement de 2000 de la population et de l'habitat.
87	Excluding usual residents not in country at time of census.	87	À l'exclusion des résidents habituels qui ne sont pas dans le pays au moment du recensement.
88	Data based on preliminary results of the 2010 Population and Housing Census.	88	D'après les résultats préliminaires du recensement de la population et des logements de 2010.
89	Data are based on the latest register-based population estimates for 2010. Data refer to resident population which comprises Singapore citizens and permanent residents. Urban and rural breakdown not applicable as Singapore is a city-state.	89	Données basées sur les estimations démographiques les plus récentes fondées sur les registres de 2010. Les données se rapportent à la population résidente composé des citoyens de Singapour et des résidents permanents. La ventilation entre zones urbaines et zones rurales ne s'applique pas à Singapour, puisqu'il s'agit d'une ville État.
90	Data refer to total population, which comprises Singapore residents and non-residents.	90	Les données se rapportent à la population totale composé des résidents de Singapour et les non résidents.
91	The Population and Housing Census 2001 did not cover the whole area of the country due to the security problems; the Census was complete in 18 districts only; in three districts it was not possible to conduct it; and in four districts it was partially conducted.	91	Le recensement de la population et de l'habitat en 2001 n' pas couvert la totalité du pays pour des problèmes de sécurité ; le recensement à été complété seulement en 18 districts ; dans 3 districts ça n'a pas été possible de conduire le recensement et dans 4 districts il a été partiellement conduit.
92	Including Palestinian refugees.	92	Y compris les réfugiés de Palestine.

93	All persons falling within the scope of the census were enumerated on a de jure basis, except students who were enumerated on a de facto basis.
94	Data based on Address Based Population Registration System.
95	Data include non-national population.
96	Data are adjusted according to the results of 1999 and 2009 censuses.
97	Data refer to 31 December.
98	Decrease in population due to revision in administrative registers. Population statistics are compiled from registers.
99	Excluding Faeroe Islands and Greenland shown separately, if available.
100	Excluding Åland Islands.
101	Excluding diplomatic personnel outside the country and including members of alien armed forces not living in military camps and foreign diplomatic personnel not living in embassies or consulates.
102	Data of the micro census - a 1% household sample survey - refer to a single reference week in spring (usually last week in April). Excluding homeless persons. Excluding foreign military personnel and foreign diplomatic and consular personnel and their family members in the country.
103	Excluding families of military personnel, visitors and transients.
104	Data refer to 31 December. Excluding military personnel, visitors and transients.
105	Including armed forces stationed outside the country and alien armed forces in the area.
106	Excluding armed forces stationed outside the country, but including alien armed forces stationed in the area.
107	Excluding armed forces stationed outside the country, but including alien armed forces stationed in the area. Data refer to 1 January.
108	Data refer to the Vatican City State.
109	Surface area is 0.44 Km2.
110	Data refer to 15 April.
111	Data refer to 30 April.
112	Including civilian nationals temporarily outside the country.
113	Including civilian nationals temporarily outside the country. Data refer to 1 January.
114	Figures for male and female population do not add up to the figure for total population, because they exclude 119 persons of unknown sex.
115	Census results, based on compilation of continuous accounting and sample surveys.
116	Excluding Svalbard and Jan Mayen Island shown separately.
117	Population statistics are compiled from registers. Including residents temporarily outside the country.
118	Including residents temporarily outside the country.
119	Excluding civilian aliens within country, but including civilian nationals temporarily outside country.
120	Excluding Transnistria and the municipality of Bender.
121	Data refer to 1 January. Population statistics are compiled from registers.
122	Excluding data for Kosovo and Metohia.
123	Excluding data for Kosovo and Metohia. Data refer to 1 January.
124	Excluding inland water.
125	Excluding transient visitors.
126	Inhabited only during the winter season. Census data are for total population while estimates refer to Norwegian population only. Included also in the de jure population of Norway.
127	Data refer to 1 January. Data refer to Svalbard only.

93	Toutes les personnes englobées dans le recensement ont été dénombrées comme population de droit, à l'exception des étudiants qui ont été dénombrés comme population de fait.
94	Les données sont basées sur le registre national de la population basé sur l'adresse.
95	Les données comprennent non-nationaux.
96	Les données ont été ajustées à partir des résultats des recensements de la population de 1999 et 2009.
97	Les données se réfèrent au 31 décembre.
98	Diminution de la population due à la révision des registres administratifs. Les statistiques de la population sont compilées à partir des registres.
99	Non compris les Iles Féroé et le Groenland, qui font l'objet de rubriques distinctes, si disponible.
100	Non compris les Îles d'Åland.
101	Non compris le personnel diplomatique hors du pays et y compris les militaires étrangers ne vivant pas dans des camps militaires et le personnel diplomatique étranger ne vivant pas dans les ambassades ou les consulats.
102	Les données du micro recensement (enquête sur les ménages, réalisée sur un échantillon de 1 %) concernent une seule semaine de référence au printemps (habituellement la dernière semaine d'avril). Non compris les personnes sans domicile fixe. Non compris le personnel militaire étranger, le personnel diplomatique et consulaire étranger et les membres de leur famille se trouvant dans le pays.
103	Non compris les familles des militaires, ni les visiteurs et voyageurs en transit.
104	Données se rapportent au 31 décembre. Non compris les militaires, ni les visiteurs et voyageurs en transit.
105	Y compris les militaires nationaux hors du pays et les militaires étrangers en garnison sur le territoire.
106	Non compris les militaires en garnison hors du pays, mais y compris les militaires étrangers en garnison sur le territoire.
107	Non compris les militaires en garnison hors du pays, mais y compris les militaires étrangers en garnison sur le territoire. Données se rapportent au 1 janvier.
108	Les données se réfèrent à la Cité du Vatican.
109	Superficie: 0,44 Km2
110	Données se rapportent au 15 avril.
111	Données se rapportent au 30 avril.
112	Y compris les civils nationaux temporairement hors du pays.
113	Y compris les civils nationaux temporairement hors du pays. Données se rapportent au 1 janvier.
114	Les chiffres relatifs à la population masculine et féminine ne correspondent pas au chiffre de la population totale, parce que l'on en a exclu 119 personnes de sexe inconnu.
115	Les résultats du recensement, d'après les résultats des dénombrements et enquêtes par sondage continue.
116	Non compris Svalbard et Jan Mayen qui font l'objet de rubriques distinctes.
117	Les statistiques de la population sont compilées à partir des registres. Y compris les résidents se trouvant temporairement hors du pays.
118	Y compris les nationaux se trouvant temporairement hors du pays.
119	Non compris les civils étrangers dans le pays, mais y compris les civils nationaux temporairement hors du pays.
120	Les données ne tiennent pas compte de l'information sur la Transnistrie et la municipalité de Bender.
121	Données se rapportent au 1 janvier. Les statistiques de la population sont compilées à partir des registres.
122	Sans les données pour le Kosovo et Metohie.
123	Sans les données pour le Kosovo et Metohie. Données se rapportent au 1 janvier.
124	Exception faite des eaux intérieures.
125	Non compris les visiteurs en transit.
126	N'est habitée pendant la saison d'hiver. Les données de recensement se rapportent à la population totale, mais les estimations ne concernent que la population norvégienne, comprise également dans la population de droit de la Norvège.
127	Données se rapportent au 1 janvier. Données ne concernant que le Svalbard.

128	Counts for the 2001 Census are taken from "Key Statistics table 1 for the Urban/Rural classification: England and Wales" available on CD-ROM, based on the usually resident population.
129	This data has been randomly rounded to protect confidentiality. Individual figures may not add up to totals, and values for the same data may vary in different tables. Including population in off-shore, migratory and shipping.
130	Data are based on Australian Standard Geographical Classification boundaries. Intercensal estimates.
131	Excluding Niue, shown separately, which is part of Cook Islands, but because of remoteness is administered separately.
132	Including armed forces stationed in the area. Data refer to projections based on the 2000 Population Census.
133	Including armed forces stationed in the area. Data refer to projections based on the 2010 Population Census.
134	Excluding 84 square km of uninhabited islands. Land area only.
135	This data has been randomly rounded to protect confidentiality. Individual figures may not add up to totals, and values for the same data may vary in different tables.
136	Excluding diplomatic personnel and armed forces stationed outside country; also excluding alien armed forces within the country.
137	Based on the census, updated for residents missed or counted more than once by the census (net census undercount); residents temporarily overseas on census night, and births, deaths and net migration between the census night and the date of the estimate.
138	Based on the results of the 1996 population census. Data refer to national projections.

128	Les chiffres du recensement de 2001 proviennent du tableau intitulé "Key Statistics table 1 for the Urban/Rural classification: England and Wales" disponible sur CD-ROM et sont fondés sur la notion de résidence habituelle.
129	Ces données ont été arrondies de façon aléatoire afin d'en préserver la confidentialité. La somme de certains chiffres peut ne pas correspondre aux totaux indiqués et les valeurs des mêmes données peuvent varier d'un tableau à un autre. Y compris les populations extraterritoriales, les populations nomades et les populations maritimes.
130	Les données réfèrent au découpage de la nomenclature géographique normalisée d'Australie. Estimations inter-censitaires.
131	Non compris Niue, qui fait l'objet d'une rubrique distincte et qui fait partie des îles Cook, mais qui, en raison de son éloignement, est administrée séparément.
132	Y compris les militaires en garnison sur le territoire. Les données se réfèrent aux projections basées sur le recensement de la population.
133	Y compris les militaires en garnison sur le territoire. Les données se réfèrent aux projections basées sur le recensement de la population
134	Exclut des îles inhabitées d'une superficie de 84 kilomètres carrés. La superficie des terres seulement.
135	Ces données ont été arrondies de façon aléatoire afin d'en préserver la confidentialité. La somme de certains chiffres peut ne pas correspondre aux totaux indiqués et les valeurs des mêmes données peuvent varier d'un tableau à un autre.
136	Non compris le personnel diplomatique et les militaires hors du pays; non compris également les militaires étrangers en garnison dans le pays.
137	D'après le recensement, mise à jour pour les résidents omis ou dénombrés plus d'une fois par le recensement (sous-dénombrement net); résidents temporairement à l'étranger la nuit du recensement, et naissances, décès et migration nette entre la nuit du recensement et la date de l'estimation.
138	À partir des résultats du recensement de la population de 1996. Les données se réfèrent aux projections nationales.

Population in urban and rural areas, rates of growth and largest urban agglomeration population

Population urbaine, population rurale, taux d'accroissement et population de l'agglomération urbaine la plus peuplée

Region, country or area Région, pays ou zone	Year Année	Population estimates and projections Estimations de la population et projections		Annual growth rate[1] Taux d'accroissement annuel[1]		Population of largest urban agglomeration with 750,000 inhabitants or more in 2010 Population de l'agglomération urbaine la plus peuplée avec 750,000 habitants ou plus en 2010		
		Rural % Rurale %	Urban % Urbaine %	Rural % Rurale %	Urban % Urbaine %	Number (000s) Nombre (000s)	% of urban % d'urbaine	% of total % de totale
World	**2005**	**50.9[1]**	**49.1**	**0.2**	**2.1**	...	...	...
Monde	**2010**	**48.4**	**51.6**	**0.1**	**2.0**	...	...	...
Africa	**2005**	**62.7**	**37.4**	**1.7**	**3.3**	...	...	...
Afrique	**2010**	**60.8**	**39.2**	**1.6**	**3.2**	...	...	...
Algeria	2005	33.3	66.7	-2.0	3.1	2 548	11.6	7.8
Algérie	2010	28.0	72.0	-1.9	2.5	2 851	11.2	8.0
Angola	2005	46.1	53.9	0.9	4.5	3 533	39.7	21.4
Angola	2010	41.6	58.4	0.8	4.0	4 790	43.0	25.1
Benin	2005	59.0	41.0	1.8	4.5	724	23.1	9.5
Bénin	2010	55.7	44.3	1.5	4.1	882	22.5	10.0
Botswana	2005	42.7	57.3	-0.4	2.6	...	...	...
Botswana	2010	39.0	61.0	-0.7	2.1	...	...	...
Burkina Faso	2005	78.5	21.5	1.9	6.5	1 328	43.4	9.4
Burkina Faso	2010	74.3	25.7	1.8	6.0	1 911	45.2	11.6
Burundi	2005	90.6	9.4	2.6	5.4	...	...	...
Burundi	2010	89.4	10.6	1.6	4.5	...	...	...
Cameroon	2005	51.5	48.5	1.0	3.4	1 876	22.0	10.7
Cameroun	2010	48.5	51.5	0.9	3.2	2 348	23.3	12.0
Cape Verde	2005	42.3	57.7	-1.1	2.3	...	...	...
Cap-Vert	2010	38.2	61.8	-1.1	2.1	...	...	...
Central African Rep.	2005	61.9	38.1	1.6	2.2	...	...	...
Rép. centrafricaine	2010	61.2	38.8	1.6	2.6	...	...	...
Chad	2005	78.4	21.6	2.7	2.9	854	40.4	8.7
Tchad	2010	78.3	21.7	2.5	3.0	1 038	42.5	9.2
Comoros	2005	72.1	27.9	2.6	2.7	...	...	...
Comores	2010	72.0	28.0	2.4	2.8	...	...	...
Congo	2005	39.0	61.0	1.5	3.4	1 269	58.9	35.9
Congo	2010	36.8	63.2	1.0	2.8	1 557	60.9	38.5
Côte d'Ivoire	2005	53.2	46.8	0.4	3.4	3 545	42.0	19.7
Côte d'Ivoire	2010	49.4	50.6	0.7	3.6	4 151	41.6	21.0
Dem. Rep. of the Congo	2005	68.8	31.2	2.0	4.4	6 766	37.8	11.8
Rép. dém. du Congo	2010	66.3	33.7	1.8	4.2	8 415	37.8	12.8
Djibouti	2005	23.2	76.8	1.7	2.0	...	...	...
Djibouti	2010	23.0	77.0	1.5	2.0	...	...	...
Egypt	2005	57.0	43.0	1.7	1.9	10 565	33.1	14.2
Egypte	2010	56.6	43.4	1.4	2.0	11 031	31.4	13.6
Equatorial Guinea	2005	61.1	38.9	2.7	3.1	...	...	...
Guinée équatoriale	2010	60.7	39.3	2.4	3.2	...	...	...
Eritrea	2005	81.0	19.1	2.7	5.0	...	...	...
Erythrée	2010	79.1	20.9	2.3	5.0	...	...	...
Ethiopia	2005	84.3	15.7	2.0	3.5	2 634	22.6	3.6
Ethiopie	2010	83.2	16.8	1.8	3.6	2 919	21.0	3.5
Gabon	2005	16.5	83.5	-1.2	2.4	...	...	...
Gabon	2010	14.2	85.8	-0.4	2.3	...	...	...
Gambia	2005	46.9	53.1	1.2	4.1	...	...	...
Gambie	2010	43.3	56.7	1.4	3.6	...	...	...
Ghana	2005	52.3	47.7	1.0	3.8	2 008	19.5	9.3
Ghana	2010	48.8	51.2	0.9	3.5	2 469	19.8	10.1
Guinea	2005	67.2	32.9	1.3	3.2	1 432	48.2	15.8
Guinée	2010	65.0	35.0	1.8	3.9	1 715	49.1	17.2
Guinea-Bissau	2005	60.5	39.6	0.8	3.8	...	...	...
Guinée-Bissau	2010	56.8	43.2	0.9	3.6	...	...	...
Kenya	2005	78.3	21.7	2.1	4.3	2 677	34.7	7.5
Kenya	2010	76.4	23.6	2.1	4.4	3 237	33.9	8.0

Population in urban and rural areas, rates of growth and largest urban agglomeration population *(continued)*

Population urbaine, population rurale, taux d'accroissement et population de l'agglomération urbaine la plus peuplée *(suite)*

Region, country or area Région, pays ou zone	Year Année	Population estimates and projections Estimations de la population et projections				Population of largest urban agglomeration with 750,000 inhabitants or more in 2010 Population de l'agglomération urbaine la plus peuplée avec 750,000 habitants ou plus en 2010		
		Rural % Rurale %	Urban % Urbaine %	Annual growth rate[1] Taux d'accroissement annuel[1]		Number (000s) Nombre (000s)	% of urban % d'urbaine	% of total % de totale
				Rural % Rurale %	Urban % Urbaine %			
Lesotho	2005	76.7	23.3	^0.0	3.9	...	...	...
Lesotho	2010	73.2	26.8	^0.0	3.6	...	...	...
Liberia	2005	54.0	46.1	4.7	4.4	1 202	78.3	37.8
Libéria	2010	52.2	47.8	1.9	3.4	812	42.5	20.3
Libyan Arab Jamah.	2005	23.1	76.9	1.3	2.1	1 058	23.9	18.3
Jamah. arabe libyenne	2010	22.4	77.6	^0.0	1.0	1 111	22.5	17.5
Madagascar	2005	71.2	28.8	2.0	5.0	1 585	30.8	8.9
Madagascar	2010	68.1	31.9	1.9	4.7	1 900	28.7	9.2
Malawi	2005	85.0	15.1	2.9	3.6	593	30.7	4.6
Malawi	2010	84.5	15.5	3.1	4.2	738	31.9	5.0
Mali	2005	68.9	31.1	2.1	5.0	1 485	36.3	11.3
Mali	2010	65.7	34.3	1.9	4.8	1 932	36.7	12.6
Mauritania	2005	59.7	40.4	2.2	3.0	640	52.0	21.0
Mauritanie	2010	58.8	41.2	1.8	2.9	759	53.2	21.9
Mauritius[2]	2005	57.8	42.2	0.8	0.5	...	...	...
Maurice[2]	2010	58.2	41.8	0.5	0.6	...	...	...
Mayotte	2005	49.8	50.2	3.2	3.0	...	...	...
Mayotte	2010	49.9	50.1	2.9	3.1	...	...	...
Morocco	2005	45.0	55.0	0.2	1.6	2 937	17.6	9.7
Maroc	2010	43.3	56.7	0.1	1.6	3 009	16.6	9.4
Mozambique	2005	70.0	30.0	2.1	3.0	1 072	17.2	5.2
Mozambique	2010	69.0	31.0	1.9	3.1	1 132	15.6	4.8
Namibia	2005	65.0	35.0	1.0	3.4	...	...	...
Namibie	2010	62.2	37.8	0.7	3.1	...	...	...
Niger	2005	83.3	16.7	3.3	4.6	906	41.7	7.0
Niger	2010	82.4	17.6	3.2	4.9	1 222	44.7	7.9
Nigeria	2005	54.3	45.8	1.3	3.9	8 859	13.9	6.3
Nigéria	2010	51.0	49.0	1.3	3.8	10 788	13.9	6.8
Réunion	2005	7.6	92.4	-3.6	1.6	...	...	...
Réunion	2010	6.0	94.0	-2.7	1.3	...	...	...
Rwanda	2005	82.5	17.5	2.6	4.3	776	48.1	8.4
Rwanda	2010	81.2	18.8	2.5	4.5	961	48.1	9.0
Saint Helena[3]	2005	60.1	39.9	-2.1	-2.4	...	...	...
Sainte-Hélène[3]	2010	60.5	39.5	-0.9	-0.9	...	...	...
Sao Tome and Principe	2005	42.0	58.0	-0.4	2.9	...	...	...
Sao Tomé-et-Principe	2010	38.0	62.0	0.1	3.0	...	...	...
Senegal	2005	58.9	41.1	2.3	3.2	2 437	54.5	22.4
Sénégal	2010	57.7	42.3	2.1	3.3	2 926	55.7	23.5
Seychelles	2005	48.4	51.6	^0.0	1.3	...	...	...
Seychelles	2010	46.8	53.2	-0.5	1.1	...	...	...
Sierra Leone	2005	62.7	37.3	2.1	3.4	785	40.9	15.2
Sierra Leone	2010	61.1	38.9	1.5	3.0	910	39.9	15.5
Somalia	2005	64.8	35.2	1.5	3.4	1 415	48.1	16.9
Somalie	2010	62.7	37.3	1.8	3.8	1 426	41.0	15.3
South Africa	2005	40.7	59.3	-0.2	1.7	3 272	11.6	6.9
Afrique du Sud	2010	38.5	61.5	-0.7	1.2	3 763	12.2	7.5
Sudan (former)	2005	67.2	32.8	1.7	2.0	3 979	39.5	12.9
Soudan (anc.)	2010	66.9	33.1	1.9	2.6	4 516	40.6	13.4
Swaziland	2005	78.1	21.9	1.6	0.9	...	...	...
Swaziland	2010	78.7	21.3	1.4	1.2	...	...	...
Togo	2005	64.8	35.2	1.4	3.5	1 146	60.2	21.2
Togo	2010	62.5	37.5	1.2	3.3	1 453	64.2	24.1
Tunisia	2005	34.9	65.1	0.6	1.4	734	11.4	7.4
Tunisie	2010	33.9	66.1	0.4	1.3	777	11.2	7.4

Population in urban and rural areas, rates of growth and largest urban agglomeration population *(continued)*

Population urbaine, population rurale, taux d'accroissement et population de l'agglomération urbaine la plus peuplée *(suite)*

Region, country or area Région, pays ou zone	Year Année	Rural % Rurale %	Urban % Urbaine %	Annual growth rate[1] Taux d'accroissement annuel[1]		Population of largest urban agglomeration with 750,000 inhabitants or more in 2010 Population de l'agglomération urbaine la plus peuplée avec 750,000 habitants ou plus en 2010		
				Rural % Rurale %	Urban % Urbaine %	Number (000s) Nombre (000s)	% of urban % d'urbaine	% of total % de totale
Uganda	2005	86.8	13.3	2.8	5.9	1 320	35.1	4.6
Ouganda	2010	84.8	15.2	2.6	5.7	1 594	31.5	4.8
United Rep. of Tanzania	2005	75.8	24.2	2.3	4.5	2 683	28.6	6.9
Rép.-Unie de Tanzanie	2010	73.7	26.3	2.4	4.8	3 415	29.0	7.6
Western Sahara	2005	19.2	80.8	2.6	4.0	...	...	...
Sahara occidental	2010	18.2	81.8	2.1	3.5	...	...	...
Zambia	2005	63.4	36.6	2.0	3.8	1 356	32.3	11.8
Zambie	2010	61.3	38.7	2.3	4.2	1 719	33.9	13.1
Zimbabwe	2005	64.1	35.9	-0.7	1.2	1 468	32.6	11.7
Zimbabwe	2010	61.9	38.1	1.3	3.4	1 526	31.8	12.1
Northern America	**2005**	**19.3**	**80.7**	**-0.5**	**1.2**	...	...	...
Amérique septentrionale	**2010**	**18.0**	**82.0**	**-0.5**	**1.1**	...	...	...
Bermuda	2005	0.0	100.0	0.0	0.3	...	...	...
Bermudes	2010	0.0	100.0	0.0	0.2	...	...	...
Canada	2005	19.9	80.1	0.6	1.2	5 035	19.5	15.6
Canada	2010	19.4	80.6	0.4	1.1	5 485	20.0	16.1
Greenland	2005	17.1	82.9	-1.8	0.4	...	...	...
Groenland	2010	15.6	84.4	-1.9	0.3	...	...	...
Saint Pierre and Miquelon	2005	10.1	89.9	-1.8	-0.1	...	...	...
Saint-Pierre-et-Miquelon	2010	9.4	90.6	-1.4	0.1	...	...	...
United States	2005	19.3	80.7	-0.6	1.2	18 888	7.9	6.4
Etats-Unis	2010	17.9	82.1	-0.6	1.1	20 104	7.9	6.5
Latin America and the Caribbean	**2005**	**22.7**	**78.8**	**-0.3**	**1.6**	...	...	...
Amérique latine et Caraïbes	**2010**	**21.4**	**77.3**	**-0.3**	**1.4**	...	...	...
Anguilla	2005	0.0	100.0	0.0	2.5	...	...	...
Anguilla	2010	0.0	100.0	0.0	1.6	...	...	...
Antigua and Barbuda	2005	69.4	30.6	1.3	0.6	...	...	...
Antigua-et-Barbuda	2010	70.1	29.9	1.0	1.0	...	...	...
Argentina	2005	8.6	91.4	-1.5	1.1	12 586	35.6	32.5
Argentine	2010	7.7	92.3	-1.2	1.0	13 370	35.8	33.1
Aruba	2005	53.4	46.6	1.2	1.3	...	...	...
Aruba	2010	53.2	46.8	0.2	0.5	...	...	...
Bahamas	2005	16.9	83.1	0.2	1.7	...	...	...
Bahamas	2010	15.9	84.1	-0.1	1.4	...	...	...
Barbados	2005	58.8	41.2	-0.7	1.5	...	...	...
Barbade	2010	56.1	43.9	-0.7	1.4	...	...	...
Belize	2005	53.7	46.3	2.6	1.5	...	...	...
Belize	2010	55.0	45.0	2.3	1.5	...	...	...
Bolivia (Plurinational State of)	2005	35.8	64.2	0.4	2.3	1 524	26.0	16.7
Bolivie (État plurinational de)	2010	33.6	66.4	0.3	2.2	1 678	25.4	16.9
Brazil	2005	17.2	82.8	-0.9	1.3	18 330	7.4	9.9
Brésil	2010	15.7	84.3	-1.0	1.2	19 649	7.2	10.1
British Virgin Islands	2005	60.3	39.8	0.9	1.5	...	...	...
Iles Vierges britanniques	2010	59.6	40.4	0.6	1.5	...	...	...
Cayman Islands	2005	0.0	100.0	0.0	1.5	...	...	...
Iles Caïmanes	2010	0.0	100.0	0.0	0.8	...	...	...
Chile	2005	12.4	87.6	-1.3	1.3	5 605	39.2	34.4
Chili	2010	11.1	88.9	-1.1	1.1	5 959	39.1	34.8
Colombia	2005	26.4	73.6	0.3	1.9	7 353	23.2	17.1
Colombie	2010	25.0	75.0	0.2	1.7	8 502	24.5	18.4
Costa Rica	2005	38.3	61.7	0.2	2.4	1 232	46.3	28.6
Costa Rica	2010	35.8	64.2	^0.0	2.1	1 466	49.0	31.5
Cuba	2005	24.4	75.6	0.3	-0.1	2 187	25.7	19.4
Cuba	2010	24.8	75.2	^0.0	-0.1	2 128	25.1	18.9

Population in urban and rural areas, rates of growth and largest urban agglomeration population *(continued)*

Population urbaine, population rurale, taux d'accroissement et population de l'agglomération urbaine la plus peuplée *(suite)*

Region, country or area Région, pays ou zone	Year Année	Rural % Rurale %	Urban % Urbaine %	Annual growth rate[1] Taux d'accroissement annuel[1]		Population of largest urban agglomeration with 750,000 inhabitants or more in 2010 Population de l'agglomération urbaine la plus peuplée avec 750,000 habitants ou plus en 2010		
				Rural % Rurale %	Urban % Urbaine %	Number (000s) Nombre (000s)	% of urban % d'urbaine	% of total % de totale
Dominica	2005	33.1	66.9	-0.4	-0.3	...	...	...
Dominique	2010	32.9	67.1	-0.4	0.2	...	...	...
Dominican Republic	2005	34.3	65.7	-0.7	2.4	1 977	32.5	21.3
Rép. dominicaine	2010	30.9	69.1	-0.7	2.0	2 154	31.4	21.7
Ecuador	2005	36.4	63.6	-0.4	2.5	2 207	25.8	16.4
Equateur	2010	33.1	66.9	-0.5	2.1	2 273	23.5	15.7
El Salvador	2005	38.4	61.7	-1.0	1.3	1 401	37.6	23.2
El Salvador	2010	35.7	64.3	-0.8	1.4	1 570	39.5	25.4
Falkland Is. (Malvinas)	2005	29.2	70.8	-1.6	1.2	...	...	...
Iles Falkland (Malvinas)	2010	26.4	73.6	-1.6	0.9	...	...	...
French Guiana	2005	24.5	75.5	2.1	2.9	...	...	...
Guyane française	2010	23.8	76.2	1.8	2.8	...	...	...
Grenada	2005	62.7	37.3	-0.2	1.2	...	...	...
Grenade	2010	61.2	38.8	-0.2	1.2	...	...	...
Guadeloupe[4]	2005	1.6	98.4	0.5	0.7	...	...	...
Guadeloupe[4]	2010	1.6	98.4	0.1	0.5	...	...	...
Guatemala	2005	52.8	47.2	1.6	3.4	985	16.4	7.8
Guatemala	2010	50.7	49.3	1.6	3.4	1 128	15.9	7.8
Guyana	2005	71.7	28.3	0.2	0.2	...	...	...
Guyana	2010	71.7	28.3	0.1	0.5	...	...	...
Haiti	2005	55.9	44.1	-1.7	4.6	2 171	52.7	23.2
Haïti	2010	48.0	52.0	-1.7	3.7	2 143	41.3	21.4
Honduras	2005	51.4	48.7	0.8	3.2	902	27.0	13.1
Honduras	2010	48.4	51.6	0.8	3.1	1 051	26.8	13.8
Jamaica	2005	48.0	52.0	0.5	0.4	...	...	...
Jamaïque	2010	48.0	52.0	0.2	0.5	...	...	...
Martinique	2005	10.7	89.3	1.0	0.4	...	...	...
Martinique	2010	11.0	89.0	0.4	0.3	...	...	...
Mexico	2005	23.7	76.3	-0.1	1.7	18 735	23.1	17.6
Mexique	2010	22.2	77.8	-0.2	1.5	20 142	22.8	17.8
Montserrat	2005	86.5	13.5	1.0	2.0	...	...	...
Montserrat	2010	85.9	14.1	0.7	1.9	...	...	...
Netherlands Antilles[5]	2005	8.1	91.9	-1.9	1.8	...	...	...
Antilles néerlandaises[5]	2010	6.8	93.2	-2.2	0.9	...	...	...
Nicaragua	2005	44.1	55.9	0.7	1.8	909	30.0	16.8
Nicaragua	2010	42.7	57.3	0.7	1.9	954	28.8	16.5
Panama	2005	29.3	70.7	-1.2	2.7	1 221	53.3	37.7
Panama	2010	25.4	74.6	-1.0	2.2	1 389	53.0	39.5
Paraguay	2005	41.5	58.5	0.4	2.8	1 765	51.2	29.9
Paraguay	2010	38.6	61.4	0.3	2.6	2 073	52.3	32.1
Peru	2005	25.0	75.0	-0.5	1.6	8 081	39.1	29.3
Pérou	2010	23.1	76.9	-0.4	1.6	8 950	40.0	30.8
Puerto Rico	2005	2.4	97.6	-13.3	0.1	2 493	67.5	65.9
Porto Rico	2010	1.2	98.8	-9.6	0.1	2 478	66.9	66.1
Saint Kitts and Nevis	2005	67.9	32.1	1.3	1.2	...	...	...
Saint-Kitts-et-Nevis	2010	68.1	31.9	1.1	1.4	...	...	...
Saint Lucia	2005	76.9	23.1	2.3	-3.6	...	...	...
Sainte-Lucie	2010	81.7	18.3	1.8	-3.1	...	...	...
Saint Vincent-Grenadines	2005	53.0	47.0	-0.6	0.9	...	...	...
Saint Vincent-Grenadines	2010	51.1	48.9	-0.8	0.8	...	...	...
Suriname	2005	32.8	67.2	-0.4	1.6	...	...	...
Suriname	2010	30.7	69.3	-0.5	1.4	...	...	...
Trinidad and Tobago	2005	87.9	12.1	0.1	2.5	...	...	...
Trinité-et-Tobago	2010	86.6	13.4	^0.0	2.2	...	...	...

Population in urban and rural areas, rates of growth and largest urban agglomeration population *(continued)*

Population urbaine, population rurale, taux d'accroissement et population de l'agglomération urbaine la plus peuplée *(suite)*

Region, country or area Région, pays ou zone	Year Année	Population estimates and projections Estimations de la population et projections				Population of largest urban agglomeration with 750,000 inhabitants or more in 2010 Population de l'agglomération urbaine la plus peuplée avec 750,000 habitants ou plus en 2010		
		Rural % Rurale %	Urban % Urbaine %	Annual growth rate[1] Taux d'accroissement annuel[1]		Number (000s) Nombre (000s)	% of urban % d'urbaine	% of total % de totale
				Rural % Rurale %	Urban % Urbaine %			
Turks and Caicos Islands	2005	10.3	89.7	-4.0	5.4	...	...	...
Iles Turques et Caïques	2010	6.7	93.3	-6.0	1.7	...	...	...
United States Virgin Is.	2005	5.8	94.2	-4.2	0.2	...	...	...
Iles Vierges américaines	2010	4.7	95.3	-3.6	-0.1	...	...	...
Uruguay	2005	8.1	91.9	-1.1	0.4	1 622	53.1	48.8
Uruguay	2010	7.5	92.5	-0.9	0.5	1 659	53.3	49.3
Venezuela (Boliv. Rep. of)	2005	8.1	91.9	-2.1	2.0	2 938	12.0	11.0
Venezuela (Rép. boliv. du)	2010	6.7	93.3	-1.6	1.7	3 176	11.7	11.0
Asia	**2005**	**59.1**	**40.9**	**-0.1**	**2.7**	**...**	**...**	**...**
Asie	**2010**	**55.6**	**44.4**	**-0.2**	**2.4**	**...**	**...**	**...**
Afghanistan	2005	78.1	21.9	2.2	3.8	2 856	47.3	10.3
Afghanistan	2010	76.8	23.2	2.7	4.4	3 052	41.8	9.7
Armenia	2005	35.8	64.2	0.2	0.1	1 104	56.1	36.0
Arménie	2010	35.9	64.1	0.1	0.3	1 113	56.2	36.0
Azerbaijan[6]	2005	47.6	52.4	0.9	1.7	1 867	41.5	21.7
Azerbaïdjan[6]	2010	46.6	53.4	0.7	1.6	2 062	42.0	22.4
Bahrain	2005	11.6	88.4	10.7	11.1	...	...	...
Bahreïn	2010	11.4	88.6	1.5	2.2	...	...	...
Bangladesh	2005	74.4	25.6	0.5	2.8	12 615	35.0	9.0
Bangladesh	2010	72.1	27.9	0.6	3.0	14 930	36.0	10.0
Bhutan	2005	69.0	31.0	0.8	4.3	...	...	...
Bhoutan	2010	65.2	34.8	0.3	3.7	...	...	...
Brunei Darussalam	2005	26.5	73.5	0.3	2.4	...	...	...
Brunéi Darussalam	2010	24.4	75.6	0.1	2.1	...	...	...
Cambodia	2005	80.8	19.2	1.0	1.8	1 317	51.4	9.9
Cambodge	2010	80.2	19.8	1.0	2.1	1 509	53.9	10.7
China[7]	2005	57.5	42.5	-2.0	3.4	16 590	3.0	1.3
Chine[7]	2010	50.8	49.2	-2.3	2.9	19 554	3.0	1.5
China, Hong Kong SAR	2005	0.0	100.0	0.0	0.6	6 810	99.7	100.0
Chine, Hong Kong RAS	2010	0.0	100.0	0.0	1.0	7 053	100.0	100.0
China, Macao SAR	2005	0.0	100.0	0.0	2.4	...	...	...
Chine, Macao RAS	2010	0.0	100.0	0.0	2.0	...	...	...
Cyprus[8]	2005	30.6	69.4	0.8	1.6	...	...	...
Chypre[8]	2010	29.7	70.3	0.4	1.4	...	...	...
Dem. P. R. Korea	2005	40.2	59.8	0.3	0.6	2 805	19.8	11.8
R. p. dém. de Corée	2010	39.8	60.2	0.1	0.6	2 834	19.3	11.6
Georgia[9]	2005	47.5	52.5	-0.7	-0.5	1 096	46.7	24.5
Géorgie[9]	2010	47.3	52.7	-0.9	-0.4	1 117	48.7	25.7
India	2005	70.8	29.2	1.0	2.6	18 670	5.6	1.6
Inde	2010	69.1	30.9	0.8	2.5	21 935	5.8	1.8
Indonesia	2005	54.1	45.9	-0.5	2.7	8 988	8.6	4.0
Indonésie	2010	50.1	49.9	-0.6	2.5	9 630	8.0	4.0
Iran (Islamic Rep. of)	2005	32.4	67.6	0.3	1.6	7 044	15.0	10.1
Iran (Rép. islamique d')	2010	31.1	68.9	0.6	1.3	7 243	14.2	9.8
Iraq	2005	33.0	67.0	3.2	2.8	5 327	29.0	19.5
Iraq	2010	33.5	66.5	3.2	3.1	5 891	28.0	18.6
Israel	2005	8.5	91.5	1.6	2.4	3 026	50.1	45.8
Israël	2010	8.2	91.8	0.9	1.7	3 319	48.7	44.7
Japan	2005	14.0	86.0	-7.9	1.1	35 622	32.8	28.2
Japon	2010	9.5	90.5	-7.6	0.6	36 933	32.2	29.2
Jordan	2005	18.8	81.2	1.5	3.3	1 062	24.5	19.9
Jordanie	2010	17.5	82.5	0.5	2.2	1 150	22.5	18.6
Kazakhstan	2005	45.3	54.7	1.5	0.7	1 275	15.4	8.4
Kazakhstan	2010	46.3	53.7	1.3	0.9	1 400	16.3	8.7

Population in urban and rural areas, rates of growth and largest urban agglomeration population *(continued)*

Population urbaine, population rurale, taux d'accroissement et population de l'agglomération urbaine la plus peuplée *(suite)*

Region, country or area Région, pays ou zone	Year Année	Population estimates and projections Estimations de la population et projections		Annual growth rate[1] Taux d'accroissement annuel [1]		Population of largest urban agglomeration with 750,000 inhabitants or more in 2010 Population de l'agglomération urbaine la plus peuplée avec 750,000 habitants ou plus en 2010		
		Rural % Rurale %	Urban % Urbaine %	Rural % Rurale %	Urban % Urbaine %	Number (000s) Nombre (000s)	% of urban % d'urbaine	% of total % de totale
Kuwait	2005	1.8	98.2	3.1	3.8	1 582	71.2	69.9
Koweït	2010	1.8	98.2	1.7	2.4	2 318	86.2	84.7
Kyrgyzstan	2005	64.7	35.3	1.1	1.1	798	44.8	15.8
Kirghizistan	2010	64.7	35.3	0.9	1.3	831	44.1	15.6
Lao People's Dem. Rep.	2005	72.6	27.4	-0.2	5.3	580	36.8	10.1
Rép. dém. pop. lao	2010	66.9	33.1	-0.4	4.4	766	37.3	12.4
Lebanon	2005	13.4	86.6	^0.0	1.0	1 777	50.7	43.9
Liban	2010	12.9	87.1	-0.2	0.9	1 983	53.8	46.9
Malaysia [10]	2005	32.4	67.6	-1.3	3.0	1 405	8.0	5.4
Malaisie [10]	2010	28.0	72.0	-1.0	2.5	1 524	7.5	5.4
Maldives	2005	66.3	33.8	-0.6	4.8	...	...	...
Maldives	2010	60.0	40.0	-0.7	3.9	...	...	...
Mongolia	2005	37.5	62.5	-1.3	3.1	933	58.6	36.6
Mongolie	2010	32.4	67.6	-1.4	2.8	1 138	61.1	41.3
Myanmar	2005	70.6	29.4	-0.1	2.5	3 928	28.9	8.5
Myanmar	2010	67.9	32.1	-0.1	2.5	4 356	28.3	9.1
Nepal	2005	84.9	15.1	1.5	3.8	794	19.3	2.9
Népal	2010	83.3	16.7	1.3	3.6	974	19.5	3.3
Occupied Palestinian Terr. [11]	2005	26.9	73.1	1.7	2.8	...	...	...
Terr. palestinien occupé [11]	2010	25.9	74.1	1.9	3.1	...	...	...
Oman	2005	28.1	71.9	1.8	3.1	...	...	...
Oman	2010	26.8	73.2	0.9	2.2	...	...	...
Pakistan	2005	65.5	34.5	1.4	2.6	11 743	21.5	7.4
Pakistan	2010	64.1	35.9	1.2	2.7	13 500	21.7	7.8
Philippines	2005	52.0	48.0	1.5	2.0	10 761	26.2	12.6
Philippines	2010	51.4	48.6	1.2	2.2	11 654	25.7	12.5
Qatar	2005	2.6	97.5	2.4	15.5	...	...	...
Qatar	2010	1.3	98.7	-8.6	3.0	...	...	...
Republic of Korea	2005	18.7	81.4	-1.3	0.9	9 825	25.7	20.9
République de Corée	2010	17.1	82.9	-1.3	0.7	9 751	24.4	20.2
Saudi Arabia	2005	19.0	81.0	1.5	2.9	4 227	21.7	17.6
Arabie saoudite	2010	17.9	82.1	1.0	2.4	5 227	23.2	19.0
Singapore	2005	0.0	100.0	0.0	3.5	4 266	100.0	100.0
Singapour	2010	0.0	100.0	0.0	1.1	5 086	100.0	100.0
Sri Lanka	2005	84.9	15.1	1.0	0.9	...	...	...
Sri Lanka	2010	85.0	15.0	0.7	1.4	...	...	...
Syrian Arab Republic	2005	46.2	53.8	1.2	2.7	2 605	26.2	14.1
Rép. arabe syrienne	2010	44.3	55.7	0.8	2.4	3 068	27.0	15.0
Tajikistan	2005	73.6	26.4	1.3	1.3	...	...	...
Tadjikistan	2010	73.5	26.5	1.4	1.7	...	...	...
Thailand	2005	67.8	32.2	0.3	1.6	7 228	33.6	10.8
Thaïlande	2010	66.3	33.7	-0.1	1.6	8 213	35.2	11.9
Timor-Leste	2005	73.9	26.1	1.6	3.5	...	...	...
Timor-Leste	2010	72.0	28.0	2.4	4.3	...	...	...
Turkey	2005	33.2	66.8	-1.0	2.4	9 753	21.4	14.3
Turquie	2010	29.5	70.5	-2.3	2.4	10 953	21.4	15.1
Turkmenistan	2005	53.0	47.1	0.7	1.8	...	...	...
Turkménistan	2010	51.6	48.4	0.6	1.9	...	...	...
United Arab Emirates	2005	17.7	82.3	10.1	12.7	1 264	37.8	31.1
Emirats arabes unis	2010	16.0	84.0	0.3	2.5	1 835	29.1	24.4
Uzbekistan	2005	63.3	36.7	1.3	0.9	2 169	22.8	8.4
Ouzbékistan	2010	63.8	36.2	1.1	1.3	2 213	22.3	8.1
Viet Nam	2005	72.7	27.3	0.2	3.3	5 212	23.0	6.3
Viet Nam	2010	69.6	30.4	0.1	3.0	6 189	23.2	7.0

Population in urban and rural areas, rates of growth and largest urban agglomeration population *(continued)*

Population urbaine, population rurale, taux d'accroissement et population de l'agglomération urbaine la plus peuplée *(suite)*

Region, country or area Région, pays ou zone	Year Année	Rural % Rurale %	Urban % Urbaine %	Annual growth rate[1] Taux d'accroissement annuel[1] Rural % Rurale %	Urban % Urbaine %	Population of largest urban agglomeration with 750,000 inhabitants or more in 2010 Population de l'agglomération urbaine la plus peuplée avec 750,000 habitants ou plus en 2010 Number (000s) Nombre (000s)	% of urban % d'urbaine	% of total % de totale
Yemen	2005	71.1	28.9	2.3	4.9	1 757	29.4	8.5
Yémen	2010	68.3	31.7	2.2	4.8	2 293	30.0	9.5
Europe	**2005**	**28.4**	**71.6**	**-0.6**	**0.5**	...	...	...
Europe	**2010**	**27.3**	**72.7**	**-0.7**	**0.4**	...	...	...
Albania	2005	53.2	46.8	-1.8	2.6	...	...	...
Albanie	2010	47.7	52.3	-2.0	2.3	...	...	...
Andorra	2005	9.7	90.3	6.3	1.2	...	...	...
Andorre	2010	12.2	87.8	5.5	0.9	...	...	...
Austria	2005	33.5	66.5	-0.2	0.7	1 641	30.0	19.9
Autriche	2010	32.5	67.5	-0.5	0.5	1 708	30.2	20.3
Belarus	2005	27.7	72.4	-2.2	0.1	1 775	25.0	18.1
Bélarus	2010	25.4	74.6	-2.0	0.2	1 847	25.8	19.2
Belgium	2005	2.7	97.3	-0.7	0.6	1 858	18.3	17.8
Belgique	2010	2.5	97.5	-0.9	0.3	1 933	18.5	18.0
Bosnia and Herzegovina	2005	54.7	45.3	-1.0	1.0	...	...	...
Bosnie-Herzégovine	2010	52.3	47.7	-1.3	0.9	...	...	...
Bulgaria	2005	29.8	70.2	-2.3	^0.0	1 169	21.5	15.1
Bulgarie	2010	27.5	72.5	-2.8	0.1	1 175	21.6	15.7
Channel Islands [12]	2005	69.4	30.7	0.5	0.9	...	...	...
Iles Anglo-Normandes [12]	2010	68.9	31.1	^0.0	0.6	...	...	...
Croatia	2005	43.6	56.4	-0.7	0.2	...	...	...
Croatie	2010	42.5	57.5	-0.9	0.3	...	...	...
Czech Republic	2005	26.3	73.7	0.7	0.5	1 213	16.1	11.9
République tchèque	2010	26.5	73.5	0.4	0.2	1 265	16.4	12.1
Denmark	2005	14.1	85.9	-0.9	0.7	1 127	24.2	20.8
Danemark	2010	13.2	86.8	-0.7	0.5	1 192	24.8	21.5
Estonia	2005	30.6	69.4	-0.1	-0.1	...	...	...
Estonie	2010	30.5	69.5	-0.3	0.0	...	...	...
Faeroe Islands	2005	60.2	39.8	-0.2	0.8	...	...	...
Iles Féroé	2010	59.1	40.9	0.1	1.0	...	...	...
Finland [13]	2005	17.1	82.9	-0.3	0.6	1 067	24.5	20.4
Finlande [13]	2010	16.4	83.6	-0.5	0.5	1 122	25.0	20.9
France	2005	18.5	81.6	-3.9	1.5	10 105	20.3	16.6
France	2010	14.8	85.2	-3.3	1.1	10 516	19.7	16.7
Germany	2005	26.7	73.4	-0.4	0.1	3 392	5.6	4.1
Allemagne	2010	26.2	73.8	-0.7	^0.0	3 450	5.7	4.2
Gibraltar	2005	0.0	100.0	0.0	0.1	...	...	...
Gibraltar	2010	0.0	100.0	0.0	0.1	...	...	...
Greece	2005	39.7	60.3	-0.2	0.6	3 251	48.2	29.1
Grèce	2010	38.8	61.2	-0.4	0.6	3 382	48.6	29.8
Holy See	2005	0.0	100.0	0.0	-1.4	...	...	...
Saint-Siège	2010	0.0	100.0	0.0	0.1	...	...	...
Hungary	2005	33.6	66.4	-1.8	0.6	1 700	25.4	16.9
Hongrie	2010	31.0	69.0	-1.7	0.5	1 731	25.1	17.3
Iceland	2005	7.0	93.0	-0.2	1.6	...	...	...
Islande	2010	6.4	93.6	-0.6	1.3	...	...	...
Ireland	2005	39.5	60.5	0.7	1.9	1 037	41.3	25.0
Irlande	2010	38.1	61.9	0.3	1.6	1 102	39.8	24.7
Isle of Man	2005	48.8	51.2	1.0	0.5	...	...	...
Ile de Man	2010	49.4	50.6	0.5	0.4	...	...	...
Italy	2005	32.4	67.6	0.2	0.8	3 345	8.4	5.7
Italie	2010	31.8	68.2	-0.4	0.5	3 306	8.0	5.5
Latvia	2005	32.0	68.0	-0.3	-0.6	...	...	...
Lettonie	2010	32.3	67.7	-0.4	-0.4	...	...	...

8

Population in urban and rural areas, rates of growth and largest urban agglomeration population *(continued)*

Population urbaine, population rurale, taux d'accroissement et population de l'agglomération urbaine la plus peuplée *(suite)*

Region, country or area Région, pays ou zone	Year Année	Population estimates and projections Estimations de la population et projections		Annual growth rate[1] Taux d'accroissement annuel[1]		Population of largest urban agglomeration with 750,000 inhabitants or more in 2010 Population de l'agglomération urbaine la plus peuplée avec 750,000 habitants ou plus en 2010		
		Rural % Rurale %	Urban % Urbaine %	Rural % Rurale %	Urban % Urbaine %	Number (000s) Nombre (000s)	% of urban % d'urbaine	% of total % de totale
Liechtenstein	2005	85.3	14.7	0.8	0.4	...	...	...
Liechtenstein	2010	85.6	14.4	0.8	0.5	...	...	...
Lithuania	2005	33.4	66.6	-0.8	-0.4	...	...	...
Lituanie	2010	33.0	67.0	-0.8	-0.3	...	...	...
Luxembourg	2005	16.1	83.9	0.5	2.4	...	...	...
Luxembourg	2010	14.8	85.2	-0.2	1.6	...	...	...
Malta	2005	6.4	93.7	-3.2	0.6	...	...	...
Malte	2010	5.3	94.7	-2.8	0.5	...	...	...
Monaco	2005	0.0	100.0	0.0	0.1	...	...	...
Monaco	2010	0.0	100.0	0.0	^0.0	...	...	...
Montenegro	2005	37.8	62.2	-0.3	0.4	...	...	...
Monténégro	2010	36.9	63.1	-0.5	0.4	...	...	...
Netherlands	2005	19.8	80.2	-2.4	1.0	1 023	7.8	6.3
Pays-Bas	2010	17.3	82.7	-2.1	0.7	1 049	7.6	6.3
Norway[14]	2005	22.5	77.5	-0.4	1.5	818	22.9	17.7
Norvège[14]	2010	20.9	79.1	-0.7	1.0	898	23.2	18.4
Poland	2005	38.5	61.5	0.3	-0.1	1 689	7.2	4.4
Pologne	2010	39.1	60.9	0.2	^0.0	1 718	7.4	4.5
Portugal	2005	42.4	57.6	-1.2	1.2	2 747	45.3	26.1
Portugal	2010	39.5	60.5	-1.4	0.9	2 825	43.7	26.5
Republic of Moldova[15]	2005	56.8	43.2	-2.4	0.6	...	...	...
République de Moldova[15]	2010	53.1	46.9	-2.1	0.8	...	...	...
Romania	2005	47.2	52.8	-0.3	-0.3	1 931	16.8	8.9
Roumanie	2010	47.2	52.8	-0.3	-0.2	1 935	17.1	9.0
Russian Federation	2005	27.1	72.9	-0.7	0.1	10 755	10.3	7.5
Fédération de Russie	2010	26.3	73.7	-0.8	0.1	11 472	10.9	8.0
San Marino	2005	6.0	94.0	0.6	0.8	...	...	...
Saint-Marin	2010	5.9	94.1	0.2	0.7	...	...	...
Serbia[16]	2005	45.6	54.4	-0.7	0.6	1 125	21.0	11.4
Serbie[16]	2010	44.0	56.0	-0.9	0.5	1 133	20.5	11.5
Slovakia	2005	44.4	55.6	0.5	-0.1	...	...	...
Slovaquie	2010	45.2	54.8	0.3	0.1	...	...	...
Slovenia	2005	49.5	50.5	0.5	0.1	...	...	...
Slovénie	2010	50.0	50.0	0.3	0.2	...	...	...
Spain[17]	2005	23.3	76.7	0.7	1.4	5 619	16.9	13.0
Espagne[17]	2010	22.7	77.3	^0.0	0.8	6 405	18.0	13.9
Sweden	2005	15.7	84.3	-0.2	0.9	1 248	16.4	13.8
Suède	2010	14.9	85.1	-0.5	0.7	1 360	17.0	14.5
Switzerland	2005	26.5	73.5	0.5	0.7	1 128	20.7	15.2
Suisse	2010	26.4	73.6	0.1	0.5	1 183	21.0	15.4
TFYR of Macedonia	2005	41.0	59.1	0.2	0.3	...	...	...
L'ex-R.Y. Macédoine	2010	40.8	59.2	-0.2	0.3	...	...	...
Ukraine	2005	32.2	67.8	-1.2	-0.4	2 673	8.4	5.7
Ukraine	2010	31.3	68.7	-1.2	-0.3	2 805	9.0	6.2
United Kingdom	2005	21.0	79.0	0.1	0.7	8 552	18.0	14.2
Royaume-Uni	2010	20.5	79.5	0.0	0.8	8 923	18.1	14.4
Oceania	**2005**	**29.6**	**70.4**	**1.6**	**1.8**	**...**	**...**	**...**
Océanie	**2010**	**29.3**	**70.7**	**1.4**	**1.5**	**...**	**...**	**...**
American Samoa	2005	8.7	91.3	-2.7	2.0	...	...	...
Samoa américaines	2010	7.0	93.0	-1.9	1.9	...	...	...
Australia[18]	2005	11.8	88.2	0.2	1.9	4 260	23.7	20.9
Australie[18]	2010	11.0	89.0	-0.1	1.5	4 479	22.6	20.1
Cook Islands	2005	29.0	71.0	-0.7	1.5	...	...	...
Iles Cook	2010	26.7	73.3	-0.4	0.9	...	...	...

Population in urban and rural areas, rates of growth and largest urban agglomeration population *(continued)*

Population urbaine, population rurale, taux d'accroissement et population de l'agglomération urbaine la plus peuplée *(suite)*

Region, country or area Région, pays ou zone	Year Année	Population estimates and projections Estimations de la population et projections		Annual growth rate[1] Taux d'accroissement annuel[1]		Population of largest urban agglomeration with 750,000 inhabitants or more in 2010 Population de l'agglomération urbaine la plus peuplée avec 750,000 habitants ou plus en 2010		
		Rural % Rurale %	Urban % Urbaine %	Rural % Rurale %	Urban % Urbaine %	Number (000s) Nombre (000s)	% of urban % d'urbaine	% of total % de totale
Fiji	2005	50.1	49.9	0.1	1.7	...	...	...
Fidji	2010	48.2	51.8	0.0	1.6			
French Polynesia	2005	48.2	51.8	1.4	1.1	...	...	...
Polynésie française	2010	48.6	51.4	1.0	1.1			
Guam	2005	6.9	93.1	1.1	1.3	...	...	...
Guam	2010	6.8	93.2	0.7	1.2			
Kiribati	2005	56.5	43.6	1.5	1.7	...	...	...
Kiribati	2010	56.2	43.8	1.3	1.8			
Marshall Islands	2005	30.0	70.0	-0.3	1.2	...	...	...
Iles Marshall	2010	28.5	71.5	0.5	2.0			
Micronesia (Fed. States of)	2005	77.7	22.3	0.3	0.5	...	...	...
Micronésie (Etats féd. de)	2010	77.5	22.5	0.4	1.0			
Nauru	2005	0.0	100.0	0.0	0.3	...	...	...
Nauru	2010	0.0	100.0	0.0	0.6			
New Caledonia	2005	36.8	63.2	2.3	1.2	...	...	...
Nouvelle-Calédonie	2010	38.1	61.9	1.9	1.2			
New Zealand	2005	14.0	86.1	0.9	1.1	1 189	33.4	28.8
Nouvelle-Zélande	2010	13.8	86.2	0.7	1.1	1 407	37.4	32.2
Niue	2005	64.8	35.2	-3.5	-1.5	...	...	...
Nioué	2010	62.5	37.5	-3.5	-1.6			
Northern Mariana Islands	2005	9.2	90.8	-3.3	-1.9	...	...	...
Iles Mariannes du Nord	2010	8.7	91.3	0.4	1.9			
Palau	2005	22.3	77.7	-5.3	2.0	...	...	...
Palaos	2010	16.6	83.4	-4.3	1.7			
Papua New Guinea	2005	87.4	12.6	2.4	2.1	...	...	...
Papouasie-Nvl-Guinée	2010	87.6	12.4	2.1	2.7			
Samoa	2005	78.8	21.2	0.6	-0.8	...	...	...
Samoa	2010	79.9	20.1	0.7	-0.5			
Solomon Islands	2005	82.2	17.8	2.2	5.0	...	...	...
Iles Salomon	2010	80.0	20.0	1.9	4.7			
Tokelau	2005	100.0	0.0	-1.3	0.0	...	...	...
Tokélaou	2010	100.0	0.0	0.3	0.0			
Tonga	2005	76.9	23.2	0.6	0.8	...	...	...
Tonga	2010	76.6	23.4	0.3	0.8			
Tuvalu	2005	51.9	48.1	-0.5	1.1	...	...	...
Tuvalu	2010	49.9	50.1	-0.6	1.0			
Vanuatu	2005	76.9	23.1	2.1	3.8	...	...	...
Vanuatu	2010	75.4	24.6	2.0	3.6			
Wallis and Futuna Islands	2005	100.0	0.0	-1.0	0.0	...	...	...
Iles Wallis et Futuna	2010	100.0	0.0	-0.7	0.0			

Source:
United Nations Population Division, New York, *World Urbanization Prospects: The 2011 Revision.*

Source:
Organisation des Nations Unies, Division de statistique, New York, *"World Urbanization Prospects:The 2011 Revision."*

1 Annual rates of growth calculated for the periods 2005 - 2010 and 2010 - 2015.
2 Including Agalega, Rodrigues and Saint Brandon.
3 Including Ascension and Tristan da Cunha.
4 Including Saint-Barthélemy and Saint-Martin (French part).
5 Comprising Bonaire, Curaçao, Saba, St. Eustatius and Dutch part of St. Martin.
6 Including Nagorno-Karabakh.
7 For statistical purposes, the data for China do not include those for the

1 Ces taux d'accroissement annuel ont été calculés pour les périodes 2005 à 2010 et 2010 à 2015.
2 Y compris Agalega, Rodrigues et Saint Brandon.
3 Y compris Ascension et Tristan da Cunha.
4 Y compris Saint Barthélémy et Saint Martin.
5 Comprend Bonaire, Curaçao, Saba, Saint-Eustache et la partie néederlandaise de Saint-Martin.
6 Y compris le Haut-Karabakh.
7 Pour la présentation des statistiques, les données pour la Chine ne

Population in urban and rural areas, rates of growth and largest urban agglomeration population *(continued)*

Population urbaine, population rurale, taux d'accroissement et population de l'agglomération urbaine la plus peuplée *(suite)*

Hong Kong Special Administrative Region (Hong Kong SAR) and Macao Special Administrative Region (Macao SAR).

8	Including Northern-Cyprus.
9	Including Abkhazia and South Ossetia
10	Including Sabah and Sarawak.
11	Including East Jerusalem.
12	Refers to Guernsey and Jersey.
13	Including Aland Islands.
14	Including Svalbard and Jan Mayen Islands.
15	Including Transnistria.
16	Including Kosovo.
17	Including Canary Islands, Ceuta and Melilla.
18	Including Christmas Island, Cocos (Keeling) Islands and Norfolk Island.

comprennent pas la Région Administrative Spéciale de Hong Kong (Hong Kong RAS) et la Région Administrative Spéciale de Macao (Macao RAS).

8	Y compris la partie nord de Chypre.
9	Y compris l'Abkhazie et l'Ossétie du Sud.
10	Y compris Sabah et Sarawak.
11	Y compris Jérusalem-Est.
12	Se rapporte à Guernsey and Jersey.
13	Y compris les Îles d'Åland.
14	Y compris îles Svalbard et Jan Mayen.
15	Y compris la Transnistrie.
16	Y compris Kosovo.
17	Y compris les Iles Canaries, Ceuta et Melilla.
18	Y compris les îles Christmas, Cocos (Keeling) et Norfolk.

Proportion of seats held by women in national parliament
Percentage, as of 31 January 2012

Proportion de sièges occupés par les femmes au parlement national
Pourcentage, données disponibles en 31 janvier 2012

Country or area	1990	2000	2005	2006	2007	2008	2009	2010	2011	2012	Pays ou zone
Afghanistan	3.7	...	...	27.3	27.3	27.7	27.7	27.3	27.7	27.7	Afghanistan
Albania	28.8	5.2	6.4	7.1	7.1	7.1	7.1	16.4	16.4	15.7	Albanie
Algeria	2.4	3.2	6.2	6.2	6.2	7.7	7.7	7.7	7.7	8.0	Algérie
Andorra	...	7.1	14.3	28.6	28.6	25.0	25.0	35.7	35.7	50.0	Andorre
Angola	14.5	15.5	15.0	15.0	15.0	15.0	37.3	38.6	38.6	38.2	Angola
Antigua and Barbuda	0.0	...	10.5	10.5	10.5	10.5	10.5	10.5	10.5	10.5	Antigua-et-Barbuda
Argentina	6.3	28.0	33.7	36.2	35.0	40.0	40.0	38.5	38.5	37.4	Argentine
Armenia	35.6	3.1	5.3	5.3	5.3	9.2	8.4	9.2	9.2	8.4	Arménie
Australia	6.1	22.4	24.7	24.7	24.7	26.7	26.7	27.3	24.7	24.7	Australie
Austria	11.5	26.8	33.9	33.9	32.2	32.8	27.3	27.9	27.9	27.9	Autriche
Azerbaijan	...	12.0	10.5	12.0	11.3	11.4	11.4	11.4	16.0	16.0	Azerbaïdjan
Bahamas	4.1	15.0	20.0	20.0	20.0	12.2	12.2	12.2	12.2	12.2	Bahamas
Bahrain	...	...	0.0	0.0	2.5	2.5	2.5	2.5	2.5	10.0	Bahreïn
Bangladesh	10.3	9.1	2.0	14.8[1,2]	...	...	6.3[3]	18.6	18.6	19.7	Bangladesh
Barbados	3.7	10.7	13.3	13.3	13.3	10.0	10.0	10.0	10.0	10.0	Barbade
Belarus	...	4.5	29.4	29.1	29.1	29.1	31.8	31.8	31.8	31.8	Bélarus
Belgium	8.5	23.3	34.7	34.7	34.7	35.3	35.3	38.0	39.3	38.0	Belgique
Belize	0.0	6.9	6.7	6.7	6.7	3.3	0.0	0.0	0.0	0.0	Belize
Benin	2.9	6.0	7.2	7.2	7.2	10.8	10.8	10.8	10.8	8.4	Bénin
Bhutan	2.0	2.0	9.3	9.3	2.7	2.7	8.5	8.5	8.5	8.5	Bhoutan
Bolivia (Plurin. State of)	9.2	11.5	19.2	16.9	16.9	16.9	16.9	22.3	25.4	25.4	Bolivie (État plurin. de)
Bosnia and Herzegovina	...	28.6	16.7	16.7	14.3	11.9	11.9	19.0	16.7	21.4	Bosnie-Herzégovine
Botswana	5.0	...	11.1	11.1	11.1	11.1	11.1	7.9	7.9	7.9	Botswana
Brazil	5.3	5.7	8.6	8.6	8.8	9.0	9.0	8.8	8.6	8.6	Brésil
Bulgaria	21.0	10.8	26.3	22.1	22.1	21.7	21.7	20.8	20.8	20.8	Bulgarie
Burkina Faso	...	8.1	11.7	11.7	11.7	15.3	15.3	15.3	15.3	15.3	Burkina Faso
Burundi	...	6.0	18.4	30.5	30.5	30.5	30.5	31.4	32.1	30.5	Burundi
Cambodia	...	8.2	9.8	9.8	9.8	19.5	16.3	21.1	21.1	20.3	Cambodge
Cameroon	14.4	5.6	8.9	8.9	8.9	13.9	13.9	13.9	13.9	13.9	Cameroun
Canada	13.3	20.6	21.1	20.8	20.8	21.3	22.1	22.1	22.1	24.8	Canada
Cape Verde	12.0	11.1	11.1	15.3	15.3	18.1	18.1	18.1	18.1	20.8	Cap-Vert
Central African Rep.	3.8	7.3	...	10.5	10.5	10.5	10.5	9.6	...	12.5	Rép. centrafricaine
Chad	...	2.4	6.5	6.5	6.5	5.2	5.2	5.2	5.2	12.8	Tchad
Chile	...	10.8	12.5	15.0	15.0	15.0	15.0	14.2	14.2	14.2	Chili
China	21.3	21.8	20.2	20.3	20.3	20.6	21.3	21.3	21.3	21.3	Chine
Colombia	4.5	11.8	12.0	12.1	8.4	8.4	8.4	8.4	12.7	12.1	Colombie
Comoros	0.0	...	3.0	3.0	3.0	3.0	3.0	3.0	3.0	3.0	Comores
Congo	14.3	12.0	8.5	8.5	8.5	7.3	7.3	7.3	7.3	7.3	Congo
Costa Rica	10.5	19.3	35.1	35.1	38.6	36.8	36.8	36.8	38.6	38.6	Costa Rica
Côte d'Ivoire	5.7	...	8.5	8.5	8.5	8.9	8.9	8.9	8.9	11.0	Côte d'Ivoire
Croatia	...	...	21.7	21.7	21.7	20.9	20.9	23.5	23.5	23.8	Croatie
Cuba	33.9	27.6	36.0	36.0	36.0	43.2	43.2	43.2	43.2	45.2	Cuba
Cyprus	1.8	5.4	16.1	16.1	14.3	14.3	14.3	12.5	12.5	10.7	Chypre
Czech Republic	...	15.0	17.0	17.0	15.5	15.5	15.5	15.5	22.0	22.0	République tchèque
Dem. P. R. Korea	21.1	20.1	20.1	20.1	20.1	20.1	20.1	15.6	15.6	15.6	R. p. dém. de Corée

9

Proportion of seats held by women in national parliament *(continued)*
Percentage, as of 31 January 2012

Proportion de sièges occupés par les femmes au parlement national *(suite)*
Pourcentage, données disponibles en 31 janvier 2012

Country or area	1990	2000	2005	2006	2007	2008	2009	2010	2011	2012	Pays ou zone
Dem. Rep. of the Congo	5.4	...	12.0	12.0	8.4	8.4	8.4	8.4	8.4	8.9	Rép. dém. du Congo
Denmark	30.7	37.4	38.0	36.9	36.9	38.0	38.0	38.0	38.0	39.1	Danemark
Djibouti	0.0	0.0	10.8	10.8	10.8	13.8	13.8	13.8	13.8	13.8	Djibouti
Dominica	10.0	9.4	19.4	12.9	12.9	16.1	18.8	14.3	12.5	12.5	Dominique
Dominican Republic	7.5	16.1	17.3	17.3	19.7	19.7	19.7	19.7	20.8	20.8	Rép. dominicaine
Ecuador	4.5	17.4	16.0	16.0	25.0	25.0	27.6[4]	32.3	32.3	32.3	Equateur
Egypt	3.9	2.0	2.9	2.0	2.0	1.8	1.8	1.8	12.7	2.0	Egypte
El Salvador	11.7	16.7	10.7	10.7	16.7	16.7	19.0	19.0	19.0	19.0	El Salvador
Equatorial Guinea	13.3	5.0	18.0	18.0	18.0	18.0	6.0	10.0	10.0	10.0	Guinée équatoriale
Eritrea	...	14.7	22.0	22.0	22.0	22.0	22.0	22.0	22.0	22.0	Erythrée
Estonia	...	17.8	18.8	18.8	18.8	20.8	20.8	22.8	22.8	19.8	Estonie
Ethiopia	...	2.0	7.7	21.4	21.9	21.9	21.9	21.9	27.8	27.8	Ethiopie
Fiji	...	11.3	8.5	8.5[5]	...	...	...	...	...	...	Fidji
Finland	31.5	37.0	37.5	37.5	38.0	41.5	41.5	40.0	40.0	42.5	Finlande
France	6.9	10.9	12.2	12.2	12.2	18.2	18.2	18.9	18.9	18.9	France
Gabon	13.3	8.3	9.2	9.2	12.5	16.7	16.7	14.7	14.7	15.8	Gabon
Gambia	7.8	2.0	13.2	13.2	9.4	9.4	9.4	7.5	7.5	7.5	Gambie
Georgia	...	7.2	9.4	9.4	9.4	9.4	6.0	5.1	6.5	6.6	Géorgie
Germany	...	30.9	32.8	31.8	31.6	31.6	32.2	32.8	32.8	32.9	Allemagne
Ghana	...	9.0	10.9	10.9	10.9	10.9	7.9	8.3	8.3	8.3	Ghana
Greece	6.7	6.3	14.0	13.0	13.0	14.7	14.7	17.3	17.3	18.7	Grèce
Grenada	...	...	26.7	26.7	26.7	26.7	13.3	13.3	13.3	13.3	Grenade
Guatemala	7.0	7.1	8.2	8.2	8.2	12.0	12.0	12.0	12.0	13.3	Guatemala
Guinea	...	8.8	19.3	19.3	19.3	19.3[6]	...	...	...	...	Guinée
Guinea-Bissau	20.0	...	14.0	14.0	14.0	14.0	10.0	10.0	10.0	10.0	Guinée-Bissau
Guyana	36.9	18.5	30.8	30.8	29.0	29.0	30.0	30.0	30.0	31.3	Guyana
Haiti	...	3.6	3.6	3.6	4.1	4.1	4.1	4.1	11.1	4.2	Haïti
Honduras	10.2	9.4	5.5	23.4	23.4	23.4	23.4	18.0	18.0	19.5	Honduras
Hungary	20.7	8.3	9.1	9.1	10.4	11.1	11.1	11.1	9.1	8.8	Hongrie
Iceland	20.6	34.9	30.2	33.3	33.3	33.3	33.3	42.9	42.9	39.7	Islande
India	5.0	9.0	8.3	8.3	8.3	9.1	9.1	10.8	10.8	11.0	Inde
Indonesia	12.4	...	11.3	11.3	11.3	11.6	11.6	18.0	18.0	18.2	Indonésie
Iran (Islamic Rep. of)	1.5	4.9	4.1	4.1	4.1	4.1	2.8	2.8	2.8	2.8	Iran (Rép. islamique d')
Iraq	10.8	6.4	...	25.5	25.5	25.5	25.5	25.5	25.2	25.2	Iraq
Ireland	7.8	12.0	13.3	13.3	13.3	13.3	13.3	13.9	13.9	15.1	Irlande
Israel	6.7	11.7	15.0	15.0	14.2	14.2	14.2	19.2	19.2	20.0	Israël
Italy	12.9	11.1	11.5	11.5	17.3	17.3	21.3	21.3	21.3	21.6	Italie
Jamaica	5.0	13.3	11.7	11.7	11.7	13.3	13.3	13.3	13.3	12.7	Jamaïque
Japan	1.4	4.6	7.1	9.0	9.4	9.4	9.4	11.3	11.3	10.8	Japon
Jordan	0.0	0.0	5.5	5.5	5.5	6.4	6.4	6.4	10.8	10.8	Jordanie
Kazakhstan	...	10.4	10.4	10.4	10.4	15.9	15.9	17.8	17.8	24.3	Kazakhstan
Kenya	1.1	3.6	7.1	7.1	7.3	7.2[7]	9.8	9.8	9.8	9.8	Kenya
Kiribati	0.0	4.9	4.8	4.8	7.1	4.3	4.3	4.3	4.3	8.7	Kiribati
Kuwait	...	0.0	0.0	1.5[8]	1.5[9]	1.5[10]	3.1[11]	7.7	7.7	7.7	Koweït
Kyrgyzstan	...	1.4	10.0	0.0	0.0	25.6	25.6	25.6	23.3	23.3	Kirghizistan
Lao People's Dem. Rep.	6.3	21.2	22.9	22.9	25.2	25.2	25.2	25.2	25.2	25.0	Rép. dém. pop. lao

Proportion of seats held by women in national parliament *(continued)*
Percentage, as of 31 January 2012
Proportion de sièges occupés par les femmes au parlement national *(suite)*
Pourcentage, données disponibles en 31 janvier 2012

Country or area	1990	2000	2005	2006	2007	2008	2009	2010	2011	2012	Pays ou zone
Latvia	...	17.0	21.0	21.0	19.0	20.0	20.0	22.0	20.0	23.0	Lettonie
Lebanon	0.0	2.3	2.3	4.7	4.7	4.7	4.7	3.1	3.1	3.1	Liban
Lesotho	...	3.8	11.7	11.7	11.8	25.0	25.0	24.2	24.2	24.2	Lesotho
Liberia	...	...	5.3	12.5	12.5	12.5	12.5	12.5	12.5	9.6	Libéria
Libyan Arab Jamah.	...	...	...	4.7	7.7	7.7	7.7	7.7	7.7	...	Jamah. arabe libyenne
Liechtenstein	4.0	4.0	12.0	24.0	24.0	24.0	24.0	24.0	24.0	24.0	Liechtenstein
Lithuania	...	17.5	22.0	22.0	24.8	22.7	17.7	19.1	19.1	19.1	Lituanie
Luxembourg	13.3	16.7	23.3	23.3	23.3	23.3	23.3	20.0	20.0	25.0	Luxembourg
Madagascar	6.5	8.0	6.9	6.9	6.9	7.9	7.9[5]	...	12.5	17.5	Madagascar
Malawi	9.8	8.3	14.0	13.6	13.6	13.0	13.0	20.8	20.8	22.3	Malawi
Malaysia	5.1	...	9.1	9.1	9.1	10.0	10.8	9.9	9.9	10.4	Malaisie
Maldives	6.3	...	12.0	12.0	12.0	12.0	12.0	6.5	6.5	6.5	Maldives
Mali	...	12.2	10.2	10.2	10.2	10.2	10.2	10.2	10.2	10.2	Mali
Malta	2.9	9.2	9.2	9.2	9.2	9.2	8.7	8.7	8.7	8.7	Malte
Marshall Islands	...	...	3.0	3.0	3.0	3.0	3.0	3.0	3.0	3.0	Iles Marshall
Mauritania	...	3.8	3.7	...	17.9	22.1	22.1	22.1	22.1	22.1	Mauritanie
Mauritius	7.1	7.6	5.7	17.1	17.1	17.1	17.1	17.1	18.8	18.8	Maurice
Mexico	12.0	18.2	22.6	24.2	22.6	23.2	23.2	27.6	26.2	26.2	Mexique
Micronesia (Fed. States of)	...	0.0	0.0	0.0	0.0	0.0	0.0	0.0	0.0	0.0	Micronésie (Etats féd. de)
Monaco	11.1	22.2	20.8	20.8	20.8	20.8	25.0	26.1	26.1	19.0	Monaco
Mongolia	24.9	7.9	6.8	6.7	6.6	6.6	4.1	3.9	3.9	3.9	Mongolie
Montenegro	...	...	...	...	8.6	11.1	11.1	11.1	11.1	12.3	Monténégro
Morocco	0.0	0.6	10.8	10.8	10.8	10.5	10.5	10.5	10.5	17.0	Maroc
Mozambique	15.7	...	34.8	34.8	34.8	34.8	34.8	39.2	39.2	39.2	Mozambique
Myanmar	...	...	...	...	...	...	...	...	4.3	3.5	Myanmar
Namibia	6.9	22.2	25.0	26.9	26.9	26.9	26.9	26.9[12]	24.4	24.4	Namibie
Nauru	5.6	0.0	0.0	0.0	0.0	0.0	0.0	0.0	0.0	0.0	Nauru
Nepal	6.1	5.9[13]	...	...	17.3[14]	17.3[14]	33.2	33.2	33.2	33.2	Népal
Netherlands	21.3	36.0	36.7	36.7	36.7	39.3	41.3	42.0	40.7	40.7	Pays-Bas
New Zealand	14.4	29.2	28.3	32.2	32.2	33.1	33.6	33.6	33.6	32.2	Nouvelle-Zélande
Nicaragua	14.8	9.7	20.7	20.7	18.5	18.5	18.5	20.7	20.7	40.2	Nicaragua
Niger	5.4	1.2	12.4	12.4	12.4	12.4	12.4	9.7	...	13.3	Niger
Nigeria	...	...	4.7	6.4	6.1	7.0	7.0	7.0	7.0	6.8	Nigéria
Norway	35.8	36.4	38.2	37.9	37.9	36.1	36.1	39.6	39.6	39.6	Norvège
Oman	...	...	2.4	2.4	2.4	0.0	0.0	0.0	0.0	1.2	Oman
Pakistan	10.1	...	21.3	21.3	21.3	21.1	22.5	22.2	22.2	22.5	Pakistan
Palau	...	0.0	0.0	0.0	0.0	0.0	0.0	0.0	0.0	0.0	Palaos
Panama	7.5	...	16.7	16.7	16.7	16.7	16.7	8.5	8.5	8.5	Panama
Papua New Guinea	0.0	1.8	0.9	0.9	0.9	0.9	0.9	0.9	0.9	0.9	Papouasie-Nvl-Guinée
Paraguay	5.6	2.5	10.0	10.0	10.0	10.0	12.5	12.5	12.5	12.5	Paraguay
Peru	5.6	10.8	18.3	18.3	29.2	29.2	29.2	27.5	27.5	21.5	Pérou
Philippines	9.1	12.4	15.3	15.7	15.3	20.5	20.5	21.0	22.1	22.9	Philippines
Poland	13.5	13.0	20.2	20.4	20.4	20.4	20.2	20.0	20.0	23.7	Pologne
Portugal	7.6	18.7	19.1	21.3	21.3	28.3	28.3	27.4	27.4	28.7	Portugal
Qatar	...	...	...	0.0	0.0	0.0	0.0	0.0	0.0	0.0	Qatar
Republic of Korea	2.0	3.7	13.0	13.4	13.4	14.4	13.7	14.7	14.7	14.7	République de Corée

Proportion of seats held by women in national parliament *(continued)*
Percentage, as of 31 January 2012

Proportion de sièges occupés par les femmes au parlement national *(suite)*
Pourcentage, données disponibles en 31 janvier 2012

Country or area	1990	2000	2005	2006	2007	2008	2009	2010	2011	2012	Pays ou zone
Republic of Moldova	...	8.9	15.8	21.8	21.8	21.8	21.8	23.8	18.8	19.8	République de Moldova
Romania	34.4	7.3	11.4	11.2	11.2	9.4	11.4	11.4	11.4	11.2	Roumanie
Russian Federation	...	7.7	9.8	9.8	9.8	14.0	14.0	14.0	14.0	13.6	Fédération de Russie
Rwanda	17.1	17.1	48.8	48.8	48.8	48.8	56.3	56.3	56.3	56.3	Rwanda
Saint Kitts and Nevis	6.7	13.3	0.0	0.0	0.0	6.7	6.7	6.7	6.7	6.7	Saint-Kitts-et-Nevis
Saint Lucia	0.0	11.1	11.1	11.1	5.6[15]	11.1	11.1	11.1	11.1	16.7	Sainte-Lucie
Saint Vincent-Grenadines	9.5	4.8	22.7	18.2	18.2	18.2	18.2	21.7	14.3	17.4	Saint Vincent-Grenadines
Samoa	0.0	8.2	6.1	6.1	6.1	8.2	8.2	8.2	8.2	4.1	Samoa
San Marino	11.7	13.3	16.7	16.7	11.7	11.7	15.0	16.7	16.7	18.3	Saint-Marin
Sao Tome and Principe	11.8	9.1	9.1	9.1	7.3	1.8	7.3	7.3	18.2	18.2	Sao Tomé-et-Principe
Saudi Arabia	...	...	0.0	0.0	0.0	0.0	0.0	0.0	0.0	0.0	Arabie saoudite
Senegal	12.5	12.1	19.2	19.2	19.2	22.0	22.0	22.7	22.7	22.7	Sénégal
Serbia	...	...	...	...	20.4	20.4	21.6	21.6	21.6	22.0	Serbie
Serbia and Montenegro	...	5.1	7.9	7.9	...	...	...	...	...	...	Serbie-et-Monténégro
Seychelles	16.0	23.5	29.4	29.4	29.4	23.5	23.5	23.5	23.5	43.8	Seychelles
Sierra Leone	...	8.8	14.5	14.5	14.5	13.2	13.2	13.2	13.2	12.9	Sierra Leone
Singapore	4.9	4.3	16.0	16.0	24.5	24.5	24.5	23.4	23.4	22.2	Singapour
Slovakia	...	12.7	16.7	16.7	20.0	19.3	19.3	18.0	15.3	16.0	Slovaquie
Slovenia	...	7.8	12.2	12.2	12.2	12.2	13.3	14.4	14.4	32.2	Slovénie
Solomon Islands	0.0	2.0	0.0	0.0	0.0	0.0	0.0	0.0	0.0	0.0	Iles Salomon
Somalia	4.0	...	...	8.0	7.8	8.2[16]	...	6.9	6.8	6.8	Somalie
South Africa	2.8	30.0	32.8	32.8	32.8	33.0	33.0	44.5	44.5	42.3	Afrique du Sud
Spain	14.6	21.6	36.0	36.0	36.0	36.6	36.3	36.6	36.6	36.0	Espagne
Sri Lanka	4.9	4.9	4.9	4.9	4.9	5.8	5.8	5.8	5.3	5.8	Sri Lanka
Sudan	...	...	9.7	14.7	17.8	18.1	18.1	18.9	25.6	24.6	Soudan
Suriname	7.8	15.7	19.6	25.5	25.5	25.5	25.5	25.5	9.8	11.8	Suriname
Swaziland	3.6	3.1	10.8	10.8	10.8	10.8	13.8	13.6	13.6	13.6	Swaziland
Sweden	38.4	42.7	45.3	45.3	47.3	47.0	47.0	46.4	45.0	44.7	Suède
Switzerland	14.0	22.5	25.0	25.0	25.0	28.5	28.5	29.0	29.0	28.5	Suisse
Syrian Arab Republic	9.2	10.4	12.0	12.0	12.0	12.0	12.4	12.4	12.4	12.4	Rép. arabe syrienne
Tajikistan	...	2.8	12.7	17.5	17.5	17.5	17.5	17.5	19.0	19.0	Tadjikistan
Thailand	2.8	5.6	8.8	10.8	8.7	11.7	11.7	13.3	13.3	15.8	Thaïlande
TFYR of Macedonia	...	7.5	19.2	19.2	28.3	29.2	31.7	32.5	32.5	30.9	L'ex-R.Y. Macédoine
Timor-Leste	...	...	25.3	25.3	25.3	29.2	29.2	29.2	29.2	32.3	Timor-Leste
Togo	5.2	...	6.2	7.4	8.6	11.1	11.1	11.1	11.1	11.1	Togo
Tonga	0.0	...	0.0	3.4	3.3	3.3	3.1[17]	3.1	0.0	3.6	Tonga
Trinidad and Tobago	16.7	11.1	19.4	19.4	19.4	26.8	26.8	26.8	28.6	28.6	Trinité-et-Tobago
Tunisia	4.3	11.5	22.8	22.8	22.8	22.8	22.8	27.6	27.6	26.7	Tunisie
Turkey	1.3	4.2	4.4	4.4	4.4	9.1	9.1	9.1	9.1	14.2	Turquie
Turkmenistan	26.0	26.0	...	16.0	16.0	16.0	16.8	16.8	16.8	16.8	Turkménistan
Tuvalu	7.7	0.0	0.0	0.0	0.0	0.0	0.0	0.0	0.0	6.7	Tuvalu
Uganda	12.2	17.9	23.9	23.9	29.8	30.7	30.7	31.5	31.3	35.0	Ouganda
Ukraine	...	7.8	5.3	5.3	8.7	8.2	8.2	8.0	8.0	8.0	Ukraine
United Arab Emirates	0.0	0.0	0.0	0.0	22.5	22.5	22.5	22.5	22.5	17.5	Emirats arabes unis
United Kingdom	6.3	18.4	18.1	19.7	19.7	19.5	19.5	19.5	22.0	22.3	Royaume-Uni
United Rep. of Tanzania	...	16.4	21.4	30.4	30.4	30.4	30.4	30.7	36.0	36.0	Rép.-Unie de Tanzanie

Proportion of seats held by women in national parliament *(continued)*
Percentage, as of 31 January 2012

Proportion de sièges occupés par les femmes au parlement national *(suite)*
Pourcentage, données disponibles en 31 janvier 2012

Country or area	1990	2000	2005	2006	2007	2008	2009	2010	2011	2012	Pays ou zone
United States	6.6	13.3	14.9	15.2	16.3	16.8	17.0	16.8	16.8	16.8	Etats-Unis
Uruguay	6.1	12.1	12.1	11.1	11.1	12.1	12.1	14.1	15.2	12.1	Uruguay
Uzbekistan	...	6.8	17.5	17.5	17.5	17.5	17.5	22.0	22.0	22.0	Ouzbékistan
Vanuatu	4.3	0.0	3.8	3.8	3.8	3.8	3.8	3.8	3.8	1.9	Vanuatu
Venezuela (Boliv. Rep. of)	10.0	12.1	9.7	17.4	18.0	18.6	18.6	17.5	17.0	17.0	Venezuela (Rép. boliv. du)
Viet Nam	17.7	26.0	27.3	27.3	27.3	25.8	25.8	25.8	25.8	24.4	Viet Nam
Yemen	4.1	0.7	0.3	0.3	0.3	0.3	0.3	0.3	0.3	0.3	Yémen
Zambia	6.6	10.1	12.0	12.7	14.6	15.2	15.2	14.0	14.0	11.5	Zambie
Zimbabwe	11.0	14.0	10.0	16.0	16.7	16.0	15.2	15.0	15.0	15.0	Zimbabwe

Source:
International Parliamentary Union (IPU), Geneva, *Women in National Parliaments 2012.*

Source:
Union interparlementaire, Genève, *Les femmes dans les parlements 2012.*

1   In 2004, the number of seats in parliament was raised from 300 to 345, with the addition of 45 reserved seats for women. These reserved seats were filled in September and October 2005, being allocated to political parties in proportion to their share of the national vote received in the 2001 election.

2   The parliament was dissolved on 27 October 2006, in view of elections that are yet to take place. Women held 52 of the 345 seats (15%) in the outgoing parliament.

3   This figure excludes the 45 reserved seats for women which were not yet filled in January 2009.

4   Data refers to the composition of the Legislative and Oversight Commission which assumed legislative and oversight functions in October 2008. The Commission is to be replaced by a new 124-member National Assembly, as provided for in the new Constitution of 2008, when elections are held in 2009.

5   Parliament has been dissolved or suspended for an indefinite period.

6   The parliament was dissolved following the December 2008 coup.

7   Situation for 1 January 2008 for directly elected members endorsed by the electoral commission. The additional twelve appointed seats and two ex-officio seats had yet to be filled.

8   In June 2005, a woman was appointed Minister for the first time in the country's history. As Cabinet Ministers also sit in Parliament, there was therefore one woman in Parliament.

9   No woman candidate was elected in the 2006 elections. One woman was appointed to the 16-member cabinet. As cabinet ministers also sit in parliament, there is therefore one woman out of a total of 65 members.

10   No woman candidate was elected in the 2006 elections. One woman was appointed to the 16-member cabinet sworn in July 2006. A new cabinet sworn in March 2007 included two women. As cabinet ministers also sit in parliament, there are two women out of a total of 65.

11   No woman candidate was elected in the 2008 elections. Two women were appointed to the 16-member cabinet sworn in June 2008. As cabinet ministers also sit in parliament, there are two women out of a total of 65 members. Four women were elected to the parliament in 2009.

12   Figure excludes 11 members yet to be sworn in.

13   The parliament (elected in the parliamentary elections in 1999) was dissolved on 22 May 2002. Women held 12 of the 205 (5.9%) seats in the outgoing parliament.

1   En 2004, le nombre de sièges parlementaires est passé de 300 à 345, les nouveaux sièges étant réservés aux femmes. Les sièges réservés ont été pourvus en septembre et en octobre 2005, au prorata des voix obtenues par les partis politiques lors des élections nationales de 2001.

2   Le parlement où les femmes occupaient 52 des 345 sièges (15%) a été dissous le 27 octobre 2006 en vue des élections à venir.

3   Ce chiffre exclut les 45 sièges réservés aux femmes toujours vacants en janvier 2009.

4   Les données se réfèrent à la composition de la Commission législative et de contrôle en charge d'assurer les principales fonctions de la branche législative depuis octobre 2008. Après les élections qui seront tenues en 2009, la Commission législative et de contrôle sera remplacée par une nouvelle Assemblée nationale composée de 124 membres comme le prévoyait la nouvelle Constitution de 2008.

5   Le Parlement a été dissous ou suspendu pour une durée indéterminée.

6   L'Assemblée nationale a été dissoute après le coup d'État de décembre 2008.

7   Au 1er janvier 2008, la situation des membres directement élus et approuvés par la commission électorale est la suivante: les sièges des 12 membres nommés et 2 des membres de droits restent vacants.

8   En juin 2005, pour la première fois de son histoire, une femme fut nommée ministre. Comme les ministres du gouvernement siègent de droit au Parlement, il y avait donc une femme au Parlement.

9   Aucune femme n'a été élue en 2006. Une femme a été nommée parmi les 16 membres du gouvernement. Les ministres siégeant également au Parlement, le Parlement compte donc une femme sur un total de 65 membres.

10   Aucune femme n'a été élue en 2006. Une femme a été nommée parmi les 16 membres du gouvernement qui ont prêté serment en juillet 2006. Un nouveau gouvernement dont les membres ont prêté serment en mars 2007 inclut deux femmes. Les ministres siégeant également au Parlement, le Parlement compte donc deux femmes sur un total de 65 membres.

11   Aucune femme n'a été élue en 2008. Deux femmes ont été nommées parmi les 16 membres du gouvernement qui ont prêté serment en juin 2008. Les ministres siégeant également au Parlement, le Parlement compte donc deux femmes sur un total de 65 membres. Quatre femmes ont été élues au Parlement en 2009.

12   Ce chiffre ne tient pas compte de 11 membres qui n'avaient pas encore été assermentés.

13   Le parlement élu aux élections de 1999 a été dissous le 22 mai 2002. Les femmes y occupaient 12 des 205 sièges, soit 5.9%.

Proportion of seats held by women in national parliament *(continued)*
Percentage, as of 31 January 2012

Proportion de sièges occupés par les femmes au parlement national *(suite)*
Pourcentage, données disponibles en 31 janvier 2012

14	After the promulgation of the interim constitution in January 2007, the House of Representatives dissolved itself in favour of a 330-member interim legislature, called the Legislative Parliament. This interim legislature comprises all members of the previous parliament and other appointed members. It was replaced by an elected unicameral Constituent Assembly in April 2008.
15	No woman was elected in the 2006 elections. However one woman was appointed Speaker of the House and therefore became a member of the House.
16	Based on a peace agreement signed in Djibouti in November 2008, the statutory number of the Transitional Federal Parliament (TFP) increased from 275 to 550 members. On 28 January 2009, 200 of the 275 new TFP members were sworn in, bringing the total number of members to 475. However, the final composition, including the number of women members, is not yet available.
17	No women were elected in 2008, however one woman was appointed to the Cabinet. As cabinet ministers also sit in parliament, there is one woman out of a total of 32 members.

14 Après la promulgation de la constitution provisoire en janvier 2007, la Chambre des représentants a prononcé sa dissolution au profit d'une législature provisoire de 330 membres, baptisée Parlement législatif. Cet organe provisoire se compose de tous les membres du parlement précédent, ainsi que de membres nommés. Il a été remplacé en avril 2008 par une Assemblée constituante monocamérale.

15 Aucune femme n'a été élue en 2006. Une femme a cependant été nommée à la présidence de la chambre des députés et est donc devenue membre de cette dernière.

16 Suite à un accord de paix signé à Djibouti en novembre 2008, le nombre réglementaire de membres du Parlement transitoire fédéral (PTF) a été porté de 275 à 550. Le 28 janvier 2009, 200 des 275 nouveaux membres du PTF ont prêté serment, ce qui ramène le nombre total de membres à 475. Cependant, la composition finale ainsi que le nombre de femmes y siégeant n'est pas encore disponible.

17 Aucune femme n'a été élue en 2008. Cependant, une femme a été nommée au Gouvernement. Les ministres siégeant également au Parlement, le Parlement compte donc une femme sur un total de 32 membres.

Share of women in wage employment in the non-agricultural sector
Percentage of total employment

Proportion de femmes salariées dans le secteur non agricole
Pourcentage d'emploi total

Country or area	1990	2000	2003	2004	2005	2006	2007	2008	2009	2010	Pays ou zone
Afghanistan [1]	...	...	17.8	18.5	25.9	18.0	17.6	18.4	...	...	Afghanistan [1]
Albania [2]	...	28.9	33.0	...	...	...	...	...	...	...	Albanie [2]
Algeria	...	...	14.2[2]	14.5[2]	14.7[2]	15.0[2]	16.8[2]	15.0[2]	15.3[3]	15.1[3]	Algérie
American Samoa [2]	41.7	...									Samoa américaines [2]
Andorra	...	...	45.6	45.7	45.8	46.1	46.6	46.8	47.3	...	Andorre
Antigua and Barbuda [4]	...	...	50.6	50.6	50.6	50.6	50.6	50.6	...	...	Antigua-et-Barbuda [4]
Argentina	37.1	42.6	45.5	44.8	45.1	45.0				...	Argentine
Armenia	...	...	*45.0	*43.4	*41.2	*41.5	41.4	*40.4	43.1[2]	...	Arménie
Aruba	...	48.3	...	...	...	...	48.6			...	Aruba
Australia	*43.7	46.3	47.0	46.7	47.0	47.1	47.0	47.1	47.5	47.1	Australie
Austria	*41.5[2]	*43.7[2]	45.5	46.2	46.6	46.6	46.3	47.0	47.8	47.8	Autriche
Azerbaijan	...	47.6	46.2	44.9	46.5	46.1	44.6	43.6	44.0	43.9	Azerbaïdjan
Bahamas	...	...	50.1[4]	50.4[4]	50.0[4]	49.7[4]	48.8[4]	*49.2[3]	*50.2[3]	...	Bahamas
Bahrain	7.6	12.4	12.8	11.5	11.0	10.3	9.8	9.6	9.6	10.0	Bahreïn
Bangladesh [2]	...	24.7	21.6	...	20.1	...	...	...	...	...	Bangladesh [2]
Barbados	*46.8[4]	49.9[2]	51.1[2]	51.3[2]	*52.0[4]	*51.2[4]	*50.4[4]	*50.7[4]	...	...	Barbade
Belarus	*55.4[3]	55.9	*56.3[3]	*56.2[3]	*56.1[3]	*56.0[3]	*56.0[3]	*56.0[3]	*55.8[3]	...	Bélarus
Belgium	*38.7[3]	*43.4[3]	44.4	44.7	45.3	45.7	46.0	46.6	46.9	47.2	Belgique
Belize	...	...	...	...	36.5[2]	*35.9[3]	*37.7[3]	...	...	...	Belize
Bermuda	48.7	49.8	48.9	48.7	48.6	48.5	48.7	...	...	...	Bermudes
Bhutan [2]	...	...	...	...	...	...	...	...	26.8	...	Bhoutan [2]
Bolivia (Plurin. State of) [2]	*35.2	*38.6	...	*36.1	*37.7	*42.4	*38.1	...	36.5	...	Bolivie (État plur. de) [2]
Bosnia and Herzegovina	...	...	...	...	...	*38.7[2]	*38.2[2]	39.3	40.5	41.0	Bosnie-Herzégovine
Botswana	33.5	*42.9	40.8	39.5	42.6	43.6	43.4	...	41.6	41.4	Botswana
Brazil	*35.1	40.3	*41.4	*41.6	*41.5	*41.8	*41.6			...	Brésil
British Virgin Islands [3]	...	49.8	50.4	49.3	49.1	...	...	...	...	...	Iles Vierges britan. [3]
Brunei Darussalam	...	30.3	30.3	...	...	...	...	...	...	...	Brunéi Darussalam
Bulgaria	...	52.8	53.1	52.7	52.2	51.4	49.1	48.7	48.9	49.2	Bulgarie
Burkina Faso	23.0[2]	23.2[1]	23.6[1]	24.8[1]	25.4[1]	26.5[1]	26.5[1]	...	...	...	Burkina Faso
Burundi [2]	14.3	...	...	...	...	...	...	...	...	...	Burundi [2]
Cambodia	...	41.1[2]	...	*43.5[3]	...	...	...	...	...	...	Cambodge
Cameroon [2]	...	...	...	...	...	...	...	...	...	26.4	Cameroun [2]
Canada	46.9	48.3	49.2	49.4	49.4	49.5	49.8	49.9	50.4	50.2	Canada
Cape Verde [2]	...	38.9	...	...	...	...	...	...	...	...	Cap-Vert [2]
Cayman Islands	...	*51.2[3]	*54.2[3]	*52.2[3]	*49.5[3]	49.4[2]	49.3[2]	50.5[2]	...	...	Iles Caïmanes
Central African Rep. [3]	...	...	46.8	...	...	...	...	...	...	...	Rép. centrafricaine [3]
Chad	3.8	...	...	...	...	...	...	...	...	...	Tchad
Chile	*37.3[4]	32.8	33.5	*34.2[4]	*34.4[4]	34.9	35.5	36.2	*36.9[3]	37.6	Chili
China	37.8	...	...	...	...	...	...	...	...	...	Chine
China, Hong Kong SAR	41.2	44.8	46.8	47.3	47.8	47.9	48.2	48.6	49.6	49.5	Chine, Hong Kong RAS
China, Macao SAR	42.7	48.9	49.0	49.4	49.5	48.1	48.1	...	50.0	50.1	Chine, Macao RAS
Colombia	*41.8[4]	48.8	48.8	48.3	47.4	46.6	47.5	47.5	46.3	46.4	Colombie
Congo *[5]	26.1	...	...	...	...	...	...	...	...	...	Congo *[5]
Cook Islands	38.4	...	...	...	...	...	...	...	...	...	Iles Cook
Costa Rica	37.2	39.3	39.5	38.5	39.6	40.7	41.1	41.5	42.8	43.3	Costa Rica

10 Share of women in wage employment in the non-agricultural sector *(continued)*
Percentage of total employment
Proportion de femmes salariées dans le secteur non agricole *(suite)*
Pourcentage d'emploi total

Country or area	1990	2000	2003	2004	2005	2006	2007	2008	2009	2010	Pays ou zone
Croatia	*43.2	47.0	46.1	45.7	45.9	46.9	45.5	45.8	47.1	47.0	Croatie
Cuba	...	43.3	42.8	42.6	42.6	42.7	43.7	43.4	44.8	44.8	Cuba
Cyprus	...	44.4	49.3	48.2	47.7	48.1	49.1	48.7	48.3	48.8	Chypre
Czech Republic	*51.0	46.5	46.8	47.1	46.6	46.4	46.3	46.0	45.9	46.1	République tchèque
Dem. P. R. Korea *[5]	40.7	...	...	...	...	...	...	...	...	...	R. p. dém. de Corée *[5]
D. R. of the Congo *[5]	25.9	...	...	...	...	...	...	...	...	...	R. dém. du Congo *[5]
Denmark	*48.0[3]	48.5	48.3	48.8	48.7	48.8	49.0	49.3	49.5	50.0	Danemark
Dominican Republic	...	*37.3[2]	*39.0[2]	38.0	37.7	39.3	38.8	...	40.6	41.8	Rép. dominicaine
Ecuador	*30.9[2]	*39.3[2]	...	39.2[6]	40.2[6]	38.7[6]	...	...	...	...	Equateur
Egypt	20.5	19.0	19.9	18.8	17.7	18.1	19.0	*18.0[4]	*18.1[3]	...	Egypte
El Salvador	*45.5[4]	49.1	47.9	47.8	48.5	48.6	48.0	...	...	...	El Salvador
Equatorial Guinea *[5]	10.5	...	...	...	...	...	...	...	...	...	Guinée équatoriale *[5]
Estonia	52.3	51.7	51.5	52.2	52.6	52.5	52.3	51.8	53.9	54.0	Estonie
Ethiopia	...	...	...	40.6	*43.8[3]	*47.3[3]	...	...	39.7	41.6	Ethiopie
Faeroe Islands [4]	...	...	...	...	45.8	...	...	...	...	...	Iles Féroé [4]
Fiji	29.9	33.2	...	...	*29.6[2]	...	...	...	...	...	Fidji
Finland	50.6	50.3	50.6	50.7	50.9	51.0	51.0	50.7	51.5	51.3	Finlande
France	*44.7	*47.4	48.2	48.3	48.6	48.9	49.3	49.2	49.6	49.7	France
French Guiana [2]	36.1	...	...	...	...	...	...	...	...	...	Guyane française [2]
French Polynesia [2]	...	42.4	42.2	42.7	42.5	42.8	42.7	...	...	...	Polynésie française [2]
Gabon [2]	...	...	...	...	...	...	...	...	...	34.5	Gabon [2]
Georgia	...	...	48.9	50.3	48.5	*48.5[2]	*47.8[2]	*46.2[2]	46.7[2]	48.5[2]	Géorgie
Germany	...	45.1	46.4	46.6	46.6	46.9	46.9	46.8	47.6	47.8	Allemagne
Ghana [2]	...	31.7	...	...	...	...	...	...	...	...	Ghana [2]
Gibraltar	34.5	39.7	41.6	41.5	41.9	41.5	41.0	...	41.2	...	Gibraltar
Greece	35.0	39.1	40.1	40.9	41.0	41.6	42.0	42.2	43.0	43.4	Grèce
Greenland [3]	...	48.8	49.4	49.5	49.3	...	...	...	...	...	Groenland [3]
Guam	...	45.6	42.4	43.3	44.5	44.6	44.1	43.3	43.1	42.9	Guam
Guatemala	36.8[4]	...	...	...	...	...	...	...	...	30.0[2]	Guatemala
Guinea [1]	...	24.2	25.6	26.0	28.5	28.7	28.8	28.5	...	...	Guinée [1]
Guinea-Bissau *[5]	10.8	...	...	...	...	...	...	...	...	...	Guinée-Bissau *[5]
Haiti [2]	44.2	...	...	...	...	...	...	...	...	...	Haïti [2]
Honduras	*41.4[4]	...	*40.6[2]	*42.5[2]	41.5	*42.2[2]	*41.9[2]	...	...	...	Honduras
Hungary	...	48.6	49.1	48.9	48.7	48.3	48.0	48.4	48.5	49.2	Hongrie
Iceland	...	52.2	52.5	51.8	52.2	50.9	50.0	49.4	51.1	51.7	Islande
India	12.7	16.6	17.6	17.9	18.1	...	...	...	...	...	Inde
Indonesia	29.2	31.7	29.5	29.0	30.3	31.3	30.9	32.4	...	...	Indonésie
Iran (Islamic Rep. of)	10.5	13.6	12.1	13.0	16.1	...	...	...	15.1[2]	15.2[2]	Iran (Rép. islam. d')
Iraq	...	...	...	16.0	...	15.3	...	12.1	...	...	Iraq
Ireland	41.7	46.3	47.4	47.5	47.7	47.5	48.2	49.2	51.8	52.1	Irlande
Israel	43.0	48.3	48.9	48.7	49.3	49.0	49.0	*49.3[2]	49.8	50.0	Israël
Italy	*35.9[4]	39.8	41.2	42.7	42.6	42.8	43.0	43.5	43.9	44.3	Italie
Jamaica	*47.3[3]	45.0[2]	46.3[2]	45.2[2]	45.6[2]	45.8[2]	46.3[2]	48.2[2]	...	...	Jamaïque
Japan	38.0	40.0	40.8	41.2	41.3	41.6	41.6	41.8	42.3	42.6	Japon
Jordan	...	14.4	13.9	...	13.7	15.5	15.8	15.7	...	...	Jordanie
Kazakhstan	...	...	48.7	49.4	49.1	49.9	50.1	50.0	...	...	Kazakhstan

10

Share of women in wage employment in the non-agricultural sector *(continued)*
Percentage of total employment
Proportion de femmes salariées dans le secteur non agricole *(suite)*
Pourcentage d'emploi total

Country or area	1990	2000	2003	2004	2005	2006	2007	2008	2009	2010	Pays ou zone
Kenya	21.4	...	...	...	...	...	...	...	...	...	Kenya
Kiribati[2]	...	36.8	...	...	38.5	...	...	...	...	...	Kiribati[2]
Kyrgyzstan	...	45.8	47.3	49.4	51.9	52.2	50.8	*51.5[3]	*50.6[3]	...	Kirghizistan
Lao People's Dem. Rep.	20.3	...	...	...	32.1	...	...	...	...	...	Rép. dém. pop. lao
Latvia	...	53.1	53.3	53.2	53.4	52.8	52.0	52.7	54.2	54.2	Lettonie
Liechtenstein	...	38.7[4]	38.9[4]	39.1[4]	39.4[4]	...	...	...	43.7	43.7	Liechtenstein
Lithuania	*55.4	53.2	53.2	53.3	53.0	52.9	53.0	...	54.3	54.4	Lituanie
Luxembourg	...	...	40.6	41.9	42.4	43.2	*43.8[2]	*43.3[2]	43.7[2]	44.0[2]	Luxembourg
Madagascar	...	...	*37.2[2]	...	37.7	...	...	...	...	...	Madagascar
Malawi	10.5	...	...	...	...	...	...	...	...	...	Malawi
Malaysia	...	*37.9[2]	37.9	38.3	38.5	38.7	39.0	39.2	...	...	Malaisie
Maldives[2]	15.8	40.6	...	...	...	30.0	...	...	...	...	Maldives[2]
Mali[2]	...	...	...	34.6	...	...	...	...	...	...	Mali[2]
Malta	...	32.7	33.5	33.1	33.8	34.6	35.7	35.9	36.4	...	Malte
Martinique[3]	45.4	...	...	...	...	...	...	50.8	...	...	Martinique[3]
Mauritania	...	35.8	...	...	...	...	...	...	...	...	Mauritanie
Mauritius	37.4	38.6	38.4	37.5	36.9	37.2	37.2	37.0	36.9	37.6	Maurice
Mexico	...	37.3	36.9	37.5	39.1	39.3	39.4	39.4	39.7	39.4	Mexique
Monaco[3]	...	39.2	...	...	...	...	...	...	...	...	Monaco[3]
Mongolia	...	48.6[2]	*49.3[4]	*51.2[4]	*51.2[4]	*52.0[4]	*51.2[4]	*51.1[4]	52.6	52.7	Mongolie
Montenegro	...	44.0	...	...	43.4[2]	...	...	...	46.3[2]	...	Monténégro
Morocco[2]	...	...	23.2	22.9	22.8	21.0	20.7	20.8	...	...	Maroc[2]
Mozambique *[5]	11.4	...	...	...	...	...	...	...	...	...	Mozambique *[5]
Myanmar[2]	30.7	...	...	...	...	...	...	...	...	...	Myanmar[2]
Namibia[2]	...	42.8	...	41.4	...	...	...	...	...	...	Namibie[2]
Netherlands	37.7	43.9	45.7	45.7	46.2	46.7	47.3	47.7	47.8	48.2	Pays-Bas
Netherlands Antilles	...	49.9[2]	*50.2[3]	*52.2[3]	*51.9[3]	*51.2[3]	*51.8[3]	*51.0[3]	...	...	Antilles néerlandaises
New Zealand	47.8	49.8	50.6	50.0	50.0	50.1	49.9	50.2	50.6	50.7	Nouvelle-Zélande
Nicaragua	...	...	39.5[2]	38.6[2]	38.3[2]	38.6[2]	*38.1[3]	...	...	...	Nicaragua
Niger	...	...	...	...	25.4	27.2	30.4	36.1	...	...	Niger
Nigeria[2]	...	18.6	20.8	21.0	21.1	...	...	...	...	...	Nigéria[2]
Northern Mariana Islands[4]	44.0	...	...	...	...	...	...	...	...	...	Iles Mariann. du Nord[4]
Norway	*47.0[4]	48.2	49.1	49.2	49.0	49.3	49.2	49.1	49.6	49.4	Norvège
Occupied Palestinian Terr.	...	13.5	16.8	17.9	16.1	17.1	17.0	17.9	18.8	17.2	Terr. Pales. occupé
Oman	18.7	24.5	...	...	...	...	...	*21.9	...	...	Oman
Pakistan	*7.7[4]	13.0[2]	13.6[2]	13.9[2]	13.9[2]	13.4[2]	13.2[2]	12.6[2]	...	...	Pakistan
Palau	*39.5[3]	39.6[4]	...	...	...	...	...	...	...	...	Palaos
Panama	...	43.0	44.0	43.6	43.4	42.5	43.1	42.2	42.1	42.9	Panama
Papua New Guinea	27.9	32.1	...	...	...	...	...	...	...	...	Papouasie-Nvl-Guinée
Paraguay	41.0	*39.3[3]	*38.9[3]	*40.0[3]	*40.1[3]	*38.7[3]	40.2	39.5	...	...	Paraguay
Peru	...	33.3	36.0	34.8	35.1	34.9	36.8	37.5	...	...	Pérou
Philippines	...	40.9	41.3	40.7	41.4	41.9	41.9	41.7	41.9	41.9	Philippines
Poland	...	46.9	47.7	47.2	46.7	46.6	46.7	47.3	47.6	...	Pologne
Portugal	42.5	45.7	46.9	47.4	47.3	47.3	47.6	47.6	48.7	49.0	Portugal
Puerto Rico	46.5	39.6	40.1	*39.9[2]	*40.5[2]	*40.8[2]	*41.5[2]	*41.7[2]	43.8[2]	46.3[2]	Porto Rico
Qatar	...	...	*15.5[4]	...	14.6[2]	12.3[2]	...	9.8[2]	12.1[2]	...	Qatar

10
Share of women in wage employment in the non-agricultural sector *(continued)*
Percentage of total employment
Proportion de femmes salariées dans le secteur non agricole *(suite)*
Pourcentage d'emploi total

Country or area	1990	2000	2003	2004	2005	2006	2007	2008	2009	2010	Pays ou zone
Republic of Korea	38.1	40.1	41.2	41.6	41.8	42.0	42.1	*42.2[2]	*42.1[2]	42.6[2]	République de Corée
Republic of Moldova	...	52.8	54.6	54.6	54.9	53.5	54.6	54.1	54.3	55.0	Rép. de Moldova
Romania	*41.9[2]	45.5	45.3	46.5	46.2	46.6	46.1	45.8	45.7	45.8	Roumanie
Russian Federation	...	50.4	51.0	50.9	50.9	51.2	51.0	50.6	50.9	50.7	Fédération de Russie
Rwanda	...	33.0	...	...	...	...	...	...	...	...	Rwanda
Saint Helena [4]	...	...	...	...	...	...	...	47.6	...	...	Sainte-Hélène [4]
Saint Lucia	...	49.4[2]	*45.9[4]	*47.5[4]	...	...	...	...	...	...	Sainte-Lucie
San Marino	40.4	...	41.9	42.2	42.1	42.1	42.2	42.2	43.1	43.7	Saint-Marin
Saudi Arabia	...	14.0	...	...	...	*14.6[3]	*14.7[3]	*14.6[3]	16.0	...	Arabie saoudite
Serbia	...	44.0	...	43.9	41.6	43.5	43.9	44.0	43.7	...	Serbie
Sierra Leone	...	...	...	23.2	...	...	...	...	...	...	Sierra Leone
Singapore [2]	...	...	43.5	44.0	...	44.8	45.1	45.7	45.4	...	Singapour [2]
Slovakia	*46.8	48.9	48.7	48.5	48.1	47.2	47.4	47.7	47.8	48.7	Slovaquie
Slovenia	*47.8	48.0	47.4	47.6	47.4	47.9	46.8	47.4	47.9	47.8	Slovénie
Somalia *[5]	21.7	...	...	...	...	...	...	...	...	...	Somalie *[5]
South Africa	...	*41.1[4]	*41.6[4]	*40.8[4]	*41.4[4]	*41.3[4]	42.0[2]	44.0[2]	45.0	44.5	Afrique du Sud
Spain	32.3	38.9	40.7	41.5	42.3	43.0	43.7	44.9	46.5	47.3	Espagne
Sri Lanka	...	*30.2[2]	30.0	31.0	31.9	32.2	31.0	*30.8[2]	*31.0[2]	...	Sri Lanka
Sudan (former)	22.2	...	...	...	...	...	...	...	...	...	Soudan (anc.)
Suriname	*41.0[2]	...	...	*38.1[2]	...	...	...	...	...	36.3	Suriname
Sweden	50.5	50.6	50.9	50.9	50.5	50.3	50.1	49.9	50.2	49.8	Suède
Switzerland	*43.4[4]	45.7	46.9	47.1	47.1	46.9	46.8	47.9	47.8	47.1	Suisse
Syrian Arab Republic	...	...	*16.1[4]	...	...	...	16.3	...	15.3	...	Rép. arabe syrienne
Tajikistan	...	40.0	41.1	39.8	39.4	37.1	...	...	...	...	Tadjikistan
Thailand	41.9[2]	44.1[2]	44.5[2]	44.0[2]	45.4[2]	45.1[2]	45.0[2]	45.4[2]	*45.5[4]	...	Thaïlande
TFYR of Macedonia	38.3	41.6	44.1	43.2	42.6	42.6	43.0	41.9	*42.2[2]	*42.2[2]	L'ex-R.Y. Macédoine
Togo *[5]	41.0	...	...	...	...	...	...	...	...	...	Togo *[5]
Trinidad and Tobago	35.6	40.0	41.9	43.5	43.9	...	...	...	...	...	Trinité-et-Tobago
Tunisia *[3]	...	24.3	25.0	...	...	...	...	...	...	...	Tunisie *[3]
Turkey	...	*19.5[2]	*21.0[2]	*20.4[2]	20.9[2]	21.5[2]	22.4[2]	23.0[2]	23.0	23.0	Turquie
Turks and Caicos Islands [2]	...	...	41.0	42.2	41.6	40.5	38.1	...	...	...	Iles Turques et Caïq. [2]
Tuvalu [2]	...	...	39.1	33.9	...	...	...	...	...	...	Tuvalu [2]
Uganda [4]	...	...	39.0	...	...	...	...	...	...	...	Ouganda [4]
Ukraine	46.6	52.9	54.4	55.1	54.9	54.6	54.7	54.6	...	...	Ukraine
United Arab Emirates	...	...	...	...	...	...	...	20.1	...	...	Emirats arabes unis
United Kingdom	*44.0[2]	46.0	46.0	46.3	46.3	46.4	46.1	46.3	46.9	...	Royaume-Uni
United Rep. of Tanzania	...	...	...	...	...	30.5	...	...	...	...	Rép.-Unie de Tanzanie
United States	46.6	47.4	47.7	47.5	47.3	47.3	47.4	47.7	48.3	48.3	Etats-Unis
Uruguay	42.3	46.4	*48.1[2]	...	*48.8[2]	*45.1[2]	*45.5[2]	...	...	...	Uruguay
Uzbekistan *[3]	...	37.1	37.0	40.6	40.3	40.3	39.4	...	...	...	Ouzbékistan *[3]
Vanuatu [2]	...	...	...	37.5	37.9	38.3	37.8	38.9	...	...	Vanuatu [2]
Venezuela (Bol.. Rep. of) [4]	35.2	39.8	42.2	42.1	41.6	41.0	41.4	41.6	...	...	Venezuela (R. bol. du) [4]
Viet Nam [2]	...	40.7	40.1	40.4	...	...	...	...	...	...	Viet Nam [2]
Yemen	...	7.0	*6.1	6.0	...	6.3	6.2	...	...	...	Yémen
Zambia [2]	16.6	22.0	...	...	...	...	...	...	...	...	Zambie [2]
Zimbabwe	15.4	20.4	...	...	...	...	...	...	...	...	Zimbabwe

10

Share of women in wage employment in the non-agricultural sector *(continued)*
Percentage of total employment

Proportion de femmes salariées dans le secteur non agricole *(suite)*
Pourcentage d'emploi total

Source:
International Labour Organization (ILO), Geneva, the ILO labour statistics database, last accessed August 2012.

Source:
Bureau international du Travail (BIT), Genève, la base de données du BIT, dernier accès août 2012.

1	Employment in public sector.
2	Total paid employment.
3	Total employment.
4	Total employment in non-agriculture.
5	Economically active population in non-agriculture.
6	Urban areas.

1	Emploi dans le secteur public.
2	Emplois rémunérés (total).
3	Emploi total.
4	Population active totale dans le secteur non agricole.
5	Population active dans le secteur non agricole.
6	Régions urbaines.

Country or area	1991	2004	2005	2006	2007	2008	2009	2010	Pays ou zone
Afghanistan									**Afghanistan**
Primary education	0.55	0.44	0.59	0.63	0.63	0.65	0.67	0.69	Enseignement primaire
Secondary education	0.51	0.21	0.33	0.37	0.38	0.43	0.49	0.51	Enseignement secondaire
Tertiary education	...	0.28	...	...	...	...	0.24	...	Enseignement supérieur
Albania									**Albanie**
Primary education	1.01	0.99	...	...	...	1.00	0.99	0.99	Enseignement primaire
Secondary education	0.93	0.96	...	...	...	0.98	1.00	0.98	Enseignement secondaire
Tertiary education	1.13	1.57	...	...	...	...	...	...	Enseignement supérieur
Algeria									**Algérie**
Primary education	0.85	0.93	0.93	0.93	0.94	0.94	0.94	0.94	Enseignement primaire
Secondary education	0.79	1.07	*1.08	...	...	...	1.02	...	Enseignement secondaire
Tertiary education	...	1.08	1.28	1.26	1.40	...	1.44	1.46	Enseignement supérieur
Andorra									**Andorre**
Primary education	...	0.96	0.95	0.98	0.97	0.97	0.99	1.01	Enseignement primaire
Secondary education	...	1.08	1.11	1.10	1.08	1.07	1.06	1.05	Enseignement secondaire
Tertiary education	...	0.96	1.05	1.16	...	1.43	...	...	Enseignement supérieur
Angola									**Angola**
Primary education	0.91	...	...	...	...	0.86	0.85	0.81	Enseignement primaire
Secondary education	...	...	...	...	...	0.77	0.77	0.69	Enseignement secondaire
Tertiary education	...	...	...	...	...	...	...	0.82	Enseignement supérieur
Anguilla *									**Anguilla ***
Primary education	...	1.03	1.06	0.99	0.98	1.00	...	...	Enseignement primaire
Secondary education	...	1.00	0.97	1.02	1.02	0.95	...	...	Enseignement secondaire
Tertiary education	...	4.23	3.11	4.86	4.96	5.01	...	...	Enseignement supérieur
Antigua and Barbuda									**Antigua-et-Barbuda**
Primary education	...	...	...	...	0.95	0.94	0.95	0.92	Enseignement primaire
Secondary education	...	...	...	...	0.98	0.95	1.00	1.01	Enseignement secondaire
Tertiary education	...	...	...	...	...	...	2.21	2.58	Enseignement supérieur
Argentina									**Argentine**
Primary education	...	0.99	0.99	0.98	0.99	0.99	0.99	...	Enseignement primaire
Secondary education	...	1.10	1.11	1.12	1.13	1.14	1.12	...	Enseignement secondaire
Tertiary education	...	1.42	1.46	1.52	1.52	1.52	1.51	...	Enseignement supérieur
Armenia									**Arménie**
Primary education	...	1.02	1.03	1.03	1.02	1.02	1.03	1.02	Enseignement primaire
Secondary education	...	1.01	1.02	1.03	1.04	1.04	1.02	1.02	Enseignement secondaire
Tertiary education	...	1.21	1.22	1.19	1.20	1.32	1.28	1.28	Enseignement supérieur
Aruba									**Aruba**
Primary education	...	0.92	0.94	0.96	0.95	0.95	0.96	0.97	Enseignement primaire
Secondary education	...	1.00	1.00	0.99	1.01	1.04	1.01	1.01	Enseignement secondaire
Tertiary education	...	1.47	1.44	1.46	1.35	1.33	1.35	1.30	Enseignement supérieur
Australia									**Australie**
Primary education	1.00	1.00	1.00	1.00	1.00	1.00	0.99	0.99	Enseignement primaire
Secondary education	...	0.96	0.99	0.98	0.98	0.98	0.96	0.95	Enseignement secondaire
Tertiary education	1.19	1.23	1.25	1.27	1.28	1.30	1.33	1.35	Enseignement supérieur
Austria									**Autriche**
Primary education	1.00	1.00	1.00	0.99	0.99	0.99	0.99	0.99	Enseignement primaire
Secondary education	0.92	0.94	0.95	0.96	0.96	0.96	0.96	0.96	Enseignement secondaire
Tertiary education	0.87	1.18	1.20	1.21	1.20	1.18	1.18	...	Enseignement supérieur
Azerbaijan									**Azerbaïdjan**
Primary education	0.99	0.96	0.95	0.94	1.00	0.99	0.99	0.99	Enseignement primaire
Secondary education	1.01	0.95	0.95	0.96	...	0.98	1.02	0.98	Enseignement secondaire
Tertiary education	0.67	0.85	0.87	0.91	0.83	0.78	0.97	0.98	Enseignement supérieur
Bahamas									**Bahamas**
Primary education	...	*0.99	0.99	0.99	0.99	0.99	1.03	1.02	Enseignement primaire
Secondary education	...	*0.99	0.99	1.00	1.03	1.02	1.02	1.05	Enseignement secondaire
Bahrain									**Bahreïn**
Primary education	1.01	0.96	0.96	0.99	...	...	...	...	Enseignement primaire
Secondary education	1.04	1.01	1.02	1.04	...	...	...	...	Enseignement secondaire
Tertiary education	1.38	...	...	...	...	...	...	...	Enseignement supérieur

Ratio of girls to boys in primary, secondary and tertiary education *(continued)*
Rapport filles/garçons dans l'enseignement primaire, secondaire et supérieur *(suite)*

Country or area	1991	2004	2005	2006	2007	2008	2009	2010	Pays ou zone
Bangladesh									**Bangladesh**
Secondary education	...	1.04	1.08	1.07	1.07	1.14	1.09	1.13	Enseignement secondaire
Tertiary education	...	0.48	0.53	0.56	0.56	0.56	0.61	...	Enseignement supérieur
Barbados									**Barbade**
Primary education	...	1.06	1.07	1.05	1.07	1.05	1.04	1.02	Enseignement primaire
Secondary education	...	1.09	1.07	1.11	1.10	1.11	1.10	1.09	Enseignement secondaire
Tertiary education	...	...	...	...	2.35	...	2.41	2.38	Enseignement supérieur
Belarus									**Bélarus**
Primary education	...	0.97	0.97	0.98	0.99	1.00	1.00	1.00	Enseignement primaire
Secondary education	...	1.02	1.02	1.02	1.02	...	...	...	Enseignement secondaire
Tertiary education	...	1.37	1.36	1.37	1.41	1.43	1.44	1.43	Enseignement supérieur
Belgium									**Belgique**
Primary education	1.01	1.00	1.00	0.99	1.00	1.00	1.00	...	Enseignement primaire
Secondary education	1.01	0.97	0.97	0.97	0.96	0.97	0.97	...	Enseignement secondaire
Tertiary education	0.97	1.20	1.23	1.24	1.26	1.26	1.25	...	Enseignement supérieur
Belize									**Belize**
Primary education	0.92	0.87	0.86	0.87	0.88	0.88	0.89	0.91	Enseignement primaire
Secondary education	1.00	1.03	...	...	...	...	...	...	Enseignement secondaire
Tertiary education	...	1.52	1.59	1.67	1.64	1.62	1.66	1.57	Enseignement supérieur
Benin									**Bénin**
Primary education	0.49	0.74	0.76	0.79	...	0.83	0.85	0.87	Enseignement primaire
Secondary education	...	0.45	*0.54	...	...	...	...	...	Enseignement secondaire
Tertiary education	0.14	...	...	...	...	...	0.38	...	Enseignement supérieur
Bermuda									**Bermudes**
Primary education	...	1.06	1.05	1.07	...	...	...	*1.00	Enseignement primaire
Secondary education	...	1.16	1.13	1.09	...	...	...	1.18	Enseignement secondaire
Tertiary education	...	1.98	1.90	2.38	2.51	2.65	2.65	2.12	Enseignement supérieur
Bhutan									**Bhoutan**
Primary education	...	...	0.97	0.98	...	1.01	1.02	1.02	Enseignement primaire
Secondary education	...	...	0.88	0.92	...	0.94	1.00	1.01	Enseignement secondaire
Tertiary education	...	...	0.67	0.61	0.56	0.58	...	0.61	Enseignement supérieur
Bolivia (Plurinational State of)									**Bolivie (État plurinational de)**
Primary education	...	*1.00	...	1.00	1.00	0.99	0.99	...	Enseignement primaire
Secondary education	...	...	...	0.96	0.97	0.98	0.99	...	Enseignement secondaire
Tertiary education	...	...	...	...	0.84	...	...	...	Enseignement supérieur
Bosnia and Herzegovina									**Bosnie-Herzégovine**
Primary education	...	...	...	...	1.02	1.01	1.02	1.02	Enseignement primaire
Secondary education	...	...	...	...	1.03	1.02	1.02	1.03	Enseignement secondaire
Tertiary education	...	...	...	...	...	1.29	1.30	1.31	Enseignement supérieur
Botswana									**Botswana**
Primary education	1.07	0.98	0.99	0.98	0.97	0.97	0.96	...	Enseignement primaire
Secondary education	1.18	*1.05	1.05	1.06	1.05	*1.07	*1.06	...	Enseignement secondaire
Tertiary education	0.73	1.10	1.13	1.15	...	...	...	...	Enseignement supérieur
Brazil									**Brésil**
Primary education	...	0.93	0.94	...	...	...	...	...	Enseignement primaire
Secondary education	...	1.10	1.10	...	...	...	...	...	Enseignement secondaire
Tertiary education	1.06	1.32	1.29	...	...	...	...	...	Enseignement supérieur
British Virgin Islands									**Îles Vierges britanniques**
Primary education	...	0.96	0.96	0.97	0.96	...	*0.96	0.94	Enseignement primaire
Secondary education	...	1.06	1.18	1.13	1.11	...	*1.03	1.03	Enseignement secondaire
Tertiary education	...	2.33	*2.28	...	...	...	*1.64	...	Enseignement supérieur
Brunei Darussalam									**Brunéi Darussalam**
Primary education	0.96	1.00	1.00	0.99	0.99	1.00	1.01	1.01	Enseignement primaire
Secondary education	1.08	1.03	1.03	1.03	1.03	1.03	1.03	1.03	Enseignement secondaire
Tertiary education	...	1.94	2.01	2.00	1.87	1.97	1.73	1.79	Enseignement supérieur
Bulgaria									**Bulgarie**
Primary education	0.98	0.99	0.99	0.99	0.99	1.00	1.00	1.00	Enseignement primaire
Secondary education	1.00	0.96	0.96	0.96	0.96	0.97	0.96	0.95	Enseignement secondaire
Tertiary education	1.10	1.17	1.15	1.21	1.22	1.30	1.31	1.31	Enseignement supérieur

11

Ratio of girls to boys in primary, secondary and tertiary education *(continued)*
Rapport filles/garçons dans l'enseignement primaire, secondaire et supérieur *(suite)*

Country or area	1991	2004	2005	2006	2007	2008	2009	2010	Pays ou zone
Burkina Faso									**Burkina Faso**
Primary education	0.64	0.79	0.80	0.82	0.84	0.87	0.89	0.91	Enseignement primaire
Secondary education	...	*0.70	0.71	0.73	0.73	0.74	0.75	0.76	Enseignement secondaire
Tertiary education	0.30	...	0.45	0.46	0.46	0.49	0.48	0.48	Enseignement supérieur
Burundi									**Burundi**
Primary education	0.84	0.83	0.86	0.91	0.93	0.95	0.97	0.99	Enseignement primaire
Secondary education	0.58	0.75	*0.74	*0.74	0.72	*0.71	0.72	0.72	Enseignement secondaire
Tertiary education	0.36	0.38	*0.38	*0.43	...	...	...	0.54	Enseignement supérieur
Cambodia									**Cambodge**
Primary education	...	0.92	0.93	0.93	0.93	0.94	0.94	0.95	Enseignement primaire
Secondary education	...	*0.69	*0.74	0.78	0.82	*0.85	...	*0.90	Enseignement secondaire
Tertiary education	...	0.46	0.46	0.49	0.55	0.53	...	...	Enseignement supérieur
Cameroon									**Cameroun**
Primary education	0.86	0.85	*0.84	0.84	0.86	0.86	0.86	0.86	Enseignement primaire
Secondary education	0.71	0.79	0.79	0.79	...	0.80	0.83	*0.83	Enseignement secondaire
Tertiary education	...	*0.64	0.66	0.72	0.79	0.79	0.79	0.81	Enseignement supérieur
Canada									**Canada**
Primary education	0.98	*0.99	0.99	0.99	0.99	1.00	...	...	Enseignement primaire
Secondary education	1.00	...	0.98	0.98	0.98	0.98	...	...	Enseignement secondaire
Tertiary education	1.23	...	...	...	...	...	...	...	Enseignement supérieur
Cape Verde									**Cap-Vert**
Primary education	...	0.95	0.95	0.95	0.94	0.93	0.92	0.92	Enseignement primaire
Secondary education	...	1.10	1.09	1.16	1.20	1.11	1.19	1.20	Enseignement secondaire
Tertiary education	...	1.14	1.08	1.13	1.26	1.31	1.35	1.29	Enseignement supérieur
Cayman Islands									**Iles Caïmanes**
Primary education	...	0.99	0.99	0.97	0.98	0.97	...	...	Enseignement primaire
Secondary education	...	1.08	0.95	1.00	1.02	1.13	...	...	Enseignement secondaire
Tertiary education	...	...	...	2.50	2.34	2.24	...	...	Enseignement supérieur
Central African Rep.									**Rép. centrafricaine**
Primary education	0.64	0.66	0.69	0.69	0.70	0.70	0.71	0.71	Enseignement primaire
Secondary education	0.41	...	...	...	...	...	0.56	0.58	Enseignement secondaire
Tertiary education	0.15	...	...	0.28	...	0.35	0.43	0.32	Enseignement supérieur
Chad									**Tchad**
Primary education	0.45	0.66	0.68	0.68	0.70	0.70	0.71	0.73	Enseignement primaire
Secondary education	...	0.33	*0.34	0.36	0.45	0.41	0.41	0.42	Enseignement secondaire
Tertiary education	...	0.14	0.06	...	...	0.15	0.17	*0.17	Enseignement supérieur
Chile									**Chili**
Primary education	0.98	0.95	0.96	0.95	0.95	0.95	0.95	...	Enseignement primaire
Secondary education	1.02	1.01	1.01	1.02	1.02	1.03	1.03	...	Enseignement secondaire
Tertiary education	...	0.95	0.96	1.00	1.01	1.03	1.06	...	Enseignement supérieur
China									**Chine**
Primary education	0.91	...	...	1.04	1.03	1.03	1.03	1.03	Enseignement primaire
Secondary education	0.75	...	...	1.03	1.04	1.05	1.07	1.04	Enseignement secondaire
Tertiary education	...	0.89	0.91	0.96	1.00	1.04	1.07	1.10	Enseignement supérieur
China, Hong Kong SAR									**Chine, Hong Kong RAS**
Primary education	...	0.98	0.98	0.98	0.99	0.99	1.01	1.02	Enseignement primaire
Secondary education	...	0.99	1.00	1.00	1.00	1.01	1.01	1.02	Enseignement secondaire
Tertiary education	...	1.01	0.99	0.97	*0.99	*1.01	*1.01	1.04	Enseignement supérieur
China, Macao SAR									**Chine, Macao RAS**
Primary education	0.96	0.95	0.96	0.98	0.97	0.98	0.99	1.00	Enseignement primaire
Secondary education	...	1.04	1.03	1.02	1.00	0.97	0.96	0.93	Enseignement secondaire
Tertiary education	0.48	0.63	0.70	0.81	0.92	0.96	0.96	0.99	Enseignement supérieur
Colombia									**Colombie**
Primary education	1.02	0.99	0.98	0.98	0.99	0.99	1.00	0.98	Enseignement primaire
Secondary education	1.19	1.11	1.11	1.11	1.11	1.10	1.10	1.10	Enseignement secondaire
Tertiary education	1.07	1.08	1.08	1.09	1.09	0.99	1.05	1.09	Enseignement supérieur
Comoros									**Comores**
Primary education	0.73	0.88	*0.88	...	0.90	0.92	...	...	Enseignement primaire
Secondary education	...	0.76	*0.76	...	...	...	...	...	Enseignement secondaire
Tertiary education	...	*0.77	...	...	...	...	0.71	0.74	Enseignement supérieur

Country or area	1991	2004	2005	2006	2007	2008	2009	2010	Pays ou zone
Congo									**Congo**
Primary education	0.92	0.94	0.94	0.91	0.94	0.94	0.94	0.95	Enseignement primaire
Secondary education *	...	0.85	...	...	...	...	...	...	Enseignement secondaire *
Tertiary education	0.22	...	...	...	...	...	0.21	...	Enseignement supérieur
Cook Islands									**Iles Cook**
Primary education	...	*0.98	1.03	...	0.99	...	1.07	1.02	Enseignement primaire
Secondary education	...	*1.12	1.13	...	1.13	...	1.13	1.10	Enseignement secondaire
Costa Rica									**Costa Rica**
Primary education	0.99	0.99	0.98	0.99	0.99	0.99	0.99	0.99	Enseignement primaire
Secondary education	1.06	1.06	1.06	1.06	1.05	1.06	1.06	1.06	Enseignement secondaire
Tertiary education		1.26	*1.26	...	...	...	...	...	Enseignement supérieur
Côte d'Ivoire									**Côte d'Ivoire**
Primary education	0.71	...	...	0.79	0.79	0.79	0.81	...	Enseignement primaire
Tertiary education	...	...	...	*0.49	0.50	...	...	...	Enseignement supérieur
Croatia									**Croatie**
Primary education	...	...	1.00	1.00	1.00	1.00	1.00	1.00	Enseignement primaire
Secondary education	...	...	1.03	1.03	1.03	1.03	1.04	1.07	Enseignement secondaire
Tertiary education	...	...	1.21	1.23	1.22	1.25	1.27	1.34	Enseignement supérieur
Cuba									**Cuba**
Primary education	0.97	0.96	0.96	0.97	0.97	0.97	0.98	0.98	Enseignement primaire
Secondary education	1.15	1.02	1.02	1.02	1.00	1.00	0.99	0.99	Enseignement secondaire
Tertiary education	1.40	*1.72	1.71	1.62	1.83	1.67	1.67	1.65	Enseignement supérieur
Cyprus									**Chypre**
Primary education	...	1.00	1.00	1.00	0.99	0.99	0.99	0.99	Enseignement primaire
Secondary education	...	1.03	1.02	1.02	1.02	1.01	1.01	1.00	Enseignement secondaire
Tertiary education	...	0.98	1.13	1.05	0.99	0.96	0.87	0.86	Enseignement supérieur
Czech Republic									**République tchèque**
Primary education	1.00	0.99	0.98	0.99	0.99	0.99	0.99	...	Enseignement primaire
Secondary education	0.97	1.01	1.01	1.01	1.01	1.01	1.01	...	Enseignement secondaire
Tertiary education	0.81	1.10	1.16	1.22	1.27	1.32	1.38	...	Enseignement supérieur
Dem. Rep. of the Congo									**Rép. dém. du Congo**
Primary education	0.75	...	...	...	0.82	0.84	0.86	0.87	Enseignement primaire
Secondary education	...	...	...	...	0.53	0.56	0.56	0.58	Enseignement secondaire
Tertiary education	...	...	...	...	0.35	0.36	0.31	...	Enseignement supérieur
Denmark									**Danemark**
Primary education	1.00	1.00	1.00	1.00	1.00	1.00	1.00	...	Enseignement primaire
Secondary education	1.01	1.05	1.03	1.03	1.03	1.03	1.02	...	Enseignement secondaire
Tertiary education	1.14	1.41	1.39	1.39	1.40	1.43	1.45	...	Enseignement supérieur
Djibouti									**Djibouti**
Primary education	0.72	0.79	0.82	0.81	0.86	0.88	0.89	...	Enseignement primaire
Secondary education	...	0.69	0.66	0.67	0.70	0.70	0.73	...	Enseignement secondaire
Tertiary education	0.00	0.82	0.73	0.68	0.69	...	0.69	...	Enseignement supérieur
Dominica									**Dominique**
Primary education	0.98	1.00	1.00	0.99	0.97	0.97	0.97	0.98	Enseignement primaire
Secondary education	*1.08	1.09	1.08	1.07	1.09	1.04	1.12	1.09	Enseignement secondaire
Tertiary education	0.81	...	...	...	...	3.35	...	...	Enseignement supérieur
Dominican Republic									**Rép. dominicaine**
Primary education	...	0.95	0.95	0.95	0.94	0.93	0.86	0.88	Enseignement primaire
Secondary education	...	1.17	1.19	1.20	1.20	1.19	1.13	1.12	Enseignement secondaire
Tertiary education *	...	1.59	...	...	...	...	...	...	Enseignement supérieur *
Ecuador									**Equateur**
Primary education	...	1.00	1.00	1.00	1.00	*1.01	1.01	...	Enseignement primaire
Secondary education	...	1.00	1.01	1.01	1.01	*1.03	...	...	Enseignement secondaire
Tertiary education	...	...	...	...	...	1.15	...	...	Enseignement supérieur
Egypt									**Egypte**
Primary education	0.83	*0.96	0.94	0.94	0.95	...	0.96	*0.96	Enseignement primaire
Secondary education	0.79	*0.94	...	...	...	...	0.96	0.96	Enseignement secondaire
Tertiary education	0.59	*0.77	...	...	...	...	...	0.91	Enseignement supérieur
El Salvador									**El Salvador**
Primary education	0.99	0.97	0.97	0.97	1.00	0.97	0.97	0.95	Enseignement primaire
Secondary education	1.12	1.02	1.03	1.04	1.04	1.03	1.02	1.01	Enseignement secondaire
Tertiary education	...	*1.14	1.16	1.17	1.18	1.17	1.16	1.16	Enseignement supérieur

11

Ratio of girls to boys in primary, secondary and tertiary education *(continued)*
Rapport filles/garçons dans l'enseignement primaire, secondaire et supérieur *(suite)*

Country or area	1991	2004	2005	2006	2007	2008	2009	2010	Pays ou zone
Equatorial Guinea									**Guinée équatoriale**
Primary education	...	...	0.95	...	...	0.95	0.96	0.97	Enseignement primaire
Tertiary education	0.15	...	...	...	...	...	...	...	Enseignement supérieur
Eritrea									**Erythrée**
Primary education	0.95	0.80	0.81	0.81	0.83	0.82	0.83	0.84	Enseignement primaire
Secondary education	...	0.56	0.59	0.60	0.71	*0.71	0.71	0.76	Enseignement secondaire
Tertiary education	...	0.15	...	...	...	...	0.32	0.33	Enseignement supérieur
Estonia									**Estonie**
Primary education	0.97	0.97	0.97	0.98	0.99	0.99	0.99	...	Enseignement primaire
Secondary education	...	1.02	1.01	1.02	1.02	1.03	1.02	...	Enseignement secondaire
Tertiary education	1.08	1.68	1.66	1.67	1.63	1.68	1.70	...	Enseignement supérieur
Ethiopia									**Ethiopie**
Primary education	0.66	0.77	0.83	0.86	0.88	0.89	0.91	0.91	Enseignement primaire
Secondary education	0.76	0.57	0.60	0.63	0.67	0.72	0.77	0.82	Enseignement secondaire
Tertiary education	0.22	0.33	0.32	0.32	0.34	0.31	0.40	0.36	Enseignement supérieur
Fiji									**Fidji**
Primary education	1.00	0.99	...	0.99	0.98	1.00	0.98	...	Enseignement primaire
Secondary education	0.97	1.07	...	1.09	1.11	1.07	1.09	...	Enseignement secondaire
Tertiary education	...	1.20	*1.19	...	...	...	...	...	Enseignement supérieur
Finland									**Finlande**
Primary education	0.99	0.99	0.99	1.00	1.00	0.99	0.99	0.99	Enseignement primaire
Secondary education	1.19	1.05	1.05	1.04	1.04	1.05	1.05	1.05	Enseignement secondaire
Tertiary education	1.13	1.20	1.21	1.22	1.23	1.24	1.23	1.22	Enseignement supérieur
France									**France**
Primary education	0.99	0.99	0.99	0.99	0.99	0.99	0.99	0.99	Enseignement primaire
Secondary education	1.06	1.00	1.00	1.00	1.00	1.00	1.00	1.01	Enseignement secondaire
Tertiary education	1.17	1.26	1.27	1.27	1.28	1.27	1.28	...	Enseignement supérieur
Gabon *									**Gabon ***
Primary education	...	0.99	...	...	...	...	...	...	Enseignement primaire
Gambia									**Gambie**
Primary education	...	1.00	1.03	1.04	1.04	1.06	1.04	1.02	Enseignement primaire
Secondary education	0.49	...	...	...	...	*0.92	*0.95	*0.95	Enseignement secondaire
Tertiary education	...	0.22	...	...	...	...	...	...	Enseignement supérieur
Georgia									**Géorgie**
Primary education	1.00	0.95	0.97	1.02	0.98	1.00	1.01	1.03	Enseignement primaire
Secondary education	0.97	0.99	0.97	*0.99	...	0.95	...	...	Enseignement secondaire
Tertiary education	0.91	1.03	1.03	1.12	1.11	1.20	1.24	1.25	Enseignement supérieur
Germany									**Allemagne**
Primary education	...	1.00	1.00	1.00	1.00	1.00	1.00	1.00	Enseignement primaire
Secondary education	...	0.98	0.98	0.97	0.98	0.97	0.95	0.95	Enseignement secondaire
Ghana									**Ghana**
Primary education	0.86	0.95	0.97	0.99	0.99	0.99	0.99	...	Enseignement primaire
Secondary education	...	0.84	*0.84	0.86	0.88	0.89	0.90	...	Enseignement secondaire
Tertiary education	0.30	...	0.56	0.53	0.54	0.45	0.62	...	Enseignement supérieur
Greece									**Grèce**
Primary education	0.99	0.99	1.00	1.00	1.00	...	...	...	Enseignement primaire
Secondary education	0.98	1.00	0.98	0.97	0.95	...	...	...	Enseignement secondaire
Tertiary education	...	1.17	1.14	1.13	1.10	...	...	...	Enseignement supérieur
Grenada									**Grenade**
Primary education	...	0.96	*0.97	...	0.98	0.95	0.94	1.00	Enseignement primaire
Secondary education	1.16	1.08	1.02	...	0.97	0.91	1.00	1.03	Enseignement secondaire
Tertiary education	...	...	...	...	...	...	1.36	...	Enseignement supérieur
Guatemala									**Guatemala**
Primary education	0.87	0.92	0.92	0.93	0.94	0.94	...	0.96	Enseignement primaire
Secondary education	...	0.90	0.91	0.91	0.92	0.93	...	0.93	Enseignement secondaire
Tertiary education	...	...	...	...	1.00	...	...	...	Enseignement supérieur
Guinea									**Guinée**
Primary education	0.48	0.79	0.82	0.84	0.85	0.85	0.85	0.84	Enseignement primaire
Secondary education	0.34	0.46	*0.51	0.53	*0.57	0.59	*0.59	...	Enseignement secondaire
Tertiary education	0.07	0.19	0.24	0.28	*0.33	0.33	...	...	Enseignement supérieur
Guinea-Bissau									**Guinée-Bissau**
Primary education	...	...	...	...	...	...	...	0.94	Enseignement primaire

Ratio of girls to boys in primary, secondary and tertiary education *(continued)*
Rapport filles/garçons dans l'enseignement primaire, secondaire et supérieur *(suite)*

Country or area	1991	2004	2005	2006	2007	2008	2009	2010	Pays ou zone
Guyana									**Guyana**
Primary education	0.96	*0.99	1.02	1.04	1.03	1.04	1.03	1.04	Enseignement primaire
Secondary education	...	*1.05	1.03	...	1.00	1.08	1.07	1.11	Enseignement secondaire
Tertiary education	...	1.84	2.04	2.16	2.13	1.44	2.11	2.52	Enseignement supérieur
Honduras									**Honduras**
Primary education	1.01	0.99	0.99	0.99	1.00	1.00	...	1.00	Enseignement primaire
Secondary education	1.23	...	...	...	1.25	1.27	...	1.23	Enseignement secondaire
Tertiary education	0.79	*1.41	...	...	...	1.51	...	...	Enseignement supérieur
Hungary									**Hongrie**
Primary education	0.99	0.98	0.98	0.98	0.98	0.98	0.99	...	Enseignement primaire
Secondary education	1.01	0.99	0.99	0.99	0.99	0.98	0.99	...	Enseignement secondaire
Tertiary education	1.06	1.40	1.46	1.46	1.45	1.43	1.37	...	Enseignement supérieur
Iceland									**Islande**
Primary education	...	0.98	0.98	0.99	1.00	1.00	1.00	...	Enseignement primaire
Secondary education	0.96	1.03	1.02	1.03	1.06	1.03	1.03	...	Enseignement secondaire
Tertiary education	1.39	1.87	1.91	1.87	1.87	1.89	1.87	...	Enseignement supérieur
India									**Inde**
Primary education	0.76	*0.96	0.96	0.95	0.97	1.00	...	...	Enseignement primaire
Secondary education	...	*0.81	*0.82	*0.83	0.86	0.88	0.91	0.92	Enseignement secondaire
Tertiary education	0.54	0.67	0.71	0.72	0.70	...	0.68	0.73	Enseignement supérieur
Indonesia									**Indonésie**
Primary education	0.97	0.98	*0.97	0.96	0.96	0.97	0.97	1.02	Enseignement primaire
Secondary education	0.82	0.99	*0.99	1.00	1.00	0.99	0.99	1.00	Enseignement secondaire
Tertiary education	...	0.79	*0.79	*0.91	0.99	0.92	0.96	0.89	Enseignement supérieur
Iran (Islamic Rep. of)									**Iran (Rép. islamique d')**
Primary education	0.90	0.97	0.98	0.98	0.99	...	0.99	1.01	Enseignement primaire
Secondary education	0.74	0.96	0.96	0.97	1.01	0.98	0.94	0.86	Enseignement secondaire
Tertiary education	0.37	1.08	1.06	1.08	1.12	1.15	1.07	1.01	Enseignement supérieur
Iraq									**Iraq**
Primary education	0.85	0.84	...	...	0.84	...	...	...	Enseignement primaire
Secondary education	...	0.67	...	...	0.75	...	...	...	Enseignement secondaire
Tertiary education	...	0.60	*0.60	...	...	...	...	...	Enseignement supérieur
Ireland									**Irlande**
Primary education	1.01	0.99	1.00	0.99	1.00	1.00	1.00	1.00	Enseignement primaire
Secondary education	1.09	1.08	1.09	1.08	1.08	1.07	1.06	1.05	Enseignement secondaire
Tertiary education	0.89	1.26	1.24	1.25	1.27	1.23	1.22	...	Enseignement supérieur
Israel									**Israël**
Primary education	1.03	1.00	1.01	1.01	1.01	1.01	1.01	...	Enseignement primaire
Secondary education	1.05	1.00	0.99	1.00	1.00	1.02	1.02	...	Enseignement secondaire
Tertiary education	1.01	1.32	1.33	1.27	1.31	1.29	1.30	...	Enseignement supérieur
Italy									**Italie**
Primary education	1.00	0.99	0.99	0.99	1.00	1.00	0.99	0.99	Enseignement primaire
Secondary education	1.00	0.99	0.99	0.99	0.98	0.98	0.98	0.99	Enseignement secondaire
Tertiary education	0.94	1.34	1.36	1.39	1.41	1.41	1.41	...	Enseignement supérieur
Jamaica									**Jamaïque**
Primary education	1.00	0.99	0.98	...	0.97	0.96	0.96	0.95	Enseignement primaire
Secondary education	1.06	1.02	1.04	...	1.05	1.05	1.01	1.03	Enseignement secondaire
Tertiary education	...	...	...	...	...	2.24	2.29	2.28	Enseignement supérieur
Japan									**Japon**
Primary education	1.00	1.00	1.00	1.00	1.00	1.00	1.00	1.00	Enseignement primaire
Secondary education	1.02	1.00	1.00	1.00	1.00	1.00	1.00	1.00	Enseignement secondaire
Tertiary education	0.65	0.89	0.89	0.88	0.88	0.88	0.89	0.89	Enseignement supérieur
Jordan									**Jordanie**
Primary education	1.00	1.01	1.01	1.02	1.02	1.01	...	1.00	Enseignement primaire
Secondary education	1.02	1.02	1.03	1.03	1.04	1.04	...	1.06	Enseignement secondaire
Tertiary education	1.12	1.13	1.08	1.14	1.12	1.12	1.12	1.16	Enseignement supérieur
Kazakhstan									**Kazakhstan**
Primary education	...	1.01	1.01	1.01	1.01	1.01	1.00	1.00	Enseignement primaire
Secondary education	...	0.98	0.98	0.98	0.99	0.98	0.97	0.97	Enseignement secondaire
Tertiary education	...	1.39	1.43	1.42	1.43	1.43	1.44	1.44	Enseignement supérieur

11

Ratio of girls to boys in primary, secondary and tertiary education *(continued)*
Rapport filles/garçons dans l'enseignement primaire, secondaire et supérieur *(suite)*

Country or area	1991	2004	2005	2006	2007	2008	2009	2010	Pays ou zone
Kenya									**Kenya**
Primary education	0.97	0.94	0.96	0.97	0.99	0.98	0.98	...	Enseignement primaire
Secondary education	...	*0.93	*0.95	0.93	0.87	0.92	0.90	...	Enseignement secondaire
Tertiary education	...	0.60	*0.60	...	...	...	0.70	...	Enseignement supérieur
Kiribati									**Kiribati**
Primary education	1.01	1.03	1.02	1.00	1.03	1.04	1.04	...	Enseignement primaire
Secondary education	1.07	1.18	1.14	1.19	1.18	1.11	...	...	Enseignement secondaire
Kuwait									**Koweït**
Primary education	0.96	1.02	1.01	1.03	1.03	1.03	...	...	Enseignement primaire
Secondary education	...	1.07	1.06	1.05	1.03	1.07	...	...	Enseignement secondaire
Tertiary education *	...	2.20	...	...	...	...	...	...	Enseignement supérieur *
Kyrgyzstan									**Kirghizistan**
Primary education	...	1.00	0.99	0.99	0.99	1.00	1.00	0.99	Enseignement primaire
Secondary education	1.02	1.00	1.00	1.00	1.00	1.00	1.00	0.99	Enseignement secondaire
Tertiary education	...	1.18	1.24	1.26	1.29	1.34	1.30	...	Enseignement supérieur
Lao People's Dem. Rep.									**Rép. dém. pop. lao**
Primary education	0.79	0.88	0.88	0.89	0.89	0.90	...	0.93	Enseignement primaire
Secondary education	...	0.75	0.76	0.78	0.79	0.81	...	0.83	Enseignement secondaire
Tertiary education	...	0.62	0.71	0.68	0.72	0.78	...	0.77	Enseignement supérieur
Latvia									**Lettonie**
Primary education	1.00	0.96	0.96	0.96	0.96	0.96	0.98	0.99	Enseignement primaire
Secondary education	1.02	0.99	1.00	1.00	1.02	1.02	1.01	0.98	Enseignement secondaire
Tertiary education	1.28	1.72	1.79	1.80	1.85	1.88	1.82	1.75	Enseignement supérieur
Lebanon									**Liban**
Primary education	...	...	...	0.98	0.97	0.97	0.98	0.97	Enseignement primaire
Secondary education	...	...	...	1.10	1.12	1.11	1.11	1.12	Enseignement secondaire
Tertiary education	...	1.10	1.13	1.15	1.20	1.23	1.19	1.19	Enseignement supérieur
Lesotho									**Lesotho**
Primary education	1.22	1.00	1.00	1.00	0.99	0.98	1.00	0.98	Enseignement primaire
Secondary education	1.43	*1.27	1.27	1.28	*1.33	*1.36	*1.40	1.38	Enseignement secondaire
Tertiary education	1.36	...	1.34	1.25	...	...	...	...	Enseignement supérieur
Liberia									**Libéria**
Primary education	...	...	...	...	0.92	0.91	...	...	Enseignement primaire
Libyan Arab Jamah.									**Jamah. arabe libyenne**
Primary education	...	0.97	0.99	0.96	...	...	...	...	Enseignement primaire
Secondary education	...	...	*1.19	1.18	...	...	...	...	Enseignement secondaire
Liechtenstein									**Liechtenstein**
Primary education	...	0.99	...	1.03	0.99	0.96	1.02	0.94	Enseignement primaire
Secondary education	...	1.09	...	1.12	1.09	1.08	1.01	1.03	Enseignement secondaire
Tertiary education	...	0.37	...	0.43	0.47	0.52	0.49	0.62	Enseignement supérieur
Lithuania									**Lituanie**
Primary education	0.93	0.99	0.99	0.99	0.99	0.98	0.98	0.99	Enseignement primaire
Secondary education	...	0.99	0.99	1.00	1.00	1.00	1.00	0.98	Enseignement secondaire
Tertiary education	...	1.55	1.56	1.55	1.56	1.55	1.51	1.52	Enseignement supérieur
Luxembourg									**Luxembourg**
Primary education	1.08	1.00	1.00	1.00	1.00	1.01	...	...	Enseignement primaire
Secondary education	...	1.05	1.06	1.04	1.03	1.02	...	...	Enseignement secondaire
Tertiary education	...	...	...	1.13	...	0.97	...	...	Enseignement supérieur
Madagascar									**Madagascar**
Primary education	0.98	0.96	0.96	0.96	0.97	0.97	0.98	0.98	Enseignement primaire
Secondary education	...	...	*0.96	0.95	0.95	0.95	*0.94	...	Enseignement secondaire
Tertiary education	0.82	0.90	0.89	0.87	0.88	0.89	0.90	0.91	Enseignement supérieur
Malawi									**Malawi**
Primary education	0.87	1.03	1.03	1.04	1.04	1.03	1.03	1.04	Enseignement primaire
Secondary education	0.61	0.81	0.82	0.84	0.84	0.85	0.88	0.91	Enseignement secondaire
Tertiary education	0.35	*0.55	*0.55	*0.51	0.51	...	...	0.62	Enseignement supérieur
Malaysia									**Malaisie**
Primary education	1.00	1.00	1.00	...	...	...	...	...	Enseignement primaire
Secondary education	1.05	1.12	1.10	1.08	1.07	1.08	1.07	...	Enseignement secondaire
Tertiary education	...	1.27	1.30	1.25	1.30	1.30	1.29	...	Enseignement supérieur

Country or area	1991	2004	2005	2006	2007	2008	2009	2010	Pays ou zone
Maldives									**Maldives**
Primary education	...	0.98	0.98	0.97	0.97	0.97	0.97	...	Enseignement primaire
Secondary education *	...	1.13	...	...	...	...	...	...	Enseignement secondaire *
Tertiary education	...	*2.30	...	...	...	1.08	...	...	Enseignement supérieur
Mali									**Mali**
Primary education	0.61	0.79	0.80	0.82	0.83	0.85	0.86	0.87	Enseignement primaire
Secondary education	0.52	0.60	*0.62	0.62	0.67	0.65	0.67	0.70	Enseignement secondaire
Tertiary education	0.16	0.54	*0.54	...	*0.47	0.47	0.42	0.42	Enseignement supérieur
Malta									**Malte**
Primary education	0.97	0.98	0.97	...	0.99	1.00	1.01	1.01	Enseignement primaire
Secondary education	0.93	0.93	0.96	...	1.02	0.97	0.88	0.89	Enseignement secondaire
Tertiary education	0.83	1.33	1.36	...	1.42	1.45	1.37	1.36	Enseignement supérieur
Marshall Islands									**Iles Marshall**
Primary education	...	0.95	1.26	1.00	0.99	1.01	1.00	...	Enseignement primaire
Secondary education	...	1.04	1.00	1.01	1.00	1.06	1.03	...	Enseignement secondaire
Mauritania									**Mauritanie**
Primary education	0.76	1.01	1.04	1.03	1.04	1.05	1.05	1.05	Enseignement primaire
Secondary education	0.48	0.86	0.88	0.85	*0.87	*0.88	*0.83	*0.85	Enseignement secondaire
Tertiary education	0.17	0.32	0.34	0.36	...	0.41	0.41	0.41	Enseignement supérieur
Mauritius									**Maurice**
Primary education	1.01	1.00	1.00	1.00	1.00	1.00	1.00	1.01	Enseignement primaire
Secondary education	...	0.98	*0.98	*0.98	*0.98	*0.99	*1.00	*1.00	Enseignement secondaire
Tertiary education	0.72	*0.97	*1.04	*1.01	*1.18	*1.24	...	...	Enseignement supérieur
Mexico									**Mexique**
Primary education	0.97	0.99	0.98	0.98	0.98	0.98	0.99	0.99	Enseignement primaire
Secondary education	1.00	1.05	1.05	1.06	1.06	1.07	1.08	1.07	Enseignement secondaire
Tertiary education	...	0.98	0.99	0.98	0.98	0.98	0.98	0.97	Enseignement supérieur
Micronesia (Fed. States of)									**Micronésie (Etats féd. de)**
Primary education	...	0.98	0.97	...	1.01	...	...	...	Enseignement primaire
Secondary education	...	1.06	1.08	...	...	...	...	...	Enseignement secondaire
Mongolia									**Mongolie**
Primary education	0.99	0.99	1.00	1.00	1.00	0.99	0.99	0.98	Enseignement primaire
Secondary education	1.10	1.11	1.11	1.10	...	...	1.08	1.07	Enseignement secondaire
Tertiary education	...	1.65	1.62	1.57	1.55	1.57	1.55	1.53	Enseignement supérieur
Montenegro									**Monténégro**
Primary education	...	1.00	1.00	0.99	1.00	1.00	0.98	0.98	Enseignement primaire
Secondary education	...	1.00	1.02	1.02	1.01	1.14	1.01	1.01	Enseignement secondaire
Tertiary education	...	1.60	1.55	1.52	1.37	1.24	1.28	1.24	Enseignement supérieur
Montserrat									**Montserrat**
Primary education	...	0.97	1.04	*1.00	1.12	...	...	...	Enseignement primaire
Secondary education	...	1.10	1.10	*0.98	1.02	...	...	...	Enseignement secondaire
Morocco									**Maroc**
Primary education	0.69	0.91	0.90	0.90	0.91	0.91	0.93	0.94	Enseignement primaire
Secondary education	0.72	0.83	*0.84	...	*0.86	...	...	...	Enseignement secondaire
Tertiary education	0.58	0.82	0.80	0.81	0.89	0.88	0.87	...	Enseignement supérieur
Mozambique									**Mozambique**
Primary education	0.74	0.83	0.84	0.86	0.87	0.88	0.90	0.90	Enseignement primaire
Secondary education	0.56	0.70	0.69	0.72	0.73	0.75	0.79	0.82	Enseignement secondaire
Tertiary education	...	0.46	0.50	...	...	...	...	...	Enseignement supérieur
Myanmar									**Myanmar**
Primary education	0.96	1.01	1.01	1.00	...	1.00	0.99	1.00	Enseignement primaire
Secondary education	0.98	0.94	0.98	0.99	1.01	...	1.03	1.06	Enseignement secondaire
Tertiary education	...	...	...	...	1.38	...	...	...	Enseignement supérieur
Namibia									**Namibie**
Primary education	1.04	1.01	1.01	1.01	1.00	0.99	0.99	...	Enseignement primaire
Secondary education	1.23	1.13	1.14	1.17	1.18	...	...	...	Enseignement secondaire
Tertiary education	1.76	...	0.88	0.88	...	1.32	...	...	Enseignement supérieur
Nauru									**Nauru**
Primary education	...	1.02	1.05	0.99	1.04	1.06	...	...	Enseignement primaire
Secondary education	...	1.20	1.13	1.18	1.17	1.20	...	...	Enseignement secondaire

Ratio of girls to boys in primary, secondary and tertiary education *(continued)*
Rapport filles/garçons dans l'enseignement primaire, secondaire et supérieur *(suite)*

Country or area	1991	2004	2005	2006	2007	2008	2009	2010	Pays ou zone
Nepal									**Népal**
Primary education	0.63	...	...	...	...	...	...	...	Enseignement primaire
Secondary education	0.46	...	*0.86	*0.89	...	...	...	...	Enseignement secondaire
Tertiary education	0.33	0.40	...	...	...	...	...	...	Enseignement supérieur
Netherlands									**Pays-Bas**
Primary education	1.03	0.97	0.98	0.98	0.98	0.98	0.99	0.99	Enseignement primaire
Secondary education	0.92	0.98	0.98	0.98	0.98	0.98	0.99	0.99	Enseignement secondaire
Tertiary education	0.83	1.07	1.07	1.08	1.10	1.11	1.12	...	Enseignement supérieur
New Zealand									**Nouvelle-Zélande**
Primary education	0.99	0.99	0.99	0.99	1.00	1.00	1.00	1.00	Enseignement primaire
Secondary education	1.01	1.06	1.06	1.04	1.02	1.05	1.03	1.05	Enseignement secondaire
Tertiary education	1.13	1.44	1.45	1.48	1.46	1.46	1.45	1.46	Enseignement supérieur
Nicaragua									**Nicaragua**
Primary education	1.06	0.98	0.97	0.97	0.98	0.98	...	0.98	Enseignement primaire
Secondary education	...	1.13	1.13	1.13	1.13	1.13	...	1.10	Enseignement secondaire
Tertiary education	0.96	...	...	...	...	...	...	...	Enseignement supérieur
Niger									**Niger**
Primary education	0.61	0.71	0.73	0.74	0.75	0.78	0.80	0.82	Enseignement primaire
Secondary education	0.37	0.61	0.63	0.63	0.61	0.60	...	0.66	Enseignement secondaire
Tertiary education	...	0.31	0.34	0.29	0.33	0.36	0.35	0.37	Enseignement supérieur
Nigeria									**Nigéria**
Primary education	0.81	0.84	0.85	0.86	0.89	0.89	0.90	0.91	Enseignement primaire
Secondary education	...	0.81	0.84	0.82	0.78	0.84	0.88	0.88	Enseignement secondaire
Tertiary education	...	*0.71	0.71	...	...	...	...	...	Enseignement supérieur
Niue									**Nioué**
Primary education	...	1.03	0.89	...	...	...	...	...	Enseignement primaire
Secondary education	...	1.73	1.78	...	...	...	...	...	Enseignement secondaire
Norway									**Norvège**
Primary education	1.00	1.00	1.00	1.01	1.00	1.00	1.00	1.00	Enseignement primaire
Secondary education	1.03	1.03	1.01	1.00	0.99	0.98	0.98	0.98	Enseignement secondaire
Tertiary education	1.19	1.52	1.52	1.54	1.58	1.62	1.64	1.63	Enseignement supérieur
Occupied Palestinian Terr.									**Terr. palestinien occupé**
Primary education	...	1.00	0.99	1.00	1.00	1.00	1.00	0.98	Enseignement primaire
Secondary education	...	1.04	1.05	1.06	1.06	*1.07	1.07	1.08	Enseignement secondaire
Tertiary education	...	1.01	1.02	1.16	1.21	1.21	1.30	1.34	Enseignement supérieur
Oman									**Oman**
Primary education	0.92	...	...	...	...	...	0.97	...	Enseignement primaire
Secondary education	0.81	...	...	...	...	...	0.99	...	Enseignement secondaire
Tertiary education	0.97	1.07	1.03	1.05	1.21	...	1.35	1.39	Enseignement supérieur
Pakistan									**Pakistan**
Primary education	...	0.72	0.75	0.77	0.81	0.81	0.82	0.82	Enseignement primaire
Secondary education	0.47	*0.77	*0.77	0.77	0.75	0.75	0.78	0.76	Enseignement secondaire
Tertiary education	...	0.77	0.85	0.83	0.83	0.83	...	...	Enseignement supérieur
Palau									**Palaos**
Primary education	...	0.97	...	...	*1.03	...	...	...	Enseignement primaire
Secondary education	...	1.02	...	...	...	...	...	...	Enseignement secondaire
Panama									**Panama**
Primary education	...	0.97	0.97	0.97	0.97	0.97	0.97	0.97	Enseignement primaire
Secondary education	...	1.07	1.07	1.09	1.08	1.08	1.08	1.07	Enseignement secondaire
Tertiary education	...	1.66	1.63	1.62	1.59	1.54	1.53	...	Enseignement supérieur
Papua New Guinea									**Papouasie-Nvl-Guinée**
Primary education	0.85	0.87	0.85	0.85	...	0.89	...	...	Enseignement primaire
Secondary education	0.67	...	...	...	...	...	...	...	Enseignement secondaire
Paraguay									**Paraguay**
Primary education	0.97	0.97	0.97	0.97	0.97	0.97	0.97	...	Enseignement primaire
Secondary education	1.05	1.02	1.03	1.03	1.04	1.04	1.05	...	Enseignement secondaire
Tertiary education	...	1.34	1.13	...	1.34	1.35	1.43	...	Enseignement supérieur
Peru									**Pérou**
Primary education	0.97	0.99	1.00	0.99	1.00	1.00	1.00	1.00	Enseignement primaire
Secondary education	0.94	0.98	0.97	0.98	0.99	0.99	0.98	0.98	Enseignement secondaire
Tertiary education	...	*1.02	*1.02	*1.06	...	...	...	1.09	Enseignement supérieur

11

Ratio of girls to boys in primary, secondary and tertiary education *(continued)*
Rapport filles/garçons dans l'enseignement primaire, secondaire et supérieur *(suite)*

Country or area	1991	2004	2005	2006	2007	2008	2009	2010	Pays ou zone
Philippines									**Philippines**
Primary education	1.00	0.99	0.99	0.99	0.99	0.98	0.98	...	Enseignement primaire
Secondary education	...	1.11	1.12	1.12	1.11	1.09	1.08	...	Enseignement secondaire
Tertiary education	...	1.28	1.23	1.25	...	1.25	...	...	Enseignement supérieur
Poland									**Pologne**
Primary education	0.99	0.99	0.99	0.99	0.99	0.99	0.99	...	Enseignement primaire
Secondary education	1.05	1.01	0.99	0.98	0.98	0.99	0.99	...	Enseignement secondaire
Tertiary education	1.33	1.40	1.40	1.40	1.40	1.41	1.43	...	Enseignement supérieur
Portugal									**Portugal**
Primary education	0.95	0.95	0.95	0.95	0.94	0.94	0.97	...	Enseignement primaire
Secondary education	1.16	1.10	1.10	1.09	1.07	1.05	1.04	...	Enseignement secondaire
Tertiary education	1.29	1.32	1.30	1.28	1.22	1.20	1.19	...	Enseignement supérieur
Puerto Rico									**Porto Rico**
Primary education	...	...	...	...	...	...	1.04	1.04	Enseignement primaire
Secondary education	...	...	...	...	...	...	1.03	1.06	Enseignement secondaire
Tertiary education	...	...	...	...	1.60	1.56	1.56	1.48	Enseignement supérieur
Qatar									**Qatar**
Primary education	0.94	0.83	0.87	0.96	0.93	0.97	0.99	1.00	Enseignement primaire
Secondary education	1.21	...	...	...	...	1.30	1.29	1.21	Enseignement secondaire
Tertiary education	3.48	4.09	*3.69	*3.71	4.43	4.84	5.42	5.38	Enseignement supérieur
Republic of Korea									**République de Corée**
Primary education	1.01	0.99	0.99	0.99	0.99	0.99	0.99	0.99	Enseignement primaire
Secondary education	0.97	0.99	0.99	0.99	0.99	0.99	0.99	0.99	Enseignement secondaire
Tertiary education	0.49	0.64	0.65	0.66	0.67	0.69	0.70	0.72	Enseignement supérieur
Republic of Moldova									**République de Moldova**
Primary education	1.00	0.99	0.99	0.99	0.98	0.98	0.98	1.00	Enseignement primaire
Secondary education	1.09	1.05	1.04	1.04	1.03	1.03	1.02	1.02	Enseignement secondaire
Tertiary education	...	1.35	1.46	1.38	1.39	1.45	1.39	1.34	Enseignement supérieur
Romania									**Roumanie**
Primary education	1.00	0.99	0.99	0.99	0.99	0.99	0.99	0.99	Enseignement primaire
Secondary education	0.99	1.01	1.01	1.00	0.99	0.99	0.99	0.99	Enseignement secondaire
Tertiary education	0.93	1.26	1.26	1.30	1.33	1.34	1.34	1.35	Enseignement supérieur
Russian Federation									**Fédération de Russie**
Primary education	1.00	...	0.99	1.00	1.00	1.00	1.00	...	Enseignement primaire
Secondary education	...	0.99	0.99	0.98	0.98	0.97	0.98	...	Enseignement secondaire
Tertiary education	1.23	1.36	1.37	1.36	1.36	1.36	1.35	...	Enseignement supérieur
Rwanda									**Rwanda**
Primary education	0.99	1.02	1.03	1.04	1.03	1.03	1.02	1.02	Enseignement primaire
Secondary education	0.82	0.90	0.88	*0.90	0.90	0.91	0.95	1.02	Enseignement secondaire
Tertiary education	...	0.62	...	...	...	...	0.76	0.77	Enseignement supérieur
Saint Kitts and Nevis									**Saint-Kitts-et-Nevis**
Primary education	...	1.03	1.02	...	1.00	1.02	1.02	1.00	Enseignement primaire
Secondary education	...	*1.11	*1.05	...	1.01	1.06	1.08	0.99	Enseignement secondaire
Tertiary education	...	...	...	...	...	2.10	...	...	Enseignement supérieur
Saint Lucia									**Sainte-Lucie**
Primary education	0.95	0.95	0.96	0.92	0.95	0.97	0.97	0.96	Enseignement primaire
Secondary education	1.46	1.09	1.17	1.17	1.11	1.05	1.03	0.99	Enseignement secondaire
Tertiary education	...	3.38	2.72	5.31	2.33	2.24	2.57	2.57	Enseignement supérieur
Saint Vincent-Grenadines									**Saint Vincent-Grenadines**
Primary education	0.99	0.96	0.91	...	0.95	0.92	0.93	0.93	Enseignement primaire
Secondary education	1.24	*1.08	1.25	...	1.12	1.12	1.04	1.02	Enseignement secondaire
Samoa									**Samoa**
Primary education	...	1.00	...	...	1.01	...	1.00	1.02	Enseignement primaire
Secondary education	...	1.13	*1.13	...	...	...	1.15	1.14	Enseignement secondaire
San Marino									**Saint-Marin**
Primary education	...	...	...	...	...	...	1.01	*1.13	Enseignement primaire
Secondary education	...	...	...	...	...	...	1.04	*1.02	Enseignement secondaire
Sao Tome and Principe									**Sao Tomé-et-Principe**
Primary education	...	0.97	0.97	*0.97	0.99	0.98	1.01	1.00	Enseignement primaire
Secondary education	...	1.04	1.07	*1.10	1.07	1.07	1.12	1.03	Enseignement secondaire
Tertiary education	...	...	...	...	...	...	0.93	0.98	Enseignement supérieur

11

Ratio of girls to boys in primary, secondary and tertiary education *(continued)*
Rapport filles/garçons dans l'enseignement primaire, secondaire et supérieur *(suite)*

Country or area	1991	2004	2005	2006	2007	2008	2009	2010	Pays ou zone
Saudi Arabia									**Arabie saoudite**
Primary education	...	...	1.00	...	0.99	0.99	0.98	0.99	Enseignement primaire
Secondary education	...	...	0.93	...	...	*0.89	*0.90	0.95	Enseignement secondaire
Tertiary education	1.00	1.50	1.45	1.41	1.25	1.25	1.24	1.12	Enseignement supérieur
Senegal									**Sénégal**
Primary education	0.73	0.95	0.97	0.99	1.00	1.03	1.05	1.06	Enseignement primaire
Secondary education	...	0.72	0.75	*0.76	*0.78	0.79	...	0.88	Enseignement secondaire
Tertiary education	...	...	...	0.46	0.53	0.55	0.59	*0.60	Enseignement supérieur
Serbia									**Serbie**
Primary education	...	*1.01	1.01	1.00	1.00	1.00	0.99	0.99	Enseignement primaire
Secondary education	...	*1.03	1.03	1.04	1.03	1.03	1.03	1.02	Enseignement secondaire
Tertiary education	...	...	...	...	1.29	1.30	1.29	1.30	Enseignement supérieur
Seychelles									**Seychelles**
Primary education	0.98	0.99	0.97	...	1.02	1.02	1.01	1.00	Enseignement primaire
Secondary education	0.98	1.10	1.06	...	1.11	1.14	1.13	1.09	Enseignement secondaire
Slovakia									**Slovaquie**
Primary education	...	0.99	0.99	0.99	0.99	0.99	0.99	0.99	Enseignement primaire
Secondary education	...	1.01	1.01	1.01	1.01	1.01	1.01	1.01	Enseignement secondaire
Tertiary education	...	1.22	1.29	1.42	1.49	1.58	1.59	1.55	Enseignement supérieur
Slovenia									**Slovénie**
Primary education	...	1.00	0.99	0.99	0.99	0.99	0.99	...	Enseignement primaire
Secondary education	...	1.00	1.00	1.00	0.99	0.99	1.00	...	Enseignement secondaire
Tertiary education	1.32	1.39	1.44	1.48	1.47	1.46	1.45	...	Enseignement supérieur
Solomon Islands									**Iles Salomon**
Primary education	0.87	*0.96	0.96	0.97	0.97	...	...	...	Enseignement primaire
Secondary education	0.60	*0.84	0.84	0.84	0.84	...	...	...	Enseignement secondaire
Somalia									**Somalie**
Primary education	...	...	...	...	0.55	...	...	...	Enseignement primaire
Secondary education *	...	...	...	...	0.46	...	...	...	Enseignement secondaire *
South Africa									**Afrique du Sud**
Primary education	0.99	0.96	0.96	0.96	0.96	0.96	0.96	...	Enseignement primaire
Secondary education	1.17	1.07	1.06	*1.06	*1.05	*1.04	1.05	...	Enseignement secondaire
Tertiary education	0.83	...	...	...	...	...	...	...	Enseignement supérieur
Spain									**Espagne**
Primary education	0.99	0.99	0.99	0.98	0.99	0.99	0.99	0.99	Enseignement primaire
Secondary education	1.07	1.06	1.06	1.06	1.06	1.06	1.04	1.02	Enseignement secondaire
Tertiary education	1.09	1.22	1.22	1.22	1.23	1.23	1.24	...	Enseignement supérieur
Sri Lanka									**Sri Lanka**
Primary education	0.96	...	*1.00	1.00	1.00	1.00	1.00	1.00	Enseignement primaire
Secondary education	1.09	*1.01	...	...	...	...	...	...	Enseignement secondaire
Tertiary education	...	...	...	...	...	...	...	1.92	Enseignement supérieur
Suriname									**Suriname**
Primary education	1.02	...	0.97	0.96	0.94	0.96	0.95	...	Enseignement primaire
Secondary education	1.18	...	1.29	1.32	1.33	1.28	1.23	...	Enseignement secondaire
Swaziland									**Swaziland**
Primary education	0.99	0.94	0.94	0.94	0.93	...	0.92	0.92	Enseignement primaire
Secondary education	...	0.98	1.02	1.02	0.91	...	1.01	1.00	Enseignement secondaire
Tertiary education	0.75	1.08	1.06	0.98	...	...	...	...	Enseignement supérieur
Sweden									**Suède**
Primary education	1.00	1.00	1.00	1.00	1.00	0.99	0.99	0.99	Enseignement primaire
Secondary education	1.05	1.03	1.00	1.00	0.99	0.99	0.99	0.99	Enseignement secondaire
Tertiary education	1.22	1.54	1.54	1.54	1.57	1.59	1.59	1.54	Enseignement supérieur
Switzerland									**Suisse**
Primary education	1.01	1.00	1.00	1.00	1.00	1.00	1.00	1.00	Enseignement primaire
Secondary education	0.94	0.94	0.94	0.94	0.95	0.96	0.96	0.97	Enseignement secondaire
Tertiary education	0.54	0.83	0.87	0.90	0.92	0.99	1.01	0.99	Enseignement supérieur
Syrian Arab Republic									**Rép. arabe syrienne**
Primary education	0.90	0.95	0.96	0.97	0.97	0.97	0.97	0.98	Enseignement primaire
Secondary education	0.73	0.93	0.94	0.95	0.98	1.00	1.01	1.01	Enseignement secondaire
Tertiary education	0.65	...	...	...	...	...	...	...	Enseignement supérieur

11

Ratio of girls to boys in primary, secondary and tertiary education *(continued)*
Rapport filles/garçons dans l'enseignement primaire, secondaire et supérieur *(suite)*

Country or area	1991	2004	2005	2006	2007	2008	2009	2010	Pays ou zone
Tajikistan									**Tadjikistan**
Primary education	0.98	0.96	0.96	0.96	0.96	0.96	0.96	0.96	Enseignement primaire
Secondary education	...	0.84	0.83	0.83	0.84	0.87	0.88	0.87	Enseignement secondaire
Tertiary education	...	0.33	0.35	0.37	0.38	0.39	0.41	0.41	Enseignement supérieur
Thailand									**Thaïlande**
Primary education	0.98	0.98	0.97	0.99	0.98	0.99	0.99	...	Enseignement primaire
Secondary education	0.97	1.08	*1.06	1.08	1.09	1.09	1.09	1.08	Enseignement secondaire
Tertiary education	...	1.19	1.14	1.08	1.24	1.22	1.24	1.31	Enseignement supérieur
TFYR of Macedonia									**L'ex-R.Y. Macédoine**
Primary education	...	1.00	1.00	1.00	1.01	1.02	1.01	1.01	Enseignement primaire
Secondary education	...	0.98	0.98	...	0.98	0.97	0.98	0.99	Enseignement secondaire
Tertiary education	1.11	1.41	1.39	1.39	1.27	1.21	1.19	1.18	Enseignement supérieur
Timor-Leste									**Timor-Leste**
Primary education	...	0.93	0.92	...	...	0.95	0.95	0.96	Enseignement primaire
Secondary education	...	0.98	1.00	...	...	1.00	0.99	1.01	Enseignement secondaire
Tertiary education	...	...	...	...	...	...	0.70	...	Enseignement supérieur
Togo									**Togo**
Primary education	0.65	0.84	0.85	0.86	0.86	0.88	0.85	0.90	Enseignement primaire
Secondary education	0.34	0.51	0.53	0.54	*0.53	...	...	...	Enseignement secondaire
Tertiary education	0.16	...	...	...	...	...	...	...	Enseignement supérieur
Tonga									**Tonga**
Primary education	1.00	0.95	0.97	0.96	0.96	...	...	...	Enseignement primaire
Secondary education	1.02	*1.05	...	1.00	...	...	...	...	Enseignement secondaire
Tertiary education *	...	1.60	...	...	...	...	...	...	Enseignement supérieur *
Trinidad and Tobago									**Trinité-et-Tobago**
Primary education	1.00	0.97	0.97	...	0.97	0.97	0.96	0.97	Enseignement primaire
Secondary education	1.03	1.07	...	...	...	*1.07	...	...	Enseignement secondaire
Tertiary education	0.77	1.27	*1.28	...	...	...	...	...	Enseignement supérieur
Tunisia									**Tunisie**
Primary education	0.88	0.95	0.95	0.95	0.95	0.95	0.96	...	Enseignement primaire
Secondary education	0.78	...	1.08	*1.07	...	1.06	*1.06	...	Enseignement secondaire
Tertiary education	0.66	1.32	1.36	1.38	1.47	1.46	1.51	...	Enseignement supérieur
Turkey									**Turquie**
Primary education	0.91	0.95	0.95	0.96	0.97	0.98	0.98	...	Enseignement primaire
Secondary education	0.61	0.78	0.84	0.84	0.85	0.89	0.91	...	Enseignement secondaire
Tertiary education	0.51	0.72	0.74	0.75	0.76	0.78	0.79	...	Enseignement supérieur
Turks and Caicos Islands *									**Iles Turques et Caïques ***
Primary education	...	1.03	1.04	...	...	...	...	...	Enseignement primaire
Secondary education	...	0.98	0.94	...	...	...	...	...	Enseignement secondaire
Tertiary education	...	...	...	...	...	0.90	...	...	Enseignement supérieur
Tuvalu									**Tuvalu**
Primary education	...	1.03	0.96	0.95	...	...	...	...	Enseignement primaire
Uganda									**Ouganda**
Primary education	0.81	0.97	0.98	0.99	1.00	1.00	1.01	1.01	Enseignement primaire
Secondary education	...	0.79	*0.79	*0.81	0.80	0.83	*0.82	*0.85	Enseignement secondaire
Tertiary education	0.38	0.62	...	0.76	...	0.79	0.79	...	Enseignement supérieur
Ukraine									**Ukraine**
Primary education	1.00	0.99	1.00	1.00	1.00	1.00	1.00	1.01	Enseignement primaire
Secondary education	1.04	0.99	0.92	0.98	0.99	0.98	0.98	0.98	Enseignement secondaire
Tertiary education	...	1.22	1.23	1.23	1.24	1.25	1.26	1.25	Enseignement supérieur
United Arab Emirates									**Emirats arabes unis**
Primary education	0.97	1.00	1.02	1.03	...	...	...	...	Enseignement primaire
Secondary education	1.20	1.03	1.01	1.01	...	...	...	...	Enseignement secondaire
Tertiary education	4.35	...	...	...	...	...	...	...	Enseignement supérieur
United Kingdom									**Royaume-Uni**
Primary education	1.01	1.00	1.00	1.00	1.00	1.00	1.00	...	Enseignement primaire
Secondary education	1.04	1.03	1.03	1.03	1.02	1.02	1.02	...	Enseignement secondaire
Tertiary education	0.96	1.37	1.39	1.41	1.41	1.41	1.40	...	Enseignement supérieur
United Rep. of Tanzania									**Rép.-Unie de Tanzanie**
Primary education	0.98	0.96	0.96	0.97	0.98	0.99	1.00	1.02	Enseignement primaire
Secondary education	0.77	...	...	...	...	...	...	...	Enseignement secondaire
Tertiary education	0.19	0.41	*0.48	...	...	...	...	0.82	Enseignement supérieur

Country or area	1991	2004	2005	2006	2007	2008	2009	2010	Pays ou zone
United States									**Etats-Unis**
Primary education	0.98	*1.00	0.99	1.01	1.00	1.00	1.01	0.99	Enseignement primaire
Secondary education	1.02	1.02	1.02	0.99	1.01	1.00	1.01	1.01	Enseignement secondaire
Tertiary education	1.25	1.41	1.42	1.43	1.42	1.41	1.41	1.41	Enseignement supérieur
Uruguay									**Uruguay**
Primary education	0.99	0.97	0.98	0.97	0.97	0.97	0.97	...	Enseignement primaire
Secondary education	...	1.15	1.15	1.16	0.99	1.13	...	...	Enseignement secondaire
Tertiary education	...	...	...	1.68	1.75	1.74	1.74	...	Enseignement supérieur
Uzbekistan									**Ouzbékistan**
Primary education	0.98	0.98	0.98	0.98	0.98	0.98	0.98	0.97	Enseignement primaire
Secondary education	...	0.96	0.97	0.97	0.98	0.98	0.99	0.99	Enseignement secondaire
Tertiary education	...	0.78	0.70	0.70	0.71	0.68	0.70	...	Enseignement supérieur
Vanuatu									**Vanuatu**
Primary education	0.96	0.97	0.97	0.97	0.95	0.97	0.95	0.95	Enseignement primaire
Secondary education	0.81	0.87	...	...	...	1.04	1.09	1.02	Enseignement secondaire
Tertiary education *	...	0.60	...	...	...	...	...	...	Enseignement supérieur *
Venezuela (Boliv. Rep. of)									**Venezuela (Rép. boliv. du)**
Primary education	0.99	0.98	0.98	0.98	0.97	0.97	0.97	0.97	Enseignement primaire
Secondary education	1.24	1.14	1.13	1.12	1.12	1.10	1.09	1.10	Enseignement secondaire
Tertiary education	...	...	...	...	...	1.69	...	...	Enseignement supérieur
Viet Nam									**Viet Nam**
Primary education	...	0.94	0.94	0.96	0.96	...	0.96	0.94	Enseignement primaire
Secondary education	...	0.96	0.98	0.99	1.02	1.05	1.05	1.09	Enseignement secondaire
Tertiary education	...	*0.71	0.71	0.95	1.00	0.98	0.99	1.00	Enseignement supérieur
Yemen									**Yémen**
Primary education	...	0.71	0.74	...	...	0.81	...	0.82	Enseignement primaire
Secondary education	...	0.47	0.49	...	...	*0.57	...	*0.62	Enseignement secondaire
Tertiary education	...	0.37	0.37	0.39	0.42	...	...	...	Enseignement supérieur
Zambia									**Zambie**
Primary education	...	0.96	0.96	0.98	0.97	0.98	0.99	1.01	Enseignement primaire
Zimbabwe									**Zimbabwe**
Primary education	0.97	...	...	...	...	...	...	...	Enseignement primaire
Secondary education	0.79	...	...	...	...	...	...	...	Enseignement secondaire
Tertiary education	...	...	...	...	...	...	...	0.80	Enseignement supérieur

Source:
United Nations Educational, Scientific and Cultural Organization (UNESCO) Institute for Statistics, Montreal, the UNESCO Institute for Statistics (UIS) database, last accessed July 2012.

Source:
L'Institut de statistique de l'Organisation des Nations Unies pour l'éducation, la science et la culture (UNESCO), Montréal, la base de données de l'institut de statistique de l'UNESCO (ISU), dernier accès juillet 2012.

12

Education at the primary, secondary and tertiary levels
Number of students enrolled and percentage female

Enseignement primaire, secondaire et supérieur
Nombre d'élèves inscrits et pourcentage de sexe féminin

Country or area Pays ou zone	Year [t] Année [t]	Primary education Enseignement primaire		Secondary education Enseignement secondaire		Tertiary education Enseignement supérieur	
		Total	% F	Total	% F	Total	% F
Afghanistan	2005	4 318 819	35.7	651 453	23.4	...	...
Afghanistan	2006	4 669 110	37.2	1 006 841	25.4	...	...
	2007	4 718 077	36.9	1 035 782	26.1	...	...
	2008	4 974 836	37.8	1 425 009	28.6	...	...
	2009	4 945 632	38.6	1 716 190	31.3	95 185	18.0
	2010	5 279 326	39.3	2 044 157	32.0	...	...
Albania	2008	255 425	48.0	406 553	48.0	...	...
Albanie	2009	236 102	47.6	354 587	48.6	...	...
	2010	224 781	47.6	355 871	47.8	...	...
Algeria	2005	4 361 744	47.0	3 755 821 [1]	50.7 [1]	792 121	55.2
Algérie	2006	4 196 580	47.0	...	...	817 968	54.8
	2007	4 086 925	47.2	...	...	901 562	57.4
	2008	3 942 242	47.3	...	...	...	...
	2009	3 252 664	47.3	4 585 189	49.4	1 149 666	58.1
	2010	3 312 440	47.3	...	...	1 144 271	58.3
Andorra	2005	4 085	46.9	3 737	50.3	342	50.9
Andorre	2006	4 332	47.4	3 843	49.9	401	53.1
	2007	4 427	47.2	3 819	49.4	...	...
	2008	4 492	47.2	3 851	49.2	459	57.5
	2009	4 474	47.6	3 914	48.9	...	...
	2010	4 367	48.2	4 059	48.3	...	...
Angola	2005	...	...	...	...	48 184	...
Angola	2006	...	...	458 111 [1]	...	48 694	...
	2007 [1]	3 558 605	48.4	581 540	...	...	...
	2008	3 930 051	46.1	646 180	43.7	...	...
	2009	4 046 266	45.8	711 232	43.5	...	...
	2010	4 273 006	44.7	850 334	40.8	66 251	45.4
Anguilla	2005	1 449	50.8	1 024	50.5	33	75.8
Anguilla	2006	1 512	48.9	998	51.6	47	83.0
	2007	1 558	48.6	1 001	51.6	54	83.3
	2008	1 610	49.3	1 008	49.9	54	83.3
	2009	1 590	48.6	1 027	49.9	...	...
	2010	1 620	48.6	1 045	50.3	...	...
Antigua and Barbuda	2007	11 569	48.9	7 838	51.1	...	...
Antigua-et-Barbuda	2008	11 562	48.3	8 628	50.2	...	...
	2009	11 276	48.3	8 557	51.2	1 037	70.6
	2010	11 254	47.3	8 436	51.2	1 170	73.6
Argentina	2005	4 651 255	48.8	3 476 306	51.9	2 082 577	58.7
Argentine	2006	4 685 696	48.8	3 481 085	52.1	2 202 032	59.7
	2007	4 700 176	48.8	3 483 089	52.3	2 208 291	59.7
	2008	4 716 102	48.9	3 530 995	52.4	2 287 874	59.7
	2009	4 702 112	48.8	3 636 717	52.1	2 387 049	59.5
Armenia	2005	125 149	48.2	364 234	49.6	86 629	55.5
Arménie	2006	121 502	47.8	355 790	49.6	99 293	54.5
	2007	127 546	47.2	336 877	49.7	107 398	54.7
	2008	121 841	46.7	309 439	49.2	149 211	57.0
	2009	114 528	46.8	304 116	48.4	154 639	56.1
	2010	117 140	46.6	281 424	48.2	155 145	55.9
Aruba	2005	10 250	48.3	7 116	50.7	2 106	59.8
Aruba	2006	10 390	48.8	7 439	50.4	2 094	60.3
	2007	10 346	48.6	7 853	50.9	2 232	58.4
	2008	10 012	48.5	7 270	51.3	2 242	58.0
	2009	9 944	48.6	7 439	50.4	2 196	58.3
	2010	9 858	48.9	7 342	50.2	2 330	57.2

Country or area Pays ou zone	Year[t] Année[t]	Primary education Enseignement primaire		Secondary education Enseignement secondaire		Tertiary education Enseignement supérieur	
		Total	% F	Total	% F	Total	% F
Australia	2005	1 934 941	48.6	2 496 917	47.6	1 024 589	54.5
Australie	2006	1 938 861	48.6	2 536 684	47.4	1 040 153	54.9
	2007	1 973 456	48.6	2 511 214	47.6	1 083 715	55.1
	2008	1 977 837	48.6	2 538 385	47.5	1 117 804	55.3
	2009	1 991 715	48.6	2 255 457	47.6	1 199 845	55.8
Austria	2005	362 822	48.7	781 292	47.5	244 410	53.7
Autriche	2006	355 293	48.5	782 981	47.7	253 139	53.8
	2007	347 249	48.4	777 792	47.8	260 975	53.7
	2008	337 448	48.3	770 792	47.7	284 791	53.3
	2009	331 565	48.5	762 981	47.6	308 150	53.2
Azerbaijan	2005	568 097	47.7	1 069 980	47.9	128 634	46.7
Azerbaïdjan	2006	538 339	47.1	1 051 591	47.6	131 507	47.5
	2007	512 976	47.2	...	...	135 164	45.7
	2008	496 697	46.9	1 151 357	47.8	141 896	44.3
	2009	490 242	46.5	1 114 356	48.7	180 276	49.6
	2010	481 551	46.4	1 062 674	47.4	180 727	49.4
Bahamas	2005	37 050	49.1	32 089	49.7	...	...
Bahamas	2006	35 921	49.1	32 709	49.8	...	...
	2007	37 122	49.1	34 217	50.4	...	...
	2008	36 833	49.1	34 399	50.1	...	...
	2009	34 865	49.8	34 274	50.1	...	...
	2010	33 977	49.6	34 406	50.8	...	...
Bahrain	2005	83 299	48.7	71 645	50.0	...	...
Bahreïn	2006	89 721	48.8	73 767	49.7	...	...
	2008	86 084	48.8	77 928	49.5	...	...
	2009	88 281	48.8	79 162	49.6	...	...
	2010	90 993	48.8	79 919	49.6	35 848	45.9
Bangladesh	2005	16 219 478	50.1	10 109 395	50.6	911 600	33.5
Bangladesh	2006	16 396 870	50.4	10 250 862	50.4	1 053 566	34.8
	2007	16 312 907	50.7	10 444 714	50.3	1 145 401	34.9
	2008	16 001 605[2]	50.5[2]	10 036 889	52.0	1 294 535	35.1
	2009	16 539 389[2]	50.2[2]	10 907 065	50.9	1 582 175	37.0
	2010	16 987 106[2]	50.5[2]	11 394 831	51.6	...	...
Barbados	2005	22 249	49.2	21 418	49.4	...	...
Barbade	2006	22 461	48.7	20 855	50.2	...	...
	2007	22 584	49.3	20 651	50.0	11 405	68.0
	2008[2]	22 849	49.0	20 337	50.3	...	...
	2009	22 727[2]	49.0[2]	19 928[2]	50.0[2]	14 324	68.7
	2010	22 659[2]	49.2[2]	19 497[2]	49.6[2]	13 232	68.5
Belarus	2005	379 577	47.8	928 488	49.1	528 508	56.8
Bélarus	2006	367 736	48.1	878 943	49.1	544 328	56.8
	2007	361 493	48.2	823 253	49.2	556 526	57.5
	2008	362 304	48.5	...	...	576 679	57.8
	2009	362 110	48.5	...	...	586 434	57.8
	2010	357 796	48.6	...	...	606 033	57.6
Belgium	2005	738 580	48.8	814 539	48.0	389 547	54.4
Belgique	2006	732 808	48.8	821 996	48.1	394 427	54.7
	2007	732 411	48.9	825 293	48.0	393 687	54.9
	2008	733 052	48.9	817 258	48.2	401 652	55.0
	2009	731 603	48.9	810 411	48.2	425 219	54.8
Belize	2005	50 389	48.4	28 885	50.9	4 571	60.8
Belize	2006	51 497	48.6	30 084	50.7	4 931	62.1
	2007	51 898	49.0	30 475	51.0	5 362	61.9
	2008	51 994	48.6	31 120	51.4	5 775	61.7
	2009	52 629	48.7	31 721	51.4	6 972	62.6
	2010	52 650	48.7	32 780	51.7	7 043	61.7

Country or area Pays ou zone	Year[t] Année[t]	Primary education Enseignement primaire		Secondary education Enseignement secondaire		Tertiary education Enseignement supérieur	
		Total	% F	Total	% F	Total	% F
Benin	2005	1 318 140	43.6	435 449[1]	35.4[1]	42 197	...
Bénin	2006	1 356 818	44.4	...	...	42 603	...
	2008	1 601 146	45.5	...	...	...	...
	2009	1 719 390	46.0	...	...	...	...
	2010	1 787 940	46.5	...	...	...	...
Bermuda	2005	4 760	50.4	4 756	52.4	639	65.1
Bermudes	2006	4 678	51.0	4 518	51.5	689	70.0
	2007	...	...	...	...	886	71.1
	2008	...	...	...	...	948	72.2
	2009	...	...	...	...	969	72.1
	2010	4 473	49.1	4 418	53.4	834	67.4
Bhutan	2005	99 458	48.7	42 144	47.1	3 553	34.8
Bhoutan	2006	102 225	48.9	45 035	47.8	3 820	33.7
	2007	...	...	...	...	4 190	33.0
	2008	106 100	49.5	52 098	48.2	5 051	34.7
	2009	108 842	49.7	56 543	49.5	...	...
	2010	110 369	49.9	60 036	49.9	5 499	36.6
Bolivia (Plurinational State of)	2006	1 508 194	49.0	1 043 127	48.1	...	...
Bolivie (État plurinational de)	2007	1 512 002	49.0	1 052 014	48.4	352 554[2]	45.0[2]
	2008	1 508 389	48.9	1 059 641	48.6	...	...
	2009	1 480 516	48.7	1 060 755	48.9	...	...
Bosnia and Herzegovina	2007	198 800	48.8	333 304	49.2	99 414	...
Bosnie-Herzégovine	2008	181 917	48.7	338 971	49.0	104 938	55.9
	2009	173 647	48.9	334 355	48.9	105 488	56.0
	2010	175 271	48.9	322 766	49.0	105 137	55.9
Botswana	2005	329 191	49.3	171 265	50.9	15 710	52.8
Botswana	2006	330 417	49.1	174 843	51.1	16 239	53.2
	2007	327 617	48.9	177 615	51.0	...	...
Brazil	2005	18 661 105	47.6	24 863 112	51.6	4 572 297	55.9
Brésil	2007	17 996 083	47.2	23 423 870	51.7	5 272 877	55.7
	2008	17 812 436	47.2	23 645 669	51.7	5 958 135	55.8
	2009	17 451 886	47.2	23 616 942	51.6	6 115 138	57.0
British Virgin Islands	2005	2 898	48.2	1 882	54.2	1 200[1]	68.8[1]
Iles Vierges britanniques	2006	2 923	48.3	1 959	53.0	...	...
	2007	3 044	48.8	1 921	53.8	...	...
	2009	3 128	49.0	1 942	51.6	1 211	64.7
	2010	3 201	48.6	2 029	50.5	...	...
Brunei Darussalam	2005	46 012	47.9	43 900	48.8	5 023	66.5
Brunéi Darussalam	2006	46 086	47.7	45 887	48.9	5 094	66.1
	2007	45 972	47.7	46 173	48.8	5 284	64.5
	2008	45 125	47.9	46 826	48.6	5 607	65.6
	2009	44 681	48.1	48 119	48.5	6 107	62.6
	2010	44 215	48.3	48 724	48.6	5 776	63.3
Bulgaria	2005	290 017	48.4	685 640	47.7	237 909	52.1
Bulgarie	2006	273 045	48.3	662 510	47.7	243 464	53.5
	2007	267 584	48.3	633 343	47.7	258 692	53.7
	2008	262 701	48.5	593 321	47.9	264 463	55.3
	2009	261 007	48.6	554 835	47.8	274 247	55.6
Burkina Faso	2005	1 270 837	43.7	295 412	40.7	27 942	30.7
Burkina Faso	2006	1 390 571	44.2	319 749	41.3	30 472	31.0
	2007	1 561 258	44.8	352 376	41.6	33 459	30.9
	2008	1 742 439	45.6	423 543	41.8	41 779	32.7
	2009	1 906 279	46.1	467 658	41.9	47 587	32.1
	2010	2 047 630	46.8	537 988	42.5	51 166	31.9
Burundi	2005	1 036 859	46.2	171 110[1]	42.5[1]	16 915	27.7[1]
Burundi	2006	1 324 937	47.7	192 296[1]	42.6[1]	17 953	30.5[1]
	2007	1 490 844	48.2	209 945	41.9	19 296	...
	2008	1 603 116	48.7	243 202[1]	41.4[1]	21 856	...
	2009	1 739 450	49.2	288 956	42.0	24 290	...
	2010	1 849 861	49.7	337 577	41.9	29 269	35.4

Country or area Pays ou zone	Year[t] Année[t]	Primary education Enseignement primaire		Secondary education Enseignement secondaire		Tertiary education Enseignement supérieur	
		Total	% F	Total	% F	Total	% F
Cambodia	2005	2 695 372	47.2	722 478[1]	41.9[1]	56 810	31.5
Cambodge	2006	2 582 250	47.3	811 797	43.3	75 989	32.8
	2007	2 479 644	47.2	875 120	44.2	92 340	35.2
	2008	2 340 606	47.4	929 121[1]	44.9[1]	122 633	34.4
	2009	2 289 759	47.4	940 244[1]	...	...	...
	2010	2 272 527	47.8	949 195[1]	46.3[1]	...	...
Cameroon	2005	2 977 781	45.2	784 203	43.8	99 864[2]	39.5[2]
Cameroun	2006	2 998 135	45.2	698 444	43.9	120 298	41.8
	2007	3 120 357	45.9	...	...	132 134	43.9
	2008	3 201 477	45.9	1 127 691	44.1	147 631	44.1
	2009	3 350 662	46.1	1 268 655	45.2	174 144	43.9
	2010	3 510 396	46.0	1 283 075[1]	45.2[1]	220 331	44.7
Canada	2005	2 320 738	48.6	2 601 926	48.1	...	...
Canada	2006	2 305 211	48.6	2 632 432	48.2	...	...
	2007	2 260 819	48.7	2 657 320	48.2	...	...
	2008	2 200 335	48.7	2 668 134	48.2	...	...
Cape Verde	2005	82 952	48.5	50 758	52.0	3 910	51.0
Cap-Vert	2006	81 434	48.6	61 465	53.5	4 567	52.1
	2007	78 801	48.3	60 783	54.2	5 289	54.6
	2008	76 299	48.2	61 906	52.4	6 658	55.5
	2009	73 548	47.9	60 769	54.1	8 465	56.3
	2010	71 134	47.9	61 677	54.3	10 144	55.2
Cayman Islands	2005	3 240	48.4	2 824	47.8	...	...
Iles Caïmanes	2006	3 461	48.0	2 899	49.0	567	71.6
	2007	3 706	48.2	3 010	49.5	626	70.0
	2008	3 736	47.9	3 198	51.9	912	68.9
Central African Rep.	2005	412 381	41.1	...	...	6 270[1]	...
Rép. centrafricaine	2006	418 825	41.0	...	...	4 462	22.5
	2007	494 985	41.4	...	...	...	...
	2008	584 078	41.7	83 831	36.7	9 473	26.4
	2009	608 075	41.8	93 341	36.2	10 427	30.5
	2010	636 871	41.9	86 462	37.2	11 158	24.5
Chad	2005	1 262 393	40.1	245 286[1]	25.5[1]	12 373	6.0
Tchad	2006	1 296 486	40.2	262 714	26.2	...	...
	2007	1 324 298	40.9	314 470	30.8	...	...
	2008	1 529 711	41.1	369 812	29.0	18 990	12.7
	2009	1 671 205	41.2	421 686	29.0	20 394	14.7
	2010	1 679 661	42.1	448 754	29.1	22 130[1]	14.7[1]
Chile	2005	1 720 951	48.0	1 630 099	49.5	663 694	48.1
Chili	2006	1 694 765	48.0	1 633 868	49.6	661 142	49.2
	2007	1 679 017	47.8	1 611 631	49.8	753 398	49.4
	2008	1 656 810	47.8	1 588 836	49.8	804 981	49.9
	2009	1 611 682	47.9	1 528 200	49.8	876 243	50.7
China[3]	2005	...	...	...	...	20 601 219	46.0
Chine[3]	2006	109 000 000	46.8	101 000 000	47.7	23 360 535	47.1
	2007	107 000 000	46.6	102 000 000	47.7	25 346 279	47.9
	2008	106 000 000	46.5	101 000 000	47.8	26 691 696	48.8
	2009	104 000 000	46.4	100 000 000	48.0	29 295 841	49.2
	2010	101 000 000	46.2	99 218 082	47.1	31 046 735	49.7
China, Hong Kong SAR	2005	451 171	48.0	498 354	48.9	152 294	51.0
Chine, Hong Kong RAS	2006	429 892	48.0	500 708	48.8	155 324	50.5
	2007	414 501	47.9	510 284	48.8	194 236	50.5
	2008	389 937	47.8	513 787	48.7	252 615	50.6
	2009	369 047	47.9	511 872	48.7	254 273	50.0
	2010	348 549	47.9	508 269	48.5	264 761	50.5

Education at the primary, secondary and tertiary levels *(continued)*
Number of students enrolled and percentage female
Enseignement primaire, secondaire et supérieur *(suite)*
Nombre d'élèves inscrits et pourcentage de sexe féminin

Country or area Pays ou zone	Year[t] Année[t]	Primary education Enseignement primaire		Secondary education Enseignement secondaire		Tertiary education Enseignement supérieur	
		Total	% F	Total	% F	Total	% F
China, Macao SAR	2005	37 401	46.8	46 539	49.4	23 420	42.8
Chine, Macao RAS	2006	17 496	47.2	46 393	49.3	23 291	45.9
	2007	32 932	46.9	45 410	49.2	23 868	48.8
	2008	30 487	47.1	41 271	49.2	25 407	49.8
	2009	27 483	47.3	39 328	49.3	28 805	50.1
	2010	25 326	47.6	38 222	48.7	29 476	51.1
Colombia	2005	5 298 257	48.5	4 297 228	51.6	1 223 594	51.3
Colombie	2006	5 296 190	48.6	4 509 406	51.7	1 314 972	51.5
	2007	5 292 476	48.8	4 684 033	51.7	1 372 674	51.5
	2008	5 285 523	48.8	4 772 189	51.4	1 487 186	49.1
	2009	5 299 258	48.9	4 992 062	51.5	1 570 447	50.5
	2010	5 084 972	48.5	5 079 732	51.4	1 674 420	51.6
Comoros	2005[1]	106 700	46.2	43 349	42.5	...	...
Comores	2007	104 518	46.5	...	...	2 598[2]	...
	2008	111 115	47.1	...	...	...	...
	2009	...	...	...	...	4 594	41.0
	2010	...	...	...	...	5 091	42.0
Congo	2005	597 304	47.9	...	...	...	...
Congo	2006	617 010	47.2	...	...	...	...
	2007	621 702	48.0	...	...	...	...
	2008	628 081	48.0	...	...	...	...
	2009	671 683	48.0	...	...	23 397	17.3
	2010	705 093	48.3	...	...	20 383	...
Cook Islands	2005	2 201	48.1	1 899	49.2	...	...
Iles Cook	2007	2 031	46.9	1 951	50.1	...	...
	2008	2 016	...	1 999	...	...	...
	2009	1 939	49.1	1 928	50.6	...	...
	2010	1 841	48.4	1 893	49.8	...	...
Costa Rica	2005	542 087	48.3	347 244	50.0	110 717[1]	54.3[1]
Costa Rica	2006	546 542	48.3	374 428	50.1	...	...
	2007	536 436	48.4	377 924	49.8	...	...
	2008	534 816	48.4	380 813	50.0	...	...
	2009	531 665	48.4	405 584	50.1	...	...
	2010	520 609	48.4	413 686	50.0	...	...
Côte d'Ivoire	2006	2 111 975	44.1	...	...	149 261[1]	32.7[1]
Côte d'Ivoire	2007	2 179 801	44.1	...	...	156 772	33.3
	2008	2 356 240	44.1	...	...	...	...
	2009	2 383 359	44.7	...	...	...	...
Croatia	2005	196 253	48.7	400 123	49.7	134 658	53.8
Croatie	2006	194 748	48.6	395 836	49.7	136 646	54.1
	2007	190 693	48.7	392 952	49.7	139 996	54.1
	2008	182 296	48.7	391 637	49.7	143 410	54.6
	2009	174 192	48.6	391 437	49.8	139 069	55.0
Cuba	2005	895 045	47.8	937 493	49.1	471 858	62.1[2]
Cuba	2006	889 834	47.9	928 342	49.1	681 629	60.8
	2007	883 132	47.9	898 833	48.7	864 846	63.6
	2008	871 444	48.0	865 602	48.6	987 250	61.4
	2009	868 477	48.1	826 088	48.5	970 895	61.3
	2010	852 744	48.1	808 904	48.4	800 873	61.0
Cyprus	2005	61 247	48.7	64 293	49.2	20 078	52.0
Chypre	2006	59 710	48.8	64 714	49.2	20 587	50.9
	2007	57 785	48.6	64 853	49.3	22 227	50.1
	2008	56 799	48.8	64 966	49.2	25 688	49.0
	2009	55 837	48.6	64 557	49.1	30 986	46.8
Czech Republic	2005	502 831	48.3	975 284	49.2	336 307	52.6
République tchèque	2006	473 269	48.4	966 280	49.1	338 009	53.8
	2007	462 820	48.5	937 026	49.1	363 277	54.7
	2008	459 899	48.4	903 691	49.0	392 540	55.5
	2009	460 486	48.5	868 328	49.0	416 847	56.5

12

Education at the primary, secondary and tertiary levels *(continued)*
Number of students enrolled and percentage female
Enseignement primaire, secondaire et supérieur *(suite)*
Nombre d'élèves inscrits et pourcentage de sexe féminin

Country or area Pays ou zone	Year[t] Année[t]	Primary education Enseignement primaire		Secondary education Enseignement secondaire		Tertiary education Enseignement supérieur	
		Total	% F	Total	% F	Total	% F
Dem. Rep. of the Congo	2007	8 839 888	44.8	2 815 175	34.6	237 836	25.9[2]
Rép. dém. du Congo	2008	9 973 365	45.5	3 129 488[2]	35.5[2]	308 739	26.1
	2009	10 244 086	45.9	3 398 550	35.8	377 867	23.6
	2010	10 572 422	46.3	3 484 459	36.4	...	...
Denmark	2005	414 103	48.7	464 952	49.5	232 255	57.4
Danemark	2006	415 793	48.7	463 617	49.4	228 893	57.4
	2007	415 793	48.7	475 140	49.4	232 194	57.6
	2008	410 400	48.9	484 199	49.4	230 707	58.0
	2009	406 622	48.8	493 144	49.2	234 574	58.2
Djibouti	2005	50 651	44.6	30 142	39.5	1 696	41.7
Djibouti	2006	53 745	44.4	30 265	39.8	1 928	40.0
	2007	56 667	45.8	34 972	40.8	2 192	40.4
	2008	56 395	46.5	41 159	40.7	...	...
	2009	55 546	46.7	42 690	42.0	3 159	40.6
Dominica	2005	9 441	48.7	7 476	50.0	...	...
Dominique	2006	8 912	48.7	7 475	49.7	...	...
	2007	8 643	48.5	7 481	50.0	...	...
	2008	8 369	48.7	7 309	49.0	229	76.0
	2009	8 231	48.8	7 214	50.9	...	...
	2010	8 138	48.9	6 766	50.6	...	...
Dominican Republic	2005	1 289 745	47.9	808 352	53.9	...	...
Rép. dominicaine	2006	1 234 450	47.9	794 000	54.1	...	...
	2007	1 355 085	47.5	920 494	54.1	...	...
	2008	1 305 661	47.4	909 331	53.7	...	...
	2009	1 333 468	45.5	934 126	52.5	...	...
	2010	1 317 802	46.0	904 527	52.4	...	...
Ecuador	2005	1 997 624	49.0	1 053 175	49.4	...	...
Equateur	2006	2 006 430	48.9	1 103 258	49.5	...	...
	2007	2 039 168	49.0	1 141 866	49.5	...	...
	2008	...	...	...	...	534 522	52.9
	2009	2 008 015	49.4	1 344 263	50.3	...	...
Egypt	2005	9 563 627	47.3	...	...	2 397 387	...
Egypte	2006	9 794 591	47.4	...	...	2 440 748	...
	2007	9 988 181	47.6	...	...	2 501 349	...
	2008	...	...	...	...	2 488 434	...
	2009	10 407 187	47.8	...	...	...	...
El Salvador	2005	1 045 484	48.2	524 202	50.0	122 431	54.7
El Salvador	2006	1 035 100	48.2	529 057	50.3	124 956	54.7
	2007	1 075 041	49.1	536 017	50.3	132 246	54.8
	2008	993 795	48.2	539 277	50.1	138 615	54.6
	2009	963 524	48.1	555 645	49.8	143 849	54.4
	2010	939 726	47.8	577 111	49.6	150 012	54.2
Equatorial Guinea	2005	75 809	48.7	...	...	...	...
Guinée équatoriale	2008	81 099	48.6	...	...	...	...
	2009	82 417	48.8	...	...	...	...
	2010	85 061	49.1	...	...	...	...
Eritrea	2005	377 512	44.4	216 944	37.2	...	...
Erythrée	2006	364 263	44.4	227 786	37.6	...	...
	2007	331 855	45.1	218 369	41.4	...	...
	2008	314 034	44.8	229 079[1]	41.5[1]	...	...
	2009	300 129	45.0	240 892	41.5	9 949	24.5
	2010	286 021	45.2	248 082	43.1	10 198	25.0
Estonia	2005	85 539	47.9	124 493	49.1	67 760	61.5
Estonie	2006	79 589	48.0	120 246	49.3	68 286	61.6
	2007	76 026	48.3	114 108	49.3	68 767	61.1
	2008	74 629	48.2	106 059	49.4	68 168	61.7
	2009	73 563	48.2	99 562	49.1	68 399	61.9

Education at the primary, secondary and tertiary levels *(continued)*
Number of students enrolled and percentage female

Enseignement primaire, secondaire et supérieur *(suite)*
Nombre d'élèves inscrits et pourcentage de sexe féminin

Country or area Pays ou zone	Year [t] Année [t]	Primary education Enseignement primaire		Secondary education Enseignement secondaire		Tertiary education Enseignement supérieur	
		Total	% F	Total	% F	Total	% F
Ethiopia	2005	10 019 729	45.1	2 488 465	37.3	191 212	24.4
Ethiopie	2006	10 971 581	46.1	2 992 589	38.5	180 286	24.2
	2007	12 174 719	46.5	3 430 129	40.0	255 454	25.7
	2008	13 379 059	46.9	3 696 385	41.9	264 822	23.8
	2009	13 570 558	47.5	3 882 551	43.4	320 827	28.5
	2010	13 635 289	47.5	4 206 700	44.9	434 659	26.5
Fiji	2005[1]	...	...	...	...	12 717	53.1
Fidji	2006	109 702	48.0	100 243	50.7	...	...
	2007	103 641	47.8	99 098	51.1	...	...
	2008	102 543	48.1	98 561	50.2	...	...
	2009	100 967	47.9	97 937	50.8	...	...
Finland	2005	381 785	48.9	430 596	50.0	305 996	53.6
Finlande	2006	372 128	48.9	432 565	50.0	308 966	53.9
	2007	364 902	48.9	432 607	50.1	309 163	54.0
	2008	357 403	48.8	431 233	50.2	309 648	54.2
	2009	351 095	48.8	428 332	50.2	296 691	54.0
France	2005	4 015 490	48.5	6 036 192	49.0	2 187 383	55.2
France	2006	4 051 861	48.5	5 993 897	48.9	2 201 201	55.3
	2007	4 105 628	48.5	5 940 366	48.9	2 179 505	55.3
	2008	4 139 284	48.5	5 899 298	48.9	2 164 538	55.2
	2009	4 152 622	48.5	5 861 961	48.9	2 172 855	55.2
Gambia	2005	205 347	50.4	...	...	...	...
Gambie	2006	207 474	50.8	...	...	...	...
	2007	218 638	50.8	...	...	...	...
	2008	220 931	51.2	116 924[1]	48.3[1]	6 489	...
	2009	235 826	50.7	123 022	49.0[1]	...	...
	2010	229 013	50.3	124 397[1]	48.8[1]	...	...
Georgia	2005	338 222	48.3	316 430	48.8	174 255	50.4
Géorgie	2006	326 597	48.8	314 427	49.8[1]	144 991	52.4
	2007	322 249	47.2	321 171	...	141 303	52.0
	2008	311 265	47.0	305 388	48.7	129 926	54.1[1]
	2009	298 935	46.9	341 649	...	95 225	54.9
	2010	289 137	47.1	...	...	105 696	55.3
Germany	2005	3 306 136	48.7	8 289 699	48.2	...	...
Allemagne	2006	3 329 349	48.7	8 285 301	48.0	...	...
	2007	3 311 285	48.7	7 981 848	48.2	...	...
	2008	3 236 158	48.6	7 907 105	48.1	...	...
	2009	3 150 822	48.6	7 740 935	47.5	...	...
Ghana	2005	2 929 536	47.9	1 370 261[1]	44.5[1]	119 559	34.9
Ghana	2006	3 130 575	48.5	1 454 097	44.9	110 184	33.7
	2007	3 367 157	48.5	1 617 803	45.7	140 017	34.2
	2008	3 625 178	48.6	1 723 734	45.9	...	...
	2009	3 659 116	48.6	1 836 311	46.1	203 376	37.3
Gibraltar	2008	3 211	48.7	1 674	47.4	...	...
Gibraltar	2009	3 255	48.8	1 657	47.1	...	...
Greece	2005	650 242	48.5	715 537	47.7	646 587	51.1
Grèce	2006	645 324	48.6	704 515	47.7	653 003	50.9
	2007	639 083	48.6	682 012	47.1	602 858	50.4
Grenada	2005	16 072[1]	48.7[1]	13 675[2]	50.1[2]	...	...
Grenade	2007	13 733	48.7	13 060	49.0	...	...
	2008	13 873	47.7	12 469	47.3	...	...
	2009	14 186	47.5	11 031	49.7	6 689	57.1
	2010	13 663	48.0	11 500	50.3	...	...
Guatemala	2005	2 345 301	47.6	754 496	47.6	...	...
Guatemala	2006	2 405 041	47.7	809 131	47.8	...	...
	2007	2 448 976	47.9	864 154	48.0	233 885	50.8
	2008	2 500 575	48.0	902 796	48.3	...	...
	2010	2 659 776	48.3	982 650	48.1	...	...

12

Education at the primary, secondary and tertiary levels *(continued)*
Number of students enrolled and percentage female
Enseignement primaire, secondaire et supérieur *(suite)*
Nombre d'élèves inscrits et pourcentage de sexe féminin

Country or area Pays ou zone	Year[t] Année[t]	Primary education Enseignement primaire		Secondary education Enseignement secondaire		Tertiary education Enseignement supérieur	
		Total	% F	Total	% F	Total	% F
Guinea	2005	1 206 743	44.1	420 057[1]	32.9[1]	23 788	18.6
Guinée	2006	1 258 038	44.8	482 825	34.0	42 711	21.4
	2007	1 317 791	45.2	530 590[1]	35.3[1]	68 261	24.4[1]
	2008	1 364 491	45.2	530 705	36.2	80 222	24.4
	2009	1 389 685	45.3	560 494[1]	36.3[1]	...	...
	2010	1 453 355	44.8	...	...	...	...
Guinea-Bissau	2005	252 488	...	50 507	...	3 122	...
Guinée-Bissau	2006	269 287	...	55 176	...	3 689	...
	2010	278 890	48.3	...	...	...	...
Guyana	2005	116 756	49.0	70 615	50.0	7 278	67.6
Guyana	2006	110 503	49.0	...	...	7 370	68.7
	2007	109 243	48.7	72 970	48.8	7 532	68.1
	2008	107 456	48.8	74 673	50.3	7 306	58.7
	2009	100 760	48.7	78 397	49.9	7 124	49.0
	2010	99 241	48.8	80 676	50.6	7 939	70.8
Honduras	2005	1 231 533	49.1	...	...	...	...
Honduras	2006	1 293 333	49.0	...	...	...	...
	2007	1 308 119	49.1	554 297	55.0	...	...
	2008	1 276 495	49.0	566 938	55.3	147 740[2]	60.0[2]
	2010	1 274 904	49.0	655 294	54.3	...	...
Hungary	2005	430 561	48.3	960 215	48.7	436 012	58.4
Hongrie	2006	415 858	48.3	948 856	48.7	438 702	58.5
	2007	399 250	48.2	937 323	48.7	431 572	58.3
	2008	394 246	48.3	924 414	48.5	413 715	58.0
	2009	389 510	48.4	913 392	48.5	397 679	56.8
Iceland	2005	30 785	48.3	33 323	49.3	15 169	64.9
Islande	2006	30 421	48.6	33 900	49.5	15 721	64.3
	2007	30 084	49.0	34 434	50.2	15 821	64.1
	2008	29 945	49.1	35 075	49.7	16 631	64.4
	2009	29 860	49.1	35 075	49.6	16 919	64.3
India	2005	139 000 000	46.7	89 461 794	43.0[1]	11 777 296	39.4
Inde	2006	139 000 000	46.6	91 529 430	43.3[1]	12 852 684	39.9
	2007	140 000 000	47.0	96 049 060	44.0	14 862 962	39.1
	2008	145 000 000	...	102 000 000	44.6	17 211 215	...
	2009	...	...	...	...	18 648 923	38.6
Indonesia	2005	29 149 746	48.3[1]	15 993 187	49.0[1]	3 660 270[1]	43.7[1]
Indonésie	2006	28 982 708	48.2	16 797 809	49.3	3 657 429	47.3
	2007	29 796 705	48.1	18 716 929	49.4	3 806 629	49.3
	2008	29 498 266	48.4	18 314 900	49.0	4 419 577	47.4
	2009	29 901 051	48.3	19 520 704	49.0	4 859 409	48.5
	2010	30 341 821	49.5	19 975 916	49.3	5 001 048	46.7
Iran (Islamic Rep. of)	2005	6 206 718	48.2	9 066 410	48.1	2 126 274	51.0
Iran (Rép. islamique d')	2006	6 006 553	48.2	8 805 028	48.2	2 398 811	51.6
	2007	5 827 851	48.4	8 323 213	49.1	2 828 528	52.4
	2008	5 725 620	...	8 187 132	48.2	3 391 852	52.9
	2009	5 654 969	48.5	7 929 346	47.3	3 349 741	51.0
	2010	...	...	...	...	3 790 859	49.5
Iraq	2005[1]	...	...	...	...	424 908	36.2
Iraq	2007	4 864 350	44.4	2 037 509	41.4	...	...
Ireland	2005	454 060	48.5	317 337	51.0	186 561	54.9
Irlande	2006	461 588	48.5	313 479	50.6	186 044	55.1
	2007	475 836	48.5	316 015	50.6	190 349	55.2
	2008	486 921	48.7	318 382	50.4	178 518	54.2
	2009	498 838	48.8	326 543	50.2	182 609	53.9
Israel	2005	784 663	48.9	610 341	48.7	310 937	56.0
Israël	2006	802 555	49.0	613 366	48.6	310 014	55.1
	2007	826 314	48.9	615 973	48.8	327 108	55.8
	2008	841 394	48.9	614 711	49.1	325 246	55.6
	2009	861 013	48.9	618 959	49.1	342 707	55.7

Education at the primary, secondary and tertiary levels *(continued)*
Number of students enrolled and percentage female

Enseignement primaire, secondaire et supérieur *(suite)*
Nombre d'élèves inscrits et pourcentage de sexe féminin

Country or area Pays ou zone	Year[t] Année[t]	Primary education Enseignement primaire		Secondary education Enseignement secondaire		Tertiary education Enseignement supérieur	
		Total	% F	Total	% F	Total	% F
Italy	2005	2 771 247	48.3	4 507 408	48.4	2 014 998	56.6
Italie	2006	2 790 254	48.3	4 531 571	48.4	2 029 023	56.9
	2007	2 820 150	48.3	4 553 163	48.3	2 033 642	57.2
	2008	2 830 056	48.3	4 575 124	48.3	2 013 856	57.4
	2009	2 819 193	48.3	4 575 921	48.4	2 011 713	57.7
Jamaica	2005	326 411	48.8	246 332	50.1	...	...
Jamaïque	2007	310 021	49.0	257 186	50.4	...	...
	2008	315 129	48.9	262 608	50.4	61 139	68.6
	2009	312 262	48.7	266 933	49.6	61 509	68.8
	2010	299 344	48.7	265 175	50.1	71 352	68.7
Japan	2005	7 231 854	48.8	7 710 439	48.8	4 038 302	45.9
Japon	2006	7 229 135	48.8	7 561 241	48.8	4 084 861	45.7
	2007	7 220 111	48.8	7 427 059	48.8	4 032 625	45.6
	2008	7 166 285	48.8	7 355 678	48.8	3 938 632	45.7
	2009	7 156 039	48.8	7 299 966	48.9	3 874 224	45.8
Jordan	2005	804 904	48.9	625 682	49.2	217 823	50.3
Jordanie	2006	805 457	49.3	649 242	49.5	220 103	51.6
	2007	807 702	49.3	670 836	49.5	231 657	51.3
	2008	817 160	49.0	700 342	49.6	254 752	51.3
	2009	...	...	...	...	266 881	51.3
Kazakhstan	2005	1 023 974	48.8	2 039 911	48.5	753 181	58.1
Kazakhstan	2006	972 931	48.8	1 982 190	48.4	780 783	58.0
	2007	947 807	48.8	1 874 213	48.6	772 600	58.2
	2008	956 019	48.8	1 778 106	48.4	719 802	58.2
	2009	950 976	48.8	1 740 549	48.2	635 241	58.3
	2010	957 919	48.9	1 713 837	48.2	610 264	58.3
Kenya	2005	6 075 706	48.7	2 468 483[1]	48.6	113 532[1]	37.3[1]
Kenya	2006	6 101 390	49.0	2 583 755	48.1	...	...
	2007	6 687 510	49.4	2 729 040	46.5	...	...
	2008	6 868 810	49.2	3 106 919	47.6	...	...
	2009	7 150 259	49.2	3 204 379	47.3	167 983	41.2
Kiribati	2005	16 133	49.4	11 522	51.8	...	...
Kiribati	2006	16 087	48.9	11 420	52.8	...	...
	2007	15 764	49.8	11 535	52.7	...	...
	2008	16 123	50.1	11 583	51.2	...	...
	2009	15 566	50.0	...	...	...	...
Kuwait	2005	202 826	48.5	248 895	49.7	...	...
Koweït	2006	203 423	48.8	236 410	49.8	...	...
	2007	211 576	48.7	247 233	48.9	...	...
	2008	208 608	48.8	249 879	49.6	...	...
	2009	210 665	48.9	255 101	49.3	...	...
	2010	213 750	48.8	258 184	50.0	...	...
Kyrgyzstan	2005	434 155	48.7	721 205	49.5	220 460	55.3
Kirghizistan	2006	423 930	48.8	718 585	49.5	233 463	55.6
	2007	407 669	48.8	713 613	49.5	239 380	56.1
	2008	399 833	48.8	696 833[2]	49.4[2]	296 267	57.1
	2009	392 485	48.9	678 785[2]	49.3[2]	294 349	56.4
	2010	390 711	48.8	664 201[2]	49.0[2]	...	...
Lao People's Dem. Rep.	2005	890 821	46.0	393 856	42.5	47 424	41.2
Rép. dém. pop. lao	2006	891 881	46.1	395 382	43.0	56 716	40.0
	2007	891 807	46.4	403 833	43.4	75 003	41.5
	2008	900 817	46.6	412 375	43.9	89 457	43.2
Latvia	2005	84 369	47.9	271 631	49.0	130 706	63.2
Lettonie	2006	78 796	47.9	258 432	49.1	131 125	63.3
	2007	121 345	47.8	195 745	49.6	129 497	63.9
	2008	117 129	47.8	182 805	49.6	127 760	64.4
	2009	114 236	48.1	158 325	49.3	125 360	63.7
	2010	113 691	48.5	147 375	48.5	112 567	62.7

Country or area Pays ou zone	Year [t] Année [t]	Primary education Enseignement primaire		Secondary education Enseignement secondaire		Tertiary education Enseignement supérieur	
		Total	% F	Total	% F	Total	% F
Lebanon	2005	...	...	...	...	165 730	52.8
Liban	2006	470 988	48.5	381 466	51.6	173 123	53.2
	2007	473 134	48.4	384 162	52.0	187 055	54.0
	2008	467 311	48.4	384 726	51.8	196 682	54.7
	2009	464 442	48.5	391 087	51.8	199 656	53.7
	2010	461 719	48.4	383 226	52.0	202 345	53.7
Lesotho	2005	422 278	49.6	94 460	55.8	7 918	56.9
Lesotho	2006	424 855	49.6	93 996	56.0	8 500	55.2
	2007	400 943	49.4	101 738[1]	56.8[1]	...	...
	2008	396 456	49.3	107 208[1]	57.3[1]	...	...
	2009	389 424	49.6	115 805[1]	58.0[1]	...	...
	2010	388 678	49.1	123 307	57.7	...	...
Liberia	2007	538 450	47.2	...	...	...	...
Libéria	2008	539 887	46.9	...	...	...	...
Libyan Arab Jamah.	2005	713 902	48.4	701 536	53.3[1]	...	...
Jamah. arabe libyenne	2006	755 338	47.7	732 614	52.9	...	...
Liechtenstein	2005	2 242	50.0	2 048	50.9	527	28.8
Liechtenstein	2006	2 247	50.7	2 032	51.8	636	30.3
	2007	2 244	50.8	2 014	51.1	673	31.8
	2008	2 158	50.0	2 078	51.4	800	33.0
	2009	2 133	50.5	2 087	50.2	754	31.7
Lithuania	2005	158 105	48.6	423 706	48.8	195 405	60.1
Lituanie	2006	150 422	48.4	410 507	48.9	198 868	59.9
	2007	143 814	48.3	393 889	48.9	199 855	60.0
	2008	135 719	48.1	376 683	48.9	204 767	59.9
	2009	129 496	48.1	358 395	48.8	210 744	59.2
Luxembourg	2005	35 016	48.8	35 946	50.4	...	...
Luxembourg	2006	35 431	48.9	37 009	50.0	2 692	51.6
	2007	35 668	48.7	38 209	49.8	...	...
	2008	35 630	49.0	39 349	49.6	3 011	48.3
Madagascar	2005	3 597 731	48.9	621 173[1]	49.0[1]	44 948	47.0
Madagascar	2006	3 698 906	49.0	726 998	48.7	49 680	46.5
	2007	3 837 343	49.2	833 568	48.8	58 313	47.0
	2008	4 020 322	49.2	945 245	48.6	62 069	47.2
	2009	4 323 981	49.4	1 022 464[1]	48.5	68 460	47.5
	2010	4 241 916	49.4	...	...	74 444	47.8
Malawi	2005	2 868 038	50.2	516 462	44.7	5 810	35.3[1]
Malawi	2006	2 933 557	50.5	565 467	45.5	6 298[1]	33.6[1]
	2007	2 943 248	50.4	574 003	45.2	6 458	33.6
	2008	3 197 928	50.2	636 416	45.6	...	...
	2009	3 250 111	50.3	666 679	46.4	...	...
	2010	3 417 404	50.4	692 157	47.3	10 296	38.0
Malaysia	2005	3 202 008	48.6	2 489 117	51.3	696 760	56.0
Malaisie	2006	3 133 399	48.6	2 516 116	50.9	737 267	54.8
	2007	3 103 579	48.5	2 499 165	50.6	805 136	55.8
	2008	3 053 378	48.5	2 537 203	50.7	922 239	55.8
	2009	3 000 676	48.5	2 546 102	50.6	1 000 694	55.6
Maldives	2005	57 873	47.8	...	...	...	...
Maldives	2006	54 770	47.7	...	...	...	...
	2007	50 270	47.8	...	...	...	...
	2008	47 082	47.8	...	...	...	...
	2009	44 675	48.1	...	...	...	...
Mali	2005	1 505 903	43.4[1]	429 716	37.5	33 222	34.6[1]
Mali	2006	1 609 979	44.0	474 976	37.5	...	...
	2007	1 716 956	44.4	533 849	39.1	66 094[1]	31.1[1]
	2008	1 823 037	44.8	612 012	38.6	67 839	31.1
	2009	1 926 242	45.1	686 071	39.0	76 667	28.9
	2010	2 018 551	45.5	758 285	40.2	81 188	28.7

Education at the primary, secondary and tertiary levels *(continued)*
Number of students enrolled and percentage female
Enseignement primaire, secondaire et supérieur *(suite)*
Nombre d'élèves inscrits et pourcentage de sexe féminin

Country or area Pays ou zone	Year[t] Année[t]	Primary education Enseignement primaire		Secondary education Enseignement secondaire		Tertiary education Enseignement supérieur	
		Total	% F	Total	% F	Total	% F
Malta	2005	29 596	48.0	40 541	47.6	9 441	56.3
Malte	2007	27 782	48.5	36 977	49.0	9 811	57.4
	2008	26 771	48.7	37 247	47.9	9 472	57.9
	2009	24 674	48.9	39 682	45.5	10 352	56.5
Marshall Islands	2005	8 055	54.3	5 260	48.9	...	...
Iles Marshall	2006	8 270	48.4	5 369	49.1	...	...
	2007	8 215	47.9	5 369	49.1	...	...
	2008	8 342	48.4	5 358	50.8	...	...
	2009	8 398	48.1	5 229	50.0	...	...
Mauritania	2005	443 615	50.0	92 796	45.9	8 758	24.5
Mauritanie	2006	465 970	49.8	98 946[2]	45.0[2]	10 157	25.6
	2007	483 776	50.0	102 130[1]	45.6[1]	11 794	...
	2008	473 688	50.3	98 263[1]	45.8[1]	12 004	28.2
	2009	512 998	50.4	107 624[1]	44.6[1]	12 519	28.2
	2010	531 383	50.4	111 468[1]	45.0[1]	14 536	28.2
Mauritius	2005	123 562	49.2	128 759[1]	49.0[1]	20 514[1]	50.3[1]
Maurice	2006	121 387	49.2	134 401[1]	48.9[1]	22 221[1]	49.7[1]
	2007	119 310	49.2	135 929[1]	48.9[1]	22 971[1]	53.5[1]
	2008	119 022	49.0	134 832[1]	49.0[1]	25 578[1]	54.8[1]
	2009	117 922	49.2	134 270[1]	49.3[1]	...	...
	2010	117 432	49.2	132 555[1]	49.2[1]	...	...
Mexico	2005	14 700 005	48.8	10 564 404	51.2	2 384 858	50.3
Mexique	2006	14 595 195	48.7	10 883 455	51.3	2 446 726	50.3
	2007	14 631 498	48.8	11 122 276	51.3	2 528 664	50.3
	2008	14 699 146	48.8	11 444 055	51.4	2 623 367	50.3
	2009	14 861 232	48.8	11 474 843	51.5	2 705 190	50.2
Micronesia (Fed. States of)	2005	18 793	48.1	13 634	49.3	...	...
Micronésie (Etats féd. de)	2007	18 512	49.0	...	...	...	...
Monaco	2008	1 852	47.5	3 015	48.0	...	...
Monaco	2009	1 837	48.9	3 017	48.3	...	...
	2010	1 820	50.7	2 999	49.3	...	...
Mongolia	2005	251 205	49.5	339 249	52.4	123 824	61.4
Mongolie	2006	249 622	49.5	329 264	52.1	138 019	60.7
	2007	239 262	49.4	...	...	142 411	60.5
	2008	239 663	49.2	...	...	151 533	60.9
	2009	252 604	49.2	305 791	51.3	162 217	60.6
	2010	273 966	49.0	...	...	165 769	60.3
Montenegro	2005	37 812	48.3	68 471	49.1	11 011	60.2
Monténégro	2006	38 740	48.1	68 218	49.0	12 903	59.8
	2007	39 123	48.2	67 683	48.7	16 173	57.2
	2008	39 580	48.2	67 015	51.8	19 395	54.5
	2009	37 269	47.8	68 135	48.7	22 738	55.2
	2010	35 264	47.8	69 619	48.6	23 786	54.3
Montserrat	2005	509	46.2	298	49.3	...	...
Montserrat	2006	508	45.9	328	46.3	...	...
	2007	497	49.3	347	46.4	...	...
	2008	...	...	...	...	51	80.4
	2009	485	48.9	358	48.0	56	82.1
	2010	...	...	...	...	61	85.2
Morocco	2005	4 022 600	46.4	1 952 456[1]	45.1[1]	366 879	45.1
Maroc	2006	3 943 831	46.3	2 061 046	...	384 595	45.2
	2007	3 939 177	46.5	2 173 454	45.5[1]	369 142	47.6
	2008	3 878 640	46.7	...	...	401 093	47.3
	2009	3 850 994	47.0	...	...	418 833	46.9
	2010	3 945 201	47.2	...	...	...	...

12

Education at the primary, secondary and tertiary levels *(continued)*
Number of students enrolled and percentage female
Enseignement primaire, secondaire et supérieur *(suite)*
Nombre d'élèves inscrits et pourcentage de sexe féminin

Country or area Pays ou zone	Year [t] Année [t]	Primary education Enseignement primaire		Secondary education Enseignement secondaire		Tertiary education Enseignement supérieur	
		Total	% F	Total	% F	Total	% F
Mozambique	2005	3 942 829	45.7	305 877	40.8	28 298	33.1
Mozambique	2006	4 165 580	46.2	367 962	41.8	...	...
	2007	4 560 905	46.4	443 974	42.2	...	...
	2008	4 899 652	46.7	512 266	42.8	...	...
	2009	5 071 878	47.2	598 424	44.1	...	...
	2010	5 277 868	47.3	671 902	45.0	...	...
Myanmar	2005	4 948 198	49.9	2 589 312	49.1	...	...
Myanmar	2006	4 969 445	49.6	2 696 307	49.3	...	...
	2007	5 013 582	...	2 686 198	49.9	507 660	57.9
	2008	5 109 630	49.6	2 828 868	...	...	...
	2009	5 094 623	49.3	2 812 866	50.3	...	...
	2010	5 125 942	49.5	2 852 447	51.1	...	...
Namibia	2005	404 198	49.8	148 104	53.1	13 566	46.7
Namibie	2006	402 529	49.8	151 805	53.7	13 185	46.7
	2007	409 508	49.6	158 162	53.9	...	...
	2008	407 402	49.5	...	...	19 707	56.8
	2009	406 920	49.4	...	...	...	...
Nauru	2005	1 812	48.2	600	50.7	...	...
Nauru	2006	1 393	47.1	815	51.7	...	...
	2007	1 235	48.6	689	51.4	...	...
	2008	1 254	49.7	816	51.5	...	...
Nepal	2005	4 030 045	46.3	2 054 165	44.7[1]	...	...
Népal	2006	4 502 697	47.4	1 983 561[1]	45.5[1]	...	...
	2007	4 515 059	48.3	1 998 990[1]	46.2[1]	254 792	...
	2008	4 418 713	48.9	2 305 166	46.7	...	...
	2009	4 782 313	49.5	...	...	289 262	39.7
	2010	4 900 665	50.1	...	...	376 869	40.7
Netherlands	2005	1 277 990	48.2	1 410 547	48.4	564 983	51.0
Pays-Bas	2006	1 277 478	48.2	1 423 262	48.4	579 622	51.1
	2007	1 280 571	48.3	1 444 057	48.4	590 121	51.5
	2008	1 285 543	48.3	1 460 503	48.4	602 286	51.7
	2009	1 290 029	48.4	1 462 461	48.4	618 502	51.8
New Zealand	2005	352 845	48.5	526 152	50.2	239 983	58.7
Nouvelle-Zélande	2006	350 810	48.6	522 326	49.8	237 784	59.0
	2007	349 080	48.7	526 974	49.3	242 650	58.7
	2008	348 160	48.8	514 563	49.8	244 355	58.4
	2009	347 674	48.8	542 798	49.4	263 028	57.9
	2010	348 492	48.9	512 195	49.9	266 232	58.1
Nicaragua	2005	945 089	48.4	437 853	52.7	...	...
Nicaragua	2006	966 206	48.4	448 258	52.6	...	...
	2007	952 964	48.5	470 520	52.4	...	...
	2008	944 341	48.4	462 198	52.6	...	...
	2010	923 745	48.5	465 201	51.7	...	...
Niger	2005	1 064 056	40.8	181 641	39.1	10 799	29.6
Niger	2006	1 126 073	41.0	216 961	38.8	11 208	26.6
	2007	1 235 065	41.5	213 991	37.9	10 869	28.5
	2008	1 389 194	42.7	232 498	37.6	12 823	29.6
	2009	1 554 102	43.1	256 555	37.8	15 992	29.0
	2010	1 726 452	43.8	303 348	39.8	17 096	29.8
Nigeria	2005	22 115 432	44.9	6 397 581	44.6	1 391 527	40.7
Nigéria	2006	22 861 884	45.4	6 436 449	44.2	...	...
	2007	21 513 996	46.0	6 068 160	42.8	...	...
	2008	19 979 638	46.1	6 888 700	44.7	...	...
	2009	20 080 986	46.3	7 827 318	45.7	...	...
	2010	20 681 805	46.6	9 056 768	45.8	...	...
Niue							
Nioué	2005	178	50.6	206	48.1	...	...

Education at the primary, secondary and tertiary levels *(continued)*
Number of students enrolled and percentage female

Enseignement primaire, secondaire et supérieur *(suite)*
Nombre d'élèves inscrits et pourcentage de sexe féminin

Country or area Pays ou zone	Year [t] Année [t]	Primary education Enseignement primaire		Secondary education Enseignement secondaire		Tertiary education Enseignement supérieur	
		Total	% F	Total	% F	Total	% F
Norway Norvège	2005	429 652	48.7	403 026	48.9	213 940	59.6
	2006	429 680	48.8	412 311	48.5	214 711	59.7
	2007	430 747	48.7	419 698	48.3	215 237	60.2
	2008	429 585	48.8	423 598	48.1	212 672	60.8
	2009	426 769	48.8	425 141	48.0	219 282	61.1
Occupied Palestinian Terr. Terr. palestinien occupé	2005	387 138	48.8	656 797	50.1	138 139	49.5
	2006	381 904	49.0	685 585	50.3	150 128	52.7
	2007	383 559	49.0	701 715	50.5	169 373	53.7
	2008	390 051	48.8	707 892	50.7	180 905	53.9
	2009	395 205	48.8	713 921	50.6	182 565	55.6
	2010	402 866	48.5	710 936	50.9	196 625	56.3
Oman Oman	2005	...	...	...	...	48 483	50.8
	2006	...	...	...	...	55 956	50.5
	2007	...	...	...	...	61 548	50.7
	2008	...	...	...	...	63 262	...
	2009	302 037	48.3	321 670	48.0	75 715	49.8
	2010	...	...	...	...	78 063	50.0
Pakistan Pakistan	2005	17 257 947	41.8	7 994 299[1]	42.3[1]	782 621	45.1
	2006	16 687 658	42.4	8 421 015	42.3	820 347	44.5
	2007	17 979 190	43.6	9 145 084	41.8	954 698[2]	44.5[2]
	2008	18 175 801	43.8	9 339 991	41.8	973 792[2]	44.5[2]
	2009	18 468 096	44.1	9 432 977	42.8	...	...
	2010	18 756 348	44.0	9 685 181	42.1	...	...
Palau Palaos	2005[1]	...	...	2 282	...	...	...
	2007	1 544	47.8[1]	2 448	...	...	...
Panama Panama	2005	430 152	48.2	256 224	50.8	126 242	61.2
	2006	436 945	48.3	257 378	51.0	130 838	60.9
	2007	446 176	48.3	260 694	50.8	132 660	60.6
	2008	445 107	48.2	266 760	50.9	134 290	59.7
	2009	440 627	48.2	274 809	51.0	135 209	59.6
	2010	439 746	48.1	283 747	50.6	...	...
Papua New Guinea Papouasie-Nvl-Guinée	2005	531 759	44.4	...	...	...	...
	2006	532 250	44.3	...	...	...	...
	2008	600 557	45.4	...	...	...	...
Paraguay Paraguay	2005	933 995	48.4	529 309	49.9	156 167[1]	52.3[1]
	2006	914 138	48.4	529 329	50.1	...	...
	2007	894 422	48.3	532 103	50.1	180 637	56.7
	2008	872 906	48.3	543 056	50.3	...	...
	2009	852 168	48.3	549 482	50.3	236 194	58.2
Peru Pérou	2005	4 077 361	49.1	2 469 618	48.6	909 315[1]	50.0[1]
	2006	4 026 316	49.0	2 539 939	48.9	952 437[1]	50.9[1]
	2007	3 993 965	49.0	2 603 890	48.9	...	...
	2008	3 854 764	49.1	2 609 081	49.0	...	...
	2009	3 787 409	49.0	2 659 945	48.7	...	...
Philippines Philippines	2005	13 083 744	48.6	6 352 482	51.7	2 402 649	54.2
	2006	13 006 648	48.5	6 301 582	51.6	2 483 988	54.5
	2007	13 145 210	48.5	6 365 985	51.4	...	...
	2008	13 411 286	48.5	6 509 273	51.1	2 651 466	54.4
	2009	13 686 643	48.3	6 766 952	50.9	...	...
Poland Pologne	2005	2 723 661	48.6	3 444 903	48.6	2 118 081	57.5
	2006	2 602 020	48.6	3 316 939	48.4	2 145 687	57.4
	2007	2 484 820	48.5	3 205 849	48.5	2 146 926	57.4
	2008	2 375 205	48.5	3 085 019	48.6	2 165 980	57.6
	2009	2 294 369	48.5	2 958 193	48.7	2 149 998	57.9
Portugal Portugal	2005	752 739	47.6	669 529	51.2	380 937	55.7
	2006	750 493	47.6	661 748	51.0	367 312	55.2
	2007	753 646	47.5	680 338	50.7	366 729	54.0
	2008	754 142	47.4	691 701	50.2	376 917	53.5
	2009	743 662	48.0	709 519	49.9	373 002	53.4

Education at the primary, secondary and tertiary levels *(continued)*
Number of students enrolled and percentage female
Enseignement primaire, secondaire et supérieur *(suite)*
Nombre d'élèves inscrits et pourcentage de sexe féminin

Country or area Pays ou zone	Year[t] Année[t]	Primary education Enseignement primaire		Secondary education Enseignement secondaire		Tertiary education Enseignement supérieur	
		Total	% F	Total	% F	Total	% F
Puerto Rico	2007	...	...	...	...	211 458	61.1
Porto Rico	2008	...	...	...	...	227 546	60.4
	2009	303 833	48.9	301 186	50.0	235 618	60.4
	2010	299 746	48.8	290 991	50.5	249 372	59.1
Qatar	2005	69 991	48.7	55 705	49.4	9 699[1]	68.2[1]
Qatar	2006	70 927	48.8	58 787	49.2	10 161[1]	67.6[1]
	2007	75 451	48.7	61 226	49.5	11 132	65.2
	2008	78 123	49.0	66 084	48.9	12 545	63.7
	2009	84 645	48.9	66 584	48.9	13 133	64.2
	2010	88 723	48.8	68 924	49.1	13 846	63.0
Republic of Korea	2005	4 031 496	47.2	3 786 224	47.1	3 210 184	37.1
République de Corée	2006	3 933 186	47.4	3 864 005	46.9	3 204 036	37.5
	2007	3 837 696	47.6	3 917 400	46.8	3 208 591	38.0
	2008	3 679 629	47.7	3 958 781	46.9	3 204 310	38.5
	2009	3 481 714	47.7	3 986 079	47.0	3 219 216	38.9
Republic of Moldova	2005	184 159	48.5	394 469	50.1	130 350	58.7
République de Moldova	2006	171 024	48.6	381 543	50.1	143 750	57.4
	2007	160 528	48.5	367 636	49.9	148 449[2]	57.3[2]
	2008	151 736	48.3	347 202	49.8	143 601	58.3
	2009	145 369	48.3	328 418	49.7	135 147	57.3
	2010	141 197	48.5	307 619	49.6	130 168	56.4
Romania	2005	970 295	48.4	2 089 646	49.2	738 806	54.6
Roumanie	2006	938 095	48.4	2 013 016	49.0	834 969	55.4
	2007	917 829	48.5	1 954 077	48.7	928 175	56.1
	2008	865 175	48.3	1 934 151	48.6	1 056 622	56.3
	2009	855 707	48.4	1 861 830	48.6	1 098 188	56.3
Russian Federation	2005	5 308 605	48.8	12 433 155	48.7	9 003 208	57.1
Fédération de Russie	2006	5 164 735	48.9	11 548 337	48.5	9 167 277	56.9
	2007	5 010 284	48.8	10 797 816	48.4	9 370 428	56.8
	2008	4 968 710	48.9	10 087 007	48.2	9 446 408	56.8
	2009	5 015 307	48.9	9 613 548	48.3	9 330 115	56.6
Rwanda	2005	1 857 841	50.9	218 517	47.2	27 787	...
Rwanda	2006	2 019 991	51.3	239 629	47.8[1]	37 149	...
	2007	2 150 430	50.9	266 518	47.6	41 013	...
	2008	2 190 270	50.9	288 036	47.8	45 128	...
	2009	2 264 672	50.8	346 518	49.1	55 213	43.5
	2010	2 299 326	50.7	425 587	50.7	62 734	43.8
Saint Kitts and Nevis	2005	6 350	49.8	3 939[1]	50.7[1]	...	...
Saint-Kitts-et-Nevis	2007	6 172	49.4	4 522	49.6	...	...
	2008	6 474	49.8	4 396	50.8	859	67.3
	2009	6 334	49.8	4 270	51.3	...	...
	2010	6 255	49.4	4 308	49.3	...	...
Saint Lucia	2005	23 573	48.6	13 786	54.3	2 197	73.8
Sainte-Lucie	2006	24 046	47.8	14 377	53.9	1 628	84.6
	2007	22 028	48.6	15 146	52.5	1 438	70.7
	2008	20 938	49.1	16 014	50.9	2 577	69.7
	2009	20 187	49.0	16 234	50.5	2 796	72.4
	2010	19 483	48.8	16 017	49.4	1 973	72.3
Saint Vincent-Grenadines	2005	17 858	47.0	9 780	55.2	...	...
Saint Vincent-Grenadines	2007	15 928	48.3	11 238	52.4	...	...
	2008	15 532	47.4	11 641	52.3	...	...
	2009	14 909	47.8	11 704	50.4	...	...
	2010	14 435	47.7	11 426	50.1	...	...
Samoa	2005[1]	...	...	24 242	50.7	...	...
Samoa	2007	30 199	48.0	...	...	...	...
	2009	29 663	47.5	25 429	51.2	...	...
	2010	30 871	48.1	25 998	50.8	...	...
San Marino	2008	1 573	47.6	2 223	48.7	929	57.4
Saint-Marin	2009	1 568	47.6	2 286	48.8	...	...
	2010	1 577	50.3	2 334	48.2	937	58.2

12

Education at the primary, secondary and tertiary levels *(continued)*
Number of students enrolled and percentage female
Enseignement primaire, secondaire et supérieur *(suite)*
Nombre d'élèves inscrits et pourcentage de sexe féminin

Country or area Pays ou zone	Year [t] Année [t]	Primary education Enseignement primaire		Secondary education Enseignement secondaire		Tertiary education Enseignement supérieur	
		Total	% F	Total	% F	Total	% F
Sao Tome and Principe	2005	30 468	48.6	8 091	51.1	...	...
Sao Tomé-et-Principe	2006[1]	31 066	48.6	8 235	51.8	...	...
	2007	31 397	49.3	8 997	51.2	...	...
	2008	32 584	49.0	8 518	51.1	...	...
	2009	33 789	49.7	9 668	52.2	704	47.6
	2010	33 982	49.4	10 045	50.1	766	48.8
Saudi Arabia	2005	3 097 604[2]	49.0[2]	2 609 567[2]	48.0[2]	603 771	58.0
Arabie saoudite	2006	...	...	...	...	636 445	57.9
	2007	3 173 807	48.8[2]	2 826 049	...	674 412	54.7
	2008	3 211 387	48.7	2 891 649	46.3[1]	714 877	54.7
	2009	3 255 243	48.6	2 989 910[1]	46.5[1]	757 770	54.7
	2010	3 321 066	49.1	3 036 438	47.9	903 567	52.4
Senegal	2005	1 444 163	48.6	405 899	42.5	59 127[2]	...
Sénégal	2006	1 473 464	49.2	447 425[1]	42.8[1]	62 539	31.6
	2007	1 572 178	49.6	519 064[1]	43.3[1]	71 211	34.6
	2008	1 618 303	50.2	582 101	43.9	91 359	35.3
	2009	1 652 585	50.6	...	...	94 371	37.0
	2010	1 695 007	50.9	725 208	46.3	92 106[2]	37.3[1]
Serbia	2005	324 490	48.8	632 761	49.5	...	...
Serbie	2006	312 469	48.8	622 854	49.6	...	...
	2007	297 816	48.7	615 135	49.4	238 710	55.3
	2008	289 785	48.8	608 456	49.4	237 598	55.4
	2009	282 395	48.6	603 834	49.4	235 940	55.2
	2010	283 161	48.6	590 830	49.2	226 772	55.3
Seychelles	2005	9 204	48.3	7 894	49.9	...	...
Seychelles	2007	8 864	49.3	7 816	50.1	...	...
	2008	8 744	49.5	7 542	50.5	...	...
	2009	8 624	49.5	7 487	50.1	...	...
	2010	8 670	49.7	7 248	49.2	...	...
Singapore	2007	301 101	48.1	232 100	48.2	...	...
Singapour	2008	299 704	48.2	231 144	48.2	183 627	48.5
	2009	294 602	48.3	232 003	48.2	198 634	49.1
	2010	...	...	...	...	213 446	49.6
Slovakia	2005	242 459	48.5	662 659	49.2	181 419	55.3
Slovaquie	2006	235 378	48.5	640 120	49.1	197 943	57.7
	2007	230 536	48.6	617 109	49.1	217 952	58.9
	2008	224 769	48.6	591 482	49.1	229 477	60.3
	2009	217 805	48.6	568 629	49.1	234 997	60.5
Slovenia	2005	93 156	48.4	181 299	48.7	112 228	57.8
Slovénie	2006	93 274	48.4	174 330	48.7	114 794	58.4
	2007	107 848	48.3	152 720	48.5	115 944	58.3
	2008	107 295	48.4	147 463	48.5	115 445	58.1
	2009	107 104	48.4	142 349	48.5	114 391	58.0
Solomon Islands	2005	75 082	46.8	22 487	43.5	...	...
Iles Salomon	2006	80 649	47.1	26 345	43.5	...	...
	2007	83 232	47.1	27 332	43.5	...	...
Somalia							
Somalie	2007	457 132	35.5	86 929[1]	31.5[1]	...	...
South Africa	2005	7 314 449	48.7	4 657 674	51.4	...	...
Afrique du Sud	2006	7 256 518	48.7	4 790 382[1]	51.3[1]	...	...
	2007	7 312 258	48.8	4 815 932[1]	51.0[1]	...	...
	2008	7 231 660	48.8	4 671 139[1]	50.8[1]	...	...
	2009	7 128 500	48.7	4 687 958	51.0	...	...
Spain	2005	2 484 903	48.3	3 107 816	50.1	1 809 353	53.7
Espagne	2006	2 501 205	48.3	3 091 036	50.1	1 789 254	53.9
	2007	2 555 757	48.3	3 080 161	50.2	1 777 498	54.0
	2008	2 625 414	48.4	3 069 321	50.0	1 781 019	54.0
	2009	2 684 078	48.4	3 065 017	49.7	1 800 834	54.1

Country or area Pays ou zone	Year [t] Année [t]	Primary education Enseignement primaire		Secondary education Enseignement secondaire		Tertiary education Enseignement supérieur	
		Total	% F	Total	% F	Total	% F
Sri Lanka	2005 [1]	1 635 308	49.1	...	...	...	...
Sri Lanka	2006	1 611 763	49.0	...	...	...	...
	2007	1 621 617	49.0	...	...	...	...
	2008	1 631 430	49.1	...	...	...	...
	2009	1 619 244	49.1	...	...	...	...
	2010	1 720 806	49.1	...	...	252 949	65.1
Sudan (former)	2005	3 278 090	45.6	1 369 735	47.5	...	...
Soudan (anc.)	2006	3 880 705	45.6	1 446 539	48.1	...	...
	2007	3 959 310	45.3	1 462 798	47.2	...	...
	2008	4 351 957	46.0	1 579 567	46.9	...	...
	2009	4 744 468	46.5	1 837 456	46.0	...	...
Suriname	2005	65 527	48.3	45 818	55.8	...	...
Suriname	2006	66 121	48.3	46 725	56.3	...	...
	2007	65 020	47.9	47 235	56.6	...	...
	2008	69 604	48.3	48 134	55.5	...	...
	2009	71 074	48.2	47 221	54.4	...	...
Swaziland	2005	221 596	48.0	71 124	49.9	5 897	52.0
Swaziland	2006	229 686	47.9	77 169	50.1	5 692	49.8
	2007	232 572	47.9	83 049	47.1	...	...
	2009	231 349	47.6	83 089	49.9	...	...
	2010	241 237	47.5	88 787	49.6	...	...
Sweden	2005	658 461	48.7	735 494	48.6	426 723	59.6
Suède	2006	626 847	48.7	750 567	48.5	422 614	59.6
	2007	601 120	48.6	760 491	48.5	413 710	59.9
	2008	584 726	48.6	764 264	48.6	406 879	60.3
	2009	573 416	48.6	751 826	48.5	422 580	60.1
Switzerland	2005	524 222	48.6	574 783	47.3	199 696	46.0
Suisse	2006	517 056	48.5	584 073	47.3	204 999	46.9
	2007	510 804	48.5	592 454	47.5	213 112	47.6
	2008	505 382	48.5	598 957	47.6	224 469	49.3
	2009	499 435	48.5	601 033	47.7	233 488	49.7
Syrian Arab Republic	2005	2 252 145	47.8	2 389 383	47.4	...	...
Rép. arabe syrienne	2006	2 279 545	47.8	2 464 688	47.7	...	...
	2007	2 310 168	47.8	2 549 444	48.2	...	...
	2008	2 356 403	47.9	2 626 228	48.5	...	...
	2009	2 383 223	47.9	2 664 335	48.7	...	...
	2010	2 429 450	47.9	2 731 825	48.7	...	...
Tajikistan	2005	693 078	48.2	984 410	44.8	119 317	25.9
Tadjikistan	2006	687 900	48.0	998 928	44.7	133 385	26.8
	2007	680 308	48.2	1 012 275	45.0	147 294	27.4
	2008	692 247	48.1	1 019 250	45.9	155 420	28.2
	2009	686 290	48.1	1 023 371	46.1	157 452	29.0
	2010	682 090	48.1	1 031 723	45.6	159 137	29.1
Thailand	2005	5 974 615	48.1	4 533 173	50.5 [1]	2 359 127	52.4
Thaïlande	2006	5 843 512	48.4	4 530 029	50.8	2 338 572	51.0
	2007	5 703 756	48.4	4 789 339	51.1	2 503 572	54.5
	2008	5 564 622	48.4	4 728 761	51.0	2 430 047	54.0
	2009	5 370 546	48.4	4 769 211	51.1	2 417 262	54.3
	2010	...	...	4 807 093	50.8	2 426 577	55.8
TFYR of Macedonia	2005	110 149	48.3	214 005	48.0	49 364	56.7
L'ex-R.Y. Macédoine	2006	105 045	48.2	...	...	48 368	56.7
	2007	100 911	48.2	208 364	47.8	58 199	54.5
	2008	115 082	48.4	203 853	47.6	65 504	53.2
	2009	112 477	48.3	199 064	47.8	65 200	53.0
Timor-Leste	2005	177 970	46.9	74 822	48.7	...	...
Timor-Leste	2008	206 576	47.5	78 655	48.9	...	...
	2009	218 294	47.6	96 067	48.6	16 727	40.0
	2010	230 175	47.9	101 501	49.0	...	...

12
Education at the primary, secondary and tertiary levels *(continued)*
Number of students enrolled and percentage female
Enseignement primaire, secondaire et supérieur *(suite)*
Nombre d'élèves inscrits et pourcentage de sexe féminin

Country or area Pays ou zone	Year [t] Année [t]	Primary education Enseignement primaire		Secondary education Enseignement secondaire		Tertiary education Enseignement supérieur	
		Total	% F	Total	% F	Total	% F
Togo Togo	2005	996 707	45.9	404 470	34.7	...	...
	2006	1 051 872	46.3	430 064	35.3	28 076[1]	...
	2007	1 021 617	46.4	408 964	34.6[1]	32 502	...
	2008	1 055 372	46.7	...	...	...	...
	2009	1 224 916[1]	46.0	...	...	...	...
	2010	1 286 653	47.4	...	...	...	...
Tonga Tonga	2005	17 032	47.3	...	...	...	...
	2006	16 941	47.1	13 938	48.4	...	...
	2007	16 892	47.0	...	...	...	...
Trinidad and Tobago Trinité-et-Tobago	2005	129 703[2]	48.6[2]	...	...	16 920[1]	55.6[1]
	2007	130 242	48.5	...	...	...	...
	2008	130 880	48.5	95 275[1]	51.1[1]	...	...
	2009[2]	130 914	48.4	...	...	...	...
	2010	131 350	48.5	...	...	...	...
Tunisia Tunisie	2005	1 184 301	47.7	1 239 468	51.1	311 569	57.2
	2006	1 134 414	47.7	1 247 046	51.0[1]	325 325	57.5
	2007	1 068 822	47.7	1 268 219	...	326 185	59.0
	2008	1 036 445	47.8	1 259 240	50.6	350 828	58.8
	2009	1 025 044	48.0	1 201 632	50.5[1]	360 172	59.5
Turkey Turquie	2005	6 678 265	47.9	6 345 057	44.7	2 106 351	41.9
	2006	6 705 994	48.1	6 631 883	45.0	2 342 898	42.4
	2007	6 769 452	48.3	6 822 949	45.3	2 453 664	42.6
	2008	6 760 145	48.4	6 708 970	46.1	2 532 622	43.1
	2009	6 591 608	48.6	7 100 959	46.9	2 924 281	43.6
Turks and Caicos Islands Iles Turques et Caïques	2005	2 220	51.1	1 686[1]	47.8[1]	...	...
	2008	...	...	...	...	2	50.0
	2009	2 891	48.6	2 095	51.8	...	...
Tuvalu Tuvalu	2005	1 450	48.3	...	...	...	...
	2006	1 460	47.9	...	...	...	...
Uganda Ouganda	2005	7 223 879	49.6	765 797[1]	44.4[1]	...	...
	2006	7 363 721	49.8	855 120[1]	44.9[1]	92 605	43.3
	2007	7 537 971	49.9	1 031 520	44.9	...	...
	2008	7 963 979	49.9	1 175 648	45.6	107 728	44.3
	2009	8 297 774	50.0	1 277 543[1]	45.3[1]	123 887	44.3
	2010	8 374 648	50.1	1 305 514[1]	46.1[1]	...	...
Ukraine Ukraine	2005	1 945 715	48.6	4 042 827	46.8[2]	2 604 875	54.1
	2006	1 753 689	48.6	3 896 263	48.4[2]	2 740 342	54.2[2]
	2007	1 647 847	48.7[2]	3 708 736	48.7[2]	2 819 248	54.3
	2008	1 573 458	48.8[2]	3 498 524	48.3[2]	2 847 713	54.4[2]
	2009	1 531 943	48.7	3 288 557	48.3[2]	2 798 693	54.8
	2010	1 540 282	48.8	3 132 972	48.2[2]	2 635 004	54.5
United Arab Emirates Emirats arabes unis	2005	262 807	48.5	284 978	48.9	...	...
	2006	272 331	48.5	298 447	49.0	...	...
	2007	284 034	48.5	311 013[1]	48.7[1]	...	...
	2009	304 250	48.2	324 027[1]	48.5[1]	87 006	59.6
	2010	326 588	48.6	336 652[1]	49.5[1]	...	...
United Kingdom Royaume-Uni	2005	4 634 991	48.7	5 760 887	49.3	2 287 541	57.2
	2006	4 517 618	48.9	5 357 793	49.3	2 336 111	57.3
	2007	4 409 184	48.9	5 306 369	49.2	2 362 815	57.2
	2008	4 465 021	48.7	5 356 450	49.2	2 329 494	57.2
	2009	4 416 474	48.7	5 429 636	49.1	2 415 222	57.0
United Rep. of Tanzania Rép.-Unie de Tanzanie	2005	7 541 208	48.9	...	...	51 554[1]	32.5[1]
	2006	7 959 884	49.1	...	...	...	...
	2007	8 316 925	49.3	...	...	...	...
	2008	8 626 825	49.3	...	...	...	...
	2009	8 441 553	49.7	...	...	...	...
	2010	8 419 305	50.1	...	...	85 113	45.1

12

Education at the primary, secondary and tertiary levels *(continued)*
Number of students enrolled and percentage female
Enseignement primaire, secondaire et supérieur *(suite)*
Nombre d'élèves inscrits et pourcentage de sexe féminin

Country or area Pays ou zone	Year [t] Année [t]	Primary education Enseignement primaire		Secondary education Enseignement secondaire		Tertiary education Enseignement supérieur	
		Total	% F	Total	% F	Total	% F
United States	2005	24 454 602	48.5	24 431 934	49.2	17 272 044	57.2
Etats-Unis	2006	24 319 033	49.0	24 552 317	48.6	17 487 475	57.4
	2007	24 492 041	48.8	24 731 027	48.9	17 758 870	57.3
	2008	24 676 574	48.9	24 692 888	48.6	18 248 124	57.2
	2009	24 586 434	49.0	24 524 564	49.1	19 102 814	57.1
	2010	24 393 002	48.7	24 192 786	49.0	20 427 709	57.1
Uruguay	2005	365 536	48.4	323 087	52.6	...	...
Uruguay	2006	365 388	48.3	323 027	52.8	113 368	61.9
	2007	359 439	48.3	294 852	48.8	158 841	62.9
	2008	353 560	48.2	281 593	52.2	162 968	62.8
	2009	348 691	48.1	288 491	...	161 459	62.7
Uzbekistan	2005	2 383 326	48.6	4 515 852	48.4	265 957	40.7
Ouzbékistan	2006	2 277 191	48.6	4 542 174	48.5	280 837	40.9
	2007	2 164 897	48.5	4 598 037	48.7	288 550	41.0
	2008	2 071 317	48.6	4 497 372	48.8	299 010	39.9
	2009	1 995 747	48.6	4 506 226	48.9	300 782	40.5
	2010	1 970 922	48.5	4 448 978	48.8	...	...
Vanuatu	2005	38 530	47.7	...	...	...	...
Vanuatu	2006	37 060	47.8	...	...	...	...
	2007	37 817	47.4	...	...	...	...
	2008	38 658	47.7	16 734	49.4	...	...
	2009	38 762	47.2	17 877	50.5	...	...
	2010	41 834	47.3	20 256	48.8	...	...
Venezuela (Boliv. Rep. of)	2005	3 449 290	48.4	2 028 388	52.1	...	...
Venezuela (Rép. boliv. du)	2006	3 452 062	48.4	2 104 857	51.9	...	...
	2007	3 521 139	48.3	2 174 619	51.8	...	...
	2008	3 439 199	48.3	2 224 214	51.4	2 109 331	62.1[1]
	2009	3 461 820	48.2	2 252 421	51.2	2 123 041	...
	2010	3 457 754	48.2	2 254 935	51.3		
Viet Nam	2005	7 773 484	47.5	9 939 319	48.6	1 354 543	40.9
Viet Nam	2006	7 317 813	47.9	9 975 113	48.8	1 427 046	48.2
	2007	7 041 312	47.8	9 845 407	49.5	1 587 609	49.3
	2008	6 871 795	...	9 543 007	50.2	1 654 846	48.8
	2009	6 745 016	47.9	9 095 812	50.2	1 774 321	49.0
	2010	6 922 624	47.3	8 799 835	51.1	2 020 413	49.2
Yemen	2005	3 219 564	41.6	1 455 206	32.1	201 043	26.1
Yémen	2006	...	...	...	...	200 853	27.2
	2007	...	...	...	...	236 972	28.7
	2008	3 282 457	43.6	1 479 157[1]	35.4[1]	...	...
	2010	3 426 991	44.0	1 561 888[1]	37.5[1]	...	...
Zambia	2005	2 572 846	48.7	...	...	...	...
Zambie	2006	2 678 610	49.3	...	...	...	...
	2007	2 790 312	49.1	...	...	...	...
	2008	2 909 436	49.3	...	...	...	...
	2009	2 840 540	49.5	...	...	...	...
	2010	2 899 131	50.1	...	...	...	...
Zimbabwe Zimbabwe	2010	...	...	...	...	94 611	45.0

Source:
United Nations Educational, Scientific and Cultural Organization (UNESCO) Institute for Statistics, Montreal, the UNESCO Institute for Statistics (UIS) database, May 2012.

[t] Data relate to the calendar year in which the academic year ends.

1   UIS estimation.
2   National estimation.

Source :
L'Institut de statistique de l'Organisation des Nations Unies pour l'éducation, la science et la culture (UNESCO), Montréal, la base de données de l'institut de statistique de l'UNESCO (ISU), mai 2012.

[t] Les données se réfèrent à l'année civile durant laquelle l'année scolaire se termine.

1   Estimation de l'ISU.
2   Estimation nationale.

12

Education at the primary, secondary and tertiary levels *(continued)*
Number of students enrolled and percentage female

Enseignement primaire, secondaire et supérieur *(suite)*
Nombre d'élèves inscrits et pourcentage de sexe féminin

3   For statistical purposes, the data for China do not include those for the Hong Kong Special Administrative Region (Hong Kong SAR) and Macao Special Administrative Region (Macao SAR).

3   Pour la présentation des statistiques, les données pour la Chine ne comprennent pas la Région Administrative Spéciale de Hong Kong (Hong Kong RAS) et la Région Administrative Spéciale de Macao (Macao RAS).

Public expenditure on education
Percentage of GNI and of government expenditure

Dépenses publiques afférentes à l'éducation
Pourcentage par rapport au RNB et aux dépenses du gouvernement

Country or area	As % of Gross National Income (GNI) En % du Revenu National Brut (RNB)				As % of total government expenditure En % des dépenses totales du gouvernement				Pays ou zone
	2007	2008	2009	2010	2007	2008	2009	2010	
Algeria	...	4.4	...	...	...	20.3	...	...	Algérie
Andorra	2.6	3.2	3.1	...	...	...	...	...	Andorre
Anguilla	...	3.4	...	...	...	10.7	...	...	Anguilla
Antigua and Barbuda	...	...	2.6	...	...	...	9.8	...	Antigua-et-Barbuda
Argentina	5.0	5.5	6.2	...	13.5	14.0	14.0	...	Argentine
Armenia+	2.9	3.1	3.8	3.1	15.0	14.0	13.0	...	Arménie
Aruba	5.2	5.4	6.0	...	17.3	19.5	20.5	...	Aruba
Australia	4.7	4.6	5.2	...	13.7	12.9	...	...	Australie
Austria	5.4	5.5	...	...	11.1	11.2	...	...	Autriche
Azerbaijan	3.0	2.7	3.5	...	11.9	9.1	10.9	...	Azerbaïdjan
Bahrain	3.1	3.1	...	...	11.6	11.7	...	...	Bahreïn
Bangladesh	2.4	2.2	2.1	...	15.8	14.0	14.1	...	Bangladesh
Barbados	7.7	7.5	7.5	...	...	15.7	14.3	...	Barbade
Belarus	5.2	...	4.6	...	9.3	...	8.9	...	Bélarus
Belgium	6.0	6.3	...	...	12.4	12.9	...	...	Belgique
Belize	...	6.6	6.9	...	...	18.7	...	...	Belize
Benin	3.6	4.1	4.5	...	15.9	19.3	18.2	...	Bénin
Bermuda	...	...	2.1	1.9	...	...	13.4	13.4	Bermudes
Bhutan	...	5.3	5.4	4.5	...	...	11.0	9.4	Bhoutan
Botswana	8.6	...	8.2	...	21.0	...	16.2	...	Botswana
Brazil	5.2	5.5	...	...	16.1	...	...	...	Brésil
British Virgin Islands	3.4	...	3.3	...	14.7	...	13.7	13.6	Iles Vierges britanniques
Brunéi Darussalam	...	...	...	2.0	...	...	...	8.6	Brunéi Darussalam
Bulgaria	4.2	4.7	...	...	10.0	12.4	...	...	Bulgarie
Burkina Faso	4.6	...	...	...	21.8	...	...	...	Burkina Faso
Burundi	...	7.2	8.3	9.4	...	22.3	23.4	25.1	Burundi
Cambodia	1.7	...	...	2.8	12.4	...	...	...	Cambodge
Cameroon	3.3	3.0	3.7	3.5	19.5	17.0	19.2	17.9	Cameroun
Canada	5.0	4.8	...	...	...	...	...	...	Canada
Cape Verde	6.3	6.6	5.9	5.9	16.4	16.7	15.9	14.4	Cap-Vert
Central African Rep.	1.3	1.3	1.3	1.2	12.0	11.7	12.5	12.0	Rép. centrafricaine
Chad	...	...	3.5	3.1	...	...	12.6	10.1	Tchad
Chili	3.8	4.3	4.9	...	18.2	...	...	...	Chili
China, Hong Kong SAR	3.5	3.3	4.3	3.5	23.2	23.0	24.1	20.2	Chine, Hong Kong RAS
China, Macao SAR	2.1	2.6	2.9	...	16.2	14.0	13.0	...	Chine, Macao RAS
Columbia	4.2	4.1	4.9	5.0	12.6	14.9	...	...	Colombie
Comores	...	7.6	...	...	...	...	...	...	Comores
Congo	...	...	...	8.3	...	...	...	...	Congo
Costa Rica	4.9	5.2	6.5	...	...	22.8	23.1	...	Costa Rica
Côte d'Ivoire	4.6	4.8	...	...	21.7	24.6	...	...	Côte d'Ivoire
Croatia	4.1	4.5	...	...	...	...	...	...	Croatie

Public expenditure on education *(continued)*
Percentage of GNI and of government expenditure
Dépenses publiques afférentes à l'éducation *(suite)*
Pourcentage par rapport au RNB et aux dépenses du gouvernement

Country or area	As % of Gross National Income (GNI) En % du Revenu National Brut (RNB)				As % of total government expenditure En % des dépenses totales du gouvernement				Pays ou zone
	2007	2008	2009	2010	2007	2008	2009	2010	
Cuba	12.1	13.8	13.6	...	20.6	18.5	17.5	18.4	Cuba
Cyprus	7.5	7.9	...	...	16.4	17.4	...	...	Chypre
République tchèque	4.5	4.3	...	...	9.9	9.5	...	...	République tchèque
Denmark	7.7	7.6	...	...	15.4	15.0	...	...	Danemark
Djibouti	7.6	...	...	...	22.8	...	...	...	Djibouti
Dominica	3.4	4.0	3.7	3.7	10.7	11.3	10.2	9.3	Dominique
Dominican Rep.	2.3	...	...	...	11.0	...	...	...	Rép. dominicaine
Egypt	3.7	3.7	...	...	12.6	11.9	...	...	Egypte
El Salvador	3.1[1]	3.8	...	3.3	13.1[1]	...	...	...	El Salvador
Estonia	5.1	6.0	...	...	13.9	14.2	...	...	Estonie
Ethiopia	5.5	5.5	4.6	4.7	23.3	22.8	23.6	25.4	Ethiopie
Fiji	6.0	4.3	4.5	...	20.4	15.6	14.7	...	Fidji
Finland	5.9	6.1	...	...	12.5	12.4	...	...	Finlande
France	5.5	5.5	...	...	10.7	10.6	...	...	France
Gambia	...	4.4	4.0	5.4	...	16.4	16.0	22.8	Gambie
Georgia	2.7	3.0	3.3[1]	...	7.8	7.2	7.7[1]	...	Géorgie
Germany	4.4	4.5	...	...	10.3	10.4	...	...	Allemagne
Ghana	5.5	5.8	5.4	5.6	24.2	22.4	24.0	24.4	Ghana
Guatemala	3.1	3.3	...	...	...	...	...	...	Guatemala
Guinea	...	2.8	...	...	...	19.2	...	...	Guinée
Guyana	3.8	...	3.4	3.7	12.5	...	13.2	16.7	Guyana
Hungary	5.7	5.5	...	...	10.5	10.4	...	...	Hongrie
Iceland	7.7	9.6	...	...	18.8	13.9	...	...	Islande
Indonesia	3.7	2.9	...	4.7	18.7	17.9	...	26.0	Indonésie
Iran (Islamic Rep. of)	5.6	4.8	4.7	4.7	19.5	20.0	20.9	19.8	Iran (Rép. islamique d')
Ireland	5.6	6.6	...	...	13.5	13.4	...	...	Irlande
Israel	5.9	6.0	...	...	13.0	13.7	...	...	Israël
Italy	4.3	4.7	...	...	9.0	9.4	...	...	Italie
Jamaica	5.8	6.5	6.2	6.4[2]	...	...	...	11.5[2]	Jamaïque
Japan	3.4	3.3	...	3.7	9.4	9.4	...	...	Japon
Kazakhstan	3.2	...	3.4	...	...	...	...	...	Kazakhstan
Kenya	...	...	...	6.7	...	...	...	17.2	Kenya
Korea, Republic of	4.2	4.8	...	...	14.8	15.8	...	...	Corée, République de
Kyrgyzstan	6.6	6.1	6.5	...	25.6	24.7	...	...	Kirghizistan
Lao People's Dem. Rep.	3.1	2.4	...	3.3	15.8	12.2	...	13.2	Rép. dém. pop. lao
Latvia	5.2	5.8	5.2	...	14.0	14.7	...	...	Lettonie
Lebanon	2.5	1.9	1.8	...	9.6	8.1	7.2	...	Liban
Lesotho	...	10.3	...	...	...	23.7	...	...	Lesotho
Liberia	...	3.5	...	...	...	12.1	...	...	Libéria
Liechtenstein	2.1	2.4	...	...	...	...	...	...	Liechtenstein
Lithuania	4.9	5.1	...	...	13.4	13.1	...	...	Lituanie
Madagascar	3.4	2.9	3.2	...	16.4	13.4	...	...	Madagascar
Malawi	...	...	...	4.7	...	...	...	12.1	Malawi
Malaysia	4.6	4.2	5.9	...	18.2	17.2	18.9	...	Malaisie

Country or area	As % of Gross National Income (GNI) En % du Revenu National Brut (RNB)				As % of total government expenditure En % des dépenses totales du gouvernement				Pays ou zone
	2007	2008	2009	2010	2007	2008	2009	2010	
Maldives	5.7	6.0	9.2	...	14.8	12.0	16.0	...	Maldives
Mali	...	4.0	4.6	4.6	...	17.4	22.3	22.0	Mali
Malta	6.5	6.0	...	...	14.8	13.3	...	...	Malte
Mauritania	...	4.0	...	4.3	...	15.6	...	15.3	Mauritanie
Mauritius	3.4	3.1	3.1	...	12.6	12.7	11.4	...	Maurice
Mexico	4.9	5.0	...	...	21.6	...	...	...	Mexique
Monaco	...	...	1.2	...	...	...	6.6	6.4	Monaco
Mongolia	4.8	...	5.4	5.9	13.3	...	14.6	...	Mongolie
Montserrat	6.8	6.6	6.3	...	8.3	8.6	8.4	...	Montserrat
Morocco	...	5.7	5.5	...	...	25.7	...	...	Maroc
Namibia	...	6.6	...	8.1	...	22.4	...	...	Namibie
Nauru [1]	...	...	...	...	7.5	...	...	...	Nauru [1]
Nepal	...	3.8	4.6	4.7	...	19.1	19.5	20.2	Népal
Netherlands	5.2	5.6	...	...	11.7	11.9	...	...	Pays-Bas
New Zealand	6.5	6.1	6.9	7.6	17.9	16.1	...	...	Nouvelle-Zélande
Niger	4.0	3.7	4.7	3.9	...	16.2	19.3	16.9	Niger
Norway	6.8	6.6	...	...	16.5	16.1	...	...	Norvège
Oman	...	...	4.7	...	...	...	...	...	Oman
Pakistan	2.8	2.9	2.6	2.3	11.2	...	11.2	9.9	Pakistan
Panama	...	4.1	...	...	...	...	...	...	Panama
Paraguay	4.1	...	...	...	11.9	...	...	...	Paraguay
Peru	2.7	2.9	2.7	...	16.4	20.7	16.4	...	Pérou
Philippines	2.6	2.7	...	...	15.9	17.0	...	...	Philippines
Poland	5.1	5.2	...	...	11.7	11.8	...	...	Pologne
Portugal	...	5.1	...	...	...	11.0	...	...	Portugal
Qatar	...	2.4	...	...	...	8.2	...	...	Qatar
Republic of Moldova	7.6	7.5	9.0	8.4	19.8	19.8	21.0	22.3	République de Moldova
Romania	4.3	...	...	...	11.8	...	...	...	Roumanie
Russian Federation	...	4.2	...	...	...	...	...	...	Fédération de Russie
Rwanda	4.4	3.9	...	5.0	19.0	20.4	...	18.2	Rwanda
Saint Kitts and Nevis	4.7	...	...	...	10.7	...	...	...	Saint-Kitts-et-Nevis
Saint Lucia	...	6.0	4.2	4.6[1]	...	13.0	10.3	10.9[1]	Sainte-Lucie
Saint Vincent-Gren.	5.9	...	5.6	5.0	...	...	13.8	10.2	Saint Vincent-Gren
Samoa	...	5.8	...	...	...	13.4	...	...	Samoa
Saudi Arabia	6.3	5.5	...	...	19.8	19.3	...	...	Arabie saoudite
Senegal	...	5.1[2]	5.6	5.7	...	19.0[2]	24.0	...	Sénégal
Serbia	4.8	5.0	5.1	...	8.9	9.3	9.5	...	Serbie
Sierra Leone	3.4[2]	3.2[2]	4.3	...	18.8[2]	14.9[2]	18.1	...	Sierra Leone
Singapore	...	2.7	3.2	3.3	...	15.3	11.6	10.3	Singapour
Slovakia	3.7	3.7	...	...	10.5	10.3	...	...	Slovaquie
Slovenia	5.3	5.4	...	...	12.2	11.8	...	...	Slovénie
South Africa	5.3	5.3	5.7	6.1	17.1	16.2	16.9	19.2	Afrique du Sud
Spain	4.5	4.8	...	...	11.1	11.2	...	...	Espagne
Sri Lanka	...	...	2.1	...	...	...	8.1	...	Sri Lanka

Public expenditure on education *(continued)*
Percentage of GNI and of government expenditure

Dépenses publiques afférentes à l'éducation *(suite)*
Pourcentage par rapport au RNB et aux dépenses du gouvernement

Country or area	As % of Gross National Income (GNI) En % du Revenu National Brut (RNB)				As % of total government expenditure En % des dépenses totales du gouvernement				Pays ou zone
	2007	2008	2009	2010	2007	2008	2009	2010	
Swaziland	...	7.4	7.1	7.6	...	21.7	18.0	16.0	Swaziland
Sweden	6.4	6.5	...	...	12.7	13.0	...	...	Suède
Switzerland	5.1	5.8	...	...	16.1	16.7	...	...	Suisse
Syrian Arab Republic	5.0	...	...	...	16.7	...	...	...	Rép. arabe syrienne
Tajikistan	3.5	3.5	...	4.1	18.2	18.7	...	14.8	Tadjikistan
Thailand	4.0	3.9	4.3	3.9	20.9	20.5	20.3	22.3	Thaïlande
Timor-Leste	...	2.0	3.9	3.6	...	11.7	15.5	11.7	Timor-Leste
Togo	4.3	3.9	4.6	5.0	17.2	15.8	17.6	...	Togo
Tunisia	6.8	6.6	...	...	22.5	22.7	...	...	Tunisie
Uganda	...	3.8	3.2	...	...	18.9	15.0	...	Ouganda
Ukraine	5.4	...	...	...	20.2	...	...	...	Ukraine
United Arab Emirates	0.7	0.8	1.0	...	24.8	27.2	23.4	...	Emirats arabes unis
United Kingdom	5.4	5.3	...	...	11.8	11.1	...	...	Royaume-Uni
United Rep. of Tanzania	...	6.8	...	6.2	...	27.5	...	18.3	Rép.-Unie de Tanzanie
United States	5.3	5.5	...	...	14.1	13.8	...	...	Etats-Unis
Vanuatu	...	7.0	5.4	...	...	28.1	23.7	...	Vanuatu
Venezuela (Bol. Rep. of)	3.7	...	...	...	...	...	...	...	Venezuela (Rép. Bol. du)
Viet Nam	...	5.5	...	...	...	19.8	...	...	Viet Nam
Yemen	...	5.6	...	...	...	16.0	...	...	Yémen
Zambia	1.7	1.5	...	...	...	...	...	...	Zambie
Zimbabwe	...	...	...	2.7	...	...	...	8.3	Zimbabwe

Source:
United Nations Educational, Scientific and Cultural Organization (UNESCO) Institute for Statistics, Montreal, the UNESCO Institute for Statistics (UIS) database, last accessed July 2012.

1 National estimation.
2 UIS estimation.

Source:
L'Institut de statistique de l'Organisation des Nations Unies pour l'éducation, la science et la culture (UNESCO), Montréal, la base de données de l'institut de statistique de l'UNESCO (ISU), dernier accès juillet 2012.

1 Estimation nationale.
2 Estimation de l'ISU.

Food supply
Calories, protein and fat: average supply per capita per day

Disponibilités alimentaires
Calories, protéine et lipides : disponibilités moyennes par habitant, par jour

Region, country or area	Calories (number) Calories (nombre)			Protein (grams) Protéine (grammes)			Fat (grams) Lipides (grammes)			Region, pays ou zone
	1990	2000	2009	1990	2000	2009	1990	2000	2009	
World	**2 627**	**2 732**	**2 831**	**71**	**75**	**79**	**68**	**75**	**82**	**Monde**
Africa	**2 278**	**2 421**	**2 560**	**59**	**62**	**67**	**47**	**50**	**55**	**Afrique**
Algeria	2 855	2 922	3 239	76	79	90	72	68	66	Algérie
Angola	1 643	1 811	2 079	39	40	46	45	39	49	Angola
Benin	2 236	2 395	2 592	52	59	64	43	46	44	Bénin
Botswana	2 219	2 117	2 164	69	66	62	57	50	57	Botswana
Burkina Faso	2 270	2 371	2 647	70	72	80	47	53	59	Burkina Faso
Burundi	1 893	1 674	1 604	59	46	43	14	11	19	Burundi
Cameroon	2 018	2 133	2 457	48	55	62	42	45	41	Cameroun
Cape Verde	2 396	2 386	2 644	62	63	73	68	69	81	Cap-Vert
Central African Rep.	1 890	1 948	2 181	40	46	51	60	59	73	Rép. centrafricaine
Chad	1 629	1 954	2 074	47	62	64	39	61	51	Tchad
Comoros	2 318	2 025	2 139	55	47	49	52	49	52	Comores
Congo	2 004	2 171	2 056	42	43	41	42	54	41	Congo
Côte d'Ivoire	2 489	2 550	2 670	54	50	54	47	52	53	Côte d'Ivoire
Djibouti	1 693	1 969	2 419	46	48	59	29	47	67	Djibouti
Egypt	3 154	3 318	3 349	84	93	97	55	56	57	Egypte
Eritrea	1 475[1]	1 506	1 640	46[1]	48	51	24[1]	23	21	Erythrée
Ethiopia	1 516[1]	1 808	2 097	43[1]	51	61	16[1]	17	24	Ethiopie
Gabon	2 418	2 685	2 745	67	77	83	46	56	55	Gabon
Gambia	2 394	2 350	2 643	52	54	63	55	71	67	Gambie
Ghana	1 719	2 472	2 934	40	51	60	36	39	46	Ghana
Guinea	2 540	2 490	2 652	57	54	56	46	56	58	Guinée
Guinea-Bissau	2 249	2 372	2 476	45	47	45	58	56	64	Guinée-Bissau
Kenya	2 010	2 059	2 092	56	57	59	46	47	51	Kenya
Lesotho	2 273	2 327	2 371	65	65	68	34	33	30	Lesotho
Liberia	2 136	2 191	2 261	39	40	38	40	55	56	Libéria
Libyan Arab Jamah.	3 222	3 175	3 157	83	79	80	89	94	93	Jamah. arabe libyenne
Madagascar	2 266	2 073	2 117	53	48	49	33	28	26	Madagascar
Malawi	1 927	2 209	2 318	53	57	62	27	30	40	Malawi
Mali	2 205	2 217	2 624	62	62	73	52	47	56	Mali
Mauritania	2 540	2 713	2 856	79	78	85	65	69	84	Mauritanie
Mauritius	2 725	2 877	2 993	69	78	85	74	84	84	Maurice
Morocco	3 073	3 056	3 264	86	82	90	57	60	69	Maroc
Mozambique	1 807	1 979	2 112	32	37	39	37	39	37	Mozambique
Namibia	2 061	2 226	2 151	59	68	60	34	52	52	Namibie
Niger	2 146	2 171	2 489	58	63	81	35	43	58	Niger
Nigeria	2 153	2 611	2 711	49	59	62	52	59	67	Nigéria
Rwanda	1 741	1 867	2 188	43	43	55	15	16	28	Rwanda
Sao Tome and Principe	2 233	2 374	2 734	51	52	63	79	66	78	Sao Tomé-et-Principe
Senegal	2 316	2 243	2 479	69	64	62	48	65	73	Sénégal
Seychelles	2 191	2 432	2 426	70	73	79	50	74	61	Seychelles
Sierra Leone	1 990	1 989	2 162	41	43	50	56	45	55	Sierra Leone
South Africa	2 830	2 894	3 017	74	77	84	67	71	86	Afrique du Sud

14

Food supply *(continued)*
Calories, protein and fat: average supply per capita per day
Disponibilités alimentaires
Calories, protéine et lipides : disponibilités moyennes par habitant, par jour

Region, country or area	Calories (number) Calories (nombre)			Protein (grams) Protéine (grammes)			Fat (grams) Lipides (grammes)			Region, pays ou zone
	1990	2000	2009	1990	2000	2009	1990	2000	2009	
Sudan (former)	1 934	2 165	2 326	59	69	72	54	68	67	Soudan (anc.)
Swaziland	2 338	2 362	2 249	58	62	58	47	46	45	Swaziland
Togo	2 161	2 208	2 363	51	52	55	44	43	51	Togo
Tunisia	3 124	3 236	3 314	83	91	95	87	92	82	Tunisie
Uganda	2 309	2 270	2 260	54	49	49	34	33	47	Ouganda
United Rep. of Tanzania	2 157	1 999	2 137	54	53	55	33	32	42	Rép.-Unie de Tanzanie
Zambia	2 055	1 864	1 879	52	47	47	33	32	38	Zambie
Zimbabwe	2 008	1 985	2 219	51	46	56	49	52	61	Zimbabwe
Northern America	**3 459**	**378**	**366**	**107**	**115**	**112**	**139**	**155**	**155**	**Amérique septent.**
Antigua and Barbuda	2 467	2 155	2 373	82	71	85	98	75	86	Antigua-et-Barbuda
Bahamas	2 714	2 785	2 750	83	93	88	87	94	98	Bahamas
Barbados	3 068	2 832	3 021	93	81	91	108	91	100	Barbade
Belize	2 461	2 560	2 680	65	68	68	64	64	65	Belize
Bermuda	2 791	2 646	2 716	99	86	86	124	106	124	Bermudes
Canada	3 019	3 515	3 399	96	107	103	127	148	145	Canada
Costa Rica	2 802	2 825	2 886	69	75	75	72	79	90	Costa Rica
Cuba	2 930	3 046	3 258	69	70	85	86	53	66	Cuba
Dominica	2 963	3 081	3 147	76	92	96	84	86	83	Dominique
Dominican Republic	2 084	2 322	2 491	47	50	59	66	79	77	Rép. dominicaine
El Salvador	2 318	2 561	2 574	56	65	71	50	58	59	El Salvador
Grenada	2 496	2 220	2 456	68	59	76	83	80	90	Grenade
Guatemala	2 350	2 096	2 244	60	55	61	44	47	59	Guatemala
Haiti	1 731	1 931	1 979	42	43	44	29	43	41	Haïti
Honduras	2 317	2 435	2 694	55	60	66	56	67	72	Honduras
Jamaica	2 642	2 729	2 807	69	71	77	71	81	86	Jamaïque
Mexico	3 033	3 158	3 146	80	90	90	77	86	93	Mexique
Netherlands Antilles	2 586	3 087	3 102	82	102	89	81	92	83	Antilles néerlandaises
Nicaragua	1 741	2 148	2 517	47	53	67	39	48	59	Nicaragua
Panama	2 305	2 195	2 606	59	63	75	70	67	71	Panama
Saint Kitts and Nevis	2 611	2 513	2 546	72	77	73	84	81	81	Saint-Kitts-et-Nevis
Saint Lucia	2 497	2 720	2 710	75	89	89	59	81	77	Sainte-Lucie
Saint Vincent-Grenad.	2 354	2 528	2 914	60	68	86	72	64	84	Saint Vincent-Grenad.
Trinidad and Tobago	2 635	2 696	2 751	63	62	68	66	73	76	Trinité-et-Tobago
United States	3 507	3 804	3 688	108	116	113	140	156	156	Etats-Unis
America, South	**2 579**	**2 782**	**2 951**	**65**	**77**	**83**	**73**	**89**	**96**	**Amérique du Sud**
Argentina	2 913	3 268	2 918	92	105	93	100	117	109	Argentine
Bolivia (Plurin. State of)	1 977	2 121	2 172	52	57	61	39	42	47	Bolivie (État plurin. de)
Brazil	2 721	2 882	3 173	66	80	89	78	100	111	Brésil
Chile	2 536	2 808	2 908	70	79	89	63	83	81	Chili
Colombia	2 394	2 662	2 717	56	65	69	59	70	73	Colombie
Ecuador	2 131	2 221	2 267	47	55	57	73	76	88	Equateur
Guyana	2 386	2 814	2 718	59	82	74	31	61	52	Guyana
Paraguay	2 423	2 596	2 518	67	73	65	68	93	88	Paraguay
Peru	2 028	2 379	2 563	52	65	71	41	45	43	Pérou
Suriname	2 388	2 457	2 548	62	55	56	45	61	67	Suriname

14
Food supply *(continued)*
Calories, protein and fat: average supply per capita per day
Disponibilités alimentaires
Calories, protéine et lipides : disponibilités moyennes par habitant, par jour

Region, country or area	Calories (number) Calories (nombre)			Protein (grams) Protéine (grammes)			Fat (grams) Lipides (grammes)			Region, pays ou zone
	1990	2000	2009	1990	2000	2009	1990	2000	2009	
Uruguay	2 509	2 844	2 808	76	89	79	84	94	74	Uruguay
Venezuela (Boliv. Rep. of)	2 394	2 484	3 014	59	67	84	71	72	97	Venezuela (Rép. boliv. du)
Asia	**2 421**	**2 591**	**2 706**	**62**	**70**	**75**	**50**	**62**	**72**	**Asie**
Armenia	2 230[2]	2 280	2 806	65[2]	66	88	36[2]	47	84	Arménie
Azerbaijan	2 314[2]	2 444	3 072	70[2]	71	90	39[2]	40	58	Azerbaïdjan
Bangladesh	2 153	2 309	2 481	47	50	58	18	28	28	Bangladesh
Brunei Darussalam	2 786	2 884	3 088	80	85	81	77	79	100	Brunéi Darussalam
Cambodia	1 841	2 129	2 382	44	52	62	22	29	37	Cambodge
China	2 562	2 867	3 036	66	86	94	55	80	96	Chine
Cyprus	2 685	2 677	2 678	85	85	80	101	110	117	Chypre
Dem. P. R. Korea	2 377	2 135	2 078	76	62	57	47	35	33	R. p. dém. de Corée
Georgia	1 849[2]	2 378	2 743	57[2]	70	74	31[2]	45	63	Géorgie
India	2 185	2 264	2 321	53	54	57	40	46	50	Inde
Indonesia	2 266	2 431	2 646	47	53	59	41	43	55	Indonésie
Iran (Islamic Rep. of)	3 010	3 137	3 143	79	86	90	66	63	81	Iran (Rép. islamique d')
Israel	3 398	3 539	3 569	113	120	125	112	128	150	Israël
Japan	2 945	2 902	2 723	97	97	90	83	90	87	Japon
Jordan	2 724	2 687	2 977	72	72	78	66	79	96	Jordanie
Kazakhstan	3 044[2]	2 396	3 284	93[2]	76	103	80[2]	72	101	Kazakhstan
Kuwait	2 281	3 490	3 681	64	101	116	67	119	126	Koweït
Kyrgyzstan	2 671[2]	2 401	2 791	81[2]	83	87	68[2]	50	65	Kirghizistan
Lao People's Dem. Rep.	2 044	2 146	2 377	49	57	65	23	27	38	Rép. dém. pop. lao
Lebanon	2 965	3 056	3 153	74	83	87	95	110	106	Liban
Malaysia	2 656	2 864	2 902	63	76	79	90	84	85	Malaisie
Maldives	2 318	2 510	2 720	75	102	99	43	61	63	Maldives
Mongolia	2 244	2 165	2 434	75	81	80	81	80	88	Mongolie
Myanmar	1 938	2 174	2 493	48	57	82	40	43	71	Myanmar
Nepal	2 161	2 257	2 443	55	58	62	35	37	46	Népal
Occupied Palest. Terr.	...	2 141	2 130	...	59	58	...	60	50	Terr. Palest. occupé
Pakistan	2 324	2 374	2 423	59	61	63	56	64	75	Pakistan
Philippines	2 290	2 412	2 580	52	55	61	41	51	52	Philippines
Republic of Korea	2 956	3 090	3 200	83	87	90	58	78	96	République de Corée
Saudi Arabia	2 885	3 126	3 076	80	84	86	87	92	78	Arabie saoudite
Sri Lanka	2 166	2 332	2 426	47	53	58	43	45	44	Sri Lanka
Syrian Arab Republic	2 896	3 103	3 212	74	74	84	82	110	117	Rép. arabe syrienne
Tajikistan	2 092[2]	1 912	2 106	58[2]	50	55	54[2]	42	58	Tadjikistan
Thailand	2 069	2 650	2 862	49	63	63	40	52	55	Thaïlande
Timor-Leste	1 837	1 902	2 076	54	51	56	32	33	43	Timor-Leste
Turkey	3 766	3 636	3 666	109	105	106	94	99	106	Turquie
Turkmenistan	2 787[2]	2 608	2 878	82[2]	79	93	69[2]	68	83	Turkménistan
United Arab Emirates	3 335	3 271	3 245	108	107	103	113	96	90	Emirats arabes unis
Uzbekistan	2 728[2]	2 376	2 618	80[2]	67	78	71[2]	66	69	Ouzbékistan
Viet Nam	1 902	2 269	2 690	45	56	75	26	40	69	Viet Nam
Yemen	2 020	2 073	2 109	55	57	57	41	41	42	Yémen

14

Food supply *(continued)*
Calories, protein and fat: average supply per capita per day
Disponibilités alimentaires
Calories, protéine et lipides : disponibilités moyennes par habitant, par jour

Region, country or area	Calories (number) Calories (nombre)			Protein (grams) Protéine (grammes)			Fat (grams) Lipides (grammes)			Region, pays ou zone
	1990	2000	2009	1990	2000	2009	1990	2000	2009	
Europe	**3 378**	**3 248**	**3 362**	**104**	**97**	**102**	**125**	**121**	**129**	**Europe**
Albania	2 656	2 842	2 903	81	94	96	64	81	96	Albanie
Austria	3 509	3 809	3 800	102	111	107	156	166	171	Autriche
Belarus	3 133[2]	2 990	3 186	97[2]	87	90	96[2]	97	123	Bélarus
Belgium	...	3 724	3 721	...	96	99	...	163	164	Belgique
Belgium-Luxembourg	3 544	...	...	104	...	...	155	...	...	Belgique-Luxembourg
Bosnia and Herzegovina	2 419[2]	2 681	3 070	70[2]	74	89	35[2]	59	77	Bosnie-Herzégovine
Bulgaria	3 133	2 816	2 791	96	86	78	102	93	101	Bulgarie
Croatia	2 412[2]	2 532	3 130	62[2]	66	85	71[2]	80	124	Croatie
Czech Republic	3 040[1]	3 076	3 305	93[1]	90	92	116[1]	112	142	République tchèque
Denmark	3 129	3 312	3 378	98	105	108	129	133	138	Danemark
Estonia	2 530[2]	3 061	3 163	103[2]	88	92	79[2]	89	90	Estonie
Finland	3 147	3 165	3 240	99	102	110	124	124	134	Finlande
France	3 515	3 608	3 531	116	118	110	161	170	166	France
Germany	3 321	3 423	3 549	98	96	102	142	146	146	Allemagne
Greece	3 539	3 608	3 661	112	118	116	139	139	154	Grèce
Hungary	3 702	3 392	3 477	101	91	88	153	143	150	Hongrie
Iceland	3 055	3 155	3 376	112	124	132	124	130	147	Islande
Ireland	3 617	3 718	3 617	112	116	111	136	139	130	Irlande
Italy	3 584	3 720	3 627	110	116	112	151	158	158	Italie
Latvia	3 275[2]	2 769	2 923	111[2]	77	86	95[2]	92	116	Lettonie
Lithuania	2 993[2]	3 201	3 486	100[2]	107	126	85[2]	77	108	Lituanie
Luxembourg	...	3 514	3 637	...	106	115	...	151	150	Luxembourg
Malta	3 078	3 422	3 438	95	112	111	106	109	114	Malte
Montenegro	...	...	2 887	...	...	77	...	...	123	Monténégro
Netherlands	3 269	3 200	3 261	96	106	107	140	140	136	Pays-Bas
Norway	3 154	3 352	3 453	98	104	108	128	137	142	Norvège
Poland	3 350	3 423	3 392	101	100	101	110	114	115	Pologne
Portugal	3 393	3 534	3 617	102	113	119	123	133	148	Portugal
Republic of Moldova	2 571[2]	2 432	2 707	69[2]	60	69	80[2]	68	76	Rép. de Moldova
Romania	3 149	3 170	3 487	97	96	112	103	92	107	Roumanie
Russian Federation	2 927[2]	2 889	3 172	92[2]	85	100	81[2]	76	95	Fédération de Russie
Serbia	...	...	2 823	...	...	80	...	...	88	Serbie
Serbia and Montenegro	2 985[2]	2 654	...	88[2]	77	...	124[2]	115	...	Serbie-et-Monténégro
Slovakia	2 784[1]	2 797	2 881	79[1]	72	73	100[1]	97	107	Slovaquie
Slovenia	2 670[2]	3 056	3 275	77[2]	103	103	94[2]	108	126	Slovénie
Spain	3 279	3 375	3 239	105	111	106	139	153	151	Espagne
Sweden	2 974	3 101	3 125	96	102	108	122	123	128	Suède
Switzerland	3 424	3 442	3 454	97	94	95	155	150	153	Suisse
TFYR of Macedonia	2 418[2]	2 801	2 957	70[2]	73	77	60[2]	85	109	L'ex-R.Y. Macédoine
Ukraine	3 366[2]	2 896	3 198	94[2]	80	88	92[2]	72	95	Ukraine
United Kingdom	3 244	3 372	3 432	94	100	104	137	141	142	Royaume-Uni
Oceania	**3 142**	**3 010**	**3 211**	**105**	**96**	**98**	**126**	**126**	**138**	**Océanie**
Australia	3 177	3 014	3 261	110	101	102	128	132	147	Australie
Fiji	2 677	2 847	2 996	69	73	73	97	96	102	Fidji

14 Disponibilités alimentaires
Calories, protéine et lipides : disponibilités moyennes par habitant, par jour

Region, country or area	Calories (number) Calories (nombre)			Protein (grams) Protéine (grammes)			Fat (grams) Lipides (grammes)			Region, pays ou zone
	1990	2000	2009	1990	2000	2009	1990	2000	2009	
French Polynesia	2 810	2 791	2 942	84	92	98	101	114	128	Polynésie française
Kiribati	2 587	2 763	2 866	63	69	74	92	103	103	Kiribati
New Caledonia	2 814	2 742	2 826	78	77	84	100	108	114	Nouvelle-Calédonie
New Zealand	3 254	3 153	3 172	101	88	94	133	113	120	Nouvelle-Zélande
Samoa	2 616	2 753	2 997	71	75	80	117	125	143	Samoa
Solomon Islands	2 125	2 366	2 439	52	52	55	46	45	49	Iles Salomon
Vanuatu	2 580	2 700	2 841	61	64	67	103	97	102	Vanuatu

Source:
Food and Agriculture Organization of the United Nations (FAO), Rome, FAOSTAT database, last accessed February 2013.

Source:
Organisation des Nations Unies pour l'alimentation et l'agriculture (FAO), Rome, les données des FAOSTAT, dernier accès février 2013.

1   The data is from 1993.
2   The data is from 1992.

1   Les données sont pour 1993.
2   Les données sont pour 1992.

Population below the minimum level of dietary energy consumption
Population undernourished, total in millions and percentage

Population n'atteignant pas le niveau minimal d'apport calorique
Population sous-alimentée, total en milliers et pourcentage

Country or area	Millions - Millions				Percentage - Pourcentage				Pays ou zone
	1990-1992	1995-1997	2000-2002	2006-2008	1990-1992	1995-1997	2000-2002	2006-2008	
Albania	^0	^0	^0	^0	5[1]	5[1]	5[1]	5[1]	Albanie
Algeria	^0	2	1	^0	5[1]	5[1]	5[1]	5[1]	Algérie
Angola	7	8	8	7	67	61	52	41	Angola
Antigua and Barbuda	^0	^0	^0	^0	12	29	35	21	Antigua-et-Barbuda
Argentina	^0	^0	^0	^0	5[1]	5[1]	5[1]	5[1]	Argentine
Armenia	2	1	1	1	45	36	28	21	Arménie
Australia	^0	^0	^0	^0	5[1]	5[1]	5[1]	5[1]	Australie
Austria	^0	^0	^0	^0	5[1]	5[1]	5[1]	5[1]	Autriche
Azerbaijan	2	2	1	^0	27	27	11	5[1]	Azerbaïdjan
Bahamas	^0	^0	^0	^0	7	8	5[1]	6	Bahamas
Bangladesh	44	54	42	41	38	41	30	26	Bangladesh
Barbados	^0	^0	^0	^0	5[1]	5[1]	5[1]	5[1]	Barbade
Belarus	^0	^0	^0	^0	5[1]	5[1]	5[1]	5[1]	Bélarus
Belgium	^0	^0	^0	^0	5[1]	5[1]	5[1]	5[1]	Belgique
Belize	^0	^0	^0	^0	7	8	7	5[1]	Belize
Benin	1	1	1	1	20	18	15	12	Bénin
Bermuda	...	...	...	...	5[1]	5[1]	5[1]	5[1]	Bermudes
Bolivia (Plurin. State of)	2	2	2	3	29	24	22	27	Bolivie (État plurin. de)
Bosnia and Herzegovina	^0	^0	^0	^0	5[1]	5[1]	5[1]	5[1]	Bosnie-Herzégovine
Botswana	^0	^0	1	1	19	23	27	25	Botswana
Brazil	17	17	16	12	11	10	9	6	Brésil
Brunei Darussalam	^0	^0	^0	^0	5[1]	5[1]	5[1]	5[1]	Brunéi Darussalam
Bulgaria	^0	^0	^0	^0	5[1]	5[1]	5[1]	5[1]	Bulgarie
Burkina Faso	1	1	1	1	14	12	12	8	Burkina Faso
Burundi	3	4	4	5	44	56	59	62	Burundi
Cambodia	4	5	4	4	38	40	29	25	Cambodge
Cameroon	4	5	4	4	33	34	26	22	Cameroun
Canada	^0	^0	^0	^0	5[1]	5[1]	5[1]	5[1]	Canada
Cape Verde	^0	^0	^0	^0	12	14	15	11	Cap-Vert
Central African Rep.	1	2	2	2	44	47	43	40	Rép. centrafricaine
Chad	4	4	4	4	60	53	43	39	Tchad
Chile	1	^0	^0	^0	7	5[1]	5[1]	5[1]	Chili
China[2]	210	142	133	130	18	12	10	10	Chine[2]
Colombia	5	4	4	4	15	11	10	9	Colombie
Comoros	^0	^0	^0	^0	38	47	54	47	Comores
Congo	1	1	1	1	42	41	20	13	Congo
Costa Rica	^0	^0	^0	^0	5[1]	5[1]	5[1]	5[1]	Costa Rica
Côte d'Ivoire	2	3	3	3	15	17	17	14	Côte d'Ivoire
Croatia	^0	^0	^0	^0	5[1]	5[1]	5[1]	5[1]	Croatie
Cuba	1	2	^0	^0	6	14	5[1]	5[1]	Cuba
Cyprus	^0	^0	^0	^0	5[1]	5[1]	5[1]	5[1]	Chypre
Czech Republic	^0	^0	^0	^0	5[1]	5[1]	5[1]	5[1]	République tchèque
Dem. P. R. Korea	4	7	8	8	21	30	34	35	R. p. dém. de Corée
Denmark	^0	^0	^0	^0	5[1]	5[1]	5[1]	5[1]	Danemark
Djibouti	^0	^0	^0	^0	60	50	40	26	Djibouti

15

Population below the minimum level of dietary energy consumption *(continued)*
Population undernourished, total in millions and percentage

Population n'atteignant pas le niveau minimal d'apport calorique *(suite)*
Population sous-alimentée, en milliers et pourcentage

Country or area	Millions - Millions				Percentage - Pourcentage				Pays ou zone
	1990-1992	1995-1997	2000-2002	2006-2008	1990-1992	1995-1997	2000-2002	2006-2008	
Dominica	^0	^0	^0	^0	5[1]	5[1]	5[1]	5[1]	Dominique
Dominican Republic	2	2	2	2	28	26	25	24	Rép. dominicaine
Ecuador	2	2	2	2	23	16	17	15	Equateur
Egypt	^0	^0	^0	^0	5[1]	5[1]	5[1]	5[1]	Egypte
El Salvador	1	1	^0	1	13	12	7	9	El Salvador
Eritrea	2[3]	2	3	3	67[3]	64	70	65	Erythrée [3]
Estonia	^0	^0	^0	^0	10	5[1]	5[1]	5[1]	Estonie
Ethiopia	35[3]	36	33	33	69[3]	62	48	41	Ethiopie
Fiji	^0	^0	^0	^0	8	5[1]	5[1]	5[1]	Fidji
Finland	^0	^0	^0	^0	5[1]	5[1]	5[1]	5[1]	Finlande
France	^0	^0	^0	^0	5[1]	5[1]	5[1]	5[1]	France
French Polynesia	^0	^0	^0	^0	10	5[1]	5[1]	5[1]	Polynésie française
Gabon	^0	^0	^0	^0	6	5[1]	5[1]	5[1]	Gabon
Gambia	^0	^0	^0	^0	14	23	21	19	Gambie
Georgia	3	1	1	^0	58	19	12	6	Géorgie
Germany	^0	^0	^0	^0	5[1]	5[1]	5[1]	5[1]	Allemagne
Ghana	4	2	2	1	28	13	9	5[1]	Ghana
Greece	^0	^0	^0	^0	5[1]	5[1]	5[1]	5[1]	Grèce
Grenada	^0	^0	^0	^0	13	18	24	21	Grenade
Guatemala	1	2	3	3	15	20	22	22	Guatemala
Guinea	1	2	2	2	20	19	20	16	Guinée
Guinea-Bissau	^0	^0	^0	^0	22	26	25	22	Guinée-Bissau
Guyana	^0	^0	^0	^0	20	11	7	8	Guyana
Haiti	5	5	5	6	63	60	53	57	Haïti
Honduras	1	1	1	1	19	16	14	12	Honduras
Hungary	^0	^0	^0	^0	5[1]	5[1]	5[1]	5[1]	Hongrie
Iceland	^0	^0	^0	^0	5[1]	5[1]	5[1]	5[1]	Islande
India	177	167	208	225	20	17	20	19	Inde
Indonesia	29	22	30	30	16	11	15	13	Indonésie
Iran (Islamic Rep. of)	^0	^0	^0	^0	5[1]	5[1]	5[1]	5[1]	Iran (Rép. islamique d')
Ireland	^0	^0	^0	^0	5[1]	5[1]	5[1]	5[1]	Irlande
Israel	^0	^0	^0	^0	5[1]	5[1]	5[1]	5[1]	Israël
Italy	^0	^0	^0	^0	5[1]	5[1]	5[1]	5[1]	Italie
Jamaica	^0	^0	^0	^0	11	6	5[1]	5[1]	Jamaïque
Japan	^0	^0	^0	^0	5[1]	5[1]	5[1]	5[1]	Japon
Jordan	^0	^0	^0	^0	5[1]	5[1]	5[1]	5[1]	Jordanie
Kazakhstan	^0	^0	1	^0	5[1]	5[1]	8	5[1]	Kazakhstan
Kenya	8	9	11	12	33	32	33	33	Kenya
Kiribati	^0	^0	^0	^0	8	6	5[1]	5[1]	Kiribati
Kuwait	^0	^0	^0	^0	20	5	6	5	Koweït
Kyrgyzstan	1	1	1	1	17	13	17	11	Kirghizistan
Lao People's Dem. Rep.	1	1	1	1	31	29	26	22	Rép. dém. pop. lao
Latvia	^0	^0	^0	^0	5[1]	5[1]	5[1]	5[1]	Lettonie
Lebanon	^0	^0	^0	^0	5[1]	5[1]	5[1]	5[1]	Liban
Lesotho	^0	^0	^0	^0	15	16	14	14	Lesotho
Liberia	1	1	1	1	30	32	36	32	Libéria
Libyan Arab Jamah.	^0	^0	^0	^0	5[1]	5[1]	5[1]	5[1]	Jamah. arabe libyenne
Lithuania	^0	^0	^0	^0	5[1]	5[1]	5[1]	5[1]	Lituanie

15

Population below the minimum level of dietary energy consumption *(continued)*
Population undernourished, total in millions and percentage

Population n'atteignant pas le niveau minimal d'apport calorique *(suite)*
Population sous-alimentée, en milliers et pourcentage

Country or area	Millions - Millions				Percentage - Pourcentage				Pays ou zone
	1990-1992	1995-1997	2000-2002	2006-2008	1990-1992	1995-1997	2000-2002	2006-2008	
Luxembourg	^0	^0	^0	^0	5[1]	5[1]	5[1]	5[1]	Luxembourg
Madagascar	2	4	4	5	21	26	28	25	Madagascar
Malawi	4	4	4	4	43	36	30	27	Malawi
Malaysia	^0	^0	^0	^0	5[1]	5[1]	5[1]	5[1]	Malaisie
Maldives	^0	^0	^0	^0	9	9	8	10	Maldives
Mali	2	3	2	2	27	25	18	12	Mali
Malta	^0	^0	^0	^0	5[1]	5[1]	5[1]	5[1]	Malte
Mauritania	^0	^0	^0	^0	12	9	8	8	Mauritanie
Mauritius	^0	^0	^0	^0	7	7	5[1]	5[1]	Maurice
Mexico	^0	^0	^0	^0	5[1]	5[1]	5[1]	5[1]	Mexique
Mongolia	1	1	1	1	28	33	27	27	Mongolie
Montenegro	^0	^0	^0	^0	5[1]	5[1]	5[1]	5[1]	Monténégro
Morocco	2	2	2	^0	6	6	6	5[1]	Maroc
Mozambique	8	8	9	8	59	47	46	38	Mozambique
Namibia	1	1	^0	^0	32	30	21	18	Namibie
Nepal	4	4	5	5	21	20	18	17	Népal
Netherlands	^0	^0	^0	^0	5[1]	5[1]	5[1]	5[1]	Pays-Bas
Netherlands Antilles	^0	^0	^0	^0	8	5[1]	5[1]	5[1]	Antilles néerlandaises
New Caledonia	^0	^0	^0	^0	8	9	8	8	Nouvelle-Calédonie
New Zealand	^0	^0	^0	^0	5[1]	5[1]	5[1]	5[1]	Nouvelle-Zélande
Nicaragua	2	2	1	1	50	38	25	19	Nicaragua
Niger	3	4	3	2	37	37	27	16	Niger
Nigeria	16	11	12	9	16	10	9	6	Nigéria
Norway	^0	^0	^0	^0	5[1]	5[1]	5[1]	5[1]	Norvège
Occ. Palestinian Terr.	^0	^0	1	1	10	10	15	21	Terr. palestinien occ.
Pakistan	30	27	36	43	25	20	24	25	Pakistan
Panama	1	1	1	1	18	20	19	15	Panama
Paraguay	1	1	1	1	16	10	10	10	Paraguay
Peru	6	5	5	5	27	21	18	16	Pérou
Philippines	15	14	15	12	24	20	18	13	Philippines
Poland	^0	^0	^0	^0	5[1]	5[1]	5[1]	5[1]	Pologne
Portugal	^0	^0	^0	^0	5[1]	5[1]	5[1]	5[1]	Portugal
Republic of Korea	^0	^0	^0	^0	5[1]	5[1]	5[1]	5[1]	République de Corée
Republic of Moldova	^0	^0	^0	^0	5[1]	5[1]	5[1]	5[1]	Rép. de Moldova
Romania	^0	^0	^0	^0	5[1]	5[1]	5[1]	5[1]	Roumanie
Russian Federation	^0	^0	^0	^0	5[1]	5[1]	5[1]	5[1]	Fédération de Russie
Rwanda	3	3	3	3	44	53	38	32	Rwanda
Saint Kitts and Nevis	^0	^0	^0	^0	11	16	14	16	Saint-Kitts-et-Nevis
Saint Lucia	^0	^0	^0	^0	9	7	8	8	Sainte-Lucie
St. Vincent-Grenadines	^0	^0	^0	^0	16	16	9	5	St. Vincent-Grenadines
Samoa	^0	^0	^0	^0	9	10	5[1]	5[1]	Samoa
Sao Tome and Principe	^0	^0	^0	^0	14	15	8	5[1]	Sao Tomé-et-Principe
Saudi Arabia	^0	^0	^0	^0	5[1]	5[1]	5[1]	5[1]	Arabie saoudite
Senegal	2	2	3	2	22	26	26	19	Sénégal
Serbia	^0	^0	^0	^0	5[1]	5[1]	5[1]	5[1]	Serbie
Serbia and Montenegro	^0	^0	^0	^0	5[1]	5[1]	5[1]	5[1]	Serbie-et-Monténégro
Seychelles	^0	^0	^0	^0	11	10	8	8	Seychelles
Sierra Leone	2	2	2	2	45	39	43	35	Sierra Leone

15 Population below the minimum level of dietary energy consumption *(continued)*
Population undernourished, total in millions and percentage

Population n'atteignant pas le niveau minimal d'apport calorique *(suite)*
Population sous-alimentée, en milliers et pourcentage

Country or area	Millions - Millions				Percentage - Pourcentage				Pays ou zone
	1990-1992	1995-1997	2000-2002	2006-2008	1990-1992	1995-1997	2000-2002	2006-2008	
Slovakia	^0	^0	^0	^0	5[1]	5[1]	5[1]	5[1]	Slovaquie
Slovenia	^0	^0	^0	^0	5[1]	5[1]	5[1]	5[1]	Slovénie
Solomon Islands	^0	^0	^0	^0	21	13	12	11	Iles Salomon
South Africa	^0	^0	^0	^0	5[1]	5[1]	5[1]	5[1]	Afrique du Sud
Spain	^0	^0	^0	^0	5[1]	5[1]	5[1]	5[1]	Espagne
Sri Lanka	5	5	4	4	28	25	20	20	Sri Lanka
Sudan	11	9	10	9	39	29	28	22	Soudan
Suriname	^0	^0	^0	^0	14	13	15	15	Suriname
Swaziland	^0	^0	^0	^0	12	21	18	19	Swaziland
Sweden	^0	^0	^0	^0	5[1]	5[1]	5[1]	5[1]	Suède
Switzerland	^0	^0	^0	^0	5[1]	5[1]	5[1]	5[1]	Suisse
Syrian Arab Republic	^0	^0	^0	^0	5[1]	5[1]	5[1]	5[1]	Rép. arabe syrienne
Tajikistan	2	2	3	2	34	42	46	26	Tadjikistan
Thailand	15	11	12	11	26	18	18	16	Thaïlande
TFYR of Macedonia	^0	^0	^0	^0	5[1]	5[1]	5[1]	5[1]	L'ex-R.Y. Macédoine
Timor-Leste	^0	^0	^0	^0	39	32	28	31	Timor-Leste
Togo	2	2	2	2	43	36	36	30	Togo
Trinidad and Tobago	^0	^0	^0	^0	11	14	11	11	Trinité-et-Tobago
Tunisia	^0	^0	^0	^0	5[1]	5[1]	5[1]	5[1]	Tunisie
Turkey	^0	^0	^0	^0	5[1]	5[1]	5[1]	5[1]	Turquie
Turkmenistan	^0	^0	^0	^0	9	9	9	7	Turkménistan
Uganda	4	5	5	7	19	23	19	22	Ouganda
Ukraine	^0	^0	^0	^0	5[1]	5[1]	5[1]	5[1]	Ukraine
United Arab Emirates	^0	^0	^0	^0	5[1]	5[1]	5[1]	5[1]	Emirats arabes unis
United Kingdom	^0	^0	^0	^0	5[1]	5[1]	5[1]	5[1]	Royaume-Uni
United Rep. of Tanzania	8	13	14	14	29	42	40	34	Rép.-Unie de Tanzanie
United States	^0	^0	^0	^0	5[1]	5[1]	5[1]	5[1]	Etats-Unis
Uruguay	^0	^0	^0	^0	5[1]	5[1]	5[1]	5[1]	Uruguay
Uzbekistan	1	1	5	3	5[1]	5[1]	19	11	Ouzbékistan
Vanuatu	^0	^0	^0	^0	10	9	8	5[1]	Vanuatu
Venezuela (Bol. Rep. of)	2	3	3	2	10	14	13	7	Venezuela (Rép. bol. du)
Viet Nam	21	17	13	10	31	22	17	11	Viet Nam
Yemen	4	5	6	7	30	31	31	30	Yémen
Zambia	3	4	5	5	35	38	43	44	Zambie
Zimbabwe	4	5	5	4	40	44	41	30	Zimbabwe

Source:
Food and Agricultural Organization of the United Nations (FAO), Rome, FAOSTAT database last accessed July 2012

1　Data less than 5%.
2　Data include those for Hong Kong Special Administrative Region (Hong Kong SAR), Macao Special Administrative Region (Macao SAR) and Taiwan Province of China.
3　Eritrea and Ethiopia were not separate entities in 1990-1992 but estimates of the number and proportion of undernourished in the former Ethiopia PDR are included in regional and sub-regional aggregates for that period.

Source:
Organisation des Nations Unies pour l'alimentation et l'agriculture (FAO), Rome, la base de données FAOSTAT, dernier accès juillet 2012.

1　Les données représentent moins de 5%.
2　Les données comprennent les chiffres pour la Région Administrative Spéciale de Hong Kong (Hong Kong RAS), la Région Administrative Spéciale de Macao (Macao RAS) et la province de Taiwan.
3　L'Érythrée et l'Éthiopie n'étaient pas des entités distinctes en 1990-1992 mais les effectifs et les proportions estimatifs de personnes sous alimentées dans l'ex-République démocratique populaire d'Éthiopie sont inclus dans les chiffres globaux de la sous-région et de la région de la période.

Cellular mobile telephone subscribers
Number (thousands) and per 100 inhabitants

Abonnés au téléphone mobile
Nombre (milliers) et pour 100 habitants

Country or area	2004	2005	2006	2007	2008	2009	2010	2011	Pays ou zone
Afghanistan									**Afghanistan**
Number (thousands)	600	1 200	2 520	4 668	7 899	10 500[1]	13 000[1]	17 558	Nombre (en milliers)
Per 100 inhabitants	2	4	9	16	26	34[1]	41[1]	54	Pour 100 habitants
Albania									**Albanie**
Number (thousands)	1 260	1 530	1 910	2 322	#1 860[2]	2 464[1]	2 692[1]	3 100	Nombre (en milliers)
Per 100 inhabitants	40	49	61	73	#58[2]	77[1]	84[1]	96	Pour 100 habitants
Algeria									**Algérie**
Number (thousands)	4 882	13 661	20 998	27 563	27 031	32 730	32 780	35 616	Nombre (en milliers)
Per 100 inhabitants	15	42	63	81	79	94	92	99	Pour 100 habitants
American Samoa									**Samoa américaines**
Number (thousands)	2	...	...	...	...	...	...	...	Nombre (en milliers)
Per 100 inhabitants	4	...	...	...	...	...	...	...	Pour 100 habitants
Andorra									**Andorre**
Number (thousands)	58	65	69	64	64	65	65	65	Nombre (en milliers)
Per 100 inhabitants	78	83	86	78	78	77	77	75	Pour 100 habitants
Angola									**Angola**
Number (thousands)	740	1 611	3 055[3]	4 962	6 773	8 109	8 909[1]	9 491[1]	Nombre (en milliers)
Per 100 inhabitants	5	10	18[3]	28	38	44	47[1]	48[1]	Pour 100 habitants
Anguilla									**Anguilla**
Number (thousands)	7[4]	13[4]	17	24	26	25	26	26	Nombre (en milliers)
Per 100 inhabitants	55[4]	96[4]	122	163	180	165	167	166	Pour 100 habitants
Antigua and Barbuda									**Antigua-et-Barbuda**
Number (thousands)	54	86	110	112	137	135[5]	168	163	Nombre (en milliers)
Per 100 inhabitants	65	102	130	131	157	154[5]	189	182	Pour 100 habitants
Argentina									**Argentine**
Number (thousands)	13 512	22 156	31 510	40 402	46 509	52 483	53 700[1]	55 000[1]	Nombre (en milliers)
Per 100 inhabitants	35	57	81	103	117	131	133[1]	135[1]	Pour 100 habitants
Armenia									**Arménie**
Number (thousands)	203	318	1 260	1 876	1 442	2 192	3 865	3 211[6]	Nombre (en milliers)
Per 100 inhabitants	7	10	41	61	47	71	125	104[6]	Pour 100 habitants
Aruba									**Aruba**
Number (thousands)	98	103	109	114	121	128[1]	132[1]	...	Nombre (en milliers)
Per 100 inhabitants	99	102	106	109	114	120[1]	123[1]	...	Pour 100 habitants
Australia									**Australie**
Number (thousands)	16 480	18 420	19 760	21 260	22 120[7]	22 200	22 500	24 490	Nombre (en milliers)
Per 100 inhabitants	82	90	95	101	103[7]	101	101	108	Pour 100 habitants
Austria									**Autriche**
Number (thousands)	7 992	8 665	9 281[8]	9 912[8]	10 816	11 434	12 241	13 023	Nombre (en milliers)
Per 100 inhabitants	98	105	112[8]	119[8]	130	137	146	155	Pour 100 habitants
Azerbaijan									**Azerbaïdjan**
Number (thousands)	1 457	2 242	3 324	4 519	6 548	7 757	9 100	10 120	Nombre (en milliers)
Per 100 inhabitants	17	26	38	51	73	86	99	109	Pour 100 habitants
Bahamas									**Bahamas**
Number (thousands)	186	228	253	374	358[9]	359	428	299[10]	Nombre (en milliers)
Per 100 inhabitants	59	71	78	114	107[9]	106	125	86[10]	Pour 100 habitants
Bahrain									**Bahreïn**
Number (thousands)	650	767	907	1 116	1 441	1 402	1 567	1 694	Nombre (en milliers)
Per 100 inhabitants	97	106	112	121	137	120	124	128	Pour 100 habitants
Bangladesh									**Bangladesh**
Number (thousands)	2 782	9 000	19 131	34 370[11]	44 640	52 430[12]	68 650	85 000[1]	Nombre (en milliers)
Per 100 inhabitants	2	6	13	24[11]	31	36[12]	46	56[1]	Pour 100 habitants
Barbados									**Barbade**
Number (thousands)	200	206	237	258	289	337	350	348	Nombre (en milliers)
Per 100 inhabitants	74	76	87	95	106	124	128	127	Pour 100 habitants
Belarus									**Bélarus**
Number (thousands)	2 239	4 100	5 960	6 960	8 128	9 686	10 333	10 695	Nombre (en milliers)
Per 100 inhabitants	23	42	61	72	84	101	108	112	Pour 100 habitants
Belgium									**Belgique**
Number (thousands)	9 132	9 605	9 847	10 738	11 342[13]	11 775[13]	12 154[13]	12 541	Nombre (en milliers)
Per 100 inhabitants	88	92	94	102	107[13]	110[13]	113[13]	117	Pour 100 habitants

16

Cellular mobile telephone subscribers *(continued)*
Number (thousands) and per 100 inhabitants
Abonnés au téléphone mobile *(suite)*
Nombre (milliers) et pour 100 habitants

Country or area	2004	2005	2006	2007	2008	2009	2010	2011	Pays ou zone
Belize									**Belize**
Number (thousands)	75[1]	96[1]	118[1]	118	160	162	194[14]	203[15]	Nombre (en milliers)
Per 100 inhabitants	27[1]	34[1]	41[1]	40	53	53	62[14]	64[15]	Pour 100 habitants
Benin									**Bénin**
Number (thousands)	459	596	1 056	2 052	3 625	5 033	7 075	7 765	Nombre (en milliers)
Per 100 inhabitants	6	8	13	25	43	59	80	85	Pour 100 habitants
Bermuda									**Bermudes**
Number (thousands)	49	53	60	69[1]	79[1]	85[1]	88[1]	...	Nombre (en milliers)
Per 100 inhabitants	77	82	93	107[1]	122[1]	131[1]	136[1]	...	Pour 100 habitants
Bhutan									**Bhoutan**
Number (thousands)	19	36	82	149	253	339[16]	394[16]	484[16]	Nombre (en milliers)
Per 100 inhabitants	3	5	12	22	36	47[16]	54[16]	66[16]	Pour 100 habitants
Bolivia (Plurin. State of)									**Bolivie (État plurinational de)**
Number (thousands)	1 801	2 421	2 876	3 254	5 039	6 464	7 179	8 353	Nombre (en milliers)
Per 100 inhabitants	20	26	31	34	52	66	72	83	Pour 100 habitants
Bosnia and Herzegovina									**Bosnie-Herzégovine**
Number (thousands)	1 407	1 594	1 888	2 450	3 179	3 257	3 110	3 171	Nombre (en milliers)
Per 100 inhabitants	37	42	50	65	84	86	83	85	Pour 100 habitants
Botswana									**Botswana**
Number (thousands)	523	564	823	1 152	1 486	1 874	2 363	2 900	Nombre (en milliers)
Per 100 inhabitants	28	30	43	60	76	95	118	143	Pour 100 habitants
Brazil									**Brésil**
Number (thousands)	65 605	86 210	99 919	120 980	150 641	173 959	202 944	242 232	Nombre (en milliers)
Per 100 inhabitants	36	46	53	64	79	90	104	123	Pour 100 habitants
British Virgin Islands									**Iles Vierges britanniques**
Number (thousands)	...	...	...	21	23	46	47	...	Nombre (en milliers)
Per 100 inhabitants	...	...	...	92	101	200	201	...	Pour 100 habitants
Brunei Darussalam									**Brunéi Darussalam**
Number (thousands)	202	233	301	366	399	413	435	443	Nombre (en milliers)
Per 100 inhabitants	57	64	81	97	104	105	109	109	Pour 100 habitants
Bulgaria									**Bulgarie**
Number (thousands)	4 730	6 245	8 253	9 897	10 429	10 455	10 200	10 475	Nombre (en milliers)
Per 100 inhabitants	61	81	107	130	137	139	136	141	Pour 100 habitants
Burkina Faso									**Burkina Faso**
Number (thousands)	396	634	1 017	1 858	3 024	3 824	5 708	7 682	Nombre (en milliers)
Per 100 inhabitants	3	4	7	12	19	24	35	45	Pour 100 habitants
Burundi									**Burundi**
Number (thousands)	101	153	200[1]	270	481	838	1 151[1]	1 240[1]	Nombre (en milliers)
Per 100 inhabitants	1	2	3[1]	4	6	10	14[1]	14[1]	Pour 100 habitants
Cambodia									**Cambodge**
Number (thousands)	862	1 062	1 722	2 583	4 237	6 268	8 151	10 000	Nombre (en milliers)
Per 100 inhabitants	7	8	13	19	31	45	58	70	Pour 100 habitants
Cameroon									**Cameroun**
Number (thousands)	1 531	2 253	3 136	4 536[1]	6 161	8 004	8 637	10 487	Nombre (en milliers)
Per 100 inhabitants	9	13	17	25[1]	33	42	44	52	Pour 100 habitants
Canada									**Canada**
Number (thousands)	15 020	17 017	18 749	20 277	22 093	23 812	24 037[17]	25 858[1]	Nombre (en milliers)
Per 100 inhabitants	47	53	57	61	66	71	71[17]	75[1]	Pour 100 habitants
Cape Verde									**Cap-Vert**
Number (thousands)	66	82	109	152[1]	278	291	372	396	Nombre (en milliers)
Per 100 inhabitants	14	17	23	32[1]	57	59	75	79	Pour 100 habitants
Cayman Islands									**Iles Caïmanes**
Number (thousands)	34	81[18]	93[18]	101[18]	98[19]	109[18]	100[18]	95[18]	Nombre (en milliers)
Per 100 inhabitants	67	155[18]	172[18]	186[18]	178[19]	195[18]	178[18]	168[18]	Pour 100 habitants
Central African Rep.									**Rép. centrafricaine**
Number (thousands)	60	100	110[1]	200[1]	250[1]	680	979	1 124	Nombre (en milliers)
Per 100 inhabitants	2	2	3[1]	5[1]	6[1]	16	22	25	Pour 100 habitants
Chad									**Tchad**
Number (thousands)	123	210	466	918[1]	1 600	2 281	2 875	3 666	Nombre (en milliers)
Per 100 inhabitants	1	2	5	9[1]	15	21	26	32	Pour 100 habitants

Country or area	2004	2005	2006	2007	2008	2009	2010	2011	Pays ou zone
Chile									**Chili**
Number (thousands)	9 261	10 570	12 451	13 955	14 797	16 450	19 852	22 400	Nombre (en milliers)
Per 100 inhabitants	57	65	76	84	88	97	116	130	Pour 100 habitants
China [20]									**Chine** [20]
Number (thousands)	334 824	393 406	461 058	547 306	641 245	747 214	859 003	986 253	Nombre (en milliers)
Per 100 inhabitants	26	30	35	41	48	56	64	73	Pour 100 habitants
China, Hong Kong SAR									**Chine, Hong Kong RAS**
Number (thousands)	8 214	8 544	9 444	10 752[21]	11 580	12 597	13 794	14 931	Nombre (en milliers)
Per 100 inhabitants	121	125	138	156[21]	167	180	196	210	Pour 100 habitants
China, Macao SAR									**Chine, Macao RAS**
Number (thousands)	432	533	636	794	933	1 037	1 122	1 353	Nombre (en milliers)
Per 100 inhabitants	92	111	129	157	180	195	206	243	Pour 100 habitants
Colombia									**Colombie**
Number (thousands)	10 401	21 850	29 763	33 941	41 365	42 160	44 478	46 200	Nombre (en milliers)
Per 100 inhabitants	25	51	68	77	92	92	96	98	Pour 100 habitants
Comoros									**Comores**
Number (thousands)	8	16	37	62	92	123	165	216	Nombre (en milliers)
Per 100 inhabitants	1	2	6	9	13	17	22	29	Pour 100 habitants
Congo									**Congo**
Number (thousands)	384	558	917	1 288[1]	1 807[1]	2 171[1]	3 799	3 885	Nombre (en milliers)
Per 100 inhabitants	11	16	25	35[1]	47[1]	51[1]	99	94	Pour 100 habitants
Costa Rica									**Costa Rica**
Number (thousands)	923	1 101	1 444	1 508	1 887	1 950	3 035	4 358	Nombre (en milliers)
Per 100 inhabitants	22	26	33	34	42	42	65	92	Pour 100 habitants
Côte d'Ivoire									**Côte d'Ivoire**
Number (thousands)	1 674	2 349	4 065	7 468	10 449	13 184	15 599	17 416	Nombre (en milliers)
Per 100 inhabitants	9	13	22	40	55	68	79	86	Pour 100 habitants
Croatia									**Croatie**
Number (thousands)	2 836	3 650	4 395	5 035	#4 555[2]	4 675[1]	4 928[1]	5 115	Nombre (en milliers)
Per 100 inhabitants	64	82	99	114	#103[2]	106[1]	112[1]	116	Pour 100 habitants
Cuba									**Cuba**
Number (thousands)	76	136	153	198	332	621	1 003	1 315	Nombre (en milliers)
Per 100 inhabitants	1	1	1	2	3	6	9	12	Pour 100 habitants
Cyprus									**Chypre**
Number (thousands)	658	783	868	988	1 017	978	1 034	1 091	Nombre (en milliers)
Per 100 inhabitants	65	76	83	93	94	90	94	98	Pour 100 habitants
Czech Republic									**République tchèque**
Number (thousands)	10 783	11 776	12 406	13 229	13 780	14 258[22]	#12 775[23]	12 810	Nombre (en milliers)
Per 100 inhabitants	106	115	121	128	133	137[22]	#122[23]	122	Pour 100 habitants
Dem. P. R. Korea									**R. p. dém. de Corée**
Number (thousands)	0	0	0	0	0	69[12]	432	1 000[1]	Nombre (en milliers)
Per 100 inhabitants	0	0	0	0	0	^0[12]	2	4[1]	Pour 100 habitants
Dem. Rep. of the Congo									**Rép. dém. du Congo**
Number (thousands)	1 991[24]	2 746[24]	4 415[24]	6 592[24]	9 938[24]	#9 459[25]	11 820	15 673	Nombre (en milliers)
Per 100 inhabitants	4[24]	5[24]	7[24]	11[24]	16[24]	#15[25]	18	23	Pour 100 habitants
Denmark									**Danemark**
Number (thousands)	5 167	5 449	5 828	6 308[7]	6 557	6 834	6 981	7 047	Nombre (en milliers)
Per 100 inhabitants	96	101	107	115[7]	119	124	126	126	Pour 100 habitants
Djibouti									**Djibouti**
Number (thousands)	34	44	45	70	113	129	166	193	Nombre (en milliers)
Per 100 inhabitants	4	5	5	8	13	15	19	21	Pour 100 habitants
Dominica									**Dominique**
Number (thousands)	42	52	72	89	91	99	*106	111[1]	Nombre (en milliers)
Per 100 inhabitants	61	75	104	130	134	145	*156	164[1]	Pour 100 habitants
Dominican Republic									**Rép. dominicaine**
Number (thousands)	2 534	3 623	4 606	5 513	7 210	8 630	8 893	8 771	Nombre (en milliers)
Per 100 inhabitants	28	39	49	58	75	88	90	87	Pour 100 habitants
Ecuador									**Equateur**
Number (thousands)	3 544	6 246	8 485	9 940	11 684	13 242	14 781	15 333	Nombre (en milliers)
Per 100 inhabitants	27	47	62	72	83	93	102	105	Pour 100 habitants

16

Cellular mobile telephone subscribers *(continued)*
Number (thousands) and per 100 inhabitants
Abonnés au téléphone mobile *(suite)*
Nombre (milliers) et pour 100 habitants

Country or area	2004	2005	2006	2007	2008	2009	2010	2011	Pays ou zone
Egypt									**Egypte**
Number (thousands)	7 643	13 630	18 001	30 094	41 287	55 352	70 661	83 425	Nombre (en milliers)
Per 100 inhabitants	10	18	24	39	53	69	87	101	Pour 100 habitants
El Salvador									**El Salvador**
Number (thousands)	1 833	2 412	3 852	6 137	6 951	7 566	7 700[26]	7 837[1]	Nombre (en milliers)
Per 100 inhabitants	30	40	63	101	113	123	124[26]	126[1]	Pour 100 habitants
Equatorial Guinea									**Guinée équatoriale**
Number (thousands)	62	97	120[1]	150[1]	180[1]	200[1]	399	426[1]	Nombre (en milliers)
Per 100 inhabitants	10	16	19[1]	23[1]	27[1]	29[1]	57	59[1]	Pour 100 habitants
Eritrea									**Erythrée**
Number (thousands)	20	40	62	84	109	141	185	242	Nombre (en milliers)
Per 100 inhabitants	^0	1	1	2	2	3	4	4	Pour 100 habitants
Estonia									**Estonie**
Number (thousands)	1 256	1 445	1 659	1 682	1 624	1 571	1 653[27]	1 863[28]	Nombre (en milliers)
Per 100 inhabitants	93	107	123	125	121	117	123[27]	139[28]	Pour 100 habitants
Ethiopia									**Ethiopie**
Number (thousands)	156	411	867	1 208	1 955	4 052	6 854	14 127	Nombre (en milliers)
Per 100 inhabitants	^0	1	1	2	2	5	8	17	Pour 100 habitants
Faeroe Islands									**Iles Féroé**
Number (thousands)	41	42	50	52	55	57	59	...	Nombre (en milliers)
Per 100 inhabitants	86	87	103	107	113	117	122	...	Pour 100 habitants
Falkland Is. (Malvinas)									**Iles Falkland (Malvinas)**
Number (thousands)	^0	1	2	3	3	3	3	3	Nombre (en milliers)
Per 100 inhabitants	^0	26	77	100	100	108	108	111	Pour 100 habitants
Fiji									**Fidji**
Number (thousands)	142[29]	205[29]	285[29]	530[29]	600[29]	640	698[30]	727[30]	Nombre (en milliers)
Per 100 inhabitants	17[29]	25[29]	34[29]	63[29]	71[29]	75	81[30]	84[30]	Pour 100 habitants
Finland									**Finlande**
Number (thousands)	4 988	5 270	5 670	6 080	6 830	7 700	8 390	8 940	Nombre (en milliers)
Per 100 inhabitants	95	100	108	115	128	144	156	166	Pour 100 habitants
France									**France**
Number (thousands)	44 544	48 088	51 662	55 358	57 972	59 600	63 200	66 300	Nombre (en milliers)
Per 100 inhabitants	74	79	84	90	93	95	101	105	Pour 100 habitants
French Guiana									**Guyane française**
Number (thousands)	98	...	...	...	...	218	...	...	Nombre (en milliers)
Per 100 inhabitants	50	...	...	...	...	97	...	...	Pour 100 habitants
French Polynesia									**Polynésie française**
Number (thousands)	96	120	152	175	187	208	216	223	Nombre (en milliers)
Per 100 inhabitants	38	47	59	67	71	78	80	81	Pour 100 habitants
Gabon									**Gabon**
Number (thousands)	489[31]	737[31]	898[31]	1 169[31]	1 300[31]	1 373[1]	1 610	1 800[1]	Nombre (en milliers)
Per 100 inhabitants	36[31]	54[31]	64[31]	82[31]	90[31]	93[1]	107	117[1]	Pour 100 habitants
Gambia									**Gambie**
Number (thousands)	175	247	404	800	1 166	1 313	1 478	1 581[1]	Nombre (en milliers)
Per 100 inhabitants	12	16	26	50	71	78	86	89[1]	Pour 100 habitants
Georgia									**Géorgie**
Number (thousands)	841	1 174	1 704	2 600	2 755	2 837[1]	#3 980[32]	4 431	Nombre (en milliers)
Per 100 inhabitants	19	26	38	59	63	65[1]	#91[32]	102	Pour 100 habitants
Germany									**Allemagne**
Number (thousands)	71 322	79 271	85 652[33]	96 233[34]	105 523[34]	105 000[34]	104 560[34]	108 700[34]	Nombre (en milliers)
Per 100 inhabitants	86	96	104[33]	117[34]	128[34]	127[34]	127[34]	132[34]	Pour 100 habitants
Ghana									**Ghana**
Number (thousands)	1 695	2 875	5 207	7 604	11 570	15 109	17 437	21 166	Nombre (en milliers)
Per 100 inhabitants	8	13	23	33	50	63	71	85	Pour 100 habitants
Gibraltar									**Gibraltar**
Number (thousands)	18	20[1]	22[1]	24[1]	26[1]	29	30[1]	33[35]	Nombre (en milliers)
Per 100 inhabitants	64	69[1]	75[1]	82[1]	89[1]	98	103[1]	111[35]	Pour 100 habitants
Greece									**Grèce**
Number (thousands)	9 324	10 260	10 980	12 295	13 799	13 295	12 293	12 128	Nombre (en milliers)
Per 100 inhabitants	84	92	98	109	122	117	108	106	Pour 100 habitants

16 Cellular mobile telephone subscribers *(continued)*
Number (thousands) and per 100 inhabitants
Abonnés au téléphone mobile *(suite)*
Nombre (milliers) et pour 100 habitants

Country or area	2004	2005	2006	2007	2008	2009	2010	2011	Pays ou zone
Greenland									**Groenland**
Number (thousands)	39	46	54	66	56	53	57	59	Nombre (en milliers)
Per 100 inhabitants	68	81	94	116	97	93	100	103	Pour 100 habitants
Grenada									**Grenade**
Number (thousands)	43	47	46[36]	51[36]	60[36]	114	122	...	Nombre (en milliers)
Per 100 inhabitants	42	46	45[36]	50[36]	58[36]	110	117	...	Pour 100 habitants
Guam									**Guam**
Number (thousands)	98	...	...	...	...	...	...	...	Nombre (en milliers)
Per 100 inhabitants	59	...	...	...	...	...	...	...	Pour 100 habitants
Guatemala									**Guatemala**
Number (thousands)	3 168	4 510	7 179	11 898	14 949	17 307	18 068	20 716	Nombre (en milliers)
Per 100 inhabitants	26	35	55	89	109	123	126	140	Pour 100 habitants
Guernsey									**Guernesey**
Number (thousands)	44	...	...	...	...	...	...	...	Nombre (en milliers)
Per 100 inhabitants	79	...	...	...	...	...	...	...	Pour 100 habitants
Guinea									**Guinée**
Number (thousands)	155	189	...	2 000	2 750[1]	3 489	4 000	4 500[1]	Nombre (en milliers)
Per 100 inhabitants	2	2	...	21	29[1]	36	40	44[1]	Pour 100 habitants
Guinea-Bissau									**Guinée-Bissau**
Number (thousands)	39	99	157	296	500	560	...	402[1]	Nombre (en milliers)
Per 100 inhabitants	3	7	11	21	34	38	...	26[1]	Pour 100 habitants
Guyana									**Guyana**
Number (thousands)	172	281	400[1]	539	448	514	555	519[37]	Nombre (en milliers)
Per 100 inhabitants	23	38	53[1]	72	60	68	74	69[37]	Pour 100 habitants
Haiti									**Haïti**
Number (thousands)	400	500[1]	1 200	2 500	3 200[1]	3 648[1]	4 000	4 200[1]	Nombre (en milliers)
Per 100 inhabitants	4	5[1]	13	26	33[1]	37[1]	40	41[1]	Pour 100 habitants
Honduras									**Honduras**
Number (thousands)	707	1 281	2 241	4 185	6 211	8 391	9 505	8 062[38]	Nombre (en milliers)
Per 100 inhabitants	10	19	32	58	85	113	125	104[38]	Pour 100 habitants
Hungary									**Hongrie**
Number (thousands)	8 727[21]	9 320	9 966	11 030	12 224	11 792	12 012	11 690	Nombre (en milliers)
Per 100 inhabitants	86[21]	92	99	110	122	118	120	117	Pour 100 habitants
Iceland									**Islande**
Number (thousands)	290	283	302	326	337[39]	340[39]	341	344	Nombre (en milliers)
Per 100 inhabitants	99	95	100	107	108[39]	108[39]	107	106	Pour 100 habitants
India									**Inde**
Number (thousands)	52 220	90 140	166 050	233 620[11]	346 890[11]	525 090[11]	752 190[11]	893 862[11]	Nombre (en milliers)
Per 100 inhabitants	5	8	14	20[11]	29[11]	43[11]	61[11]	72[11]	Pour 100 habitants
Indonesia									**Indonésie**
Number (thousands)	30 337	46 910	63 803	93 387	140 578[12]	163 677	211 290	236 799	Nombre (en milliers)
Per 100 inhabitants	14	21	28	40	60[12]	69	88	98	Pour 100 habitants
Iran (Islamic Rep. of)									**Iran (Rép. islamique d')**
Number (thousands)	5 076	8 511[40]	15 385	29 770	43 000	52 555[1]	54 052	56 043	Nombre (en milliers)
Per 100 inhabitants	7	12[40]	22	42	59	72[1]	73	75	Pour 100 habitants
Iraq									**Iraq**
Number (thousands)	574	1 533	9 345	14 021	17 529	20 117	23 264	25 519[1]	Nombre (en milliers)
Per 100 inhabitants	2	6	33	48	59	65	73	78[1]	Pour 100 habitants
Ireland									**Irlande**
Number (thousands)	3 860	4 270	4 690	4 971[41]	5 048[42]	4 704[43]	4 701[11]	4 906[11]	Nombre (en milliers)
Per 100 inhabitants	94	103	111	116[41]	116[42]	107[43]	105[11]	108[11]	Pour 100 habitants
Israel									**Israël**
Number (thousands)	7 222	7 757	8 404	8 902[1]	8 982	9 022[1]	9 111[1]	9 200	Nombre (en milliers)
Per 100 inhabitants	112	117	124	129[1]	127	124[1]	123[1]	122	Pour 100 habitants
Italy									**Italie**
Number (thousands)	62 750	71 500	80 418	89 801	90 341	88 024	90 600	92 300	Nombre (en milliers)
Per 100 inhabitants	108	122	136	151	151	146	150	152	Pour 100 habitants
Jamaica									**Jamaïque**
Number (thousands)	1 838	1 981	2 275	2 684	2 723	2 956	3 182	2 975	Nombre (en milliers)
Per 100 inhabitants	69	74	84	99	100	108	116	108	Pour 100 habitants

Cellular mobile telephone subscribers *(continued)*
Number (thousands) and per 100 inhabitants

Abonnés au téléphone mobile *(suite)*
Nombre (milliers) et pour 100 habitants

Country or area	2004	2005	2006	2007	2008	2009	2010	2011	Pays ou zone
Japan									**Japon**
Number (thousands)	91 474[44]	96 484[44]	99 826[44]	107 339[44]	110 395[11,45]	116 295[45]	123 287[11,45]	129 868	Nombre (en milliers)
Per 100 inhabitants	72[44]	76[44]	79[44]	85[44]	87[11,45]	92[45]	97[11,45]	103	Pour 100 habitants
Jersey									**Jersey**
Number (thousands)	84	...	...	...	...	...	...	...	Nombre (en milliers)
Per 100 inhabitants	95	...	...	...	...	...	...	...	Pour 100 habitants
Jordan									**Jordanie**
Number (thousands)	1 624	3 138	4 343	4 772	5 314	6 014	6 620	7 483	Nombre (en milliers)
Per 100 inhabitants	31	59	79	84	91	100	107	118	Pour 100 habitants
Kazakhstan									**Kazakhstan**
Number (thousands)	2 447	5 398	7 776	12 323	14 911	17 063	19 403	23 103	Nombre (en milliers)
Per 100 inhabitants	16	36	51	80	95	108	121	143	Pour 100 habitants
Kenya									**Kenya**
Number (thousands)	2 546	4 612	7 340	11 349	16 304	19 365	24 969	26 981	Nombre (en milliers)
Per 100 inhabitants	7	13	20	30	42	49	62	65	Pour 100 habitants
Kiribati									**Kiribati**
Number (thousands)	1	1	1[1]	1[1]	1[1]	10	11	14	Nombre (en milliers)
Per 100 inhabitants	1	1	1[1]	1[1]	1[1]	10	11	14	Pour 100 habitants
Kuwait									**Koweït**
Number (thousands)	2 000	2 277	2 530	2 774	2 907[1]	3 876[1]	4 400[1]	...	Nombre (en milliers)
Per 100 inhabitants	91	101	108	113	114[1]	146[1]	161[1]	...	Pour 100 habitants
Kyrgyzstan									**Kirghizistan**
Number (thousands)	263	542	1 262	2 168	3 394	4 487	5 275	5 653[1]	Nombre (en milliers)
Per 100 inhabitants	5	11	25	42	65	85	99	105[1]	Pour 100 habitants
Lao People's Dem. Rep.									**Rép. dém. pop. lao**
Number (thousands)	204	658	1 010	1 478	2 022	3 235	4 003	5 481	Nombre (en milliers)
Per 100 inhabitants	4	11	17	25	34	53	65	87	Pour 100 habitants
Latvia									**Lettonie**
Number (thousands)	1 537	1 872	2 184	2 217[1]	2 299	2 304	2 306[1]	2 309[1]	Nombre (en milliers)
Per 100 inhabitants	66	81	95	97[1]	101	102	102[1]	103[1]	Pour 100 habitants
Lebanon									**Liban**
Number (thousands)	884[1]	994[1]	1 106[1]	1 260	1 427[1]	2 390	2 875	3 350[1]	Nombre (en milliers)
Per 100 inhabitants	22[1]	25[1]	27[1]	30	34[1]	57	68	79[1]	Pour 100 habitants
Lesotho									**Lesotho**
Number (thousands)	196	250	358	456[1]	593	661[1]	987	1 051[1]	Nombre (en milliers)
Per 100 inhabitants	10	12	17	22[1]	28	31[1]	45	48[1]	Pour 100 habitants
Liberia									**Libéria**
Number (thousands)	94	160	280[1]	563[1]	855[46]	1 085[46]	1 571[47]	2 030[47]	Nombre (en milliers)
Per 100 inhabitants	3	5	8[1]	16[1]	23[46]	28[46]	39[47]	49[47]	Pour 100 habitants
Libyan Arab Jamah.									**Jamah. arabe libyenne**
Number (thousands)	500	2 000	3 928	4 500[1]	7 379	9 534	10 900[1]	10 000[1]	Nombre (en milliers)
Per 100 inhabitants	9	35	67	75[1]	120	152	172[1]	156[1]	Pour 100 habitants
Liechtenstein									**Liechtenstein**
Number (thousands)	26	28	29	32	34[1]	35[1]	36[1]	37	Nombre (en milliers)
Per 100 inhabitants	74	79	82	91	96[1]	98[1]	99[1]	102	Pour 100 habitants
Lithuania									**Lituanie**
Number (thousands)	3 051[48]	4 353[48]	4 718[48]	4 912[48]	5 023[48]	4 961[48]	4 891[48]	5 004[1]	Nombre (en milliers)
Per 100 inhabitants	89[48]	127[48]	139[48]	145[48]	149[48]	148[48]	147[48]	151[1]	Pour 100 habitants
Luxembourg									**Luxembourg**
Number (thousands)	470[49]	510	713	685	707	720	727	765	Nombre (en milliers)
Per 100 inhabitants	104[49]	112	153	144	145	145	143	148	Pour 100 habitants
Madagascar									**Madagascar**
Number (thousands)	334	510	1 046	2 218	4 835	6 284	7 712	8 160	Nombre (en milliers)
Per 100 inhabitants	2	3	6	12	25	31	37	38	Pour 100 habitants
Malawi									**Malawi**
Number (thousands)	222	421	620[1]	1 051	1 508	2 486	3 117	3 856	Nombre (en milliers)
Per 100 inhabitants	2	3	5[1]	8	11	17	21	25	Pour 100 habitants
Malaysia									**Malaisie**
Number (thousands)	14 611	19 545	19 464	23 347	27 713	30 144	33 859	36 661	Nombre (en milliers)
Per 100 inhabitants	57	75	73	86	101	108	119	127	Pour 100 habitants

16
Cellular mobile telephone subscribers *(continued)*
Number (thousands) and per 100 inhabitants
Abonnés au téléphone mobile *(suite)*
Nombre (milliers) et pour 100 habitants

Country or area	2004	2005	2006	2007	2008	2009	2010	2011	Pays ou zone
Maldives									**Maldives**
Number (thousands)	113	204	271	314	436	458	494	530	Nombre (en milliers)
Per 100 inhabitants	39	69	91	103	142	147	156	166	Pour 100 habitants
Mali									**Mali**
Number (thousands)	407	762	1 513	2 531	3 439	4 461	7 440	10 822	Nombre (en milliers)
Per 100 inhabitants	3	6	11	18	24	30	48	68	Pour 100 habitants
Malta									**Malte**
Number (thousands)	306	324	347	369	386	422	456	522	Nombre (en milliers)
Per 100 inhabitants	75	79	84	89	93	102	109	125	Pour 100 habitants
Marshall Islands									**Iles Marshall**
Number (thousands)	1	1	1[1]	2[1]	2[1]	3[1]	4[1]	...	Nombre (en milliers)
Per 100 inhabitants	1	1	2[1]	3[1]	4[1]	6[1]	7[1]	...	Pour 100 habitants
Mauritania									**Mauritanie**
Number (thousands)	522	746	1 060	1 414	2 092	2 182	2 745	3 283	Nombre (en milliers)
Per 100 inhabitants	18	24	34	44	63	65	79	93	Pour 100 habitants
Mauritius									**Maurice**
Number (thousands)	548	657	772	929	1 033	1 087	1 191	1 294	Nombre (en milliers)
Per 100 inhabitants	44	52	61	73	80	84	92	99	Pour 100 habitants
Mexico									**Mexique**
Number (thousands)	38 451	47 129	55 395	66 559	75 303	83 194	91 363[50]	94 565[50]	Nombre (en milliers)
Per 100 inhabitants	37	44	51	61	68	74	81[50]	82[50]	Pour 100 habitants
Micronesia (Fed. States of)									**Micronésie (Etats féd. de)**
Number (thousands)	13	14	19	27	28[1]	28[1]	28	...	Nombre (en milliers)
Per 100 inhabitants	12	13	17	25	25[1]	25[1]	25	...	Pour 100 habitants
Monaco									**Monaco**
Number (thousands)	16	17	18	20	22	23	23	30	Nombre (en milliers)
Per 100 inhabitants	45	49	52	58	62	65	66	86	Pour 100 habitants
Mongolia									**Mongolie**
Number (thousands)	429	557	775	1 195	1 763	2 249	2 510	2 942	Nombre (en milliers)
Per 100 inhabitants	17	22	30	46	66	83	91	105	Pour 100 habitants
Montenegro									**Monténégro**
Number (thousands)	484	543	644	703[1]	1 158	1 294	1 170[1]	...	Nombre (en milliers)
Per 100 inhabitants	77	87	103	112[1]	184	205	185[1]	...	Pour 100 habitants
Montserrat									**Montserrat**
Number (thousands)	2	...	4	4	3	3	4	4	Nombre (en milliers)
Per 100 inhabitants	41	...	75	61	51	52	71	70	Pour 100 habitants
Morocco									**Maroc**
Number (thousands)	9 337	12 393	16 005	20 029	22 816	25 311	31 982	36 554	Nombre (en milliers)
Per 100 inhabitants	31	41	52	65	73	80	100	113	Pour 100 habitants
Mozambique									**Mozambique**
Number (thousands)	708	1 504	2 339	3 080	4 405	5 971	7 224	7 855	Nombre (en milliers)
Per 100 inhabitants	3	7	11	14	20	26	31	33	Pour 100 habitants
Myanmar									**Myanmar**
Number (thousands)	92	129	214	248	367	502	594[1]	1 244	Nombre (en milliers)
Per 100 inhabitants	^0	^0	^0	1	1	1	1[1]	3	Pour 100 habitants
Namibia									**Namibie**
Number (thousands)	286	449	609	800	1 052	1 217[1]	1 535[51]	2 439	Nombre (en milliers)
Per 100 inhabitants	14	22	29	37	48	54[1]	67[51]	105	Pour 100 habitants
Nauru									**Nauru**
Number (thousands)	...	...	...	...	...	...	6[52]	7	Nombre (en milliers)
Per 100 inhabitants	...	...	...	...	...	...	60[52]	65	Pour 100 habitants
Nepal									**Népal**
Number (thousands)	117	227	1 157	3 269[53]	4 200	5 598[54]	9 196	13 354[11]	Nombre (en milliers)
Per 100 inhabitants	^0	1	4	12[53]	15	19[54]	31	44[11]	Pour 100 habitants
Netherlands									**Pays-Bas**
Number (thousands)	14 800	15 834	17 296	19 285	20 627	20 149	19 179[55]	19 835[56]	Nombre (en milliers)
Per 100 inhabitants	91	97	106	117	125	122	115[55]	...	Pour 100 habitants
Netherlands Antilles									**Antilles néerlandaises**
Number (thousands)	200	...	...	...	...	...	...	...	Nombre (en milliers)
Per 100 inhabitants	109	...	...	...	...	...	...	...	Pour 100 habitants

16

Cellular mobile telephone subscribers *(continued)*
Number (thousands) and per 100 inhabitants
Abonnés au téléphone mobile *(suite)*
Nombre (milliers) et pour 100 habitants

Country or area	2004	2005	2006	2007	2008	2009	2010	2011	Pays ou zone
New Caledonia									**Nouvelle-Calédonie**
Number (thousands)	116	134	155[1]	176	196	210	221	227	Nombre (en milliers)
Per 100 inhabitants	51	58	66[1]	74	81	85	88	89	Pour 100 habitants
New Zealand									**Nouvelle-Zélande**
Number (thousands)	3 027	3 530	3 802	4 251[57]	4 620[12]	4 700[58]	4 710[2]	4 820[2]	Nombre (en milliers)
Per 100 inhabitants	74	85	91	100[57]	108[12]	109[58]	108[2]	109[2]	Pour 100 habitants
Nicaragua									**Nicaragua**
Number (thousands)	739	1 119	1 830	2 502	3 108	3 345	3 962	4 822	Nombre (en milliers)
Per 100 inhabitants	14	21	33	45	55	59	68	82	Pour 100 habitants
Niger									**Niger**
Number (thousands)	172	324	483	900[1]	1 898	2 599[59]	3 806	4 340	Nombre (en milliers)
Per 100 inhabitants	1	2	4	6[1]	13	17[59]	25	27	Pour 100 habitants
Nigeria									**Nigéria**
Number (thousands)	9 147	18 587	32 322	#40 396[60]	62 988	74 518	87 298	95 167	Nombre (en milliers)
Per 100 inhabitants	7	13	23	#27[60]	42	48	55	59	Pour 100 habitants
Northern Mariana Islands									**Iles Mariannes du Nord**
Number (thousands)	20	...	...	...	...	...	...	...	Nombre (en milliers)
Per 100 inhabitants	30	...	...	...	...	...	...	...	Pour 100 habitants
Norway									**Norvège**
Number (thousands)	4 525	4 754	4 869	5 038	5 211	5 360	5 649	5 750[1]	Nombre (en milliers)
Per 100 inhabitants	99	103	104	107	109	111	116	117[1]	Pour 100 habitants
Occupied Palestinian Terr.									**Terr. palestinien occupé**
Number (thousands)	437	568	822	1 021	1 314	1 800	...	...	Nombre (en milliers)
Per 100 inhabitants	13	16	23	27	34	46	...	...	Pour 100 habitants
Oman									**Oman**
Number (thousands)	806	1 333	1 818	2 500	3 219	3 971	4 606	4 809	Nombre (en milliers)
Per 100 inhabitants	34	55	73	98	122	146	166	169	Pour 100 habitants
Pakistan									**Pakistan**
Number (thousands)	5 023	12 771	34 507	62 857[11]	88 020	94 342	99 186	108 895	Nombre (en milliers)
Per 100 inhabitants	3	8	21	38[11]	53	55	57	62	Pour 100 habitants
Palau									**Palaos**
Number (thousands)	4	6	8	11	12	13	15	15[61]	Nombre (en milliers)
Per 100 inhabitants	20	30	42	53	58	63	71	75[61]	Pour 100 habitants
Panama									**Panama**
Number (thousands)	1 260	1 749	2 174	3 011	3 915	6 067	6 646	7 281[50]	Nombre (en milliers)
Per 100 inhabitants	40	54	66	90	115	175	189	204[50]	Pour 100 habitants
Papua New Guinea									**Papouasie-Nvl-Guinée**
Number (thousands)	48	75	100[1]	300[62]	874[63]	1 418[63]	1 909[63]	2 400[1]	Nombre (en milliers)
Per 100 inhabitants	1	1	2[1]	5[62]	13[63]	21[63]	28[63]	34[1]	Pour 100 habitants
Paraguay									**Paraguay**
Number (thousands)	1 749	1 887	3 233	4 694	5 791	5 619[64]	5 921	6 529	Nombre (en milliers)
Per 100 inhabitants	30	32	54	77	93	89[64]	92	99	Pour 100 habitants
Peru									**Pérou**
Number (thousands)	4 093	5 583	9 120[1]	15 417	20 952	24 700	29 115[65]	32 461[65]	Nombre (en milliers)
Per 100 inhabitants	15	20	33[1]	55	74	86	100[65]	110[65]	Pour 100 habitants
Philippines									**Philippines**
Number (thousands)	32 936	34 779	42 869	57 345	68 117	75 587	79 896	87 256	Nombre (en milliers)
Per 100 inhabitants	39	41	49	65	76	82	86	92	Pour 100 habitants
Poland									**Pologne**
Number (thousands)	23 096	29 166	36 745	41 389	43 926	44 807	46 952	49 200[1]	Nombre (en milliers)
Per 100 inhabitants	61	76	96	108	115	117	123	128[1]	Pour 100 habitants
Portugal									**Portugal**
Number (thousands)	10 571	11 447	12 226	13 477	14 049	11 795[66]	12 210	12 285	Nombre (en milliers)
Per 100 inhabitants	101	109	116	127	132	111[66]	114	115	Pour 100 habitants
Puerto Rico									**Porto Rico**
Number (thousands)	1 848	1 993	2 199	2 432	2 544	2 712	2 934	3 108	Nombre (en milliers)
Per 100 inhabitants	49	53	58	65	68	72	78	83	Pour 100 habitants
Qatar									**Qatar**
Number (thousands)	490[67]	717[67]	920[67]	1 264[67]	1 429[23]	1 949[23]	2 186[68]	2 302[68]	Nombre (en milliers)
Per 100 inhabitants	69[67]	87[67]	94[67]	107[67]	102[23]	122[23]	124[68]	123[68]	Pour 100 habitants

16

Cellular mobile telephone subscribers *(continued)*
Number (thousands) and per 100 inhabitants
Abonnés au téléphone mobile *(suite)*
Nombre (milliers) et pour 100 habitants

Country or area	2004	2005	2006	2007	2008	2009	2010	2011	Pays ou zone
Republic of Korea									**République de Corée**
Number (thousands)	36 586	38 342	40 197	44 369	45 607	47 944	50 767	52 507	Nombre (en milliers)
Per 100 inhabitants	78	82	85	93	96	100	105	109	Pour 100 habitants
Republic of Moldova									**République de Moldova**
Number (thousands)	787	1 090	1 358	1 883	2 423	2 785	3 165	3 715	Nombre (en milliers)
Per 100 inhabitants	21	29	37	51	67	77	89	105	Pour 100 habitants
Romania									**Roumanie**
Number (thousands)	10 215	13 354	15 991[69]	20 400[69]	24 470[69]	25 100	24 400	23 400[50]	Nombre (en milliers)
Per 100 inhabitants	47	61	74[69]	94[69]	113[69]	117	114	109[50]	Pour 100 habitants
Russian Federation									**Fédération de Russie**
Number (thousands)	73 722	120 000	150 674[70]	171 200	199 522	230 500	237 689	256 117	Nombre (en milliers)
Per 100 inhabitants	51	83	105[70]	119	139	161	166	179	Pour 100 habitants
Rwanda									**Rwanda**
Number (thousands)	137	223	314	635	1 323	2 429	3 549	4 446	Nombre (en milliers)
Per 100 inhabitants	2	2	3	7	13	24	33	41	Pour 100 habitants
Saint Kitts and Nevis									**Saint-Kitts-et-Nevis**
Number (thousands)	29	51[11]	51	65	75	76	80	...	Nombre (en milliers)
Per 100 inhabitants	60	104[11]	102	128	146	146	153	...	Pour 100 habitants
Saint Lucia									**Sainte-Lucie**
Number (thousands)	101	106	106	147	175	190	198	217	Nombre (en milliers)
Per 100 inhabitants	62	64	63	87	103	110	114	123	Pour 100 habitants
Saint Vincent-Grenadines									**Saint Vincent-Grenadines**
Number (thousands)	72	71	88	110	130	121[71]	132	132	Nombre (en milliers)
Per 100 inhabitants	66	65	80	101	119	111[71]	121	121	Pour 100 habitants
Samoa									**Samoa**
Number (thousands)	16	24	46	86[72]	124[1]	151[1]	167[1]	...	Nombre (en milliers)
Per 100 inhabitants	9	13	25	47[72]	68[1]	83[1]	91[1]	...	Pour 100 habitants
San Marino									**Saint-Marin**
Number (thousands)	17	17	17	18	24	30	31	35	Nombre (en milliers)
Per 100 inhabitants	57	57	57	56	78	96	97	112	Pour 100 habitants
Sao Tome and Principe									**Sao Tomé-et-Principe**
Number (thousands)	8	12	18	30	50	64[1]	103	115	Nombre (en milliers)
Per 100 inhabitants	5	8	12	19	32	39[1]	62	68	Pour 100 habitants
Saudi Arabia									**Arabie saoudite**
Number (thousands)	9 176	14 164	19 700	28 400	36 000	44 864	51 564	53 706	Nombre (en milliers)
Per 100 inhabitants	40	59	79	111	138	167	188	191	Pour 100 habitants
Senegal									**Sénégal**
Number (thousands)	1 121	1 730	2 983	3 631	5 389	6 901	8 344	9 353	Nombre (en milliers)
Per 100 inhabitants	11	16	27	32	46	57	67	73	Pour 100 habitants
Serbia									**Serbie**
Number (thousands)	4 730	5 511	6 644	8 453	9 619	9 912	9 915	10 182	Nombre (en milliers)
Per 100 inhabitants	48	68	82	104	119	122	122	125	Pour 100 habitants
Seychelles									**Seychelles**
Number (thousands)	54	59	70	77[12]	93[73]	111[74]	118[75]	127[76]	Nombre (en milliers)
Per 100 inhabitants	66	70	83	91[12]	109[73]	129[74]	136[75]	146[76]	Pour 100 habitants
Sierra Leone									**Sierra Leone**
Number (thousands)	...	...	...	776[1]	1 009	1 160[1]	2 000[77]	2 137[1]	Nombre (en milliers)
Per 100 inhabitants	...	...	...	14[1]	18	20[1]	34[77]	36[1]	Pour 100 habitants
Singapore									**Singapour**
Number (thousands)	3 991[11]	4 385	4 789	5 924	6 415	6 880	7 385	7 755[78]	Nombre (en milliers)
Per 100 inhabitants	96[11]	103	109	129	134	139	145	149[78]	Pour 100 habitants
Slovakia									**Slovaquie**
Number (thousands)	4 275[79]	4 540[79]	4 893[79]	6 068[79]	#5 520[80]	5 498	5 925	5 983	Nombre (en milliers)
Per 100 inhabitants	79[79]	84[79]	90[79]	112[79]	#101[80]	101	108	109	Pour 100 habitants
Slovenia									**Slovénie**
Number (thousands)	1 849	1 759[81]	1 820	1 928	2 055	2 100	2 122	2 169	Nombre (en milliers)
Per 100 inhabitants	93	88[81]	91	96	102	104	105	107	Pour 100 habitants
Solomon Islands									**Iles Salomon**
Number (thousands)	3	6	7[1]	11[1]	30[1]	50[1]	150[1]	275	Nombre (en milliers)
Per 100 inhabitants	1	1	1[1]	2[1]	6[1]	10[1]	28[1]	50	Pour 100 habitants

Country or area	2004	2005	2006	2007	2008	2009	2010	2011	Pays ou zone
Somalia									**Somalie**
Number (thousands)	500	500	550[1]	600[1]	627[1]	641[1]	648[1]	655[1]	Nombre (en milliers)
Per 100 inhabitants	6	6	6[1]	7[1]	7[1]	7[1]	7[1]	7[1]	Pour 100 habitants
South Africa									**Afrique du Sud**
Number (thousands)	20 839	33 960	39 662	*42 300	45 000	46 436[1]	50 372	64 000[1]	Nombre (en milliers)
Per 100 inhabitants	44	71	82	*87	91	93[1]	100	127[1]	Pour 100 habitants
Spain									**Espagne**
Number (thousands)	38 623	42 694	45 695	48 422	49 623	51 084	51 601	53 067	Nombre (en milliers)
Per 100 inhabitants	90	98	104	109	110	112	112	114	Pour 100 habitants
Sri Lanka									**Sri Lanka**
Number (thousands)	2 211	3 362	5 412	7 983	11 082	16 305	17 359	18 319	Nombre (en milliers)
Per 100 inhabitants	11	17	27	39	54	79	83	87	Pour 100 habitants
Sudan (former)									**Soudan (anc.)**
Number (thousands)	1 049[82]	1 828[82]	4 683[82]	8 218[82]	11 991[82]	15 340	18 093	25 107	Nombre (en milliers)
Per 100 inhabitants	3[82]	5[82]	12[82]	20[82]	29[82]	36	42	56	Pour 100 habitants
Suriname									**Suriname**
Number (thousands)	213	233	320	380[1]	657[1]	764	890[1]	947[1]	Nombre (en milliers)
Per 100 inhabitants	43	47	63	74[1]	128[1]	147	170[1]	179[1]	Pour 100 habitants
Swaziland									**Swaziland**
Number (thousands)	145	200	250	380[1]	532	664	726	767	Nombre (en milliers)
Per 100 inhabitants	13	18	22	34[1]	46	57	61	64	Pour 100 habitants
Sweden									**Suède**
Number (thousands)	8 785[3]	9 104	9 607	10 117	10 014	10 440	10 885	11 194[83]	Nombre (en milliers)
Per 100 inhabitants	98[3]	101	106	110	108	112	116	119[83]	Pour 100 habitants
Switzerland									**Suisse**
Number (thousands)	6 275	6 834	7 436	8 209	8 897	9 323	9 644	*10 017	Nombre (en milliers)
Per 100 inhabitants	85	92	100	109	117	122	126	*130	Pour 100 habitants
Syrian Arab Republic									**Rép. arabe syrienne**
Number (thousands)	2 346	2 950	4 675	6 235	7 056	10 022	11 799	13 117	Nombre (en milliers)
Per 100 inhabitants	13	16	25	32	36	50	58	63	Pour 100 habitants
Tajikistan									**Tadjikistan**
Number (thousands)	135	265	2 150	2 133	3 674	4 900[1]	5 941	6 324[1]	Nombre (en milliers)
Per 100 inhabitants	2	4	33	32	55	72[1]	86	91[1]	Pour 100 habitants
Thailand									**Thaïlande**
Number (thousands)	27 379	31 137	40 723	52 974	61 837	65 952	71 624	78 668	Nombre (en milliers)
Per 100 inhabitants	41	47	61	78	91	96	104	113	Pour 100 habitants
TFYR of Macedonia									**L'ex-R.Y. Macédoine**
Number (thousands)	986	1 131	1 264	1 794	1 968	1 943	2 153	2 257	Nombre (en milliers)
Per 100 inhabitants	48	55	62	88	96	94	105	109	Pour 100 habitants
Timor-Leste									**Timor-Leste**
Number (thousands)	26	33	49[1]	78[72]	125	351	601[1]	614	Nombre (en milliers)
Per 100 inhabitants	3	3	5[1]	7[72]	12	32	53[1]	53	Pour 100 habitants
Togo									**Togo**
Number (thousands)	333	434	708	1 190	1 550	2 187	2 452	3 105	Nombre (en milliers)
Per 100 inhabitants	6	8	13	21	27	37	41	50	Pour 100 habitants
Tonga									**Tonga**
Number (thousands)	16[1]	30[1]	30[1]	47	50	53[1]	54[1]	55	Nombre (en milliers)
Per 100 inhabitants	16[1]	30[1]	30[1]	45	49	51[1]	52[1]	53	Pour 100 habitants
Trinidad and Tobago									**Trinité-et-Tobago**
Number (thousands)	651	924	1 519	1 510[84]	1 806	1 846	1 894	1 825	Nombre (en milliers)
Per 100 inhabitants	50	70	115	114[84]	136	138	141	136	Pour 100 habitants
Tunisia									**Tunisie**
Number (thousands)	3 736	5 681	7 339	7 843	8 602	9 797	11 114	12 388	Nombre (en milliers)
Per 100 inhabitants	38	57	73	77	84	95	106	117	Pour 100 habitants
Turkey									**Turquie**
Number (thousands)	34 708	43 609	52 663	61 976	65 824	62 780	61 770	65 322	Nombre (en milliers)
Per 100 inhabitants	52	64	76	89	93	87	85	89	Pour 100 habitants
Turkmenistan									**Turkménistan**
Number (thousands)	50	105[1]	217[70]	382	1 135	2 133	3 198	3 511[1]	Nombre (en milliers)
Per 100 inhabitants	1	2[1]	5[70]	8	23	43	63	69[1]	Pour 100 habitants

Cellular mobile telephone subscribers *(continued)*
Number (thousands) and per 100 inhabitants
Abonnés au téléphone mobile *(suite)*
Nombre (milliers) et pour 100 habitants

Country or area	2004	2005	2006	2007	2008	2009	2010	2011	Pays ou zone
Tuvalu									**Tuvalu**
Number (thousands)	1	1	2	2	...	1[85]	2	2	Nombre (en milliers)
Per 100 inhabitants	5	13	16	18	...	10[85]	16	22	Pour 100 habitants
Uganda									**Ouganda**
Number (thousands)	1 165	1 315	2 009	4 195[1]	8 555	9 384	12 828	16 697	Nombre (en milliers)
Per 100 inhabitants	4	5	7	14[1]	27	29	38	48	Pour 100 habitants
Ukraine									**Ukraine**
Number (thousands)	13 735	30 014	49 076	55 240	55 681	54 943	53 920	55 567	Nombre (en milliers)
Per 100 inhabitants	29	64	105	119	121	120	119	123	Pour 100 habitants
United Arab Emirates									**Emirats arabes unis**
Number (thousands)	3 683	4 534	5 519	7 732	9 358	10 672	10 926	11 727	Nombre (en milliers)
Per 100 inhabitants	101	111	118	143	151	154	145	149	Pour 100 habitants
United Kingdom									**Royaume-Uni**
Number (thousands)	59 688	65 472	70 078	73 836[12]	76 735	80 255	81 115	81 612	Nombre (en milliers)
Per 100 inhabitants	100	109	116	121[12]	125	130	131	131	Pour 100 habitants
United Rep. of Tanzania									**Rép.-Unie de Tanzanie**
Number (thousands)	1 942	2 964	5 609	8 252	13 007[3]	17 469	20 984	25 666	Nombre (en milliers)
Per 100 inhabitants	5	8	14	20	31[3]	40	47	56	Pour 100 habitants
United States									**Etats-Unis**
Number (thousands)	184 819	203 700	229 600	249 300	261 300	274 300	278 900[86]	331 600[1]	Nombre (en milliers)
Per 100 inhabitants	63	69	77	82	86	89	90[86]	106[1]	Pour 100 habitants
United States Virgin Is. [1]									**Iles Vierges américaines** [1]
Number (thousands)	64	80	...	...	...	...	...	...	Nombre (en milliers)
Per 100 inhabitants	59	73	...	...	...	...	...	...	Pour 100 habitants
Uruguay									**Uruguay**
Number (thousands)	600	1 155	2 330	3 004	3 508[87]	4 112[87]	4 437[87]	4 757[87]	Nombre (en milliers)
Per 100 inhabitants	18	35	70	90	105[87]	122[87]	132[87]	141[87]	Pour 100 habitants
Uzbekistan									**Ouzbékistan**
Number (thousands)	544	720	2 530[1]	5 691	12 375	16 418	20 952[1]	25 442	Nombre (en milliers)
Per 100 inhabitants	2	3	10[1]	21	46	61	76[1]	92	Pour 100 habitants
Vanuatu									**Vanuatu**
Number (thousands)	11	13	15[1]	26[72]	36[1]	126	285[1]	...	Nombre (en milliers)
Per 100 inhabitants	5	6	7[1]	12[72]	16[1]	54	119[1]	...	Pour 100 habitants
Venezuela (Boliv. Rep. of)									**Venezuela (Rép. boliv. du)**
Number (thousands)	8 421	12 496	18 789	23 820	27 414	28 124	27 880	28 782[50]	Nombre (en milliers)
Per 100 inhabitants	32	47	69	86	98	99	96	98[50]	Pour 100 habitants
Viet Nam									**Viet Nam**
Number (thousands)	4 960	9 593	18 892	45 024	74 872	98 224	111 570	127 318	Nombre (en milliers)
Per 100 inhabitants	6	12	22	53	87	113	127	143	Pour 100 habitants
Yemen									**Yémen**
Number (thousands)	1 476	2 278	2 978	4 349	6 445	8 313	11 085	11 668	Nombre (en milliers)
Per 100 inhabitants	7	11	14	20	28	36	46	47	Pour 100 habitants
Zambia									**Zambie**
Number (thousands)	464	950	1 663	2 639	3 539	4 407	5 447	8 165	Nombre (en milliers)
Per 100 inhabitants	4	8	14	22	29	35	42	61	Pour 100 habitants
Zimbabwe									**Zimbabwe**
Number (thousands)	426	647	849	1 226	1 655	3 991	7 700	9 200	Nombre (en milliers)
Per 100 inhabitants	3	5	7	10	13	32	61	72	Pour 100 habitants

Source:
International Telecommunication Union (ITU), Geneva, the ITU database, last accessed July 2012.

Source:
Union internationale des télécommunications (UIT), Genève, la base de données de l'UIT, dernier accès juillet 2012.

1	ITU estimate.
2	Measured using subscriptions active in the last 90 days.
3	June.
4	Active subscribers.
5	Decrease due to purge of subscribers whose services are dormant for 6 months or more.
6	Break in comparability due to adjustment in activity criterion to 3 months.

1	Estimation de l'UIT.
2	Mesuré en utilisant les abonnements actifs au cours des 90 derniers jours.
3	Juin.
4	Abonnés actifs.
5	Diminution expliquée par l'élimination des abonnés dont les comptes ont été inactifs pendant au moins 6 mois.
6	Rupture de comparabilité due au changement de critère d'activité à 3 mois.

16

Cellular mobile telephone subscribers *(continued)*
Number (thousands) and per 100 inhabitants
Abonnés au téléphone mobile *(suite)*
Nombre (milliers) et pour 100 habitants

7	Includes subscriptions via data cards or USB modems.		7	Comprend les abonnements mobiles à large bande par clé (3G ou 4G) ou modem USB.
8	Includes subscribers to public mobile data services.		8	Y compris les abonnés aux services mobiles de données sur réseau public.
9	Change from TDMA to GSM platform caused decrease in the number of subscriptions.		9	Le changement de la plateforme TDMA à celle du GSM a causé une baisse du nombre d'abonnements.
10	The reduction is a result of 1) a clean up of SIM's during the Months of February and March 2011. 2) The reclassification by the country of active subscriptions from 90 to 60 days.		10	La baisse est le résultat de 1) l'élimination de cartes SIMS pendant les mois de février et mars 2011 2) le reclassement par le pays des abonnements actifs de 90 à 60 jours.
11	December.		11	Décembre.
12	September.		12	Septembre.
13	Number of active clients (yearly reports mobile network operators, MVNO included).		13	Nombre de clients actifs (rapports annuels des opérateurs de téléphonie mobile, MVNO compris).
14	Includes Mobile GSM and AMPS Post and Pre Mobile Base at December 2010.		14	Y compris Mobile GSM et AMPS Post et Pre Mobile Base en décembre 2010.
15	Includes Mobile GSM and AMPS Post and Pre Mobile Base at December 2011		15	Y compris Mobile GSM et AMPS Post et Pre Mobile Base en décembre 2011.
16	Both Bhutan Telecom and Tashi Cell provide mobile-cellular services.		16	Buthan Telecom and Tashi Cell sont les deux fournisseurs de téléphonie mobile.
17	Third quarter.		17	Troisième trimestre.
18	Year-end mobile handsets in operation.		18	Téléphones portables en fonctionnement à la fin de l'année.
19	Year-end mobile handsets in operation. Reduction explained by high fluctuation of temporary residents.		19	Téléphones portables en fonctionnement à la fin de l'année. La diminution s'explique par les effectifs très variables de résidents temporaires.
20	For statistical purposes, the data for China do not include those for the Hong Kong Special Administrative Region (Hong Kong SAR), Macao Special Administrative Region (Macao SAR) and Taiwan Province of China.		20	Pour la présentation des statistiques, les données pour la Chine ne comprennent pas la Région Administrative Spéciale de Hong Kong (Hong Kong RAS), la Région Administrative Spéciale de Macao (Macao RAS) et la province de Taiwan.
21	November.		21	Novembre.
22	The stated data corresponds to the "old" methodology, the corrected data in accordance with to the used (new) methodology is 10 666 711.		22	Ces données reflètent la méthodologie antérieure. Selon la nouvelle méthodologie, les correctes données sont 10 666 711.
23	Active subscriptions only (active during the past 3 months).		23	Abonnements actifs seulement (actifs au cours des 3 derniers mois).
24	Including non-active subscriptions.		24	Y compris les abonnements inactifs.
25	Break in comparability since from 2009 on only active subscriptions are taken into consideration.		25	Rupture de comparabilité, du fait que depuis 2009 ne sont pris en compte que les abonnements actifs.
26	Estimate based on June 2010 data.		26	Estimation basée sur les données de juin 2010.
27	Excluding 1 890 000 prepaid cards that are used to provide travel SIM service.		27	Non compris 1 890 000 cartes SIM prépayées destinées a être utilisées en voyage.
28	Excluding 2 209 181 prepaid cards that are used to provide travel SIM service.		28	Non compris 2 209 181 cartes SIM prépayées destinées a être utilisées en voyage.
29	Data refer to March of following year.		29	Les données se réfèrent à mars de l'année suivante.
30	30 June.		30	30 juin.
31	Includes inactive subscribers.		31	Y compris les abonnés inactifs.
32	Break in methodology: active subscriptions in the last quarter. Previously active subscriptions in the last month.		32	Rupture de méthodologie: abonnement actifs durant le dernier trimestre. Auparavant, les abonnements actifs au cours du dernier mois.
33	Including data services.		33	Inclus les services mobiles de données
34	Excluding Data-only SIM cards.		34	Non compris les cartes SIM "data-only".
35	Updated figure by the Gibraltar Regulatory Authority on 27 June 2011.		35	Chiffres mis à jour le 27 juin 2011 par L'Autorité Regulatoire de Gibraltar.
36	Refers only to C&W.		36	Se réfère à C&W seulement.
37	Decrease as a result of closure of inactive accounts and active blocking of international bypass SIMs.		37	baisse due à la fermeture des comptes inactifs et le filtrage actif des cartes internationales SIMS débloquées.
38	Decrease mostly due to exclusion of inactive accounts by one of the main operators.		38	Baisse due à l'exclusion des comptes inactifs par l'un des principaux opérateurs.
39	Including NMT.		39	Y compris NMT.
40	October.		40	Octobre.
41	Excluding mobile broadband (HSDPA) subscriptions.		41	À l'exclusion des abonnements au très haut débit mobile (HSDPA).
42	Please note that this number may be overestimated. Data refers to as at the end of December.		42	Le nombre peut être surestimé. Les données sont celles de fin décembre.
43	Decrease in the number of subscriptions was due to change in the definition of prepaid subscriptions (now includes only those that have done an event (outgoing call, SMSs, MMS, Internet usage, etc)) that decrements their balance in the previous 90 days. Data refers to December.		43	La baisse du nombre d'abonnements est due à une modification de la définition des abonnements prépayés. Ceux-ci incluent maintenant seulement ceux qui ont fait une action (appel sortant, SMS, MMS, utilisation de l'Internet, etc) entraînant une diminution du solde au cours des derniers 90 jours. Les données concernent le mois de décembre.
44	Including Personal Handy System (PHS) subscriptions.		44	Y compris les abonnements au système PHS (Personal Handy System).

16

Cellular mobile telephone subscribers *(continued)*
Number (thousands) and per 100 inhabitants
Abonnés au téléphone mobile *(suite)*
Nombre (milliers) et pour 100 habitants

45	Including Personal Handy System PHS and data cards (undividable).	45	Y compris le système PHS et clés (données impossibles à ventiler).
46	Figure obtained from four mobile operators who provided mobile services in the country.	46	Chiffre obtenu des quatre opérateurs de téléphonie mobile dans le pays.
47	Figure obtained from all five mobile operators currently providing service in the country.	47	Chiffre obtenu de l'ensemble des cinq opérateurs de téléphonie mobile assurant actuellement des services dans le pays.
48	Active mobile subscriptions.	48	Abonnements mobiles actifs.
49	Only active from this year on.	49	Seulement actif à partir de cette année.
50	Preliminary data.	50	Données préliminaires.
51	MTC only.	51	MTC seulement.
52	Digicel is now providing Island-wide GSM services.	52	Digicel assure désormais des services GSM dans toute l'île.
53	Refer to SNLP subscribers only.	53	Abonnés à SNPL seulement.
54	March 2010.	54	Mars 2010.
55	July 2010, lower than previous years due to the removal of inactive SIM-cards out of the administrative system of operators.	55	Juillet 2010, chiffres inférieurs aux précédents du fait que les cartes SIM inactives ont été éliminées du système administratif des opérateurs.
56	Based on 2011 third quarter information.	56	Basé sur les informations du troisième trimestre 2011.
57	Telecom NZ and Vodafone NZ subscribers.	57	Abonnés à Telecom NZ et Vodafone NZ.
58	Measured using subscriptions active in the last 180 days.	58	Mesuré en utilisant les abonnements actifs au cours des 180 derniers jours.
59	Based on Zain market share.	59	Basé sur la part de marché de Zain.
60	Includes active GSM & CDMA mobile lines.	60	Y compris les lignes mobiles GSM et AMRC actives.
61	Unaudited.	61	non vérifié.
62	Refers to mid-year; Pacific Economic Survey 2008.	62	Enquête économique sur le Pacifique.
63	GSM.	63	GSM.
64	Decrease due to database updating, excluding inactive accounts.	64	Baisse due à la mise à jour de la base de données qui exclue les comptes inactifs.
65	Including also subscriptions providing only data services (due to difficulties to disaggregate the information at this point).	65	Comprend également les abonnements ne comportant que des services de transmission de données (du fait qu'il est difficile pour le moment de séparer ces services).
66	The 2009 figure is not available. Data refers to 1st quarter 2010.	66	Les chiffres ne sont pas disponibles pour 2009. Les données se réfèrent donc au premier trimestre 2010.
67	Active and non-active subscriptions.	67	abonnements actifs et inactifs.
68	Active subscriptions.	68	Abonnements actifs.
69	Active (last 6 months) SIM cards.	69	Cartes SIM actives (6 derniers mois).
70	On basis of MTS (Moscow TeleSystems) Annual Report.	70	Basé sur le rapport annuel de MTS (Moscow TeleSystems).
71	Decrease due to a change in policy. Inactive accounts for 3 months are being deactivated.	71	Baisse due à une modification des contrats: les comptes inactifs pendant 3 mois sont désactivés.
72	Refers to mid-year.	72	Données en milieu d'année.
73	January 2009.	73	Janvier 2009.
74	January 2010.	74	Janvier 2010.
75	January 2011.	75	Janvier 2011.
76	Data refer to 31 December.	76	Les données se réfèrent au 31 décembre.
77	Data as at February 2011. This includes multiple subscriptions by single individuals.	77	Données de février 2011, y compris les abonnements multiples souscrits par un même abonné.
78	As at December 2011.	78	Données en décembre 2011.
79	No distinction made between active or non-active subscribers.	79	Aucune distinction entre abonnés actifs et abonnés non-actifs.
80	Break in comparability from 1 January 2008, only active mobile subscribers are counted. Active subscribers are those that have used at least one payable service in the last 90 days.	80	Rupture de comparabilité à compter du 1er janvier 2008, seuls sont comptés les abonnés actifs au téléphone mobile. Les abonnés actifs sont ceux qui ont utilisé au moins un service facturable au cours des derniers 90 jours.
81	New methodology of active subscribers.	81	Nouvelle méthode de décompte des abonnés actifs.
82	Canar counted as fixed line.	82	Canar comptabilisé comme ligne fixe.
83	July.	83	Juillet.
84	Only one telecom provider.	84	Un seul fournisseur d'accès télécom.
85	Natural disasters impacted telecommunication network.	85	Les désastres naturels ont impacté les réseaux de télécommunication.
86	June 2010. The FCC has changed how it collects this data going back to 2005.	86	Juin 2010. La Commission fédérale des communications a modifié la manière dont elle collecte ces données depuis 2005.
87	Including data dedicated subscriptions.	87	Y compris les abonnements aux services d'accès aux données.

Country or area	2005	2006	2007	2008	2009	2010	2011	Pays ou zone
Afghanistan								**Afghanistan**
Number (thousands)	1	...	...	...	2	...	...	Nombre (milliers)
Per 100 inhabitants ^	0	...	...	...	0	...	...	Pour 100 habitants ^
Albania								**Albanie**
Number (thousands)	...	...	40	84	105	112	140	Nombre (milliers)
Per 100 inhabitants	...	...	1	3	3	3	4	Pour 100 habitants
Algeria								**Algérie**
Number (thousands)	190	...	...	...	...	...	...	Nombre (milliers)
Per 100 inhabitants	1	...	...	...	...	...	...	Pour 100 habitants
Andorra								**Andorre**
Number (thousands)	17	...	27	29	32	28	26	Nombre (milliers)
Per 100 inhabitants	22	...	33	36	38	33	30	Pour 100 habitants
Angola								**Angola**
Number (thousands)	45	95	100	107	320	...	...	Nombre (milliers)
Per 100 inhabitants	^0	1	1	1	2	...	...	Pour 100 habitants
Anguilla								**Anguilla**
Number (thousands)	2[1]	3[1]	3	4	...	...	...	Nombre (milliers)
Per 100 inhabitants	16[1]	20[1]	23	25	...	...	...	Pour 100 habitants
Antigua and Barbuda								**Antigua-et-Barbuda**
Number (thousands)	9	...	...	13	14	15	15	Nombre (milliers)
Per 100 inhabitants	11	...	...	15	16	16	16	Pour 100 habitants
Argentina								**Argentine**
Number (thousands)	2 417	2 742	3 415	3 737	3 850[2]	3 995[2]	...	Nombre (milliers)
Per 100 inhabitants	6	7	9	9	10[2]	10[2]	...	Pour 100 habitants
Armenia								**Arménie**
Number (thousands)	...	...	...	78	79	97	164	Nombre (milliers)
Per 100 inhabitants	...	...	...	3	3	3	5	Pour 100 habitants
Aruba								**Aruba**
Number (thousands)	...	...	16	18	...	...	...	Nombre (milliers)
Per 100 inhabitants	...	...	15	17	...	...	...	Pour 100 habitants
Australia								**Australie**
Number (thousands)	5 980[3]	6 650[3]	...	6 375[4]	5 983[4]	6 092[4]	5 970[4]	Nombre (milliers)
Per 100 inhabitants	29[3]	32[3]	...	30[4]	27[4]	27[4]	26[4]	Pour 100 habitants
Austria								**Autriche**
Number (thousands)	1 772	2 380	2 521[5]	2 047	2 149	*2 305	2 461	Nombre (milliers)
Per 100 inhabitants	22	29	30[5]	25	26	*27	29	Pour 100 habitants
Azerbaijan								**Azerbaïdjan**
Number (thousands)	73	101	217	410	522	871	1 318	Nombre (milliers)
Per 100 inhabitants	1	1	2	5	6	9	14	Pour 100 habitants
Bahamas								**Bahamas**
Number (thousands)	27	29	30[6]	36	39	25[7]	...	Nombre (milliers)
Per 100 inhabitants	9	9	9[6]	11	11	7[7]	...	Pour 100 habitants
Bahrain								**Bahreïn**
Number (thousands)	50	57	73	77	76	68	183	Nombre (milliers)
Per 100 inhabitants	7	7	8	7	7	5	14	Pour 100 habitants
Bangladesh								**Bangladesh**
Number (thousands)	123	150	...	...	830	940	1 150	Nombre (milliers)
Per 100 inhabitants	^0	^0	...	...	1	1	1	Pour 100 habitants
Barbados								**Barbade**
Number (thousands)	...	...	66	...	61	...	...	Nombre (milliers)
Per 100 inhabitants	...	...	24	...	22	...	...	Pour 100 habitants
Belarus								**Bélarus**
Number (thousands)	38	407	1 758	1 598	1 630	2 044	2 313	Nombre (milliers)
Per 100 inhabitants	^0	4	18	17	17	21	24	Pour 100 habitants
Belgium								**Belgique**
Number (thousands)	2 283[8]	2 559[8]	2 862[8]	3 056	3 205	3 416	3 544	Nombre (milliers)
Per 100 inhabitants	22[8]	24[8]	27[8]	29	30	32	33	Pour 100 habitants

Fixed (wired) internet subscriptions *(continued)*
Number (thousands) and per 100 inhabitants
Abonnements à l'internet fixe (filaire) *(suite)*
Nombre (milliers) et pour 100 habitants

Country or area	2005	2006	2007	2008	2009	2010	2011	Pays ou zone
Belize								**Belize**
Number (thousands)	7	8	9	9	9	9	...	Nombre (milliers)
Per 100 inhabitants	2	3	3	3	3	3	...	Pour 100 habitants
Benin								**Bénin**
Number (thousands)	7	8	9	...	...	...	...	Nombre (milliers)
Per 100 inhabitants ^	0	0	0	...	...	...	...	Pour 100 habitants ^
Bermuda								**Bermudes**
Number (thousands)	31	38	...	...	...	...	...	Nombre (milliers)
Per 100 inhabitants	48	59	...	...	...	...	...	Pour 100 habitants
Bhutan								**Bhoutan**
Number (thousands)	4	6	6[6]	6	7	10	14	Nombre (milliers)
Per 100 inhabitants	1	1	1[6]	1	1	1	2	Pour 100 habitants
Bolivia (Plurin. State of)								**Bolivie (État plurin. de)**
Number (thousands)	72	116	198	124	130	114	117	Nombre (milliers)
Per 100 inhabitants	1	1	2	1	1	1	1	Pour 100 habitants
Bosnia and Herzegovina								**Bosnie-Herzégovine**
Number (thousands)	181	238	274	336	399	522	515	Nombre (milliers)
Per 100 inhabitants	5	6	7	9	11	14	14	Pour 100 habitants
Botswana								**Botswana**
Number (thousands)	...	...	...	10	12	14	16	Nombre (milliers)
Per 100 inhabitants	...	...	...	1	1	1	1	Pour 100 habitants
Brazil								**Brésil**
Number (thousands)	4 364	5 922	8 711	27 523	22 909	20 909	22 898	Nombre (milliers)
Per 100 inhabitants	2	3	5	14	12	11	12	Pour 100 habitants
British Virgin Islands								**Iles Vierges britanniques**
Number (thousands)	...	...	...	...	11	11	...	Nombre (milliers)
Per 100 inhabitants	...	...	...	...	47	47	...	Pour 100 habitants
Brunei Darussalam								**Brunéi Darussalam**
Number (thousands)	18	19[9]	20[9]	24[9]	26	27[9]	27[9]	Nombre (milliers)
Per 100 inhabitants	5	5[9]	5[9]	6[9]	7	7[9]	7[9]	Pour 100 habitants
Bulgaria								**Bulgarie**
Number (thousands)	207	467[10]	648	828	962[11]	1 091	1 228	Nombre (milliers)
Per 100 inhabitants	3	6[10]	8	11	13[11]	15	16	Pour 100 habitants
Burkina Faso								**Burkina Faso**
Number (thousands)	8	9	12	15	23	29	31	Nombre (milliers)
Per 100 inhabitants ^	0	0	0	0	0	0	0	Pour 100 habitants ^
Burundi								**Burundi**
Number (thousands)	...	^0	1	4	18	38	...	Nombre (milliers)
Per 100 inhabitants ^	...	0	0	0	0	0	...	Pour 100 habitants ^
Cambodia								**Cambodge**
Number (thousands)	9	11	15	19	...	...	47	Nombre (milliers)
Per 100 inhabitants ^	0	0	0	0	...	...	0	Pour 100 habitants ^
Cameroon								**Cameroun**
Number (thousands)	15	25	...	...	...	...	...	Nombre (milliers)
Per 100 inhabitants ^	0	0	...	...	...	...	...	Pour 100 habitants ^
Canada								**Canada**
Number (thousands)	8 880[12]	9 481	10 163	10 714	10 580	10 993	11 250	Nombre (milliers)
Per 100 inhabitants	28[12]	29	31	32	31	32	33	Pour 100 habitants
Cape Verde								**Cap-Vert**
Number (thousands)	7	13	11	9	13	17	22	Nombre (milliers)
Per 100 inhabitants	1	3	2	2	3	3	4	Pour 100 habitants
Central African Rep.								**Rép. centrafricaine**
Number (thousands)	3	...	...	...	^0	^0	0	Nombre (milliers)
Per 100 inhabitants	^0	...	...	...	^0	^0	0	Pour 100 habitants
Chad								**Tchad**
Number (thousands)	...	...	...	...	5	...	...	Nombre (milliers)
Per 100 inhabitants ^	...	...	...	...	0	...	...	Pour 100 habitants ^
Chile								**Chili**
Number (thousands)	906	1 188[6]	1 332	1 439	1 695	1 820	2 025	Nombre (milliers)
Per 100 inhabitants	6	7[6]	8	9	10	11	12	Pour 100 habitants

Country or area	2005	2006	2007	2008	2009	2010	2011	Pays ou zone
China								**Chine**
Number (thousands)	73 012	77 363	85 889	95 214	111 522	...	...	Nombre (milliers)
Per 100 inhabitants	6	6	7	7	8	...	...	Pour 100 habitants
China, Hong Kong SAR								**Chine, Hong Kong RAS**
Number (thousands)	2 630[13]	2 692[13]	2 866[13]	2 572[13]	2 723[14]	2 922[14]	3 059	Nombre (milliers)
Per 100 inhabitants	39[13]	39[13]	42[13]	37[13]	39[14]	41[14]	43	Pour 100 habitants
China, Macao SAR								**Chine, Macao RAS**
Number (thousands)	89	105	122	124	128	133	138	Nombre (milliers)
Per 100 inhabitants	18	21	24	24	24	24	25	Pour 100 habitants
Colombia								**Colombie**
Number (thousands)	688	888	1 381	1 880[6]	2 266	2 676	3 297	Nombre (milliers)
Per 100 inhabitants	2	2	3	4[6]	5	6	7	Pour 100 habitants
Comoros								**Comores**
Number (thousands)	1	1	1	2	2	...	...	Nombre (milliers)
Per 100 inhabitants ^	0	0	0	0	0	...	...	Pour 100 habitants ^
Congo								**Congo**
Number (thousands)	...	...	...	...	1	2	2	Nombre (milliers)
Per 100 inhabitants ^	...	...	...	...	0	0	0	Pour 100 habitants ^
Costa Rica								**Costa Rica**
Number (thousands)	...	114	157	183	272	...	453	Nombre (milliers)
Per 100 inhabitants	...	3	4	4	6	...	10	Pour 100 habitants
Côte d'Ivoire								**Côte d'Ivoire**
Number (thousands)	18	...	...	...	...	...	50	Nombre (milliers)
Per 100 inhabitants ^	0	...	...	...	...	...	0	Pour 100 habitants ^
Croatia								**Croatie**
Number (thousands)	954	1 070	1 177[6]	1 361	1 498	1 497	1 192[15]	Nombre (milliers)
Per 100 inhabitants	21	24	27[6]	31	34	34	27[15]	Pour 100 habitants
Cuba								**Cuba**
Number (thousands)	...	16	34[6]	...	40	40	...	Nombre (milliers)
Per 100 inhabitants ^	...	0	0[6]	...	0	0	...	Pour 100 habitants ^
Cyprus [16]								**Chypre** [16]
Number (thousands)	91	106	131	160	191	207	212	Nombre (milliers)
Per 100 inhabitants	9	10	12	15	18	19	19	Pour 100 habitants
Czech Republic								**République tchèque**
Number (thousands)	2 352[17]	1 408	1 592	1 794	1 369[18]	1 530	1 669	Nombre (milliers)
Per 100 inhabitants	23[17]	14	15	17	13[18]	15	16	Pour 100 habitants
Dem. Rep. of the Congo								**Rép. dém. du Congo**
Number (thousands)	24	34	48	67	73	76	30	Nombre (milliers)
Per 100 inhabitants ^	0	0	0	0	0	0	0	Pour 100 habitants ^
Denmark								**Danemark**
Number (thousands)	1 809[19]	2 044	2 080	2 113	2 158	2 216	2 240	Nombre (milliers)
Per 100 inhabitants	33[19]	38	38	38	39	40	40	Pour 100 habitants
Djibouti								**Djibouti**
Number (thousands)	4	4	5	6	9	12	15	Nombre (milliers)
Per 100 inhabitants	^0	^1	1	1	1	1	2	Pour 100 habitants
Dominica								**Dominique**
Number (thousands)	...	...	...	...	...	9	...	Nombre (milliers)
Per 100 inhabitants	...	...	...	...	...	13	...	Pour 100 habitants
Dominican Republic								**Rép. dominicaine**
Number (thousands)	135	184	264	321	328	379	436	Nombre (milliers)
Per 100 inhabitants	1	2	3	3	3	4	4	Pour 100 habitants
Ecuador								**Equateur**
Number (thousands)	137	206	300[6]	306	349	485	639	Nombre (milliers)
Per 100 inhabitants	1	2	2[6]	2	2	3	4	Pour 100 habitants
Egypt								**Egypte**
Number (thousands)	2 552[20]	2 556[20]	2 679[20]	2 505[20]	2 290	2 117	2 166	Nombre (milliers)
Per 100 inhabitants	3[20]	3[20]	3[20]	3[20]	3	3	3	Pour 100 habitants
El Salvador								**El Salvador**
Number (thousands)	127	70	95	126	151	...	...	Nombre (milliers)
Per 100 inhabitants	2	1	2	2	2	...	...	Pour 100 habitants

17
Fixed (wired) internet subscriptions *(continued)*
Number (thousands) and per 100 inhabitants
Abonnements à l'internet fixe (filaire) *(suite)*
Nombre (milliers) et pour 100 habitants

Country or area	2005	2006	2007	2008	2009	2010	2011	Pays ou zone
Equatorial Guinea								**Guinée équatoriale**
Number (thousands)	1	...	...	...	...	...	...	Nombre (milliers)
Per 100 inhabitants ^	0	...	...	...	...	...	...	Pour 100 habitants ^
Eritrea								**Erythrée**
Number (thousands)	5	5	5	6	7	7	7	Nombre (milliers)
Per 100 inhabitants ^	0	0	0	0	0	0	0	Pour 100 habitants ^
Estonia								**Estonie**
Number (thousands)	197	259	284	325	343	338	349	Nombre (milliers)
Per 100 inhabitants	15	19	21	24	26	25	26	Pour 100 habitants
Ethiopia								**Ethiopie**
Number (thousands)	18	26	32	36	75	72	151	Nombre (milliers)
Per 100 inhabitants ^	0	0	0	0	0	0	0	Pour 100 habitants ^
Faeroe Islands								**Iles Féroé**
Number (thousands)	12	13	14	16	16	16	...	Nombre (milliers)
Per 100 inhabitants	25	27	30	33	33	34	...	Pour 100 habitants
Falkland Is. (Malvinas)								**Iles Falkland (Malvinas)**
Number (thousands)	1	1	1[6]	1[21]	1[21]	1[21]	...	Nombre (milliers)
Per 100 inhabitants	32	34	34[6]	37[21]	38[21]	39[21]	...	Pour 100 habitants
Fiji								**Fidji**
Number (thousands)	13	...	14[6]	29	28	39	39	Nombre (milliers)
Per 100 inhabitants	2	...	2[6]	3	3	5	4	Pour 100 habitants
France								**France**
Number (thousands)	13 217	15 252	17 250	18 810	20 504	21 820	23 060	Nombre (milliers)
Per 100 inhabitants	22	25	28	30	33	35	37	Pour 100 habitants
French Polynesia								**Polynésie française**
Number (thousands)	19	22	25	29	30	...	...	Nombre (milliers)
Per 100 inhabitants	7	8	10	11	11	...	...	Pour 100 habitants
Gabon								**Gabon**
Number (thousands)	9	10	11[6]	14	20	22	...	Nombre (milliers)
Per 100 inhabitants	1	1	1[6]	1	1	1	...	Pour 100 habitants
Gambia								**Gambie**
Number (thousands)	...	...	4	...	...	...	...	Nombre (milliers)
Per 100 inhabitants ^	...	...	0	...	...	...	...	Pour 100 habitants ^
Georgia								**Géorgie**
Number (thousands)	178	162	88	100	176	254	325	Nombre (milliers)
Per 100 inhabitants	4	4	2	2	4	6	8	Pour 100 habitants
Germany [6]								**Allemagne** [6]
Number (thousands)	20 000	...	...	...	...	...	...	Nombre (milliers)
Per 100 inhabitants	24	...	...	...	...	...	...	Pour 100 habitants
Ghana								**Ghana**
Number (thousands)	11	22	25	29	...	53	63	Nombre (milliers)
Per 100 inhabitants ^	0	0	0	0	...	0	0	Pour 100 habitants ^
Gibraltar								**Gibraltar**
Number (thousands)	...	...	...	...	11	11	12	Nombre (milliers)
Per 100 inhabitants	...	...	...	...	36	38	41	Pour 100 habitants
Greece								**Grèce**
Number (thousands)	882	955	1 262	1 744	2 032	2 314	2 510	Nombre (milliers)
Per 100 inhabitants	8	9	11	15	18	20	22	Pour 100 habitants
Greenland								**Groenland**
Number (thousands)	...	...	10	12	12	12	12	Nombre (milliers)
Per 100 inhabitants	...	...	18	21	22	22	21	Pour 100 habitants
Grenada								**Grenade**
Number (thousands)	6	7	...	11[21]	12	14	...	Nombre (milliers)
Per 100 inhabitants	5	7	...	10[21]	12	14	...	Pour 100 habitants
Guinea-Bissau								**Guinée-Bissau**
Number (thousands)	...	...	...	1	1	...	...	Nombre (milliers)
Per 100 inhabitants ^	...	...	...	0	0	...	...	Pour 100 habitants ^
Guyana								**Guyana**
Number (thousands)	48	...	...	...	...	16	...	Nombre (milliers)
Per 100 inhabitants	6	...	...	...	...	2	...	Pour 100 habitants

Country or area	2005	2006	2007	2008	2009	2010	2011	Pays ou zone
Haiti								**Haïti**
Number (thousands)	...	...	100	...	...	...	...	Nombre (milliers)
Per 100 inhabitants	...	...	1	...	...	...	...	Pour 100 habitants
Honduras								**Honduras**
Number (thousands)	26	29	36	59	72	...	...	Nombre (milliers)
Per 100 inhabitants	^0	^0	1	1	1	...	...	Pour 100 habitants
Hungary								**Hongrie**
Number (thousands)	977	1 292	1 445	1 706	1 903	2 073	2 221	Nombre (milliers)
Per 100 inhabitants	10	13	14	17	19	21	22	Pour 100 habitants
Iceland								**Islande**
Number (thousands)	87	98	106	111	111	112	115	Nombre (milliers)
Per 100 inhabitants	29	33	35	36	35	35	35	Pour 100 habitants
India								**Inde**
Number (thousands)	6 935	12 609	13 490	12 850	15 240[6]	18 690	22 390	Nombre (milliers)
Per 100 inhabitants	1	1	1	1	1[6]	2	2	Pour 100 habitants
Indonesia								**Indonésie**
Number (thousands)	1 853	2 702	1 573	1 707	...	...	...	Nombre (milliers)
Per 100 inhabitants	1	1	1	1	...	...	...	Pour 100 habitants
Iran (Islamic Rep. of)								**Iran (Rép. islamique d')**
Number (thousands)	...	...	...	...	...	...	5 240	Nombre (milliers)
Per 100 inhabitants	...	...	...	...	...	...	7	Pour 100 habitants
Iraq								**Iraq**
Number (thousands)	...	^0	^0	3	...	^0	...	Nombre (milliers)
Per 100 inhabitants ^	...	0	0	0	...	0	...	Pour 100 habitants ^
Ireland								**Irlande**
Number (thousands)	926	1 037	1 086	1 129	1 104[22]	1 075[22]	1 089[22]	Nombre (milliers)
Per 100 inhabitants	22	25	25	26	25[22]	24[22]	24[22]	Pour 100 habitants
Israel								**Israël**
Number (thousands)	1 677	1 890	...	1 714	...	...	1 879[23]	Nombre (milliers)
Per 100 inhabitants	25	28	...	24	...	...	25[23]	Pour 100 habitants
Italy								**Italie**
Number (thousands)	17 700[24,25]	11 778[24]	12 199[24]	11 283[24]	12 300	13 400[26]	...	Nombre (milliers)
Per 100 inhabitants	30[24,25]	20[24]	21[24]	19[24]	20	22[26]	...	Pour 100 habitants
Jamaica								**Jamaïque**
Number (thousands)	...	74	96	104	115	...	...	Nombre (milliers)
Per 100 inhabitants	...	3	4	4	4	...	...	Pour 100 habitants
Japan[27]								**Japon**[27]
Number (thousands)	...	...	...	...	36 057	37 679	38 715	Nombre (milliers)
Per 100 inhabitants	...	...	...	...	28	30	31	Pour 100 habitants
Jordan								**Jordanie**
Number (thousands)	197	206	228	229	245	248	208	Nombre (milliers)
Per 100 inhabitants	4	4	4	4	4	4	3	Pour 100 habitants
Kazakhstan								**Kazakhstan**
Number (thousands)	302	310	683	700[6]	757	1 543	1 262	Nombre (milliers)
Per 100 inhabitants	2	2	4	4[6]	5	10	8	Pour 100 habitants
Kenya								**Kenya**
Number (thousands)	80	187	...	11[28]	8[28]	12	...	Nombre (milliers)
Per 100 inhabitants	^0	1	...	^0[28]	^0[28]	^0	...	Pour 100 habitants
Kuwait								**Koweït**
Number (thousands)	283	...	...	...	...	...	...	Nombre (milliers)
Per 100 inhabitants	13	...	...	...	...	...	...	Pour 100 habitants
Kyrgyzstan								**Kirghizistan**
Number (thousands)	14	18	20	31	48	69	115	Nombre (milliers)
Per 100 inhabitants	^0	^0	^0	1	1	1	2	Pour 100 habitants
Lao People's Dem. Rep.								**Rép. dém. pop. lao**
Number (thousands)	6[29]	5[29]	5[29]	13	16	...	...	Nombre (milliers)
Per 100 inhabitants ^	0[29]	0[29]	0[29]	0	0	...	...	Pour 100 habitants ^
Latvia								**Lettonie**
Number (thousands)	73	116	321[6]	...	...	...	...	Nombre (milliers)
Per 100 inhabitants	3	5	14[6]	...	...	...	...	Pour 100 habitants

17
Fixed (wired) internet subscriptions *(continued)*
Number (thousands) and per 100 inhabitants
Abonnements à l'internet fixe (filaire) *(suite)*
Nombre (milliers) et pour 100 habitants

Country or area	2005	2006	2007	2008	2009	2010	2011	Pays ou zone
Lebanon								**Liban**
Number (thousands)	230	310	260	315	...	...	469	Nombre (milliers)
Per 100 inhabitants	6	8	6	8	...	...	11	Pour 100 habitants
Lesotho								**Lesotho**
Number (thousands)	3	...	1	1	3	10	...	Nombre (milliers)
Per 100 inhabitants ^	0	...	0	0	0	0	...	Pour 100 habitants ^
Liberia[6]								**Libéria**[6]
Number (thousands)	...	...	15	...	...	...	...	Nombre (milliers)
Per 100 inhabitants ^	...	...	0	...	...	...	...	Pour 100 habitants ^
Libyan Arab Jamah.								**Jamah. arabe libyenne**
Number (thousands)	...	82	...	723	772	...	...	Nombre (milliers)
Per 100 inhabitants	...	1	...	12	12	...	...	Pour 100 habitants
Liechtenstein								**Liechtenstein**
Number (thousands)	16	16	17	...	...	...	...	Nombre (milliers)
Per 100 inhabitants	45	45	47	...	...	...	...	Pour 100 habitants
Lithuania								**Lituanie**
Number (thousands)	257[30]	380	513	594	636	685	...	Nombre (milliers)
Per 100 inhabitants	8[30]	11	15	18	19	21	...	Pour 100 habitants
Luxembourg								**Luxembourg**
Number (thousands)	119	131	157	143	156	168	...	Nombre (milliers)
Per 100 inhabitants	26	28	33	29	31	33	...	Pour 100 habitants
Madagascar								**Madagascar**
Number (thousands)	10	20	11	11	8	9	18	Nombre (milliers)
Per 100 inhabitants ^	0	0	0	0	0	0	0	Pour 100 habitants ^
Malawi								**Malawi**
Number (thousands)	15	...	85	106	150	305	450	Nombre (milliers)
Per 100 inhabitants	^0	...	1	1	1	2	3	Pour 100 habitants
Malaysia								**Malaisie**
Number (thousands)	4 155	4 489	4 931	5 222	5 592	...	...	Nombre (milliers)
Per 100 inhabitants	16	17	18	19	20	...	...	Pour 100 habitants
Maldives								**Maldives**
Number (thousands)	5	8	12	18	18	17	21	Nombre (milliers)
Per 100 inhabitants	2	3	4	6	6	5	7	Pour 100 habitants
Mali								**Mali**
Number (thousands)	...	6	7	10	20	24	37	Nombre (milliers)
Per 100 inhabitants ^	...	0	0	0	0	0	0	Pour 100 habitants ^
Malta								**Malte**
Number (thousands)	89	95	100	103	110	122	129	Nombre (milliers)
Per 100 inhabitants	22	23	24	25	27	29	31	Pour 100 habitants
Mauritania								**Mauritanie**
Number (thousands)	2	4	6	10	8	7	7	Nombre (milliers)
Per 100 inhabitants ^	0	0	0	0	0	0	0	Pour 100 habitants ^
Mauritius								**Maurice**
Number (thousands)	86	82	88	89	101	99	127	Nombre (milliers)
Per 100 inhabitants	7	7	7	7	8	8	10	Pour 100 habitants
Mexico								**Mexique**
Number (thousands)	3 882	4 806	5 757	8 129	9 679	11 354[31]	11 992	Nombre (milliers)
Per 100 inhabitants	4	4	5	7	9	10[31]	10	Pour 100 habitants
Micronesia (Fed. States of)								**Micronésie (Etats féd. de)**
Number (thousands)	2	1	1	...	...	...	...	Nombre (milliers)
Per 100 inhabitants	2	1	1	...	...	...	...	Pour 100 habitants
Monaco								**Monaco**
Number (thousands)	10	11	13	...	...	14	16	Nombre (milliers)
Per 100 inhabitants	28	32	35	...	...	39	45	Pour 100 habitants
Mongolia								**Mongolie**
Number (thousands)	9	11	17	37	49	75[6]	90[6]	Nombre (milliers)
Per 100 inhabitants	^0	^0	1	1	2	3[6]	3[6]	Pour 100 habitants
Montenegro								**Monténégro**
Number (thousands)	81	89	...	...	...	...	...	Nombre (milliers)
Per 100 inhabitants	13	14	...	...	...	...	...	Pour 100 habitants

Country or area	2005	2006	2007	2008	2009	2010	2011	Pays ou zone
Montserrat								**Montserrat**
Number (thousands)	...	1	1	...	...	...	...	Nombre (milliers)
Per 100 inhabitants	...	14	16	...	...	...	...	Pour 100 habitants
Morocco								**Maroc**
Number (thousands)	262	400	483	489	480	500	592	Nombre (milliers)
Per 100 inhabitants	1	1	2	2	2	2	2	Pour 100 habitants
Mozambique								**Mozambique**
Number (thousands)	...	...	...	...	14	...	16	Nombre (milliers)
Per 100 inhabitants ^	...	...	...	...	0	...	0	Pour 100 habitants ^
Myanmar								**Myanmar**
Number (thousands)	6	16	18	21	...	...	15	Nombre (milliers)
Per 100 inhabitants ^	0	0	0	0	...	...	0	Pour 100 habitants ^
Namibia								**Namibie**
Number (thousands)	60	75	90[6]	...	...	...	...	Nombre (milliers)
Per 100 inhabitants	3	4	4[6]	...	...	...	...	Pour 100 habitants
Nepal								**Népal**
Number (thousands)	45	63	80	...	...	128[22]	...	Nombre (milliers)
Per 100 inhabitants ^	0	0	0	...	...	0[22]	...	Pour 100 habitants ^
Netherlands								**Pays-Bas**
Number (thousands)	5 600[6]	5 970[6]	5 618[6]	5 805	6 130	6 330	...	Nombre (milliers)
Per 100 inhabitants	34[6]	36[6]	34[6]	35	37	38	...	Pour 100 habitants
New Caledonia								**Nouvelle-Calédonie**
Number (thousands)	19	20[6]	22	27	33	...	...	Nombre (milliers)
Per 100 inhabitants	8	8[6]	9	11	13	...	...	Pour 100 habitants
New Zealand								**Nouvelle-Zélande**
Number (thousands)	1 156[32]	1 283[32]	1 449[32]	1 504[32]	1 400	1 400	1 400	Nombre (milliers)
Per 100 inhabitants	28[32]	31[32]	34[32]	35[32]	32	32	32	Pour 100 habitants
Nicaragua								**Nicaragua**
Number (thousands)	23	24	...	...	...	...	...	Nombre (milliers)
Per 100 inhabitants ^	0	0	...	...	...	...	...	Pour 100 habitants ^
Niger								**Niger**
Number (thousands)	4	...	...	...	...	4	16	Nombre (milliers)
Per 100 inhabitants ^	0	...	...	...	...	0	0	Pour 100 habitants ^
Nigeria								**Nigéria**
Number (thousands)	...	...	...	116	188	222	...	Nombre (milliers)
Per 100 inhabitants ^	...	...	...	0	0	0	...	Pour 100 habitants ^
Norway								**Norvège**
Number (thousands)	1 421	1 513	1 602	1 610	1 668	1 723	1 786	Nombre (milliers)
Per 100 inhabitants	31	32	34	34	35	35	36	Pour 100 habitants
Occupied Palestinian Terr.								**Terr. palestinien occupé**
Number (thousands)	78	79	102	103	115	...	...	Nombre (milliers)
Per 100 inhabitants	2	2	3	3	3	...	...	Pour 100 habitants
Oman								**Oman**
Number (thousands)	54	63	71[33]	80	78	74	89	Nombre (milliers)
Per 100 inhabitants	2	3	3[33]	3	3	3	3	Pour 100 habitants
Pakistan								**Pakistan**
Number (thousands)	2 100	2 400	3 500[6]	3 500	3 700	3 236	2 882	Nombre (milliers)
Per 100 inhabitants	1	1	2[6]	2	2	2	2	Pour 100 habitants
Palau								**Palaos**
Number (thousands)	1	1	1	1	1	1	1	Nombre (milliers)
Per 100 inhabitants	7	6	6	6	5	5	6	Pour 100 habitants
Panama								**Panama**
Number (thousands)	82	127	166	208	244	285	290	Nombre (milliers)
Per 100 inhabitants	3	4	5	6	7	8	8	Pour 100 habitants
Paraguay								**Paraguay**
Number (thousands)	60	65	74	105	157	106	...	Nombre (milliers)
Per 100 inhabitants	1	1	1	2	2	2	...	Pour 100 habitants
Peru								**Pérou**
Number (thousands)	833	...	...	...	824	925	1 197	Nombre (milliers)
Per 100 inhabitants	3	...	...	...	3	3	4	Pour 100 habitants

Fixed (wired) internet subscriptions *(continued)*
Number (thousands) and per 100 inhabitants
Abonnements à l'internet fixe (filaire) *(suite)*
Nombre (milliers) et pour 100 habitants

Country or area	2005	2006	2007	2008	2009	2010	2011	Pays ou zone
Philippines								**Philippines**
Number (thousands)	1 440	2 000	2 596	3 546	3 600	4 320	5 184	Nombre (milliers)
Per 100 inhabitants	2	2	3	4	4	5	5	Pour 100 habitants
Poland								**Pologne**
Number (thousands)	2 686	3 244	...	4 365[34]	5 036[34]	4 963[34]	...	Nombre (milliers)
Per 100 inhabitants	7	9	...	11[34]	13[34]	13[34]	...	Pour 100 habitants
Portugal								**Portugal**
Number (thousands)	1 436	1 580	1 612	1 644[35]	1 945[36]	2 156	2 266	Nombre (milliers)
Per 100 inhabitants	14	15	15	15[35]	18[36]	20	21	Pour 100 habitants
Puerto Rico								**Porto Rico**
Number (thousands)	...	...	...	513	512	576	568[37]	Nombre (milliers)
Per 100 inhabitants	...	...	...	14	14	15	15[37]	Pour 100 habitants
Qatar								**Qatar**
Number (thousands)	53	70	87	115	146	150	167	Nombre (milliers)
Per 100 inhabitants	6	7	7	8	9	9	9	Pour 100 habitants
Republic of Korea								**République de Corée**
Number (thousands)	12 188	14 041	14 710	15 474	16 348	17 194	17 859	Nombre (milliers)
Per 100 inhabitants	26	30	31	32	34	36	37	Pour 100 habitants
Republic of Moldova								**République de Moldova**
Number (thousands)	61	94	110	156	204	269	355	Nombre (milliers)
Per 100 inhabitants	2	3	3	4	6	8	10	Pour 100 habitants
Romania								**Roumanie**
Number (thousands)	790[38]	1 430	2 122[39]	2 490[39]	2 800[39]	3 000[39]	3 260[39]	Nombre (milliers)
Per 100 inhabitants	4[38]	7	10[39]	12[39]	13[39]	14[39]	15[39]	Pour 100 habitants
Russian Federation								**Fédération de Russie**
Number (thousands)	19 056	24 778	...	...	...	...	19 427	Nombre (milliers)
Per 100 inhabitants	13	17	...	...	...	...	14	Pour 100 habitants
Rwanda								**Rwanda**
Number (thousands)	3	4	6	8	12	17	17	Nombre (milliers)
Per 100 inhabitants ^	0	0	0	0	0	0	0	Pour 100 habitants ^
Saint Helena[21]								**Sainte-Hélène**[21]
Number (thousands)	1	1	1	1	1	1	1	Nombre (milliers)
Per 100 inhabitants	11	13	13	14	16	19	22	Pour 100 habitants
Saint Lucia								**Sainte-Lucie**
Number (thousands)	...	9	12	16	19	21	22	Nombre (milliers)
Per 100 inhabitants	...	5	7	10	11	12	12	Pour 100 habitants
Saint Vincent-Grenadines								**Saint Vincent-Grenadines**
Number (thousands)	5	7	9[6]	10[6]	12	13	14	Nombre (milliers)
Per 100 inhabitants	5	6	8	9	11	12	13	Pour 100 habitants
San Marino								**Saint-Marin**
Number (thousands)	6	6	6	7	...	...	...	Nombre (milliers)
Per 100 inhabitants	18	19	19	21	...	...	...	Pour 100 habitants
Sao Tome and Principe								**Sao Tomé-et-Principe**
Number (thousands)	1	...	...	1	1	1	1	Nombre (milliers)
Per 100 inhabitants	1	...	...	1	1	1	1	Pour 100 habitants
Saudi Arabia								**Arabie saoudite**
Number (thousands)	1 263[40]	1 648[40]	1 722[40]	1 832[40]	1 882	1 898	1 871	Nombre (milliers)
Per 100 inhabitants	5[40]	7[40]	7[40]	7[40]	7	7	7	Pour 100 habitants
Senegal								**Sénégal**
Number (thousands)	21[41]	30[41]	39[41]	48[41]	60	79	93	Nombre (milliers)
Per 100 inhabitants	^0[41]	^0[41]	^0[41]	^0[41]	^0	1	1	Pour 100 habitants
Serbia								**Serbie**
Number (thousands)	757	1 005	1 012	850	843	918	972	Nombre (milliers)
Per 100 inhabitants	9	12	12	10	10	11	12	Pour 100 habitants
Seychelles								**Seychelles**
Number (thousands)	4	5	5[42]	5[43]	6[44]	8[45]	11[46]	Nombre (milliers)
Per 100 inhabitants	5	6	6[42]	6[43]	7[44]	9[45]	12[46]	Pour 100 habitants
Singapore[47]								**Singapour**[47]
Number (thousands)	2 255	2 303	1 928	1 122	1 247	1 334	1 386	Nombre (milliers)
Per 100 inhabitants	53	52	42	24	25	26	27	Pour 100 habitants

Country or area	2005	2006	2007	2008	2009	2010	2011	Pays ou zone
Slovakia								**Slovaquie**
Number (thousands)	294	395	544	576	674	732	780	Nombre (milliers)
Per 100 inhabitants	5	7	10	11	12	13	14	Pour 100 habitants
Slovenia								**Slovénie**
Number (thousands)	398	407	417	455	465	487	499	Nombre (milliers)
Per 100 inhabitants	20	20	21	23	23	24	25	Pour 100 habitants
Solomon Islands								**Iles Salomon**
Number (thousands)	2	...	...	...	...	...	...	Nombre (milliers)
Per 100 inhabitants ^	0	...	...	...	...	...	...	Pour 100 habitants ^
Spain								**Espagne**
Number (thousands)	6 234	7 507	8 592	9 394	9 860	10 660	11 108	Nombre (milliers)
Per 100 inhabitants	14	17	19	21	22	23	24	Pour 100 habitants
Sri Lanka								**Sri Lanka**
Number (thousands)	115	135	202	246	250	298	...	Nombre (milliers)
Per 100 inhabitants	1	1	1	1	1	1	...	Pour 100 habitants
Sudan (former)								**Soudan (anc.)**
Number (thousands)	...	44	...	...	...	27	32	Nombre (milliers)
Per 100 inhabitants ^	...	0	...	...	...	0	0	Pour 100 habitants ^
Suriname								**Suriname**
Number (thousands)	7	8	10[6]	11[6]	13	...	24	Nombre (milliers)
Per 100 inhabitants	1	2	2[6]	2[6]	2	...	5	Pour 100 habitants
Swaziland								**Swaziland**
Number (thousands)	21	21	...	20	4	4	5	Nombre (milliers)
Per 100 inhabitants	2	2	...	2	^0	^0	^0	Pour 100 habitants
Sweden								**Suède**
Number (thousands)	3 289[48]	3 595[48]	3 577	3 389	3 282	3 231	...	Nombre (milliers)
Per 100 inhabitants	36[48]	40[48]	39	37	35	34	...	Pour 100 habitants
Switzerland								**Suisse**
Number (thousands)	2 585	2 827	2 800	2 760	2 847	2 990	3 150[49]	Nombre (milliers)
Per 100 inhabitants	35	38	37	36	37	39	41[49]	Pour 100 habitants
Syrian Arab Republic								**Rép. arabe syrienne**
Number (thousands)	216	309	629	744	851	986	...	Nombre (milliers)
Per 100 inhabitants	1	2	3	4	4	5	...	Pour 100 habitants
Thailand								**Thaïlande**
Number (thousands)	...	...	1 298	...	...	...	3 846	Nombre (milliers)
Per 100 inhabitants	...	...	2	...	...	...	6	Pour 100 habitants
TFYR of Macedonia								**L'ex-R.Y. Macédoine**
Number (thousands)	108[50]	166[50]	274[25,50]	288	222	239	260	Nombre (milliers)
Per 100 inhabitants	5[50]	8[50]	13[25,50]	14	11	12	13	Pour 100 habitants
Timor-Leste								**Timor-Leste**
Number (thousands)	1	1	1	1	1	...	...	Nombre (milliers)
Per 100 inhabitants ^	0	0	0	0	0	...	...	Pour 100 habitants ^
Togo								**Togo**
Number (thousands)	...	...	64	65	60	61	...	Nombre (milliers)
Per 100 inhabitants	...	...	1	1	1	1	...	Pour 100 habitants
Tokelau								**Tokélaou**
Number (thousands) ^	0	...	...	...	...	...	...	Nombre (milliers) ^
Per 100 inhabitants	12	...	...	...	...	...	...	Pour 100 habitants
Tonga								**Tonga**
Number (thousands)	2	2	4	4	...	...	...	Nombre (milliers)
Per 100 inhabitants	2	2	4	4	...	...	...	Pour 100 habitants
Trinidad and Tobago								**Trinité-et-Tobago**
Number (thousands)	65[6]	81	82[51]	114	145	150	157	Nombre (milliers)
Per 100 inhabitants	5[6]	6	6[51]	9	11	11	12	Pour 100 habitants
Tunisia								**Tunisie**
Number (thousands)	150	179	253	281	414	543	604	Nombre (milliers)
Per 100 inhabitants	2	2	3	3	4	5	6	Pour 100 habitants
Turkey								**Turquie**
Number (thousands)	2 253	3 180	4 879	5 829	6 456	7 224	7 652	Nombre (milliers)
Per 100 inhabitants	3	5	7	8	9	10	10	Pour 100 habitants

17

Fixed (wired) internet subscriptions *(continued)*
Number (thousands) and per 100 inhabitants
Abonnements à l'internet fixe (filaire) *(suite)*
Nombre (milliers) et pour 100 habitants

Country or area	2005	2006	2007	2008	2009	2010	2011	Pays ou zone
Tuvalu								**Tuvalu**
Number (thousands)	1	1	1[6]	...	...	...	...	Nombre (milliers)
Per 100 inhabitants	5	7	8[6]	...	...	...	...	Pour 100 habitants
Uganda								**Ouganda**
Number (thousands)	10	11	16	22	30	134	89	Nombre (milliers)
Per 100 inhabitants ^	0	0	0	0	0	0	0	Pour 100 habitants ^
Ukraine								**Ukraine**
Number (thousands)	3 750	...	1 375	1 905	2 649	3 661	4 178	Nombre (milliers)
Per 100 inhabitants	8	...	3	4	6	8	9	Pour 100 habitants
United Arab Emirates								**Emirats arabes unis**
Number (thousands)	529	683	904	1 200	1 404	1 375	1 324	Nombre (milliers)
Per 100 inhabitants	13	15	17	19	20	18	17	Pour 100 habitants
United Kingdom								**Royaume-Uni**
Number (thousands)	16 320	16 956	18 300	18 573	19 238	19 133[52]	20 438[52]	Nombre (milliers)
Per 100 inhabitants	27	28	30	30	31	31[52]	33[52]	Pour 100 habitants
United Rep. of Tanzania								**Rép.-Unie de Tanzanie**
Number (thousands)	92	129	181	252	398	487[25]	...	Nombre (milliers)
Per 100 inhabitants	^0	^0	^0	1	1	1[25]	...	Pour 100 habitants
United States								**Etats-Unis**
Number (thousands)	...	...	77 987	...	83 998	86 125	...	Nombre (milliers)
Per 100 inhabitants	...	...	26	...	27	28	...	Pour 100 habitants
Uruguay								**Uruguay**
Number (thousands)	175	199	231	271	301	367	455	Nombre (milliers)
Per 100 inhabitants	5	6	7	8	9	11	13	Pour 100 habitants
Uzbekistan								**Ouzbékistan**
Number (thousands)	...	1 700	2 015	2 469	2 737	...	...	Nombre (milliers)
Per 100 inhabitants	...	6	8	9	10	...	...	Pour 100 habitants
Vanuatu								**Vanuatu**
Number (thousands)	2	...	...	...	3[6]	2	2	Nombre (milliers)
Per 100 inhabitants	1	...	...	...	1[6]	1	1	Pour 100 habitants
Venezuela (Boliv. Rep. of)								**Venezuela (Rép. boliv. du)**
Number (thousands)	637	760	1 003	1 473	1 574[53]	1 917[53]	2 038[31,53]	Nombre (milliers)
Per 100 inhabitants	2	3	4	5	6[53]	7[53]	7[31,53]	Pour 100 habitants
Viet Nam								**Viet Nam**
Number (thousands)	2 906	4 059	5 241	6 700	...	...	...	Nombre (milliers)
Per 100 inhabitants	3	5	6	8	...	...	...	Pour 100 habitants
Wallis and Futuna Islands								**Iles Wallis et Futuna**
Number (thousands)	1	1	...	...		...	...	Nombre (milliers)
Per 100 inhabitants	4	4	...	...	...	...	...	Pour 100 habitants
Yemen								**Yémen**
Number (thousands)	109	156	216	306	456	582	...	Nombre (milliers)
Per 100 inhabitants	1	1	1	1	2	2	...	Pour 100 habitants
Zambia								**Zambie**
Number (thousands)	...	9	13	18	18	17	15	Nombre (milliers)
Per 100 inhabitants ^	...	0	0	0	0	0	0	Pour 100 habitants ^
Zimbabwe								**Zimbabwe**
Number (thousands)	96	97	100	100	41	45	54	Nombre (milliers)
Per 100 inhabitants	1	1	1	1	^0	^0	^0	Pour 100 habitants

Source:
International Telecommunication Union (ITU), Geneva, the ITU database, last accessed March 2013.

Source:
Union internationale des télécommunications (UIT), Genève, la base de données de l'UIT, dernier accès mars 2013.

1 High speed internet.
2 ITU calculation as per data reported in sub-indicators.
3 March.
4 Internet activity survey. December.
5 Regular users of internet. Age 14+
6 ITU estimate.

1 Internet haut débit.
2 Selon les calculs de l'UIT fondés sur les données communiquées dans les sous-indicateurs.
3 Mars.
4 Enquête sur les activités liées à Internet. Décembre.
5 Utilisateurs réguliers d'Internet. Âge : 14 ans et plus.
6 Estimation de l'UIT.

7	Reduction due to purging of system of non-active accounts.	7	Diminution liée à la suppression des comptes inactifs.
8	Active subscribers.	8	Abonnés actifs.
9	ITU research based on AITI website.	9	Recherches de l'UIT fondées sur le site Web de l'AITI.
10	Data by the licensed operators providing Internet and some of the ISPs providing services on free regime (part of the non-licensed ISPs have not provided information to CRC).	10	Données communiquées par les opérateurs détenteurs d'une licence et par certains fournisseurs d'accès Internet opérant dans le cadre du régime libre (certains fournisseurs ne détenant pas une licence n'ont pas communiqué de données à la Commission de réglementation des communications).
11	Information provided by 93% of all ISPs.	11	Données communiquées par 93 % de tous les fournisseurs d'accès Internet.
12	Retail subscribers.	12	Particuliers
13	Estimated number of customer accounts based on returns from licensed Internet Service Providers.	13	Estimations (comptes clients) fondées sur les données communiquées par les fournisseurs d'accès Internet détenteurs d'une licence.
14	Based on the number of registered Internet customer accounts for both dial-up and broadband access.	14	Nombre de comptes clients ouverts : lignes commutées et haut débit.
15	Break in comparability: from this year excluding inactive dial-up subscriptions.	15	Discontinuité dans la comparabilité : à partir de cette année, il n'est plus tenu compte des abonnements inactifs (accès par lignes commutées).
16	The figures include the subscribers of all companies that offer internet services.	16	Y compris les abonnés des sociétés qui offrent des services Internet.
17	Data includes CDMA subscriptions because it is often used as fixed-wireless service.	17	Les données comprennent les abonnements AMRC (accès multiple par code de répartition) car ils sont souvent utilisés comme service fixe sans fil.
18	The decrease is due to the exclusion of FWA which is now included in terrestrial wireless subscriptions.	18	La diminution s'explique par le retrait des accès fixes sans fil, désormais comptabilisés parmi les abonnements à des services d'accès terrestres sans fil.
19	Active within last 3 months.	19	Usagers actifs pendant les trois derniers mois.
20	Egypt has a subscription-free Internet model that offers Internet access at a price of local call.	20	L'Égypte propose un accès à Internet sans abonnement pour le prix d'un appel local.
21	Cable and Wireless	21	Câble et sans fil.
22	December.	22	Décembre.
23	Excluding dial-up.	23	Accès par lignes commutées non pris en compte.
24	Home plus office active users.	24	Particuliers et usagers actifs sur le lieu d'exercice de leur profession.
25	June.	25	Juin.
26	In terms of BB lines (excl. internet dial-up subs.).	26	Large bande (exception faite des abonnés à des services Internet par lignes commutées).
27	The number is based on total subscriptions of operators with over fifty thousand subscriptions.	27	Nombre fondé sur le nombre total d'abonnements souscrits auprès d'opérateurs comptant plus de 50 000 abonnés.
28	Decline was due to subscribers switching to wireless technologies.	28	La diminution s'explique par les abonnés qui optent pour des technologies sans fil.
29	Laotel only.	29	Laotel uniquement.
30	Only fixed Internet access subscriptions are included.	30	Ne comprend que les abonnements à Internet par ligne fixe.
31	Preliminary.	31	Chiffres préliminaires.
32	March. Including wireless, cable, satellite and other connection types.	32	Mars. Comprend les connexions sans fil, câblées, par satellite et d'autres types de connexions.
33	Including estimated pre-paid Internet subscribers.	33	Y compris les abonnés à Internet bénéficiant de services prépayés (estimations).
34	Including all subscriptions that used Internet in the past year.	34	Y compris tous les abonnés qui se sont servis d'Internet pendant l'année écoulée.
35	Active usage one month.	35	Usagers actifs pendant un mois.
36	Break in comparability: from this year data refer to number of lines and not number of clients.	36	Discontinuité dans la comparabilité : à partir de cette année, les données font référence au nombre de lignes et non plus au nombre de clients.
37	As of December 31, 2011. Excludes unregulated providers.	37	Au 31 décembre 2011. Ne comprend pas les fournisseurs non réglementés.
38	Previously, mobile connections were included.	38	Les abonnements mobiles étaient précédemment comptabilisés.
39	Radio and satellite are not included.	39	Les accès par radio et par satellite ne sont pas comptabilisés.
40	Estimate from Communication and Information Technology Commission.	40	Estimations émanant de la Commission nationale de l'informatique et des communications.
41	Only Telecom Plus subscribers.	41	Les données ne portent que sur les abonnés de Telecom Plus.
42	January 2008	42	Janvier 2008
43	January 2009.	43	Janvier 2009.
44	January 2010.	44	Janvier 2010.
45	January 2011.	45	Janvier 2011.
46	31 December 2011	46	31 décembre 2011.
47	No differentiation between active and non-active subscriptions.	47	Aucune distinction n'est faite entre les abonnés actifs et les abonnés inactifs.
48	Modem including ISDN.	48	Accès par modem, y compris RNIS.
49	Provisional data.	49	Données provisoires.
50	Excluding cable modem internet subscribers.	50	Ne comprend pas les abonnés à Internet utilisant un câblo-modem.
51	September.	51	Septembre.
52	Excludes corporate connections.	52	Ne comprend pas les connexions d'entreprise.
53	Including cable modem, DSL, TDM, WLL and Dial-up.	53	Y compris les types d'accès suivants : câblo-modem, DSL, multiplexage temporel, sans fil et lignes commutées.

18

Cinema infrastructure
Number of indoor cinemas, screens and seats

Exploitation cinématographique
Nombre de salles de cinemas, d'ecrans et de places

| Country or area
Pays ou zone | Year
Année | Indoor cinemas - Salles de cinéma | | Screens - Écrans | | Number
of seats
Nombre de
places |
		Number Nombre	Per million inhabitants Par millions d'habitants	Number Nombre	Per capita Par habitant	
Africa · Afrique						
Algeria	2007	...	...	10	0.03	...
Algérie	2009	...	...	19	0.06	...
Burkina Faso	2007	10	0.81	10	0.08	10 000
Burkina Faso	2008	10	0.79	10	0.08	10 000
	2009	10	0.76	10	0.08	10 000
Cameroon	2006	3	0.20	...	...	...
Cameroun	2007	3	0.20	3	0.02	...
	2008	3	0.19	3	0.02	...
Egypt	2007	114	1.68	232	0.34	83 891
Egypte	2008	116	1.68	250	0.36	86 659
	2009	116	1.65	237	0.34	83 683
Ethiopia [1]						
Ethiopie [1]	2008	19	...	...	...	...
Gabon	2007	3	2.44	3	0.24	1 300
Gabon	2008	3	2.39	3	0.24	1 300
	2009	3	2.34	3	0.23	1 300
Mauritius	2007	...	...	26	2.23	...
Maurice	2008	...	...	26	2.21	...
	2009	...	...	26	2.19	...
Morocco	2007	78	2.80	104	0.37	55 949
Maroc	2008	70	2.49	95	0.34	50 862
	2009	53	1.87	77	0.27	39 770
Mozambique	2007	4	0.22	4	0.02	2 709
Mozambique	2008	4	0.22	4	0.02	2 709
	2009	4	0.21	4	0.02	2 709
Namibia	2005	4	2.23	...	...	...
Namibie	2006	3	1.64	...	...	...
Niger	2007	3	0.27	3	0.03	2 523
Niger	2008	3	0.26	3	0.03	2 523
	2009	3	0.25	3	0.03	2 523
Nigeria	2007	53	0.44	100[2]	0.08[2]	30 000[2]
Nigéria	2008	53	0.43	100[2]	0.08[2]	30 000[2]
	2009	53	0.41	100[2]	0.08[2]	30 000[2]
South Africa	2007	...	...	831	1.92	...
Afrique du Sud	2008	...	...	836	1.90	...
	2009	...	...	846	1.91	...
Tunisia						
Tunisie	2007	...	...	27	0.29	...
America, North · Amérique du Nord						
Canada	2006	...	...	2 831	9.53	...
Canada	2007	672	22.41	...	...	...
	2008	681	22.51	...	...	...
Costa Rica	2007	...	...	94	2.34	...
Costa Rica	2008[3]	...	...	115	2.81	...
	2009[3]	...	...	115	2.77	...
Cuba	2007	296	28.66	296	2.87	...
Cuba	2008	307	29.68	307	2.97	...
	2009	313	30.22	313	3.02	...
Dominican Republic	2007	21	2.51	120	1.44	25 566
Rép. dominicaine	2008	23	2.71	123	1.45	26 111
	2009	23	2.67	123	1.43	26 111

Communication and culture — Communication et culture   131

Cinema infrastructure *(continued)*
Number of indoor cinemas, screens and seats
Exploitation cinématographique *(suite)*
Nombre de salles de cinemas, d'ecrans et de places

Country or area Pays ou zone	Year Année	Indoor cinemas - Salles de cinéma		Screens - Écrans		Number of seats Nombre de places
		Number Nombre	Per million inhabitants Par millions d'habitants	Number Nombre	Per capita Par habitant	
Mexico	2007	522	5.41	4 204	4.36	...
Mexique	2008	530	5.41	4 499	4.60	880 803
	2009	559	5.63	4 568	4.60	884 661
Saint Kitts and Nevis	2008	1	21.86	7	15.30	...
Saint-Kitts-et-Nevis	2009	1	21.56	7	15.09	...
Saint Vincent-Grenadines	2005	2	20.52	...	...	...
Saint Vincent-Grenadines	2006	2	20.45	...	...	...
United States	2007	6 277	23.25	40 077	14.85	...
Etats-Unis	2008	6 269	23.03	40 194	14.77	...
	2009	6 039	22.00	39 717	14.47	...
America, South · Amérique du Sud						
Argentina	2007	289	8.23	821	2.34	221 915
Argentine	2008	275	7.77	825	2.33	214 514
	2009	280	7.84	832	2.33	219 856
Bolivia (Plurinational State of)	2007[2]	14	1.72	...	...	...
Bolivie (État plurinational de)	2008[2]	17	2.04	40	0.48	...
	2009	19	2.24	71[2]	0.84[2]	...
Brazil	2007	783	4.58	2 160	1.26	...
Brésil	2008	816	4.72	2 278	1.32	...
	2009	647	3.70	2 120	1.21	...
Chile	2007	52	3.45	280	1.86	63 908
Chili	2008	55	3.61	299	1.96	66 978
	2009	55	3.57	301	1.96	66 583
Colombia	2007	...	...	439	1.11	...
Colombie	2008	...	...	472	1.18	...
	2009	138	3.39	562	1.38	111 862
Guyana	2007	3	4.52	3	0.45	...
Guyana	2008	3	4.47	3	0.45	...
	2009	2	2.95	2	0.29	...
Paraguay	2006	...	...	27	0.52	...
Paraguay	2009	...	...	27	0.49	...
Peru	2007	...	...	291	1.17	...
Pérou	2008	...	...	285	1.13	...
	2009	...	...	227	0.89	...
Uruguay	2007	...	...	70	2.36	...
Uruguay	2008	...	...	70	2.35	...
	2009	...	...	70	2.34	...
Venezuela (Boliv. Rep. of)	2007	...	...	405	1.66	...
Venezuela (Rép. boliv. du)	2008	...	...	414	1.66	...
	2009	...	...	443	1.75	...
Asia · Asie						
Azerbaijan	2007	17	2.12	24	0.30	9 836
Azerbaïdjan	2008	14	1.72	19	0.23	5 181
	2009	9	1.10	14	0.17	3 402
Bahrain						
Bahreïn	2009	...	...	52	4.82	...
Cambodia	2007	14	1.16	15	0.12	4 500
Cambodge	2008	10	0.82	11	0.09	3 500
	2009	8	0.64	8	0.06	3 000
China	2006	...	...	37 753	3.10	...
Chine	2007	...	...	36 112	2.95	...

Cinema infrastructure
Number of indoor cinemas, screens and seats *(continued)*
Exploitation cinématographique *(suite)*
Nombre de salles de cinemas, d'ecrans et de places

Country or area Pays ou zone	Year Année	Indoor cinemas - Salles de cinéma		Screens - Écrans		Number of seats Nombre de places
		Number Nombre	Per million inhabitants Par millions d'habitants	Number Nombre	Per capita Par habitant	
China, Hong Kong SAR	2006	...	...	212	3.30	...
Chine, Hong Kong RAS	2008	...	...	221	3.40	...
	2009	...	...	198	3.03	
China, Macao SAR	2007	3	6.29	5	1.05	2 727
Chine, Macao RAS	2008	3	6.15	5	1.02	2 727
	2009	3	6.01	5	1.00	2 727
Cyprus	2007	...	...	33	3.38	...
Chypre	2008	...	...	31	3.14	...
	2009	8	8.00	36	3.60	...
Georgia	2007	23	5.69	32	0.79	5 041
Géorgie	2008	23	5.74	32	0.80	4 652
	2009	23	5.77	32	0.80	4 652
India	2007		...	10 189	0.98	
Inde	2008	...	...	10 120	0.96	...
	2009	...	...	10 070	0.94	...
Indonesia	2007	...	...	681	0.33	...
Indonésie	2008	...	...	712	0.34	...
	2009	...	...	726	0.34	...
Iran (Islamic Rep. of)	2007	181	2.78	240	0.37	118 000
Iran (Rép. islamique d')	2008	182	2.77	247	0.38	114 000
	2009	226	3.40	247	0.37	108 960
Israel	2007	53	8.76	...	...	46 796
Israël	2008	54	8.72	...	...	48 313
	2009	50	7.89	...	...	44 565
Japan	2007	703	6.16	3 221	2.82	...
Japon	2008	691	6.07	3 359	2.95	...
	2009	678	5.97	3 396	2.99	...
Jordan Jordanie	2007	...	...	24	0.49	...
Kazakhstan	2007	77	5.54	111	0.80	26 302
Kazakhstan	2008	77	5.51	129	0.92	27 341
	2009	83	5.90	171	1.22	32 178
Korea, Republic of	2007	314	7.06	1 975	4.44	365 034
Corée, République de	2008	309	6.92	2 004	4.49	362 657
	2009	305	6.82	2 055	4.59	360 796
Kuwait Koweït	2008	...	...	58	2.53	...
Kyrgyzstan	2007	51	11.16	53	1.16	14 607
Kirghizistan	2008	50	10.86	52	1.13	16 220
	2009	22	4.74	24	0.52	9 503
Lao People's Dem. Rep.	2007	3	0.58	4	0.08	...
Rép. dém. pop. lao	2008	4	0.76	6	0.11	1 192
	2009	4	0.74	6	0.11	1 192
Lebanon	2007	46	12.19	177	4.69	31 350
Liban	2008	47	12.36	185	4.87	32 550
	2009	48	12.54	185	4.83	33 750
Malaysia	2007	76	3.17	353	1.47	78 496
Malaisie	2008	91	3.72	453	1.85	92 642
	2009	93	3.73	485	1.94	101 165
Mongolia	2007	33	13.96	...	...	...
Mongolie	2008	30	12.57	...	...	...
	2009	52	21.56	...	...	...
Myanmar	2007	149	3.50	149	0.35	...
Myanmar	2008	132	3.07	132	0.31	...
	2009	124	2.87	124	0.29	...

18

Cinema infrastructure *(continued)*
Number of indoor cinemas, screens and seats
Exploitation cinématographique *(suite)*
Nombre de salles de cinemas, d'ecrans et de places

| Country or area
Pays ou zone | Year
Année | Indoor cinemas - Salles de cinéma | | Screens - Écrans | | Number
of seats
Nombre de
places |
		Number Nombre	Per million inhabitants Par millions d'habitants	Number Nombre	Per capita Par habitant	
Occupied Palestinian Terr. Terr. palestinien occupé	2007	...	...	2	0.06	...
Oman	2007	7	3.05	...	...	...
Oman	2008	7	2.97	...	...	...
	2009	7	2.89	...	...	...
Pakistan	2007	284	1.98	312	0.22	124 800
Pakistan	2008	239	1.64	302	0.21	120 800
	2009	228	1.54	319	0.21	127 600
Philippines	2007	...	...	765	1.00	...
Philippines	2008	...	...	770	0.98	...
	2009	...	...	770	0.96	...
Qatar	2007	12	10.88	30	2.72	...
Qatar	2008	25	19.02	43	3.27	...
	2009	25	16.56	...	...	5 200
Singapore	2007	...	...	175	4.08	40 000
Singapour	2008	...	...	174	3.89	37 000
	2009	...	...	176	3.80	37 000
Thailand	2007	...	...	704	1.13	...
Thaïlande	2008	...	...	737	1.18	...
	2009	...	...	752	1.19	...
Turkey	2007	...	...	1 464	2.31	220 020
Turquie	2008	...	...	1 575	2.46	244 551
	2009	484	7.46	1 810	2.79	247 616
United Arab Emirates	2006	...	...	202	4.64	...
Emirats arabes unis	2007	...	...	226	4.46	...
	2009	...	...	236	3.61	...
Europe · Europe						
Andorra	2005	2	28.01	...	...	...
Andorre	2006	2	27.32	...	...	...
Austria	2007	163	21.66	570	7.57	102 138
Autriche	2008	164	21.72	577	7.64	103 507
	2009	160	21.11	577	7.61	103 880
Belarus	2007	138	15.38	...	...	...
Bélarus	2008	137	15.40	...	...	...
	2009	138	15.63	...	...	...
Belgium	2007	103	10.91	513	5.43	112 316
Belgique	2008	97	10.23	491	5.18	107 154
	2009	94	9.87	481	5.05	106 404
Bulgaria	2007	57	8.13	114	1.63	25 301
Bulgarie	2008	32	4.61	95	1.37	21 425
	2009	30	4.35	104	1.51	22 657
Croatia	2007	79	19.37	114	2.80	33 153
Croatie	2008	70	17.24	112	2.76	30 266
	2009	65	16.08	107	2.65	28 001
Czech Republic	2007	528	55.85	681	7.20	155 202
République tchèque	2008	511	53.83	689	7.26	152 566
	2009	516	54.11	695	7.29	150 925
Denmark	2007	167	33.98	394	8.02	58 960
Danemark	2008	164	33.19	397	8.03	58 400
	2009	163	32.81	400	8.05	58 200
Estonia	2007	11	9.00	...	...	...
Estonie	2008	10	8.23	...	...	...
	2009	12	9.92	...	...	...

Cinema infrastructure
Number of indoor cinemas, screens and seats *(continued)*
Exploitation cinématographique *(suite)*
Nombre de salles de cinemas, d'ecrans et de places

Country or area Pays ou zone	Year Année	Indoor cinemas - Salles de cinéma		Screens - Écrans		Number of seats Nombre de places
		Number Nombre	Per million inhabitants Par millions d'habitants	Number Nombre	Per capita Par habitant	
Finland	2007	192	40.25	309	6.48	54 517
Finlande	2008	189	39.50	313	6.54	54 357
	2009	174	36.25	300	6.25	52 229
France	2007	1 928	35.21	5 202	9.50	1 039 253
France	2008	1 950	35.47	5 292	9.63	1 052 895
	2009	1 939	35.12	5 342	9.68	1 058 936
Germany	2007	1 812	24.09	4 832	6.42	836 505
Allemagne	2008	1 793	23.90	4 810	6.41	831 913
	2009	1 744	23.31	4 734	6.33	819 320
Greece	2005	...	...	490	4.79	...
Grèce	2006	...	...	500	4.88	...
	2007	...	...	540	5.27	...
Hungary	2007	184	20.06	400	4.36	78 655
Hongrie	2008	182	19.90	418	4.57	81 591
	2009	171	18.75	408	4.47	78 789
Iceland	2007	20	73.01	43	15.70	6 913
Islande	2008	18	64.76	41	14.75	6 446
	2009	17	60.29	40	14.19	...
Ireland	2007	...	...	426	11.05	77 175
Irlande	2008	...	...	435	11.16	77 430
	2009	70	17.77	442	11.22	77 989
Italy	2007	1 165	21.82	3 087	5.78	...
Italie	2008	1 129	21.04	3 141	5.85	...
	2009	1 104	20.48	3 208	5.95	...
Latvia	2007	14	6.71	46	2.20	10 440
Lettonie	2008	15	7.24	50	2.41	11 793
	2009	17	8.27	55	2.67	12 993
Lithuania	2007	44	14.14	78	2.51	20 551
Lituanie	2008	43	13.94	80	2.59	20 174
	2009	42	13.73	84	2.75	20 613
Luxembourg	2007	...	...	26	6.02	4 792
Luxembourg	2008	13	29.44	33	7.47	6 390
	2009	13	28.81	33	7.31	6 195
Malta	2007	7	18.32	42	10.99	10 820[2]
Malte	2008	7	18.29	42	10.97	10 820[2]
	2009	7	18.26	42	10.95	10 820[2]
Netherlands	2007	230	15.51	696	4.69	115 299
Pays-Bas	2008	235	15.77	717	4.81	119 079
	2009	242	16.17	751	5.02	122 747
Norway	2007	212	50.35	417	9.90	79 897
Norvège	2008	210	49.28	424	9.95	79 177
	2009	212	49.17	422	9.79	78 716
Poland	2007	496	14.08	1 008	2.86	244 174
Pologne	2008	483	13.73	1 043	2.97	249 533
	2009	448	12.76	1 061	3.02	248 181
Portugal	2007	176	18.31	546	5.68	109 820
Portugal	2008	182	18.89	572	5.94	113 792
	2009	174	18.02	577	5.98	110 914
Republic of Moldova	2007	...	...	34	1.00	...
République de Moldova	2008	...	...	32	0.95	...
	2009	...	...	37	1.12	...
Romania	2007	72	3.60	117	0.58	43 057
Roumanie	2008	75	3.77	136	0.68	46 782
	2009	74	3.73	182	0.92	...

18

Cinema infrastructure *(continued)*
Number of indoor cinemas, screens and seats
Exploitation cinématographique *(suite)*
Nombre de salles de cinemas, d'ecrans et de places

| Country or area
Pays ou zone | Year
Année | Indoor cinemas - Salles de cinéma | | Screens - Écrans | | Number
of seats
Nombre de
places |
		Number Nombre	Per million inhabitants Par millions d'habitants	Number Nombre	Per capita Par habitant	
Russian Federation	2007	691	5.23	1 576	1.19	...
Fédération de Russie	2008	769	5.85	1 910	1.45	...
	2009	807	6.16	2 133	1.63	...
Serbia [2]	2007	108	12.05	126	1.41	51 829
Serbie [2]	2008	101	11.26	124	1.38	44 782
	2009	83	9.24	109	1.21	40 076
Slovakia	2007	190	37.82	234	4.66	89 952
Slovaquie	2008	181	36.00	235	4.67	57 973
	2009	198	39.34	255	5.07	58 447
Slovenia	2007	54	29.20	103	5.57	21 133
Slovénie	2008	57	30.85	109	5.90	24 457
	2009	48	25.99	99	5.36	21 567
Spain	2007	907	22.57	4 296	10.69	970 776
Espagne	2008	868	21.39	4 140	10.20	947 857
	2009	851	20.78	4 082	9.97	...
Sweden	2007	550	67.71	933	11.49	146 985
Suède	2008	514	62.76	848	10.35	133 757
	2009	461	55.80	848	10.26	132 298
Switzerland	2007	307	45.09	550	8.08	...
Suisse	2008	307	44.82	564	8.23	...
	2009	302	43.85	559	8.12	...
TFYR of Macedonia	2007	16	8.45	27	1.43	6 686
L'ex-R.Y. Macédoine	2008	14	7.37	26	1.37	5 672
	2009	10	5.26	18	0.95	4 294
Ukraine	2007	...	...	3 033	7.11	861 961
Ukraine	2008	...	...	2 479	5.87	693 566
	2009	...	...	2 241	5.36	584 563
United Kingdom	2007	727	13.32	3 514	6.44	765 652
Royaume-Uni	2008	726	13.24	3 610	6.58	782 070
	2009	723	13.12	3 651	6.63	783 629
Oceania · Océanie						
Australia	2007	485 [2]	25.50 [2]	1 941	10.21	457 000
Australie	2008	493 [2]	25.49 [2]	1 980	10.24	462 000
	2009	492 [2]	25.03 [2]	1 989	10.12	463 000
Fiji	2007	2	2.70	10	1.35	2 017
Fidji	2008	2	2.67	10	1.33	2 017
	2009	2	2.64	10 [E]	1.32	2 017

Source:
United Nations Educational, Scientific and Cultural Organization
(UNESCO) Institute for Statistics, Montreal, the UNESCO Institute
for Statistics (UIS) database, last accessed January 2012.

Source:
L'Institut de statistique de l'Organisation des Nations Unies pour l'éducation, la
science et la culture (UNESCO), Montréal, la base de données de l'Institut de
statistique de l'UNESCO (ISU), dernier accès janvier 2012.

1   Partial data.
2   National estimation.
3   UIS estimation.

1   Données partielles.
2   Estimation nationale.
3   Estimation de l'ISU.

Part Three

Economic activity

Part Three of the *Yearbook* presents statistical series on production and consumption for a wide range of economic activities, and other basic series on major economic topics, for all countries or areas of the world for which data are available. Included are basic tables on national accounts, finance, labour force, prices, a wide range of agricultural, mined and manufactured commodities, energy, environment, research and development personnel and expenditure. International economic topics such as external trade are covered in Part Four.

Troisième partie

Activité économique

La troisième partie de l'*Annuaire* présente, pour une large gamme d'activités économiques, des séries statistiques sur la production et la consommation, et, pour tous les pays ou zones du monde pour lesquels des données sont disponibles, d'autres séries fondamentales ayant trait à des questions économiques importantes. Y figurent des tableaux de base consacrés à la comptabilité nationale, aux finances, à la main-d'œuvre, aux prix, à un large éventail de produits agricoles, miniers et manufacturés, à l'énergie, à l'environnement, au personnel employé à des travaux de recherche et développement et dépenses de recherche et développement. Les questions économiques internationales comme le commerce extérieur sont traitées dans la quatrième partie.

Gross domestic product and gross domestic product per capita
In millions of US dollars at current and constant 2005 prices; per capita US dollars; real rates of growth

Produit intérieur brut et produit intérieur brut par habitant
En millions de dollars É.-U. aux prix courants et constants de 2005; par habitant en dollars É.U. ; taux de croissance réels

Country or area	2004	2005	2006	2007	2008	2009	2010	Pays ou zone
World								**Monde**
GDP at current prices	42 275 025	45 744 751	49 602 912	55 885 941	61 232 771	57 960 080	63 063 973	**PIB aux prix courants**
GDP per capita	6 600	7 057	7 562	8 420	9 119	8 533	9 178	**PIB par habitant**
GDP at constant prices	44 179 360	45 744 751	47 633 185	49 556 513	50 232 991	49 062 202	51 040 463	**PIB aux prix constants**
Growth rates	4.1	3.5	4.1	4.0	1.4	-2.3	4.0	**Taux de croissance**
Afghanistan								**Afghanistan**
GDP at current prices	5 700	6 840	8 166	10 120	10 789	12 490	15 676	PIB aux prix courants
GDP per capita	214	248	287	347	362	408	499	PIB par habitant
GDP at constant prices	5 973	6 840	7 605	8 835	9 037	9 092	9 840	PIB aux prix constants
Growth rates	9.4	14.5	11.2	16.2	2.3	0.6	8.2	Taux de croissance
Albania								**Albanie**
GDP at current prices	7 307	8 159	8 993	10 701	12 970	12 041	11 783	PIB aux prix courants
GDP per capita	2 338	2 597	2 849	3 376	4 077	3 771	3 677	PIB par habitant
GDP at constant prices	7 714	8 159	8 602	9 110	9 808	10 133	10 488	PIB aux prix constants
Growth rates	5.7	5.8	5.4	5.9	7.7	3.3	3.5	Taux de croissance
Algeria								**Algérie**
GDP at current prices	85 333	103 234	117 208	135 119	171 392	137 892	158 650	PIB aux prix courants
GDP per capita	2 634	3 139	3 510	3 985	4 978	3 945	4 473	PIB par habitant
GDP at constant prices	98 224	103 234	105 299	108 458	111 061	113 726	117 517	PIB aux prix constants
Growth rates	5.1	5.1	2.0	3.0	2.4	2.4	3.3	Taux de croissance
Andorra								**Andorre**
GDP at current prices	2 890	3 179	3 478	3 942	4 127	3 731	3 491	PIB aux prix courants
GDP per capita	38 381	40 821	43 541	48 431	49 981	44 591	41 138	PIB par habitant
GDP at constant prices	2 984	3 179	3 341	3 341	3 205	3 055	2 952	PIB aux prix constants
Growth rates	8.1	6.6	5.1	^0.0	-4.1	-4.7	-3.4	Taux de croissance
Angola								**Angola**
GDP at current prices	19 775	30 629	41 789	60 449	84 179	75 493	82 470	PIB aux prix courants
GDP per capita	1 239	1 858	2 457	3 449	4 667	4 069	4 322	PIB par habitant
GDP at constant prices	25 395	30 629	36 315	44 522	50 666	51 882	53 656	PIB aux prix constants
Growth rates	11.2	20.6	18.6	22.6	13.8	2.4	3.4	Taux de croissance
Anguilla								**Anguilla**
GDP at current prices	149	170	219	274	290	216	211	PIB aux prix courants
GDP per capita	11 391	12 504	15 600	19 021	19 709	14 355	13 750	PIB par habitant
GDP at constant prices	157	170	214	253	257	191	184	PIB aux prix constants
Growth rates	21.6	8.3	26.2	18.3	1.3	-25.5	-3.8	Taux de croissance
Antigua and Barbuda								**Antigua-et-Barbuda**
GDP at current prices	815	867	1 011	1 155	1 203	1 132	1 118	PIB aux prix courants
GDP per capita	9 843	10 330	11 899	13 445	13 850	12 890	12 602	PIB par habitant
GDP at constant prices	832	867	982	1 071	1 073	982	941	PIB aux prix constants
Growth rates	7.0	4.2	13.3	9.1	0.2	-8.5	-4.1	Taux de croissance
Argentina								**Argentine**
GDP at current prices	153 129	183 196	214 267	262 451	328 468	308 740	370 263	PIB aux prix courants
GDP per capita	3 994	4 736	5 491	6 667	8 271	7 706	9 162	PIB par habitant
GDP at constant prices	167 794	183 196	198 706	215 900	230 492	232 451	253 746	PIB aux prix constants
Growth rates	9.0	9.2	8.5	8.7	6.8	0.9	9.2	Taux de croissance
Armenia								**Arménie**
GDP at current prices	3 577	4 900	6 384	9 206	11 662	8 648	9 371	PIB aux prix courants
GDP per capita	1 168	1 598	2 080	2 995	3 787	2 803	3 031	PIB par habitant
GDP at constant prices	4 304	4 900	5 547	6 310	6 748	5 793	5 915	PIB aux prix constants
Growth rates	10.5	13.9	13.2	13.7	6.9	-14.2	2.1	Taux de croissance
Aruba								**Aruba**
GDP at current prices	2 228	2 331	2 424	2 615	2 745	2 502	2 456	PIB aux prix courants
GDP per capita	22 497	23 080	23 604	25 093	26 017	23 467	22 851	PIB par habitant
GDP at constant prices	2 308	2 331	2 345	2 355	2 297	2 110	2 033	PIB aux prix constants
Growth rates	7.4	1.0	0.6	0.4	-2.5	-8.1	-3.7	Taux de croissance
Australia								**Australie**
GDP at current prices	681 335	764 765	822 029	992 191	1 052 897	1 001 935	1 271 945	PIB aux prix courants
GDP per capita	33 891	37 482	39 627	46 979	48 941	45 746	57 119	PIB par habitant
GDP at constant prices	741 904	764 765	792 023	822 374	834 285	853 266	874 477	PIB aux prix constants
Growth rates	3.0	3.1	3.6	3.8	1.4	2.3	2.5	Taux de croissance

Gross domestic product and gross domestic product per capita *(continued)*
In millions of US dollars at current and constant 2005 prices; per capita US dollars; real rates of growth

Produit intérieur brut et produit intérieur brut par habitant *(suite)*
En millions de dollars É.-U. aux prix courants et constants de 2005; par habitant en dollars É.-U. ; taux de croissance réels

Country or area	2004	2005	2006	2007	2008	2009	2010	Pays ou zone
Austria								**Autriche**
GDP at current prices	291 430	304 984	324 954	375 042	414 174	381 775	379 047	PIB aux prix courants
GDP per capita	35 603	37 048	39 278	45 133	49 650	45 614	45 159	PIB par habitant
GDP at constant prices	297 834	304 984	316 176	327 893	332 471	319 804	327 206	PIB aux prix constants
Growth rates	2.6	2.4	3.7	3.7	1.4	-3.8	2.3	Taux de croissance
Azerbaijan								**Azerbaïdjan**
GDP at current prices	8 680	13 246	20 982	33 049	48 851	44 292	51 797	PIB aux prix courants
GDP per capita	1 024	1 542	2 411	3 747	5 462	4 885	5 638	PIB par habitant
GDP at constant prices	10 475	13 246	17 809	22 270	24 664	26 946	28 283	PIB aux prix constants
Growth rates	10.2	26.4	34.5	25.1	10.8	9.3	5.0	Taux de croissance
Bahamas								**Bahamas**
GDP at current prices	7 094	7 706	7 966	8 319	8 240	7 807	7 702	PIB aux prix courants
GDP per capita	22 541	24 130	24 580	25 296	24 696	23 072	22 462	PIB par habitant
GDP at constant prices	7 453	7 706	7 900	8 024	7 907	7 483	7 554	PIB aux prix constants
Growth rates	0.9	3.4	2.5	1.6	-1.4	-5.4	0.9	Taux de croissance
Bahrain								**Bahreïn**
GDP at current prices	11 235	13 459	15 852	18 472	22 151	19 319	22 945	PIB aux prix courants
GDP per capita	16 725	18 569	19 536	19 954	21 049	16 518	18 184	PIB par habitant
GDP at constant prices	12 479	13 459	14 354	15 557	16 539	17 052	17 821	PIB aux prix constants
Growth rates	5.6	7.9	6.6	8.4	6.3	3.1	4.5	Taux de croissance
Bangladesh								**Bangladesh**
GDP at current prices	55 950	57 628	60 309	68 599	79 568	89 050	99 689	PIB aux prix courants
GDP per capita	404	410	424	477	547	606	670	PIB par habitant
GDP at constant prices	54 389	57 628	61 448	65 398	69 447	73 434	77 891	PIB aux prix constants
Growth rates	6.3	6.0	6.6	6.4	6.2	5.7	6.1	Taux de croissance
Barbados								**Barbade**
GDP at current prices	3 203	3 685	3 885	4 038	3 988	3 895	3 963	PIB aux prix courants
GDP per capita	11 865	13 623	14 331	14 865	14 652	14 280	14 497	PIB par habitant
GDP at constant prices	3 547	3 685	3 818	3 963	3 955	3 737	3 719	PIB aux prix constants
Growth rates	4.8	3.9	3.6	3.8	-0.2	-5.5	-0.5	Taux de croissance
Belarus								**Bélarus**
GDP at current prices	23 142	30 210	36 962	45 276	60 752	49 271	54 713	PIB aux prix courants
GDP per capita	2 344	3 075	3 781	4 654	6 276	5 113	5 702	PIB par habitant
GDP at constant prices	27 604	30 210	33 230	36 081	39 777	39 839	42 847	PIB aux prix constants
Growth rates	11.4	9.4	10.0	8.6	10.2	0.2	7.6	Taux de croissance
Belgium								**Belgique**
GDP at current prices	361 689	377 253	399 800	459 339	507 020	472 878	469 347	PIB aux prix courants
GDP per capita	34 922	36 225	38 167	43 586	47 822	44 356	43 815	PIB par habitant
GDP at constant prices	370 831	377 253	387 446	398 682	402 496	391 062	399 921	PIB aux prix constants
Growth rates	3.3	1.7	2.7	2.9	1.0	-2.8	2.3	Taux de croissance
Belize								**Belize**
GDP at current prices	1 055	1 115	1 214	1 277	1 359	1 349	1 401	PIB aux prix courants
GDP per capita	3 839	3 968	4 228	4 356	4 541	4 417	4 496	PIB par habitant
GDP at constant prices	1 082	1 115	1 177	1 181	1 225	1 225	1 259	PIB aux prix constants
Growth rates	4.6	3.1	5.6	0.3	3.8	^0.0	2.7	Taux de croissance
Benin								**Bénin**
GDP at current prices	4 051	4 358	4 705	5 512	6 634	6 585	6 558	PIB aux prix courants
GDP per capita	548	571	598	679	794	766	741	PIB par habitant
GDP at constant prices	4 237	4 358	4 522	4 731	4 968	5 101	5 231	PIB aux prix constants
Growth rates	3.1	2.9	3.8	4.6	5.0	2.7	2.6	Taux de croissance
Bermuda								**Bermudes**
GDP at current prices	4 464	4 846	5 387	5 860	6 068	5 715	6 015	PIB aux prix courants
GDP per capita	69 860	75 568	83 748	90 846	93 847	88 197	92 625	PIB par habitant
GDP at constant prices	4 605	4 846	5 155	5 373	5 356	4 925	4 998	PIB aux prix constants
Growth rates	3.6	5.2	6.4	4.2	-0.3	-8.1	1.5	Taux de croissance
Bhutan								**Bhoutan**
GDP at current prices	703	819	898	1 196	1 258	1 265	1 486	PIB aux prix courants
GDP per capita	1 094	1 242	1 331	1 737	1 793	1 772	2 047	PIB par habitant
GDP at constant prices	764	819	875	1 032	1 080	1 153	1 230	PIB aux prix constants
Growth rates	5.9	7.1	6.8	17.9	4.7	6.7	6.7	Taux de croissance

19

Gross domestic product and gross domestic product per capita *(continued)*
In millions of US dollars at current and constant 1990 prices; per capita US dollars; real rates of growth

Produit intérieur brut et produit intérieur brut par habitant *(suite)*
En millions de dollars É.-U. aux prix courants et constants de 1990 ; par habitant en dollars É.-U. ; taux de croissance réels

Country or area	2004	2005	2006	2007	2008	2009	2010	Pays ou zone
Bolivia (Plurin. State of)								**Bolivie (État plurin. de)**
GDP at current prices	8 773	9 549	11 452	13 120	16 674	17 340	19 640	PIB aux prix courants
GDP per capita	977	1 044	1 231	1 386	1 734	1 774	1 978	PIB par habitant
GDP at constant prices	9 145	9 549	10 007	10 464	11 107	11 480	11 954	PIB aux prix constants
Growth rates	4.2	4.4	4.8	4.6	6.1	3.4	4.1	Taux de croissance
Bosnia and Herzegovina								**Bosnie-Herzégovine**
GDP at current prices	10 123	10 909	12 361	15 240	18 512	17 050	16 837	PIB aux prix courants
GDP per capita	2 677	2 885	3 269	4 033	4 905	4 525	4 478	PIB par habitant
GDP at constant prices	10 503	10 909	11 560	12 276	12 977	12 595	12 696	PIB aux prix constants
Growth rates	6.3	3.9	6.0	6.2	5.7	-2.9	0.8	Taux de croissance
Botswana								**Botswana**
GDP at current prices	10 049	10 256	11 256	12 376	13 473	11 474	14 857	PIB aux prix courants
GDP per capita	5 425	5 468	5 921	6 421	6 892	5 790	7 403	PIB par habitant
GDP at constant prices	10 081	10 256	10 782	11 300	11 624	11 050	11 845	PIB aux prix constants
Growth rates	6.0	1.7	5.1	4.8	2.9	-4.9	7.2	Taux de croissance
Brazil								**Brésil**
GDP at current prices	663 733	882 044	1 089 254	1 366 854	1 653 353	1 593 018	2 088 966	PIB aux prix courants
GDP per capita	3 610	4 743	5 795	7 202	8 632	8 243	10 716	PIB par habitant
GDP at constant prices	855 028	882 044	916 947	972 802	1 023 023	1 016 428	1 092 556	PIB aux prix constants
Growth rates	5.7	3.2	4.0	6.1	5.2	-0.6	7.5	Taux de croissance
British Virgin Islands								**Iles Vierges britanniques**
GDP at current prices	746	870	934	1 011	992	876	909	PIB aux prix courants
GDP per capita	34 350	39 565	41 968	44 905	43 575	38 095	39 113	PIB par habitant
GDP at constant prices	761	870	882	888	902	941	983	PIB aux prix constants
Growth rates	3.8	14.3	1.4	0.7	1.5	4.3	4.5	Taux de croissance
Brunei Darussalam								**Brunéi Darussalam**
GDP at current prices	7 872	9 531	11 470	12 247	14 394	10 733	13 024	PIB aux prix courants
GDP per capita	22 116	26 249	30 975	32 442	37 415	27 391	32 648	PIB par habitant
GDP at constant prices	9 495	9 531	9 951	9 966	9 773	9 600	9 993	PIB aux prix constants
Growth rates	0.5	0.4	4.4	0.2	-1.9	-1.8	4.1	Taux de croissance
Bulgaria								**Bulgarie**
GDP at current prices	25 283	28 894	33 210	42 115	51 824	48 569	47 702	PIB aux prix courants
GDP per capita	3 246	3 734	4 319	5 512	6 827	6 439	6 365	PIB par habitant
GDP at constant prices	27 167	28 894	30 776	32 760	34 788	32 883	32 932	PIB aux prix constants
Growth rates	6.7	6.4	6.5	6.4	6.2	-5.5	0.2	Taux de croissance
Burkina Faso								**Burkina Faso**
GDP at current prices	4 839	5 463	5 816	6 756	8 398	8 358	8 559	PIB aux prix courants
GDP per capita	351	385	398	449	541	523	520	PIB par habitant
GDP at constant prices	5 027	5 463	5 804	6 043	6 430	6 638	7 023	PIB aux prix constants
Growth rates	4.5	8.7	6.3	4.1	6.4	3.2	5.8	Taux de croissance
Burundi								**Burundi**
GDP at current prices	954	1 117	1 273	1 356	1 312	1 321	1 481	PIB aux prix courants
GDP per capita	136	154	170	176	165	162	177	PIB par habitant
GDP at constant prices	1 107	1 117	1 178	1 253	1 307	1 351	1 404	PIB aux prix constants
Growth rates	4.4	0.9	5.5	6.4	4.3	3.4	3.9	Taux de croissance
Cambodia								**Cambodge**
GDP at current prices	5 338	6 293	7 275	8 639	10 352	10 402	11 272	PIB aux prix courants
GDP per capita	405	471	538	632	749	744	797	PIB par habitant
GDP at constant prices	5 557	6 293	6 971	7 682	8 197	8 204	8 694	PIB aux prix constants
Growth rates	10.3	13.3	10.8	10.2	6.7	0.1	6.0	Taux de croissance
Cameroon								**Cameroun**
GDP at current prices	15 775	16 588	17 953	20 432	23 322	23 381	23 649	PIB aux prix courants
GDP per capita	919	945	1 000	1 113	1 243	1 219	1 207	PIB par habitant
GDP at constant prices	16 215	16 588	17 123	17 680	18 190	18 473	19 027	PIB aux prix constants
Growth rates	3.7	2.3	3.2	3.3	2.9	1.6	3.0	Taux de croissance
Canada								**Canada**
GDP at current prices	992 228	1 133 757	1 278 607	1 424 067	1 502 678	1 337 577	1 577 040	PIB aux prix courants
GDP per capita	31 062	35 119	39 187	43 183	45 088	39 720	46 361	PIB par habitant
GDP at constant prices	1 100 531	1 133 757	1 165 763	1 191 410	1 199 616	1 166 389	1 203 888	PIB aux prix constants
Growth rates	3.1	3.0	2.8	2.2	0.7	-2.8	3.2	Taux de croissance

19 Gross domestic product and gross domestic product per capita *(continued)*
In millions of US dollars at current and constant 2005 prices; per capita US dollars; real rates of growth
Produit intérieur brut et produit intérieur brut par habitant *(suite)*
En millions de dollars É.-U. aux prix courants et constants de 2005; par habitant en dollars É.-U. ; taux de croissance réels

Country or area	2004	2005	2006	2007	2008	2009	2010	Pays ou zone
Cape Verde								**Cap-Vert**
GDP at current prices	924	972	1 108	1 331	1 531	1 549	1 609	PIB aux prix courants
GDP per capita	1 980	2 055	2 316	2 756	3 142	3 151	3 244	PIB par habitant
GDP at constant prices	912	972	1 071	1 163	1 235	1 279	1 348	PIB aux prix constants
Growth rates	4.3	6.5	10.1	8.6	6.2	3.6	5.4	Taux de croissance
Cayman Islands								**Iles Caïmanes**
GDP at current prices	2 662	3 042	3 207	3 516	3 559	3 353	3 208	PIB aux prix courants
GDP per capita	52 945	58 195	59 708	64 303	64 373	60 126	57 048	PIB par habitant
GDP at constant prices	2 856	3 042	3 182	3 282	3 256	2 999	2 879	PIB aux prix constants
Growth rates	0.9	6.5	4.6	3.2	-0.8	-7.9	-4.0	Taux de croissance
Central African Rep.								**Rép. centrafricaine**
GDP at current prices	1 270	1 350	1 473	1 697	1 983	1 981	1 984	PIB aux prix courants
GDP per capita	321	336	360	408	468	459	451	PIB par habitant
GDP at constant prices	1 319	1 350	1 405	1 468	1 532	1 560	1 611	PIB aux prix constants
Growth rates	2.7	2.4	4.0	4.5	4.4	1.8	3.3	Taux de croissance
Chad								**Tchad**
GDP at current prices	4 415	5 873	6 300	7 008	8 354	6 895	8 166	PIB aux prix courants
GDP per capita	466	600	625	676	784	630	727	PIB par habitant
GDP at constant prices	5 443	5 873	5 883	5 892	5 912	5 928	6 228	PIB aux prix constants
Growth rates	33.7	7.9	0.2	0.1	0.3	0.3	5.1	Taux de croissance
Chile								**Chili**
GDP at current prices	95 653	118 250	146 774	164 317	170 741	160 859	203 443	PIB aux prix courants
GDP per capita	5 929	7 254	8 912	9 879	10 166	9 487	11 888	PIB par habitant
GDP at constant prices	112 022	118 250	123 678	129 367	134 105	131 850	138 703	PIB aux prix constants
Growth rates	6.0	5.6	4.6	4.6	3.7	-1.7	5.2	Taux de croissance
China [1]								**Chine** [1]
GDP at current prices	1 942 781	2 283 671	2 787 254	3 494 351	4 531 831	5 050 543	5 739 358	PIB aux prix courants
GDP per capita	1 520	1 777	2 158	2 691	3 472	3 850	4 354	PIB par habitant
GDP at constant prices	2 051 815	2 283 671	2 573 697	2 939 162	3 221 321	3 517 683	3 883 522	PIB aux prix constants
Growth rates	10.1	11.3	12.7	14.2	9.6	9.2	10.4	Taux de croissance
China, Hong Kong SAR								**Chine, Hong Kong RAS**
GDP at current prices	165 886	177 772	189 932	207 087	215 365	209 285	224 459	PIB aux prix courants
GDP per capita	24 367	26 105	27 796	30 132	31 093	29 949	31 824	PIB par habitant
GDP at constant prices	166 014	177 772	190 251	202 407	207 075	201 566	215 615	PIB aux prix constants
Growth rates	8.5	7.1	7.0	6.4	2.3	-2.7	7.0	Taux de croissance
China, Macao SAR								**Chine, Macao RAS**
GDP at current prices	10 015	11 502	14 210	17 659	20 149	20 738	27 177	PIB aux prix courants
GDP per capita	21 304	23 893	28 809	34 919	38 863	39 040	49 990	PIB par habitant
GDP at constant prices	10 617	11 502	13 163	15 097	15 523	15 763	19 888	PIB aux prix constants
Growth rates	26.4	8.3	14.4	14.7	2.8	1.5	26.2	Taux de croissance
Colombia								**Colombie**
GDP at current prices	117 082	146 566	162 590	207 416	244 465	234 693	288 086	PIB aux prix courants
GDP per capita	2 762	3 405	3 721	4 677	5 432	5 141	6 223	PIB par habitant
GDP at constant prices	139 978	146 566	156 383	167 174	173 103	175 617	183 182	PIB aux prix constants
Growth rates	5.3	4.7	6.7	6.9	3.5	1.5	4.3	Taux de croissance
Comoros								**Comores**
GDP at current prices	362	387	403	465	530	535	541	PIB aux prix courants
GDP per capita	579	602	610	685	761	748	737	PIB par habitant
GDP at constant prices	371	387	392	394	398	405	413	PIB aux prix constants
Growth rates	-0.2	4.2	1.2	0.5	1.0	1.8	2.1	Taux de croissance
Congo								**Congo**
GDP at current prices	4 649	6 087	7 731	7 436	10 176	8 196	10 775	PIB aux prix courants
GDP per capita	1 349	1 723	2 131	1 993	2 653	2 079	2 665	PIB par habitant
GDP at constant prices	5 655	6 087	6 467	6 364	6 741	7 247	7 878	PIB aux prix constants
Growth rates	3.6	7.6	6.2	-1.6	5.9	7.5	8.7	Taux de croissance
Cook Islands								**Iles Cook**
GDP at current prices	178	183	188	228	233	207	248	PIB aux prix courants
GDP per capita	9 357	9 409	9 556	11 477	11 661	10 247	12 212	PIB par habitant
GDP at constant prices	185	183	192	191	185	178	174	PIB aux prix constants
Growth rates	2.2	-1.1	5.0	-0.2	-3.5	-3.6	-2.4	Taux de croissance

Gross domestic product and gross domestic product per capita *(continued)*
In millions of US dollars at current and constant 1990 prices; per capita US dollars; real rates of growth
Produit intérieur brut et produit intérieur brut par habitant *(suite)*
En millions de dollars É.-U. aux prix courants et constants de 1990 ; par habitant en dollars É.-U. ; taux de croissance réels

Country or area	2004	2005	2006	2007	2008	2009	2010	Pays ou zone
Costa Rica								**Costa Rica**
GDP at current prices	18 595	19 965	22 526	26 322	29 838	29 241	35 891	PIB aux prix courants
GDP per capita	4 390	4 633	5 141	5 912	6 598	6 370	7 704	PIB par habitant
GDP at constant prices	18 855	19 965	21 718	23 441	24 079	23 768	24 760	PIB aux prix constants
Growth rates	4.3	5.9	8.8	7.9	2.7	-1.3	4.2	Taux de croissance
Côte d'Ivoire								**Côte d'Ivoire**
GDP at current prices	15 701	16 354	18 144	19 696	23 281	23 043	22 780	PIB aux prix courants
GDP per capita	885	907	990	1 056	1 226	1 191	1 154	PIB par habitant
GDP at constant prices	16 065	16 354	16 550	16 931	17 574	17 574	18 026	PIB aux prix constants
Growth rates	1.6	1.8	1.2	2.3	3.8	0.0	2.6	Taux de croissance
Croatia								**Croatie**
GDP at current prices	41 003	44 821	49 855	59 336	69 911	63 435	60 852	PIB aux prix courants
GDP per capita	9 215	10 090	11 244	13 406	15 823	14 382	13 820	PIB par habitant
GDP at constant prices	42 982	44 821	47 033	49 413	50 485	47 460	46 895	PIB aux prix constants
Growth rates	4.1	4.3	4.9	5.1	2.2	-6.0	-1.2	Taux de croissance
Cuba								**Cuba**
GDP at current prices	38 203	42 644	52 742	58 604	60 806	62 279	64 220	PIB aux prix courants
GDP per capita	3 400	3 789	4 682	5 201	5 397	5 530	5 704	PIB par habitant
GDP at constant prices	38 349	42 644	47 790	51 260	53 370	54 144	55 262	PIB aux prix constants
Growth rates	5.8	11.2	12.1	7.3	4.1	1.4	2.1	Taux de croissance
Cyprus [2]								**Chypre** [2]
GDP at current prices	15 640	16 902	18 406	21 742	25 132	23 413	22 957	PIB aux prix courants
GDP per capita	21 218	22 298	23 876	27 686	31 693	29 277	28 364	PIB par habitant
GDP at constant prices	16 274	16 902	17 600	18 497	19 160	18 805	19 019	PIB aux prix constants
Growth rates	4.2	3.9	4.1	5.1	3.6	-1.9	1.1	Taux de croissance
Czech Republic								**République tchèque**
GDP at current prices	113 977	130 066	148 374	180 479	225 427	196 151	197 674	PIB aux prix courants
GDP per capita	11 172	12 726	14 463	17 499	21 723	18 789	18 839	PIB par habitant
GDP at constant prices	121 839	130 066	139 198	147 181	151 742	144 617	148 578	PIB aux prix constants
Growth rates	4.7	6.8	7.0	5.7	3.1	-4.7	2.7	Taux de croissance
Dem. Rep. of the Congo								**Rép. dém. du Congo**
GDP at current prices	6 511	7 166	8 824	10 029	11 933	11 147	13 230	PIB aux prix courants
GDP per capita	117	125	149	165	191	174	201	PIB par habitant
GDP at constant prices	6 647	7 166	7 566	8 040	8 533	8 770	9 400	PIB aux prix constants
Growth rates	6.7	7.8	5.6	6.3	6.1	2.8	7.2	Taux de croissance
Denmark								**Danemark**
GDP at current prices	244 728	257 676	274 377	311 418	341 467	308 925	309 866	PIB aux prix courants
GDP per capita	45 318	47 546	50 412	56 941	62 115	55 915	55 830	PIB par habitant
GDP at constant prices	251 525	257 676	266 423	270 641	267 606	253 665	258 095	PIB aux prix constants
Growth rates	2.3	2.4	3.4	1.6	-1.1	-5.2	1.7	Taux de croissance
Djibouti								**Djibouti**
GDP at current prices	666	709	769	848	983	1 049	1 140	PIB aux prix courants
GDP per capita	839	877	933	1 010	1 148	1 203	1 283	PIB par habitant
GDP at constant prices	687	709	799	839	880	929	971	PIB aux prix constants
Growth rates	3.0	3.2	12.7	5.0	5.0	5.5	4.5	Taux de croissance
Dominica								**Dominique**
GDP at current prices	367	362	388	419	462	480	476	PIB aux prix courants
GDP per capita	5 311	5 246	5 643	6 119	6 780	7 069	7 021	PIB par habitant
GDP at constant prices	363	362	378	400	431	427	436	PIB aux prix constants
Growth rates	3.3	-0.5	4.4	6.0	7.7	-0.9	2.1	Taux de croissance
Dominican Republic								**Rép. dominicaine**
GDP at current prices	21 582	33 542	35 660	41 013	45 523	46 598	51 576	PIB aux prix courants
GDP per capita	2 364	3 621	3 794	4 303	4 710	4 756	5 195	PIB par habitant
GDP at constant prices	30 699	33 542	37 122	40 268	42 384	43 848	47 247	PIB aux prix constants
Growth rates	1.3	9.3	10.7	8.5	5.3	3.5	7.8	Taux de croissance
Ecuador								**Equateur**
GDP at current prices	32 646	36 942	41 705	45 504	54 209	52 022	58 910	PIB aux prix courants
GDP per capita	2 471	2 751	3 058	3 286	3 856	3 648	4 073	PIB par habitant
GDP at constant prices	34 936	36 942	38 698	39 486	42 346	42 499	43 859	PIB aux prix constants
Growth rates	8.8	5.7	4.8	2.0	7.2	0.4	3.2	Taux de croissance

Gross domestic product and gross domestic product per capita *(continued)*
In millions of US dollars at current and constant 2005 prices; per capita US dollars; real rates of growth
Produit intérieur brut et produit intérieur brut par habitant *(suite)*
En millions de dollars É.-U. aux prix courants et constants de 2005; par habitant en dollars É.-U. ; taux de croissance réels

Country or area	2004	2005	2006	2007	2008	2009	2010	Pays ou zone
Egypt								**Egypte**
GDP at current prices	79 191	94 461	107 747	132 165	164 844	187 978	215 272	PIB aux prix courants
GDP per capita	1 087	1 273	1 426	1 718	2 105	2 358	2 654	PIB par habitant
GDP at constant prices	90 418	94 461	100 926	108 079	115 812	121 239	127 480	PIB aux prix constants
Growth rates	4.1	4.5	6.8	7.1	7.2	4.7	5.1	Taux de croissance
El Salvador								**El Salvador**
GDP at current prices	15 798	17 094	18 551	20 105	21 431	20 661	21 215	PIB aux prix courants
GDP per capita	2 620	2 825	3 054	3 295	3 496	3 354	3 426	PIB par habitant
GDP at constant prices	16 506	17 094	17 763	18 445	18 679	18 094	18 352	PIB aux prix constants
Growth rates	1.9	3.6	3.9	3.8	1.3	-3.1	1.4	Taux de croissance
Equatorial Guinea								**Guinée équatoriale**
GDP at current prices	4 774	7 206	8 525	10 703	15 668	9 968	11 803	PIB aux prix courants
GDP per capita	8 095	11 856	13 624	16 622	23 656	14 635	16 852	PIB par habitant
GDP at constant prices	6 618	7 206	7 589	9 353	10 779	11 272	11 180	PIB aux prix constants
Growth rates	32.6	8.9	5.3	23.2	15.2	4.6	-0.8	Taux de croissance
Eritrea								**Erythrée**
GDP at current prices	1 109	1 098	1 211	1 318	1 380	1 873	2 254	PIB aux prix courants
GDP per capita	257	245	261	275	279	367	429	PIB par habitant
GDP at constant prices	1 071	1 098	1 088	1 103	995	1 031	1 050	PIB aux prix constants
Growth rates	1.5	2.6	-1.0	1.4	-9.8	3.6	1.8	Taux de croissance
Estonia								**Estonie**
GDP at current prices	12 031	13 903	16 808	21 990	23 854	19 235	18 958	PIB aux prix courants
GDP per capita	8 922	10 330	12 506	16 375	17 773	14 337	14 135	PIB par habitant
GDP at constant prices	12 772	13 903	15 307	16 454	15 850	13 590	13 898	PIB aux prix constants
Growth rates	6.3	8.9	10.1	7.5	-3.7	-14.3	2.3	Taux de croissance
Ethiopia								**Ethiopie**
GDP at current prices	10 035	12 286	15 134	19 182	25 866	28 476	26 928	PIB aux prix courants
GDP per capita	138	165	199	247	326	351	325	PIB par habitant
GDP at constant prices	10 987	12 286	13 617	15 177	16 814	18 292	20 566	PIB aux prix constants
Growth rates	13.6	11.8	10.8	11.5	10.8	8.8	12.4	Taux de croissance
Fiji								**Fidji**
GDP at current prices	2 785	3 006	3 102	3 405	3 565	2 825	3 052	PIB aux prix courants
GDP per capita	3 401	3 655	3 747	4 076	4 226	3 314	3 546	PIB par habitant
GDP at constant prices	2 852	3 006	3 064	3 048	3 045	2 954	2 957	PIB aux prix constants
Growth rates	0.8	5.4	1.9	-0.5	-0.1	-3.0	0.1	Taux de croissance
Finland								**Finlande**
GDP at current prices	188 918	195 626	207 796	246 128	271 947	240 701	238 731	PIB aux prix courants
GDP per capita	36 149	37 302	39 460	46 523	51 153	45 062	44 502	PIB par habitant
GDP at constant prices	190 081	195 626	204 252	215 359	217 477	199 586	206 858	PIB aux prix constants
Growth rates	4.1	2.9	4.4	5.4	1.0	-8.2	3.6	Taux de croissance
France [3]								**France** [3]
GDP at current prices	2 055 678	2 136 555	2 255 706	2 582 392	2 831 795	2 624 503	2 559 850	PIB aux prix courants
GDP per capita	32 937	34 002	35 669	40 586	44 245	40 773	39 546	PIB par habitant
GDP at constant prices	2 098 231	2 136 555	2 189 262	2 239 291	2 237 485	2 176 406	2 208 616	PIB aux prix constants
Growth rates	2.5	1.8	2.5	2.3	-0.1	-2.7	1.5	Taux de croissance
French Polynesia								**Polynésie française**
GDP at current prices	5 327	5 463	5 638	6 353	6 995	6 815	6 679	PIB aux prix courants
GDP per capita	21 169	21 434	21 844	24 309	26 440	25 458	24 669	PIB par habitant
GDP at constant prices	5 395	5 463	5 526	5 643	5 743	5 834	5 926	PIB aux prix constants
Growth rates	2.2	1.3	1.2	2.1	1.8	1.6	1.6	Taux de croissance
Gabon								**Gabon**
GDP at current prices	7 756	9 459	10 297	12 341	16 825	15 382	18 771	PIB aux prix courants
GDP per capita	5 770	6 901	7 370	8 668	11 601	10 411	12 469	PIB par habitant
GDP at constant prices	8 957	9 459	9 233	9 754	9 923	9 882	10 432	PIB aux prix constants
Growth rates	-0.4	5.6	-2.4	5.6	1.7	-0.4	5.6	Taux de croissance
Gambia								**Gambie**
GDP at current prices	579	630	656	803	985	907	1 001	PIB aux prix courants
GDP per capita	396	419	424	504	602	539	579	PIB par habitant
GDP at constant prices	635	630	640	670	707	751	797	PIB aux prix constants
Growth rates	9.2	-0.9	1.6	4.7	5.6	6.3	6.1	Taux de croissance

Gross domestic product and gross domestic product per capita *(continued)*
In millions of US dollars at current and constant 1990 prices; per capita US dollars; real rates of growth
Produit intérieur brut et produit intérieur brut par habitant *(suite)*
En millions de dollars É.-U. aux prix courants et constants de 1990 ; par habitant en dollars É.-U. ; taux de croissance réels

Country or area	2004	2005	2006	2007	2008	2009	2010	Pays ou zone
Georgia								**Géorgie**
GDP at current prices	5 126	6 411	7 745	10 173	12 795	10 767	11 665	PIB aux prix courants
GDP per capita	1 134	1 432	1 743	2 304	2 912	2 462	2 680	PIB par habitant
GDP at constant prices	5 850	6 411	7 013	7 878	8 060	7 756	8 250	PIB aux prix constants
Growth rates	5.9	9.6	9.4	12.3	2.3	-3.8	6.4	Taux de croissance
Germany								**Allemagne**
GDP at current prices	2 726 341	2 766 254	2 902 749	3 323 810	3 623 688	3 298 634	3 280 334	PIB aux prix courants
GDP per capita	33 037	33 514	35 169	40 281	43 937	40 029	39 857	PIB par habitant
GDP at constant prices	2 747 443	2 766 254	2 868 605	2 962 381	2 994 470	2 840 943	2 945 784	PIB aux prix constants
Growth rates	1.2	0.7	3.7	3.3	1.1	-5.1	3.7	Taux de croissance
Ghana								**Ghana**
GDP at current prices	14 233	17 198	20 410	24 758	28 528	25 978	32 520	PIB aux prix courants
GDP per capita	674	795	921	1 090	1 226	1 090	1 333	PIB par habitant
GDP at constant prices	16 195	17 198	17 981	19 143	20 757	21 585	23 251	PIB aux prix constants
Growth rates	5.4	6.2	4.6	6.5	8.4	4.0	7.7	Taux de croissance
Greece								**Grèce**
GDP at current prices	230 039	240 076	262 053	304 900	341 188	321 795	301 065	PIB aux prix courants
GDP per capita	20 636	21 468	23 357	27 088	30 216	28 411	26 504	PIB par habitant
GDP at constant prices	234 723	240 076	253 383	260 975	260 565	252 096	243 230	PIB aux prix constants
Growth rates	4.4	2.3	5.5	3.0	-0.2	-3.3	-3.5	Taux de croissance
Greenland								**Groenland**
GDP at current prices	1 645	1 703	1 789	2 032	2 228	2 016	2 022	PIB aux prix courants
GDP per capita	28 838	29 770	31 224	35 457	38 878	35 181	35 293	PIB par habitant
GDP at constant prices	1 669	1 703	1 747	1 764	1 744	1 654	1 682	PIB aux prix constants
Growth rates	2.7	2.0	2.6	1.0	-1.1	-5.2	1.7	Taux de croissance
Grenada								**Grenade**
GDP at current prices	594	697	701	759	830	761	776	PIB aux prix courants
GDP per capita	5 800	6 788	6 804	7 344	8 002	7 311	7 429	PIB par habitant
GDP at constant prices	622	697	684	715	721	661	664	PIB aux prix constants
Growth rates	-6.5	12.0	-1.9	4.5	0.9	-8.3	0.4	Taux de croissance
Guatemala								**Guatemala**
GDP at current prices	23 965	27 211	30 231	34 113	39 136	37 683	41 473	PIB aux prix courants
GDP per capita	1 932	2 140	2 319	2 554	2 859	2 685	2 882	PIB par habitant
GDP at constant prices	26 352	27 211	28 675	30 483	31 483	31 655	32 481	PIB aux prix constants
Growth rates	3.2	3.3	5.4	6.3	3.3	0.5	2.6	Taux de croissance
Guinea								**Guinée**
GDP at current prices	3 662	2 937	2 821	4 209	3 778	4 441	4 267	PIB aux prix courants
GDP per capita	412	325	307	449	395	455	427	PIB par habitant
GDP at constant prices	2 852	2 937	2 965	3 018	3 166	3 157	3 217	PIB aux prix constants
Growth rates	2.3	3.0	1.0	1.8	4.9	-0.3	1.9	Taux de croissance
Guinea-Bissau								**Guinée-Bissau**
GDP at current prices	524	573	579	693	848	862	817	PIB aux prix courants
GDP per capita	391	419	415	487	583	581	539	PIB par habitant
GDP at constant prices	551	573	589	614	638	688	699	PIB aux prix constants
Growth rates	2.2	4.0	2.8	4.1	4.0	7.9	1.6	Taux de croissance
Guyana								**Guyana**
GDP at current prices	1 256	1 315	1 458	1 740	1 923	2 026	2 260	PIB aux prix courants
GDP per capita	1 689	1 763	1 949	2 320	2 558	2 690	2 996	PIB par habitant
GDP at constant prices	1 342	1 315	1 383	1 480	1 509	1 559	1 615	PIB aux prix constants
Growth rates	3.3	-2.0	5.1	7.0	2.0	3.3	3.6	Taux de croissance
Haiti								**Haïti**
GDP at current prices	3 354	3 807	4 470	5 472	5 872	5 937	6 123	PIB aux prix courants
GDP per capita	364	407	472	569	603	602	613	PIB par habitant
GDP at constant prices	3 739	3 807	3 892	4 023	4 057	4 174	3 963	PIB aux prix constants
Growth rates	-3.5	1.8	2.3	3.3	0.8	2.9	-5.1	Taux de croissance
Honduras								**Honduras**
GDP at current prices	8 871	9 757	10 918	12 361	13 882	14 176	15 400	PIB aux prix courants
GDP per capita	1 316	1 418	1 556	1 727	1 901	1 903	2 026	PIB par habitant
GDP at constant prices	9 200	9 757	10 398	11 041	11 509	11 263	11 576	PIB aux prix constants
Growth rates	6.2	6.1	6.6	6.2	4.2	-2.1	2.8	Taux de croissance

Gross domestic product and gross domestic product per capita *(continued)*
In millions of US dollars at current and constant 2005 prices; per capita US dollars; real rates of growth
Produit intérieur brut et produit intérieur brut par habitant *(suite)*
En millions de dollars É.-U. aux prix courants et constants de 2005; par habitant en dollars É.-U. ; taux de croissance réels

Country or area	2004	2005	2006	2007	2008	2009	2010	Pays ou zone
Hungary								**Hongrie**
GDP at current prices	101 926	110 322	112 533	136 102	154 234	126 632	128 629	PIB aux prix courants
GDP per capita	10 081	10 937	11 181	13 553	15 390	12 660	12 884	PIB par habitant
GDP at constant prices	106 115	110 322	114 621	114 753	115 779	107 907	109 265	PIB aux prix constants
Growth rates	4.8	4.0	3.9	0.1	0.9	-6.8	1.3	Taux de croissance
Iceland								**Islande**
GDP at current prices	13 251	16 286	16 651	20 428	16 851	12 113	12 574	PIB aux prix courants
GDP per capita	45 226	54 884	55 319	66 820	54 241	38 389	39 278	PIB par habitant
GDP at constant prices	15 188	16 286	17 053	18 074	18 303	17 082	16 399	PIB aux prix constants
Growth rates	7.8	7.2	4.7	6.0	1.3	-6.7	-4.0	Taux de croissance
India								**Inde**
GDP at current prices	715 459	837 299	947 684	1 205 950	1 283 209	1 353 215	1 722 328	PIB aux prix courants
GDP per capita	637	734	819	1 027	1 078	1 120	1 406	PIB par habitant
GDP at constant prices	765 923	837 299	914 932	1 004 750	1 054 309	1 150 303	1 251 603	PIB aux prix constants
Growth rates	8.3	9.3	9.3	9.8	4.9	9.1	8.8	Taux de croissance
Indonesia								**Indonésie**
GDP at current prices	256 837	285 869	364 571	432 216	510 229	539 356	707 448	PIB aux prix courants
GDP per capita	1 143	1 258	1 586	1 859	2 172	2 272	2 949	PIB par habitant
GDP at constant prices	270 471	285 869	301 594	323 995	340 018	355 575	377 282	PIB aux prix constants
Growth rates	5.0	5.7	5.5	7.4	4.9	4.6	6.1	Taux de croissance
Iran (Islamic Rep. of)								**Iran (Rép. islamique d')**
GDP at current prices	170 673	205 586	243 672	312 141	366 295	352 420	386 670	PIB aux prix courants
GDP per capita	2 477	2 948	3 452	4 370	5 067	4 819	5 227	PIB par habitant
GDP at constant prices	195 324	205 586	218 136	236 179	238 629	238 791	241 248	PIB aux prix constants
Growth rates	5.1	5.3	6.1	8.3	1.0	0.1	1.0	Taux de croissance
Iraq								**Iraq**
GDP at current prices [4]	16 837	18 164	20 660	21 561	23 487	25 908	28 141	PIB aux prix courants [4]
GDP per capita [4]	633	664	734	744	788	843	889	PIB par habitant [4]
GDP at constant prices [4]	17 399	18 164	20 010	20 285	21 626	23 637	25 354	PIB aux prix constants [4]
Growth rates	54.2	4.4	10.2	1.4	6.6	9.3	7.3	Taux de croissance
Ireland								**Irlande**
GDP at current prices	186 947	203 280	223 671	259 955	263 654	223 098	206 600	PIB aux prix courants
GDP per capita	45 757	48 888	52 922	60 578	60 570	50 564	46 220	PIB par habitant
GDP at constant prices	192 976	203 280	214 078	225 172	218 479	203 198	202 325	PIB aux prix constants
Growth rates	4.5	5.3	5.3	5.2	-3.0	-7.0	-0.4	Taux de croissance
Israel								**Israël**
GDP at current prices	126 572	133 968	145 479	167 112	201 660	194 865	217 445	PIB aux prix courants
GDP per capita	19 559	20 284	21 536	24 149	28 434	26 837	29 312	PIB par habitant
GDP at constant prices	127 661	133 968	141 463	149 239	155 250	156 550	164 136	PIB aux prix constants
Growth rates	4.8	4.9	5.6	5.5	4.0	0.8	4.8	Taux de croissance
Italy								**Italie**
GDP at current prices	1 727 825	1 777 694	1 863 381	2 116 203	2 296 498	2 111 157	2 051 290	PIB aux prix courants
GDP per capita	29 655	30 299	31 539	35 569	38 344	35 041	33 877	PIB par habitant
GDP at constant prices	1 766 111	1 777 694	1 813 888	1 840 774	1 816 417	1 721 646	1 743 957	PIB aux prix constants
Growth rates	1.5	0.7	2.0	1.5	-1.3	-5.2	1.3	Taux de croissance
Jamaica								**Jamaïque**
GDP at current prices	10 135	11 163	11 920	12 825	13 877	12 327	13 428	PIB aux prix courants
GDP per capita	3 803	4 163	4 421	4 734	5 101	4 514	4 899	PIB par habitant
GDP at constant prices	11 006	11 163	11 438	11 601	11 538	11 187	11 061	PIB aux prix constants
Growth rates	1.0	1.4	2.5	1.4	-0.5	-3.0	-1.1	Taux de croissance
Japan								**Japon**
GDP at current prices	4 605 939	4 552 191	4 362 578	4 377 961	4 879 838	5 032 983	5 458 873	PIB aux prix courants
GDP per capita	36 468	36 016	34 496	34 604	38 562	39 770	43 141	PIB par habitant
GDP at constant prices	4 465 818	4 552 191	4 645 032	4 754 787	4 699 380	4 403 902	4 578 543	PIB aux prix constants
Growth rates	2.7	1.9	2.0	2.4	-1.2	-6.3	4.0	Taux de croissance
Jordan								**Jordanie**
GDP at current prices	11 411	12 589	15 645	17 765	22 698	25 092	27 504	PIB aux prix courants
GDP per capita	2 190	2 357	2 847	3 135	3 881	4 164	4 445	PIB par habitant
GDP at constant prices	11 640	12 589	13 586	14 739	15 861	16 230	16 732	PIB aux prix constants
Growth rates	8.6	8.1	7.9	8.5	7.6	2.3	3.1	Taux de croissance

19

Gross domestic product and gross domestic product per capita *(continued)*
In millions of US dollars at current and constant 1990 prices; per capita US dollars; real rates of growth

Produit intérieur brut et produit intérieur brut par habitant *(suite)*
En millions de dollars É.-U. aux prix courants et constants de 1990 ; par habitant en dollars É.-U. ; taux de croissance réels

Country or area	2004	2005	2006	2007	2008	2009	2010	Pays ou zone
Kazakhstan								**Kazakhstan**
GDP at current prices	43 152	57 124	81 004	104 850	133 442	115 309	146 908	PIB aux prix courants
GDP per capita	2 867	3 765	5 290	6 775	8 524	7 279	9 167	PIB par habitant
GDP at constant prices	52 073	57 124	63 167	68 659	70 914	71 773	76 805	PIB aux prix constants
Growth rates	9.6	9.7	10.6	8.7	3.3	1.2	7.0	Taux de croissance
Kenya								**Kenya**
GDP at current prices	16 095	18 739	22 504	27 165	30 519	30 580	32 483	PIB aux prix courants
GDP per capita	464	526	616	725	794	775	802	PIB par habitant
GDP at constant prices	17 693	18 739	19 924	21 329	21 644	22 216	23 450	PIB aux prix constants
Growth rates	5.1	5.9	6.3	7.0	1.5	2.6	5.6	Taux de croissance
Kiribati								**Kiribati**
GDP at current prices	99	106	107	127	136	124	146	PIB aux prix courants
GDP per capita	1 100	1 148	1 143	1 341	1 404	1 266	1 468	PIB par habitant
GDP at constant prices	106	106	109	108	112	110	109	PIB aux prix constants
Growth rates	-0.7	^0.0	3.2	-0.5	3.4	-2.3	-0.4	Taux de croissance
Korea, Dem. P. R.								**Corée, R. p. dém. de**
GDP at current prices	11 168	13 031	13 764	14 375	13 337	12 035	12 278[4]	PIB aux prix courants
GDP per capita	473	548	576	598	552	496	504[4]	PIB par habitant
GDP at constant prices	12 559	13 031	12 898	12 745	13 139	13 020	13 117[4]	PIB aux prix constants
Growth rates	2.1	3.8	-1.0	-1.2	3.1	-0.9	0.7	Taux de croissance
Korea, Republic of								**Corée, République de**
GDP at current prices	721 976	844 866	951 773	1 049 239	931 405	834 060	1 014 369	PIB aux prix courants
GDP per capita	15 417	17 959	20 136	22 090	19 512	17 389	21 052	PIB par habitant
GDP at constant prices	812 706	844 866	888 618	933 990	955 456	958 509	1 017 571	PIB aux prix constants
Growth rates	4.6	4.0	5.2	5.1	2.3	0.3	6.2	Taux de croissance
Kosovo								**Kosovo**
GDP at current prices	3 616	3 734	3 914	4 645	5 642	5 435	5 590	PIB aux prix courants
GDP per capita	1 487	1 546	1 615	1 895	2 265	2 180	2 241	PIB par habitant
GDP at constant prices	3 596	3 734	3 862	4 104	4 388	4 514	4 695	PIB aux prix constants
Growth rates	-0.9	3.8	3.4	6.3	6.9	2.9	4.0	Taux de croissance
Kuwait								**Koweït**
GDP at current prices	59 437	80 798	101 559	114 635	147 380	105 902	124 331	PIB aux prix courants
GDP per capita	27 146	35 688	43 190	46 832	57 834	40 019	45 430	PIB par habitant
GDP at constant prices	73 048	80 798	85 020	88 727	93 134	88 304	90 039	PIB aux prix constants
Growth rates	10.2	10.6	5.2	4.4	5.0	-5.2	2.0	Taux de croissance
Kyrgyzstan								**Kirghizistan**
GDP at current prices	2 212	2 460	2 834	3 803	5 140	4 690	4 616	PIB aux prix courants
GDP per capita	441	488	557	740	988	890	865	PIB par habitant
GDP at constant prices	2 465	2 460	2 537	2 753	2 985	3 071	3 029	PIB aux prix constants
Growth rates	7.0	-0.2	3.1	8.5	8.4	2.9	-1.4	Taux de croissance
Lao People's Dem. Rep.								**Rép. dém. pop. lao**
GDP at current prices	2 397	2 739	3 325	4 214	5 285	5 585	6 496	PIB aux prix courants
GDP per capita	423	476	569	710	878	914	1 048	PIB par habitant
GDP at constant prices	2 554	2 739	2 967	3 508	3 781	4 065	4 380	PIB aux prix constants
Growth rates	6.9	7.3	8.3	18.2	7.8	7.5	7.7	Taux de croissance
Latvia								**Lettonie**
GDP at current prices	13 735	15 938	19 854	28 651	33 453	25 854	24 014	PIB aux prix courants
GDP per capita	5 922	6 913	8 658	12 557	14 729	11 433	10 663	PIB par habitant
GDP at constant prices	14 473	15 938	17 716	19 416	18 780	15 451	15 399	PIB aux prix constants
Growth rates	8.9	10.1	11.2	9.6	-3.3	-17.7	-0.3	Taux de croissance
Lebanon								**Liban**
GDP at current prices	21 465	21 861	22 438	25 057	29 933	34 528	39 248	PIB aux prix courants
GDP per capita	5 369	5 394	5 476	6 060	7 183	8 227	9 284	PIB par habitant
GDP at constant prices	21 675	21 861	22 006	23 685	25 887	27 958	30 055	PIB aux prix constants
Growth rates	7.5	0.9	0.7	7.6	9.3	8.0	7.5	Taux de croissance
Lesotho								**Lesotho**
GDP at current prices	1 235	1 355	1 415	1 581	1 601	1 720	2 129	PIB aux prix courants
GDP per capita	603	656	678	751	752	800	981	PIB par habitant
GDP at constant prices	1 323	1 355	1 419	1 482	1 552	1 599	1 638	PIB aux prix constants
Growth rates	2.3	2.4	4.7	4.5	4.7	3.0	2.4	Taux de croissance

19

Gross domestic product and gross domestic product per capita *(continued)*
In millions of US dollars at current and constant 2005 prices; per capita US dollars; real rates of growth
Produit intérieur brut et produit intérieur brut par habitant *(suite)*
En millions de dollars É.-U. aux prix courants et constants de 2005; par habitant en dollars É.-U. ; taux de croissance réels

Country or area	2004	2005	2006	2007	2008	2009	2010	Pays ou zone
Liberia								**Libéria**
GDP at current prices	527	578	642	697	751	832	873	PIB aux prix courants
GDP per capita	170	182	194	200	205	217	219	PIB par habitant
GDP at constant prices	549	578	623	682	730	764	803	PIB aux prix constants
Growth rates	2.6	5.3	7.8	9.4	7.1	4.6	5.1	Taux de croissance
Libyan Arab Jamah.								**Jamah. arabe libyenne**
GDP at current prices	33 293	45 451	55 077	62 668	81 376	58 762	71 945	PIB aux prix courants
GDP per capita	5 890	7 878	9 345	10 405	13 233	9 383	11 321	PIB par habitant
GDP at constant prices	41 211	45 451	48 504	50 971	52 358	51 968	54 132	PIB aux prix constants
Growth rates	4.4	10.3	6.7	5.1	2.7	-0.7	4.2	Taux de croissance
Liechtenstein								**Liechtenstein**
GDP at current prices	3 454	3 658	4 000	4 601	5 073	4 797	5 145	PIB aux prix courants
GDP per capita	100 520	105 440	114 305	130 478	142 830	134 104	142 781	PIB par habitant
GDP at constant prices	3 490	3 658	3 986	4 357	4 232	4 040	4 124	PIB aux prix constants
Growth rates	3.0	4.8	9.0	9.3	-2.9	-4.5	2.1	Taux de croissance
Lithuania								**Lituanie**
GDP at current prices	22 656	26 100	30 240	39 319	47 552	37 002	36 478	PIB aux prix courants
GDP per capita	6 601	7 641	8 900	11 636	14 153	11 075	10 975	PIB par habitant
GDP at constant prices	24 213	26 100	28 138	30 895	31 794	27 077	27 466	PIB aux prix constants
Growth rates	7.4	7.8	7.8	9.8	2.9	-14.8	1.4	Taux de croissance
Luxembourg								**Luxembourg**
GDP at current prices	34 091	37 659	42 552	51 312	57 768	51 945	53 330	PIB aux prix courants
GDP per capita	75 609	82 370	91 395	107 863	118 673	104 384	105 095	PIB par habitant
GDP at constant prices	35 720	37 659	39 532	42 156	42 474	40 223	41 300	PIB aux prix constants
Growth rates	4.4	5.4	5.0	6.6	0.8	-5.3	2.7	Taux de croissance
Madagascar								**Madagascar**
GDP at current prices	4 364	5 039	5 515	7 343	9 413	8 552	8 739	PIB aux prix courants
GDP per capita	251	282	299	387	482	425	422	PIB par habitant
GDP at constant prices	4 817	5 039	5 292	5 622	6 023	5 774	5 805	PIB aux prix constants
Growth rates	5.3	4.6	5.0	6.2	7.1	-4.1	0.5	Taux de croissance
Malawi								**Malawi**
GDP at current prices	2 625	2 755	3 117	3 648	4 220	4 897	5 325	PIB aux prix courants
GDP per capita	210	215	236	268	301	339	357	PIB par habitant
GDP at constant prices	2 668	2 755	2 884	3 161	3 424	3 731	3 980	PIB aux prix constants
Growth rates	15.8	3.3	4.7	9.6	8.3	8.9	6.7	Taux de croissance
Malaysia								**Malaisie**
GDP at current prices	124 749	137 954	156 601	186 774	222 574	192 917	237 797	PIB aux prix courants
GDP per capita	4 875	5 286	5 890	6 904	8 093	6 902	8 373	PIB par habitant
GDP at constant prices	130 971	137 954	146 023	155 485	162 960	160 294	171 826	PIB aux prix constants
Growth rates	6.8	5.3	5.8	6.5	4.8	-1.6	7.2	Taux de croissance
Maldives								**Maldives**
GDP at current prices	776	750	915	1 054	1 260	1 319	1 480	PIB aux prix courants
GDP per capita	2 668	2 540	3 057	3 474	4 097	4 230	4 685	PIB par habitant
GDP at constant prices	789	750	919	975	1 008	918	1 025	PIB aux prix constants
Growth rates	11.3	-5.0	22.5	6.1	3.4	-8.9	11.6	Taux de croissance
Mali								**Mali**
GDP at current prices	4 982	5 486	6 123	7 145	8 738	8 964	9 204	PIB aux prix courants
GDP per capita	390	416	450	510	604	601	599	PIB par habitant
GDP at constant prices	5 169	5 486	5 774	6 023	6 322	6 605	6 899	PIB aux prix constants
Growth rates	2.3	6.1	5.3	4.3	5.0	4.5	4.5	Taux de croissance
Malta								**Malte**
GDP at current prices	5 644	5 981	6 390	7 514	8 554	8 099	8 163	PIB aux prix courants
GDP per capita	13 860	14 612	15 545	18 211	20 665	19 506	19 599	PIB par habitant
GDP at constant prices	5 769	5 981	6 114	6 375	6 654	6 477	6 653	PIB aux prix constants
Growth rates	-0.5	3.7	2.2	4.3	4.4	-2.7	2.7	Taux de croissance
Marshall Islands								**Iles Marshall**
GDP at current prices	132	139	145	156	166	163	166	PIB aux prix courants
GDP per capita	2 549	2 678	2 784	2 975	3 140	3 060	3 069	PIB par habitant
GDP at constant prices	137	139	141	142	144	141	142	PIB aux prix constants
Growth rates	6.7	2.0	0.9	1.3	1.4	-2.1	0.5	Taux de croissance

Gross domestic product and gross domestic product per capita *(continued)*
In millions of US dollars at current and constant 1990 prices; per capita US dollars; real rates of growth
Produit intérieur brut et produit intérieur brut par habitant *(suite)*
En millions de dollars É.-U. aux prix courants et constants de 1990 ; par habitant en dollars É.-U. ; taux de croissance réels

Country or area	2004	2005	2006	2007	2008	2009	2010	Pays ou zone
Mauritania								**Mauritanie**
GDP at current prices	1 889	2 184	3 041	3 357	3 704	3 083	3 913	PIB aux prix courants
GDP per capita	637	717	971	1 045	1 124	913	1 131	PIB par habitant
GDP at constant prices	2 005	2 184	2 597	2 639	2 661	2 703	2 829	PIB aux prix constants
Growth rates	5.7	9.0	18.9	1.6	0.8	1.6	4.7	Taux de croissance
Mauritius								**Maurice**
GDP at current prices	6 579	6 489	6 732	7 792	9 641	8 865	9 729	PIB aux prix courants
GDP per capita	5 281	5 163	5 314	6 108	7 510	6 864	7 488	PIB par habitant
GDP at constant prices	6 396	6 489	6 782	7 180	7 576	7 806	8 121	PIB aux prix constants
Growth rates	4.3	1.5	4.5	5.9	5.5	3.0	4.0	Taux de croissance
Mexico								**Mexique**
GDP at current prices	758 580	846 095	949 063	1 033 177	1 091 981	879 099	1 032 224	PIB aux prix courants
GDP per capita	7 212	7 946	8 801	9 460	9 871	7 847	9 101	PIB par habitant
GDP at constant prices	819 261	846 095	888 897	918 794	929 983	871 546	922 307	PIB aux prix constants
Growth rates	4.1	3.3	5.1	3.4	1.2	-6.3	5.8	Taux de croissance
Micronesia (Fed. States of)								**Micronésie (Etats féd. de)**
GDP at current prices	240	250	255	257	263	280	297	PIB aux prix courants
GDP per capita	2 201	2 285	2 318	2 339	2 387	2 528	2 678	PIB par habitant
GDP at constant prices	245	250	250	245	239	241	248	PIB aux prix constants
Growth rates	-3.2	2.1	0.2	-2.1	-2.4	0.7	3.1	Taux de croissance
Monaco								**Monaco**
GDP at current prices	4 118	4 280	4 663	5 974	6 581	5 561	5 424	PIB aux prix courants
GDP per capita	116 718	121 386	132 234	169 270	186 243	157 179	153 177	PIB par habitant
GDP at constant prices	4 203	4 280	4 517	5 175	5 192	4 602	4 670	PIB aux prix constants
Growth rates	2.5	1.8	5.5	14.6	0.3	-11.4	1.5	Taux de croissance
Mongolia								**Mongolie**
GDP at current prices	1 992	2 523	3 414	4 235	5 623	4 584	6 192	PIB aux prix courants
GDP per capita	792	991	1 321	1 614	2 108	1 690	2 247	PIB par habitant
GDP at constant prices	2 353	2 523	2 739	3 019	3 289	3 247	3 454	PIB aux prix constants
Growth rates	10.6	7.3	8.6	10.2	8.9	-1.3	6.4	Taux de croissance
Montenegro								**Monténégro**
GDP at current prices	2 073	2 257	2 696	3 669	4 520	4 141	4 111	PIB aux prix courants
GDP per capita	3 307	3 601	4 299	5 842	7 184	6 569	6 510	PIB par habitant
GDP at constant prices	2 167	2 257	2 450	2 712	2 899	2 735	2 803	PIB aux prix constants
Growth rates	4.4	4.2	8.6	10.7	6.9	-5.7	2.5	Taux de croissance
Montserrat								**Montserrat**
GDP at current prices	41	43	45	46	50	53	55	PIB aux prix courants
GDP per capita	7 698	7 696	7 837	7 921	8 519	8 941	9 343	PIB par habitant
GDP at constant prices	43	43	41	41	44	45	46	PIB aux prix constants
Growth rates	6.8	0.4	-5.9	1.5	6.7	3.6	1.3	Taux de croissance
Morocco[5]								**Maroc**[5]
GDP at current prices	56 948	59 524	65 640	75 223	88 879	91 374	91 542	PIB aux prix courants
GDP per capita	1 893	1 959	2 138	2 426	2 838	2 888	2 865	PIB par habitant
GDP at constant prices	57 802	59 524	64 143	65 878	69 559	73 001	75 410	PIB aux prix constants
Growth rates	4.8	3.0	7.8	2.7	5.6	4.9	3.3	Taux de croissance
Mozambique								**Mozambique**
GDP at current prices	5 698	6 579	7 096	8 036	9 891	9 674	9 533	PIB aux prix courants
GDP per capita	281	317	333	368	443	423	408	PIB par habitant
GDP at constant prices	6 069	6 579	7 150	7 670	8 194	8 713	9 324	PIB aux prix constants
Growth rates	7.9	8.4	8.7	7.3	6.8	6.3	7.0	Taux de croissance
Myanmar								**Myanmar**
GDP at current prices	10 254	11 931	13 852	18 233	25 859	32 805	42 027	PIB aux prix courants
GDP per capita	223	258	297	389	547	689	876	PIB par habitant
GDP at constant prices	10 505	11 931	13 491	15 109	16 657	18 394	20 310	PIB aux prix constants
Growth rates	13.6	13.6	13.1	12.0	10.2	10.4	10.4	Taux de croissance
Namibia								**Namibie**
GDP at current prices	6 607	7 261	7 979	8 811	8 958	9 183	11 701	PIB aux prix courants
GDP per capita	3 233	3 491	3 766	4 081	4 071	4 096	5 125	PIB par habitant
GDP at constant prices	7 082	7 261	7 775	8 193	8 542	8 481	8 852	PIB aux prix constants
Growth rates	12.3	2.5	7.1	5.4	4.3	-0.7	4.4	Taux de croissance

19

Gross domestic product and gross domestic product per capita *(continued)*
In millions of US dollars at current and constant 2005 prices; per capita US dollars; real rates of growth
Produit intérieur brut et produit intérieur brut par habitant *(suite)*
En millions de dollars É.-U. aux prix courants et constants de 2005; par habitant en dollars É.-U. ; taux de croissance réels

Country or area	2004	2005	2006	2007	2008	2009	2010	Pays ou zone
Nauru								**Nauru**
GDP at current prices	28	26	25	23	42	54	63	PIB aux prix courants
GDP per capita	2 737	2 600	2 506	2 276	4 081	5 312	6 190	PIB par habitant
GDP at constant prices	29	26	21	19	37	30	30	PIB aux prix constants
Growth rates	-1.9	-9.8	-20.3	-10.8	95.6	-18.2	0.0	Taux de croissance
Nepal								**Népal**
GDP at current prices	7 286	8 259	8 990	10 959	11 692	12 742	16 020	PIB aux prix courants
GDP per capita	273	303	323	386	404	433	535	PIB par habitant
GDP at constant prices	8 009	8 259	8 566	8 858	9 399	9 814	10 261	PIB aux prix constants
Growth rates	4.7	3.1	3.7	3.4	6.1	4.4	4.6	Taux de croissance
Netherlands								**Pays-Bas**
GDP at current prices	609 890	638 471	677 692	782 567	870 812	793 430	779 310	PIB aux prix courants
GDP per capita	37 589	39 157	41 378	47 591	52 766	47 915	46 910	PIB par habitant
GDP at constant prices	625 667	638 471	660 142	686 023	698 399	673 699	685 082	PIB aux prix constants
Growth rates	2.2	2.0	3.4	3.9	1.8	-3.5	1.7	Taux de croissance
Netherlands Antilles								**Antilles néerlandaises**
GDP at current prices	3 104	3 277	3 436	3 636	3 944	3 966	4 078	PIB aux prix courants
GDP per capita	16 904	17 622	18 210	18 957	20 227	20 029	20 321	PIB par habitant
GDP at constant prices	3 242	3 277	3 346	3 453	3 536	3 518	3 518	PIB aux prix constants
Growth rates	1.2	1.1	2.1	3.2	2.4	-0.5	0.0	Taux de croissance
New Caledonia								**Nouvelle-Calédonie**
GDP at current prices	5 884	6 236	6 973	8 808	9 124	8 754	8 861	PIB aux prix courants
GDP per capita	25 893	26 987	29 675	36 866	37 562	35 455	35 319	PIB par habitant
GDP at constant prices	6 019	6 236	6 592	6 868	6 965	7 132	7 379	PIB aux prix constants
Growth rates	3.9	3.6	5.7	4.2	1.4	2.4	3.5	Taux de croissance
New Zealand								**Nouvelle-Zélande**
GDP at current prices	100 775	113 058	109 376	133 949	130 426	117 365	141 406	PIB aux prix courants
GDP per capita	24 705	27 348	26 136	31 648	30 489	27 151	32 372	PIB par habitant
GDP at constant prices	109 500	113 058	115 575	118 880	117 613	118 536	121 298	PIB aux prix constants
Growth rates	3.6	3.2	2.2	2.9	-1.1	0.8	2.3	Taux de croissance
Nicaragua								**Nicaragua**
GDP at current prices	4 465	4 872	5 230	5 662	6 372	6 214	6 551	PIB aux prix courants
GDP per capita	834	898	952	1 018	1 131	1 088	1 132	PIB par habitant
GDP at constant prices	4 672	4 872	5 074	5 259	5 404	5 325	5 563	PIB aux prix constants
Growth rates	5.3	4.3	4.2	3.6	2.8	-1.5	4.5	Taux de croissance
Niger								**Niger**
GDP at current prices	2 897	3 369	3 647	4 284	5 403	5 319	5 549	PIB aux prix courants
GDP per capita	231	259	271	307	374	355	358	PIB par habitant
GDP at constant prices	3 136	3 369	3 564	3 676	4 028	3 992	4 290	PIB aux prix constants
Growth rates	-0.8	7.4	5.8	3.1	9.6	-0.9	7.5	Taux de croissance
Nigeria								**Nigéria**
GDP at current prices	87 845	112 248	145 430	166 451	208 065	169 408	196 410	PIB aux prix courants
GDP per capita	644	803	1 015	1 133	1 381	1 097	1 240	PIB par habitant
GDP at constant prices	108 510	112 248	120 703	126 851	129 810	119 064	122 349	PIB aux prix constants
Growth rates	33.7	3.4	7.5	5.1	2.3	-8.3	2.8	Taux de croissance
Norway								**Norvège**
GDP at current prices	258 579	302 013	336 732	387 536	445 193	370 671	413 056	PIB aux prix courants
GDP per capita	56 372	65 324	72 124	82 070	93 157	76 680	84 589	PIB par habitant
GDP at constant prices	293 960	302 013	308 901	318 583	319 646	314 184	315 275	PIB aux prix constants
Growth rates	3.9	2.7	2.3	3.1	0.3	-1.7	0.3	Taux de croissance
Occupied Palestinian Terr.								**Terr. palestinien occupé**
GDP at current prices	4 198	4 634	4 619	5 182	6 247	6 764	7 349	PIB aux prix courants
GDP per capita	1 205	1 303	1 270	1 390	1 633	1 721	1 820	PIB par habitant
GDP at constant prices	4 267	4 634	4 393	4 629	4 958	5 327	5 674	PIB aux prix constants
Growth rates	12.0	8.6	-5.2	5.4	7.1	7.4	6.5	Taux de croissance
Oman								**Oman**
GDP at current prices	24 674	30 905	36 804	41 901	60 567	46 865	57 850	PIB aux prix courants
GDP per capita	10 374	12 721	14 777	16 360	22 968	17 280	20 791	PIB par habitant
GDP at constant prices	29 719	30 905	32 614	34 808	39 277	39 719	41 391	PIB aux prix constants
Growth rates	3.4	4.0	5.5	6.7	12.8	1.1	4.2	Taux de croissance

Gross domestic product and gross domestic product per capita *(continued)*
In millions of US dollars at current and constant 1990 prices; per capita US dollars; real rates of growth
Produit intérieur brut et produit intérieur brut par habitant *(suite)*
En millions de dollars É.-U. aux prix courants et constants de 1990 ; par habitant en dollars É.-U. ; taux de croissance réels

Country or area	2004	2005	2006	2007	2008	2009	2010	Pays ou zone
Pakistan								**Pakistan**
GDP at current prices	96 821	109 213	126 481	142 793	145 478	155 716	174 150	PIB aux prix courants
GDP per capita	621	688	783	868	869	913	1 003	PIB par habitant
GDP at constant prices	101 435	109 213	115 960	122 550	124 506	128 983	134 328	PIB aux prix constants
Growth rates	7.4	7.7	6.2	5.7	1.6	3.6	4.1	Taux de croissance
Palau								**Palaos**
GDP at current prices	134	145	158	170	187	204	222	PIB aux prix courants
GDP per capita	6 744	7 267	7 880	8 457	9 252	10 008	10 822	PIB par habitant
GDP at constant prices	137	145	149	152	151	155	159	PIB aux prix constants
Growth rates	4.9	5.5	3.0	2.1	-1.0	2.9	2.5	Taux de croissance
Panama								**Panama**
GDP at current prices	14 179	15 465	17 137	19 794	23 002	24 080	26 777	PIB aux prix courants
GDP per capita	4 456	4 776	5 202	5 907	6 752	6 956	7 614	PIB par habitant
GDP at constant prices	14 427	15 465	16 783	18 816	20 835	21 382	22 978	PIB aux prix constants
Growth rates	7.5	7.2	8.5	12.1	10.7	2.6	7.5	Taux de croissance
Papua New Guinea								**Papouasie-Nvl-Guinée**
GDP at current prices	4 177	4 866	5 528	6 341	8 000	8 060	9 796	PIB aux prix courants
GDP per capita	702	798	885	991	1 222	1 202	1 428	PIB par habitant
GDP at constant prices	4 682	4 866	4 978	5 334	5 687	5 998	6 421	PIB aux prix constants
Growth rates	0.6	3.9	2.3	7.2	6.6	5.5	7.1	Taux de croissance
Paraguay								**Paraguay**
GDP at current prices	6 950	7 473	9 275	12 222	16 873	14 240	17 886	PIB aux prix courants
GDP per capita	1 201	1 267	1 544	1 997	2 708	2 245	2 771	PIB par habitant
GDP at constant prices	7 265	7 473	7 797	8 325	8 810	8 471	9 764	PIB aux prix constants
Growth rates	4.1	2.9	4.3	6.8	5.8	-3.8	15.3	Taux de croissance
Peru								**Pérou**
GDP at current prices	69 701	79 389	92 319	107 524	129 107	130 355	157 324	PIB aux prix courants
GDP per capita	2 559	2 881	3 313	3 817	4 536	4 532	5 411	PIB par habitant
GDP at constant prices	74 316	79 389	85 534	93 120	102 209	103 078	112 100	PIB aux prix constants
Growth rates	5.0	6.8	7.7	8.9	9.8	0.9	8.8	Taux de croissance
Philippines								**Philippines**
GDP at current prices	91 371	103 072	122 211	149 360	174 195	168 335	199 591	PIB aux prix courants
GDP per capita	1 089	1 205	1 403	1 685	1 932	1 836	2 140	PIB par habitant
GDP at constant prices	98 372	103 072	108 476	115 653	120 456	121 839	131 138	PIB aux prix constants
Growth rates	6.7	4.8	5.2	6.6	4.2	1.1	7.6	Taux de croissance
Poland								**Pologne**
GDP at current prices	252 769	303 912	341 597	425 129	529 391	430 546	469 393	PIB aux prix courants
GDP per capita	6 621	7 963	8 949	11 132	13 852	11 256	12 263	PIB par habitant
GDP at constant prices	293 303	303 912	322 838	344 743	362 417	368 237	382 761	PIB aux prix constants
Growth rates	5.3	3.6	6.2	6.8	5.1	1.6	3.9	Taux de croissance
Portugal								**Portugal**
GDP at current prices	184 795	191 176	201 060	231 742	251 925	234 199	228 859	PIB aux prix courants
GDP per capita	17 589	18 132	19 008	21 846	23 689	21 976	21 438	PIB par habitant
GDP at constant prices	189 740	191 176	193 929	198 556	198 539	193 563	196 251	PIB aux prix constants
Growth rates	1.6	0.8	1.4	2.4	^0.0	-2.5	1.4	Taux de croissance
Puerto Rico								**Porto Rico**
GDP at current prices	82 809	86 157	88 405	92 606	95 211	96 261	99 202	PIB aux prix courants
GDP per capita	21 836	22 781	23 430	24 594	25 329	25 645	26 461	PIB par habitant
GDP at constant prices	86 289	86 157	84 064	83 014	80 608	78 937	77 544	PIB aux prix constants
Growth rates	0.8	-0.2	-2.4	-1.2	-2.9	-2.1	-1.8	Taux de croissance
Qatar								**Qatar**
GDP at current prices	31 734	44 530	60 882	79 712	115 270	97 798	127 333	PIB aux prix courants
GDP per capita	44 374	54 240	62 230	67 656	82 568	61 209	72 398	PIB par habitant
GDP at constant prices	41 427	44 530	56 184	66 289	77 998	87 324	104 255	PIB aux prix constants
Growth rates	20.8	7.5	26.2	18.0	17.7	12.0	19.4	Taux de croissance
Republic of Moldova								**République de Moldova**
GDP at current prices	2 598	2 988	3 408	4 401	6 055	5 439	5 809	PIB aux prix courants
GDP per capita	679	793	917	1 199	1 666	1 510	1 626	PIB par habitant
GDP at constant prices	2 780	2 988	3 131	3 225	3 478	3 270	3 497	PIB aux prix constants
Growth rates	7.4	7.5	4.8	3.0	7.8	-6.0	6.9	Taux de croissance

19 Gross domestic product and gross domestic product per capita *(continued)*
In millions of US dollars at current and constant 2005 prices; per capita US dollars; real rates of growth
Produit intérieur brut et produit intérieur brut par habitant *(suite)*
En millions de dollars É.-U. aux prix courants et constants de 2005; par habitant en dollars É.-U. ; taux de croissance réels

Country or area	2004	2005	2006	2007	2008	2009	2010	Pays ou zone
Romania								**Roumanie**
GDP at current prices	75 795	99 173	122 696	170 617	204 339	164 344	161 629	PIB aux prix courants
GDP per capita	3 470	4 555	5 653	7 883	9 465	7 631	7 522	PIB par habitant
GDP at constant prices	95 218	99 173	106 982	113 740	122 099	114 070	111 921	PIB aux prix constants
Growth rates	8.5	4.2	7.9	6.3	7.3	-6.6	-1.9	Taux de croissance
Russian Federation								**Fédération de Russie**
GDP at current prices	590 940	764 016	989 932	1 299 703	1 660 848	1 221 989	1 479 823	PIB aux prix courants
GDP per capita	4 095	5 311	6 898	9 070	11 601	8 542	10 351	PIB par habitant
GDP at constant prices	718 221	764 016	826 310	896 836	943 901	870 144	905 248	PIB aux prix constants
Growth rates	7.2	6.4	8.2	8.5	5.2	-7.8	4.0	Taux de croissance
Rwanda								**Rwanda**
GDP at current prices	2 089	2 581	3 111	3 741	4 712	5 262	5 655	PIB aux prix courants
GDP per capita	232	281	330	385	471	510	532	PIB par habitant
GDP at constant prices	2 362	2 581	2 814	3 031	3 381	3 585	3 854	PIB aux prix constants
Growth rates	7.4	9.3	9.0	7.7	11.5	6.1	7.5	Taux de croissance
Saint Kitts and Nevis								**Saint-Kitts-et-Nevis**
GDP at current prices	400	439	487	509	570	545	550	PIB aux prix courants
GDP per capita	8 232	8 922	9 782	10 093	11 161	10 530	10 494	PIB par habitant
GDP at constant prices	415	439	463	472	492	454	448	PIB aux prix constants
Growth rates	7.6	5.6	5.5	2.0	4.3	-7.7	-1.5	Taux de croissance
Saint Lucia								**Sainte-Lucie**
GDP at current prices	802	847	942	1 018	1 083	1 062	1 164	PIB aux prix courants
GDP per capita	4 904	5 125	5 642	6 029	6 349	6 160	6 677	PIB par habitant
GDP at constant prices	780	847	879	896	903	869	873	PIB aux prix constants
Growth rates	2.5	8.5	3.8	1.9	0.8	-3.8	0.4	Taux de croissance
Saint Vincent-Grenadines								**Saint Vincent-Grenadines**
GDP at current prices	523	551	611	685	699	672	675	PIB aux prix courants
GDP per capita	4 813	5 070	5 610	6 278	6 404	6 153	6 172	PIB par habitant
GDP at constant prices	541	551	605	625	634	620	603	PIB aux prix constants
Growth rates	6.1	2.0	9.7	3.4	1.4	-2.2	-2.8	Taux de croissance
Samoa								**Samoa**
GDP at current prices	385	435	452	552	546	525	612	PIB aux prix courants
GDP per capita	2 142	2 415	2 501	3 045	3 004	2 876	3 343	PIB par habitant
GDP at constant prices	413	435	437	467	451	443	450	PIB aux prix constants
Growth rates	4.5	5.3	0.5	6.8	-3.4	-1.7	1.5	Taux de croissance
San Marino								**Saint-Marin**
GDP at current prices	1 317	1 375	1 469	1 688	1 844	1 531	1 487	PIB aux prix courants
GDP per capita	44 325	45 392	47 817	54 425	59 113	48 818	47 171	PIB par habitant
GDP at constant prices	1 344	1 375	1 428	1 478	1 463	1 272	1 289	PIB aux prix constants
Growth rates	4.6	2.3	3.9	3.5	-1.1	-13.0	1.3	Taux de croissance
Sao Tome and Principe								**Sao Tomé-et-Principe**
GDP at current prices	111	123	135	144	182	198	212	PIB aux prix courants
GDP per capita	737	808	872	915	1 140	1 218	1 283	PIB par habitant
GDP at constant prices	120	123	138	142	155	163	170	PIB aux prix constants
Growth rates	4.5	3.1	12.3	2.4	9.4	4.8	4.5	Taux de croissance
Saudi Arabia								**Arabie saoudite**
GDP at current prices	250 339	315 583	356 630	384 942	476 305	372 663	434 666	PIB aux prix courants
GDP per capita	10 784	13 127	14 381	15 093	18 203	13 901	15 836	PIB par habitant
GDP at constant prices	298 979	315 583	325 548	332 115	346 159	346 706	359 749	PIB aux prix constants
Growth rates	5.3	5.6	3.2	2.0	4.2	0.2	3.8	Taux de croissance
Senegal								**Sénégal**
GDP at current prices	8 031	8 708	9 359	11 285	13 287	12 756	12 841	PIB aux prix courants
GDP per capita	759	801	838	983	1 127	1 054	1 033	PIB par habitant
GDP at constant prices	8 244	8 708	8 922	9 363	9 666	9 879	10 298	PIB aux prix constants
Growth rates	5.9	5.6	2.5	4.9	3.2	2.2	4.2	Taux de croissance
Serbia[6]								**Serbie**[6]
GDP at current prices	23 646	25 231	29 221	38 952	47 761	40 148	37 713	PIB aux prix courants
GDP per capita	3 168	3 391	3 943	5 277	6 498	5 457	5 123	PIB par habitant
GDP at constant prices	23 891	25 231	26 546	28 378	29 944	29 014	29 523	PIB aux prix constants
Growth rates	8.3	5.6	5.2	6.9	5.5	-3.1	1.8	Taux de croissance

Gross domestic product and gross domestic product per capita *(continued)*
In millions of US dollars at current and constant 1990 prices; per capita US dollars; real rates of growth

Produit intérieur brut et produit intérieur brut par habitant *(suite)*
En millions de dollars É.-U. aux prix courants et constants de 1990 ; par habitant en dollars É.-U. ; taux de croissance réels

Country or area	2004	2005	2006	2007	2008	2009	2010	Pays ou zone
Seychelles								**Seychelles**
GDP at current prices	864	928	1 015	1 018	921	788	991	PIB aux prix courants
GDP per capita	10 461	11 113	12 037	11 984	10 763	9 155	11 451	PIB par habitant
GDP at constant prices	870	928	1 016	1 113	1 099	1 107	1 212	PIB aux prix constants
Growth rates	-2.0	6.7	9.5	9.6	-1.3	0.7	9.5	Taux de croissance
Sierra Leone								**Sierra Leone**
GDP at current prices	1 418	1 491	1 646	1 954	2 156	2 118	2 064	PIB aux prix courants
GDP per capita	286	289	309	357	384	369	352	PIB par habitant
GDP at constant prices	1 386	1 491	1 586	1 653	1 731	1 815	1 904	PIB aux prix constants
Growth rates	9.6	7.5	6.4	4.3	4.7	4.9	4.9	Taux de croissance
Singapore								**Singapour**
GDP at current prices	112 697	125 429	145 332	177 329	189 384	183 332	222 699	PIB aux prix courants
GDP per capita	27 090	29 402	32 955	38 677	39 685	37 069	43 783	PIB par habitant
GDP at constant prices	116 806	125 429	136 345	148 309	150 515	149 356	170 969	PIB aux prix constants
Growth rates	9.2	7.4	8.7	8.8	1.5	-0.8	14.5	Taux de croissance
Slovakia								**Slovaquie**
GDP at current prices	42 178	47 895	55 796	74 966	94 395	87 374	87 263	PIB aux prix courants
GDP per capita	7 794	8 844	10 290	13 803	17 348	16 026	15 976	PIB par habitant
GDP at constant prices	44 907	47 895	51 893	57 338	60 716	57 734	60 184	PIB aux prix constants
Growth rates	5.1	6.7	8.3	10.5	5.9	-4.9	4.2	Taux de croissance
Slovenia								**Slovénie**
GDP at current prices	33 838	35 718	38 945	47 304	54 608	49 053	46 906	PIB aux prix courants
GDP per capita	16 936	17 840	19 406	23 507	27 058	24 235	23 110	PIB par habitant
GDP at constant prices	34 342	35 718	37 807	40 405	41 855	38 503	39 034	PIB aux prix constants
Growth rates	4.4	4.0	5.8	6.9	3.6	-8.0	1.4	Taux de croissance
Solomon Islands								**Iles Salomon**
GDP at current prices	364	429	471	516	608	598	642	PIB aux prix courants
GDP per capita	796	914	976	1 039	1 192	1 140	1 193	PIB par habitant
GDP at constant prices	381	429	447	475	509	485	519	PIB aux prix constants
Growth rates	8.1	12.8	4.0	6.4	7.1	-4.7	7.1	Taux de croissance
Somalia								**Somalie**
GDP at current prices	1 984	2 316	2 390	2 483	2 600	2 012	1 071	PIB aux prix courants
GDP per capita	243	277	280	284	291	221	115	PIB par habitant
GDP at constant prices	2 248	2 316	2 371	2 433	2 496	2 561	2 627	PIB aux prix constants
Growth rates	3.0	3.0	2.4	2.6	2.6	2.6	2.6	Taux de croissance
South Africa								**Afrique du Sud**
GDP at current prices	219 093	247 052	261 007	286 169	275 279	282 754	363 704	PIB aux prix courants
GDP per capita	4 639	5 169	5 400	5 859	5 582	5 683	7 255	PIB par habitant
GDP at constant prices	234 668	247 052	260 896	275 422	285 271	280 473	288 441	PIB aux prix constants
Growth rates	4.6	5.3	5.6	5.6	3.6	-1.7	2.8	Taux de croissance
Spain								**Espagne**
GDP at current prices	1 044 299	1 130 170	1 234 768	1 441 942	1 593 913	1 464 088	1 407 322	PIB aux prix courants
GDP per capita	24 438	26 044	28 052	32 327	35 306	32 080	30 543	PIB par habitant
GDP at constant prices	1 090 746	1 130 170	1 175 587	1 217 606	1 228 075	1 182 360	1 180 660	PIB aux prix constants
Growth rates	3.3	3.6	4.0	3.6	0.9	-3.7	-0.1	Taux de croissance
Sri Lanka								**Sri Lanka**
GDP at current prices	20 662	24 406	28 280	32 350	40 714	41 977	49 549	PIB aux prix courants
GDP per capita	1 054	1 230	1 410	1 596	1 989	2 031	2 375	PIB par habitant
GDP at constant prices	22 972	24 406	26 278	28 064	29 734	30 787	33 252	PIB aux prix constants
Growth rates	5.4	6.2	7.7	6.8	6.0	3.5	8.0	Taux de croissance
Sudan								**Soudan**
GDP at current prices	26 646	35 183	45 264	57 216	64 833	65 852	79 480	PIB aux prix courants
GDP per capita	710	916	1 150	1 417	1 565	1 550	1 825	PIB par habitant
GDP at constant prices	33 153	35 183	38 489	42 165	45 446	49 172	51 663	PIB aux prix constants
Growth rates	6.5	6.1	9.4	9.6	7.8	8.2	5.1	Taux de croissance
Suriname[7]								**Suriname**[7]
GDP at current prices	1 477	1 785	2 136	2 425	3 065	3 252	3 682	PIB aux prix courants
GDP per capita	2 994	3 574	4 231	4 754	5 951	6 255	7 018	PIB par habitant
GDP at constant prices	1 717	1 785	1 865	1 966	2 067	2 130	2 224	PIB aux prix constants
Growth rates	8.0	3.9	4.5	5.4	5.1	3.1	4.4	Taux de croissance

Gross domestic product and gross domestic product per capita *(continued)*
In millions of US dollars at current and constant 2005 prices; per capita US dollars; real rates of growth
Produit intérieur brut et produit intérieur brut par habitant *(suite)*
En millions de dollars É.-U. aux prix courants et constants de 2005; par habitant en dollars É.-U. ; taux de croissance réels

Country or area	2004	2005	2006	2007	2008	2009	2010	Pays ou zone
Swaziland								**Swaziland**
GDP at current prices	2 429	2 596	2 959	3 069	3 020	3 161	3 927	PIB aux prix courants
GDP per capita	2 217	2 349	2 648	2 709	2 625	2 706	3 311	PIB par habitant
GDP at constant prices	2 538	2 596	2 680	2 786	2 799	2 833	2 889	PIB aux prix constants
Growth rates	3.1	2.3	3.2	4.0	0.5	1.2	2.0	Taux de croissance
Sweden								**Suède**
GDP at current prices	362 090	370 580	399 076	462 513	486 159	403 613	458 725	PIB aux prix courants
GDP per capita	40 331	41 042	43 899	50 485	52 632	43 347	48 906	PIB par habitant
GDP at constant prices	359 225	370 580	386 504	399 314	396 864	375 700	397 080	PIB aux prix constants
Growth rates	4.2	3.2	4.3	3.3	-0.6	-5.3	5.7	Taux de croissance
Switzerland								**Suisse**
GDP at current prices	362 992	372 477	391 233	434 118	503 215	492 261	527 920	PIB aux prix courants
GDP per capita	49 311	50 233	52 385	57 716	66 447	64 591	68 880	PIB par habitant
GDP at constant prices	362 894	372 477	385 999	400 067	408 450	400 779	411 657	PIB aux prix constants
Growth rates	2.5	2.6	3.6	3.6	2.1	-1.9	2.7	Taux de croissance
Syrian Arab Republic								**Rép. arabe syrienne**
GDP at current prices	24 546	28 397	32 698	40 212	52 494	54 078	59 834	PIB aux prix courants
GDP per capita	1 363	1 536	1 728	2 081	2 665	2 697	2 931	PIB par habitant
GDP at constant prices	26 735	28 397	29 830	31 523	32 934	34 914	36 043	PIB aux prix constants
Growth rates	6.9	6.2	5.0	5.7	4.5	6.0	3.2	Taux de croissance
Tajikistan								**Tadjikistan**
GDP at current prices	2 076	2 312	2 830	3 719	5 161	4 979	5 613	PIB aux prix courants
GDP per capita	325	358	434	563	771	734	816	PIB par habitant
GDP at constant prices	2 167	2 312	2 465	2 656	2 857	2 972	3 166	PIB aux prix constants
Growth rates	10.3	6.7	6.6	7.8	7.6	4.0	6.5	Taux de croissance
Thailand								**Thaïlande**
GDP at current prices	161 340	176 352	207 089	246 977	272 578	263 711	318 850	PIB aux prix courants
GDP per capita	2 442	2 644	3 078	3 643	3 993	3 838	4 613	PIB par habitant
GDP at constant prices	168 589	176 352	185 333	194 682	199 519	194 870	210 077	PIB aux prix constants
Growth rates	6.3	4.6	5.1	5.0	2.5	-2.3	7.8	Taux de croissance
TFYR of Macedonia								**L'ex-R.Y. Macédoine**
GDP at current prices	5 514	5 987	6 558	8 160	9 834	9 314	9 138	PIB aux prix courants
GDP per capita	2 712	2 937	3 210	3 984	4 791	4 528	4 434	PIB par habitant
GDP at constant prices	5 737	5 987	6 288	6 675	7 005	6 941	7 062	PIB aux prix constants
Growth rates	4.6	4.4	5.0	6.1	5.0	-0.9	1.8	Taux de croissance
Timor-Leste [8]								**Timor-Leste** [8]
GDP at current prices	339	350	353	453	562	704	794	PIB aux prix courants
GDP per capita	348	346	339	427	521	640	706	PIB par habitant
GDP at constant prices	329	350	330	360	399	451	478	PIB aux prix constants
Growth rates	4.2	6.2	-5.8	9.1	11.0	12.9	6.1	Taux de croissance
Togo								**Togo**
GDP at current prices	1 937	2 110	2 219	2 531	3 168	3 162	3 162	PIB aux prix courants
GDP per capita	366	390	401	448	548	536	525	PIB par habitant
GDP at constant prices	2 084	2 110	2 193	2 238	2 291	2 373	2 462	PIB aux prix constants
Growth rates	2.5	1.2	3.9	2.1	2.4	3.6	3.7	Taux de croissance
Tonga								**Tonga**
GDP at current prices	239	259	292	310	341	320	369	PIB aux prix courants
GDP per capita	2 379	2 566	2 879	3 031	3 309	3 087	3 543	PIB par habitant
GDP at constant prices	261	259	259	257	264	261	262	PIB aux prix constants
Growth rates	1.0	-0.8	0.1	-0.9	2.6	-1.0	0.3	Taux de croissance
Trinidad and Tobago								**Trinité-et-Tobago**
GDP at current prices	13 280	15 982	18 369	21 642	27 179	19 623	20 397	PIB aux prix courants
GDP per capita	10 133	12 150	13 912	16 325	20 419	14 684	15 205	PIB par habitant
GDP at constant prices	15 048	15 982	18 093	18 953	19 402	18 715	19 186	PIB aux prix constants
Growth rates	8.0	6.2	13.2	4.8	2.4	-3.5	2.5	Taux de croissance
Tunisia								**Tunisie**
GDP at current prices	31 184	32 272	34 377	38 910	44 815	43 528	44 252	PIB aux prix courants
GDP per capita	3 177	3 256	3 432	3 841	4 373	4 200	4 222	PIB par habitant
GDP at constant prices	31 031	32 272	34 097	36 229	37 843	39 034	40 476	PIB aux prix constants
Growth rates	6.0	4.0	5.7	6.3	4.5	3.1	3.7	Taux de croissance

Gross domestic product and gross domestic product per capita *(continued)*
In millions of US dollars at current and constant 1990 prices; per capita US dollars; real rates of growth
Produit intérieur brut et produit intérieur brut par habitant *(suite)*
En millions de dollars É.-U. aux prix courants et constants de 1990 ; par habitant en dollars É.-U. ; taux de croissance réels

Country or area	2004	2005	2006	2007	2008	2009	2010	Pays ou zone
Turkey								**Turquie**
GDP at current prices	392 156	482 986	530 917	647 140	730 325	614 570	734 440	PIB aux prix courants
GDP per capita	5 833	7 088	7 687	9 246	10 297	8 554	10 095	PIB par habitant
GDP at constant prices	445 552	482 986	516 280	540 383	543 944	517 694	564 315	PIB aux prix constants
Growth rates	9.4	8.4	6.9	4.7	0.7	-4.8	9.0	Taux de croissance
Turkmenistan								**Turkménistan**
GDP at current prices	10 646[4]	12 436[4]	14 248[4]	16 289[4]	19 098	19 947	23 130	PIB aux prix courants
GDP per capita	2 267[4]	2 619[4]	2 967[4]	3 352[4]	3 883	4 006	4 587	PIB par habitant
GDP at constant prices	11 001[4]	12 436[4]	13 799[4]	15 325[4]	17 585	18 656	20 376	PIB aux prix constants
Growth rates	5.0	13.0	11.0	11.1	14.7	6.1	9.2	Taux de croissance
Turks and Caicos Islands								**Iles Turques et Caïques**
GDP at current prices	486	579	722	829	975	1 160	1 381	PIB aux prix courants
GDP per capita	17 225	18 953	22 151	24 084	27 122	31 124	36 000	PIB par habitant
GDP at constant prices	506	579	682	759	856	972	1 107	PIB aux prix constants
Growth rates	11.4	14.4	17.9	11.2	12.8	13.5	13.9	Taux de croissance
Tuvalu								**Tuvalu**
GDP at current prices	22	22	23	28	30	27	31	PIB aux prix courants
GDP per capita	2 278	2 289	2 411	2 884	3 028	2 716	3 187	PIB par habitant
GDP at constant prices	23	22	24	25	25	25	26	PIB aux prix constants
Growth rates	-1.3	-4.1	6.6	4.9	1.3	1.5	1.6	Taux de croissance
Uganda								**Ouganda**
GDP at current prices	8 436	10 040	11 011	13 549	16 377	16 843	17 015	PIB aux prix courants
GDP per capita	307	353	375	447	523	520	509	PIB par habitant
GDP at constant prices	9 127	10 040	10 748	11 614	12 826	13 391	13 729	PIB aux prix constants
Growth rates	5.8	10.0	7.0	8.1	10.4	4.4	2.5	Taux de croissance
Ukraine								**Ukraine**
GDP at current prices	64 881	86 142	107 753	142 719	179 992	117 227	137 936	PIB aux prix courants
GDP per capita	1 372	1 836	2 313	3 084	3 914	2 564	3 035	PIB par habitant
GDP at constant prices	83 856	86 142	92 471	99 815	102 115	87 044	90 700	PIB aux prix constants
Growth rates	12.1	2.7	7.3	7.9	2.3	-14.8	4.2	Taux de croissance
United Arab Emirates								**Emirats arabes unis**
GDP at current prices	147 824	180 617	222 106	258 150	314 845	270 335	297 648	PIB aux prix courants
GDP per capita	40 411	44 385	47 634	47 757	50 727	38 960	39 625	PIB par habitant
GDP at constant prices	172 254	180 617	198 509	204 888	211 638	208 232	211 214	PIB aux prix constants
Growth rates	9.6	4.9	9.9	3.2	3.3	-1.6	1.4	Taux de croissance
United Kingdom								**Royaume-Uni**
GDP at current prices	2 201 417	2 280 538	2 444 581	2 812 877	2 635 954	2 171 385	2 253 552	PIB aux prix courants
GDP per capita	36 757	37 881	40 381	46 191	43 022	35 220	36 327	PIB par habitant
GDP at constant prices	2 233 943	2 280 538	2 339 994	2 421 102	2 394 401	2 289 685	2 330 011	PIB aux prix constants
Growth rates	3.0	2.1	2.6	3.5	-1.1	-4.4	1.8	Taux de croissance
United Rep. of Tanzania [9]								**Rép.-Unie de Tanzanie** [9]
GDP at current prices	12 826	14 142	14 331	16 826	20 715	21 368	22 502	PIB aux prix courants
GDP per capita	349	375	370	421	504	505	516	PIB par habitant
GDP at constant prices	13 171	14 142	15 095	16 174	17 377	18 423	19 682	PIB aux prix constants
Growth rates	7.8	7.4	6.7	7.1	7.4	6.0	6.8	Taux de croissance
United States								**Etats-Unis**
GDP at current prices	11 797 800	12 564 300	13 314 500	13 961 800	14 219 300	13 863 600	14 447 100	PIB aux prix courants
GDP per capita	40 120	42 330	44 446	46 188	46 622	45 058	46 546	PIB par habitant
GDP at constant prices	12 189 400	12 564 300	12 898 400	13 144 400	13 097 200	12 635 200	13 017 000	PIB aux prix constants
Growth rates	3.5	3.1	2.7	1.9	-0.4	-3.5	3.0	Taux de croissance
Uruguay								**Uruguay**
GDP at current prices	13 686	17 363	19 802	23 877	31 177	31 322	40 265	PIB aux prix courants
GDP per capita	4 121	5 226	5 951	7 158	9 318	9 329	11 952	PIB par habitant
GDP at constant prices	16 157	17 363	18 114	19 442	21 114	21 659	23 493	PIB aux prix constants
Growth rates	5.0	7.5	4.3	7.3	8.6	2.6	8.5	Taux de croissance
Uzbekistan								**Ouzbékistan**
GDP at current prices	12 087	14 396	17 378	22 358	28 723	32 971	39 173	PIB aux prix courants
GDP per capita	470	555	663	844	1 071	1 215	1 427	PIB par habitant
GDP at constant prices	13 454	14 396	15 447	16 914	18 437	19 930	21 624	PIB aux prix constants
Growth rates	7.7	7.0	7.3	9.5	9.0	8.1	8.5	Taux de croissance

19

Gross domestic product and gross domestic product per capita *(continued)*
In millions of US dollars at current and constant 2005 prices; per capita US dollars; real rates of growth

Produit intérieur brut et produit intérieur brut par habitant *(suite)*
En millions de dollars É.-U. aux prix courants et constants de 2005; par habitant en dollars É.-U. ; taux de croissance réels

Country or area	2004	2005	2006	2007	2008	2009	2010	Pays ou zone
Vanuatu								**Vanuatu**
GDP at current prices	364	393	438	528	593	590	710	PIB aux prix courants
GDP per capita	1 770	1 862	2 019	2 373	2 602	2 525	2 963	PIB par habitant
GDP at constant prices	374	393	422	450	477	494	519	PIB aux prix constants
Growth rates	4.5	5.2	7.4	6.5	6.2	3.5	5.0	Taux de croissance
Venezuela (Boliv. Rep. of)								**Venezuela (Rép. boliv. du)**
GDP at current prices	112 451	145 513	183 478	230 364	311 131	326 133	391 307	PIB aux prix courants
GDP per capita	4 292	5 457	6 763	8 349	11 089	11 435	13 503	PIB par habitant
GDP at constant prices	131 904	145 513	159 879	173 874	181 180	175 224	172 851	PIB aux prix constants
Growth rates	18.3	10.3	9.9	8.8	4.2	-3.3	-1.4	Taux de croissance
Viet Nam								**Viet Nam**
GDP at current prices	45 428	52 917	60 913	71 016	91 094	97 180	103 902	PIB aux prix courants
GDP per capita	552	636	725	835	1 060	1 118	1 183	PIB par habitant
GDP at constant prices	48 798	52 917	57 272	62 115	66 035	69 550	74 268	PIB aux prix constants
Growth rates	7.8	8.4	8.2	8.5	6.3	5.3	6.8	Taux de croissance
Yemen								**Yémen**
GDP at current prices	14 348	17 872	20 903	23 727	28 707	27 663	34 569	PIB aux prix courants
GDP per capita	716	866	982	1 081	1 269	1 186	1 437	PIB par habitant
GDP at constant prices	16 873	17 872	18 557	19 370	20 272	21 226	22 927	PIB aux prix constants
Growth rates	5.0	5.9	3.8	4.4	4.7	4.7	8.0	Taux de croissance
Zambia								**Zambie**
GDP at current prices	5 440	7 271	10 886	11 541	14 641	12 805	16 201	PIB aux prix courants
GDP per capita	486	634	926	957	1 183	1 006	1 238	PIB par habitant
GDP at constant prices	6 910	7 271	7 723	8 210	8 703	9 234	9 890	PIB aux prix constants
Growth rates	6.2	5.2	6.2	6.3	6.0	6.1	7.1	Taux de croissance
Zanzibar								**Zanzibar**
GDP at current prices	316	350	407	473	625	666	661	PIB aux prix courants
GDP per capita	304	326	356	415	532	549	528	PIB par habitant
GDP at constant prices	334	350	371	395	415	443	472	PIB aux prix constants
Growth rates	6.5	4.9	6.0	6.6	5.1	6.7	6.5	Taux de croissance
Zimbabwe								**Zimbabwe**
GDP at current prices	6 420	6 223	6 102	6 023	5 495	5 626	7 204	PIB aux prix courants
GDP per capita	510	495	487	483	441	451	573	PIB par habitant
GDP at constant prices	6 486	6 223	5 997	5 801	5 526	5 928	6 462	PIB aux prix constants
Growth rates	-3.6	-4.1	-3.6	-3.3	-4.7	7.3	9.0	Taux de croissance

Source:
United Nations Statistics Division, New York, national accounts estimates main aggregates database, last accessed January 2012.

Source:
Organisation des Nations Unies, Division de statistique, New York, la base de données d'estimation des comptes nationaux, dernier accès janvier 2012.

1   For statistical purposes, the data for China do not include those for the Hong Kong Special Administrative Region (Hong Kong SAR) and Macao Special Administrative Region (Macao SAR).

2   Excludes northern Cyprus.
3   Includes Guadeloupe, Martinique, Réunion and French Guiana.
4   Price-adjusted rates of exchange (PARE) are used for selected years for conversion to US dollars due to large distortions in the dollar levels of per capita GDP with the use of IMF market exchange rates.

5   Including Western Sahara.
6   Excluding Kosovo and Metohia.
7   Excluding the informal sector.
8   Refers to non-oil GDP
9   Tanzania mainland only.

1   Pour la présentation des statistiques, les données pour la Chine ne comprennent pas la Région Administrative Spéciale de Hong Kong (Hong Kong RAS) et la Région Administrative Spéciale de Macao (Macao RAS).

2   Exclu Chypre du nord.
3   Y compris Guadeloupe, Martinique, Réunion et Guyane française.
4   Pour certaines années, on utilise les Taux de change corrigés des prix (TCCP) pour effectuer la conversion en dollars des États-Unis, en raison des aberrations importantes relevées dans les niveaux du PNB exprimés en dollars après conversion à l'aide des taux de change du marché communiqués par le FMI.

5   Y compris les données de Sahara occidental.
6   Non compris Kosovo et Metohia.
7   Non compris le secteur informel.
8   PIB non dérivés du pétrole.
9   Tanzanie continentale seulement.

Implicit price deflators of gross domestic product
Index base: 2005 = 100

Déflateurs implicites des prix de produit intérieur brut
Indice base : 2005 = 100

Country or area Pays ou zone	Year Année	GDP at current prices PIB aux prix courants		GDP at constant prices PIB aux prix constants	GDP implicit price deflators PIB déflateurs implicites des prix		Exchange rates Taux de change
		National currency Monnaie nationale	US dollars Dollars É.-U.	National currency Monnaie nationale	National currency Monnaie nationale	US dollars Dollars É.-U.	
Afghanistan Afghanistan	2000	49.4	51.6	44.9	110.2	115.1	95.7
	2008	160.2	157.7	132.1	121.2	119.4	101.5
	2009	185.3	182.6	132.9	139.4	137.4	101.5
	2010	215.2	229.2	143.9	149.6	159.3	93.9
Albania Albanie	2000	64.2	44.6	75.2	85.4	59.3	143.9
	2008	133.6	159.0	120.2	111.1	132.3	84.0
	2009	140.4	147.6	124.2	113.0	118.8	95.1
	2010	150.3	144.4	128.6	116.9	112.4	104.1
Algeria Algérie	2000	54.5	53.1	78.8	69.1	67.3	102.7
	2008	146.3	166.0	107.6	136.0	154.3	88.1
	2009	132.4	133.6	110.2	120.2	121.3	99.1
	2010	155.8	153.7	113.8	136.8	135.0	101.4
Andorra Andorre	2000	58.9	43.6	68.6	85.9	63.6	135.0
	2008	110.2	129.8	100.8	109.3	128.8	84.9
	2009	105.1	117.4	96.1	109.3	122.1	89.5
	2010	103.1	109.8	92.8	111.1	118.3	93.9
Angola Angola	2000	3.4	29.8	61.1	5.6	48.8	11.5
	2008	236.6	274.8	165.4	143.0	166.1	86.1
	2009	224.3	246.5	169.4	132.4	145.5	91.0
	2010	283.9	269.3	175.2	162.1	153.7	105.5
Anguilla Anguilla	2000	63.6	63.6	73.2	87.0	87.0	100.0
	2008	171.1	171.1	151.3	113.1	113.1	100.0
	2009	127.3	127.3	112.8	112.9	112.9	100.0
	2010	124.4	124.4	108.5	114.7	114.7	100.0
Antigua and Barbuda Antigua-et-Barbuda	2000	76.6	76.6	81.5	94.1	94.1	100.0
	2008	138.8	138.8	123.8	112.2	112.2	100.0
	2009	130.6	130.6	113.2	115.3	115.3	100.0
	2010	129.0	129.0	108.6	118.8	118.8	100.0
Argentina Argentine	2000	53.4	155.2	90.6	59.0	171.3	34.4
	2008	194.2	179.3	125.8	154.3	142.5	108.3
	2009	215.3	168.5	126.9	169.7	132.8	127.8
	2010	271.2	202.1	138.5	195.8	145.9	134.2
Armenia Arménie	2000	46.0	39.0	56.2	81.8	69.4	117.9
	2008	159.1	238.0	137.7	115.5	172.8	66.9
	2009	140.1	176.5	118.2	118.5	149.3	79.4
	2010	156.1	191.2	120.7	129.4	158.4	81.6
Aruba Aruba	2000	80.4	80.4	94.2	85.3	85.3	100.0
	2008	117.8	117.8	98.5	119.5	119.5	100.0
	2009	107.3	107.3	90.5	118.6	118.6	100.0
	2010	105.4	105.4	87.2	120.8	120.8	100.0
Australia Australie	2000	70.8	53.7	84.3	84.0	63.8	131.7
	2008	125.3	137.7	109.1	114.9	126.2	91.0
	2009	128.3	131.0	111.6	115.0	117.4	97.9
	2010	138.5	166.3	114.4	121.1	145.5	83.3
Austria Autriche	2000	85.0	63.0	92.0	92.4	68.4	135.0
	2008	115.3	135.8	109.0	105.8	124.6	84.9
	2009	112.1	125.2	104.9	106.9	119.4	89.5
	2010	116.7	124.3	107.3	108.8	115.8	93.9
Azerbaijan Azerbaïdjan	2000	37.7	39.8	53.2	70.9	74.9	94.7
	2008	320.5	368.8	186.2	172.1	198.1	86.9
	2009	284.3	334.4	203.4	139.8	164.4	85.0
	2010	332.0	391.1	213.5	155.5	183.1	84.9

Country or area Pays ou zone	Year Année	GDP at current prices PIB aux prix courants		GDP at constant prices PIB aux prix constants	GDP implicit price deflators PIB déflateurs implicites des prix		Exchange rates Taux de change
		National currency Monnaie nationale	US dollars Dollars É.-U.	National currency Monnaie nationale	National currency Monnaie nationale	US dollars Dollars É.-U.	
Bahamas	2000	82.1	82.1	92.1	89.1	89.1	100.0
Bahamas	2008	106.9	106.9	102.6	104.2	104.2	100.0
	2009	101.3	101.3	97.1	104.3	104.3	100.0
	2010	99.9	99.9	98.0	102.0	102.0	100.0
Bahrain	2000	59.6	59.6	74.7	79.9	79.9	100.0
Bahreïn	2008	164.6	164.6	122.9	133.9	133.9	100.0
	2009	143.5	143.5	126.7	113.3	113.3	100.0
	2010	170.5	170.5	132.4	128.8	128.8	100.0
Bangladesh	2000	64.0	78.9	76.8	83.3	102.8	81.1
Bangladesh	2008	147.2	138.1	120.5	122.2	114.6	106.6
	2009	165.8	154.5	127.4	130.2	121.3	107.3
	2010	187.3	173.0	135.2	138.6	128.0	108.3
Barbados	2000	79.1	79.1	91.8	86.1	86.1	100.0
Barbade	2008	108.2	108.2	107.3	100.8	100.8	100.0
	2009	105.7	105.7	101.4	104.2	104.2	100.0
	2010	107.5	107.5	100.9	106.6	106.6	100.0
Belarus	2000	14.0	34.5	69.7	20.1	49.5	40.7
Bélarus	2008	199.5	201.1	131.7	151.5	152.7	99.2
	2009	211.2	163.1	131.9	160.2	123.7	129.5
	2010	250.5	181.1	141.8	176.6	127.7	138.3
Belgium	2000	83.3	61.7	92.4	90.1	66.7	135.0
Belgique	2008	114.1	134.4	106.7	106.9	126.0	84.9
	2009	112.2	125.4	103.7	108.3	120.9	89.5
	2010	116.8	124.4	106.0	110.2	117.4	93.9
Belize	2000	74.6	74.6	76.9	97.0	97.0	100.0
Belize	2008	121.9	121.9	109.9	110.9	110.9	100.0
	2009	121.0	121.0	109.9	110.1	110.1	100.0
	2010	125.7	125.7	112.9	111.3	111.3	100.0
Benin	2000	73.1	54.1	81.8	89.3	66.2	135.0
Bénin	2008	129.2	152.2	114.0	113.4	133.5	84.9
	2009	135.3	151.1	117.0	115.6	129.1	89.5
	2010	141.3	150.5	120.0	117.7	125.4	93.9
Bermuda	2000	72.6	72.6	83.4	87.0	87.0	100.0
Bermudes	2008	125.2	125.2	110.5	113.3	113.3	100.0
	2009	117.9	117.9	101.6	116.1	116.1	100.0
	2010	124.1	124.1	103.1	120.4	120.4	100.0
Bhutan	2000	54.7	53.6	68.3	80.0	78.5	101.9
Bhoutan	2008	151.5	153.6	131.9	114.9	116.5	98.7
	2009	169.5	154.5	140.8	120.4	109.7	109.8
	2010	188.2	181.5	150.2	125.3	120.8	103.7
Bolivia (Plurinational State of)	2000	67.4	87.9	85.9	78.5	102.4	76.7
Bolivie (État plurinational de)	2008	156.7	174.6	116.3	134.7	150.1	89.7
	2009	158.0	181.6	120.2	131.5	151.0	87.0
	2010	179.0	205.7	125.2	143.0	164.3	87.0
Bosnia and Herzegovina	2000	68.7	50.9	81.1	84.7	62.8	135.0
Bosnie-Herzégovine	2008	144.1	169.7	119.0	121.1	142.7	84.9
	2009	139.9	156.3	115.5	121.2	135.4	89.5
	2010	144.9	154.3	116.4	124.5	132.6	93.9
Botswana	2000	54.8	54.9	77.4	70.9	71.0	99.8
Botswana	2008	175.5	131.4	113.3	154.9	115.9	133.6
	2009	156.6	111.9	107.8	145.4	103.8	140.0
	2010	192.6	144.9	115.5	166.7	125.4	132.9

Country or area Pays ou zone	Year Année	GDP at current prices PIB aux prix courants		GDP at constant prices PIB aux prix constants	GDP implicit price deflators PIB déflateurs implicites des prix		Exchange rates Taux de change
		National currency Monnaie nationale	US dollars Dollars É.-U.	National currency Monnaie nationale	National currency Monnaie nationale	US dollars Dollars É.-U.	
Brazil	2000	54.9	73.1	87.2	63.0	83.9	75.2
Brésil	2008	141.2	187.5	116.0	121.7	161.6	75.3
	2009	148.3	180.6	115.2	128.7	156.7	82.1
	2010	171.2	236.8	123.9	138.2	191.2	72.3
British Virgin Islands	2000	86.3	86.3	95.3	90.5	90.5	100.0
Iles Vierges britanniques	2008	114.0	114.0	103.6	110.0	110.0	100.0
	2009	100.7	100.7	108.1	93.2	93.2	100.0
	2010	104.5	104.5	113.0	92.5	92.5	100.0
Brunei Darussalam	2000	65.2	63.0	90.3	72.3	69.8	103.6
Brunéi Darussalam	2008	128.6	151.0	102.5	125.4	147.3	85.2
	2009	98.4	112.6	100.7	97.7	111.8	87.4
	2010	111.9	136.6	104.9	106.8	130.3	81.9
Bulgaria	2000	60.2	44.7	76.6	78.7	58.3	134.9
Bulgarie	2008	152.4	179.4	120.4	126.5	149.0	84.9
	2009	150.2	168.1	113.8	132.0	147.7	89.4
	2010	154.9	165.1	114.0	136.0	144.9	93.9
Burkina Faso	2000	65.1	48.2	73.4	88.6	65.6	135.0
Burkina Faso	2008	130.5	153.7	117.7	110.9	130.6	84.9
	2009	137.0	153.0	121.5	112.7	125.9	89.5
	2010	147.1	156.7	128.6	114.4	121.9	93.9
Burundi	2000	59.4	89.1	90.1	65.9	98.9	66.6
Burundi	2008	128.8	117.5	117.0	110.1	100.4	109.6
	2009	134.5	118.3	121.0	111.2	97.8	113.7
	2010	150.6	132.6	125.7	119.9	105.5	113.6
Cambodia	2000	54.7	58.3	64.0	85.5	91.1	93.9
Cambodge	2008	163.0	164.5	130.3	125.1	126.3	99.1
	2009	167.2	165.3	130.4	128.2	126.8	101.1
	2010	182.7	179.1	138.2	132.2	129.7	102.0
Cameroon	2000	75.6	56.0	83.4	90.7	67.2	135.0
Cameroun	2008	119.4	140.6	109.7	108.9	128.2	84.9
	2009	126.2	141.0	111.4	113.3	126.6	89.5
	2010	133.9	142.6	114.7	116.7	124.3	93.9
Canada	2000	78.4	63.9	88.2	88.9	72.5	122.6
Canada	2008	116.7	132.5	105.8	110.3	125.3	88.1
	2009	111.3	118.0	102.9	108.2	114.7	94.3
	2010	118.3	139.1	106.2	111.4	131.0	85.0
Cape Verde	2000	74.9	55.5	77.0	97.3	72.1	135.0
Cap-Vert	2008	133.8	157.6	127.1	105.3	124.0	84.9
	2009	142.7	159.4	131.6	108.4	121.1	89.5
	2010	155.4	165.5	138.7	112.0	119.3	93.9
Cayman Islands	2000	74.9	74.9	89.2	83.9	83.9	100.0
Iles Caïmanes	2008	113.7	117.0	107.0	106.3	109.3	97.2
	2009	107.1	110.2	98.6	108.7	111.8	97.2
	2010	102.5	105.5	94.6	108.3	111.4	97.2
Central African Rep.	2000	91.4	67.7	102.3	89.4	66.2	135.0
Rép. centrafricaine	2008	124.7	146.9	113.5	109.9	129.5	84.9
	2009	131.4	146.8	115.5	113.7	127.0	89.5
	2010	138.0	146.9	119.4	115.6	123.1	93.9
Chad	2000	31.8	23.6	50.1	63.5	47.1	135.0
Tchad	2008	120.8	142.2	100.7	120.0	141.3	84.9
	2009	105.1	117.4	100.9	104.1	116.3	89.5
	2010	130.6	139.0	106.0	123.1	131.1	93.9

Country or area Pays ou zone	Year Année	GDP at current prices PIB aux prix courants		GDP at constant prices PIB aux prix constants	GDP implicit price deflators PIB déflateurs implicites des prix		Exchange rates Taux de change
		National currency Monnaie nationale	US dollars Dollars É.-U.	National currency Monnaie nationale	National currency Monnaie nationale	US dollars Dollars É.-U.	
Chile	2000	61.3	63.6	81.4	75.3	78.1	96.4
Chili	2008	134.8	144.4	113.4	118.8	127.3	93.3
	2009	136.3	136.0	111.5	122.2	122.0	100.2
	2010	156.8	172.0	117.3	133.7	146.7	91.2
China [1]	2000	52.8	52.2	62.8	84.1	83.2	101.0
Chine [1]	2008	168.3	198.5	141.1	119.3	140.7	84.8
	2009	184.4	221.2	154.0	119.7	143.6	83.4
	2010	207.7	251.3	170.1	122.1	147.8	82.6
China, Hong Kong SAR	2000	95.3	95.1	81.7	116.7	116.5	100.2
Chine, Hong Kong RAS	2008	121.3	121.2	116.5	104.1	104.0	100.1
	2009	117.3	117.7	113.4	103.5	103.8	99.7
	2010	126.1	126.3	121.3	104.0	104.1	99.9
China, Macao SAR	2000	54.9	54.8	57.7	95.1	94.9	100.2
Chine, Macao RAS	2008	175.4	175.2	135.0	130.0	129.8	100.1
	2009	179.7	180.3	137.1	131.1	131.6	99.7
	2010	236.0	236.3	172.9	136.5	136.7	99.9
Colombia	2000	61.3	68.1	83.7	73.2	81.4	90.0
Colombie	2008	141.4	166.8	118.1	119.7	141.2	84.8
	2009	149.5	160.1	119.8	124.8	133.6	93.4
	2010	160.8	196.6	125.0	128.7	157.3	81.8
Comoros	2000	70.4	52.2	87.2	80.7	59.8	135.0
Comores	2008	116.3	137.0	102.7	113.2	133.3	84.9
	2009	123.8	138.3	104.6	118.4	132.3	89.5
	2010	131.3	139.8	106.8	122.9	130.9	93.9
Congo	2000	71.4	52.9	82.0	87.1	64.6	135.0
Congo	2008	141.9	167.2	110.8	128.2	151.0	84.9
	2009	120.5	134.6	119.1	101.2	113.1	89.5
	2010	166.2	177.0	129.4	128.4	136.8	93.9
Cook Islands	2000	77.8	50.2	88.3	88.1	56.8	155.0
Iles Cook	2008	128.1	127.9	101.1	126.7	126.5	100.2
	2009	127.5	113.1	97.5	130.7	116.0	112.7
	2010	133.3	135.7	95.1	140.1	142.7	98.2
Costa Rica	2000	51.5	79.9	81.9	63.0	97.6	64.5
Costa Rica	2008	164.6	149.5	120.6	136.5	123.9	110.1
	2009	175.7	146.5	119.1	147.6	123.0	120.0
	2010	197.3	179.8	124.0	159.1	145.0	109.7
Côte d'Ivoire	2000	88.2	65.3	99.9	88.3	65.4	135.0
Côte d'Ivoire	2008	120.9	142.4	107.5	112.5	132.5	84.9
	2009	126.1	140.9	107.5	117.4	131.1	89.5
	2010	130.8	139.3	110.2	118.7	126.4	93.9
Croatia	2000	66.8	48.0	80.4	83.1	59.7	139.1
Croatie	2008	129.4	156.0	112.6	114.9	138.5	83.0
	2009	125.7	141.5	105.9	118.7	133.7	88.8
	2010	125.5	135.8	104.6	119.9	129.8	92.4
Cuba	2000	71.7	71.7	78.3	91.6	91.6	100.0
Cuba	2008	142.6	142.6	125.2	113.9	113.9	100.0
	2009	146.0	146.0	127.0	115.0	115.0	100.0
	2010	150.6	150.6	129.6	116.2	116.2	100.0
Cyprus [2]	2000	72.8	54.3	85.4	85.3	63.6	134.1
Chypre [2]	2008	128.0	148.7	113.4	112.9	131.2	86.1
	2009	125.8	138.5	111.3	113.0	124.5	90.8
	2010	129.3	135.8	112.5	114.9	120.7	95.2

Country or area Pays ou zone	Year Année	GDP at current prices PIB aux prix courants		GDP at constant prices PIB aux prix constants	GDP implicit price deflators PIB déflateurs implicites des prix		Exchange rates Taux de change
		National currency Monnaie nationale	US dollars Dollars É.-U.	National currency Monnaie nationale	National currency Monnaie nationale	US dollars Dollars É.-U.	
Czech Republic	2000	72.8	45.2	81.8	89.0	55.2	161.1
République tchèque	2008	123.5	173.3	116.7	105.9	148.6	71.3
	2009	120.0	150.8	111.2	107.9	135.6	79.6
	2010	121.2	152.0	114.2	106.1	133.0	79.7
Dem. Rep. of the Congo	2000	8.8	73.5[3]	81.2	10.8	90.6[3]	11.9
Rép. dém. du Congo	2008	196.5	166.5	119.1	165.0	139.8	118.0
	2009	265.8	155.6	122.4	217.2	127.1	170.9
	2010	351.8	184.6	131.2	268.2	140.7	190.6
Denmark	2000	83.7	62.1	94.0	89.1	66.1	134.8
Danemark	2008	112.7	132.5	103.9	108.5	127.6	85.0
	2009	107.2	119.9	98.4	108.9	121.8	89.4
	2010	112.8	120.3	100.2	112.6	120.1	93.8
Djibouti	2000	78.6	78.6	94.2	83.4	83.4	100.0
Djibouti	2008	138.7	138.7	124.3	111.6	111.6	100.0
	2009	148.1	148.1	131.1	113.0	113.0	100.0
	2010	160.9	160.9	137.0	117.4	117.4	100.0
Dominica	2000	89.7	89.7	91.8	97.7	97.7	100.0
Dominique	2008	127.8	127.8	119.1	107.3	107.3	100.0
	2009	132.8	132.8	118.1	112.5	112.5	100.0
	2010	131.6	131.6	120.5	109.2	109.2	100.0
Dominican Republic	2000	38.1	70.5	84.1	45.3	83.9	54.0
Rép. dominicaine	2008	154.5	135.7	126.4	122.3	107.4	113.9
	2009	164.6	138.9	130.7	125.9	106.3	118.5
	2010	186.5	153.8	140.9	132.4	109.2	121.3
Ecuador	2000	44.1	44.1	77.7	56.8	56.8	100.0
Equateur	2008	146.7	146.7	114.6	128.0	128.0	100.0
	2009	140.8	140.8	115.0	122.4	122.4	100.0
	2010	159.5	159.5	118.7	134.3	134.3	100.0
Egypt	2000	60.9	101.3	83.5	72.9	121.4	60.1
Egypte	2008	164.1	174.5	122.6	133.8	142.3	94.0
	2009	190.9	199.0	128.4	148.8	155.1	96.0
	2010	221.0	227.9	135.0	163.8	168.9	97.0
El Salvador	2000	76.8	76.8	89.0	86.3	86.3	100.0
El Salvador	2008	125.4	125.4	109.3	114.7	114.7	100.0
	2009	120.9	120.9	105.9	114.2	114.2	100.0
	2010	124.1	124.1	107.4	115.6	115.6	100.0
Equatorial Guinea	2000	22.1	16.3	29.9	73.7	54.6	135.0
Guinée équatoriale	2008	184.6	217.5	149.6	123.4	145.4	84.9
	2009	123.8	138.3	156.4	79.2	88.4	89.5
	2010	153.8	163.8	155.2	99.1	105.6	93.9
Eritrea	2000	40.3	64.3	88.1	45.7	73.0	62.6
Erythrée	2008	125.7	125.7	90.6	138.7	138.7	100.1
	2009	170.6	170.5	93.9	181.7	181.6	100.1
	2010	205.3	205.2	95.6	214.8	214.7	100.1
Estonia	2000	55.1	40.9	70.8	77.8	57.7	134.9
Estonie	2008	145.8	171.6	114.0	127.9	150.5	85.0
	2009	123.8	138.4	97.8	126.6	141.5	89.5
	2010	127.9	136.4	100.0	128.0	136.4	93.8
Ethiopia	2000	62.6	66.0	73.2	85.5	90.2	94.8
Ethiopie	2008	233.2	210.5	136.9	170.4	153.8	110.8
	2009	315.0	231.8	148.9	211.6	155.7	135.9
	2010	360.1	219.2	167.4	215.1	130.9	164.3

| Country or area
Pays ou zone | Year
Année | GDP at current prices
PIB aux prix courants | | GDP at constant prices
PIB aux prix constants | GDP implicit price deflators
PIB déflateurs implicites des prix | | Exchange rates
Taux de change |
		National currency Monnaie nationale	US dollars Dollars É.-U.	National currency Monnaie nationale	National currency Monnaie nationale	US dollars Dollars É.-U.	
Fiji	2000	72.1	57.3	91.1	79.2	62.9	125.9
Fidji	2008	111.8	118.6	101.3	110.4	117.1	94.3
	2009	108.8	94.0	98.3	110.7	95.6	115.8
	2010	114.8	101.5	98.4	116.8	103.2	113.1
Finland	2000	84.0	62.2	87.9	95.6	70.8	135.0
Finlande	2008	118.0	139.0	111.2	106.2	125.1	84.9
	2009	110.2	123.0	102.0	108.0	120.6	89.5
	2010	114.6	122.0	105.7	108.4	115.4	93.9
France[4]	2000	83.8	62.1	92.4	90.7	67.2	135.0
France[4]	2008	112.5	132.5	104.7	107.5	126.6	84.9
	2009	110.0	122.8	101.9	108.0	120.6	89.5
	2010	112.5	119.8	103.4	108.8	115.9	93.9
French Polynesia	2000	85.1	63.0	90.2	94.3	69.9	135.0
Polynésie française	2008	108.7	128.0	105.1	103.4	121.8	84.9
	2009	111.7	124.8	106.8	104.6	116.8	89.5
	2010	114.7	122.3	108.5	105.8	112.7	93.8
Gabon	2000	78.3	58.0	92.1	85.0	63.0	135.0
Gabon	2008	151.0	177.9	104.9	144.0	169.6	84.9
	2009	145.6	162.6	104.5	139.4	155.7	89.5
	2010	186.3	198.5	110.3	169.0	179.9	93.9
Gambia	2000	55.7	124.4	85.0	65.5	146.3	44.8
Gambie	2008	121.5	156.4	112.3	108.2	139.3	77.7
	2009	134.3	144.1	119.4	112.6	120.7	93.2
	2010	149.9	159.0	126.6	118.4	125.6	94.3
Georgia	2000	52.0	47.7	70.2	74.1	67.9	109.0
Géorgie	2008	164.1	199.6	125.7	130.6	158.8	82.2
	2009	154.8	167.9	121.0	127.9	138.8	92.2
	2010	178.9	182.0	128.7	139.0	141.4	98.3
Germany	2000	92.1	68.2	97.1	94.8	70.3	135.0
Allemagne	2008	111.2	131.0	108.3	102.7	121.0	84.9
	2009	106.8	119.3	102.7	103.9	116.1	89.5
	2010	111.4	118.6	106.5	104.6	111.4	93.9
Ghana	2000	27.9	46.4	77.5	36.0	59.9	60.1
Ghana	2008	193.6	165.9	120.7	160.4	137.4	116.7
	2009	234.8	151.1	125.5	187.1	120.4	155.5
	2010	296.6	189.1	135.2	219.4	139.9	156.9
Greece	2000	70.6	52.9	82.0	86.1	64.5	133.4
Grèce	2008	120.7	142.1	108.5	111.2	130.9	84.9
	2009	120.0	134.0	105.0	114.3	127.7	89.5
	2010	117.8	125.4	101.3	116.2	123.8	93.9
Greenland	2000	84.6	62.7	95.6	88.4	65.6	134.8
Groenland	2008	111.3	130.9	102.5	108.6	127.7	85.0
	2009	105.9	118.4	97.1	109.0	121.9	89.4
	2010	111.4	118.8	98.8	112.7	120.2	93.8
Grenada	2000	74.5	74.5	89.7	83.1	83.1	100.0
Grenade	2008	119.0	119.0	103.4	115.1	115.1	100.0
	2009	109.1	109.1	94.8	115.1	115.1	100.0
	2010	111.3	111.3	95.2	116.9	116.9	100.0
Guatemala	2000	64.3	63.2	86.2	74.6	73.4	101.7
Guatemala	2008	142.4	143.8	115.7	123.1	124.3	99.0
	2009	148.1	138.5	116.3	127.3	119.0	106.9
	2010	160.9	152.4	119.4	134.8	127.7	105.6

Implicit price deflators of gross domestic product *(continued)*
Index base: 2005 = 100

Déflateurs implicites des prix de produit intérieur brut *(suite)*
Indice base : 2005 = 100

Country or area Pays ou zone	Year Année	GDP at current prices PIB aux prix courants		GDP at constant prices PIB aux prix constants	GDP implicit price deflators PIB déflateurs implicites des prix		Exchange rates Taux de change
		National currency Monnaie nationale	US dollars Dollars É.-U.	National currency Monnaie nationale	National currency Monnaie nationale	US dollars Dollars É.-U.	
Guinea	2000	52.1	108.7	86.0	60.6	126.4	47.9
Guinée	2008	194.1	128.6	107.8	180.1	119.3	150.9
	2009	206.7	151.2	107.5	192.3	140.7	136.7
	2010	252.3	145.3	109.5	230.4	132.6	173.7
Guinea-Bissau	2000	87.4	64.8	93.2	93.9	69.5	135.0
Guinée-Bissau	2008	125.6	147.9	111.3	112.8	132.9	84.9
	2009	134.6	150.3	120.1	112.1	125.2	89.5
	2010	133.9	142.6	122.0	109.8	116.9	93.9
Guyana	2000	78.9	86.4	96.5	81.7	89.5	91.3
Guyana	2008	148.9	146.2	114.7	129.8	127.4	101.9
	2009	157.1	154.0	118.5	132.6	129.9	102.0
	2010	172.4	171.8	122.8	140.4	139.9	100.3
Haiti	2000	46.2	88.2	102.8	44.9	85.8	52.3
Haïti	2008	149.1	154.2	106.6	139.9	144.7	96.7
	2009	158.8	156.0	109.6	144.9	142.2	101.9
	2010	158.9	160.8	104.1	152.7	154.5	98.8
Honduras	2000	58.0	73.7	79.7	72.9	92.5	78.8
Honduras	2008	142.8	142.3	118.0	121.1	120.6	100.4
	2009	145.8	145.3	115.4	126.3	125.9	100.3
	2010	158.4	157.8	118.6	133.5	133.0	100.3
Hungary	2000	59.5	42.1	81.5	72.9	51.6	141.4
Hongrie	2008	120.6	139.8	105.0	114.9	133.2	86.2
	2009	116.4	114.8	97.8	119.0	117.4	101.4
	2010	121.5	116.6	99.0	122.7	117.7	104.2
Iceland	2000	66.7	53.4	81.2	82.2	65.8	124.8
Islande	2008	144.5	103.5	112.4	128.6	92.1	139.6
	2009	146.0	74.4	104.9	139.2	70.9	196.3
	2010	149.9	77.2	100.7	148.8	76.7	194.1
India	2000	56.9	55.9	71.4	79.8	78.3	101.9
Inde	2008	151.2	153.3	125.9	120.1	121.7	98.7
	2009	177.4	161.6	137.4	129.1	117.6	109.8
	2010	213.3	205.7	149.5	142.7	137.6	103.7
Indonesia	2000	50.1	57.7	79.4	63.1	72.7	86.8
Indonésie	2008	178.4	178.5	118.9	150.0	150.1	99.9
	2009	202.0	188.7	124.4	162.4	151.7	107.1
	2010	231.5	247.5	132.0	175.4	187.5	93.6
Iran (Islamic Rep. of)	2000	32.4	50.6	75.6	42.8	66.9	63.9
Iran (Rép. islamique d')	2008	187.4	178.2	116.1	161.5	153.5	105.2
	2009	188.6	171.4	116.2	162.4	147.6	110.0
	2010	215.2	188.1	117.4	183.4	160.3	114.4
Iraq	2000	75.8	93.0[3]	97.5	77.7	95.4[3]	81.5
Iraq	2008	243.2	129.3[3]	119.1	204.3	108.6[3]	188.1
	2009	179.7	142.6[3]	130.1	138.1	109.6[3]	126.0
	2010	226.5	154.9[3]	139.6	162.2	111.0[3]	146.2
Ireland	2000	64.8	48.0	78.6	82.4	61.0	135.0
Irlande	2008	110.1	129.7	107.5	102.5	120.7	84.9
	2009	98.3	109.8	100.0	98.3	109.8	89.5
	2010	95.4	101.6	99.5	95.9	102.1	93.9
Israel	2000	84.7	93.2	90.3	93.9	103.3	90.9
Israël	2008	120.4	150.5	115.9	103.9	129.9	80.0
	2009	127.5	145.5	116.9	109.1	124.5	87.6
	2010	135.2	162.3	122.5	110.4	132.5	83.3

Country or area Pays ou zone	Year Année	GDP at current prices PIB aux prix courants		GDP at constant prices PIB aux prix constants	GDP implicit price deflators PIB déflateurs implicites des prix		Exchange rates Taux de change
		National currency Monnaie nationale	US dollars Dollars É.-U.	National currency Monnaie nationale	National currency Monnaie nationale	US dollars Dollars É.-U.	
Italy	2000	83.3	61.7	95.7	87.1	64.5	135.0
Italie	2008	109.7	129.2	102.2	107.3	126.4	84.9
	2009	106.3	118.8	96.9	109.8	122.6	89.5
	2010	108.4	115.4	98.1	110.4	117.6	93.9
Jamaica	2000	55.4	80.3	93.0	59.6	86.3	69.0
Jamaïque	2008	145.2	124.3	103.4	140.5	120.3	116.8
	2009	155.8	110.4	100.2	155.5	110.2	141.1
	2010	169.1	120.3	99.1	170.7	121.4	140.6
Japan	2000	100.3	102.5	93.7	107.0	109.4	97.8
Japon	2008	100.5	107.2	103.2	97.4	103.8	93.8
	2009	93.9	110.6	96.7	97.0	114.3	84.9
	2010	95.5	119.9	100.6	95.0	119.2	79.6
Jordan	2000	67.2	67.2	73.4	91.5	91.5	100.0
Jordanie	2008	180.5	180.3	126.0	143.2	143.1	100.1
	2009	199.6	199.3	128.9	154.8	154.6	100.1
	2010	218.8	218.5	132.9	164.6	164.4	100.1
Kazakhstan	2000	34.3	32.0	61.1	56.1	52.5	107.0
Kazakhstan	2008	211.5	233.6	124.1	170.4	188.2	90.5
	2009	224.1	201.9	125.6	178.3	160.7	111.0
	2010	285.2	257.2	134.5	212.1	191.3	110.9
Kenya	2000	67.8	67.3	83.1	81.6	81.0	100.8
Kenya	2008	149.1	162.9	115.5	129.1	141.0	91.6
	2009	167.1	163.2	118.6	140.9	137.7	102.4
	2010	180.2	173.3	125.1	144.0	138.5	104.0
Kiribati	2000	83.3	63.2	94.7	88.0	66.8	131.7
Kiribati	2008	116.9	128.4	106.2	110.0	120.9	91.0
	2009	115.1	117.6	103.7	111.0	113.4	97.9
	2010	115.2	138.4	103.3	111.6	134.1	83.3
Korea, Dem. P. R.	2000	1.3	81.4	88.3	1.4	92.2	1.6
Corée, R. p. dém. de	2008	102.9	102.4	100.8	102.1	101.5	100.6
	2009	92.9	92.4	99.9	92.9	92.4	100.6
	2010	93.1	94.2[3]	100.7	92.5	93.6[3]	98.8
Korea, Republic of	2000	69.7	63.1	80.3	86.8	78.6	110.4
Corée, République de	2008	118.6	110.2	113.1	104.9	97.5	107.6
	2009	123.1	98.7	113.5	108.5	87.0	124.7
	2010	135.6	120.1	120.4	112.5	99.7	112.9
Kosovo	2000	62.2	46.1	81.2	76.6	56.8	135.0
Kosovo	2008	128.3	151.1	117.5	109.2	128.6	84.9
	2009	130.3	145.5	120.9	107.8	120.4	89.5
	2010	140.6	149.7	125.7	111.8	119.1	93.9
Kuwait	2000	49.0	46.7	67.7	72.4	69.0	105.1
Koweït	2008	167.9	182.4	115.3	145.7	158.2	92.1
	2009	129.2	131.1	109.3	118.2	119.9	98.6
	2010	151.0	153.9	111.4	135.5	138.1	98.2
Kyrgyzstan	2000	64.8	55.7	83.1	78.0	67.1	116.3
Kirghizistan	2008	186.3	208.9	121.3	153.6	172.2	89.2
	2009	199.4	190.6	124.8	159.8	152.7	104.6
	2010	210.3	187.6	123.1	170.8	152.4	112.1
Lao People's Dem. Rep.	2000	44.7	60.4	73.6	60.7	82.0	74.0
Rép. dém. pop. lao	2008	158.3	192.9	138.0	114.7	139.8	82.1
	2009	162.9	203.9	148.4	109.8	137.4	79.9
	2010	184.0	237.1	159.9	115.1	148.3	77.6

Country or area Pays ou zone	Year Année	GDP at current prices PIB aux prix courants		GDP at constant prices PIB aux prix constants	GDP implicit price deflators PIB déflateurs implicites des prix		Exchange rates Taux de change
		National currency Monnaie nationale	US dollars Dollars É.-U.	National currency Monnaie nationale	National currency Monnaie nationale	US dollars Dollars É.-U.	
Latvia	2000	52.4	48.8	67.4	77.8	72.4	107.4
Lettonie	2008	178.7	209.9	117.8	151.7	178.1	85.1
	2009	145.2	162.2	96.9	149.8	167.3	89.5
	2010	141.5	150.7	96.6	146.5	155.9	93.9
Lebanon	2000	76.3	76.3	83.2	91.8	91.8	100.0
Liban	2008	136.9	136.9	118.4	115.6	115.6	100.0
	2009	158.0	158.0	127.9	123.5	123.5	100.0
	2010	179.5	179.5	137.5	130.6	130.6	100.0
Lesotho	2000	62.1	56.9	87.0	71.4	65.5	109.1
Lesotho	2008	153.4	118.1	114.5	134.0	103.2	129.9
	2009	169.1	126.9	118.0	143.4	107.6	133.3
	2010	180.9	157.1	120.9	149.7	130.0	115.1
Liberia	2000	91.3	91.3	126.3	72.3	72.3	100.0
Libéria	2008	129.9	129.9	126.3	102.9	102.9	100.0
	2009	143.9	143.9	132.1	109.0	109.0	100.0
	2010	151.0	151.0	138.9	108.7	108.7	100.0
Libyan Arab Jamah.	2000	33.1	84.6	77.4	42.8	109.3	39.2
Jamah. arabe libyenne	2008	167.4	179.0	115.2	145.4	155.4	93.5
	2009	123.9	129.3	114.3	108.3	113.1	95.8
	2010	152.6	158.3	119.1	128.2	132.9	96.4
Liechtenstein	2000	92.1	67.9	96.1	95.9	70.7	135.6
Liechtenstein	2008	120.6	138.7	115.7	104.3	119.9	87.0
	2009	114.6	131.1	110.4	103.8	118.7	87.4
	2010	117.8	140.6	112.7	104.5	124.7	83.8
Lithuania	2000	63.5	44.1	68.7	92.4	64.1	144.2
Lituanie	2008	154.8	182.2	121.8	127.1	149.6	85.0
	2009	127.0	141.8	103.7	122.4	136.7	89.6
	2010	131.3	139.8	105.2	124.8	132.8	94.0
Luxembourg	2000	72.7	53.8	83.8	86.7	64.2	135.0
Luxembourg	2008	130.2	153.4	112.8	115.5	136.0	84.9
	2009	123.5	137.9	106.8	115.6	129.1	89.5
	2010	133.0	141.6	109.7	121.3	129.1	93.9
Madagascar	2000	52.0	77.0	89.4	58.2	86.1	67.6
Madagascar	2008	159.3	186.8	119.5	133.3	156.3	85.3
	2009	165.8	169.7	114.6	144.7	148.1	97.7
	2010	181.0	173.5	115.2	157.1	150.6	104.3
Malawi	2000	43.8	87.2	88.9	49.3	98.1	50.3
Malawi	2008	181.8	153.2	124.3	146.2	123.2	118.7
	2009	211.9	177.8	135.4	156.5	131.3	119.2
	2010	245.2	193.3	144.5	169.7	133.8	126.9
Malaysia	2000	68.2	68.0	79.3	86.0	85.7	100.3
Malaisie	2008	142.1	161.3	118.1	120.3	136.6	88.1
	2009	130.2	139.8	116.2	112.0	120.4	93.1
	2010	146.6	172.4	124.6	117.7	138.4	85.1
Maldives	2000	76.6	83.3	79.0	96.9	105.4	92.0
Maldives	2008	168.1	168.1	134.5	125.0	125.0	100.0
	2009	175.9	175.9	122.5	143.6	143.6	100.0
	2010	197.4	197.4	136.7	144.4	144.4	100.0
Mali	2000	65.3	48.4	73.4	89.0	66.0	135.0
Mali	2008	135.2	159.3	115.2	117.3	138.2	84.9
	2009	146.3	163.4	120.4	121.5	135.7	89.5
	2010	157.5	167.8	125.8	125.3	133.4	93.9

Country or area Pays ou zone	Year Année	GDP at current prices PIB aux prix courants		GDP at constant prices PIB aux prix constants	GDP implicit price deflators PIB déflateurs implicites des prix		Exchange rates Taux de change
		National currency Monnaie nationale	US dollars Dollars É.-U.	National currency Monnaie nationale	National currency Monnaie nationale	US dollars Dollars É.-U.	
Malta	2000	83.9	66.2	95.7	87.7	69.2	126.7
Malte	2008	121.2	143.0	111.3	109.0	128.6	84.8
	2009	121.0	135.4	108.3	111.8	125.1	89.4
	2010	128.0	136.5	111.2	115.0	122.7	93.7
Marshall Islands	2000	77.4	77.4	82.5	93.7	93.7	100.0
Iles Marshall	2008	119.1	119.1	103.7	114.9	114.9	100.0
	2009	117.3	117.3	101.5	115.5	115.5	100.0
	2010	119.0	119.0	102.1	116.6	116.6	100.0
Mauritania	2000	53.3	59.2	79.7	66.8	74.3	90.0
Mauritanie	2008	152.1	169.6	121.8	124.9	139.2	89.7
	2009	139.5	141.1	123.7	112.7	114.1	98.8
	2010	184.0	179.1	129.5	142.1	138.3	102.7
Mauritius	2000	64.0	71.9	85.0	75.2	84.5	89.0
Maurice	2008	143.3	148.6	116.8	122.8	127.3	96.5
	2009	148.0	136.6	120.3	123.1	113.6	108.4
	2010	156.5	149.9	125.2	125.0	119.8	104.4
Mexico	2000	65.3	75.3	91.1	71.7	82.6	86.8
Mexique	2008	131.8	129.1	109.9	119.9	117.4	102.1
	2009	128.8	103.9	103.0	125.1	100.9	124.0
	2010	141.5	122.0	109.0	129.8	111.9	116.0
Micronesia (Fed. States of)	2000	93.4	93.4	97.4	95.9	95.9	100.0
Micronésie (Etats féd. de)	2008	105.4	105.4	95.7	110.1	110.1	100.0
	2009	111.9	111.9	96.3	116.2	116.2	100.0
	2010	119.0	119.0	99.3	119.8	119.8	100.0
Monaco	2000	83.8	62.1	92.4	90.7	67.2	135.0
Monaco	2008	130.5	153.8	121.3	107.6	126.8	84.9
	2009	116.3	129.9	107.5	108.2	120.8	89.5
	2010	119.0	126.7	109.1	109.0	116.1	93.9
Mongolia	2000	40.3	45.1	73.1	55.1	61.7	89.3
Mongolie	2008	215.5	222.8	130.3	165.4	171.0	96.7
	2009	216.7	181.7	128.7	168.4	141.2	119.3
	2010	276.7	245.4	136.9	202.1	179.3	112.8
Montenegro	2000	58.7	43.5	87.1	67.4	50.0	135.0
Monténégro	2008	170.0	200.3	128.5	132.4	155.9	84.9
	2009	164.2	183.5	121.2	135.5	151.4	89.5
	2010	171.0	182.1	124.2	137.7	146.7	93.9
Montserrat	2000	80.7	80.7	97.0	83.2	83.2	100.0
Montserrat	2008	116.2	116.2	101.8	114.1	114.1	100.0
	2009	122.3	122.3	105.5	116.0	116.0	100.0
	2010	128.7	128.7	106.8	120.5	120.5	100.0
Morocco[5]	2000	74.6	62.2	78.4	95.1	79.3	119.9
Maroc[5]	2008	130.5	149.3	116.9	111.7	127.8	87.4
	2009	139.5	153.5	122.6	113.8	125.2	90.9
	2010	145.3	153.8	126.7	114.7	121.4	94.5
Mozambique	2000	43.3	65.5	65.5	66.1	100.0	66.0
Mozambique	2008	158.4	150.4	124.6	127.2	120.7	105.4
	2009	175.5	147.1	132.5	132.5	111.0	119.3
	2010	213.4	144.9	141.7	150.6	102.2	147.3
Myanmar	2000	20.8	61.0	54.6	38.1	111.7	34.1
Myanmar	2008	237.9	216.7	139.6	170.4	155.2	109.8
	2009	274.8	275.0	154.2	178.2	178.4	99.9
	2010	328.3	352.3	170.2	192.8	206.9	93.2

Implicit price deflators of gross domestic product *(continued)*
Index base: 2005 = 100
Déflateurs implicites des prix de produit intérieur brut *(suite)*
Indice base : 2005 = 100

| Country or area
Pays ou zone | Year
Année | GDP at current prices
PIB aux prix courants | | GDP at constant prices
PIB aux prix constants | GDP implicit price deflators
PIB déflateurs implicites
des prix | | Exchange rates
Taux de change |
		National currency Monnaie nationale	US dollars Dollars É.-U.	National currency Monnaie nationale	National currency Monnaie nationale	US dollars Dollars É.-U.	
Namibia	2000	58.7	53.8	78.6	74.7	68.5	109.1
Namibie	2008	160.3	123.4	117.6	136.2	104.9	129.9
	2009	168.5	126.5	116.8	144.3	108.3	133.3
	2010	185.5	161.1	121.9	152.2	132.2	115.1
Nauru	2000	105.6	80.1	137.4	76.8	58.3	131.7
Nauru	2008	143.9	158.0	139.1	103.5	113.6	91.0
	2009	202.0	206.3	113.8	177.5	181.3	97.9
	2010	201.0	241.4	113.8	176.6	212.2	83.3
Nepal	2000	69.1	69.4	84.3	82.0	82.3	99.6
Népal	2008	138.4	141.6	113.8	121.6	124.4	97.8
	2009	167.6	154.3	118.8	141.1	129.8	108.7
	2010	198.8	194.0	124.2	160.0	156.1	102.5
Netherlands	2000	81.4	60.3	93.7	86.9	64.4	135.0
Pays-Bas	2008	115.8	136.4	109.4	105.9	124.7	84.9
	2009	111.3	124.3	105.5	105.4	117.8	89.5
	2010	114.6	122.1	107.3	106.8	113.8	93.9
Netherlands Antilles	2000	87.2	87.2	94.4	92.3	92.3	100.0
Antilles néerlandaises	2008	120.4	120.4	107.9	111.6	111.6	100.0
	2009	121.0	121.0	107.4	112.7	112.7	100.0
	2010	124.4	124.4	107.4	115.9	115.9	100.0
New Caledonia	2000	73.8	54.7	84.8	87.1	64.5	135.0
Nouvelle-Calédonie	2008	124.3	146.3	111.7	111.3	131.0	84.9
	2009	125.7	140.4	114.4	109.9	122.8	89.5
	2010	133.3	142.1	118.3	112.7	120.1	93.8
New Zealand	2000	73.2	47.2	82.9	88.2	56.9	155.0
Nouvelle-Zélande	2008	115.6	115.4	104.0	111.1	110.9	100.2
	2009	117.0	103.8	104.9	111.6	99.0	112.7
	2010	122.8	125.1	107.3	114.5	116.6	98.2
Nicaragua	2000	61.3	80.8	85.6	71.6	94.4	75.8
Nicaragua	2008	151.4	130.8	110.9	136.5	117.9	115.8
	2009	155.0	127.5	109.3	141.8	116.7	121.6
	2010	171.6	134.5	114.2	150.3	117.8	127.6
Niger	2000	69.2	51.3	80.2	86.3	63.9	135.0
Niger	2008	136.2	160.4	119.6	113.9	134.1	84.9
	2009	141.3	157.9	118.5	119.3	133.3	89.5
	2010	154.7	164.7	127.3	121.5	129.4	93.9
Nigeria	2000	32.0	41.3	60.5	53.0	68.4	77.5
Nigéria	2008	167.4	185.4	115.7	144.7	160.3	90.3
	2009	171.2	150.9	106.1	161.4	142.3	113.4
	2010	200.2	175.0	109.0	183.7	160.5	114.4
Norway	2000	76.1	55.7	89.6	85.0	62.2	136.6
Norvège	2008	129.1	147.4	105.8	121.9	139.3	87.5
	2009	119.8	122.7	104.0	115.2	118.0	97.6
	2010	128.3	136.8	104.4	122.9	131.0	93.8
Occupied Palestinian Terr.	2000	90.5	90.5	90.3	100.2	100.2	100.0
Terr. palestinien occupé	2008	134.8	134.8	107.0	126.0	126.0	100.0
	2009	145.9	145.9	115.0	127.0	127.0	100.0
	2010	158.6	158.6	122.4	129.5	129.5	100.0
Oman	2000	62.9	62.9	86.0	73.2	73.2	100.0
Oman	2008	196.0	196.0	127.1	154.2	154.2	100.0
	2009	151.6	151.6	128.5	118.0	118.0	100.0
	2010	187.2	187.2	133.9	139.8	139.8	100.0

20

Implicit price deflators of gross domestic product *(continued)*
Index base: 2005 = 100
Déflateurs implicites des prix de produit intérieur brut *(suite)*
Indice base : 2005 = 100

| Country or area
Pays ou zone | Year
Année | GDP at current prices
PIB aux prix courants | | GDP at constant prices
PIB aux prix constants | GDP implicit price deflators
PIB déflateurs implicites des prix | | Exchange rates
Taux de change |
		National currency Monnaie nationale	US dollars Dollars É.-U.	National currency Monnaie nationale	National currency Monnaie nationale	US dollars Dollars É.-U.	
Pakistan Pakistan	2000	58.9	65.3	78.4	75.1	83.3	90.1
	2008	157.6	133.2	114.0	138.2	116.8	118.3
	2009	195.8	142.6	118.1	165.8	120.7	137.3
	2010	228.3	159.5	123.0	185.6	129.7	143.2
Palau Palaos	2000	82.9	82.9	93.7	88.5	88.5	100.0
	2008	129.4	129.4	104.1	124.3	124.3	100.0
	2009	140.8	140.8	107.1	131.4	131.4	100.0
	2010	153.1	153.1	109.8	139.5	139.5	100.0
Panama Panama	2000	75.1	75.1	81.0	92.8	92.8	100.0
	2008	148.7	148.7	134.7	110.4	110.4	100.0
	2009	155.7	155.7	138.3	112.6	112.6	100.0
	2010	173.2	173.2	148.6	116.5	116.5	100.0
Papua New Guinea Papouasie-Nvl-Guinée	2000	64.5	71.9	89.9	71.8	80.0	89.7
	2008	143.1	164.4	116.9	122.5	140.7	87.0
	2009	147.1	165.6	123.3	119.4	134.4	88.8
	2010	171.2	201.3	132.0	129.7	152.6	85.0
Paraguay Paraguay	2000	53.6	94.9	88.1	60.8	107.7	56.4
	2008	159.5	225.8	117.9	135.3	191.5	70.6
	2009	153.1	190.5	113.4	135.1	168.1	80.4
	2010	183.8	239.3	130.7	140.6	183.2	76.8
Peru Pérou	2000	71.1	67.2	81.4	87.4	82.5	105.9
	2008	144.3	162.6	128.8	112.1	126.3	88.7
	2009	150.0	164.2	129.8	115.6	126.5	91.4
	2010	169.9	198.2	141.2	120.3	140.3	85.7
Philippines Philippines	2000	63.1	78.6	79.9	78.9	98.4	80.2
	2008	136.0	169.0	116.9	116.4	144.6	80.5
	2009	141.4	163.3	118.2	119.6	138.2	86.6
	2010	158.6	193.6	127.2	124.6	152.2	81.9
Poland Pologne	2000	75.7	56.4	85.9	88.1	65.6	134.3
	2008	129.7	174.2	119.3	108.8	146.1	74.5
	2009	136.6	141.7	121.2	112.8	116.9	96.4
	2010	143.9	154.5	125.9	114.3	122.6	93.2
Portugal Portugal	2000	82.6	61.2	96.1	86.0	63.7	135.0
	2008	111.9	131.8	103.9	107.7	126.9	84.9
	2009	109.7	122.5	101.3	108.3	121.0	89.5
	2010	112.4	119.7	102.7	109.5	116.6	93.9
Puerto Rico Porto Rico	2000	80.3	80.3	95.5	84.1	84.1	100.0
	2008	110.5	110.5	93.6	118.1	118.1	100.0
	2009	111.7	111.7	91.6	122.0	122.0	100.0
	2010	115.1	115.1	90.0	127.9	127.9	100.0
Qatar Qatar	2000	39.9	39.9	67.2	59.3	59.3	100.0
	2008	258.9	258.9	175.2	147.8	147.8	100.0
	2009	219.6	219.6	196.1	112.0	112.0	100.0
	2010	286.0	286.0	234.1	122.1	122.1	100.0
Republic of Moldova République de Moldova	2000	42.6	43.1	71.0	59.9	60.7	98.7
	2008	167.1	202.6	116.4	143.6	174.1	82.5
	2009	160.5	182.0	109.4	146.7	166.4	88.2
	2010	190.8	194.4	117.0	163.1	166.1	98.2
Romania Roumanie	2000	28.0	37.6	75.7	37.0	49.7	74.5
	2008	178.1	206.0	123.1	144.7	167.4	86.5
	2009	173.4	165.7	115.0	150.8	144.1	104.7
	2010	177.8	163.0	112.9	157.5	144.4	109.1

Country or area Pays ou zone	Year Année	GDP at current prices PIB aux prix courants		GDP at constant prices PIB aux prix constants	GDP implicit price deflators PIB déflateurs implicites des prix		Exchange rates Taux de change
		National currency Monnaie nationale	US dollars Dollars É.-U.	National currency Monnaie nationale	National currency Monnaie nationale	US dollars Dollars É.-U.	
Russian Federation	2000	33.8	34.0	74.3	45.5	45.7	99.5
Fédération de Russie	2008	191.0	217.4	123.5	154.6	176.0	87.9
	2009	179.5	159.9	113.9	157.6	140.4	112.2
	2010	208.0	193.7	118.5	175.5	163.5	107.4
Rwanda	2000	48.0	68.6	69.1	69.4	99.4	69.9
Rwanda	2008	179.0	182.6	131.0	136.7	139.4	98.0
	2009	207.7	203.9	138.9	149.5	146.8	101.9
	2010	227.9	219.1	149.3	152.6	146.7	104.0
Saint Kitts and Nevis	2000	75.0	75.0	84.9	88.4	88.4	100.0
Saint-Kitts-et-Nevis	2008	130.0	130.0	112.2	115.8	115.8	100.0
	2009	124.2	124.2	103.6	119.9	119.9	100.0
	2010	125.3	125.3	102.0	122.9	122.9	100.0
Saint Lucia	2000	82.6	82.6	88.6	93.3	93.3	100.0
Sainte-Lucie	2008	127.9	127.9	106.7	119.9	119.9	100.0
	2009	125.4	125.4	102.6	122.3	122.3	100.0
	2010	137.4	137.4	103.0	133.4	133.4	100.0
Saint Vincent-Grenadines	2000	72.1	72.1	85.5	84.3	84.3	100.0
Saint Vincent-Grenadines	2008	126.8	126.8	115.0	110.2	110.2	100.0
	2009	121.9	121.9	112.5	108.4	108.4	100.0
	2010	122.4	122.4	109.4	111.9	111.9	100.0
Samoa	2000	64.4	53.1	77.1	83.5	68.8	121.3
Samoa	2008	122.4	125.5	103.7	118.1	121.1	97.6
	2009	121.5	120.5	101.8	119.3	118.4	100.8
	2010	126.3	140.7	103.3	122.2	136.1	89.8
San Marino	2000	76.0	56.3	84.9	89.4	66.3	135.0
Saint-Marin	2008	113.8	134.1	106.4	107.0	126.1	84.9
	2009	99.6	111.3	92.5	107.7	120.3	89.5
	2010	101.6	108.2	93.7	108.4	115.4	93.9
Sao Tome and Principe	2000	47.1	62.3	82.7	56.9	75.3	75.6
Sao Tomé-et-Principe	2008	205.8	147.8	125.8	163.6	117.5	139.2
	2009	246.7	160.7	131.9	187.0	121.8	153.5
	2010	294.8	172.2	137.8	213.9	125.0	171.2
Saudi Arabia	2000	59.8	59.7	83.0	72.0	71.9	100.1
Arabie saoudite	2008	151.1	150.9	109.7	137.7	137.6	100.1
	2009	118.2	118.1	109.9	107.6	107.5	100.1
	2010	137.8	137.7	114.0	120.9	120.8	100.1
Senegal	2000	72.5	53.7	79.6	91.1	67.5	135.0
Sénégal	2008	129.6	152.6	111.0	116.7	137.5	84.9
	2009	131.1	146.5	113.4	115.6	129.1	89.5
	2010	138.5	147.5	118.3	117.1	124.7	93.9
Serbia [6]	2000	22.8	34.6	77.8	29.3	44.5	66.0
Serbie [6]	2008	158.1	189.3	118.7	133.2	159.5	83.5
	2009	161.2	159.1	115.0	140.2	138.4	101.3
	2010	174.1	149.5	117.0	148.8	127.7	116.5
Seychelles	2000	86.1	82.9	103.1	83.5	80.4	103.9
Seychelles	2008	170.6	99.2	118.5	144.1	83.8	172.0
	2009	210.1	84.9	119.3	176.2	71.2	247.5
	2010	227.7	106.7	130.6	174.3	81.7	213.3
Sierra Leone	2000	45.0	62.1	54.8	82.1	113.3	72.4
Sierra Leone	2008	149.2	144.6	116.1	128.5	124.5	103.2
	2009	166.5	142.1	121.8	136.7	116.7	117.2
	2010	187.0	138.5	127.7	146.4	108.4	135.0

Country or area Pays ou zone	Year Année	GDP at current prices PIB aux prix courants		GDP at constant prices PIB aux prix constants	GDP implicit price deflators PIB déflateurs implicites des prix		Exchange rates Taux de change
		National currency Monnaie nationale	US dollars Dollars É.-U.	National currency Monnaie nationale	National currency Monnaie nationale	US dollars Dollars É.-U.	
Singapore	2000	77.9	75.2	79.2	98.4	95.0	103.6
Singapour	2008	128.4	151.0	120.0	107.0	125.8	85.0
	2009	127.7	146.2	119.1	107.3	122.8	87.4
	2010	145.5	177.6	136.3	106.7	130.3	81.9
Slovakia	2000	63.2	42.6	78.7	80.3	54.1	148.4
Slovaquie	2008	135.7	197.1	126.8	107.1	155.5	68.9
	2009	127.5	182.4	120.5	105.8	151.3	69.9
	2010	133.6	182.2	125.7	106.3	145.0	73.3
Slovenia	2000	64.6	55.9	83.7	77.2	66.8	115.5
Slovénie	2008	129.8	152.9	117.2	110.8	130.5	84.9
	2009	122.9	137.3	107.8	114.0	127.4	89.5
	2010	123.3	131.3	109.3	112.8	120.2	93.9
Solomon Islands	2000	53.2	78.7	86.0	61.9	91.5	67.6
Iles Salomon	2008	145.7	141.6	118.5	123.0	119.5	102.9
	2009	148.9	139.2	112.9	131.9	123.3	107.0
	2010	160.2	149.6	120.9	132.5	123.7	107.1
Somalia	2000	55.6	88.6	85.4	65.1	103.7	62.8
Somalie	2008	106.1	112.3	107.8	98.4	104.2	94.5
	2009	111.4	86.9	110.6	100.7	78.6	128.2
	2010	96.8	46.3	113.5	85.3	40.8	209.2
South Africa	2000	58.7	53.8	82.9	70.8	64.9	109.1
Afrique du Sud	2008	144.8	111.4	115.5	125.4	96.5	129.9
	2009	152.5	114.5	113.5	134.3	100.8	133.3
	2010	169.5	147.2	116.8	145.2	126.1	115.1
Spain	2000	69.4	51.4	85.2	81.4	60.3	135.0
Espagne	2008	119.7	141.0	108.7	110.2	129.8	84.9
	2009	116.0	129.6	104.6	110.9	123.8	89.5
	2010	116.9	124.5	104.5	111.9	119.2	93.9
Sri Lanka	2000	52.5	68.5	82.1	63.9	83.4	76.6
Sri Lanka	2008	179.8	166.8	121.8	147.6	136.9	107.8
	2009	196.7	172.0	126.1	156.0	136.4	114.4
	2010	228.4	203.0	136.3	167.6	149.0	112.5
Sudan	2000	39.3	37.2	71.8	54.7	51.8	105.6
Soudan	2008	158.1	184.3	129.2	122.4	142.7	85.8
	2009	176.8	187.2	139.8	126.5	133.9	94.5
	2010	223.8	225.9	146.8	152.4	153.8	99.1
Suriname	2000	25.7[7]	53.0	78.3	32.8[7]	67.7	48.4
Suriname	2008	172.6[7]	171.8	115.8	149.0[7]	148.3	100.5
	2009	183.1[7]	182.2	119.4	153.4[7]	152.7	100.5
	2010	207.4[7]	206.3	124.6	166.4[7]	165.5	100.5
Swaziland	2000	64.6	59.2	89.4	72.2	66.2	109.1
Swaziland	2008	151.1	116.3	107.8	140.2	107.9	129.9
	2009	162.3	121.8	109.1	148.7	111.6	133.3
	2010	174.2	151.3	111.3	156.5	135.9	115.1
Sweden	2000	81.8	66.7	87.6	93.4	76.2	122.6
Suède	2008	115.7	131.2	107.1	108.0	122.5	88.2
	2009	111.6	108.9	101.4	110.0	107.4	102.4
	2010	119.4	123.8	107.2	111.4	115.5	96.5
Switzerland	2000	91.0	67.1	93.7	97.1	71.6	135.6
Suisse	2008	117.5	135.1	109.7	107.2	123.2	87.0
	2009	115.5	132.2	107.6	107.3	122.8	87.4
	2010	118.7	141.7	110.5	107.4	128.2	83.8

Country or area Pays ou zone	Year Année	GDP at current prices PIB aux prix courants		GDP at constant prices PIB aux prix constants	GDP implicit price deflators PIB déflateurs implicites des prix		Exchange rates Taux de change
		National currency Monnaie nationale	US dollars Dollars É.-U.	National currency Monnaie nationale	National currency Monnaie nationale	US dollars Dollars É.-U.	
Syrian Arab Republic	2000	60.1	69.3	78.2	76.8	88.6	86.7
Rép. arabe syrienne	2008	162.3	184.9	116.0	140.0	159.4	87.8
	2009	167.2	190.4	123.0	136.0	154.9	87.8
	2010	183.4	210.7	126.9	144.5	166.0	87.0
Tajikistan	2000	24.8	37.2	63.0	39.4	59.1	66.6
Tadjikistan	2008	245.7	223.2	123.6	198.8	180.6	110.1
	2009	286.2	215.3	128.6	222.7	167.5	132.9
	2010	342.9	242.7	136.9	250.5	177.3	141.3
Thailand	2000	69.4	69.6	78.0	89.0	89.2	99.7
Thaïlande	2008	128.0	154.6	113.1	113.2	136.6	82.8
	2009	127.5	149.5	110.5	115.4	135.3	85.3
	2010	142.4	180.8	119.1	119.6	151.8	78.8
TFYR of Macedonia	2000	80.1	59.9	92.5	86.6	64.8	133.7
L'ex-R.Y. Macédoine	2008	139.5	164.3	117.0	119.3	140.4	85.0
	2009	139.2	155.6	115.9	120.1	134.2	89.5
	2010	144.0	152.6	118.0	122.0	129.4	94.3
Timor-Leste	2000	90.4[8]	90.4	88.6	102.0[8]	102.0	100.0
Timor-Leste	2008	160.7[8]	160.7	114.1	140.9[8]	140.9	100.0
	2009	201.2[8]	201.2	128.8	156.2[8]	156.2	100.0
	2010	226.9[8]	226.9	136.7	166.0[8]	166.0	100.0
Togo	2000	82.8	61.3	94.3	87.8	65.1	135.0
Togo	2008	127.4	150.1	108.6	117.4	138.3	84.9
	2009	134.2	149.9	112.5	119.3	133.2	89.5
	2010	140.7	149.9	116.7	120.6	128.5	93.9
Tonga	2000	65.9	72.8	90.7	72.6	80.3	90.5
Tonga	2008	131.4	131.5	101.8	129.1	129.1	100.0
	2009	129.2	123.4	100.8	128.2	122.4	104.7
	2010	133.5	142.3	101.1	132.0	140.8	93.8
Trinidad and Tobago	2000	51.0	51.0	67.8	75.3	75.3	100.0
Trinité-et-Tobago	2008	169.8	170.1	121.4	139.9	140.1	99.8
	2009	123.3	122.8	117.1	105.3	104.9	100.4
	2010	128.9	127.6	120.0	107.4	106.3	101.0
Tunisia	2000	70.3	66.5	80.7	87.1	82.5	105.7
Tunisie	2008	131.9	138.9	117.3	112.5	118.4	95.0
	2009	140.4	134.9	121.0	116.1	111.5	104.1
	2010	151.3	137.1	125.4	120.6	109.3	110.3
Turkey	2000	25.7	55.2	80.0	32.1	69.0	46.5
Turquie	2008	146.5	151.2	112.6	130.1	134.3	96.9
	2009	146.8	127.2	107.2	137.0	118.7	115.4
	2010	170.1	152.1	116.8	145.6	130.2	111.9
Turkmenistan	2000	28.7	39.7	78.0	36.8	50.9	72.4
Turkménistan	2008	244.6	153.6	141.4	172.9	108.6	159.2
	2009	318.3	160.4	150.0	212.2	106.9	198.4
	2010	369.1	186.0	163.9	225.2	113.5	198.4
Turks and Caicos Islands	2000	55.2	55.2	66.3	83.3	83.3	100.0
Iles Turques et Caïques	2008	168.6	168.6	148.0	113.9	113.9	100.0
	2009	200.5	200.5	168.0	119.4	119.4	100.0
	2010	238.6	238.6	191.4	124.7	124.7	100.0
Tuvalu	2000	72.8	55.3	94.8	76.8	58.3	131.7
Tuvalu	2008	121.6	133.5	113.2	107.4	117.9	91.0
	2009	117.5	120.0	114.9	102.3	104.4	97.9
	2010	117.5	141.2	116.8	100.7	120.9	83.3

20

Implicit price deflators of gross domestic product *(continued)*
Index base: 2005 = 100
Déflateurs implicites des prix de produit intérieur brut *(suite)*
Indice base : 2005 = 100

| Country or area Pays ou zone | Year Année | GDP at current prices PIB aux prix courants | | GDP at constant prices PIB aux prix constants | GDP implicit price deflators PIB déflateurs implicites des prix | | Exchange rates Taux de change |
		National currency Monnaie nationale	US dollars Dollars É.-U.	National currency Monnaie nationale	National currency Monnaie nationale	US dollars Dollars É.-U.	
Uganda Ouganda	2000	58.3	63.2	72.7	80.3	86.9	92.4
	2008	157.6	163.1	127.7	123.4	127.7	96.6
	2009	191.3	167.8	133.4	143.4	125.8	114.0
	2010	204.4	169.5	136.7	149.5	123.9	120.6
Ukraine Ukraine	2000	38.5	36.3	68.9	55.9	52.7	106.2
	2008	214.8	209.0	118.5	181.2	176.3	102.8
	2009	206.9	136.1	101.1	204.8	134.7	152.0
	2010	248.0	160.1	105.3	235.5	152.1	154.9
United Arab Emirates Emirats arabes unis	2000	57.8	57.8	77.0	75.0	75.0	100.0
	2008	174.3	174.3	117.2	148.8	148.8	100.0
	2009	149.7	149.7	115.3	129.8	129.8	100.0
	2010	164.8	164.8	116.9	140.9	140.9	100.0
United Kingdom Royaume-Uni	2000	77.8	64.8	86.8	89.7	74.6	120.2
	2008	114.3	115.6	105.0	108.9	110.1	98.9
	2009	111.1	95.2	100.4	110.7	94.8	116.7
	2010	116.3	98.8	102.2	113.8	96.7	117.7
United Rep. of Tanzania[9] Rép.-Unie de Tanzanie[9]	2000	51.1	72.0	71.1	71.8	101.2	70.9
	2008	155.2	146.5	122.9	126.3	119.2	106.0
	2009	176.7	151.1	130.3	135.7	116.0	117.0
	2010	202.2	159.1	139.2	145.3	114.3	127.1
United States Etats-Unis	2000	78.8	78.8	88.8	88.7	88.7	100.0
	2008	113.2	113.2	104.2	108.6	108.6	100.0
	2009	110.3	110.3	100.6	109.7	109.7	100.0
	2010	115.0	115.0	103.6	111.0	111.0	100.0
Uruguay Uruguay	2000	65.0	131.5	99.1	65.6	132.7	49.4
	2008	153.7	179.6	121.6	126.4	147.7	85.6
	2009	166.3	180.4	124.7	133.3	144.6	92.2
	2010	190.0	231.9	135.3	140.5	171.4	82.0
Uzbekistan Ouzbékistan	2000	20.5	95.6	76.3	26.8	125.2	21.4
	2008	237.1	199.5	128.1	185.1	155.8	118.8
	2009	302.1	229.0	138.4	218.2	165.4	131.9
	2010	388.3	272.1	150.2	258.5	181.2	142.7
Vanuatu Vanuatu	2000	87.2	69.2	95.0	91.7	72.8	126.0
	2008	140.0	150.9	121.4	115.3	124.3	92.8
	2009	146.7	150.1	125.6	116.8	119.5	97.7
	2010	156.2	180.6	131.9	118.5	136.9	86.5
Venezuela (Boliv. Rep. of) Venezuela (Rép. boliv. du)	2000	26.2	80.5	88.2	29.7	91.3	32.5
	2008	219.7	213.8	124.5	176.4	171.7	102.7
	2009	230.3	224.1	120.4	191.2	186.1	102.7
	2010	332.7	268.9	118.8	280.1	226.4	123.7
Viet Nam Viet Nam	2000	52.6	58.9	69.6	75.6	84.6	89.3
	2008	177.0	172.1	124.8	141.8	138.0	102.8
	2009	197.6	183.7	131.4	150.4	139.7	107.6
	2010	236.0	196.4	140.4	168.2	139.9	120.2
Yemen Yémen	2000	47.4	56.2	79.4	59.8	70.8	84.4
	2008	167.6	160.6	113.4	147.7	141.6	104.3
	2009	163.9	154.8	118.8	138.0	130.3	105.9
	2010	220.8	193.4	128.3	172.2	150.8	114.2
Zambia Zambie	2000	31.0	44.5	79.2	39.2	56.2	69.7
	2008	169.0	201.4	119.7	141.2	168.2	83.9
	2009	199.1	176.1	127.0	156.8	138.7	113.1
	2010	239.5	222.8	136.0	176.1	163.8	107.5

20

Implicit price deflators of gross domestic product *(continued)*
Index base: 2005 = 100
Déflateurs implicites des prix de produit intérieur brut *(suite)*
Indice base : 2005 = 100

Country or area Pays ou zone	Year Année	GDP at current prices PIB aux prix courants		GDP at constant prices PIB aux prix constants	GDP implicit price deflators PIB déflateurs implicites des prix		Exchange rates Taux de change
		National currency Monnaie nationale	US dollars Dollars É.-U.	National currency Monnaie nationale	National currency Monnaie nationale	US dollars Dollars É.-U.	
Zanzibar	2000	48.3	68.1	71.3	67.7	95.5	70.9
Zanzibar	2008	189.5	178.8	118.8	159.5	150.5	106.0
	2009	222.7	190.4	126.7	175.7	150.3	117.0
	2010	240.3	189.1	134.9	178.1	140.1	127.1
Zimbabwe	2000	121.3	121.3	124.5	97.4	97.4	100.0
Zimbabwe	2008	88.3	88.3	88.8	99.4	99.4	100.0
	2009	90.4	90.4	95.3	94.9	94.9	100.0
	2010	115.8	115.8	103.8	111.5	111.5	100.0

Source:
United Nations Statistics Division, New York, national accounts estimates main aggregates database, last accessed January 2012.

1 For statistical purposes, the data for China do not include those for the Hong Kong Special Administrative Region (Hong Kong SAR), Macao Special Administrative Region (Macao SAR) and Taiwan Province of China.
2 Excludes northern Cyprus.
3 Price-adjusted rates of exchange (PARE) are used for selected years for conversion to US dollars due to large distortions in the dollar levels of per capita GDP with the use of IMF market exchange rates.
4 Includes Guadeloupe, Martinique, Réunion and French Guiana.
5 Including Western Sahara.
6 Excluding Kosovo and Metohia.
7 Excluding the informal sector.
8 Refers to non-oil GDP.
9 Tanzania mainland only.

Source:
Organisation des Nations Unies, Division de statistique, New York, la base de données d'estimation des comptes nationaux, dernier accès janvier 2012.

1 Pour la présentation des statistiques, les données pour la Chine ne comprennent pas la Région Administrative Spéciale de Hong Kong (Hong Kong RAS), la Région Administrative Spéciale de Macao (Macao RAS) et la province de Taiwan.
2 Exclu Chypre du nord.
3 Pour certaines années, on utilise les Taux de change corrigés des prix (TCCP) pour effectuer la conversion en dollars des États-Unis, en raison des aberrations importantes relevées dans les niveaux du PNB exprimés en dollars après conversion à l'aide des taux de change du marché communiqués par le FMI.
4 Y compris Guadeloupe, Martinique, Réunion et Guyane française.
5 Y compris les données de Sahara occidental.
6 Non compris Kosovo et Metohia.
7 Non compris le secteur informel.
8 PIB non dérivés du pétrole.
9 Tanzanie continentale seulement.

Gross domestic product by type of expenditure in current prices
Percentage distribution

Dépenses imputées au produit intérieur brut aux prix courants
Répartition en pourcentage

Country or area Pays ou zone	Year Année	GDP in current prices (mil. nat.cur.) PIB aux prix courants (millions monnaie nat.)	Household final consumption[1] expenditure Consom. finale des ménages[1]	Govt. final consumption expenditure Consom. finale des admin. publiques	Gross fixed capital formation[2] Formation brute de capital fixe[2]	Changes in inventories Variation des stocks	Exports of goods and services Exportations de biens et services	Imports of goods and services Importations de biens et services
Afghanistan	2008	542 167	97.9	10.0	27.6	...	17.2	52.7
Afghanistan	2009	627 394	98.2	13.9	17.5	...	14.4	44.1
	2010	728 572	81.5	35.9	26.5	...	19.8	63.8
Albania	2008	1 088 132	79.4	10.2	38.2	-1.1	29.4	56.1
Albanie	2009	1 143 610	87.0	9.6	29.0	...	28.7	54.4
	2010	1 224 662	86.5	9.5	25.1	...	35.6	56.7
Algeria	2008	11 069 000	28.8	13.2	27.7	9.5	47.9	28.7
Algérie	2009	10 017 500	37.4	16.4	38.1	8.7	35.2	35.8
	2010	11 782 912	35.2	15.4	32.7	8.5	40.6	32.1
Andorra	2008	2 818	57.2	19.5	28.7	0.4	26.5	32.2
Andorre	2009	2 686	56.6	21.1	24.0	0.4	23.4	25.5
	2010	2 636	58.4	20.8	22.5	0.5	26.3	28.4
Angola	2008	6 316 200	33.1	26.2	15.8	...	75.6	50.8
Angola	2009	5 988 700	50.8	36.2	17.1	...	58.4	62.6
	2010	7 579 500	45.4	30.2	10.3	...	60.3	54.7
Anguilla	2008	784	88.1	14.6	62.7	...	46.8	112.2
Anguilla	2009	583	80.9	20.1	39.1	...	48.3	88.3
	2010	570	88.3	15.8	52.8	...	49.1	105.9
Antigua and Barbuda	2008	3 249	30.5	18.8	79.2	...	49.1	77.5
Antigua-et-Barbuda	2009	3 056	25.5	19.4	75.8	...	47.5	68.2
	2010	3 018	22.9	17.4	72.0	...	49.7	60.2
Argentina	2008	1 032 758	57.6	13.4	23.3	1.8	24.5	20.7
Argentine	2009	1 145 458	58.3	15.2	20.9	0.3	21.4	16.0
	2010	1 442 655	57.3	14.9	22.0	2.5	21.7	18.4
Armenia	2008	3 568 228	71.6	10.2	39.8	1.1	15.1	40.7
Arménie	2009	3 141 651	80.4	13.3	36.4	-1.7	15.5	43.0
	2010	3 501 638	80.9	13.1	33.1	0.3	19.8	45.2
Aruba	2008	4 914	55.3	22.0	31.6	1.6	67.7	78.2
Aruba	2009	4 478	56.8	23.6	28.3	2.0	64.9	75.5
	2010	4 397	58.7	24.9	28.7	...	61.7	74.0
Australia	2008	1 255 241	53.5	17.6	28.3	-0.1	22.7	22.1
Australie	2009	1 284 670	54.3	18.2	28.1	-0.1	19.8	20.2
	2010	1 386 617	52.8	18.3	27.4	0.2	20.9	19.8
Austria	2008	282 746	52.8	18.7	22.1	0.7	59.3	53.5
Autriche	2009	274 818	54.5	19.8	21.3	-0.2	50.4	45.7
	2010	286 197	54.6	19.4	21.1	0.6	54.0	49.7
Azerbaijan	2008	40 137	33.4	8.5	18.6	0.1	65.8	23.5
Azerbaïdjan	2009	35 602	42.8	11.1	18.8	0.1	51.6	23.1
	2010	41 575	43.9	9.6	16.9	0.1	55.1	21.1
Bahamas	2008	8 240	70.3	13.0	23.5	1.1	46.2	54.0
Bahamas	2009	7 807	69.4	14.8	22.5	1.2	40.0	47.8
	2010	7 702	72.7	14.9	20.5	1.2	42.0	51.2
Bahrain	2008	8 329	30.4	13.3[3]	32.7	1.2	95.9	73.5
Bahreïn	2009	7 264	34.8	15.5[3]	26.6	0.6	81.3	58.8
	2010	8 627	35.0	12.4[3]	28.9	0.5	81.3	59.3
Bangladesh	2008	5 458 224	74.4	5.3	24.2	...	20.3	28.8
Bangladesh	2009	6 147 952	74.7	5.3	24.4	...	19.4	26.6
	2010	6 943 243	75.4	5.4	24.9	...	18.5	24.9
Barbados	2008	7 976	73.4	16.7	18.7	0.2	52.4	61.1
Barbade	2009	7 790	75.2	17.0	15.1	-0.2	45.7	53.2
	2010	7 925	73.8	16.4	18.0	...	45.6	53.7

Gross domestic product by type of expenditure in current prices *(continued)*
Percentage distribution

Dépenses imputées au produit intérieur brut aux prix courants *(suite)*
Répartition en pourcentage

			% of Gross domestic product – en % du Produit intérieur brut					
Country or area Pays ou zone	Year Année	GDP in current prices (mil. nat.cur.) PIB aux prix courants (millions monnaie nat.)	Household final consumption[1] expenditure Consom. finale des ménages[1]	Govt. final consumption expenditure Consom. finale des admin. publiques	Gross fixed capital formation[2] Formation brute de capital fixe[2]	Changes in inventories Variation des stocks	Exports of goods and services Exportations de biens et services	Imports of goods and services Importations de biens et services
Belarus	2008	129 790 773	52.0	16.5	33.3	4.3	60.9	68.7
Bélarus	2009	137 442 181	55.4	16.9	35.9	1.4	50.5	61.8
	2010	162 963 584	55.6	16.1	38.7	1.9	54.6	68.3
Belgium	2008	346 130	52.0	23.1	22.4	1.7	84.6	83.7
Belgique	2009	340 398	52.8	24.6	20.9	-1.0	72.4	69.6
	2010	354 378	52.9	24.2	20.2	^0.0	80.0	77.3
Belize	2008	2 717	64.7	15.8	25.5	1.8	62.1	70.0
Belize	2009	2 698	66.9	17.2	22.0	...	54.0	59.9
	2010	2 802	63.1	16.6	17.8	...	57.8	55.7
Benin	2008	2 970 544	75.2	11.9	20.3	0.4	19.8	27.5
Bénin	2009	3 109 410	76.1	12.0	21.0	0.3	15.8	25.1
	2010	3 248 233	76.6	11.9	20.5	0.5	15.1	24.7
Bermuda	2008	6 068	74.8	19.9	18.9	1.0	40.8	55.4
Bermudes	2009	5 715	74.7	19.8	18.8	1.0	42.1	56.4
	2010	6 015	74.9	20.0	19.0	1.0	41.0	55.9
Bhutan	2008	54 713	39.8	19.0	38.7	1.1	46.6	57.7
Bhoutan	2009	61 223	37.9	21.4	41.3	-0.1	64.8	72.0
	2010	67 958	37.6	19.5	42.3	5.6	65.1	75.1
Bolivia (Plurinational State of)	2008	120 694	62.2	13.3[4]	17.3	0.3	44.9	38.0
Bolivie (État plurinational de)	2009	121 727	65.5	14.7[4]	16.5	0.5	35.7	32.9
	2010	137 876	62.3	13.8[4]	16.6	0.4	41.2	34.3
Bosnia and Herzegovina	2008	24 717	91.9	22.5	30.6	1.6	36.8	69.5
Bosnie-Herzégovine	2009	24 004	91.1	24.0	24.8	-0.5	31.9	55.3
	2010	24 864	80.6	20.7	20.3	...	36.7	58.3
Botswana	2008	91 981	34.7	18.9	23.1	7.7	42.0	38.2
Botswana	2009	82 096	44.7	24.5	28.5	2.1	32.0	43.4
	2010	100 935	42.3	21.0	25.8	2.1	32.6	39.7
Brazil	2008	3 031 864	58.9	20.2	19.1	1.6	13.7	13.5
Brésil	2009	3 185 125	61.7	21.8	17.0	-0.4	11.1	11.2
	2010	3 674 964	60.6	21.2	18.5	0.8	11.2	12.2
British Virgin Islands	2008	992	36.7	9.1	24.0	-1.7	109.5	77.5
Iles Vierges britanniques	2009	876	36.6	9.0	24.0	-1.7	109.7	77.5
	2010	909	36.5	9.0	24.0	-1.7	109.7	77.5
Brunei Darussalam	2008	20 398	17.7	17.1	13.7	^0.0	78.3	27.6
Brunéi Darussalam	2009	15 611	24.4	23.3	17.6	^0.0	72.8	35.8
	2010	17 756	20.7	21.0	14.7	^0.0	73.0	30.4
Bulgaria	2008	69 295	66.4	16.6	33.6	3.9	58.2	78.7
Bulgarie	2009	68 322	63.2	16.3	28.9	0.5	47.5	56.3
	2010	70 474	61.2	15.8	23.5	1.4	57.8	59.7
Burkina Faso	2008	3 760 764	70.9	21.3	20.4	3.8	9.8	26.3
Burkina Faso	2009	3 946 747	69.5	21.1	22.0	1.9	12.1	26.5
	2010	4 239 151	65.2	21.2	27.1	2.4	16.7	30.5
Burundi	2008	1 555 730	86.1	18.0	14.4	0.5	6.1	23.6
Burundi	2009	1 625 129	86.8	18.0	14.4	0.5	4.8	22.9
	2010	1 819 705	84.7	19.3	13.4	0.4	6.0	23.3
Cambodia	2008	41 968 385	79.4	5.6	17.3	1.4	65.5	67.8
Cambodge	2009	43 056 732	76.2	8.0	20.1	1.3	59.9	63.0
	2010	47 047 985	75.2	8.4	16.0	1.2	66.1	66.4
Cameroon	2008	10 443 829	75.1	10.8	17.6	0.6	24.1	28.2
Cameroun	2009	11 040 255	75.2	11.3	17.8	0.7	16.0	21.0
	2010	11 712 607	74.7	11.5	17.6	0.7	17.5	22.3
Canada	2008	1 603 418	55.5	19.7	22.9	0.4	35.1	33.6
Canada	2009	1 528 985	58.8	22.1	21.3	-0.5	28.8	30.4
	2010	1 624 608	57.9	21.8	22.1	0.1	29.4	31.3

Gross domestic product by type of expenditure in current prices *(continued)*
Percentage distribution

Dépenses imputées au produit intérieur brut aux prix courants *(suite)*
Répartition en pourcentage

			% of Gross domestic product – en % du Produit intérieur brut					
Country or area Pays ou zone	Year Année	GDP in current prices (mil. nat.cur.) PIB aux prix courants (millions monnaie nat.)	Household final consumption[1] expenditure Consom. finale des ménages[1]	Govt. final consumption expenditure Consom. finale des admin. publiques	Gross fixed capital formation[2] Formation brute de capital fixe[2]	Changes in inventories Variation des stocks	Exports of goods and services Exportations de biens et services	Imports of goods and services Importations de biens et services
Cape Verde	2008	115 286	76.4	18.7	51.4	0.6	21.8	68.8
Cap-Vert	2009	122 979	73.4	18.7	57.1	0.7	22.9	72.9
	2010	133 965	60.0	18.9	68.2	0.8	24.7	71.6
Cayman Islands	2008	2 883	63.4	14.6	22.4	...	61.9	61.3
Iles Caïmanes	2009	2 716	63.4	14.6	22.4	...	61.9	61.3
	2010	2 598	63.4	14.6	22.4	...	61.9	61.3
Central African Rep.	2008	888 099	90.7	7.8	11.6	...	11.7	21.9
Rép. centrafricaine	2009	935 532	91.5	8.4	11.3	...	10.2	21.4
	2010	982 524	91.2	8.1	11.4	...	11.0	21.7
Chad	2008	3 740 949	26.8	23.2	15.1	0.8	55.1	21.1
Tchad	2009	3 255 857	32.5	29.8	21.4	1.1	44.5	28.9
	2010	4 044 652	25.8	24.3	22.5	1.0	49.1	24.1
Chile	2008	89 205 487	59.3	11.9	24.6	0.6	44.7	41.1
Chili	2009	90 219 527	59.6	13.8	21.0	-2.2	39.0	31.2
	2010	103 806 380	57.3	13.1	20.9	1.5	40.5	33.3
China[5]	2008	31 490 130	35.1	13.3	40.7	3.3	34.9	27.2
Chine[5]	2009	34 502 360	35.1	12.9	45.4	2.3	26.4	22.0
	2010	38 857 000	35.0	13.1	46.9	2.4	27.0	23.0
China, Hong Kong SAR	2008	1 677 011	61.0	8.3	19.9	0.5	212.4	202.2
Chine, Hong Kong RAS	2009	1 622 322	62.4	8.8	19.9	1.4	195.1	187.6
	2010	1 743 858	62.2	8.4	21.5	2.2	223.0	217.4
China, Macao SAR	2008	161 599	27.4	8.7	31.1	0.8	96.8	64.8
Chine, Macao RAS	2009	165 576	27.8	9.7	19.3	0.1	93.7	50.7
	2010	217 480	23.3	8.1	12.6	0.1	107.0	51.1
Colombia	2008	481 037 000	63.6	15.2	23.0	0.4	18.0	20.2
Colombie	2009	508 532 000	63.6	15.9	22.8	-0.1	16.0	18.1
	2010	546 951 000	62.8	16.2[1]	22.4	0.8	15.8	18.0
Comoros	2008	178 047	104.3	15.3	13.7	...	14.0	48.4
Comores	2009	189 586	105.9	15.3	11.9	...	13.2	47.9
	2010	201 028	104.6	14.7	16.5	...	13.2	50.8
Congo	2008	4 556 900	27.9	9.8	39.0	0.3	92.3	69.3
Congo	2009	3 869 849	34.1	12.1	49.1	0.3	74.4	70.0
	2010	5 336 498	29.2	9.1	44.9	...	78.4	61.6
Cook Islands	2008	332	47.5	33.1	15.5	...	80.3	76.3
Iles Cook	2009	330	46.4	32.0	15.1	...	81.5	74.9
	2010	346	47.3	31.8	15.4	...	82.8	77.4
Costa Rica	2008	15 701 760	67.8	14.4	23.6	4.0	45.4	55.2
Costa Rica	2009	16 763 545	66.7	16.9	22.2	-6.3	42.5	41.9
	2010	18 819 111	64.8	17.8	19.7	0.2	38.2	40.7
Côte d'Ivoire	2008	10 425 300	66.9	14.7	10.0	1.2	49.0	41.8
Côte d'Ivoire	2009	10 880 700	64.5	14.3	8.3	1.2	49.8	38.2
	2010	11 282 549	65.8	15.0	7.8	1.1	49.2	38.7
Croatia	2008	345 015	58.3[6]	19.3	27.7	3.0	41.7	49.9
Croatie	2009	335 189	56.4[6]	20.5	24.9	2.2	35.4	39.4
	2010	334 564	56.7[6]	20.5	21.6	1.8	38.3	38.8
Cuba	2008	60 806	49.1	39.9[1]	10.8	4.0	20.6	24.4
Cuba	2009	62 279	48.2	38.5[1]	9.3	1.1	17.9	14.9
	2010	64 220	49.7	37.9[1]	9.9	1.9	19.6	19.0
Cyprus	2008	17 157	69.8	17.6	22.9	0.7	46.0	57.0
Chypre	2009	16 853	66.2	19.5	20.5	-0.6	40.9	46.5
	2010	17 334	67.3	19.4	18.6	0.2	43.0	48.5
Czech Republic	2008	3 848 411	48.9	19.7	26.9	2.1	64.5	62.1
République tchèque	2009	3 739 225	50.3	21.7	24.9	-0.9	59.7	55.7
	2010	3 775 237	50.3	21.4	24.6	0.5	67.9	64.7

Gross domestic product by type of expenditure in current prices *(continued)*
Percentage distribution
Dépenses imputées au produit intérieur brut aux prix courants *(suite)*
Répartition en pourcentage

Country or area Pays ou zone	Year Année	GDP in current prices (mil. nat.cur.) PIB aux prix courants (millions monnaie nat.)	Household final consumption[1] expenditure Consom. finale des ménages[1]	Govt. final consumption expenditure Consom. finale des admin. publiques	Gross fixed capital formation[2] Formation brute de capital fixe[2]	Changes in inventories Variation des stocks	Exports of goods and services Exportations de biens et services	Imports of goods and services Importations de biens et services
Dem. P. R. Korea	2008	1 853 815	105.3[7]	...	...	...	5.9	11.1
R. p. dém. de Corée	2009	1 672 886	105.3[7]	...	...	...	5.9	11.2
	2010	1 677 102	105.2[7]	...	...	...	5.9	11.1
Dem. Rep. of the Congo	2008	6 674 000	79.0	12.1	21.5	...	60.0	74.7
Rép. dém. du Congo	2009	9 026 700	85.1	12.1	19.1	...	45.4	61.2
	2010	11 949 300	71.9	9.7	26.4	...	68.2	76.7
Denmark	2008	1 740 843	48.3	26.7	21.0	0.9	55.1	51.9
Danemark	2009	1 656 108	49.1	30.0	18.3	-1.2	47.9	44.1
	2010	1 742 708	49.0	29.4	16.8	-0.4	50.6	45.0
Djibouti	2008	174 617	70.8	19.8	16.9	...	35.8	57.0
Djibouti	2009	186 471	78.6	19.5	17.7	...	34.6	56.7
	2010	202 586	77.4	18.6	17.3	...	32.8	54.0
Dominica	2008	1 248	92.4	13.8	20.9	...	35.1	62.2
Dominique	2009	1 296	85.8	16.8	19.7	...	32.2	54.6
	2010	1 284	81.9	17.6	24.7	...	32.8	54.1
Dominican Republic	2008	1 576 163	87.8	7.6	18.2	0.1	25.5	39.2
Rép. dominicaine	2009	1 678 763	85.4	7.8	14.7	0.1	22.3	30.3
	2010	1 901 897	87.6	7.7	16.3	0.1	22.3	34.0
Ecuador	2008	54 209	61.1	11.0	24.0	3.9	37.9	37.8
Equateur	2009	52 022	66.8	12.3	24.2	-0.9	29.5	32.0
	2010	58 910	68.4	12.5	25.8	-0.6	32.3	38.4
Egypt	2008	895 515	72.3	10.9	22.3	0.1	33.0	38.6
Egypte	2009	1 042 252	76.1	11.4	18.9	0.3	25.0	31.6
	2010	1 206 600	74.7	11.2	18.6	0.3	21.4	26.1
El Salvador	2008	21 431	98.4	9.2	15.2	...	26.9	49.7
El Salvador	2009	20 661	91.4	10.6	13.4	...	23.2	38.7
	2010	21 215	93.3	10.9	13.3	...	26.2	43.6
Equatorial Guinea	2008	7 016 363	5.5	2.8	30.5	^0.0	95.7	34.4
Guinée équatoriale	2009	4 706 881	8.0	4.8	70.5	^0.0	89.2	72.4
	2010	5 845 969	7.4	4.3	61.1	9.6	89.5	68.9
Eritrea	2008	21 220	82.6	26.4	12.7	...	4.4	26.1
Erythrée	2009	28 801	86.9	20.0	9.1	...	4.5	20.5
	2010	34 659	80.6	21.6	12.3	...	4.4	18.9
Estonia	2008	255 105	54.4	19.2	29.7	0.7	70.8	75.1
Estonie	2009	216 542	53.6	22.0	21.5	-2.7	64.8	58.9
	2010	223 829	52.1	20.9	18.8	0.7	79.4	72.6
Ethiopia	2008	248 303	85.0	9.8	22.4	...	11.4	30.8
Ethiopie	2009	335 380	85.4	8.2	22.7	...	10.5	28.7
	2010	383 364	86.2	8.3	22.4	...	13.6	33.0
Fiji	2008	5 683	90.7	14.9	14.6	1.9	52.2	74.3
Fidji	2009	5 531	79.0	18.0	15.6	2.1	47.1	61.7
	2010	5 839	79.7	18.0	15.5	2.1	47.6	61.4
Finland	2008	185 651	51.4	22.5	21.5	0.9	46.8	43.1
Finlande	2009	173 267	54.3	25.0	19.7	-1.2	37.1	35.5
	2010	180 253	54.6	24.6	18.8	-0.3	40.3	39.0
France	2008	1 933 195	56.9	23.3	21.4	0.6	27.0	29.1
France	2009	1 889 231	58.0	24.7	19.8	-0.7	23.3	25.2
	2010	1 932 802	58.2	24.8	19.3	^0.0	25.5	27.8
French Polynesia	2008	570 029	94.6	7.4	17.2	0.1	12.1	38.9
Polynésie française	2009	585 513	94.1	7.3	17.2	0.2	12.2	38.4
	2010	601 460	94.7	7.3	17.1	0.1	12.3	39.0
Gabon	2008	7 534 200	27.4	10.9	21.2	0.7	61.8	22.1
Gabon	2009	7 263 300	29.6	12.3	22.9	0.6	57.4	22.8
	2010	9 297 000	24.7	10.4	24.0	0.5	62.3	21.1

Gross domestic product by type of expenditure in current prices *(continued)*
Percentage distribution

Dépenses imputées au produit intérieur brut aux prix courants *(suite)*
Répartition en pourcentage

			% of Gross domestic product – en % du Produit intérieur brut					
Country or area Pays ou zone	Year Année	GDP in current prices (mil. nat.cur.) PIB aux prix courants (millions monnaie nat.)	Household final consumption[1] expenditure Consom. finale des ménages[1]	Govt. final consumption expenditure Consom. finale des admin. publiques	Gross fixed capital formation[2] Formation brute de capital fixe[2]	Changes in inventories Variation des stocks	Exports of goods and services Exportations de biens et services	Imports of goods and services Importations de biens et services
Gambia	2008	21 857	73.3	8.0	29.1	2.9	7.2	27.9
Gambie	2009	24 164	73.2	7.7	28.3	2.8	13.2	28.7
	2010	26 970	73.2	7.7	27.5	2.8	10.0	24.6
Georgia	2008	19 075	76.9	25.9	21.5	4.5	28.6	58.4
Géorgie	2009	17 986	81.6	24.5	15.3	-2.3	29.7	48.9
	2010	20 791	76.0	21.0	17.3	2.3	34.8	52.3
Germany	2008	2 473 800	56.1	18.3	18.7	0.7	48.1	41.8
Allemagne	2009	2 374 500	58.4	20.0	17.3	-0.8	41.9	37.0
	2010	2 476 800	57.5	19.7	17.6	-0.2	46.8	41.4
Ghana	2008	30 179	86.1	11.2	21.5	...	25.0	44.5
Ghana	2009	36 598	77.5	11.7	20.1	0.6	29.3	42.3
	2010	46 232	77.6	9.5	19.0	0.7	29.3	41.1
Greece	2008	232 920	72.6	18.1	22.1	1.5	24.1	38.6
Grèce	2009	231 642	72.6	20.4	19.1	-0.7	19.2	30.5
	2010	227 318	74.5	18.2	16.6	-0.4	21.5	30.4
Greenland	2008	11 360	30.7	52.4	30.8	...	21.8	40.3
Groenland	2009	10 807	30.3	52.8	31.7	...	17.8	36.0
	2010	11 373	31.3	53.0	30.5	...	18.9	39.9
Grenada	2008	2 241	89.8	14.9	26.9	...	22.9	54.5
Grenade	2009	2 055	83.5	15.9	23.6	...	23.0	45.9
	2010	2 096	97.7	16.2	16.7	...	21.8	51.1
Guatemala	2008	295 871	89.3	9.0	17.9	-1.5	24.7	39.4
Guatemala	2009	307 552	86.1	10.2	15.0	-2.1	24.0	33.2
	2010	334 182	84.5	10.0	15.8	...	25.1	35.8
Guinea	2008	20 780 430	78.2	6.1	21.3	0.7	33.7	40.1
Guinée	2009	22 124 955	80.9	8.5	16.4	^0.0	24.2	30.0
	2010	27 008 508	76.1	12.3	18.0	^0.0	32.8	39.2
Guinea-Bissau	2008	379 633	94.8	12.1	8.6	0.1	15.4	31.0
Guinée-Bissau	2009	406 816	90.0	14.8	8.4	0.1	14.9	28.2
	2010	404 763	88.5	9.5	7.2	0.1	18.1	29.3
Guyana	2008	391 505	93.4	15.4	24.0	...	52.2	85.0
Guyana	2009	413 112	82.3	16.2	26.6	...	46.0	71.1
	2010	453 216	86.7	15.3	25.8	...	50.9	78.8
Haiti	2008	229 623	106.3	12.3	15.1	...	13.9	46.8
Haïti	2009	244 572	104.0	13.7	14.3	...	15.5	46.0
	2010	244 687	126.7	13.1	13.1	...	13.2	61.5
Honduras	2008	262 417	79.9	17.1	33.7	2.4	51.3	84.4
Honduras	2009	267 851	80.6	18.5	22.5	-2.7	40.8	59.7
	2010	290 991	79.6	18.2	23.4	-0.5	43.9	64.6
Hungary	2008	26 545 649	54.2	21.8	21.7	1.8	81.7	81.2
Hongrie	2009	25 622 866	54.5	22.7	20.7	-2.7	77.6	72.7
	2010	26 747 662	53.3	21.8	18.0	0.4	86.6	80.0
Iceland	2008	1 481 986	53.3	24.8	24.5	0.2	44.4	47.1
Islande	2009	1 497 672	51.0	26.5	14.0	^0.0	52.6	44.2
	2010	1 537 106	51.3	26.0	13.0	-0.2	56.0	46.0
India	2008	55 826 230	58.4	11.0	33.3	2.0	23.8	28.9
Inde	2009	65 502 710	57.7	12.0	32.5	3.3	19.8	25.0
	2010	78 756 266	57.2	11.5	31.5	3.3	21.5	24.8
Indonesia	2008	4 948 690 000	60.6	8.4	27.7	0.1	29.8	28.8
Indonésie	2009	5 603 870 000	58.7	9.6	31.1	-0.1	24.2	21.4
	2010	6 422 920 000	56.7	9.1	32.2	0.3	24.6	23.0
Iran (Islamic Rep. of)	2008	3 453 621 396	48.8	9.9	26.8	8.1	28.8	22.4
Iran (Rép. islamique d')	2009	3 476 375 847	51.7	11.2	23.3	9.7	23.9	19.8
	2010	3 964 986 983	51.0	10.7	23.2	9.5	25.1	19.3

Gross domestic product by type of expenditure in current prices *(continued)*
Percentage distribution

Dépenses imputées au produit intérieur brut aux prix courants *(suite)*
Répartition en pourcentage

Country or area Pays ou zone	Year Année	GDP in current prices (mil. nat.cur.) PIB aux prix courants (millions monnaie nat.)	% of Gross domestic product – en % du Produit intérieur brut					
			Household final consumption[1] expenditure Consom. finale des ménages[1]	Govt. final consumption expenditure Consom. finale des admin. publiques	Gross fixed capital formation[2] Formation brute de capital fixe[2]	Changes in inventories Variation des stocks	Exports of goods and services Exportations de biens et services	Imports of goods and services Importations de biens et services
Iraq	2008	129 852 309	37.8	20.1	17.9	0.5	60.9	37.2
Iraq	2009	95 937 989	40.1	55.3	25.7	...	62.3	83.4
	2010	120 892 919	34.6	42.9	24.3	...	65.0	66.7
Ireland	2008	179 990	51.2	18.6	21.9	-0.3	83.4	74.4
Irlande	2009	160 596	50.9	19.9	15.7	-1.4	90.9	75.4
	2010	155 992	50.8	18.9	11.6	-0.5	101.1	82.0
Israel	2008	723 562	58.0	24.5	18.4	0.4	40.3	41.6
Israël	2009	766 273	56.9	24.0	17.0	-0.3	34.7	32.3
	2010	813 021	58.2	23.9	17.8	-1.9	36.9	34.9
Italy	2008	1 567 761	59.3	20.2	20.9	0.3	28.7	29.4
Italie	2009	1 519 702	60.0	21.5	19.2	-0.3	23.9	24.3
	2010	1 548 816	60.4	21.2	19.6	0.6	26.8	28.6
Jamaica	2008	1 009 674	90.0	15.4	24.3	0.4	41.1	71.1
Jamaïque	2009	1 083 448	81.6	15.7	20.9	0.2	34.3	52.7
	2010	1 175 630	82.8	15.1	17.9	0.2	29.9	45.6
Japan	2008	504 377 600	57.8	18.5	23.1	0.5	17.6	17.4
Japon	2009	470 936 700	59.4	20.1	21.2	-1.0	12.6	12.3
	2010	479 179 200	59.1	20.1	20.5	-0.4	15.2	14.1
Jordan	2008	16 108	79.0	21.5	27.6	2.0	54.7	84.7
Jordanie	2009	17 816	73.7	20.1	25.8	1.8	43.6	65.6
	2010	19 528	76.1	17.4	24.8	1.8	44.3	65.1
Kazakhstan	2008	16 052 919	43.5	10.2	26.8	0.7	57.3	37.1
Kazakhstan	2009	17 007 647	47.4	11.7	27.8	1.6	42.0	33.8
	2010	21 647 666	45.2	10.9	24.3	1.1	44.3	29.4
Kenya	2008	2 111 173	75.0	16.5	19.4	-0.2	27.6	41.7
Kenya	2009	2 365 453	78.2	15.8	19.1	0.3	24.2	36.6
	2010	2 551 161	77.8	16.7	19.9	-0.6	27.5	37.9
Kiribati	2008	162	133.9	51.5	57.8	0.3	16.2	159.7
Kiribati	2009	159	133.5	51.3	57.6	0.3	16.9	159.6
	2010	159	135.8	52.2	58.6	0.3	18.2	165.1
Kosovo	2008	3 851	95.3	17.5	24.4	4.1	14.8	56.0
Kosovo	2009	3 912	92.3	17.1	26.2	3.6	15.6	54.9
	2010	4 221	93.6	17.9	24.2	4.0	15.2	54.8
Kuwait	2008	39 620	28.1	13.4	18.5	-0.9	66.8	25.9
Koweït	2009	30 477	33.5	18.5	17.9	^0.0	59.5	29.4
	2010	35 634	30.4	16.7	19.0	^0.0	60.1	26.3
Kyrgyzstan	2008	187 992	92.5	17.5	27.2	1.8	53.6	92.6
Kirghizistan	2009	201 223	78.3	18.4	28.6	-1.3	54.7	78.7
	2010	212 177	83.9	19.0	28.1	0.3	57.7	89.2
Lao People's Dem. Rep.	2008	46 214 712	66.2	8.3	37.1	...	32.7	44.4
Rép. dém. pop. lao	2009	47 562 167	72.7	9.4	31.1	...	25.8	38.1
	2010	53 722 196	54.8	9.2	37.1	...	28.3	32.9
Latvia	2008	16 085	62.5	20.0	29.7	1.6	43.1	56.8
Lettonie	2009	13 070	61.4	19.6	21.6	-1.1	43.9	45.4
	2010	12 739	63.0	17.5	19.5	1.4	53.8	55.2
Lebanon	2008	45 124 000	83.9	14.7	29.6	1.0	24.6	53.8
Liban	2009	52 051 000	75.1	18.0	33.6	1.1	21.4	47.2
	2010	59 165 938	78.6	15.9	29.8	1.0	21.4	46.5
Lesotho	2008	13 223	93.8	37.9	28.5	0.2	57.1	117.4
Lesotho	2009	14 577	95.2	40.7	27.8	1.2	46.2	113.1
	2010	15 590	94.8	39.8	29.9	1.3	44.3	112.6
Liberia	2008	751	202.3	19.3	20.0	...	31.1	172.6
Libéria	2009	832	184.5	15.1	20.0	...	29.3	148.8
	2010	873	204.9	16.3	20.0	...	29.6	170.8

Gross domestic product by type of expenditure in current prices *(continued)*
Percentage distribution

Dépenses imputées au produit intérieur brut aux prix courants *(suite)*
Répartition en pourcentage

Country or area Pays ou zone	Year Année	GDP in current prices (mil. nat.cur.) PIB aux prix courants (millions monnaie nat.)	Household final consumption[1] expenditure Consom. finale des ménages[1]	Govt. final consumption expenditure Consom. finale des admin. publiques	Gross fixed capital formation[2] Formation brute de capital fixe[2]	Changes in inventories Variation des stocks	Exports of goods and services Exportations de biens et services	Imports of goods and services Importations de biens et services
Libyan Arab Jamah.	2008	99 569	35.6	12.5	9.1	0.4	69.2	26.7
Jamah. arabe libyenne	2009	73 660	36.6	12.6	9.3	0.4	68.1	27.0
	2010	90 770	36.1	12.5	9.2	0.4	68.7	26.9
Liechtenstein	2008	5 495	56.6	10.9	21.3	-0.2	56.4	45.1
Liechtenstein	2009	5 220	58.1	11.6	20.6	-1.3	51.7	40.7
	2010	5 365	58.0	11.5	20.8	-1.6	53.6	42.2
Lithuania	2008	112 084	65.7	19.2	25.4	1.5	59.6	71.4
Lituanie	2009	91 914	69.1	22.0	17.2	-6.8	54.4	55.9
	2010	95 074	64.4	20.5	16.4	0.1	68.3	69.5
Luxembourg	2008	39 437	32.4	14.8	20.4	0.4	174.7	142.6
Luxembourg	2009	37 393	34.9	16.9	17.7	-0.6	161.0	129.8
	2010	40 267	33.5	16.6	18.0	0.7	165.0	133.8
Madagascar	2008	16 080 899	80.8	9.3	40.3	...	26.5	56.9
Madagascar	2009	16 729 377	85.4	9.5	31.7	...	25.0	51.6
	2010	18 264 414	86.3	9.4	18.8	...	26.5	41.0
Malawi	2008	592 955	89.3	9.8	22.6	2.7	22.5	46.8
Malawi	2009	691 317	89.3	9.8	22.6	2.7	22.5	46.8
	2010	799 992	86.6	10.0	22.3	2.5	23.3	44.9
Malaysia	2008	742 470	45.2	12.4	19.6	-0.3	103.2	80.0
Malaisie	2009	679 938	49.9	14.1	20.2	-5.8	96.4	74.9
	2010	765 965	48.0	12.7	20.3	1.1	97.3	79.5
Maldives	2008	16 131	26.1	40.4	58.3	^0.0	74.7	99.5
Maldives	2009	16 879	24.6	40.0	57.4	^0.0	77.3	99.3
	2010	18 941	26.2	38.9	56.7	^0.0	76.5	98.3
Mali	2008	3 912 771	63.8	17.6	18.3	1.9	22.9	24.5
Mali	2009	4 232 905	62.2	17.3	20.4	0.9	21.6	22.4
	2010	4 558 440	61.7	17.3	21.2	1.3	22.7	24.2
Malta	2008	5 840	62.9	20.8	17.0	0.8	87.8	89.3
Malte	2009	5 830	64.2	21.3	15.0	-0.3	78.8	79.0
	2010	6 164	61.7	21.0	16.6	-2.7	88.2	84.8
Marshall Islands	2008	166	91.1	54.1	56.8	...	12.4	114.5
Iles Marshall	2009	163	91.1	54.1	56.8	...	12.4	114.5
	2010	166	91.1	54.1	56.8	...	12.4	114.5
Mauritania	2008	882 347	61.0	24.8	25.5	11.3	51.8	74.3
Mauritanie	2009	808 898	69.6	27.9	28.4	-6.6	48.1	67.2
	2010	1 066 975	60.4	23.6	30.6	-7.2	56.7	65.5
Mauritius	2008	274 316	73.2	12.7	24.6	2.7	52.9	66.1
Maurice	2009	283 329	73.7	14.0	26.3	-4.8	48.8	58.1
	2010	299 489	73.6	13.7	24.6	0.5	49.9	62.2
Mexico	2008	12 153 436	64.6	10.8	22.2	4.8	28.1	30.4
Mexique	2009	11 879 676	65.9	12.0	21.6	2.1	27.7	29.2
	2010	13 043 195	64.9	11.7	20.4	4.9	30.4	31.9
Micronesia (Fed. States of)	2008	263	73.8	51.3	31.2	2.0	20.3	78.6
Micronésie (Etats féd. de)	2009	280	73.7	51.2	31.2	2.0	16.6	74.7
	2010	297	73.4	51.0	31.0	2.0	17.0	74.3
Monaco	2008	4 493	56.9	23.3	21.4	0.6	27.0	29.1
Monaco	2009	4 003	58.0	24.7	19.8	-0.7	23.3	25.2
	2010	4 095	58.2	24.8	19.3	^0.0	25.5	27.8
Mongolia	2008	6 555 569	56.2	14.6	36.2	7.4	54.0	67.2
Mongolie	2009	6 590 637	58.4	14.1	28.9	5.5	50.3	57.5
	2010	8 414 505	54.5	13.5	35.6	5.9	47.1	59.4
Montenegro	2008	3 086	91.2	22.6	38.2	2.4	39.5	94.0
Monténégro	2009	2 981	84.0	22.2	26.8	0.4	32.1	65.4
	2010	3 104	82.2	23.4	21.1	1.7	34.7	63.1

Gross domestic product by type of expenditure in current prices *(continued)*
Percentage distribution

Dépenses imputées au produit intérieur brut aux prix courants *(suite)*
Répartition en pourcentage

Country or area Pays ou zone	Year Année	GDP in current prices (mil. nat.cur.) PIB aux prix courants (millions monnaie nat.)	Household final consumption[1] expenditure Consom. finale des ménages[1]	Govt. final consumption expenditure Consom. finale des admin. publiques	Gross fixed capital formation[2] Formation brute de capital fixe[2]	Changes in inventories Variation des stocks	Exports of goods and services Exportations de biens et services	Imports of goods and services Importations de biens et services
Montserrat	2008	135	93.6	56.1	27.2	...	35.8	112.7
Montserrat	2009	142	84.7	55.4	32.0	...	32.4	104.6
	2010	150	85.5	55.3	29.8	...	35.7	106.4
Morocco	2008	688 843	58.1	17.2	33.0	5.1	37.5	50.9
Maroc	2009	736 206	57.0	18.0	30.7	5.3	28.6	39.5
	2010	766 460	57.7	17.7	31.0	3.0	33.1	42.7
Mozambique	2008	240 358	80.1	12.4	16.5	1.1	30.2	40.3
Mozambique	2009	266 213	80.5	12.9	16.5	-1.6	27.7	36.1
	2010	323 750	83.9	12.9	21.9	0.0	30.6	49.2
Myanmar	2008	29 227 535	79.0	3.6	15.7	-0.1	0.1	0.1
Myanmar	2009	33 760 900	74.9	3.9	19.3	-0.1	0.1	0.1
	2010	40 334 986	69.4	3.9	22.8	0.2	0.1	0.1
Namibia	2008	74 000	55.3	20.5	25.4	2.4	52.4	52.8
Namibie	2009	77 812	58.8	24.4	24.9	2.4	44.4	53.3
	2010	85 667	54.5	25.4	24.0	2.3	43.5	48.2
Nauru	2008	50	133.9	51.5	57.8	0.3	16.2	159.7
Nauru	2009	70	133.5	51.3	57.6	0.3	16.9	159.6
	2010	69	135.8	52.2	58.6	0.3	18.2	165.1
Nepal	2008	815 658	80.3	9.9	21.9	8.4	12.8	33.3
Népal	2009	988 053	79.8	10.8	21.4	10.3	12.4	34.7
	2010	1 171 905	82.0	10.6	20.2	14.8	9.8	37.4
Netherlands	2008	594 481	45.5	25.7	20.5	^0.0	76.3	68.0
Pays-Bas	2009	571 145	45.9	28.7	19.4	-0.7	68.8	62.0
	2010	588 414	45.4	28.5	18.3	0.4	78.1	70.6
Netherlands Antilles	2008	7 060	66.2	16.7	36.4	1.2	79.7	100.2
Antilles néerlandaises	2009	7 100	63.3	16.9	34.8	-0.2	78.1	92.9
	2010	7 300	64.6	17.0	35.6	-0.3	78.0	95.0
New Caledonia	2008	743 583	62.3	25.2	42.6	...	18.6	48.6
Nouvelle-Calédonie	2009	752 116	62.8	25.5	37.5	...	15.5	41.3
	2010	797 861	60.6	24.6	39.2	...	20.5	44.9
New Zealand	2008	185 561	58.5	20.1	21.7	0.7	30.8	32.1
Nouvelle-Zélande	2009	187 802	59.0	20.4	19.6	-0.7	27.9	26.5
	2010	197 208	58.2	20.4	19.0	0.6	28.3	26.8
Nicaragua	2008	123 442	85.7	20.2	32.3	0.5	35.4	74.2
Nicaragua	2009	126 386	83.4	19.2	27.2	-2.6	35.2	62.3
	2010	139 916	84.0	16.8	27.4	0.1	41.3	69.6
Niger	2008	2 419 654	70.9	15.0	30.9	1.2	17.7	35.7
Niger	2009	2 511 762	74.2	16.5	32.9	-0.3	19.1	42.4
	2010	2 748 221	69.3	15.0	40.2	0.9	18.8	44.2
Nigeria	2008	24 665 244	63.9	12.7	8.3	^0.0	39.9	24.8
Nigéria	2009	25 225 140	74.8	12.7	12.1	^0.0	30.8	30.4
	2010	29 498 163	59.5	14.5	13.6	^0.0	45.6	33.1
Norway	2008	2 510 887	39.4	19.6	21.8	0.3	48.5	29.6
Norvège	2009	2 330 902	43.6	22.9	22.5	-2.5	41.6	28.1
	2010	2 496 178	43.0	22.4	20.3	1.0	41.9	28.6
Occupied Palestinian Terr.	2008	6 247	110.2	20.6	18.6	0.7	15.4	65.4
Terr. palestinien occupé	2009	6 764	109.5	22.5	18.7	0.2	13.6	64.5
	2010	7 349	113.6	21.8	26.1	...	13.7	75.2
Oman	2008	23 288	30.9	14.2	29.5	4.0	58.8	37.4
Oman	2009	18 020	40.6	19.9	33.6	-5.2	52.6	41.5
	2010	22 243	35.3	17.6	28.7	-4.5	55.3	37.7
Pakistan	2008	10 242 799	76.5	12.5	20.5	1.6	12.9	23.9
Pakistan	2009	12 723 987	81.3	8.1	16.6	1.6	12.9	20.4
	2010	14 836 536	82.5	8.0	13.8	1.6	13.6	19.4

Gross domestic product by type of expenditure in current prices *(continued)*
Percentage distribution

Dépenses imputées au produit intérieur brut aux prix courants *(suite)*
Répartition en pourcentage

Country or area Pays ou zone	Year Année	GDP in current prices (mil. nat.cur.) PIB aux prix courants (millions monnaie nat.)	% of Gross domestic product – en % du Produit intérieur brut					
			Household final consumption[1] expenditure Consom. finale des ménages[1]	Govt. final consumption expenditure Consom. finale des admin. publiques	Gross fixed capital formation[2] Formation brute de capital fixe[2]	Changes in inventories Variation des stocks	Exports of goods and services Exportations de biens et services	Imports of goods and services Importations de biens et services
Palau Palaos	2008	187	49.6	35.6	18.9	2.7	71.9	78.6
	2009	204	49.4	35.0	19.1	2.7	72.3	78.6
	2010	222	49.5	34.6	18.7	2.6	71.1	76.6
Panama Panama	2008	23 002	52.8	10.4	26.5	1.1	85.2	76.0
	2009	24 080	46.0	10.8	24.6	1.0	81.5	63.9
	2010	26 777	58.1	11.3	26.8	0.7	76.0	72.8
Papua New Guinea Papouasie-Nvl-Guinée	2008	21 601	51.4	16.4	13.6	1.8	75.9	59.1
	2009	22 207	67.8	17.6	13.6	1.7	55.7	56.5
	2010	25 837	76.7	16.5	13.6	1.5	61.5	69.7
Paraguay Paraguay	2008	73 621 700	77.5	9.7	17.6	0.4	50.4	55.6
	2009	70 705 315	77.6	11.8	15.4	0.4	47.4	52.7
	2010	84 836 335	74.9	12.2	16.5	0.4	53.1	57.1
Peru Pérou	2008	377 562	62.9	8.8	26.1	1.2	27.2	26.2
	2009	392 565	63.7	10.1	24.0	-1.5	23.6	19.7
	2010	444 460	60.7	9.5	26.3	0.1	25.4	22.0
Philippines Philippines	2008	7 720 903	74.3	8.8	19.7[8]	-0.4	36.9	39.4
	2009	8 026 143	74.7	9.9	19.0[8]	-2.4	32.2	33.4
	2010	9 003 480	71.6	9.7	20.5[8]	^0.0	34.8	36.6
Poland Pologne	2008	1 275 432	61.6	18.5	22.3	1.6	39.9	43.9
	2009	1 343 366	61.1	18.4	21.2	-0.8	39.5	39.4
	2010	1 415 362	61.4	18.9	19.9	1.1	42.3	43.5
Portugal Portugal	2008	171 983	66.8	20.1	22.6	0.6	32.5	42.5
	2009	168 587	65.8	21.8	20.0	-0.1	28.0	35.5
	2010	172 799	66.7	21.4	19.1	-0.1	30.9	38.1
Puerto Rico Porto Rico	2008	95 211	58.2	11.7	10.2	0.4	77.8	58.3
	2009	96 261	59.4	11.3	9.1	0.4	77.9	58.1
	2010	99 202	58.8	11.4	10.4	0.4	79.5	60.5
Qatar Qatar	2008	419 582	17.8	11.4	38.4	1.0	50.6	28.1
	2009	355 986	22.1	15.8	40.3	-0.4	47.0	31.4
	2010	463 492	22.0	13.5	35.0	-0.4	52.0	28.6
Republic of Korea République de Corée	2008	1 026 451 800	54.7	15.3	29.4	1.8	53.0	54.2
	2009	1 065 036 800	54.1	16.0	28.9	-2.6	49.7	46.0
	2010	1 172 803 400	52.5	15.4	28.6	0.5	52.4	49.6
Republic of Moldova République de Moldova	2008	62 922	93.1	20.4	34.0	5.2	40.8	93.6
	2009	60 430	89.7	23.8	22.6	0.6	36.9	73.5
	2010	71 849	93.2	21.8	22.7	1.0	39.6	78.2
Romania Roumanie	2008	514 700	64.9	16.9	31.9	-0.7	30.4	43.5
	2009	501 139	62.1	18.5	24.4	0.9	30.6	36.6
	2010	513 641	62.6	16.4	22.7	3.7	35.8	41.2
Russian Federation Fédération de Russie	2008	41 276 849	48.9	17.8	22.3	3.2	31.3	22.1
	2009	38 786 372	54.7	21.0	22.0	-3.1	28.0	20.5
	2010	44 939 153	51.9	19.5	21.9	0.9	30.0	21.7
Rwanda Rwanda	2008	2 576 925	78.4	14.7	22.7	...	14.5	30.2
	2009	2 990 274	82.5	15.2	21.6	...	10.1	29.4
	2010	3 281 667	83.3	15.4	21.0	...	10.8	30.6
Saint Kitts and Nevis Saint-Kitts-et-Nevis	2008	1 540	63.3	17.1	39.6	1.1	46.3	67.4
	2009	1 471	74.4	19.6	39.6	...	35.2	68.7
	2010	1 485	67.4	19.6	38.1	...	35.4	62.7
Saint Lucia Sainte-Lucie	2008	2 925	78.7	14.5	33.7	...	48.9	75.7
	2009	2 868	61.3	16.8	31.0	...	51.2	60.4
	2010	3 142	60.2	16.5	34.5	...	51.0	62.2
Saint Vincent-Grenadines Saint Vincent-Grenadines	2008	1 888	85.7	16.7	29.3	...	30.1	61.6
	2009	1 815	87.0	17.9	24.2	...	28.6	57.7
	2010	1 822	88.8	16.2	25.5	...	27.2	57.7

Gross domestic product by type of expenditure in current prices *(continued)*
Percentage distribution

Dépenses imputées au produit intérieur brut aux prix courants *(suite)*
Répartition en pourcentage

Country or area Pays ou zone	Year Année	GDP in current prices (mil. nat.cur.) PIB aux prix courants (millions monnaie nat.)	% of Gross domestic product – en % du Produit intérieur brut					
			Household final consumption[1] expenditure Consom. finale des ménages[1]	Govt. final consumption expenditure Consom. finale des admin. publiques	Gross fixed capital formation[2] Formation brute de capital fixe[2]	Changes in inventories Variation des stocks	Exports of goods and services Exportations de biens et services	Imports of goods and services Importations de biens et services
Samoa	2008	1 444	92.9	21.5	8.5	0.2	30.8	53.8
Samoa	2009	1 433	92.5	21.1	9.0	0.2	31.1	53.9
	2010	1 489	92.9	20.3	8.8	0.2	30.8	53.0
San Marino	2008	1 259	37.7	3.4	34.0	...	223.4	206.8
Saint-Marin	2009	1 102	43.0	3.9	24.7	...	214.3	190.4
	2010	1 123	39.1	3.5	35.1	...	213.2	198.9
Sao Tome and Principe	2008	2 677 725	117.7	14.3	26.7	-5.0	9.8	63.6
Sao Tomé-et-Principe	2009	3 209 535	117.2	13.9	23.4	-5.0	9.0	58.5
	2010	3 835 453	115.3	14.3	26.1	-5.0	9.4	60.0
Saudi Arabia	2008	1 786 143	27.8	19.3	19.5	2.7	67.8	37.1
Arabie saoudite	2009	1 397 488	36.7	24.9	24.5	2.7	54.2	43.1
	2010	1 629 998	34.1	22.5	21.1	1.0	56.8	35.4
Senegal	2008	5 950 154	80.5	13.3	27.1	5.6	26.3	52.8
Sénégal	2009	6 023 208	78.9	13.9	23.7	3.4	23.2	43.1
	2010	6 359 666	75.2	14.6	27.3	2.5	24.5	44.1
Serbia	2008	2 661 387	77.0	20.1	23.8	6.0	31.4	58.3
Serbie	2009	2 713 206	79.9	19.9	18.8	-1.0	29.5	47.2
	2010	2 931 424	79.9	19.3	18.6	-1.0	35.7	52.5
Seychelles	2008	8 710	76.1	28.7	40.1	...	107.8	152.8
Seychelles	2009	10 726	71.7	31.0	29.3	...	105.2	137.2
	2010	11 621	60.2	27.3	52.4	...	89.4	132.2
Sierra Leone	2008	6 427 146	70.8	14.4	6.2	33.9	13.1	38.3
Sierra Leone	2009	7 170 143	70.8	14.4	6.2	33.9	13.1	38.3
	2010	8 052 359	71.3	16.3	8.1	44.3	17.7	46.1
Singapore	2008	267 952	39.7	10.8	28.3	1.9	233.4	212.5
Singapour	2009	266 659	40.1	10.7	28.6	-2.3	199.9	176.3
	2010	303 652	37.9	10.7	25.0	-1.2	211.1	183.0
Slovakia	2008	66 932	57.1	17.6	24.8	2.8	83.4	85.7
Slovaquie	2009	62 896	61.0	20.0	20.8	-0.9	70.8	71.6
	2010	65 887	58.3	19.6	22.2	1.2	81.1	82.4
Slovenia	2008	37 280	53.2	18.1	28.8	3.1	67.1	70.4
Slovénie	2009	35 311	55.8	20.3	23.4	-0.9	58.4	57.0
	2010	35 416	56.0	20.8	21.6	1.0	65.4	64.9
Solomon Islands	2008	4 712	62.3	38.9	18.3	1.2	44.3	67.2
Iles Salomon	2009	4 815	61.7	39.0	18.2	1.2	39.3	57.6
	2010	5 180	70.1	40.1	19.3	1.0	44.0	74.6
Somalia	2008	37 455 600	72.6	8.7	20.1	0.1	0.3	1.7
Somalie	2009	39 342 786	72.6	8.7	20.0	0.1	0.3	1.7
	2010	34 171 032	72.7	8.7	19.9	0.1	0.3	1.7
South Africa	2008	2 274 139	61.5	18.9	23.1	-0.5	35.6	38.6
Afrique du Sud	2009	2 395 969	60.8	21.1	22.2	-2.6	27.4	28.3
	2010	2 662 757	59.2	21.5	19.6	-0.3	27.4	27.5
Spain	2008	1 088 124	57.2	19.5	28.7	0.4	26.5	32.2
Espagne	2009	1 053 914	56.6	21.1	24.0	0.4	23.4	25.5
	2010	1 062 591	58.4	20.8	22.5	0.5	26.3	28.4
Sri Lanka	2008	4 410 682	70.0	16.2	25.3	1.8	24.8	38.5
Sri Lanka	2009	4 825 085	64.3	17.7	23.8	0.6	21.4	27.9
	2010	5 602 321	65.8	15.6	25.9	1.5	21.7	30.8
Sudan	2008	135 512	69.5	7.8	18.4	2.8	18.8	17.2
Soudan	2009	151 561	70.8	8.7	18.8	4.6	12.7	15.6
	2010	191 824	70.8	7.8	18.5	4.0	13.6	14.6
Suriname	2008	8 414[9]	16.8	4.8	79.5	...	63.6	62.7
Suriname	2009	8 926[9]	15.7	4.5	76.7	...	51.5	50.4
	2010	10 108[9]	15.0	4.3	68.3	...	58.8	51.9

Country or area Pays ou zone	Year Année	GDP in current prices (mil. nat.cur.) PIB aux prix courants (millions monnaie nat.)	Household final consumption[1] expenditure Consom. finale des ménages[1]	Govt. final consumption expenditure Consom. finale des admin. publiques	Gross fixed capital formation[2] Formation brute de capital fixe[2]	Changes in inventories Variation des stocks	Exports of goods and services Exportations de biens et services	Imports of goods and services Importations de biens et services
Swaziland	2008	24 947	84.9	13.4	11.1	...	59.4	68.7
Swaziland	2009	26 788	88.2	13.7	10.3	...	55.5	67.7
	2010	28 753	81.5	25.0	8.9	...	50.3	65.7
Sweden	2008	3 204 320	47.0	26.1	20.0	0.2	53.5	46.8
Suède	2009	3 089 181	49.4	27.8	17.8	-1.5	48.4	41.9
	2010	3 306 271	48.4	27.2	17.9	0.6	50.0	44.1
Switzerland	2008	545 028	56.6	10.9	21.3	-0.2	56.4	45.1
Suisse	2009	535 650	58.1	11.6	20.6	-1.3	51.7	40.7
	2010	550 571	58.0	11.5	20.8	-1.6	53.6	42.2
Syrian Arab Republic	2008	2 445 061	56.9	11.2	16.7	15.0	36.9	36.8
Rép. arabe syrienne	2009	2 519 152	59.9	12.0	17.9	12.3	29.1	31.2
	2010	2 762 614	59.0	10.0	19.7	13.5	35.1	35.6
Tajikistan	2008	17 707	87.6	9.3	24.5	2.0	32.7	79.1
Tadjikistan	2009	20 628	86.3	12.5	26.3	-1.5	24.5	61.5
	2010	24 711	111.2	9.7	18.4	0.0	15.2	54.5
Tanganyika	2008	24 781 679	66.4	17.4	29.4	0.4[10]	25.1[10]	...
Tanganyika	2009	28 212 646	65.5	17.5	28.4	0.5[10]	23.2[10]	...
	2010	32 284 384	65.1	17.5	27.9	0.5[10]	23.6[10]	...
Thailand	2008	9 080 466	55.1	12.3	27.5	1.7	76.4	73.9
Thaïlande	2009	9 041 551	55.2	13.4	24.1	-2.9	68.4	57.8
	2010	10 102 986	53.7	12.9	24.7	1.3	71.3	63.9
TFYR of Macedonia	2008	411 728	80.3	18.2	26.8	...	50.9	76.2
L'ex-R.Y. Macédoine	2009	410 734	76.5	19.1	19.9	6.0	39.0	60.6
	2010	424 762	76.7	18.8	19.5	3.8	47.6	66.3
Timor-Leste	2008	562[11]	106.6	50.2	23.5	...	11.8	92.3
Timor-Leste	2009	704[11]	105.7	49.7	21.6	...	11.7	88.9
	2010	794[11]	103.9	49.2	21.9	...	11.7	86.7
Togo	2008	1 418 529	85.7	13.4	14.3	3.3	35.9	52.6
Togo	2009	1 493 274	82.8	14.2	16.7	2.0	37.8	53.4
	2010	1 566 187	85.2	12.0	17.7	0.9	38.9	54.7
Tonga	2008	661	100.1	18.5	26.0	0.3	13.5	57.3
Tonga	2009	650	100.1	19.9	26.3	0.9	14.0	63.2
	2010	672	99.0	19.1	24.7	4.7	13.4	60.0
Trinidad and Tobago	2008	170 938	46.5	9.8	10.0	1.4	65.8	37.9
Trinité-et-Tobago	2009	124 116	63.6	14.2	11.1	1.5	47.4	38.4
	2010	129 753	53.6	14.8	11.2	1.5	56.6	39.7
Tunisia	2008	55 219	61.4	16.2	23.7	1.8	55.7	58.8
Tunisie	2009	58 775	61.9	16.5	24.4	0.2	45.0	47.9
	2010	63 342	62.7	16.6	24.7	1.4	48.7	54.0
Turkey	2008	950 534	69.9	12.8	19.9	1.9	23.9	28.3
Turquie	2009	952 559	71.5	14.7	16.9	-1.9	23.3	24.4
	2010	1 103 750	71.3	14.3	18.7	1.2	21.1	26.6
Turkmenistan	2008	43 683	51.4	8.3	13.5	...	72.5	45.7
Turkménistan	2009	56 850	48.9	9.9	11.4	...	75.6	45.9
	2010	65 921	45.5	9.1	14.4	...	74.5	43.4
Turks and Caicos Islands	2008	975	52.9	17.9	44.3	...	60.8	75.9
Iles Turques et Caïques	2009	1 160	53.8	18.1	46.1	...	62.2	80.3
	2010	1 381	54.0	17.8	45.9	...	62.0	79.7
Tuvalu	2008	35	35.4	72.3	77.3	...	1.7	86.7
Tuvalu	2009	34	35.1	70.4	76.6	...	1.7	83.8
	2010	34	35.5	70.7	77.4	...	1.7	85.2
Uganda	2008	28 176 384	81.3	10.0	20.1	0.3	20.0	31.6
Ouganda	2009	34 195 733	76.4	9.5	21.0	...	24.0	30.9
	2010	36 539 165	75.7	9.9	21.4	^0.0	23.4	30.7

| | | % of Gross domestic product – en % du Produit intérieur brut | | | | | | |

Gross domestic product by type of expenditure in current prices *(continued)*
Percentage distribution
Dépenses imputées au produit intérieur brut aux prix courants *(suite)*
Répartition en pourcentage

Country or area Pays ou zone	Year Année	GDP in current prices (mil. nat.cur.) PIB aux prix courants (millions monnaie nat.)	% of Gross domestic product – en % du Produit intérieur brut					
			Household final consumption[1] expenditure Consom. finale des ménages[1]	Govt. final consumption expenditure Consom. finale des admin. publiques	Gross fixed capital formation[2] Formation brute de capital fixe[2]	Changes in inventories Variation des stocks	Exports of goods and services Exportations de biens et services	Imports of goods and services Importations de biens et services
Ukraine Ukraine	2008	948 056	62.2	17.8	26.4	1.5	46.9	54.9
	2009	913 345	64.5	20.2	18.4	-1.3	46.4	48.1
	2010	1 094 607	63.3	20.1	19.1	0.3	50.2	53.0
United Arab Emirates Emirats arabes unis	2008	1 156 267	62.5	5.8	21.2	1.3	79.0	69.8
	2009	992 805	61.7	9.0	22.3	1.6	74.7	69.2
	2010	1 093 114	59.5	8.3	23.8	1.5	75.3	68.2
United Kingdom Royaume-Uni	2008	1 433 870	63.7	22.0	16.9	0.1	29.5	32.2
	2009	1 393 854	64.2	23.5	15.0	-0.8	28.4	30.2
	2010	1 458 452	64.3	23.2	14.9	0.5	30.0	32.7
United Rep. of Tanzania [12] Rép.-Unie de Tanzanie [12]	2008	24 781 379	66.4	17.4	29.4	0.4[10]	25.1[10]	38.8
	2009	28 212 646	65.5	17.5	28.4	0.5[10]	23.2[10]	35.2
	2010	32 284 384	65.1	17.5	27.9	0.5[10]	23.6[10]	34.7
United States Etats-Unis	2008	14 219 300	70.6	16.9	17.8	-0.3	13.0	18.0
	2009	13 863 600	71.2	17.6	15.3	-1.2	11.4	14.2
	2010	14 447 100	70.9	17.5	14.7	0.5	12.7	16.3
Uruguay Uruguay	2008	653 136	70.4	11.9	20.4	1.8	29.1	33.7
	2009	706 883	68.9	13.0	18.8	-1.6	26.7	25.8
	2010	807 685	68.6	12.7	18.8	-0.9	25.9	25.0
Uzbekistan Ouzbékistan	2008	37 746 700	52.9	17.3	24.7	...	42.5	39.8
	2009	48 097 000	56.2	17.8	26.1	...	36.4	36.4
	2010	61 831 200	56.1	17.3	23.9	...	39.5	37.6
Vanuatu Vanuatu	2008	60 133	62.2	15.6	33.0	1.2	49.9	61.0
	2009	63 024	63.7	15.3	27.0	1.0	50.0	57.4
	2010	67 121	62.9	15.7	27.8	1.0	50.1	57.0
Venezuela (Boliv. Rep. of) Venezuela (Rép. boliv. du)	2008	667 997	53.0	11.5	20.4	5.5	30.7	21.1
	2009	700 208	64.2	13.3	22.1	2.7	18.3	20.5
	2010	1 011 774	56.8	10.8	17.5	3.3	28.7	17.2
Viet Nam Viet Nam	2008	1 485 038 468	67.4	6.1	34.6	5.1	77.9	93.1
	2009	1 658 389 370	66.5	6.3	34.5	3.6	68.3	78.7
	2010	1 980 914 000	66.5	6.5	35.6	3.3	74.4	88.2
Yemen Yémen	2008	5 734 669	68.1	12.5	19.5	4.7	33.6	38.4
	2009	5 611 297	83.6	13.2	20.9	-2.5	24.0	33.7
	2010	7 558 609	81.0	10.5	17.9	-2.1	25.7	29.0
Zambia Zambie	2008	54 839 439	59.9	22.1	19.7	1.4	35.3	37.4
	2009	64 615 578	65.1	9.8	20.2	1.5	35.6	32.2
	2010	77 717 920	53.2	10.1	22.5	1.4	47.7	34.9
Zanzibar Zanzibar	2008	748 057	66.4	17.4	18.9	0.5	25.1	38.8
	2009	879 420	65.5	17.5	19.6	0.3	23.2	35.2
	2010	948 666	66.6	18.1	20.9	0.3	24.2	38.3
Zimbabwe Zimbabwe	2008	5 495	120.5	2.1	3.8	1.9	42.4	70.8
	2009	5 626	101.1	14.3	11.7	1.7	28.3	57.1
	2010	7 204	106.6	6.6	7.0	1.9	36.9	58.9

Source:
United Nations Statistics Division, New York, national accounts main aggregates database, last accessed February 2012.

Source:
Organisation des Nations Unies, Division de statistique, New York, la base de données sur les comptes nationaux, dernier accès février 2012.

1   Including "Non-profit institutions serving households" (NPISHs) final consumption expenditure.
2   Including acquisitions less disposals of valuables.
3   Including Goverment investment in the Production Activitives.

1   Y compris la consommation finale des institutions sans but lucratif au service des ménages.
2   Y compris les acquisitions moins cessions d'objets de valeur.
3   Y compris les investissements du gouvernement dans les activités de production.

Gross domestic product by type of expenditure in current prices *(continued)*
Percentage distribution

Dépenses imputées au produit intérieur brut aux prix courants *(suite)*
Répartition en pourcentage

4	Excludes individual consumption of general government.
5	For statistical purposes, the data for China do not include those for the Hong Kong Special Administrative Region (Hong Kong SAR), Macao Special Administrative Region (Macao SAR) and Taiwan Province of China.
6	Includes net value of direct purchases between residents abroad and non-residents from domestic market.
7	Final consumption expenditure.
8	Includes intellectual property products.
9	Excluding the informal sector.
10	Valued c.i.f. instead of f.o.b.
11	Refers to non-oil GDP.
12	Tanganyika only.

4	Non compris la consommation individuelle de l'administrations publique.
5	Pour la présentation des statistiques, les données pour la Chine ne comprennent pas la Région Administrative Spéciale de Hong Kong (Hong Kong RAS), la Région Administrative Spéciale de Macao (Macao RAS) et la province de Taiwan.
6	Y compris la valeur nette entre les achats directs effectués à l'étranger par les ménages résidents et ceux des ménages non résident sur le marché intérieur.
7	Dépenses de consommation finale.
8	Y compris les produits soumis à des droits de propriété intellectuelle.
9	Non compris le secteur informel.
10	Valeur c.a.f (coût, assurance et fret) au lieu de la valeur f.a.b (franco à bord).
11	PIB non dérivés du pétrole.
12	Tanganyika seulement.

Value added by industries at current prices
Total and percentage distribution

Valeur ajoutée par branche d'activité aux prix courants
Total et répartition en pourcentage

Country or area Pays ou zone	Year Année	Value added, gross (mil. nat. cur) Valeur ajoutée, brute (mil. mon. nat.)	% of Value added - % de la valeur ajoutée						
			Agriculture, hunting, forestry and fishing Agriculture, chasse, sylviculture et pêche	Mining, manufactu- ring and utilities Activités extractives, Activités de fabrication, électricité, gaz et eau	Manu- facturing Activités de fabri- cation	Construc- tion Construc- tion	Wholesale, retail, trade, restaurants and hotels Commerce, restaurants et hôtels	Transport, storage & commu- nication Transports, entrepôts et commu- nications	Other activities Autres activités
Afghanistan	2008	504 786	32.9	17.4	16.8	9.9	11.9	10.2	17.8
Afghanistan	2009	591 369	33.3	14.2	13.6	8.5	8.4	18.9	16.7
	2010	683 015	35.0	16.2	15.6	9.1	10.4	12.9	16.5
Albania	2008	972 532[1]	18.5	9.8	8.1	14.9	21.2	9.6	25.9
Albanie	2009	1 024 047[1]	18.9	9.3	7.6	14.2	21.2	9.8	26.5
	2010	1 098 525[1]	18.8	9.5	7.9	14.7	21.2	9.7	26.1
Algeria	2008	10 709 736[1]	6.6	52.6	3.7	8.1	10.2	8.5	14.0
Algérie	2009	9 567 204[1]	9.6	39.2	4.7	10.3	13.2	10.1	17.7
	2010	11 354 875[1]	7.9	47.8	4.2	8.8	11.3	9.4	14.8
Andorra	2008	2 565	0.4	5.1	4.1	12.1	26.1	4.3	52.1
Andorre	2009	2 442	0.4	5.2	4.1	11.6	25.6	4.0	53.2
	2010	2 399	0.4	5.1	4.1	9.7	25.9	4.4	54.5
Angola	2008	6 162 100	6.8	64.0	4.9	5.2	13.8	4.2	6.1
Angola	2009	5 841 500	10.5	52.8	6.2	7.7	16.3	4.9	7.8
	2010	7 391 500	10.1	53.3	6.3	8.1	16.2	4.9	7.4
Anguilla [2]	2008	678[1]	1.4	7.4	1.9	26.5	21.2	13.2	30.4
Anguilla [2]	2009	537[1]	1.8	7.6	1.6	15.5	22.3	13.3	39.6
	2010	498[1]	1.6	7.6	1.8	21.7	23.0	13.2	33.0
Antigua and Barbuda	2008	2 947[1,2]	2.9	6.8	1.7	20.2	17.3	18.0	34.9
Antigua-et-Barbuda	2009	2 842[1,2]	3.3	6.9	1.6	18.8	16.0	18.7	36.4
	2010	2 750[1,2]	3.0	6.7	1.7	19.2	16.7	18.3	36.1
Argentina	2008	947 208[1]	9.8	26.3	21.2	6.0	14.5	8.5	34.9
Argentine	2009	1 057 644[1]	7.5	26.1	21.2	5.7	14.8	8.2	37.7
	2010	1 323 199[1]	10.0	25.3	20.5	5.6	14.7	8.1	36.2
Armenia	2008	3 217 959[1]	18.1	14.7	9.8	28.1	13.3	7.5	18.3
Arménie	2009	2 859 677[1]	18.6	14.7	9.6	20.4	14.7	7.9	23.7
	2010	3 165 668[1]	19.3	16.4	10.5	19.0	15.2	7.5	22.7
Aruba	2008	4 646[1]	0.4[3]	13.4[4]	3.9[5]	6.5	21.1	8.3	50.3
Aruba	2009	4 262[1]	0.5[3]	12.6[4]	4.2[5]	5.4	18.5	9.1	54.1
	2010	4 176[1]	0.4[3]	13.0[4]	4.1[5]	6.6	20.0	8.5	51.4
Australia	2008	1 171 901	2.4	21.3	9.3	7.7	11.4	8.6	48.7
Australie	2009	1 197 781	2.3	19.8	9.3	7.9	11.5	8.5	50.0
	2010	1 285 049	2.5	20.4	10.0	7.6	11.8	8.7	49.1
Austria	2008	256 534	1.7	23.2	20.4	7.1	17.3	6.4	44.4
Autriche	2009	247 996	1.5	21.8	18.6	7.3	17.2	6.3	45.8
	2010	257 803	1.5	22.3	19.2	6.9	17.1	6.3	45.9
Azerbaijan	2008	38 029[1]	5.9	61.8	5.0	7.4	6.7	7.1	11.2
Azerbaïdjan	2009	33 360[1]	6.5	52.4	5.9	7.7	8.2	9.3	15.9
	2010	39 065[1]	5.7	55.9	5.8	8.0	8.2	8.4	13.8
Bahamas	2008	8 070[1]	2.1	6.9	3.9	6.3	25.2	8.6	51.0
Bahamas	2009	7 713[1]	1.9	7.1	4.0	6.6	22.5	9.2	52.7
	2010	7 541[1]	2.1	7.3	4.2	6.8	24.6	8.9	50.4
Bahrain	2008	9 063[1]	0.3	42.5	14.9	4.7	9.0	5.3	38.2
Bahreïn	2009	7 996[1]	0.4	36.3	13.4	4.1	9.2	6.5	43.6
	2010	9 198[1]	0.4	40.2	16.0	3.7	8.7	6.2	40.9
Bangladesh	2008	5 259 755	19.0	20.2	17.9	8.3	15.6	10.8	26.1
Bangladesh	2009	5 939 242	18.7	20.2	17.9	8.4	15.6	10.8	26.2
	2010	6 714 660	18.6	20.2	17.9	8.3	15.7	10.7	26.6
Barbados	2008	6 655[1]	2.3	9.6	8.0	7.0	29.4	8.1	43.6
Barbade	2009	6 558[1]	2.5	9.8	7.7	5.3	30.2	8.0	44.3
	2010	6 628[1]	2.4	10.0	8.0	6.3	29.9	8.4	43.1
Belarus	2008	112 981 722[1]	9.6	34.4	32.8	10.7	12.7	10.0	22.5
Bélarus	2009	121 901 010[1]	9.1	31.3	29.5	11.6	12.4	11.0	24.7
	2010	147 177 907[1]	8.9	31.9	30.3	12.2	12.7	10.5	23.8
Belgium	2008	308 339	0.7	17.7	15.7	5.5	14.5	8.3	53.4
Belgique	2009	303 366	0.7	16.3	14.4	5.4	13.8	7.9	55.9
	2010	314 502	0.7	16.6	14.6	5.3	13.9	7.9	55.6

Value added by industries at current prices *(continued)*
Percentage distribution

Valeur ajoutée par branche d'activité aux prix courants *(suite)*
Répartition en pourcentage

Country or area / Pays ou zone	Year / Année	Value added, gross (mil. nat. cur) Valeur ajoutée, brute (mil. mon. nat.)	Agriculture, hunting, forestry and fishing / Agriculture, chasse, sylviculture et pêche	Mining, manufacturing and utilities Activités extractives, Activités de fabrication, électricité, gaz et eau	Manu-facturing Activités de fabri-cation	Construc-tion Construc-tion	Wholesale, retail, trade, restaurants and hotels Commerce, restaurants et hôtels	Transport, storage & commu-nication Transports, entrepôts et commu-nications	Other activities Autres activités
Belize	2008	2 484[1]	11.6	16.7	13.7	5.0	20.9	11.4	34.5
Belize	2009	2 460[1]	12.2	16.5	12.6	4.2	20.9	11.7	34.5
	2010	2 554[1]	11.8	16.6	12.9	4.3	21.0	11.8	34.5
Benin	2008	2 725 542[1]	35.2	9.1	7.8	4.6	19.1	9.2	22.8
Bénin	2009	2 859 313[1]	35.2	9.5	8.1	4.7	18.4	9.0	23.2
	2010	2 976 547[1]	35.4	9.8	8.4	4.6	18.0	8.9	23.3
Bermuda	2008	6 432[1]	0.8	2.9[4]	1.4	5.8[3]	11.6	4.6	74.4
Bermudes	2009	5 894[1]	0.8	3.0[4]	1.3	5.4[3]	11.3	4.8	74.9
	2010	6 331[1]	0.8	3.0[4]	1.5	5.5[3]	12.0	5.0	73.8
Bhutan	2008	53 100	19.0	32.7	8.7	11.8	6.2	10.1	20.3
Bhoutan	2009	59 519	18.8	30.6	8.4	12.6	5.8	10.1	22.2
	2010	66 008	19.0	31.5	8.5	12.8	6.0	9.8	20.9
Bolivia (Plur. State of)	2008	97 370[1]	12.9	34.0	13.8	2.9	11.6	10.4	28.2
Bolivie (État plur. de)	2009	102 116[1]	13.3	31.9	13.9	3.0	11.6	10.5	29.8
	2010	115 934[1]	12.4	32.7	13.4	3.2	11.7	10.7	29.4
Bosnia and Herzegovina	2008	20 793[1]	8.9	21.0	13.6	6.4	18.3	8.0	37.4
Bosnie-Herzégovine	2009	20 588[1]	8.6	20.2	12.6	6.2	17.6	8.0	39.5
	2010	20 881[1]	9.1	20.5	13.3	6.2	17.9	8.1	38.3
Botswana	2008	88 359[1]	2.3	48.6	3.5	4.0	11.4	3.9	29.8
Botswana	2009	78 284[1]	2.5	34.8	4.3	5.5	14.5	5.2	37.6
	2010	95 873[1]	2.5	39.9	4.0	5.4	13.7	4.6	34.0
Brazil	2008	2 580 110	5.9	23.0	16.6	4.9	20.3	8.8	37.1
Brésil	2009	2 740 733	6.1	20.5	15.8	4.9	20.7	8.8	38.9
	2010	3 135 643	5.8	21.6	15.8	5.3	20.4	8.7	38.3
British Virgin Islands	2008	997[1]	1.0	4.7	2.7	7.1	27.8	11.5	48.0
Iles Vierges brit.	2009	877[1]	1.1	5.4	3.1	7.2	26.6	11.0	48.8
	2010	916[1]	1.0	4.9	2.8	7.3	27.3	11.3	48.3
Brunei Darussalam[6]	2008	20 397	0.6	71.5	13.7	2.6	3.0	2.6	19.6
Brunéi Darussalam[6]	2009	15 611	0.9	62.1	14.0	3.3	4.3	3.6	25.9
	2010	17 756	0.8	67.3	12.7	2.9	3.5	3.0	22.5
Bulgaria	2008	57 733	6.9	22.0	15.8	8.4	14.2	10.2	38.3
Bulgarie	2009	58 695	4.8	22.1	15.8	8.5	14.6	10.3	39.6
	2010	60 646	5.3	23.2	16.4	8.1	13.8	9.8	39.9
Burkina Faso	2008	3 519 842[1]	40.2	10.4	8.4	5.1	12.0	5.2	27.2
Burkina Faso	2009	3 695 760[1]	40.3	10.5	8.2	5.3	11.4	5.9	26.7
	2010	3 963 076[1]	37.6	11.2	9.2	5.4	12.0	5.6	28.2
Burundi	2008	1 470 902	39.2	14.8	13.0	11.3	8.2	5.5	21.1
Burundi	2009	1 610 136	39.7	14.7	13.0	11.3	8.3	5.2	20.9
	2010	1 732 654	40.1	15.2	13.3	9.3	8.4	5.6	21.5
Cambodia	2008	39 435 369[1]	34.9	17.3	16.3	6.5	14.3	7.9	19.2
Cambodge	2009	40 448 461[1]	35.7	16.4	15.4	6.7	14.4	8.0	19.0
	2010	44 165 337[1]	36.1	16.7	15.7	6.4	14.7	8.1	18.1
Cameroon	2008	9 693 537[1]	23.3	25.5	14.9	3.3	22.1	6.6	19.2
Cameroun	2009	10 244 479[1]	23.3	25.0	16.1	4.7	20.9	6.4	19.6
	2010	10 096 205[1]	24.9	27.6	16.4	4.0	23.6	7.0	12.9
Canada	2008	1 499 001	1.8	23.4	12.4	7.1	14.2	7.2	46.4
Canada	2009	1 423 361	1.7	21.6	11.1	6.8	14.1	7.2	48.6
	2010	1 514 253	1.6	21.8	11.4	7.2	14.2	7.2	48.1
Cape Verde	2008	105 862[1]	7.8	7.3	3.3	11.1	23.9	22.7	27.2
Cap-Vert	2009	113 743[1]	7.7	7.6	3.0	12.7	23.7	22.0	26.4
	2010	123 193[1]	7.8	7.2	3.2	11.4	24.4	22.3	27.0
Cayman Islands	2008	3 168[1]	0.3	4.1	0.9	4.7	12.1	7.0	71.9
Iles Caïmanes	2009	2 940[1]	0.3	4.4	0.8	3.6	11.9	7.4	72.3
	2010	2 842[1]	0.3	4.4	0.8	4.3	11.9	7.1	72.1
Central African Rep.	2008	837 699	53.9	10.9	8.5	4.3	12.9[7]	5.6	12.4
Rép. centrafricaine	2009	874 732	53.3	10.7	8.2	4.4	13.1	5.6	13.0
	2010	911 524	53.4	10.4	7.7	4.4	13.2	5.7	12.9
Chad	2008	3 658 798	20.2	52.6	5.6	1.2	11.0	1.6	13.3
Tchad	2009	3 164 422	20.5	43.5	6.2	2.1	13.3	2.0	18.6
	2010	3 943 158	19.1	49.5	5.3	2.0	11.7	1.7	15.9

Value added by industries at current prices *(continued)*
Percentage distribution

Valeur ajoutée par branche d'activité aux prix courants *(suite)*
Répartition en pourcentage

			% of Value added - % de la valeur ajoutée						
Country or area Pays ou zone	Year Année	Value added, gross (mil. nat. cur) Valeur ajoutée, brute (mil. mon. nat.)	Agriculture, hunting, forestry and fishing Agriculture, chasse, sylviculture et pêche	Mining, manufacturing and utilities Activités extractives, Activités de fabrication, électricité, gaz et eau	Manu-facturing Activités de fabri-cation	Construc-tion Construc-tion	Wholesale, retail, trade, restaurants and hotels Commerce, restaurants et hôtels	Transport, storage & commu-nication Transports, entrepôts et commu-nications	Other activities Autres activités
Chile Chili	2008 2009 2010	84 398 467[1,8] 86 502 197[1,8] 100 230 552[1,8]	3.5 3.5 3.2	35.4 33.5 34.8	13.1 13.0 11.5	8.5 7.9 8.2	9.5 9.4 9.4	7.6 7.6 7.6	35.6 38.1 36.9
China[9] Chine[9]	2008 2009 2010	31 404 630 34 090 450 40 120 200	10.7 10.3 10.1	41.5 39.7 40.7	32.7 32.3 32.4	6.0 6.6 6.1	10.4 10.6 10.5	5.2 4.9 5.3	26.2 27.9 27.3
China, Hong Kong SAR Chine, Hong Kong RAS	2008 2009 2010	1 592 898 1 550 850 1 676 349	0.1[10] 0.1[10] 0.1[10]	4.4[11] 4.1[11] 4.4[11]	2.0 1.8 1.9	3.0 3.2 2.9	28.1[12] 26.7[12] 27.2[12]	9.2 9.4 9.8	55.2[13,14] 56.5[13,14] 55.6[13,14]
China, Macao SAR Chine, Macao RAS	2008 2009 2010	115 263 113 678 155 663	... ...	3.2 2.8 3.4	2.0 1.5 2.2	13.8 8.3 12.5	11.8 13.9 11.8	3.4 3.7 3.7	67.7 71.3 68.6
Colombia Colombie	2008 2009 2010	439 561 000 467 731 000 502 101 362	7.5 7.3 7.1	28.0 27.2 28.3	15.2 15.1 15.2	7.6 8.4 8.1	12.7 12.5 12.7	7.2 7.1 6.9	36.9 37.5 36.9
Comoros Comores	2008 2009 2010	186 495 198 325 210 187	48.3 48.2 48.2	5.6 5.7 5.7	4.1 4.1 4.1	4.8 4.8 4.8	16.1 15.8 15.7	10.5 11.0 11.2	14.7 14.5 14.4
Congo Congo	2008 2009 2010	4 475 900 3 783 379 5 233 659	4.3 5.3 4.2	72.4 64.2 71.6	4.1 5.3 4.1	3.1 4.2 3.4	6.0 8.0 6.4	4.5 5.9 4.7	9.7 12.4 9.7
Cook Islands Iles Cook	2008 2009 2010	345[1,6] 348[1,6] 360[1,6]	4.9 4.8 5.1	5.6 5.7 5.5	3.4[3] 3.6[3] 3.5[3]	3.5 4.2 3.7	38.7 34.2 36.4	15.1 17.0 15.9	32.3 34.1 33.3
Costa Rica Costa Rica	2008 2009 2010	14 750 404 16 057 293 17 777 676	6.9 7.0 7.3	21.4 19.9 21.3	19.3 16.9 18.9	5.9 6.1 5.8	19.1 17.2 18.4	9.7 8.9 9.4	37.1 41.0 37.9
Côte d'Ivoire Côte d'Ivoire	2008 2009 2010	9 482 693 9 862 295 10 227 546	27.0 28.5 27.4	23.4 22.3 22.8	16.8 16.4 16.5	5.1 4.4 4.8	14.9 15.1 15.0	4.3 4.3 4.4	25.3 25.5 25.6
Croatia Croatie	2008 2009 2010	296 086 290 648 288 356	5.2 5.4 5.5	19.5 18.4 19.0	16.5 15.5 16.2	8.4 8.0 6.7	16.6 15.4 15.5	7.7 7.4 7.3	42.7 45.5 46.0
Cuba Cuba	2008 2009 2010	50 472 51 716 53 105	5.0 5.1 5.0	14.2 13.9 14.0	10.9 10.7 10.6	6.5 6.5 6.5	15.4 14.8 15.7	9.4 9.5 9.4	49.6 50.3 49.5
Cyprus Chypre	2008 2009 2010	15 157 15 145 15 618	2.3 2.4 2.4	9.3 9.5 9.3	6.9 6.7 6.4	13.2 10.4 9.5	19.1 18.1 18.2	9.0 9.3 9.2	47.0 50.5 51.3
Czech Republic République tchèque	2008 2009 2010	3 321 373 3 257 952 3 296 126	2.5 2.3 2.4	31.0 30.3 30.5	24.7 23.6 24.5	6.6 7.4 7.2	14.7 14.0 14.0	10.5 10.1 10.1	34.6 35.9 35.9
Dem. P. R. Korea R. p. dém. de Corée	2008 2009 2010	1 855 669 1 671 213 1 677 661	21.6 20.9 21.2	38.0 38.9 37.6	22.5 22.1 21.5	8.3 8.0 8.4	... ...	... ...	32.2 32.1 32.8
Dem. Rep. of the Congo Rép. dém. du Congo	2008 2009 2010	6 546 363 9 048 293 11 802 959	40.2 42.9 41.7	22.5 19.2 21.2	5.5 5.5 5.6	5.5 4.8 5.3	17.9 18.4 17.8	4.5 4.8 4.6	9.4 9.9 9.4
Denmark Danemark	2008 2009 2010	1 486 431 1 423 387 1 498 381	1.0 0.9 1.2	20.3 17.6 17.8	14.3 13.2 12.3	5.4 4.9 4.3	13.4 12.2 13.0	7.9 7.1 7.7	52.0 57.3 56.0
Djibouti Djibouti	2008 2009 2010	134 433 157 341 168 477	4.1 3.9 3.9	8.4 7.8 7.6	2.6 2.3 2.4	9.5 11.9 12.1	19.3 18.7 18.7	26.8 27.8 28.4	31.9 29.9 29.4
Dominica Dominique	2008 2009 2010	1 062[1] 1 106[1] 1 094	13.5 13.2 13.0	9.8 8.3 9.7	3.6 2.6 3.4	5.9 5.1 5.3	15.2 15.5 14.8	13.6 16.8 14.9	42.1 41.1 42.4
Dominican Republic Rép. dominicaine	2008 2009 2010	1 509 373[1] 1 604 447[1] 1 813 083[1]	6.1 6.0 6.0	25.1 26.0 25.6	22.4 23.7 23.3	6.1 5.3 5.4	20.4 18.8 19.2	11.8 10.9 11.3	30.5 32.9 32.6

Country or area Pays ou zone	Year Année	Value added, gross (mil. nat. cur) Valeur ajoutée, brute (mil. mon. nat.)	% of Value added - % de la valeur ajoutée						
			Agriculture, hunting, forestry and fishing Agriculture, chasse, sylviculture et pêche	Mining, manufacturing and utilities Activités extractives, Activités de fabrication, électricité, gaz et eau	Manu-facturing Activités de fabri-cation	Construc-tion Construc-tion	Wholesale, retail, trade, restaurants and hotels Commerce, restaurants et hôtels	Transport, storage & communication Transports, entrepôts et commu-nications	Other activities Autres activités
Ecuador	2008	53 394[1]	6.5	31.7	11.7	10.0	12.8	10.1	29.0
Equateur	2009	50 271[1]	7.0	25.4	11.8	10.9	13.9	10.8	32.0
	2010	57 666[1]	6.8	29.0	11.7	10.1	13.3	10.3	30.5
Egypt	2008	855 366[2]	13.2	33.6	16.3	4.3	14.7	10.8	23.4
Egypte	2009	994 152[2]	13.6	33.1	16.6	4.4	14.9	10.2	23.8
	2010	1 150 620[2]	14.0	33.0	16.9	4.6	15.1	9.6	23.8
El Salvador	2008	20 425[1]	12.1	23.0	20.7	4.0	21.3	8.9	30.8
El Salvador	2009	19 894[1]	11.9	22.1	19.7	4.0	20.8	8.3	32.8
	2010	20 438[1]	12.2	22.2	19.8	3.8	20.8	8.3	32.8
Equatorial Guinea	2008	7 397 595	1.5	95.0	0.3	1.5	0.5	0.1	1.5
Guinée équatoriale	2009	4 605 600	2.7	89.1	0.4	4.2	1.1	0.2	2.9
	2010	5 998 692	2.0	92.8	0.3	2.4	0.7	0.1	2.0
Eritrea	2008	20 603	14.4	7.3	5.6	15.0	20.5	13.1	29.6
Erythrée	2009	28 006	14.4	7.3	5.6	15.0	20.5	13.2	29.7
	2010	33 516	17.7	7.1	5.6	14.1	19.8	12.7	28.6
Estonia	2008	227 075	3.0	19.8	15.4	9.9	14.9	12.5	39.9
Estonie	2009	186 934	2.8	19.8	14.3	7.0	13.3	13.1	44.1
	2010	195 522	3.3	22.8	16.4	5.7	13.0	13.5	41.7
Ethiopia	2008	233 175[1]	50.2	5.9	4.0	5.2	15.8	4.0	18.9
Ethiopie	2009	318 785[1]	50.4	5.3	3.7	5.0	17.8	4.0	17.5
	2010	357 795[1]	46.3	6.0	4.0	4.4	18.6	4.5	20.3
Fiji	2008	4 859[2]	14.3	15.6	14.4	3.0	17.3	14.4	35.4
Fidji	2009	4 763[2]	13.4	16.5	15.2	3.2	17.4	15.2	34.3
	2010	4 798[2]	12.6	18.3	16.7	3.4	18.0	15.0	32.7
Finland	2008	161 504	2.9	25.0	22.4	7.3	11.8	7.9	45.2
Finlande	2009	148 770	2.7	21.2	18.2	7.0	11.5	8.0	49.6
	2010	156 944	2.9	22.4	18.8	6.6	11.8	8.1	48.3
France	2008	1 735 078	2.0	13.6	11.9	6.7	12.5	6.4	58.8
France	2009	1 704 550	1.7	12.4	10.6	6.4	12.4	6.6	60.4
	2010	1 737 990	2.0	13.4	11.7	6.5	12.4	6.4	59.3
French Polynesia	2008	538 291	2.4	9.0	7.0[15]	5.2	23.6	7.4	52.4
Polynésie française	2009	552 553	2.4	8.9	6.9[15]	5.2	23.6	7.4	52.5
	2010	567 655	2.5	9.0	7.0[15]	5.2	23.5	7.4	52.4
Gabon	2008	7 265 200	2.8	65.6	5.0	3.6	13.0	4.2	10.9
Gabon	2009	6 847 200	3.1	60.9	5.0	4.5	14.2	4.7	12.6
	2010	8 602 221	2.6	67.9	3.7	3.2	11.8	3.9	10.6
Gambia	2008	20 300[1]	26.7	8.6	6.1	4.2	30.6	11.5	18.5
Gambie	2009	22 728[1]	30.1	7.7	5.3	4.0	26.9	11.2	20.2
	2010	25 134[1]	32.1	7.3	4.9	4.0	24.2	11.9	20.5
Georgia	2008	16 745[1]	9.3	15.3	11.9	6.3	18.4	10.8	40.0
Géorgie	2009	15 771[1]	9.2	15.2	11.3	6.4	17.1	11.1	41.1
	2010	18 296[1]	8.3	16.7	12.7	6.2	18.8	11.5	38.5
Germany	2008	2 224 800	0.9	25.6	22.7	4.0	12.0	5.8	51.6
Allemagne	2009	2 140 610	0.8	22.2	19.1	4.3	11.8	5.7	55.3
	2010	2 239 550	0.9	23.8	20.7	4.1	11.6	5.6	54.0
Ghana	2008	28 664	31.0	11.7	7.9	8.7	12.0	13.6	23.1
Ghana	2009	35 663	31.8	10.2	7.0	8.8	12.1	12.4	24.8
	2010	43 133	29.9	10.0	6.8	8.6	12.3	12.5	26.6
Greece	2008	209 662	3.1	13.1	10.0	5.1	23.4	11.1	44.3
Grèce	2009	210 605	3.1	13.3	10.3	4.5	23.6	9.5	46.0
	2010	203 199	3.3	13.8	10.8	4.1	23.1	10.2	45.6
Greenland	2008	11 228	5.9	12.8	9.9	8.5	10.8	6.1	55.8
Groenland	2009	10 688	6.0	13.0	10.0	8.3	10.7	6.3	55.7
	2010	11 239	5.9	13.0	10.0	8.4	10.8	6.2	55.8
Grenada	2008	1 956[1]	4.2	8.9	3.8	11.0	12.5	13.6	49.8
Grenade	2009	1 809[1]	5.2	8.5	3.8	6.2	11.6	14.8	53.6
	2010	1 816[1]	5.3	9.3	4.5	4.6	10.8	14.0	56.0
Guatemala	2008	283 783[1]	11.6	23.5	19.3	5.4	21.7	7.8	30.0
Guatemala	2009	297 478[1]	12.1	23.3	19.3	4.8	21.3	7.9	30.7
	2010	320 404[1]	11.9	23.4	19.3	5.2	21.3	7.7	30.5

Value added by industries at current prices *(continued)*
Percentage distribution
Valeur ajoutée par branche d'activité aux prix courants *(suite)*
Répartition en pourcentage

Country or area Pays ou zone	Year Année	Value added, gross (mil. nat. cur) Valeur ajoutée, brute (mil. mon. nat.)	% of Value added - % de la valeur ajoutée						
			Agriculture, hunting, forestry and fishing Agriculture, chasse, sylviculture et pêche	Mining, manufactu- ring and utilities Activités extractives, Activités de fabrication, électricité, gaz et eau	Manu- facturing Activités de fabri- cation	Construc- tion Construc- tion	Wholesale, retail, trade, restaurants and hotels Commerce, restaurants et hôtels	Transport, storage & commu- nication Transports, entrepôts et commu- nications	Other activities Autres activités
Guinea	2008	19 006 160	25.0	31.5	6.8	10.9	17.1	5.6	10.0
Guinée	2009	20 222 916	25.9	28.9	7.4	11.4	17.7	5.9	10.2
	2010	24 446 528	22.5	33.5	7.0	11.0	17.1	5.7	10.3
Guinea-Bissau	2008	365 418[1]	47.5	12.6	12.1	1.0	19.6	4.9	14.5
Guinée-Bissau	2009	383 111[1]	43.2	12.4	11.9	1.0	22.8	5.2	15.5
	2010	381 058[1]	45.3	12.9	12.5	0.4	22.0	6.0	13.5
Guyana	2008	360 732[1]	21.7	23.8	8.0	9.7	11.8	10.5	22.5
Guyana	2009	372 648[1]	19.9	23.3	7.4	9.8	13.6	10.8	22.7
	2010	409 569[1]	17.4	24.0	6.6	10.2	14.6	10.9	22.9
Haiti	2008	230 616	19.8	10.3	9.7	22.5	20.0	12.1	15.3
Haïti	2009	245 382	20.3	10.5	9.8	22.6	19.7	12.0	14.9
	2010	250 926	20.9	9.4	8.6	24.2	18.7	12.0	14.8
Honduras	2008	256 486[1]	12.4	20.1	18.2	6.4	17.8	7.0	36.2
Honduras	2009	262 786[1]	11.2	19.2	17.2	6.1	16.9	7.2	39.4
	2010	285 295[1]	11.8	19.5	17.4	5.5	16.9	7.2	39.1
Hungary	2008	22 829 176	4.3	24.9	21.7	4.4	13.1	8.2	45.2
Hongrie	2009	21 264 020	3.4	25.2	22.2	4.6	13.5	8.4	44.9
	2010	22 202 696	3.6	27.1	23.7	4.1	13.0	8.1	44.2
Iceland[2]	2008	1 279 132	6.3	18.0	13.1	9.2	11.2	6.3	49.1
Islande[2]	2009	1 313 737	7.2	20.2	15.2	5.0	11.7	6.8	49.1
	2010	1 317 800	6.4	17.5	13.0	8.5	11.7	6.7	49.1
India	2008	53 661 441	17.5	19.9	15.6	8.5	16.8	7.8	29.6
Inde	2009	62 287 740	17.6	19.1	14.9	8.1	16.2	7.8	31.3
	2010	73 069 905	19.0	18.2	14.2	8.1	16.3	7.3	31.1
Indonesia	2008	4 948 687 600[16]	14.5	39.6	27.8	8.5	14.0	6.3	17.2
Indonésie	2009	5 603 865 900[16]	15.3	37.8	26.4	9.9	13.3	6.3	17.5
	2010	6 422 919 200[16]	15.3	36.8	24.8	10.3	13.7	6.5	17.4
Iran (Islamic Rep. of)	2008	3 473 497 965	9.8	38.9	11.3	4.1	11.1	8.1	28.0
Iran (Rép. islamique d')	2009	3 509 947 682	9.4	39.5	11.2	4.0	10.9	8.2	27.9
	2010	4 012 740 128	9.2	40.0	11.2	4.0	10.8	8.2	27.8
Iraq	2008	158 443 584[1]	3.8	58.1	1.7	4.2	5.3	5.4	23.3
Iraq	2009	140 159 107[1]	4.4	44.0	2.4	5.0	8.2	10.1	28.2
	2010	173 046 330[1]	5.0	46.4	2.3	3.5	8.6	11.2	25.3
Ireland	2008	159 244	2.3	23.2	21.3	7.2	10.8	4.3	52.2
Irlande	2009	143 590	2.1	25.1	23.1	4.3	10.8	4.3	53.4
	2010	140 568	2.5	27.8	25.5	3.1	10.6	4.2	51.8
Israel	2008	666 398[1]	1.9	16.7	15.1[3]	5.0	10.9	6.9	58.7
Israël	2009	702 721[1]	2.1	16.5	14.6[3]	4.9	9.9	6.9	59.8
	2010	746 919[1]	1.9	16.8	15.1[3]	4.9	10.5	7.0	58.9
Italy	2008	1 408 984	2.0	20.9	18.2	6.1	14.9	7.3	48.8
Italie	2009	1 367 681	1.9	19.0	16.4	6.2	15.0	7.3	50.6
	2010	1 386 942	1.9	19.4	16.8	6.0	14.9	7.3	50.6
Jamaica	2008	923 577[1]	5.2	14.5	8.6	8.1	23.7	10.6	37.9
Jamaïque	2009	997 707[1]	5.9	13.4	8.7	7.7	23.4	10.1	39.6
	2010	1 063 721[1]	5.8	13.6	8.4	7.7	23.8	9.8	39.4
Japan	2008	517 094 900[1]	1.4	21.7	19.9	5.8	13.4[12,17]	6.6	51.1[14,18]
Japon	2009	480 925 000[1]	1.4	20.0	17.6	6.1	12.7[12,17]	6.2	53.7[14,18]
	2010	491 205 130[1]	1.4	21.4	19.4	5.9	13.1[12,17]	6.4	51.8[14,18]
Jordan	2008	15 235[1]	2.5	25.9	18.7	4.6	10.4	12.1	44.5
Jordanie	2009	16 733[1]	2.8	24.9	18.7	5.2	9.7	13.0	44.6
	2010	18 354[1]	2.6	24.8	18.8	4.8	10.3	12.8	44.7
Kazakhstan	2008	15 679 033[1]	5.4	32.9	12.1	8.3	13.4	11.3	28.7
Kazakhstan	2009	16 765 046[1]	6.2	31.0	11.0	8.0	13.2	11.2	30.4
	2010	20 954 294[1]	4.5	33.9	11.8	8.0	14.4	11.5	27.7
Kenya	2008	1 877 087[1]	25.6	15.3	12.2	4.3	12.7	11.5	30.7
Kenya	2009	2 108 235[1]	26.8	14.3	11.1	4.6	12.9	11.1	30.3
	2010	2 252 788[1]	25.0	14.8	11.3	4.9	13.5	11.1	30.8
Kiribati	2008	158[1]	26.1	6.7	5.5	2.0	5.9	10.9	48.5
Kiribati	2009	157[1]	25.1	6.2	5.1	2.2	5.1	11.7	49.6
	2010	147[1]	26.3	6.4	5.4	2.2	6.7	12.4	46.0

Country or area Pays ou zone	Year Année	Value added, gross (mil. nat. cur) Valeur ajoutée, brute (mil. mon. nat.)	% of Value added - % de la valeur ajoutée						
			Agriculture, hunting, forestry and fishing Agriculture, chasse, sylviculture et pêche	Mining, manufactu- ring and utilities Activités extractives, Activités de fabrication, électricité, gaz et eau	Manu- facturing Activités de fabri- cation	Construc- tion Construc- tion	Wholesale, retail, trade, restaurants and hotels Commerce, restaurants et hôtels	Transport, storage & commu- nication Transports, entrepôts et commu- nications	Other activities Autres activités
Kosovo	2008	3 278	13.7	15.4	14.6[19]	10.7	12.6	4.8	42.9
Kosovo	2009	3 313	13.9	15.2	14.4[19]	11.0	12.5	4.8	42.5
	2010	3 557	14.1	15.0	14.2[19]	11.2	12.5	4.7	42.6
Kuwait	2008	41 185[1]	0.2	62.3	4.3	1.6	3.4	6.4	26.1
Koweït	2009	32 003[1]	0.2	53.3	4.9	1.8	4.4	8.6	31.7
	2010	37 146[1]	0.2	55.8	5.1	1.6	4.7	8.4	29.3
Kyrgyzstan	2008	168 672[1]	26.2	16.9	14.7	5.9	19.7	8.8	22.6
Kirghizistan	2009	185 717[1]	20.3	18.4	15.4	7.3	19.7	9.5	24.9
	2010	197 140[1]	20.0	20.8	17.2	6.1	18.7	9.8	24.6
Lao People's Dem. Rep.	2008	44 086 007[1]	31.5	22.2	9.1	5.0	20.5	4.8	16.1
Rép. dém. pop. lao	2009	45 899 549[1]	31.6	20.5	10.5	4.9	21.1	5.0	16.9
	2010	51 394 720[1]	32.0	21.7	9.5	5.1	20.6	4.8	15.9
Latvia	2008	14 432	3.0	15.1	10.8	10.1	18.8	12.2	40.7
Lettonie	2009	11 795	3.8	15.8	10.9	8.0	16.9	15.4	40.2
	2010	11 421	4.5	18.7	13.4	5.9	18.2	16.1	36.6
Lebanon	2008	45 123 000	5.6	4.8	8.8[3]	13.0	26.6[20]	7.2	42.8
Liban	2009	45 544 270	5.2	6.6	8.8[3]	10.7	24.3[20]	8.1	45.2
	2010	56 699 596	5.7	6.2	8.8[3]	11.7	24.5[20]	7.8	44.2
Lesotho	2008	12 595[1]	7.6	31.9	18.7	4.2	8.9	5.9	41.5
Lesotho	2009	13 806[1]	8.2	26.6	15.6	4.6	8.0	6.0	46.6
	2010	14 726[1]	8.0	29.6	18.6	4.5	8.7	6.2	43.0
Liberia	2008	723	70.7	8.5	7.1	3.2	6.2	6.7	4.7
Libéria	2009	801	72.0	8.1	6.7	3.1	6.0	6.4	4.5
	2010	841	72.0	8.1	6.7	3.1	6.0	6.4	4.5
Libyan Arab Jamah.	2008	116 409[1]	1.9	74.9	4.2	4.8	3.2	3.3	11.9
Jamah. arabe libyenne	2009	91 398[1]	2.6	64.7	6.0	7.7	4.5	4.5	16.0
	2010	107 087[1]	2.2	70.2	4.9	5.7	3.8	3.9	14.2
Liechtenstein	2008	5 839[1]	1.3	22.2	20.1	5.4	15.9	6.2	49.0
Liechtenstein	2009	5 453[1]	1.2	20.8	18.6	5.6	15.7	6.2	50.6
	2010	5 626[1]	1.1	21.5	19.2	5.7	15.8	6.3	49.7
Lithuania	2008	99 905	3.7	21.6	18.1	10.0	18.4	12.2	34.1
Lituanie	2009	82 428	3.4	20.5	16.4	6.4	18.3	13.8	37.6
	2010	84 898	3.4	22.3	18.2	5.7	18.3	15.2	35.2
Luxembourg	2008	35 681	0.3	8.8	7.8	5.4	11.5	9.4	64.5
Luxembourg	2009	33 806	0.3	6.7	5.5	5.8	11.0	8.8	67.6
	2010	36 561	0.3	7.3	6.1	5.5	10.7	8.6	67.7
Madagascar	2008	14 637 942[1]	24.5	16.0	14.6	4.8	10.3	21.2	23.2
Madagascar	2009	15 592 403[1]	28.8	15.8	14.4	4.2	11.0	19.6	20.6
	2010	17 040 432[1]	27.6	15.8	14.3	3.8	10.9	20.7	21.3
Malawi	2008	590 149[1]	29.7	13.1	10.5	3.4	20.1	6.6	27.1
Malawi	2009	678 632[1]	30.1	13.2	10.6	3.4	20.7	6.6	26.1
	2010	786 153[1]	29.9	13.3	10.6	3.3	21.0	6.6	26.0
Malaysia	2008	754 528[1]	10.0	44.4	25.8	2.7	13.4	6.1	23.3
Malaisie	2009	693 709[1]	9.3	39.7	25.0	3.2	14.5	6.7	26.5
	2010	780 047[1]	10.4	40.4	25.6	3.2	14.2	6.5	25.2
Maldives	2008	14 965[1]	5.2	7.4	5.6	9.5	38.2	9.9	29.8
Maldives	2009	16 778[1]	5.4	7.1	5.3	5.1	38.2	9.4	34.8
	2010	17 694[1]	5.0	6.8	5.0	5.4	39.9	9.2	33.8
Mali	2008	3 559 429[1]	39.7	14.7	5.8	5.4	15.7	6.2	18.3
Mali	2009	3 824 962[1]	38.9	15.3	5.7	5.7	16.0	6.1	18.1
	2010	4 094 243[1]	40.1	14.1	5.6	5.8	16.1	6.0	17.9
Malta	2008	5 176	1.8	17.1	15.6	4.2	16.5	9.9	50.4
Malte	2009	5 092	2.1	15.8	13.3	3.9	15.2	9.2	54.0
	2010	5 431	1.9	15.8	13.4	3.5	15.0	8.6	55.2
Marshall Islands	2008	160[1,2]	10.0	7.9	4.4	11.3	17.5	5.3	47.9
Iles Marshall	2009	158[1,2]	10.0	7.9	4.4	11.3	17.5	5.3	47.9
	2010	160[1,2]	10.0	7.9	4.4	11.3	17.5	5.3	47.9
Mauritania	2008	833 498[1]	21.5	34.6	6.6	6.4	10.0	5.9	21.6
Mauritanie	2009	767 030[1]	24.1	28.0	7.2	6.1	10.5	6.9	24.4
	2010	1 008 243[1]	23.6	31.4	6.7	6.5	9.6	6.3	22.6

Value added by industries at current prices *(continued)*
Percentage distribution

Valeur ajoutée par branche d'activité aux prix courants *(suite)*
Répartition en pourcentage

				% of Value added - % de la valeur ajoutée					
Country or area Pays ou zone	Year Année	Value added, gross (mil. nat. cur) Valeur ajoutée, brute (mil. mon. nat.)	Agriculture, hunting, forestry and fishing Agriculture, chasse, sylviculture et pêche	Mining, manufacturing and utilities Activités extractives, Activités de fabrication, électricité, gaz et eau	Manu-facturing Activités de fabri-cation	Construc-tion Construc-tion	Wholesale, retail, trade, restaurants and hotels Commerce, restaurants et hôtels	Transport, storage & commu-nication Transports, entrepôts et commu-nications	Other activities Autres activités
Mauritius Maurice	2008 2009 2010	243 115 252 590 266 526	4.1 3.9 3.6	21.3 21.5 20.7	19.4 19.2 18.5	6.8 6.9 6.9	19.8 18.0 18.5	9.8 9.6 9.6	38.2 40.1 40.7
Mexico Mexique	2008 2009 2010	12 082 396[1] 11 598 471[1] 12 766 027[1]	3.4 3.6 3.6	29.4 26.7 27.5	18.0[21] 17.7[21] 17.7[21]	7.2 7.1 6.6	18.5 18.5 19.7	9.0 9.0 9.1	32.6 35.1 33.6
Micronesia (Fed. States of) Micronésie (Etats féd. de)	2008 2009 2010	249[1] 262[1] 277[1]	27.4 26.3 26.0	1.0 2.4 2.0	0.5 0.5 0.5	3.0 5.0 6.0	17.1 15.5 15.4	6.4 6.5 6.6	45.0 44.4 44.1
Monaco Monaco	2008 2009 2010	4 493 4 003 4 095	... ...	4.8[22] 4.8[22] 5.1[22]	4.8[23] 4.8[23] 5.1[23]	... ...	39.2 39.6 39.8	5.3 5.7 5.4	50.8 49.9 49.7
Mongolia Mongolie	2008 2009 2010	5 882 752 5 998 869 7 410 889	21.4 19.6 16.2	31.5 30.9 36.1	7.5 7.2 7.3	2.1 1.4 1.5	8.7 8.0 10.0	10.2 12.0 12.0	26.1 28.2 24.2
Montenegro Monténégro	2008 2009 2010	2 477 2 473 2 511	9.3 10.0 9.5	13.5 13.6 13.5	6.7 5.9 6.5	7.7 6.5 7.2	20.8 20.6 21.2	11.7 11.5 11.5	37.1 37.9 37.2
Montserrat Montserrat	2008 2009 2010	130 137 142	1.2 1.6 1.2	7.9 8.1 8.1	0.7 0.7 0.7	8.0 9.5 9.1	5.5 5.1 5.2	10.2 9.6 10.4	67.1 66.2 66.1
Morocco Maroc	2008 2009 2010	652 957[1] 688 767[1] 720 323[1]	13.9 15.6 14.2	22.9 20.5 20.9	13.5 15.3 14.4	5.9 6.7 6.3	13.3 12.9 13.4	6.9 7.0 7.1	37.1 37.5 38.1
Mozambique Mozambique	2008 2009 2010	225 665[1] 248 725[1] 304 006[1]	28.5 28.8 28.1	20.8 19.9 21.0	14.9 13.9 14.6	3.0 3.0 3.0	16.5 16.7 16.5	9.8 10.0 9.9	21.3 21.5 21.5
Myanmar Myanmar	2008 2009 2010	29 227 535 33 760 900 40 331 469	40.3 38.2 36.4	18.4 19.9 21.3	16.8 18.2 19.6	4.2 4.5 4.6	21.1 20.4 19.9	12.8 13.5 13.8	3.2 3.5 4.0
Namibia Namibie	2008 2009 2010	69 259[1] 72 287[1] 79 922[1]	9.2 9.3 9.9	33.0 27.9 29.7	13.6 14.5 14.7	4.4 4.0 3.8	12.9 14.0 13.6	4.9 5.1 5.3	35.6 39.7 37.8
Nauru[6] Nauru[6]	2008 2009 2010	50 70 69	5.3 4.1 6.2	33.6 47.7 31.5	14.3 24.9 13.3	4.4 3.4 4.1	17.6 13.1 20.2	12.3 9.2 6.8	26.8 22.5 31.2
Nepal Népal	2008 2009 2010	779 443[1] 938 672[1] 1 096 037[1]	31.7 33.0 35.0	9.9 9.1 8.5	7.3 7.0 6.4	7.0 6.8 6.5	15.0 14.7 14.9	9.9 9.9 8.7	26.7 26.6 26.5
Netherlands Pays-Bas	2008 2009 2010	529 319 509 619 529 139	1.8 1.7 2.0	19.8 17.9 18.4	13.7 12.6 13.2	5.8 6.0 5.3	14.5 13.8 14.0	6.7 6.5 6.5	51.5 54.1 53.8
Netherlands Antilles Antilles néerlandaises	2008 2009 2010	6 511[1] 6 559[1] 6 735[1]	0.7[3] 0.7[3] 0.7[3]	9.8[4] 10.0[4] 9.9[4]	6.7 6.4 6.3	6.1 5.7 5.8	19.6 18.0 18.1	11.2 10.3 10.3	52.7 55.3 55.2
New Caledonia Nouvelle-Calédonie	2008 2009 2010	682 287[1] 690 341[1] 735 115[1]	1.7 1.7 1.6	15.9 13.2 18.1	14.1[3] 11.3[3] 16.3[3]	12.3 12.5 11.3	13.0[17] 13.0[17] 12.5[17]	6.9 7.3 7.0	50.3[18] 52.5[18] 49.6[18]
New Zealand Nouvelle-Zélande	2008 2009 2010	178 818[1,6] 180 734[1,6] 189 896[1,6]	5.4 5.5 5.5	18.7 18.6 18.6	14.7 14.6 14.7	5.4 5.4 5.4	14.7 14.6 14.7	7.1 7.1 7.1	48.8 48.9 48.7
Nicaragua Nicaragua	2008 2009 2010	115 587 119 046 129 299	19.0 18.7 20.3	21.7 22.2 23.7	17.5 18.1 18.8	5.8 5.3 4.6	14.4 14.5 14.6	5.7 5.7 5.6	33.5 33.7 31.2
Niger Niger	2008 2009 2010	2 272 384[1] 2 345 181[1] 2 570 313[1]	46.0 42.6 44.2	12.6 13.3 13.4	5.2 5.5 5.2	2.6 2.7 2.6	14.2 14.9 14.1	6.5 6.8 6.6	18.1 19.8 19.0
Nigeria Nigéria	2008 2009 2010	24 296 329 24 794 240 29 205 783	31.4 35.4 35.2	38.6 31.5 36.0	2.3 2.4 2.2	1.3 1.4 1.4	14.1 16.1 16.4	6.9 7.0 2.7	7.7 8.6 8.4

Value added by industries at current prices *(continued)*
Percentage distribution

Valeur ajoutée par branche d'activité aux prix courants *(suite)*
Répartition en pourcentage

			% of Value added - % de la valeur ajoutée						
Country or area Pays ou zone	Year Année	Value added, gross (mil. nat. cur) Valeur ajoutée, brute (mil. mon. nat.)	Agriculture, hunting, forestry and fishing Agriculture, chasse, sylviculture et pêche	Mining, manufacturing and utilities Activités extractives, Activités de fabrication, électricité, gaz et eau	Manu-facturing Activités de fabri-cation	Construc-tion Construc-tion	Wholesale, retail, trade, restaurants and hotels Commerce, restaurants et hôtels	Transport, storage & communication Transports, entrepôts et commu-nications	Other activities Autres activités
Norway Norvège	2008 2009 2010	2 259 795 2 075 422 2 221 590	1.2 1.3 1.6	40.5 34.1 35.7	9.1 9.9 9.3	4.9 4.9 4.9	9.3 9.5 8.8	6.6 7.1 6.5	37.5 43.1 42.5
Occupied Palestinian Terr. Terr. palestinien occupé	2008 2009 2010	5 307[1] 5 648[1] 6 224[1]	6.7 6.6 6.6	16.6 16.6 18.0	12.4 11.9 13.9	4.5 4.7 6.4	17.8 19.3 16.0	10.9 11.0 8.8	43.6 41.9 44.2
Oman Oman	2008 2009 2010	23 509[1] 18 420[1] 22 618[1]	1.0 1.4 1.2	61.7 51.4 56.8	10.5 10.1 9.7	4.8 6.4 5.3	9.5 10.4 9.4	5.0 5.9 5.3	18.0 24.6 22.0
Pakistan Pakistan	2008 2009 2010	9 921 584[2] 12 110 462[2] 14 066 515[2]	20.3 21.6 21.2	24.2 22.3 22.9	19.7 17.1 17.7	2.6 2.4 2.5	18.4 17.4 17.5	11.7 13.1 13.1	22.8 23.2 22.7
Palau Palaos	2008 2009 2010	181[1] 200[1] 218[1]	3.2 3.2 3.2	3.8 3.7 3.7	0.3 0.4 0.4	20.3 16.7 17.2	34.4 32.5 33.0	7.6 8.4 8.4	30.7 35.5 34.5
Panama Panama	2008 2009 2010	22 163[1] 23 115[1] 25 694[1]	5.3 5.8 5.6	10.3 10.8 10.5	6.4 6.5 6.4	6.7 6.3 6.2	18.4 17.9 18.2	19.2 18.1 18.4	40.1 41.0 41.0
Papua New Guinea Papouasie-Nvl-Guinée	2008 2009 2010	21 102[1] 20 260[1] 25 261[1]	32.8 35.6 31.9	35.8 32.1 31.0	5.9 6.6 5.9	10.6 14.0 13.7	6.6 0.8 7.4	2.1 3.0 3.0	12.2 14.5 13.0
Paraguay Paraguay	2008 2009 2010	66 698 676 63 786 077 76 803 793	26.1 21.4 23.9	15.6 16.3 16.0	13.9 14.4 14.1	6.7 7.3 6.6	21.9 21.2 21.9	7.8 8.1 8.2	22.0 25.8 23.4
Peru Pérou	2008 2009 2010	344 638 362 646 407 772	7.2 7.3 7.2	29.2 26.7 28.7	15.9 14.0 15.3	7.0 7.5 7.0	18.0 18.5 18.0	9.4 9.6 9.4	29.2 30.5 29.7
Philippines[6] Philippines[6]	2008 2009 2010	7 720 903 8 026 143 9 003 480	13.2 13.1 12.3	27.5 26.0 26.5	22.8 21.3 21.4	5.4 5.7 6.1	17.1 16.9 17.4	7.1 7.0 6.5	29.7 31.3 31.2
Poland Pologne	2008 2009 2010	1 116 476 1 193 691 1 246 427	3.7 3.7 3.5	24.3 24.3 24.6	18.6 18.5 18.5	7.3 7.5 7.1	19.1 19.8 20.1	7.1 7.2 7.4	38.5 37.6 37.3
Portugal Portugal	2008 2009 2010	149 311 148 294 151 385	2.4 2.4 2.4	17.3 16.8 17.0	13.7 12.8 13.0	7.3 6.5 6.5	18.2 18.2 18.6	8.6 8.2 8.1	46.2 47.9 47.5
Puerto Rico[6] Porto Rico[6]	2008 2009 2010	96 566 97 448 100 368	0.6 0.7 0.7	45.8 46.0 45.4	43.6 43.8 43.1	1.7 1.5 1.7	12.6 12.7 12.7	4.1 4.1 4.2	35.2 35.0 35.4
Qatar Qatar	2008 2009 2010	426 191[1] 363 024[1] 470 426[1]	0.1 0.1 0.1	65.1 53.7 61.9	10.5 9.3 10.5	6.4 7.0 5.1	5.5 8.2 6.9	3.5 4.5 3.9	19.5 26.5 22.1
Republic of Korea République de Corée	2008 2009 2010	919 688 000 960 361 604 1 057 801 371	2.7 2.8 2.6	29.5 30.0 32.8	27.9 27.8 30.5	7.0 6.9 6.5	12.5 12.0 11.8	7.3 7.3 7.1	41.1 41.1 39.2
Republic of Moldova République de Moldova	2008 2009 2010	53 083[1] 51 794[1] 61 383[1]	10.4 9.9 14.0	16.5 15.5 15.5	13.4 12.3 12.4	5.9 4.1 3.8	16.9 16.9 16.6	14.3 14.0 13.4	36.0 39.6 36.8
Romania Roumanie	2008 2009 2010	458 536 447 847 455 924	7.4 7.1 6.7	25.8 27.2 29.7	22.4 23.4 25.6	11.9 11.0 10.0	13.8 13.5 13.7	11.2 10.5 10.1	29.8 30.7 29.8
Russian Federation Fédération de Russie	2008 2009 2010	35 182 698 33 804 091 38 682 285	4.4 4.7 4.0	29.8 27.5 31.0	17.5 14.5 16.4	6.3 6.2 5.7	21.3 19.2 19.2	9.3 9.6 9.7	28.9 32.9 30.3
Rwanda Rwanda	2008 2009 2010	2 412 997[1] 2 805 567[1] 3 082 217[1]	34.6 36.1 34.3	7.8 7.6 8.0	6.6 6.8 7.1	8.0 7.8 8.0	17.1 15.9 16.2	8.1 8.0 8.3	24.3 24.7 25.2
Saint Kitts and Nevis Saint-Kitts-et-Nevis	2008 2009 2010	1 392[1] 1 336[1] 1 351[1]	2.5 2.5 2.5	10.3 10.1 10.3	7.9 7.5 7.9	13.5 10.1 12.4	19.1 18.2 18.7	15.5 15.5 15.2	39.0 43.7 41.0

Value added by industries at current prices *(continued)*
Percentage distribution

Valeur ajoutée par branche d'activité aux prix courants *(suite)*
Répartition en pourcentage

Country or area Pays ou zone	Year Année	Value added, gross (mil. nat. cur) Valeur ajoutée, brute (mil. mon. nat.)	% of Value added - % de la valeur ajoutée						
			Agriculture, hunting, forestry and fishing Agriculture, chasse, sylviculture et pêche	Mining, manufacturing and utilities Activités extractives, Activités de fabrication, électricité, gaz et eau	Manu-facturing Activités de fabri-cation	Construc-tion Construc-tion	Wholesale, retail, trade, restaurants and hotels Commerce, restaurants et hôtels	Transport, storage & commu-nication Transports, entrepôts et commu-nications	Other activities Autres activités
Saint Lucia Sainte-Lucie	2008	2 627[1]	4.4	8.8	4.6	9.1	23.3	17.6	36.8
	2009	2 570[1]	4.1	9.0	4.2	7.3	22.1	18.3	39.2
	2010	2 810[1]	3.2	8.4	3.8	7.9	25.4	17.4	37.8
Saint Vincent-Grenadines Saint Vincent-Grenadines	2008	1 602[1]	6.6	9.5	4.8	9.8	19.0	14.6	40.5
	2009	1 538[1]	7.0	10.3	5.4	9.5	16.9	14.5	41.8
	2010	1 559[1]	7.1	10.3	5.6	8.9	16.5	14.4	42.8
Samoa Samoa	2008	1 461[1]	11.5	15.8	11.2	12.4	22.6	13.4	24.3
	2009	1 452[1]	11.7	13.5	8.5	12.2	23.3	14.0	25.4
	2010	1 509[1]	9.6	14.9	9.8	12.9	23.4	13.8	25.5
San Marino Saint-Marin	2008	1 131	2.0	20.9	18.2	6.1	14.9	7.3	48.8
	2009	992	1.9	19.0	16.4	6.2	15.0	7.3	50.6
	2010	1 006	1.9	19.4	16.8	6.0	14.9	7.3	50.6
Sao Tome and Principe Sao Tomé-et-Principe	2008	2 594 676[1]	18.0	11.3	8.0	9.1	25.1	13.1	23.5
	2009	3 217 352[1]	17.1	9.4	6.7	8.3	26.4	14.1	24.7
	2010	3 753 308[1]	17.6	10.1	7.1	8.8	25.6	13.4	24.5
Saudi Arabia Arabie saoudite	2008	1 790 029[1,6]	2.3	66.3	8.3	3.8	4.5	3.0	20.2
	2009	1 403 890[1,6]	3.0	54.5	10.5	4.8	6.1	4.1	27.6
	2010	1 635 595[1,6]	2.6	57.4	10.1	4.4	5.4	3.7	26.6
Senegal Sénégal	2008	5 215 598	15.7	17.9	14.1	5.0	21.0	12.7	27.7
	2009	5 301 192	16.7	18.4	14.1	4.7	20.0	12.5	27.7
	2010	5 552 713	15.4	18.3	14.2	5.1	20.7	12.6	27.9
Serbia Serbie	2008	2 289 885[1]	10.7	21.8	16.8	5.4	13.5	8.7	39.9
	2009	2 326 513[1]	9.6	22.2	16.3	4.7	12.5	8.9	42.2
	2010	2 549 876[1]	11.7	18.4	13.9	2.9	13.3	18.7	35.1
Seychelles Seychelles	2008	7 720[1]	2.8	10.9	9.7[24]	6.3	29.3	13.7	37.0
	2009	9 531[1]	2.6	10.4	8.9[24]	6.0	31.0	12.7	37.3
	2010	9 838[1]	2.7	10.4	8.8[24]	5.4	29.7	11.9	39.9
Sierra Leone Sierra Leone	2008	6 174 965[1]	58.7	5.1	2.1	1.6	9.5	6.9	18.2
	2009	6 855 996[1]	58.2	4.0	1.8	1.3	9.7	7.5	19.4
	2010	7 681 939[1]	58.5	3.7	1.8	1.4	9.4	7.4	19.6
Singapore Singapour	2008	253 720	^0.0[25]	22.2[26]	20.7	4.5	19.9	13.9	39.5
	2009	252 753	^0.0[25]	22.9[26]	21.4	5.4	18.6	12.4	40.7
	2010	285 918	^0.0[25]	23.7[26]	22.2	4.5	18.7	12.2	40.8
Slovakia Slovaquie	2008	60 803	4.2	29.0	23.1	9.7	17.5	7.1	32.5
	2009	57 337	3.9	25.7	19.6	9.5	17.1	7.3	36.6
	2010	60 209	3.8	25.8	20.6	9.0	17.0	7.2	37.2
Slovenia Slovénie	2008	32 716	2.4	25.3	21.3	8.4	15.2	9.7	39.0
	2009	30 788	2.4	23.1	19.0	8.0	15.1	9.5	42.0
	2010	30 822	2.5	23.6	19.4	6.4	14.8	9.8	42.9
Solomon Islands Iles Salomon	2008	4 687[1]	28.9	8.4	6.0	2.2	10.2	9.0	41.3
	2009	4 785[1]	29.4	8.1	5.9	2.2	10.4	8.5	41.4
	2010	4 787[1]	28.4	8.0	5.9	2.1	10.8	8.9	41.9
Somalia Somalie	2008	32 901 701[1]	60.2	3.2	2.5	4.2	10.6	9.4	12.4
	2009	34 560 415[1]	60.2	3.2	2.5	4.2	10.6	9.4	12.5
	2010	30 035 567[1]	60.2	3.2	2.5	4.2	10.6	9.4	12.5
South Africa Afrique du Sud	2008	2 044 267	3.1	28.8	16.7	3.6	13.3	9.2	42.1
	2009	2 176 599	2.9	27.1	15.2	4.0	13.5	9.2	43.4
	2010	2 406 938	2.5	27.0	14.6	3.8	13.9	9.1	43.6
Spain Espagne	2008	996 011	2.7	17.0	14.5	11.4	17.8	6.6	44.4
	2009	979 699	2.7	15.3	12.7	10.8	17.9	6.8	46.6
	2010	972 403	2.7	15.6	13.2	10.1	18.4	6.9	46.4
Sri Lanka Sri Lanka	2008	4 067 197[2]	15.2	22.7	18.4	7.8	18.0	13.2	23.1
	2009	4 519 010[2]	14.1	22.2	18.0	8.0	17.0	13.5	25.3
	2010	5 246 943[2]	14.1	22.2	18.0	8.0	17.0	13.5	25.3
Sudan Soudan	2008	130 159[1]	31.7	25.7	7.5	4.0	14.1	11.6	12.9
	2009	143 803[1]	34.2	19.9	8.3	4.5	15.3	12.4	13.8
	2010	182 656[1]	33.4	23.1	7.8	4.2	14.8	10.8	13.7
Suriname Suriname	2008	6 714[1]	5.9	39.5	22.0	4.3	13.2	8.0	29.3
	2009	7 108[1]	5.8	39.8	22.4	4.5	13.1	7.6	29.2
	2010	8 059[1]	5.7	39.9	22.5	4.5	13.2	7.5	29.1

Country or area Pays ou zone	Year Année	Value added, gross (mil. nat. cur) Valeur ajoutée, brute (mil. mon. nat.)	Agriculture, hunting, forestry and fishing Agriculture, chasse, sylviculture et pêche	Mining, manufacturing and utilities Activités extractives, Activités de fabrication, électricité, gaz et eau	Manufacturing Activités de fabrication	Construction Construction	Wholesale, retail, trade, restaurants and hotels Commerce, restaurants et hôtels	Transport, storage & communication Transports, entrepôts et communications	Other activities Autres activités
Swaziland	2008	18 938[1]	7.7	42.5	41.3	2.9	10.7	7.2	29.0
Swaziland	2009	20 585[1]	7.7	42.6	41.4	2.6	10.2	7.0	29.9
	2010	21 945[1]	7.7	42.4	41.1	3.0	10.8	7.1	29.0
Sweden	2008	2 809 850	1.8	21.6	17.7	5.2	12.5	7.1	51.9
Suède	2009	2 691 388	1.8	19.4	15.5	5.2	12.4	7.1	54.1
	2010	2 880 732	1.9	21.1	16.4	5.5	12.5	7.1	51.9
Switzerland	2008	514 155	1.3	22.2	20.1	5.4	15.9	6.2	49.0
Suisse	2009	505 894	1.2	20.8	18.6	5.6	15.7	6.2	50.6
	2010	519 533	1.1	21.5	19.2	5.7	15.8	6.3	49.7
Syrian Arab Republic[6]	2008	2 445 061	18.7	31.2	4.1	3.1	21.1	9.3	16.7
Rép. arabe syrienne[6]	2009	2 519 152	22.6	24.0	4.5	3.0	23.1	10.0	17.3
	2010	2 762 614	20.2	28.6	4.5	3.2	20.9	9.7	17.3
Tajikistan	2008	15 645[1]	22.5	16.1	16.1[15]	11.7	22.8	11.4	15.5
Tadjikistan	2009	18 585[1]	20.6	15.9	15.9[15]	11.3	23.4	12.2	16.7
	2010	22 008[1]	21.7	17.6	17.6[15]	10.7	21.6	11.5	17.0
Thailand	2008	9 080 466[16]	11.6	41.2	34.8	2.9	19.0	7.1	18.2
Thaïlande	2009	9 041 551[16]	11.5	40.6	34.2	2.7	18.9	7.2	19.1
	2010	10 102 986[16]	12.4	42.0	35.6	2.7	17.9	6.8	18.3
TFYR of Macedonia	2008	357 448	11.6	24.1	19.8	5.7	15.7	9.3	33.7
L'ex-R.Y. Macédoine	2009	358 945	11.1	21.8	16.4	6.0	16.7	9.2	35.2
	2010	370 959	12.1	20.9	16.8	6.4	15.4	8.7	36.5
Timor-Leste	2008	562	30.8	4.7	2.7	9.3	7.1	7.9	40.3
Timor-Leste	2009	704	30.5	4.4	2.5	9.2	7.0	7.3	41.6
	2010	794	29.6	4.4	2.5	9.4	7.0	7.4	42.3
Togo	2008	1 273 860[1]	45.4	17.1	9.4	3.1[27]	10.3[28]	5.8	18.3
Togo	2009	1 341 432[1]	47.7	15.3	8.8	2.5[27]	8.7[28]	5.9	20.1
	2010	1 374 520[1]	46.6	14.5	8.4	3.7[27]	10.4[28]	5.3	19.5
Tonga	2008	566[1]	18.7	11.8	8.4	6.8	14.0	4.6	44.0
Tonga	2009	579[1]	19.3	11.3	7.9	7.0	15.2	4.4	42.8
	2010	600[1]	19.9	10.5	7.4	6.9	15.2	4.3	43.1
Trinidad and Tobago	2008	170 095[1]	0.4	54.6	23.1	8.5	12.7	4.5	19.4
Trinité-et-Tobago	2009	124 566[1]	0.6	41.9	17.9	11.0	14.7	5.6	26.2
	2010	128 457[1]	0.6	42.7	19.3	10.0	14.6	6.0	26.1
Tunisia	2008	52 080[1,2]	8.3	28.9	19.1	4.4	13.4	13.1	31.9
Tunisie	2009	54 710[1,2]	8.9	26.2	18.2	4.7	13.9	13.3	32.9
	2010	58 835[1,2]	7.9	26.9	17.7	4.8	14.1	13.2	33.2
Turkey	2008	854 585[1]	8.5	22.0	18.0	5.2	16.4	15.5	32.5
Turquie	2009	864 450[1]	9.1	21.1	16.5	4.2	15.2	14.3	36.2
	2010	985 622[1]	9.4	21.5	17.4	4.6	15.4	14.6	34.4
Turkmenistan	2008	43 020	12.3	44.6	44.6[15]	9.0	4.0	6.1	23.9
Turkménistan	2009	55 955	12.3	44.6	44.6[15]	8.9	4.0	6.1	24.0
	2010	64 990	14.6	40.3	40.3[15]	8.1	4.4	6.6	26.0
Turks and Caicos Islands	2008	903[1]	1.1	7.0	1.9	14.5	33.2	8.9	35.3
Iles Turques et Caïques	2009	1 074[1]	1.0	6.8	1.9	15.3	33.1	8.5	35.3
	2010	1 278[1]	1.0	6.8	1.9	15.4	33.1	8.5	35.2
Tuvalu	2008	33	23.2	1.9	1.2	7.4	13.9	5.7	48.0
Tuvalu	2009	34	20.6	2.2	1.0	7.5	11.3	8.0	50.3
	2010	32	21.6	2.2	0.9	7.2	12.2	7.4	49.4
Uganda	2008	26 526 184[1]	22.9	12.4	7.7	13.0	19.7	7.3	24.6
Ouganda	2009	32 050 811[1]	24.3	12.6	8.1	12.1	21.3	6.6	23.1
	2010	34 277 745[1]	23.1	12.5	7.7	12.7	20.1	6.9	24.6
Ukraine	2008	860 714[1]	7.6	28.8	19.1	3.4	16.4	10.1	33.7
Ukraine	2009	847 330[1]	7.8	25.3	16.7	2.5	16.3	11.5	36.6
	2010	1 012 318[1]	7.8[29]	26.3	16.5	3.2	15.1[7]	12.1	35.5[30]
United Arab Emirates	2008	1 201 547[1,6]	0.8	45.7	8.3	10.2	14.1	7.4	21.9
Emirats arabes unis	2009	1 039 525[1,6]	0.9	39.7	9.7	11.3	14.8	8.9	24.4
	2010	1 141 257[1,6]	0.8	42.0	9.3	11.2	14.3	8.7	23.0
United Kingdom	2008	1 295 663	0.8	16.2	11.6	6.5	14.1	7.0	55.6
Royaume-Uni	2009	1 257 626	0.7	15.0	11.1	6.2	14.0	6.9	57.2
	2010	1 298 005	0.7	15.7	11.5	6.1	13.8	6.8	56.9

Value added by industries at current prices *(continued)*
Percentage distribution
Valeur ajoutée par branche d'activité aux prix courants *(suite)*
Répartition en pourcentage

			% of Value added - % de la valeur ajoutée						
Country or area Pays ou zone	Year Année	Value added, gross (mil. nat. cur) Valeur ajoutée, brute (mil. mon. nat.)	Agriculture, hunting, forestry and fishing Agriculture, chasse, sylviculture et pêche	Mining, manufacturing and utilities Activités extractives, Activités de fabrication, électricité, gaz et eau	Manu- facturing Activités de fabri- cation	Construc- tion Construc- tion	Wholesale, retail, trade, restaurants and hotels Commerce, restaurants et hôtels	Transport, storage & commu- nication Transports, entrepôts et commu- nications	Other activities Autres activités
United Rep. of Tanzania[31] Rép.-Unie de Tanzanie[31]	2008	22 712 089[1]	29.4	14.5	8.5	8.4	15.5	7.3	25.0
	2009	25 838 764[1]	28.4	15.3	9.4	8.7	15.4	7.8	24.5
	2010	29 581 028[1]	29.2	14.8	8.8	8.5	15.5	7.4	24.7
United States[6] Etats-Unis[6]	2008	14 369 500	1.1	16.6	12.6	4.5	14.6	5.7	57.6
	2009	14 113 315	1.0	15.7	12.3	3.9	14.4	5.6	59.5
	2010	14 601 646	1.1	16.3	12.7	4.4	14.7	5.7	57.9
Uruguay Uruguay	2008	585 547[1]	10.4	18.9	17.8	7.2	16.8	8.1	38.6
	2009	635 976[1]	9.2	18.1	16.1	7.8	16.0	7.7	41.1
	2010	724 912[1]	9.2	18.5	14.6	8.0	16.0	7.5	40.8
Uzbekistan Ouzbékistan	2008	33 662 198	22.8	27.2	22.7[3]	6.4	10.4	12.5	20.7
	2009	45 314 302	20.8	29.2	24.5[3]	7.0	10.3	12.3	20.4
	2010	56 737 243	23.0	28.1	23.5[3]	6.7	10.2	12.0	20.0
Vanuatu Vanuatu	2008	53 937[1]	22.4	6.9	4.4	3.3	21.3	11.1	35.0
	2009	57 727[1]	21.5	5.3	3.3	5.5	21.4	11.9	34.4
	2010	63 220[1]	19.5	6.4	3.9	4.0	22.3	12.9	34.9
Venezuela (Boliv. Rep. of) Venezuela (Rép. bol. du)	2008	624 968	4.0	46.7	15.0	8.1	11.9	6.3	23.1
	2009	646 671	4.0	45.6	14.6	8.4	12.2	6.4	23.4
	2010	939 243	4.0	45.0	14.6	8.6	12.5	6.5	23.5
Viet Nam Viet Nam	2008	1 485 038 488	22.2	33.4	20.4	6.4	18.1	4.5	15.4
	2009	1 658 390 370	20.9	33.6	20.1	6.7	18.8	4.4	15.7
	2010	1 980 914 000	20.6	34.1	19.7	7.0	18.7	4.3	15.3
Yemen Yémen	2008	5 893 904[1]	10.1	36.7	7.8	5.0	17.4	9.8	21.0
	2009	5 746 838[1]	10.0	37.5	7.5	4.8	16.3	10.6	20.7
	2010	7 744 492[1]	10.1	36.9	7.5	4.9	16.8	10.3	21.0
Zambia Zambie	2008	53 712 501	20.2	16.1	9.6	16.4	18.9	4.2	24.2
	2009	64 423 637	20.9	14.7	9.3	18.4	17.8	3.7	24.6
	2010	78 027 211	19.7	15.9	8.8	20.0	16.8	3.9	23.7
Zanzibar Zanzibar	2008	655 731	35.0	8.0	5.0	8.3	18.3	9.1	21.3
	2009	773 566	35.0	7.4	4.7	7.5	17.7	12.7	19.8
	2010	833 329	37.3	7.5	4.8	6.9	18.0	10.4	20.1
Zimbabwe Zimbabwe	2008	5 499[1]	20.3	26.2	11.6	0.9	26.2	10.6	15.8
	2009	4 889[1]	17.9	28.2	16.9	0.7	12.6	17.5	23.2
	2010	6 875[1]	21.6	31.4	11.8	1.5	16.6	10.6	18.4

Source:
United Nations Statistics Division, New York, national accounts database, last accessed January 2012

Source:
Organisation des Nations Unies, Division de statistique, New York, la base de données sur les comptes nationaux, dernier accès janvier 2012.

1   Including Financial intermediation services indirectly measured (FISIM).

2   At factor cost.
3   Including mining and quarrying.
4   Excluding mining and quarrying.
5   Oil refining included in "Other activities".
6   At producers' prices.
7   Excludes Hotels and restaurants.
8   At producers' prices (includes Other Taxes on Production, less Subsidies; and Taxes on fuel and tobacco).

9   For statistical purposes, the data for China do not include those for the Hong Kong Special Administrative Region (Hong Kong SAR), Macao Special Administrative Region (Macao SAR) and Taiwan Province of China.
10   Excluding hunting and forestry.

1   Y compris les Services d'intermédiation financière mesurés indirectement (SIFMI).
2   Au coût des facteurs.
3   Y compris les industries extractives.
4   Non compris les industries extractives.
5   Le raffinage du pétrole y compris dans "Autres activités".
6   Aux prix à la production.
7   Non compris les hôtels et restaurants.
8   Aux prix à la production (y compris les autres taxes à la production, déduction faite des subventions, et les taxes sur les carburants et le tabac).
9   Pour la présentation des statistiques, les données pour la Chine ne comprennent pas la Région Administrative Spéciale de Hong Kong (Hong Kong RAS), la Région Administrative Spéciale de Macao (Macao RAS) et la province de Taiwan.
10   Non compris la chasse et la sylviculture.

11	Includes waste management.	11	Y compris la gestion des déchets.
12	Excluding repair of motor vehicles, motorcycles and personal and household goods.	12	Non compris les réparations de véhicules à moteur, de motocycles et d'articles personnels et ménagers.
13	Excludes waste management.	13	Gestion des déchets non-compris.
14	Includes repair of motor vehicles, motorcycles and personal and household goods.	14	Y compris les réparations de véhicules à moteur, de motocycles et d'articles personnels et ménagers.
15	Including mining and quarrying, electricity, gas and water.	15	Y compris les industries extractives, l'électricité, le gaz et l'eau.
16	Refers to gross domestic product.	16	Concerné le produit intérieur brut.
17	Excludes hotels and restaurants, since those items are included in item "Other activities".	17	Non compris les hôtels et restaurants, car ils sont compris dans "Autres activités".
18	Includes hotels and restaurants.	18	Y compris les hôtels et restaurants.
19	Including electricity, gas and water.	19	Y compris l'électricité, le gaz, et l'eau.
20	Restaurants and Hotels and repair of motor vehicles and household goods are included in "Other Activities".	20	Les restaurants, les hôtels et les réparations d'articles personnels et ménagers sont inclus dans "autres activités".
21	Basic petroleum manufacturing is included in mining and quarrying.	21	Les industries extractives y compris la fabrication de produits pétroliers de base.
22	Including construction.	22	Y compris la construction.
23	Includes mining and quarrying; electricity, gas and water supply, and construction.	23	Y compris les activités extractives; les activités de production et distribution d'électricité, de gaz et d'eau et la construction.
24	Includes mining and handicrafts.	24	Y compris l'extraction et l'artisanat.
25	Including quarrying.	25	Y compris les carrières.
26	Excluding quarrying.	26	Non compris les carrières.
27	Refers to buildings and public works.	27	Se rapportent aux bâtiments et aux travaux publics.
28	Refers to trade only.	28	Se rapporte seulement au commerce
29	Excluding fishing.	29	Non compris la pêche.
30	Includes fishing, fishery; activity of hotel and restaurants; provision of communal and individual services; cultural and sporting activity.	30	Y compris la pêche, l'industrie de la pêche, les activités des hôtels et des restaurants, la mise à disposition de services collectifs ou individuels, les affaires culturelles et sportives.
31	Tanzania mainland only.	31	Tanzanie continentale seulement.

# Index numbers of industrial production
2005 = 100

# Indices de la production industrielle
2005 = 100

Country or area and industry [ISIC Rev. 4] Pays ou zone et industrie [CITI Rév. 4]	2003	2004	2006	2007	2008	2009	2010	2011
Africa · Afrique								
Algeria[1] Algérie[1]								
Total industry - Total, industrie	93.5	93.9	96.7	97.0	98.7	99.1	96.7	97.0
Total mining - Total, industries extractives	87.1	86.1	116.7	125.9	138.3	143.0	138.3	125.2
Total manufacturing - Total, industries manufacturières	105.9	103.5	90.7	87.2	88.9	90.4	85.5	84.3
Food, beverages and tobacco - Aliments, boissons et tabac	129.4	109.2	88.9	87.1	93.0	84.4	81.7	98.7
Textiles, wearing apparel, leather, footwear - Textiles, habillement, cuir et chaussures	107.4	99.2	77.4	65.2	60.0	60.6	55.9	49.7
Chemicals, petroleum, rubber and plastic products - Produits chimiques, pétroliers, caoutchouc et plastiques	110.7	99.2	97.1	99.2	103.8	109.1	129.2	123.7
Basic metals - Métaux de base	112.7	112.5	100.3	100.3	133.9	204.3	109.4	57.1
Electricity - Electricité	86.3	91.3	103.4	109.5	118.2	126.6	133.7	144.6
Benin[1] Bénin[1]								
Total industry - Total, industrie	100.7	98.3	104.8	112.8	120.4	128.7	134.4	...
Cameroon[1] Cameroun[1]								
Total industry - Total, industrie	93.6	97.9	102.5	103.8	107.1	103.3	102.3	104.6
Total manufacturing - Total, industries manufacturières	94.6	98.7	103.2	104.4	107.5	102.9	101.4	103.6
Food, beverages and tobacco - Aliments, boissons et tabac	108.2	106.6	100.4	105.2	128.8	131.4	151.8	168.6
Textiles - Textiles	72.3	79.3	58.9	66.5	60.0	53.0	52.4	53.6
Chemicals, petroleum, rubber and plastic products - Produits chimiques, pétroliers, caoutchouc et plastiques	90.7	92.8	118.1	111.3	98.4	102.0	97.5	102.6
Basic metals - Métaux de base	101.4	110.1	105.7	102.9	104.3	100.7	121.8	109.2
All machinery and transport equipment - Fabrication de machines et de matériel de transport	122.9	91.0	90.5	359.5	321.9	233.3	309.8	287.8
Electricity, gas and water - Electricité, gaz et eau	91.6	97.6	103.3	105.8	111.2	111.8	115.7	119.7
Central African Rep.[1] Rép. centrafricaine[1]								
Total industry - Total, industrie	...	...	136.1	182.7	193.3	143.0	126.3	136.0
Chad[1] Tchad[1]								
Total industry - Total, industrie	92.6	94.9	92.1	88.0	80.8	77.2	...	...
Congo[1] Congo[1]								
Total industry - Total, industrie	...	85.8	101.1	104.9	106.4	158.9	...	...
Total manufacturing - Total, industries manufacturières	...	85.1	97.8	102.7	107.7	...	...	...
Food and beverages - Aliments et boissons	...	98.4	121.1	137.4	153.8	199.1	...	...
Chemicals, petroleum, rubber and plastic products - Produits chimiques, pétroliers, caoutchouc et plastiques	...	81.7	101.7	100.1	75.5	93.7	...	...
Electricity and water - Electricité et eau	...	89.9	109.1	120.6	98.2	114.2	...	...
Côte d'Ivoire[1] Côte d'Ivoire[1]								
Total industry - Total, industrie	85.3	88.0	105.7	101.3	102.2	106.3	103.3	95.7
Total mining - Total, industries extractives	87.3	90.3	241.0	201.2	188.1	...	...	...
Total manufacturing - Total, industries manufacturières	90.9	93.3	91.9	93.7	95.3	97.7	99.4	88.9
Electricity and water - Electricité et eau	90.1	94.3	99.4	98.8	101.8	...	...	...
Egypt[1] Egypte[1]								
Total industry - Total, industrie	80.1	90.2	117.9	121.9	136.8	131.8	...	...
Total mining - Total, industries extractives	73.5	89.1	121.5	118.9	145.5	143.8	...	...
Total manufacturing - Total, industries manufacturières	85.7	91.0	115.4	125.4	129.6	120.5	129.8	129.4
Food, beverages and tobacco - Aliments, boissons et tabac	94.6	95.2	104.3	114.6	119.9	110.7	127.8	127.7
Textiles, wearing apparel, leather, footwear - Textiles, habillement, cuir et chaussures	111.4	101.5	114.3	116.9	138.3	135.4	144.6	151.6
Chemicals, petroleum, rubber and plastic products - Produits chimiques, pétroliers, caoutchouc et plastiques	89.2	83.4	141.6	164.9	172.2	122.5	144.3	151.9
Basic metals - Métaux de base	138.1	110.5	127.3	135.3	110.2	118.4	102.5	84.2
Electricity - Electricité	87.0	92.9	107.0	114.9	123.7	129.7	141.2	143.6
Ethiopia[1,2] Ethiopie[1,2]								
Total industry - Total, industrie	84.8	90.2	109.9	120.5	130.2	140.8	155.4	...
Total mining - Total, industries extractives	94.1	96.0	107.2	113.6	110.1	124.1	178.9	...
Total manufacturing - Total, industries manufacturières	83.2	88.7	110.6	119.8	132.2	144.2	158.5	...
Electricity and water - Electricité et eau	87.0	92.7	108.8	123.7	129.7	136.1	143.0	...

Country or area and industry [ISIC Rev. 4] Pays ou zone et industrie [CITI Rév. 4]	2003	2004	2006	2007	2008	2009	2010	2011
Gabon[1] Gabon[1]								
Total industry - Total, industrie	92.4	94.7	105.9	112.0	119.5	114.0	...	...
Total manufacturing - Total, industries manufacturières	90.8	92.5	103.8	112.4	120.3	...	...	...
Food, beverages and tobacco - Aliments, boissons et tabac	90.8	90.4	106.3	117.3	124.8	...	...	...
Chemicals and petroleum products - Produits chimiques et pétroliers	97.1	93.9	100.2	117.7	122.0	...	...	...
Electricity and water - Electricité et eau	94.2	96.9	108.2	111.5	118.7	...	...	...
Kenya[1] Kenya[1]								
Total industry - Total, industrie	86.4	92.7	106.0	113.2	114.2	118.3	126.4	129.7
Total mining - Total, industries extractives	70.1	88.3	108.8	110.5	140.3	120.3	144.4	163.2
Total manufacturing - Total, industries manufacturières	87.0	92.8	105.8	113.3	112.7	118.3	125.6	127.3
Food, beverages and tobacco - Aliments, boissons et tabac	85.2	94.9	105.5	121.5	120.4	121.8	129.8	132.0
Textiles, wearing apparel, leather, footwear - Textiles, habillement, cuir et chaussures	84.6	76.3	115.0	117.3	118.5	135.7	157.1	156.1
Chemicals, petroleum, rubber and plastic products - Produits chimiques, pétroliers, caoutchouc et plastiques	92.2	101.9	108.7	123.1	125.8	139.8	148.6	166.0
Fabricated metal products; machinery and equipment, electrical machinery and apparatus - Ouvrage en métaux, machines et matériel, machines et appareils électriques	96.6	100.9	103.7	96.7	86.6	89.5	75.2	68.8
Electricity - Electricité	87.5	93.6	106.3	114.0	116.4	117.3	125.8	136.3
Madagascar[1] Madagascar[1]								
Total industry - Total, industrie	85.9	89.1	107.2	115.8	124.5	...	...	...
Total mining - Total, industries extractives	83.4	86.9	108.3	117.5	126.8	...	...	...
Total manufacturing - Total, industries manufacturières	86.6	89.9	115.0	123.6	134.6	...	...	...
Food, beverages and tobacco - Aliments, boissons et tabac	84.2	86.1	111.8	117.7	127.1	...	...	...
Textiles, wearing apparel, leather, footwear - Textiles, habillement, cuir et chaussures	77.7	79.6	109.6	121.6	133.8	...	...	...
Chemicals, petroleum, rubber and plastic products - Produits chimiques, pétroliers, caoutchouc et plastiques	111.9	116.7	100.6	101.6	102.7	...	...	...
Fabricated metal products; machinery and equipment, electrical machinery and apparatus - Ouvrage en métaux, machines et matériel, machines et appareils électriques	75.6	77.6	98.8	107.2	115.7	...	...	...
Electricity, gas and water - Electricité, gaz et eau	81.2	83.8	105.6	114.2	128.0	...	...	...
Malawi[1] Malawi[1]								
Total industry - Total, industrie	95.0	102.5	102.9	...	...	...	...	...
Total manufacturing - Total, industries manufacturières	99.9	108.6	101.0	112.5	78.5	151.1	...	...
Food, beverages and tobacco - Aliments, boissons et tabac	79.3	112.0	101.2	281.4	327.5	386.7	...	...
Textiles, wearing apparel, leather, footwear - Textiles, habillement, cuir et chaussures	59.6	86.1	83.0	75.0	64.1	57.9	...	...
Chemicals, petroleum, rubber and plastic products - Produits chimiques, pétroliers, caoutchouc et plastiques	136.9	128.5	89.4	84.3	80.4	78.3	...	...
Fabricated metal products, excluding machinery and equipment - Fabrication d'ouvrages en métaux, machines et matériel, machines et appareils électriques	62.5	61.8	126.1	160.3	222.7	292.4	...	...
Electricity and water - Electricité et eau	86.7	91.9	106.8	110.2	114.1	118.9	...	...
Mali[1] Mali[1]								
Total industry - Total, industrie	97.4	94.9	100.3	85.9	76.0	81.1	74.0	82.4
Total mining - Total, industries extractives	109.9	87.9	101.6	83.1	79.0	69.1	51.9	49.9
Total manufacturing - Total, industries manufacturières	93.5	99.2	114.6	106.1	91.7	124.1	118.7	141.4
Food, beverages and tobacco - Aliments, boissons et tabac	80.3	96.9	136.1	117.5	62.7	174.4	187.0	243.3
Textiles and wearing apparel - Textiles et habillement	111.6	80.7	67.2	91.9	92.3	110.1	110.9	89.4
Chemicals, petroleum, rubber and plastic products - Produits chimiques, pétroliers, caoutchouc et plastiques	97.0	121.5	108.0	130.8	163.3	146.5	110.1	120.4
Basic metals - Métaux de base	106.0	93.4	98.6	96.3	83.7	95.2	94.2	112.6
Electricity, gas and water - Electricité, gaz et eau	81.3	90.2	106.6	105.5	125.9	133.0	146.4	157.7
Mauritius[1] Maurice[1]								
Total industry - Total, industrie	106.4	106.6	104.0	105.6	109.2	111.7	112.1	116.9
Total mining - Total, industries extractives	103.3	103.8	109.1	99.1	121.1	106.3	105.7	100.8
Total manufacturing - Total, industries manufacturières	108.5	108.0	103.9	105.3	108.7	111.3	113.6	116.1
Food, beverages and tobacco - Aliments, boissons et tabac	99.7	101.0	106.9	98.1	105.6	111.1	115.3	112.1
Textiles, wearing apparel, leather, footwear - Textiles, habillement, cuir et chaussures	130.0	116.8	101.6	108.9	109.3	109.5	109.2	116.9

23 Index numbers of industrial production *(continued)*
2005 = 100
Indices de la production industrielle *(suite)*
2005 = 100

Country or area and industry [ISIC Rev. 4] Pays ou zone et industrie [CITI Rév. 4]	2003	2004	2006	2007	2008	2009	2010	2011
Chemicals and chemical products - Produits chimiques	156.3	126.9	98.2	115.9	125.9	126.3	128.9	138.1
Basic metals - Métaux de base	111.0	135.6	134.6	94.1	99.1	84.4	88.5	69.5
Electricity, gas and water - Electricité, gaz et eau	92.6	96.3	103.9	107.5	114.1	114.2	118.6	123.3
Morocco[1] Maroc[1]								
Total industry - Total, industrie	88.7	93.5	105.2	108.8	110.9	110.2	114.9	118.6
Total mining - Total, industries extractives	86.1	93.7	108.5	112.8	110.7	96.3	111.5	116.1
Total manufacturing[2] - Total, industries manufacturières [2]	90.5	94.9	105.2	110.0	112.3	112.6	114.8	117.6
Food, beverages and tobacco - Aliments, boissons et tabac	90.1	94.9	99.2	100.4	105.2	106.2	106.4	110.0
Textiles, wearing apparel, leather, footwear - Textiles, habillement, cuir et chaussures	94.7	95.0	101.1	103.1	102.1	101.5	104.9	105.7
Chemicals, petroleum, rubber and plastic products - Produits chimiques, pétroliers, caoutchouc et plastiques	84.4	95.3	103.8	106.1	110.5	107.9	113.2	116.1
Basic metals - Métaux de base	92.0	90.5	105.0	112.8	104.7	108.2	101.3	101.4
Electricity - Electricité	80.4	86.0	103.5	100.1	103.1	106.1	117.6	125.2
Namibia[1] Namibie[1]								
Total industry - Total, industrie	85.4	98.4	111.7	117.2	117.0	102.4	115.1	...
Total mining - Total, industries extractives	77.4	112.2	127.6	128.3	124.6	72.9	90.8	...
Total manufacturing - Total, industries manufacturières	92.7	93.0	102.7	111.5	113.8	120.2	131.2	...
Electricity and water - Electricité et eau	75.2	80.4	105.6	110.3	108.5	108.4	112.2	...
Senegal[1] Sénégal[1]								
Total industry - Total, industrie	88.0	98.2	94.3	103.0	93.4	100.2	103.6	110.4
Total mining - Total, industries extractives	129.4	117.4	68.0	67.6	77.6	88.3	94.4	111.6
Total manufacturing - Total, industries manufacturières	84.6	97.9	95.2	105.0	92.4	100.0	102.1	109.3
Food, beverages and tobacco - Aliments, boissons et tabac	71.6	93.4	117.9	128.3	106.4	114.2	114.3	115.2
Textiles, wearing apparel, leather, footwear - Textiles, habillement, cuir et chaussures	134.7	108.0	94.3	103.0	50.1	73.8	33.4	34.5
Chemicals, petroleum, rubber and plastic products - Produits chimiques, pétroliers, caoutchouc et plastiques	109.2	110.5	53.7	64.0	58.0	58.6	59.4	66.9
Electricity and water - Electricité et eau	90.2	91.2	100.6	106.5	106.5	107.0	116.8	115.8
South Africa[1] Afrique du Sud[1]								
Total industry - Total, industrie	94.1	97.7	103.1	106.3	105.2	93.9	98.7	100.4
Total mining - Total, industries extractives	95.2	98.8	98.7	97.8	92.3	86.2	91.5	91.3
Total manufacturing - Total, industries manufacturières	93.4	97.1	104.8	109.6	110.4	96.2	100.9	103.5
Food and beverages - Aliments et boissons	87.6	94.0	100.6	105.2	109.6	111.8	116.5	119.2
Textiles, wearing apparel, leather, footwear - Textiles, habillement, cuir et chaussures	99.3	103.2	102.1	105.2	104.8	90.5	84.8	81.7
Chemicals, petroleum, rubber and plastic products - Produits chimiques, pétroliers, caoutchouc et plastiques	94.4	97.8	103.2	110.8	118.2	105.1	112.0	114.2
Basic metals - Métaux de base	101.3	104.9	108.0	108.3	97.3	79.3	86.4	88.0
Electricity - Electricité	95.6	99.9	103.6	107.6	105.5	101.9	106.0	107.2
Swaziland[1] Swaziland[1]								
Total industry - Total, industrie	94.4	99.2	102.2	...	...	...	...	...
Total mining - Total, industries extractives	116.8	128.2	116.6	...	...	...	...	...
Total manufacturing - Total, industries manufacturières	94.1	99.1	102.0	...	...	...	...	...
Electricity, gas and water - Electricité, gaz et eau	98.7	96.3	105.1	...	...	...	...	...
Togo Togo								
Total industry - Total, industrie	...	101.5	113.8	121.9	110.5	120.0	123.8	126.2
Total mining - Total, industries extractives	...	109.8	127.8	159.7	145.9	157.5	175.7	180.5
Total manufacturing - Total, industries manufacturières	...	94.9	103.4	106.6	104.7	110.6	103.0	115.9
Food and beverages - Aliments et boissons	...	77.6	115.1	125.7	128.0	143.4	135.2	156.0
Textiles and wearing apparel - Textiles et habillement	...	171.9	112.7	157.6	138.5	92.5	50.1	73.6
Chemicals, rubber and plastic products - Produits chimiques, caoutchouc et plastiques	...	119.6	74.3	53.3	43.1	37.7	35.2	44.8
Basic metals - Métaux de base	...	113.0	75.5	70.1	65.4	58.9	53.9	68.7
Fabricated metals - Fabrication d'ouvrages en métaux (sauf machines et matériel)	...	111.5	50.1	61.7	46.8	37.0	27.0	88.0
Electricity, gas, steam and air conditioning supply - Electricité, gaz, vapeur, et distribution de l'air conditionné	...	111.8	129.6	127.8	91.1	108.8	130.7	100.9

Country or area and industry [ISIC Rev. 4] Pays ou zone et industrie [CITI Rév. 4]	2003	2004	2006	2007	2008	2009	2010	2011
Tunisia[1] Tunisie[1]								
Total industry - Total, industrie	95.3	99.2	103.1	112.7	116.4	111.1	119.7	...
Total mining - Total, industries extractives	94.4	98.7	94.4	112.8	107.1	107.3	...	...
Total manufacturing - Total, industries manufacturières	95.8	99.6	104.5	113.1	118.3	111.3	...	...
Food, beverages and tobacco - Aliments, boissons et tabac	93.9	101.1	104.9	108.7	110.6	108.2	...	...
Textiles, wearing apparel, leather, footwear - Textiles, habillement, cuir et chaussures	107.6	106.5	98.0	103.4	107.0	91.9	...	...
Chemicals, petroleum, rubber and plastic products - Produits chimiques, pétroliers, caoutchouc et plastiques	106.0	102.6	97.5	98.3	99.1	101.8	...	...
Basic metals - Métaux de base	84.2	82.1	111.8	131.8	145.9	107.1	...	...
Electricity and water - Electricité et eau	92.5	95.7	104.0	108.6	113.1	117.0	...	...
Uganda[1] Ouganda[1]								
Total industry - Total, industrie	87.4	96.9	100.1	107.6	113.2	130.4	134.1	139.1
Total manufacturing - Total, industries manufacturières	86.8	96.7	102.3	113.5	118.0	138.2	142.8	148.4
Food, beverages and tobacco - Aliments, boissons et tabac	98.5	104.5	103.9	117.1	127.5	141.5	142.1	146.1
Textiles, wearing apparel, leather, footwear - Textiles, habillement, cuir et chaussures	187.7	214.9	125.4	118.1	119.4	120.2	125.1	140.7
Chemicals, petroleum, rubber and plastic products - Produits chimiques, pétroliers, caoutchouc et plastiques	82.0	99.9	100.1	103.2	107.3	129.2	124.5	145.2
Basic metals - Métaux de base	74.5	93.6	105.9	113.3	106.3	99.5	109.1	122.7
Electricity [2] - Electricité [2]	92.1	98.1	83.2	60.8	76.5	69.7	66.3	66.5
United Rep. of Tanzania[1] Rép.- Unie de Tanzanie[1]								
Total manufacturing - Total, industries manufacturières	91.4	96.9	119.6	123.5	202.9	187.8	...	...
Food, beverages and tobacco - Aliments, boissons et tabac	77.9	87.2	132.8	132.7	176.4	204.8	...	...
Chemicals, rubber and plastic products - Produits chimiques, caoutchouc et plastiques	96.0	82.6	130.9	97.5	132.9	171.4	...	...
Basic metals - Métaux de base	90.5	93.6	114.0	128.9	191.8	233.7	...	...
Textiles, leather and footwear - Textiles, cuir et chaussures	161.5	161.6	159.0	159.7	243.3	168.8	...	...
Zambia[1] Zambie[1]								
Total industry - Total, industrie	84.8	92.2	108.6	114.8	120.9	128.3	140.7	140.2
Total mining - Total, industries extractives	75.3	87.7	110.9	119.7	132.3	144.7	162.4	183.1
Total manufacturing - Total, industries manufacturières	91.1	96.1	105.0	110.2	112.1	113.9	121.5	116.6
Food, beverages and tobacco - Aliments, boissons et tabac	91.2	96.5	109.2	117.4	120.9	127.1	136.4	150.0
Textiles and wearing apparel - Textiles et habillement	104.9	103.0	92.8	74.8	57.2	45.8	19.9	5.9
Chemicals, petroleum, rubber and plastic products - Produits chimiques, pétroliers, caoutchouc et plastiques	90.8	96.9	104.0	108.4	115.5	114.8	118.0	115.0
Basic metals - Métaux de base	99.0	102.0	99.7	95.0	116.8	111.1	108.9	64.9
Electricity - Electricité	97.2	94.2	113.1	113.8	111.1	120.5	131.1	159.5
Zimbabwe[1] Zimbabwe[1]								
Total industry - Total, industrie	108.1	97.3	103.8	...	...	...	...	...
Total manufacturing - Total, industries manufacturières	111.0	97.7	106.5	...	...	...	...	...
Food, beverages and tobacco - Aliments, boissons et tabac	111.9	101.0	99.5	...	...	...	...	...
Textiles, wearing apparel, leather, footwear - Textiles, habillement, cuir et chaussures	81.5	91.3	132.5	...	...	...	...	...
Chemicals, petroleum, rubber and plastic products - Produits chimiques, pétroliers, caoutchouc et plastiques	103.5	101.7	80.5	...	...	...	...	...
Electricity - Electricité	85.7	94.6	82.9	...	...	...	...	...

America, North · Amérique du Nord

	2003	2004	2006	2007	2008	2009	2010	2011
Barbados[1] Barbade[1]								
Total industry - Total, industrie	96.0	98.3	101.4	101.0	99.3	89.6	88.0	84.7
Total mining - Total, industries extractives	84.4	92.5	96.9	91.2	84.0	52.7	58.2	50.3
Total manufacturing - Total, industries manufacturières	95.7	98.0	99.1	98.0	96.1	84.1	80.6	77.0
Food, beverages and tobacco - Aliments, boissons et tabac	100.4	100.3	94.7	97.9	99.1	88.7	91.1	85.8
Wearing apparel - Habillement	99.6	102.0	88.1	81.3	47.6	56.7	32.1	43.7
Chemicals and chemical products - Produits chimiques	84.2	94.8	97.0	94.2	97.4	74.2	73.9	66.6
Electricity, gas and water - Electricité, gaz et eau	98.8	100.6	108.3	110.9	110.2	111.2	113.6	111.9
Belize[1] Belize[1]								
Total industry - Total, industrie	99.2	100.5	125.6	...	...	...	...	...
Total manufacturing - Total, industries manufacturières	90.8	100.4	90.6	...	...	...	...	...
Food, beverages and tobacco - Aliments, boissons et tabac	91.1	99.8	89.1	...	...	...	...	...
Wearing apparel - Habillement	91.8	112.5	103.0	...	...	...	...	...

Country or area and industry [ISIC Rev. 4] Pays ou zone et industrie [CITI Rév. 4]	2003	2004	2006	2007	2008	2009	2010	2011
Chemicals and chemical products - Produits chimiques	96.1	98.1	102.0	...	...	...	...	...
Electricity and water - Electricité et eau	102.1	100.5	138.1	...	...	...	...	...
Canada[1] Canada[1]								
Total industry - Total, industrie	96.4	98.1	99.5	98.8	93.5	83.9	88.2	92.1
Total mining - Total, industries extractives	97.5	99.1	102.7	103.7	100.9	92.7	98.0	102.2
Total manufacturing - Total, industries manufacturières	96.4	98.4	98.6	96.5	89.7	78.6	83.0	85.6
Food, beverages and tobacco - Aliments, boissons et tabac	97.0	97.2	101.4	99.2	99.4	100.4	101.8	101.0
Textiles, wearing apparel, leather, footwear - Textiles, habillement, cuir et chaussures	125.7	113.5	90.3	77.4	64.9	54.3	57.0	56.9
Chemicals, petroleum, rubber and plastic products - Produits chimiques, pétroliers, caoutchouc et plastiques	101.3	102.1	97.7	95.1	89.5	79.6	83.0	84.6
Basic metals - Métaux de base	91.7	97.3	99.6	97.3	96.7	72.5	81.7	83.2
Electricity, gas and water - Electricité, gaz et eau	94.3	95.1	99.3	103.9	103.1	99.2	101.9	112.3
Costa Rica[1] Costa Rica[1]								
Total industry - Total, industrie	87.2	90.8	110.3	117.5	113.1	104.5	110.7	113.6
Total manufacturing - Total, industries manufacturières	86.8	90.3	110.8	118.6	113.6	104.1	111.2	114.4
Food and beverages - Aliments et boissons	95.2	94.9	103.5	110.6	110.9	108.8	112.7	112.9
Textiles, wearing apparel, leather, footwear - Textiles, habillement, cuir et chaussures	94.4	97.8	93.4	96.1	97.7	95.7	97.8	99.8
Chemicals, petroleum, rubber and plastic products - Produits chimiques, pétroliers, caoutchouc et plastiques	100.4	101.8	103.4	109.3	113.3	98.5	110.1	117.4
Electricity and water - Electricité et eau	90.8	94.4	106.0	108.6	108.8	107.4	110.9	112.1
Cuba[1] Cuba[1]								
Total industry - Total, industrie	99.0	98.9	103.2	107.5	107.0	101.1	102.3	...
Total mining - Total, industries extractives	114.4	105.9	112.1	108.7	96.8	98.2	112.8	...
Total manufacturing - Total, industries manufacturières	97.2	97.9	101.9	106.3	106.6	99.2	101.6	...
Food, beverages and tobacco - Aliments, boissons et tabac	93.3	98.0	103.1	110.4	115.1	108.3	109.3	...
Textiles, wearing apparel, leather, footwear - Textiles, habillement, cuir et chaussures	118.6	111.7	90.4	84.9	105.0	96.7	93.6	...
Chemicals, petroleum, rubber and plastic products - Produits chimiques, pétroliers, caoutchouc et plastiques	106.8	98.5	96.5	101.9	186.1	91.4	104.6	...
Basic metals - Métaux de base	93.4	98.3	95.8	98.2	95.6	100.4	99.6	...
Electricity, gas and water - Electricité, gaz et eau	103.0	101.9	107.3	115.1	115.6	115.9	101.6	...
Dominican Republic[1] Rép. dominicaine[1]								
Total industry - Total, industrie	93.6	94.3	103.6	106.4	108.6	106.5	114.0	121.1
Total mining - Total, industries extractives	94.6	95.3	111.0	109.4	76.3	36.7	37.7	67.8
Total manufacturing - Total, industries manufacturières	91.8	94.0	103.2	105.7	108.5	107.2	114.9	122.0
Electricity and water - Electricité et eau	125.2	95.4	109.9	116.7	128.7	132.6	139.8	134.7
El Salvador[1] El Salvador[1]								
Total industry - Total, industrie	97.6	98.2	102.3	104.8	107.1	103.7	105.6	107.8
Total mining - Total, industries extractives	113.1	94.7	104.4	102.2	94.7	80.3	71.3	79.4
Total manufacturing - Total, industries manufacturières	97.4	98.3	102.2	104.7	107.2	104.0	106.0	108.2
Food and beverages - Aliments et boissons	94.2	97.0	102.9	107.3	109.0	107.8	109.8	112.7
Textiles, wearing apparel, leather, footwear - Textiles, habillement, cuir et chaussures	92.7	95.3	103.8	105.4	108.5	108.2	113.4	119.1
Chemicals, petroleum, rubber and plastic products - Produits chimiques, pétroliers, caoutchouc et plastiques	97.9	96.6	103.1	109.2	111.6	102.0	100.9	105.6
Electricity - Electricité	92.7	93.8	106.2	109.1	114.2	112.8	115.3	117.2
Guatemala[1] Guatemala[1]								
Total industry - Total, industrie	93.7	97.6	104.0	107.9	109.8	109.2	113.0	117.5
Total mining - Total, industries extractives	117.4	103.3	117.6	133.9	128.2	132.5	137.1	165.2
Total manufacturing - Total, industries manufacturières	92.9	97.5	103.8	106.9	109.1	108.1	111.7	115.2
Food, beverages and tobacco - Aliments, boissons et tabac	95.0	97.2	102.9	106.8	109.9	111.8	115.3	118.9
Textiles, wearing apparel, leather, footwear - Textiles, habillement, cuir et chaussures	81.3	97.7	102.7	102.8	102.7	93.2	97.8	95.8
Chemicals, petroleum, rubber and plastic products - Produits chimiques, pétroliers, caoutchouc et plastiques	95.7	96.6	102.9	107.3	110.9	112.4	117.4	123.3
Electricity and water - Electricité et eau	94.0	98.2	103.0	109.8	111.2	111.9	117.3	124.0

Country or area and industry [ISIC Rev. 4] Pays ou zone et industrie [CITI Rév. 4]	2003	2004	2006	2007	2008	2009	2010	2011
Haiti[1] Haïti[1]								
Total industry - Total, industrie	91.3	92.0	100.6	102.4	104.7	118.9	103.9	...
Total manufacturing - Total, industries manufacturières	92.5	93.0	104.0	105.3	107.5	119.2	103.9	...
Food, beverages and tobacco - Aliments, boissons et tabac	88.4	86.2	100.0	97.5	101.7	116.0	85.6	...
Textiles, wearing apparel, leather, footwear - Textiles, habillement, cuir et chaussures	93.1	98.4	101.4	101.2	103.7	118.0	116.4	...
Chemicals, petroleum, rubber and plastic products - Produits chimiques, pétroliers, caoutchouc et plastiques	95.8	96.8	104.5	114.0	100.8	99.2	92.1	...
Basic metals - Métaux de base	107.8	99.4	105.8	114.4	120.4	127.2	92.7	...
Electricity - Electricité	80.2	83.7	68.9	74.6	77.8	116.3	104.6	...
Honduras[1] Honduras[1]								
Total industry - Total, industrie	88.6	93.8	103.2	106.5	109.5	99.7	103.8	110.1
Total mining - Total, industries extractives	90.2	96.3	116.4	122.7	137.2	115.5	106.0	106.6
Total manufacturing - Total, industries manufacturières	91.4	96.5	102.0	105.1	107.6	96.5	101.3	107.9
Food, beverages and tobacco - Aliments, boissons et tabac	93.9	98.1	105.6	108.2	111.4	111.3	113.1	122.5
Textiles, wearing apparel, leather, footwear - Textiles, habillement, cuir et chaussures	88.7	96.3	91.0	91.8	99.3	81.1	90.9	91.9
Chemicals, petroleum, rubber and plastic products - Produits chimiques, pétroliers, caoutchouc et plastiques	92.7	96.6	102.7	105.4	98.0	96.2	98.2	95.2
Basic metals - Métaux de base	70.7	88.3	99.3	109.8	115.4	89.5	77.6	93.9
Electricity, gas and water - Electricité, gaz et eau	64.5	70.4	109.9	115.2	119.3	122.8	125.0	129.1
Mexico[1] Mexique[1]								
Total industry[3] - Total, industrie[3]	93.7	97.2	105.7	107.9	107.7	99.4	105.6	109.7
Total mining - Total, industries extractives	99.0	100.3	101.4	101.2	99.5	96.6	97.8	95.9
Total manufacturing - Total, industries manufacturières	92.9	96.6	105.9	107.8	107.0	96.5	105.9	111.4
Food, beverages and tobacco - Aliments, boissons et tabac	92.8	96.6	102.7	105.4	107.1	106.7	108.2	110.8
Textiles and wearing apparel - Textiles et habillement	101.2	102.6	100.6	96.8	95.1	86.1	92.1	89.8
Chemicals, petroleum, rubber and plastic products - Produits chimiques, pétroliers, caoutchouc et plastiques	93.6	98.1	103.4	104.9	103.2	98.5	98.7	99.7
Basic metals - Métaux de base	90.8	94.3	103.5	101.9	101.4	83.8	94.8	99.3
Electricity, gas and water - Electricité, gaz et eau	94.3	98.0	112.2	116.2	113.6	115.6	127.6	134.8
Nicaragua[1] Nicaragua[1]								
Total industry - Total, industrie	92.2	98.6	104.2	109.0	106.9	107.9	118.2	126.9
Total mining - Total, industries extractives	89.6	108.8	101.3	94.6	88.8	79.7	124.8	157.6
Total manufacturing - Total, industries manufacturières	92.4	98.3	104.7	110.8	107.8	109.0	117.8	125.0
Food, beverages and tobacco - Aliments, boissons et tabac	86.8	95.4	106.6	116.1	117.4	121.9	132.0	142.3
Wearing apparel, leather and footwear - Fabrication d'articles d'habillement, fabrication de cuir et d'articles de cuir	98.6	102.6	96.2	102.2	85.0	72.3	88.5	87.7
Chemicals, petroleum, rubber and plastic products - Produits chimiques, pétroliers, caoutchouc et plastiques	82.4	90.5	96.9	95.1	93.0	94.9	82.1	89.8
Electricity and water - Electricité et eau	91.9	96.4	102.4	104.4	108.6	112.7	118.1	125.7
Panama[1] Panama[1]								
Total industry - Total, industrie	93.7	96.6	105.9	114.1	122.8	124.6	128.1	136.5
Total mining - Total, industries extractives	88.6	99.4	116.9	144.9	189.9	198.6	213.1	252.2
Total manufacturing - Total, industries manufacturières	96.6	97.2	105.7	111.0	116.7	114.3	114.1	118.0
Food and beverages - Aliments et boissons	95.7	96.8	104.6	108.5	111.4	113.3	112.8	115.5
Textiles, wearing apparel, leather, footwear - Textiles, habillement, cuir et chaussures	146.8	114.5	96.3	95.8	98.9	96.2	94.8	98.9
Chemicals, petroleum, rubber and plastic products - Produits chimiques, pétroliers, caoutchouc et plastiques	105.5	97.4	104.0	105.8	106.6	101.3	106.1	105.6
Basic metals - Métaux de base	96.2	105.0	99.4	101.3	99.3	92.0	91.9	91.4
Electricity and water - Electricité et eau	89.1	94.6	103.1	111.5	115.8	124.5	132.6	141.3
Trinidad and Tobago[1] Trinité- et- Tobago[1]								
Total industry - Total, industrie	85.6	90.8	109.1	122.2	131.2	145.7	158.7	160.7
Total mining - Total, industries extractives	94.1	94.9	104.8	95.4	93.8	95.0	91.4	86.9
Total manufacturing - Total, industries manufacturières	81.7	87.3	111.1	134.1	147.9	174.6	195.8	200.9
Food, beverages and tobacco - Aliments, boissons et tabac	61.0	89.9	104.5	132.6	157.3	163.3	171.8	170.7
Chemicals and petroleum products - Produits chimiques et pétroliers	66.8	74.7	90.9	91.2	109.3	106.0	93.3	96.5
Basic metals - Métaux de base	119.0	113.8	118.1	119.7	93.7	246.9	371.4	451.8
Textiles, leather and footwear - Textiles, cuir et chaussures	81.5	89.0	104.3	105.6	122.9	124.3	146.4	145.2
Electricity, gas and water - Electricité, gaz et eau	100.1	100.3	113.2	113.0	118.1	128.7	134.9	129.9

Country or area and industry [ISIC Rev. 4] Pays ou zone et industrie [CITI Rév. 4]	2003	2004	2006	2007	2008	2009	2010	2011
United States Etats- Unis								
Total industry - Total, industrie	94.3	96.6	102.4	105.4	101.3	89.1	94.4	98.6
Total mining - Total, industries extractives	101.8	101.2	102.5	103.1	104.1	98.7	103.8	110.3
Total manufacturing - Total, industries manufacturières	93.3	95.9	102.7	105.9	100.9	86.9	92.4	96.8
Food, beverages and tobacco - Aliments, boissons et tabac	96.3	96.4	99.6	98.7	95.2	93.9	94.0	95.0
Textiles, wearing apparel, leather, footwear - Textiles, habillement, cuir et chaussures	106.6	100.1	93.5	80.0	67.8	52.1	54.8	55.2
Petroleum, chemicals, pharmaceuticals, rubber and plastic - Pétroliers, produits chimiques, pharmaceutiques, caoutchouc et plastiques	93.8	97.6	102.2	105.3	99.0	92.1	93.4	96.0
Basic metals - Métaux de base	94.3	102.6	102.9	105.0	105.0	77.7	95.3	101.6
Fabricated metals, computer, electronic and optical products, electrical equipment, machinery and transport equipment - Fabrication d'ouvrages en métaux produits électroniques et optiques, appareils électriques, fabrication de machines et de matériel de transport	89.8	93.5	106.3	115.0	112.6	92.9	103.0	112.0
Electricity, gas, steam and air conditioning supply - Electricité, gaz, vapeur, et distribution de l'air conditionné	96.6	98.0	99.4	102.7	102.7	100.1	103.7	103.4
America, South · Amérique du Sud								
Argentina [1] Argentine [1]								
Total industry - Total, industrie	80.7	91.8	109.2	118.8	125.3	126.0	140.6	155.6
Total manufacturing - Total, industries manufacturières	80.3	91.6	109.3	119.4	125.9	126.6	141.8	157.3
Food, beverages and tobacco - Aliments, boissons et tabac	84.0	93.0	105.6	116.4	126.5	135.2	149.4	164.1
Textiles, wearing apparel, leather, footwear - Textiles, habillement, cuir et chaussures	81.7	91.8	106.3	116.3	113.4	110.5	130.6	147.5
Chemicals, petroleum, rubber and plastic products - Produits chimiques, pétroliers, caoutchouc et plastiques	87.9	94.3	109.4	115.6	117.9	124.4	134.9	144.4
Basic metals - Métaux de base	84.9	93.3	109.6	112.4	124.6	110.7	139.0	147.7
Electricity - Electricité	88.0	94.9	107.3	108.3	115.3	114.8	119.3	124.9
Bolivia (Plurinational State of) [1] Bolivie (État plurinational de) [1]								
Total industry - Total, industrie	94.0	93.3	107.6	114.2	145.1	154.9	153.8	...
Total mining - Total, industries extractives	95.1	88.9	106.3	116.7	188.3	206.9	198.4	206.4
Total manufacturing - Total, industries manufacturières	93.6	96.8	108.9	112.6	114.9	117.9	120.8	126.2
Food, beverages and tobacco - Aliments, boissons et tabac	99.9	99.7	110.5	114.8	113.1	119.8	...	...
Textiles, wearing apparel, leather, footwear - Textiles, habillement, cuir et chaussures	88.6	88.2	106.5	94.1	94.3	91.6	...	...
Chemicals, petroleum, rubber and plastic products - Produits chimiques, pétroliers, caoutchouc et plastiques	85.4	100.8	103.9	112.8	122.5	117.6	...	...
Basic metals - Métaux de base	100.1	101.0	100.8	84.2	85.1	105.3	...	...
Fabricated metal products, excluding machinery and equipment - Fabrication d'ouvrages en métaux, machines et matériel, machines et appareils électriques	120.6	126.5	120.0	125.8	126.0	118.7	...	...
Electricity, gas and water - Electricité, gaz et eau	91.8	94.5	106.5	112.3	116.4	123.6	132.6	...
Brazil [1] Brésil [1]								
Total industry - Total, industrie	89.5	97.0	102.9	109.0	112.4	104.1	115.0	115.4
Total mining - Total, industries extractives	87.0	90.8	107.4	113.9	117.9	107.6	122.0	124.7
Total manufacturing - Total, industries manufacturières	89.7	97.3	102.5	108.7	112.0	103.9	114.6	114.8
Food, beverages and tobacco - Aliments, boissons et tabac	93.4	98.2	103.2	106.2	106.4	107.0	113.4	113.7
Textiles, wearing apparel, leather, footwear - Textiles, habillement, cuir et chaussures	98.4	103.4	98.3	100.5	98.5	91.1	96.5	86.3
Chemicals, petroleum, rubber and plastic products - Produits chimiques, pétroliers, caoutchouc et plastiques	94.1	98.6	101.2	105.4	106.2	104.3	109.4	109.1
Basic metals - Métaux de base	98.7	102.0	102.8	109.8	113.4	93.5	110.0	109.4
Chile [1] Chili [1]								
Total industry - Total, industrie	89.3	97.7	102.3	106.5	104.2	101.1	101.6	104.1
Total mining - Total, industries extractives	91.6	100.8	100.7	104.7	99.3	99.5	99.5	98.6
Total manufacturing - Total, industries manufacturières	87.2	94.9	103.3	107.5	107.8	100.6	101.2	106.6
Food, beverages and tobacco - Aliments, boissons et tabac	88.9	95.5	110.9	113.8	115.8	105.7	103.9	109.3
Textiles, wearing apparel, leather, footwear - Textiles, habillement, cuir et chaussures	99.1	106.2	91.2	83.8	69.8	56.8	58.6	48.1

23 Index numbers of industrial production *(continued)*
2005 = 100
Indices de la production industrielle *(suite)*
2005 = 100

Country or area and industry [ISIC Rev. 4] Pays ou zone et industrie [CITI Rév. 4]	2003	2004	2006	2007	2008	2009	2010	2011
Chemicals, petroleum, rubber and plastic products - Produits chimiques, pétroliers, caoutchouc et plastiques	82.8	88.4	99.4	101.7	103.8	102.2	105.8	108.9
Basic metals - Métaux de base	74.2	93.9	93.8	103.9	93.1	83.4	71.1	77.0
Electricity - Electricité	87.7	94.8	105.5	111.9	113.6	113.1	116.6	123.6
Colombia[1] Colombie[1]								
Total industry - Total, industrie	93.0	96.9	108.1	115.7	115.7	116.4	123.6	132.5
Total mining - Total, industries extractives	97.9	97.9	104.6	107.0	114.5	127.0	142.2	162.5
Total manufacturing - Total, industries manufacturières	90.5	96.2	110.8	121.5	117.8	112.5	118.0	123.6
Food, beverages and tobacco - Aliments, boissons et tabac	101.9	101.1	109.1	116.1	116.1	116.7	118.9	126.8
Textiles, wearing apparel, leather, footwear - Textiles, habillement, cuir et chaussures	93.3	100.8	107.0	119.7	109.6	91.3	106.8	113.9
Chemicals, petroleum, rubber and plastic products - Produits chimiques, pétroliers, caoutchouc et plastiques	91.8	98.3	102.0	108.2	107.9	103.5	109.7	114.1
Basic metals - Métaux de base	79.7	90.1	104.9	109.0	101.1	96.1	98.9	92.4
Electricity, gas and water - Electricité, gaz et eau	94.4	98.2	104.0	107.7	109.1	112.7	113.0	115.1
Ecuador[1] Equateur[1]								
Total industry - Total, industrie	81.0	96.0	104.7	102.8	107.8	105.2	107.3	114.2
Total mining - Total, industries extractives	71.5	98.3	103.6	95.0	95.0	91.8	92.1	95.4
Total manufacturing - Total, industries manufacturières	90.5	91.8	108.6	119.8	124.8	122.6	132.5	139.4
Food, beverages and tobacco - Aliments, boissons et tabac	92.3	91.0	111.5	123.5	124.4	123.4	130.8	...
Textiles, wearing apparel, leather, footwear - Textiles, habillement, cuir et chaussures	90.8	93.3	100.1	108.3	107.9	104.4	116.6	...
Chemicals, petroleum, rubber and plastic products - Produits chimiques, pétroliers, caoutchouc et plastiques	94.8	95.7	96.6	114.6	99.3	100.1	92.5	...
Basic metals - Métaux de base	104.6	93.5	118.2	113.6	114.5	99.2	117.3	...
Fabricated metal products; machinery and equipment, electrical machinery and apparatus - Ouvrage en métaux, machines et matériel, machines et appareils électriques	84.5	85.3	116.4	139.3	167.4	152.3	186.5	...
Electricity and water - Electricité et eau	108.1	103.5	114.1	134.0	150.0	141.6	152.2	162.6
Paraguay[1] Paraguay[1]								
Total industry - Total, industrie	92.1	96.3	104.7	104.5	107.6	107.8	114.1	...
Total mining - Total, industries extractives	90.3	92.7	97.8	101.2	106.3	109.4	99.6	...
Total manufacturing - Total, industries manufacturières	91.9	95.8	104.2	103.0	105.9	105.3	111.7	...
Food, beverages and tobacco - Aliments, boissons et tabac	93.6	96.8	104.6	103.3	105.5	108.6	112.1	...
Textiles, wearing apparel, leather, footwear - Textiles, habillement, cuir et chaussures	98.2	103.8	104.0	104.2	92.2	88.2	90.3	...
Chemicals, petroleum, rubber and plastic products - Produits chimiques, pétroliers, caoutchouc et plastiques	166.5	140.2	75.3	66.1	68.5	73.1	78.1	...
Basic metals - Métaux de base	88.8	96.0	98.9	100.7	101.9	97.2	97.2	...
All machinery and transport equipment - Fabrication de machines et de matériel de transport	87.2	83.4	122.0	144.0	158.4	141.6	157.2	...
Electricity and water - Electricité et eau	93.4	100.3	108.4	114.9	118.9	124.6	130.9	...
Peru[1] Pérou[1]								
Total industry - Total, industrie	87.2	93.0	105.7	114.9	124.8	119.1	130.5	136.2
Total mining - Total, industries extractives	87.7	92.3	101.4	104.1	112.1	112.8	112.6	112.4
Total manufacturing - Total, industries manufacturières	86.6	93.1	107.6	119.5	130.4	120.9	137.4	145.1
Food and beverages - Aliments et boissons	88.8	94.2	108.3	118.8	129.7	129.6	134.8	149.5
Textiles, wearing apparel, leather, footwear - Textiles, habillement, cuir et chaussures	87.5	97.1	97.3	104.2	96.1	72.9	99.4	103.8
Chemicals, petroleum, rubber and plastic products - Produits chimiques, pétroliers, caoutchouc et plastiques	83.9	89.1	108.0	120.9	129.8	134.1	147.5	151.0
Basic metals - Métaux de base	96.7	98.4	103.9	97.2	106.4	88.1	85.2	89.2
Electricity and water - Electricité et eau	90.7	94.7	106.9	116.0	125.0	126.5	136.3	146.3
Uruguay[1] Uruguay[1]								
Total manufacturing - Total, industries manufacturières	72.3	89.0	109.3	115.7	129.7	124.6	129.0	129.6
Food, beverages and tobacco - Aliments, boissons et tabac	70.9	86.0	109.5	116.7	121.6	123.4	125.4	128.7
Textiles, wearing apparel, leather, footwear - Textiles, habillement, cuir et chaussures	80.4	96.5	99.0	107.2	98.4	76.3	75.6	83.2
Chemicals, petroleum, rubber and plastic products - Produits chimiques, pétroliers, caoutchouc et plastiques	82.5	100.5	97.7	94.4	113.4	108.6	112.6	101.6
Basic metals - Métaux de base	69.8	89.5	117.6	126.6	118.6	93.1	102.0	109.3

23 Index numbers of industrial production *(continued)*
2005 = 100
Indices de la production industrielle *(suite)*
2005 = 100

Country or area and industry [ISIC Rev. 4] Pays ou zone et industrie [CITI Rév. 4]	2003	2004	2006	2007	2008	2009	2010	2011
Venezuela (Boliv. Rep. of)[1] Venezuela (Rép. boliv. du)[1]								
Total industry - Total, industrie	75.6	90.3	107.9	108.3	110.4	104.7	100.8	103.6
Total mining - Total, industries extractives	85.0	97.0	107.2	108.5	102.2	91.7	79.8	83.9
Total manufacturing - Total, industries manufacturières	69.7	89.8	110.1	117.7	119.3	105.1	102.5	104.3
Food, beverages and tobacco - Aliments, boissons et tabac	86.0	93.2	112.0	122.4	127.3	123.9	131.5	124.7
Textiles, wearing apparel, leather, footwear - Textiles, habillement, cuir et chaussures	56.7	90.3	103.8	110.8	117.2	100.6	111.8	111.4
Chemicals, petroleum, rubber and plastic products - Produits chimiques, pétroliers, caoutchouc et plastiques	80.5	102.3	98.0	109.6	108.8	103.1	106.6	105.2
Basic metals - Métaux de base	81.6	99.7	105.5	112.5	100.6	61.6	38.7	44.6
Electricity - Electricité	86.2	92.7	106.6	108.9	113.6	118.5	110.8	116.8

Asia · Asie

	2003	2004	2006	2007	2008	2009	2010	2011
Armenia[1] Arménie[1]								
Total industry - Total, industrie	90.8	93.0	99.1	101.7	103.4	95.7	104.9	...
Total mining - Total, industries extractives	94.9	104.8	106.2	109.7	109.5	121.2	149.8	...
Total manufacturing - Total, industries manufacturières	91.5	91.0	98.0	99.4	100.0	91.2	101.7	...
Food, beverages and tobacco - Aliments, boissons et tabac	91.3	94.4	103.1	109.8	117.3	111.8	128.4	...
Textiles, wearing apparel, leather, footwear - Textiles, habillement, cuir et chaussures	108.5	132.2	105.5	106.4	106.4	82.1	95.8	...
Chemicals, petroleum, rubber and plastic products - Produits chimiques, pétroliers, caoutchouc et plastiques	43.6	65.6	93.6	117.7	108.8	91.9	90.4	...
Basic metals - Métaux de base	76.7	75.1	104.8	119.3	108.0	129.9	138.2	...
Electricity, gas and water - Electricité, gaz et eau	77.1	87.9	97.8	105.4	109.5	95.0	86.1	...
Azerbaijan Azerbaïdjan								
Total industry - Total, industrie	...	...	139.3	176.2	185.8	205.4	209.0	194.4
Total mining - Total, industries extractives	...	...	144.7	186.8	196.7	221.3	223.8	205.2
Total manufacturing - Total, industries manufacturières	...	...	106.9	114.7	122.3	112.9	123.5	132.3
Food, beverages and tobacco - Aliments, boissons et tabac	...	...	103.4	108.6	109.6	111.3	114.4	118.4
Textiles, wearing apparel, leather, footwear - Textiles, habillement, cuir et chaussures	...	...	81.5	72.5	56.4	54.0	57.2	72.8
Chemicals, petroleum, rubber and plastic products - Produits chimiques, pétroliers, caoutchouc et plastiques	...	...	104.9	101.7	113.8	95.1	107.1	112.8
Basic metals - Métaux de base	...	...	115.0	75.8	87.8	29.8	43.0	81.7
Fabricated metals, computer, electronic and optical products, electrical equipment, machinery - Fabrication d'ouvrages en métaux, produits électroniques et optiques, appareils électriques, fabrication de machines	...	...	179.2	278.3	319.2	178.5	...	...
Electricity, gas, steam and air conditioning supply - Electricité, gaz, vapeur, et distribution de l'air conditionné	...	...	110.2	102.6	111.3	97.5	105.4	114.3
Bahrain[1] Bahreïn[1]								
Total industry - Total, industrie	...	...	99.4	104.3	109.9	108.6	116.8	...
Total mining - Total, industries extractives	...	...	100.0	102.8	105.8	104.0	106.9	...
Total manufacturing - Total, industries manufacturières	...	...	98.0	104.4	112.0	110.9	123.6	...
Electricity and water - Electricité et eau	...	...	109.1	119.3	130.4	136.0	143.8	...
Bangladesh[1,3] Bangladesh[1,3]								
Total industry - Total, industrie	86.4	92.6	110.6	119.6	129.1	138.4	148.4	173.2
Total mining - Total, industries extractives	87.8	94.3	109.5	117.2	125.0	134.4	147.2	147.4
Total manufacturing - Total, industries manufacturières	86.4	94.0	108.6	119.7	131.1	140.0	148.9	181.1
Food, beverages and tobacco - Aliments, boissons et tabac	90.8	93.0	107.2	113.0	113.5	112.1	122.3	146.4
Textiles, wearing apparel, leather, footwear - Textiles, habillement, cuir et chaussures	81.6	86.2	115.6	129.7	145.0	154.1	160.7	180.3
Chemicals, petroleum, rubber and plastic products - Produits chimiques, pétroliers, caoutchouc et plastiques	98.4	97.9	98.6	104.4	97.7	95.6	100.5	96.3
Basic metals - Métaux de base	86.4	88.3	106.8	119.4	128.7	148.7	87.3	115.9
All machinery and transport equipment - Fabrication de machines et de matériel de transport	79.8	82.2	105.0	110.6	112.3	118.4	132.2	123.8
Electricity - Electricité	86.6	92.9	104.1	106.7	114.0	120.1	132.8	145.7
Brunei Darussalam[1] Brunéi Darussalam[1]								
Total industry - Total, industrie	103.3	102.5	103.3	96.4	90.7	86.0	87.5	...
Total mining - Total, industries extractives	103.5	102.8	104.3	95.9	86.9	84.0	85.4	...

Country or area and industry [ISIC Rev. 4] Pays ou zone et industrie [CITI Rév. 4]	2003	2004	2006	2007	2008	2009	2010	2011
Total manufacturing - Total, industries manufacturières	103.2	102.0	100.8	97.7	100.5	90.6	92.0	...
Electricity and water - Electricité et eau	95.7	96.0	100.1	102.8	103.7	110.3	115.3	...
China, Hong Kong SAR Chine, Hong Kong RAS								
Total industry - Total, industrie	...	...	101.3	100.9	96.5	93.2	94.5	95.7
Total manufacturing - Total, industries manufacturières	...	...	102.3	100.8	94.0	86.2	89.3	89.9
Food, beverages and tobacco - Aliments, boissons et tabac	...	...	109.7	125.0	128.2	127.1	135.1	144.5
Textiles and wearing apparel - Textiles et habillement	...	...	98.5	85.1	69.0	50.1	44.6	39.6
Basic metals - Métaux de base	...	...	96.9	85.7	76.7	68.8	75.6	68.5
Electricity, gas, steam and air conditioning supply - Electricité, gaz, vapeur, et distribution de l'air conditionné	93.5	97.0	100.3	101.0	99.2	100.6	99.9	101.8
China, Macao SAR[1] Chine, Macao RAS[1]								
Total industry - Total, industrie	113.6	112.7	92.9	87.5	64.9	50.3	45.3	45.1
Total manufacturing - Total, industries manufacturières	135.9	127.9	99.0	93.8	63.5	29.3	30.6	38.7
Textiles and wearing apparel - Textiles et habillement	140.2	134.2	95.7	91.2	61.0	15.3	9.6	7.3
Cyprus[4] Chypre[4]								
Total industry - Total, industrie	97.8	99.6	100.4	105.3	109.9	99.7	98.0	90.1
Total mining - Total, industries extractives	92.0	96.3	99.4	106.8	115.8	94.2	103.4	94.9
Total manufacturing - Total, industries manufacturières	99.0	100.7	99.3	104.2	108.7	96.2	93.2	85.7
Food, beverages and tobacco - Aliments, boissons et tabac	...	...	92.8	96.1	98.3	94.1	93.4	87.0
Textiles, wearing apparel, leather, footwear - Textiles, habillement, cuir et chaussures	...	...	96.1	87.6	75.9	59.5	53.5	51.0
Petroleum, chemicals, pharmaceuticals, rubber and plastic - Pétroliers, produits chimiques, pharmaceutiques, caoutchouc et plastiques	...	...	104.2	115.2	125.8	115.5	126.0	123.7
Basic metals - Métaux de base	...	...	110.4	117.2	122.2	106.2	99.9	91.8
Electricity, gas, steam and air conditioning supply - Electricité, gaz, vapeur, et distribution de l'air conditionné	93.0	94.9	106.2	110.1	114.9	118.1	120.5	110.8
Georgia[1] Géorgie[1]								
Total industry - Total, industrie	70.9	74.4	131.8	140.9	133.2	117.9	137.0	166.6
Total mining - Total, industries extractives	123.5	99.9	102.7	108.4	119.3	116.2	121.3	114.3
Total manufacturing - Total, industries manufacturières	65.2	71.1	135.8	146.0	136.5	119.0	141.1	174.4
Electricity, gas and water - Electricité, gaz et eau	102.0	92.7	108.0	109.3	110.7	109.2	108.9	118.6
India[1,5] Inde[1,5]								
Total industry - Total, industrie	82.4	92.1	112.9	130.5	133.7	140.8	152.4	156.7
Total mining - Total, industries extractives	93.7	97.8	105.2	110.0	112.8	122.6	128.2	125.6
Total manufacturing - Total, industries manufacturières	80.1	90.7	115.0	136.1	139.4	146.2	159.3	164.0
Food, beverages and tobacco - Aliments, boissons et tabac	86.4	90.1	113.5	124.8	116.6	115.1	122.3	139.1
Textiles, wearing apparel, leather, footwear - Textiles, habillement, cuir et chaussures	80.2	92.7	110.6	118.5	112.5	118.0	125.3	122.5
Chemicals, petroleum, rubber and plastic products - Produits chimiques, pétroliers, caoutchouc et plastiques	87.8	98.4	110.2	118.2	118.5	122.4	124.7	126.1
Basic metals - Métaux de base	82.0	86.5	114.7	135.2	137.5	140.5	152.9	166.2
Electricity - Electricité	90.4	95.1	107.2	114.1	117.2	124.3	131.2	141.9
Indonesia[1] Indonésie[1]								
Total industry - Total, industrie	99.5	99.1	104.2	111.7	122.4	118.5	140.3	163.3
Total mining - Total, industries extractives	103.4	99.3	110.1	119.6	137.9	128.8	167.7	207.5
Total manufacturing - Total, industries manufacturières	95.6	98.8	98.4	103.9	107.0	108.3	113.3	119.6
Food, beverages and tobacco - Aliments, boissons et tabac	75.0	85.0	106.7	116.5	125.2	145.9	154.1	167.6
Textiles, wearing apparel, leather, footwear - Textiles, habillement, cuir et chaussures	114.8	116.4	121.7	116.9	111.1	105.4	107.7	116.2
Chemicals, petroleum, rubber and plastic products - Produits chimiques, pétroliers, caoutchouc et plastiques	87.9	94.7	114.1	139.7	134.1	137.9	144.4	155.1
Basic metals - Métaux de base	96.5	102.8	122.1	136.9	145.5	137.6	142.1	165.2
Electricity - Electricité	88.7	94.3	104.5	111.7	117.3	123.1	133.3	143.4
Iran (Islamic Rep. of)[1] Iran (Rép. islamique d')[1]								
Total manufacturing - Total, industries manufacturières	86.8	88.6	109.1	120.9	...	...	...	...
Food and beverages - Aliments et boissons	56.0	58.0	102.5	112.0	...	...	...	...
Textiles, wearing apparel, leather, footwear - Textiles, habillement, cuir et chaussures	96.5	94.7	97.2	104.3	...	...	...	...
Chemicals, petroleum, rubber and plastic products - Produits chimiques, pétroliers, caoutchouc et plastiques	61.2	65.7	113.9	124.2	...	...	...	...

23
Index numbers of industrial production *(continued)*
2005 = 100
Indices de la production industrielle *(suite)*
2005 = 100

Country or area and industry [ISIC Rev. 4] Pays ou zone et industrie [CITI Rév. 4]	2003	2004	2006	2007	2008	2009	2010	2011
Israel[1] Israël[1]								
Total industry - Total, industrie	90.3	96.4	109.8	114.8	123.2	115.8	124.9	127.4
Total mining - Total, industries extractives	100.8	97.9	99.7	98.7	99.3	89.1	99.9	92.7
Total manufacturing - Total, industries manufacturières	89.9	96.3	110.1	115.1	123.9	116.6	125.5	128.4
Food, beverages and tobacco - Aliments, boissons et tabac	97.8	99.5	102.1	105.0	103.5	102.1	104.8	108.5
Textiles - Textiles	99.1	99.5	103.9	97.6	96.3	83.4	86.3	81.1
Chemicals, petroleum, rubber and plastic products - Produits chimiques, pétroliers, caoutchouc et plastiques	85.3	94.7	119.7	120.2	153.2	140.1	166.1	162.4
Basic metals - Métaux de base	90.8	97.8	100.3	106.6	99.4	82.5	93.2	98.9
Fabricated metal products, excluding machinery and equipment - Fabrication d'ouvrages en métaux, machines et matériel, machines et appareils électriques	95.1	97.0	110.5	115.4	121.8	103.9	115.9	126.2
Japan Japon								
Total industry - Total, industrie	94.2	98.6	104.3	107.1	103.9	82.2	95.1	92.6
Total mining - Total, industries extractives	97.0	97.0	102.6	106.6	103.1	93.6	90.0	90.8
Total manufacturing - Total, industries manufacturières	94.2	98.7	104.5	107.4	103.8	81.0	94.5	92.1
Food and beverages - Aliments et boissons	99.9	101.1	98.3	100.7	101.4	103.6	104.4	105.1
Textiles, wearing apparel, leather, footwear - Textiles, habillement, cuir et chaussures	116.8	108.7	95.3	89.9	81.9	67.3	66.3	66.3
Chemicals, petroleum, rubber and plastic products - Produits chimiques, pétroliers, caoutchouc et plastiques	97.6	99.3	100.3	101.6	96.4	83.2	91.4	88.5
Basic metals - Métaux de base	97.2	100.5	102.8	105.5	102.4	73.5	93.4	90.1
Fabricated metals, computer, electronic and optical products, electrical equipment, machinery - Fabrication d'ouvrages en métaux produits électroniques et optiques, appareils électriques, fabrication de machines	89.9	96.9	106.9	111.3	107.2	76.6	95.0	91.2
Electricity and gas - Electricité et gaz	94.1	97.2	102.0	103.9	104.7	96.9	103.0	98.8
Jordan[1] Jordanie[1]								
Total industry - Total, industrie	81.0	90.7	105.8	109.2	110.6	108.8	105.4	105.1
Total mining - Total, industries extractives	105.3	101.3	91.7	90.5	100.3	71.6	99.9	116.4
Total manufacturing - Total, industries manufacturières	78.7	89.6	106.3	108.8	109.5	110.9	104.8	102.5
Food, beverages and tobacco - Aliments, boissons et tabac	73.5	84.5	105.6	101.2	106.4	125.9	128.2	124.9
Textiles, wearing apparel, leather, footwear - Textiles, habillement, cuir et chaussures	80.7	99.3	106.7	95.2	105.3	103.6	97.8	129.8
Chemicals, petroleum, rubber and plastic products - Produits chimiques, pétroliers, caoutchouc et plastiques	81.9	92.4	103.9	103.7	104.3	105.5	105.5	102.9
Basic metals - Métaux de base	78.3	86.0	83.4	88.6	84.5	75.6	72.7	79.1
Electricity - Electricité	82.2	93.0	116.9	138.0	139.6	128.3	121.9	127.4
Kazakhstan[1] Kazakhstan[1]								
Total industry - Total, industrie	86.5	95.5	107.2	112.6	114.9	...	...	...
Total mining - Total, industries extractives	85.8	97.3	107.0	109.8	115.6	...	...	...
Total manufacturing - Total, industries manufacturières	85.1	93.0	108.1	116.6	113.5	...	...	...
Food, beverages and tobacco - Aliments, boissons et tabac	78.9	86.2	107.2	114.5	113.8	...	...	...
Textiles and wearing apparel - Textiles et habillement	84.8	87.7	102.7	83.8	95.2	...	...	...
Chemicals and petroleum products - Produits chimiques et pétroliers	85.4	90.9	104.4	119.2	126.2	...	...	...
Metal and Metal Products, except machinery and equipment - Métallurgie et travail des métaux	101.6	106.3	106.8	110.9	109.4	...	...	...
All machinery and transport equipment - Fabrication de machines et de matériel de transport	60.9	80.2	119.4	136.8	126.7	...	...	...
Electricity, gas and water - Electricité, gaz et eau	93.9	95.8	102.8	112.2	119.5	...	...	...
Kyrgyzstan[1] Kirghizistan[1]								
Total industry - Total, industrie	98.1	109.6	88.0	89.5	65.6	61.8	69.1	77.8
Total mining - Total, industries extractives	69.8	103.0	97.0	100.3	108.6	117.2	114.7	145.9
Total manufacturing - Total, industries manufacturières	101.1	112.5	82.7	81.5	54.3	50.4	55.2	61.5
Food, beverages and tobacco - Aliments, boissons et tabac	96.2	100.6	108.2	112.9	114.5	126.7	123.9	120.9
Textiles and wearing apparel - Textiles et habillement	63.1	88.3	119.1	151.5	168.0	117.4	168.3	251.5
Chemicals and chemical products - Produits chimiques	80.6	115.2	89.4	126.3	132.2	75.2	91.1	147.1
Metal and Metal Products, except machinery and equipment - Métallurgie et travail des métaux	137.9	131.3	64.2	64.1	101.8	92.3	98.5	101.9

Country or area and industry [ISIC Rev. 4] Pays ou zone et industrie [CITI Rév. 4]	2003	2004	2006	2007	2008	2009	2010	2011
All machinery and transport equipment - Fabrication de machines et de matériel de transport	130.7	127.9	96.1	81.3	110.8	92.2	119.2	115.1
Electricity, gas and water - Electricité, gaz et eau	90.2	98.8	104.9	116.9	107.2	110.2	156.1	168.2
Malaysia[1] Malaisie[1]								
Total industry - Total, industrie	86.0	96.1	104.9	107.3	108.1	99.9	107.1	108.4
Total mining - Total, industries extractives	93.7	99.5	96.2	98.3	99.1	95.5	94.0	87.1
Total manufacturing - Total, industries manufacturières	83.4	95.1	109.0	111.5	112.2	101.0	112.2	117.3
Food, beverages and tobacco - Aliments, boissons et tabac	90.0	93.4	104.6	110.6	120.5	121.2	127.0	136.4
Textiles, wearing apparel, leather, footwear - Textiles, habillement, cuir et chaussures	104.1	94.6	102.2	100.3	100.3	80.4	83.8	92.5
Chemicals, petroleum, rubber and plastic products - Produits chimiques, pétroliers, caoutchouc et plastiques	85.3	91.6	109.1	111.8	113.2	111.5	118.0	127.4
Basic metals - Métaux de base	106.6	105.6	105.6	122.9	119.4	91.6	110.9	112.4
Electricity - Electricité	87.4	94.6	105.1	109.2	110.5	111.4	121.2	123.6
Mongolia[1] Mongolie[1]								
Total industry - Total, industrie	93.6	105.1	108.3	119.8	118.2	96.1	111.0	109.7
Total mining - Total, industries extractives	76.2	88.8	103.6	104.9	104.7	101.7	110.6	109.8
Total manufacturing - Total, industries manufacturières	122.4	133.0	130.1	179.8	172.2	85.6	114.7	110.9
Food and beverages - Aliments et boissons	99.9	102.3	113.5	151.2	161.5	117.9	128.6	110.9
Textiles, wearing apparel, leather, footwear - Textiles, habillement, cuir et chaussures	223.3	225.6	168.2	179.9	141.3	91.4	101.6	173.0
Chemicals and chemical products - Produits chimiques	142.2	162.0	117.0	172.4	264.1	130.6	125.1	149.7
Basic metals - Métaux de base	45.4	72.9	154.9	346.1	252.1	35.9	147.5	91.0
Electricity, gas and water - Electricité, gaz et eau	90.1	96.3	101.3	104.9	110.7	101.5	105.9	105.7
Occupied Palestinian Terr.[1] Terr. palestinien occupé[1]								
Total industry - Total, industrie	85.2	92.3	84.3	88.2	96.5	87.4	94.1	101.2
Total mining - Total, industries extractives	97.1	92.4	91.4	51.0	52.7	55.4	57.4	57.4
Total manufacturing - Total, industries manufacturières	83.1	93.6	85.4	89.2	91.1	91.3	86.5	93.4
Electricity and water - Electricité et eau	90.2	87.1	78.5	93.9	128.0	81.0	132.3	142.4
Oman[1] Oman[1]								
Total industry - Total, industrie	98.6	97.4	96.1	95.7	104.3	113.9	...	...
Total mining - Total, industries extractives	102.5	99.0	95.6	91.1	99.2	107.5	...	...
Total manufacturing - Total, industries manufacturières	90.8	92.5	110.2	124.3	136.8	153.0	...	...
Electricity and water - Electricité et eau	81.4	92.4	89.1	95.4	105.0	117.1	...	...
Pakistan[1,6] Pakistan[1,6]								
Total industry - Total, industrie	79.6	92.2	108.2	113.7	107.0	107.8	108.4	...
Total mining - Total, industries extractives	87.1	95.9	101.7	105.4	100.0	104.2	103.2	...
Total manufacturing - Total, industries manufacturières	77.5	91.6	109.5	116.1	109.1	109.5	111.2	...
Food, beverages and tobacco - Aliments, boissons et tabac	83.3	93.3	101.6	102.8	103.7	97.7	98.3	...
Textiles - Textiles	83.9	95.4	111.6	117.3	120.0	107.2	105.9	...
Chemicals and chemical products - Produits chimiques	75.7	95.2	97.2	100.4	102.0	105.7	96.3	...
Electricity - Electricité	87.1	92.1	106.5	105.3	99.3	99.1	92.8	...
Philippines[1] Philippines[1]								
Total industry - Total, industrie	95.9	97.7	91.8	89.8	89.9	82.4	99.5	101.1
Total mining - Total, industries extractives	88.3	92.7	97.3	120.7	119.4	144.4	173.7	184.4
Total manufacturing - Total, industries manufacturières	96.9	97.9	90.1	86.0	86.2	76.0	93.6	94.6
Food, beverages and tobacco - Aliments, boissons et tabac	100.4	94.2	98.6	93.4	97.5	88.5	91.4	84.5
Textiles, wearing apparel, leather, footwear - Textiles, habillement, cuir et chaussures	224.3	94.6	85.6	67.8	73.5	48.6	43.9	42.6
Chemicals, petroleum, rubber and plastic products - Produits chimiques, pétroliers, caoutchouc et plastiques	105.5	92.9	93.8	93.3	89.3	73.1	90.3	98.3
Basic metals - Métaux de base	100.0	126.8	136.4	111.1	101.6	91.7	114.1	103.0
Fabricated metal products; machinery and equipment, electrical machinery and apparatus - Ouvrage en métaux, machines et matériel, machines et appareils électriques	107.3	113.4	72.7	73.7	67.2	63.3	84.7	79.5
Electricity and water - Electricité et eau	91.9	98.4	100.7	104.1	103.6	103.9	113.9	115.7
Qatar[1] Qatar[1]								
Total industry - Total, industrie	81.4	94.3	110.4	124.1	141.6	150.1	190.9	217.5
Total mining - Total, industries extractives	80.3	94.8	111.7	127.1	143.9	150.4	193.7	224.2
Total manufacturing - Total, industries manufacturières	86.6	92.2	104.7	111.8	132.9	151.2	185.0	193.3
Electricity and water - Electricité et eau	79.2	92.9	110.1	113.8	127.8	127.3	129.7	160.7

23
Index numbers of industrial production *(continued)*
2005 = 100
Indices de la production industrielle *(suite)*
2005 = 100

Country or area and industry [ISIC Rev. 4] Pays ou zone et industrie [CITI Rév. 4]	2003	2004	2006	2007	2008	2009	2010	2011
Republic of Korea République de Corée								
Total industry - Total, industrie	85.2	94.0	108.4	115.9	119.8	119.7	139.2	148.7
Total mining - Total, industries extractives	112.4	108.4	95.8	91.5	82.3	87.9	81.5	80.8
Total manufacturing - Total, industries manufacturières	84.9	94.0	108.7	116.4	120.3	120.0	140.1	149.9
Food, beverages and tobacco - Aliments, boissons et tabac	99.8	102.4	102.0	102.9	102.3	100.8	105.8	107.2
Textiles, wearing apparel, leather, footwear - Textiles, habillement, cuir et chaussures	113.4	106.3	104.1	105.8	103.9	98.7	105.8	106.7
Petroleum, chemicals, pharmaceuticals, rubber and plastic - Pétroliers, produits chimiques, pharmaceutiques, caoutchouc et plastiques	93.0	97.2	104.3	110.4	111.1	112.1	120.7	125.1
Basic metals - Métaux de base	94.8	99.7	103.7	108.4	110.0	99.7	119.7	128.4
Fabricated metals, computer, electronic and optical products, electrical equipment, machinery - Fabrication d'ouvrages en métaux produits électroniques et optiques, appareils électriques, fabrication de machines	79.8	91.7	112.9	123.7	130.5	132.5	161.4	176.7
Electricity, gas, steam and air conditioning supply - Electricité, gaz, vapeur, et distribution de l'air conditionné	88.2	93.3	104.1	108.8	114.5	116.5	127.5	132.9
Saudi Arabia[1] Arabie saoudite[1]								
Total industry - Total, industrie	89.2	95.0	102.5	101.6	106.5	101.3	104.9	112.2
Total mining - Total, industries extractives	89.5	95.4	100.5	96.5	100.6	91.9	93.9	97.9
Total manufacturing - Total, industries manufacturières	88.2	94.2	107.1	113.2	120.0	121.8	128.2	144.1
Electricity, gas and water - Electricité, gaz et eau	89.1	94.9	106.4	110.8	118.1	126.2	136.2	141.9
Singapore Singapour								
Total industry - Total, industrie	80.8	91.5	111.3	117.9	113.2	108.8	139.9	150.3
Total manufacturing - Total, industries manufacturières	80.2	91.3	111.9	118.6	113.5	108.8	141.2	152.2
Food, beverages and tobacco - Aliments, boissons et tabac	91.9	93.4	103.9	115.6	124.6	118.8	126.7	131.4
Textiles, wearing apparel, leather, footwear - Textiles, habillement, cuir et chaussures	121.0	117.6	91.2	81.3	62.8	41.2	30.1	28.5
Petroleum, chemicals, pharmaceuticals, rubber and plastic - Pétroliers, produits chimiques, pharmaceutiques, caoutchouc et plastiques	79.9	92.9	114.3	114.8	108.5	111.0	152.1	185.8
Basic metals - Métaux de base	72.0	85.6	117.9	107.3	129.6	109.3	120.7	118.1
Fabricated metals, computer, electronic and optical products, electrical equipment, machinery - Fabrication d'ouvrages en métaux produits électroniques et optiques, appareils électriques, fabrication de machines	77.8	89.3	112.3	120.5	116.6	106.8	134.7	131.8
Electricity - Electricité	90.9	93.7	101.3	105.9	106.5	107.6	116.8	118.4
Sri Lanka[1] Sri Lanka[1]								
Total industry - Total, industrie	93.1	96.2	103.9	109.4	114.3	117.3	126.1	...
Total manufacturing - Total, industries manufacturières	93.7	96.5	103.6	109.1	114.4	117.8	126.5	...
Food, beverages and tobacco - Aliments, boissons et tabac	91.9	95.3	105.9	112.3	119.5	126.3	134.9	...
Textiles, wearing apparel, leather, footwear - Textiles, habillement, cuir et chaussures	88.5	95.8	103.8	110.2	111.4	111.1	120.7	...
Chemicals, petroleum, rubber and plastic products - Produits chimiques, pétroliers, caoutchouc et plastiques	83.6	87.8	107.7	115.4	133.4	135.9	153.3	...
Basic metals - Métaux de base	86.8	94.1	106.1	113.1	117.4	118.1	124.4	...
Electricity - Electricité	87.9	93.0	107.1	111.9	112.9	112.7	122.1	...
Syrian Arab Republic[1] Rép. arabe syrienne[1]								
Total industry - Total, industrie	115.4	104.4	100.0	96.7	93.4	93.4	97.8	...
Total mining - Total, industries extractives	139.7	109.0	96.2	88.5	85.9	91.0	93.6	...
Total manufacturing - Total, industries manufacturières	91.6	101.9	103.7	103.7	99.1	98.1	97.2	...
Food, beverages and tobacco - Aliments, boissons et tabac	98.7	106.4	107.5	109.0	116.7	118.0	122.3	...
Textiles, wearing apparel, leather, footwear - Textiles, habillement, cuir et chaussures	97.8	100.0	96.2	93.2	84.3	88.7	93.5	...
Chemicals, petroleum, rubber and plastic products - Produits chimiques, pétroliers, caoutchouc et plastiques	94.3	107.0	106.1	102.9	94.1	91.8	91.5	...
Basic metals - Métaux de base	97.9	89.4	95.7	84.0	70.2	64.9	59.6	...
Fabricated metal products; machinery and equipment, electrical machinery and apparatus - Ouvrage en métaux, machines et matériel, machines et appareils électriques	102.0	101.3	102.8	86.8	93.6	82.5	92.3	...
Electricity and water - Electricité et eau	81.9	88.8	103.5	106.3	112.6	118.9	127.3	...

Country or area and industry [ISIC Rev. 4] Pays ou zone et industrie [CITI Rév. 4]	2003	2004	2006	2007	2008	2009	2010	2011
Tajikistan[1] Tadjikistan[1]								
Total industry - Total, industrie	80.3	90.1	105.6	115.5	111.4	104.2	113.8	...
Total mining - Total, industries extractives	100.0	99.0	106.8	112.1	110.1	110.8	128.6	...
Total manufacturing - Total, industries manufacturières	76.8	89.8	105.3	116.3	112.0	103.0	110.8	...
Electricity, gas and water - Electricité, gaz et eau	97.7	95.4	105.3	111.5	103.8	101.5	106.0	...
Thailand[1] Thaïlande[1]								
Total manufacturing - Total, industries manufacturières	82.6	91.8	106.4	115.0	119.5	110.9	126.8	115.1
Food, beverages and tobacco - Aliments, boissons et tabac	96.2	94.6	105.8	109.5	109.7	104.6	109.8	114.1
Textiles, wearing apparel, leather, footwear - Textiles, habillement, cuir et chaussures	94.8	98.8	96.2	95.5	88.0	76.0	80.3	67.2
Chemicals, petroleum, rubber and plastic products - Produits chimiques, pétroliers, caoutchouc et plastiques	94.1	101.6	102.4	101.9	100.4	98.0	106.1	105.0
Basic metals - Métaux de base	95.4	105.3	99.6	99.7	92.0	82.4	96.0	90.2
Turkey Turquie								
Total industry - Total, industrie	...	...	107.3	114.7	114.0	102.5	116.0	126.2
Total mining - Total, industries extractives	...	...	107.6	116.3	125.9	124.9	127.5	131.3
Total manufacturing - Total, industries manufacturières	...	...	107.2	114.4	112.7	99.9	114.3	124.8
Food, beverages and tobacco - Aliments, boissons et tabac	...	...	106.0	108.9	113.3	112.6	118.2	124.2
Textiles, wearing apparel, leather, footwear - Textiles, habillement, cuir et chaussures	...	...	100.6	102.1	91.3	81.8	90.8	90.9
Petroleum, chemicals, pharmaceuticals, rubber and plastic - Pétroliers, produits chimiques, pharmaceutiques, caoutchouc et plastiques	...	...	108.4	116.8	115.8	110.3	122.8	132.8
Basic metals - Métaux de base	...	...	113.9	126.1	123.5	104.5	115.8	123.3
Fabricated metals, computer, electronic and optical products, electrical equipment, machinery - Fabrication d'ouvrages en métaux produits électroniques et optiques, appareils électriques, fabrication de machines	...	...	108.0	117.9	118.4	93.1	119.3	140.2
Electricity, gas, steam and air conditioning supply - Electricité, gaz, vapeur, et distribution de l'air conditionné	...	...	108.6	118.1	122.6	119.8	129.8	141.0
Uzbekistan[1] Ouzbékistan[1]								
Total industry - Total, industrie	85.2	93.2	110.8	...	...	...	...	...
Viet Nam[1] Viet Nam[1]								
Total industry - Total, industrie	...	...	...	...	131.7	141.0	156.1	166.7
Total mining - Total, industries extractives	...	...	...	...	99.8	109.3	107.6	109.1
Total manufacturing - Total, industries manufacturières	...	...	...	...	143.6	148.6	167.2	182.4
Food, beverages and tobacco - Aliments, boissons et tabac	...	...	...	...	140.4	140.9	158.6	176.5
Textiles, wearing apparel, leather, footwear - Textiles, habillement, cuir et chaussures	...	...	...	...	134.6	132.2	140.4	174.0
Chemicals, petroleum, rubber and plastic products - Produits chimiques, pétroliers, caoutchouc et plastiques	...	...	...	...	118.6	125.4	142.2	160.9
Basic metals - Métaux de base	...	...	...	...	132.5	161.8	183.2	210.7
Fabricated metal products; machinery and equipment, electrical machinery and apparatus - Ouvrage en métaux, machines et matériel, machines et appareils électriques	...	...	...	...	179.4	162.6	152.3	166.8
Electricity, gas and water - Electricité, gaz et eau	...	...	...	...	150.1	189.7	225.6	244.2
Europe · Europe								
Albania[1] Albanie[1]								
Total industry - Total, industrie	98.2	100.2	104.0	90.8	117.9	116.5	139.6	121.1
Total mining - Total, industries extractives	102.8	105.2	116.7	136.5	156.7	153.1	241.7	386.1
Total manufacturing - Total, industries manufacturières	86.8	90.4	105.7	113.0	132.0	152.3	172.4	196.8
Food, beverages and tobacco - Aliments, boissons et tabac	90.7	102.7	122.2	124.8	149.9	149.4	158.9	161.6
Textiles, wearing apparel, leather, footwear - Textiles, habillement, cuir et chaussures	99.4	100.4	114.1	106.6	128.1	159.5	181.6	183.6
Chemicals, petroleum, rubber and plastic products - Produits chimiques, pétroliers, caoutchouc et plastiques	66.2	73.4	78.4	69.9	73.3	122.5	77.4	119.1
Basic metals and metal products - Métaux de base et produits métalliques	100.7	80.8	82.3	113.9	126.6	109.2	145.6	167.0
Electricity, gas and water - Electricité, gaz et eau	112.8	112.4	100.1	61.2	89.6	72.7	87.7	39.5

Country or area and industry [ISIC Rev. 4] Pays ou zone et industrie [CITI Rév. 4]	2003	2004	2006	2007	2008	2009	2010	2011
Austria Autriche								
Total industry - Total, industrie	89.9	96.2	107.2	113.2	116.4	102.5	109.8	117.6
Total mining - Total, industries extractives	107.4	102.0	110.7	110.7	118.3	110.3	115.4	107.9
Total manufacturing - Total, industries manufacturières	89.0	96.2	107.1	113.8	116.1	100.7	108.1	115.8
Food, beverages and tobacco - Aliments, boissons et tabac	96.1	97.6	105.2	106.9	106.3	102.0	104.9	106.6
Textiles, wearing apparel, leather, footwear - Textiles, habillement, cuir et chaussures	115.4	106.4	96.4	96.2	89.5	76.6	80.2	72.5
Petroleum, chemicals, pharmaceuticals, rubber and plastic - Pétroliers, produits chimiques, pharmaceutiques, caoutchouc et plastiques	87.5	93.6	108.9	118.6	124.9	114.3	120.0	127.0
Basic metals - Métaux de base	88.0	96.2	110.1	116.5	117.6	86.5	108.1	118.8
Fabricated metals, computer, electronic and optical products, electrical equipment, machinery - Fabrication d'ouvrages en métaux produits électroniques et optiques, appareils électriques, fabrication de machines	83.8	94.4	108.0	118.0	121.8	101.0	109.8	121.9
Electricity, gas, steam and air conditioning supply - Electricité, gaz, vapeur, et distribution de l'air conditionné	94.2	94.7	107.3	108.2	118.5	116.2	123.5	135.2
Belarus[1] Bélarus[1]								
Total industry - Total, industrie	78.1	90.5	111.2	120.8	134.5	130.3	145.6	158.8
Total mining - Total, industries extractives	85.0	92.7	103.1	104.8	106.0	109.2	119.9	121.8
Total manufacturing - Total, industries manufacturières	77.8	90.5	112.5	123.8	138.9	135.1	150.6	166.9
Electricity, gas and water - Electricité, gaz et eau	89.4	100.7	101.6	99.3	103.2	93.5	107.1	100.7
Belgium Belgique								
Total industry - Total, industrie	93.4	97.9	103.2	108.6	110.0	96.7	105.0	109.2
Total mining - Total, industries extractives	94.4	93.9	103.6	109.6	113.1	96.1	101.4	103.2
Total manufacturing - Total, industries manufacturières	93.8	98.8	103.4	108.9	110.8	95.5	104.4	109.7
Food, beverages and tobacco - Aliments, boissons et tabac	95.8	98.6	103.3	106.2	111.8	111.4	113.0	116.8
Textiles, wearing apparel, leather, footwear - Textiles, habillement, cuir et chaussures	105.3	104.0	102.5	102.6	92.5	75.5	77.9	74.3
Petroleum, chemicals, pharmaceuticals, rubber and plastic - Pétroliers, produits chimiques, pharmaceutiques, caoutchouc et plastiques	95.9	101.3	103.4	103.3	105.8	93.0	107.0	113.7
Basic metals - Métaux de base	96.6	97.7	109.7	106.3	112.5	82.6	99.0	100.2
Fabricated metals, computer, electronic and optical products, electrical equipment, machinery - Fabrication d'ouvrages en métaux produits électroniques et optiques, appareils électriques, fabrication de machines	90.1	97.6	100.8	115.1	116.2	91.0	99.3	103.7
Electricity, gas, steam and air conditioning supply - Electricité, gaz, vapeur, et distribution de l'air conditionné	90.0	89.3	101.9	105.7	101.3	108.4	111.2	104.6
Bosnia and Herzegovina[1] Bosnie- Herzégovine[1]								
Total industry - Total, industrie	...	...	112.5	119.9	128.7	130.6	135.4	143.0
Total mining - Total, industries extractives	...	...	108.6	107.2	120.9	117.9	113.7	131.4
Total manufacturing - Total, industries manufacturières	...	...	117.4	128.4	135.6	139.3	146.4	153.7
Food, beverages and tobacco - Aliments, boissons et tabac	...	...	107.9	108.1	113.3	125.4	116.0	105.3
Textiles, wearing apparel, leather, footwear - Textiles, habillement, cuir et chaussures	...	...	100.2	98.2	102.1	100.6	109.8	120.3
Chemicals, petroleum, rubber and plastic products - Produits chimiques, pétroliers, caoutchouc et plastiques	...	...	88.4	104.3	135.5	276.2	308.1	354.1
Basic metals - Métaux de base	...	...	154.1	160.5	166.3	137.1	174.5	193.0
Electricity and gas - Electricité et gaz	...	...	102.1	105.3	115.4	115.5	119.7	122.1
Bulgaria Bulgarie								
Total industry - Total, industrie	82.1	93.3	106.2	116.5	117.2	94.9	97.2	103.0
Total mining - Total, industries extractives	86.0	101.0	100.8	92.8	87.8	74.6	75.6	81.8
Total manufacturing - Total, industries manufacturières	79.7	92.8	108.7	119.0	119.9	93.1	96.7	101.7
Food, beverages and tobacco - Aliments, boissons et tabac	83.3	95.6	100.3	112.3	119.7	107.6	106.3	104.0
Textiles, wearing apparel, leather, footwear - Textiles, habillement, cuir et chaussures	90.6	101.8	110.7	116.1	101.4	73.6	68.9	69.9
Basic metals - Métaux de base	60.1	95.5	110.5	110.8	111.8	95.7	97.2	103.8
Chemicals, pharmaceuticals, rubber and plastic products - Produits chimiques, pharmaceutiques, caoutchouc et plastiques	85.9	91.8	100.6	109.1	116.5	86.1	96.9	106.7

23
Index numbers of industrial production *(continued)*
2005 = 100
Indices de la production industrielle *(suite)*
2005 = 100

Country or area and industry [ISIC Rev. 4] Pays ou zone et industrie [CITI Rév. 4]	2003	2004	2006	2007	2008	2009	2010	2011
Fabricated metals, computer, electronic and optical products, electrical equipment, machinery - Fabrication d'ouvrages en métaux produits électroniques et optiques, appareils électriques, fabrication de machines	77.0	85.2	111.2	127.6	134.4	100.3	109.5	121.2
Electricity, gas, steam and air conditioning supply - Electricité, gaz, vapeur, et distribution de l'air conditionné	90.2	91.9	98.7	117.4	120.2	112.5	110.0	118.7
Croatia Croatie								
Total industry - Total, industrie	92.5	95.5	104.0	109.4	110.7	100.4	99.0	97.8
Total mining - Total, industries extractives	106.5	103.1	110.3	113.5	111.4	99.4	90.3	85.8
Total manufacturing - Total, industries manufacturières	91.4	94.5	104.0	110.0	111.2	99.4	97.3	97.1
Food, beverages and tobacco - Aliments, boissons et tabac	90.8	93.7	104.1	109.1	111.7	104.2	104.4	106.1
Textiles, wearing apparel, leather, footwear - Textiles, habillement, cuir et chaussures	128.3	107.7	98.5	102.7	101.1	83.5	90.3	91.2
Petroleum, chemicals, pharmaceuticals, rubber and plastic - Pétroliers, produits chimiques, pharmaceutiques, caoutchouc et plastiques	97.7	102.1	94.1	99.6	92.7	89.3	87.5	81.2
Basic metals - Métaux de base	76.1	95.5	103.6	103.3	112.6	84.5	89.3	87.7
Fabricated metals, computer, electronic and optical products, electrical equipment, machinery - Fabrication d'ouvrages en métaux produits électroniques et optiques, appareils électriques, fabrication de machines	85.5	89.6	104.5	112.8	113.7	92.7	82.6	79.5
Electricity and gas - Electricité et gaz	95.7	101.1	102.0	102.7	106.6	109.0	116.0	107.9
Czech Republic République tchèque								
Total industry - Total, industrie	87.5	96.4	108.2	119.5	117.3	101.5	111.8	118.9
Total mining - Total, industries extractives	105.5	103.3	100.0	98.9	95.9	95.0	94.7	96.3
Total manufacturing - Total, industries manufacturières	84.3	95.1	109.5	123.0	121.2	102.7	114.5	123.4
Food and beverages - Aliments et boissons	100.1	103.4	103.0	107.6	99.0	93.3	90.9	88.7
Textiles, wearing apparel, leather, footwear - Textiles, habillement, cuir et chaussures	101.0	98.8	98.2	102.0	89.9	77.2	79.2	84.8
Petroleum, chemicals, pharmaceuticals, rubber and plastic - Pétroliers, produits chimiques, pharmaceutiques, caoutchouc et plastiques	77.4	91.0	107.9	118.4	119.4	105.9	114.0	120.2
Basic metals - Métaux de base	100.9	112.2	108.0	97.3	101.7	73.8	89.8	94.7
Fabricated metals, computer, electronic and optical products, electrical equipment, machinery - Fabrication d'ouvrages en métaux produits électroniques et optiques, appareils électriques, fabrication de machines	77.5	90.1	116.2	137.3	136.4	111.5	133.1	150.3
Electricity, gas, steam and air conditioning supply - Electricité, gaz, vapeur, et distribution de l'air conditionné	101.0	102.0	103.1	104.8	100.0	96.1	101.1	98.5
Denmark Danemark								
Total industry - Total, industrie	99.0	97.6	104.1	102.1	101.0	85.8	87.3	88.9
Total mining - Total, industries extractives	91.1	95.7	93.9	84.6	83.2	74.9	71.6	65.3
Total manufacturing - Total, industries manufacturières	99.0	97.0	105.5	106.6	106.3	88.0	90.1	94.3
Food, beverages and tobacco - Aliments, boissons et tabac	103.9	100.9	101.6	100.5	99.3	92.4	93.9	92.1
Textiles, wearing apparel, leather, footwear - Textiles, habillement, cuir et chaussures	146.7	104.6	100.0	89.5	80.2	68.4	70.4	72.3
Basic metals - Métaux de base	111.0	102.3	103.5	113.2	114.8	71.3	79.2	85.5
Chemicals, pharmaceuticals, rubber and plastic products - Produits chimiques, pharmaceutiques, caoutchouc et plastiques	98.6	90.4	100.4	98.0	95.5	83.7	89.4	94.4
Fabricated metals, computer, electronic and optical products, electrical equipment, machinery - Fabrication d'ouvrages en métaux produits électroniques et optiques, appareils électriques, fabrication de machines	97.2	97.9	108.5	115.8	118.1	92.4	93.3	102.4
Electricity, gas, steam and air conditioning supply - Electricité, gaz, vapeur, et distribution de l'air conditionné	119.6	108.7	115.8	100.3	91.1	91.3	98.8	94.0
Estonia Estonie								
Total industry - Total, industrie	83.8	91.2	108.3	116.4	109.9	84.6	104.9	121.4
Total mining - Total, industries extractives	98.9	90.1	109.3	120.8	111.3	99.8	112.9	122.1
Total manufacturing - Total, industries manufacturières	80.1	89.4	110.5	117.1	111.9	83.3	102.7	123.3
Food and beverages - Aliments et boissons	89.4	94.2	106.9	108.4	102.3	93.4	91.8	94.2

23 Index numbers of industrial production *(continued)*
2005 = 100
Indices de la production industrielle *(suite)*
2005 = 100

Country or area and industry [ISIC Rev. 4] Pays ou zone et industrie [CITI Rév. 4]	2003	2004	2006	2007	2008	2009	2010	2011
Textiles, wearing apparel, leather, footwear - Textiles, habillement, cuir et chaussures	114.7	108.0	102.9	98.9	89.8	68.9	74.1	83.7
Petroleum, chemicals, pharmaceuticals, rubber and plastic - Pétroliers, produits chimiques, pharmaceutiques, caoutchouc et plastiques	78.3	89.8	116.3	124.5	124.7	80.3	94.4	106.0
Basic metals - Métaux de base	141.0	110.3	101.7	163.2	142.5	75.0	111.9	111.2
Fabricated metals, computer, electronic and optical products, electrical equipment, machinery - Fabrication d'ouvrages en métaux produits électroniques et optiques, appareils électriques, fabrication de machines	65.1	79.9	116.3	132.5	141.2	101.9	162.7	251.9
Electricity, steam and air conditioning supply - Production et distribution d'électricité, de gaz	98.9	101.0	96.3	111.6	98.8	86.8	114.3	111.2
Finland Finlande								
Total industry - Total, industrie	94.6	100.0	109.5	110.8	116.0	94.4	99.6	100.5
Total mining - Total, industries extractives	104.9	82.2	127.8	99.6	101.8	90.1	93.6	99.6
Total manufacturing - Total, industries manufacturières	92.8	98.9	108.6	115.0	117.2	93.4	98.0	100.0
Food and beverages - Aliments et boissons	100.9	101.9	100.0	101.2	101.3	98.0	101.2	101.2
Textiles, wearing apparel, leather, footwear - Textiles, habillement, cuir et chaussures	102.7	100.5	101.8	99.4	92.2	76.4	85.3	86.4
Basic metals - Métaux de base	105.0	109.2	103.3	94.9	90.8	70.2	91.1	94.1
Fabricated metals, machinery and transport equipment.	92.4	94.3	109.9	118.9	122.4	88.8	90.3	97.2
Electricity, gas, steam and air conditioning supply - Electricité, gaz, vapeur, et distribution de l'air conditionné	111.6	113.4	116.1	114.4	105.3	104.7	116.6	106.2
France[7] France[7]								
Total industry - Total, industrie	98.0	100.1	100.5	101.8	99.3	86.3	90.7	92.9
Total mining - Total, industries extractives	103.0	102.9	103.0	103.7	101.5	89.7	89.0	89.1
Total manufacturing - Total, industries manufacturières	98.1	100.1	100.7	102.4	99.3	85.3	89.3	92.7
Food, beverages and tobacco - Aliments, boissons et tabac	100.8	100.6	100.9	103.1	102.7	100.7	101.7	105.4
Textiles, wearing apparel, leather, footwear - Textiles, habillement, cuir et chaussures	127.1	116.5	90.6	86.9	77.3	60.2	62.3	60.8
Petroleum, chemicals, pharmaceuticals, rubber and plastic - Pétroliers, produits chimiques, pharmaceutiques, caoutchouc et plastiques	94.8	98.1	101.8	105.3	102.8	93.6	98.6	100.7
Basic metals - Métaux de base	101.8	104.6	102.4	100.9	95.3	68.3	79.0	81.6
Fabricated metals, computer, electronic and optical products, electrical equipment, machinery - Fabrication d'ouvrages en métaux produits électroniques et optiques, appareils électriques, fabrication de machines	96.5	99.7	100.7	102.9	99.2	79.0	84.1	88.3
Electricity, gas, steam and air conditioning supply - Electricité, gaz, vapeur, et distribution de l'air conditionné	96.6	99.4	98.6	97.1	99.0	94.6	101.9	94.9
Germany Allemagne								
Total industry - Total, industrie	93.1	97.0	105.3	111.4	112.1	93.7	104.2	111.9
Total mining - Total, industries extractives	104.3	102.1	95.5	124.0	110.2	92.9	85.4	79.1
Total manufacturing - Total, industries manufacturières	92.6	96.7	105.8	112.4	113.5	93.9	105.2	114.4
Food, beverages and tobacco - Aliments, boissons et tabac	95.4	96.8	101.5	103.1	101.8	100.8	102.0	103.4
Textiles, wearing apparel, leather, footwear - Textiles, habillement, cuir et chaussures	109.1	106.4	95.0	94.3	86.8	73.5	79.2	80.5
Petroleum, chemicals, pharmaceuticals, rubber and plastic - Pétroliers, produits chimiques, pharmaceutiques, caoutchouc et plastiques	92.9	96.5	103.8	108.8	106.9	95.5	106.0	109.5
Basic metals - Métaux de base	95.0	99.6	108.0	111.8	110.6	80.6	97.5	102.2
Fabricated metals, computer, electronic and optical products, electrical equipment, machinery - Fabrication d'ouvrages en métaux produits électroniques et optiques, appareils électriques, fabrication de machines	90.7	95.9	107.4	116.6	119.1	92.7	107.3	121.5
Electricity, gas, steam and air conditioning supply - Electricité, gaz, vapeur, et distribution de l'air conditionné	97.4	100.2	101.4	97.8	96.2	91.6	95.6	88.5
Greece Grèce								
Total industry - Total, industrie	101.1	101.7	100.9	103.2	98.8	89.3	83.8	76.6
Total mining - Total, industries extractives	108.4	107.9	97.2	96.8	92.5	81.6	76.3	76.4
Total manufacturing - Total, industries manufacturières	101.2	101.8	102.0	104.2	99.3	88.3	83.8	76.1
Food, beverages and tobacco - Aliments, boissons et tabac	98.4	102.4	100.2	104.3	104.2	101.0	95.3	91.9

23 Index numbers of industrial production *(continued)*
2005 = 100
Indices de la production industrielle *(suite)*
2005 = 100

Country or area and industry [ISIC Rev. 4] Pays ou zone et industrie [CITI Rév. 4]	2003	2004	2006	2007	2008	2009	2010	2011
Textiles, wearing apparel, leather, footwear - Textiles, habillement, cuir et chaussures	130.2	119.8	91.7	96.3	79.2	59.8	45.5	35.1
Petroleum, chemicals, pharmaceuticals, rubber and plastic - Pétroliers, produits chimiques, pharmaceutiques, caoutchouc et plastiques	98.7	98.6	104.9	109.5	105.9	102.4	104.8	95.0
Basic metals - Métaux de base	91.8	97.7	105.5	107.5	100.7	82.5	92.5	98.3
Fabricated metals, computer, electronic and optical products, electrical equipment, machinery - Fabrication d'ouvrages en métaux produits électroniques et optiques, appareils électriques, fabrication de machines	105.6	106.5	103.9	104.0	98.3	77.6	69.8	61.2
Electricity, gas, steam and air conditioning supply - Electricité, gaz, vapeur, et distribution de l'air conditionné	98.7	99.4	98.3	101.8	98.9	94.7	86.0	78.4
Hungary Hongrie								
Total industry - Total, industrie	87.6	93.9	109.8	118.3	118.4	97.5	107.7	113.3
Total mining - Total, industries extractives	94.7	103.8	115.1	95.1	128.6	114.3	89.2	103.4
Total manufacturing - Total, industries manufacturières	85.5	92.9	110.9	120.2	119.4	97.5	109.1	115.4
Food, beverages and tobacco - Aliments, boissons et tabac	114.4	106.6	101.7	98.8	91.8	88.7	88.3	90.3
Textiles, wearing apparel, leather, footwear - Textiles, habillement, cuir et chaussures	116.5	110.0	102.7	103.5	91.6	70.3	68.4	84.3
Petroleum, chemicals, pharmaceuticals, rubber and plastic - Pétroliers, produits chimiques, pharmaceutiques, caoutchouc et plastiques	87.7	94.1	106.9	111.2	111.4	98.9	107.9	114.7
Basic metals - Métaux de base	97.9	104.8	114.8	107.6	103.3	54.0	65.0	69.6
Fabricated metals, computer, electronic and optical products, electrical equipment, machinery - Fabrication d'ouvrages en métaux produits électroniques et optiques, appareils électriques, fabrication de machines	79.0	90.0	114.4	128.8	129.7	101.5	117.8	127.8
Electricity, gas, steam and air conditioning supply - Electricité, gaz, vapeur, et distribution de l'air conditionné	103.4	101.7	100.3	104.2	109.1	96.4	97.4	96.3
Ireland Irlande								
Total industry - Total, industrie	94.9	96.3	103.1	108.4	105.7	101.3	108.9	109.0
Total mining - Total, industries extractives	98.5	98.7	101.9	98.6	92.2	80.4	75.1	61.2
Total manufacturing - Total, industries manufacturières	94.8	96.1	103.3	109.0	105.8	101.8	110.0	110.6
Food and beverages - Aliments et boissons	92.9	98.9	101.5	104.1	101.0	96.8	100.0	102.3
Textiles, wearing apparel, leather, footwear - Textiles, habillement, cuir et chaussures	119.8	117.7	77.7	65.4	61.7	52.2	48.8	40.7
Basic metals - Métaux de base	93.1	88.0	104.7	119.7	122.2	73.7	87.0	83.5
Chemicals, pharmaceuticals, rubber and plastic products - Produits chimiques, pharmaceutiques, caoutchouc et plastiques	110.6	101.2	103.8	111.6	107.1	122.4	144.4	146.3
Fabricated metals, computer, electronic and optical products, electrical equipment, machinery - Fabrication d'ouvrages en métaux produits électroniques et optiques, appareils électriques, fabrication de machines	87.9	96.0	109.0	114.5	113.5	81.3	66.5	64.7
Electricity, gas, steam and air conditioning supply - Electricité, gaz, vapeur, et distribution de l'air conditionné	94.8	98.6	100.6	104.2	108.7	101.5	105.2	102.9
Italy Italie								
Total industry - Total, industrie	101.3	102.1	103.1	105.8	102.3	83.3	88.9	88.4
Total mining - Total, industries extractives	94.9	92.9	98.2	92.0	84.6	74.3	73.2	74.4
Total manufacturing - Total, industries manufacturières	101.8	102.5	103.3	106.3	102.7	82.9	88.9	88.4
Food and beverages - Aliments et boissons	98.5	99.0	101.6	102.5	102.2	101.1	103.3	101.3
Textiles, wearing apparel, leather, footwear - Textiles, habillement, cuir et chaussures	113.9	109.2	104.9	109.1	105.4	93.6	99.2	91.3
Petroleum, chemicals, pharmaceuticals, rubber and plastic - Pétroliers, produits chimiques, pharmaceutiques, caoutchouc et plastiques	100.5	101.8	103.0	104.9	100.7	89.4	93.3	91.4
Basic metals - Métaux de base	95.2	99.5	107.0	107.2	100.7	70.6	84.7	89.9

23 Index numbers of industrial production *(continued)*
2005 = 100
Indices de la production industrielle *(suite)*
2005 = 100

Country or area and industry [ISIC Rev. 4] Pays ou zone et industrie [CITI Rév. 4]	2003	2004	2006	2007	2008	2009	2010	2011
Fabricated metals, computer, electronic and optical products, electrical equipment, machinery - Fabrication d'ouvrages en métaux produits électroniques et optiques, appareils électriques, fabrication de machines	102.1	103.0	104.2	109.1	105.4	75.0	82.9	84.5
Electricity, gas, steam and air conditioning supply - Electricité, gaz, vapeur, et distribution de l'air conditionné	94.2	97.7	102.1	101.8	102.5	93.3	95.6	93.4
Latvia Lettonie								
Total industry - Total, industrie	87.1	93.4	106.5	107.9	104.1	85.4	98.0	107.5
Total mining - Total, industries extractives	75.9	84.5	109.8	123.6	120.7	98.3	111.7	121.1
Total manufacturing - Total, industries manufacturières	87.1	92.9	106.4	106.7	103.0	82.2	95.7	106.9
Food - Aliments	88.2	93.5	104.7	104.0	103.3	90.2	89.7	90.6
Textiles and wearing apparel - Textiles et habillement	93.5	92.1	106.2	107.6	94.4	56.4	67.6	78.3
Basic metals - Métaux de base	96.9	102.8	103.0	105.3	99.4	89.4	106.1	106.3
Chemicals, pharmaceuticals, rubber and plastic products - Produits chimiques, pharmaceutiques, caoutchouc et plastiques	74.5	84.9	120.2	122.8	123.5	107.6	115.0	114.9
Fabricated metals, computer, electronic and optical products, electrical equipment, machinery - Fabrication d'ouvrages en métaux produits électroniques et optiques, appareils électriques, fabrication de machines	84.6	83.6	117.3	130.2	142.6	87.0	114.4	153.6
Electricity and gas - Electricité et gaz	88.6	97.3	106.7	111.4	106.9	99.2	107.4	108.5
Lithuania Lituanie								
Total industry - Total, industrie	85.1	94.1	106.0	108.5	114.0	97.4	103.4	110.3
Total mining - Total, industries extractives	126.2	112.5	98.4	98.3	90.1	58.4	64.0	70.6
Total manufacturing - Total, industries manufacturières	81.7	92.1	107.6	110.2	117.5	99.2	107.3	118.5
Food, beverages and tobacco - Aliments, boissons et tabac	86.6	89.3	113.1	128.6	126.4	114.7	114.8	122.3
Textiles, wearing apparel, leather, footwear - Textiles, habillement, cuir et chaussures	107.8	103.5	104.5	102.1	85.3	65.0	78.2	95.0
Petroleum, chemicals, pharmaceuticals, rubber and plastic - Pétroliers, produits chimiques, pharmaceutiques, caoutchouc et plastiques	79.1	91.9	103.0	100.6	120.4	109.9	119.8	126.1
Basic metals - Métaux de base	94.7	78.6	89.9	129.0	234.6	211.4	220.5	282.2
Fabricated metals, computer, electronic and optical products, electrical equipment, machinery - Fabrication d'ouvrages en métaux produits électroniques et optiques, appareils électriques, fabrication de machines	72.7	89.5	114.8	130.4	121.7	84.7	97.9	112.7
Electricity, gas, steam and air conditioning supply - Electricité, gaz, vapeur, et distribution de l'air conditionné	93.8	100.2	100.1	102.4	102.0	96.2	92.3	79.0
Luxembourg Luxembourg								
Total industry - Total, industrie	92.7	97.9	101.9	101.3	96.3	80.9	89.4	87.4
Total mining - Total, industries extractives	102.3	103.5	79.1	81.0	79.6	71.0	56.2	68.0
Total manufacturing - Total, industries manufacturières	91.7	97.7	101.7	101.4	96.4	79.7	88.2	86.8
Food - Aliments	...	...	102.1	108.6	106.1	107.5	...	...
Electricity, gas, steam and air conditioning supply - Electricité, gaz, vapeur, et distribution de l'air conditionné	102.5	99.0	106.6	103.2	97.8	94.4	105.9	95.8
Malta Malte								
Total industry - Total, industrie	...	...	107.0	115.0	112.0	94.1	101.8	103.5
Total mining - Total, industries extractives	...	...	88.5	116.4	74.6	70.9	54.9	52.0
Total manufacturing - Total, industries manufacturières	...	...	107.6	116.0	113.1	94.1	102.7	104.4
Food, beverages and tobacco - Aliments, boissons et tabac	...	...	103.2	105.5	107.7	101.1	91.7	93.6
Textiles, wearing apparel, leather, footwear - Textiles, habillement, cuir et chaussures	...	...	72.6	58.7	55.0	43.3	46.7	48.9
Basic metals - Métaux de base	...	...	497.1	183.9	262.8	157.0	144.7	280.7
Chemicals, pharmaceuticals, rubber and plastic products - Produits chimiques, pharmaceutiques, caoutchouc et plastiques	...	...	133.1	158.7	152.0	126.8	151.7	150.2
Fabricated metals, computer, electronic and optical products, electrical equipment, machinery - Fabrication d'ouvrages en métaux produits électroniques et optiques, appareils électriques, fabrication de machines	...	...	113.4	122.8	118.7	98.8	122.7	125.5
Electricity, gas, steam and air conditioning supply - Electricité, gaz, vapeur, et distribution de l'air conditionné	...	...	100.9	102.5	101.6	96.7	94.3	96.8

23

Index numbers of industrial production *(continued)*
2005 = 100
Indices de la production industrielle *(suite)*
2005 = 100

Country or area and industry [ISIC Rev. 4] Pays ou zone et industrie [CITI Rév. 4]	2003	2004	2006	2007	2008	2009	2010	2011
Montenegro[1] Monténégro[1]								
Total industry - Total, industrie	...	...	101.0	101.0	99.1	67.1	78.9	70.7
Total mining - Total, industries extractives	...	...	102.9	104.4	123.0	42.4	67.2	71.5
Total manufacturing - Total, industries manufacturières	...	...	100.1	109.4	97.1	59.5	57.8	61.7
Food, beverages and tobacco - Aliments, boissons et tabac	...	...	102.8	102.5	124.5	110.4	100.5	97.9
Wearing apparel, leather and footwear - Fabrication d'articles d'habillement, fabrication de cuir et d'articles de cuir	...	...	123.2	148.7	222.8	73.2	22.1	16.8
Chemicals, petroleum, rubber and plastic products - Produits chimiques, pétroliers, caoutchouc et plastiques	...	...	65.2	94.7	61.7	87.2	95.2	72.9
Basic metals - Métaux de base	...	...	104.4	113.5	100.6	46.2	39.8	45.0
Electricity, gas and water - Electricité, gaz et eau	...	...	103.1	74.8	98.7	96.4	145.6	98.0
Netherlands Pays- Bas								
Total industry - Total, industrie	95.8	100.5	102.0	106.5	106.9	98.6	106.1	106.3
Total mining - Total, industries extractives	109.6	121.6	97.4	97.3	105.3	97.6	109.0	100.2
Total manufacturing - Total, industries manufacturières	94.3	97.9	103.5	109.7	108.1	98.8	105.7	109.2
Food, beverages and tobacco - Aliments, boissons et tabac	95.4	96.3	102.1	105.1	102.9	102.7	104.6	106.4
Textiles, wearing apparel, leather, footwear - Textiles, habillement, cuir et chaussures	113.2	99.4	102.6	109.8	106.8	92.7	104.8	107.6
Petroleum, chemicals, pharmaceuticals, rubber and plastic - Pétroliers, produits chimiques, pharmaceutiques, caoutchouc et plastiques	93.2	98.9	104.0	110.1	106.3	103.9	108.1	108.1
Basic metals - Métaux de base	91.3	103.1	102.5	109.7	109.8	84.2	109.9	107.8
Fabricated metals, computer, electronic and optical products, electrical equipment, machinery - Fabrication d'ouvrages en métaux produits électroniques et optiques, appareils électriques, fabrication de machines	91.9	97.2	104.7	114.7	113.8	91.8	106.3	115.4
Electricity, gas, steam and air conditioning supply - Electricité, gaz, vapeur, et distribution de l'air conditionné	84.2	84.8	97.5	95.4	98.9	98.8	104.8	91.6
Norway Norvège								
Total industry - Total, industrie	101.1	100.5	97.4	96.5	97.1	93.1	88.2	84.3
Total mining - Total, industries extractives	104.7	103.3	95.5	91.2	90.5	87.9	80.3	74.0
Total manufacturing - Total, industries manufacturières	96.1	97.6	105.4	111.2	114.8	107.7	110.5	112.1
Food and beverages - Aliments et boissons	102.5	103.5	100.6	103.2	104.4	105.3	104.9	102.3
Textiles, wearing apparel, leather, footwear - Textiles, habillement, cuir et chaussures	107.3	100.6	107.5	104.3	87.5	74.7	64.4	66.6
Basic metals - Métaux de base	92.6	101.3	102.5	104.7	102.2	80.8	93.5	86.3
Chemicals, pharmaceuticals, rubber and plastic products - Produits chimiques, pharmaceutiques, caoutchouc et plastiques	96.5	98.8	100.2	104.5	105.5	94.9	114.4	112.0
Fabricated metals, computer, electronic and optical products, electrical equipment, machinery - Fabrication d'ouvrages en métaux produits électroniques et optiques, appareils électriques, fabrication de machines	95.2	94.6	112.5	123.4	137.3	134.4	131.4	138.6
Electricity, gas, steam and air conditioning supply - Electricité, gaz, vapeur, et distribution de l'air conditionné	78.9	80.2	88.3	99.6	103.7	95.9	91.0	93.7
Poland Pologne								
Total industry - Total, industrie	...	...	111.0	120.4	123.4	118.0	129.7	138.6
Total mining - Total, industries extractives	...	...	100.9	97.8	98.6	85.7	87.3	89.2
Total manufacturing - Total, industries manufacturières	...	...	114.3	126.7	130.6	126.2	141.3	152.6
Food, beverages and tobacco - Aliments, boissons et tabac	...	...	108.1	115.0	114.5	121.4	126.6	133.8
Textiles, wearing apparel, leather, footwear - Textiles, habillement, cuir et chaussures	...	...	107.0	115.1	107.6	98.5	102.7	113.6
Petroleum, chemicals, pharmaceuticals, rubber and plastic - Pétroliers, produits chimiques, pharmaceutiques, caoutchouc et plastiques	...	...	112.9	121.1	124.2	120.9	132.8	144.2
Basic metals - Métaux de base	...	...	114.8	123.9	117.6	89.0	107.7	120.7
Fabricated metals, computer, electronic and optical products, electrical equipment, machinery - Fabrication d'ouvrages en métaux produits électroniques et optiques, appareils électriques, fabrication de machines	...	...	120.8	143.3	154.4	148.8	169.3	183.1
Electricity, gas, steam and air conditioning supply - Electricité, gaz, vapeur, et distribution de l'air conditionné	...	...	100.3	102.6	102.0	96.9	97.4	98.4

23

Index numbers of industrial production *(continued)*
2005 = 100
Indices de la production industrielle *(suite)*
2005 = 100

Country or area and industry [ISIC Rev. 4] Pays ou zone et industrie [CITI Rév. 4]	2003	2004	2006	2007	2008	2009	2010	2011
Portugal Portugal								
Total industry - Total, industrie	108.2	103.6	103.1	103.0	98.8	90.5	92.0	90.2
Total mining - Total, industries extractives	95.1	105.0	89.5	100.5	105.9	84.7	78.9	79.4
Total manufacturing - Total, industries manufacturières	110.0	106.8	102.9	104.0	99.9	89.8	91.7	90.8
Food, beverages and tobacco - Aliments, boissons et tabac	96.1	98.7	103.8	108.4	105.8	109.8	110.8	107.9
Textiles, wearing apparel, leather, footwear - Textiles, habillement, cuir et chaussures	116.6	110.4	97.3	94.7	86.8	78.3	79.3	74.3
Petroleum, chemicals, pharmaceuticals, rubber and plastic - Pétroliers, produits chimiques, pharmaceutiques, caoutchouc et plastiques	94.8	96.2	101.6	104.2	98.6	91.0	99.3	95.7
Basic metals - Métaux de base	95.8	98.6	110.6	114.0	117.6	126.7	145.2	157.8
Fabricated metals, computer, electronic and optical products, electrical equipment, machinery - Fabrication d'ouvrages en métaux produits électroniques et optiques, appareils électriques, fabrication de machines	118.1	111.7	108.7	108.8	107.2	83.5	82.0	84.1
Electricity, gas, steam and air conditioning supply - Electricité, gaz, vapeur, et distribution de l'air conditionné	101.2	86.3	107.0	98.4	91.3	95.6	96.2	89.1
Republic of Moldova République de Moldova								
Total industry [1] - Total, industrie [1]	86.4	93.4	95.2	94.0	95.3	75.2	82.2	88.3
Total mining [1] - Total, industries extractives [1]	77.6	95.9	127.9	133.7	140.1	98.9	105.9	124.0
Total manufacturing [1] - Total, industries manufacturières [1]	85.8	93.8	93.5	91.8	92.8	71.7	79.5	86.6
Food, beverages and tobacco [1] - Aliments, boissons et tabac [1]	90.7	95.5	81.5	75.1	81.3	67.7	76.2	77.4
Textiles, wearing apparel, leather, footwear [1] - Textiles, habillement, cuir et chaussures [1]	80.1	94.8	107.8	109.0	101.0	76.7	82.7	92.5
Chemicals, petroleum, rubber and plastic products [1] - Produits chimiques, pétroliers, caoutchouc et plastiques [1]	74.8	83.8	122.2	128.7	131.7	100.6	105.0	104.9
Basic metals [1] - Métaux de base [1]	60.6	67.2	121.8	125.1	161.8	123.1	137.7	128.6
Manufacture of all metal products and machinery - Fabrication des métaux et machines	97.6	99.3	99.2	98.5	96.2	94.6	98.0	...
Electricity, gas and water [1] - Electricité, gaz et eau [1]	90.1	90.2	105.0	104.6	103.1	96.1	96.7	92.2
Romania Roumanie								
Total industry - Total, industrie	100.5	102.9	109.2	120.5	123.8	116.9	123.4	130.3
Total mining - Total, industries extractives	101.3	102.1	102.4	100.8	100.8	88.7	82.6	86.3
Total manufacturing - Total, industries manufacturières	100.4	103.7	112.5	126.1	130.1	121.6	128.9	136.1
Food, beverages and tobacco - Aliments, boissons et tabac	102.9	102.2	108.3	127.2	136.5	132.9	124.2	126.0
Textiles, wearing apparel, leather, footwear - Textiles, habillement, cuir et chaussures	122.4	118.3	100.4	93.0	78.0	59.7	61.5	60.5
Petroleum, chemicals, pharmaceuticals, rubber and plastic - Pétroliers, produits chimiques, pharmaceutiques, caoutchouc et plastiques	93.4	97.6	109.7	122.6	134.2	120.0	124.1	130.8
Basic metals - Métaux de base	89.1	99.3	101.4	103.1	87.1	55.8	71.1	76.2
Fabricated metals, computer, electronic and optical products, electrical equipment, machinery - Fabrication d'ouvrages en métaux produits électroniques et optiques, appareils électriques, fabrication de machines	90.1	97.2	119.5	139.3	148.1	146.0	164.4	175.9
Electricity, gas, steam and air conditioning supply - Electricité, gaz, vapeur, et distribution de l'air conditionné	100.7	98.5	92.3	96.3	96.6	103.4	111.8	118.8
Russian Federation [1] Fédération de Russie [1]								
Total industry - Total, industrie	88.1	95.2	106.3	113.5	114.2	103.6	112.1	117.4
Total mining - Total, industries extractives	92.3	98.6	102.8	106.2	106.6	106.0	109.8	111.9
Total manufacturing - Total, industries manufacturières	84.1	93.0	108.4	119.8	120.4	102.1	114.1	121.5
Food, beverages and tobacco - Aliments, boissons et tabac	89.6	93.7	107.5	115.7	117.9	117.1	123.3	124.6
Textiles, wearing apparel, leather, footwear - Textiles, habillement, cuir et chaussures	103.7	98.7	112.8	112.8	108.6	94.0	106.5	111.1
Chemicals, petroleum, rubber and plastic products - Produits chimiques, pétroliers, caoutchouc et plastiques	91.6	95.3	106.9	112.6	115.2	111.4	121.1	126.5
Basic metals - Métaux de base	94.2	97.4	108.7	109.9	102.5	88.5	99.0	104.2
Electricity, gas and water - Electricité, gaz et eau	98.0	99.1	103.4	102.8	103.4	99.4	103.4	103.5
Serbia Serbie								
Total industry - Total, industrie	93.3	97.5	103.7	107.6	109.4	99.8	100.3	104.7
Total mining - Total, industries extractives	95.7	96.5	104.2	104.4	109.9	105.7	111.8	123.5
Total manufacturing - Total, industries manufacturières	93.3	101.0	104.5	109.4	110.6	92.8	96.4	96.0

23

Index numbers of industrial production *(continued)*
2005 = 100
Indices de la production industrielle *(suite)*
2005 = 100

Country or area and industry [ISIC Rev. 4] Pays ou zone et industrie [CITI Rév. 4]	2003	2004	2006	2007	2008	2009	2010	2011
Food, beverages and tobacco - Aliments, boissons et tabac	91.1	94.2	104.9	110.2	109.4	102.2	103.6	100.9
Textiles, wearing apparel, leather, footwear - Textiles, habillement, cuir et chaussures	114.9	109.6	97.6	87.3	77.5	57.4	60.1	57.9
Petroleum, chemicals, pharmaceuticals, rubber and plastic - Pétroliers, produits chimiques, pharmaceutiques, caoutchouc et plastiques	81.3	97.6	101.4	111.4	110.8	86.6	96.6	96.5
Basic metals - Métaux de base	57.9	82.1	122.7	120.2	124.4	88.6	107.2	103.5
Fabricated metals, computer, electronic and optical products, electrical equipment, machinery - Fabrication d'ouvrages en métaux produits électroniques et optiques, appareils électriques, fabrication de machines	118.0	129.0	88.4	95.5	104.5	82.4	80.2	83.8
Electricity, gas, steam and air conditioning supply - Electricité, gaz, vapeur, et distribution de l'air conditionné	92.9	92.9	102.4	105.7	107.8	108.7	103.9	114.0
Slovakia Slovaquie								
Total industry - Total, industrie	97.3	100.8	115.7	135.2	139.5	119.7	141.6	151.7
Total mining - Total, industries extractives	108.9	116.8	96.8	111.7	99.7	101.3	101.7	98.0
Total manufacturing - Total, industries manufacturières	98.0	101.4	121.0	146.7	150.8	127.3	152.8	166.3
Food, beverages and tobacco - Aliments, boissons et tabac	101.0	103.4	101.2	99.3	97.9	92.6	93.1	99.0
Textiles, wearing apparel, leather, footwear - Textiles, habillement, cuir et chaussures	103.9	102.8	152.5	150.3	148.4	131.6	140.1	157.2
Petroleum, chemicals, pharmaceuticals, rubber and plastic - Pétroliers, produits chimiques, pharmaceutiques, caoutchouc et plastiques	92.9	99.4	108.6	121.2	120.3	119.4	124.6	135.1
Basic metals - Métaux de base	122.2	116.2	108.9	109.1	90.9	76.9	92.4	89.4
Fabricated metals, computer, electronic and optical products, electrical equipment, machinery - Fabrication d'ouvrages en métaux produits électroniques et optiques, appareils électriques, fabrication de machines	90.5	96.8	141.2	204.3	224.8	180.6	237.4	265.5
Electricity and gas - Electricité et gaz	93.0	96.2	97.2	92.8	100.2	92.3	102.9	101.6
Slovenia Slovénie								
Total industry - Total, industrie	91.9	96.6	105.6	113.0	115.9	95.6	101.6	103.6
Total mining - Total, industries extractives	111.0	97.6	107.5	113.5	119.8	116.3	129.1	118.6
Total manufacturing - Total, industries manufacturières	92.2	96.2	106.2	115.2	118.2	96.2	102.5	104.5
Food and beverages - Aliments et boissons	113.1	101.3	100.0	98.7	91.1	85.7	85.3	90.2
Textiles, wearing apparel, leather, footwear - Textiles, habillement, cuir et chaussures	121.9	107.2	98.0	90.3	81.8	47.9	48.3	53.3
Chemicals, petroleum, rubber and plastic products - Produits chimiques, pétroliers, caoutchouc et plastiques	86.8	96.5	106.4	115.5	124.0	104.0	119.8	105.9
Basic metals - Métaux de base	105.1	96.9	119.6	127.5	87.5	61.5	67.4	74.8
Fabricated metals, computer, electronic and optical products, electrical equipment, machinery - Fabrication d'ouvrages en métaux produits électroniques et optiques, appareils électriques, fabrication de machines	82.6	93.5	106.6	116.7	128.3	103.6	114.5	117.1
Electricity and gas - Electricité et gaz	85.0	101.6	99.1	88.0	89.9	83.9	85.5	89.7
Spain Espagne								
Total industry - Total, industrie	98.2	100.0	103.7	106.2	98.6	82.5	83.3	81.8
Total mining - Total, industries extractives	109.4	104.2	102.9	103.7	89.5	67.8	70.8	60.5
Total manufacturing - Total, industries manufacturières	98.8	100.3	104.0	106.5	98.2	81.5	82.0	80.9
Food, beverages and tobacco - Aliments, boissons et tabac	97.2	98.6	100.1	101.7	101.1	99.1	99.3	98.6
Textiles, wearing apparel, leather, footwear - Textiles, habillement, cuir et chaussures	120.8	112.8	96.4	92.4	81.7	65.2	64.3	61.2
Petroleum, chemicals, pharmaceuticals, rubber and plastic - Pétroliers, produits chimiques, pharmaceutiques, caoutchouc et plastiques	97.2	99.0	102.9	104.7	102.7	95.1	100.0	99.3
Basic metals - Métaux de base	96.2	102.2	106.1	106.9	99.8	75.5	84.1	84.5
Fabricated metals, computer, electronic and optical products, electrical equipment, machinery - Fabrication d'ouvrages en métaux produits électroniques et optiques, appareils électriques, fabrication de machines	98.8	100.4	106.7	112.1	102.4	77.0	76.0	75.4
Electricity, gas, steam and air conditioning supply - Electricité, gaz, vapeur, et distribution de l'air conditionné	89.8	96.1	100.6	102.7	103.8	95.9	98.7	95.1

23 Index numbers of industrial production *(continued)*
2005 = 100
Indices de la production industrielle *(suite)*
2005 = 100

Country or area and industry [ISIC Rev. 4] Pays ou zone et industrie [CITI Rév. 4]	2003	2004	2006	2007	2008	2009	2010	2011
Sweden Suède								
Total industry - Total, industrie	92.3	97.6	103.2	106.7	103.8	84.8	92.9	98.7
Total mining - Total, industries extractives	87.2	95.0	101.2	107.8	108.3	91.2	116.8	121.6
Total manufacturing - Total, industries manufacturières	93.3	97.9	104.8	108.3	104.7	84.3	92.0	98.5
Food and beverages - Aliments et boissons	98.0	99.6	101.0	101.1	103.0	103.5	101.5	95.7
Petroleum, chemicals, pharmaceuticals, rubber and plastic - Pétroliers, produits chimiques, pharmaceutiques, caoutchouc et plastiques	94.6	100.0	107.7	97.7	93.8	85.6	92.1	100.3
Basic metals - Métaux de base	97.8	103.5	96.1	96.8	90.8	61.7	73.6	77.4
Fabricated metals, computer, electronic and optical products, electrical equipment, machinery - Fabrication d'ouvrages en métaux produits électroniques et optiques, appareils électriques, fabrication de machines	88.9	95.2	106.4	115.9	112.9	79.6	91.2	103.6
Electricity, gas, steam and air conditioning supply - Electricité, gaz, vapeur, et distribution de l'air conditionné	86.1	96.1	91.0	94.0	95.5	86.9	94.3	95.2
Switzerland[1] Suisse[1]								
Total industry - Total, industrie	93.2	97.4	107.8	118.1	119.6	110.3	117.0	118.2
Total mining - Total, industries extractives	101.2	105.5	109.7	116.4	108.4	111.3	126.1	121.6
Total manufacturing - Total, industries manufacturières	92.5	96.9	108.3	119.2	120.8	110.6	117.7	119.5
Food, beverages and tobacco - Aliments, boissons et tabac	97.8	99.2	103.7	108.8	112.8	108.7	110.5	111.8
Textiles, wearing apparel, leather, footwear - Textiles, habillement, cuir et chaussures	94.3	99.8	104.0	120.1	110.8	91.0	92.6	103.6
Chemicals, petroleum, rubber and plastic products - Produits chimiques, pétroliers, caoutchouc et plastiques	90.5	96.3	110.3	118.9	119.5	120.1	125.3	120.0
Basic metals - Métaux de base	119.0	107.4	98.6	109.1	100.8	94.7	114.3	120.4
Electricity, gas and water - Electricité, gaz et eau	102.9	102.4	102.0	104.3	106.2	105.4	108.0	102.1
TFYR of Macedonia L'ex- R.Y. Macédoine								
Total industry - Total, industrie	...	...	105.5	108.6	113.5	104.8	101.0	103.2
Total mining - Total, industries extractives	...	...	111.1	122.3	133.8	117.2	112.7	121.0
Total manufacturing - Total, industries manufacturières	...	...	106.4	112.2	118.8	106.5	98.5	103.9
Food, beverages and tobacco - Aliments, boissons et tabac	...	...	102.0	106.9	113.8	111.2	117.1	121.3
Textiles, wearing apparel, leather, footwear - Textiles, habillement, cuir et chaussures	...	...	105.0	91.8	76.5	66.0	66.1	69.8
Petroleum, chemicals, pharmaceuticals, rubber and plastic - Pétroliers, produits chimiques, pharmaceutiques, caoutchouc et plastiques	...	...	100.7	98.8	109.3	101.5	91.7	83.1
Basic metals - Métaux de base	...	...	117.8	155.8	147.4	84.1	110.8	118.5
Fabricated metal products; machinery and equipment, electrical machinery and apparatus - Ouvrage en métaux, machines et matériel, machines et appareils électriques	...	...	106.7	123.7	158.0	165.5	102.4	129.7
Electricity, gas, steam and air conditioning supply - Electricité, gaz, vapeur, et distribution de l'air conditionné	...	...	100.8	91.2	88.4	96.1	109.9	97.7
Ukraine[1] Ukraine[1]								
Total industry - Total, industrie	87.0	97.3	105.8	114.1	107.9	84.3	93.8	101.0
Total mining - Total, industries extractives	92.8	96.7	105.9	108.6	104.0	92.9	96.4	103.3
Total manufacturing - Total, industries manufacturières	85.7	97.4	105.7	116.6	109.3	80.3	91.5	99.0
Food - Aliments	78.1	88.0	109.6	118.6	116.6	110.3	115.2	115.1
Textiles, wearing apparel, leather, footwear - Textiles, habillement, cuir et chaussures	86.5	98.8	97.4	95.0	85.3	63.5	69.2	75.1
Chemicals, petroleum, rubber and plastic products - Produits chimiques, pétroliers, caoutchouc et plastiques	92.2	100.9	97.2	103.3	93.1	79.6	90.3	96.5
Metal and Metal Products, except machinery and equipment - Métallurgie et travail des métaux	90.3	101.4	109.0	117.0	102.6	82.1	92.5	100.9
All machinery and transport equipment - Fabrication de machines et de matériel de transport	71.5	92.5	111.5	136.8	139.7	78.9	109.4	129.9
Electricity, gas and water - Electricité, gaz et eau	98.8	97.7	106.5	108.8	106.9	95.0	104.1	109.6
United Kingdom Royaume- Uni								
Total industry - Total, industrie	101.2	101.5	100.3	100.6	97.9	88.8	91.2	90.8
Total mining - Total, industries extractives	118.2	109.3	92.5	90.1	84.5	76.9	73.6	63.1
Total manufacturing - Total, industries manufacturières	98.0	100.1	101.8	102.7	100.3	90.5	93.9	95.9
Food, beverages and tobacco - Aliments, boissons et tabac	97.6	99.2	99.2	98.7	96.5	94.9	98.5	104.7

23

Index numbers of industrial production *(continued)*
2005 = 100
Indices de la production industrielle *(suite)*
2005 = 100

Country or area and industry [ISIC Rev. 4] Pays ou zone et industrie [CITI Rév. 4]	2003	2004	2006	2007	2008	2009	2010	2011
Textiles, wearing apparel, leather, footwear - Textiles, habillement, cuir et chaussures	115.3	102.5	100.1	98.5	98.8	89.3	92.3	93.4
Petroleum, chemicals, pharmaceuticals, rubber and plastic - Pétroliers, produits chimiques, pharmaceutiques, caoutchouc et plastiques	100.7	101.0	100.4	100.4	100.4	90.4	88.9	87.6
Basic metals - Métaux de base	93.8	99.0	100.0	101.2	97.5	73.0	79.9	80.9
Fabricated metals, computer, electronic and optical products, electrical equipment, machinery - Fabrication d'ouvrages en métaux produits électroniques et optiques, appareils électriques, fabrication de machines	97.4	100.6	102.9	105.5	102.5	86.5	96.9	101.8
Electricity, gas, steam and air conditioning supply - Electricité, gaz, vapeur, et distribution de l'air conditionné	98.5	100.0	100.4	100.9	101.2	96.4	99.5	95.4

Oceania · Océanie

Australia [2]   Australie [2]

Total industry - Total, industrie	99.0	98.7	100.9	105.2	108.4	106.8	110.3	110.4
Total mining - Total, industries extractives	97.9	95.0	101.9	110.6	112.8	115.8	122.9	124.6
Total manufacturing - Total, industries manufacturières	100.1	101.2	99.6	101.5	105.6	99.4	100.6	99.5
Food, beverages and tobacco - Aliments, boissons et tabac	99.1	99.2	99.2	100.2	100.6	97.2	104.1	102.9
Textiles, wearing apparel, leather, footwear - Textiles, habillement, cuir et chaussures	131.6	130.9	97.4	97.6	97.0	85.2	53.8	42.5
Petroleum, chemicals, pharmaceuticals, rubber and plastic - Pétroliers, produits chimiques, pharmaceutiques, caoutchouc et plastiques	102.2	99.8	97.4	94.6	94.8	84.6	89.2	91.0
Basic metals - Métaux de base	103.1	105.5	105.4	124.9	147.0	146.7	138.4	142.4
Fabricated metals, computer, electronic and optical products, electrical equipment, machinery - Fabrication d'ouvrages en métaux produits électroniques et optiques, appareils électriques, fabrication de machines	97.3	100.0	99.8	98.8	101.0	94.8	97.8	96.3
Electricity and gas - Electricité et gaz	97.1	99.0	103.3	104.2	107.0	111.5	113.2	113.9

Fiji [1]   Fidji [1]

Total industry - Total, industrie	102.5	114.4	103.3	102.1	97.8	94.6	101.1	104.4
Total mining - Total, industries extractives	119.8	137.6	75.8	26.4	53.9	34.9	59.6	53.7
Total manufacturing - Total, industries manufacturières	106.5	119.6	104.3	103.3	98.1	94.9	102.9	106.3
Food, beverages and tobacco - Aliments, boissons et tabac	97.3	98.9	106.6	105.8	104.1	95.2	100.7	103.8
Wearing apparel, leather and footwear - Fabrication d'articles d'habillement, fabrication de cuir et d'articles de cuir	106.1	104.0	96.0	98.0	89.1	92.2	95.3	120.5
Chemicals, petroleum, rubber and plastic products - Produits chimiques, pétroliers, caoutchouc et plastiques	105.2	103.3	101.4	97.7	91.1	99.4	111.1	105.0
Basic metals - Métaux de base	...	...	140.5	105.8	110.6	87.7	86.6	97.1
Fabricated metal products; machinery and equipment, electrical machinery and apparatus - Ouvrage en métaux, machines et matériel, machines et appareils électriques	107.3	105.0	110.8	98.6	86.7	96.7	97.3	98.1
Electricity and water - Electricité et eau	90.8	98.7	105.9	114.4	107.0	106.5	112.7	118.6

New Zealand [8]   Nouvelle- Zélande [8]

Total industry - Total, industrie	98.1	101.1	99.2	107.6	106.4	107.0	113.4	116.0
Total mining - Total, industries extractives	123.3	105.0	104.4	98.9	143.1	136.5	141.3	143.3
Total manufacturing [9] - Total, industries manufacturières [9]	94.9	97.3	101.0	97.7	99.0	93.5	87.8	87.4
Food, beverages and tobacco - Aliments, boissons et tabac	93.4	99.0	103.6	100.0	101.7	100.4	96.0	91.9
Textiles, wearing apparel, leather, footwear - Textiles, habillement, cuir et chaussures	105.7	98.3	97.9	100.8	98.5	92.0	90.3	78.2
Basic metals - Métaux de base	93.6	97.7	100.9	95.9	101.1	92.5	78.4	83.7

Source:
United Nations Statistics Division, New York, the index numbers of industrial production database, last accessed November 2012.

Source:
Organisation des Nations Unies, Division de statistique, New York, la base de données pour les indices de la production industrielle, dernier accès novembre 2012.

1   Data classified according to ISIC Rev. 3.
2   Twelve months ending 30 June of the year stated.
3   Including construction.
4   For government controlled areas.

1   Données classifiées selon la CITI, Rév. 3.
2   Période de douze mois finissant le 30 juin de l'année indiquée.
3   Y compris la construction.
4   Pour les zones contrôlées par le gouvernement.

23

Index numbers of industrial production *(continued)*
2005 = 100

Indices de la production industrielle *(suite)*
2005 = 100

5	Twelve months beginning 1 April of the year stated.	5	Période de 12 mois commençant le 1er avril de l'année indiquée.
6	Twelve months beginning 1 July of the year stated.	6	Période de 12 mois commençant le 1er juillet de l'année indiquée.
7	Excludes the Overseas Departments (French Guiana, Guadeloupe, Martinique, Mayotte and Réunion).	7	Non compris les départements d'outre-mer (Guyane française, Guadeloupe, Martinique, Mayotte et Réunion).
8	Twelve months ending 31 March of the year stated.	8	Période de 12 mois finissant le 31 mars de l'année indiquée.
9	Excludes repair and installation of machinery and equipment.	9	Non compris la réparation et installation de machines et de matériel.

Country or area	2003	2004	2005	2006	2007	2008	2009	2010	2011	Pays ou zone
Albania	6.50	5.25	5.00	5.50	6.25	6.25	5.25	5.00	...	Albanie
Algeria	4.50	4.00	4.00	4.00	4.00	4.00	4.00	4.00	4.00	Algérie
Angola	150.00	95.00	95.00	14.00	19.57	19.57	30.00	25.00	20.00	Angola
Anguilla	6.50	6.50	6.50	6.50	6.50	6.50	6.50	6.50	6.50	Anguilla
Antigua and Barbuda	6.50	6.50	6.50	6.50	6.50	6.50	6.50	6.50	6.50	Antigua-et-Barbuda
Aruba	5.00	5.00	5.00	5.00	5.00	5.00	3.00	1.00	1.00	Aruba
Australia	4.81	5.25	5.46	5.81	6.39	6.67	3.28	4.35	4.69	Australie
Azerbaijan	7.00	7.00	9.00	9.50	13.00	8.00	2.00	3.00	5.25	Azerbaïdjan
Bahamas	5.75	5.75	5.25	5.25	5.25	5.25	5.25	5.25	4.50	Bahamas
Bahrain	...	...	...	...	4.00	0.75	0.50	0.50	...	Bahreïn
Bangladesh	5.00	5.00	5.00	5.00	5.00	5.00	5.00	5.00	5.00	Bangladesh
Barbados	7.50	7.50	10.00	12.00	12.00	10.00	7.00	7.00	...	Barbade
Belarus	28.00	17.00	11.00	10.00	10.00	12.00	13.50	10.50	45.00	Bélarus
Belize	12.00	12.00	12.00	12.00	12.00	12.00	12.00	18.00	11.00	Belize
Benin	4.50	4.00	4.00	4.25	4.25	4.75	4.25	4.25	4.25	Bénin
Bolivia (Plurinational State of)	7.50	6.00	5.25	5.25	6.50	13.00	3.00	3.00	...	Bolivie (État plurinational de)
Botswana	14.25	14.25	14.50	15.00	14.50	15.00	10.00	9.50	9.50	Botswana
Brazil	16.50	17.75	18.00	13.25	11.25	13.75	8.75	10.75	11.00	Brésil
Bulgaria	2.83	2.37	2.05	3.26	4.58	5.77	0.55	0.18	0.22	Bulgarie
Burkina Faso	4.50	4.00	4.00	4.25	4.25	4.75	4.25	4.25	4.25	Burkina Faso
Burundi	14.50	14.50	14.50	11.07	10.12	10.08	10.00	11.25	...	Burundi
Cameroon	6.00	6.00	5.50	5.25	5.25	4.75	4.25	4.00	4.00	Cameroun
Canada	2.75	2.50	3.25	4.25	4.25	1.50	0.25	1.00	1.00	Canada
Cape Verde	8.50	8.50	8.50	8.50	8.50	7.50	7.50	7.50	...	Cap-Vert
Central African Rep.	6.00	6.00	5.50	5.25	5.25	4.75	4.25	4.00	4.00	Rép. centrafricaine
Chad	6.00	6.00	5.50	5.25	5.25	4.75	4.25	4.00	4.00	Tchad
Chile	2.45	2.25	4.50	5.25	6.00	8.25	0.50	3.12	5.25	Chili
China	2.70	3.33	3.33	3.33	3.33	2.79	2.79	3.25	3.25	Chine
China, Hong Kong SAR	2.50	3.75	5.75	6.75	5.75	0.50	0.50	0.50	0.50	Chine, Hong Kong RAS
Colombia	12.00	11.25	10.75	9.50	11.50	11.50	5.50	5.00	6.75	Colombie
Comoros	3.83	3.55	3.59	4.34	5.36	5.36	2.22	1.93	...	Comores
Congo	6.00	6.00	5.50	5.25	5.25	4.75	4.25	4.00	4.00	Congo
Costa Rica	26.00	26.00	27.00	24.75	17.00	25.00	23.00	21.50	22.00	Costa Rica
Côte d'Ivoire	4.50	4.00	4.00	4.25	4.25	4.75	4.25	4.25	4.25	Côte d'Ivoire
Croatia	4.50	4.50	4.50	4.50	9.00	9.00	9.00	9.00	7.00	Croatie
Cyprus	4.50	5.50	4.25	4.50	5.00	...	...	...	...	Chypre
Czech Republic	2.00	2.50	2.00	2.50	3.50	2.25	1.00	0.75	0.75	République tchèque
Dem. Rep. of the Congo	...	...	...	40.00	22.50	40.00	70.00	22.00	...	Rép. dém. du Congo
Denmark	2.00	2.00	2.25	3.50	4.00	3.50	1.00	0.75	0.75	Danemark
Dominica	6.50	6.50	6.50	6.50	6.50	6.50	6.50	6.50	6.50	Dominique
Ecuador	11.67	10.23	9.96	9.54	...	9.14	9.19	8.68	8.17	Equateur
Egypt	10.00	10.00	10.00	9.00	9.00	11.50	8.50	8.50	...	Egypte
Equatorial Guinea	6.00	6.00	5.50	5.25	5.25	4.75	4.25	4.00	4.00	Guinée équatoriale
Euro Area	3.00	3.00	3.25	4.50	5.00	3.00	1.75	1.75	1.75	Zone euro
Fiji	1.25	1.75	2.25	4.25	...	...	...	2.50	0.50	Fidji
Gabon	6.00	6.00	5.50	5.25	5.25	4.75	4.25	4.00	4.00	Gabon
Gambia	29.00	28.00	14.00	9.00	10.00	11.00	9.00	10.00	...	Gambie

24

Rates of discount of central banks *(continued)*
Per cent per annum, end of period
Taux d'escompte des banques centrales *(suite)*
Pour cent par année, fin de la période

Country or area	2003	2004	2005	2006	2007	2008	2009	2010	2011	Pays ou zone
Georgia	...	...	...	...	...	9.00	5.00	7.50	7.25	Géorgie
Ghana	21.50	18.50	15.50	12.50	13.50	17.00	18.00	13.50	12.50	Ghana
Grenada	6.50	6.50	6.50	6.50	6.50	6.50	6.50	6.50	6.50	Grenade
Guinea	16.25	16.25	22.25	...	...	...	...	...	...	Guinée
Guinea-Bissau	4.50	4.00	4.00	4.25	4.25	4.75	4.25	4.25	4.25	Guinée-Bissau
Guyana	5.50	6.00	6.00	6.75	6.50	6.75	6.75	6.25	...	Guyana
Hungary	12.50	9.50	6.00	8.00	7.50	10.00	6.25	5.75	7.00	Hongrie
Iceland	7.70	10.25	12.00	15.25	15.25	22.00	14.55	5.50	5.75	Islande
India	6.00	6.00	6.00	6.00	6.00	6.00	6.00	6.00	...	Inde
Indonesia	8.31	7.43	12.75	9.75	8.00	9.25	6.50	6.50	6.00	Indonésie
Iran (Islamic Rep. of)	11.68	...	...	...	...	...	...	...	...	Iran (Rép. islamique d')
Iraq	...	6.00	6.33	10.42	20.00	16.75	8.83	6.25	...	Iraq
Israel	5.20	3.90	4.44	5.00	4.00	2.50	1.01	2.00	...	Israël
Japan	0.10	0.10	0.10	0.40	0.75	0.30	0.30	0.30	0.30	Japon
Jordan	2.50	3.75	6.50	7.50	7.00	6.25	4.75	4.25	4.50	Jordanie
Kazakhstan	7.00	7.00	8.00	9.00	11.00	10.50	7.00	7.00	7.50	Kazakhstan
Republic of Korea	2.50	2.00	2.00	2.75	3.25	1.75	1.25	1.25	...	République de Corée
Kuwait	3.25	4.75	6.00	6.25	6.25	3.75	3.00	2.50	2.50	Koweït
Lao People's Dem. Rep.	20.00	20.00	20.00	20.00	12.67	7.67	4.75	4.33	...	Rép. dém. pop. lao
Latvia	3.00	4.00	4.00	5.00	6.00	6.00	4.00	3.50	3.50	Lettonie
Lebanon	20.00	20.00	12.00	12.00	12.00	12.00	10.00	10.00	...	Liban
Lesotho	15.00	13.00	13.00	10.76	12.82	14.05	10.66	9.52	...	Lesotho
Libyan Arab Jamah.	5.00	4.00	4.00	4.00	4.00	5.00	3.00	3.00	...	Jamah. arabe libyenne
Lithuania	...	...	3.02	3.79	4.85	4.73	2.06	1.75	2.00	Lituanie
Malawi	35.00	25.00	25.00	20.00	15.00	15.00	15.00	13.00	...	Malawi
Malaysia	...	2.70	3.00	3.50	3.50	3.25	2.00	2.75	3.00	Malaisie
Maldives	19.00	18.00	18.00	12.00	13.00	13.00	13.00	16.00	16.00	Maldives
Mali	4.50	4.00	4.00	4.25	4.25	4.75	4.25	4.25	4.25	Mali
Malta	3.00	3.00	3.25	3.75	...	...	...	...	...	Malte
Mauritania	11.00	11.00	14.00	14.00	12.00	12.00	9.00	9.00	...	Mauritanie
Mexico	...	...	...	...	...	8.25	4.50	4.50	4.50	Mexique
Mongolia	11.47	15.75	4.75	6.42	9.85	14.78	10.82	10.99	14.25	Mongolie
Montserrat	6.50	6.50	6.50	6.50	6.50	6.50	6.50	6.50	6.50	Montserrat
Morocco	3.25	3.25	3.25	3.25	3.25	3.32	3.31	3.25	3.25	Maroc
Mozambique	9.95	9.95	9.95	9.95	9.95	9.95	9.95	9.95	...	Mozambique
Myanmar	10.00	10.00	10.00	12.00	12.00	12.00	12.00	12.00	...	Myanmar
Namibia	7.75	7.50	7.00	9.00	10.50	10.00	7.00	6.00	...	Namibie
Nepal	5.50	5.50	6.00	6.25	6.25	6.50	6.50	7.00	7.00	Népal
New Zealand	5.00	6.50	7.25	7.25	8.25	5.00	2.50	3.00	2.50	Nouvelle-Zélande
Niger	4.50	4.00	4.00	4.25	4.25	4.75	4.25	4.25	4.25	Niger
Nigeria	15.00	15.00	13.00	10.00	9.50	9.75	6.00	6.25	12.00	Nigéria
Norway	4.25	3.75	4.25	5.50	6.25	4.00	1.75	2.00	1.99	Norvège
Oman	7.50	0.69	3.12	3.63	1.98	0.91	0.05	0.07	0.10	Oman
Pakistan	7.50	7.50	9.00	9.50	10.00	15.00	12.50	14.00	12.00	Pakistan
Papua New Guinea	15.50	12.67	9.67	8.13	7.38	7.00	6.92	6.00	6.35	Papouasie-Nvl-Guinée
Paraguay	20.00	20.00	20.00	20.00	20.00	20.00	20.00	20.00	...	Paraguay
Peru	3.25	3.75	4.00	5.25	5.75	7.25	2.05	3.80	5.05	Pérou
Philippines	5.53	8.36	5.70	5.04	4.28	6.00	3.50	4.00	4.50	Philippines
Poland	5.25	6.50	4.50	4.00	5.00	5.00	3.50	3.50	4.50	Pologne

24 Rates of discount of central banks *(continued)*
Per cent per annum, end of period
Taux d'escompte des banques centrales *(suite)*
Pour cent par année, fin de la période

Country or area	2003	2004	2005	2006	2007	2008	2009	2010	2011	Pays ou zone
Qatar	1.33	2.60	4.50	5.50	5.50	5.50	5.50	5.50	4.50	Qatar
Republic of Moldova	14.00	14.50	12.50	14.50	16.00	14.00	5.00	7.00	9.50	République de Moldova
Russian Federation	16.00	13.00	12.00	11.00	10.00	13.00	8.75	7.75	8.00	Fédération de Russie
Rwanda	14.50	14.50	12.50	12.50	12.50	11.25	6.00	5.47	...	Rwanda
Saint Kitts and Nevis	6.50	6.50	6.50	6.50	6.50	6.50	6.50	6.50	6.50	Saint-Kitts-et-Nevis
Saint Lucia	6.50	6.50	6.50	6.50	6.50	6.50	6.50	6.50	6.50	Sainte-Lucie
Saint Vincent-Grenadines	6.50	6.50	6.50	6.50	6.50	6.50	6.50	6.50	6.50	Saint Vincent-Grenadines
Sao Tome and Principe	14.50	14.50	18.20	28.00	28.00	28.00	16.00	15.00	15.00	Sao Tomé-et-Principe
Saudi Arabia	1.25	2.25	4.25	4.70	4.00	1.50	0.25	0.25	0.25	Arabie saoudite
Senegal	4.50	4.00	4.00	4.25	4.25	4.75	4.25	4.25	4.25	Sénégal
Serbia	10.63	16.30	19.16	15.35	9.57	17.75	9.92	11.17	9.82	Serbie
Seychelles	4.67	3.51	3.87	4.44	5.13	...	...	...	...	Seychelles
Singapore	0.64	0.88	2.15	3.23	2.30	0.84	0.27	0.22	0.19	Singapour
Slovakia	6.00	4.00	3.00	4.75	4.25	...	...	...	...	Slovaquie
Slovenia	7.25	5.00	5.00	4.50	...	...	...	...	...	Slovénie
South Africa	8.00	7.50	7.00	9.00	11.00	11.50	7.00	5.50	5.50	Afrique du Sud
Sri Lanka	15.00	15.00	15.00	15.00	15.00	15.00	15.00	15.00	...	Sri Lanka
Swaziland	8.00	7.50	7.00	9.00	11.00	11.00	6.50	5.50	5.50	Swaziland
Sweden	3.00	2.00	1.50	2.50	3.50	2.00	0.50	0.50	1.91	Suède
Switzerland	0.75	1.25	1.50	2.50	3.25	1.00	0.75	0.75	0.25	Suisse
Syrian Arab Republic	5.00	5.00	5.00	5.00	5.00	5.00	5.00	5.00	...	Rép. arabe syrienne
Tajikistan	15.00	10.00	9.00	12.00	15.00	13.50	8.00	8.25	...	Tadjikistan
Thailand	1.25	2.00	4.00	5.00	3.25	2.75	1.25	2.00	3.25	Thaïlande
TFYR of Macedonia	6.50	6.50	6.50	6.50	6.50	6.50	6.50	5.00	4.00	L'ex-R.Y. Macédoine
Togo	4.50	4.00	4.00	4.25	4.25	4.75	4.25	4.25	4.25	Togo
Trinidad and Tobago	7.00	7.00	8.00	10.00	10.00	10.75	7.25	5.75	...	Trinité-et-Tobago
Turkey	43.00	38.00	23.00	27.00	25.00	25.00	15.00	14.00	17.00	Turquie
Uganda	25.62	16.15	14.36	16.30	14.68	19.42	9.65	11.97	29.00	Ouganda
Ukraine	7.00	9.00	9.50	8.50	8.00	12.00	10.25	7.75	7.75	Ukraine
United Kingdom	3.75	4.75	4.50	5.00	5.50	2.00	0.50	0.50	...	Royaume-Uni
United Rep. of Tanzania	12.34	14.42	19.33	20.07	16.40	15.99	3.70	7.58	...	Rép.-Unie de Tanzanie
United States	1.00	2.25	4.25	5.25	4.25	0.13	0.13	0.13	0.13	Etats-Unis
Uruguay	46.27	10.00	10.00	10.00	10.00	20.00	20.00	20.00	...	Uruguay
Vanuatu	6.50	6.50	6.25	6.00	6.00	6.00	6.00	...	...	Vanuatu
Venezuela (Boliv. Rep. of)	28.50	28.50	28.50	28.50	28.50	33.50	29.50	29.50	29.50	Venezuela (Rép. boliv. du)
Viet Nam	5.00	5.00	5.00	6.50	6.50	10.25	8.00	9.00	15.00	Viet Nam
Zambia	14.35	16.68	14.81	8.79	11.73	14.49	8.39	7.17	9.71	Zambie
Zimbabwe	300.00	110.00	540.00	500.00	975.00	...	...	...	...	Zimbabwe

Source: International Monetary Fund (IMF), Washington, D.C., the International Financial Statistics database, last accessed March 2012.

Source: Fonds monétaire international (FMI), Washington, D.C., la base de données de Statistiques Financières Internationales, dernier accès mars 2012.

Short-term interest rates
Treasury bill and money market rates: per cent per annum

Taux d'intérêt à court terme
Taux des bons du trésor et du marché monétaire : pour cent par année

Country or area	2003	2004	2005	2006	2007	2008	2009	2010	2011	Pays ou zone
Afghanistan										**Afghanistan**
Money market	...	...	...	2.50	5.65	...	...	2.01	0.20	Marché monétaire
Albania										**Albanie**
Treasury bill	8.81	6.79	5.52	5.49	5.93	6.24	6.27	5.83	5.46	Bons du trésor
Algeria										**Algérie**
Money market	2.74	1.64	1.43	2.05	3.13	3.27	3.68	3.22	2.14	Marché monétaire
Treasury bill	1.67	0.87	0.75	2.14	0.96	0.33	0.67	0.31	0.21	Bons du trésor
Anguilla										**Anguilla**
Money market	6.07	4.67	4.01	4.76	5.24	4.92	6.03	6.36	5.68	Marché monétaire
Antigua and Barbuda										**Antigua-et-Barbuda**
Money market	6.07	4.67	4.01	4.76	5.24	4.92	6.03	6.36	5.68	Marché monétaire
Treasury bill	7.00	7.00	7.00	6.52	6.33	6.02	6.38	6.25	6.50	Bons du trésor
Argentina										**Argentine**
Money market	3.74	1.96	4.11	7.20	8.67	10.07	10.23	9.09	9.98	Marché monétaire
Armenia										**Arménie**
Money market [1]	7.51	4.18	3.17	4.34	4.47	6.75	6.25	6.58	7.69	Marché monétaire [1]
Treasury bill	11.91	5.27	4.05	4.87	6.09	7.69	9.42	10.59	9.53	Bons du trésor
Aruba [2]										**Aruba [2]**
Money market	0.18	0.11	0.51	2.27	2.53	0.45	0.05	0.05	0.05	Marché monétaire
Australia										**Australie**
Money market	4.81	5.25	5.46	5.81	6.39	6.67	3.28	4.35	4.69	Marché monétaire
Treasury bill	...	...	...	...	...	...	3.15	4.44	4.56	Bons du trésor
Azerbaijan [3]										**Azerbaïdjan [3]**
Treasury bill	8.00	4.62	7.52	10.04	10.64	10.48	3.31	1.83	2.28	Bons du trésor
Bahamas										**Bahamas**
Treasury bill	1.78	0.56	0.14	0.87	2.66	2.73	2.62	2.28	1.25	Bons du trésor
Bahrain										**Bahreïn**
Money market [4]	1.24	1.74	3.63	5.25	5.12	3.09	1.82	0.38	...	Marché monétaire [4]
Treasury bill	1.13	1.56	3.57	5.04	4.86	2.53	1.06	0.83	0.96	Bons du trésor
Barbados [5]										**Barbade [5]**
Treasury bill	1.41	1.20	4.62	5.96	5.65	4.20	3.76	3.30	3.41	Bons du trésor
Belgium										**Belgique**
Treasury bill	2.23	1.97	2.02	2.73	3.80	3.63	0.58	0.32	0.78	Bons du trésor
Belize [6]										**Belize [6]**
Treasury bill	3.22	3.22	3.22	3.22	3.22	3.22	3.22	3.04	2.42	Bons du trésor
Benin [7]										**Bénin [7]**
Money market	4.95	4.95	4.95	4.95	3.93	3.94	3.47	3.31	3.29	Marché monétaire
Bolivia (Plurinational State of)										**Bolivie (État pl. de)**
Money market	4.07	4.05	3.53	3.80	4.27	7.68	3.55	0.90	1.87	Marché monétaire
Treasury bill [8]	9.92	7.41	4.96	4.56	6.04	8.31	2.86	0.07	0.46	Bons du trésor [8]
Brazil										**Brésil**
Money market	23.37	16.24	19.12	15.28	11.98	12.36	10.06	9.80	11.66	Marché monétaire
Treasury bill	22.11	17.14	18.76	14.38	11.50	13.68	9.70	10.93	11.66	Bons du trésor
Bulgaria										**Bulgarie**
Money market [9]	1.95	1.95	2.02	2.79	4.03	5.16	2.01	0.18	0.20	Marché monétaire [9]
Treasury bill	2.81	2.64	2.23	2.58	3.79	4.06	4.67	2.56	...	Bons du trésor
Burkina Faso [7]										**Burkina Faso [7]**
Money market	4.95	4.95	4.95	4.95	3.93	3.94	3.47	3.31	3.29	Marché monétaire
Burundi [10]										**Burundi [10]**
Treasury bill	16.55	14.95	7.92	8.84	...	...	...	...	...	Bons du trésor
Canada										**Canada**
Money market [11]	2.93	2.25	2.66	4.02	4.34	2.96	0.39	0.60	1.00	Marché monétaire [11]
Treasury bill	2.87	2.22	2.73	4.03	4.15	2.39	0.35	0.60	0.92	Bons du trésor
Cape Verde [12]										**Cap-Vert [12]**
Treasury bill	5.81	6.42	4.07	2.70	3.41	3.41	3.52	3.89	3.96	Bons du trésor
Chile										**Chili**
Money market	2.72	1.88	3.48	5.02	5.36	7.11	1.95	1.40	4.67	Marché monétaire
China, Hong Kong SAR										**Chine, Hong Kong RAS**
Money market	0.07	0.13	4.25	3.94	1.88	0.23	0.13	0.13	0.13	Marché monétaire
Treasury bill	-0.08	0.07	3.65	3.29	1.96	0.05	0.07	0.28	0.22	Bons du trésor

Short-term interest rates *(continued)*
Treasury bill and money market rates: per cent per annum
Taux d'intérêt à court terme *(suite)*
Taux des bons du trésor et du marché monétaire : pour cent par année

Country or area	2003	2004	2005	2006	2007	2008	2009	2010	2011	Pays ou zone
China, Macao SAR [9]										Chine, Macao RAS [9]
Money market	0.11	0.27	4.09	3.91	3.27	0.30	0.11	0.25	0.38	Marché monétaire
Colombia [13]										Colombie [13]
Money market	6.95	7.01	6.18	6.49	8.66	9.73	5.65	3.15	4.03	Marché monétaire
Côte d'Ivoire [7]										Côte d'Ivoire [7]
Money market	4.95	4.95	4.95	4.95	3.93	3.94	3.47	3.31	3.29	Marché monétaire
Croatia [14]										Croatie [14]
Money market	3.19	5.08	3.25	2.46	5.11	6.08	7.53	1.01	1.04	Marché monétaire
Cyprus										Chypre
Money market	3.35	4.01	3.27	2.90	4.01	...	...	...	...	Marché monétaire
Treasury bill [15]	3.51	4.44	4.34	2.56	3.59	...	...	...	...	Bons du trésor [15]
Czech Republic										République tchèque
Money market [16]	2.08	2.56	2.17	2.55	4.11	3.63	1.54	1.22	1.17	Marché monétaire [16]
Treasury bill [17]	2.04	2.57	1.96	2.51	3.55	3.62	1.29	0.84	0.78	Bons du trésor [17]
Dem. Rep. of the Congo										Rép. dém. du Congo
Money market	...	...	...	...	26.22	17.60	62.21	35.92	14.79	Marché monétaire
Denmark										Danemark
Money market	2.38	2.16	2.20	3.18	4.33	4.88	1.81	0.70	1.06	Marché monétaire
Dominica										Dominique
Money market	6.07	4.67	4.01	4.76	5.24	4.92	6.03	6.33	5.68	Marché monétaire
Treasury bill	6.40	6.40	6.40	6.40	6.40	6.40	6.40	6.40	6.40	Bons du trésor
Dominican Republic [18]										Rép. dominicaine [18]
Money market	24.24	36.76	12.57	10.60	8.24	12.24	8.08	6.25	8.29	Marché monétaire
Egypt [19]										Egypte [19]
Treasury bill	6.90	9.90	8.57	9.53	6.85	11.37	9.84	9.28	13.95	Bons du trésor
El Salvador [20]										El Salvador [20]
Money market	3.86	4.36	5.18	6.00	5.25	...	...	...	...	Marché monétaire
Estonia										Estonie
Money market	2.92	2.50	2.38	3.16	4.87	6.66	5.93	1.57	...	Marché monétaire
Ethiopia										Ethiopie
Treasury bill	1.31	0.56	0.25	0.08	0.93	0.68	...	...	...	Bons du trésor
Euro Area										Zone euro
Money market	2.26	2.05	2.12	3.01	3.98	3.78	0.70	0.48	0.82	Marché monétaire
Fiji										Fidji
Money market [21]	0.87	0.89	1.28	4.42	5.00	1.25	1.31	1.00	...	Marché monétaire [21]
Treasury bill [22]	1.01	1.52	1.94	7.45	4.55	0.23	6.07	3.45	2.20	Bons du trésor [22]
Finland										Finlande
Money market	2.33	2.11	2.18	3.08	4.28	4.63	1.23	0.81	1.39	Marché monétaire
France										France
Treasury bill	2.28	2.02	2.07	2.89	3.86	3.62	0.65	0.38	0.69	Bons du trésor
Georgia										Géorgie
Money market [23]	16.88	11.87	7.71	9.46	7.42	14.77	10.00	48.00	14.00	Marché monétaire [23]
Treasury bill [24]	44.26	19.16	...	...	...	...	5.98	9.55	9.68	Bons du trésor [24]
Germany										Allemagne
Money market [25]	2.32	2.05	2.09	2.84	3.86	3.82	0.63	0.38	0.81	Marché monétaire [25]
Treasury bill [26]	1.98	2.00	2.03	3.08	3.81	...	...	...	...	Bons du trésor [26]
Ghana										Ghana
Money market [27]	24.71	15.73	14.70	10.57	12.00	15.64	21.50	...	...	Marché monétaire [27]
Treasury bill [28]	27.25	16.57	14.89	9.95	9.66	16.96	23.76	...	...	Bons du trésor [28]
Greece [29]										Grèce [29]
Treasury bill	2.34	2.27	2.33	3.44	4.45	4.81	1.62	1.35	2.01	Bons du trésor
Grenada										Grenade
Money market	6.07	4.67	4.01	4.76	5.24	4.94	6.03	6.36	5.68	Marché monétaire
Treasury bill	6.50	5.50	5.50	6.25	6.38	6.25	6.33	6.21	5.94	Bons du trésor
Guatemala										Guatemala
Money market	6.65	6.16	6.54	6.56	...	...	...	...	...	Marché monétaire
Guinea-Bissau [30]										Guinée-Bissau [30]
Money market	4.95	4.95	4.95	4.95	3.93	3.94	3.47	3.31	3.29	Marché monétaire
Guyana										Guyana
Treasury bill	3.04	3.62	3.79	3.95	3.94	3.99	4.31	3.87	...	Bons du trésor
Hungary [31]										Hongrie [31]
Treasury bill	8.22	11.33	6.95	6.87	7.67	8.90	8.48	5.37	6.02	Bons du trésor

25

Short-term interest rates *(continued)*
Treasury bill and money market rates: per cent per annum
Taux d'intérêt à court terme *(suite)*
Taux des bons du trésor et du marché monétaire : pour cent par année

Country or area	2003	2004	2005	2006	2007	2008	2009	2010	2011	Pays ou zone
Iceland										**Islande**
Money market[32]	5.14	6.22	9.05	12.41	13.96	16.05	11.15	6.92	3.94	Marché monétaire[32]
Treasury bill[33]	4.93	6.04	8.80	13.41	15.13	17.88	11.38	6.65	4.28	Bons du trésor[33]
India[34]										**Inde[34]**
Money market	...	...	...	...	15.29	11.55	4.49	6.51	8.80	Marché monétaire
Indonesia[35]										**Indonésie[35]**
Money market	7.76	5.38	6.78	9.18	6.02	8.48	7.16	6.01	5.62	Marché monétaire
Iraq[36]										**Iraq[36]**
Treasury bill	...	...	7.07	9.48	21.00	17.67	7.43	6.31	9.49	Bons du trésor
Ireland[37]										**Irlande[37]**
Money market	2.08	2.13	2.40	3.64	4.71	2.99	0.48	0.81	1.14	Marché monétaire
Israel										**Israël**
Treasury bill	7.00	4.78	4.34	5.54	4.33	3.90	1.39	2.19	3.05	Bons du trésor
Italy										**Italie**
Money market	2.33	2.10	2.18	3.09	4.29	4.67	1.28	1.02	2.73	Marché monétaire
Treasury bill	2.19	2.08	2.17	3.18	4.04	3.76	0.96	1.13	2.79	Bons du trésor
Jamaica										**Jamaïque**
Money market[38]	25.53	12.79	10.96	9.37	9.04	10.78	8.79	5.44	3.59	Marché monétaire[38]
Treasury bill	25.94	15.47	13.39	12.79	12.56	15.89	19.95	9.26	6.59	Bons du trésor
Japan										**Japon**
Money market[39]	^0.00	^0.00	^0.00	0.12	0.47	0.46	0.11	0.09	0.08	Marché monétaire[39]
Treasury bill[40]	^0.00	^0.00	^0.00	0.42	0.55	0.36	0.12	0.13	0.10	Bons du trésor[40]
Jordan										**Jordanie**
Money market	2.58	2.18	3.59	5.55	5.70	4.94	3.33	2.19	2.56	Marché monétaire
Kazakhstan[41]										**Kazakhstan[41]**
Treasury bill	5.86	3.28	3.28	3.28	7.01	7.00	7.00	7.00	7.00	Bons du trésor
Kenya										**Kenya**
Treasury bill	3.73	2.96	8.44	6.81	6.80	7.70	7.38	3.60	8.72	Bons du trésor
Kuwait										**Koweït**
Money market[42]	2.47	2.14	2.83	5.62	4.88	2.80	1.60	0.91	0.94	Marché monétaire[42]
Treasury bill[43]	2.33	1.75	1.99	...	...	...	0.92	0.64	0.83	Bons du trésor[43]
Kyrgyzstan										**Kirghizistan**
Money market	4.65	4.78	3.24	2.83	3.18	7.62	7.32	4.54	...	Marché monétaire
Treasury bill[44]	7.21	4.94	4.40	4.75	4.90	13.16	10.57	4.59	8.32	Bons du trésor[44]
Lao People's Dem. Rep.										**Rép. dém. pop. lao**
Treasury bill	24.87	20.37	18.61	18.34	18.36	12.26	9.52	7.97	...	Bons du trésor
Latvia										**Lettonie**
Money market	2.86	3.25	2.49	3.24	5.07	4.09	3.92	0.73	0.31	Marché monétaire
Treasury bill	3.24	3.43	2.56	4.13	4.23	6.99	10.42	2.43	1.12	Bons du trésor
Lebanon										**Liban**
Treasury bill	6.46	5.25	5.22	5.22	5.22	5.21	4.91	4.10	3.93	Bons du trésor
Lesotho										**Lesotho**
Treasury bill	11.96	8.52	7.23	6.87	7.81	9.75	7.75	6.24	5.35	Bons du trésor
Libyan Arab Jamah.[45]										**Jam. arabe lib.[45]**
Money market	4.00	4.00	...	...	...	...	...	...	...	Marché monétaire
Lithuania										**Lituanie**
Money market	1.79	1.53	1.97	2.76	4.18	3.95	0.88	0.22	0.75	Marché monétaire
Treasury bill	2.61	2.25	2.36	2.95	4.23	5.35	8.54	2.80	2.40	Bons du trésor
Madagascar										**Madagascar**
Money market[46]	10.50	16.50	16.50	14.50	11.00	11.50	9.50	9.50	9.50	Marché monétaire[46]
Treasury bill	11.94	12.95	18.84	21.16	11.84	8.81	7.62	9.33	9.58	Bons du trésor
Malawi[47]										**Malawi[47]**
Treasury bill	39.27	28.58	24.40	19.27	13.95	11.29	10.15	7.16	6.56	Bons du trésor
Malaysia										**Malaisie**
Money market[48]	2.74	2.70	2.72	3.38	3.50	3.47	2.12	2.45	2.88	Marché monétaire[48]
Treasury bill[49]	2.79	2.40	2.48	3.23	3.43	3.39	2.05	2.58	2.92	Bons du trésor[49]
Maldives[50]										**Maldives[50]**
Treasury bill	...	...	...	...	5.50	6.00	6.00	4.90	5.44	Bons du trésor
Mali[7]										**Mali[7]**
Money market	4.95	4.95	4.95	4.95	3.93	3.94	3.47	3.31	3.29	Marché monétaire
Malta[51]										**Malte[51]**
Treasury bill	3.29	2.94	3.18	3.49	4.25	4.54	1.23	0.81	1.39	Bons du trésor

25

Short-term interest rates *(continued)*
Treasury bill and money market rates: per cent per annum
Taux d'intérêt à court terme *(suite)*
Taux des bons du trésor et du marché monétaire : pour cent par année

Country or area	2003	2004	2005	2006	2007	2008	2009	2010	2011	Pays ou zone
Mauritania [52]										**Mauritanie** [52]
Treasury bill	7.65	7.22	11.84	11.50	10.43	11.09	8.66	8.55	...	Bons du trésor
Mauritius [53]										**Maurice** [53]
Money market	3.22	1.33	2.45	5.59	8.52	7.52	4.63	3.07	2.33	Marché monétaire
Mexico										**Mexique**
Money market	6.83	7.15	9.59	7.51	7.66	8.28	5.93	4.91	4.82	Marché monétaire
Treasury bill	6.23	6.82	9.20	7.19	7.19	7.68	5.43	4.40	4.24	Bons du trésor
Mongolia										**Mongolie**
Treasury bill	...	10.39	13.73	6.73	6.82	...	...	...	...	Bons du trésor
Montenegro [54]										**Monténégro** [54]
Treasury bill	...	10.39	6.03	1.15	0.56	...	4.18	3.21	2.57	Bons du trésor
Montserrat										**Montserrat**
Money market	6.07	4.67	4.01	4.76	5.24	4.92	6.03	6.36	5.68	Marché monétaire
Morocco [55]										**Maroc** [55]
Money market	3.22	2.39	2.78	2.58	3.31	3.37	3.26	3.29	3.29	Marché monétaire
Mozambique										**Mozambique**
Money market	13.34	9.87	6.35	15.25	15.15	12.84	8.66	10.24	14.06	Marché monétaire
Treasury bill [56]	15.32	12.37	9.10	15.05	15.16	13.76	10.59	11.99	15.24	Bons du trésor [56]
Namibia										**Namibie**
Money market	10.03	6.93	6.93	7.12	8.61	9.37	7.75	...	...	Marché monétaire
Treasury bill	10.51	7.78	7.09	7.26	8.59	9.64	8.19	6.46	5.62	Bons du trésor
Nepal [57]										**Népal** [57]
Treasury bill	3.85	2.40	2.20	1.98	3.59	4.72	6.35	6.82	0.80	Bons du trésor
Netherlands Antilles [58]										**Ant. néerlandaises** [58]
Treasury bill	2.80	3.86	3.52	5.39	6.04	4.40	1.35	...	...	Bons du trésor
New Zealand										**Nouvelle-Zélande**
Money market	5.33	5.77	6.76	7.30	7.93	7.55	2.82	2.62	2.50	Marché monétaire
Treasury bill [59]	5.21	5.85	6.52	7.05	7.55	7.01	2.83	2.78	2.55	Bons du trésor [59]
Niger [7]										**Niger** [7]
Money market	4.95	4.95	4.95	4.95	3.93	3.94	3.47	3.31	3.29	Marché monétaire
Nigeria [60]										**Nigéria** [60]
Treasury bill	14.79	14.34	7.63	9.99	6.85	8.20	3.79	3.85	...	Bons du trésor
Norway										**Norvège**
Money market	4.45	2.17	2.26	3.12	...	6.06	...	...	...	Marché monétaire
Oman [61]										**Oman** [61]
Money market	...	0.66	2.25	3.40	1.47	0.29	0.08	0.10	0.11	Marché monétaire
Pakistan										**Pakistan**
Money market [62]	2.14	2.70	6.83	8.89	9.30	12.33	11.96	11.69	12.47	Marché monétaire [62]
Treasury bill [63]	1.87	2.49	7.18	8.54	8.99	11.37	12.52	12.55	13.12	Bons du trésor [63]
Panama										**Panama**
Money market	1.50	1.90	3.13	5.06	5.05	2.57	0.42	0.28	0.30	Marché monétaire
Papua New Guinea										**Pap.-Nvl-Guinée**
Money market [9]	13.58	7.79	4.36	3.29	3.00	5.50	7.67	7.00	6.98	Marché monétaire [9]
Treasury bill [64]	18.69	8.85	3.81	4.01	4.67	6.19	7.08	4.64	4.14	Bons du trésor [64]
Paraguay [65]										**Paraguay** [65]
Money market	13.02	1.33	2.29	8.33	3.93	4.50	8.94	1.85	...	Marché monétaire
Peru [9]										**Pérou** [9]
Money market	2.51	3.00	3.34	4.51	4.99	6.54	1.24	2.98	4.24	Marché monétaire
Philippines										**Philippines**
Money market	6.97	7.05	7.31	7.84	7.02	5.48	4.54	4.20	4.54	Marché monétaire
Treasury bill [36]	5.87	7.32	6.13	5.29	3.38	5.17	4.16	3.52	1.34	Bons du trésor [36]
Poland										**Pologne**
Money market	5.69	5.67	5.34	4.10	4.42	5.75	3.18	3.08	4.10	Marché monétaire
Treasury bill	5.38	6.60	4.90	4.19	4.70	6.27	4.56	4.00	...	Bons du trésor
Qatar										**Qatar**
Money market	...	2.09	3.13	4.77	4.38	1.06	2.09	1.70	0.46	Marché monétaire
Republic of Korea [66]										**Rép. de Corée** [66]
Money market	4.00	3.65	3.33	4.19	4.77	4.78	1.98	2.16	3.09	Marché monétaire
Republic of Moldova										**Rép. de Moldova**
Money market	11.51	13.21	6.26	9.38	12.35	16.01	10.93	5.58	8.44	Marché monétaire
Treasury bill	15.77	12.29	3.75	7.43	13.52	18.89	11.82	7.13	11.71	Bons du trésor

25

Short-term interest rates *(continued)*
Treasury bill and money market rates: per cent per annum
Taux d'intérêt à court terme *(suite)*
Taux des bons du trésor et du marché monétaire : pour cent par année

Country or area	2003	2004	2005	2006	2007	2008	2009	2010	2011	Pays ou zone
Romania										**Roumanie**
Money market[67]	18.95	20.01	8.99	8.34	7.55	11.37	10.92	5.44	4.80	Marché monétaire[67]
Treasury bill[47]	15.07	...	...	...	7.11	10.42	10.90	7.21	7.32	Bons du trésor[47]
Russian Federation										**Féd. de Russie**
Money market	3.77	3.33	2.68	3.43	4.43	5.48	7.78	3.07	3.93	Marché monétaire
Treasury bill	5.35	...	...	...	...	...	...	...	...	Bons du trésor
Rwanda										**Rwanda**
Money market[9]	10.13	11.02	8.28	8.26	7.21	7.13	...	6.89	...	Marché monétaire[9]
Treasury bill	11.18	12.52	8.35	9.86	7.24	...	...	7.44	...	Bons du trésor
Saint Kitts and Nevis										**St.-Kitts-et-Nevis**
Money market	6.07	4.67	4.01	4.76	5.24	4.92	6.03	6.37	5.68	Marché monétaire
Treasury bill	7.17	7.00	7.00	7.00	7.00	7.00	6.85	6.75	6.75	Bons du trésor
Saint Lucia										**Sainte-Lucie**
Money market	6.07	4.67	4.01	4.76	5.24	4.92	6.03	6.36	5.68	Marché monétaire
Treasury bill	5.44	5.50	4.64	5.17	5.65	5.60	5.20	4.50	4.45	Bons du trésor
Saint Vincent-Grenadines										**St. Vin.-Grenadines**
Money market	6.07	4.67	4.01	4.76	5.24	4.92	6.03	6.36	5.68	Marché monétaire
Treasury bill	5.73	4.60	4.85	5.62	5.75	5.56	5.67	4.92	4.16	Bons du trésor
Saudi Arabia										**Arabie saoudite**
Money market	...	...	...	...	...	...	...	0.74	...	Marché monétaire
Treasury bill	...	...	...	...	...	...	...	0.38	...	Bons du trésor
Senegal										**Sénégal**
Money market	4.95	4.95	4.95	4.95	3.93	3.94	3.47	3.31	3.29	Marché monétaire
Serbia										**Serbie**
Money market	12.69	12.86	20.51	16.51	10.31	15.55	11.01	13.10	11.04	Marché monétaire
Treasury bill[68]	20.02	21.17	14.58	10.24	4.42	9.61	10.34	14.16	11.51	Bons du trésor[68]
Seychelles[69]										**Seychelles[69]**
Treasury bill	4.61	3.17	3.34	3.70	3.92	7.07	12.97	3.04	4.23	Bons du trésor
Sierra Leone[70]										**Sierra Leone[70]**
Treasury bill	15.68	26.14	22.98	17.71	18.41	15.48	10.47	17.21	24.05	Bons du trésor
Singapore										**Singapour**
Money market[71]	0.74	1.05	2.30	3.46	2.72	1.30	0.69	0.56	0.41	Marché monétaire[71]
Treasury bill[72]	0.65	0.96	2.06	2.96	2.35	0.91	0.34	0.34	0.29	Bons du trésor[72]
Slovakia										**Slovaquie**
Money market	6.08	3.82	3.02	4.83	4.25	4.15	...	...	...	Marché monétaire
Slovenia										**Slovénie**
Money market	5.59	4.40	3.73	3.38	4.08	4.27	0.90	0.57	1.18	Marché monétaire
Treasury bill	6.53	4.17	3.66	3.30	3.90	3.88	1.14	...	...	Bons du trésor
Solomon Islands										**Iles Salomon**
Treasury bill	5.85	6.00	4.53	3.41	3.17	3.20	4.00	3.71	2.53	Bons du trésor
South Africa										**Afrique du Sud**
Money market	10.93	7.15	6.62	7.19	9.22	11.32	8.15	6.19	5.29	Marché monétaire
Treasury bill	10.67	7.53	6.91	7.34	9.12	10.81	7.85	6.42	5.49	Bons du trésor
Spain										**Espagne**
Money market[34]	2.31	2.04	2.09	2.83	3.85	3.85	0.68	0.45	1.02	Marché monétaire[34]
Treasury bill	2.21	2.17	2.19	3.26	4.07	3.71	1.00	1.69	3.04	Bons du trésor
Sri Lanka										**Sri Lanka**
Money market[73]	9.68	8.87	10.15	12.89	30.88	21.22	11.67	9.02	...	Marché monétaire[73]
Treasury bill[74]	8.09	7.71	9.03	10.98	16.60	18.91	12.93	8.57	...	Bons du trésor[74]
Swaziland										**Swaziland**
Money market[75]	6.98	4.12	3.47	4.40	6.67	8.17	5.40	3.85	2.85	Marché monétaire[75]
Treasury bill[76]	10.61	7.94	7.08	7.54	9.03	10.77	7.93	6.60	6.07	Bons du trésor[76]
Sweden										**Suède**
Money market[77]	3.29	2.28	1.85	2.37	3.66	4.38	0.77	0.67	2.07	Marché monétaire[77]
Treasury bill[78]	3.03	2.11	1.72	2.33	3.55	3.91	0.40	0.50	1.65	Bons du trésor[78]
Switzerland										**Suisse**
Money market[79]	0.09	0.55	0.63	1.94	2.00	0.01	0.05	0.04	0.07	Marché monétaire[79]
Treasury bill[80]	0.16	0.37	0.71	1.36	2.16	1.33	0.00	0.03	-0.14	Bons du trésor[80]
Thailand										**Thaïlande**
Money market	1.31	1.23	2.62	4.64	3.75	3.28	1.21	1.25	2.80	Marché monétaire
Treasury bill	1.35	1.30	2.67	4.66	3.48	3.19	1.24	1.44	2.87	Bons du trésor

25 Short-term interest rates *(continued)*
Treasury bill and money market rates: per cent per annum
Taux d'intérêt à court terme *(suite)*
Taux des bons du trésor et du marché monétaire : pour cent par année

Country or area	2003	2004	2005	2006	2007	2008	2009	2010	2011	Pays ou zone
Togo[30]										**Togo**[30]
Money market	4.95	4.95	4.95	4.95	3.93	3.94	3.47	3.31	3.29	Marché monétaire
Trinidad and Tobago										**Trinité-et-Tobago**
Treasury bill	4.71	4.77	4.86	6.07	6.91	7.01	2.69	0.85	...	Bons du trésor
Tunisia[81]										**Tunisie**[81]
Money market	5.14	5.00	5.00	5.07	5.24	5.21	4.30	4.43	4.03	Marché monétaire
Turkey										**Turquie**
Money market[82]	36.16	21.42	14.73	15.59	17.24	16.00	9.24	5.81	2.99	Marché monétaire[82]
Treasury bill[83]	34.90	22.08	15.49	18.37	17.65	...	...	...	...	Bons du trésor[83]
Uganda[84]										**Ouganda**[84]
Treasury bill	16.87	9.02	8.50	8.12	9.05	9.08	...	5.01	14.61	Bons du trésor
Ukraine										**Ukraine**
Money market	7.90	6.34	4.16	3.58	2.27	13.71	12.64	3.42	7.11	Marché monétaire
United Kingdom										**Royaume-Uni**
Money market[85]	3.59	4.29	4.70	4.77	5.67	4.68	0.53	0.48	0.52	Marché monétaire[85]
Treasury bill[83]	3.55	4.43	4.55	4.65	5.52	4.30	0.53	0.50	0.49	Bons du trésor[83]
United Rep. of Tanzania[86]										**Rep.-Un. de Tanzanie**[86]
Treasury bill	6.26	8.35	10.67	11.64	13.38	8.11	7.14	3.87	6.37	Bons du trésor
United States										**Etats-Unis**
Money market[87]	1.13	1.35	3.21	4.96	5.02	1.93	0.16	0.18	0.10	Marché monétaire[87]
Treasury bill[88]	1.01	1.37	3.15	4.72	4.41	1.46	0.16	0.13	0.06	Bons du trésor[88]
Uruguay										**Uruguay**
Money market	20.76	3.57	1.25	1.60	4.11	9.80	8.60	6.31	7.58	Marché monétaire
Treasury bill	32.53	14.75	4.14	4.54	7.11	...	11.87	9.06	8.77	Bons du trésor
Vanuatu										**Vanuatu**
Money market	5.50	5.50	5.50	5.50	5.50	5.78	5.61	...	...	Marché monétaire
Venezuela (Boliv. Rep. of)										**Venezuela (Rép. bol. du)**
Money market	13.23	4.38	2.62	5.26	8.72	11.09	10.03	5.36	4.93	Marché monétaire
Viet Nam[89]										**Viet Nam**[89]
Treasury bill	5.83	5.69	6.13	4.73	4.15	12.13	8.04	...	12.35	Bons du trésor
Yemen[90]										**Yémen**[90]
Treasury bill	12.92	13.84	14.89	15.65	15.86	15.20	13.47	20.92	22.88	Bons du trésor
Zambia[91]										**Zambie**[91]
Treasury bill	29.98	12.60	16.32	10.37	11.95	13.47	15.39	6.28	9.55	Bons du trésor
Zimbabwe										**Zimbabwe**
Money market[92]	110.05	129.58	...	...	...	...	...	...	...	Marché monétaire[92]
Treasury bill[93]	52.73	125.68	185.11	322.36	248.77	...	...	...	...	Bons du trésor[93]

Source:
International Monetary Fund (IMF), Washington, D.C., the database on International Financial Statistics, last accessed May 2012.

Source:
Fonds monétaire international (FMI), Washington, D.C., la base de données de Statistiques Financières Internationales, dernier accès mai 2012.

1	Loan-amount-weighted average rate of interbank loans and deposits.	1 Taux moyen des prêts et dépôts interbancaires pondéré en fonction du montant des prêts.
2	Rate paid on seven-day interbank advances.	2 Taux des avances interbancaires à sept jours.
3	Weighted average rate on three-month treasury bills sold at auction.	3 Taux moyen pondéré des bons du Trésor à trois mois mis en adjudication.
4	Rate offered on three-month interbank deposits.	4 Taux des dépôts interbancaires à trois mois.
5	Average tender rate for three-month treasury bills.	5 Taux moyen de soumission pour les bons du Trésor à trois mois.
6	Discount rate on treasury bills.	6 Taux d'escompte des bons du Trésor.
7	Overnight advances.	7 Taux des avances à un jour.
8	Rate on 91-day treasury bills denominated in national currency auctioned by the CBB.	8 Taux des bons du Trésor à 91 jours (en monnaie nationale) mis en adjudication par la Banque centrale de Bolivie.
9	Interbank.	9 Interbancaire.
10	Rate on one-month treasury bills.	10 Taux des bons du Trésor à un mois.
11	Overnight rate.	11 Taux à un jour.
12	Average yield on 182-day treasury bills denominated in national currency.	12 Rendement moyen des bons du Trésor à 182 jours exprimés en monnaie nationale.
13	Weighted average rate on loans between financial corporations.	13 Taux moyen pondéré des prêts entre établissements financiers.
14	Short-term rate determined on the Zagreb Money Market.	14 Taux à court terme déterminé sur le marché monétaire de Zagreb.
15	Weighted average rate on 13-week treasury bills sold at auctions	15 Taux moyen pondéré des bons du Trésor à 13 semaines mis en

25 Short-term interest rates *(continued)*
Treasury bill and money market rates: per cent per annum
Taux d'intérêt à court terme *(suite)*
Taux des bons du trésor et du marché monétaire : pour cent par année

	during the month.		adjudication pendant le mois.
16	Average rate on treasury bills. † Beginning in April 1993 average rate of three issues of 91-day treasury bills. The rate is determined through securities auctions by the CBL.	16	Taux moyen des bons du Trésor. † À partir d'avril 1993, taux moyen de trois émissions de bons du Trésor à 91 jours. Le taux est déterminé sur la base des mises en adjudication effectuées par la CBL.
17	Rate on the three-month interbank deposits.	17	Taux des dépôts bancaires à trois mois.
18	Simple average of rates at which multiple banks borrow funds in the interbank market.	18	Moyenne simple des taux auxquels diverses banques empruntent sur le marché interbancaire.
19	Weighted average based on the last auction of the month.	19	Moyenne pondérée fondée sur la dernière mise en adjudication pendant le mois.
20	Average of rates on 1- to 7-day loans between commercial banks.	20	Moyenne des taux des prêts consentis entre banques commerciales sur des périodes comprises entre 1 et 7 jours.
21	Weighted average rate of interbank overnight loans.	21	Taux moyen pondéré des prêts interbancaires au jour le jour.
22	Weighted average rate on 91-day treasury bills.	22	Taux moyen pondéré des bons du Trésor à 91 jours.
23	Weighted average rate on loans determined in the interbank credit auction market. The rate is weighted by the loan amounts.	23	Taux moyen pondéré des prêts déterminé sur le marché d'enchères interbancaires. Le taux est pondéré sur la base du montant des prêts.
24	Weighted average rate on treasury bills. The rate is weighted by issuance amounts.	24	Taux moyen pondéré des bons du Trésor. Taux pondéré en fonction du montant des titres émis.
25	Period averages of ten daily average quotations for overnight credit.	25	Moyennes périodiques établies à partir de 10 cotations quotidiennes pour le crédit au jour le jour.
26	Rate on 12-month Federal debt register claims.	26	Taux des créances sur 12 mois inscrites au registre de la dette fédérale.
27	Weighted average rate on interbank loans. The rate is weighted by loan amounts.	27	Taux moyen pondéré des prêts interbancaires. Taux pondéré en fonction du montant des prêts.
28	Rate of discount on 91-day treasury bills.	28	Taux d'escompte des bons du Trésor à 91 jours.
29	12 months.	29	Douze mois.
30	Rate paid on overnight interbank advances.	30	Taux des avances interbancaires au jour le jour.
31	Weighted average yield on 90-day Treasury bills sold at auctions.	31	Rendement moyen pondéré des bons du Trésor à 90 jours vendus par voie d'adjudication.
32	End-of-month yield on the interbank overnight market.	32	Taux en fin de mois sur le marché interbancaire au jour le jour.
33	Yield set by the government in the primary market. † Beginning in November 1992, annualized secondary market yield on 90-day treasury bills.	33	Rendement fixé par le gouvernement sur le marché primaire. † À compter de novembre 1992, rendement annualisé des bons du Trésor à 90 jours sur le marché secondaire.
34	Call money rate.	34	Taux de l'argent au jour le jour.
35	Rate on one-day loans between commercial banks.	35	Taux des prêts à un jour entre banques commerciales.
36	91 days.	36	Quatre-vingt-onze jours.
37	Rate on one-month fixed interbank deposits (data refer to closing rates).	37	Taux des dépôts interbancaires à un mois (taux de clôture).
38	Average rate on overnight interbank transactions in national currency.	38	Taux moyen des transactions interbancaires au jour le jour, en monnaie nationale.
39	Rate for collateral and overnight loans in the Tokyo Call Money Market.	39	Taux des prêts garantis et des prêts au jour le jour sur le marché monétaire au jour le jour de Tokyo.
40	Average yield on 3-month treasury discount bills.	40	Taux de rendement moyen des bons du Trésor à prime d'émission à trois mois.
41	Yield based on treasury bill prices established at the last auction of the month.	41	Rendement fondé sur les prix des bons du Trésor établis lors de la dernière mise en adjudication pendant le mois.
42	Average of daily bid and offer quotations for the interbank rate on three-month deposits in national currency. The rate is freely determined by the market. The rate on certificates of deposit fluctuates in line with, but is generally slightly lower than, the interbank deposit rate. Rates on time deposits with commercial banks are market determined and also vary with the interbank rate.	42	Moyenne des soumissions quotidiennes pour le taux interbancaire des dépôts à trois mois, en monnaie nationale. Le taux est librement déterminé par le marché. Le taux des certificats de dépôt est calé sur le taux de dépôt interbancaire, mais de façon générale il se situe légèrement en dessous. Les taux des dépôts à terme auprès de banques commerciales sont déterminés par le marché et suivent aussi les fluctuations du taux interbancaire.
43	Average of maximum acceptable interest rates set by the CBK for three-month treasury bills sold at weekly auctions.	43	Moyenne des taux d'intérêt maximaux acceptables fixés par la banque centrale du Kenya pour les bons du Trésor à trois mois mis en adjudication toutes les semaines.
44	Weighted average rate on 3-month treasury bills sold in the primary market.	44	Taux moyen pondéré des bons du Trésor à trois mois négociés sur le marché primaire.
45	Maximum rate on interbank call loans.	45	Taux maximal des prêts interbancaires au jour le jour.
46	Highest rate charged on overnight interbank loans.	46	Taux le plus élevé appliqué aux prêts interbancaires au jour le jour.
47	Rate on 91-day Treasury bills.	47	Taux des bons du Trésor à 91 jours.
48	Weighted average overnight interbank rate. Monthly rates refer to the average for the trading days of the month. Daily rates are calculated as the average of interbank deposit rates for the day, with individual rates weighted by the volume of transactions.	48	Moyenne pondérée des taux interbancaires au jour le jour. Les taux mensuels font référence à la moyenne des taux des jours de bourse du mois. Les taux quotidiens correspondent à la moyenne des taux de rémunération des dépôts pour la journée, les taux individuels étant pondérés en fonction du volume des transactions.

49	Average discount rate on three-month treasury bills.	49	Taux d'escompte moyen des bons du Trésor à trois mois.
50	Rate on 28-day treasury bills in national currency announced by the MMA.	50	Taux des bons du Trésor à 28 jours (en monnaie nationale) annoncés par l'Autorité monétaire des Maldives.
51	Weighted average rate on three-month Treasury bills sold through weekly auctions.	51	Taux moyen pondéré des bons du Trésor à trois mois vendus par voie d'adjudications hebdomadaires.
52	Weighted average rate of accepted bids on treasury bills at weekly auctions.	52	Taux moyen pondéré des soumissions retenues pour les bons du Trésor lors des mises en adjudication hebdomadaires.
53	Interbank deposits at call.	53	Dépôts interbancaires au jour le jour.
54	Yield on newly issued 182-day Treasury bills from the latest auction.	54	Rendement des bons du Trésor à 182 jours nouvellement émis depuis la dernière mise en adjudication.
55	Data refer to the interbank lending rate.	55	Taux prêteur interbancaire.
56	Average yield on 91-day treasury bills denominated in national currency.	56	Rendement moyen des bons du Trésor à 91 jours exprimés en monnaie nationale.
57	Weighted average yield on 91-day treasury bills.	57	Rendement moyen pondéré des bons du Trésor à 91 jours.
58	Interest rate on three-month treasury bills.	58	Taux d'intérêt des bons du Trésor à trois mois.
59	Tender rate on three-month treasury bills.	59	Taux de soumission des bons du Trésor à trois mois.
60	Rate on new issues of treasury bills.	60	Taux des nouvelles émissions de bons du Trésor.
61	Rate charged on overnight inter-bank lending in national currency.	61	Taux appliqué aux prêts interbancaires au jour le jour exprimés en monnaie nationale.
62	Monthly average of daily minimum and maximum call-money rates.	62	Moyenne mensuelle des taux minimaux et maximaux quotidiens de l'argent au jour le jour.
63	Weighted average yield on six-month treasury securities. † Prior to July 1996, rate on six-month Federal Treasury Bill. Since July 1996, rate on six-month Federal Treasury Bond (STFB), which replaced the six-month Federal Treasury Bill.	63	Rendement moyen pondéré des titres du Trésor des États-Unis à six mois. † Avant juillet 1996, taux des bons du Trésor fédéral à court terme (échéance à six mois). Depuis juillet 1996, taux des bons du Trésor à long terme (échéance à six mois), qui ont remplacé les bons du Trésor à court terme.
64	Rate on 182-day treasury bills. Data refer to the second Thursday of the month. † Beginning in August 1994, weighted average rate on 182-day treasury bills in national currency at the last auction of the month.	64	Taux des bons du Trésor à 182 jours. Les données font référence au deuxième jeudi du mois. † À partir d'août 1994, taux moyen pondéré des bons du Trésor à 182 jours, en monnaie nationale, fixé pendant la dernière adjudication du mois.
65	Average rate on loans between financial corporations in national currency.	65	Taux moyen des prêts entre établissements financiers, en monnaie nationale.
66	Average daily rate on call money, weighted by the volume of transactions.	66	Taux moyen quotidien de l'argent au jour le jour pondéré en fonction du volume de transactions.
67	Daily average rate on deposits between commercial banks in national currency.	67	Taux moyen quotidien des dépôts entre banques commerciales, en monnaie nationale.
68	Average monthly yield on three-month Treasury bills weighted by volume.	68	Rendement mensuel moyen des bons du Trésor à trois mois pondéré en fonction du volume.
69	Average rate on 91- and 365-day treasury bills.	69	Taux moyens des bons du Trésor à 91 jours et 365 jours.
70	Coupon rate on new issues of treasury bills.	70	Taux d'intérêt nominal des nouvelles émissions de bons du Trésor.
71	Rate refers to the modes of the three-month interbank rates quoted by money brokers. Monthly data refer to the rates on the last Friday (or working day closest to the last Friday) of the month.	71	Le taux correspond aux modes de la série des taux interbancaires à trois mois soumis par les courtiers du marché monétaire. Les données mensuelles font référence aux taux en vigueur le dernier vendredi (ou le jour ouvré le plus proche du dernier vendredi) du mois.
72	Rate refers to modes of closing bid prices quoted by the Singapore Government Securities (SGS) primary dealers on three-monthtrasury bills. Beginning in January 2001, the average bid rate quoted by the SGS primary dealers. Monthly data refer to the rates on the last Friday, or working day closest to the last Friday, of the month.	72	Le taux correspond aux modes des cours de clôture soumis par les spécialistes en valeurs du Trésor SGS (Singapore Government Securities) en ce qui concerne les bons du Trésor à trois mois. Depuis janvier 2001, il s'agit du taux de soumission moyen des spécialistes SGS. Les données mensuelles font référence aux taux en vigueur le dernier vendredi (ou le jour ouvré le plus proche du dernier vendredi) du mois.
73	Maximum advance rate charged by commercial banks on interbank call loans.	73	Taux maximal appliqué par les banques commerciales aux prêts interbancaires au jour le jour.
74	Discount rate in the secondary market. Beginning in August 1996, discount rate in the primary market.	74	Taux d'escompte sur le marché secondaire. À compter d'août 1996, taux d'escompte sur le marché primaire.
75	Interbank call deposit rate.	75	Taux de rémunération des dépôts interbancaires au jour le jour.
76	Yield on treasury bills with 91-days maturity auctioned by the CBS.	76	Rendement des bons du Trésor à 91 jours mis en adjudication par la Banque centrale du Swaziland.
77	Relates to the monthly average of daily rates for day-to-day interbank loans.	77	Moyenne mensuelle des taux quotidiens des prêts interbancaires au jour le jour.
78	Rate on three-month treasury discount notes.	78	Taux des bons du Trésor à prime d'émission à trois mois.
79	End-of-period rate of interest on overnight Swiss franc deposits in international markets.	79	Taux d'intérêt de fin de période appliqué aux dépôts au jour le jour sur les marchés internationaux (en francs suisses).
80	Monthly average rate of interest on Federal Debt Register Claims.	80	Taux d'intérêt mensuel moyen des créances inscrites au registre de la dette fédérale.

81	Upper margin of interest on overnight interbank deposits.
82	Weighted average annualized rate in the overnight interbank money market.
83	Weighted average auction rate on three-month Treasury bills.
84	Rate on the 91-day treasury bills.
85	Data refer to the interbank offer rate for overnight deposits.
86	Rate on three-month treasury bills.
87	Federal funds rate.
88	Interbank borrowing rate.
89	Average monthly yield on 360-day treasury bills sold at auction.
90	Simple annualized rate on three-month treasury bills.
91	Average rate on treasury bills.
92	Rate charged by discount houses to buy three-month bankers' acceptances.
93	Yield on 91-day treasury bills.

81	Marge supérieure des taux d'intérêt des dépôts interbancaires au jour le jour.
82	Taux moyen pondéré annualisé sur le marché monétaire interbancaire au jour le jour.
83	Taux moyen pondéré d'adjudication des bons du Trésor à trois mois.
84	Taux des bons du Trésor à 91 jours.
85	Correspond au taux de vente pour les dépôts interbancaires au jour le jour.
86	Taux des bons du Trésor à trois mois.
87	Taux des fonds fédéraux.
88	Taux des prêts interbancaires.
89	Rendement mensuel moyen des bons du Trésor à 360 jours vendus par voie d'adjudication.
90	Taux simple annualisé des bons du Trésor à trois mois.
91	Taux moyen des bons du Trésor.
92	Taux pratiqué par les chambres de compensation dans le cadre des achats d'acceptations bancaires à trois mois.
93	Rendement des bons du Trésor à 91 jours.

Employment by economic activity
Total employment and persons employed by ISIC 3 categories (thousands)

Emploi par activité économique
Emploi total et personnes employées par branches de la CITI rév. 3 (milliers)

Country or area & Pays ou zone &	Year Année	Sex Sexe	Total employment Emploi total	ISIC Rev. 3 Tabulation categories + CITI Rév. 3 Catégories de classement +						
				Categ. A Catég. A	Categ. B Catég. B	Categ. C Catég. C	Categ. D Catég. D	Categ. E Catég. E	Categ. F Catég. F	Categ. G Catég. G
Albania	2004	MF	931.0	545.0[1]	...	6.0	56.0	13.0	52.0	64.0
Albanie	2005	MF	932.1	545.0[1]	...	6.0	56.0	12.0	52.0	64.0
	2006	MF	935.0	542.0[1]	...	5.0	58.0	10.0	53.0	68.0
Algeria [3,4]	2001	M	5 345.2	1 132.4	69.4	111.0	406.8	99.1	643.8	761.6
Algérie [3,4]	2001	F	883.6	109.1	1.2	8.5	225.0	10.8	6.2	27.3
	2003	M	5 751.0	1 303.1	5.8	78.7	406.3	93.4	790.4	853.7
	2003	F	933.0	101.5	1.3	4.2	210.3	11.1	9.5	27.2
	2004	M	6 439.2	1 289.3	24.1	125.9	489.0	74.6	956.6	1 129.0
	2004	F	1 356.1	295.9	6.9	9.2	357.7	4.5	11.0	45.4
Anguilla [4,5,6]	2001	M	3.0	^0.0	0.1	^0.0	0.1	0.1	0.8	0.3
Anguilla [4,5,6]	2001	F	2.6	^0.0	^0.0	0.0	0.1	0.0	0.0	0.3
Antigua and Barbuda [4]	2006	M	18.6	0.5	0.3	0.1	1.0	0.5	3.3	2.5
Antigua-et-Barbuda [4]	2006	F	18.5	0.2	^0.0	^0.0	0.7	0.1	0.1	2.8
	2007	M	19.0	0.6	0.3	0.1	1.0	0.5	3.4	2.5
	2007	F	18.8	0.2	^0.0	^0.0	0.7	0.1	0.1	2.9
	2008	M	19.3	0.6	0.3	0.1	1.1	0.5	3.4	2.6
	2008	F	19.1	0.2	^0.0	^0.0	0.7	0.1	0.1	2.9
Argentina [7,8]	2004[9]	M	5 446.9	65.7	8.4	30.6	925.4	33.8	717.8	1 230.0
Argentine [7,8]	2004[9]	F	3 968.0	32.0	2.9	2.6	435.0	10.2	14.0	715.7
	2005[9]	M	5 557.3	74.5	6.4	23.2	947.2	44.0	801.1	1 227.0
	2005[9]	F	4 081.4	25.3	1.0	7.7	412.5	5.0	21.9	724.8
	2006[10]	M	5 786.7	59.2	8.2	34.1	988.3	38.1	854.8	1 263.5
	2006[10]	F	4 253.8	13.6	0.8	5.7	422.3	6.0	29.9	755.2
Armenia [5]	2006	M	593.0	274.2	0.2	6.3	71.3	18.7	27.1	68.0
Arménie [5]	2006	F	499.4	230.1	...	1.3	39.2	4.1	2.6	37.9
	2007	M	571.4	248.6	0.2	7.2	67.8	18.6	28.5	66.5
	2007	F	530.1	258.1	0.0	1.4	35.9	4.2	2.6	39.6
	2008	M	570.9	224.5	0.4	6.9	61.1	19.7	57.2	68.2
	2008	F	546.7	268.5	0.1	1.4	33.8	4.8	3.2	45.0
Aruba [4,11]	2000	M	22.5	0.1	0.0	^0.0	1.9	0.4	3.6	3.2
Aruba [4,11]	2000	F	19.4	^0.0	^0.0	^0.0	0.5	0.1	0.3	3.9
	2007	M	27.2	0.3	...	^0.0	2.6	0.6	5.7	3.1
	2007	F	24.4	0.1	...	...	0.6	0.1	0.8	4.2
Australia [4,12]	2009	M	5 937.0	251.0[1,13]	...	142.0[14]	738.0	107.0	876.0	810.0[15]
Australie [4,12]	2009	F	4 984.0	113.0[1,13]	...	22.0[14]	277.0	28.0	119.0	814.0[15]
	2010	M	6 130.0	254.0[1,13]	...	160.0[14]	738.0	114.0	905.0	811.0[15]
	2010	F	5 085.0	119.0[1,13]	...	29.0[14]	260.0	30.0	119.0	821.0[15]
	2011	M	6 212.0	228.0[1,13]	...	188.0[14]	717.0	113.0	919.0	825.0[15]
	2011	F	5 187.0	100.0[1,13]	...	35.0[14]	251.0	38.0	119.0	825.0[15]
Austria [4]	2009	M	2 186.0	117.0[1,13]	...	8.0	449.0	38.0[18]	306.0	296.0[19]
Autriche [4]	2009	F	1 892.0	97.0[1,13]	...	2.0	160.0	3.0[18]	48.0	351.0[19]
	2010	M	2 197.0	119.0[1,13]	...	9.0	458.0	37.0[18]	299.0	292.0[19]
	2010	F	1 899.0	96.0[1,13]	...	1.0	166.0	4.0[18]	41.0	333.0[19]
	2011	M	2 228.0	122.0[1,13]	...	9.0	482.0	36.0[18]	312.0	287.0[19]
	2011	F	1 916.0	97.0[1,13]	...	2.0	172.0	13.0[18]	52.0	342.0[19]
Azerbaijan [4,22]	2006	M	2 105.7	752.9	8.8	54.7	98.4	46.8	217.4	312.9
Azerbaïdjan [4,22]	2006	F	1 880.2	811.9	2.6	6.0	49.2	5.6	14.4	433.1
	2007	M	2 020.5	708.7	1.7	38.9	141.7	34.0	216.8	186.8
	2007	F	1 993.5	834.3	2.7	5.2	52.3	6.1	11.9	472.7
	2008	M	2 048.3	785.0	3.6	35.2	114.6	32.5	187.4	206.7
	2008	F	2 007.7	816.4	0.9	10.1	80.9	12.1	19.2	450.7

26

Employment by economic activity *[cont.]*
Total employment and persons employed by ISIC 3 categories (thousands)
Emploi par activité économique *[suite]*
Emploi total et personnes employées par branches de la CITI rév. 3 (milliers)

ISIC Rev. 3 **Tabulation categories** +
CITI Rév. 3 **Catégories de classement** +

Categ. H / Catég. H	Categ. I / Catég. I	Categ. J / Catég. J	Categ. K / Catég. K	Categ. L / Catég.L	Categ. M / Catég. M	Categ. N / Catég. N	Categ. O / Catég. O	Categ. P / Catég. P	Categ. Q / Catég. Q	Country or area & / Pays ou zone &
17.0	20.0	81.0[2]	...	...	48.0	27.0	...	...	...	Albania
15.0	19.0	90.0[2]	...	...	47.0	24.0	...	...	...	Albanie
16.0	19.0	90.0[2]	...	...	48.0	25.0	...	...	...	
78.4	322.5	55.0	50.5	926.3	403.4	128.6	126.7	23.4	6.3	Algeria [3,4]
4.2	17.4	13.1	9.5	81.9	206.9	88.5	60.0	12.2	1.9	Algérie [3,4]
97.6	384.5	49.5	53.6	958.6	400.3	143.2	124.0	4.6	2.4	
4.9	20.9	18.1	14.4	112.6	227.5	101.9	59.4	7.6	0.5	
154.6	419.8	46.1	56.0	990.1	372.4	135.2	141.8	19.2	2.8	
10.2	16.2	22.8	16.4	114.2	261.6	100.3	67.1	15.7	1.1	
0.6	0.3	0.1	0.2	0.3	0.1	^0.0	0.1	^0.0	...	Anguilla [4,5,6]
1.0	0.1	0.1	0.1	0.4	0.2	0.1	0.1	0.1	...	Anguilla [4,5,6]
2.2	2.0	0.4	0.9	2.3	0.4	0.3	1.3	0.3	0.3	Antigua and Barbuda [4]
3.3	1.1	0.8	0.7	2.5	1.5	1.6	1.7	1.2	0.2	Antigua-et-Barbuda [4]
2.3	2.0	0.4	0.9	2.4	0.4	0.3	1.3	0.3	0.3	
3.4	1.1	0.8	0.7	2.5	1.5	1.6	1.7	1.2	0.2	
2.3	2.1	0.4	0.9	2.4	0.5	0.3	1.3	0.3	0.3	
3.5	1.1	0.8	0.8	2.6	1.5	1.6	1.7	1.2	0.2	
167.6	561.5	92.0	436.2	466.2	154.9	196.6	287.6	53.1	...	Argentina [7,8]
153.5	86.4	51.8	240.2	306.7	557.4	455.9	242.3	649.3	...	Argentine [7,8]
171.2	548.3	93.0	459.4	429.7	174.6	173.8	311.2	56.4	2.1	
144.3	100.6	69.8	283.3	299.0	561.8	454.5	269.7	684.6	1.4	
213.9	557.4	95.9	528.3	444.4	185.9	163.5	317.1	18.2	2.0	
167.0	86.6	93.5	281.5	324.3	620.9	426.7	229.6	778.8	0.2	
3.8	33.4	3.1	13.8	19.5	23.9	11.4	18.3	...	...	Armenia [5]
3.9	15.2	3.5	9.5	15.4	76.9	37.4	22.5	...	...	Arménie [5]
3.9	33.0	4.0	16.1	20.8	25.0	11.9	19.4	...	...	
4.5	14.6	4.8	10.2	17.1	76.3	38.3	22.6	...	...	
5.8	36.4	4.5	15.6	21.5	23.7	8.5	17.0	...	...	
6.6	15.2	6.1	11.2	18.2	77.9	36.1	19.3	...	...	
3.5	1.9	0.5	2.1	2.1	0.5	0.4	1.7	0.1	^0.0	Aruba [4,11]
4.1	1.0	1.0	1.6	1.4	1.0	1.5	1.1	1.8	^0.0	Aruba [4,11]
3.6	2.0	0.5	3.5	2.1	0.6	0.8	1.7	0.1	...	
5.1	0.9	1.4	3.4	1.9	1.0	2.3	1.5	1.1	^0.0	
325.0	448.0	187.0	88.0	360.5[16]	250.0[17]	251.0	215.7	...	...	Australia [4,12]
413.0	142.0	210.0	96.0	314.6[16]	567.0[17]	949.0	193.1	...	...	Australie [4,12]
340.0	452.0	193.0	98.0	368.7[16]	256.0[17]	262.0	217.6	...	...	
417.0	128.0	205.0	98.0	328.8[16]	599.0[17]	993.0	192.8	...	...	
346.0	456.0	199.0	100.0	380.3[16]	263.0[17]	281.0	222.3	...	...	
439.0	129.0	225.0	99.0	343.3[16]	596.0[17]	1 036.0	183.7	...	...	
96.0	157.0[20]	74.0[21]	12.0	156.0	75.0	84.0	28.0	1.0	...	Austria [4]
159.0	46.0[20]	70.0[21]	19.0	121.0	178.0	305.0	71.0	9.0	...	Autriche [4]
96.0	153.0[20]	77.0[21]	15.0	154.0	80.0	88.0	32.0	1.0	5.0	
157.0	44.0[20]	72.0[21]	23.0	125.0	181.0	308.0	75.0	10.0	3.0	
96.0	158.0[20]	83.0[21]	16.0	155.0	76.0	87.0	29.0	9.0	...	
155.0	48.0[20]	68.0[21]	24.0	120.0	181.0	298.0	75.0	9.0	...	
32.8	138.1	30.3	15.2	101.4	122.3	47.7	87.5	31.1	7.5	Azerbaijan [4,22]
15.7	16.4	23.6	4.7	38.9	229.8	118.4	71.2	36.9	1.8	Azerbaïdjan [4,22]
21.4	178.4	9.4	54.4	167.7	120.4	51.5	88.1	...	0.7	
5.7	25.1	8.4	75.3	107.9	213.9	129.2	43.0	...	...	
11.7	143.7	10.5	95.4	198.3	96.6	52.1	74.5	...	0.5	
11.7	23.3	24.6	99.4	51.2	214.7	128.4	64.1	...	...	

26

Employment by economic activity *[cont.]*
Total employment and persons employed by ISIC 3 categories (thousands)
Emploi par activité économique *[suite]*
Emploi total et personnes employées par branches de la CITI rév. 3 (milliers)

Country or area [&] Pays ou zone [&]	Year Année	Sex Sexe	Total employment Emploi total	ISIC Rev. 3 Tabulation categories [+] CITI Rév. 3 Catégories de classement [+]						
				Categ. A Catég. A	Categ. B Catég. B	Categ. C Catég. C	Categ. D Catég. D	Categ. E Catég. E	Categ. F Catég. F	Categ. G Catég. G
Bahamas [4,5]	2006[6]	M	86.0	3.8[1]	...	2.0[24]	4.9	...	19.4	12.0
Bahamas [4,5]	2006[6]	F	80.5	0.4[1]	...	0.5[24]	2.5	...	1.2	12.5
	2007[23]	M	89.6	3.7[1]	...	2.3[24]	4.1	...	19.9	12.8
	2007[23]	F	81.9	0.2[1]	...	0.6[24]	2.4	...	1.4	12.1
	2008[23]	M	90.8	4.5[1]	...	2.3[24]	4.0	...	18.4	12.3
	2008[23]	F	84.1	0.6[1]	...	0.4[24]	2.2	...	1.0	12.1
Bahrain [4,23]	2001	M	231.5	2.2	2.2	2.6	42.7	2.4	26.0	31.1
Bahreïn [4,23]	2001	F	59.9	0.1	^0.0	0.2	7.2	0.1	0.4	3.4
Bangladesh [4,27]	2000[28]	M	32 369.0	17 256.0[1]	...	107.0	2 346.0	116.0	999.0	5 769.0[15,29]
Bangladesh [4,27]	2000[28]	F	19 395.0	14 914.0[1]	...	188.0	1 436.0	18.0	100.0	506.0[15,29]
	2003	M	34 478.0	16 132.0	1 027.0	80.0	2 637.0	90.0	1 445.0	5 894.0
	2003	F	9 844.0	5 754.0	17.0	2.0	1 706.0	8.0	97.0	214.0
	2005	M	36 080.0	14 168.0	916.0	44.0	3 926.0	73.0	1 421.0	6 705.0
	2005	F	11 277.0	7 504.0	179.0	7.0	1 298.0	3.0	104.0	403.0
Barbados [31]	2009	M	65.0	...	...	...	...	...	...	...
Barbade [31]	2009	F	63.0	...	...	...	...	...	...	...
	2010	M	66.0	2.0[1,13]	...	12.0[32]	5.0	2.0[33]	...	10.0[19]
	2010	F	62.0	1.0[1,13]	...	1.0[32]	4.0	1.0[33]	...	10.0[19]
	2011	M	66.0	3.0[1,13]	...	13.0[32]	5.0	2.0[33]	...	9.0[19]
	2011	F	62.0	1.0[1,13]	...	1.0[32]	4.0	1.0[33]	...	11.0[19]
Belgium [4]	2009	M	2 429.0	46.0[1,13]	...	...	498.0	48.0[18]	292.0	298.0[19]
Belgique [4]	2009	F	1 991.0	20.0[1,13]	...	...	158.0	...	24.0	274.0[19]
	2010	M	2 458.0	43.0[1,13]	...	...	488.0	55.0[18]	297.0	320.0[19]
	2010	F	2 031.0	18.0[1,13]	...	...	165.0	14.0[18]	25.0	270.0[19]
	2011	M	2 462.0	40.0[1,13]	...	...	488.0	52.0[18]	305.0	314.0[19]
	2011	F	2 047.0	18.0[1,13]	...	...	154.0	12.0[18]	32.0	274.0[19]
Belize [23,36,37]	1999	M	53.7	19.8[1]	...	0.3	4.7	0.9	4.4	7.4
Belize [23,36,37]	1999	F	24.1	1.5[1]	...	^0.0	2.6	0.1	0.1	4.9
	2005	M	64.9	16.7	1.5	0.2	6.4	0.8	6.7	10.3
	2005	F	33.7	0.8	0.3	^0.0	3.2	0.2	0.2	6.6
Bermuda [4,6]	2000	M	19.0	0.4	0.1	0.1	0.8	0.3	3.6	2.4
Bermudes [4,6]	2000	F	17.9	^0.0	^0.0	^0.0	0.4	0.1	0.2	2.4
Bhutan [4,6]	2005	M	158.1	51.5	...	2.2	3.3	3.7	28.3	3.5
Bhoutan [4,6]	2005	F	90.7	57.1	...	0.6	1.6	0.4	2.6	3.3
Bolivia (Plurinational State of) [7,40]	2005	M	2 356.0	887.9[41]	11.8[42]	59.9	295.2	11.0	253.9	244.0
Bolivie (État plurinational de) [7,40]	2005	F	1 901.1	741.9[41]	2.0[42]	11.2	170.3	2.9	21.4	385.4
	2006	M	2 505.6	981.8[41]	8.8[42]	50.8	279.9	12.6	245.1	257.1
	2006	F	2 044.7	803.2[41]	3.6[42]	4.7	197.9	0.4	3.0	390.2
	2007	M	2 577.0	871.5[41]	13.1[42]	70.6	331.4	13.1	310.3	266.7
	2007	F	2 095.4	801.5[41]	0.2[42]	1.7	183.6	2.3	5.9	406.9
Botswana [36,40,43]	2000	M	269.4	58.9[1]	...	10.0	19.8	2.0	39.0	25.3
Botswana [36,40,43]	2000	F	214.0	36.4[1]	...	1.2	22.8	0.2	5.9	38.3
	2003	M	245.4	70.1[1]	...	11.3	18.3	3.5	35.7	20.9
	2003	F	217.0	28.0[1]	...	2.5	26.2	0.9	6.2	40.7
	2006	M	281.8	98.8[1]	...	12.5	16.0	2.6	23.1	27.9
	2006	F	257.4	62.6[1]	...	1.7	20.0	1.5	4.5	49.5
Brazil [3,7,44]	2005	M	50 493.7	11 581.9	373.0	292.9	7 687.4	299.1	5 494.4	9 566.3
Brésil [3,7,44]	2005	F	36 696.0	5 805.0	71.0	25.0	4 649.0	60.0	148.0	5 937.0
	2006	M	51 400.0	11 226.0	345.0	314.0	7 831.0	325.0	5 665.0	9 637.0
	2006	F	37 918.0	5 638.0	54.0	28.0	4 665.0	71.0	172.0	6 110.0
	2007	M	52 363.0	10 934.0	316.1	342.9	8 320.5	297.3	5 920.9	9 958.6
	2007	F	38 423.0	5 273.0	55.6	35.6	4 784.6	65.4	186.2	6 350.3

ISIC Rev. 3 Tabulation categories [+]
CITI Rév. 3 Catégories de classement [+]

Categ. H Catég. H	Categ. I Catég. I	Categ. J Catég. J	Categ. K Catég. K	Categ. L Catég.L	Categ. M Catég. M	Categ. N Catég. N	Categ. O Catég. O	Categ. P Catég. P	Categ. Q Catég. Q	Country or area [&] Pays ou zone [&]
10.8	7.3	7.9[25]	...	17.6[26]	...	...	...	...	...	Bahamas [4,5]
15.8	3.9	10.5[25]	...	33.2[26]	...	...	...	...	...	Bahamas [4,5]
11.5	9.3	8.0[25]	...	17.7[26]	...	...	...	...	...	
15.9	4.0	12.2[25]	...	33.0[26]	...	...	...	...	...	
11.0	9.3	8.3[25]	...	20.2[26]	...	...	...	...	...	
16.3	4.9	11.8[25]	...	34.6[26]	...	...	...	...	...	
11.2	11.6	4.6	14.7	48.1	5.7	3.2	8.8	7.7	1.6	Bahrain [4,23]
1.9	2.1	1.9	1.6	4.3	7.8	4.4	1.8	21.9	0.5	Bahreïn [4,23]
...	2 432.0	357.0[25,30]	...	...	...	...	1 243.0	...	...	Bangladesh [4,27]
...	77.0	77.0[25,30]	...	...	...	...	1 726.0	...	...	Bangladesh [4,27]
530.0	2 989.0	204.0	186.0	903.0	867.0	357.0	1 136.0	...	...	
33.0	25.0	19.0	7.0	85.0	318.0	146.0	1 413.0	...	...	
661.0	3 910.0	392.0	227.0	778.0	964.0	241.0	1 654.0	...	...	
51.0	66.0	115.0	11.0	104.0	343.0	122.0	968.0	...	...	
...	...	...	...	...	...	...	...	...	...	Barbados [31]
...	...	...	...	...	...	...	...	...	...	Barbade [31]
5.0	5.0[20]	2.0[21]	...	4.0	3.0	2.0	2.0	1.0	...	
8.0	2.0[20]	5.0[21]	...	4.0	5.0	5.0	2.0	4.0	...	
5.0	7.0[20]	2.0[21]	...	4.0	2.0	2.0	1.0	2.0	...	
8.0	2.0[20]	3.0[21]	...	5.0	4.0	4.0	3.0	4.0	...	
76.0	319.0[34]	82.0[30]	11.0[35]	220.0	122.0	132.0	28.0	2.0	21.0	Belgium [4]
67.0	88.0[34]	76.0[30]	10.0[35]	198.0	272.0	458.0	64.0	32.0	22.0	Belgique [4]
75.0	319.0[34]	87.0[30]	13.0[35]	213.0	127.0	132.0	33.0	3.2	23.0	
68.0	101.0[34]	71.0[30]	10.0[35]	195.0	287.0	477.0	65.0	35.0	20.0	
79.0	319.0[34]	83.0[30]	12.0[35]	209.0	125.0	137.0	30.0	...	20.0	
70.0	91.0[34]	78.0[30]	12.0[35]	192.0	288.0	477.0	68.0	34.0	19.0	
2.5	3.7	0.8	1.2	3.4	2.3[38]	...	1.7	0.5	...	Belize [23,36,37]
3.3	0.5	0.7	0.3	1.6	4.7[38]	...	1.5	2.4	...	Belize [23,36,37]
3.2	5.4	0.6	1.5	4.6	2.1	0.7	2.2	1.5	0.3	
5.5	0.9	1.0	0.6	2.2	4.1	2.0	1.7	4.3	0.3	
2.4	1.8	0.8	1.7	1.4	0.4	0.5	0.8	0.1	^0.0	Bermuda [4,6]
1.9	1.0	2.0	1.9	1.1	1.3	1.9	1.0	0.8	^0.0	Bermudes [4,6]
2.1	7.4	1.6	...	16.0	5.0	1.7	31.7[39]	...	...	Bhutan [4,6]
1.9	0.6	0.7	...	1.5	2.8	0.9	17.0[39]	...	...	Bhoutan [4,6]
38.5	231.2	4.1	65.6	62.5	91.4	21.7	70.6	3.1	3.8	Bolivia (Plurinational State of) [7,40]
132.8	25.1	9.1	39.0	28.6	101.3	42.4	82.4	105.2	0.2	Bolivie (État plurinational de) [7,40]
48.0	216.9	13.6	101.2	81.3	93.6	33.8	72.3	8.2	0.5	
138.7	34.6	9.8	50.8	33.9	124.3	63.1	75.2	111.4	...	
33.8	242.2	17.3	94.1	107.7	92.0	39.9	66.5	5.9	0.3	
125.5	30.2	10.9	42.7	44.4	131.0	69.6	82.6	154.9	1.7	
2.4	10.8	2.0	11.7	47.6	18.3	4.4	11.0	2.8	0.2	Botswana [36,40,43]
7.4	3.0	2.3	6.1	25.7	24.3	7.8	11.0	18.4	0.1	Botswana [36,40,43]
3.8	9.4	1.5	9.2	36.2	14.2	4.5	4.0	2.4	0.2	
10.9	3.2	3.4	5.1	31.0	24.5	9.5	5.5	19.2	...	
3.8	10.5	3.0	15.6	34.5	15.2	5.4	5.2	7.2	0.5	
10.9	5.6	5.4	9.7	25.6	28.1	8.6	5.3	18.0	0.4	
1 587.1	3 441.6	501.4	3 286.6	2 634.2	1 037.4	702.0	1 369.8	453.0	3.0	Brazil [3,7,44]
1 600.0	525.0	506.0	1 650.0	1 633.0	3 647.0	2 275.0	1 932.0	6 214.0	4.0	Brésil [3,7,44]
1 644.0	3 535.0	539.0	3 541.0	2 766.0	1 054.0	760.0	1 556.0	460.0	1.0	
1 751.0	529.0	531.0	1 890.0	1 685.0	3 802.0	2 402.0	2 245.0	6 322.0	2.0	
1 615.1	3 779.7	603.1	3 520.3	2 777.9	1 127.3	764.2	1 490.9	418.3	2.4	
1 735.8	594.3	578.3	1 979.0	1 726.2	3 924.9	2 563.0	2 220.4	6 313.4	1.0	

Employment by economic activity *[cont.]*
Total employment and persons employed by ISIC 3 categories (thousands)
Emploi par activité économique *[suite]*
Emploi total et personnes employées par branches de la CITI rév. 3 (milliers)

Country or area & Pays ou zone &	Year Année	Sex Sexe	Total employment Emploi total	ISIC Rev. 3 Tabulation categories[+] CITI Rév. 3 Catégories de classement[+]						
				Categ. A Catég. A	Categ. B Catég. B	Categ. C Catég. C	Categ. D Catég. D	Categ. E Catég. E	Categ. F Catég. F	Categ. G Catég. G
Brunei Darussalam [4,45]	2001	M	85.8	1.3	0.5	3.2	7.8	2.2	11.4	8.5
Brunéi Darussalam [4,45]	2001	F	60.4	0.2	^0.0	0.8	4.7	0.4	0.9	4.4
Bulgaria [4,31]	2009	M	1 732.0	149.0[1,13]	...	27.0	358.0	58.0[18]	294.0	242.0[19]
Bulgarie [4,31]	2009	F	1 521.0	82.0[1,13]	...	7.0	356.0	18.0[18]	29.0	286.0[19]
	2010	M	1 608.0	132.0[1,13]	...	27.0	324.0	60.0[18]	246.0	240.0[19]
	2010	F	1 445.0	76.0[1,13]	...	6.0	314.0	16.0[18]	22.0	291.0[19]
	2011	M	1 536.0	132.0[1,13]	...	23.0	300.0	61.0[18]	205.0	244.0[19]
	2011	F	1 413.0	69.0[1,13]	...	5.0	301.0	22.0[18]	20.0	295.0[19]
Cambodia [7,46]										
Cambodge [7,46]	2004	MF	6 560.6	2 577.6	31.5	3.9	218.3	0.2	8.9	404.8
Canada [4,47]	2009	M	8 761.0	223.0[48]	259.0[49,50]	...	1 277.0	110.0[51]	1 032.0	1 353.0[52]
Canada [4,47]	2009	F	8 052.0	93.0[48]	59.0[49,50]	...	505.0	38.0[51]	129.0	1 299.2[52]
	2010	M	8 912.0	212.0[48]	271.0[49,50]	...	1 262.0	113.0[51]	1 088.0	1 345.6[52]
	2010	F	8 130.0	89.0[48]	58.0[49,50]	...	482.0	35.0[51]	130.0	1 332.3[52]
	2011	M	9 085.0	216.0[48]	276.0[49,50]	...	1 252.0	105.0[51]	1 121.0	1 369.8[52]
	2011	F	8 221.0	90.0[48]	62.0[49,50]	...	508.0	35.0[51]	141.0	1 300.2[52]
Cayman Islands [4,22]	2006[23]	M	18.4	0.6[1]	...	0.6[24]	0.2	...	6.0	2.3
Iles Caïmanes [4,22]	2006[23]	F	16.6	0.2[1]	...	0.1[24]	0.2	...	0.4	2.0
	2007[11]	M	18.3	0.6[1]	...	0.4[24]	0.5	...	5.2	1.8
	2007[11]	F	16.8	0.0[1]	...	0.2[24]	0.1	...	0.4	1.8
	2008[11]	M	19.4	0.6[1]	...	0.6[54]	...	0.4	5.3	2.1
	2008[11]	F	18.1	0.1[1]	...	0.1[54]	...	0.2	0.5	2.6
Chile [4]	2010	M	4 361.0	574.0	40.0	189.0	566.0	52.0	547.0	817.0
Chili [4]	2010	F	2 769.0	137.0	5.0	14.0	237.0	7.0	25.0	691.0
	2011	M	4 520.0	574.0	44.0	206.0	605.0	51.0	578.0	818.0
	2011	F	2 967.0	146.0	5.0	15.0	255.0	10.0	31.0	740.0
China [55,56,57]	2005	M	70 794.0	2 806.0[1]	...	3 962.0	18 134.0	2 086.0	7 924.0	3 017.0
Chine [55,56,57]	2005	F	43 246.0	1 657.0[1]	...	1 130.0	13 975.0	913.0	1 342.0	2 423.0
	2006	M	72 675.0	2 717.0[1]	...	4 147.0	18 876.0	2 112.0	8 506.0	2 854.0
	2006	F	44 457.0	1 635.0[1]	...	1 150.0	14 640.0	913.0	1 381.0	2 303.0
	2007	M	74 841.0	2 690.0[1]	...	4 253.0	19 704.0	2 127.0	9 084.0	2 781.0
	2007	F	45 403.0	1 573.0[1]	...	1 097.0	14 950.0	907.0	1 424.0	2 288.0
China, Macao SAR	2008[37]	M	172.0	^0.0[59]	...	...	11.0	1.0	34.0	19.0
Chine, Macao RAS	2008[37]	F	151.0	^0.0[59]	...	...	13.0	^0.0	5.0	20.0
	2010[58]	M	162.0	^0.0[59]	...	...	8.0	1.0	24.0	20.0
	2010[58]	F	157.0	^0.0[59]	...	...	8.0	^0.0	4.0	22.0
	2011[58]	M	169.0	^1.0[59]	...	...	7.0	1.0	24.0	22.0
	2011[58]	F	164.0	^0.0[59]	...	...	6.0	^0.0	3.0	24.0
Colombia [60]	2009	M	11 093.0	2 975.0[1]	...	150.0	1 333.0	61.0	942.0	...
Colombie [60]	2009	F	7 334.0	454.0[1]	...	34.0	1 085.0	18.0	26.0	...
	2010	M	11 406.0	2 996.0[1]	...	188.0	1 346.0	72.0	993.0	...
	2010	F	7 734.0	501.0[1]	...	42.0	1 125.0	20.0	33.0	...
	2011	M	11 875.0	3 065.0[1]	...	200.0	1 426.0	85.0	1 100.0	...
	2011	F	8 144.0	569.0[1]	...	44.0	1 178.0	24.0	45.0	...
Costa Rica [43,63]	2006	M	1 172.6	218.6	8.7	4.1	166.9	17.5	124.7	227.5
Costa Rica [43,63]	2006	F	657.3	28.4	0.5	0.6	77.0	4.6	2.0	124.7
	2007	M	1 222.6	209.8	9.0	2.3	170.6	16.7	146.5	237.3
	2007	F	703.1	34.9	0.9	0.3	81.0	4.4	5.3	129.2
	2008	M	1 229.5	205.1	6.2	1.8	155.3	21.9	148.3	242.8
	2008	F	728.2	30.0	0.4	0.4	84.3	6.1	4.1	134.8
Croatia [4,31]	2009	M	869.0	111.0[1,13]	...	8.0	174.0	32.0[18]	129.0	107.0[19]
Croatie [4,31]	2009	F	736.0	111.0[1,13]	...	1.0	102.0	6.0[18]	12.0	124.0[19]
	2010	M	830.0	114.0[1,13]	...	10.0	166.0	33.0[18]	108.0	90.0[19]
	2010	F	711.0	116.0[1,13]	...	2.0	87.0	7.0[18]	8.0	113.0[19]
	2011	M	813.0	119.0[1,13]	...	9.0	163.0	34.0[18]	97.0	90.0[19]
	2011	F	680.0	110.0[1,13]	...	2.0	90.0	2.0[18]	9.0	107.0[19]

ISIC Rev. 3 Tabulation categories [+]
CITI Rév. 3 Catégories de classement [+]

Categ. H Catég. H	Categ. I Catég. I	Categ. J Catég. J	Categ. K Catég. K	Categ. L Catég.L	Categ. M Catég. M	Categ. N Catég. N	Categ. O Catég. O	Categ. P Catég. P	Categ. Q Catég. Q	Country or area [&] Pays ou zone [&]
3.8	3.4	5.1[25]	...	38.7	...	...	...	...	...	Brunei Darussalam [4,45]
3.3	1.4	3.1[25]		41.1	...	...	...	...	...	Brunéi Darussalam [4,45]
60.0	185.0[34]	21.0[21]	...	136.0	36.0	33.0	19.0	...	...	Bulgaria [4,31]
109.0	74.0[34]	40.0[21]	8.0	99.0	155.0	131.0	29.0	...	...	Bulgarie [4,31]
61.0	176.0[34]	19.0[21]	...	126.0	33.0	31.0	20.0	...	...	
99.0	72.0[34]	34.0[21]	...	101.0	151.0	128.0	30.0	...	...	
59.0	171.0[34]	19.0[21]	...	124.0	36.0	29.0	20.0	...	...	
97.0	67.0[34]	33.0[21]	...	101.0	154.0	124.0	28.0	...	...	
										Cambodia [7,46]
25.1	5.2	3.0	4.8	17.5	33.1	11.9	42.7	14.5	3.0	Cambodge [7,46]
430.0	609.2[20]	466.0[25,30]	...	468.0[53]	395.0	336.0	357.0	...	...	Canada [4,47]
627.0	197.0[20]	626.0[25,30]	...	463.0[53]	794.0	1 614.0	430.0	...	...	Canada [4,47]
441.0	615.6[20]	476.0[25,30]	...	472.0[53]	404.0	363.0	354.0	...	...	
617.0	190.0[20]	620.0[25,30]	...	484.0[53]	814.0	1 668.0	399.0	...	...	
456.0	640.6[20]	473.0[25,30]	...	474.0[53]	416.0	372.0	352.0	...	...	
638.0	203.0[20]	611.0[25,30]	...	498.0[53]	804.0	1 720.0	407.0	...	...	
1.6	0.9	1.0	2.1	1.2	0.6[38]	...	1.1	0.3	...	Cayman Islands [4,22]
2.2	0.6	2.2	2.3	1.2	1.9[38]	...	0.7	2.7	...	Iles Caïmanes [4,22]
1.6	1.0	1.2	2.1	1.5	0.7[38]	...	1.2	0.2	...	
1.9	1.0	2.1	2.1	1.0	2.1[38]	...	0.9	2.6	^0.0	
2.1	0.9	1.4	2.5	1.1	0.7[38]	...	1.0	0.3	...	
2.2	0.8	2.4	2.5	1.0	2.3[38]	...	1.0	2.4	...	
102.0	440.0	64.0	270.0	238.0	153.0	89.0	132.0	88.0	1.0	Chile [4]
139.0	83.0	64.0	175.0	152.0	337.0	212.0	97.0	392.0	1.0	Chili [4]
110.0	459.0	57.0	299.0	243.0	165.0	92.0	136.0	82.0	1.0	
150.0	83.0	66.0	194.0	157.0	350.0	230.0	111.0	425.0	1.0	
823.0	4 429.0	1 873.0	3 988.0	9 039.0	7 700.0	2 080.0	724.0	...	...	China [55,56,57]
989.0	1 710.0	1 720.0	1 939.0	3 369.0	7 132.0	3 009.0	501.0	...	...	Chine [55,56,57]
844.0	4 480.0	1 888.0	4 224.0	9 170.0	7 706.0	2 125.0	717.0	...	...	
995.0	1 647.0	1 786.0	2 037.0	3 486.0	7 338.0	3 129.0	507.0	...	...	
850.0	4 538.0	1 968.0	4 434.0	9 352.0	7 732.0	2 187.0	729.0	...	...	
1 008.0	1 693.0	1 929.0	2 137.0	3 560.0	7 477.0	3 241.0	521.0	...	...	
21.0	12.0	3.0	14.0	13.0	4.0	2.0	38.0	^0.0	...	China, Macao SAR
21.0	4.0	5.0	9.0	7.0	8.0	4.0	41.0	13.0	...	Chine, Macao RAS
20.0	14.0	3.0	17.0	14.0	4.0	3.0	33.0	1.0	...	
23.0	4.0	4.0	11.0	8.0	8.0	5.0	43.0	16.0	...	
21.0	13.0	3.0	18.0	12.0	4.0	3.0	36.0	1.0	...	
24.0	4.0	5.0	11.0	9.0	9.0	6.0	45.0	17.0	^0.0	
2 463.0[61]	1 241.0	99.0	635.0	1 184.0[62]	...	...	...	...	...	Colombia [60]
2 306.0[61]	295.0	122.0	556.0	2 434.0[62]	...	...	...	...	...	Colombie [60]
2 542.0[61]	1 308.0	113.0	632.0	1 211.0[62]	...	...	...	...	...	
2 484.0[61]	307.0	126.0	573.0	2 520.0[62]	...	...	...	...	...	
2 657.0[61]	1 355.0	107.0	677.0	1 201.0[62]	...	...	...	...	...	
2 629.0[61]	305.0	131.0	626.0	2 593.0[62]	...	...	...	...	...	
41.8	104.0	23.3	73.4	55.8	30.6	23.8	34.1	14.2	0.9	Costa Rica [43,63]
56.0	14.5	14.9	34.8	30.7	77.8	38.7	31.7	116.9	1.7	Costa Rica [43,63]
44.3	108.8	25.8	84.3	54.6	34.3	23.3	35.9	14.1	0.8	
64.0	16.9	23.7	37.3	34.1	76.4	40.7	36.8	114.4	0.4	
41.7	119.6	26.3	88.7	58.6	31.0	23.1	43.5	8.4	1.2	
58.6	23.5	27.1	48.8	35.2	81.5	41.6	37.6	110.6	1.5	
40.0	99.5[34]	11.0[30]	...	53.0	21.0	19.0	...	...	...	Croatia [4,31]
47.0	31.1[34]	23.0[30]	...	49.0	71.0	81.0	...	...	...	Croatie [4,31]
40.0	101.4[34]	11.0[30]	...	50.0	19.0	19.0	...	...	...	
49.0	32.6[34]	23.0[30]	...	46.0	73.0	81.0	...	...	...	
39.0	99.2[34]	10.0[30]	...	48.0	20.0	19.0	...	...	...	
41.0	26.7[34]	24.0[30]	...	43.0	69.0	74.0	...	...	...	

Country or area [&] Pays ou zone [&]	Year Année	Sex Sexe	Total employment Emploi total	ISIC Rev. 3 Tabulation categories [+] CITI Rév. 3 Catégories de classement [+]						
				Categ. A Catég. A	Categ. B Catég. B	Categ. C Catég. C	Categ. D Catég. D	Categ. E Catég. E	Categ. F Catég. F	Categ. G Catég. G
Cyprus [4,31] Chypre [4,31]	2009	M	210.0	10.0[1,13]	...	...	23.0	4.0[18]	40.0	41.0[19]
	2009	F	171.0	5.0[1,13]	...	...	12.0	1.0[18]	4.0	31.0[19]
	2010	M	211.0	10.0[1,13]	...	...	21.0	3.0[18]	39.0	41.0[19]
	2010	F	174.0	5.0[1,13]	...	...	12.0	0.0[18]	4.0	32.0[19]
	2011	M	205.0	10.0[1,13]	...	1.0	19.0	4.0[18]	41.0	39.0[19]
	2011	F	170.0	4.0[1,13]	...	...	10.0	1.0[18]	4.0	31.0[19]
Czech Republic [4,31] République tchèque [4,31]	2009	M	2 824.0	107.0[1,13]	...	45.0	805.0	90.0[18]	456.0	297.0[19]
	2009	F	2 111.0	47.0[1,13]	...	8.0	438.0	21.0[18]	41.0	334.0[19]
	2010	M	2 798.0	111.0[1,13]	...	40.0	818.0	84.0[18]	430.0	267.0[19]
	2010	F	2 087.0	40.0[1,13]	...	8.0	418.0	23.0[18]	35.0	326.0[19]
	2011	M	2 794.0	106.0[1,13]	...	41.0	855.0	84.0[18]	399.0	273.0[19]
	2011	F	2 110.0	39.0[1,13]	...	6.0	439.0	25.0[18]	34.0	329.0[19]
Denmark [4] Danemark [4]	2009	M	1 454.0	57.0[1,13]	...	...	244.0	25.0[18]	157.0	237.0[19]
	2009	F	1 316.0	15.0[1,13]	...	...	110.0	5.0[18]	17.0	180.0[19]
	2010	M	1 415.0	54.0[1,13]	...	...	240.0	22.0[18]	146.0	221.0[19]
	2010	F	1 292.0	11.0[1,13]	...	...	100.0	2.0[18]	12.0	176.0[19]
	2011	M	1 421.0	54.0[1,13]	...	...	242.0	24.0[18]	148.0	215.0[19]
	2011	F	1 282.0	11.0[1,13]	...	...	101.0	8.0[18]	11.0	177.0[19]
Dominica [4,6,28] Dominique [4,6,28]	1999	M	17.1	5.8[1]	...	...	1.3	0.3	2.1	2.2[29]
	1999	F	10.9	1.8[1]	...	^0.0	1.1	0.1	^0.0	2.8[29]
	2001	M	15.0	4.4[1]	...	0.2	1.1	0.3	2.4	2.1[29]
	2001	F	9.8	0.8[1]	...	...	0.8	^0.1	^0.1	3.1[29]
Dominican Republic [7] Rép. dominicaine [7]	2005	M	2 175.4	436.2	11.3	5.8	335.6	17.2	207.1	460.7
	2005	F	1 103.7	30.9	...	0.1	151.3	9.0	6.4	247.8
	2006	M	2 272.0	478.5	11.6	3.1	332.1	21.2	236.0	477.3
	2006	F	1 197.9	25.3	...	0.5	157.6	5.5	5.2	244.8
	2007	M	2 336.8	477.0	12.7	5.8	345.1	22.1	239.4	487.2
	2007	F	1 214.1	25.2	0.2	0.2	149.5	8.7	7.4	245.3
Ecuador [7,46,56] Equateur [7,46,56]	2004	M	2 288.5	247.5	34.2	14.6	335.6	17.3	239.9	589.5
	2004	F	1 570.1	73.3	3.3	1.5	203.4	5.6	8.8	506.7
	2005	M	2 327.8	218.7	38.4	10.6	361.4	15.4	249.4	597.3
	2005	F	1 564.0	54.8	12.7	0.1	175.7	3.4	9.4	501.6
	2006	M	2 416.5	222.8	42.2	14.2	368.3	15.7	278.2	623.0
	2006	F	1 615.1	62.2	6.8	1.6	187.2	3.6	11.9	528.8
Egypt [5,64,65] Egypte [5,64,65]	2006	M	16 559.4	4 529.7	160.5	49.5	2 188.3	229.2	1 806.9	1 964.6
	2006	F	3 884.2	1 679.2	1.3	3.8	192.5	21.2	16.0	207.3
	2007	M	17 090.0	4 587.7	144.2	34.8	2 190.4	245.9	2 051.5	2 048.8
	2007	F	4 634.3	2 153.5	0.6	0.7	221.8	36.4	26.6	258.2
	2008	M	18 041.0	4 932.0	150.0	35.0	2 365.0	277.0	2 243.0	2 124.0
	2008	F	4 466.0	2 034.0	1.0	2.0	202.0	20.0	25.0	263.0
El Salvador [7,57] El Salvador [7,57]	2005	M	1 330.7	399.3	11.3	2.2	181.1	5.5	127.0	277.1[29]
	2005	F	952.9	45.1	0.8	^0.0	188.1	0.9	2.3	397.0[29]
	2006	M	1 342.0	381.7	11.6	2.0	185.4	7.8	152.7	273.0[29]
	2006	F	995.1	46.1	1.4	...	183.1	1.2	5.0	425.8[29]
	2007	M	1 401.8	385.2	11.6	3.7	201.4	9.2	144.7	288.3[29]
	2007	F	1 017.3	37.1	2.0	...	202.3	1.0	3.8	432.3[29]
Estonia Estonie	2009	M	288.0	16.0[1,13]	...	...	64.0	...	52.0	32.0[19]
	2009	F	308.0	8.0[1,13]	...	...	50.0	...	6.0	52.0[19]
	2010	M	275.0	16.0[1,13]	...	...	62.0	6.0[67]	45.0	30.0[19]
	2010	F	296.0	8.0[1,13]	...	...	46.0	2.0[67]	3.0	50.0[19]
	2011	M	301.0	19.0[1,13]	...	...	72.0	...	53.0	32.0[19]
	2011	F	308.0	7.0[1,13]	...	...	49.0	...	6.0	50.0[19]

ISIC Rev. 3 Tabulation categories[+]
CITI Rév. 3 Catégories de classement[+]

Categ. H / Catég. H	Categ. I / Catég. I	Categ. J / Catég. J	Categ. K / Catég. K	Categ. L / Catég.L	Categ. M / Catég. M	Categ. N / Catég. N	Categ. O / Catég. O	Categ. P / Catég. P	Categ. Q / Catég. Q	Country or area[&] / Pays ou zone[&]
14.0	17.0[34]	8.0[30]	1.0	18.0	7.0	5.0	4.0	0.0	2.0	Cyprus [4,31]
14.0	7.7[34]	11.0[30]	1.0	11.0	18.0	11.0	7.0	17.0	1.0	Chypre [4,31]
14.0	16.8[34]	8.0[30]	1.0	18.0	8.0	5.0	4.0	1.0	1.0	
14.0	7.2[34]	11.0[30]	1.0	11.0	19.0	11.0	6.0	20.0	1.0	
13.0	16.2[34]	8.0[30]	1.0	16.0	8.0	4.0	5.0	1.0	1.0	
13.0	7.4[34]	11.0[30]	1.0	10.0	21.0	11.0	6.0	20.0	0.0	
82.0	327.2[34]	45.0[30]	20.0[35]	168.0	67.0	60.0	34.0	2.0	...	Czech Republic [4,31]
104.0	189.5[34]	66.0[30]	21.0[35]	154.0	228.0	266.0	58.0	9.0	...	République tchèque [4,31]
83.0	325.2[34]	49.0[30]	19.0[35]	173.0	71.0	69.0	32.0	2.0	...	
108.0	193.1[34]	67.0[30]	21.0[35]	156.0	225.0	271.0	61.0	14.0	...	
82.0	322.8[34]	52.0[30]	22.0[35]	165.0	70.0	61.0	29.0	3.0	...	
105.0	188.6[34]	72.0[30]	20.0[35]	151.0	227.0	266.0	60.0	15.0	...	
41.0	185.0[34]	46.0[30]	17.0[35]	81.0	90.0	92.0	26.0	1.0	...	Denmark [4]
49.0	60.0[34]	47.0[30]	9.0[35]	95.0	129.0	415.0	39.0	5.0	...	Danemark [4]
39.0	179.0[34]	44.0[30]	18.0[35]	72.0	94.0	96.0	29.0	1.0	...	
49.0	59.0[34]	43.0[30]	9.0[35]	85.0	137.0	422.0	41.0	5.0	...	
43.0	184.0[34]	43.0[30]	17.0[35]	70.0	101.0	97.0	24.0	...	...	
52.0	56.0[34]	42.0[30]	10.0[35]	82.0	141.0	412.0	42.0	...	...	
...	1.4	1.6[25]	...	...	...	...	3.6	...	...	Dominica [4,6,28]
...	0.5	1.0[25]	...	...	...	...	3.6	...	...	Dominique [4,6,28]
...	1.2	0.5[25]	...	...	...	...	2.8	...	...	
...	0.3	0.7[25]	...	...	...	...	3.9	...	...	
88.6	215.5	34.5	66.3	44.2	29.2	100.3	18.9	0.5	...	Dominican Republic [7]
103.3	23.0	27.8	31.1	106.7	74.8	114.0	132.7	1.0	...	Rép. dominicaine [7]
100.4	230.1	31.8	60.6	95.0	42.1	27.1	110.0	15.0	...	
113.0	18.1	34.3	26.4	54.1	110.2	76.2	160.5	165.6	0.9	
104.5	234.4	33.1	62.6	105.8	55.4	28.2	103.9	19.5	0.2	
117.8	23.1	40.5	31.4	46.8	114.5	68.2	159.0	175.1	1.3	
62.2	233.9	26.3	138.0	124.9	100.6	47.4	68.5	7.0	1.2	Ecuador [7,46,56]
108.9	30.9	22.8	51.8	49.0	162.4	90.4	107.6	143.4	0.2	Equateur [7,46,56]
71.0	244.6	26.2	144.1	125.6	91.7	46.9	65.0	20.9	0.4	
119.8	35.5	25.7	55.6	42.6	167.2	85.1	93.7	180.8	0.3	
85.3	251.7	25.2	146.7	126.4	100.2	42.3	64.6	9.7	...	
140.1	40.7	22.7	54.0	43.9	180.7	73.7	98.2	158.0	0.9	
394.5	1 300.7	133.7	374.6	1 475.8	1 140.8	261.2	472.5	34.3	2.1	Egypt [5,64,65]
16.9	56.6	41.3	57.2	425.9	829.1	284.3	35.0	10.7	0.4	Egypte [5,64,65]
358.5	1 398.6	145.1	389.1	1 515.1	1 165.8	261.5	486.5	36.6	0.5	
12.3	53.8	49.8	62.6	459.4	914.0	311.6	52.0	15.0	0.5	
451.0	1 517.0	127.0	383.0	1 443.0	1 124.0	266.0	529.0	53.0	2.0	
11.0	58.0	39.0	65.0	447.0	918.0	317.0	46.0	13.0	1.0	
...	95.7	73.7[25]	...	62.4	27.3	58.3[66]	...	9.7	...	El Salvador [7,57]
...	10.8	34.5[25]	...	26.0	58.4	100.3[66]	...	88.6	...	El Salvador [7,57]
...	96.6	64.0[25]	...	67.0	28.9	60.2[66]	...	11.2	...	
...	8.2	36.0[25]	...	25.2	52.8	104.6[66]	...	105.8	...	
...	94.7	76.3[25]	...	73.2	34.0	65.5[66]	...	13.8	...	
...	8.6	38.0[25]	...	25.5	56.0	112.9[66]	...	97.9	...	
5.0	44.0[34]	3.0[30]	...	14.0	12.0	3.0	3.0	...	...	Estonia
15.0	20.0[34]	9.0[30]	...	22.0	50.0	30.0	8.0	...	...	Estonie
5.0	39.0[34]	3.0[30]	4.0[68]	16.0	9.0	5.0	2.0	...	...	
14.0	17.0[34]	6.0[30]	6.0[68]	24.0	47.0	30.0	9.0	...	...	
...	43.0[34]	3.0[30]	4.0[68]	18.0	8.0	...	2.0	...	...	
15.0	22.0[34]	7.0[30]	7.0[68]	22.0	49.0	30.0	8.0	...	...	

26

Employment by economic activity *[cont.]*
Total employment and persons employed by ISIC 3 categories (thousands)
Emploi par activité économique *[suite]*
Emploi total et personnes employées par branches de la CITI rév. 3 (milliers)

Country or area [&] Pays ou zone [&]	Year Année	Sex Sexe	Total employment Emploi total	ISIC Rev. 3 Tabulation categories [+] CITI Rév. 3 Catégories de classement [+]						
				Categ. A Catég. A	Categ. B Catég. B	Categ. C Catég. C	Categ. D Catég. D	Categ. E Catég. E	Categ. F Catég. F	Categ. G Catég. G
Ethiopia [5,7,56]	2004[23]	M	1 625.6	168.3[1]	...	9.2	236.9	21.6	141.2	325.4
Ethiopie [5,7,56]	2004[23]	F	1 228.8	56.8[1]	...	0.8	207.6	7.3	17.6	297.6
	2006[63]	M	1 913.2	224.8[1]	...	11.9	290.7	30.0	179.9	450.6
	2006[63]	F	1 923.6	106.2[1]	...	1.4	294.9	8.6	29.0	422.0
Faeroe Islands [3,28,58]	2005	M	15.0	3.0[1]	...	...	...	...	2.0	1.0
Iles Féroé [3,28,58]	2005	F	12.0	1.0[1]	...	...	...	...	...	2.0
Finland [31,70]	2009	M	1 255.0	79.0[1,13]	...	5.0	281.0	21.0[18]	160.0	149.0[19]
Finlande [31,70]	2009	F	1 202.0	34.0[1,13]	...	^0.0	99.0	4.0[18]	14.0	147.0[19]
	2010	M	1 259.0	75.0[1,13]	...	7.0	266.0	21.0[18]	157.0	148.0[19]
	2010	F	1 188.0	33.0[1,13]	...	1.0	96.0	6.0[18]	15.0	151.0[19]
	2011	M	1 278.0	76.0[1,13]	...	5.0	269.0	19.0[18]	162.0	150.0[19]
	2011	F	1 196.0	29.0[1,13]	...	1.0	91.0	5.0[18]	14.0	154.0[19]
France [4,31]	2009	M	13 463.0	521.0[1,13]	...	...	2 515.0	306.0[18]	1 690.0	1 782.0[19]
France [4,31]	2009	F	12 177.0	232.0[1,13]	...	...	995.0	73.0[18]	184.0	1 618.0[19]
	2010	M	13 495.0	530.0[1,13]	...	...	2 395.0	321.0[18]	1 718.0	1 786.0[19]
	2010	F	12 199.0	220.0[1,13]	...	...	974.0	80.0[18]	180.0	1 565.0[19]
	2011	M	13 538.0	519.0[1,13]	...	...	2 388.0	296.0[18]	1 697.0	1 765.0[19]
	2011	F	12 240.0	234.0[1,13]	...	...	1 011.0	87.0[18]	191.0	1 479.0[19]
French Polynesia [4,46]	2002	M	53.4	3.4	3.1	0.3	4.8	0.5	7.4	6.8
Polynésie française [4,46]	2002	F	34.4	1.0	0.8	^0.0	2.4	0.1	0.4	4.7
Georgia [4,5]	2005	M	915.2	473.5	...	5.2	60.1	18.1	42.4	107.9
Géorgie [4,5]	2005	F	829.4	474.3	...	0.6	29.7	5.3	0.7	80.3
	2006	M	920.5	491.9	...	2.5	54.8	14.8	53.7	86.6
	2006	F	826.8	474.5	...	0.9	26.7	3.7	1.2	81.5
	2007	M	888.1	448.5	...	4.3	60.6	14.7	66.5	88.4
	2007	F	816.2	462.1	...	0.4	22.1	3.5	4.6	80.5
Germany [4,31]	2009	M	20 816.0	427.0[1,13]	...	91.0	5 734.0	433.0[18]	2 242.0	2 436.0[19]
Allemagne [4,31]	2009	F	17 655.0	220.0[1,13]	...	13.0	2 114.0	128.0[18]	324.0	2 761.0[19]
	2010	M	20 892.0	421.0[1,13]	...	85.0	5 654.0	433.0[18]	2 253.0	2 471.0[19]
	2010	F	17 846.0	213.0[1,13]	...	11.0	2 092.0	128.0[18]	333.0	2 793.0[19]
	2011	M	21 403.0	433.0[1,13]	...	88.0	5 757.0	463.0[18]	2 310.0	2 514.0[19]
	2011	F	18 334.0	215.0[1,13]	...	11.0	2 141.0	133.0[18]	334.0	2 845.0[19]
Greece [4,31]	2009	M	2 718.0	320.0[1,13]	...	14.0	382.0	48.0[18]	357.0	468.0[19]
Grèce [4,31]	2009	F	1 791.0	216.0[1,13]	...	1.0	131.0	11.0[18]	12.0	347.0[19]
	2010	M	2 627.0	325.0[1,13]	...	13.0	354.0	48.0[18]	311.0	461.0[19]
	2010	F	1 762.0	224.0[1,13]	...	1.0	116.0	11.0[18]	11.0	334.0[19]
	2011	M	2 441.0	298.0[1,13]	...	11.0	315.0	39.0[18]	239.0	439.0[19]
	2011	F	1 649.0	209.0[1,13]	...	1.0	102.0	12.0[18]	10.0	317.0[19]
Guatemala [5,7]	2006	M	3 338.7	1 462.6[1]	...	7.3	438.5	11.1	349.1	522.3[29]
Guatemala [5,7]	2006	F	2 051.8	328.8[1]	...	0.2	416.3	1.3	5.8	704.6[29]
Guyana [4]	2002	M	169.2	40.8	5.3	8.8	23.5	1.8	15.9	22.3
Guyana [4]	2002	F	70.4	4.8	0.3	0.7	7.1	0.5	0.3	15.6
Hungary [4,31]	2009	M	2 045.0	129.0[1,13]	...	9.0	497.0	65.0[18]	273.0	260.0[19]
Hongrie [4,31]	2009	F	1 737.0	45.0[1,13]	...	1.0	296.0	19.0[18]	21.0	295.0[19]
	2010	M	2 023.0	129.0[1,13]	...	11.0	483.0	65.0[18]	255.0	252.0[19]
	2010	F	1 759.0	40.0[1,13]	...	1.0	302.0	20.0[18]	22.0	294.0[19]
	2011	M	2 057.0	138.0[1,13]	...	10.0	503.0	65.0[18]	245.0	259.0[19]
	2011	F	1 755.0	46.0[1,13]	...	2.0	304.0	23.0[18]	18.0	291.0[19]
Iceland [31,58]	2009	M	88.0	6.0[1,13]	...	...	13.0	...	11.0	13.0[19]
Islande [31,58]	2009	F	79.0	2.0[1,13]	...	...	5.0	...	1.0	9.0[19]
	2010	M	86.0	7.0[1,13]	...	...	13.0	...	10.0	11.0[19]
	2010	F	79.0	2.0[1,13]	...	...	5.0	...	1.0	9.0[19]
	2011	M	86.0	8.0[1,13]	...	...	13.0	...	9.0	12.0[19]
	2011	F	80.0	2.0[1,13]	...	...	5.0	...	1.0	10.0[19]

26

Employment by economic activity *[cont.]*
Total employment and persons employed by ISIC 3 categories (thousands)
Emploi par activité économique *[suite]*
Emploi total et personnes employées par branches de la CITI rév. 3 (milliers)

ISIC Rev. 3 Tabulation categories [+]
CITI Rév. 3 Catégories de classement [+]

Categ. H / Catég. H	Categ. I / Catég. I	Categ. J / Catég. J	Categ. K / Catég. K	Categ. L / Catég.L	Categ. M / Catég. M	Categ. N / Catég. N	Categ. O / Catég. O	Categ. P / Catég. P	Categ. Q / Catég. Q	Country or area & / Pays ou zone &
53.4	108.7	16.4	34.4	139.3	137.7[38]	...	197.9	22.4	12.4	Ethiopia 5,7,56
202.2	10.7	5.2	11.5	61.6	95.5[38]	...	57.9	192.2	3.4	Ethiopie 5,7,56
73.8	143.7	31.2	38.6	184.2	175.0[38]	...	48.7	13.4	15.6	
296.2	10.9	13.2	17.8	84.4	139.4[38]	...	300.8	188.2	9.5	
...	2.0	1.0[25,30,69]	...	...	...	...	4.0	...	...	Faeroe Islands 3,28,58
...	...	1.0[25,30,69]	...	...	...	...	7.0	...	...	Iles Féroé 3,28,58
23.0	177.0[34]	18.0[30]	11.0	51.0	54.0	43.0	23.0	5.0	...	Finland 31,70
62.0	70.0[34]	33.0[30]	8.0	65.0	110.0	345.0	52.0	4.0	...	Finlande 31,70
24.0	186.0[34]	18.0[30]	12.0	51.0	58.0	44.0	24.0	4.0	...	
58.0	65.0[34]	31.0[30]	9.0	66.0	116.0	335.0	51.0	4.0	...	
24.0	182.0[34]	20.0[30]	11.0	54.0	60.0	51.0	22.0	3.0	...	
58.0	65.0[34]	33.0[30]	11.0	63.0	118.0	345.0	51.0	5.0	...	
475.0	1 462.0[34]	368.0[30]	144.0	1 211.0	580.0	683.0	213.0	90.0	...	France 4,31
429.0	610.0[34]	505.0[30]	163.0	1 401.0	1 165.0	2 586.0	469.0	506.0	...	France 4,31
501.0	1 463.0[34]	386.0[30]	133.0	1 222.0	565.0	726.0	208.0	99.0	...	
465.0	614.0[34]	478.0[30]	173.0	1 357.0	1 186.0	2 641.0	512.0	494.0	...	
497.0	1 487.0[34]	370.0[30]	141.0	1 226.0	582.0	728.0	225.0	103.0	...	
486.0	604.0[34]	497.0[30]	177.0	1 287.0	1 150.0	2 682.0	503.0	506.0	...	
3.3	3.7	0.6	2.2	11.8	2.2	1.3	1.8	0.4	...	French Polynesia 4,46
4.4	2.0	0.9	1.5	6.2	3.9	2.9	1.6	1.7	...	Polynésie française 4,46
7.6	57.9	7.2	15.8	56.1	29.6	12.0	18.1	0.6	2.9	Georgia 4,5
8.7	11.3	6.1	10.1	25.7	101.2	46.0	20.1	8.6	0.4	Géorgie 4,5
4.8	70.3	8.4	16.4	55.4	23.4	12.8	22.1	1.6	0.9	
12.1	7.5	5.9	10.5	23.1	108.8	39.4	19.8	10.1	1.4	
7.0	65.7	8.0	21.6	47.6	21.2	9.3	22.2	1.4	1.1	
11.0	6.0	9.3	13.1	16.7	103.0	50.6	21.7	9.8	1.8	
618.0	2 166.0[34]	660.0[30]	136.0	1 475.0	764.0	1 048.0	352.0	12.0	...	Germany 4,31
870.0	879.0[34]	663.0[30]	140.0	1 296.0	1 606.0	3 479.0	788.0	191.0	...	Allemagne 4,31
628.0	2 173.0[34]	652.0[30]	133.0	1 498.0	739.0	1 094.0	343.0	11.0	...	
860.0	878.0[34]	669.0[30]	134.0	1 309.0	1 633.0	3 591.0	775.0	197.0	...	
650.0	2 258.0[34]	647.0[30]	138.0	1 460.0	755.0	1 127.0	357.0	14.0	...	
900.0	894.0[34]	664.0[30]	137.0	1 326.0	1 711.0	3 728.0	778.0	213.0	...	
167.0	241.0[34]	56.0[30]	5.0	233.0	117.0	75.0	37.0	3.0	...	Greece 4,31
147.0	60.0[34]	56.0[30]	3.0	143.0	208.0	156.0	49.0	85.0	...	Grèce 4,31
164.0	237.0[34]	58.0[30]	3.0	232.0	111.0	80.0	41.0	4.0	...	
141.0	59.0[34]	57.0[30]	3.0	140.0	210.0	165.0	47.0	86.0	...	
162.0	216.0[34]	59.0[30]	3.0	235.0	108.0	86.0	37.0	4.0	...	
133.0	59.0[34]	55.0[30]	3.0	125.0	200.0	154.0	49.0	69.0	...	
...	146.6	129.3[25]	...	87.7	73.2	103.2 66	...	...	8.0	Guatemala 5,7
...	14.1	46.9[25]	...	27.8	146.6	354.2 66	...	...	5.2	Guatemala 5,7
2.0	15.0	1.4	4.6	8.7	3.1	1.3	6.5	1.3	0.2	Guyana 4
3.6	1.9	1.7	2.9	6.4	10.0	4.3	3.2	4.9	0.3	Guyana 4
69.0	250.0[34]	31.0[30]	9.0	138.0	70.0	54.0	27.0	...	...	Hungary 4,31
88.0	96.0[34]	65.0[30]	11.0	152.0	245.0	191.0	57.0	...	...	Hongrie 4,31
68.0	260.0[34]	28.0[30]	9.0	147.0	75.0	53.0	25.0	...	...	
91.0	95.0[34]	63.0[30]	11.0	157.0	246.0	203.0	57.0	...	...	
67.0	255.0[34]	34.0[30]	10.0	151.0	74.0	57.0	24.0	...	...	
99.0	95.0[34]	59.0[30]	11.0	147.0	242.0	201.0	55.0	...	...	
4.0	12.0[34]	3.0[30]	...	4.0	4.0	4.0	...	...	...	Iceland 31,58
4.0	5.0[34]	5.0[30]	...	5.0	15.0	15.0	3.0	...	...	Islande 31,58
4.0	11.0[34]	3.0[30]	...	4.0	5.0	4.0	1.0	...	...	
4.0	5.0[34]	5.0[30]	...	4.0	15.0	17.0	3.0	...	...	
3.0	11.0[34]	3.0[30]	...	3.0	4.0	4.0	2.0	...	...	
5.0	5.0[34]	5.0[30]	...	4.0	14.0	16.0	3.0	...	...	

Country or area [&] Pays ou zone [&]	Year Année	Sex Sexe	Total employment Emploi total	ISIC Rev. 3 Tabulation categories [+] CITI Rév. 3 Catégories de classement [+]						
				Categ. A Catég. A	Categ. B Catég. B	Categ. C Catég. C	Categ. D Catég. D	Categ. E Catég. E	Categ. F Catég. F	Categ. G Catég. G
Indonesia [28]	2009	M	104 678.0	42 321.0[1]	...	1 147.0	12 728.0	216.0	5 049.0	21 892.0[29]
Indonésie [28]	2010	M	107 807.0	42 160.0[1]	...	1 222.0	13 438.0	221.0	5 219.0	22 353.0[29]
	2011	M	110 476.0	40 902.0[1]	...	1 409.0	14 119.0	248.0	5 965.0	23 318.0[29]
Iran (Islamic Rep. of) [7]	2006	M	16 871.8	3 519.7	81.9	130.5	2 688.4	181.0	2 344.8	2 862.8
Iran (Rép. islamique d') [7]	2006	F	3 969.6	1 225.2	0.5	8.7	1 219.3	9.7	22.5	168.4
	2007	M	17 230.0	3 454.5	77.6	123.8	2 744.9	187.7	2 577.8	2 850.1
	2007	F	3 862.5	1 276.0	1.5	4.3	1 089.4	8.4	23.1	167.2
	2008	M	17 119.0	3 232.0	76.0	123.0	2 630.0	171.0	2 763.0	2 821.0
	2008	F	3 381.0	1 034.0	2.0	5.0	882.0	9.0	27.0	160.0
Iraq	2006	M	5 224.0	1 129.0	21.1	41.6	338.9	72.7	654.8	925.6
Iraq	2006	F	1 333.2	796.7	1.7	1.8	37.4	4.0	10.1	36.2
	2007	M	6 028.4	722.7	10.0	79.9	470.3	122.8	788.7	1 077.5
	2007	F	1 088.3	343.5	...	4.5	51.9	7.7	8.5	40.2
	2008	M	6 176.9	1 036.8	19.7	28.0	340.4	150.9	814.7	1 124.5
	2008	F	1 429.2	723.1	2.0	4.4	29.0	10.7	8.8	42.7
Ireland [4,31]	2009	M	1 046.0	87.0[1,13]	...	7.0	157.0	19.0[18]	145.0	132.0[19]
Irlande [4,31]	2009	F	882.0	9.0[1,13]	...	1.0	67.0	5.0[18]	11.0	142.0[19]
	2010	M	990.0	76.0[1,13]	...	6.0	149.0	18.0[18]	111.0	134.0[19]
	2010	F	858.0	9.0[1,13]	...	1.0	61.0	5.0[18]	9.0	134.0[19]
	2011	M	966.0	74.0[1,13]	...	5.0	144.0	18.0[18]	100.0	135.0[19]
	2011	F	842.0	9.0[1,13]	...	^0.0	63.0	4.0[18]	7.0	130.0[19]
Israel [4]	2009	M	1 502.0	39.0	...	...	297.0	14.0	135.0	219.0
Israël [4]	2009	F	1 339.0	9.0	...	...	118.0	5.0	9.0	157.0
	2010	M	1 552.0	37.0	...	...	299.0	16.0	146.0	226.0
	2010	F	1 386.0	11.0	...	...	118.0	4.0	12.0	163.0
	2011	M	1 604.0	34.0	...	...	298.0	18.0	152.0	232.0
	2011	F	1 421.0	8.0	...	...	119.0	5.0	10.0	171.0
Italy [4,31]	2009	M	13 789.0	603.0[1,13]	...	29.0	3 240.0	262.0[18]	1 849.0	2 041.0[19]
Italie [4,31]	2009	F	9 236.0	246.0[1,13]	...	4.0	1 208.0	52.0[18]	114.0	1 373.0[19]
	2010	M	13 634.0	612.0[1,13]	...	30.0	3 128.0	275.0[18]	1 840.0	1 998.0[19]
	2010	F	9 238.0	254.0[1,13]	...	6.0	1 137.0	53.0[18]	109.0	1 353.0[19]
	2011	M	13 619.0	602.0[1,13]	...	34.0	3 160.0	286.0[18]	1 724.0	1 953.0[19]
	2011	F	9 349.0	248.0[1,13]	...	5.0	1 151.0	56.0[18]	123.0	1 347.0[19]
Jamaica [37]	2008	M	661.0	170.0[1]	...	8.0	56.0	6.0	104.0	100.0
Jamaïque [37]	2008	F	501.0	47.0[1]	...	2.0	30.0	2.0	5.0	124.0
	2009	M	639.0	180.0[1]	...	4.0	50.0	6.0	92.0	97.0
	2009	F	487.0	47.0[1]	...	1.0	28.0	2.0	4.0	118.0
	2010	M	623.0	177.0[1]	...	3.0	47.0	5.0	86.0	97.0
	2010	F	472.0	45.0[1]	...	1.0	27.0	2.0	3.0	115.0
Japan [4,71]	2009	M	36 435.0	1 403.0	150.0	33.0	7 505.0	300.0[72]	4 425.0	5 250.0[15]
Japon [4,71]	2009	F	23 677.5	1 018.0	55.0	...	3 220.0	40.0[72]	743.0	5 305.0[15]
	2010	M	36 150.0	1 375.0	132.5	28.0	7 343.0	300.0[72]	4 288.0	5 288.0[15]
	2010	F	26 412.5	973.0	47.5	8.0	3 145.0	40.0[72]	693.0	5 283.0[15]
	2011	M	34 535.0	1 240.0	125.0	23.0	7 020.0	255.0[72]	4 070.0	5 013.0[15]
	2011	F	25 232.5	835.0	37.5	8.0	2 953.0	33.0[72]	660.0	5 048.0[15]
Latvia [4,31]	2009	M	478.0	55.0[1,13]	...	...	73.0	19.0[18]	71.0	59.0[19]
Lettonie [4,31]	2009	F	505.0	30.0[1,13]	...	...	63.0	8.0[18]	9.0	104.0[19]
	2010	M	455.0	55.0[1,13]	...	...	75.0	19.0[18]	59.0	52.0[19]
	2010	F	486.0	28.0[1,13]	...	...	54.0	3.0[18]	7.0	98.0[19]
	2011	M	479.0	64.0[1,13]	...	...	76.0	11.0[18]	62.0	59.0[19]
	2011	F	492.0	27.0[1,13]	...	...	56.0	3.0[18]	9.0	93.0[19]

Employment by economic activity *[cont.]*
Total employment and persons employed by ISIC 3 categories (thousands)
Emploi par activité économique *[suite]*
Emploi total et personnes employées par branches de la CITI rév. 3 (milliers)

ISIC Rev. 3 Tabulation categories [+]
CITI Rév. 3 Catégories de classement [+]

Categ. H / Catég. H	Categ. I / Catég. I	Categ. J / Catég. J	Categ. K / Catég. K	Categ. L / Catég.L	Categ. M / Catég. M	Categ. N / Catég. N	Categ. O / Catég. O	Categ. P / Catég. P	Categ. Q / Catég. Q	Country or area [&] / Pays ou zone [&]
...	6 033.0	1 486.0[25]	...	...	...	...	13 807.0	...	...	Indonesia [28]
...	5 718.0	1 690.0[25]	...	...	...	...	15 786.0	...	...	Indonésie [28]
...	5 332.0	2 346.0[25]	...	...	...	...	16 836.0	...	...	
177.4	1 867.4	235.5	358.1	1 212.3	668.5	239.5	281.0	11.5	0.7	Iran (Islamic Rep. of) [7]
9.6	42.8	42.3	65.4	110.8	656.6	213.1	153.7	17.6	0.7	Iran (Rép. islamique d') [7]
180.3	1 938.4	243.6	367.7	1 249.4	665.1	259.2	291.3	6.6	0.8	
12.8	37.6	37.9	70.0	104.1	656.0	201.5	150.3	21.3	0.0	
194.0	2 021.0	243.0	444.0	1 216.0	618.0	243.0	303.0	5.0	1.0	
17.0	46.0	41.0	77.0	116.0	601.0	204.0	140.0	14.0	1.0	
52.9	606.7	19.8	35.2	656.5	275.7	106.2	282.9	0.6	3.8	Iraq
...	9.8	7.1	5.4	70.9	280.3	40.0	29.8	0.8	0.9	Iraq
102.7	683.7	18.2	239.2	630.9	260.8	155.0	477.8	...	...	
2.6	23.9	8.2	46.7	46.7	352.1	41.8	43.0	...	...	
60.3	595.2	11.9	32.2	904.5	339.5	162.6	543.2	6.2	6.3	
2.3	12.9	8.9	2.9	98.8	347.3	55.6	75.3	3.5	1.0	
54.0	128.0[34]	42.0[30]	5.0	54.0	39.0	41.0	13.0	1.0	...	Ireland [4,31]
66.0	39.0	55.0[30]	4.0	53.0	108.0	189.0	31.0	7.0	...	Irlande [4,31]
53.0	126.0[34]	44.0[30]	5.0	55.0	40.0	43.0	12.0	1.0	...	
67.0	39.0	48.0[30]	4.0	51.0	110.0	192.0	31.0	6.0	...	
50.0	128.0[34]	41.0[30]	6.0	54.0	36.0	44.0	13.0	1.0	...	
60.0	39.0	51.0[30]	4.0	49.0	107.0	192.0	30.0	6.0	...	
77.0	128.0	42.0	239.0	68.0	85.0	66.0	71.0	5.0	...	Israel [4]
55.0	57.0	68.0	174.0	64.0	272.0	223.0	71.0	47.0	...	Israël [4]
73.0	131.0	45.0	248.0	76.0	90.0	66.0	76.0	6.0	...	
61.0	60.0	71.0	181.0	59.0	278.0	238.0	71.0	50.0	...	
79.0	135.0	49.0	253.0	86.0	89.0	66.0	76.0	5.0	...	
60.0	62.0	69.0	177.0	61.0	297.0	241.0	78.0	47.0	...	
574.0	1 244.0[34]	378.0[30]	74.0[68]	941.0	396.0	505.0	300.0	44.0	13.0	Italy [4,31]
593.0	383.0[34]	271.0[30]	59.0[68]	480.0	1 180.0	1 149.0	470.0	427.0	10.0	Italie [4,31]
590.0	1 219.0[34]	378.0[30]	78.0[68]	928.0	369.0	519.0	293.0	50.0	6.0	
601.0	384.0[34]	285.0[30]	62.0[68]	481.0	1 170.0	1 132.0	483.0	494.0	6.0	
607.0	1 268.0[34]	367.0[30]	86.0[68]	949.0	366.0	532.0	281.0	77.0	6.0	
612.0	372.0[34]	288.0[30]	60.0[68]	489.0	1 176.0	1 162.0	452.0	584.0	6.0	
33.0	65.0	7.0	29.0	29.0	15.0	6.0	21.0	12.0	3.0	Jamaica [37]
48.0	18.0	15.0	21.0	26.0	50.0	25.0	35.0	51.0	4.0	Jamaïque [37]
34.0	60.0	8.0	27.0	26.0	16.0	6.0	21.0	10.0	2.0	
45.0	17.0	17.0	21.0	25.0	51.0	23.0	36.0	50.0	2.0	
32.0	59.0	8.0	29.0	27.0	15.0	5.0	19.0	11.0	1.0	
43.0	15.0	16.0	23.0	27.0	51.0	20.0	35.0	47.0	2.0	
1 480.0	4 275.0[73]	803.0[30]	695.0	1 700.0	1 295.0	1 505.0	2 680.0	...	...	Japan [4,71]
2 320.0	1 130.0[73]	850.0[30]	405.0	...	1 570.0	4 700.0	1 950.0	...	...	Japon [4,71]
1 528.0	4 308.0[73]	775.0[30]	695.0	1 680.0	1 290.0	1 578.0	2 663.0	...	...	
2 343.0	1 145.0[73]	848.0[30]	400.0	...	1 585.0	4 948.0	1 883.0	...	...	
1 425.0	4 108.0[73]	750.0[30]	683.0	1 625.0	1 243.0	1 585.0	2 550.0	...	...	
2 230.0	1 078.0[73]	800.0[30]	398.0	...	1 563.0	4 895.0	1 795.0	...	...	
...	77.0[34]	6.0[30]	8.0	32.0	17.0	7.0	8.0	...	...	Latvia [4,31]
20.0	34.0[34]	14.0[30]	...	38.0	76.0	40.0	16.0	...	...	Lettonie [4,31]
6.0	78.0[34]	6.0[30]	10.0	31.0	13.0	6.0	...	...	...	
23.0	33.0[34]	12.0[30]	8.0	32.0	84.0	41.0	14.0	...	...	
...	79.0[34]	7.0[30]	10.0	27.0	18.0	7.0	...	...	...	
22.0	35.0[34]	14.0[30]	9.0	35.0	83.0	41.0	15.0	...	...	

Employment by economic activity *[cont.]*
Total employment and persons employed by ISIC 3 categories (thousands)
Emploi par activité économique *[suite]*
Emploi total et personnes employées par branches de la CITI rév. 3 (milliers)

26

Country or area & Pays ou zone &	Year Année	Sex Sexe	Total employment Emploi total	ISIC Rev. 3 Tabulation categories [+] CITI Rév. 3 Catégories de classement [+]						
				Categ. A Catég. A	Categ. B Catég. B	Categ. C Catég. C	Categ. D Catég. D	Categ. E Catég. E	Categ. F Catég. F	Categ. G Catég. G
Lithuania [4,31] Lituanie [4,31]	2009	M	680.0	79.0[1,13]	...	...	120.0	22.0[18]	107.0	112.0[19]
	2009	F	736.0	51.0[1,13]	...	...	106.0	9.0[18]	15.0	138.0[19]
	2010	M	640.0	74.0[1,13]	...	...	113.0	18.0[18]	81.0	106.0[19]
	2010	F	703.0	48.0[1,13]	...	...	95.0	4.0[18]	12.0	137.0[19]
	2011	M	667.0	71.0[1,13]	...	...	117.0	19.0[18]	84.0	110.0[19]
	2011	F	704.0	46.0[1,13]	...	...	96.0	...	9.0	137.0[19]
Luxembourg [4,31] Luxembourg [4,31]	2009	M	124.0	2.0[1,13]	...	...	11.0	...	11.0	12.0[19]
	2009	F	93.0	1.0[1,13]	...	...	3.0	...	...	9.0[19]
	2010	M	125.0	2.0[1,13]	...	...	10.0	...	12.0	10.0[19]
	2010	F	96.0	1.0[1,13]	...	...	3.0	...	2.0	8.0[19]
	2011	M	127.0	2.0[1,13]	...	...	11.0	...	13.0	11.0[19]
	2011	F	97.0	1.0[1,13]	...	...	2.0	...	...	9.0[19]
Madagascar [22,74] Madagascar [22,74]	2003	M	4 135.7	3 110.1	61.8	4.5	227.0	18.1	54.6	167.7
	2003	F	3 962.8	3 118.4	25.8	9.7	222.3	0.5	6.0	252.9
	2005	M	4 841.8	3 875.7	68.1	10.4	205.3	21.4	12.0	173.9
	2005	F	4 728.6	3 869.6	30.9	8.5	62.2	6.1	0.9	296.6
Malaysia [5,65] Malaisie [5,65]	2006	M	6 618.6	1 013.9	123.2	35.9	1 270.4	63.4	834.4	1 081.0
	2006	F	3 656.8	361.4	5.0	6.1	812.4	12.0	74.5	569.6
	2007	M	6 747.1	1 064.5	115.4	33.7	1 196.6	52.0	854.5	1 120.2
	2007	F	3 791.0	372.8	5.4	5.7	780.7	8.8	68.0	592.0
	2008	M	6 851.1	1 027.5	117.4	44.6	1 182.6	50.1	914.7	1 119.5
	2008	F	3 808.5	338.2	4.7	9.8	762.2	10.3	83.4	609.9
Maldives [40] Maldives [40]	2000	M	57.4[43]	1.1[43]	9.2[43]	0.4[43]	4.3[43]	1.0[43]	3.6[43]	4.8[43]
	2000	F	28.9[43]	1.4[43]	0.1[43]	^0.0[43]	6.8[43]	0.1[43]	0.1[43]	1.0[43]
	2006[4]	M	69.7	1.5	8.2	0.3	6.8	1.1	5.7	7.4
	2006[4]	F	40.5	2.7	0.2	^0.0	12.5	0.2	0.2	4.3
Mali [4] Mali [4]	2004	M	1 388.3	657.7	33.3	8.4	136.1	5.1	97.5	266.1
	2004	F	982.5	291.7	2.0	3.0	136.4	0.0	4.7	402.1
Malta [4,31] Malte [4,31]	2009	M	107.0	2.0[1,13]	...	...	18.0	3.0	11.0	17.0[19]
	2009	F	54.0	^0.0[1,13]	...	...	5.0	0.2	1.0	8.0[19]
	2010	M	108.0	2.0[1,13]	...	...	18.0	2.0	11.0	18.0[19]
	2010	F	56.0	^0.0[1,13]	...	...	6.0	0.5	1.0	8.0[19]
	2011	M	110.0	...	...	...	19.0	...	11.0	16.0[19]
	2011	F	58.0	...	...	...	6.0	...	1.0	9.0[19]
Mauritius [58] Maurice [58]	2009	M	342.0	...	...	54.0	...	...	54.0	47.0
	2009	F	183.0	...	...	41.0	...	...	2.0	27.0
	2010	M	346.0	...	...	52.0	54.0	...	56.0	46.0
	2010	F	190.0	...	...	38.0	37.0	...	2.0	29.0
	2011	M	344.0	...	...	51.0	51.0	...	55.0	50.0
	2011	F	193.0	...	...	38.0	38.0	...	2.0	33.0
Mexico [37,76] Mexique [37,76]	2006	M	26 597.9	5 141.3	157.2	147.9	4 357.5	150.2	3 352.0	5 380.2
	2006	F	15 599.9	724.4	10.1	16.2	2 721.2	36.1	100.5	4 214.7
	2007	M	26 841.0	4 938.0	134.4	164.8	4 400.5	182.4	3 473.8	5 389.5
	2007	F	16 066.0	692.1	7.9	21.1	2 729.2	38.0	112.0	4 431.4
	2008	M	27 401.7	4 971.8	121.0	162.3	4 448.3	174.1	3 522.1	5 483.6
	2008	F	16 465.0	657.1	8.7	20.9	2 779.8	32.1	119.1	4 490.8
Mongolia [57,58] Mongolie [57,58]	2006	M	491.8	207.0[1]	...	26.8	21.4	16.3	31.4	64.5
	2006	F	518.1	184.4[1]	...	15.1	25.6	13.7	24.9	96.1
	2007	M	504.2	204.6[1]	...	29.5	21.9	18.2	34.2	65.7
	2007	F	519.9	181.0[1]	...	14.6	26.0	12.9	25.8	96.5
	2008	M	512.7	200.6[1]	...	29.9	22.7	18.2	38.2	66.9
	2008	F	529.0	177.0[1]	...	16.6	24.8	11.9	28.6	102.8
Montenegro [4] Monténégro [4]	2009	M	122.0	9.0[1]	...	18.0[54]	...	4.0	13.0	22.0
	2009	F	91.0	5.0[1]	...	6.0[54]	...	1.0	...	24.0
	2010	M	119.0	7.0[1]	...	18.0[54]	...	4.0	12.0	22.0
	2010	F	89.0	4.0[1]	...	6.0[54]	...	2.0	...	25.0
	2011[31]	M	110.0	7.0[1]	...	...	11.0	7.3[18]	10.0	20.0
	2011[31]	F	85.0	4.0[1]	...	0.3	5.0	1.0[18]	...	23.0

	ISIC Rev. 3 Tabulation categories [+]									
	CITI Rév. 3 Catégories de classement [+]									
Categ. H Catég. H	Categ. I Catég. I	Categ. J Catég. J	Categ. K Catég. K	Categ. L Catég.L	Categ. M Catég. M	Categ. N Catég. N	Categ. O Catég. O	Categ. P Catég. P	Categ. Q Catég. Q	Country or area [&] Pays ou zone [&]
6.0	81.0[34]	5.0[30]	6.0	42.0	28.0	11.0	8.0	...	...	Lithuania [4,31]
29.0	35.0[34]	17.0[30]	6.0	43.0	121.0	81.0	20.0	...	...	Lituanie [4,31]
7.0	81.0[34]	...	7.0	40.0	30.0	13.0	9.0	...	...	
26.0	34.0[34]	17.0[30]	7.0	42.0	118.0	79.0	18.0	...	...	
7.0	92.0[34]	...	7.0	40.0	32.0	12.0	12.0	...	...	
28.0	37.0[34]	15.0[30]	7.0	43.0	115.0	80.0	19.0	...	...	
4.0	15.0[34]	17.0[30]	...	15.0	7.0	7.0	1.0	0.2	6.0	Luxembourg [4,31]
3.0	3.0[34]	11.0[30]	...	9.0	11.0	16.0	3.0	4.0	5.0	Luxembourg [4,31]
3.0	14.0[34]	16.0[30]	...	16.0	7.0	5.0	...	0.1	6.0	
3.0	4.0[34]	11.0[30]	...	10.0	11.0	16.0	2.0	5.0	6.0	
4.0	14.0[34]	17.0[30]	...	17.0	6.0	5.0	1.0	0.2	7.0	
4.0	4.0[34]	11.0[30]	...	9.0	12.0	17.0	2.0	4.0	7.0	
21.0	108.1	4.4[25]	...	144.3	33.1	8.8	172.3	...	...	Madagascar [22,74]
26.7	9.1	1.3[25]	...	61.3	33.1	5.6	190.2	...	...	Madagascar [22,74]
30.5	80.8	2.7	...	133.6	18.5	5.1	203.8	...	...	
33.5	5.4	1.4	...	68.8	26.0	4.8	313.9	...	...	
385.5	449.9	120.5	317.8	486.5	209.7	70.6	135.2	19.6	1.0	Malaysia [5,65]
335.8	89.8	121.8	190.6	187.6	390.4	152.6	111.9	235.0	0.2	Malaisie [5,65]
397.7	450.2	142.2	343.5	514.6	221.7	74.9	144.9	19.5	1.0	
363.0	88.0	140.0	214.7	201.5	411.0	164.0	121.7	253.2	0.7	
403.4	487.0	134.2	342.7	536.4	226.1	76.2	158.4	29.4	0.9	
380.2	96.3	141.8	210.6	214.7	430.4	176.5	115.8	223.6	0.2	
9.2[43]	7.2[43]	1.1[25,43]	...	9.7[4,75]	...	...	...	...	...	Maldives [40]
0.5[43]	0.7[43]	0.6[25,43]	...	8.4[4,75]	...	...	...	...	...	Maldives [40]
10.6	6.2	0.3	0.9	11.7	2.7	1.3	2.1	...	0.1	
1.5	0.9	0.3	0.3	4.3	7.1	2.8	1.1	...	0.1	
1.4	51.8	4.4	3.5	33.3	35.6	11.4	23.8	18.8	...	Mali [4]
6.3	3.5	0.0	0.6	6.6	18.3	9.5	11.5	85.1	0.9	Mali [4]
9.0	13.0[34]	3.0[30]	...	10.0	5.0	5.0	1.0	...	...	Malta [4,31]
5.0	3.0[34]	4.0[30]	...	5.0	9.0	7.0	2.0	...	...	Malte [4,31]
9.0	12.0[34]	3.0[30]	...	10.0	5.0	6.0	1.0	...	...	
4.0	1.0[34]	4.0[30]	...	4.0	9.0	8.0	2.0	...	...	
9.0	13.0[34]	3.0[30]	...	10.0	5.0	6.0	...	...	...	
4.0	3.0[34]	4.0[30]	...	5.0	10.0	8.0	2.0	...	...	
...	...	...	...	...	...	...	...	...	...	Mauritius [58]
...	...	...	...	...	...	...	...	...	...	Maurice [58]
...	...	...	...	...	...	...	...	...	...	
...	...	...	...	...	...	...	...	...	...	
...	...	...	...	...	...	...	...	...	...	
...	...	...	...	...	...	...	...	...	...	
1 041.9	1 802.8	190.8	1 245.0	1 329.6	846.2	366.4	736.9	142.9	0.9	Mexico [37,76]
1 473.1	198.6	171.7	680.2	702.5	1 406.2	794.9	632.5	1 613.5	1.9	Mexique [37,76]
1 142.4	1 742.0	215.8	1 322.3	1 316.2	910.2	372.3	781.5	144.6	3.1	
1 528.1	201.0	187.8	727.3	725.1	1 409.2	840.3	592.4	1 713.7	4.1	
1 177.4	1 820.8	209.3	1 378.2	1 386.9	916.9	411.4	837.3	151.2	3.5	
1 659.3	213.5	196.6	811.0	785.1	1 409.1	841.5	632.1	1 700.6	0.3	
10.3	25.8	6.8	6.0	26.2	20.4	12.4	11.8	5.0	...	Mongolia [57,58]
20.7	15.4	10.0	6.0	20.7	41.6	26.9	11.1	5.6	...	Mongolie [57,58]
10.8	28.8	7.1	6.8	27.3	20.9	12.7	10.3	5.4	...	
21.6	15.3	10.3	7.7	21.2	43.9	27.5	9.4	6.2	...	
11.9	30.2	7.9	5.8	29.0	21.6	13.9	10.0	5.9	...	
22.6	16.1	11.9	6.2	21.9	44.6	28.4	9.7	5.9	...	
9.0	13.0	...	4.0	11.0	4.0	3.0	10.0[77]	...	...	Montenegro [4]
9.0	5.0	...	3.0	9.0	9.0	10.0	7.0[77]	...	...	Monténégro [4]
8.0	14.0	...	5.0	11.0	5.0	2.0	10.0[77]	...	...	
10.0	...	3.0	3.0	8.0	9.0	10.0	6.0[77]	...	...	
8.0	11.0[34]	...	...	11.0	4.0	3.0	...	...	...	
6.0	2.0[34]	...	...	9.0	...	7.0	...	...	...	

Employment by economic activity *[cont.]*
Total employment and persons employed by ISIC 3 categories (thousands)
Emploi par activité économique *[suite]*
Emploi total et personnes employées par branches de la CITI rév. 3 (milliers)

26

Country or area & Pays ou zone &	Year Année	Sex Sexe	Total employment Emploi total	ISIC Rev. 3 Tabulation categories + CITI Rév. 3 Catégories de classement +						
				Categ. A Catég. A	Categ. B Catég. B	Categ. C Catég. C	Categ. D Catég. D	Categ. E Catég. E	Categ. F Catég. F	Categ. G Catég. G
Morocco[4] Maroc[4]	2006	M	7 233.3	2 651.8[1]	...	39.3	760.8	39.2	783.1	1 461.6[29]
	2006	F	2 694.4	1 651.6[1]	...	0.6	381.2	3.6	6.5	140.8[29]
	2007	M	7 323.7	2 596.3[1]	...	873.1[78]	...	...	832.4	1 321.6[29]
	2007	F	2 732.6	1 638.8[1]	...	405.9[78]	...	...	6.4	113.7[29]
	2008	M	7 453.5	2 547.8[1]	...	891.1[78]	...	...	897.7	1 342.2[29]
	2008	F	2 735.8	1 620.5[1]	...	416.1[78]	...	...	6.0	114.8[29]
Namibia[80] Namibie[80]	2000	M	226.8	69.8	4.7	3.2	11.4	3.7	20.7	17.2
	2000	F	205.0	56.7	3.1	0.7	11.6	0.5	1.0	21.7
	2004	M	216.7	65.0	7.9	5.9	12.1	5.0	18.3	27.0
	2004	F	168.7	37.6	4.8	1.7	11.7	1.1	1.3	26.9
Nepal Népal	1999[4]	M	4 736.0	3 164.0	12.0	6.0	366.0	24.0	292.0	283.0
	1999[4]	F	4 727.0	4 026.0	1.0	2.0	186.0	2.0	52.0	125.0
	2001[7,81]	M	5 606.8	3 370.6	7.2	10.3	457.0	33.2	235.3	521.6
	2001[7,81]	F	4 293.4	3 125.6	1.2	5.7	415.3	115.0	51.1	342.1
Netherlands[4,31] Pays-Bas[4,31]	2009	M	4 648.0	155.0[1,13]	...	10.0	651.0	57.0[18]	449.0	601.0[19]
	2009	F	3 948.0	64.0[1,13]	...	1.0	196.0	18.0[18]	45.0	545.0[19]
	2010	M	4 526.0	167.0[1,13]	...	8.0	619.0	54.0[18]	415.0	566.0[19]
	2010	F	3 844.0	66.0[1,13]	...	1.0	182.0	15.0[18]	41.0	530.0[19]
	2011	M	4 499.0	150.0[1,13]	...	6.0	590.0	52.0[18]	397.0	567.0[19]
	2011	F	3 870.0	59.0[1,13]	...	1.0	176.0	14.0[18]	41.0	534.0[19]
Netherlands Antilles[4,11,82] Antilles néerlandaises[4,11,82]	2006	MF	52.1	0.5[1]	...	^0.0	3.5	0.8	3.9	9.5
	2007	MF	54.0	0.7[1]	...	0.1	3.8	0.8	4.0	9.2
	2008	MF	56.5	0.6[1]	...	0.1	3.9	0.8	5.1	9.8
New Caledonia[37] Nouvelle-Calédonie[37]	2006	MF	73.5	2.1[1]	...	1.1	6.9	0.8	6.9	8.7
	2007	MF	77.5	2.2[1]	...	1.2	7.4	0.8	7.6	9.0
	2008	MF	82.1	2.2[1]	...	1.2	8.2	0.8	8.1	9.4

Country or area & Pays ou zone &	Year Année	Sex Sexe	Total employment	Categ. A	Categ. B	Categ. C	Categ. D	Categ. E	Categ. F	Categ. G
Nepal Népal	1999[4]	M	4 736.0	3 164.0	12.0	6.0	366.0	24.0	292.0	283.0
	1999[4]	F	4 727.0	4 026.0	1.0	2.0	186.0	2.0	52.0	125.0
	2001[7,81]	M	5 606.8	3 370.6	7.2	10.3	457.0	33.2	235.3	521.6
	2001[7,81]	F	4 293.4	3 125.6	1.2	5.7	415.3	115.0	51.1	342.1
Netherlands[4,31] Pays-Bas[4,31]	2009	M	4 648.0	155.0[1,13]	...	10.0	651.0	57.0[18]	449.0	601.0[19]
	2009	F	3 948.0	64.0[1,13]	...	1.0	196.0	18.0[18]	45.0	545.0[19]
	2010	M	4 526.0	167.0[1,13]	...	8.0	619.0	54.0[18]	415.0	566.0[19]
	2010	F	3 844.0	66.0[1,13]	...	1.0	182.0	15.0[18]	41.0	530.0[19]
	2011	M	4 499.0	150.0[1,13]	...	6.0	590.0	52.0[18]	397.0	567.0[19]
	2011	F	3 870.0	59.0[1,13]	...	1.0	176.0	14.0[18]	41.0	534.0[19]
Netherlands Antilles[4,11,82] Antilles néerlandaises[4,11,82]	2006	MF	52.1	0.5[1]	...	^0.0	3.5	0.8	3.9	9.5
	2007	MF	54.0	0.7[1]	...	0.1	3.8	0.8	4.0	9.2
	2008	MF	56.5	0.6[1]	...	0.1	3.9	0.8	5.1	9.8
New Caledonia[37] Nouvelle-Calédonie[37]	2006	MF	73.5	2.1[1]	...	1.1	6.9	0.8	6.9	8.7
	2007	MF	77.5	2.2[1]	...	1.2	7.4	0.8	7.6	9.0
	2008	MF	82.1	2.2[1]	...	1.2	8.2	0.8	8.1	9.4

Country or area & Pays ou zone &	Year Année	Sex Sexe	Total employment	Categ. A	Categ. B	Categ. C	Categ. D	Categ. E	Categ. F	Categ. G
New Zealand[4,12] Nouvelle-Zélande[4,12]	2009	M	1 149.0	99.0[1,13]	...	6.0[14]	177.0	12.0[83]	158.0	210.0[15,29,84]
	2009	F	1 016.0	44.0[1,13]	...	...	73.0	3.0[83]	23.0	226.0[15,29,84]
	2010	M	1 161.0	105.0[1,13]	...	6.0[14]	176.0	13.0[83]	156.0	214.0[15,29,84]
	2010	F	1 019.0	45.0[1,13]	...	...	72.0	4.0[83]	23.0	226.0[15,29,84]
	2011	M	1 178.0	105.0[1,13]	...	7.0[14]	179.0	12.0[83]	151.0	218.0[15,29,84]
	2011	F	1 038.0	48.0[1,13]	...	^0.0[14]	71.0	5.0[83]	21.0	225.0[15,29,84]
Nicaragua[7] Nicaragua[7]	2004	M	1 239.3	509.2	11.0	4.8	135.5	6.1	94.3	199.1
	2004	F	733.8	77.2	0.6	0.8	119.3	0.7	1.0	193.5
	2005	M	1 296.6	523.6	12.2	4.2	157.5	7.4	90.9	201.0
	2005	F	784.3	64.5	0.9	1.2	144.8	1.8	1.7	218.3
	2006	M	1 303.5	528.7	14.5	5.9	153.1	5.3	99.1	195.6
	2006	F	786.3	64.9	1.0	0.8	136.1	1.2	1.7	213.5

ISIC Rev. 3 Tabulation categories [+]
CITI Rév. 3 Catégories de classement [+]

Categ. H Catég. H	Categ. I Catég. I	Categ. J Catég. J	Categ. K Catég. K	Categ. L Catég.L	Categ. M Catég. M	Categ. N Catég. N	Categ. O Catég. O	Categ. P Catég. P	Categ. Q Catég. Q	Country or area [&] Pays ou zone [&]
...	367.7	105.0[25]	...	1 016.2[75]	...	...	...	...	...	Morocco [4]
...	27.1	47.4[25]	...	433.3[75]	...	...	...	...	...	Maroc [4]
...	371.9	1 317.6[79]	...	...	...	...	...	...	...	
...	29.9	534.7[79]	...	...	...	...	...	...	...	
...	419.3	1 341.6[79]	...	...	...	...	...	...	...	
...	31.9	542.1[79]	...	...	...	...	...	...	...	
3.0	12.2	2.5	17.9	15.4	11.7	3.0	24.3	4.8	0.2	Namibia [80]
4.7	2.1	2.4	21.4	9.0	18.8	10.1	22.0	17.5	0.2	Namibie [80]
5.9	12.7	3.5	5.3	20.2	12.3	3.5	7.5	4.1	0.1	
7.2	3.1	4.1	4.1	10.5	18.9	10.5	5.2	20.0	0.0	
63.0	130.0	17.0	25.0	64.0	126.0	26.0	51.0	80.0	6.0	Nepal
52.0	6.0	2.0	6.0	6.0	37.0	7.0	6.0	209.0	1.0	Népal
79.1	155.8	39.9	25.9	265.5	169.1	43.6	62.0	62.9	54.6	
41.7	5.8	6.8	4.1	35.6	59.3	18.2	10.6	42.3	3.7	
160.0	547.0[34]	130.0[30]	38.0	340.0	229.0	253.0	61.0	0.3	...	Netherlands [4,31]
175.0	180.0[34]	111.0[30]	34.0	228.0	363.0	1 125.0	123.0	6.0	...	Pays-Bas [4,31]
164.0	524.0[34]	119.0[30]	36.0	328.0	212.0	237.0	59.0	0.2	...	
174.0	161.0[34]	98.0[30]	26.0	214.0	358.0	1 123.0	117.0	4.0	...	
163.0	517.0[34]	125.0[30]	35.0	331.0	210.0	233.0	49.0	1.0	...	
179.0	161.0[34]	95.0[30]	25.0	212.0	354.0	1 142.0	113.0	3.0	...	
4.2	3.1	3.9	5.2	4.8	2.6	4.4	3.6	2.0	0.1	Netherlands Antilles [4,11,82]
4.4	3.5	4.1	5.6	5.3	2.8	4.6	3.3	1.8	0.1	Antilles néerlandaises [4,11,82]
4.5	4.1	4.1	6.0	4.7	2.5	4.3	3.6	2.1	^0.0	
3.6	4.9	1.7	5.3	...	0.2	1.6	2.1	3.7	...	New Caledonia [37]
4.0	4.9	1.7	5.5	...	0.2	1.7	2.3	3.7	...	Nouvelle-Calédonie [37]
4.3	5.3	1.8	6.2	...	0.2	1.8	2.6	3.7	...	
63.0	130.0	17.0	25.0	64.0	126.0	26.0	51.0	80.0	6.0	Nepal
52.0	6.0	2.0	6.0	6.0	37.0	7.0	6.0	209.0	1.0	Népal
79.1	155.8	39.9	25.9	265.5	169.1	43.6	62.0	62.9	54.6	
41.7	5.8	6.8	4.1	35.6	59.3	18.2	10.6	42.3	3.7	
160.0	547.0[34]	130.0[30]	38.0	340.0	229.0	253.0	61.0	0.3	...	Netherlands [4,31]
175.0	180.0[34]	111.0[30]	34.0	228.0	363.0	1 125.0	123.0	6.0	...	Pays-Bas [4,31]
164.0	524.0[34]	119.0[30]	36.0	328.0	212.0	237.0	59.0	0.2	...	
174.0	161.0[34]	98.0[30]	26.0	214.0	358.0	1 123.0	117.0	4.0	...	
163.0	517.0[34]	125.0[30]	35.0	331.0	210.0	233.0	49.0	1.0	...	
179.0	161.0[34]	95.0[30]	25.0	212.0	354.0	1 142.0	113.0	3.0	...	
4.2	3.1	3.9	5.2	4.8	2.6	4.4	3.6	2.0	0.1	Netherlands Antilles [4,11,82]
4.4	3.5	4.1	5.6	5.3	2.8	4.6	3.3	1.8	0.1	Antilles néerlandaises [4,11,82]
4.5	4.1	4.1	6.0	4.7	2.5	4.3	3.6	2.1	^0.0	
3.6	4.9	1.7	5.3	...	0.2	1.6	2.1	3.7	...	New Caledonia [37]
4.0	4.9	1.7	5.5	...	0.2	1.7	2.3	3.7	...	Nouvelle-Calédonie [37]
4.3	5.3	1.8	6.2	...	0.2	1.8	2.6	3.7	...	
...	91.0[73]	30.0[30]	21.0	...	51.0[17]	38.0	5.0	...	...	New Zealand [4,12]
...	44.0[73]	39.0[30]	18.0	...	133.0[17]	182.0	3.0	...	...	Nouvelle-Zélande [4,12]
...	91.0[73]	26.0[30]	19.0	...	53.0[17]	40.0	5.0	...	...	
...	43.0[73]	37.0[30]	18.0	...	136.0[17]	183.0	3.0	...	...	
...	96.0[73]	27.0[30]	20.0	...	54.0[17]	42.0	4.0	...	...	
...	44.0[73]	39.0[30]	17.0	...	147.0[17]	188.0	3.0	...	...	
20.9	74.6	8.1	33.9	44.5	26.8	19.5	32.3	16.7	2.1	Nicaragua [7]
53.0	5.4	8.7	10.0	23.8	59.7	36.4	52.6	89.6	1.5	Nicaragua [7]
16.3	80.6	8.8	40.4	47.4	28.6	18.7	34.4	18.4	5.9	
45.4	7.5	8.3	12.6	23.4	60.4	32.6	57.3	100.3	3.3	
18.1	82.3	7.5	42.1	44.6	28.5	19.6	33.0	22.6	3.1	
53.9	6.7	8.4	11.9	29.1	66.0	34.7	56.2	94.8	5.0	

26

Employment by economic activity *[cont.]*
Total employment and persons employed by ISIC 3 categories (thousands)
Emploi par activité économique *[suite]*
Emploi total et personnes employées par branches de la CITI rév. 3 (milliers)

Country or area [&] Pays ou zone [&]	Year Année	Sex Sexe	Total employment Emploi total	ISIC Rev. 3 Tabulation categories [+] CITI Rév. 3 Catégories de classement [+]						
				Categ. A Catég. A	Categ. B Catég. B	Categ. C Catég. C	Categ. D Catég. D	Categ. E Catég. E	Categ. F Catég. F	Categ. G Catég. G
Norway [31,58]	2009	M	1 309.0	53.0[1,13]	...	36.0	195.0	24.0[18]	166.0	183.0[19]
Norvège [31,58]	2009	F	1 190.0	14.0[1,13]	...	10.0	53.0	7.0[18]	14.0	163.0[19]
	2010	M	1 315.0	52.0[1,13]	...	37.0	183.0	24.0[18]	165.0	184.0[19]
	2010	F	1 186.0	12.0[1,13]	...	8.0	54.0	6.0[18]	15.0	162.0[19]
	2011	M	1 332.0	49.0[1,13]	...	43.0	180.0	26.0[18]	175.0	183.0[19]
	2011	F	1 204.0	11.0[1,13]	...	11.0	58.0	6.0[18]	15.0	166.0[19]
Occupied Palestinian Terr. [4,85]	2006	M	546.0	64.9	0.9	2.2	70.3	2.4	73.7	106.2
Terr. palestinien occupé [4,85]	2006	F	120.4	41.2	...	...	10.2	0.1	0.2	8.5
	2007	M	538.0	56.6	1.5	1.5	69.9	2.2	72.4	107.1
	2007	F	127.6	45.9	...	...	12.0	...	0.3	9.3
	2008	M	525.7	52.4	0.7	1.4	...	2.7	70.1	103.4
	2008	F	121.3	33.4	...	^0.0	...	0.1	0.6	8.1
Oman [5,43,86]	2000	M	243.1	8.9	7.2	7.8	9.4	1.1	7.8	14.2
Oman [5,43,86]	2000	F	38.6	2.0	^0.0	0.7	4.5	^0.0	0.2	2.4
Palau [58]	2007	MF	12.1	0.2	0.2	^0.0	0.4	...	1.2	1.9
Palaos [58]	2008	MF	11.7	0.1	0.1	^0.0	0.4	...	1.0	1.8
Panama [4]	2008[45]	M	879.0	201.0	10.0	3.0	75.0	6.0	134.0	152.0
Panama [4]	2008[45]	F	517.0	37.0	^0.0	^0.0	50.0	2.0	4.0	107.0
	2009	M	903.0	204.0[1]	11.0	3.0	80.0	7.0[18]	136.0	146.0[19]
	2009	F	539.0	39.0[1]	1.0	^0.0	50.0	2.0[18]	5.0	110.0[19]
	2011[31]	M	916.0	206.0[1,13]	...	2.0	70.0	11.0[18]	145.0	147.0[19]
	2011[31]	F	565.0	40.0[1,13]	...	0.3	45.0	4.0[18]	8.0	117.0[19]
Papua New Guinea [7,63]										
Papouasie-Nvl-Guinée [7,63]	2000	MF	2 345.0	1 666.0	30.0	9.3	25.6	2.2	48.3	353.2
Paraguay [7,87]	2007	M	1 653.6	551.2[1]	...	8.6	226.8	8.0	153.9	355.4[29]
Paraguay [7,87]	2007	F	1 062.8	249.4[1]	...	...	92.5	0.8	1.0	284.1[29]
	2008	M	1 726.4	537.2[1]	...	6.4	238.4	8.8	173.5	364.4[29]
	2008	F	1 084.1	208.0[1]	...	0.2	101.8	2.0	0.6	309.5[29]
Peru [37,56]	2006	M	4 821.9	567.1	41.3	89.0	730.5	21.4	420.0	795.2
Pérou [37,56]	2006	F	3 872.1	290.2	0.7	5.1	405.2	4.9	11.6	1 240.0
	2007	M	5 015.0	468.2	58.0	88.8	800.7	19.0	459.9	791.9
	2007	F	4 182.8	230.3	0.7	8.4	491.6	2.0	9.9	1 295.7
	2008	M	5 142.8	473.7	57.2	91.7	805.6	29.8	494.7	751.4
	2008	F	4 302.7	237.0	1.7	7.1	511.0	6.0	17.3	1 350.0
Philippines [4,88]	2006	M	20 013.0	7 382.0	1 327.0	124.0	1 653.0	107.0	1 648.0	2 464.0
Philippines [4,88]	2006	F	12 622.0	2 872.0	101.0	14.0	1 400.0	21.0	29.0	3 738.0
	2007	M	20 542.0	7 437.0	1 327.0	135.0	1 684.0	112.0	1 742.0	2 526.0
	2007	F	13 018.0	2 905.0	117.0	14.0	1 375.0	23.0	36.0	3 828.0
	2008	M	20 959.0	7 666.0	1 316.0	146.0	1 622.0	110.0	1 798.0	2 565.0
	2008	F	13 129.0	2 937.0	110.0	12.0	1 304.0	20.0	36.0	3 880.0
Poland [4,31]	2009	M	8 722.0	1 165.0[1,13]	...	200.0	2 031.0	269.0[18]	1 232.0	1 068.0[19]
Pologne [4,31]	2009	F	7 146.0	942.0[1,13]	...	21.0	1 028.0	77.0[18]	76.0	1 264.0[19]
	2010	M	8 746.0	1 150.0[1,13]	...	210.0	1 975.0	262.0[18]	1 205.0	1 076.0[19]
	2010	F	7 214.0	900.0[1,13]	...	20.0	986.0	74.0[18]	80.0	1 300.0[19]
	2011	M	8 892.0	1 175.0[1,13]	...	226.0	2 017.0	264.0[18]	1 232.0	1 069.0[19]
	2011	F	7 239.0	870.0[1,13]	...	29.0	1 008.0	71.0[18]	86.0	1 308.0[19]
Portugal [4,31]	2009	M	2 688.0	294.0[1,13]	...	16.0	505.0	40.0[18]	479.0	419.0[19]
Portugal [4,31]	2009	F	2 367.0	271.0[1,13]	...	1.0	346.0	11.0[18]	27.0	344.0[19]
	2010	M	2 645.0	293.0[1,13]	...	18.0	491.0	38.0[18]	451.0	414.0[19]
	2010	F	2 334.0	249.0[1,13]	...	2.0	335.0	2.0[18]	31.0	323.0[19]
	2011	M	2 575.0	284.0[1,13]	...	17.0	486.0	42.0[18]	414.0	380.0[19]
	2011	F	2 263.0	195.0[1,13]	...	2.0	328.0	7.0[18]	26.0	329.0[19]

Employment by economic activity *[cont.]*
Total employment and persons employed by ISIC 3 categories (thousands)

26 Emploi par activité économique *[suite]*
Emploi total et personnes employées par branches de la CITI rév. 3 (milliers)

ISIC Rev. 3 Tabulation categories[+]
CITI Rév. 3 Catégories de classement[+]

Categ. H / Catég. H	Categ. I / Catég. I	Categ. J / Catég. J	Categ. K / Catég. K	Categ. L / Catég.L	Categ. M / Catég. M	Categ. N / Catég. N	Categ. O / Catég. O	Categ. P / Catég. P	Categ. Q / Catég. Q	Country or area [&] / Pays ou zone [&]
25.0	170.0[34]	28.0[30]	17.0	77.0	70.0	91.0	19.0	...	...	Norway [31,58]
43.0	58.0[34]	26.0[30]	9.0	71.0	136.0	428.0	31.0	...	...	Norvège [31,58]
27.0	175.0[34]	28.0[30]	16.0	77.0	76.0	96.0	15.0	0.3	...	
42.0	57.0[34]	24.0[30]	8.0	72.0	132.0	434.0	32.0	2.3	...	
27.0	182.0[34]	29.0[30]	13.0	74.0	77.0	103.0	14.0	...	...	
40.0	58.0[34]	23.0[30]	7.0	71.0	135.0	445.0	34.0	...	...	
13.1	37.2	3.3	8.9	92.7	34.2	15.1	15.6	0.2	5.3	Occupied Palestinian Terr. [4,85]
0.4	1.1	1.2	2.3	6.2	33.5	9.3	3.8	0.2	2.0	Terr. palestinien occupé [4,85]
12.9	36.9	3.2	9.6	92.6	34.4	15.9	16.1	^0.0	5.1	
0.5	0.5	1.0	1.8	7.0	33.6	8.6	4.5	0.1	2.3	
18.7	31.3	3.8	...	94.4	32.6	16.7	14.3	0.3	4.6	
0.9	0.8	1.1	...	7.4	38.5	10.6	4.9	0.2	1.8	
2.3	19.5	4.7	1.9	133.6	17.8	5.2	1.2	^0.0	^0.0	Oman [5,43,86]
0.2	0.8	1.4	1.1	3.3	16.0	5.4	0.2	...	0.1	Oman [5,43,86]
1.7	0.9	0.2	0.7	3.0	0.6	0.1	0.3	0.9	^0.0	Palau [58]
1.7	0.9	0.1	0.7	3.0	0.6	0.1	0.3	0.8	^0.0	Palaos [58]
27.0	86.0	11.0	41.0	46.0	25.0	17.0	37.0	8.0	^0.0	Panama [4]
42.0	12.0	17.0	29.0	34.0	48.0	36.0	31.0	67.0	^0.0	Panama [4]
28.0	94.0	10.0[30]	45.0	47.0	23.0	19.0	41.0	8.0	^0.0	
47.0	15.0	17.0[30]	32.0	36.0	49.0	41.0	30.0	63.0	^0.0	
30.0	96.0[34]	13.0[30]	6.0[35]	54.0	27.0	15.0	19.0	9.0	1.0	
44.0	19.0[34]	21.0[30]	4.0[35]	44.0	59.0	41.0	30.0	59.0	1.0	
										Papua New Guinea [7,63]
4.4	24.5	3.7	27.5	32.0	27.1	12.3	31.4	15.5	0.2	Papouasie-Nvl-Guinée [7,63]
...	85.7	65.7[25]	...	198.1[75]	...	...	...	...	...	Paraguay [7,87]
...	15.8	38.6[25]	...	380.3[75]	...	...	...	...	...	Paraguay [7,87]
...	101.5	78.5[25]	...	217.7[75]	...	...	...	...	...	
...	16.9	42.3[25]	...	402.3[75]	...	...	...	...	...	
155.3	670.1	43.2	305.8	276.0	227.3	67.4	382.4	29.1	0.7	Peru [37,56]
475.7	80.6	31.3	121.0	120.4	318.4	133.7	186.4	446.9	...	Pérou [37,56]
174.1	738.0	41.1	316.6	316.1	258.7	86.4	370.5	26.4	0.4	
506.4	102.4	28.3	166.4	121.5	391.6	162.0	216.6	447.9	1.2	
172.7	797.4	51.6	331.2	311.7	248.8	101.0	402.3	21.9	...	
557.4	109.6	40.8	155.2	111.5	392.7	169.5	232.2	401.5	2.2	
402.0	2 329.0	148.0	508.0	927.0	249.0	99.0	405.0	239.0	2.0	Philippines [4,88]
484.0	154.0	196.0	275.0	558.0	750.0	260.0	396.0	1 374.0	...	Philippines [4,88]
409.0	2 428.0	156.0	578.0	950.0	259.0	101.0	434.0	262.0	2.0	
498.0	170.0	203.0	307.0	601.0	776.0	272.0	415.0	1 478.0	...	
436.0	2 425.0	156.0	624.0	1 023.0	269.0	114.0	426.0	262.0	1.0	
518.0	165.0	211.0	329.0	653.0	802.0	277.0	407.0	1 467.0	1.0	
105.0	907.0[34]	131.0[30]	68.0	511.0	269.0	158.0	90.0	3.0	...	Poland [4,31]
224.0	300.0[34]	240.0[30]	88.0	510.0	958.0	723.0	139.0	17.0	...	Pologne [4,31]
111.0	907.0[34]	128.0[30]	77.0	523.0	277.0	170.0	90.0	4.0	...	
239.0	295.0[34]	243.0[30]	97.0	526.0	977.0	765.0	157.0	20.0	...	
117.0	921.0[34]	132.0[30]	69.0	529.0	278.0	169.0	88.0	3.0	...	
238.0	295.0[34]	257.0[30]	101.0	535.0	950.0	755.0	156.0	22.0	...	
119.0	207.0[34]	50.0[30]	15.0	211.0	81.0	50.0	31.0	1.0	...	Portugal [4,31]
176.0	63.0[34]	39.0[30]	19.0	124.0	276.0	272.0	65.0	149.0	...	Portugal [4,31]
114.0	216.0[34]	50.0[30]	12.0	199.0	85.0	59.0	30.0	2.0	...	
178.0	67.0[34]	38.0[30]	15.0	114.0	284.0	290.0	74.0	142.0	...	
115.0	199.0[34]	58.0[30]	13.0	197.0	86.0	71.0	31.0	2.0	...	
176.0	57.0[34]	47.0[30]	12.0	115.0	282.0	296.0	65.0	134.0	...	

Country or area & Pays ou zone &	Year Année	Sex Sexe	Total employment Emploi total	ISIC Rev. 3 Tabulation categories [+] CITI Rév. 3 Catégories de classement [+]						
				Categ. A Catég. A	Categ. B Catég. B	Categ. C Catég. C	Categ. D Catég. D	Categ. E Catég. E	Categ. F Catég. F	Categ. G Catég. G
Qatar [4,11]	2004	M	373.1	10.2	1.8	16.9	39.7	4.2	116.6	52.3
Qatar [4,11]	2004	F	64.5	^0.0	^0.0	1.1	0.4	0.1	0.4	2.1
	2006	M	452.6	12.5	3.2	25.9	62.0	4.4	124.7	67.6
	2006	F	76.7	...	...	1.3	0.7	0.2	0.8	2.3
	2007	M	726.8	15.9	3.6	41.3	71.0	5.1	306.2	98.3
	2007	F	100.8	...	...	2.4	0.9	0.4	1.1	3.3
Republic of Korea [4,71]	2009	M	13 734.0	910.0[1]	...	21.0[14]	2 676.0	81.0[89]	1 557.0	1 968.0[90]
République de Corée [4,71]	2009	F	9 771.0	738.0[1]	...	1.0[14]	1 160.0	15.0[89]	163.0	1 632.0[90]
	2010	M	13 915.0	884.0[1]	...	20.0[14]	2 791.0	67.0[89]	1 587.0	1 946.0[90]
	2010	F	9 914.0	683.0[1]	...	1.0[14]	1 237.0	12.0[89]	166.0	1 634.0[90]
	2011	M	14 153.0	859.0[1]	...	17.0[14]	2 817.0	63.0[89]	1 595.0	2 028.0[90]
	2011	F	10 091.0	683.0[1]	...	1.0[14]	1 274.0	13.0[89]	156.0	1 610.0[90]
Republic of Moldova [4]	2008	M	629.0	212.0[1]	...	...	88.0	...	73.0	...
République de Moldova [4]	2008	F	622.0	177.0[1]	...	...	75.0	...	10.0	...
	2009	M	598.0	188.0[1]	...	...	86.0	...	64.0	...
	2009	F	587.0	146.0[1]	...	...	69.0	...	9.0	...
	2011	M	593.0	183.0[1]	...	...	87.0	...	61.0	...
	2011	F	581.0	140.0[1]	...	...	66.0	...	6.0	...
Romania [4]	2009	M	5 101.0	1 417.0[1,13]	...	87.0	970.0	151.0[18]	658.0	533.0[19]
Roumanie [4]	2009	F	4 143.0	1 272.0[1,13]	...	14.0	781.0	46.0[18]	68.0	624.0[19]
	2010	M	5 111.0	1 486.0[1,13]	...	81.0	941.0	142.0[18]	641.0	512.0[19]
	2010	F	4 128.0	1 294.0[1,13]	...	14.0	706.0	49.0[18]	64.0	622.0[19]
	2011	M	5 026.0	1 370.0[1,13]	...	74.0	962.0	147.0[18]	622.0	526.0[19]
	2011	F	4 112.0	1 243.0[1,13]	...	12.0	710.0	47.0[18]	59.0	639.0[19]
Russian Federation [93]	2009	M	35 059.0	3 648.0[1]	...	1 098.0	6 160.0	1 582.0	4 054.0	...
Fédération de Russie [93]	2009	F	34 226.0	2 192.0[1]	...	279.0	4 346.0	653.0	852.0	...
	2010	M	35 500.0	3 562.0[1]	...	1 129.0	6 238.0	1 630.0	4 231.0	...
	2010	F	34 303.0	1 966.0[1]	...	292.0	4 344.0	658.0	803.0	...
	2011	M	35 989.0	3 548.0[1]	...	1 172.0	6 272.0	1 654.0	4 329.0	...
	2011	F	34 742.0	2 038.0[1]	...	294.0	4 274.0	637.0	769.0	...
Saint Helena [80,95]	2008	M	1.2	0.1	^0.0	^0.0	^0.1	0.1	0.2	0.1
Sainte-Hélène [80,95]	2008	F	1.0	^0.0	^0.0	^0.0	^0.0	...	^0.0	0.2
Saint Lucia [4]	2002	M	32.1	4.4	0.4	...	2.0	0.5	4.6	3.4
Sainte-Lucie [4]	2002	F	26.4	2.3	^0.0	...	2.5	0.1	0.3	5.2
	2003	M	36.5	5.4	0.6	...	2.3	0.5	4.7	4.7
	2003	F	27.4	2.3	^0.0	...	2.3	0.1	0.2	5.7
	2004	M	34.8	5.9	0.7	...	2.3	0.4	4.8	4.4
	2004	F	27.4	2.6	0.1	...	2.4	0.1	0.2	5.4
Samoa [4]	2001	M	35.1	15.4	2.2	...	2.8[96]	0.8	1.6	1.5
Samoa [4]	2001	F	15.2	2.1	0.3	...	4.5[96]	0.1	0.1	1.3
San Marino [4,57]	2006	M	12.2	0.1	...	...	4.4	...	1.6	1.7
Saint-Marin [4,57]	2006	F	8.5	^0.0	...	...	1.8	...	0.1	1.5
	2007	M	12.7	0.1	...	...	4.6	...	1.6	1.8
	2007	F	8.8	^0.0	...	...	1.8	...	0.1	1.6
	2008	M	13.0	0.1	...	...	4.6	...	1.6	1.9
	2008	F	9.0	^0.0	...	...	1.8	...	0.1	1.7
Saudi Arabia [4]	2006[23]	M	6 461.5	295.2[1]	...	102.1	495.7	79.5	835.4	1 200.3
Arabie saoudite [4]	2006[23]	F	1 061.5	4.3[1]	...	0.1	9.4	...	1.5	9.8
	2007	M	6 679.8	328.3[1]	...	97.8	561.4	76.9	865.3	1 239.7
	2007	F	1 075.6	4.6[1]	...	2.0	10.0	0.4	2.6	10.8
	2008	M	6 894.5	342.5[1]	...	102.8	506.3	72.3	883.5	1 285.1
	2008	F	1 092.5	0.5[1]	...	1.5	10.6	^0.0	2.1	9.7

ISIC Rev. 3 Tabulation categories[+]
CITI Rév. 3 Catégories de classement[+]

Categ. H Catég. H	Categ. I Catég. I	Categ. J Catég. J	Categ. K Catég. K	Categ. L Catég.L	Categ. M Catég. M	Categ. N Catég. N	Categ. O Catég. O	Categ. P Catég. P	Categ. Q Catég. Q	Country or area [&] Pays ou zone [&]
9.7	13.1	3.5	11.2	47.3	7.5	5.4	9.0	23.9	1.0	Qatar [4,11]
0.6	2.2	1.3	0.7	6.2	12.4	6.2	1.2	29.4	0.2	Qatar [4,11]
13.9	21.0	4.5	15.1	40.6	7.6	8.2	10.0	29.7	1.5	
1.1	2.8	1.6	0.8	6.4	15.1	8.5	2.0	32.8	0.2	
14.1	32.8	6.5	27.3	45.2	9.5	8.2	10.3	29.0	1.5	
2.1	3.1	2.6	1.1	7.4	16.7	12.9	2.5	43.8	0.2	
643.0	1 153.0[91]	384.0[30]	537.0[92]	661.0	599.0	223.0	629.0	6.0	9.0	Republic of Korea [4,71]
1 294.0	94.0[91]	382.0[30]	407.0[92]	370.0	1 233.0	774.0	583.0	140.0	3.0	République de Corée [4,71]
641.0	1 171.0[91]	416.0[30]	584.0[92]	610.0	590.0	229.0	641.0	7.0	10.0	
1 248.0	109.0[91]	391.0[30]	439.0[92]	350.0	1 209.0	923.0	576.0	143.0	3.0	
632.0	1 213.0[91]	421.0[30]	604.0[92]	622.0	547.0	248.0	667.0	6.0	9.0	
1 221.0	119.0[91]	425.0[30]	482.0[92]	329.0	1 139.0	1 063.0	595.0	147.0	4.0	
87.0[61]	53.0	...	...	75.0[62]	...	...	...	...	...	Republic of Moldova [4]
122.0[61]	18.0	...	...	173.0[62]	...	...	...	...	...	République de Moldova [4]
94.0[61]	51.0	...	...	77.0[62]	...	...	...	...	...	
124.0[61]	17.0	...	...	172.0[62]	...	...	...	...	...	
94.0[61]	51.0	...	...	76.0[62]	...	...	...	...	...	
129.0[61]	16.0	...	...	174.0[62]	...	...	...	...	...	
60.0	441.0[34]	42.0[30]	8.0	303.0	99.0	84.0	51.0	...	...	Romania [4]
105.0	137.0[34]	81.0[30]	...	187.0	287.0	311.0	49.0	20.8	...	Roumanie [4]
73.0	445.0[34]	44.0[30]	10.0	288.0	96.0	83.0	51.0	...	...	
107.0	125.0[34]	88.0[30]	10.0	183.0	289.0	320.0	60.0	35.1	...	
74.0	443.0[34]	51.0[30]	...	286.0	100.0	87.0	56.0	...	...	
112.0	119.0[34]	94.0[30]	11.0	180.0	292.0	314.0	69.0	42.3	...	
4 293.0[61]	4 698.0	2 981.0[25]	...	3 387.0	1 222.0	1 103.0	832.0[94]	...	...	Russian Federation [93]
7 691.0[61]	1 828.0	2 729.0[25]	...	2 171.0	5 284.0	4 376.0	1 827.0[94]	...	...	Fédération de Russie [93]
4 413.0[61]	4 685.0	3 026.0[25]	...	3 436.0	1 219.0	1 091.0	840.0[94]	...	...	
7 829.0[61]	1 815.0	2 733.0[25]	...	2 287.0	5 346.0	4 394.0	1 836.0[94]	...	...	
4 581.0[61]	4 819.0	3 218.0[25]	...	3 263.0	1 196.0	1 085.0	852.0[94]	...	...	
8 133.0[61]	1 841.0	2 864.0[25]	...	2 240.0	5 309.0	4 431.0	1 911.0[94]	...	...	
^0.0	0.2	^0.0	0.1	0.1	^0.0	^0.0	0.1	^0.0	^0.0	Saint Helena [80,95]
^0.0	^0.0	^0.0	0.1	0.1	0.1	0.2	0.1	^0.0	...	Sainte-Hélène [80,95]
2.9	2.4	0.3	0.9	3.2	0.5	0.1	0.9	0.5	...	Saint Lucia [4]
3.3	0.8	0.6	0.7	3.7	1.4	0.2	0.5	1.5	...	Sainte-Lucie [4]
3.3	3.1	0.6	1.1	3.6	0.6	0.1	0.8	0.5	...	
3.4	1.1	0.6	1.0	3.7	1.5	0.5	0.8	1.6	...	
3.0	2.5	0.4	1.5	3.7	0.2	0.1	1.1	0.2	...	
3.7	0.8	0.7	1.1	4.5	0.9	0.3	0.9	1.7	...	
0.8	1.6	0.5	0.2	2.1	0.9	0.3	1.6	2.0	0.2	Samoa [4]
0.8	0.3	0.6	0.1	1.2	1.5	0.5	0.5	0.9	0.3	Samoa [4]
0.1	0.3	0.5	1.5	1.3	0.1	0.4	0.3	...	...	San Marino [4,57]
0.1	0.2	0.4	1.2	1.1	0.5	0.8	0.7	...	...	Saint-Marin [4,57]
0.1	0.3	0.5	1.7	1.7	^0.0	^0.0	0.3	...	...	
0.1	0.2	0.4	1.2	2.3	^0.0	0.1	0.8	...	...	
0.1	0.4	0.5	1.7	1.7	^0.0	0.1	0.3	...	...	
0.1	0.2	0.5	1.3	2.3	^0.0	0.1	0.8	...	...	
239.8	289.5	81.5	245.3	1 394.8	490.2	235.2	162.3	307.0	7.9	Saudi Arabia [4]
1.5	1.8	5.1	7.3	31.2	417.0	90.3	6.9	474.6	0.7	Arabie saoudite [4]
236.8	324.8	77.0	250.1	1 387.1	513.5	244.2	160.5	301.9	14.5	
2.4	7.0	4.6	3.2	34.7	407.2	89.2	7.9	488.8	0.1	
248.5	356.3	82.0	303.2	1 470.7	514.2	274.2	153.6	290.9	8.4	
3.7	1.8	5.7	4.8	29.5	392.9	82.5	7.5	539.1	0.6	

Country or area [&] Pays ou zone [&]	Year Année	Sex Sexe	Total employment Emploi total	ISIC Rev. 3 Tabulation categories[+] CITI Rév. 3 Catégories de classement[+]						
				Categ. A Catég. A	Categ. B Catég. B	Categ. C Catég. C	Categ. D Catég. D	Categ. E Catég. E	Categ. F Catég. F	Categ. G Catég. G
Senegal [4] Sénégal [4]	2006 2006	M F	2 048.1 1 104.8	631.9 354.6	66.5 10.4	11.5 2.6	203.7 41.7	18.5 3.3	179.7 6.9	388.0 397.9
Serbia Serbie	2009 2011[31]	MF MF	2 616.4 2 253.2	623.0[13] 478.0[1]	2.0 ...	27.0 31.0	451.0 387.0	47.0 67.6	137.0 119.0	372.0 301.0[19]
Sierra Leone [7,57] Sierra Leone [7,57]	2004 2004	M F	987.2 945.8	617.9 654.3	33.3 17.8	59.3 9.7	7.4 2.0	7.1 1.2	28.2 10.8	102.2 167.3
Singapore [4,31] Singapour [4,31]	2009 2010 2011	MF MF MF	2 957.0 3 064.0 3 178.0	... ...	... ...	... ...	549.0 542.0 536.0	... ...	377.0 388.0 402.0	402.0 407.0 414.0
Slovakia [4,31] Slovaquie [4,31]	2009 2009 2010 2010 2011 2011	M F M F M F	1 326.0 1 040.0 1 285.0 1 033.0 1 310.0 1 041.0	64.0[1,13] 21.0[1,13] 57.0[1,13] 18.0[1,13] 57.0[1,13] 15.0[1,13]	... ...	10.0 1.0 13.0 1.0 11.0 0.0	359.0 206.0 336.0 194.0 370.0 198.0	53.0[18] 11.0[18] 46.0[18] 12.0[18] 46.0[18] 9.0[18]	245.0 12.0 247.0 11.0 229.0 15.0	132.0[19] 181.0[19] 127.0[19] 179.0[19] 129.0[19] 175.0[19]
Slovenia [4,31] Slovénie [4,31]	2009 2009 2010 2010 2011 2011	M F M F M F	531.0 450.0 523.0 443.0 506.0 430.0	49.0[1,13] 40.0[1,13] 47.0[1,13] 38.0[1,13] 46.0[1,13] 34.0[1,13]	... ...	3.0 ... 4.0 ^0.0 5.0 ^0.0	152.0 86.0 153.0 81.0 148.0 69.0	14.0[18] 4.0[18] 14.0[18] 2.0[18] 15.0[18] 4.0[18]	56.0 7.0 52.0 6.0 49.0 5.0	55.0[19] 66.0[19] 54.0[19] 63.0[19] 51.0[19] 61.0[19]
South Africa [65] Afrique du Sud [65]	2009[28] 2009[28] 2010 2010 2011 2011	M F M F M F	7 562.0 5 894.0 7 390.0 5 671.0 7 482.0 5 783.0	467.0[1,13] 219.0[1,13] 422.0[1,13] 217.0[1,13] 413.0[1,13] 201.0[1,13]	... ...	278.0 40.0 337.0 36.0 278.0 34.0	1 255.0 599.0 1 159.0 581.0 1 170.0 596.0	77.0 21.0 70.0 21.0 66.0 20.0	1 005.0 128.0 944.0 116.0 941.0 114.0	1 524.0[29] 1 451.0[29] ... ...
Spain [31,58] Espagne [31,58]	2009 2009 2010 2010 2011 2011	M F M F M F	10 646.0 8 242.0 10 290.0 8 167.0 9 991.0 8 113.0	581.0[1,13] 205.0[1,13] 589.0[1,13] 204.0[1,13] 561.0[1,13] 199.0[1,13]	... ...	42.0 4.0 42.0 3.0 37.0 4.0	1 879.0 641.0 1 766.0 604.0 1 731.0 574.0	173.0[18] 37.0[18] 163.0[18] 32.0[18] 173.0[18] 36.0[18]	1 744.0 145.0 1 514.0 137.0 1 290.0 103.0	1 484.0[19] 1 490.0[19] 1 472.0[19] 1 438.0[19] 1 466.0[19] 1 462.0[19]
Sri Lanka [7] Sri Lanka [7]	2008 2008 2009 2010 2010	M F M M F	4 663.0 2 511.0 4 609.0 4 770.0 2 465.0	1 389.0[1] 947.0[1] 1 382.0[1] 1 411.0[1] 942.0[1]	... ...	510.0[99] 23.0[99] 502.0[99] 487.0[99] 20.0[99]	716.0 639.0 677.0 675.0 595.0	... ...	... ...	680.0 244.0 669.0 730.0 256.0
Suriname [4,45] Suriname [4,45]	2004 2004	M F	101.9 54.8	10.1[1] 2.5[1]	... ...	8.4 0.9	8.1 2.9	1.4 0.2	13.5 0.5	15.7 9.3
Sweden [4,31] Suède [4,31]	2009 2009 2010 2010 2011 2011	M F M F M F	2 359.0 2 140.0 2 401.0 2 145.0 2 443.0 2 199.0	77.0[1,13] 21.0[1,13] 76.0[1,13] 20.0[1,13] 74.0[1,13] 19.0[1,13]	... ...	8.0 1.0 7.0 1.0 7.0 2.0	427.0 133.0 419.0 130.0 427.0 131.0	33.0[18] 9.0[18] 34.0[18] 10.0[18] 35.0[18] 10.0[18]	272.0 21.0 282.0 23.0 288.0 24.0	311.0[19] 239.0[19] 318.0[19] 241.0[19] 319.0[19] 247.0[19]
Switzerland [4,31] Suisse [4,31]	2010 2010 2011 2011	M F M F	2 328.0 1 953.0 2 378.0 1 988.0	93.0[1,13] 47.0[1,13] 93.0[1,13] 55.0[1,13]	... ...	3.0 ^0.0 4.0 1.0	447.0 160.0 452.0 155.0	30.0[18] 8.0[18] 34.0[18] 7.0[18]	227.0 29.0 243.0 31.0	291.0[19] 292.0[19] 298.0[19] 301.0[19]
Syrian Arab Republic [4] Rép. arabe syrienne [4]	2008 2008 2009 2009 2010 2010	M F M F M F	4 166.0 672.0 4 374.0 625.0 4 404.0 651.0	642.0 168.0 636.0 122.0 643.0 144.0	... ...	... ...	729.0 53.0 765.0 53.0 801.0 57.0	... ...	680.0 7.0 801.0 7.0 818.0 3.0	... ...

ISIC Rev. 3 Tabulation categories [+]
CITI Rév. 3 Catégories de classement [+]

Categ. H / Catég. H	Categ. I / Catég. I	Categ. J / Catég. J	Categ. K / Catég. K	Categ. L / Catég.L	Categ. M / Catég. M	Categ. N / Catég. N	Categ. O / Catég. O	Categ. P / Catég. P	Categ. Q / Catég. Q	Country or area [&] / Pays ou zone [&]
12.2	135.9	11.8	...	118.7[97]	...	...	...	...	3.3	Senegal [4]
16.4	5.8	4.9	...	39.0[97]	...	...	...	...	3.7	Sénégal [4]
73.0	149.0	55.0	92.0	129.0	153.0	175.0	123.0	7.0	1.1	Serbia
62.0	168.0[34]	44.0[30]	3.0	119.0	150.0	144.0	36.0	12.0	2.0	Serbie
2.6	14.4	4.0	5.5	21.1	23.3	9.9	44.4	4.0	2.5	Sierra Leone [7,57]
2.3	1.3	2.9	5.3	4.9	11.3	10.0	39.1	4.3	1.3	Sierra Leone [7,57]
176.0	281.0[34]	160.0[30]	71.0[35]	195.0	...	86.0	331.0	...	...	Singapore [4,31]
185.0	291.0[34]	173.0[30]	79.0[35]	658.0	...	92.0	346.0	...	...	Singapour [4,31]
198.0	308.0[34]	177.0[30]	82.0[35]	211.0	...	98.0	342.0	...	...	
45.0	150.0[34]	15.0[30]	7.0[35]	91.0	34.0	24.0	12.0	0.5	...	Slovakia [4,31]
62.0	50.0[34]	35.0[30]	6.0[35]	87.0	128.0	125.0	23.0	5.0	...	Slovaquie [4,31]
41.0	149.0[34]	17.0[30]	7.0[35]	97.0	32.0	25.0	10.0	0.5	...	
63.0	52.0[34]	31.0[30]	7.0[35]	92.0	133.0	132.0	22.0	4.0	...	
39.0	156.0[34]	18.0[30]	6.0[35]	93.0	33.0	27.0	9.0	1.0	...	
62.0	55.0[34]	36.0[30]	5.0[35]	100.0	131.0	133.0	20.0	6.0	...	
18.0	67.0[34]	10.0[30]	...	29.0	16.0	12.0	6.0	...	...	Slovenia [4,31]
23.0	21.0[34]	18.0[30]	2.0	32.0	57.0	42.0	9.0	...	...	Slovénie [4,31]
20.0	63.0[34]	9.0[30]	...	30.0	17.0	11.0	4.0	...	...	
26.0	21.0[34]	17.0[30]	1.0	29.0	60.0	45.0	10.0	...	...	
16.0	62.0[34]	12.0[30]	2.0	30.0	17.0	10.0	3.0	...	...	
27.0	20.0[34]	18.0[30]	1.0	29.0	62.0	45.0	10.0	...	...	
...	602.0	977.0[25,30]	...	...	...	...	132.0	...	...	South Africa [65]
...	162.0	780.0[25,30]	...	...	...	...	...	...	...	Afrique du Sud [65]
1 520.0 [61]	618.0	980.0[25]	...	1 147.0[62]	...	...	122.0	261.3[98]	...	
1 407.0 [61]	157.0	676.0[25]	...	1 580.0[62]	...	...	...	881.8[98]	...	
1 581.0 [61]	616.0	989.0[25]	...	1 187.0[62]	...	...	137.0	252.8[98]	...	
1 164.0 [61]	146.0	733.0[25]	...	1 663.0[62]	...	...	...	864.8[98]	...	
635.0	1 081.0[34]	262.0[30]	42.0	809.0	403.0	311.0	132.0	65.0	...	Spain [31,58]
786.0	345.0[34]	212.0[30]	48.0	558.0	757.0	1 013.0	284.0	660.0	...	Espagne [31,58]
625.0	1 089.0[34]	252.0[30]	44.0	817.0	405.0	311.0	122.0	63.0	...	
745.0	327.0[34]	212.0[30]	40.0	589.0	777.0	1 053.0	260.0	683.0	...	
637.0	1 061.0[34]	238.0[30]	45.0	816.0	403.0	326.0	137.0	63.0	...	
755.0	331.0[34]	212.0[30]	51.0	597.0	774.0	1 101.0	250.0	633.0	...	
...	...	162.6[25]	...	345.0	88.0	...	...	...	...	Sri Lanka [7]
...	...	73.0[25]	...	118.0	211.0	...	...	...	...	Sri Lanka [7]
...	...	145.0[25]	...	347.0	91.0	...	...	...	...	
...	...	177.0[25]	...	355.0	84.0	...	...	...	...	
...	...	79.0[25]	...	135.0	636.0	...	...	...	...	
1.9	7.6	1.4	4.5	16.3	1.8	1.6	5.0	...	...	Suriname [4,45]
2.9	1.1	1.3	1.9	11.7	6.6	5.2	4.9	...	...	Suriname [4,45]
66.0	308.0[34]	44.0[30]	42.0	115.0	124.0	123.0	45.0	...	...	Sweden [4,31]
78.0	111.0[34]	54.0[30]	25.0	152.0	355.0	576.0	70.0	...	...	Suède [4,31]
70.0	312.0[34]	46.0[30]	41.0	119.0	132.0	125.0	45.0	...	...	
82.0	110.0[34]	52.0[30]	23.0	154.0	361.0	573.0	68.0	...	...	
63.0	322.0[34]	46.0[30]	40.0	126.0	136.0	130.0	42.0	...	...	
81.0	111.0[34]	52.0[30]	25.0	153.0	367.0	591.0	71.0	...	...	
72.0	226.0[34]	144.0[30]	17.0	114.0	113.0	124.0	39.0	6.0	6.0	Switzerland [4,31]
99.0	93.0[34]	92.0[30]	25.0	91.0	187.0	398.0	89.0	30.0	3.0	Suisse [4,31]
73.0	226.0[34]	152.0[30]	17.0	112.0	112.0	130.0	41.0	6.0	7.0	
101.0	90.0[34]	96.0[30]	24.0	95.0	188.0	408.0	92.0	31.0	4.0	
756.0 [61]	345.0	105.0[25]	...	908.0[62]	...	...	...	...	...	Syrian Arab Republic [4]
38.0 [61]	13.0	18.0[25]	...	376.0[62]	...	...	...	...	...	Rép. arabe syrienne [4]
781.0 [61]	366.0	93.0[25]	...	931.0[62]	...	...	...	...	...	
38.0 [61]	14.0	19.0[25]	...	371.0[62]	...	...	...	...	...	
861.0 [61]	383.0	114.0[25]	...	876.0[62]	...	...	...	...	...	
42.0 [61]	11.0	19.0[25]	...	375.0[62]	...	...	...	...	...	

Country or area & Pays ou zone &	Year Année	Sex Sexe	Total employment Emploi total	ISIC Rev. 3 Tabulation categories[+] CITI Rév. 3 Catégories de classement[+]						
				Categ. A Catég. A	Categ. B Catég. B	Categ. C Catég. C	Categ. D Catég. D	Categ. E Catég. E	Categ. F Catég. F	Categ. G Catég. G
Tajikistan [4]	2004	M	1 441.7	602.3	...	10.3	80.1	15.9	285.0	153.8
Tadjikistan [4]	2004	F	1 010.8	758.7	...	1.5	34.4	1.4	11.0	48.3
Thailand [4]	2009	M	20 489.0	8 043.0	364.0	39.0	2 526.0	85.0	1 953.0	3 122.0
Thaïlande [4]	2009	F	17 217.0	6 185.0	100.0	12.0	2 848.0	17.0	350.0	2 926.0
	2010	M	20 652.0	7 951.0	330.0	33.0	2 578.0	86.0	1 989.0	3 210.0
	2010	F	17 385.0	6 168.0	98.0	7.0	2 771.0	20.0	367.0	3 027.0
	2011	M	20 814.0	8 095.0	326.0	40.0	2 597.0	124.0	2 007.0	3 120.0
	2011	F	17 650.0	6 362.0	100.0	10.0	2 763.0	39.0	364.0	3 002.0
TFYR of Macedonia [4]	2006	M	352.0	70.0	...	4.0	65.0	14.0	40.0	45.0
L'ex-R.Y. Macédoine [4]	2006	F	218.0	44.0	...	^0.0	58.0	2.0	3.0	28.0
	2007	M	359.0	67.0	...	5.0	65.0	13.0	35.0	48.0
	2007	F	231.0	40.0	...	0.0	61.0	2.0	3.0	35.0
	2008	M	373.0	73.0	...	6.0	68.0	13.0	37.0	51.0
	2008	F	236.0	47.0	...	^0.0	61.0	2.0	2.0	35.0
Tonga [4]	2003	M	20.4	9.5	0.9	0.1	0.9	0.4	1.4	1.3
Tonga [4]	2003	F	14.1	0.5	0.2	...	7.6	0.2	^0.0	1.6
Trinidad and Tobago [4,28]	2006	M	348.5	21.1[1]	...	16.0	37.8	6.4	82.8	46.0[29]
Trinité-et-Tobago [4,28]	2006	F	237.7	4.7[1]	...	4.4	17.7	1.3	13.9	60.6[29]
	2007	M	354.2	18.2[1]	...	18.6	39.2	5.6	88.7	45.6[29]
	2007	F	233.6	4.2[1]	...	4.2	14.9	1.6	14.3	62.7[29]
	2008	M	353.5	18.4[1]	...	16.6	40.3	6.1	91.9	43.7[29]
	2008	F	245.9	4.5[1]	...	4.5	14.8	1.8	16.6	64.5[29]
Turkey [4,31]	2009	M	15 402.0	2 656.0[1,13]	...	96.0	3 022.0	103.0[18]	1 265.0	2 779.0[19]
Turquie [4,31]	2009	F	5 868.0	2 225.0[1,13]	...	3.0	845.0	9.0[18]	40.0	602.0[19]
	2010	M	16 169.0	2 828.0[1,13]	...	110.0	3 263.0	153.0[18]	1 376.0	2 697.0[19]
	2010	F	6 424.0	2 527.0[1,13]	...	4.0	950.0	12.0[18]	56.0	629.0[19]
	2011	M	17 131.0	3 076.0[1,13]	...	122.0	3 379.0	198.0[18]	1 620.0	2 787.0[19]
	2011	F	6 969.0	2 746.0[1,13]	...	...	987.0	14.0[18]	54.0	689.0[19]
Turks and Caicos Islands 4	2005	MF	17.4	0.1	0.2	0.1	0.2	0.3	2.4	1.3
Iles Turques et Caïques 4	2006	MF	18.2	0.2	0.2	^0.0	0.2	0.2	3.2	1.5
	2007	MF	19.6	0.1	0.1	^0.0	0.2	0.2	4.3	1.7
Uganda 7	2003	M	4 618.0	2 771.2	78.7	18.5	337.4	4.6	115.8	637.9
Ouganda 7	2003	F	4 642.0	3 507.1	4.6	9.3	227.5	4.7	4.9	436.3
United Arab Emirates	2000	M	1 553.0	129.5	10.8	39.4	167.7	17.4	337.8	231.9
Emirats arabes unis	2000	F	226.0	0.1	^0.0	1.3	27.3	0.1	2.3	14.8
	2005[4,57]	M	2 158.7	115.8	5.4	43.3	188.5	23.3	712.4	305.0
	2005[4,57]	F	321.2	0.3	^0.0	1.7	11.1	1.1	6.0	29.2
	2008[4,95]	M	1 501.3	72.0	5.9	33.2	149.1	23.5	219.2	278.3
	2008[4,95]	F	344.9	0.5	0.1	2.7	11.3	1.7	8.7	22.1
United Kingdom 31,58	2009	M	15 448.0	246.0[1,13]	...	93.0	2 110.0	292.0[18]	2 112.0	2 071.0[19]
Royaume-Uni 31,58	2009	F	13 474.0	75.0[1,13]	...	16.0	682.0	82.0[18]	251.0	1 929.0[19]
	2010	M	15 491.0	269.0[1,13]	...	88.0	2 187.0	292.0[18]	1 974.0	2 105.0[19]
	2010	F	13 451.0	82.0[1,13]	...	15.0	664.0	76.0[18]	240.0	1 895.0[19]
	2011	M	15 576.0	264.0[1,13]	...	91.0	2 162.0	327.0[18]	1 950.0	2 092.0[19]
	2011	F	13 502.0	89.0[1,13]	...	11.0	675.0	82.0[18]	242.0	1 898.0[19]
United Rep. of Tanzania	2001[7,100,101]	M	...	6 698.6	...	15.5	161.7	13.5	147.5	565.5[15,29]
Rép.-Unie de Tanzanie	2001[7,100,101]	F	...	7 191.2	...	13.8	83.8	1.2	4.2	697.5[15,29]
	2006[4]	M	8 779.8	6 064.8	184.6	90.8	332.9	13.5	204.8	907.7
	2006[4]	F	9 164.7	7 120.3	25.0	14.1	232.2	3.5	6.7	665.0

26

Employment by economic activity *[cont.]*
Total employment and persons employed by ISIC 3 categories (thousands)
Emploi par activité économique *[suite]*
Emploi total et personnes employées par branches de la CITI rév. 3 (milliers)

ISIC Rev. 3 Tabulation categories [+]
CITI Rév. 3 Catégories de classement [+]

Categ. H / Catég. H	Categ. I / Catég. I	Categ. J / Catég. J	Categ. K / Catég. K	Categ. L / Catég.L	Categ. M / Catég. M	Categ. N / Catég. N	Categ. O / Catég. O	Categ. P / Catég. P	Categ. Q / Catég. Q	Country or area [&] / Pays ou zone [&]
12.2	59.7	14.7	14.5	59.2	59.0	21.1	46.8	2.4	...	Tajikistan [4]
11.6	4.8	4.2	2.1	11.5	63.8	41.6	10.4	1.0	...	Tadjikistan [4]
906.0	959.0	166.0	430.0	868.0	447.0	172.0	368.0	31.0	1.0	Thailand [4]
1 687.0	182.0	210.0	314.0	481.0	686.0	527.0	470.0	206.0	2.0	Thaïlande [4]
940.0	929.0	159.0	431.0	961.0	497.0	175.0	339.0	31.0	...	
1 714.0	179.0	208.0	334.0	528.0	749.0	526.0	471.0	203.0	2.0	
910.0	891.0	172.0	409.0	1 035.0	495.0	175.0	362.0	40.0	...	
1 636.0	184.0	224.0	341.0	561.0	792.0	504.0	546.0	207.0	...	
13.0	26.0	3.0	7.0	28.0	15.0	10.0	13.0	0.1	0.3	TFYR of Macedonia [4]
6.0	4.0	4.0	8.0	12.0	19.0	23.0	6.0	0.3	0.7	L'ex-R.Y. Macédoine [4]
12.0	30.0	5.0	8.0	29.0	13.0	10.0	16.0	0.9	0.8	
6.0	6.0	5.0	8.0	12.0	21.0	23.0	9.0	0.6	1.1	
13.0	31.0	3.0	10.0	31.0	14.0	9.0	13.0	0.3	0.6	
6.0	6.0	5.0	7.0	12.0	19.0	24.0	8.0	0.5	0.2	
0.2	1.2	0.2	0.2	1.9	0.7	0.3	1.0	0.3	^0.1	Tonga [4]
0.4	0.4	0.3	0.1	0.7	1.1	0.4	0.3	0.4	^0.0	Tonga [4]
...	33.2	22.2[25]	...	...	...	...	82.0	...	...	Trinidad and Tobago [4,28]
...	9.5	25.9[25]	...	...	...	...	99.1	...	...	Trinité-et-Tobago [4,28]
...	32.9	23.9[25]	...	...	...	...	81.4	...	...	
...	8.6	25.7[25]	...	...	...	...	97.2	...	...	
...	33.7	23.9[25]	...	...	...	...	78.4	...	...	
...	7.5	28.6[25]	...	...	...	...	101.1	...	...	
890.0	1 039.0[34]	156.0[30]	53.0	1 031.0	516.0	264.0	497.0	184.0	...	Turkey [4,31]
161.0	105.0[34]	117.0[30]	10.0	175.0	451.0	327.0	114.0	405.0	3.5	Turquie [4,31]
917.0	1 103.0[34]	158.0[30]	47.0	1 099.0	541.0	259.0	474.0	173.0	...	
168.0	10.0[34]	115.0[30]	14.0	191.0	477.0	331.0	109.0	399.0	...	
935.0	979.0[34]	157.0[30]	126.0	1 136.0	593.0	279.0	480.0	146.0	...	
204.0	66.0[34]	123.0[30]	28.0	202.0	513.0	413.0	115.0	407.0	...	
2.9	0.7	0.5	1.6	2.3	0.5[38]	...	1.0	1.6	...	Turks and Caicos Islands [4]
3.7	0.7	0.5	2.0	2.8	0.8[38]	...	1.0	0.9	...	Iles Turques et Caïques [4]
4.1	0.8	0.5	2.4	2.3	0.8[38]	...	1.2	0.4	...	
64.4	171.3	...	27.7	64.8	157.2	37.0	92.5	39.5	...	Uganda [7]
176.4	4.6	...	9.3	9.3	83.6	37.1	55.7	71.6	...	Ouganda [7]
56.5	119.9	18.4	40.9	225.4	32.4	17.0	51.1	54.6	1.3	United Arab Emirates
5.4	6.3	4.4	4.4	10.0	37.2	16.2	2.7	92.8	0.4	Emirats arabes unis
88.1	151.3	27.1	115.3	201.1	32.9	23.4	49.2	60.4	1.7	
12.3	16.1	9.5	12.5	17.4	37.1	21.0	7.3	133.8	0.5	
63.9	119.0	41.3	132.8	154.2	38.2	24.3	50.2	90.5	2.9	
8.6	13.6	17.4	15.1	16.1	45.7	24.3	9.1	146.1	0.9	
622.0	1 905.0[34]	635.0[30]	123.0	989.0	816.0	810.0	290.0	22.0	31.0	United Kingdom [31,58]
737.0	589.0[34]	593.0[30]	141.0	971.0	2 122.0	2 942.0	458.0	43.0	13.0	Royaume-Uni [31,58]
662.0	1 873.0[34]	622.0[30]	123.0	979.0	854.0	807.0	290.0	18.0	25.0	
756.0	577.0[34]	543.0[30]	157.0	917.0	2 223.0	2 993.0	435.0	47.0	16.0	
667.0	1 916.0[34]	656.0[30]	144.0	920.0	848.0	845.0	303.0	20.0	33.0	
776.0	574.0[34]	534.0[30]	153.0	921.0	2 183.0	3 061.0	452.0	47.0	18.0	
...	111.6	22.2[25,30]	...	...	...	...	622.8	...	...	United Rep. of Tanzania
...	7.6	4.3[25,30]	...	...	...	...	559.9	...	...	Rép.-Unie de Tanzanie
98.5	245.0	11.3	69.0	157.4	126.9	46.1	88.3	138.2	...	
279.0	13.1	6.2	13.0	27.3	98.7	59.1	38.2	563.3	...	

Country or area & Pays ou zone &	Year Année	Sex Sexe	Total employment Emploi total	Categ. A Catég. A	Categ. B Catég. B	Categ. C Catég. C	Categ. D Catég. D	Categ. E Catég. E	Categ. F Catég. F	Categ. G Catég. G
United States [5,58]	2006	M	77 502.0	1 663.0[1]	...	598.0	11 543.0	926.0	10 618.0	11 802.0
Etats-Unis [5,58]	2006	F	66 925.0	543.0[1]	...	89.0	4 834.0	259.0	1 131.0	9 526.0
	2007	M	78 254.0	1 604.0[1]	...	635.0	11 416.0	936.0	10 738.0	11 524.0
	2007	F	67 792.0	490.0[1]	...	101.0	4 885.0	257.0	1 119.0	9 414.0
	2008	M	77 486.0	1 650.0[1]	...	714.0	11 249.0	987.0	9 905.0	11 327.0
	2008	F	67 876.0	518.0[1]	...	105.0	4 655.0	239.0	1 069.0	9 258.0
Uruguay [37,40]	2005[56]	M	620.1	44.3[59]	...	...	107.2[102]	...	73.2	152.2[29]
Uruguay [37,40]	2005[56]	F	494.4	7.4[59]	...	...	62.0[102]	...	1.5	103.0[29]
	2006	M	822.4	126.7[59]	...	...	138.0[102]	...	88.5	184.3[29]
	2006	F	591.0	30.5[59]	...	...	71.6[102]	...	2.1	123.9[29]
	2007	M	852.9	132.9[59]	...	...	143.5[102]	...	99.3	183.5[29]
	2007	F	629.0	30.4[59]	...	...	76.4[102]	...	2.9	135.8[29]
Uzbekistan Ouzbékistan	1999	MF	8 885.0	3 421.0[1]	...	1 142.0[78]	...	...	583.0	734.0[29]
Venezuela (Boliv. Rep. of) [4,5,8,28]	2006	M	6 894.0	939.4[1]	...	66.9	936.6	39.5	1 009.0	1 289.8[29]
Venezuela (Rép. boliv. du) [4,5,8,28]	2006	F	4 223.0	76.7[1]	...	11.0	414.3	10.9	48.7	1 330.2[29]
	2007	M	7 073.0	924.0[1]	...	86.2	966.2	39.2	1 059.2	1 308.2[29]
	2007	F	4 418.9	77.9[1]	...	16.5	452.2	12.3	50.5	1 395.5[29]
	2008	M	7 264.4	920.1[1]	...	91.2	985.4	42.8	1 099.9	1 340.2[29]
	2008	F	4 598.6	85.8[1]	...	15.6	431.0	11.9	53.9	1 468.8[29]
Viet Nam [4,63]	2002	M	20 356.0	11 461.0	948.6	156.5	1 972.1	97.8	1 357.3	1 521.5
Viet Nam [4,63]	2002	F	19 807.0	12 185.0	323.3	87.8	2 078.8	20.3	133.6	2 785.0
	2003	M	20 959.2	11 072.5	1 023.1	194.7	2 203.6	103.9	1 631.8	1 673.1
	2003	F	20 216.5	12 164.2	311.3	127.4	2 308.0	24.3	164.7	2 834.2
	2004	M	21 649.0	11 041.0	1 059.3	182.7	2 429.1	117.6	1 774.1	1 778.0
	2004	F	20 666.0	12 027.0	370.0	112.2	2 520.8	24.1	182.5	2 918.0
Yemen [4]	1999	M	2 731.6	1 146.5	31.4	16.7	112.5	11.0	236.9	382.3
Yémen [4]	1999	F	890.1	781.3	...	1.0	23.0	0.8	1.3	11.9
Zambia [28,43,103]	2000	M	1 557.0	1 014.9[1]	...	34.6	56.6	11.0	36.8	106.6[29]
Zambie [28,43,103]	2000	F	1 256.0	999.2[1]	...	1.8	20.9	1.1	1.5	83.8[29]

Source:
International Labour Office (ILO), Geneva, the ILO labour statistics
database, last accessed January 2013.

Source:
Bureau international du travail (BIT), Genève, la base de données du
BIT, dernier accès janvier 2013.

ISIC Rev. 3 Tabulation categories [+]
CITI Rév. 3 Catégories de classement [+]

Categ. H / Catég. H	Categ. I / Catég. I	Categ. J / Catég. J	Categ. K / Catég. K	Categ. L / Catég.L	Categ. M / Catég. M	Categ. N / Catég. N	Categ. O / Catég. O	Categ. P / Catég. P	Categ. Q / Catég. Q	Country or area [&] / Pays ou zone [&]
4 452.0	4 722.0	3 035.0	10 184.0	3 563.0	3 892.0	3 632.0	6 873.0[39]	...	...	United States [5,58]
5 023.0	1 547.0	4 219.0	7 920.0	2 961.0	8 630.0	13 784.0	6 459.0[39]	...	...	Etats-Unis [5,58]
4 525.0	4 836.0	3 030.0	10 613.0	3 720.0	3 962.0	3 794.0	6 922.0[39]	...	...	
5 057.0	1 621.0	4 276.0	8 190.0	3 026.0	8 866.0	14 040.0	6 449.0[39]	...	...	
4 592.0	4 954.0	3 056.0	10 524.0	3 707.0	3 994.0	3 805.0	7 022.0[39]	...	...	
5 203.0	1 547.0	4 223.0	7 965.0	3 056.0	9 174.0	14 429.0	6 436.0[39]	...	...	
...	49.1	64.0[25]	...	56.4	14.4	19.6	32.3[77]	7.4	...	Uruguay [37,40]
...	12.4	40.0[25]	...	29.7	53.3	61.5	32.0[77]	91.6	...	Uruguay [37,40]
...	61.5	61.1[25]	...	70.9	18.9	24.8	35.5[77]	11.2	...	
...	14.3	40.6[25]	...	33.6	59.5	68.9	33.7[77]	111.6	...	
...	68.5	67.4[25]	...	62.5	19.8	25.2	38.7[77]	11.6	...	
...	15.4	47.0[25]	...	31.8	64.4	72.0	36.0[77]	116.6	...	
										Uzbekistan
...	372.0	50.0[25]	...	...	...	...	1 968.0	...	...	Ouzbékistan
...	819.5	355.6[25]	...	...	...	...	1 421.5	...	...	Venezuela (Boliv. Rep. of) [4,5,8,28]
...	94.1	195.4[25]	...	...	...	...	2 301.1	...	...	Venezuela (Rép. boliv. du) [4,5,8,28]
...	898.4	366.4[25]	...	...	...	...	1 409.0	...	...	
...	96.0	223.2[25]	...	...	...	...	2 085.9	...	...	
...	943.1	386.2[25]	...	...	...	...	1 440.1	...	...	
...	99.4	227.8[25]	...	...	...	...	2 193.7	...	...	
145.3	1 117.4	59.0	113.8	432.4	318.7	115.6	468.7	69.2	0.9	Viet Nam [4,63]
375.7	149.9	71.0	70.6	157.6	739.9	163.3	343.3	121.0	1.1	Viet Nam [4,63]
195.3	1 150.5	74.0	144.4	457.5	335.1	135.1	480.2	84.1	0.4	
447.9	146.8	74.5	74.2	162.6	762.9	171.0	308.6	132.9	1.0	
176.1	1 128.2	80.8	142.6	516.0	359.6	140.1	624.6	97.4	1.8	
418.9	164.7	78.2	76.6	182.9	825.4	187.9	431.8	143.7	1.4	
42.0	121.0	9.3	18.0	347.7	171.0	31.8	49.1	3.4	0.3	Yemen [4]
0.9	1.5	1.7	0.9	10.3	38.2	10.6	4.0	2.2	0.3	Yémen [4]
...	50.0	19.8[25]	...	...	...	...	228.9	...	...	Zambia [28,43,103]
...	3.8	9.3[25]	...	...	...	...	134.4	...	...	Zambie [28,43,103]

[+] Tabulation categories of ISIC Rev. 3 :

A. Agriculture, hunting and forestry.
B. Fishing.
C. Mining and quarrying.
D. Manufacturing.
E. Electricity, gas and water supply.
F. Construction.
G. Wholesale and retail trade, repair of motor vehicles, motor cycles and personal and household goods.
H. Hotels and restaurants.
I. Transport, storage and communications.
J. Financial intermediation.
K. Real estate, renting and business activities.
L. Public administration and defence; compulsory social security.
M. Education.
N. Health and social work.
O. Other community, social and personal service activities.
P. Private households with employed persons.
Q. Extra-territorial organizations and bodies.

[+] Catégories de classement de la CITI Rév. 3

A. Agriculture, chasse et sylviculture.
B. Pêche.
C. Activités extractives.
D. Activités de fabrication.
E. Production et distribution d'électricité, de gaz et d'eau.
F. Construction.
G. Commerce de gros et de détail; réparation de véhicules automobiles, de motocycles et de biens personnels et domestiques.
H. Hôtels et restaurants.
I. Transports, entreposage et communications.
J. Intermédiation financière.
K. Immobilier, locations et activités de services aux entreprises.
L. Administration publique et défense; sécurité sociale obligatoire.
M. Education.
N. Santé et action sociale.
O. Autres activités de services collectifs, sociaux et personnels.
P. Ménages privés employant du personnel domestique.
Q. Organisations et organismes extraterritoriaux.

& Data for most countries are collected from labour force surveys. The following countries are exceptions, with sources as follows:

& Les données pour la plupart des pays sont extraites d'enquêtes par sondage sur la main-d'œuvre, sauf les pays ci-dessous dont les sources sont les suivantes :

Household surveys:
Madagascar
Senegal

Enquêtes auprès des ménages:
Madagascar
Sénégal

Official estimates:
Mongolia
San Marino

Evaluations officielles:
Mongolie
Saint-Marin

Population census:
Anguilla
Aruba
Bahrain
Bermuda
Bhutan
Brunei Darussalam
Chile
French Polynesia
Guyana
Isle of Man
Kuwait
Maldives
Nepal
New Caledonia
Niue
Palau
Papua New Guinea
Saint Helena
Samoa
Sierra Leone
Suriname

Recensement de la population:
Anguilla
Aruba
Bahreïn
Bermudes
Bhoutan
Brunéi Darussalam
Chili
Polynésie française
Guyana
Ile de Man
Koweït
Maldives
Népal
Nouvelle-Calédonie
Nioué
Palaos
Papouasie-Nouvelle-Guinée
Sainte Hélène
Samoa
Sierra-Leone
Suriname

1	Tabulation categories A-B.	1	Catégories de classement A à B.
2	Tabulation categories J-L and O-Q	2	Catégories de classement J à L et O à Q
3	September.	3	Septembre.
4	Persons aged 15 years and over.	4	Personnes âgées de 15 ans et plus.
5	Excluding armed forces.	5	Non compris les militaires.
6	May.	6	Mai.
7	Persons aged 10 years and over.	7	Personnes âgées de 10 ans et plus.
8	Second semester.	8	Second semestre.
9	28 urban agglomerations.	9	28 agglomérations urbaines.
10	31 urban agglomerations.	10	31 agglomérations urbaines.
11	October.	11	Octobre.
12	Data classified according to ANZSIC.	12	Données classifiées selon l'ANZSIC.
13	Excluding hunting.	13	Non compris la chasse.
14	Excluding quarrying.	14	Non compris les carrières.
15	Excluding repair of motor vehicles, motorcycles and personal and household goods.	15	Non compris les réparations de véhicules à moteur, de motocycles et d'articles personnels et ménagers.
16	Excluding compulsory social security and defence.	16	Non compris la sécurité sociale obligatoire et la défense.
17	Including teacher training.	17	Y compris la formation des enseignants.
18	Includes steam, air conditioning supply, sewerage, waste management and remediation activities.	18	Y compris la vapeur, la distribution de climatisation, le système d'évacuation, la gestion des déchets et la dépollution.
19	Excluding personal and household goods.	19	Ne comprend pas les biens personnels et ménagers.
20	Excluding communications.	20	Non compris les communications.
21	Includes insurance activities.	21	Y compris les activités d'assurance.
22	Excluding armed forces and conscripts.	22	Non compris compris les forces armées et les conscrits.
23	April.	23	Avril.
24	Tabulation categories C and E.	24	Catégories de classement C et E.
25	Tabulation categories J-K.	25	Catégories de classement J à K.

26	Tabulation categories L-P.	26	Catégories de classement L à P.
27	Year ending in June of the year indicated.	27	Année se terminant en juin de l'année indiquée.
28	Data classified according to ISIC Rev. 2.	28	Données classifiées selon la CITI, Rév. 2.
29	Tabulation categories G-H.	29	Catégories de classement G à H.
30	Includes insurance.	30	Y compris l'assurance.
31	Data classified according to ISIC Rev. 4.	31	Données classifiées selon la CITI, Rév. 4.
32	Tabulation categories C and F.	32	Catégories de classement C et F.
33	Includes air conditioning supply and steam.	33	Comprend la distribution de climatisation et de vapeur.
34	Including information service activities.	34	Y compris les activités de service d'information.
35	Excludes renting and business activity.	35	Ne comprend pas les activités commerciales et de location.
36	Including the armed forces.	36	Y compris les forces armées.
37	Persons aged 14 years and over.	37	Personnes âgées de 14 ans et plus.
38	Tabulation categories M-N.	38	Catégories de classement M à N.
39	Tabulation categories O-X. (Additional category X, not shown separately in the table, comprises activities which are not classifiable by economic activity).	39	Catégories de classement O à X. (la catégorie supplémentaire X, qui ne figure pas dans le tableau, comprend les activités qui ne peuvent être classeés dans une activité économique).
40	Excluding conscripts.	40	Non compris les conscrits.
41	Excluding forestry.	41	Non compris sylviculture.
42	Including forestry.	42	Y compris l'exploitation forestière.
43	Persons aged 12 years and over.	43	Personnes âgées de 12 ans et plus.
44	Excluding rural population of Rondônia, Acre, Amazonas, Roraima, Pará and Amapá.	44	Non compris la population rurale de Rondônia, Acre, Amazonas, Roraima, Pará et Amapá.
45	August.	45	Août.
46	November.	46	Novembre.
47	Data aggregated according to the North American Industry Classification System (NAICS).	47	Les données sont classifiées selon le Système de classification des industries de l'Amérique du Nord (SCIAN).
48	Excluding hunting and forestry.	48	Non compris la chasse et la sylviculture.
49	Tabulation categories B and C	49	Catégories de classement B à C.
50	Includes forestry, oil and gas.	50	Y compris la sylviculture,le pétrole et le gaz.
51	Data refer to utilities only.	51	Les données se référent uniquement au service public.
52	Refers to trade only.	52	Se rapporte seulement au commerce
53	Public administration only.	53	Administration publique seulemente.
54	Tabulation categories C-D.	54	Catégories de classement C à D.
55	State-owned units, urban collective-owned units and other ownership units.	55	Unités d'Etat, unités collectives urbaines et autres.
56	Urban areas.	56	Régions urbaines.
57	December.	57	Décembre.
58	Persons aged 16 years and over.	58	Personnes âgées de 16 ans et plus.
59	Tabulation categories A-C.	59	Catégories de classement A à C.
60	Persons aged 12 and over in urban areas and 10 and over in rural areas.	60	Personnes âgées de plus de 12 ans dans les zones urbaines ou de plus de 10 ans dans les zones rurales.
61	Including trade.	61	Y compris commerce.
62	Tabulation categories L-O.	62	Catégories de classement L à O.
63	July.	63	Juillet.
64	May and November.	64	Mai et novembre.
65	Persons aged 15 to 64 years.	65	Personnes âgées de 15 à 64 ans.
66	Tabulation categories N and O.	66	Catégories de classement N et O.
67	Excludes water; includes steam and air conditioning supply.	67	Ne comprend pas l'eau; comprend la distribution de climatisation et de vapeur.
68	Excluding business services.	68	Non compris les services aux entreprises.
69	Excluding rent.	69	Non compris le groupe "Loyer".
70	Persons aged 15 to 74 years.	70	Personnes âgées de 15 à 74 ans.
71	Data classifed according to NSIC.	71	Données classifiées selon l'NSIC.
72	Includes heat.	72	Y compris le chauffage.
73	Includes information and postal activities, excludes storage.	73	Y compris les informations et les activités postales; non compris les entrepôts.
74	Persons aged 6 years and over.	74	Personnes âgées de 6 ans et plus.
75	Tabulation categories L-Q.	75	Catégories de classement L à Q.
76	Second quarter.	76	Deuxième trimestre.
77	Tabulation categories O and Q.	77	Catégories de classement O et Q.
78	Tabulation categories C-E.	78	Catégories de classement C à E.
79	Tabulation categories J-Q.	79	Catégories de classement J à Q.
80	Persons aged 15 to 69 years.	80	Personnes âgées de 15 à 69 ans.
81	June.	81	Juin.
82	Curaçao.	82	Curaçao.
83	Includes waste management.	83	Y compris la gestion des déchets.

84	Excluding restaurants.		84	Non compris les restaurants.
85	West Bank and Gaza.		85	Cisjordanie et Gaza.
86	Omanis.		86	Omanais.
87	Fourth quarter.		87	Quatrième trimestre.
88	Excluding regular military living in barracks.		88	Non compris les militaires de carrière vivant dans des casernes.
89	Includes steam.		89	Y compris la vapeur.
90	Wholesale and retail trade only.		90	Commerce de gros et de détail seulement.
91	Transportation only.		91	Transports uniquement.
92	Excludes real estate.		92	Non compris immobilières.
93	Persons aged 15 to 72 years.		93	Personnes âgées de 15 à 72 ans.
94	Tabulation categories O-Q.		94	Catégories de classement O à Q.
95	February.		95	Février.
96	Including home-made handicrafts.		96	Y compris l'artisanat fait main.
97	Tabulation categories L-N.		97	Catégories de classement L à N.
98	Tabulation categories P-Q.		98	Catégories de classement P à Q.
99	Tabulation categories C, E and F.		99	Catégories de classement C, E et F.
100	Tanganyika only.		100	Tanganyika seulement.
101	March.		101	Mars.
102	Tabulation categories D-E.		102	Catégories de classement D à E.
103	The data refer to the usually active population.		103	Les données se réfèrent à la population habituellement active.

Wages in manufacturing
By hour, day, week or month, and by gender

Salaires dans les industries manufacturières
Par heure, jour, semaine ou mois, et par sexe

Country or area § Pays ou zone §	2003	2004	2005	2006	2007	2008	2009	2010
Albania (lek) Albanie (lek)								
MF(I) - month mois	16 572.0	17 559.0	18 333.0	19 750.0	...	...	27 655.0	28 066.0
Andorra (euro) Andorre (euro)								
MF(I) - month mois	1 508.9	1 585.9	1 680.3	1 801.6	1 902.5	...	...	...
M(I) - month mois	1 700.3	1 801.3	1 938.4	2 043.3	2 141.5	2 206.0	...	...
F(I) - month mois	1 189.8	1 255.2	1 309.8	1 407.9	1 534.2	1 561.2	...	...
Argentina (Argentine peso) Argentine (peso argentin)								
MF(I) - month mois	...	...	...	...	...	...	1 800.0	2 100.0
M(I) - month mois	...	...	...	...	...	...	1 900.0	2 200.0
F(I) - month mois	...	...	...	...	...	...	1 400.0	2 000.0
MF(II) - hour heure [1,2]	5.1	6.3	7.6	9.7	...	...	...	...
Armenia (dram) Arménie (dram)								
MF(I) - month mois	41 881.0	48 191.0	54 536.0	61 490.0	71 834.0	83 491.0	92 528.0	100 502.0
M(I) - month mois	...	...	...	78 214.0	88 692.0	106 651.0	...	114 106.0
F(I) - month mois	...	...	...	46 410.0	54 844.0	65 520.0	...	72 064.0
Aruba (Aruban florin) Aruba (florin de Aruba)								
MF(I) - month mois	...	...	...	...	...	...	...	3 636.0
M(I) - month mois	...	...	...	...	...	...	...	3 893.0
F(I) - month mois	...	...	...	...	...	...	...	2 802.0
Australia [3,4] (Australian dollar) Australie [3,4] (dollar australien)								
MF(I) - hour heure	...	22.8	...	25.4	...	...	...	...
M(I) - hour heure	...	23.4	...	26.1	...	...	...	...
F(I)- hour heure	...	19.9	...	23.6	...	...	...	...
Austria (euro) Autriche (euro)								
MF(I) - hour heure [5,6]	13.8	14.0	14.4	14.9	15.3	15.8	...	...
MF(I) - month mois	2 618.0	...	...	...	...	...	2 900.0	2 900.0
M(I) - month mois	2 941.0	...	...	...	...	...	3 300.0	3 300.0
F(I) - month mois	1 809.0	...	...	...	...	...	1 900.0	1 900.0
MF(II) - month mois	2 093.0	...	...	...	...	...	...	...
M(II) - month mois	2 303.0	...	...	...	...	...	...	...
F(II) - month mois	1 444.0	...	...	...	...	...	...	...
MF(V) - month mois	3 436.0	...	...	...	...	...	...	...
M(V) - month mois	4 132.0	...	...	...	...	...	...	...
F(V) - month mois	2 198.0	...	...	...	...	...	...	...
Azerbaijan (manat) Azerbaïdjan (manat)								
MF(I) - month mois	445 436.5	491 330.2	115.0[7]	141.0	192.3	251.8	267.5	320.5
M(I) - month mois	...	...	...	...	...	253.9	295.5	360.1
F(I) - month mois	...	...	...	...	...	151.4	178.6	191.1
Bahrain (Bahrain dinar) Bahreïn (dinar de Bahreïn)								
MF(I) - month mois	230.0[8,9]	234.0[8,9]	228.0[8,9]	219.0[8,9]	225.0[8,9]	...	270.0	274.0
M(I) - month mois	250.0[8,9]	249.0[8,9]	239.0[8,9]	226.0[8,9]	230.0[8,9]	...	271.0	276.0
F(I) - month mois	125.0[8,9]	138.0[8,9]	145.0[8,9]	155.0[8,9]	177.0[8,9]	...	197.0	261.0
MF(VI) - month mois [8,9]	...	...	...	...	...	253.0	...	...
M(VI) - month mois [8,9]	...	...	...	...	...	254.0	...	...
F(VI) - month mois [8,9]	...	...	...	...	...	252.0	...	...
Belarus (Belarussian rouble) Bélarus (rouble bélarussien)								
MF(I) - month mois	337.0[10,11,12]	467.0[10,11,12]	616.0[10,11,12]	728.0[10,11,12]	881.0[10,11,12]	937.0[10,11,12]	1 018 168.0	1 297 748.0
M(I) - month mois	...	...	...	...	...	...	1 349 060.0	1 972 878.0
F(I) - month mois	...	...	...	...	...	...	949 045.0	1 370 427.0
Belgium (euro) Belgique (euro)								
MF(I) - hour heure [13]	14.9	15.6	16.1	16.4	16.6	...	...	...
M(I) - hour heure [13]	15.5	16.1	16.6	16.9	17.2	...	...	...
F(I)- hour heure [13]	12.7	13.6	14.0	14.5	14.7	...	...	...
MF(I) - month mois	2 520.0[13,14]	2 609.0[13,14]	2 660.0[13,14]	2 695.0[13,14]	2 740.0[13]	...	2 930.0	...
M(I) - month mois	2 653.0[13,14]	2 737.0[13,14]	2 784.0[13]	2 815.0[13]	2 869.0[13]	...	3 040.0	...
F(I) - month mois	2 051.0[13]	2 160.0[13]	2 218.0[13]	2 251.0[13]	2 279.0[13]	...	2 518.0	...
MF(II) - hour heure [13,14]	13.1	13.5	...	...	...	...	...	...
M(II) - hour heure [13,14]	13.6	14.0	...	...	...	...	...	...
F(II) - hour heure [13,14]	10.8	11.3	...	...	...	...	...	...

Country or area § Pays ou zone §	2003	2004	2005	2006	2007	2008	2009	2010
MF(II) - month mois [13,14]	2 256.0	2 316.0	2 328.0	2 405.0	...	...	...	...
M(II) - month mois [13,14]	2 275.0	2 333.0	2 396.0	2 465.0	...	...	...	...
F(II) - month mois [13,14]	1 831.0	1 893.0	1 901.0	1 999.0	...	...	...	...
MF(V) - hour heure [13,14]	18.5	19.4	...	...	...	...	...	...
M(V) - hour heure [13,14]	20.2	21.1	...	...	...	...	...	...
F(V) - hour heure [13,14]	14.9	15.8	...	...	...	...	...	...
MF(V) - month mois [13,14]	3 292.0	3 395.0	3 479.0	3 541.0	...	...	...	...
M(V) - month mois [13,14]	3 496.0	3 590.0	...	...	...	...	...	...
F(V) - month mois [13,14]	2 422.0	2 735.0	...	...	...	...	...	...
Bermuda (Bermuda dollar) Bermudes (dollar des Bermudes)								
MF(I) - month mois	...	4 167.0[15]	3 561.0[15]	3 692.0[15]	3 950.0[15]	...	3 886.9	5 129.3
M(I) - month mois	...	4 333.0[15]	3 691.0[15]	3 792.0[15]	4 101.0[15]	...	3 827.1	5 301.9
F(I) - month mois	...	2 375.0[15]	3 347.0[15]	3 490.0[15]	3 740.0[15]	...	4 117.9	4 779.8
Bolivia (Plurinational State of) (boliviano) Bolivie (État plurinational de) (boliviano)								
MF(I) - month mois	...	...	...	...	...	...	1 745.0	...
M(I) - month mois	...	...	...	...	...	...	1 879.5	...
F(I) - month mois	...	...	...	...	...	...	1 244.5	...
Bosnia and Herzegovina [16] (convertible marka) Bosnie-Herzégovine [16] (marka convertible)								
MF(I) - month mois	...	...	...	672.8	...	...	...	...
Botswana [17] (pula) Botswana [17] (pula)								
MF(I) - month mois	...	...	...	1 590.0	2 174.0	2 271.0	...	...
M(I) - month mois	...	...	...	2 053.0	...	2 814.0	...	...
F(I) - month mois	...	...	...	1 134.0	...	1 538.0	...	...
Bulgaria (lev) Bulgarie (lev)								
MF(I) - month mois	246.0[18]	262.0[18]	289.0[18]	320.0[18]	383.0[18]	474.0[18]	511.0	550.0
M(I) - month mois	293.0[18]	311.0[18]	343.0[18]	378.0[18]	452.0[18]	...	601.0	646.0
F(I) - month mois	203.0[18]	216.0[18]	237.0[18]	264.0[18]	315.0[18]	...	421.0	454.0
Canada (Canadian dollar) Canada (dollar canadien)								
MF(I) - month mois	...	...	...	...	...	...	887.4	907.4
M(I) - month mois	...	...	...	...	...	...	955.9	976.8
F(I) - month mois	...	...	...	...	...	...	724.9	734.9
MF(I) - week semaine [19]	837.4	860.6	895.4	904.7	939.6	947.4	...	...
MF(II) - hour heure [19,20]	19.4	20.0	20.5	20.5	21.6	22.0	...	...
Chile (Chilean peso) Chili (peso chilien)								
MF(I) - hour heure	...	...	...	...	...	...	...	2 473.0
MF(I) - month mois [21,22]	221 860.0[23]	229 575.0[23]	242 160.0[23]	300 948.0	315 408.0	351 684.0	...	...
China [24] (yuan) Chine [24] (yuan)								
MF(I) - month mois	1 041.3	1 169.4	1 313.1	1 497.2	1 740.3	2 016.0	...	...
China, Hong Kong SAR (Hong Kong dollar) Chine, Hong Kong RAS (dollar de Hong Kong)								
MF(I) - month mois	10 000.0[25,26]	9 500.0[25,26]	9 800.0[25,26]	...	10 300.0[25,26]	...	10 500.0	11 000.0
M(I) - month mois	...	...	11 000.0[25,26]	...	12 000.0[25,26]	...	12 000.0	12 000.0
F(I) - month mois	...	...	7 000.0[25,26]	...	7 500.0[25,26]	...	7 500.0	8 000.0
China, Macao SAR (Macao pataca) Chine, Macao RAS (pataca de Macao)								
MF(I) - month mois	4 010.0[27]	4 178.0[27]	4 390.0[27]	4 652.0[27]	4 990.0[27]	5 447.0[27]	4 500.0	5 300.0
M(I) - month mois	5 335.0[27]	5 750.0[27]	5 961.0[27]	6 193.0[27]	6 716.0[27]	7 072.0[27]	6 000.0	7 000.0
F(I) - month mois [27]	3 584.0	3 689.0	3 860.0	4 074.0	4 272.0	4 689.0	...	...
MF(VI) - month mois [25]	2 834.0	2 983.0	3 101.0	3 140.0	4 000.0	4 000.0	...	...
M(VI) - month mois [25]	4 363.0	4 829.0	4 765.0	5 462.0	6 500.0	5 300.0	...	...
F(VI) - month mois [25]	2 542.0	2 652.0	2 795.0	2 698.0	3 100.0	3 500.0	...	...
Colombia [28,29,30] (Colombian peso) Colombie [28,29,30] (peso colombien)								
MF(I) - month mois	442 510.0	468 406.0	506 020.0	608 137.0	694 244.0	...	...	...
M(I) - month mois	531 791.0	557 571.0	605 537.0	707 408.0	847 898.0	...	...	...
F(I) - month mois	347 588.0	365 782.0	394 964.0	473 334.0	505 713.0	...	...	...
Costa Rica (Costa Rican colón) Costa Rica (colón costa-ricien)								
MF(I) - hour heure [31]	...	...	953.0	993.3	1 210.2	1 272.1	...	...
M(I) - hour heure [31]	...	...	1 006.1	1 028.5	1 325.5	1 345.6	...	...
F(I)- hour heure [31]	...	...	793.6	890.3	923.4	1 091.4	...	...
MF(I) - month mois	...	...	393 518.0[31]	...	...	136 829.0[31]	...	334 229.0
M(I) - month mois	...	...	410 986.0[31]	...	...	146 547.0[31]	...	339 074.0
F(I) - month mois	...	...	335 824.0[31]	...	...	114 086.0[31]	...	321 842.0
Croatia (kuna) Croatie (kuna)								
MF(I) - month mois	4 952.0[32]	5 189.0[32]	5 452.0[32]	5 833.0[32]	6 161.0[32]	6 455.0[32]	6 536.0	6 530.0

Wages in manufacturing *(continued)*
By hour, day, week or month, and by gender
Salaires dans les industries manufacturières *(suite)*
Par heure, jour, semaine ou mois, et par sexe

Country or area § Pays ou zone §	2003	2004	2005	2006	2007	2008	2009	2010
M(I) - month mois	5 412.0[32]	5 680.0[32]	5 969.0[32]	6 377.0[32]	6 734.0[32]	7 048.0[32]	7 087.0	7 062.0
F(I) - month mois	4 196.0[32]	4 359.0[32]	4 560.0[32]	4 874.0[32]	5 148.0[32]	5 357.0[32]	5 499.0	5 524.0
Cuba (Cuban peso) Cuba (peso cubain)								
MF(I) - month mois	275.0[33]	290.0[33]	338.0[33]	404.0[33]	433.0[33]	430.0[33]	449.0	433.0
Cyprus (Cyprus pound) Chypre (livre chypriote)								
MF(I) - hour heure [13,21,34]	4.6	4.8	4.9	5.0	...	...	...	...
M(I) - hour heure [13,21,34]	5.4	5.7	5.8	5.7	...	...	...	...
F(I)- hour heure [13,21,34]	3.4	3.5	3.6	3.7	...	...	...	...
MF(I) - month mois	...	...	...	...	...	...	1 542.0	1 575.0
M(I) - month mois	...	...	...	...	...	...	1 731.0	1 758.0
F(I) - month mois	...	...	...	...	...	...	1 181.0	1 222.0
MF(II) - hour heure [13,21,34]	4.1	4.2	4.3	4.9	...	...	...	...
M(II) - hour heure [13,21,34]	4.8	5.0	5.1	5.3	...	...	...	...
F(II) - hour heure [13,21,34]	2.9	2.9	3.0	3.2	...	...	...	...
MF(II) - week semaine [13,21,34]	165.7	169.4	171.8	200.6	...	...	...	...
M(II) - week semaine [13,21,34]	194.9	203.3	202.9	223.1	...	...	...	...
F(II) - week semaine [13,21,34]	113.5	108.8	115.6	125.1	...	...	...	...
MF(V) - month mois [13,21,34]	876.6	928.4	936.8	887.2	...	...	...	...
M(V) - month mois [13,21,34]	1 038.9	1 108.2	1 105.0	1 035.1	...	...	...	...
F(V) - month mois [13,21,34]	641.1	667.5	692.9	654.8	...	...	...	...
Czech Republic (Czech koruna) République tchèque (couronne tchèque)								
MF(I) - month mois	15 329.0	16 560.0	17 337.0	18 482.0	...	...	24 653.0	25 241.0
M(I) - month mois	...	...	...	...	...	...	27 696.0	28 259.0
F(I) - month mois	...	...	...	...	...	...	19 099.0	19 737.0
MF(II) - month mois [35]	13 049.0	14 095.0	14 662.0	...	...	...	...	...
M(II) - month mois [35]	15 112.0	16 323.0	16 980.0	...	...	...	...	...
F(II) - month mois [35]	9 881.0	10 674.0	11 103.0	...	...	...	...	...
Denmark [9,36] (Danish krone) Danemark [9,36] (couronne danoise)								
MF(I) - hour heure	215.3	217.2	226.6	235.6	248.8	...	...	...
M(I) - hour heure	223.8	226.1	235.5	244.6	258.5	...	...	...
F(I)- hour heure	194.5	196.8	204.7	213.4	223.7	...	...	...
Dominican Republic (Dominican peso) Rép. dominicaine (peso dominicain)								
MF(I) - hour heure	32.7	50.8	81.1	85.4	85.4	86.1	...	...
MF(I) - month mois	...	...	...	...	...	...	11 111.0	11 745.0
M(I) - month mois	...	...	...	...	...	...	11 702.0	12 405.0
F(I) - month mois	...	...	...	...	...	...	9 551.0	10 106.0
Ecuador (U.S. dollar) Equateur (dollar des Etats-Unis)								
MF(I) - month mois	338.2	370.6	...	...	...	...	...	...
Egypt [8,13] (Egyptian pound) Egypte [8,13] (livre égyptienne)								
MF(II) - week semaine	150.0	162.0	179.0	203.0	220.0	...	...	...
M(II) - week semaine	157.0	168.0	187.0	210.0	231.0	...	...	...
F(II) - week semaine	104.0	126.0	134.0	159.0	153.0	...	...	...
El Salvador (El Salvadoran colón) El Salvador (cólon salvadorien)								
MF(I) - month mois	209.6	211.3	229.0	235.1	...	...	...	...
M(I) - month mois	249.6	261.8	280.6	284.8	...	...	...	...
F(I) - month mois	171.2	162.5	178.1	181.3	...	...	...	...
MF(II) - hour heure [37]	1.3	1.4	1.5	1.2	1.3	1.6	...	...
M(II) - hour heure [37]	1.5	1.7	1.5	1.4	1.3	1.7	...	...
F(II) - hour heure [37]	1.2	1.2	1.2	1.1	1.1	1.4	...	...
Estonia [38] (Estonian kroon) Estonie [38] (couronne estonienne)								
MF(I) - month mois	6 403.0	7 012.0	7 760.0	9 158.0	11 047.7	12 366.4	...	...
Ethiopia (Ethiopian birr) Ethiopie (birr éthiopien)								
MF(I) - month mois	...	...	...	...	...	...	628.5	685.1
M(I) - month mois	...	...	...	...	...	...	717.9	788.9
F(I) - month mois	...	...	...	...	...	...	458.6	504.5
Finland (euro) Finlande (euro)								
MF(I) - month mois	2 463.0[14,28,39]	2 564.0[14,28,39]	2 641.0[14,28,39]	2 788.0[14,28,39]	2 915.0[14,28,39]	3 024.0[14,28,39]	3 115.0	3 194.0
M(I) - month mois	2 581.0[14,28,39]	2 685.0[14,28,39]	2 772.0[14,28,39]	2 921.0[14,28,39]	3 048.0[14,28,39]	3 160.0[14,28,39]	3 245.0	3 317.0
F(I) - month mois	2 160.0[14,28,39]	2 252.0[14,28,39]	2 315.0[14,28,39]	2 447.0[14,28,39]	2 568.0[14,28,39]	2 690.0[14,28,39]	2 760.0	2 844.0
MF(II) - hour heure [9,28]	...	...	13.9	14.5	15.1	15.3	...	...
M(II) - hour heure [9,28]	...	...	14.4	15.1	15.7	15.9	...	...
F(II) - hour heure [9,28]	...	...	12.2	12.6	13.1	...	...	...

27

Wages in manufacturing *(continued)*
By hour, day, week or month, and by gender
Salaires dans les industries manufacturières *(suite)*
Par heure, jour, semaine ou mois, et par sexe

Country or area § Pays ou zone §	2003	2004	2005	2006	2007	2008	2009	2010
France (euro) France (euro)								
MF(I) - hour heure [40]	15.9	16.4	16.8	17.3	17.9	...	...	...
M(I) - hour heure [40]	16.8	17.3	17.7	18.2	18.8	...	...	...
F(I)- hour heure [40]	13.5	14.0	14.5	15.0	15.6	...	...	...
MF(II) - hour heure	12.0	12.3	12.6	12.9	13.3	...	...	...
M(II) - hour heure	12.4	12.8	13.0	13.4	13.8	...	...	...
F(II) - hour heure	10.3	10.7	11.0	11.3	11.7	...	...	...
French Polynesia (CFP franc) Polynésie française (franc CFP)								
M(I) - month mois	213 876.0	...	...	...	...	...	...	...
F(I) - month mois	186 653.0	...	...	...	...	...	...	...
Georgia (lari) Géorgie (lari)								
MF(I) - month mois	152.5	183.9	212.1	260.5	357.7	...	447.9	510.6
M(I) - month mois	174.9	210.2	243.5	293.7	411.0	...	507.6	577.2
F(I) - month mois	108.4	132.2	147.7		246.4	...	332.0	373.2
Germany (euro) Allemagne (euro)								
MF(I) - hour heure	...	...	...	...	19.1	19.5	...	...
M(I) - hour heure	...	...	...	...	20.0	20.5	...	...
F(I)- hour heure	...	...	...	...	15.3	15.6	...	...
MF(I) - month mois	...	...	...	...	...	...	3 533.0	3 708.0
M(I) - month mois	...	...	...	...	...	...	3 713.0	3 898.0
F(I) - month mois	...	...	...	...	...	...	2 774.0	2 906.0
MF(II) - hour heure	15.1	15.4	15.6	15.7[41]	...	...	...	...
M(II) - hour heure	15.7	16.0	16.2	16.4[41]	...	...	...	...
F(II) - hour heure	11.6	11.9	12.0	12.1[41]	...	...	...	...
Greece (euro) Grèce (euro)								
MF(I) - month mois	...	...	...	1 800.7	...	...	...	...
Guam [9,10] (US dollar) Guam [9,10] (dollar des Etats-Unis)								
MF(II) - hour heure	12.2	12.5	12.3	14.9	14.4	13.1	...	...
Guatemala (quetzal) Guatemala (quetzal)								
MF(I) - month mois	1 911.4	2 100.1	2 199.7	2 482.1	2 579.4	2 737.2		
Guyana [42] (Guyana dollar) Guyana [42] (dollar guyanais)								
MF(I) - month mois	29 678.0	47 800.0	...	55 615.0	47 150.0	...	...	...
Hungary [14,43] (forint) Hongrie [14,43] (forint)								
MF(I) - month mois	124 770.0	136 992.0	147 234.0	156 812.7	171 564.5	184 184.8	...	...
M(I) - month mois	140 244.0	153 396.0	164 230.0	175 199.4	191 594.8	...	...	...
F(I) - month mois	102 585.0	112 946.0	121 082.0	128 302.2	139 856.3	...	...	...
Iceland (Icelandic króna) Islande (couronne islandaise)								
MF(I) - hour heure	1 404.0	1 494.0	1 622.0	1 762.0	1 946.0	2 033.0	...	...
M(I) - hour heure	1 568.0	1 670.0	1 812.0	1 961.0	2 131.0	2 216.0	...	...
F(I)- hour heure	1 122.0	1 200.0	1 312.0	1 425.0	1 597.0	1 675.0	...	...
MF(I) - month mois [44]	283 000.0	304 000.0	331 000.0	361 000.0	390 000.0	407 000.0	...	...
M(I) - month mois [44]	312 000.0	335 000.0	365 000.0	398 000.0	426 000.0	443 000.0	...	...
F(I) - month mois [44]	212 000.0	231 000.0	254 000.0	272 000.0	303 000.0	318 000.0	...	...
India [23,45] (Indian rupee) Inde [23,45] (roupie indienne)								
MF(II) - month mois	1 078.9	1 731.8	1 234.4	3 525.9	...	...	...	...
Indonesia (Indonesian rupiah) Indonésie (roupie indonésien)								
MF(I) - month mois	...	...	...	...	...	...	1 120 901.0	1 196 521.0
M(I) - month mois	...	...	...	...	...	...	1 261 702.0	1 333 731.0
F(I) - month mois	...	...	...	...	...	...	910 940.0	979 225.0
Ireland (euro) Irlande (euro)								
MF(I) - week semaine [8,46]	603.5	632.8	659.4	678.3	...	...	...	...
MF(II) - hour heure [17,47]	12.9	13.6	14.0	14.5	...	...	...	...
M(II) - hour heure [8,48]	13.8	14.4	14.8	15.3	...	...	...	...
F(II) - hour heure [8,48]	10.7	11.1	11.6	12.3	...	...	...	...
MF(II) - week semaine [8,48]	511.8	534.2	557.6	575.2	...	...	...	...
M(II) - week semaine [8,48]	564.9	588.9	609.9	624.5	...	...	...	...
F(II) - week semaine [8,48]	393.8	406.8	430.2	451.1	...	...	...	...
Isle of Man [49] (pound sterling) Ile de Man [49] (livre sterling)								
MF(I) - hour heure	9.7	10.4	10.6	11.0	12.0	12.9	...	...
M(I) - hour heure	11.0	10.3	10.9	11.1	12.7	12.6	...	...
F(I)- hour heure	7.5	10.7	9.2	10.7	9.0	14.2	...	...
MF(I) - week semaine	409.6	412.4	441.0	445.8	482.4	540.0	...	...

27

Wages in manufacturing *(continued)*
By hour, day, week or month, and by gender
Salaires dans les industries manufacturières *(suite)*
Par heure, jour, semaine ou mois, et par sexe

Country or area § Pays ou zone §	2003	2004	2005	2006	2007	2008	2009	2010
M(I) - week semaine	504.5	455.4	468.0	463.2	518.2	545.4	...	...
F(I) - week semaine	253.9	265.2	325.0	401.1	323.0	...	...	...
Israel (new sheqel) **Israël (nouveau sheqel)**								
MF(I) - month mois	...	...	...	...	...	...	9 197.0	9 368.0
M(I) - month mois	...	...	...	...	...	...	9 900.0	10 351.0
F(I) - month mois	...	...	...	...	...	...	7 472.0	7 035.0
MF(II) - month mois [50]	...	...	9 915.0	10 377.0	10 694.0	10 982.0	...	...
Jamaica (Jamaican dollar) **Jamaïque (dollar jamaïcain)**								
MF(I) - week semaine	7 162.0	7 910.0	8 617.0	9 080.0	9 819.0	10 895.0	12 863.0	13 603.8
Japan (yen) **Japon (yen)**								
MF(I) - month mois	296 500.0[8,9,49,51]	293 100.0[8,9,49,51]	292 100.0[8,9,49,51]	299 600.0[8,9,49,51]	296 800.0[8,9,49,51]	293 400.0[8,9,49,51]	287 400.0	292 300.0
M(I) - month mois	327 800.0[8,9,49,51]	323 100.0[8,9,49,51]	323 800.0[8,9,49,51]	332 300.0[8,9,49,51]	328 500.0[8,9,49,51]	322 600.0[8,9,49,51]	315 100.0	318 600.0
F(I) - month mois	195 800.0[8,49,51]	194 100.0[8,9,49,51]	190 900.0[8,9,49,51]	194 600.0[8,9,49,51]	197 700.0[8,9,49,51]	198 000.0[8,9,49,51]	196 600.0	199 400.0
Jersey [49,52,53,54] (pound) **Jersey [49,52,53,54] (livre)**								
MF(I) - week semaine	470.0	490.0	520.0	530.0	550.0	570.0	...	...
Jordan [13] (Jordan dinar) **Jordanie [13] (dinar jordanien)**								
MF(I) - month mois	198.0	186.0	203.0	211.0	237.0	267.0	...	...
M(I) - month mois	208.0	201.0	222.0	234.0	254.0	289.0	...	...
F(I) - month mois	136.0	130.0	136.0	142.0	174.0	181.0	...	...
Kazakhstan (tenge) **Kazakhstan (tenge)**								
MF(I) - month mois	24 823.0	30 234.0	35 412.0	43 617.0	54 415.0	65 874.0	68 959.0	78 764.0
M(I) - month mois	27 515.0	33 541.5	39 536.4	48 460.0	60 528.9	73 456.8	76 764.0	87 377.0
F(I) - month mois	19 382.0	23 432.5	27 247.3	33 432.1	41 452.5	49 763.9	52 032.0	59 658.0
Kyrgyzstan (Kyrgyz som) **Kirghizistan (som kirghize)**								
MF(I) - month mois	3 182.6	3 758.6	4 229.6	6 211.0	6 254.0	...	...	...
Latvia (lats) **Lettonie (lats)**								
MF(I) - month mois	159.3[55]	176.4[55]	200.3[55]	239.6[55]	315.0[55]	394.0[55]	406.6	391.2
M(I) - month mois	172.8[55]	192.1[55]	217.9[55]	263.1[55]	350.3[55]	430.2[55]	446.3	429.8
F(I) - month mois	142.0[55]	155.9[55]	177.3[55]	209.0[55]	269.7[55]	346.7[55]	353.6	339.5
Lithuania [56] (litas) **Lituanie [56] (litas)**								
MF(I) - hour heure [57]	6.6	6.9	7.6	8.9	11.0	12.8	...	...
M(I) - hour heure [57]	7.5	7.7	8.6	10.2	12.7	14.9	...	...
F(I)- hour heure [57]	5.8	5.9	6.5	7.5	9.0	10.4	...	...
MF(I) - month mois	1 016.0	1 085.0	1 184.0	1 387.0	1 727.0	2 035.0	...	...
Luxembourg (euro) **Luxembourg (euro)**								
MF(I) - month mois	...	...	...	...	...	...	44 692.0	45 291.0
M(I) - month mois	...	...	...	...	...	...	46 145.0	46 808.0
F(I) - month mois	...	...	...	...	...	...	36 513.0	36 776.0
MF(II) - hour heure [13]	13.5	14.2	14.7	14.7	14.8	15.1	...	...
M(II) - hour heure [13]	14.0	14.7	15.2	15.2	15.3	15.6	...	...
F(II) - hour heure [13]	10.2	10.6	11.1	11.0	11.1	11.4	...	...
MF(V) - month mois [13]	4 090.0	4 189.0	4 334.0	4 374.0	4 506.0	4 650.0	...	...
M(V) - month mois [13]	4 412.0	4 510.0	4 663.0	4 710.0	4 876.0	5 007.0	...	...
F(V) - month mois [13]	2 911.0	3 030.0	3 185.0	3 229.0	3 280.0	3 489.0	...	...
Madagascar (Malagasy ariary) **Madagascar (ariary malgache)**								
MF(I) - hour heure	...	...	2 033.0	...	...	...	...	...
M(I) - hour heure	...	...	2 106.0	...	...	...	...	...
F(I)- hour heure	...	...	1 794.0	...	...	...	...	...
Maldives (rufiyaa) **Maldives (rufiyaa)**								
MF(I) - month mois	...	...	...	...	...	...	6 608.0	6 608.0
M(I) - month mois	...	...	...	...	...	...	7 094.0	7 094.0
F(I) - month mois	...	...	...	...	...	...	4 385.0	4 385.0
Malta (Maltese lira, euro) **Malte (lire maltaise, euro)**								
MF(I) - hour heure	2.3	2.3	2.4	2.6	2.6	#6.4[58]	...	...
M(I) - hour heure	2.4	2.4	2.5	2.6	2.7	#6.6[58]	...	...
F(I)- hour heure	2.2	2.2	2.2	2.3	2.3	#5.8[58]	...	...
MF(I) - month mois	...	...	...	...	...	...	1 393.0	1 451.0
M(I) - month mois	...	...	...	...	...	...	1 516.0	1 579.0
F(I) - month mois	...	...	...	...	...	...	1 082.0	1 130.0
Mauritius (Mauritian rupee) **Maurice (roupie mauricienne)**								
MF(I) - month mois	6 668.0[8,59]	7 299.0[8,59]	7 798.0[8,59]	8 214.0[8,59]	8 622.0[8,59]	8 995.0[8,59]	9 700.0	10 700.0

27 Wages in manufacturing *(continued)*
By hour, day, week or month, and by gender
Salaires dans les industries manufacturières *(suite)*
Par heure, jour, semaine ou mois, et par sexe

Country or area § Pays ou zone §	2003	2004	2005	2006	2007	2008	2009	2010
M(I) - month mois	...	...	...	...	...	...	12 600.0	13 800.0
F(I) - month mois	...	...	...	...	...	...	6 100.0	6 600.0
Mexico (Mexican peso) Mexique (peso mexicain)								
MF(I) - hour heure	19.4	...	...	...	...	...	...	...
M(I) - hour heure	21.2	...	...	...	...	...	...	...
F(I)- hour heure	15.7	...	...	...	...	...	...	...
MF(I) - month mois [60,61]	3 757.3	3 887.9	4 140.3	4 422.6	4 689.2	4 679.3	...	...
M(I) - month mois [60,61]	4 176.6	4 273.8	4 625.6	4 839.5	5 242.5	5 172.2	...	...
F(I) - month mois [60,61]	2 911.7	3 114.6	3 217.5	3 628.3	3 651.1	3 715.3	...	...
MF(II) - hour heure	26.9	...	...	...	...	...	...	...
Mongolia [11] (togrog) Mongolie [11] (togrog)								
MF(I) - month mois	82.7	92.8	100.5	124.1	160.2	268.0	271.9	326.2
M(I) - month mois	86.9	98.1	114.9	142.7	189.4	315.9	299.0	374.6
F(I) - month mois	75.6	89.1	88.9	105.2	135.6	225.2	243.4	276.5
Montenegro (euro) Monténégro (euro)								
MF(I) - month mois	...	...	...	...	530.0	615.0	611.0	699.0
Netherlands [10,62] (euro) Pays-Bas [10,62] (euro)								
MF(I) - hour heure	17.8	18.2	18.5	...	...	...	...	...
M(I) - hour heure	18.5	18.9	19.1	...	...	...	...	...
F(I)- hour heure	14.7	15.4	15.6	...	...	...	...	...
MF(I) - month mois [14]	2 572.0	2 637.0	2 689.0	...	...	...	...	...
M(I) - month mois [14]	2 634.0	2 692.0	2 740.0	...	...	...	...	...
F(I) - month mois [14]	2 123.0	2 221.0	2 282.0	...	...	...	...	...
New Zealand (New Zealand dollar) Nouvelle-Zélande (dollar néo-zélandais)								
MF(I) - hour heure [53,63,64]	18.5	19.3	19.6	20.5	21.5	22.4	...	...
M(I) - hour heure [53,63,64]	19.5	20.2	20.5	21.5	22.5	23.6	...	...
F(I)- hour heure [53,63,64]	15.5	16.6	16.8	17.6	18.5	19.2	...	...
MF(I) - month mois	...	...	...	...	...	...	4 240.0	4 350.0
M(I) - month mois	...	...	...	...	...	...	4 630.0	4 750.0
F(I) - month mois	...	...	...	...	...	...	3 270.0	3 340.0
Nicaragua (córdoba) Nicaragua (córdoba)								
MF(I) - hour heure	13.5	13.5	13.7	13.9	...	...	...	...
MF(I) - month mois	3 279.0	3 283.0	3 331.0	3 393.0	...	...	4 339.0	4 581.0
Norway (Norwegian krone) Norvège (couronne norvégienne)								
MF(I) - month mois	26 944.0[13,14,65]	27 920.0[13,14,65]	28 908.0[13,14,65]	30 162.0[13,14,65]	31 983.0[13,14,65]	33 977.0[13,14,65]	35 600.0	36 900.0
M(I) - month mois	27 625.0[13,14,62]	28 588.0[13,14,62]	29 513.0[13,14,62]	30 767.0[13,14,62]	32 710.0[13,14,62]	34 638.0[13,14,62]	36 400.0	37 600.0
F(I) - month mois	24 260.0[13,14,62]	25 290.0[13,14,62]	26 432.0[13,14,62]	27 649.0[13,14,62]	29 124.0[13,14,62]	31 301.0[13,14,62]	32 400.0	33 700.0
Occupied Palestinian Terr. [66,67,68] (new shekel) Terr. palestinien occupé [66,67,68] (nouveau shekel)								
MF(I) - day jour	68.5	66.8	74.0	77.7	71.1	81.4	...	...
M(I) - day jour	71.7	70.9	77.8	81.8	76.4	86.6	...	...
F(I) - day jour	41.6	30.8	40.8	44.5	40.4	43.4	...	...
Panama (balboa) Panama (balboa)								
MF(I) - month mois	...	...	...	...	...	...	500.4	483.8
M(I) - month mois	...	...	...	...	...	...	510.2	501.7
F(I) - month mois	...	...	...	...	...	...	463.1	422.0
MF(VI) - hour heure [25,68,69]	1.7	1.9	2.2	2.2	2.2	2.0	...	...
M(VI)- hour heure [25,68,69]	1.7	1.9	2.1	2.1	2.2	2.1	...	...
F(VI) - hour heure [25,68,69]	1.8	2.1	2.7	2.7	2.1	2.0	...	...
Paraguay (guaraní) Paraguay (guaraní)								
MF(I) - month mois	816 428.0[23]	...	...	...	5 399.1[11,28]	5 907.1[11,28]	1 435 441.0	1 491 498.0
M(I) - month mois	966 821.0[23]	...	...	...	5 550.4[11,28]	5 827.6[11,28]	1 445 467.0	1 481 175.0
F(I) - month mois	514 766.0[23]	...	...	...	4 745.9[11,28]	6 303.2[11,28]	1 395 611.0	1 539 724.0
Peru (new sol) Pérou (nouveau sol)								
MF(I) - month mois	...	...	...	...	...	...	1 208.4	1 172.0
M(I) - month mois	...	...	...	...	...	...	1 287.3	1 282.6
F(I) - month mois	...	...	...	...	...	...	1 010.6	906.5
Philippines (Philippine peso) Philippines (peso philippin)								
MF(I) - day jour	237.4	239.4	246.6	265.0	277.2	289.6	299.9	310.5
M(I) - day jour	246.3	247.7	254.0	270.5	290.9	299.1	309.7	319.7
F(I) - day jour	225.0	227.4	236.5	257.4	257.9	275.8	284.8	296.4
MF(I) - month mois [70,71,72]	11 166.0	...	12 973.0	13 872.0	...	15 625.0	...	...

Wages in manufacturing *(continued)*
By hour, day, week or month, and by gender

Salaires dans les industries manufacturières *(suite)*
Par heure, jour, semaine ou mois, et par sexe

Country or area § Pays ou zone §	2003	2004	2005	2006	2007	2008	2009	2010
Poland (zloty) Pologne (zloty)								
MF(I) - month mois	1 980.7[73]	2 053.7[73]	2 123.6[73]	2 246.0[73]	2 450.7[73]	2 706.3[73]	...	3 185.2
M(I) - month mois	...	...	...	...	...	...	...	3 448.2
F(I) - month mois	...	...	...	...	...	...	...	2 668.2
Portugal (euro) Portugal (euro)								
MF(I) - month mois	775.0	806.0	837.0	868.0	893.0	932.0	962.7	977.7
M(I) - month mois	905.0	934.0	968.2	1 008.0	1 026.0	1 065.0	1 099.7	1 119.6
F(I) - month mois	596.0	622.0	648.4	675.0	696.0	729.0	756.4	768.9
MF(II) - hour heure	3.7	3.8	3.9	4.0	4.1	4.3	...	...
M(II) - hour heure	4.2	4.4	4.5	4.6	4.7	4.8	...	...
F(II) - hour heure	2.9	3.0	3.0	3.1	3.2	3.3	...	...
Puerto Rico (US dollar) Porto Rico (dollar des Etats-Unis)								
MF(II) - hour heure[59]	10.5	10.8	11.1	11.5	11.9	12.1	...	...
MF(II) - week semaine	427.8	444.4	452.9	464.9	488.4	490.9	...	...
Qatar (Qatar riyal) Qatar (riyal qatarien)								
MF(I) - month mois	...	...	...	3 677.0[13]	5 060.0[13]	...	7 166.0	...
M(I) - month mois	...	...	...	3 688.0[13]	5 027.0[13]	...	7 116.0	...
F(I) - month mois	...	...	...	4 092.0[13]	7 118.0[13]	...	9 457.0	...
Republic of Korea (Korean won) République de Corée (won coréen)								
MF(I) - month mois	2 018.0[11,74]	2 209.0[11,74]	2 387.6[11,74]	2 522.5[11,74]	2 688.0[11,74]	2 758.7[11,74]	2 162 857.0	2 274 189.0
M(I) - month mois	2 304.6[11,74]	2 521.4[11,74]	2 715.7[11,74]	2 847.4[11,74]	3 025.6[11,74]	...	2 380 222.0	2 491 680.0
F(I) - month mois	1 291.2[11,74]	1 382.8[11,74]	1 525.4[11,74]	1 643.2[11,74]	1 742.1[11,74]	...	1 505 057.0	1 615 354.0
Republic of Moldova (Moldovan leu) République de Moldova (leu moldove)								
MF(I) - month mois	1 216.1[35]	1 417.8[35]	1 651.6[35]	1 914.5[35]	2 314.1[35]	2 762.8[35]	2 800.8	3 079.8
Romania (Romanian leu) Roumanie (leu roumain)								
MF(I) - month mois	5 804 147.0	7 196 971.0	#829.0[75]	950.0	1 146.0	...	1 528.0	1 675.0
M(I) - month mois	6 662 800.0	8 167 249.0	#945.0[75]	1 087.0	1 302.0	...	1 713.0	1 869.0
F(I) - month mois	4 915 058.0	6 203 325.0	#710.0[75]	807.0	976.0	...	1 320.0	1 458.0
Russian Federation (ruble) Fédération de Russie (ruble)								
MF(I) - month mois	...	...	8 421.0	10 199.0	12 879.0	16 050.0	16 583.0	19 078.0
Saint Lucia[76] (EC dollar) Sainte-Lucie[76] (dollar des Caraïbes orientales)								
M(II) - hour heure[77]	7.0	...	...	...	...	...	...	...
F(II) - hour heure[77]	5.0	...	...	...	...	...	...	...
M(V) - hour heure	14.5	...	...	...	...	...	...	...
F(V) - hour heure	11.7	...	...	...	...	...	...	...
San Marino (euro) Saint-Marin (euro)								
MF(I) - month mois	1 922.1	1 900.0	1 933.6	2 021.1	...	...	...	...
Saudi Arabia (Saudi Arabian riyal) Arabie saoudite (riyal saoudien)								
MF(I) - month mois	...	...	...	...	...	...	3 276.0	...
M(I) - month mois	...	...	...	...	...	...	3 301.0	...
F(I) - month mois	...	...	...	...	...	...	1 805.0	...
Serbia (dinar) Serbie (dinar)								
MF(I) - month mois	12 996.0[78]	16 065.0[78]	20 366.0[78]	25 830.0[78]	30 620.0[78]	36 540.0[78]	34 998.0	40 101.0
Serbia and Montenegro[78,79] (new dinar) Serbie-et-Monténégro[78,79] (nouveau dinar)								
MF(I) - month mois	12 996.0	16 065.0	20 366.0	...	...	...	...	...
Seychelles (Seychelles rupee) Seychelles (roupie seychelloises)								
MF(I) - month mois	2 986.0	3 042.0	3 314.0	3 350.0	3 306.0	4 100.0	...	...
Singapore (Singapore dollar) Singapour (dollar singapourien)								
MF(I) - month mois	3 265.0	3 350.0	#3 495.0	3 618.0	3 764.0	3 955.0	3 966.0	4 263.0
M(I) - month mois	3 881.0	3 969.0	#4 111.0	4 218.0	4 359.0	4 559.0	4 510.0	4 869.0
F(I) - month mois	2 374.0	2 442.0	#2 563.0	2 682.0	2 815.0	2 974.0	3 048.0	3 253.0
Slovakia (Slovak koruna, euro) Slovaquie (couronne slovaque, euro)								
MF(I) - month mois	14 873.0[80]	16 378.0[80]	17 604.0[80]	18 817.0[80]	20 024.0[80]	21 449.0[80]	#740.0	789.0
M(I) - month mois	...	...	...	...	...	...	#838.0	887.0
F(I) - month mois	...	...	...	...	...	...	#588.0	627.0
Slovenia (tolar, euro) Slovénie (tolar, euro)								
MF(I) - month mois	211 060.0[81,82]	226 029.0[81,82]	238 985.0[81,82]	252 162.0[81,82]	#1 123.6[82]	1 208.2[82]	1 241.0	1 357.0
M(I) - month mois	...	...	...	...	...	...	1 309.0	1 425.0
F(I) - month mois	...	...	...	...	...	...	1 107.0	1 220.0
Spain (euro) Espagne (euro)								
MF(I) - hour heure[83]	11.5	12.0	12.4	12.9	13.4	14.1	...	...

27

Wages in manufacturing *(continued)*
By hour, day, week or month, and by gender
Salaires dans les industries manufacturières *(suite)*
Par heure, jour, semaine ou mois, et par sexe

Country or area § Pays ou zone §	2003	2004	2005	2006	2007	2008	2009	2010
MF(I) - month mois	...	...	...	...	...	...	1 992.0	...
M(I) - month mois	...	...	...	...	...	...	2 112.0	...
F(I) - month mois	...	...	...	...	...	...	1 644.0	...
Sri Lanka (Sri Lanka rupee) Sri Lanka (roupie sri-lankaise)								
MF(I) - month mois	...	...	...	...	...	...	11 096.0	12 234.0
M(I) - month mois	...	...	...	...	...	...	13 634.0	14 557.0
F(I) - month mois	...	...	...	...	...	...	8 067.0	9 337.0
MF(II) - day jour [84]	306.3	309.0	336.5	356.1	412.2	432.6	...	...
M(II) - day jour [84]	311.2	312.1	338.1	357.5	419.0	489.2	...	...
F(II) - day jour [84]	253.0	270.0	327.9	346.2	394.4	376.0	...	...
MF(II) - hour heure [84]	33.2	35.5	36.9	39.9	45.4	49.9	...	...
M(II) - hour heure [84]	33.6	35.8	37.1	40.0	46.1	55.2	...	...
F(II) - hour heure [84]	28.9	31.2	35.1	39.1	43.0	44.6	...	...
Sweden [9,17,85] (Swedish krona) Suède [9,17,85] (couronne suédoise)								
MF(II) - hour heure	122.0[34]	126.1[34]	129.9[34]	133.8[34]	139.5[34]	145.2[86]	...	...
M(II) - hour heure	124.1[34]	128.4[34]	132.2[34]	136.1[34]	142.1[34]	147.7[86]	...	...
F(II) - hour heure	112.9[34]	116.8[34]	119.9[34]	124.1[34]	128.6[34]	134.4[86]	...	...
Switzerland (Swiss franc) Suisse (franc suisse)								
MF(I) - month mois	...	6 349.0[87]	...	6 527.0[87]	...	6 752.0[87]	...	6 901.5
M(I) - month mois	...	6 726.0[87]	...	6 915.0[87]	...	7 146.0[87]	...	7 277.4
F(I) - month mois	...	5 162.0[87]	...	5 353.0[87]	...	5 616.0[87]	...	5 792.9
Syrian Arab Republic (Syrian pound) Rép. arabe syrienne (livre syrienne)								
MF(V) - month mois	...	...	7 418.0	8 066.0	8 721.0	9 895.0	...	...
M(V) - month mois	...	...	7 517.0	8 168.0	8 817.0	10 071.0	...	...
F(V) - month mois	...	...	6 147.0	6 769.0	7 413.0	7 989.0	...	...
TFYR of Macedonia [67] (TFYR Macedonian denar) L'ex-R.Y. Macédoine [67] (denar de l'ex-R.Y. Macédoine)								
MF(I) - month mois	10 028.0	10 486.0	10 298.0	10 624.0	11 653.0	12 613.0	...	...
Turkey (new Turkish Lira) Turquie (nouveau livre turque)								
MF(I) - day jour	36 069.1	42 629.9	46 184.1	...	...	...	...	...
MF(I) - hour heure	4 809.2	5 684.0	6 157.9	...	...	...	...	...
MF(I) - month mois	865 658.0	1 023 118.0	1 108 419.0	...	...	...	...	#1 468.0[88]
M(I) - month mois	...	...	...	...	...	...	...	1 530.0
F(I) - month mois	...	...	...	...	...	...	...	1 233.0
Uganda (Uganda shilling) Ouganda (shilling ougandais)								
MF(I) - month mois	...	...	...	...	...	...	267 299.1	...
Ukraine (hryvnia) Ukraine (hryvnia)								
MF(I) - month mois	552.9	700.0	905.1	1 137.3	1 456.4	1 849.0	1 856.0	2 281.0
M(I) - month mois	640.8	809.0	1 042.3	1 302.1	1 667.0	2 103.2	2 090.0	2 558.0
F(I) - month mois	443.5	562.9	727.0	920.0	1 175.3	1 503.5	1 535.0	1 887.0
United Arab Emirates (UAE dirham) Emirats arabes unis (dirham des EAU)								
MF(I) - month mois	...	...	...	...	...	...	6 783.5	...
M(I) - month mois	...	...	...	...	...	...	6 710.8	...
F(I) - month mois	...	...	...	...	...	...	7 852.9	...
United Kingdom (pound sterling) Royaume-Uni (livre sterling)								
MF(I) - hour heure [14]	10.3	10.5	11.2	11.4	11.7	12.3	...	...
M(I) - hour heure [14]	10.8	11.0	11.6	11.8	12.3	12.9	...	...
F(I)- hour heure [14]	8.6	9.2	10.0	10.1	10.1	10.7	...	...
MF(I) - month mois	...	...	...	...	...	...	2 341.0	2 371.0
M(I) - month mois	...	...	...	...	...	...	2 511.0	2 555.0
F(I) - month mois	...	...	...	...	...	...	1 708.0	1 696.0
MF(I) - week semaine [14]	431.0	437.0	467.0	477.0	491.0	513.0	...	...
M(I) - week semaine [14]	456.0	462.0	486.0	495.0	517.0	521.0	...	...
F(I) - week semaine [14]	340.0	348.0	393.0	406.0	401.0	425.0	...	...
United States [9,89,90] (US dollar) Etats-Unis [9,89,90] (dollar des Etats-Unis)								
MF(I) - hour heure	15.7	16.1	16.6	16.8	17.3	17.7	...	...
United States Virgin Is. (US dollar) Iles Vierges américaines (dollar des Etats-Unis)								
MF(II) - hour heure	23.4	23.4	23.5	26.5	26.4	28.1	...	...
Uruguay [91] (Uruguayan peso) Uruguay [91] (peso uruguayen)								
MF(I) - hour heure	...	...	...	...	90.5	100.5	...	...
Venezuela (Boliv. Rep. of) (bolívar) Venezuela (Rép. boliv. du) (bolívar)								
MF(I) - month mois	...	...	...	...	...	...	1 532.0	1 899.0

27 Wages in manufacturing *(continued)*
By hour, day, week or month, and by gender
Salaires dans les industries manufacturières *(suite)*
Par heure, jour, semaine ou mois, et par sexe

Country or area § Pays ou zone §	2003	2004	2005	2006	2007	2008	2009	2010
M(I) - month mois	...	...	...	...	...	...	1 562.0	1 929.0
F(I) - month mois	...	...	...	...	...	...	1 442.0	1 803.0
Zimbabwe (Zimbabwe dollar) **Zimbabwe (dollar zimbabwéen)**								
MF(I) - month mois	...	...	...	...	...	...	234.2	...

Source:
International Labour Office (ILO), Geneva, the ILO labour statistics database, last accessed March 2013.

§   I.   Employees.
     II.   Wage earners.
     III.   Skilled wage earners.
     IV.   Unskilled wage earners.
     V.   Salaried employees.
     VI.   Total employment.

Data are classified according to ISIC Rev. 3 unless indicated otherwise.

1   Local units with 10 or more workers.
2   Production and related workers.
3   Full-time adult non-managerial employees.
4   May.
5   Including mining and quarrying.
6   Per hour paid.
7   New denomination of AZM; 1 AZN=5000 AZM.
8   Establishments with 10 or more persons employed.
9   Private sector.
10   December.
11   Figures in thousands.
12   New denomination of the rouble: 1 new rouble = 1000 old roubles.

13   October.
14   Full-time employees only.
15   Last week of Aug. of each year.
16   Data refer to the Federation of Bosnia and Herzegovina.
17   September.
18   Employees under labour contract.
19   Including overtime.
20   Employees paid by the hour.
21   Including family allowances and the value of payments in kind.

22   April.
23   Data classified according to ISIC Rev. 2.
24   State-owned units, urban collective-owned units and other ownership units.
25   Median.
26   Including outworkers.
27   Third quarter.
28   Fourth quarter.
29   Persons aged 10 years and over.
30   Excluding armed forces.
31   Main occupation; July of each year.
32   Excluding employees in craft and trade.
33   State sector (civilian).
34   Adults.
35   Enterprises with 20 or more employees.
36   Excluding young people aged less than 18 years and trainees.
37   Urban areas.
38   Enterprises with 50 or more employees, state-owned and municipal enterprises, institutions and organisations.
39   From 2003: excl. seasonal and end-of-year bonuses.

Source:
Bureau international du Travail (BIT), Genève, la base de données du BIT, dernier accès Mars 2013.

§   I.   Salariés.
     II.   Ouvriers.
     III.   Ouvriers qualifiés.
     IV.   Ouvriers non qualifiés.
     V.   Employés.
     VI.   Emploi total.

Sauf indication contraire, les données sont classifiées selon la CITI, Rév. 3.

1   Unités locales occupant 10 ouvriers et plus.
2   Ouvriers à la production et assimilés.
3   Salariés adultes à plein temps, non compris les cadres dirigeants.
4   Mai.
5   Y compris les industries extractives.
6   Salaire horaire.
7   Nouvelle dénomination de l'AZM; 1 AZN = 5000 AZM.
8   Etablissements occupant 10 personnes et plus.
9   Secteur privé.
10   Décembre.
11   Données en milliers.
12   Nouvelle dénomination du rouble: 1 nouveau rouble = 1000 anciens roubles.

13   Octobre.
14   Salariés à plein temps seulement.
15   Dernière semaine d'août de chaque année.
16   Les données se réfèrent à la Fédération de Bosnie et Herzégovine.
17   Septembre.
18   Salariés sous contrat de travail.
19   Y compris les heures supplémentaires.
20   Salariés rémunérés à l'heure.
21   Y compris les allocations familiales et la valeur des paiements en nature.

22   Avril.
23   Données classifiées selon la CITI, Rév. 2.
24   Unités d'Etat, unités collectives urbaines et autres.
25   Médiane.
26   Y compris les travailleurs externes.
27   Troisième trimestre.
28   Quatrième trimestre.
29   Personnes âgées de 10 ans et plus.
30   Non compris les militaires.
31   Occupation principale; juillet de chaque année.
32   Non compris les salariés dans l'artisanat et dans le commerce.
33   Secteur d'Etat (civils).
34   Adultes.
35   Entreprises occupant 20 salariés et plus.
36   Non compris les jeunes gens âgés de moins de 18 ans et les apprentis.
37   Régions urbaines.
38   Entreprises occupant 50 salariés et plus, entreprises d'Etat et municipales, institutions et organisations.
39   A partir de 2003: non compris les primes saisonnières et de fin d'année.

40	Including managerial staff and intermediary occupations.		40	Y compris les cadres et les professions intermédiaires.
41	Series discontinued.		41	Série arrêtée.
42	July.		42	Juillet.
43	Enterprises with 5 or more employees.		43	Entreprises occupant 5 salariés et plus.
44	Full-time adult employees.		44	Salariés adultes à plein temps.
45	The wage threshold for inclusion in these series varies in time which may explain part of the fluctuations in the series.		45	Le seuil de salaire pour l'inclusion dans ces séries varie dans le temps, cela explique en partie les fluctuations des séries.
46	Adult and non-adult rates of pay.		46	Taux de rémunération des adultes et des mineurs.
47	Including juveniles.		47	Y compris les jeunes gens.
48	Wage-earners on adult rates of pay.		48	Salariés rémunérés sur la base du taux de rémunération des adultes.
49	June.		49	Juin.
50	Israeli workers only.		50	Travailleurs israéliens seulement.
51	Regular scheduled cash earnings.		51	Gains en espèce tarifés réguliers.
52	Approximate levels since survey aims at measuring changes; excl. bonuses.		52	Niveaux approximatifs étant donné que l'enquête vise à mesurer l'évolution; non compris les primes.
53	Full-time equivalent employees.		53	Salariés en équivalents à plein temps.
54	Excluding bonuses.		54	Non compris les primes.
55	First quarter.		55	Premier trimestre.
56	All employees converted into full-time units.		56	Ensemble des salariés convertis en unités à plein temps.
57	Excluding individual unincorporated enterprises.		57	Non compris les entreprises individuelles non constituées en société.
58	Euros; 1 Euro=0.429300 MTL.		58	Euros; 1 Euro=0.429300 MTL.
59	March.		59	Mars.
60	Second quarter.		60	Deuxième trimestre.
61	Persons aged 14 years and over.		61	Personnes âgées de 14 ans et plus.
62	Excluding overtime payments.		62	Non compris la rémunération des heures supplémentaires.
63	Establishments with the equivalent of more than 0.5 full-time paid employees.		63	Etablissements occupant plus de l'équivalent de 0.5 salarié à plein temps.
64	February.		64	Février.
65	Only remuneration in cash; excl. overtime payments.		65	Seulement rémunération en espèces; non compris les paiements pour heures supplémentaires.
66	West Bank and Gaza.		66	Cisjordanie et Gaza.
67	Net earnings.		67	Gains nets.
68	Persons aged 15 years and over.		68	Personnes âgées de 15 ans et plus.
69	August.		69	Août.
70	Excluding bonuses and gratuities.		70	Non compris les primes et gratifications.
71	Establishments with 20 or more persons employed.		71	Entreprises occupant 20 salariés et plus.
72	Computed on the basis of annual wages.		72	Calculés sur la base de salaires annuels.
73	Including the value of payments in kind.		73	Y compris la valeur des paiements en nature.
74	Establishments with 5 or more regular employees.		74	Etablissements occupant 5 salariés stables et plus.
75	New denomination: 1 leu = 10 000 old lei.		75	Nouvelle dénomination: 1 leu = 1,000 anciens lei.
76	Unweighted survey results.		76	Résultats d'enquête non pondérés.
77	Minimum rates.		77	Taux minima.
78	Excluding Kosovo and Metohia.		78	Non compris Kosovo et Metohia.
79	Excluding Montenegro.		79	Non compris Monténégro.
80	Excluding enterprises with less than 20 employees.		80	Non compris les entreprises occupant moins de 20 salariés.
81	Prior to 2007: SIT; 1 Euro = 239.64 SIT.		81	Avant 2007: SIT; 1 Euro=239.64 SIT.
82	Excluding family allowances and the value of payments in kind.		82	Non compris les allocations familiales et la valeur des paiements en nature.
83	Including overtime payments and irregular gratuities.		83	Y compris la rémunération des heures supplémentaires et les prestations versées irrégulièrement.
84	March and September.		84	Mars et septembre.
85	Excluding holidays, sick-leave and overtime payments.		85	Non compris les versements pour les vacances, congés maladie ainsi que la rémunération des heures supplémentaires.
86	Data classified according to ISIC Rev. 4.		86	Données classifiées selon la CITI, Rév. 4.
87	Standardised monthly earnings (40 hours x 4 1/3 weeks).		87	Gains mensuels standardisés (40 heures x 4 1/3 semaines).
88	Denomination change.		88	Changement de dénomination.
89	National classification not strictly compatible with ISIC.		89	Classification nationale non strictement compatible avec la CITI.
90	Not all employees covered; only production and non-supervisory workers.		90	Salariés inclus: seuls les travailleurs de production à l'exception du personnel d'encadrement.
91	Index base : July 2008 = 100		91	Base de l'indice: 2008 juillet = 100

Consumer price indices
General and food (Index base: 2000 = 100)

Indices des prix à la consommation
Généraux et alimentation (Indices base : 2000 = 100)

Country or area	City - Ville	2006	2007	2008	2009	2010	2011	Pays ou zone
Albania								**Albanie**
General		119.5	123.0	127.1	130.0	134.6	139.2	Généraux
Food		115.6	119.0	124.3	130.4	136.7	143.2	Alimentation
Algeria								**Algérie**
General		118.8	123.5	128.9	140.1	145.9	154.3	Généraux
Food		119.3	126.7	134.6	...	157.1	166.5	Alimentation
Andorra								**Andorre**
General (2001 = 100)		117.1	120.1	125.6	124.2	126.2	129.3	Généraux (2001 = 100)
Food (2001 = 100)		115.4	116.8	122.6	122.4	123.3	125.1	Alimentation (2001 = 100)
Angola	Luanda							**Angola**
General		2 091.6	2 347.7	2 640.5	3 003.0	3 437.5	3 901.1	Généraux
Anguilla								**Anguilla**
General (2001 = 100)		122.7	129.1	137.9	136.9	138.3	146.9	Généraux (2001 = 100)
Food (2001 = 100)		111.9	118.9	136.9	143.2	144.8	150.3	Alimentation (2001 = 100)
Antigua and Barbuda								**Antigua-et-Barbuda**
General		111.9	114.1	119.4	119.1	...	...	Généraux
Food		110.7	116.1	122.1	131.2	...	...	Alimentation
Argentina	Buenos Aires							**Argentine**
General		179.4	195.2	211.9	225.5	248.8	273.1	Généraux
Food		205.5	228.5	243.9	250.9	287.0	311.9	Alimentation
Armenia								**Arménie**
General		121.1	126.5	137.8	142.5	154.2	165.2	Généraux
Food		132.0	140.9	156.5	155.1	169.7	189.1	Alimentation
Aruba								**Aruba**
General		121.0	127.5	139.0	136.0	138.8	144.8	Généraux
Food		122.3	139.0	154.5	161.7	158.0	164.7	Alimentation
Australia								**Australie**
General		120.2	123.0	128.3	130.7	134.4	139.0	Généraux
Food		129.2	132.3	138.5	143.6	145.8	152.9	Alimentation
Austria								**Autriche**
General		112.3	114.7	118.3	118.9	121.1	125.1	Généraux
Food (2005 = 100)		112.5	117.1	124.5	124.8	125.4	130.7	Alimentation (2005 = 100)
Bahamas	New Providence							**Bahamas**
General		112.8	115.6	120.8	123.3	124.6	128.9	Généraux
Food		116.4	120.6	128.6	134.8	133.5	123.1	Alimentation
Bahrain								**Bahreïn**
General		107.1	...	114.4	117.6	119.9	119.5	Généraux
Food		103.3	...	119.8	130.6	137.0	139.7	Alimentation
Bangladesh								**Bangladesh**
General		135.3	147.6	160.7	169.4	183.2	202.8	Généraux
Food		137.5	151.9	168.7	177.9	195.9	221.0	Alimentation
Barbados								**Barbade**
General		120.8	125.7	135.8	140.8	149.0	163.0	Généraux
		132.8	142.2	161.4	172.2	178.6	193.2	Alimentation
Belarus								**Bélarus**
General		411.2	445.9	512.0	578.3	622.9	...	Généraux
Food		380.1	417.4	491.1	559.8	29 099.4[1]	...	Alimentation
Belgium								**Belgique**
General		113.0	115.1	120.3	120.2	122.8	127.2	Généraux
Food		115.0	119.1	126.1	127.4	129.4	132.5	Alimentation
Belize								**Belize**
General		118.2	120.9	128.6	127.2	128.3	...	Généraux
		116.6	122.7	139.0	141.2	137.0	...	Alimentation
Benin	Cotonou							**Bénin**
General		119.2	120.8	130.3	133.2	133.7	137.4	Généraux
Food		113.6	112.6	132.9	140.3	141.6	149.6	Alimentation
Bermuda								**Bermudes**
General		119.5	124.1	130.0	132.4	135.6	139.2	Généraux
Food		113.6	117.6	124.1	130.9	134.7	137.8	Alimentation

Country or area	City - Ville	2006	2007	2008	2009	2010	2011	Pays ou zone
Bhutan								**Bhoutan**
General		122.6	129.0	139.8	145.8	156.1	169.9	Généraux
Food		114.2	123.5	138.2	150.7	163.9	180.6	Alimentation
Bolivia (Plurin. State of)								**Bolivie (État plurin. de)**
General		121.6	132.2	150.7	155.8	159.7	175.4	Généraux
Food		122.2	138.9	...	172.4	127.8	145.6	Alimentation
Bosnia and Herzegovina								**Bosnie-Herzégovine**
General (2005 = 100)		106.1	107.7	115.7	115.3	117.7	122.0	Généraux (2005 = 100)
Food (2005 = 100)		108.3	111.4	124.8	123.7	122.8	130.2	Alimentation (2005 = 100)
Botswana								**Botswana**
General		163.0	174.5	196.6	212.5	227.2	246.4	Généraux
Food		155.2	172.7	207.7	237.4	246.1	263.0	Alimentation
Brazil								**Brésil**
General		157.8	163.5	172.8	181.2	190.4	203.0	Généraux
Food		151.0	161.2	182.3	192.9	204.6	222.7	Alimentation
Brunei Darussalam								**Brunéi Darussalam**
General		...	101.0	103.8	...	105.1	107.1	Généraux
Food		...	104.7	109.9	...	111.6	116.6	Alimentation
Bulgaria								**Bulgarie**
General		139.0	150.7	169.3	174.0	178.2	185.8	Généraux
Food		123.4	140.0	163.4	162.3	161.7	172.9	Alimentation
Burkina Faso	Ouagadougou							**Burkina Faso**
General		118.8	118.5	131.1	134.5	131.4	135.0	Généraux
Food		119.7	117.9	145.4	149.1	152.7	162.0	Alimentation
Cambodia	Phnom Penh							**Cambodge**
General		119.5	126.5	151.4	159.0	165.3	174.4	Généraux
Food (2008=100)		124.2	136.6	100.0	99.7	104.0	110.7	Alimentation (2008 = 100)
Cameroon								**Cameroun**
General		116.2	117.2	123.5	127.2	128.9	132.7	Généraux
Canada								**Canada**
General		114.4	116.9	119.7	120.0	122.1	125.7	Généraux
Food		116.8	119.9	124.1	130.1	132.0	137.0	Alimentation
Cape Verde								**Cap-Vert**
General		110.6	115.5	123.4	124.6	127.1	132.8	Généraux
Food (2003 = 100)		102.7	107.9	117.7	120.0	122.6	129.0	Alimentation (2003 = 100)
Cayman Islands								**Iles Caïmanes**
General		117.7	121.1	126.1	124.4	124.5	...	Généraux
Food		120.1	126.3	133.4	144.6	148.6	...	Alimentation
Central African Rep.	Bangui							**Rép. centrafricaine**
General		119.1	120.3	131.5	136.1	138.1	...	Généraux
Chad	N'Djamena							**Tchad**
General		136.1	123.7	136.3	150.0	146.8	...	Généraux
Food		153.4	138.4	161.1	175.4	168.7	...	Alimentation
Chile	Santiago							**Chili**
General (2009 = 100)		...	...	...	100.0	101.4	104.8	Généraux (2009 = 100)
Food (2009 = 100)		...	...	...	100.0	102.2	109.0	Alimentation (2009 = 100)
China								**Chine**
General		108.5	113.7	120.4	119.6	123.5	130.2	Généraux
Food		119.0	133.8	152.8	153.9	165.2	184.7	Alimentation
China, Hong Kong SAR								**Chine, Hong Kong RAS**
General		95.3	97.2	101.4	101.9	104.4	109.9	Généraux
Food		100.1	104.3	114.9	116.4	119.3	127.7	Alimentation
China, Macao SAR								**Chine, Macao RAS**
General		104.1	109.9	119.4	120.8	124.1	131.3	Généraux
Food		105.0	113.6	133.2	140.6	147.2	159.2	Alimentation
Colombia								**Colombie**
General		145.2	153.4	166.0	173.2	177.4	184.2	Généraux
Food		150.5	162.5	182.6	189.6	191.7	201.0	Alimentation
Congo[2]	Brazzaville							**Congo**[2]
General		116.8	119.9	128.7	135.1	139.2	...	Généraux
Food		105.3	112.9	122.1	131.3	143.3	145.5	Alimentation

Country or area	City - Ville	2006	2007	2008	2009	2010	2011	Pays ou zone
Cook Islands	Rarotonga							**Iles Cook**
General		122.4	125.5	135.4	144.4	144.0	...	Généraux
Food		125.2	125.5	132.9	147.2	151.5	...	Alimentation
Costa Rica								**Costa Rica**
General		189.4	207.1	234.9	253.3	267.7	280.7	Généraux
Food (2007=100)		...	100.0	123.9	134.0	140.2	148.1	Alimentation (2007 = 100)
Côte d'Ivoire [2]	Abidjan							**Côte d'Ivoire** [2]
General		119.9	122.2	130.0	131.3	132.9	139.4	Généraux
Food		117.5	123.8	137.8	142.3	109.1[3]	120.5	Alimentation
Croatia								**Croatie**
General		117.7	121.1	128.4	131.5	132.9	135.9	Généraux
Food		113.1	116.9	128.5	130.6	128.7	133.2	Alimentation
Cyprus								**Chypre**
General		117.4	120.2	125.8	126.2	129.3	133.6	Généraux
Food		126.7	133.7	143.8	150.4	149.5	155.6	Alimentation
Czech Republic								**République tchèque**
General		114.6	117.9	125.4	126.7	128.6	131.0	Généraux
Food		110.0	116.4	126.4	126.7	115.7	121.0	Alimentation
Denmark								**Danemark**
General		112.3	114.2	118.1	119.7	122.4	125.8	Généraux
Food		110.2	115.1	123.8	123.7	124.2	129.1	Alimentation
Dominican Republic								**Rép. dominicaine**
General		247.9	263.1	291.1	295.3	314.0	340.6	Généraux
Food		242.8	258.8	295.7	307.3	320.4	349.3	Alimentation
Ecuador								**Equateur**
General		181.2	185.4	200.9	211.3	218.8	228.6	Généraux
Food (2005 = 100)		105.7	109.1	127.5	135.0	141.5	151.0	Alimentation (2005 = 100)
Egypt								**Egypte**
General		143.9	157.6	186.4	208.4	231.6	254.9	Généraux
Food (2004 = 100)		115.7	130.6	162.0	188.1	225.3	260.2	Alimentation (2004 = 100)
El Salvador								**El Salvador**
General		122.8	128.4	137.7	138.5	139.7	146.9	Généraux
Food		126.3	134.2	150.5	144.0	144.1	154.2	Alimentation
Estonia								**Estonie**
General		124.4	132.6	146.4	146.3	150.6	158.1	Généraux
Food		124.2	135.8	155.0	148.9	153.4	168.1	Alimentation
Ethiopia								**Ethiopie**
General		156.6	184.8	266.8	289.4	313.0	417.0	Généraux
Food (2001 = 100)		175.2	214.3	343.0	354.4	359.7	500.6	Alimentation (2001 = 100)
Fiji								**Fidji**
General		118.1	123.7	133.4	138.2	145.9	158.6	Généraux
Food		119.2	130.8	145.8	155.5	161.8	176.5	Alimentation
Finland								**Finlande**
General		107.9	110.6	115.0	115.1	116.5	120.5	Généraux
Food		110.7	113.0	122.7	125.2	120.7	128.2	Alimentation
France								**France**
General		111.8	113.4	116.6	116.7	118.5	121.0	Généraux
Food		112.7	114.3	119.9	120.4	121.4	123.7	Alimentation
French Guiana								**Guyane française**
General		110.4	114.2	118.2	119.0	119.2	121.6	Généraux
Food		111.4	113.6	119.0	122.7	123.7	126.0	Alimentation
French Polynesia								**Polynésie française**
General		108.7	110.9	114.4	114.6	116.1	118.2	Généraux
Food (2008=100)		117.5	120.9	126.6	128.9	132.4	108.2[3]	Alimentation (2008 = 100)
Gabon [2]	Libreville							**Gabon** [2]
General		109.1	112.6	118.5	120.8	122.6	124.1	Généraux
Food		112.2	100.0[4]	107.8	111.8	116.7	121.4	Alimentation
Gambia	Banjul,Kombo St.Mary							**Gambie**
General		159.7	168.3	175.8	183.8	193.1	202.3	Généraux
Food		172.2	185.8	197.1	207.4	221.1	235.3	Alimentation

28

Consumer price indices *(continued)*
General and food (Index base: 2000 = 100)
Indices des prix à la consommation *(suite)*
Généraux et alimentation (Indices base : 2000 = 100)

Country or area	City - Ville	2006	2007	2008	2009	2010	2011	Pays ou zone
Germany								**Allemagne**
General		110.1	112.5	115.4	115.9	117.2	119.9	Généraux
Food		107.3	111.5	118.3	116.8	118.5	121.8	Alimentation
Ghana								**Ghana**
General		278.0	331.9	386.8	461.2	510.6	555.2	Généraux
Food		267.2	300.6	346.2	400.5	424.9	442.1	Alimentation
Gibraltar								**Gibraltar**
General		113.8	116.9	121.2	124.5	128.5	133.2	Généraux
Food		120.4	124.4	132.1	143.4	149.5	157.3	Alimentation
Greece								**Grèce**
General		122.0	125.5	130.7	132.3	138.6	143.2	Généraux
Food		121.8	125.7	132.5	135.0	135.1	139.3	Alimentation
Guadeloupe								**Guadeloupe**
General		114.3	115.8	118.4	118.7	122.0	125.1	Généraux
Food		115.5	118.0	122.8	125.6	128.2	129.7	Alimentation
Guam								**Guam**
General		129.8	138.6	147.1	149.7	154.0	...	Généraux
Food		150.0	154.6	168.6	179.4	177.1	187.6	Alimentation
Guatemala								**Guatemala**
General		153.2	163.7	182.3	185.7	192.8	204.8	Généraux
Food		171.9	188.9	217.5	221.9	229.5	...	Alimentation
Guinea	Conakry							**Guinée**
General		249.6	306.6	362.9	379.9	438.7	532.4	Généraux
Food		328.7	378.9	456.9	489.4	589.0	750.1	Alimentation
Guinea-Bissau	Bissau							**Guinée-Bissau**
General (2003 = 100)		106.4	111.2	122.9	120.8	122.2	128.3	Généraux (2003 = 100)
Food		105.2	111.3	129.1	128.3	99.4[3]	106.7	Alimentation
Guyana	Georgetown							**Guyana**
General		136.9	153.6	166.0	170.9	177.3	186.1	Généraux
Food		130.0	150.3	172.3	171.6	178.6	191.6	Alimentation
Haiti								**Haïti**
General		282.9	307.1	354.7	354.7	374.9	406.4	Généraux
Food		300.2	324.5	388.6	378.5	397.5	438.2	Alimentation
Honduras								**Honduras**
General		157.9	168.9	188.1	198.4	207.8	221.8	Généraux
Food		143.7	159.2	189.3	195.0	198.6	210.8	Alimentation
Iceland								**Islande**
General		130.5	137.1	154.5	173.0	182.3	189.6	Généraux
Food		115.2	113.9	132.2	155.3	161.9	168.1	Alimentation
India[5]								**Inde**[5]
General		127.7	136.1	147.5	163.1	182.7	198.9	Généraux
Food		124.7	137.0	152.3	173.1	193.8	208.1	Alimentation
Indonesia								**Indonésie**
General		176.5	187.8	207.2	216.1	227.2	239.3	Généraux
Food		161.9	180.4	210.9	225.7	247.0	268.1	Alimentation
Iran (Islamic Rep. of)								**Iran (Rép. islamique d')**
General		215.9	246.1	309.1	350.7	386.3	466.0	Généraux
Food		205.5	100.0[4]	131.0	146.5	164.8	207.8	Alimentation
Iraq								**Iraq**
General		494.3	646.8	664.0	645.4	660.2	697.4	Généraux
Food		237.4	270.4	300.0	323.0	330.1	340.1	Alimentation
Ireland								**Irlande**
General		123.5	129.5	134.8	128.7	127.5	130.8	Généraux
Food		112.7	116.0	123.5	119.2	113.8	115.1	Alimentation
Isle of Man								**Ile de Man**
General		121.0	125.8	132.3	133.1	139.8	148.2	Généraux
Food		135.1	141.2	152.3	166.5	179.0	194.4	Alimentation
Israel								**Israël**
General		110.9	111.4	116.5	120.4	123.6	127.9	Généraux
Food		115.1	119.5	133.2	135.2	138.6	143.4	Alimentation

Country or area	City - Ville	2006	2007	2008	2009	2010	2011	Pays ou zone
Italy								**Italie**
General		114.7	116.9	120.7	121.6	123.3	127.3	Généraux
Food		115.6	119.0	125.4	127.7	127.9	131.1	Alimentation
Jamaica								**Jamaïque**
General		179.8	196.8	240.1	263.2	296.4	318.7	Généraux
Food		172.0	194.8	254.6	287.7	316.8	341.2	Alimentation
Japan								**Japon**
General		98.1	98.1	99.5	98.1	97.4	97.1	Généraux
Food		98.3	98.6	101.1	101.3	101.0	100.6	Alimentation
Jersey								**Jersey**
General		126.2	131.6	137.9	138.9	142.4	148.9	Généraux
Food		117.0	122.1	138.1	143.8	148.3	157.3	Alimentation
Jordan								**Jordanie**
General		119.7	126.2	145.0	141.9	149.0	155.6	Généraux
Food		121.8	133.1	158.2	159.7	167.7	174.6	Alimentation
Kenya								**Kenya**
General (2007 = 100)		...	100.0	116.2	126.9	133.7	152.4	Généraux (2007 = 100)
Food (2007=100)		...	100.0	123.1	138.6	150.4	181.2	Alimentation (2007 = 100)
Kosovo								**Kosovo**
General (2003 = 100)		98.2	102.6	112.1	109.4	113.1	...	Généraux (2003 = 100)
Food (2003 = 100)		99.7	100.7	116.8	111.7	117.0	...	Alimentation (2003 = 100)
Kuwait								**Koweït**
General		112.1	118.3	130.8	136.0	141.5	148.2	Généraux
Food		124.0	129.9	145.0	149.6	162.1	177.7	Alimentation
Lao People's Dem. Rep.								**Rép. dém. pop. lao**
General		174.1	182.0	195.9	196.0	207.7	223.4	Généraux
Food		175.6	189.9	210.7	214.7	231.2	253.9	Alimentation
Latvia								**Lettonie**
General		129.9	143.0	165.0	170.8	169.0	176.4	Généraux
Food		141.1	160.1	189.4	189.3	188.7	204.7	Alimentation
Lesotho								**Lesotho**
General		148.4	160.6	177.8	190.5	197.8	207.6	Généraux
Food		165.9	189.9	220.0	239.7	181.0[6]	193.7	Alimentation
Lithuania								**Lituanie**
General		108.2	114.4	126.9	132.6	134.3	139.9	Généraux
Food		111.7	124.3	144.1	146.5	145.8	157.8	Alimentation
Luxembourg								**Luxembourg**
General		115.0	117.6	121.6	122.1	124.9	129.1	Généraux
Food		117.6	121.5	128.0	129.9	131.0	134.4	Alimentation
Madagascar								**Madagascar**
General		183.7	202.6	221.3	214.2	263.5	288.5	Généraux
Food		177.6	202.1	223.2	241.6	257.2	292.0	Alimentation
Malawi								**Malawi**
General		226.1	244.1	265.4	287.7	309.1	332.6	Généraux
Food		209.1	224.7	240.3	258.0	271.2	279.8	Alimentation
Malaysia								**Malaisie**
General		113.0	115.3	121.5	122.3	124.4	128.3	Généraux
Food		112.5	115.9	126.1	131.4	134.5	141.0	Alimentation
Maldives	Male							**Maldives**
General		110.0	117.5	131.6	137.6	146.1	162.5	Généraux
Food (2005 = 100)		104.0	120.8	143.9	144.6	155.4	186.4	Alimentation (2005 = 100)
Mali	Bamako							**Mali**
General		114.1	115.7	126.3	129.1	130.9	134.6	Généraux
Food		114.6	117.3	132.6	136.6	107.3[3]	112.8	Alimentation
Malta								**Malte**
General		115.9	117.4	122.3	124.9	126.8	130.2	Généraux
Food		114.2	119.2	128.7	136.9	138.3	143.7	Alimentation
Martinique								**Martinique**
General		113.9	116.7	119.9	119.5	121.4	124.5	Généraux
Food		120.5	124.5	131.2	132.3	132.6	133.2	Alimentation

Country or area	City - Ville	2006	2007	2008	2009	2010	2011	Pays ou zone
Mauritania								**Mauritanie**
General		147.9	158.7	170.4	174.1	185.1	195.6	Généraux
Food		157.3	173.9	190.6	195.5	210.5	223.9	Alimentation
Mauritius								**Maurice**
General		139.5	154.9	166.5	170.8	175.8	187.2	Généraux
Food		142.4	168.9	190.7	198.5	205.8	217.9	Alimentation
Mexico								**Mexique**
General		131.8	137.0	144.0	151.6	157.9	163.3	Généraux
Food		134.1	142.6	154.1	167.5	174.0	183.0	Alimentation
Mongolia								**Mongolie**
General (2006 = 100)		100.0	109.6	140.3	150.9	166.2	181.3	Généraux (2006 = 100)
Food (2006 = 100)		100.0	112.9	158.2	160.9	180.7	194.5	Alimentation (2006 = 100)
Morocco								**Maroc**
General		110.8	113.0	117.4	...	108.4[7]	109.4	Généraux
Food		163.1	168.3	179.8	...	114.7[7]	116.3	Alimentation
Mozambique								**Mozambique**
General		196.9	214.9	246.5	255.2	287.0	319.2	Généraux
Myanmar								**Myanmar**
General		356.5	481.3	142.5[7]	144.6	155.7	163.5	Généraux
Food		365.7	493.9	143.8[7]	143.3	153.7	159.7	Alimentation
Namibia								**Namibie**
General (2006 = 100)		119.9	127.9	141.1	153.6	160.4	168.5	Généraux (2006 = 100)
Food (2002 = 100)		119.3	133.8	156.6	173.4	179.0	188.1	Alimentation (2002 = 100)
Nepal								**Népal**
General		132.6	140.5	156.9	174.8	192.8	209.8	Généraux
Food		129.1	139.6	158.8	186.1	211.3	236.1	Alimentation
Netherlands								**Pays-Bas**
General		114.4	116.2	119.1	120.6	122.1	125.0	Généraux
Food		94.4	95.4	100.8	101.9	101.8	104.0	Alimentation
Netherlands Antilles	Curaçao							**Antilles néerlandaises**
General		113.0	116.4	124.4	126.5	130.1	133.1	Généraux
Food		133.0	145.0	171.7	...	197.5	212.6	Alimentation
New Caledonia	Nouméa							**Nouvelle-Calédonie**
General		110.7	111.8	115.1	116.2	119.3	122.2	Généraux
Food		113.0	114.5	119.1	122.3	124.8	130.2	Alimentation
New Zealand								**Nouvelle-Zélande**
General		116.8	119.6	124.4	127.0	129.9	135.1	Généraux
Food		114.4	118.8	129.0	136.9	138.1	145.5	Alimentation
Nicaragua								**Nicaragua**
General (2003 = 100)		160.9	178.8	214.2	222.1	234.3	253.2	Généraux (2003 = 100)
Food (2003 = 100)		162.5	188.9	242.8	252.2	263.8	287.7	Alimentation (2003 = 100)
Niger [2]	Niamey							**Niger** [2]
General		113.6	113.6	126.5	131.9	128.2	132.0	Généraux
Food (2006 = 100)		100.0	99.4	119.8	132.1	132.5	137.0	Alimentation (2006 = 100)
Nigeria								**Nigéria**
General		224.5	236.6	263.9	296.6	337.9	374.5	Généraux
Food		228.3	232.6	270.0	309.6	355.8	392.4	Alimentation
Norfolk Island								**Ile Norfolk**
General		134.4	140.9	148.0	152.3	156.4	...	Généraux
Food		137.3	148.4	160.9	169.8	173.7	...	Alimentation
Norway								**Norvège**
General		111.6	112.4	116.7	119.2	122.0	123.6	Généraux
Food		104.6	107.3	111.9	116.6	116.8	116.7	Alimentation
Occ. Palestinian Terr. [8]								**Terr. palestinien occupé** [8]
General		123.5	126.9	139.2	143.1	148.4	152.7	Généraux
Food		118.8	124.4	147.3	152.6	157.8	161.6	Alimentation
Oman								**Oman**
General		105.2	111.4	125.2	129.5	133.7	139.1	Généraux
Food		111.8	123.9	150.6	151.3	154.4	161.4	Alimentation
Pakistan								**Pakistan**
General		139.7	150.3	180.8	205.5	234.0	249.8	Généraux
Food		143.3	158.8	202.6	229.6	268.0	306.7	Alimentation

Country or area	City - Ville	2006	2007	2008	2009	2010	2011	Pays ou zone
Panama								**Panama**
General (2003 = 100)		105.9	110.3	119.9	122.8	127.1	134.6	Généraux (2003 = 100)
Food (2003 = 100)		107.0	114.2	131.3	138.8	142.8	151.2	Alimentation (2003 = 100)
Papua New Guinea								**Papouasie-Nvl-Guinée**
General		149.2	150.6	166.8	178.3	189.0	...	Généraux
Food		159.3	160.3	187.0	200.4	211.2	...	Alimentation
Paraguay	Asunción							**Paraguay**
General		165.4	178.7	196.9	202.1	211.5	228.9	Généraux
Food		182.5	212.5	246.1	...	268.6	304.4	Alimentation
Peru	Lima							**Pérou**
General		112.3	114.3	120.9	124.5	126.4	130.6	Généraux
Food		110.2	113.0	123.3	128.5	131.8	138.2	Alimentation
Philippines								**Philippines**
General		137.9	141.8	155.0	160.0	166.1	173.9	Généraux
Food		130.6	134.9	152.3	161.2	166.1	136.6	Alimentation
Poland								**Pologne**
General		115.8	118.6	123.6	127.9	131.2	136.9	Généraux
Food		110.6	115.9	122.5	127.8	131.1	137.4	Alimentation
Portugal								**Portugal**
General		120.4	123.3	126.4	125.2	126.9	131.6	Généraux
Food		114.2	117.0	121.1	116.9	116.7	119.1	Alimentation
Puerto Rico								**Porto Rico**
General		178.9	#121.3[9]	127.6	128.0	131.1	134.9	Généraux
Food		257.1	#118.8[9]	128.0	133.3	134.2	137.5	Alimentation
Qatar								**Qatar**
General (2002 = 100)		133.1	151.2	174.2	165.7	161.8	164.8	Généraux (2002 = 100)
Food (2002 = 100)		113.9	122.3	146.6	148.5	151.6	158.2	Alimentation (2002 = 100)
Republic of Korea								**République de Corée**
General (2005 = 100)		...	104.8	109.7	116.3	123.8	133.9	Généraux (2005 = 100)
Food (2005 = 100)		...	103.0	108.2	116.3	123.8	133.9	Alimentation (2005 = 100)
Republic of Moldova								**République de Moldova**
General (2005 = 100)		...	126.7	142.9	142.8	153.4	165.1	Généraux (2005 = 100)
Food (2005 = 100)		...	121.0	139.7	131.9	140.1	152.6	Alimentation (2005 = 100)
Réunion								**Réunion**
General		113.2	114.8	118.2	118.8	120.6	123.5	Généraux
Food		111.2	114.0	121.6	124.3	125.2	128.6	Alimentation
Romania								**Roumanie**
General		246.9	258.8	279.1	294.7	312.7	330.8	Généraux
Food		222.0	230.6	251.9	260.1	266.2	282.2	Alimentation
Rwanda	Kigali							**Rwanda**
General		150.6	164.2	189.5	210.8	214.0	103.1	Généraux
Food		171.5	185.0	215.2	248.3	254.4	271.0	Alimentation
Saint Helena								**Sainte-Hélène**
General		120.8	126.4	136.5	147.3	154.6	164.1	Généraux
Food		117.1	117.2	131.2	150.6	159.9	167.7	Alimentation
Samoa								**Samoa**
General		...	145.7	162.4	172.6	174.3	184.0	Généraux
Food		...	164.3	187.5	206.6	...	218.9	Alimentation
San Marino								**Saint-Marin**
General (2003 = 100)		105.3	107.9	112.6	115.0	118.0	121.4	Généraux (2003 = 100)
Food (2003 = 100)		115.0	120.7	130.4	133.6	138.0	146.3	Alimentation (2003 = 100)
Sao Tome and Principe								**Sao Tomé-et-Principe**
General (1996 = 100)		690.4	818.5	1 080.4	1 263.6	1 432.1	...	Généraux (1996 = 100)
Food (1996 = 100)		612.2	744.9	1 027.5	1 244.9	...	...	Alimentation (1996 = 100)
Saudi Arabia								**Arabie saoudite**
General		...	104.2	114.5	120.3	126.7	133.0	Généraux
Food		...	115.5	131.7	134.3	142.7	150.0	Alimentation
Senegal	Dakar							**Sénégal**
General		110.0	116.4	123.1	121.8	121.9	102.2	Généraux
Food (2005 = 100)		101.4	108.7	119.2	115.6	119.9	127.9	Alimentation (2005 = 100)

Country or area	City - Ville	2006	2007	2008	2009	2010	2011	Pays ou zone
Serbia								**Serbie**
General (2006 = 100)		368.6	392.4	442.8	477.3[7]	137.4	152.7	Généraux (2006 = 100)
Food (2006 = 100)		310.1	328.7	397.4	139.1[7]	142.7	163.7	Alimentation (2006 = 100)
Seychelles								**Seychelles**
General		114.6	122.1	167.3	220.4	215.1	220.6	Généraux
Food		114.3	125.6	173.8	244.6	256.9	246.8	Alimentation
Sierra Leone								**Sierra Leone**
General (2003 = 100)		142.5	160.8	182.6	199.0	238.8	277.2	Généraux (2003 = 100)
Food (2003 = 100)		141.0	159.3	186.4	203.2	243.1	295.7	Alimentation (2003 = 100)
Singapore								**Singapour**
General		104.2	106.4	113.4	113.6	116.8	122.9	Généraux
Food		106.2	109.3	117.8	120.5	122.2	125.9	Alimentation
Slovakia								**Slovaquie**
General		138.7	142.5	149.0	151.5	152.9	158.9	Généraux
Food		116.4	121.0	130.3	126.1	128.1	135.8	Alimentation
Slovenia								**Slovénie**
General		133.8	138.6	146.5	147.7	150.4	153.2	Généraux
Food		127.2	136.8	150.8	151.6	153.1	159.9	Alimentation
South Africa								**Afrique du Sud**
General		134.0	143.5	160.0	171.4	178.7	187.7	Généraux
Food (2008=100)		147.8	163.1	100.0[3]	109.5	111.0	118.9	Alimentation (2008 = 100)
Spain								**Espagne**
General (2001 = 100)		104.9	107.9	112.3	111.9	113.9	117.6	Généraux (2001 = 100)
Food (2001 = 100)		110.6	114.7	121.4	120.1	119.1	121.6	Alimentation (2001 = 100)
Sri Lanka	Colombo							**Sri Lanka**
General (2002 = 100)		181.5	163.1[6]	199.9	206.8	219.1	234.4	Généraux (2002 = 100)
Food (2002 = 100)		184.6	163.4[6]	213.3	219.2	234.2	255.9	Alimentation (2002 = 100)
Suriname	Paramaribo							**Suriname**
General (2001 = 100)		190.7	203.0	232.8	247.8	248.6	292.6	Généraux (2001 = 100)
Food (2001 = 100)		182.7	198.0	246.8	247.8	273.1	318.4	Alimentation (2001 = 100)
Swaziland								**Swaziland**
General (2007 = 100)		...	100.0	113.0	121.4	...	...	Généraux (2007 = 100)
Food (2007=100)		...	...	...	136.1	...	...	Alimentation (2007 = 100)
Sweden								**Suède**
General		109.0	111.4	115.2	114.9	116.4	119.4	Généraux
Food		106.2	108.3	115.8	119.1	120.9	122.4	Alimentation
Switzerland								**Suisse**
General		105.4	106.1	108.8	108.2	109.0	109.2	Généraux
Food		105.4	106.0	109.3	109.1	107.9	104.4	Alimentation
Syrian Arab Republic								**Rép. arabe syrienne**
General		134.1	140.1	161.4	165.9	173.2	...	Généraux
Food		138.0	150.5	181.7	182.2	190.7	...	Alimentation
Tanganyika								**Tanganyika**
General		137.5	147.2	162.3	182.1	192.0	216.4	Généraux
Food (2010=100)		148.4	158.8	178.9	210.2	100.0[10]	116.0	Alimentation (2010=100)
Thailand								**Thaïlande**
General		117.0	119.7	126.2	125.1	129.2	134.1	Généraux
Food		120.1	124.9	139.4	145.5	153.4	165.6	Alimentation
TFYR of Macedonia								**L'ex-R.Y. Macédoine**
General		112.3	114.8	124.4	123.4	125.2	...	Généraux
Food		105.0	109.1	125.8	123.7	125.0	...	Alimentation
Togo	Lomé							**Togo**
General		116.3	117.3	127.5	130.0	134.2	139.0	Généraux
Food		112.7	115.9	139.5	142.9	152.0	153.8	Alimentation
Tonga								**Tonga**
General		172.0	180.8	198.9	202.5	...	...	Généraux
Food		170.4	182.9	197.7	212.4	...	...	Alimentation
Trinidad and Tobago								**Trinité-et-Tobago**
General		137.0	147.9	165.7	177.2	195.9	205.9	Généraux
Food		244.4	287.0	361.5	407.2	497.1	549.2	Alimentation

Consumer price indices *(continued)*
General and food (Index base: 2000 = 100)

Indices des prix à la consommation *(suite)*
Généraux et alimentation (Indices base : 2000 = 100)

Country or area	City - Ville	2006	2007	2008	2009	2010	2011	Pays ou zone
Tunisia								**Tunisie**
General		118.9	122.6	128.8	133.6	139.1	143.9	Généraux
Food		121.4	124.8	132.6	138.3	147.2	152.6	Alimentation
Turkey								**Turquie**
General		417.1	453.6	501.0	532.3	577.9	615.3	Généraux
Food (2003 = 100)		123.0	138.2	155.9	168.4	186.2	197.8	Alimentation (2003 = 100)
Uganda								**Ouganda**
General		133.3	141.4	158.5	179.2	186.3	221.0	Généraux
Food		139.3	142.8	171.1	213.9	218.4	289.0	Alimentation
Ukraine								**Ukraine**
General		160.2	180.8	226.4	262.4	...	...	Généraux
Food		166.5	182.4	100.0[3]	110.9	...	...	Alimentation
United Kingdom								**Royaume-Uni**
General		116.3	121.3	126.1	125.5	131.3	138.1	Généraux
Food		109.6	114.6	125.2	131.8	136.0	144.0	Alimentation
United Rep. of Tanzania[10]								**Rép.-Unie de Tanzanie**[10]
General		137.5	147.2	162.3	182.1	192.0	216.4	Généraux
Food		148.4	158.8	178.9	210.2	100.0[11]	116.0	Alimentation
United States								**Etats-Unis**
General		117.1	120.4	125.0	124.6	126.6	130.6	Généraux
Food		116.3	120.9	127.6	129.9	130.9	135.8	Alimentation
Uruguay	Montevideo							**Uruguay**
General		172.7	186.7	201.4	215.6	230.0	249.1	Généraux
Food		176.0	202.5	230.3	245.0	261.2	288.6	Alimentation
Vanuatu								**Vanuatu**
General		114.0	118.5	124.2	129.8	133.1	134.3	Généraux
Food		111.8	116.1	125.4	134.4	140.5	141.6	Alimentation
Venezuela (Boliv. Rep. of)								**Venezuela (Rép. boliv. du)**
General (2008 = 100)		...	...	95.9	121.9	156.2	197.0	Généraux (2008 = 100)
Food (2008=100)		...	...	100.0	127.9	170.1	221.0	Alimentation (2008 = 100)
Yemen								**Yémen**
General		211.6	232.8	249.1	258.3	292.0	349.0	Généraux
Food		78.0	92.1	93.6	100.0[12]	110.4	127.1	Alimentation
Zambia								**Zambie**
General		274.1	303.3	341.1	386.8	419.6	456.0	Généraux
Food		267.1	281.1	319.9	365.5	384.3	403.2	Alimentation
Zimbabwe								**Zimbabwe**
General		1.1	76.2	...	100.0[12]	103.1	106.6	Généraux
Food		1.1	84.8	...	100.0[12]	104.0	...	Alimentation

Source:
International Labour Organization (ILO), Geneva, the ILO labour statistics database, last accessed May 2013.

Source:
Bureau international du Travail (BIT), Genève, la base de données du BIT, dernier accès mai 2013.

1	Index base: 1995 = 100.
2	African population.
3	Index base: 2008 = 100
4	Index base: 2007 = 100
5	Industrial workers.
6	Index base: 2002 = 100.
7	Index base: 2006 = 100.
8	West Bank and Gaza.
9	Series replacing former series: Methodology revised.
10	Tanganyika only.
11	Index base 2010 = 100.
12	Index base 2009 = 100.

1	Indice base: 1995 = 100.
2	Population Africaine.
3	Base de l'indice: 2008 = 100
4	Base de l'indice: 2007 = 100.
5	Ouvriers industriels.
6	Indice base : 2002 = 100.
7	Base de l'indice: 2006 = 100.
8	Cisjordanie et Gaza.
9	Série remplaçant la précédente: Méthodologie révisée.
10	Tanganyika seulement.
11	Base de l'indice: 2010 = 100.
12	Base de l'indice: 2009 = 100.

Agricultural production
Index base: 2004-06 = 100

Production agricole
Indices base : 2004-06 = 100

Region, country or area	Agriculture - Agriculture				Food - Produits alimentaires				Région, pays ou zone
	2007	2008	2009	2010	2007	2008	2009	2010	
World	**105**	**109**	**109**	**110**	**105**	**109**	**110**	**111**	**Monde**
Africa	**103**	**109**	**110**	**112**	**103**	**110**	**111**	**113**	**Afrique**
Algeria	88	94	117	124	88	94	117	124	Algérie
Angola	115	117	143	151	115	117	144	152	Angola
Benin	98	114	113	116	99	117	118	122	Bénin
Botswana	101	109	109	113	101	109	109	114	Botswana
Burkina Faso	86	109	98	112	91	109	103	119	Burkina Faso
Burundi	101	100	68	50	101	102	67	50	Burundi
Cameroon	114	119	118	123	116	122	121	126	Cameroun
Cape Verde	106	118	118	120	106	118	118	120	Cap-Vert
Central African Rep.	107	109	112	114	107	109	112	114	Rép. centrafricaine
Chad	96	103	107	102	98	106	113	106	Tchad
Comoros	98	96	96	93	98	96	96	93	Comores
Congo	104	113	118	125	104	114	118	125	Congo
Côte d'Ivoire	101	106	101	106	101	108	101	106	Côte d'Ivoire
Dem. Rep. of the Congo	101	101	102	104	101	101	102	104	Rép. dém. du Congo
Djibouti	137	142	208	208	137	142	208	208	Djibouti
Egypt	111	114	117	110	111	116	118	111	Egypte
Equatorial Guinea	112	109	111	108	110	109	116	112	Guinée équatoriale
Eritrea	118	81	100	101	118	81	100	101	Erythrée
Ethiopia	105	111	122	125	103	110	122	125	Ethiopie
Gabon	101	104	114	111	101	102	114	110	Gabon
Gambia	73	100	118	133	73	100	118	133	Gambie
Ghana	102	114	121	125	102	113	121	125	Ghana
Guinea	105	114	107	113	105	114	106	113	Guinée
Guinea-Bissau	104	108	99	120	104	108	99	120	Guinée-Bissau
Kenya	115	110	114	124	115	111	116	125	Kenya
Lesotho	107	102	98	112	107	101	98	113	Lesotho
Liberia	110	107	97	102	108	120	116	122	Libéria
Libyan Arab Jamah.	106	105	109	112	106	105	109	112	Jamah. arabe libyenne
Madagascar	108	111	118	122	108	112	119	121	Madagascar
Malawi	132	134	158	166	135	133	155	165	Malawi
Mali	106	129	143	148	114	141	156	161	Mali
Mauritania	102	102	102	113	102	102	102	113	Mauritanie
Mauritius	92	97	101	97	92	97	101	97	Maurice
Morocco	93	103	121	126	93	103	121	126	Maroc
Mozambique	101	95	110	115	99	92	111	113	Mozambique
Namibia	102	91	91	93	103	91	91	94	Namibie
Niger	116	138	120	155	116	138	120	155	Niger
Nigeria	97	104	90	89	97	104	89	89	Nigéria
Réunion	94	101	103	103	94	101	103	103	Réunion
Rwanda	107	110	130	137	107	110	129	137	Rwanda
Sao Tome and Principe	111	111	117	110	111	111	117	110	Sao Tomé-et-Principe

Region, country or area	Agriculture - Agriculture				Food - Produits alimentaires				Région, pays ou zone
	2007	2008	2009	2010	2007	2008	2009	2010	
Senegal	89	126	140	152	89	127	141	154	Sénégal
Seychelles	94	87	82	77	93	88	84	79	Seychelles
Sierra Leone	91	99	104	114	91	99	105	116	Sierra Leone
Somalia	101	98	101	114	101	97	101	114	Somalie
South Africa	103	118	117	120	103	119	117	121	Afrique du Sud
Sudan	109	114	119	119	110	116	120	120	Soudan
Swaziland	98	102	102	104	98	102	103	104	Swaziland
Togo	103	110	118	120	107	117	125	127	Togo
Tunisia	104	110	105	103	105	110	105	103	Tunisie
Uganda	102	105	107	108	102	104	107	108	Ouganda
United Rep. of Tanzania	106	107	110	110	105	107	111	110	Rép.-Unie de Tanzanie
Western Sahara	103	101	97	99	103	101	97	99	Sahara occidental
Zambia	105	106	127	143	104	104	126	144	Zambie
Zimbabwe	99	97	97	97	97	91	93	96	Zimbabwe
Americas	**106**	**107**	**106**	**109**	**107**	**108**	**107**	**110**	**Amériques**
Antigua and Barbuda	108	102	105	106	107	102	105	106	Antigua-et-Barbuda
Argentina	115	113	96	115	115	113	96	115	Argentine
Bahamas	111	107	111	111	111	107	111	111	Bahamas
Barbados	99	98	100	100	99	98	100	100	Barbade
Belize	95	92	89	91	95	92	89	91	Belize
Bermuda	108	111	108	111	108	111	108	111	Bermudes
Bolivia (Plurin. State of)	108	110	113	115	108	110	113	116	Bolivie (État plurin. de)
Brazil	110	111	110	117	111	111	110	118	Brésil
British Virgin Islands	107	97	99	101	107	97	99	101	Iles Vierges britanniques
Canada	100	106	104	102	100	106	104	102	Canada
Cayman Islands	96	87	95	103	96	87	95	103	Iles Caïmanes
Chile	104	105	103	107	104	105	103	107	Chili
Colombia	106	110	113	103	106	111	112	106	Colombie
Costa Rica	103	101	100	107	103	101	102	108	Costa Rica
Cuba	93	95	98	88	93	95	98	88	Cuba
Dominica	107	104	116	113	107	104	116	114	Dominique
Dominican Republic	111	107	116	125	110	107	117	127	Rép. dominicaine
Ecuador	104	110	114	119	105	111	115	120	Equateur
El Salvador	106	114	111	112	106	115	113	112	El Salvador
Falkland Is. (Malvinas)	100	99	94	95	103	102	102	103	Iles Falkland (Malvinas)
French Guiana	89	89	84	88	89	89	84	88	Guyane française
Greenland	104	104	102	98	104	104	103	99	Groenland
Grenada	104	97	99	93	104	97	99	94	Grenade
Guadeloupe	92	92	94	103	92	92	94	103	Guadeloupe
Guatemala	113	117	121	124	115	118	123	126	Guatemala
Guyana	98	99	102	98	98	99	102	98	Guyana
Haiti	111	100	107	107	109	100	106	108	Haïti
Honduras	104	106	103	109	104	107	104	108	Honduras
Jamaica	101	101	107	101	101	100	105	99	Jamaïque
Martinique	65	71	80	81	65	71	80	81	Martinique

Region, country or area	Agriculture - Agriculture				Food - Produits alimentaires				Région, pays ou zone
	2007	2008	2009	2010	2007	2008	2009	2010	
Mexico	105	106	103	106	105	106	104	107	Mexique
Montserrat	101	98	101	99	100	98	101	99	Montserrat
Netherlands Antilles	110	108	102	106	110	108	102	106	Antilles néerlandaises
Nicaragua	108	107	118	116	107	107	117	117	Nicaragua
Panama	110	109	104	108	110	109	104	108	Panama
Paraguay	118	115	100	141	120	119	103	146	Paraguay
Peru	111	119	121	127	111	119	122	129	Pérou
Puerto Rico	100	98	104	104	101	99	105	105	Porto Rico
Saint Kitts and Nevis	30	32	31	29	30	32	31	29	Saint-Kitts-et-Nevis
Saint Lucia	96	101	103	111	96	101	103	111	Sainte-Lucie
Saint Pierre and Miquelon	95	108	108	111	95	108	108	111	Saint-Pierre-et-Miquelon
Saint Vincent-Grenadines	108	103	114	124	108	103	114	124	Saint Vincent-Gren.
Suriname	113	115	131	137	113	115	131	137	Suriname
Trinidad and Tobago	107	88	90	89	107	88	90	89	Trinité-et-Tobago
United States	103	104	105	105	104	105	107	106	Etats-Unis
United States Virgin Is.	109	109	114	118	109	109	114	118	Iles Vierges américaines
Uruguay	102	108	112	116	102	109	112	117	Uruguay
Venezuela (Boliv. Rep. of)	115	111	108	112	116	111	108	112	Venezuela (Rép. boliv. du)
Asia	**108**	**112**	**114**	**115**	**108**	**112**	**114**	**115**	**Asie**
Afghanistan	107	99	115	116	107	99	115	116	Afghanistan
Armenia	117	120	120	101	117	120	120	101	Arménie
Azerbaijan	104	111	122	118	107	115	127	123	Azerbaïdjan
Bahrain	114	112	129	117	114	112	129	117	Bahreïn
Bangladesh	112	121	121	129	113	121	121	129	Bangladesh
Bhutan	108	93	92	95	108	93	92	95	Bhoutan
Brunei Darussalam	129	132	133	134	129	133	133	134	Brunéi Darussalam
Cambodia	120	131	136	150	121	130	136	150	Cambodge
China [1]	106	112	115	114	106	112	115	115	Chine [1]
Cyprus	91	87	86	86	91	87	86	86	Chypre
Dem. P. R. Korea	92	99	101	97	92	99	101	96	R. p. dém. de Corée
Georgia	87	75	73	65	88	76	73	65	Géorgie
India	114	116	113	119	114	116	113	118	Inde
Indonesia	108	114	121	122	107	114	121	122	Indonésie
Iran (Islamic Rep. of)	108	101	108	109	108	100	107	109	Iran (Rép. islamique d')
Iraq	100	88	90	103	100	89	90	103	Iraq
Israel	104	103	104	106	104	104	105	107	Israël
Japan	101	101	99	96	101	101	99	97	Japon
Jordan	104	108	111	122	104	108	111	122	Jordanie
Kazakhstan	116	107	123	107	117	108	124	108	Kazakhstan
Kuwait	112	110	111	114	112	110	111	114	Koweït
Kyrgyzstan	101	102	106	104	102	103	109	106	Kirghizistan
Lao People's Dem. Rep.	110	124	128	125	111	123	128	125	Rép. dém. pop. lao
Lebanon	100	103	104	106	100	103	104	106	Liban
Malaysia	104	113	112	112	105	116	117	117	Malaisie
Maldives	91	87	78	86	91	87	78	86	Maldives

29

Agricultural production *(continued)*
Index base: 2004-06 = 100
Production agricole *(suite)*
Indices base : 2004-06 = 100

Region, country or area	Agriculture - Agriculture				Food - Produits alimentaires				Région, pays ou zone
	2007	2008	2009	2010	2007	2008	2009	2010	
Mongolia	106	121	147	117	106	120	147	116	Mongolie
Myanmar	117	125	125	125	117	125	126	126	Myanmar
Nepal	101	107	112	114	101	107	112	114	Népal
Occupied Palestinian Terr.	97	99	101	103	97	99	101	103	Terr. palestinien occupé
Oman	97	97	99	118	97	97	99	118	Oman
Pakistan	106	110	113	111	108	113	115	113	Pakistan
Philippines	109	112	111	112	109	112	111	112	Philippines
Qatar	112	110	135	138	112	110	135	138	Qatar
Republic of Korea	101	105	108	101	102	105	108	101	République de Corée
Saudi Arabia	104	104	101	106	104	104	101	106	Arabie saoudite
Singapore	102	95	102	97	102	95	102	97	Singapour
Sri Lanka	103	114	111	121	103	115	113	125	Sri Lanka
Syrian Arab Republic	93	88	96	94	94	89	98	96	Rép. arabe syrienne
Tajikistan	105	110	120	126	109	118	133	140	Tadjikistan
Thailand	111	112	114	110	113	113	116	112	Thaïlande
Timor-Leste	101	110	122	125	102	112	130	131	Timor-Leste
Turkey	99	103	105	106	100	104	107	109	Turquie
Turkmenistan	119	114	114	124	120	114	119	125	Turkménistan
United Arab Emirates	88	96	98	101	88	96	98	101	Emirats arabes unis
Uzbekistan	109	116	120	127	113	120	125	135	Ouzbékistan
Viet Nam	109	113	115	119	108	113	115	117	Viet Nam
Yemen	117	122	127	138	117	122	127	138	Yémen
Europe	**97**	**102**	**102**	**98**	**97**	**102**	**102**	**98**	**Europe**
Albania	103	107	112	119	103	108	112	119	Albanie
Austria	100	102	100	97	100	102	100	98	Autriche
Belarus	107	116	117	117	107	116	117	117	Bélarus
Belgium	97	95	100	101	97	95	100	101	Belgique
Bosnia and Herzegovina	97	106	110	102	97	106	110	102	Bosnie-Herzégovine
Bulgaria	76	102	97	105	76	103	98	106	Bulgarie
Croatia	100	110	109	100	100	110	108	100	Croatie
Czech Republic	95	100	97	90	95	101	97	90	République tchèque
Denmark	101	102	102	99	101	102	102	99	Danemark
Estonia	112	108	111	106	112	108	111	106	Estonie
Faeroe Islands	102	103	103	102	102	103	103	102	Iles Féroé
Finland	102	100	101	94	102	100	101	94	Finlande
France	95	97	98	96	95	96	98	95	France
Germany	99	103	106	102	99	103	106	102	Allemagne
Greece	91	91	89	82	93	94	92	85	Grèce
Hungary	81	102	92	81	81	102	92	81	Hongrie
Iceland	108	110	109	109	109	110	109	109	Islande
Ireland	100	99	95	100	100	98	95	100	Irlande
Italy	95	96	96	93	95	96	96	93	Italie
Latvia	111	115	112	108	111	115	113	108	Lettonie
Liechtenstein	99	101	98	99	99	101	98	99	Liechtenstein
Lithuania	107	110	112	99	107	110	112	99	Lituanie

29 Agricultural production *(continued)*
Index base: 2004-06 = 100
Production agricole *(suite)*
Indices base : 2004-06 = 100

Region, country or area	Agriculture - Agriculture				Food - Produits alimentaires				Région, pays ou zone
	2007	2008	2009	2010	2007	2008	2009	2010	
Luxembourg	97	105	104	97	97	105	104	97	Luxembourg
Malta	98	106	96	97	98	106	96	97	Malte
Montenegro	93	97	98	104	93	97	99	104	Monténégro
Netherlands	102	105	108	110	102	105	108	110	Pays-Bas
Norway	100	105	100	101	100	105	100	101	Norvège
Poland	102	103	106	100	102	103	106	100	Pologne
Portugal	96	100	99	101	96	100	99	101	Portugal
Republic of Moldova	73	102	90	92	74	102	90	92	République de Moldova
Romania	77	93	91	91	77	93	91	91	Roumanie
Russian Federation	103	109	108	93	103	109	108	93	Fédération de Russie
Serbia	94	103	106	102	94	103	106	102	Serbie
Slovakia	89	102	91	82	89	102	91	82	Slovaquie
Slovenia	93	96	91	92	93	96	91	92	Slovénie
Spain	101	101	103	104	101	101	103	104	Espagne
Sweden	97	98	100	95	97	98	100	95	Suède
Switzerland	101	102	105	103	101	102	105	103	Suisse
TFYR of Macedonia	104	110	111	116	105	113	113	116	L'ex-R.Y. Macédoine
Ukraine	94	115	109	107	94	115	109	107	Ukraine
United Kingdom	98	102	101	100	98	102	101	100	Royaume-Uni
Oceania	**98**	**102**	**101**	**101**	**99**	**104**	**102**	**102**	**Océanie**
American Samoa	91	100	99	108	91	100	99	108	Samoa américaines
Australia	95	100	101	99	96	104	103	101	Australie
Cook Islands	108	107	99	106	108	107	99	106	Iles Cook
Fiji	94	93	84	82	94	93	84	82	Fidji
French Polynesia	107	115	112	130	107	115	112	130	Polynésie française
Guam	110	118	111	138	110	118	111	138	Guam
Kiribati	105	109	104	131	105	109	104	131	Kiribati
Marshall Islands	134	171	156	176	134	171	156	176	Iles Marshall
Micronesia (Fed. States of)	89	90	86	105	89	90	86	105	Micronésie (Etats féd. de)
Nauru	95	101	97	111	95	101	97	111	Nauru
New Caledonia	102	103	98	97	102	103	98	97	Nouvelle-Calédonie
New Zealand	102	101	99	103	102	102	100	104	Nouvelle-Zélande
Niue	93	103	97	104	93	103	97	104	Nioué
Papua New Guinea	108	114	110	106	108	114	110	105	Papouasie-Nvl-Guinée
Samoa	102	104	107	122	102	105	107	122	Samoa
Solomon Islands	112	120	111	119	112	121	111	119	Iles Salomon
Tokelau	107	116	108	144	107	116	108	144	Tokélaou
Tonga	101	109	108	109	101	109	108	109	Tonga
Tuvalu	99	106	104	113	99	106	104	113	Tuvalu
Vanuatu	102	104	102	110	102	104	102	110	Vanuatu
Wallis and Futuna Islands	91	97	97	101	90	97	97	101	Iles Wallis et Futuna

Source:
Food and Agriculture Organization of the United Nations (FAO),
Rome, FAOSTAT database, last accessed March 2012.

Source:
Organisation des Nations Unies pour l'alimentation et l'agriculture (FAO),
Rome, la base de données FAOSTAT, dernier accès mars 2012.

29

Agricultural production *(continued)*
Index base: 2004-06 = 100
Production agricole *(suite)*
Indices base : 2004-06 = 100

1 For statistical purposes, the data for China do not include those for the Hong Kong Special Administrative Region (Hong Kong SAR) and Macao Special Administrative Region (Macao SAR).

1 Pour la présentation des statistiques, les données pour la Chine ne comprennent pas la Région Administrative Spéciale de Hong Kong (Hong Kong RAS) et la Région Administrative Spéciale de Macao (Macao RAS).

30

Oil crops
Production: thousand metric tons

Culture oléagineuses
Production: milliers de tonnes

Region, country or area	2002	2003	2004	2005	2006	2007	2008	2009	2010	Région, pays ou zone
World	610 224	653 892	719 281	760 777	784 232	787 626	828 258	819 488	863 624	Monde
Africa	42 608	45 017	46 927	48 053	48 106	45 208	48 439	49 166	48 474	Afrique
Algeria	224	200	502	349	297	241	293	515	602	Algérie
Angola	404	436	426	447	435	443	430	489	508	Angola
Benin	1 235	1 137	1 173	1 043	830	913	877	861	851	Bénin
Botswana	11	11	11	11	10	10	13	10	6	Botswana
Burkina Faso	1 081	1 170	1 176	1 403	1 448	896	1 531	1 220	1 281	Burkina Faso
Burundi	28	32	35	35	36	37	49	46	45	Burundi
Cameroon	1 955	2 062	2 033	2 654	2 741	2 828	2 728	2 634	2 630	Cameroun
Cape Verde	6	6	6	6	6	6	6	5	5	Cap-Vert
Central African Rep.	261	250	260	252	265	279	277	285	258	Rép. centrafricaine
Chad	835	738	885	876	717	438	662	566	562	Tchad
Comoros	78	78	96	92	81	81	80	81	89	Comores
Congo	144	139	153	158	196	203	205	206	208	Congo
Côte d'Ivoire	2 436	2 277	2 301	2 321	2 280	2 307	2 306	2 751	2 486	Côte d'Ivoire
Dem. Rep. of the Congo	1 730	1 754	1 774	1 794	1 811	1 831	1 850	1 870	1 889	Rép. dém. du Congo
Egypt	1 777	1 393	1 897	1 555	1 758	1 775	1 300	1 247	1 526	Egypte
Equatorial Guinea	49	49	50	51	50	49	50	49	50	Guinée équatoriale
Eritrea	15	25	18	33	20	30	15	16	16	Erythrée
Ethiopia	315	398	570	575	620	624	763	794	889	Ethiopie
Gabon	57	58	59	59	59	61	63	45	44	Gabon
Gambia	114	137	180	152	160	116	152	165	182	Gambie
Ghana	2 166	2 588	2 901	3 011	3 196	2 545	2 954	3 138	3 101	Ghana
Guinea	1 237	1 262	1 281	1 300	1 333	1 346	1 361	1 305	1 324	Guinée
Guinea-Bissau	164	167	166	168	170	173	195	172	210	Guinée-Bissau
Kenya	173	177	198	195	209	225	191	199	210	Kenya
Liberia	242	242	243	244	242	243	243	241	241	Libéria
Libyan Arab Jamah.	172	214	203	204	203	203	203	197	202	Jamah. arabe libyenne
Madagascar	137	149	171	191	205	187	190	163	181	Madagascar
Malawi	231	305	297	269	364	443	434	493	313	Malawi
Mali	1 038	1 335	1 250	1 333	1 026	916	924	921	971	Mali
Mauritania	3	3	3	4	4	4	4	4	3	Mauritanie
Mauritius	2	3	3	3	3	3	3	2	3	Maurice
Morocco	534	946	604	819	701	747	843	956	1 596	Maroc
Mozambique	669	602	710	838	794	822	806	747	764	Mozambique
Namibia	10	8	10	9	9	8	9	8	8	Namibie
Niger	191	431	213	199	199	216	374	342	509	Niger
Nigeria	15 379	15 969	16 518	16 984	17 399	16 433	16 599	16 655	15 429	Nigéria
Réunion	2	1	2	1	2	2	2	2	2	Réunion
Rwanda	28	30	29	34	36	50	62	69	71	Rwanda
Sao Tome and Principe	42	43	35	37	47	42	47	44	44	Sao Tomé-et-Principe
Senegal	406	630	782	901	663	500	900	1 169	1 433	Sénégal
Seychelles	3	3	3	3	3	2	1	1	2	Seychelles
Sierra Leone	302	329	370	385	384	327	333	351	373	Sierra Leone
Somalia	55	57	73	84	79	83	90	101	104	Somalie
South Africa	1 458	1 010	1 153	1 106	1 133	664	1 333	1 512	1 228	Afrique du Sud
Sudan	1 765	1 611	1 636	1 361	1 481	1 321	1 396	1 856	1 487	Soudan
Swaziland	14	7	12	12	7	5	6	6	7	Swaziland
Togo	484	466	470	308	283	299	289	282	295	Togo
Tunisia	372	1 426	671	1 069	1 238	1 017	1 202	765	892	Tunisie

Region, country or area	2002	2003	2004	2005	2006	2007	2008	2009	2010	Région, pays ou zone
Uganda	680	758	765	790	839	803	876	903	952	Ouganda
United Rep. of Tanzania	1 139	1 028	1 530	1 538	1 213	1 442	1 771	1 680	1 643	Rép.-Unie de Tanzanie
Zambia	208	243	274	330	300	313	375	432	379	Zambie
Zimbabwe	549	625	749	455	521	659	772	595	374	Zimbabwe
Northern America	**101 707**	**97 327**	**120 527**	**123 190**	**122 886**	**106 391**	**113 374**	**122 851**	**127 270**	**Amérique septentrionale**
Canada	7 849	10 170	11 576	13 901	13 724	13 182	17 118	17 169	16 893	Canada
United States	93 858	87 157	108 951	109 289	109 162	93 208	96 256	105 682	110 377	Etats-Unis
Lat. Am. and the Caribbean	**103 039**	**118 772**	**117 867**	**127 796**	**130 569**	**147 761**	**150 837**	**126 305**	**163 590**	**Am. Lat. et Caraïbes**
Argentina	34 668	39 210	35 796	43 372	45 556	52 704	52 539	34 975	56 969	Argentine
Barbados	2	2	2	2	2	2	2	2	2	Barbade
Belize	2	3	1	2	2	2	2	1	1	Belize
Bolivia (Plur. State of)	1 572	1 856	1 839	1 962	1 903	1 977	1 697	1 887	1 976	Bolivie (État plurinational de)
Brazil	50 395	59 712	60 279	61 825	61 613	68 927	71 677	67 127	77 687	Brésil
Chile	25	47	50	75	85	85	115	145	112	Chili
Colombia	3 577	3 569	4 304	4 475	4 427	4 509	4 369	4 388	4 343	Colombie
Costa Rica	742	756	879	1 015	1 120	1 056	1 105	1 149	1 154	Costa Rica
Cuba	135	137	148	141	129	135	114	84	78	Cuba
Dominica	12	7	7	6	12	12	11	9	9	Dominique
Dominican Republic	361	374	372	311	298	302	329	324	338	Rép. dominicaine
Ecuador	2 097	1 933	2 318	2 383	2 446	2 596	2 625	2 646	2 597	Equateur
El Salvador	38	69	73	74	73	79	85	82	88	El Salvador
Grenada	10	11	11	7	7	7	7	6	6	Grenade
Guatemala	846	839	872	918	1 180	1 184	1 633	1 629	1 633	Guatemala
Guyana	72	72	72	72	105	73	81	80	74	Guyana
Haiti	51	53	55	57	57	75	72	59	53	Haïti
Honduras	987	1 156	1 195	1 302	1 773	1 788	1 805	1 956	1 925	Honduras
Jamaica	269	269	268	269	314	315	333	267	198	Jamaïque
Martinique	1	1	1	1	1	1	1	1	1	Martinique
Mexico	1 817	2 080	2 662	2 459	2 473	2 463	2 570	2 215	2 591	Mexique
Nicaragua	165	221	243	264	234	246	296	273	289	Nicaragua
Panama	85	86	94	98	100	124	105	108	107	Panama
Paraguay	3 782	4 762	4 477	4 720	4 506	6 744	6 958	4 446	8 137	Paraguay
Peru	445	497	596	637	682	688	676	556	538	Pérou
Puerto Rico	5	6	7	4	4	4	4	3	3	Porto Rico
Saint Kitts and Nevis	1	1	1	1	1	1	1	1	1	Saint-Kitts-et-Nevis
Saint Lucia	13	14	13	10	14	14	15	12	11	Sainte-Lucie
Saint Vincent-Grenadines	4	4	5	4	5	5	5	5	5	Saint Vincent-Grenadines
Suriname	12	12	8	7	7	9	10	11	10	Suriname
Trinidad and Tobago	22	17	18	18	18	18	18	16	14	Trinité-et-Tobago
Uruguay	228	443	562	673	783	893	863	1 121	1 874	Uruguay
Venezuela (Boliv. Rep. of)	595	554	636	631	639	721	713	722	765	Venezuela (Rép. boliv. du)
Asia	**314 763**	**339 944**	**377 249**	**402 183**	**420 076**	**428 920**	**445 958**	**447 648**	**452 056**	**Asie**
Afghanistan	143	114	103	119	101	102	98	115	135	Afghanistan
Azerbaijan	155	193	249	349	244	188	130	84	98	Azerbaïdjan
Bangladesh	443	439	445	463	463	460	522	485	565	Bangladesh
Bhutan	3	4	3	6	5	5	4	2	2	Bhoutan
Cambodia	132	178	260	332	219	251	234	267	287	Cambodge
China	72 631	70 151	82 212	78 231	78 769	79 344	85 408	81 319	79 443	Chine [1]
Cyprus	29	19	24	18	24	15	16	14	16	Chypre
Georgia	23	29	25	33	16	19	17	4	4	Géorgie
India	32 605	43 464	45 821	52 427	55 010	64 962	56 062	57 004	64 895	Inde
Indonesia	75 849	83 928	94 256	112 060	119 034	120 606	129 716	134 970	134 905	Indonésie

Oil crops *(continued)*
Production: thousand metric tons

Culture oléagineuses *(suite)*
Production: milliers de tonnes

Region, country or area	2002	2003	2004	2005	2006	2007	2008	2009	2010	Région, pays ou zone
Iran (Islamic Rep. of)	852	950	1 219	1 231	1 072	1 177	1 156	1 093	1 005	Iran (Rép. islamique d')
Iraq	247	158	156	141	128	140	115	124	163	Iraq
Israel	172	137	206	149	197	150	121	94	137	Israël
Japan	295	255	186	247	250	247	282	251	240	Japon
Jordan	181	118	161	113	147	125	94	141	172	Jordanie
Kazakhstan	846	1 088	1 128	1 202	1 162	1 160	917	1 133	1 159	Kazakhstan
Korea, Dem. P. R.	410	412	410	398	404	412	416	406	402	Corée, R. p. dém. de
Korea, Republic of	172	146	187	233	203	168	185	192	167	Corée, République de
Kyrgyzstan	241	254	296	284	274	233	224	155	195	Kirghizistan
Lao People's Dem. Rep.	38	36	34	55	59	68	61	69	70	Rép. dém. pop. lao
Lebanon	191	89	173	82	185	84	92	94	107	Liban
Malaysia	75 587	84 497	88 306	94 448	100 073	99 677	105 934	107 455	106 825	Malaisie
Maldives	23	37	36	16	3	2	^0	^0	^0	Maldives
Myanmar	2 144	2 437	2 749	2 856	3 356	3 558	3 964	4 055	3 437	Myanmar
Nepal	295	277	292	311	306	299	296	299	329	Népal
Occupied Palestinian Terr.	86	144	88	140	53	88	88	84	102	Terr. palestinien occupé
Pakistan	9 428	9 372	13 312	12 140	11 391	10 518	10 706	11 454	10 225	Pakistan
Philippines	14 527	14 772	14 850	15 312	15 463	15 407	15 933	16 341	16 214	Philippines
Saudi Arabia	7	7	10	9	9	9	8	7	6	Arabie saoudite
Sri Lanka	1 829	1 962	1 983	1 932	2 137	2 153	2 231	2 125	2 278	Sri Lanka
Syrian Arab Republic	2 308	1 931	2 746	2 350	2 361	1 645	1 962	1 972	2 259	Rép. arabe syrienne
Tajikistan	815	849	873	703	689	657	553	501	526	Tadjikistan
Thailand	7 290	8 452	8 675	8 291	10 260	9 750	12 922	11 548	11 414	Thaïlande
Timor-Leste	14	14	15	15	15	15	14	14	15	Timor-Leste
Turkey	6 857	5 584	6 561	5 866	7 111	5 703	5 596	5 412	5 134	Turquie
Turkmenistan	1 160	1 184	1 660	1 655	1 160	1 576	1 663	1 107	1 650	Turkménistan
Uzbekistan	5 060	4 599	5 740	6 063	5 867	6 010	6 217	5 269	5 391	Ouzbékistan
Viet Nam	1 606	1 597	1 745	1 848	1 796	1 874	1 935	1 919	2 016	Viet Nam
Yemen	66	67	52	54	59	62	64	66	67	Yémen
Europe	**40 677**	**46 035**	**49 783**	**51 449**	**55 365**	**52 543**	**62 170**	**64 887**	**63 091**	**Europe**
Albania	31	31	63	35	44	32	60	82	74	Albanie
Austria	263	239	288	293	315	272	320	327	349	Autriche
Belarus	92	92	185	184	146	275	555	644	407	Bélarus
Belgium	32	30	35	34	45	51	42	49	50	Belgique
Bosnia and Herzegovina	10	5	9	14	15	12	11	10	10	Bosnie-Herzégovine
Bulgaria	691	827	1 131	981	1 253	683	1 560	1 580	2 163	Bulgarie
Croatia	252	191	210	276	304	220	328	314	291	Croatie
Czech Republic	827	600	1 106	957	1 056	1 146	1 194	1 280	1 160	République tchèque
Denmark	218	354	468	342	435	589	629	635	580	Danemark
Estonia	64	69	69	83	85	134	111	136	131	Estonie
European Union (EU)	31 549	34 408	38 599	36 479	38 346	38 035	40 477	44 921	43 224	Union européenne (UE)
Finland	103	94	75	106	148	114	89	140	179	Finlande
France	5 105	5 104	5 687	6 281	5 781	6 157	6 449	7 502	6 697	France
Germany	3 918	3 728	5 376	5 153	5 423	5 387	5 217	6 379	5 763	Allemagne
Greece	4 636	3 780	4 041	4 511	4 016	3 890	3 941	3 517	2 852	Grèce
Hungary	1 079	1 189	1 585	1 498	1 618	1 614	2 216	1 928	1 604	Hongrie
Ireland	7	7	7	14	18	32	23	22	24	Irlande
Italy	4 297	4 287	5 457	4 733	4 424	4 015	4 179	4 151	4 050	Italie
Latvia	35	39	105	148	123	199	201	207	229	Lettonie
Lithuania	109	123	207	204	171	313	331	417	416	Lituanie
Luxembourg	13	13	17	15	16	18	16	18	16	Luxembourg
Montenegro	...	...	...	...	2	1	2	2	2	Monténégro

30

Oil crops *(continued)*
Production: thousand metric tons
Culture oléagineuses *(suite)*
Production: milliers de tonnes

Region, country or area	2002	2003	2004	2005	2006	2007	2008	2009	2010	Région, pays ou zone
Netherlands	7	10	14	12	16	15	13	15	14	Pays-Bas
Norway	18	11	12	11	10	10	10	7	7	Norvège
Poland	967	810	1 655	1 479	1 681	2 157	2 135	2 524	2 110	Pologne
Portugal	281	286	356	234	399	249	382	454	268	Portugal
Republic of Moldova	331	411	376	400	467	229	525	403	530	République de Moldova
Romania	1 194	1 758	1 973	1 804	2 052	1 048	1 944	1 766	2 366	Roumanie
Russian Federation	4 299	5 601	5 750	7 559	8 223	7 044	8 979	8 195	7 462	Fédération de Russie
Serbia	...	...	...	...	822	629	858	772	945	Serbie
Serbia and Montenegro	531	585	763	725	...	...	...	...	...	Serbie-et-Monténégro
Slovakia	395	327	479	455	516	469	635	597	501	Slovaquie
Slovenia	8	6	8	9	8	17	14	12	18	Slovénie
Spain	5 620	8 742	6 535	4 911	6 562	7 099	6 558	8 967	9 063	Espagne
Sweden	164	136	239	214	223	223	260	317	303	Suède
Switzerland	70	69	80	78	74	77	77	82	82	Suisse
TFYR of Macedonia	25	24	24	19	21	18	20	27	30	L'ex-R.Y. Macédoine
Ukraine	3 498	4 626	3 735	5 688	6 914	5 976	10 283	9 444	10 043	Ukraine
United Kingdom	1 486	1 830	1 661	1 991	1 939	2 131	2 002	1 966	2 302	Royaume-Uni
Oceania	**7 430**	**6 798**	**6 928**	**8 105**	**7 232**	**6 802**	**7 480**	**8 630**	**9 143**	**Océanie**
American Samoa	4	5	5	5	5	6	6	7	8	Samoa américaines
Australia	3 879	3 298	3 070	4 114	3 100	2 428	2 556	3 412	3 875	Australie
Cook Islands	5	2	2	2	3	2	2	2	2	Iles Cook
Fiji	170	130	160	188	165	150	150	150	170	Fidji
French Polynesia	87	85	80	90	87	97	105	97	134	Polynésie française
Guam	55	54	53	56	53	59	64	59	82	Guam
Kiribati	96	96	129	129	129	131	142	131	182	Kiribati
Marshall Islands	14	33	20	20	21	28	35	32	36	Iles Marshall
Micronesia (Fed. States of)	40	40	47	49	50	41	44	41	57	Micronésie (Etats féd. de)
Nauru	2	2	2	2	2	2	2	2	3	Nauru
New Caledonia	17	16	19	20	20	17	18	17	17	Nouvelle-Calédonie
New Zealand	5	6	6	6	5	4	4	5	6	Nouvelle-Zélande
Niue	2	2	2	2	2	3	3	3	4	Nioué
Papua New Guinea	2 256	2 241	2 336	2 348	2 463	2 666	3 152	3 515	3 256	Papouasie-Nvl-Guinée
Samoa	110	107	148	153	153	155	168	155	214	Samoa
Solomon Islands	392	383	468	553	599	636	650	624	665	Iles Salomon
Tokelau	3	3	3	3	3	4	4	4	5	Tokélaou
Tonga	59	59	59	59	64	59	60	60	68	Tonga
Tuvalu	2	1	2	2	2	2	2	2	2	Tuvalu
Vanuatu	232	234	316	303	302	310	311	310	352	Vanuatu
Wallis and Futuna Islands	2	2	2	2	2	3	3	3	4	Iles Wallis et Futuna

Source:
Food and Agriculture Organization of the United Nations (FAO), Rome,
FAOSTAT database, last accessed January 2012.

Source:
Organisation des Nations Unies pour l'alimentation et l'agriculture (FAO),
Rome, la base de données de la FAOSTAT, dernier accès janvier 2012.

31

Cereals
Production: thousand metric tons

Céréales
Production: milliers de tonnes

Region, country or area	2002	2003	2004	2005	2006	2007	2008	2009	2010	Région, pays ou zone
World	2 032 315	2 091 750	2 280 369	2 268 385	2 236 382	2 354 989	2 525 126	2 495 443	2 432 819	Monde
Africa	119 020	132 837	133 424	141 954	149 576	138 537	153 411	159 454	156 112	Afrique
Algeria	1 953	4 266	4 033	3 528	4 018	3 602	1 536	5 253	4 686	Algérie
Angola	717	717	717	885	678	782	742	1 030	1 030	Angola
Benin	926	1 043	1 109	1 152	933	1 075	1 268	1 508	1 555	Bénin
Botswana	35	36	21	22	39	30	36	56	61	Botswana
Burkina Faso	3 119	3 564	2 902	3 650	3 681	3 109	4 359	3 627	4 523	Burkina Faso
Burundi	282	279	280	288	286	291	291	300	313	Burundi
Cameroon	1 499	1 587	1 684	1 938	2 232	2 367	2 474	2 531	2 805	Cameroun
Cape Verde	5	12	10	4	4	3	12	7	8	Cap-Vert
Central African Rep.	193	202	210	237	227	237	236	251	239	Rép. centrafricaine
Chad	1 212	1 618	1 213	1 853	1 913	1 972	2 019	2 193	1 912	Tchad
Comoros	23	25	26	22	25	22	25	26	26	Comores
Congo	19	23	24	21	20	21	23	24	25	Congo
Côte d'Ivoire	1 330	1 334	1 378	1 425	1 442	1 244	1 408	1 430	1 461	Côte d'Ivoire
Dem. Rep. of the Congo	1 520	1 521	1 522	1 523	1 524	1 525	1 526	1 527	1 528	Rép. dém. du Congo
Egypt	20 197	20 685	20 827	22 411	22 503	21 565	23 693	22 707	19 408	Egypte
Eritrea	55	106	109	336	377	462	106	227	247	Erythrée
Ethiopia	9 002	9 533	10 697	13 365	13 390	11 846	13 012	15 502	15 638	Ethiopie
Gabon	25	32	32	36	33	34	36	47	41	Gabon
Gambia	139	205	224	206	215	151	235	311	364	Gambie
Ghana	2 155	2 041	1 830	1 948	1 919	1 673	2 297	2 607	2 907	Ghana
Guinea	1 846	1 984	2 136	2 290	2 445	2 601	3 187	2 659	2 859	Guinée
Guinea-Bissau	151	143	171	213	225	184	217	217	237	Guinée-Bissau
Kenya	3 046	3 351	3 199	3 585	3 937	3 614	2 866	2 899	4 100	Kenya
Lesotho	150	116	109	112	119	73	74	75	173	Lesotho
Liberia	110	100	110	155	164	232	295	293	296	Libéria
Libyan Arab Jamah.	217	217	218	234	213	214	214	216	218	Jamah. arabe libyenne
Madagascar	2 787	3 130	3 393	3 799	3 902	4 025	4 356	4 979	5 164	Madagascar
Malawi	1 711	2 143	1 718	1 302	2 786	3 440	2 846	3 808	4 039	Malawi
Mali	2 532	3 402	2 845	3 399	3 693	3 886	4 815	6 335	6 418	Mali
Mauritania	113	171	114	172	169	183	191	172	276	Mauritanie
Mauritius	^0	^0	^0	^0	^0	1	1	1	1	Maurice
Morocco	5 289	7 974	8 603	4 283	9 242	2 505	5 330	10 444	7 834	Maroc
Mozambique	1 361	1 511	1 325	1 139	1 747	1 454	1 601	2 547	2 506	Mozambique
Namibia	100	97	119	105	127	116	113	112	116	Namibie
Niger	3 234	3 568	2 730	3 669	4 030	3 960	4 855	3 452	5 095	Niger

Region, country or area	2002	2003	2004	2005	2006	2007	2008	2009	2010	Région, pays ou zone
Nigeria	21 373	22 736	24 321	26 031	28 864	27 171	30 209	20 983	19 512	Nigéria
Réunion	12	12	13	12	15	20	14	11	14	Réunion
Rwanda	308	298	319	413	366	357	466	651	746	Rwanda
Sao Tome and Principe	3	3	3	3	3	3	3	4	4	Sao Tomé-et-Principe
Senegal	785	1 452	1 054	1 433	988	772	1 740	1 869	1 768	Sénégal
Sierra Leone	466	496	619	825	1 157	650	751	868	1 008	Sierra Leone
Somalia	442	403	366	361	264	196	193	215	258	Somalie
South Africa	13 045	11 816	12 025	14 179	9 444	9 507	15 338	14 577	14 733	Afrique du Sud
Sudan	3 714	6 373	3 516	6 193	5 806	6 691	5 269	5 552	3 562	Soudan
Swaziland	68	70	69	75	68	27	65	62	69	Swaziland
Togo	801	807	799	833	886	878	935	1 061	1 046	Togo
Tunisia	551	2 326	2 165	2 136	1 641	2 026	1 231	2 585	1 109	Tunisie
Uganda	2 368	2 508	2 274	2 459	2 557	2 631	2 723	2 836	2 963	Ouganda
United Rep. of Tanzania	6 364	4 102	6 692	5 371	5 702	6 299	6 096	5 694	6 687	Rép.-Unie de Tanzanie
Western Sahara	3	3	2	1	2	2	1	2	0	Sahara occidental
Zambia	755	1 365	1 380	1 066	1 604	1 536	1 394	2 197	3 098	Zambie
Zimbabwe	909	1 329	2 169	1 257	1 948	1 273	692	919	1 429	Zimbabwe
Northern America	**333 176**	**397 430**	**439 805**	**417 403**	**386 910**	**463 234**	**459 572**	**468 791**	**447 117**	**Amérique septentrionale**
Canada	36 047	49 189	50 778	50 962	48 577	48 109	56 031	49 410	45 412	Canada
United States	297 129	348 241	389 026	366 440	338 333	415 125	403 541	419 381	401 704	Etats-Unis
Lat. America Carib.	**138 647**	**163 084**	**163 023**	**153 202**	**157 727**	**180 554**	**188 910**	**165 761**	**195 972**	**Amérique lat. et Carib.**
Argentina	31 844	34 588	35 883	38 165	34 204	44 187	36 760	26 382	46 204	Argentine
Belize	58	56	49	59	45	63	60	75	85	Belize
Bolivia (Plurin. State of)	1 316	1 463	1 256	1 660	1 866	1 733	2 053	1 874	2 173	Bolivie (État plurin. de)
Brazil	50 879	67 468	63 964	55 669	59 149	69 442	79 752	70 914	75 731	Brésil
Chile	3 380	3 693	3 999	3 989	3 566	2 823	3 273	3 106	3 569	Chili
Colombia	3 956	4 625	4 853	4 268	3 972	4 214	4 707	4 765	4 080	Colombie
Costa Rica	201	198	210	196	207	199	234	284	284	Costa Rica
Cuba	1 001	1 076	889	732	744	809	762	869	779	Cuba
Dominican Republic	766	656	620	634	745	780	807	884	954	Rép. dominicaine
Ecuador	2 065	2 055	2 607	2 304	2 278	2 726	2 284	2 435	2 730	Equateur
El Salvador	814	791	822	895	937	860	1 038	990	994	El Salvador
French Guiana	22	23	26	18	15	9	9	9	9	Guyane française
Guatemala	1 155	1 147	1 170	1 158	1 276	1 534	1 643	1 762	2 122	Guatemala
Guyana	446	550	505	424	472	467	511	559	513	Guyana
Haiti	376	382	398	406	415	520	420	453	437	Haïti
Honduras	579	594	502	531	563	739	623	670	589	Honduras
Jamaica	2	2	2	2	2	2	2	2	2	Jamaïque

Cereals *(continued)*
Production: thousand metric tons

Céréales *(suite)*
Production: milliers de tonnes

Region, country or area	2002	2003	2004	2005	2006	2007	2008	2009	2010	Région, pays ou zone
Mexico	28 770	31 334	32 312	29 060	32 155	34 311	36 107	31 282	34 922	Mexique
Nicaragua	911	1 002	799	964	895	864	784	914	970	Nicaragua
Panama	371	409	341	334	325	332	395	331	330	Panama
Paraguay	1 549	1 908	2 064	1 569	2 951	2 855	3 443	3 166	4 976	Paraguay
Peru	3 844	3 920	3 438	4 132	4 064	4 212	4 717	5 050	4 868	Pérou
Puerto Rico	^0	1	1	1	1	1	^0	^0	^0	Porto Rico
Saint Vincent-Grenadines	1	1	1	1	1	1	1	1	1	Saint Vincent-Grenadines
Suriname	157	194	175	164	183	179	183	229	227	Suriname
Trinidad and Tobago	7	5	5	5	5	6	6	5	6	Trinité-et-Tobago
Uruguay	1 606	1 827	2 525	2 277	2 648	2 678	3 604	4 248	3 341	Uruguay
Venezuela (Boliv. Rep. of)	2 569	3 116	3 606	3 584	4 044	4 008	4 734	4 500	5 073	Venezuela (Rép. boliv. du)
Asia	**984 876**	**1 000 089**	**1 038 288**	**1 087 038**	**1 118 311**	**1 155 301**	**1 182 364**	**1 199 848**	**1 193 348**	**Asie**
Afghanistan	3 737	4 381	3 560	5 425	4 638	5 786	3 870	6 514	5 957	Afghanistan
Armenia	412	310	460	399	215	457	420	378	325	Arménie
Azerbaijan	2 133	1 993	2 087	2 056	2 012	1 944	2 420	2 903	1 927	Azerbaïdjan
Bangladesh	39 341	40 015	37 759	41 147	42 045	44 841	48 947	49 316	51 169	Bangladesh
Bhutan	90	105	154	193	185	191	166	143	134	Bhoutan
Brunei Darussalam	^0	1	1	1	1	2	1	1	1	Brunéi Darussalam
Cambodia	3 971	5 026	4 427	6 234	6 641	7 250	7 787	8 510	9 657	Cambodge
China	399 998	376 123	413 164	429 370	452 795	457 812	479 978	483 268	497 580	Chine
Cyprus	142	165	111	70	67	64	6	55	57	Chypre
Georgia	662	742	663	680	320	419	468	374	220	Géorgie
India	206 636	236 593	229 845	239 997	242 786	260 486	267 566	248 810	234 910	Inde
Indonesia	61 075	63 024	65 314	66 675	66 064	70 445	76 575	82 029	84 776	Indonésie
Iran (Islamic Rep. of)	19 861	20 942	21 986	21 907	22 407	24 026	13 475	20 835	22 272	Iran (Rép. islamique d')
Iraq	4 125	3 516	3 308	3 697	3 772	3 736	2 201	2 616	4 312	Iraq
Israel	271	306	273	308	245	284	199	257	239	Israël
Japan	12 184	10 824	11 994	12 434	11 742	12 025	12 151	11 459	11 363	Japon
Jordan	115	80	53	102	62	50	47	61	87	Jordanie
Kazakhstan	15 929	14 741	12 339	13 740	16 461	20 090	15 530	20 764	12 116	Kazakhstan
Korea, Dem. P. R.	4 211	4 393	4 485	4 645	4 676	3 893	4 702	4 454	4 543	Corée, R. p. dém. de
Korea, Republic of	7 083	6 355	7 115	6 816	6 647	6 312	7 203	7 278	6 013	Corée, République de
Kuwait	5	3	3	4	4	3	3	4	4	Koweït
Kyrgyzstan	1 712	1 634	1 709	1 622	1 504	1 418	1 440	1 858	1 510	Kirghizistan
Lao People's Dem. Rep.	2 541	2 518	2 733	2 941	3 114	3 398	4 078	4 279	4 090	Rép. dém. pop. lao
Lebanon	140	146	165	178	190	154	178	192	178	Liban
Malaysia	2 267	2 329	2 336	2 389	2 267	2 407	2 386	2 495	2 584	Malaisie
Mongolia	126	165	139	77	139	115	213	392	355	Mongolie

Region, country or area	2002	2003	2004	2005	2006	2007	2008	2009	2010	Région, pays ou zone
Myanmar	22 684	24 152	26 053	28 967	32 301	32 937	34 134	34 284	34 836	Myanmar
Nepal	7 215	7 360	7 747	7 767	7 657	7 329	8 069	8 114	7 763	Népal
Occupied Palestinian Terr.	77	68	62	68	66	55	42	40	38	Terr. palestinien occupé
Oman	14	14	19	15	14	16	15	48	59	Oman
Pakistan	27 173	28 964	30 311	33 508	33 028	35 813	35 528	38 148	34 443	Pakistan
Philippines	17 590	18 116	19 910	19 856	21 409	22 977	23 744	23 301	22 149	Philippines
Qatar	7	7	5	7	7	8	8	10	10	Qatar
Saudi Arabia	2 853	2 949	3 189	3 007	3 043	2 960	2 432	1 586	1 784	Arabie saoudite
Sri Lanka	2 890	3 106	2 668	3 295	3 396	3 193	3 994	3 788	4 470	Sri Lanka
Syrian Arab Republic	5 932	6 227	5 281	5 631	6 302	5 011	2 685	4 739	4 689	Rép. arabe syrienne
Tajikistan	688	866	860	903	893	907	909	1 250	1 207	Tadjikistan
Thailand	32 490	33 992	33 119	34 652	33 752	36 196	36 107	36 940	36 259	Thaïlande
Timor-Leste	147	136	117	151	174	132	180	255	262	Timor-Leste
Turkey	30 831	30 807	34 045	36 354	34 637	29 250	29 280	33 570	32 741	Turquie
Turkmenistan	2 461	2 667	2 785	3 035	3 489	2 886	2 503	3 173	3 235	Turkménistan
Uzbekistan	5 535	6 106	5 860	6 531	6 632	6 749	6 706	7 358	7 416	Ouzbékistan
Viet Nam	36 960	37 707	39 581	39 622	39 706	40 248	43 305	43 324	44 598	Viet Nam
Yemen	560	418	490	562	809	1 029	714	674	1 013	Yémen
Europe	**436 597**	**355 707**	**470 400**	**428 043**	**403 620**	**391 972**	**504 621**	**465 926**	**405 725**	**Europe**
Albania	519	489	499	511	508	494	609	631	694	Albanie
Austria	4 461	4 519	5 606	5 195	4 460	4 758	5 748	5 144	5 330	Autriche
Belarus	5 710	5 117	6 590	6 089	5 685	7 014	8 713	8 154	6 730	Bélarus
Belgium	2 639	2 561	2 932	2 787	2 684	2 719	3 113	3 256	3 042	Belgique
Bosnia and Herzegovina	1 308	793	1 439	1 350	1 341	1 001	1 375	1 391	1 104	Bosnie-Herzégovine
Bulgaria	6 770	3 814	7 463	5 839	5 532	3 203	7 016	6 243	7 027	Bulgarie
Croatia	3 724	2 358	3 268	3 040	3 036	2 534	3 726	3 442	3 017	Croatie
Czech Republic	6 784	5 773	8 792	7 668	6 393	7 157	8 374	7 836	6 883	République tchèque
Denmark	8 804	9 051	8 963	9 283	8 632	8 220	9 106	10 164	8 772	Danemark
Estonia	525	506	608	760	619	879	864	873	670	Estonie
Finland	3 938	3 791	3 619	4 059	3 790	4 135	4 229	4 261	2 992	Finlande
France	69 657	54 940	70 517	64 104	61 584	59 328	70 108	70 034	65 676	France
Germany	43 391	39 320	51 110	45 980	43 475	40 632	50 105	49 809	44 413	Allemagne
Greece	4 827	4 710	5 088	5 097	4 685	4 607	5 238	4 820	4 499	Grèce
Hungary	11 703	8 770	16 779	16 212	14 467	9 653	16 841	13 590	12 304	Hongrie
Ireland	1 964	2 147	2 502	1 940	2 090	2 006	2 469	2 071	2 048	Irlande
Italy	21 248	17 864	23 283	21 423	20 207	20 351	21 613	17 392	18 996	Italie
Latvia	1 029	932	1 060	1 314	1 159	1 535	1 689	1 663	1 417	Lettonie
Lithuania	2 539	2 626	2 859	2 811	1 858	3 017	3 422	3 807	2 768	Lituanie

Cereals *(continued)*
Production: thousand metric tons

Céréales *(suite)*
Production: milliers de tonnes

Region, country or area	2002	2003	2004	2005	2006	2007	2008	2009	2010	Région, pays ou zone
Luxembourg	169	164	179	161	161	148	191	189	166	Luxembourg
Malta	12	12	14	12	12	14	16	15	15	Malte
Montenegro	...	...	...	...	14	10	16	17	16	Monténégro
Netherlands	1 740	1 820	1 823	1 775	1 675	1 520	1 963	1 994	1 804	Pays-Bas
Norway	1 143	1 287	1 445	1 298	1 169	1 202	1 387	1 055	1 145	Norvège
Poland	26 877	23 391	29 635	26 928	21 776	27 143	27 664	29 826	27 120	Pologne
Portugal	1 497	1 186	1 363	790	1 167	1 109	1 310	1 109	1 124	Portugal
Republic of Moldova	2 539	1 583	2 943	2 772	2 222	887	3 132	2 149	2 386	République de Moldova
Romania	14 357	12 966	24 402	19 350	15 760	7 816	16 827	14 874	16 710	Roumanie
Russian Federation	84 859	65 562	76 231	76 564	76 495	80 208	106 418	95 616	59 624	Fédération de Russie
Serbia	...	...	...	...	8 416	6 258	8 852	8 999	9 291	Serbie
Serbia and Montenegro	8 327	5 568	9 893	9 534	...	...	...	...	...	Serbie-et-Monténégro
Slovakia	3 196	2 491	3 798	3 585	2 929	2 793	4 137	3 333	2 633	Slovaquie
Slovenia	614	401	586	579	496	534	582	535	571	Slovénie
Spain	21 710	21 412	24 809	14 226	19 036	24 484	23 937	17 755	19 335	Espagne
Sweden	5 398	5 290	5 508	5 051	4 128	5 058	5 195	5 249	4 333	Suède
Switzerland	1 101	847	1 089	1 057	1 013	1 012	1 002	1 006	924	Suisse
TFYR of Macedonia	556	472	682	645	602	469	613	603	539	L'ex-R.Y. Macédoine
Ukraine	37 995	19 662	40 997	37 258	33 511	28 938	52 740	45 406	38 679	Ukraine
United Kingdom	22 966	21 511	22 028	20 998	20 832	19 124	24 282	21 616	20 929	Royaume-Uni
Oceania	**19 999**	**42 603**	**35 429**	**40 746**	**20 239**	**25 391**	**36 247**	**35 664**	**34 546**	**Océanie**
Australia	19 029	41 631	34 564	39 840	19 399	24 428	35 211	34 501	33 515	Australie
Fiji	14	17	15	16	14	15	12	12	9	Fidji
New Caledonia	4	6	5	6	4	6	4	3	3	Nouvelle-Calédonie
New Zealand	937	937	830	867	806	927	999	1 127	1 001	Nouvelle-Zélande
Papua New Guinea	13	10	12	13	12	12	15	16	13	Papouasie-Nvl-Guinée
Solomon Islands	2	2	3	3	3	3	3	4	4	Iles Salomon
Vanuatu	1	1	1	1	1	1	1	1	1	Vanuatu

Source:
Food and Agriculture Organization of the United Nations (FAO), Rome, the FAOSTAT database, last accessed January 2012.

Source:
Organisation des Nations Unies pour l'alimentation et l'agriculture (FAO), Rome, la base de données FAOSTAT, dernier accès janvier 2012.

Roundwood
Production (solid volume of roundwood without bark): million cubic metres

Bois rond
Production (volume solide de bois rond sans écorce) : millions de mètres cubes

Region, country or area	2004	2005	2006	2007	2008	2009	2010	2011	Région, pays ou zone
World	**3 505.6**	**3 570.8**	**3 530.2**	**3 552.5**	**3 435.5**	**3 288.7**	**3 401.3**	**3 435.4**	**Monde**
Africa	**635.0**	**650.1**	**662.4**	**667.2**	**676.2**	**681.3**	**690.0**	**690.1**	**Afrique**
Algeria	7.7	7.7	7.8	8.0	8.1	8.2	8.3	8.3	Algérie
Angola	4.6	4.7	4.8	4.8	4.9	5.0	5.1	5.1	Angola
Benin	6.4	6.4	6.6	6.6	6.6	6.7	6.7	6.7	Bénin
Botswana	0.8	0.8	0.8	0.8	0.8	0.8	0.8	0.8	Botswana
Burkina Faso	9.2	11.7	12.2	12.7	13.6	13.8	14.0	14.0	Burkina Faso
Burundi	9.2	9.4	9.6	9.7	9.8	10.0	10.7	10.7	Burundi
Cameroon	11.2	11.3	12.2	12.3	12.3	12.0	12.1	12.1	Cameroun
Cape Verde	0.2	0.2	0.2	0.2	0.2	0.2	0.2	0.2	Cap-Vert
Central African Rep.	2.8	2.9	2.8	2.8	2.8	2.7	2.6	2.7	Rép. centrafricaine
Chad	7.1	7.2	7.4	7.5	7.6	7.7	7.8	7.8	Tchad
Comoros	0.3	0.3	0.3	0.3	0.3	0.3	0.3	0.3	Comores
Congo	3.5	3.6	3.6	3.7	3.7	3.3	3.8	3.8	Congo
Côte d'Ivoire	10.3	10.0	10.1	10.3	10.3	10.4	10.4	10.4	Côte d'Ivoire
Dem. Rep. of the Congo	73.9	75.3	76.5	77.8	78.9	80.0	81.2	81.2	Rép. dém. du Congo
Djibouti	0.3	0.3	0.3	0.3	0.3	0.3	0.4	0.4	Djibouti
Egypt	17.1	17.2	17.3	17.4	17.6	17.7	17.8	17.8	Egypte
Equatorial Guinea	0.9	1.1	1.1	1.0	1.0	1.0	1.0	1.0	Guinée équatoriale
Eritrea	1.3	1.3	1.3	1.3	1.3	1.3	1.3	1.3	Erythrée
Ethiopia	96.0	97.4	98.6	100.1	101.4	102.8	104.2	104.2	Ethiopie
Gabon	4.6	4.3	4.6	4.5	4.5	4.5	4.5	4.5	Gabon
Gambia	0.8	0.8	0.8	0.8	0.8	0.8	0.8	0.8	Gambie
Ghana	32.2	33.1	34.3	35.5	36.8	37.9	39.0	39.0	Ghana
Guinea	12.3	12.3	12.4	12.4	12.5	12.6	12.6	12.6	Guinée
Guinea-Bissau	2.5	2.5	2.6	2.6	2.7	2.7	2.7	2.7	Guinée-Bissau
Kenya	22.2	26.7	27.6	27.6	27.6	27.6	27.6	27.6	Kenya
Lesotho	2.0	2.1	2.1	2.1	2.1	2.1	2.1	2.1	Lesotho
Liberia	5.9	6.1	6.4	6.6	6.9	7.2	7.5	7.5	Libéria
Libyan Arab Jamah.	1.0	1.0	1.0	1.0	1.0	1.1	1.1	1.1	Jamah. arabe libyenne
Madagascar	11.0	11.2	13.3	13.3	13.4	13.3	13.4	13.4	Madagascar
Malawi	6.5	6.5	6.6	6.6	6.7	6.7	6.8	6.8	Malawi
Mali	5.4	5.4	5.5	5.6	5.6	5.7	5.7	5.7	Mali
Mauritania	1.6	1.6	1.7	1.7	1.8	1.8	1.8	1.8	Mauritanie
Morocco	0.9	1.0	0.9	1.0	0.9	0.8	0.8	0.8	Maroc
Mozambique	18.0	18.0	18.0	18.0	18.0	18.1	18.1	18.1	Mozambique
Namibia	0.8	0.8	0.8	0.8	0.8	0.8	0.8	0.8	Namibie
Niger	3.4	3.6	3.6	3.6	3.6	3.6	3.6	3.6	Niger
Nigeria	70.3	70.7	71.0	71.4	71.8	72.2	72.6	72.6	Nigéria
Rwanda	5.5	5.5	5.5	5.5	6.2	6.2	6.2	6.2	Rwanda
Sao Tome and Principe	0.1	0.1	0.1	0.1	0.1	0.1	0.1	0.1	Sao Tomé-et-Principe
Senegal	6.0	6.1	6.1	6.1	6.2	6.2	6.2	6.2	Sénégal
Sierra Leone	5.5	5.5	5.6	5.6	5.6	5.7	5.7	5.7	Sierra Leone
Somalia	10.6	10.9	11.2	11.6	11.9	12.3	12.6	12.6	Somalie
South Africa	33.8	34.6	34.8	31.5	31.9	30.9	30.9	30.9	Afrique du Sud

32

Roundwood *(continued)*
Production (solid volume of roundwood without bark): million cubic metres
Bois rond *(suite)*
Production (volume solide de bois rond sans écorce) : millions de mètres cubes

Region, country or area	2004	2005	2006	2007	2008	2009	2010	2011	Région, pays ou zone
Sudan	...	...	...	...	...	...	...	20.9	Soudan
Sudan (former)	19.7	19.9	20.1	20.3	20.5	20.7	20.9	...	Soudan (anc.)
Swaziland	1.3	1.3	1.3	1.3	1.4	1.4	1.4	1.4	Swaziland
Togo	4.7	4.6	4.6	4.6	4.6	4.6	4.6	4.6	Togo
Tunisia	2.3	2.4	2.4	2.4	2.4	2.4	2.4	2.4	Tunisie
Uganda	39.5	40.1	40.7	41.7	42.4	43.0	43.7	43.7	Ouganda
United Rep. of Tanzania	23.8	24.0	24.2	24.4	24.7	24.9	25.1	25.1	Rép.-Unie de Tanzanie
Zambia	9.2	9.4	9.9	10.0	10.2	10.3	10.4	10.4	Zambie
Zimbabwe	9.1	8.9	9.2	9.2	9.2	9.3	9.2	9.2	Zimbabwe
Northern America	**668.8**	**670.5**	**641.0**	**589.7**	**519.7**	**448.8**	**466.0**	**469.5**	**Amérique septentrionale**
Canada	208.1	203.1	183.9	164.6	139.2	116.3	142.0	145.1	Canada
United States	461.7	467.3	457.0	425.1	380.5	332.5	324.0	324.4	Etats-Unis
Latin Am. and the Caribbean	**446.2**	**463.7**	**466.1**	**477.6**	**477.8**	**482.7**	**490.4**	**490.4**	**Am. latine et Caraïbes**
Argentina	14.9	14.2	13.9	13.6	13.5	14.4	14.4	14.4	Argentine
Bahamas	0.1	0.1	0.1	0.1	0.1	0.1	0.1	0.1	Bahamas
Belize	0.2	0.2	0.2	0.2	0.2	0.2	0.2	0.2	Belize
Bolivia (Plurinational State of)	3.0	3.1	3.2	3.2	3.2	3.2	3.3	3.3	Bolivie (État plurin. de)
Brazil	243.3	255.7	257.5	261.4	256.3	264.1	271.5	271.5	Brésil
Chile	42.6	45.6	46.7	52.6	54.8	51.0	47.2	47.2	Chili
Colombia	10.5	11.9	10.5	10.4	11.1	11.2	11.2	11.2	Colombie
Costa Rica	4.5	4.7	4.8	5.0	4.9	4.7	4.7	4.7	Costa Rica
Cuba	2.5	2.6	2.6	2.2	1.9	2.4	1.9	1.9	Cuba
Dominican Republic	0.6	0.6	0.9	0.9	0.9	0.9	0.9	0.9	Rép. dominicaine
Ecuador	6.6	6.6	5.8	6.1	6.0	6.9	7.0	7.0	Equateur
El Salvador	4.9	4.9	4.9	4.9	4.9	4.9	4.9	4.9	El Salvador
French Guiana	0.2	0.2	0.2	0.2	0.2	0.2	0.2	0.2	Guyane française
Guatemala	16.3	16.7	17.1	17.4	17.8	18.1	18.5	18.5	Guatemala
Guyana	1.3	1.4	1.4	1.4	1.3	1.3	1.4	1.4	Guyana
Haiti	2.2	2.2	2.2	2.3	2.3	2.3	2.3	2.3	Haïti
Honduras	9.6	9.6	9.5	9.5	9.3	9.1	9.1	9.1	Honduras
Jamaica	0.9	0.8	0.8	0.8	0.8	0.8	0.7	0.7	Jamaïque
Mexico	45.2	44.6	44.7	44.9	45.1	45.2	45.7	45.7	Mexique
Nicaragua	6.0	6.0	6.1	6.1	6.1	6.1	6.2	6.2	Nicaragua
Panama	1.3	1.4	1.3	1.3	1.3	1.2	1.2	1.2	Panama
Paraguay	10.0	10.1	10.2	10.3	10.4	10.5	10.6	10.6	Paraguay
Peru	8.9	9.1	9.3	9.4	9.1	8.7	8.7	8.7	Pérou
Suriname	0.2	0.2	0.2	0.2	0.2	0.3	0.3	0.3	Suriname
Trinidad and Tobago	0.1	0.1	0.1	0.1	0.1	0.1	0.1	0.1	Trinité-et-Tobago
Uruguay	5.1	5.7	6.4	7.2	9.5	8.4	11.9	11.9	Uruguay
Venezuela (Boliv. Rep. of)	5.3	5.3	5.6	6.1	6.3	6.4	6.4	6.4	Venezuela (Rép. boliv. du)
Asia	**1 051.5**	**1 046.1**	**1 037.1**	**1 035.1**	**1 045.7**	**1 029.5**	**1 033.1**	**1 033.6**	**Asie**
Afghanistan	3.2	3.2	3.3	3.3	3.3	3.4	3.4	3.4	Afghanistan
Armenia	0.1	^0.0	0.1	^0.0	^0.0	^0.0	^0.0	^0.0	Arménie
Bangladesh	28.0	27.9	27.9	27.8	27.7	27.6	27.6	27.6	Bangladesh
Bhutan	4.6	4.7	4.7	5.0	5.0	5.0	5.1	5.1	Bhoutan
Brunei Darussalam	0.1	0.1	0.1	0.1	0.1	0.1	0.1	0.1	Brunéi Darussalam

Roundwood *(continued)*
Production (solid volume of roundwood without bark): million cubic metres

Bois rond *(suite)*
Production (volume solide de bois rond sans écorce) : millions de mètres cubes

Region, country or area	2004	2005	2006	2007	2008	2009	2010	2011	Région, pays ou zone
Cambodia	9.5	9.3	9.2	9.0	8.9	8.7	8.5	8.6	Cambodge
China	305.9	302.0	298.2	290.7	296.9	292.9	291.3	291.3	Chine
Dem. P. R. Korea	7.2	7.3	7.3	7.4	7.4	7.4	7.5	7.5	R. p. dém. de Corée
Georgia	0.5	0.6	0.6	0.8	0.8	0.8	0.8	0.8	Géorgie
India	326.6	328.7	329.4	330.2	331.0	331.7	332.5	332.5	Inde
Indonesia	128.4	123.8	118.2	115.3	119.3	110.1	113.8	113.8	Indonésie
Iran (Islamic Rep. of)	0.8	0.8	0.8	0.9	0.9	0.9	0.8	0.8	Iran (Rép. islamique d')
Iraq	0.2	0.2	0.2	0.2	0.2	0.2	0.2	0.2	Iraq
Japan	15.7	16.3	16.7	17.8	17.8	16.7	17.3	17.3	Japon
Jordan	0.3	0.3	0.3	0.3	0.3	0.3	0.3	0.3	Jordanie
Kazakhstan	0.5	0.9	0.1	0.2	0.2	0.3	0.3	0.3	Kazakhstan
Lao People's Dem. Rep.	6.2	6.1	6.1	6.1	6.2	6.2	6.2	6.2	Rép. dém. pop. lao
Malaysia	28.5	28.3	26.2	28.0	25.7	23.0	22.5	22.5	Malaisie
Mongolia	0.8	0.8	0.8	0.8	0.8	0.8	0.8	0.8	Mongolie
Myanmar	41.8	42.5	42.5	42.5	42.5	42.5	42.5	42.5	Myanmar
Nepal	14.0	14.0	13.9	13.9	13.8	13.8	13.8	13.8	Népal
Pakistan	28.7	29.3	29.4	32.5	32.7	32.7	32.7	32.7	Pakistan
Philippines	16.1	16.1	16.1	15.9	16.4	16.3	16.0	16.0	Philippines
Republic of Korea	4.7	4.8	4.9	5.2	5.2	5.7	5.7	5.7	République de Corée
Saudi Arabia	0.2	0.2	0.2	0.2	0.2	0.2	0.2	0.2	Arabie saoudite
Sri Lanka	6.3	6.3	6.3	6.1	6.0	5.9	5.8	5.8	Sri Lanka
Syrian Arab Republic	0.1	0.1	0.1	0.1	0.1	0.1	0.1	0.1	Rép. arabe syrienne
Tajikistan	0.1	0.1	0.1	0.1	0.1	0.1	0.1	0.1	Tadjikistan
Thailand	28.7	28.6	28.4	28.3	28.2	28.1	28.0	28.0	Thaïlande
Timor-Leste	0.2	0.1	0.1	0.1	0.1	0.1	0.1	0.1	Timor-Leste
Turkey	16.5	16.2	18.1	18.3	19.4	19.3	20.6	21.0	Turquie
Viet Nam	26.5	26.0	26.1	27.5	27.9	27.9	27.9	27.9	Viet Nam
Yemen	0.4	0.4	0.4	0.4	0.4	0.4	0.4	0.4	Yémen
Europe	**641.6**	**679.2**	**661.9**	**719.8**	**651.6**	**585.4**	**657.8**	**687.7**	**Europe**
Albania	0.3	0.3	0.3	0.4	0.4	0.4	0.4	0.4	Albanie
Austria	16.5	16.5	19.1	21.3	21.8	16.7	17.8	18.7	Autriche
Belarus	8.6	8.7	8.8	8.8	8.8	8.8	10.4	10.4	Bélarus
Belgium	4.9	5.0	5.1	5.0	4.7	4.4	4.8	5.1	Belgique
Bosnia and Herzegovina	4.0	3.8	4.1	3.8	4.0	3.4	3.6	3.9	Bosnie-Herzégovine
Bulgaria	6.0	5.9	6.0	5.7	6.1	4.6	5.7	6.2	Bulgarie
Croatia	3.8	4.0	4.5	4.2	4.5	4.2	4.5	5.3	Croatie
Czech Republic	15.6	15.5	17.7	18.5	16.2	15.5	17.0	16.3	République tchèque
Denmark	1.5	3.0	2.4	2.6	2.8	2.8	2.7	2.6	Danemark
Estonia	6.8	5.5	5.4	4.5	4.9	5.4	7.2	7.5	Estonie
Finland	54.4	52.3	50.8	56.6	50.7	41.7	51.0	50.7	Finlande
France	52.9	52.5	53.3	54.6	52.8	54.4	55.8	53.5	France
Germany	54.5	56.9	62.3	76.7	55.4	48.1	54.4	56.1	Allemagne
Greece	1.7	1.5	1.6	1.7	1.7	1.7	1.7	1.7	Grèce
Hungary	5.7	5.9	5.9	5.6	5.3	5.2	5.7	6.1	Hongrie
Ireland	2.6	2.6	2.7	2.7	2.2	2.4	2.6	2.6	Irlande
Italy	8.7	8.7	8.6	8.1	8.7	8.1	7.8	6.3	Italie

Region, country or area	2004	2005	2006	2007	2008	2009	2010	2011	Région, pays ou zone
Latvia	12.8	12.8	12.8	12.2	8.8	10.4	12.2	13.0	Lettonie
Lithuania	6.1	6.0	5.9	6.2	5.6	5.5	7.1	8.1	Lituanie
Luxembourg	0.3	0.2	0.3	0.3	0.4	0.3	0.3	0.3	Luxembourg
Montenegro	...	...	0.5	0.5	0.5	0.4	0.4	0.4	Monténégro
Netherlands	1.0	1.1	1.1	1.0	1.1	1.0	1.1	1.2	Pays-Bas
Norway	8.8	9.7	9.8	10.5	10.3	8.9	10.4	10.7	Norvège
Poland	32.7	31.9	32.4	35.9	34.3	34.6	35.5	36.9	Pologne
Portugal	10.9	10.7	10.8	10.8	10.2	9.6	9.6	9.1	Portugal
Republic of Moldova	0.4	0.3	0.4	0.4	0.4	0.4	0.4	0.4	République de Moldova
Romania	15.8	14.5	14.0	15.3	13.7	12.6	13.1	14.4	Roumanie
Russian Federation	178.4	185.0	190.6	207.0	181.4	151.4	175.0	197.0	Fédération de Russie
Serbia	...	...	2.9	3.0	3.2	3.1	7.6	7.7	Serbie
Serbia and Montenegro	3.5	3.2	...	...	...	...	...	...	Serbie-et-Monténégro
Slovakia	7.2	9.3	7.9	8.1	9.3	9.1	9.6	9.2	Slovaquie
Slovenia	2.6	2.7	3.2	2.9	3.0	2.9	2.9	3.4	Slovénie
Spain	16.3	15.5	15.7	14.5	17.0	14.0	15.6	17.6	Espagne
Sweden	67.3	98.2	64.6	78.2	70.8	65.1	72.2	72.1	Suède
Switzerland	5.1	5.3	5.7	5.5	5.0	4.7	4.9	4.9	Suisse
TFYR of Macedonia	0.8	0.8	0.8	0.6	0.7	0.6	0.6	0.6	L'ex-R.Y. Macédoine
Ukraine	14.9	14.6	15.8	16.9	16.9	14.2	16.1	17.5	Ukraine
United Kingdom	8.3	8.5	8.4	9.0	8.4	8.6	9.7	10.0	Royaume-Uni
Oceania	**61.5**	**61.1**	**61.6**	**63.1**	**64.6**	**60.9**	**64.1**	**64.1**	**Océanie**
Australia	31.9	31.9	31.8	32.3	33.3	30.3	29.8	29.8	Australie
Fiji	0.5	0.5	0.5	0.5	0.5	0.5	0.5	0.5	Fidji
New Zealand	19.8	19.0	19.3	19.9	20.3	20.2	22.0	22.0	Nouvelle-Zélande
Papua New Guinea	7.9	8.1	8.5	8.6	8.6	8.4	10.0	10.0	Papouasie-Nvl-Guinée
Samoa	0.1	0.1	0.1	0.1	0.1	0.1	0.1	0.1	Samoa
Solomon Islands	1.2	1.3	1.2	1.6	1.7	1.2	1.6	1.6	Iles Salomon
Vanuatu	0.1	0.1	0.1	0.1	0.1	0.1	0.1	0.1	Vanuatu

Source:
Food and Agriculture Organization of the United Nations (FAO), Rome,
FAOSTAT database, last accessed August 2012.

Source:
Organisation des Nations Unies pour l'alimentation et l'agriculture (FAO), Rome, la
base de données de la FAOSTAT, dernier accès août 2012.

Country or area	Capture production Captures					Aquaculture production Production de l'aquaculture					Pays ou zone
	2006	2007	2008	2009	2010	2006	2007	2008	2009	2010	
World	90 023 515	90 305 150	89 698 988	89 630 210	88 603 826	47 290 220	49 937 426	52 946 447	55 714 357	59 872 600	Monde
Afghanistan[1]	1 000	1 000	1 000	1 000	...	...	...	...	...	...	Afghanistan [1]
Albania	5 729	5 497	5 506	5 945	6 144	1 970	2 008	1 858	2 182	2 504	Albanie
Algeria	145 762	147 362	138 861	127 513	93 607	288	405	2 780	2 163	1 759	Algérie
American Samoa	5 349	6 512	4 423	4 943	5 261	...	...	...	...	...	Samoa américaines
Angola	225 741	306 436	305 762	272 263	260 000[1]	156[1]	190[1]	190[1]	210[1]	210[1]	Angola
Anguilla	710[1]	735[1]	759	681	701	...	...	...	...	...	Anguilla
Antigua and Barbuda	3 092	3 092	3 521	2 490	2 293	...	...	...	...	...	Antigua-et-Barbuda
Argentina	1 171 980	985 409	995 083	861 973	811 749	2 528	2 957	2 700	2 610	2 665	Argentine
Armenia	350	1 065	601	619[1]	617[1]	1 056[1]	3 650[1]	5 100[1]	5 240[1]	5 000[1]	Arménie
Aruba	145	159	151	163	153	...	...	...	...	...	Aruba
Australia	197 108	188 076	181 517	171 637	171 410	49 376	55 799	58 912	64 535	69 581	Australie
Austria	360	350	350	350	350	2 503	2 539	2 087	2 141	2 167	Autriche
Azerbaijan	4 061	2 949	1 524	1 206	1 081	600[1]	900[1]	1 000[1]	1 000[1]	1 000[1]	Azerbaïdjan
Bahamas	10 598	8 382	9 117	9 018	11 611	22	0	0	2	0	Bahamas
Bahrain	15 594	15 014	14 175	16 358	13 490	2	1	2	2	3	Bahreïn
Bangladesh	1 436 496	1 494 199	1 557 754	1 821 579	1 726 586	892 049	945 812	1 005 542	1 064 285	1 308 515	Bangladesh
Barbados	1 975	2 224	3 551	3 496	3 269	2[1]	2[1]	2[1]	2[1]	2[1]	Barbade
Belarus	645	689	809	826	897	8 406	14 091	14 636	15 659	16 265	Bélarus
Belgium	23 019	24 541	22 609	21 722	22 418	128	128	126	576	539	Belgique
Belize	19 022	23 902	50 949	11 114	114 292	7 624	2 872	4 528	5 725	4 741	Belize
Benin	41 507	36 386	37 495[1]	38 928	39 791	415	178	180[1]	400	461	Bénin
Bermuda	380	424	399	416	382	...	...	...	...	...	Bermudes
Bhutan	200[1]	200[1]	180[1]	180[1]	160[1]	40	40	46[1]	46[1]	46[1]	Bhoutan
Bolivia (Pl. St. of)	6 080[1]	5 770	6 750	7 568	6 946	455[1]	585	631	775	856	Bolivie (État pl. de)
Bosnia and Herz.	2 005[1]	2 005[1]	2 005[1]	2 005[1]	2 005[1]	7 621	7 442[1]	7 589[1]	7 620[1]	7 620[1]	Bosnie-Herzégovine
Botswana	81	122	86	73[1]	60	...	...	...	...	...	Botswana
Brazil	779 113	783 177	791 892	825 412	785 369	271 697	289 048	365 357	415 686	479 399	Brésil
Brit. Ind. Ocean Terr.	21	24	34	43	40	...	...	...	...	...	Tr. Br. de l'océan Ind.
British Virgin Is. [1]	1 308	1 250	1 200	1 200	1 200	...	...	...	...	...	Iles Vierges brit.[1]
Brunei Darussalam	2 279	2 550	2 357	1 766	2 272	475	622	473	433[1]	500[1]	Brunéi Darussalam
Bulgaria	7 544	8 903	8 864	8 978	10 769	3 257	4 032	5 157	6 723	7 921	Bulgarie
Burkina Faso	9 500	10 200	11 093	11 800	14 520	200	298	405	205	300[1]	Burkina Faso
Burundi	15 750[1]	16 700[1]	17 766	17 700[1]	17 700[1]	50[1]	50[1]	50[1]	50[1]	50[1]	Burundi
Cambodia	482 500	458 500	431 000	465 000	490 094	34 200	35 260	40 000	50 000	60 000	Cambodge
Cameroon	137 232	138 612	139 200[1]	140 000[1]	140 000[1]	535[1]	625[1]	625[1]	735[1]	835[1]	Cameroun
Canada	1 079 415	1 025 604	950 370	950 498	927 622	171 451	152 516	152 153	154 154	160 924	Canada
Cape Verde	24 590	18 328	23 768	16 828	19 500[1]	...	...	...	...	...	Cap-Vert
Cayman Islands	125	125	125	125	125	...	...	...	...	...	Iles Caïmanes
Central Afric. Rep. [1]	27 000	29 000	31 000	33 000	35 000	140	140	140	140	140	Rép. centrafricaine [1]
Chad [1]	50 000	45 000	40 000	40 000	40 000	...	...	...	...	...	Tchad [1]
Channel Islands	3 468	3 566	3 228	2 649	3 373	660[1]	791	972	1 025	1 130	Iles Anglo-Norm.

33

Fish production *(continued)*
Capture and aquaculture: metric tons
Production halieutique *(suite)*
Pêche de capture et aquaculture: tonnes

Country or area	Capture production Captures					Aquaculture production Production de l'aquaculture					Pays ou zone
	2006	2007	2008	2009	2010	2006	2007	2008	2009	2010	
Chile	4 160 732	3 819 285	3 554 808	3 453 786	2 679 736	794 110[1]	779 779[1]	843 142	792 891	701 062	Chili
China [2]	14 631 018[1]	14 659 036	14 791 163	14 919 596	15 418 967	29 856 841[1]	31 415 131	32 731 371	34 779 870	36 734 215	Chine [2]
China, Hong Kong SAR	154 536	154 147	158 126	158 965	168 010	4 125	4 514	4 754	4 819	4 338	Chine, H. K. RAS
China, Macao SAR [1]	1 500	1 500	1 500	1 500	1 500	...	...	...	...	...	Chine, Macao RAS [1]
Colombia	107 527[1]	124 133[1]	113 632[1]	106 321	79 027	70 132	66 565	68 200[1]	80 623	80 367	Colombie
Comoros	15 070[1]	19 676	29 989[1]	20 450[1]	52 261[1]	...	...	...	...	...	Comores
Congo	59 082	59 216	54 104	61 218	65 186	21	25	65	56	58[1]	Congo
Cook Islands	3 913	4 302	3 753	2 695	10 019	^0	2[1]	2[1]	2[1]	2[1]	Iles Cook
Costa Rica	22 000[1]	21 735	21 750[1]	21 750[1]	21 750[1]	19 962	25 765	27 035	24 725	26 810	Costa Rica
Côte d'Ivoire	54 830	47 289	50 000[1]	44 198	71 812	866	1 290	1 290[1]	1 340[1]	1 700[1]	Côte d'Ivoire
Croatia	37 853	40 199	49 024	55 750	52 828	15 497	14 045	13 878	14 229	13 991	Croatie
Cuba	27 543	29 447	28 561	28 843	23 951	27 210	37 526	36 685	36 002	31 422	Cuba
Cyprus	2 155	2 446	2 011	1 405	1 420	2 787	2 450	2 887	3 416	4 116	Chypre
Czech Republic	4 646	4 276	4 164	4 112	3 990	20 431	20 447	20 395	20 071	20 420	République tchèque
Dem. P. R. Korea [1]	205 000	205 000	205 000	205 000	205 000	63 780	63 850	63 950	64 050	64 050	R. p. dém. de Corée [1]
Dem. Rep. of the Congo	236 588	236 000	236 000[1]	236 000[1]	236 000[1]	2 970[1]	2 970[1]	2 970[1]	2 970[1]	2 970[1]	Rép. dém. du Congo
Denmark	867 721	653 053	690 584	777 752	828 016	37 188	31 168	35 337	34 129	39 507[1]	Danemark
Djibouti	1 299	1 229	1 206	1 058	1 058[1]	...	...	...	...	...	Djibouti
Dominica	694	676	696	790	700[1]	24[1]	24[1]	34[1]	35[1]	35[1]	Dominique
Dominican Republic	12 956	13 709	15 382	14 233	14 490	980[1]	980[1]	980[1]	980[1]	980[1]	Rép. dominicaine
Ecuador	452 298	399 085	495 069	485 805	391 714	169 588	171 020[1]	172 120[1]	218 361	271 919	Equateur
Egypt	375 894	372 491	373 815	387 398	385 209	595 030	635 516	693 815	705 490	919 585	Egypte
El Salvador	43 218	48 639	32 325	30 527	36 000	3 078	3 734	3 817[1]	4 356	4 500	El Salvador
Equatorial Guinea	4 000[1]	4 533[1]	5 400[1]	7 669	7 376[1]	2[1]	2[1]	2[1]	3[1]	15	Guinée équatoriale
Eritrea	8 813	1 932	1 665	3 030	3 286	...	...	...	...	...	Erythrée
Estonia	86 490	97 836	101 037	97 422	95 398	703	772	813	654	573	Estonie
Ethiopia	9 890	13 253	16 770	17 047	18 058	25[1]	25[1]	25[1]	25[1]	25[1]	Ethiopie
Faeroe Islands	623 122	620 834	518 267	351 018	393 875	18 574	30 699	46 673	59 295	47 575	Iles Féroé
Falkland Is. (Malvinas)	75 288	72 147	81 708	62 747	99 560	2	2	0	0	0	Is. Falkland (Malvinas)
Fiji	47 419	45 963	43 410[1]	39 170[1]	41 351[1]	428	180	228	230	208	Fidji
Finland	149 445	164 682	148 636	154 751	159 157	12 891	13 025	13 439	13 627	11 772	Finlande
France	574 934	513 391	460 372	420 776	426 514	237 343	237 416	238 196	233 875	224 400[1]	France
French Guiana	4 442	4 857	3 958	4 140	4 000[1]	37	35[1]	35[1]	35[1]	35[1]	Guyane française
French Polynesia	13 409	13 148	11 985	13 374	13 015	64	46	44	39	39	Polynésie française
French South. and Antar. [1,3]	472	472	470	470	470	...	...	...	...	...	Terr. austr. et ant. [1,3]
Gabon	41 521	38 500[1]	42 500[1]	32 000[1]	32 000[1]	126	124	124	140[1]	160[1]	Gabon
Gambia	36 912	43 574	42 645	45 881	46 424	75[1]	25[1]	25[1]	25[1]	25[1]	Gambie
Georgia	9 709[1]	18 197	26 512	25 050[1]	30 594[1]	75[1]	180	466[1]	470[1]	470[1]	Géorgie
Germany	293 037	290 511	274 282	244 045	222 771	35 379	44 994	43 977	38 907	40 694	Allemagne
Ghana	375 087	330 486	359 831	321 815	351 205	2 270[1]	3 820[1]	5 594	7 154	10 200	Ghana
Greece	98 236	96 093	89 424	83 328	83 000[1]	113 384	113 297	115 068	122 011	113 486[1]	Grèce
Greenland	252 959	233 754	227 665	197 878	209 446	...	...	...	...	...	Groenland
Grenada	2 169	2 407	2 386	2 615	2 452	...	...	...	...	...	Grenade
Guadeloupe	10 100	10 100	10 100	10 000[1]	10 000[1]	12	15	18	7	11	Guadeloupe

Fish production *(continued)*
Capture and aquaculture: metric tons
Production halieutique *(suite)*
Pêche de capture et aquaculture: tonnes

Country or area	Capture production Captures					Aquaculture production Production de l'aquaculture					Pays ou zone
	2006	2007	2008	2009	2010	2006	2007	2008	2009	2010	
Guam	604	640	322	488	291	162	162	162[1]	141	129	Guam
Guatemala	17 173	17 685	22 826	19 994	21 859	16 293	16 400[1]	18 727	16 623	22 792	Guatemala
Guinea	102 811	82 074	94 515	96 127[1]	109 849[1]	2[1]	6[1]	12[1]	19[1]	20[1]	Guinée
Guinea-Bissau [1]	7 067	6 500	6 804	6 800	6 800	...	...	...	...	...	Guinée-Bissau [1]
Guyana	53 763[1]	47 448	42 168	43 605	45 186	660[1]	660	292[1]	511[1]	488	Guyana
Haiti [1]	8 300	8 300	8 300	8 300	8 300	32	52	150	150	200	Haïti [1]
Honduras	20 877[1]	15 155[1]	12 904[1]	11 302[1]	11 107[1]	55 356[1]	54 689	47 080	28 858	27 509	Honduras
Hungary	7 543	7 024	7 394	6 366	6 216	14 686	15 864	15 687	14 825	14 245	Hongrie
Iceland	1 327 079	1 399 190	1 284 034	1 141 869	1 060 640	8 241	4 823	5 098	5 165	5 050	Islande
India	3 844 837	3 859 293	4 099 227	4 066 756	4 694 968	3 180 863	3 112 240	3 851 057	3 791 920	4 648 851	Inde
Indonesia	4 800 621	5 050 340	4 997 199	5 103 603	5 380 266	1 292 899	1 392 901	1 690 221	1 733 434	2 304 828	Indonésie
Iran (Islamic Rep. of)	445 879	403 690	407 842	419 903	443 650	129 468	158 561	154 731	179 573	220 034	Iran (Rép. Islam. d')
Iraq	59 259	57 779	34 472	34 505	25 720	14 867	15 810[1]	19 246	18 732	20 320	Iraq
Ireland	211 764	214 871	205 342	269 083	318 942	53 122	57 101	44 868	47 212	46 187	Irlande
Isle of Man	1 209	3 760	2 770	3 555	4 814	...	...	...	...	...	Ile de Man
Israel	3 820	3 435	2 708[1]	2 712	2 588	22 117	21 434	20 017	19 405	19 600[1]	Israël
Italy	315 435	286 642	235 759	253 001	234 101	172 793	179 409	149 003	162 432	153 486	Italie
Jamaica	17 905[1]	16 548	13 175	16 294	15 440	8 019	5 616	5 948	5 182	4 050	Jamaïque
Japan	4 328 134	4 277 691	4 302 264	4 116 263[1]	4 044 185[1]	734 100	770 434	730 361	786 910	718 284	Japon
Jordan	497	506	500	569	486	560	509	540	440	541	Jordanie
Kazakhstan	34 724	41 366	55 706	35 028	42 953	256	170	206	303	224	Kazakhstan
Kenya	158 684	131 775	135 398	133 600	143 111	1 012	4 240	4 452	4 895	12 154	Kenya
Kiribati	25 661[1]	34 170	28 000	40 623	44 599	12	5	12	10	11	Kiribati
Kuwait	5 635	4 373	3 979	4 000[1]	4 000[1]	568	348	360[1]	360[1]	360[1]	Koweït
Kyrgyzstan	8[1]	34	8	10[1]	27	20[1]	107	92	133	319[1]	Kirghizistan
Lao People's Dem. Rep.	26 925	28 410	29 200	30 000	30 900	60 000[1]	63 250	64 300	75 001	82 100	Rép. dém. pop. lao
Latvia	140 389	155 276	157 934	163 213	164 819	565	729	584	517	549	Lettonie
Lebanon	3 811	3 811[1]	3 811[1]	3 811[1]	3 811[1]	803	803	803[1]	803[1]	803[1]	Liban
Lesotho	45	48	50	45	45	2	131	91	108	300	Lesotho
Liberia	8 894	14 488	7 890	8 000[1]	8 000[1]	13[1]	13[1]	16[1]	16[1]	20[1]	Libéria
Libyan Arab Jamah.	34 647[1]	31 921	47 645	52 110	50 000[1]	240[1]	240[1]	240[1]	240[1]	240[1]	Jam. arabe libyenne
Lithuania	154 548	187 513	182 760	172 692	149 851	2 224	3 377	3 008	3 422	3 191	Lituanie
Madagascar	133 693	147 778	120 464	131 303	128 836	11 233	11 293	10 836	6 116	6 886[1]	Madagascar
Malawi	72 787	66 500	70 019	69 325	98 299	1 500	1 500	1 700	1 620	3 163	Malawi
Malaysia	1 286 478	1 385 703	1 398 885	1 397 683	1 433 427	168 317	178 239	243 081	333 444	373 151	Malaisie
Maldives	185 299	144 508	133 338	117 061	94 953	...	...	...	...	...	Maldives
Mali	100 000[1]	100 000	100 000[1]	100 000[1]	100 000	1 000[1]	640	821	1 355[1]	2 083	Mali
Malta	1 330	1 235	1 279	1 595	1 836	1 936	2 716	2 702	2 868	2 916	Malte
Marshall Islands	43 974	61 229	35 102	46 246	59 730	...	...	...	...	...	Iles Marshall
Martinique	6 300	6 200	6 200	6 200[1]	5 000[1]	103	80	81	85[1]	85[1]	Martinique
Mauritania	165 312	223 207	195 328	216 900	276 238	...	...	...	...	...	Mauritanie
Mauritius	8 681	8 097	6 642	7 676	7 786	443	175	246	437	568	Maurice
Mayotte	5 772	11 661	12 677	15 006	20 842	140	128	88	126	150[1]	Mayotte
Mexico	1 357 195	1 472 533	1 581 272	1 611 175	1 523 889	154 451	140 062	159 309	156 957	126 240	Mexique

Fish production *(continued)*
Capture and aquaculture: metric tons
Production halieutique *(suite)*
Pêche de capture et aquaculture: tonnes

Country or area	Capture production Captures					Aquaculture production Production de l'aquaculture					Pays ou zone
	2006	2007	2008	2009	2010	2006	2007	2008	2009	2010	
Micronesia (Fed. States of)	15 292	20 723	25 295	27 706	30 871[1]	...	...	...	...	...	Micron. (Et. féd. de)
Monaco [1]	1	1	1	1	1	...	...	...	...	...[1]	Monaco [1]
Mongolia	326	185	88	90	90[1]	...	...	...	...	...	Mongolie
Montenegro	1 354	980	1 479	1 450	1 144	684[1]	691[1]	764[1]	795[1]	790[1]	Monténégro
Montserrat	49	35	31	37	24	...	...	...	...	...	Montserrat
Morocco	876 878	879 469	997 127	1 165 062	1 136 240	1 161	1 636	1 399[1]	1 477[1]	1 522	Maroc
Mozambique	101 900[1]	92 270	119 646	148 049	150 634	1 048	838	692	490[1]	864[1]	Mozambique
Myanmar	2 006 790	2 235 580	2 493 750	2 766 940	3 063 210	574 990	604 660	674 776	778 096	850 697	Myanmar
Namibia	509 570	413 333	372 822	370 348	370 000[1]	204[1]	334[1]	474[1]	536[1]	545[1]	Namibie
Nauru [1]	280	260	240	220	200	...	...	...	...	...	Nauru [1]
Nepal	20 016	20 100	21 500	21 500	21 500	25 409	26 679	27 250	26 730	28 230	Népal
Netherlands	469 101	413 621	416 797	382 242	389 357	45 553	56 761	46 816	55 641	66 945	Pays-Bas
Netherlands Antilles	6 247	4 018	16 698	18 874	18 455	...	...	...	10[1]	40[1]	Antilles néerlandaises
New Caledonia	3 146	3 507	3 720	3 554	3 771	2 365	1 923	2 103	1 920	1 220	Nouvelle-Calédonie
New Zealand	476 572	494 500	452 326	439 378	436 232	107 524	111 908	112 358	104 958	110 592	Nouvelle-Zélande
Nicaragua	29 591	27 032	29 867	35 663	37 423	11 220	11 533	16 078	18 943	16 972	Nicaragua
Niger	29 835	29 728	29 960	29 884	29 884[1]	40	40	40	70[1]	70[1]	Niger
Nigeria	552 323	530 420	601 368	598 210	616 981	84 578	85 087	143 207	152 796	200 535	Nigéria
Niue	400	302[1]	108[1]	192	113	...	...	...	...	...	Nioué
Northern Mariana Islands	221	219	168	192	243	6[1]	11[1]	16[1]	21[1]	24	Is. Mariannes du Nord
Norway	2 256 448	2 380 425	2 431 371	2 524 437	2 675 292	712 373	841 560	848 359	961 840	1 008 010	Norvège
Occupied Palestinian Terr.	2 323	2 702	2 843	1 525	1 699	17	37	65	115	280	Terr. palestinien occupé
Oman	147 668	151 744	151 910	158 551	163 927	114	96	121	118	127	Oman
Pakistan	489 421	440 056	451 414	446 362	453 264	121 826[1]	130 092[1]	135 098	138 099	140 101	Pakistan
Palau	967	985	1 007	1 000[1]	1 000[1]	5[1]	18[1]	20	12[1]	12[1]	Palaos
Panama	258 108	221 567	223 406	222 516	163 488	8 744	8 813	8 224	6 359	6 248	Panama
Papua New Guinea	253 019	247 462	222 444	229 619	224 507	690[1]	840[1]	1 122[1]	1 372[1]	1 588	Papouasie-Nvl-Guinée
Paraguay	8 000[1]	5 000[1]	1 708	1 700[1]	1 700[1]	2 250[1]	2 350[1]	2 450[1]	2 600[1]	2 957	Paraguay
Peru	7 017 491	7 210 544	7 394 538	6 914 452	4 261 091	28 393	39 531	43 119	44 317	89 021	Pérou
Philippines	2 319 120	2 499 695	2 561 337	2 602 541	2 611 720	623 369	709 715	741 142	737 397	744 695	Philippines
Pitcairn [1]	3	3	3	3	3	...	...	...	...	...	Pitcairn [1]
Poland	145 479	151 820	142 496	223 893	189 721	35 867	35 628	36 813	36 503	30 757	Pologne
Portugal	229 072	256 181	224 246	198 813	222 944	7 894	7 416	7 352	6 728	3 190	Portugal
Puerto Rico	2 042	1 675	1 793	1 702	1 898	266	44	22[1]	21[1]	17[1]	Porto Rico
Qatar	16 376	15 190	17 688	14 064	13 760	36	36	36	36	36	Qatar
Republic of Korea	1 757 508	1 869 884	1 956 566	1 858 572	1 732 928	513 568	606 122	473 794	473 060	475 561	République de Corée
Republic of Moldova	612	1 160	1 407	1 607	1 633	5 840	6 550	7 200[1]	7 820[1]	8 370[1]	Rép. de Moldova
Réunion	3 548	3 989	2 978	3 050	3 050[1]	161	160[1]	160[1]	144[1]	150[1]	Réunion
Romania	6 663	6 183	5 410	4 020	2 688	8 088	10 312	12 532	13 131	8 981	Roumanie
Russian Federation	3 284 306	3 475 883	3 383 724	3 826 129	4 069 624	105 525	105 503	115 420	116 571	120 384	Fédération de Russie
Rwanda	8 400[1]	9 050	9 050[1]	9 050[1]	9 050[1]	400[1]	388[1]	388[1]	488[1]	628[1]	Rwanda
Saint Helena	1 120	837	794	856	864	...	...	...	...	...	Sainte-Hélène
Saint Kitts and Nevis	455[1]	440[1]	425[1]	410[1]	21 099	...	...	...	...	...	Saint-Kitts-et-Nevis
Saint Lucia	1 496	1 555	1 728	1 920	1 844	0	0	0	^0	6	Sainte-Lucie

Country or area	Capture production Captures					Aquaculture production Production de l'aquaculture					Pays ou zone
	2006	2007	2008	2009	2010	2006	2007	2008	2009	2010	
Saint Pierre and Miquelon	2 876	5 204	4 621	1 761	2 043	...	...	...	...	...	St.-Pierre-et-Miquelon
Saint Vincent-Grenadines	4 764	5 225	3 942	4 058	65 626	...	...	...	...	...	St. Vin.-Grenadines
Samoa	12 435	14 091	13 899	13 279	13 000[1]	...	3	3[1]	5[1]	5[1]	Samoa
Sao Tome and Principe [1]	4 150	4 250	4 500	4 550	4 650	...	...	...	...	...	Sao Tomé-et-Principe [1]
Saudi Arabia	65 485	66 221	68 898	67 664	65 142	15 586	18 497	22 353	26 120	26 374	Arabie saoudite
Senegal	366 992	412 835	425 853	442 295	409 578	45[1]	45[1]	54	71	78	Sénégal
Serbia	2 632	2 535	3 153	3 846	4 807	4 835	6 609	7 532	7 440	8 153	Serbie
Seychelles	92 739	65 514	69 200	81 096	87 108	704	368	289	300[1]	300[1]	Seychelles
Sierra Leone	148 146	144 535	203 582	200 000[1]	200 000[1]	30[1]	30[1]	40[1]	40[1]	40[1]	Sierra Leone
Singapore	3 103	3 522	1 623	2 121	1 732	8 573	4 503	3 518	3 567	3 499	Singapour
Slovakia	1 718	1 994	1 655	1 761	1 608	1 263	1 199	1 071	823	687	Slovaquie
Slovenia	1 131	1 111	869	1 032	932	1 369	1 352	1 315	1 307	778	Slovénie
Solomon Islands [1]	39 520	31 304	27 434	27 941	35 179	...	1	1	1	1	Iles Salomon [1]
Somalia [1]	30 000	30 000	30 000	30 000	30 000	...	...	...	...	...	Somalie [1]
South Africa	618 616	678 878	644 659	512 284	623 920	3 037	2 669	3 587	3 433	3 133	Afrique du Sud
Spain	961 300	820 195	918 136	918 124	968 662	292 828	281 704	249 701	266 664	252 351	Espagne
Sri Lanka	274 025	307 280	327 404	355 694	436 355	5 652	8 233	7 474	7 549	8 058	Sri Lanka
Sudan	57 000	65 509[1]	68 595[1]	71 690	71 700[1]	1 600[1]	1 950	2 000[1]	2 200[1]	2 200[1]	Soudan
Suriname	30 621	29 627	23 811	25 831	34 402	180	52	38	41	71	Suriname
Swaziland	70[1]	70[1]	70[1]	70[1]	70[1]	...	...	...	73[1]	209	Swaziland
Sweden	269 251	238 253	231 336	203 415	212 035	7 549	5 365	7 595	8 540	10 644	Suède
Switzerland	1 422	1 377	1 582	1 687	1 653	1 214	1 214	1 214	1 244	1 256	Suisse
Syrian Arab Republic	8 264	9 456	6 996	6 607	6 635	8 902	8 425	8 595	8 697	8 610	Rép. arabe syrienne
Tajikistan	146[1]	146[1]	150[1]	150[1]	160[1]	26[1]	26[1]	26	255	517	Tadjikistan
Thailand	2 698 803	2 304 951	1 873 432	1 870 702	1 827 199	1 354 297	1 370 456	1 330 861	1 416 668	1 286 122	Thaïlande
TFYR of Macedonia	89	122	122	141	177	646	1 096	1 331	1 658	1 640	L'ex-R.Y. Macédoine
Timor-Leste	2 550[1]	2 912	3 125	3 125[1]	3 125[1]	23[1]	32	52	52[1]	52[1]	Timor-Leste
Togo	24 879	19 905	23 500[1]	27 025	27 535	50[1]	50[1]	107	107	100	Togo
Tokelau [1]	86	78	68	62	54	...	...	...	...	...	Tokélaou [1]
Tonga	2 750[1]	3 103[1]	2 593[1]	2 036[1]	2 150[1]	5	4	1	...	...	Tonga
Trinidad and Tobago	13 123	13 086	13 833	13 856	13 931	...	19	13	27	14[1]	Trinité-et-Tobago
Tunisia	111 288	103 790	97 906	97 859	97 743	2 855	3 581	3 561	4 907	5 424	Tunisie
Turkey	533 048	632 450	494 126	464 233	485 939	129 333	140 743	152 896	159 639	167 721	Turquie
Turkmenistan [1]	15 000	15 000	15 000	15 000	15 000	16	16	17	17	17	Turkménistan [1]
Turks and Caicos Islands	6 040	4 860	6 133	6 803	5 446	4	...	0	^0	...	Is. Turques et Caïques
Tuvalu	2 560[1]	2 560[1]	2 560[1]	5 097	11 324[1]	1[1]	1[1]	0	^0.	...	Tuvalu
Uganda	367 099	431 500[1]	403 500[1]	412 000[1]	413 805	32 392	51 110	52 250[1]	76 654	95 000[1]	Ouganda
Ukraine	238 734	213 508	195 449	213 173	186 021	19 181	27 965	24 337	24 083	22 965	Ukraine
United Arab Emirates	82 500[1]	78 300[1]	74 075	77 705	79 610	570[1]	570[1]	1 206	...	...	Emirats arabes unis
United Kingdom	624 569	619 691	596 007	591 064	612 655	171 848	174 203	179 187	179 093	201 091	Royaume-Uni
United Rep. of Tanzania	359 855	353 415	351 325	341 598	368 171	72	45	217	202	454	Rép.-Unie de Tanzanie
United States	4 852 284	4 767 596	4 349 853	4 222 052	4 369 540	519 413	525 215	500 053	480 273	495 499	Etats-Unis
United States Virgin Is.	1 615	1 127	1 065	1 120	847	10	10[1]	10[1]	10[1]	10[1]	Iles Vierges amér.
Uruguay	133 987	108 722	108 797	81 461	74 153	37	31	36	54	85	Uruguay

Country or area	Capture production Captures					Aquaculture production Production de l'aquaculture					Pays ou zone
	2006	2007	2008	2009	2010	2006	2007	2008	2009	2010	
Uzbekistan	1 431	1 973	2 731	6 051	4 078	3 800	4 000	4 100[1]	5 162	6 654[1]	Ouzbékistan
Vanuatu	219 124	213 242	169 770	145 278	97 807	114	31	40[1]	37	105	Vanuatu
Venezuela (Boliv. Rep. of)	315 346	347 546	296 266	288 462	274 417[1]	23 355	19 931	18 761	14 838	18 400[1]	Venezuela (R. bol. du)
Viet Nam	2 027 700	2 074 600	2 136 300	2 280 500	2 420 800	1 657 727	2 085 400	2 462 450	2 556 080	2 671 800	Viet Nam[1]
Wallis and Futuna Is.	600	650[1]	700[1]	750[1]	800[1]	...	...	...	...	...	Iles Wallis et Futuna
Yemen	229 660	179 916	127 132	159 000[1]	191 100	...	...	...	...	...	Yémen
Zambia	60 236	73 542	79 403	84 716	76 396	5 210	5 876	5 640	8 505	10 290	Zambie
Zimbabwe[1]	10 500	10 500	10 500	10 500	10 500	2 450	2 500	2 602	2 652	2 702	Zimbabwe[1]

Source:
Food and Agriculture Organization of the United Nations (FAO), Rome,
FISHSTAT database, last accessed April 2012.

1　FAO estimate.
2　For statistical purposes, the data for China do not include those for
　　the Hong Kong Special Administrative Region (Hong Kong SAR),
　　Macao Special Administrative Region (Macao SAR) and Taiwan
　　Province of China.
3　Including Amsterdam Island, Saint-Paul Island, and French scattered
　　Indian Ocean Islands in Western Indian Ocean and Kerguelen Islands
　　and Crozet Archipelago in Antarctic Indian Ocean. Catches reported
　　for Antarctic fishing areas are included with those of France.

Source:
Organisation des Nations Unies pour l'alimentation et l'agriculture (FAO),
Rome, les données des pêches de FISHSTAT, dernier accès avril 2012.

1　Estimation de la FAO.
2　Pour la présentation des statistiques, les données pour la Chine ne
　　comprennent pas la Région Administrative Spéciale de Hong Kong
　　(Hong Kong RAS), la Région Administrative Spéciale de Macao
　　(Macao RAS) et la province de Taiwan.
3　Y compris les iles des Terres australes et antarctiques françaises :
　　l'île Amsterdam, l'île Saint-Paul, les Îles éparses, les îles Kerguelen
　　et l'archipel Crozet. Les captures dans les zones antarctiques de
　　pèche sont reportées parmi celles de France.

Fertilizers
Nitrogen, phosphate and potash: thousand metric tons of plant nutrients

Engrais
Azote, phosphates et potasse : milliers de tonnes d'éléments fertilisants

Country/area and type of fertilizer	Production 2007	2008	2009	2010	Consumption - Consommation 2007	2008	2009	2010	Pays/zone et type d'engrais
Afghanistan									**Afghanistan**
Nitrogen	17.0	15.3	13.6	12.0	28.2[1]	23.2[1]	35.2[1]	33.2[1]	Azote
Albania									**Albanie**
Nitrogen	0.0	0.0	0.0	0.0	31.0	28.2	33.5	30.8	Azote
Phosphate	0.0	0.0	0.0	0.0	19.0	17.6	20.6	21.3	Phosphates
Potash	0.0	0.0	0.0	0.0	0.4	0.6	0.3	...	Potasse
Algeria									**Algérie**
Nitrogen	137.8	11.0	6.6	17.1	36.6[1]	23.1[1]	21.0[1]	45.5[1]	Azote
Phosphate	42.6	11.6	5.5	14.9	52.4[1]	20.8[1]	19.0[1]	31.4[1]	Phosphates
Potash [1]	0.0	0.0	0.0	0.0	22.7	20.4	18.8	18.3	Potasse [1]
Angola [1]									**Angola** [1]
Nitrogen	...	...	...	...	5.6	8.2	3.0	4.7	Azote
Phosphate	...	...	...	...	2.4	3.9	0.5	1.9	Phosphates
Potash	...	...	...	...	3.3	16.0	0.8	1.7	Potasse
Argentina									**Argentine**
Nitrogen	468.9	406.0	514.2	433.1	981.4[1]	762.0[1]	477.1[1]	912.7[1]	Azote
Phosphate [1]	...	...	...	...	766.2	436.4	296.9	549.3	Phosphates [1]
Potash [1]	...	...	...	...	47.1	43.4	14.2	42.4	Potasse [1]
Armenia									**Arménie**
Nitrogen [1]	...	...	...	...	6.8	8.0	13.2	10.4	Azote [1]
Phosphate [1]	...	...	...	...	0.1	^0.0	0.1	0.4	Phosphates [1]
Potash	...	...	...	...	^0.0[1]	^0.0[1]	0.0[2]	^0.0[1]	Potasse
Australia									**Australie**
Nitrogen	392.9[1]	330.5[1]	543.3[1]	545.0[1]	848.8	835.0	849.8	1 241.2[1]	Azote
Phosphate	747.9[1]	532.0[1]	534.1[1]	535.0[1]	982.2	818.3	641.0	946.2[1]	Phosphates
Potash	...	...	...	...	207.4	214.5	158.0	211.5[1]	Potasse
Austria									**Autriche**
Nitrogen	...	...	...	...	82.6	84.1	79.7	86.2	Azote
Phosphate	...	...	...	...	28.3	29.7	18.0	23.6	Phosphates
Potash	...	...	...	...	40.8	36.9	16.3	38.2	Potasse
Azerbaijan [1]									**Azerbaïdjan** [1]
Nitrogen	...	...	...	...	16.8	29.7	19.3	12.8	Azote
Phosphate	...	...	...	...	1.3	6.0	2.7	2.1	Phosphates
Potash	...	...	...	...	1.6	3.3	3.2	3.8	Potasse
Bahrain									**Bahreïn**
Nitrogen	269.0	304.1	300.8	289.3	1.1	2.3	1.2	2.5	Azote
Potash	...	...	...	...	0.1	0.1	0.1	0.1	Potasse
Bangladesh									**Bangladesh**
Nitrogen	855.6	557.0	512.8	*616.2	1 048.5	1 168.4	*1 404.8	915.0[1]	Azote
Phosphate	65.2	33.6	52.4	*68.0	256.1	82.3	*429.2	336.1[1]	Phosphates
Potash	0.0[1]	...	...	...	136.8	49.0	*298.2	246.8[1]	Potasse
Barbados [1]									**Barbade** [1]
Nitrogen	...	...	...	...	1.1	1.5	0.4	0.4	Azote
Phosphate	...	...	...	...	0.6	0.2	0.4	1.2	Phosphates
Potash	...	...	...	...	^0.0	0.1	0.2	^0.0	Potasse
Belarus									**Bélarus**
Nitrogen	749.9	728.0	731.4	771.3	447.3	523.5	553.6	529.9	Azote
Phosphate	152.4	173.5	173.8	196.0	191.0	181.0	231.7	233.7	Phosphates
Potash	5 097.4	5 066.1	2 434.6	5 185.9	566.8	605.1	773.2	733.4	Potasse
Belize [1]									**Belize** [1]
Nitrogen	...	...	...	...	2.6	1.7	5.9	2.3	Azote
Phosphate	...	...	...	...	1.6	1.6	2.7	0.9	Phosphates
Potash	...	...	...	...	0.1	0.2	0.3	0.4	Potasse
Benin									**Bénin**
Nitrogen	...	...	...	...	0.6[1]	0.4[1]	5.3[1]	^0.0	Azote
Phosphate	...	...	...	...	^0.0[1]	0.4[1]	5.3[1]	^0.0	Phosphates
Potash	...	...	...	...	^0.0[1]	^0.0[1]	5.3[1]	^0.0	Potasse

Fertilizers *(continued)*
Nitrogen, phosphate and potash: thousand metric tons of plant nutrients
Engrais *(suite)*
Azote, phosphates et potasse : milliers de tonnes d'éléments fertilisants

Country/area and type of fertilizer	Production				Consumption - Consommation				Pays/zone et type d'engrais
	2007	2008	2009	2010	2007	2008	2009	2010	
Bhutan									**Bhoutan**
Nitrogen	0.0	0.0	0.0	0.0	0.8	0.8[1]	1.6	0.7	Azote
Phosphate	0.0	0.0	0.0	0.0	0.3	0.2[1]	0.5	0.2	Phosphates
Potash	0.0	0.0	0.0	0.0	0.2	0.2[1]	0.3	0.1	Potasse
Bolivia (Plur. State of)[1]									**Bolivie (État plur. de)**[1]
Nitrogen	...	...	...	...	11.9	13.5	13.8	19.6	Azote
Phosphate	...	...	...	...	8.5	4.6	8.3	11.4	Phosphates
Potash	...	...	...	...	4.2	2.0	0.9	2.9	Potasse
Bosnia and Herzegovina[1]									**Bosnie-Herzégovine**[1]
Nitrogen	...	...	...	...	21.4	11.7	22.7	18.0	Azote
Phosphate	...	...	...	...	0.1	0.1	4.7	1.9	Phosphates
Potash	...	...	...	...	0.3	0.2	4.7	2.1	Potasse
Brazil									**Brésil**
Nitrogen	983.8	921.6	892.6	627.5	2 948.8	2 483.7	2 452.7	2 854.8	Azote
Phosphate	2 085.8	1 951.1	1 819.8	1 958.5	4 049.2	3 450.1	2 806.6	3 384.7	Phosphates
Potash	389.2	351.9	415.7	385.2	4 297.6	4 155.7	2 393.6	3 894.1	Potasse
Brunei Darussalam									**Brunéi Darussalam**
Nitrogen	0.0	0.0	0.0	0.0	0.4	0.1	0.2	0.1[1]	Azote
Phosphate	0.0	0.0	0.0	0.0	0.3	0.1	^0.0	0.1[1]	Phosphates
Potash	0.0	0.0	0.0	0.0	0.4	0.1	^0.0	^0.0[1]	Potasse
Bulgaria									**Bulgarie**
Nitrogen	262.1	282.0	282.0[1]	282.0[1]	200.1[1]	213.6[1]	370.1[1]	288.0[1]	Azote
Phosphate	202.2	174.5	174.5[1]	174.5[1]	109.4[1]	122.4[1]	158.5[1]	89.1[1]	Phosphates
Potash[1]	...	...	...	...	5.2	7.6	3.8	10.9	Potasse[1]
Burkina Faso									**Burkina Faso**
Nitrogen	...	...	...	...	23.6	30.6	28.4	41.1[1]	Azote
Phosphate	...	...	...	...	13.4	13.5	12.7	7.7[1]	Phosphates
Potash	...	...	...	...	12.6	13.2	12.7	7.7[1]	Potasse
Burundi									**Burundi**
Nitrogen	0.0	0.0	0.0	0.0	0.8[1]	1.0[1]	0.9[1]	1.2[1]	Azote
Phosphate	0.0	0.0	0.0	0.0	0.7[1]	0.4[1]	0.3[1]	1.0[1]	Phosphates
Potash	0.0	0.0	0.0	0.0	0.2[1]	0.6[1]	0.3[1]	0.8[1]	Potasse
Cambodia[1]									**Cambodge**[1]
Nitrogen	...	...	...	...	8.6	12.5	16.9	21.0	Azote
Phosphate	...	...	...	...	23.9	14.9	19.5	24.0	Phosphates
Potash	...	...	...	...	0.8	1.0	1.0	1.0	Potasse
Cameroon									**Cameroun**
Nitrogen	0.0	0.0	0.0	0.0	22.3	22.9	23.7	11.6	Azote
Phosphate	0.0	0.0	0.0	0.0	6.9	6.8	4.2	6.3	Phosphates
Potash	0.0	0.0	0.0	0.0	22.2	9.4	12.0	12.9	Potasse
Canada									**Canada**
Nitrogen	3 234.8	3 193.0	3 129.2	3 272.2	2 068.0[1]	1 909.2[1]	1 914.6[1]	1 984.1[1]	Azote
Phosphate	250.0	250.0	250.0	250.0	744.0[1]	671.4[1]	561.8[1]	620.4[1]	Phosphates
Potash	10 807.2	6 795.0	7 037.4	10 289.4	253.4[1]	250.0[1]	250.0[1]	300.0[1]	Potasse
Chile									**Chili**
Nitrogen	167.1	207.6	198.2	240.0[1]	324.4[1]	394.6[1]	345.7[1]	412.5[1]	Azote
Phosphate[1]	...	...	...	...	168.4	132.4	96.1	125.0	Phosphates[1]
Potash	499.9	676.2	759.9	950.0[1]	181.2[1]	374.7[1]	132.5[1]	99.1[1]	Potasse
China									**Chine**
Nitrogen	35 359.3	35 584.8	38 776.5	...	32 593.6[1]	33 214.9[1]	36 902.1[1]	35 069.1[1]	Azote
Phosphate	12 658.0	12 262.6	14 871.4	17 107.6	11 352.0[1]	10 870.6[1]	13 597.0[1]	16 943.0[1]	Phosphates
Potash	2 496.8	2 912.2	3 627.8	2 113.4	8 469.1[1]	6 204.1[1]	4 933.9[1]	5 385.7[1]	Potasse
Colombia									**Colombie**
Nitrogen	301.5	209.7	268.0	250.2	574.6[1]	465.2[1]	547.7[1]	526.3[1]	Azote
Phosphate	158.7	116.8	120.9	135.8	285.6[1]	206.5[1]	204.2[1]	196.5[1]	Phosphates
Potash[1]	0.0	0.0	0.0	0.0	227.2	228.3	134.6	226.4	Potasse[1]
Congo[1]									**Congo**[1]
Nitrogen	...	...	...	...	0.1	0.3	0.9	0.1	Azote
Phosphate	...	...	...	...	0.1	0.1	0.7	0.1	Phosphates
Potash	...	...	...	...	0.1	0.1	0.6	0.1	Potasse

Country/area and type of fertilizer	Production				Consumption - Consommation				Pays/zone et type d'engrais
	2007	2008	2009	2010	2007	2008	2009	2010	
Costa Rica[1]									**Costa Rica**[1]
Nitrogen	...	...	...	...	66.2	67.9	71.4	57.1	Azote
Phosphate	...	...	...	...	23.8	4.8	16.0	17.8	Phosphates
Potash	...	...	...	...	68.0	68.9	77.9	47.0	Potasse
Côte d'Ivoire[1]									**Côte d'Ivoire**[1]
Nitrogen	...	...	...	...	25.9	17.6	21.4	27.0	Azote
Phosphate	...	...	...	...	15.8	4.7	6.8	22.5	Phosphates
Potash	...	...	...	...	27.9	30.5	16.2	43.8	Potasse
Croatia									**Croatie**
Nitrogen	429.2	444.6	388.9	305.6	212.4[1]	263.4[1]	175.5[1]	66.8[1]	Azote
Phosphate	125.8	118.6	51.4	51.0[1]	77.7[1]	90.6[1]	34.8[1]	84.9[1]	Phosphates
Potash[1]	0.0	0.0	0.0	...	59.3	72.2	6.2	50.5	Potasse[1]
Cuba									**Cuba**
Nitrogen	17.5	16.9	9.8	13.7	51.8[1]	58.3[1]	28.4[1]	47.1[1]	Azote
Phosphate	1.7	3.5	0.7	1.9	22.7[1]	35.4[1]	7.4[1]	24.9[1]	Phosphates
Potash	2.6	5.2	1.1	2.8	53.0[1]	59.2[1]	15.9[1]	32.9[1]	Potasse
Cyprus									**Chypre**
Nitrogen	0.0	0.0	0.0	0.0	6.3	4.5	7.0	*8.5	Azote
Phosphate	0.0	0.0	0.0	0.0	4.5	2.2	5.1	*5.2	Phosphates
Potash	0.0	0.0	0.0	0.0	1.2	1.8	3.6	*3.1	Potasse
Czech Republic									**République tchèque**
Nitrogen	333.0[1]	333.0[1]	220.7[1]	221.0[1]	237.9	221.7	226.0	255.4[1]	Azote
Phosphate	16.0[1]	16.0[1]	16.0[1]	16.0[1]	49.0	35.2	35.1	46.1[1]	Phosphates
Potash	0.0[1]	0.0[1]	0.0[1]	0.0[1]	33.1	21.3	20.4	55.8[1]	Potasse
Dem. Rep. of the Congo									**Rép. dém. du Congo**
Nitrogen	0.0	0.0	0.0	0.0	2.9[1]	4.3[1]	2.4[1]	3.7[1]	Azote
Phosphate	0.0	0.0	0.0	0.0	0.5[1]	0.9[1]	0.5[1]	0.5[1]	Phosphates
Potash	0.0	0.0	0.0	0.0	0.8[1]	1.1[1]	0.5[1]	0.4[1]	Potasse
Denmark									**Danemark**
Nitrogen	0.0	0.0	0.0	0.0	192.9	218.2	187.0	178.7	Azote
Phosphate	0.0	0.0	0.0	0.0	40.7	40.1	20.5	28.8	Phosphates
Potash	0.0	0.0	0.0	0.0	94.8	96.5	43.4	65.6	Potasse
Dominica									**Dominique**
Nitrogen	0.0	0.0	0.0	0.0	0.6[1]	0.2[1]	0.2[1]	0.1[1]	Azote
Phosphate	0.0	0.0	0.0	0.0	0.8[1]	^0.0[1]	0.2[1]	0.1[1]	Phosphates
Potash	0.0	0.0	0.0	0.0	^0.0[1]	^0.0[1]	0.2[1]	^0.0[1]	Potasse
Dominican Republic									**Rép. dominicaine**
Nitrogen[1]	...	...	...	...	44.5	43.1	37.2	55.1	Azote[1]
Phosphate[1]	...	...	...	...	14.6	20.3	15.0	22.6	Phosphates[1]
Potash	...	...	...	...	18.7[1]	0.9[1]	0.0[2]	8.9[1]	Potasse
Ecuador[1]									**Equateur**[1]
Nitrogen	...	...	...	...	118.2	156.4	151.3	159.1	Azote
Phosphate	...	...	...	...	37.0	26.2	31.7	38.3	Phosphates
Potash	...	...	...	...	82.7	82.1	41.6	101.7	Potasse
Egypt									**Egypte**
Nitrogen	2 286.5	2 618.6	2 723.6	2 806.0	1 106.4	1 562.7	1 205.6	1 425.0[1]	Azote
Phosphate	250.8	312.1	265.0	347.3	167.2	228.1	226.7	289.3[1]	Phosphates
Potash	0.0[1]	0.0[1]	0.0[1]	0.0[1]	64.3	49.6	17.8	24.1[1]	Potasse
El Salvador									**El Salvador**
Nitrogen	0.0	0.0	0.0	...	64.9[1]	59.3[1]	56.7[1]	61.9[1]	Azote
Phosphate	0.0	0.0	0.0	...	16.1[1]	7.5[1]	12.7[1]	13.0[1]	Phosphates
Potash	0.0	0.0	0.0	...	15.1[1]	14.2[1]	3.3[1]	9.6[1]	Potasse
Eritrea[1]									**Erythrée**[1]
Nitrogen	...	...	...	...	0.7	...	0.5	0.3	Azote
Phosphate	...	...	...	...	1.7	...	1.4	...	Phosphates
Potash ^	...	...	...	...	...	...	...	0.0	Potasse ^
Estonia									**Estonie**
Nitrogen	96.4	91.8	0.8	*0.7	25.0	35.5	27.3	28.6	Azote
Phosphate	...	...	...	...	8.1	9.6	5.7	6.1	Phosphates
Potash	...	...	...	...	12.4	15.0	8.4	9.4	Potasse

34

Fertilizers *(continued)*
Nitrogen, phosphate and potash: thousand metric tons of plant nutrients
Engrais *(suite)*
Azote, phosphates et potasse : milliers de tonnes d'éléments fertilisants

Country/area and type of fertilizer	Production				Consumption - Consommation				Pays/zone et type d'engrais
	2007	2008	2009	2010	2007	2008	2009	2010	
Ethiopia									**Ethiopie**
Nitrogen	...	...	...	...	106.0	111.8	118.4	156.1	Azote
Phosphate	...	...	...	...	119.2	122.3	128.0	162.1	Phosphates
Fiji[1]									**Fidji**[1]
Nitrogen	...	...	...	...	4.0	6.8	2.8	2.4	Azote
Phosphate	...	...	...	...	^0.0	0.2	0.6	0.3	Phosphates
Potash	...	...	...	...	^0.0	^0.0	0.3	^0.0	Potasse
Finland									**Finlande**
Nitrogen	272.8	279.6	228.9	244.1	184.2[1]	223.8	172.8	211.0[1]	Azote
Phosphate	69.5	61.4	92.7	63.8	42.3[1]	42.3	62.7	25.6[1]	Phosphates
Potash	0.0[1]	0.0[1]	0.0[1]	0.0[1]	52.2[1]	28.8	8.4	43.2[1]	Potasse
France									**France**
Nitrogen	1 027.0	1 246.7	1 067.2	1 018.7	2 402.0	2 099.0	1 907.0	2 050.0	Azote
Phosphate	404.3	459.1	236.0	467.1	632.0	296.0	399.0	294.5	Phosphates
Potash	0.0[1]	0.0[1]	0.0[1]	0.0[1]	794.0	390.0	414.0	431.7	Potasse
French Polynesia[1]									**Polynésie française**[1]
Nitrogen	...	...	...	...	0.3	0.5	0.3	0.4	Azote
Phosphate	...	...	...	...	0.3	0.2	0.2	0.2	Phosphates
Potash	...	...	...	...	0.3	0.3	0.2	0.3	Potasse
Gabon[1]									**Gabon**[1]
Nitrogen	...	...	...	...	0.9	0.8	0.9	0.6	Azote
Phosphate	...	...	...	...	0.3	0.3	0.3	^0.0	Phosphates
Potash	...	...	...	...	1.7	2.3	2.7	0.4	Potasse
Gambia									**Gambie**
Nitrogen	0.0	0.0	0.0	0.0	1.5	0.8	1.4	1.8	Azote
Phosphate	0.0	0.0	0.0	0.0	0.6	0.4	0.7	0.8	Phosphates
Potash	0.0	0.0	0.0	0.0	0.6	0.4	0.7	0.8	Potasse
Georgia									**Géorgie**
Nitrogen	131.8	133.9	134.7	120.0[1]	18.5	16.9	19.1	12.9	Azote
Phosphate	0.0[1]	0.0[1]	0.0[1]	0.0[1]	0.4	0.3	0.2	1.0	Phosphates
Potash	0.0[1]	0.0[1]	0.0[1]	0.0[1]	0.3	0.1	0.1	0.1	Potasse
Germany									**Allemagne**
Nitrogen	1 504.5[1]	961.9[1]	1 224.7[1]	1 305.2[1]	1 807.2	1 550.6	1 569.1	1 786.5	Azote
Phosphate	44.0	50.0[1]	73.9[1]	80.3[1]	316.7	174.4	235.2	286.4	Phosphates
Potash	2 893.6[1]	2 408.3[1]	1 874.5[1]	2 483.3[1]	511.3	179.2	362.8	433.7	Potasse
Ghana[1]									**Ghana**[1]
Nitrogen	...	...	...	...	25.9	18.4	24.8	12.4	Azote
Phosphate	...	...	...	...	13.3	9.9	42.9	28.6	Phosphates
Potash	...	...	...	...	37.1	37.2	21.4	4.8	Potasse
Greece									**Grèce**
Nitrogen	35.1	32.0	22.0	21.0[1]	136.6[1]	175.0[1]	131.9[1]	145.8[1]	Azote
Phosphate	35.1	32.0	22.0	21.0[1]	57.9[1]	68.3[1]	46.7[1]	49.5[1]	Phosphates
Potash[1]	0.0	0.0	0.0	0.0	54.3	60.9	29.6	61.1	Potasse[1]
Guatemala[1]									**Guatemala**[1]
Nitrogen	...	...	...	...	133.1	88.3	120.5	142.1	Azote
Phosphate	...	...	...	...	55.2	25.1	28.8	65.6	Phosphates
Potash	...	...	...	...	6.8	8.5	10.9	18.5	Potasse
Guinea[1]									**Guinée**[1]
Nitrogen	...	...	...	...	3.2	2.8	1.3	2.5	Azote
Phosphate	...	...	...	...	0.1	0.5	0.4	0.1	Phosphates
Potash	...	...	...	...	0.1	0.5	0.1	0.1	Potasse
Guyana[1]									**Guyana**[1]
Nitrogen	...	...	...	...	6.4	18.3	6.7	14.1	Azote
Phosphate	...	...	...	...	7.3	5.6	1.7	2.0	Phosphates
Potash	...	...	...	...	^0.0	...	0.1	0.4	Potasse
Honduras[1]									**Honduras**[1]
Nitrogen	...	...	...	...	83.4	44.7	50.9	32.5	Azote
Phosphate	...	...	...	...	15.8	33.1	11.6	27.9	Phosphates
Potash	...	...	...	...	87.7	32.0	1.1	34.7	Potasse

Fertilizers *(continued)*
Nitrogen, phosphate and potash: thousand metric tons of plant nutrients
Engrais *(suite)*
Azote, phosphates et potasse : milliers de tonnes d'éléments fertilisants

Country/area and type of fertilizer	Production				Consumption - Consommation				Pays/zone et type d'engrais
	2007	2008	2009	2010	2007	2008	2009	2010	
Hungary									**Hongrie**
Nitrogen	223.0[1]	189.7[1]	232.2[1]	241.8[1]	320.0	294.0	275.0	281.0	Azote
Phosphate	...	...	...	...	87.0	63.0	44.0	46.0	Phosphates
Potash	...	...	...	...	100.0	74.0	48.0	58.0	Potasse
Iceland									**Islande**
Nitrogen	...	...	...	...	13.8	15.3	12.0	7.7[1]	Azote
Phosphate	...	...	...	...	6.0	5.5	3.8	5.8[1]	Phosphates
Potash	...	...	...	...	4.5	4.2	2.9	5.3[1]	Potasse
India									**Inde**
Nitrogen	10 400.4	10 430.9	11 376.7	12 051.7	14 417.7	14 863.8	15 558.4	*16 549.6	Azote
Phosphate	2 704.8	2 390.8	3 215.4	3 442.5	5 518.1	5 956.8	7 210.3	*8 017.0	Phosphates
Potash	0.0[1]	0.0[1]	0.0[1]	0.0[1]	2 635.4	3 312.8	3 638.1	*3 513.3	Potasse
Indonesia									**Indonésie**
Nitrogen	2 947.3	3 189.1	3 591.2	3 536.6[1]	2 503.3	2 675.6	2 929.0	2 784.6[1]	Azote
Phosphate	349.8	349.1	267.5	250.0[1]	385.1	353.2	507.3	511.6[1]	Phosphates
Potash	0.0[1]	0.0[1]	0.0[1]	0.0[1]	810.7	1 130.8	843.6	1 000.0[1]	Potasse
Iran (Islamic Rep. of)									**Iran (Rép. islamique d')**
Nitrogen	777.8	1 041.5	928.8	792.0	968.0[1]	1 065.2[1]	786.6[1]	390.4[1]	Azote
Phosphate	51.8	4.5	27.5	13.0	435.1[1]	362.0	343.0[1]	437.4[1]	Phosphates
Potash	0.0[1]	0.0[1]	0.0[1]	0.0[1]	115.8[1]	124.9	69.2[1]	76.4[1]	Potasse
Iraq									**Iraq**
Nitrogen	110.2	149.3	141.2	96.6	126.4[1]	164.1[1]	171.9	108.0[1]	Azote
Phosphate	18.1	22.2	...	...	59.5[1]	63.6[1]	46.4	24.4[1]	Phosphates
Potash	...	...	...	...	...	...	46.4	4.8[1]	Potasse
Ireland									**Irlande**
Nitrogen	0.0	0.0	0.0	0.0	309.0[1]	306.8[1]	362.4[1]	372.6[1]	Azote
Phosphate	0.0	0.0	0.0	0.0	60.4[1]	46.3[1]	67.2[1]	97.9[1]	Phosphates
Potash	0.0	0.0	0.0	0.0	83.8[1]	63.1[1]	90.2[1]	123.0[1]	Potasse
Israel									**Israël**
Nitrogen	111.7[1]	83.1[1]	57.4[1]	100.5[1]	59.4	45.9	36.1	30.2	Azote
Phosphate	411.3[1]	455.5[1]	249.1[1]	404.0[1]	11.3	10.1	6.2	6.2	Phosphates
Potash	2 200.0	2 300.0	2 100.0	2 100.0	34.8	26.1	18.7	24.2	Potasse
Italy									**Italie**
Nitrogen	258.4	335.8	224.2	225.0[1]	812.5	670.3	486.7	498.6	Azote
Phosphate	58.4	147.8	90.0	90.0[1]	280.4	199.2	165.7	180.3	Phosphates
Potash	0.0[1]	0.0[1]	0.0[1]	0.0[1]	271.3	206.3	152.5	185.5	Potasse
Jamaica [1]									**Jamaïque** [1]
Nitrogen	...	...	...	...	3.8	4.9	4.6	4.8	Azote
Phosphate	...	...	...	...	^0.0	1.5	2.3	2.3	Phosphates
Potash	...	...	...	...	^0.0	^0.0	0.2	0.4	Potasse
Japan									**Japon**
Nitrogen	769.9	647.2	732.2	650.3	514.5[1]	468.5[1]	553.5[1]	456.4[1]	Azote
Phosphate	296.8	236.2	346.5	255.8	593.1[1]	448.5[1]	488.4[1]	424.3[1]	Phosphates
Potash [1]	0.0	0.0	0.0	0.0	408.6	281.6	207.6	238.8	Potasse [1]
Jordan									**Jordanie**
Nitrogen	158.8	150.0	119.8	148.8	36.9[1]	22.2[1]	5.2[1]	15.8[1]	Azote
Phosphate	342.7	315.4	294.2	336.3	16.5[1]	0.0[2]	0.0[2]	7.1[1]	Phosphates
Potash	1 142.1	1 220.0	683.0	*1 200.0	88.0[1]	28.2[1]	66.7[1]	0.0[2]	Potasse
Kazakhstan									**Kazakhstan**
Nitrogen	71.2	65.7	48.0[1]	48.0[1]	37.5	16.3	29.5	22.5	Azote
Phosphate	76.6	117.8	118.0[1]	118.0[1]	20.5	14.4	26.1	13.0	Phosphates
Potash	...	...	...	...	0.9	0.2	0.8	2.3	Potasse
Kenya									**Kenya**
Nitrogen	...	...	...	...	79.4	73.1	67.4[1]	70.8[1]	Azote
Phosphate	...	...	...	...	99.1	97.7	93.2[1]	75.9[1]	Phosphates
Potash	...	...	...	...	14.3	5.7	14.7[1]	20.3[1]	Potasse
Kuwait									**Koweït**
Nitrogen	424.1	442.5	337.6	443.9	0.0[2]	14.3[1]	0.0[2]	6.4[1]	Azote
Potash [1]	...	...	...	...	...	...	0.6	2.4	Potasse [1]

Fertilizers *(continued)*
Nitrogen, phosphate and potash: thousand metric tons of plant nutrients
Engrais *(suite)*
Azote, phosphates et potasse : milliers de tonnes d'éléments fertilisants

Country/area and type of fertilizer	Production				Consumption - Consommation				Pays/zone et type d'engrais
	2007	2008	2009	2010	2007	2008	2009	2010	
Kyrgyzstan									**Kirghizistan**
Nitrogen	...	...	...	...	26.1	22.5	24.5	25.3	Azote
Phosphate	...	...	...	...	2.6	1.8	2.3	3.2	Phosphates
Latvia									**Lettonie**
Nitrogen	0.0	0.0	0.0	0.0	47.8	50.2	53.5	58.6	Azote
Phosphate	0.0	0.0	0.0	0.0	16.0	14.0	11.1	16.2	Phosphates
Potash	0.0	0.0	0.0	0.0	16.7	14.2	11.2	16.3	Potasse
Lebanon									**Liban**
Nitrogen [1]	...	...	...	...	13.2	9.8	12.6	15.1	Azote [1]
Phosphate	150.0[1]	93.8	94.3	107.4	20.9[1]	5.8[1]	6.7[1]	19.6[1]	Phosphates
Potash [1]	...	...	...	...	8.9	7.6	5.2	7.8	Potasse [1]
Libyan Arab Jamah.									**Jamah. arabe libyenne**
Nitrogen	359.3	276.9	250.0	370.0[1]	68.7[1]	42.8[1]	47.5	47.3[1]	Azote
Phosphate [1]	...	...	...	...	36.8	3.7	21.8	30.8	Phosphates [1]
Potash	...	...	...	...	1.2[1]	1.2[1]	1.2	1.2[1]	Potasse
Lithuania									**Lituanie**
Nitrogen	751.5	695.4	676.8	646.7	0.0[2]	27.3	50.0	106.7	Azote
Phosphate	437.0	405.2	442.7	404.7	90.7	77.3	47.0	54.5	Phosphates
Potash	0.0[1]	0.0[1]	0.0[1]	0.0[1]	74.6	57.0	9.7	42.6	Potasse
Luxembourg									**Luxembourg**
Nitrogen	0.0	0.0	0.0	0.0	13.3	13.3	16.8[1]	21.1[1]	Azote
Phosphate	0.0	0.0	0.0	0.0	1.7	1.1	0.7[1]	1.4[1]	Phosphates
Potash	0.0	0.0	0.0	0.0	1.9	1.1	1.3[1]	1.3[1]	Potasse
Madagascar									**Madagascar**
Nitrogen	...	...	...	...	4.4	7.6	4.4	4.5	Azote
Phosphate	...	...	...	...	2.6	2.7	1.8	1.6	Phosphates
Potash	...	...	...	...	2.6	2.9	1.7	2.4	Potasse
Malawi									**Malawi**
Nitrogen	0.1	0.2	0.2[1]	...	84.3	89.3[1]	70.7[1]	86.1[1]	Azote
Phosphate	...	...	...	...	25.4	12.5[1]	16.7[1]	16.8[1]	Phosphates
Potash	...	...	...	...	15.5	9.6[1]	15.3[1]	15.9[1]	Potasse
Malaysia									**Malaisie**
Nitrogen	638.9	837.4	1 097.0	1 000.0[1]	690.2[1]	903.0[1]	963.1[1]	998.1[1]	Azote
Phosphate [1]	...	...	...	...	85.0	67.7	67.0	202.9	Phosphates [1]
Potash [1]	...	...	...	...	942.8	894.2	355.5	900.4	Potasse [1]
Maldives									**Maldives**
Nitrogen	0.0	0.0	0.0	0.0	0.3	0.1	^0.0	^0.0	Azote
Mali									**Mali**
Nitrogen	58.0	26.4	20.9	14.0	87.3[1]	55.8[1]	30.4[1]	89.3[1]	Azote
Phosphate	74.9	0.2	6.4	21.3	84.8[1]	8.7[1]	12.4[1]	57.0[1]	Phosphates
Potash [1]	...	...	...	...	8.2	6.0	5.4	27.2	Potasse [1]
Malta [1]									**Malte** [1]
Nitrogen	...	...	...	...	0.6	0.3	0.4	0.3	Azote
Phosphate	...	...	...	...	0.1	0.1	0.1	0.1	Phosphates
Potash	...	...	...	...	0.2	0.1	0.1	0.1	Potasse
Mauritius									**Maurice**
Nitrogen	0.0	0.0	0.0	0.0	8.8	7.3[1]	7.0[1]	5.4[1]	Azote
Phosphate	0.0	0.0	0.0	0.0	2.3	6.0[1]	2.7[1]	2.5[1]	Phosphates
Potash	0.0	0.0	0.0	0.0	11.8	5.0[1]	8.5[1]	6.1[1]	Potasse
Mexico									**Mexique**
Nitrogen	308.8	359.0	323.9	328.2	1 141.9[1]	938.9[1]	1 027.4[1]	1 205.7[1]	Azote
Phosphate	98.2	108.1	201.6	216.4	376.0[1]	105.8[1]	143.0[1]	155.1[1]	Phosphates
Potash [1]	...	...	...	...	247.0	199.3	200.0	194.0	Potasse [1]
Mongolia [1]									**Mongolie** [1]
Nitrogen	...	...	...	...	6.0	6.9	7.5	11.0	Azote
Montenegro [1]									**Monténégro** [1]
Nitrogen	...	...	...	...	1.4	1.3	1.1	1.4	Azote
Phosphate	...	...	...	...	0.7	0.7	0.5	0.6	Phosphates
Potash	...	...	...	...	0.7	0.6	0.4	0.5	Potasse

34

Fertilizers *(continued)*
Nitrogen, phosphate and potash: thousand metric tons of plant nutrients
Engrais *(suite)*
Azote, phosphates et potasse : milliers de tonnes d'éléments fertilisants

Country/area and type of fertilizer	Production				Consumption - Consommation				Pays/zone et type d'engrais
	2007	2008	2009	2010	2007	2008	2009	2010	
Morocco									**Maroc**
Nitrogen	275.5	197.9	336.9	463.5	304.8	275.1	196.0[1]	136.4[1]	Azote
Phosphate	1 168.4	922.2	1 178.1	1 752.2	112.9	97.0	109.6[1]	126.2[1]	Phosphates
Potash	0.0[1]	0.0[1]	...	...	56.8	61.4	24.6[1]	32.1[1]	Potasse
Mozambique [1]									**Mozambique** [1]
Nitrogen	...	...	...	...	11.5	41.9	15.1	43.4	Azote
Phosphate	...	...	...	...	1.1	10.4	4.7	2.6	Phosphates
Potash	...	...	...	...	1.3	9.4	2.4	0.4	Potasse
Myanmar									**Myanmar**
Nitrogen	50.6	48.8	32.1	16.2	80.5[1]	62.2[1]	50.7[1]	49.9[1]	Azote
Phosphate [1]	...	...	...	...	69.0	13.4	4.5	9.1	Phosphates [1]
Potash [1]	...	...	...	...	17.4	5.8	4.4	8.6	Potasse [1]
Namibia									**Namibie**
Nitrogen [1]	...	...	...	...	1.3	0.2	1.3	...	Azote [1]
Phosphate [1]	...	...	...	...	0.3	^0.0	^0.0	...	Phosphates [1]
Potash	...	...	...	...	0.3[1]	0.0[2]	^0.0[1]	...	Potasse
Nepal									**Népal**
Nitrogen	0.0	0.0	0.0	0.0	1.9	2.9	28.3	17.8[1]	Azote
Phosphate	0.0	0.0	0.0	0.0	1.3	0.2	12.2	17.4[1]	Phosphates
Potash	0.0	0.0	0.0	0.0	0.3	0.2	2.0	2.9[1]	Potasse
Netherlands									**Pays-Bas**
Nitrogen	1 491.2	1 493.8	1 397.9	1 475.7	241.2	231.1	224.2	218.0	Azote
Phosphate	168.5	120.5	105.5	136.7	36.1	26.7	9.9	30.7	Phosphates
Potash					42.9	27.8	17.1	51.3	Potasse
New Caledonia [1]									**Nouvelle-Calédonie** [1]
Nitrogen	...	...	...	...	0.8	0.5	0.4	0.6	Azote
Phosphate	...	...	...	...	0.5	0.4	0.3	0.3	Phosphates
Potash	...	...	...	...	0.5	0.4	0.4	0.4	Potasse
New Zealand									**Nouvelle-Zélande**
Nitrogen	95.0[1]	88.8[1]	104.9[1]	101.6[1]	277.5	256.4	244.0	246.2	Azote
Phosphate	320.0[1]	189.0[1]	216.0[1]	258.8[1]	701.5	505.7	325.6	379.0	Phosphates
Potash	...	...	...	...	14.3	11.2	10.5	9.6	Potasse
Nicaragua									**Nicaragua**
Nitrogen	0.0	0.0	0.0	0.0	41.9	34.1	47.4	39.9	Azote
Phosphate	0.0	0.0	0.0	0.0	13.7	10.4	6.4	3.5	Phosphates
Potash	0.0	0.0	0.0	0.0	1.1	1.6	3.8	10.0	Potasse
Niger									**Niger**
Nitrogen	...	...	...	...	2.5	1.6	3.3	4.8	Azote
Phosphate	...	...	...	...	2.2	0.4	1.6	2.0	Phosphates
Potash	...	...	...	...	0.6	0.4	1.0	0.7	Potasse
Nigeria [1]									**Nigéria** [1]
Nitrogen	...	...	...	...	70.1	140.9	44.9	80.1	Azote
Phosphate	...	...	...	...	39.9	63.8	11.2	10.8	Phosphates
Potash	...	...	...	...	45.6	78.6	16.1	9.8	Potasse
Norway									**Norvège**
Nitrogen	497.7[1]	465.6[1]	357.7[1]	419.3[1]	106.3	101.7	96.8	63.3	Azote
Phosphate	304.7[1]	288.9[1]	186.7[1]	307.9[1]	27.7	26.2	20.5	48.3	Phosphates
Potash	0.0[1]	0.0[1]	0.0[1]	0.0[1]	53.9	52.0	42.2	49.2	Potasse
Oman									**Oman**
Nitrogen	875.4	897.9	933.3	955.4	0.9[1]	8.8[1]	15.8[1]	0.0[2]	Azote
Phosphate [1]	...	...	...	...	1.3	1.7	1.7	1.8	Phosphates [1]
Potash [1]	...	...	...	...	8.0	11.2	5.9	2.2	Potasse [1]
Pakistan									**Pakistan**
Nitrogen	2 442.4	2 544.9	2 586.3	2 710.4	2 714.1	2 820.8	3 473.8	3 270.5	Azote
Phosphate	292.6	330.5	359.3	413.8	816.0	474.4	947.8	756.7	Phosphates
Potash	0.0[1]	0.0[1]	0.0[1]	0.0[1]	43.9	24.6	17.2	37.6	Potasse
Panama									**Panama**
Nitrogen	0.0	0.0	0.0	0.0	14.5[1]	15.5[1]	17.3[1]	21.7[1]	Azote
Phosphate	0.0	0.0	0.0	0.0	1.8[1]	1.8[1]	3.8[1]	6.0[1]	Phosphates
Potash	0.0	0.0	0.0	0.0	2.1[1]	2.1[1]	4.6[1]	8.7[1]	Potasse

Fertilizers *(continued)*
Nitrogen, phosphate and potash: thousand metric tons of plant nutrients
Engrais *(suite)*
Azote, phosphates et potasse : milliers de tonnes d'éléments fertilisants

Country/area and type of fertilizer	Production				Consumption - Consommation				Pays/zone et type d'engrais
	2007	2008	2009	2010	2007	2008	2009	2010	
Papua New Guinea[1]									**Papouasie-Nvl-Guinée**[1]
Nitrogen	...	...	...	...	12.2	13.7	19.0	16.0	Azote
Phosphate	...	...	...	...	3.4	2.7	1.0	2.8	Phosphates
Potash	...	...	...	...	3.3	4.9	11.1	14.1	Potasse
Paraguay[1]									**Paraguay**[1]
Nitrogen	...	...	...	...	76.8	58.8	58.9	81.6	Azote
Phosphate	...	...	...	...	140.0	116.0	116.1	140.8	Phosphates
Potash	...	...	...	...	126.4	105.9	77.2	117.9	Potasse
Peru									**Pérou**
Nitrogen[1]	...	...	...	...	246.7	203.1	261.9	223.4	Azote[1]
Phosphate	0.4	0.3	0.4	0.0	65.6[1]	44.9[1]	99.6[1]	86.4[1]	Phosphates
Potash[1]	...	...	...	...	91.0	50.5	23.7	56.1	Potasse[1]
Philippines									**Philippines**
Nitrogen	111.4	38.4	*27.2	*5.2	520.0[1]	409.9[1]	*433.6	*586.9	Azote
Phosphate	142.0	35.6	*28.5	*5.6	205.2[1]	104.2[1]	*71.5	*70.2	Phosphates
Potash	0.0[1]	0.0[1]	0.0[1]	0.0[1]	117.6[1]	94.9[1]	*175.2	*114.3	Potasse
Poland									**Pologne**
Nitrogen	1 832.9	1 715.6	1 545.8	1 637.5	1 142.3	1 095.4	1 028.0	1 294.2[1]	Azote
Phosphate	647.7	535.7	241.1	486.4	462.3	375.3	353.0	388.4[1]	Phosphates
Potash	0.0[1]	0.0[1]	0.0[1]	0.0[1]	537.4	428.7	397.0	462.2[1]	Potasse
Portugal									**Portugal**
Nitrogen	48.7	38.2	45.9	*87.3	110.5	96.3	100.0[1]	*126.6	Azote
Phosphate	61.5	49.3	58.7	*103.0	67.5	44.8	48.0[1]	*107.3	Phosphates
Potash	0.0[1]	0.0[1]	0.0[1]	0.0[1]	51.6	39.1	40.5[1]	*26.0	Potasse
Qatar									**Qatar**
Nitrogen	1 363.4	1 378.6	1 379.1	1 384.6	70.4[1]	0.0[2]	38.2[1]	81.9[1]	Azote
Potash[1]	...	...	...	...	...	3.6	0.1	3.6	Potasse[1]
Republic of Korea									**République de Corée**
Nitrogen	372.5	348.4	463.3	512.0	347.4	311.8	245.6	215.3	Azote
Phosphate	229.3	207.5	250.6	285.3	230.2	212.6	161.1	136.8	Phosphates
Potash	0.0[1]	0.0[1]	0.0[1]	0.0[1]	238.5	220.3	170.8	141.8	Potasse
Republic of Moldova									**République de Moldova**
Nitrogen	...	...	...	...	17.2	19.9	14.6	16.4	Azote
Phosphate	...	...	...	...	2.0	1.7	1.6	2.4	Phosphates
Potash	...	...	...	...	1.0	1.1	0.8	1.3	Potasse
Romania									**Roumanie**
Nitrogen	756.2	946.1	618.1	789.6	265.5	279.9	296.1	305.8	Azote
Phosphate	0.0	...	...	...	103.3	102.4	100.6	123.3	Phosphates
Potash	0.0	...	...	...	18.4	15.7	29.6	51.5	Potasse
Russian Federation									**Fédération de Russie**
Nitrogen	7 203.0	6 890.0	7 402.0	7 624.0	1 043.8	1 209.8	1 236.8	1 192.7	Azote
Phosphate	2 807.0	2 571.0	2 575.0	3 137.0	408.9	430.9	393.2	437.0	Phosphates
Potash	7 277.0	6 738.0	4 666.0	7 197.0	280.2	291.5	270.5	263.2	Potasse
Rwanda[1]									**Rwanda**[1]
Nitrogen	...	...	...	...	2.6	2.8	0.5	0.1	Azote
Phosphate	...	...	...	...	4.3	4.3	0.5	...	Phosphates
Potash	...	...	...	...	2.0	3.6	0.5	...	Potasse
Saudi Arabia									**Arabie saoudite**
Nitrogen	1 826.6	1 712.0	1 590.7	1 701.6	256.0[1]	180.4[1]	129.3[1]	165.9[1]	Azote
Phosphate	139.1	75.5	...	115.3	132.3[1]	65.1[1]	...	119.7[1]	Phosphates
Potash	0.0	0.0	0.0	0.0[1]	21.2[1]	13.7[1]	10.8[1]	7.1[1]	Potasse
Senegal									**Sénégal**
Nitrogen	5.9	4.8	1.5	1.5[1]	1.5	1.9	9.0[1]	26.9[1]	Azote
Phosphate	22.5	41.0	1.7	2.0[1]	3.4	4.1	6.5[1]	0.2[1]	Phosphates
Potash	0.0[1]	0.0[1]	0.0[1]	...	1.3	2.4	3.6[1]	2.1[1]	Potasse
Serbia									**Serbie**
Nitrogen	155.9	93.7	87.8	84.5	313.8[1]	235.7[1]	316.9[1]	157.5[1]	Azote
Phosphate	25.5	32.7	34.1	35.5	97.3[1]	66.1[1]	94.2[1]	67.6[1]	Phosphates
Potash	16.6	28.7	33.1	35.5	95.8[1]	94.4[1]	52.6[1]	87.8[1]	Potasse

Fertilizers *(continued)*
Nitrogen, phosphate and potash: thousand metric tons of plant nutrients
Engrais *(suite)*
Azote, phosphates et potasse : milliers de tonnes d'éléments fertilisants

Country/area and type of fertilizer	Production				Consumption - Consommation				Pays/zone et type d'engrais
	2007	2008	2009	2010	2007	2008	2009	2010	
Singapore									**Singapour**
Nitrogen	...	...	...	...	9.7[1]	6.8[1]	2.5[1]	0.0[2]	Azote
Phosphate [1]	...	...	...	...	0.2	0.1	0.3	0.3	Phosphates [1]
Potash	...	...	...	...	1.4[1]	2.9[1]	0.0[2]	1.7[1]	Potasse
Slovakia									**Slovaquie**
Nitrogen	196.2[1]	167.8[1]	183.4[1]	185.0[1]	87.7	77.1	86.9	90.6[1]	Azote
Phosphate	...	...	...	...	18.4	14.7	13.2	16.5[1]	Phosphates
Potash	...	...	...	...	17.7	12.0	8.2	15.1[1]	Potasse
Slovenia									**Slovénie**
Nitrogen	0.0[1]	0.0[1]	0.0[1]	0.0[1]	29.2	24.9	28.0	27.1	Azote
Phosphate	0.0[1]	0.0[1]	0.0[1]	0.0[1]	12.7	11.9	7.2	9.8	Phosphates
Potash	0.0[1]	0.0[1]	0.0[1]	0.0[1]	14.9	14.6	7.1	12.1	Potasse
South Africa									**Afrique du Sud**
Nitrogen	154.2[1]	118.1[1]	220.5[1]	105.1[1]	439.5	424.1	*414.3	*398.2	Azote
Phosphate	162.8[1]	156.6[1]	199.2[1]	181.4[1]	192.5	185.0	*180.6	*162.3	Phosphates
Potash	...	...	...	...	136.9	111.4	*111.2	*106.4	Potasse
Spain									**Espagne**
Nitrogen	710.3	628.3	620.2	714.9	985.9	739.8	781.1	941.1	Azote
Phosphate	362.4	292.1	104.3	299.5	554.4	271.6	264.2	336.7	Phosphates
Potash	621.3	571.7	416.7	445.3	444.9	319.2	166.0	359.3	Potasse
Sri Lanka									**Sri Lanka**
Nitrogen	...	...	...	...	161.6	209.4	181.7	166.1[1]	Azote
Phosphate	10.2	8.9	10.4	10.0[1]	49.3	69.1	52.5	51.7[1]	Phosphates
Potash	...	...	...	...	77.6	95.6	75.3	59.1[1]	Potasse
Sudan (former)									**Soudan (anc.)**
Nitrogen	0.0	...	...	...	55.8[1]	55.8[1]	86.2[1]	...	Azote
Phosphate	0.0	...	...	...	2.9[1]	11.7[1]	69.2[1]	...	Phosphates
Potash	0.0	...	...	...	10.4[1]	6.8[1]	3.2[1]	...	Potasse
Suriname [1]									**Suriname** [1]
Nitrogen	...	...	...	...	5.2	14.5	7.6	9.8	Azote
Phosphate	...	...	...	...	0.7	5.7	0.8	0.9	Phosphates
Potash	...	...	...	...	1.0	5.7	0.8	0.9	Potasse
Sweden									**Suède**
Nitrogen	79.3[1]	0.0[1]	0.0[1]	0.0[1]	167.1	186.5	142.4	168.0	Azote
Phosphate	10.0[1]	0.0[1]	0.0[1]	0.0[1]	31.4	33.5	18.6	22.5	Phosphates
Potash	0.0[1]	0.0[1]	0.0[1]	0.0[1]	37.6	40.4	21.8	26.0	Potasse
Switzerland [1]									**Suisse** [1]
Nitrogen	...	...	...	...	48.6	52.9	51.1	50.9	Azote
Phosphate	...	...	...	...	16.9	15.6	11.7	16.2	Phosphates
Potash	...	...	...	...	28.0	23.8	14.7	21.5	Potasse
Syrian Arab Republic									**Rép. arabe syrienne**
Nitrogen	140.6	141.9	134.6	145.8	263.1	270.2	210.4	119.2	Azote
Phosphate	94.2	99.1	64.8	81.0	109.0	131.2	86.4	35.1	Phosphates
Potash	0.0	0.0	0.0	...	9.8	12.1	8.7	0.5	Potasse
Tajikistan									**Tadjikistan**
Nitrogen	11.3	10.6	0.0	0.0	55.3	52.2	48.2	45.5	Azote
Thailand									**Thaïlande**
Nitrogen	137.0	137.0	137.0[1]	137.0[1]	1 188.2[1]	1 195.8[1]	1 406.2[1]	1 584.9[1]	Azote
Phosphate [1]	0.0	0.0	0.0	0.0	348.5	372.6	257.2	491.5	Phosphates [1]
Potash [1]	0.0	0.0	0.0	0.0	362.6	423.4	156.4	427.9	Potasse [1]
TFYR of Macedonia									**L'ex-R.Y. Macédoine**
Nitrogen	...	...	...	...	18.9[1]	15.7[1]	17.4[1]	19.4	Azote
Phosphate	...	...	...	...	5.4[1]	4.3[1]	3.5[1]	4.5	Phosphates
Potash	...	...	...	...	4.7[1]	3.8[1]	3.0[1]	3.8	Potasse
Togo									**Togo**
Nitrogen	0.0	...	...	...	5.5[1]	0.2[1]	0.9[1]	1.1[1]	Azote
Phosphate	0.0	...	...	...	4.5[1]	0.3[1]	1.2[1]	...	Phosphates
Potash	0.0	...	...	...	4.5[1]	0.0[1]	^0.0[1]	...	Potasse
Tonga									**Tonga**
Nitrogen	0.0	0.0	0.0	0.0	^0.0[1]	0.1[1]	4.4[1]	3.2[1]	Azote
Potash	0.0	0.0	0.0	0.0	0.1[1]	^0.0[1]	0.1[1]	0.9[1]	Potasse

34

Fertilizers *(continued)*
Nitrogen, phosphate and potash: thousand metric tons of plant nutrients
Engrais *(suite)*
Azote, phosphates et potasse : milliers de tonnes d'éléments fertilisants

Country/area and type of fertilizer	Production				Consumption - Consommation				Pays/zone et type d'engrais
	2007	2008	2009	2010	2007	2008	2009	2010	
Trinidad and Tobago									**Trinité-et-Tobago**
Nitrogen	328.0	294.4	320.6	326.0[1]	0.0[2]	19.7[1]	4.7[1]	71.9[1]	Azote
Phosphate [1]	...	...	...	...	0.4	0.4	0.6	0.4	Phosphates [1]
Potash [1]	...	...	...	...	1.3	1.6	1.6	0.5	Potasse [1]
Tunisia									**Tunisie**
Nitrogen	205.0	220.1	250.3	281.0	39.3	58.8	76.5	69.2	Azote
Phosphate	834.4	864.6	855.5	934.3	34.9	38.7	41.3	44.8	Phosphates
Turkey									**Turquie**
Nitrogen	596.8	612.7	572.4	776.9[1]	1 357.1	1 133.1	1 413.8	1 343.7	Azote
Phosphate	400.0	352.6	415.6	516.1[1]	517.8	328.8	581.1	514.6	Phosphates
Potash	0.0[1]	0.0[1]	0.0[1]	0.0[1]	110.7	89.5	65.5	84.0	Potasse
Uganda [1]									**Ouganda [1]**
Nitrogen	...	...	...	...	4.0	10.6	7.1	6.4	Azote
Phosphate	...	...	...	...	2.2	5.5	4.2	2.8	Phosphates
Potash	...	...	...	...	1.4	2.8	2.6	2.4	Potasse
Ukraine									**Ukraine**
Nitrogen	2 720.3	2 532.4	2 068.9	2 079.4	578.2	735.8	702.8	748.4[1]	Azote
Phosphate	101.5[1]	132.3[1]	90.0[1]	90.0[1]	168.8	173.5	189.2	197.9[1]	Phosphates
Potash	0.0[1]	0.0[1]	0.0[1]	0.0[1]	149.5	155.5	72.6	167.3[1]	Potasse
United Arab Emirates									**Emirats arabes unis**
Nitrogen	298.3	287.7	214.4	320.2	46.1[1]	19.9[1]	64.3[1]	29.4[1]	Azote
Phosphate [1]	0.0	0.0	0.0	0.0	0.6	0.6	0.3	0.3	Phosphates [1]
Potash [1]	0.0	0.0	0.0	0.0	2.6	1.4	1.5	4.5	Potasse [1]
United Kingdom									**Royaume-Uni**
Nitrogen	408.6[1]	410.0[1]	373.5[1]	203.5[1]	1 006.0	913.0	1 016.0	*1 029.0	Azote
Phosphate	35.0[1]	46.4[1]	32.1[1]	30.0[1]	215.0	129.0	184.0	*192.0	Phosphates
Potash	427.0	427.0	427.0	400.0	325.0	208.0	251.0	*263.0	Potasse
United Rep. of Tanzania									**Rép.-Unie de Tanzanie**
Nitrogen	...	...	...	...	41.5	43.4	66.9[1]	58.3[1]	Azote
Phosphate	...	...	...	...	9.0	9.3	15.0[1]	8.1[1]	Phosphates
Potash	...	...	...	...	0.3	0.3	4.6[1]	9.9[1]	Potasse
United States									**Etats-Unis**
Nitrogen	8 516.3	7 848.3	7 684.8	8 268.5	11 585.1	10 727.0	10 898.5	*11 488.4	Azote
Phosphate	10 959.9	9 215.1	8 656.3	9 414.5	3 970.6	3 248.9	3 369.8	*3 882.5	Phosphates
Potash	1 100.0	1 200.0	840.0	900.0	4 399.1	3 367.7	3 544.5	*4 284.9	Potasse
Uruguay									**Uruguay**
Nitrogen [1]	...	...	...	...	92.6	92.6	105.2	151.5	Azote [1]
Phosphate	12.8	8.6	9.0	19.8	113.4[1]	93.2[1]	98.0[1]	112.9[1]	Phosphates
Potash	...	...	...	...	0.0[2]	4.9[1]	3.0[1]	32.0[1]	Potasse
Uzbekistan									**Ouzbékistan**
Nitrogen	874.9	916.6	919.7	900.0[1]	542.0	571.9	607.8	739.3[1]	Azote
Phosphate	149.2	148.4	153.5	150.0[1]	145.2	146.3	186.9	111.3[1]	Phosphates
Potash	...	...	...	...	37.9	29.3	36.7	35.0[1]	Potasse
Venezuela (Boliv. Rep. of)									**Venezuela (Rép. boliv. du)**
Nitrogen	732.4	835.2	621.8	658.7	207.2	293.4	263.0	285.2	Azote
Phosphate	50.7	59.0	54.0	45.3	78.3	82.4	61.3	73.1	Phosphates
Potash	0.0[1]	0.0[1]	0.0[1]	0.0[1]	74.8	104.8	107.8	102.5	Potasse
Viet Nam									**Viet Nam**
Nitrogen	443.6	431.3	439.5	479.5	1 124.7[1]	1 008.6[1]	1 529.8[1]	1 091.6[1]	Azote
Phosphate	218.1	210.9	199.2	217.1	636.3[1]	468.1[1]	690.3[1]	504.2[1]	Phosphates
Potash [1]	...	...	...	...	466.3	443.9	319.1	292.4	Potasse [1]
Yemen [1]									**Yémen [1]**
Nitrogen	...	...	...	...	26.2	17.0	13.8	23.9	Azote
Potash	...	...	...	...	3.0	1.2	0.3	1.2	Potasse
Zambia [1]									**Zambie [1]**
Nitrogen	...	...	...	...	55.8	53.2	64.2	77.6	Azote
Phosphate	...	...	...	...	11.6	8.9	6.2	8.4	Phosphates
Potash	...	...	...	...	28.0	55.9	21.1	13.2	Potasse

Country/area and type of fertilizer	Production				Consumption - Consommation				Pays/zone et type d'engrais
	2007	2008	2009	2010	2007	2008	2009	2010	
Zimbabwe [1]									**Zimbabwe** [1]
Nitrogen	37.2	37.2	37.2	37.2	57.4	51.9	65.7	71.2	Azote
Phosphate	26.0	26.0	26.0	26.0	30.3	35.2	40.6	48.1	Phosphates
Potash	...	...	...	...	20.4	17.0	10.7	18.3	Potasse

Source:
Food and Agriculture Organization of the United Nations (FAO), Rome, FAOSTAT data, last accessed September 2012.

1   FAO estimate.
2   Apparent consumption has been set to zero due to utilization from stockpiles.

Source :
Organisation des Nations Unies pour l'alimentation et l'agriculture (FAO), Rome, données FAOSTAT, dernier accès septembre 2012.

1   Estimation de la FAO.
2   La consommation apparente a été mise à zéro en raison de l'utilisation des réserves.

35

Sugar
Production and consumption: thousand metric tons; consumption per capita: kilograms

Sucre
Production et consommation : milliers de tonnes ; consommation per habitant : kilogrammes

Country or area	2004	2005	2006	2007	2008	2009	2010	Pays ou zone
World								**Monde**
Production	**147 285**	**140 681**	**152 347**	**165 659**	**161 610**	**150 474**	**156 671**	**Production**
Consumption	**146 703**	**148 227**	**153 262**	**156 536**	**162 673**	**161 269**	**164 764**	**Consommation**
Consumption per capita	**23**	**23**	**24**	**24**	**25**	**24**	**24**	**Consommation par habitant**
Afghanistan *								**Afghanistan ***
Consumption	120	145	160	185	210	225	230	Consommation
Consumption per capita	5	7	7	8	9	9	9	Consommation par habitant
Albania *								**Albanie ***
Production	3	3	5	4	4	4	4	Production
Consumption	78	80	80	85	85	88	88	Consommation
Consumption per capita	25	25	25	27	27	27	27	Consommation par habitant
Algeria *								**Algérie ***
Consumption	1 135	1 185	1 215	1 245	1 265	1 285	1 305	Consommation
Consumption per capita	35	36	36	37	36	36	36	Consommation par habitant
Angola *								**Angola ***
Consumption	205	225	245	255	265	275	280	Consommation
Consumption per capita	13	14	15	16	16	15	15	Consommation par habitant
Argentina								**Argentine**
Production	1 857	2 165	2 470	2 198	2 448	2 256	2 038	Production
Consumption	1 574	1 654	1 866	1 874	1 720	1 822	1 823	Consommation
Consumption per capita	41	42	48	48	43	44	44	Consommation par habitant
Armenia								**Arménie**
Production	0	2	2	3	4	1	33	Production
Consumption *	87	87	87	88	90	90	92	Consommation *
Consumption per capita *	27	27	27	27	28	28	28	Consommation par habitant *
Australia								**Australie**
Production	5 530	5 393	4 729	4 627	4 619	4 523	3 634	Production
Consumption	1 043	1 034	*1 035	*1 040	1 221	*1 115	1 026	Consommation
Consumption per capita	52	51	*50	*49	57	*51	46	Consommation par habitant
Azerbaijan								**Azerbaïdjan**
Production	0	2	9	10	18	13	10	Production
Consumption *	160	160	160	165	165	168	170	Consommation *
Consumption per capita *	19	19	19	19	19	19	19	Consommation par habitant *
Bahamas								**Bahamas**
Consumption	12	13	14	14	13	13	13	Consommation
Consumption per capita	38	41	42	42	39	38	38	Consommation par habitant
Bangladesh *								**Bangladesh ***
Production	125	120	145	170	110	80	95	Production
Consumption	790	880	995	1 075	1 175	1 275	1 350	Consommation
Consumption per capita	6	6	7	8	8	9	9	Consommation par habitant
Barbados								**Barbade**
Production	*35	*40	32	34	32	*30	25	Production
Consumption *	14	15	15	15	15	15	15	Consommation *
Consumption per capita *	52	54	53	55	55	54	54	Consommation par habitant *
Belarus								**Bélarus**
Production	340	*435	*480	*495	541	*570	458	Production
Consumption	*410	*410	*415	*415	*410	*420	441	Consommation
Consumption per capita	*42	*42	*43	*43	*42	*43	46	Consommation par habitant *
Belize								**Belize**
Production	125	102	120	100	86	88	97	Production
Consumption	12	12	13	14	14	14	16	Consommation
Consumption per capita	42	42	42	44	43	41	49	Consommation par habitant
Benin *								**Bénin ***
Production	4	5	10	10	10	10	10	Production
Consumption	36	37	38	40	44	50	55	Consommation
Consumption per capita	5	5	5	5	5	6	6	Consommation par habitant
Bermuda								**Bermudes**
Consumption	2	2	2	2	1	1	1	Consommation
Consumption per capita	25	25	23	23	20	20	19	Consommation par habitant

Sugar *(continued)*
Production and consumption: thousand metric tons; consumption per capita: kilograms
Sucre *(suite)*
Production et consommation : milliers de tonnes ; consommation par habitant : kilogrammes

Country or area	2004	2005	2006	2007	2008	2009	2010	Pays ou zone
Bolivia (Plurin. State of)								**Bolivie (État plurin. de)**
Production	464	*400	*370	*375	*340	*355	*400	Production
Consumption *	310	320	325	330	335	340	345	Consommation *
Consumption per capita *	34	34	34	34	33	33	33	Consommation par habitant *
Bosnia and Herzegovina *								**Bosnie-Herzégovine ***
Consumption	130	130	135	135	135	140	140	Consommation
Consumption per capita	34	34	35	35	35	36	36	Consommation par habitant
Botswana								**Botswana**
Consumption	55	60	60	65	65	70	70	Consommation
Consumption per capita	32	35	35	37	37	39	38	Consommation par habitant
Brazil								**Brésil**
Production	27 290	27 439	32 270	34 060	33 045	34 305	39 451	Production
Consumption	10 857	11 902	12 513	12 474	12 597	12 199	13 233	Consommation
Consumption per capita	59	64	66	66	66	64	69	Consommation par habitant
Brunei Darussalam								**Brunéi Darussalam**
Consumption	11	11	11	11	12	13	13	Consommation
Consumption per capita	31	30	29	28	30	32	31	Consommation par habitant
Bulgaria *[1]								**Bulgarie *[1]**
Production	3	5	4	...	...	...	...	Production
Consumption	270	275	280	...	...	...	...	Consommation
Consumption per capita	35	36	36	...	...	...	...	Consommation par habitant
Burkina Faso *								**Burkina Faso ***
Production	40	40	40	40	40	40	40	Production
Consumption	65	75	80	80	85	85	90	Consommation
Consumption per capita	5	6	6	6	6	6	6	Consommation par habitant
Burundi								**Burundi**
Production	22	23	25	24	20	22	22	Production
Consumption	27	29	29	30	30	31	32	Consommation
Consumption per capita	4	4	4	4	4	4	4	Consommation par habitant
Cameroon								**Cameroun**
Production	*125	119	126	100	*100	*110	106	Production
Consumption	*145	92	112	129	*145	*150	166	Consommation
Consumption per capita	*9	5	6	7	*8	*8	8	Consommation par habitant
Canada *								**Canada ***
Production	115	105	135	130	70	70	85	Production
Consumption	1 290	1 310	1 330	1 350	1 365	1 375	1 380	Consommation
Consumption per capita	40	41	41	41	41	41	41	Consommation par habitant
Cape Verde *								**Cap-Vert ***
Consumption	17	17	17	18	18	18	18	Consommation
Consumption per capita	36	35	35	37	36	35	35	Consommation par habitant
Central African Rep. *								**Rép. centrafricaine ***
Consumption	9	11	11	11	11	11	12	Consommation
Consumption per capita	3	4	4	4	4	4	3	Consommation par habitant
Chad								**Tchad**
Production	*30	*35	*35	35	36	*40	38	Production
Consumption	*80	*85	*90	90	88	*93	93	Consommation
Consumption per capita	*9	*10	*10	10	11	*10	8	Consommation par habitant
Chile								**Chili**
Production	401	386	372	*370	*280	*220	330	Production
Consumption	673	682	*695	*705	*725	*760	*790	Consommation
Consumption per capita	41	42	*42	*43	*43	*45	*46	Consommation par habitant
China [2]								**Chine [2]**
Production	10 912	*9 785	*10 682	*13 895	15 465	13 629	*11 600	Production
Consumption *	11 613	11 785	11 975	13 500	14 725	15 000	14 850	Consommation *
Consumption per capita *	9	9	9	10	11	11	11	Consommation par habitant *
China, Hong Kong SAR *								**Chine, Hong Kong RAS ***
Consumption	180	180	180	180	180	180	180	Consommation
Consumption per capita	27	26	26	26	26	26	26	Consommation par habitant
China, Macao SAR								**Chine, Macao RAS**
Consumption	8	8	8	7	7	7	7	Consommation
Consumption per capita	21	17	16	12	12	13	13	Consommation par habitant

Country or area	2004	2005	2006	2007	2008	2009	2010	Pays ou zone
Colombia								**Colombie**
Production	2 740	2 683	2 415	2 277	2 036	2 598	2 078	Production
Consumption	1 561	1 575	1 586	1 719	1 715[3]	1 651[3]	1 623[3]	Consommation
Consumption per capita	34	34	37	39	39	37	35	Consommation par habitant
Comoros								**Comores**
Consumption	9	9	9	10	10	10	10	Consommation
Consumption per capita	11	14	14	14	14	13	14	Consommation par habitant
Congo								**Congo**
Production	*55	63	*65	*56	*67	*70	70	Production
Consumption	*55	76	*80	80	80	*85	*85	Consommation
Consumption per capita	*18	24	*22	22	21	*22	*21	Consommation par habitant
Costa Rica								**Costa Rica**
Production	*405	398	348	373	351	305	392	Production
Consumption	*230	225	*230	235	229	231	269	Consommation
Consumption per capita	*54	53	*53	53	51	50	59	Consommation par habitant
Côte d'Ivoire *								**Côte d'Ivoire ***
Production	120	145	145	145	150	150	150	Production
Consumption	210	215	220	230	240	260	280	Consommation
Consumption per capita	11	11	11	11	12	12	13	Consommation par habitant
Croatia								**Croatie**
Production	192	221	291	216	228	*230	*220	Production
Consumption *	190	200	200	200	205	205	205	Consommation *
Consumption per capita *	43	45	45	45	46	46	46	Consommation par habitant *
Cuba								**Cuba**
Production	*2 600	*1 300	1 239	1 193	1 446	1 379	*1 250	Production
Consumption	*700	*700	741	690	692	663	*675	Consommation
Consumption per capita	*62	*62	66	61	62	59	*60	Consommation par habitant
Dem. Rep. of the Congo *								**Rép. dém. du Congo ***
Production	60	60	65	65	70	70	70	Production
Consumption	90	95	105	120	130	150	160	Consommation
Consumption per capita	2	2	2	2	2	2	2	Consommation par habitant
Djibouti								**Djibouti**
Consumption	15	16	16	16	16	17	17	Consommation
Consumption per capita	17	18	18	18	18	19	19	Consommation par habitant
Dominican Republic								**Rép. dominicaine**
Production	*530	*475	487	488	492	540	549	Production
Consumption	*360	*370	338	325	343	357	364	Consommation
Consumption per capita	*39	*38	36	34	36	37	39	Consommation par habitant
Ecuador								**Equateur**
Production	*490	*470	520	*495	*510	*510	500	Production
Consumption	*485	*488	*490	*495	*505	*520	531	Consommation
Consumption per capita	*37	*37	*37	*36	*37	*37	37	Consommation par habitant
Egypt								**Egypte**
Production	*1 489	*1 625	*1 725	1 851	1 699	*1 750	2 084	Production
Consumption	*2 600	*2 675	*2 700	*2 700	*2 700	*2 750	2 890	Consommation
Consumption per capita	*35	*37	*38	*37	*36	*36	37	Consommation par habitant
El Salvador								**El Salvador**
Production	555	633	542	560	597	518	690	Production
Consumption	212	225	240	237	239	241	238	Consommation
Consumption per capita	33	37	40	39	39	39	39	Consommation par habitant
Eritrea								**Erythrée**
Consumption	16	20	20	25	30	35	40	Consommation
Consumption per capita	4	5	4	5	6	7	8	Consommation par habitant
Ethiopia *								**Ethiopie ***
Production	325	345	360	340	340	320	320	Production
Consumption	295	320	350	370	390	415	425	Consommation
Consumption per capita	4	4	5	5	5	5	5	Consommation par habitant
European Union (EU)[1]								**Union européenne (UE)[1]**
Production	21 843	21 698	17 580	16 904	14 708	16 368	16 760	Production
Consumption	17 691	16 765	17 398	18 541	18 899	17 796	19 145	Consommation
Consumption per capita	39	36	35	38	38	36	38	Consommation par habitant

35

Sugar *(continued)*
Production and consumption: thousand metric tons; consumption per capita: kilograms
Sucre *(suite)*
Production et consommation : milliers de tonnes ; consommation par habitant : kilogrammes

Country or area	2004	2005	2006	2007	2008	2009	2010	Pays ou zone
Fiji								**Fidji**
Production	330	306	324	254	283	160	153	Production
Consumption	58[4]	55	61[4]	70[4]	52	43	44	Consommation
Consumption per capita	69	66	73	84	65	52	53	Consommation par habitant
Gabon								**Gabon**
Production	*19	*21	21	*21	*21	*24	*24	Production
Consumption	*21	*21	21	*22	*22	*24	*24	Consommation
Consumption per capita	*16	*15	15	*15	*15	*16	*16	Consommation par habitant
Gambia *								**Gambie ***
Consumption	70	70	75	75	75	78	80	Consommation
Consumption per capita	47	47	50	49	49	50	52	Consommation par habitant
Georgia *								**Géorgie ***
Consumption	135	135	135	137	138	140	141	Consommation
Consumption per capita	31	31	31	31	32	32	31	Consommation par habitant
Ghana *								**Ghana ***
Consumption	200	205	215	220	230	240	245	Consommation
Consumption per capita	10	10	10	10	10	10	11	Consommation par habitant
Gibraltar								**Gibraltar**
Consumption	2	2	1	1	1	1	1	Consommation
Consumption per capita	67	55	38	37	35	35	44	Consommation par habitant
Guatemala								**Guatemala**
Production	2 092	2 015	1 961	2 364	2 145	2 382	2 495	Production
Consumption	585	657	637	716	644	726	683	Consommation
Consumption per capita	47	52	49	54	47	52	48	Consommation par habitant
Guinea *								**Guinée ***
Production	26	25	25	25	20	25	25	Production
Consumption	110	120	125	130	140	145	150	Consommation
Consumption per capita	12	13	13	13	14	14	14	Consommation par habitant
Guinea-Bissau								**Guinée-Bissau**
Consumption	9	14	14	15	15	17	18	Consommation
Consumption per capita	7	11	10	11	11	12	12	Consommation par habitant
Guyana								**Guyana**
Production	*320	246	*255	*265	*224	*245	*220	Production
Consumption	*26	22	*25	*26	*26	*27	*27	Consommation
Consumption per capita	*35	29	*33	*34	*34	*35	*35	Consommation par habitant
Haiti *								**Haïti ***
Consumption	175	185	185	190	195	195	195	Consommation
Consumption per capita	22	23	23	23	24	24	24	Consommation par habitant
Honduras								**Honduras**
Production	357	*360	391	391	384	392	429	Production
Consumption	250	*250	*255	*265	*280	*300	*320	Consommation
Consumption per capita	36	*36	*35	*35	*35	*35	*34	Consommation par habitant
Iceland *								**Islande ***
Consumption	12	11	11	11	11	11	11	Consommation
Consumption per capita	41	37	36	35	35	35	35	Consommation par habitant
India								**Inde**
Production	14 432	15 216	22 347	29 090	25 936	15 655	21 151	Production
Consumption	19 858	20 110	20 110	20 878	22 550	24 131	22 827	Consommation
Consumption per capita	19	20	18	18	20	21	19	Consommation par habitant
Indonesia								**Indonésie**
Production	*2 225	*2 435	2 510	2 814	*2 895	*2 740	*2 450	Production
Consumption *	3 915	4 052	4 330	4 690	4 975	5 125	5 275	Consommation *
Consumption per capita *	18	18	19	21	22	22	22	Consommation par habitant *
Iran (Islamic Rep. of) *								**Iran (Rép. islamique d') ***
Production	1 310	1 300	1 425	1 250	805	890	975	Production
Consumption	2 060	2 110	2 160	2 225	2 290	2 340	2 385	Consommation
Consumption per capita	31	31	31	31	32	32	32	Consommation par habitant
Iraq *								**Iraq ***
Consumption	675	675	685	700	720	740	755	Consommation
Consumption per capita	25	24	24	24	23	23	23	Consommation par habitant

35

Sugar *(continued)*
Production and consumption: thousand metric tons; consumption per capita: kilograms
Sucre *(suite)*
Production et consommation : milliers de tonnes ; consommation par habitant : kilogrammes

Country or area	2004	2005	2006	2007	2008	2009	2010	Pays ou zone
Israel *								**Israël ***
Consumption	440	455	460	470	480	490	495	Consommation
Consumption per capita	65	66	65	66	66	66	65	Consommation par habitant
Jamaica								**Jamaïque**
Production	181	126	144	163	140	131	121	Production
Consumption	111	123	98	109	128	119	115	Consommation
Consumption per capita	42	46	37	41	48	44	43	Consommation par habitant
Japan								**Japon**
Production	976	965	909	859	960	*907	*819	Production
Consumption	2 403	2 397	2 229	2 452	2 254	2 325	*2 345	Consommation
Consumption per capita	19	19	17	19	18	18	18	Consommation par habitant
Jordan *								**Jordanie ***
Consumption	235	255	270	280	285	290	295	Consommation
Consumption per capita	44	47	48	49	49	49	48	Consommation par habitant
Kazakhstan								**Kazakhstan**
Production	40	*22	*26	*30	*15	*30	14	Production
Consumption	*450	*455	*460	*465	*470	*470	489	Consommation
Consumption per capita	*30	*30	*30	*30	*30	*30	30	Consommation par habitant
Kenya								**Kenya**
Production	562	532	517	520	563	596	569	Production
Consumption *	728	756	781	741	817	828	840	Consommation *
Consumption per capita *	22	23	21	20	22	22	21	Consommation par habitant *
Korea, Dem. P. R. *								**Corée, R. p. dém. de ***
Consumption	85	90	90	90	95	95	95	Consommation
Consumption per capita	4	4	4	4	4	4	4	Consommation par habitant
Korea, Republic of								**Corée, République de**
Consumption	1 276[5]	1 303[5]	1 181[5]	1 192[5]	1 294[5]	1 265[5]	*1 330	Consommation
Consumption per capita	27	27	24	25	27	26	*27	Consommation par habitant
Kuwait *								**Koweït ***
Consumption	85	90	90	95	95	95	97	Consommation
Consumption per capita	36	37	39	39	38	37	36	Consommation par habitant
Kyrgyzstan								**Kirghizistan**
Production	88	45	*40	*15	*20	*25	*15	Production
Consumption *	120	120	125	130	130	135	140	Consommation *
Consumption per capita *	24	24	25	26	26	26	27	Consommation par habitant *
Lao People's Dem. Rep.								**Rép. dém. pop. lao**
Production	0	0	0	0	*10	*15	*50	Production
Consumption *	35	45	45	50	50	53	55	Consommation *
Consumption per capita *	6	8	8	9	8	9	9	Consommation par habitant *
Lebanon								**Liban**
Production	0	4	*5	*5	*5	*5	*5	Production
Consumption *	150	151	145	150	150	155	155	Consommation *
Consumption per capita *	43	42	40	41	40	37	33	Consommation par habitant *
Liberia								**Libéria**
Consumption	10	15	15	16	16	18	20	Consommation
Consumption per capita	3	5	5	5	4	5	5	Consommation par habitant
Libyan Arab Jamah. *								**Jamah. arabe libyenne ***
Consumption	255	265	270	275	280	285	290	Consommation
Consumption per capita	46	47	47	47	47	47	47	Consommation par habitant
Madagascar								**Madagascar**
Production	*26	*27	*20	*20	*16	*60	60	Production
Consumption	*129	*132	*135	*140	*145	*150	155	Consommation
Consumption per capita	*8	*7	*8	*8	*8	*8	8	Consommation par habitant
Malawi								**Malawi**
Production	*255	*265	*230	*280	*310	*300	279	Production
Consumption	165	175	190	205	220	240	264	Consommation
Consumption per capita	14	14	15	16	16	17	18	Consommation par habitant
Malaysia *								**Malaisie ***
Production	80	80	55	60	35	30	25	Production
Consumption	1 215	1 225	1 250	1 275	1 295	1 325	1 395	Consommation
Consumption per capita	48	46	47	47	47	48	49	Consommation par habitant

Sugar *(continued)*
Production and consumption: thousand metric tons; consumption per capita: kilograms

Sucre *(suite)*
Production et consommation : milliers de tonnes ; consommation par habitant : kilogrammes

Country or area	2004	2005	2006	2007	2008	2009	2010	Pays ou zone
Maldives								**Maldives**
Consumption	5	6	6	6	6	6	7	Consommation
Consumption per capita	17	19	19	20	19	19	20	Consommation par habitant
Mali *								**Mali ***
Production	35	35	34	34	35	35	35	Production
Consumption	95	100	105	110	115	120	125	Consommation
Consumption per capita	8	9	9	9	9	9	9	Consommation par habitant
Mauritania *								**Mauritanie ***
Consumption	140	145	145	150	150	155	155	Consommation
Consumption per capita	45	44	42	49	48	48	46	Consommation par habitant
Mauritius								**Maurice**
Production	606	524	505	462	480	498	485	Production
Consumption	42	39	39	42	42	40	39	Consommation
Consumption per capita	34	32	32	33	33	32	31	Consommation par habitant
Mexico								**Mexique**
Production	5 672	5 619	5 412	5 420	5 940	5 181	*5 075	Production
Consumption	5 300	4 877	4 979	4 944	5 031	5 153	*4 545	Consommation
Consumption per capita	50	47	48	47	47	48	42	Consommation par habitant
Mongolia								**Mongolie**
Consumption	23	25	25	26	26	27	27	Consommation
Consumption per capita	9	10	10	10	10	10	10	Consommation par habitant
Morocco								**Maroc**
Production	*540	513	*450	*505	466	410	379	Production
Consumption	*1 150	1 163	*1 170	*1 190	1 143	1 161	1 185	Consommation
Consumption per capita	*38	39	*38	*39	37	36	37	Consommation par habitant
Mozambique								**Mozambique**
Production	205	265	243	244	250	252	282	Production
Consumption	134	135	144	169	172	185	197	Consommation
Consumption per capita	7	7	7	8	8	9	9	Consommation par habitant
Myanmar *								**Myanmar ***
Production	150	150	155	160	180	220	225	Production
Consumption	150	155	165	175	185	200	215	Consommation
Consumption per capita	3	3	3	3	3	3	4	Consommation par habitant
Namibia *								**Namibie ***
Consumption	60	65	65	70	70	75	75	Consommation
Consumption per capita	33	36	33	35	34	36	35	Consommation par habitant
Nepal *								**Népal ***
Production	140	130	135	140	140	130	130	Production
Consumption	130	135	135	140	140	145	150	Consommation
Consumption per capita	5	5	5	5	5	5	5	Consommation par habitant
Netherlands Antilles *								**Antilles néerlandaises ***
Consumption	13	13	13	13	13	13	13	Consommation
Consumption per capita	71	71	69	67	66	65	66	Consommation par habitant
New Zealand *								**Nouvelle-Zélande ***
Consumption	230	225	225	225	225	225	220	Consommation
Consumption per capita	57	55	54	53	53	52	50	Consommation par habitant
Nicaragua								**Nicaragua**
Production	*440	*470	*435	*505	*480	*520	528	Production
Consumption	*200	*205	*210	*215	*220	237	233	Consommation
Consumption per capita	*37	*38	*38	*38	*39	41	40	Consommation par habitant
Niger *								**Niger ***
Production	10	10	10	10	10	10	10	Production
Consumption	70	75	75	80	80	85	90	Consommation
Consumption per capita	6	6	6	6	6	6	6	Consommation par habitant
Nigeria								**Nigéria**
Production	0	0	*30	55	21	38	30	Production
Consumption	1 222	1 236	*1 265	*1 295	1 570	1 220	994	Consommation
Consumption per capita	9	9	*9	*9	11	9	7	Consommation par habitant
Norway *								**Norvège ***
Consumption	170	165	165	165	160	160	160	Consommation
Consumption per capita	37	35	35	35	34	33	33	Consommation par habitant

Sugar *(continued)*
Production and consumption: thousand metric tons; consumption per capita: kilograms
Sucre *(suite)*
Production et consommation : milliers de tonnes ; consommation par habitant : kilogrammes

Country or area	2004	2005	2006	2007	2008	2009	2010	Pays ou zone
Pakistan								**Pakistan**
Production	4 481	2 839	3 263	*4 355	4 997	*3 500	*3 860	Production
Consumption	4 004	4 075	3 951	*4 250	4 538	*4 625	*4 715	Consommation
Consumption per capita	29	27	25	*27	28	*28	*28	Consommation par habitant
Panama								**Panama**
Production	157	157	168	164	*175	*155	*175	Production
Consumption *	115	117	120	123	125	130	135	Consommation *
Consumption per capita *	36	37	37	37	36	38	39	Consommation par habitant *
Papua New Guinea								**Papouasie-Nvl-Guinée**
Production	46	44	*35	*35	*35	*35	*40	Production
Consumption	35	35	*35	*37	*38	*40	*40	Consommation
Consumption per capita	6	6	*6	*7	*7	*7	*7	Consommation par habitant
Paraguay								**Paraguay**
Production *	115	117	120	120	120	120	120	Production *
Consumption *	115	120	120	125	125	130	130	Consommation *
Consumption per capita	20	20	20	20	20	21	20	Consommation par habitant
Peru								**Pérou**
Production	813	695	805	*905	*1 005	*1 075	1 019	Production
Consumption	967	896	*960	*1 025	*1 100	*1 170	*1 195	Consommation
Consumption per capita	35	32	*34	*36	*38	*40	*41	Consommation par habitant
Philippines								**Philippines**
Production	2 423	2 184	2 413	2 147	2 415	2 294	1 791	Production
Consumption	2 102	2 037	2 021	1 939	2 061	2 144	2 008	Consommation
Consumption per capita	25	24	23	22	23	23	21	Consommation par habitant
Republic of Moldova								**République de Moldova**
Production	111	133	161	75	134	44	104	Production
Consumption	106	*125	*130	*105	83	69	78	Consommation
Consumption per capita	29	*35	*36	*29	23	19	21	Consommation par habitant
Romania [1]								**Roumanie** [1]
Production	*55	67	*125	...	...	...	...	Production
Consumption	584	*595	*600	...	...	...	...	Consommation
Consumption per capita	27	*28	*28	...	...	...	...	Consommation par habitant
Russian Federation								**Fédération de Russie**
Production	2 496	2 719	3 459	*3 405	3 789	3 602	2 973	Production
Consumption	*6 700	*6 600	*6 500	*6 500	6 180	5 652	5 761	Consommation
Consumption per capita	*46	*46	*46	*46	44	40	41	Consommation par habitant
Rwanda *								**Rwanda ***
Production	5	5	10	10	10	10	10	Production
Consumption	16	19	20	22	24	26	28	Consommation
Consumption per capita	2	2	2	2	2	3	3	Consommation par habitant
Saint Kitts and Nevis								**Saint-Kitts-et-Nevis**
Production	*15	*10	0	0	0	0	0	Production
Consumption *	3	3	3	3	3	3	3	Consommation *
Consumption per capita *	42	42	42	36	31	40	40	Consommation par habitant *
Samoa								**Samoa**
Production	2	2	3	3	3	3	3	Production
Consumption	4	4	4	5	5	5	5	Consommation
Consumption per capita	15	15	15	19	18	18	19	Consommation par habitant
Saudi Arabia *								**Arabie saoudite ***
Consumption	720	790	820	850	880	900	925	Consommation
Consumption per capita	32	34	35	35	36	36	36	Consommation par habitant
Senegal *								**Sénégal ***
Production	90	90	95	95	100	105	105	Production
Consumption	180	185	190	200	205	212	220	Consommation
Consumption per capita	17	17	17	18	18	17	18	Consommation par habitant
Serbia *								**Serbie ***
Production	335	415	505	490	325	450	525	Production
Consumption	315	320	325	325	330	330	335	Consommation
Consumption per capita	42	43	44	44	45	45	45	Consommation par habitant

Country or area	2004	2005	2006	2007	2008	2009	2010	Pays ou zone
Sierra Leone *								**Sierra Leone ***
Production	6	6	6	6	6	6	8	Production
Consumption	25	26	27	28	30	31	32	Consommation
Consumption per capita	5	5	5	5	5	6	6	Consommation par habitant
Singapore *								**Singapour ***
Consumption	310	310	310	310	315	315	315	Consommation
Consumption per capita	73	71	70	68	65	63	62	Consommation par habitant
Somalia *								**Somalie ***
Production	20	15	20	20	20	20	20	Production
Consumption	200	205	205	220	240	245	250	Consommation
Consumption per capita	23	25	24	25	27	27	27	Consommation par habitant
South Africa								**Afrique du Sud**
Production	2 234	2 507	2 338	2 433	2 415	2 330	2 069	Production
Consumption	1 484	1 565	1 699	1 771	1 802	1 850	1 923	Consommation
Consumption per capita	32	33	36	37	37	38	39	Consommation par habitant
Sri Lanka *								**Sri Lanka ***
Production	60	60	70	75	75	41	40	Production
Consumption	625	635	645	660	680	695	705	Consommation
Consumption per capita	32	32	32	33	34	34	34	Consommation par habitant
Sudan								**Soudan**
Production	789	728	767	743	652	819	509	Production
Consumption	624	877	910	916	1 024	1 115	1 165	Consommation
Consumption per capita	18	25	25	25	27	28	29	Consommation par habitant
Suriname *								**Suriname ***
Production	5	5	7	7	7	7	7	Production
Consumption	20	21	21	22	22	23	23	Consommation
Consumption per capita	42	42	42	43	43	44	43	Consommation par habitant
Swaziland								**Swaziland**
Production	594	653	623	631	664	628	613	Production
Consumption *	45	45	50	50	50	50	50	Consommation *
Consumption per capita *	39	39	44	52	49	49	48	Consommation par habitant *
Switzerland								**Suisse**
Production	*225	221	198	*260	273	303	218	Production
Consumption	*475	526	558	*560	530	474	386	Consommation
Consumption per capita	*64	70	75	*74	69	61	49	Consommation par habitant
Syrian Arab Republic								**Rép. arabe syrienne**
Production	*105	*110	148	*160	*155	*80	*160	Production
Consumption *	790	800	825	835	840	860	880	Consommation *
Consumption per capita *	44	44	44	44	43	43	43	Consommation par habitant *
Tajikistan *								**Tadjikistan ***
Consumption	85	105	110	115	115	118	118	Consommation
Consumption per capita	13	15	16	16	16	16	16	Consommation par habitant
Thailand								**Thaïlande**
Production	7 462	4 589	5 646	7 147	7 774	7 945	6 770	Production
Consumption	2 303	2 352	2 464	2 476	2 310	2 463	2 662	Consommation
Consumption per capita	36	36	38	38	36	39	40	Consommation par habitant
TFYR of Macedonia								**L'ex-R.Y. Macédoine**
Production	16	16	19	36	*35	*35	*35	Production
Consumption *	70	70	75	75	75	78	78	Consommation *
Consumption per capita *	34	34	37	37	37	38	38	Consommation par habitant *
Togo *								**Togo ***
Consumption	50	60	62	65	66	70	75	Consommation
Consumption per capita	10	11	12	12	12	12	13	Consommation par habitant
Trinidad and Tobago								**Trinité-et-Tobago**
Production	43	33	*25	*30	0	0	0	Production
Consumption *	75	75	75	70	70	70	70	Consommation *
Consumption per capita *	59	59	58	54	54	53	53	Consommation par habitant *
Tunisia								**Tunisie**
Consumption	335	332	362	*375	347	*365	356	Consommation
Consumption per capita	34	33	36	*37	34	*35	32	Consommation par habitant

Sugar *(continued)*
Production and consumption: thousand metric tons; consumption per capita: kilograms
Sucre *(suite)*
Production et consommation : milliers de tonnes ; consommation par habitant : kilogrammes

Country or area	2004	2005	2006	2007	2008	2009	2010	Pays ou zone
Turkey								**Turquie**
Production	2 053	2 171	2 091	1 919	2 148	2 610	2 574	Production
Consumption	1 894	1 978	2 208	1 999	2 175	2 301	2 396	Consommation
Consumption per capita	27	27	30	28	30	32	33	Consommation par habitant
Turkmenistan *								**Turkménistan ***
Production	2	3	3	4	4	4	10	Production
Consumption	75	80	85	90	95	103	105	Consommation
Consumption per capita	14	15	16	17	18	19	19	Consommation par habitant
Uganda								**Ouganda**
Production	213	211	208	197	259	312	297	Production
Consumption	257	263	260	250	292	346	319	Consommation
Consumption per capita	10	10	10	9	10	11	10	Consommation par habitant
Ukraine								**Ukraine**
Production	*1 945	*2 060	*2 800	*2 025	*1 700	1 377	1 725	Production
Consumption	*2 300	*2 350	*2 350	*2 350	*2 300	2 074	1 998	Consommation
Consumption per capita	*49	*50	*50	*50	*50	45	44	Consommation par habitant
United Arab Emirates *								**Emirats arabes unis ***
Consumption	127	140	151	163	165	168	170	Consommation
Consumption per capita	31	34	36	36	35	33	32	Consommation par habitant
United Rep. of Tanzania								**Rép.-Unie de Tanzanie**
Production	211	278	257	267	286	269	289	Production
Consumption	221	268	300	307	330	445	398	Consommation
Consumption per capita	6	7	8	8	8	11	10	Consommation par habitant
United States								**Etats-Unis**
Production	7 647	6 784	7 034	7 678	6 956	6 855	7 635	Production
Consumption	8 994	9 248	9 228	9 107	9 807	9 705	10 154	Consommation
Consumption per capita	31	31	31	30	32	32	33	Consommation par habitant
Uruguay *								**Uruguay ***
Production	7	6	6	6	7	10	15	Production
Consumption	115	115	120	120	120	123	125	Consommation
Consumption per capita	35	35	36	36	36	37	37	Consommation par habitant
Uzbekistan *								**Ouzbékistan ***
Consumption	495	505	510	510	515	520	525	Consommation
Consumption per capita	20	19	19	19	19	19	19	Consommation par habitant
Venezuela (Boliv. Rep. of)								**Venezuela (Rép. boliv. du)**
Production	694	*690	*700	*700	*690	*650	*550	Production
Consumption	1 020	*1 050	*1 070	*1 080	*1 090	*1 100	*1 110	Consommation
Consumption per capita	39	*40	*40	*39	*39	*39	*39	Consommation par habitant
Viet Nam								**Viet Nam**
Production	*1 070	875	*995	1 251	*1 065	1 053	925	Production
Consumption	*1 035	906	*1 170	1 299	*1 350	*1 155	*1 215	Consommation
Consumption per capita	*13	11	*14	15	*16	*13	*14	Consommation par habitant
Yemen *								**Yémen ***
Consumption	480	495	510	525	540	555	565	Consommation
Consumption per capita	23	24	24	24	24	24	24	Consommation par habitant
Zambia								**Zambie**
Production	245	248	*250	237	207	323	409	Production
Consumption	115	95	*115	118	116	135	161	Consommation
Consumption per capita	10	8	*10	10	9	10	12	Consommation par habitant
Zimbabwe								**Zimbabwe**
Production	456	430	446	349	291	261	335	Production
Consumption	311	295	263	234	172	187	228	Consommation
Consumption per capita	27	25	22	22	14	18	22	Consommation par habitant

Source:
International Sugar Organization (ISO), London, the ISO database and the *Sugar Yearbook 2011*.

Source:
Organisation internationale du sucre (OIS), Londres, la base de données de l'OIS et l'*Annuaire du sucre 2011*.

1   Beginning 2004, data for Cyprus, Czech Republic, Estonia, Hungary, Latvia, Lithuania, Malta, Poland, Slovakia, Slovenia are incorporated in the European Union data. From 2007 including figures of Bulgaria and Romania.

1   À partir de 2004, les données pour Chypre, République tchèque, Estonie, Hongrie, Lettonie, Lituanie, Malta, Pologne, Slovaquie, Slovénie sont inclues dans les donneés de l'Union européene. À partir de 2007, les données incluent également la Bulgarie et la Roumaine.

2	For statistical purposes, the data for China do not include those for the Hong Kong Special Administrative Region (Hong Kong SAR), Macao Special Administrative Region (Macao SAR) and Taiwan Province of China.
3	Including non-human consumption: 2008 - 107 684 tons; 2009 – 92 602 tons; 2010 - 78 058.
4	Including 10 686 tons sold to other Pacific Island nations in tons in 2004; 15 515 tons in 2006 and 13 398 tons in 2007.
5	Including sugar used for the production of mono-sodium glutamate and llysin: 2004 - 235 773 tons; 2005 - 241 101 tons; 2006 - 232 665 tons; 2007 - 223 344 tons; 2008 - 226 401 tons; 2009 - 153 447 tons. As well as estimated non-food industrial consumption: 2004 – 105 000 tons; 2005 - 105 000 tons; 2006 - 25 000 tons; 2007 - 85 000 tons; 2008 - 85 000 tons; 2009 - 100 000 tons.

2	Pour la présentation des statistiques, les données pour la Chine ne comprennent pas la Région Administrative Spéciale de Hong Kong (Hong Kong RAS), la Région Administrative Spéciale de Macao (Macao RAS) et la province de Taiwan.
3	Dont consommation non humaine: 2008 - 107 684 tonnes; 2009 – 92 602 tonnes; 2010 - 78 058.
4	Y compris 10 686 tonnes vendues aux autres îles pacifiques en 2004; 15 515 tonnes en 2006 et 13 398 tonnes en 2007.
5	Y compris la sucre utilisée pour la production du glutamate monosodium et lysine: 2004 - 235 773 tonnes; 2005 - 241 101 tonnes; 2006 - 232 665 tonnes; 2007 - 223 344 tonnes; 2008 -226 401 tonnes; 2009 - 153 447 tonnes. Ainsi qu'une consommation industrielle non-alimentaire: 2004 - 105 000 tonnes; 2005 - 105 000 tonnes; 2006 - 25 000 tonnes; 2007 - 85 000 tonnes; 2008 - 85 000 tonnes; 2009 - 100 000 tonnes.

Meat production
Thousand metric tons

Production de viande
Milliers de tonnes

Region, country or area	2003	2004	2005	2006	2007	2008	2009	2010	Région, pays ou zone
World									**Monde**
Buffalo	**2 809**	**2 935**	**3 008**	**3 136**	**3 243**	**3 241**	**3 312**	**3 412**	**Buffle**
Cattle	**57 359**	**58 393**	**59 724**	**61 746**	**63 261**	**61 201**	**61 753**	**62 325**	**Bovine**
Chicken	**65 075**	**67 898**	**70 208**	**72 320**	**76 677**	**80 786**	**82 511**	**86 205**	**Poulet**
Goat	**4 116**	**4 449**	**4 689**	**4 629**	**4 792**	**4 960**	**5 096**	**5 168**	**Chèvre**
Pig	**95 817**	**96 839**	**99 258**	**101 053**	**99 957**	**103 794**	**106 405**	**109 215**	**Porc**
Sheep	**7 782**	**7 820**	**8 029**	**8 276**	**8 570**	**8 528**	**8 536**	**8 532**	**Mouton**
Africa									**Afrique**
Buffalo	**229**	**269**	**270**	**283**	**288**	**297**	**295**	**328**	**Buffle**
Cattle	**4 566**	**4 765**	**5 124**	**5 687**	**5 813**	**6 184**	**6 387**	**6 595**	**Bovine**
Chicken	**3 138**	**3 227**	**3 371**	**3 378**	**3 729**	**3 960**	**4 156**	**4 369**	**Poulet**
Goat	**1 006**	**1 034**	**1 104**	**1 092**	**1 133**	**1 168**	**1 193**	**1 226**	**Chèvre**
Pig	**827**	**889**	**941**	**948**	**1 060**	**1 137**	**1 189**	**1 232**	**Porc**
Sheep	**1 298**	**1 323**	**1 356**	**1 421**	**1 421**	**1 468**	**1 512**	**1 560**	**Mouton**
Algeria									**Algérie**
Cattle	121	125[2]	120[1]	122[1]	123[1]	125[1]	127[1]	133[1]	Bovine
Chicken [1]	253	253	253	253	254	254	254	254	Poulet [1]
Goat [1]	12	13	13	14	14	14	14	14	Chèvre [1]
Sheep [1]	165	172	178	185	187	175	178	180	Mouton [1]
Angola									**Angola**
Cattle [1]	96	73	85	85	92	100	104	106	Bovine [1]
Chicken [1]	8	8	9	8	8	8	8	8	Poulet [1]
Goat [1]	9	9	9	10	11	11	11	11	Chèvre [1]
Pig	*28	28[1]	28[1]	*30	*31	28[1]	28[1]	33[1]	Porc
Sheep [1]	1	1	1	1	1	1	1	1	Mouton [1]
Benin [1]									**Bénin** [1]
Cattle	20	21	22	23	23	24	28	29	Bovine
Chicken	15	15	15	16	17	17	18	18	Poulet
Goat	4	5	5	5	5	5	5	5	Chèvre
Pig	4	4	4	4	4	4	4	5	Porc
Sheep	2	2	3	3	3	3	3	3	Mouton
Botswana									**Botswana**
Cattle	27	35[1]	35[1]	35[1]	35[1]	36[1]	36[1]	37[1]	Bovine
Chicken	6[1]	6[1]	5[1]	5[1]	6[1]	7	6	7[1]	Poulet
Goat [1]	4	4	5	5	5	6	6	6	Chèvre [1]
Pig	^0	^0	^0	^0	1[1]	^0	^0	^0	Porc
Sheep [1]	1	1	2	2	2	2	2	2	Mouton [1]
Burkina Faso [1]									**Burkina Faso** [1]
Cattle	96	101	106	111	116	107	110	134	Bovine
Chicken	29	30	31	32	33	34	35	35	Poulet
Goat	26	27	28	29	30	31	32	33	Chèvre
Pig	27	30	33	36	34	30	31	28	Porc
Sheep	16	16	16	17	17	18	18	19	Mouton
Burundi [1]									**Burundi** [1]
Cattle	10	10	11	12	13	13	15	16	Bovine
Chicken	6	7	7	7	7	7	7	7	Poulet
Goat	4	5	5	5	6	6	6	6	Chèvre
Pig	5	6	6	11	11	10	12	12	Porc
Sheep	1	1	1	1	1	1	1	1	Mouton
Cameroon									**Cameroun**
Cattle	90[1]	93[1]	94[1]	94[1]	94[1]	110	110	124[1]	Bovine
Chicken	30[1]	46[1]	53[1]	61[1]	65[1]	68	64	68[1]	Poulet
Goat	16[1]	16[1]	16[1]	16[1]	16[1]	18	17	20	Chèvre
Pig	16[1]	29[1]	30[1]	30[1]	31[1]	33	31	38[1]	Porc
Sheep	16[1]	16[1]	16[1]	16[1]	16[1]	13	13	16	Mouton
Cape Verde									**Cap-Vert**
Cattle	^0	^0	1[1]	1[1]	1[1]	1[1]	1[1]	1[1]	Bovine
Chicken	^0	^0	^0	^0	1[1]	1[1]	1[1]	1[1]	Poulet
Goat	^0	1[1]	1[1]	1[1]	1[1]	1[1]	1[1]	1[1]	Chèvre
Pig [1]	7	7	7	7	8	8	8	8	Porc [1]

Region, country or area	2003	2004	2005	2006	2007	2008	2009	2010	Région, pays ou zone
Central African Rep.									**Rép. centrafricaine**
Cattle	66[1]	74[2]	76[1]	78[1]	84[1]	81[1]	83[1]	85[1]	Bovine
Chicken [1]	4	4	4	4	5	5	6	6	Poulet [1]
Goat [1]	12	12	12	13	14	16	17	18	Chèvre [1]
Pig	13	14[2]	14[1]	14[1]	*13	14[1]	14[1]	16[1]	Porc
Sheep [1]	2	2	2	2	2	2	2	2	Mouton [1]
Chad									**Tchad**
Cattle [1]	78	80	82	84	86	89	91	95	Bovine [1]
Chicken [1]	5	5	5	5	5	5	5	5	Poulet [1]
Goat [1]	21	21	22	22	23	24	24	24	Chèvre [1]
Pig	^0	^0	^0	1[1]	1[1]	1[1]	1[1]	1[1]	Porc
Sheep [1]	13	13	14	14	15	15	15	15	Mouton [1]
Comoros [1]									**Comores** [1]
Cattle	1	1	1	1	1	1	1	1	Bovine
Chicken	1	1	1	1	1	1	1	1	Poulet
Congo									**Congo**
Cattle	2[1]	3[1]	4[1]	5[1]	6[1]	6	6	6[1]	Bovine
Chicken [1]	5	6	6	6	6	6	6	6	Poulet [1]
Goat	1[1]	1[1]	1[1]	1[1]	1[1]	1	1	1[1]	Chèvre
Pig	1[1]	2[1]	2[1]	2[1]	2[1]	2	2	2[1]	Porc
Côte d'Ivoire									**Côte d'Ivoire**
Cattle	26	28	30	31	29	31	34	35[1]	Bovine
Chicken	21	24	23	22	23	23	23	24[1]	Poulet
Goat	3	3	3	3	3	3	3[1]	4[1]	Chèvre
Pig	7	7	7	7	7	7	7	7[1]	Porc
Sheep	7	8	8	9	7	8	8[1]	8[1]	Mouton
Dem. Rep. of the Congo									**Rép. dém. du Congo**
Cattle	12	12	12	12	12	12	12[1]	13[1]	Bovine
Chicken	11	11	11	11	11	11	11[1]	11[1]	Poulet
Goat	18	18	18	18	18	18	18[1]	18[1]	Chèvre
Pig	24	24	24	24	24	24	24[1]	26[1]	Porc
Sheep	3	3	3	3	3	3	3[1]	3[1]	Mouton
Djibouti [1]									**Djibouti** [1]
Cattle	6	4	5	2	6	6	6	6	Bovine
Goat	2	2	2	2	3	2	2	2	Chèvre
Sheep	2	2	2	2	2	2	2	2	Mouton
Egypt									**Egypte**
Buffalo	229	269	270[1]	283[1]	288[1]	297[1]	295[1]	328[1]	Buffle
Cattle	287	325	320[1]	340[1]	393	430	447	415[1]	Bovine
Chicken	560[1]	584[1]	633[1]	616	705	629	671	685[1]	Poulet
Goat	21	17	18[1]	18[1]	20[1]	21[1]	21[1]	21[1]	Chèvre
Pig	2	2	2[1]	2[1]	3	2	1	1	Porc
Sheep	50	40	43[1]	44[1]	47[1]	44[1]	45[1]	48[1]	Mouton
Eritrea									**Erythrée**
Cattle	17[1]	*17	17[1]	17[1]	23	17	23	22[1]	Bovine
Chicken [1]	2	2	2	2	2	2	2	2	Poulet [1]
Goat [1]	6	6	7	6	6	6	6	6	Chèvre [1]
Sheep	7[1]	7[1]	7[1]	6[1]	4	4[2]	4	4[1]	Mouton
Ethiopia									**Ethiopie**
Cattle [1]	338	336	350	374	363	380	390	373	Bovine [1]
Chicken [1]	50	47	43	45	46	49	51	53	Poulet [1]
Goat [1]	36	44	49	55	65	68	65	66	Chèvre [1]
Pig	2[1]	2[1]	2[1]	2[1]	*2	*2	2[1]	2[1]	Porc
Sheep [1]	53	60	68	79	85	82	85	87	Mouton [1]
Gabon									**Gabon**
Cattle [1]	1	1	2	1	1	1	1	1	Bovine [1]
Chicken [1]	4	4	4	4	4	4	4	4	Poulet [1]
Pig [1]	3	3	3	3	3	3	3	3	Porc [1]
Sheep [1]	1	1	1	1	1	1	1	1	Mouton [1]

Region, country or area	2003	2004	2005	2006	2007	2008	2009	2010	Région, pays ou zone
Gambia									**Gambie**
Cattle [1]	4	4	4	4	4	4	4	4	Bovine [1]
Chicken [1]	1	1	1	1	1	1	1	1	Poulet [1]
Goat [1]	1	1	1	1	1	1	1	1	Chèvre [1]
Pig	^0	^0	^0	^0	1 [1]	1 [1]	1 [1]	1 [1]	Porc
Sheep [1]	1	1	1	1	1	1	1	1	Mouton [1]
Ghana									**Ghana**
Cattle	24 [1]	23	25	24	23 [1]	25 [1]	26 [1]	26 [1]	Bovine
Chicken [1]	26	28	29	31	42	44	48	49	Poulet [1]
Goat	12 [1]	12	12	11	13 [1]	14 [1]	14 [1]	14 [1]	Chèvre
Pig [1]	10	10	10	12	17	17	18	18	Porc [1]
Sheep	10 [1]	10	10	10	11 [1]	16	16	17	Mouton
Guinea									**Guinée**
Cattle	37 [1]	39 [1]	41 [1]	44	47	49	52 [1]	55 [1]	Bovine
Chicken [1]	5	5	6	6	6	7	7	8	Poulet [1]
Goat	5 [1]	6 [1]	6 [1]	7	8	8	9 [1]	9 [1]	Chèvre
Pig	2 [1]	2 [1]	2 [1]	1	1 [1]	2	2 [1]	2 [1]	Porc
Sheep	4 [1]	4 [1]	5 [1]	5	5	6	6 [1]	6 [1]	Mouton
Guinea-Bissau									**Guinée-Bissau**
Cattle	5 [1]	5 [1]	5 [1]	5 [1]	5 [1]	7	6 [1]	6 [1]	Bovine
Chicken [1]	1	1	1	2	2	2	2	2	Poulet [1]
Goat [1]	1	1	1	1	1	1	1	1	Chèvre [1]
Pig [1]	11	11	12	12	12	13	13	13	Porc [1]
Sheep [1]	1	1	1	1	1	1	1	1	Mouton [1]
Kenya									**Kenya**
Cattle	343	350	396	430	445	458	483	462	Bovine
Chicken	21	19	18	22	24	24	25	27	Poulet
Goat	36 [1]	41 [1]	42 [1]	43 [1]	45 [1]	45	46	47	Chèvre
Pig	15	15	13	17	16	16	18	15	Porc
Sheep	36	36	37	35 [1]	34 [1]	39	41	42	Mouton
Lesotho									**Lesotho**
Cattle [1]	10	10	11	3	10	10	10	10	Bovine [1]
Chicken [1]	2	2	2	2	2	2	2	2	Poulet [1]
Goat	2 [1]	2 [1]	2 [1]	2	2 [1]	2 [1]	2 [1]	2 [1]	Chèvre
Pig [1]	3	5	6	9	10	4	4	4	Porc [1]
Sheep	3 [1]	4 [1]	4 [1]	5	4 [1]	4 [1]	4 [1]	4 [1]	Mouton
Liberia [1]									**Libéria** [1]
Cattle	1	1	1	1	1	1	1	1	Bovine
Chicken	8	8	8	9	9	10	10	11	Poulet
Goat	1	1	1	1	1	1	1	1	Chèvre
Pig	4	4	4	5	6	7	8	9	Porc
Sheep	1	1	1	1	1	1	1	1	Mouton
Libyan Arab Jamah.									**Jamah. arabe libyenne**
Cattle [1]	6	6	7	9	9	11	9	9	Bovine [1]
Chicken	99 [1]	99 [1]	99 [1]	94	120	120 [1]	125 [1]	129 [1]	Poulet
Goat [1]	9	10	11	12	12	12	12	13	Chèvre [1]
Sheep [1]	24	24	24	26	25	29	29	30	Mouton [1]
Madagascar [1]									**Madagascar** [1]
Cattle	115	115	134	134	135	150	150	150	Bovine
Chicken	36	36	36	36	37	37	38	38	Poulet
Goat	6	7	6	6	6	10	10	10	Chèvre
Pig	25	28	51	53	54	55	55	55	Porc
Sheep	3	3	3	3	3	3	3	3	Mouton
Malawi									**Malawi**
Cattle	23	21 [1]	21	24	27	29	30	34 [1]	Bovine
Chicken	11	16 [1]	16	11	14	19	21	22 [1]	Poulet
Goat	10	10 [1]	10	14	17	20	21	21 [1]	Chèvre
Pig	21 [1]	22 [1]	22 [1]	21 [1]	25	34	45 [1]	45 [1]	Porc
Sheep	^0	1 [1]	1	1	1	1	1	1 [1]	Mouton

Region, country or area	2003	2004	2005	2006	2007	2008	2009	2010	Région, pays ou zone
Mali[1]									**Mali**[1]
Cattle	94	77	108	106	112	129	136	144	Bovine
Chicken	34	35	36	37	34	39	41	41	Poulet
Goat	47	50	50	53	57	63	66	69	Chèvre
Pig	2	2	2	2	2	2	3	3	Porc
Sheep	34	35	33	38	40	41	45	46	Mouton
Mauritania									**Mauritanie**
Cattle	23[1]	24[1]	25[1]	26[1]	23[1]	*26	26[1]	26[1]	Bovine
Chicken[1]	4	4	4	4	4	4	4	4	Poulet[1]
Goat[1]	14	15	15	15	15	15	15	15	Chèvre[1]
Sheep[1]	24	25	25	28	28	23	23	29	Mouton[1]
Mauritius									**Maurice**
Cattle	3[1]	3[1]	3[1]	3[1]	2	2	2	2	Bovine
Chicken	30	33	33	36	40	42	44	46	Poulet
Pig	1	1	1	1	1	1	1	1	Porc
Morocco									**Maroc**
Cattle	150	140	157	160	160	180	190	192	Bovine
Chicken	320	325	370	370	380	440	490	560	Poulet
Goat	22	23	22	23	22	22	22	23	Chèvre
Pig[1]	1	1	1	1	1	1	1	1	Porc[1]
Sheep	105	105	115	120	120	121	134	139	Mouton
Mozambique[1]									**Mozambique**[1]
Cattle	15	17	19	16	22	19	19	19	Bovine
Chicken	23	20	19	22	22	22	22	23	Poulet
Goat	24	24	24	21	22	21	22	24	Chèvre
Pig	98	107	117	85	97	91	94	97	Porc
Sheep	1	1	1	1	1	1	1	1	Mouton
Namibia									**Namibie**
Cattle	52[1]	44[1]	40[1]	36	36	36	36	37[1]	Bovine
Chicken[1]	8	9	10	10	13	11	11	12	Poulet[1]
Goat[1]	5	5	3	4	3	4	4	4	Chèvre[1]
Pig[1]	2	2	3	3	4	4	4	4	Porc[1]
Sheep	8[1]	7	10[1]	11[1]	12[1]	12[1]	12[1]	12[1]	Mouton
Niger[1]									**Niger**[1]
Cattle	149	161	170	177	192	202	220	240	Bovine
Chicken	11	12	12	11	11	11	11	12	Poulet
Goat	41	42	47	48	50	53	58	61	Chèvre
Pig	1	1	1	1	1	1	1	1	Porc
Sheep	31	35	36	37	39	35	45	48	Mouton
Nigeria[1]									**Nigéria**[1]
Cattle	267	280	261	284	287	294	298	304	Bovine
Chicken	201	211	219	232	243	243	257	257	Poulet
Goat	245	252	257	264	271	277	284	291	Chèvre
Pig	179	186	193	201	209	218	226	226	Porc
Sheep	131	134	137	141	145	145	149	149	Mouton
Réunion									**Réunion**
Cattle	2	2	2	2	2	2	2[1]	2[1]	Bovine
Chicken	14	14	14	14	14[2]	15[1]	16[1]	17[1]	Poulet
Pig	12	13	13	13	13[1]	14[1]	14[1]	12[1]	Porc
Rwanda[1]									**Rwanda**[1]
Cattle	24	23	24	29	31	37	35	36	Bovine
Chicken	2	2	2	2	2	2	2	2	Poulet
Goat	3	4	5	5	6	6	7	7	Chèvre
Pig	4	6	6	6	6	6	7	8	Porc
Sheep	1	1	1	1	1	1	2	2	Mouton
Sao Tome and Principe									**Sao Tomé-et-Principe**
Chicken[1]	1	1	1	1	1	1	1	1	Poulet[1]

Meat production *(continued)*
Thousand metric tons

Production de viande *(suite)*
Milliers de tonnes

Region, country or area	2003	2004	2005	2006	2007	2008	2009	2010	Région, pays ou zone
Senegal									**Sénégal**
Cattle	43	43	47	63	49	66	82	84	Bovine
Chicken	25	26	29	32	37	41	43[1]	49[1]	Poulet
Goat	9	10	11	13	13	14	14[1]	15[1]	Chèvre
Pig	10	9	10	10	11	11	11[1]	11[1]	Porc
Sheep	15	15	17	21	22	21	18	19	Mouton
Seychelles									**Seychelles**
Chicken [1]	1	1	1	1	1	1	1	1	Poulet [1]
Pig	1[1]	1[1]	^0	^0	^0	^0	^0	^0	Porc
Sierra Leone [1]									**Sierra Leone** [1]
Cattle	5	6	6	8	8	8	9	9	Bovine
Chicken	11	11	11	12	12	12	12	12	Poulet
Goat	1	1	1	1	1	1	2	2	Chèvre
Pig	2	2	2	2	2	2	2	2	Porc
Sheep	1	1	1	1	1	1	2	2	Mouton
Somalia									**Somalie**
Cattle	64[1]	65[1]	68[1]	66[1]	*65	66[1]	66[1]	66[1]	Bovine
Chicken [1]	4	4	4	4	4	4	4	4	Poulet [1]
Goat [1]	40	40	39	42	42	42	42	42	Chèvre [1]
Sheep [1]	48	52	53	48	48	48	48	48	Mouton [1]
South Africa									**Afrique du Sud**
Cattle	610	655	705	804	805[1]	783	768	884	Bovine
Chicken	900	906	949	971	1 125[1]	1 328	1 388	1 472	Poulet
Goat [1]	39	36	37	37	36	37	36	35	Chèvre [1]
Pig	134	145	147	151	225	296	313	338[1]	Porc
Sheep	120	120	115	117	99[1]	135	139	140	Mouton
Sudan									**Soudan**
Cattle	586[1]	700[1]	850[1]	1 163	1 169	1 369	1 442	1 505[1]	Bovine
Chicken	29[1]	37[1]	31[1]	25	26	27	29	29[1]	Poulet
Goat	138	139	186	144	146	148	150	160[1]	Chèvre
Sheep	282	285	284	303	306	332	335	349[1]	Mouton
Swaziland									**Swaziland**
Cattle [1]	13	15	14	15	15	15	15	16	Bovine [1]
Chicken [1]	12	8	8	5	5	5	5	5	Poulet [1]
Goat [1]	2	2	2	2	2	2	2	2	Chèvre [1]
Pig [1]	2	1	1	2	2	2	2	2	Porc [1]
Togo [1]									**Togo** [1]
Cattle	7	8	8	8	9	9	9	9	Bovine
Chicken	15	16	18	19	21	20	26	28	Poulet
Goat	4	4	4	4	4	4	4	4	Chèvre
Pig	7	7	8	8	9	9	9	9	Porc
Sheep	4	4	4	4	4	4	5	5	Mouton
Tunisia									**Tunisie**
Cattle	58	53	53	56	52	54	52	52[1]	Bovine
Chicken	90	96	87	79	96	103	103	113	Poulet
Goat	9	9	11	11	11	10	10	9	Chèvre
Sheep	51	52	53	56	57	51	49	50	Mouton
Uganda									**Ouganda**
Cattle [1]	110	112	116	118	122	125	129	130	Bovine [1]
Chicken [1]	59	51	53	37	44	45	46	49	Poulet [1]
Goat	29[1]	29[1]	29	30	31	31	32	32[1]	Chèvre
Pig [1]	87	95	98	102	105	108	111	113	Porc [1]
Sheep [1]	6	8	8	8	8	9	9	9	Mouton [1]
United Rep. of Tanzania [1]									**Rép.-Unie de Tanzanie** [1]
Cattle	270	265	270	281	282	285	290	292	Bovine
Chicken	48	52	52	53	49	50	48	49	Poulet
Goat	31	32	32	32	32	32	32	33	Chèvre
Pig	13	13	13	13	14	14	14	14	Porc
Sheep	11	11	12	12	12	12	12	12	Mouton
Western Sahara									**Sahara occidental**
Goat [1]	1	1	1	1	1	1	1	1	Chèvre [1]

Region, country or area	2003	2004	2005	2006	2007	2008	2009	2010	Région, pays ou zone
Zambia									**Zambie**
Cattle	59[1]	56[1]	59[1]	58[1]	58[1]	*59	*60	61[1]	Bovine
Chicken [1]	39	39	39	37	37	39	40	43	Poulet [1]
Goat [1]	7	7	8	8	8	8	8	8	Chèvre [1]
Pig [1]	11	11	11	11	13	14	15	17	Porc [1]
Sheep [1]	1	1	1	1	1	1	1	1	Mouton [1]
Zimbabwe									**Zimbabwe**
Cattle [1]	99	102	102	102	104	104	104	100	Bovine [1]
Chicken [1]	40	46	52	53	57	61	62	62	Poulet [1]
Goat [1]	15	14	14	14	15	14	13	13	Chèvre [1]
Pig [1]	29	29	29	30	30	30	31	31	Porc [1]
Sheep	1[1]	1[1]	1[1]	^0	^0	^0	^0	^0	Mouton
Northern America									**Amérique septentrionale**
Cattle	**13 242**	**12 638**	**12 660**	**13 190**	**13 258**	**13 451**	**13 143**	**13 319**	**Bovine**
Chicken	**15 650**	**16 421**	**17 041**	**17 214**	**17 658**	**18 035**	**17 370**	**18 020**	**Poulet**
Pig	**10 938**	**11 239**	**11 303**	**11 449**	**11 849**	**12 547**	**12 385**	**12 112**	**Porc**
Sheep	**108**	**106**	**103**	**101**	**100**	**98**	**97**	**92**	**Mouton**
Canada									**Canada**
Cattle	1 203	1 504	1 464	1 327	1 279	1 288	1 252	1 272	Bovine
Chicken	954	970	1 000	997	1 030	1 041	1 036	1 048	Poulet
Pig	1 882	1 936	1 920	1 898	1 898	1 948	1 943	1 926	Porc
Sheep	16	18	18	17	17	16	16	16	Mouton
United States									**Etats-Unis**
Cattle	12 039	11 135	11 196	11 863	11 979	12 163	11 891	12 047	Bovine
Chicken	14 696	15 451	16 041	16 217	16 628	16 994	16 334	16 971	Poulet
Pig	9 056	9 303	9 383	9 550	9 951	10 599	10 442	10 186	Porc
Sheep	92[2]	88	85	84	83	82	80	76	Mouton
Latin America and the Caribbean									**Amérique latine et Caraïbes**
Cattle	**14 373**	**15 449**	**16 682**	**17 324**	**17 808**	**15 192**	**15 519**	**15 228**	**Bovine**
Chicken	**14 384**	**15 829**	**15 653**	**16 466**	**17 673**	**19 350**	**19 354**	**20 360**	**Poulet**
Goat	**125**	**127**	**130**	**131**	**129**	**130**	**130**	**129**	**Chèvre**
Pig	**5 733**	**5 829**	**5 699**	**5 902**	**6 300**	**6 089**	**6 357**	**6 514**	**Porc**
Sheep	**287**	**289**	**308**	**302**	**300**	**306**	**312**	**315**	**Mouton**
Antigua and Barbuda [1]									**Antigua-et-Barbuda** [1]
Cattle	1	1	1	1	1	1	1	1	Bovine
Argentina									**Argentine**
Cattle	2 658	3 024	3 131	3 034	3 224	3 132	3 378	2 630	Bovine
Chicken	738	866	1 010	1 159	1 244	1 400	1 501	1 598	Poulet
Goat [1]	10	10	10	10	10	10	10	10	Chèvre [1]
Pig	150	160[1]	185[1]	230[1]	240[1]	274	289	281	Porc
Sheep [1]	52	45	52	50	49	46	45	46	Mouton [1]
Bahamas [1]									**Bahamas** [1]
Chicken	8	8	6	7	7	7	7	7	Poulet
Barbados									**Barbade**
Chicken	12	14	15	14	14[1]	14[1]	14[1]	14[1]	Poulet
Pig	2	2	2	3	3[1]	3[1]	3[1]	3[1]	Porc
Belize									**Belize**
Cattle	2	3	2	2	2	2	2	2[1]	Bovine
Chicken	14	14	14	14	13	13	13	13[1]	Poulet
Pig	1	1	1	1	1	1	1	1[1]	Porc
Bolivia (Plurinational State of)									**Bolivie (État plurin. de)**
Cattle	168	172	175[1]	200[1]	244	249	255	247[1]	Bovine
Chicken	135	141[1]	154[1]	140[1]	151[1]	166[1]	166[1]	168[1]	Poulet
Goat [1]	6	6	6	6	6	6	6	6	Chèvre [1]
Pig	104[1]	108[1]	108[1]	110[1]	112	114	117	118[1]	Porc
Sheep	18	18	18[1]	19[1]	20[1]	20[1]	21[1]	21[1]	Mouton
Brazil									**Brésil**
Cattle	7 230	7 774	8 592[2]	9 020[2]	9 303[2]	6 621	6 662	6 977	Bovine
Chicken	7 760	8 668	7 866	8 164	8 988	10 216	9 940	10 693	Poulet
Goat [1]	29	31	33	34	29	29	30	30	Chèvre [1]
Pig	3 059	3 110	2 800[2]	2 830[2]	2 990[2]	2 636	2 930	3 078	Porc
Sheep [1]	68	76	80	77	78	79	80	81	Mouton [1]

Region, country or area	2003	2004	2005	2006	2007	2008	2009	2010	Région, pays ou zone
Chile									**Chili**
Cattle	192	208	216	238	242	240	210	211	Bovine
Chicken	389	446	457	523	486	510	513	504	Poulet
Goat [1]	5	5	5	5	6	6	6	6	Chèvre [1]
Pig	365	373	411	468	499	522	514	498	Porc
Sheep	10	10	9	11	10	11	11	11	Mouton
Colombia									**Colombie**
Cattle	642	717	792	827	856	917	936	930[1]	Bovine
Chicken	678	709	763	850	925	1 011	1 020	1 000[1]	Poulet
Goat [1]	7	7	7	7	7	7	7	7	Chèvre [1]
Pig	124	130	128	148	177	170	179	180[1]	Porc
Sheep [1]	8	9	10	7	7	7	8	8	Mouton [1]
Costa Rica									**Costa Rica**
Cattle	74	70	81	75	81	88	93	97	Bovine
Chicken	72	84	91	98	110	107	111	105	Poulet
Pig	36	38	39	41	48	52	54	54	Porc
Cuba									**Cuba**
Cattle	56	55	60	56	54	62	65	64	Bovine
Chicken	34	36	29	31	34	33	33	34	Poulet
Goat	3	3	3	3	4	4	3	2	Chèvre
Pig	94	98	97	100	177	193	179	172	Porc
Sheep	7	7	7	7	8	9	9	9	Mouton
Dominica [1]									**Dominique** [1]
Cattle	1	1	1	1	1	1	1	1	Bovine
Dominican Republic									**Rép. dominicaine**
Cattle	69	71	73	84	101	99	102	100[1]	Bovine
Chicken	157	238	297	313	329	299	315	315[1]	Poulet
Goat [1]	1	1	1	1	1	1	1	1	Chèvre [1]
Pig	64	52	83	101	94	91	82	87[1]	Porc
Ecuador									**Equateur**
Cattle	206	207	209	211	233	248	245[1]	238[1]	Bovine
Chicken	211	208	210	300	336	330[1]	329[1]	341[1]	Poulet
Goat	1	1	1	1	1	1	1[1]	1[1]	Chèvre
Pig	154	161	162	163	189	213	180[1]	185[1]	Porc
Sheep	15	11	9	9	8	8	8[1]	8[1]	Mouton
El Salvador									**El Salvador**
Cattle	29	26	27	31	31	32	31	33	Bovine
Chicken	79	92	99	101	107	96	98	105	Poulet
Pig	8	8	11	14	9	9	8	8	Porc
Falkland Is. (Malvinas) [1]									**Iles Falkland (Malvinas)** [1]
Sheep	1	1	1	1	1	1	1	1	Mouton
French Guiana									**Guyane française**
Chicken	^0	^0	^0	^0	^0	1[1]	1[1]	1[1]	Poulet
Pig	1[1]	1[1]	^0	^0	^0	^0	^0	^0	Porc
French Polynesia									**Polynésie française**
Chicken [1]	1	1	1	1	1	1	1	1	Poulet [1]
Pig	1	1	1	1	1	1	1	1[1]	Porc
Grenada [1]									**Grenade** [1]
Chicken	1	1	1	1	1	1	1	1	Poulet
Guadeloupe									**Guadeloupe**
Cattle	3[2]	3[2]	3[2]	3[2]	3	3	3[1]	3[1]	Bovine
Chicken	1[1]	1[1]	1[2]	1[2]	1[2]	1[1]	1[1]	1[1]	Poulet
Pig	1[2]	1[2]	1	1	2	2	2[1]	2[1]	Porc
Guatemala									**Guatemala**
Cattle	*50	*63	68[1]	65[1]	69	74	75[1]	75[1]	Bovine
Chicken	155[1]	147	151	168	151[1]	166[1]	166[1]	167[1]	Poulet
Pig [1]	58	58	67	58	58	58	55	56	Porc [1]
Sheep [1]	1	1	1	1	1	1	1	1	Mouton [1]

Region, country or area	2003	2004	2005	2006	2007	2008	2009	2010	Région, pays ou zone
Guyana									**Guyana**
Cattle [1]	2	2	2	2	2	2	2	2	Bovine [1]
Chicken	24	24	23	21	25	23	23[1]	23[1]	Poulet
Pig	^0	^0	^0	1[1]	1[1]	1[1]	*1	1[1]	Porc
Sheep [1]	1	1	1	1	1	1	1	1	Mouton [1]
Haiti [1]									**Haïti** [1]
Cattle	43	43	44	44	44	44	44	45	Bovine
Chicken	8	8	8	8	8	8	8	8	Poulet
Goat	7	6	6	6	7	7	6	6	Chèvre
Pig	33	33	33	33	33	33	33	35	Porc
Sheep	1	1	1	1	1	1	1	1	Mouton
Honduras									**Honduras**
Cattle	61	64	66	68	71	74	56	59	Bovine
Chicken	117	129	141	127	134	142	145	152	Poulet
Pig	8	9	9	11	11	12	14	10	Porc
Jamaica									**Jamaïque**
Cattle	14	11	10	6	6	6	5	5	Bovine
Chicken	94	96	102	105	107	107	105	102	Poulet
Goat	1	1	1	1	1	1	1	1	Chèvre
Pig	6	7	9	8	7	9	9	8	Porc
Martinique									**Martinique**
Cattle	2	2[1]	2	2	1	1[1]	1[1]	1[1]	Bovine
Chicken	1[1]	1[1]	1	1	1	1[1]	1[1]	1[1]	Poulet
Pig	2[1]	*2	1	1	1	1	1[1]	1[1]	Porc
Mexico									**Mexique**
Cattle	1 504	1 544	1 558	1 613	1 635	1 667	1 705	1 745	Bovine
Chicken	2 116	2 280	2 437	2 464	2 542	2 581	2 636	2 681	Poulet
Goat	42	42	42	43	43	43	43	44	Chèvre
Pig	1 035	1 064	1 103	1 109	1 152	1 161	1 162	1 175	Porc
Sheep	42	44	46	48	49	51	54	55	Mouton
Montserrat [1]									**Montserrat** [1]
Cattle	1	1	1	1	1	1	1	1	Bovine
Nicaragua									**Nicaragua**
Cattle	66	75	76	85	93	96	108	121	Bovine
Chicken	62	67	71	84	90	91	90	102	Poulet
Pig	6	7	7	7	7	7	7	8	Porc
Panama									**Panama**
Cattle	61	64	66	67	65	68	75	79	Bovine
Chicken	87	87	95	96	113	115	119	126	Poulet
Pig	20	21	21	25	30	35	31	30	Porc
Paraguay									**Paraguay**
Cattle	229	215	249	300	265	276[1]	315[1]	385[1]	Bovine
Chicken [1]	37	42	42	45	28	35	36	37	Poulet [1]
Goat [1]	1	1	1	1	1	1	1	1	Chèvre [1]
Pig [1]	153	148	152	156	149	175	187	200	Porc [1]
Sheep [1]	3	3	3	3	3	3	3	3	Mouton [1]
Peru									**Pérou**
Cattle	138	146	153	163	163	163	165	172	Bovine
Chicken	578	579	656	710	770	877	964	1 020	Poulet
Goat	6	7	7	7	7	6	6	6	Chèvre
Pig	93	98	103	109	115	115	115	116	Porc
Sheep	32	34	34	34	34	33	33	34	Mouton
Puerto Rico									**Porto Rico**
Cattle	10	13	10	10[1]	10[1]	10[1]	*10	10[1]	Bovine
Chicken	47	50	50	50[1]	52[1]	52[1]	52[1]	52[1]	Poulet
Pig	9	12	11	11[1]	11[1]	12[1]	*12	12[1]	Porc
Saint Lucia [1]									**Sainte-Lucie** [1]
Chicken	1	1	2	1	2	2	2	2	Poulet
Pig	1	1	1	1	1	1	1	1	Porc

Region, country or area	2003	2004	2005	2006	2007	2008	2009	2010	Région, pays ou zone
Saint Vincent-Grenadines[1]									**Saint Vincent-Grenadines**[1]
Pig	1	1	1	1	1	1	1	1	Porc
Suriname									**Suriname**
Cattle	2	1	1	2	2	2	2	2	Bovine
Chicken	6	6	7	6	10	8	9	11	Poulet
Pig	1	2	2	2	2	2	2	2	Porc
Trinidad and Tobago									**Trinité-et-Tobago**
Cattle	1	1[1]	1[1]	1[1]	1[1]	1[1]	1[1]	1[1]	Bovine
Chicken	57	58	65[1]	68[1]	60[1]	60[1]	60[1]	57[1]	Poulet
Pig	3	3[1]	3[1]	3[1]	3[1]	3[1]	3[1]	3[1]	Porc
United States Virgin Is.									**Iles Vierges américaines**
Cattle	^0	^0	^0	^0	1[1]	*1	1[1]	1[1]	Bovine
Uruguay									**Uruguay**
Cattle	424	496	590[1]	600[2]	523	527	491	524	Bovine
Chicken[1]	31	41	52	60	50	75	73	69	Poulet[1]
Pig	17	17	20	19	21	21	17	18	Porc
Sheep	27	27	33[1]	31[1]	27	30	33	32[2]	Mouton
Venezuela (Boliv. Rep. of)									**Venezuela (Rép. boliv. du)**
Cattle	435	376	425	516	481	483	480[1]	466[1]	Bovine
Chicken	676	686	739	735	780	802	800[1]	848[1]	Poulet
Goat	5	5	6	6	6	6	6[1]	6[1]	Chèvre
Pig	120	101	126	137	154	164	165[1]	169[1]	Porc
Sheep	2	2	3	3	3	3	3[1]	3[1]	Mouton
Asia									**Asie**
Buffalo	**2 578**	**2 663**	**2 732**	**2 852**	**2 951**	**2 941**	**3 011**	**3 077**	**Buffle**
Cattle	**10 759**	**11 234**	**11 257**	**11 714**	**12 361**	**12 586**	**13 015**	**13 385**	**Bovine**
Chicken	**20 953**	**21 148**	**22 492**	**23 543**	**24 914**	**26 349**	**27 233**	**28 642**	**Poulet**
Goat	**2 844**	**3 133**	**3 302**	**3 255**	**3 384**	**3 517**	**3 620**	**3 658**	**Chèvre**
Pig	**51 990**	**53 073**	**55 606**	**57 150**	**53 829**	**57 117**	**60 002**	**61 916**	**Porc**
Sheep	**3 683**	**3 734**	**3 837**	**4 013**	**4 227**	**4 162**	**4 310**	**4 371**	**Mouton**
Afghanistan									**Afghanistan**
Cattle	137	149	141	117	137	133	135	134[1]	Bovine
Chicken[1]	28	31	32	24	18	21	21	21	Poulet[1]
Goat[1]	48	49	46	44	35	42	38	38	Chèvre[1]
Sheep[1]	74	82	88	75	66	87	100	100	Mouton[1]
Armenia									**Arménie**
Cattle	30	33	34	40	43	49	50	49	Bovine
Chicken	5	4	5	5	6	7	5	5	Poulet
Pig	12	9	9	14	13	8	9	9	Porc
Sheep	6	7	8	7	7	7	7	7	Mouton
Azerbaijan									**Azerbaïdjan**
Cattle	67	69	71	73	75	77	103	114	Bovine
Chicken	27	32	35	36	49	52	67	64	Poulet
Pig	1	2	2	1	1	1	1	1	Porc
Sheep	39	41	42	44	45	46	67	74	Mouton
Bahrain									**Bahreïn**
Cattle	1[1]	1	1[1]	1[1]	1[1]	1[1]	1[1]	1[1]	Bovine
Chicken	5	5	5	4	5	6	6	6[1]	Poulet
Sheep[1]	7	6	11	6	10	13	14	17	Mouton[1]
Bangladesh[1]									**Bangladesh**[1]
Buffalo	5	5	5	5	5	6	6	6	Buffle
Cattle	180	181	183	184	186	187	188	189	Bovine
Chicken	116	123	130	138	147	151	157	162	Poulet
Goat	147	158	169	182	195	210	225	242	Chèvre
Sheep	3	3	3	3	3	4	4	4	Mouton
Bhutan[1]									**Bhutan**[1]
Cattle	5	5	5	5	5	5	5	5	Bovine
Pig	1	1	1	1	1	1	1	1	Porc
Brunei Darussalam									**Brunéi Darussalam**
Cattle[1]	3	3	2	1	1	1	1	1	Bovine[1]
Chicken[1]	14	16	14	16	18	19	19	19	Poulet[1]

Meat production *(continued)*
Thousand metric tons

Production de viande *(suite)*
Milliers de tonnes

Region, country or area	2003	2004	2005	2006	2007	2008	2009	2010	Région, pays ou zone
Cambodia[1]									**Cambodge**[1]
Buffalo	10	9	10	10	11	10	10	10	Buffle
Cattle	54	55	57	60	61	62	65	63	Bovine
Chicken	18	18	17	17	18	19	19	20	Poulet
Pig	117	123	135	139	120	110	105	100	Porc
China[4]									**Chine**[4]
Buffalo	305[2]	330[2]	345	288[2]	307[2]	306[2]	309[2]	310[2]	Buffle
Cattle[2]	5 141	5 295	5 357	5 499	5 846	5 841	6 061	6 236	Bovine[2]
Chicken[2]	9 448	9 484	9 965	10 165	10 728	11 304	11 443	11 841	Poulet[2]
Goat[2]	1 360	1 568	1 704	1 704	1 760	1 828	1 853	1 873	Chèvre[2]
Pig	43 433	44 479	46 622	47 591	43 933	47 190	49 874	51 677	Porc
Sheep[2]	1 730	1 764	1 800	1 938	2 070	1 978	2 044	2 070	Mouton[2]
Cyprus									**Chypre**
Cattle	4	4	4	4	4	4	4	4	Bovine
Chicken	33	32	33	27	28	28	27	27	Poulet
Goat	5	4	4	4	4	4	3	2	Chèvre
Pig	54	55	55	53	55	59	58	57	Porc
Sheep	3	3	3	3	3	3	3	3	Mouton
Dem. P. R. Korea[1]									**R. p. dém. de Corée**[1]
Cattle	22	21	21	22	22	22	22	22	Bovine
Chicken	36	37	36	35	34	32	32	32	Poulet
Goat	11	11	12	13	13	14	15	15	Chèvre
Pig	163	165	168	150	130	110	110	110	Porc
Sheep	1	1	1	1	1	1	1	1	Mouton
Georgia									**Géorgie**
Cattle	50	50	49	33	31	25	29	27	Bovine
Chicken	13	15	17	11	12	13	12	12	Poulet
Pig	37	35	33	31	21	11	8	13	Porc
Sheep	8	9	10	8[2]	7[2]	7[2]	4[2]	5[2]	Mouton
India									**Inde**
Buffalo[1]	1 311	1 335	1 360	1 384	1 410	1 436	1 463	1 463	Buffle[1]
Cattle[1]	947	964	982	1 000	1 018	1 037	1 056	1 087	Bovine[1]
Chicken	936[2]	1 172[2]	1 403[2]	1 512[2]	1 713	1 815	2 026	2 300[1]	Poulet
Goat[1]	473	487	502	518	534	550	568	587	Chèvre[1]
Pig[1]	470	445	425	405	385	368	350	333	Porc[1]
Sheep[1]	229	238	246	255	265	275	286	289	Mouton[1]
Indonesia									**Indonésie**
Buffalo	41	40	38	44	42	39	35	40[1]	Buffle
Cattle	370	448	359	396	339	393	408	421[1]	Bovine
Chicken	1 118	1 191	1 126	1 260	1 296	1 350	1 409	1 650[1]	Poulet
Goat	64	57	51	65	64	66	74	76[1]	Chèvre
Pig[1]	495	484	550	589	597	637	637	637	Porc[1]
Sheep	81	66	66	75	57	47	54	55[1]	Mouton
Iran (Islamic Rep. of)									**Iran (Rép. islamique d')**
Buffalo[1]	15	17	17	18	19	19	19	19	Buffle[1]
Cattle	314	337	343[2]	356[2]	372[2]	373[2]	387[2]	392[1]	Bovine
Chicken	1 104	1 152	1 237	1 360	1 468	1 566	1 610	1 650	Poulet
Goat	113	115	122[2]	125[2]	130[2]	132[2]	137[2]	138[1]	Chèvre
Sheep	304	312	318[2]	330[2]	345[2]	346[2]	359[2]	360[1]	Mouton
Iraq									**Iraq**
Buffalo[1]	1	1	1	3	1	1	1	1	Buffle[1]
Cattle	34	43	47	41	31	43	48[1]	50[1]	Bovine
Chicken	25	46	85	60	81	49	49[1]	50[1]	Poulet
Goat[1]	4	4	5	6	11	14	15	15	Chèvre[1]
Sheep[1]	29	20	26	30	42	47	47	47	Mouton[1]
Israel									**Israël**
Cattle	91	83	90	108	105	117	104	108	Bovine
Chicken	334	350	370	402	420	440	436	450	Poulet
Goat	2	3	3	4	4	4	4	4	Chèvre
Pig	17	18	19	18	18	18	20	19	Porc
Sheep[1]	7	6	6	6	6	6	6	6	Mouton[1]

Region, country or area	2003	2004	2005	2006	2007	2008	2009	2010	Région, pays ou zone
Japan									**Japon**
Cattle	496	514	499	497	504	520	517	513	Bovine
Chicken	1 240	1 242	1 273	1 367	1 366	1 369	1 394	1 401[2]	Poulet
Pig	1 274	1 263	1 245	1 247	1 251	1 249	1 310	1 291	Porc
Jordan									**Jordanie**
Cattle	10	16	8	15	14	19	13[1]	14[1]	Bovine
Chicken	123	127	133	116	134	140	141[1]	155[1]	Poulet
Goat	2	3	2	2	3	4	4[1]	3[1]	Chèvre
Sheep	13	15	13	13	20	15	13[1]	14[1]	Mouton
Kazakhstan									**Kazakhstan**
Cattle	312	330	348	367	386	400	396	407	Bovine
Chicken	38	41	46	65	64	65	79	103	Poulet
Goat	9[2]	11[2]	13[2]	17	19	21	19	20	Chèvre
Pig	185	199	197	193	194	206	209	206	Porc
Sheep	87[2]	91[2]	94[2]	99	104	110	116	123	Mouton
Kuwait									**Koweït**
Cattle	3[1]	3[1]	2[1]	3[1]	2[3]	2[3]	3[1]	3[1]	Bovine
Chicken	37	40[1]	32	42[1]	45[1]	43[1]	43[1]	46[1]	Poulet
Goat	1[1]	1[1]	1	1[1]	1[1]	1[1]	1[1]	1[1]	Chèvre
Sheep	31[1]	30[1]	34	30[1]	32[1]	30[1]	30[1]	30[1]	Mouton
Kyrgyzstan									**Kirghizistan**
Cattle	94	95	91	91	91	93	97	99	Bovine
Chicken	6	5	5	5	5	6	4	4	Poulet
Goat	7	7	7	7[2]	7	7	8	6[2]	Chèvre
Pig	22	25	19	20	20	19	17	16	Porc
Sheep	37	38	39	39[2]	40	40	41	41[2]	Mouton
Lao People's Dem. Rep.									**Rép. dém. pop. lao**
Buffalo	18	19[1]	18[1]	18[1]	18[1]	19[1]	19[1]	19[1]	Buffle
Cattle	22	21[1]	23[1]	23[1]	24[1]	26[1]	25[1]	25[1]	Bovine
Chicken	14	15[1]	15[1]	16[1]	16[1]	17[1]	17[1]	17[1]	Poulet
Goat [1]	1	1	1	1	1	1	1	1	Chèvre [1]
Pig	36	37[1]	39[1]	43[1]	46[1]	54[1]	65[1]	73[1]	Porc
Lebanon									**Liban**
Cattle [1]	56	53	61	52	47	47	66	66	Bovine [1]
Chicken	119	129	122	132	135	136[1]	136[1]	140[1]	Poulet
Goat [1]	3	3	3	3	4	4	4	4	Chèvre [1]
Pig	1	1	1	1	1	1[1]	1[1]	1[1]	Porc
Sheep [1]	15	12	8	7	8	8	8	8	Mouton [1]
Malaysia									**Malaisie**
Buffalo [1]	4	5	5	5	4	4	4	4	Buffle [1]
Cattle [1]	20	21	22	22	22	23	23	25	Bovine [1]
Chicken	765	825	860[2]	922[2]	931[2]	1 163	1 202	1 296	Poulet
Goat [1]	1	1	1	1	1	1	1	2	Chèvre [1]
Pig	198	203	200[1]	217	200	195	206	234	Porc
Mongolia									**Mongolie**
Cattle	44	52	45	44	47	54	59	48	Bovine
Goat	19[2]	33[2]	37	33	39	48	78	49	Chèvre
Sheep	62[2]	65[2]	57	55	68	72	91	77	Mouton
Myanmar									**Myanmar**
Buffalo	18	21	24	27	29	32	40[1]	40[1]	Buffle
Cattle	97	94	106	120	130	140	143[1]	144[1]	Bovine
Chicken	380	457	561	650	726	798	800[1]	826[1]	Poulet
Goat	12	15	17	19	22	24	24[1]	25[1]	Chèvre
Pig	221	261	328	370	411	463	450[1]	459[1]	Porc
Sheep	3	4	5	5	5	5	5[1]	5[1]	Mouton
Nepal									**Népal**
Buffalo	131	134	139	142	147	152	157	162	Buffle
Cattle [1]	48	48	49	49	49	49	50	50	Bovine [1]
Chicken	15	16	15	16	16	17	17	17	Poulet
Goat	40	41	42	43	45	46	48	50	Chèvre
Pig	16	15	16	16	16	16	17	17	Porc
Sheep	3	3	3	3	3	3	3	3	Mouton

Region, country or area	2003	2004	2005	2006	2007	2008	2009	2010	Région, pays ou zone
Occupied Palestinian Terr.									**Terr. palestinien occupé**
Cattle	7[1]	5	5	5	5	5	5[1]	5[1]	Bovine
Chicken	63	57	69	54	45	47	47[1]	49[1]	Poulet
Goat[1]	5	5	5	5	5	5	5	5	Chèvre[1]
Sheep[1]	13	12	12	13	12	12	11	11	Mouton[1]
Oman									**Oman**
Cattle	4[1]	4[1]	4[1]	4[1]	*4	4[1]	5[1]	5[1]	Bovine
Chicken[1]	6	6	6	5	6	6	6	6	Poulet[1]
Goat[1]	10	14	14	14	14	14	15	15	Chèvre[1]
Sheep	12[1]	11[1]	14[1]	12	13	20[1]	20[1]	20[1]	Mouton
Pakistan									**Pakistan**
Buffalo	508	524	540	668	688	708	730	760	Buffle
Cattle	445	455	464	632	656	680	706	730	Bovine
Chicken	372	378	384	512	553	600	650	705	Poulet
Goat	345	357	370	250	256	263	270	275	Chèvre
Sheep	161	161	162	149	151	152	154	158	Mouton
Philippines									**Philippines**
Buffalo	76	80	77	84	110	99	99[1]	106[1]	Buffle
Cattle	181	179	173	167	178	180	184[2]	188[2]	Bovine
Chicken	635	658	650	658	662	741	715[2]	744[2]	Poulet
Goat	33	34	36	45	50	53	54[1]	55[1]	Chèvre
Pig	1 385	1 366	1 415	1 565	1 617	1 606	1 596[2]	1 613[2]	Porc
Qatar									**Qatar**
Chicken	5	5[1]	5[1]	5[1]	5[1]	5[1]	5[1]	6[1]	Poulet
Goat[1]	1	1	1	1	1	2	2	2	Chèvre[1]
Sheep[1]	7	6	8	8	8	9	9	9	Mouton[1]
Republic of Korea									**République de Corée**
Cattle	188	186	195	200	219	246	283	308[1]	Bovine
Chicken	383[2]	386[2]	484[2]	510[2]	513[2]	488[2]	498[2]	514[1]	Poulet
Goat[1]	3	3	3	3	2	2	2	2	Chèvre[1]
Pig	1 149[2]	960	899	1 000[2]	1 043[2]	1 056[2]	1 062[2]	1 097[2]	Porc
Saudi Arabia									**Arabie saoudite**
Cattle	22[2]	22	22	21[1]	29[1]	29[1]	32[1]	31[1]	Bovine
Chicken[2]	468	480	537	548	559	564	570	575	Poulet[2]
Goat[1]	22	24	24	21	24	18	18	16	Chèvre[1]
Sheep[1]	76	78	81	79	78	70	64	67	Mouton[1]
Singapore									**Singapour**
Chicken[1]	86	69	76	76	83	83	86	89	Poulet[1]
Pig	19	20	20	16	19	19	17	19	Porc
Sri Lanka									**Sri Lanka**
Buffalo[1]	3	4	4	4	4	4	4	5	Buffle[1]
Cattle	29	28	29	26	24	22	23	24[1]	Bovine
Chicken	88	95	97	79	100	103	99	99[1]	Poulet
Goat	1	1	1	1	1	1	1	1[1]	Chèvre
Pig	2	2	2	2	2	2	2	2[1]	Porc
Syrian Arab Republic									**Rép. arabe syrienne**
Cattle	47	48	55	60	66	64	63	66[1]	Bovine
Chicken	159	170	162	174	173	179	182	190	Poulet
Goat	7	7	7	7	8	8	8	9[1]	Chèvre
Sheep	153	161	180	187	205	185	190	198[1]	Mouton
Tajikistan									**Tadjikistan**
Cattle	25	27	27	24	25	25	26	29	Bovine
Chicken	^0	^0	^0	1	1	1	4	1	Poulet
Pig	...	...	...	3	3	3	3	3	Porc
Sheep	20	21	27	29	30	36	37	39	Mouton
Thailand									**Thaïlande**
Buffalo	33	37	44	45	41	32	34	46	Buffle
Cattle	112	116	111	118	142	173	177	177	Bovine
Chicken	1 264	869	1 007	1 069	1 107	1 158	1 154	1 220	Poulet
Goat[1]	1	1	1	1	2	1	1	1	Chèvre[1]
Pig	867	872	894	935	1 041	903	809	862	Porc

Region, country or area	2003	2004	2005	2006	2007	2008	2009	2010	Région, pays ou zone
Timor-Leste [1]									**Timor-Leste** [1]
Buffalo	1	1	1	1	1	1	1	1	Buffle
Cattle	1	1	1	1	1	1	1	1	Bovine
Chicken	1	1	1	1	1	1	1	1	Poulet
Pig	8	8	8	8	9	9	9	10	Porc
Turkey									**Turquie**
Buffalo	2	2	2	2	2	1	1	1[1]	Buffle
Cattle	290	365	322	341	432	371	325	322[2]	Bovine
Chicken	872	877	937	918	1 068	1 088	1 293	1 444	Poulet
Goat [1]	45	56	43	46	58	42	37	37	Chèvre [1]
Sheep [1]	267	273	272	288	280	278	262	259	Mouton [1]
Turkmenistan									**Turkménistan**
Cattle	101[2]	100[1]	104[1]	102[1]	138[2]	136[2]	140[2]	148[1]	Bovine
Chicken	12[2]	13[1]	14[1]	17[1]	19[2]	19[2]	20[2]	22[1]	Poulet
Goat	6[2]	7[1]	7[1]	7[1]	9[2]	10[2]	10[2]	10[1]	Chèvre
Sheep	90[2]	95[1]	90[1]	93[1]	125[2]	124[2]	128[2]	130[1]	Mouton
United Arab Emirates [1]									**Emirats arabes unis** [1]
Cattle	25	26	10	5	10	5	6	6	Bovine
Chicken	41	35	34	29	26	36	36	36	Poulet
Goat	17	22	16	29	25	37	37	37	Chèvre
Sheep	14	8	13	11	7	7	7	7	Mouton
Uzbekistan									**Ouzbékistan**
Cattle	456	494	518	552	551[2]	586[2]	623[2]	665[2]	Bovine
Chicken	16	17	21	23	22[2]	24[2]	25[2]	27[2]	Poulet
Pig	11	14	16	18	18[2]	19[2]	20[2]	21[2]	Porc
Sheep	74	70	74	84	83[2]	88[2]	93[2]	100[2]	Mouton
Viet Nam									**Viet Nam**
Buffalo	97[1]	101[1]	103[1]	103[1]	110[1]	72	79	84	Buffle
Cattle	108	120	142	159	206	227	263	279	Bovine
Chicken	373	316	322	344	359	448	529	457	Poulet
Goat [1]	6	8	9	11	11	9	9	9	Chèvre [1]
Pig	1 795	2 012[2]	2 288	2 505	2 663	2 783	3 036	3 036	Porc
Yemen									**Yémen**
Cattle	70	71	73	73	82	90	97	108	Bovine
Chicken	109	111	113	118	129	136	140	144	Poulet
Goat	22	22	23	23	26	30	32	35	Chèvre
Sheep	23	23	24	24	27	29	31	34	Mouton
Europe									**Europe**
Buffalo	**2**	**3**	**6**	**1**	**4**	**3**	**6**	**7**	**Buffle**
Cattle	**11 665**	**11 544**	**11 166**	**11 090**	**11 142**	**11 000**	**10 908**	**11 034**	**Bovine**
Chicken	**10 094**	**10 410**	**10 711**	**10 773**	**11 719**	**12 121**	**13 410**	**13 766**	**Poulet**
Goat	**126**	**136**	**131**	**126**	**128**	**125**	**127**	**129**	**Chèvre**
Pig	**25 774**	**25 275**	**25 180**	**25 078**	**26 396**	**26 402**	**26 013**	**26 968**	**Porc**
Sheep	**1 262**	**1 289**	**1 287**	**1 271**	**1 265**	**1 237**	**1 191**	**1 167**	**Mouton**
Albania									**Albanie**
Cattle	40	40[2]	41	49	50	40[2]	39[2]	41[2]	Bovine
Chicken	8	9	9	10	13	16	17	17	Poulet
Goat	7	8[2]	8[2]	7	9[2]	6[2]	6[2]	7[2]	Chèvre
Pig	9[2]	10[2]	11	11	13[2]	13[2]	13[2]	13[2]	Porc
Sheep	12	14[2]	13	14	18[2]	15[2]	16[2]	14[2]	Mouton
Austria									**Autriche**
Cattle	208	206	204	216	218	224	218	225	Bovine
Chicken	88	89	89	85	95	97	101	97	Poulet
Goat	1	1	1	1	1	1	1	1[1]	Chèvre
Pig	663[1]	657[1]	642[1]	586[1]	613[1]	533	540	542	Porc
Sheep	7	7	7	7	6	7	7	7	Mouton
Belarus									**Bélarus**
Cattle	211	224	256	272	274	269	308	309	Bovine
Chicken	87	101	115	145	165	192[2]	219[2]	258[2]	Poulet
Pig	301	299	321	346	372	376	388	398	Porc
Sheep	2	2	1	1	1	1	1	1	Mouton

Meat production *(continued)*
Thousand metric tons

Production de viande *(suite)*
Milliers de tonnes

Region, country or area	2003	2004	2005	2006	2007	2008	2009	2010	Région, pays ou zone
Belgium									**Belgique**
Cattle	275	281	267	287	288	267	255	263	Bovine
Chicken	424	468	450[1]	484[1]	448[1]	450[1]	460	461[1]	Poulet
Pig	1 026	1 054	1 013	1 001	1 061	1 056	1 082	1 124	Porc
Sheep	3	4	3	3	3	3[2]	2[2]	3[2]	Mouton
Bosnia and Herzegovina									**Bosnie-Herzégovine**
Cattle	18[1]	19	24	22	24	26	23	23	Bovine
Chicken	12[1]	16	12	14	20	29	33	38	Poulet
Pig	7[2]	8	9	10	9	9	10	13	Porc
Sheep	2[2]	1	2	2	2	2	2	2	Mouton
Bulgaria									**Bulgarie**
Cattle	29	31	30	23	22	20	22	20	Bovine
Chicken	60	71	80	87	98	91	110	86	Poulet
Goat	7	6	7	6	6	5	4	4	Chèvre
Pig	71	78	75	75	76	74	74	70	Porc
Sheep	13	14	18	18	15	16	13	13	Mouton
Croatia									**Croatie**
Cattle	28	32	33	36	33	36[2]	37[2]	38[2]	Bovine
Chicken [2]	41	39	31	30	31	31	29	22	Poulet [2]
Pig	62[2]	80[1]	112[2]	112[2]	128[2]	121[2]	131[2]	121[2]	Porc
Sheep	3	2	3[2]	3[2]	3[2]	2[2]	2[2]	2[2]	Mouton
Czech Republic									**République tchèque**
Cattle	104	97	81	80	79	80	77	74	Bovine
Chicken	198	201	213	207	201	195	188	185	Poulet
Pig	411	426	380	359	360	336	300	291	Porc
Sheep	1	1	1	2	2	2	2	2	Mouton
Denmark									**Danemark**
Cattle	147	150	136	129	130	129	128	133	Bovine
Chicken	188	187	183	166	172	176	169	186	Poulet
Pig	1 762	1 810	1 793	1 749	1 802	1 707	1 585	1 668	Porc
Sheep	2	2	2	2	2	2	2	2	Mouton
Estonia									**Estonie**
Cattle	13	15	13	15	15	14	14	12	Bovine
Chicken	14	15	14	12	12	13	15	16	Poulet
Pig	40	41	40	42	43	39	33	34	Porc
Sheep	^0	^0	^0	1	1	1	1	1	Mouton
Faeroe Islands [1]									**Iles Féroé** [1]
Sheep	1	1	1	1	1	1	1	1	Mouton
Finland									**Finlande**
Cattle	96	93	87	87	89	82	82	83	Bovine
Chicken	84	87	87	88	95	101	95	96	Poulet
Pig	193	198	204	208	213	217	206	203	Porc
Sheep	1	1	1	1	1	1	1	1	Mouton
France									**France**
Cattle	1 632	1 565	1 517	1 473	1 532	1 503	1 516	1 550	Bovine
Chicken	1 133	1 106	921	819	921	1 082	1 069	1 103	Poulet
Goat	7	7	7	7	8	11	12	12	Chèvre
Pig	2 339	2 293	2 274	2 011	2 031	2 274	2 262	2 260	Porc
Sheep	129	102	99	99	97	130	126	122	Mouton
Germany									**Allemagne**
Cattle	1 226	1 258	1 167	1 193	1 186	1 199	1 190	1 205	Bovine
Chicken	549	609	605	608	688	747	786	837	Poulet
Goat	^0	^0	^0	^0	^0	^0	1	1	Chèvre
Pig	4 239	4 323	4 500	4 663	4 985	5 122	5 265	5 488	Porc
Sheep	46	48	49	43	44	39	38	38	Mouton
Greece									**Grèce**
Cattle	62	77	72	73	76	68[2]	69[2]	70[2]	Bovine
Chicken	160	147	159	118	116	112[2]	112[2]	114[2]	Poulet
Goat	47	58	57	58	56	56[2]	54[2]	54[1]	Chèvre
Pig	111	108	109	108	102	105[2]	104[2]	100[2]	Porc
Sheep	80[1]	94	92	94	93	91[2]	90[2]	89[2]	Mouton

Meat production *(continued)*
Thousand metric tons

Production de viande *(suite)*
Milliers de tonnes

Region, country or area	2003	2004	2005	2006	2007	2008	2009	2010	Région, pays ou zone
Hungary									**Hongrie**
Cattle	61	46	32	34	35	32	30	28	Bovine
Chicken	267	253	246	211	196	217	213	221	Poulet
Pig	510	540	454	489	499	461	453	452	Porc
Sheep	1	2	1	1	1	1	1	1	Mouton
Iceland									**Islande**
Cattle	4	4	4	3	4	4	4	4	Bovine
Chicken	6	5	6	7	8	7	7	7	Poulet
Pig	6	6	5	6	6	7	6	6	Porc
Sheep	9	9	9	9	9	9	9	9	Mouton
Ireland									**Irlande**
Cattle	568	564	546	572	581	536	513	558	Bovine
Chicken	90[2]	91[2]	92[2]	90[2]	85[2]	85[1]	86[1]	83[1]	Poulet
Pig	217	204	205	209	205	204	197	215	Porc
Sheep	63[2]	72	73	70	66	59	55	48	Mouton
Italy									**Italie**
Buffalo	1	3	6	1	4	2	6	6	Buffle
Cattle	1 127	1 145	1 102	1 109	1 119	1 057	1 049	1 069	Bovine
Chicken	683	704	695	628	733	790	822	865	Poulet
Goat	3	3	3	3	2	2	2	2	Chèvre
Pig	1 590	1 590	1 515	1 559	1 603	1 606	1 628	1 673	Porc
Sheep	58	59	59	59	59	57	57	52	Mouton
Latvia									**Lettonie**
Cattle	21	22	20	21	23	21	20	18	Bovine
Chicken	12	14	17	21	21	23	23	23	Poulet
Pig	37	37	38	38	40	41	39	37	Porc
Sheep	^0	^0	^0	^0	^0	1	1	1	Mouton
Lithuania									**Lituanie**
Cattle	52	58	62	47	56	48	45	44	Bovine
Chicken	39	49	57	61	63	65	67	72[2]	Poulet
Goat	1	^0	1	^0	^0	^0	^0	^0	Chèvre
Pig	105	113	119	106	99	76	60	73	Porc
Sheep	^0	^0	^0	^0	1	1	^0	1[2]	Mouton
Luxembourg									**Luxembourg**
Cattle	17	16	17	16	16[2]	16[2]	15[2]	16[2]	Bovine
Pig	12	11	11	10	10	10	10	10	Porc
Malta									**Malte**
Cattle	1	1	1	1	1	1	2	1	Bovine
Chicken	7	6	5	4	5	5	5	4	Poulet
Pig	10	8	9	8	8	9	7	8	Porc
Montenegro									**Monténégro**
Cattle	...	...	...	4	5	5[1]	5[1]	6[1]	Bovine
Chicken [1]	...	...	...	2	2	5	5	6	Poulet [1]
Pig [1]	...	...	...	2	2	2	2	2	Porc [1]
Sheep [1]	...	...	...	1	1	1	1	1	Mouton [1]
Netherlands									**Pays-Bas**
Cattle	365	386	396	384	386	378	402	389	Bovine
Chicken	535	615	628	621	684	693	764	751	Poulet
Goat	^0	^0	^0	^0	1[1]	1[1]	1[1]	1[1]	Chèvre
Pig	1 253	1 289	1 297	1 265	1 290	1 318	1 275	1 287	Porc
Sheep	15	15	13	16	16	14	14	13	Mouton
Norway									**Norvège**
Cattle	85	87	87	88	85	86	85	84	Bovine
Chicken	43	47	50	55	63	75	71	76	Poulet
Pig	105	114	113	116	118	123	124	129	Porc
Sheep	24	26	26	25	23	24	24	24	Mouton
Poland									**Pologne**
Cattle	317	311	310	363	380	393	397	401	Bovine
Chicken	637	704	796	824	896	730	1 060	1 123[2]	Poulet
Pig	2 190	1 956	1 956	2 098	2 151	1 920	1 736	1 895	Porc
Sheep	1	2	1	1	2	1	1	1	Mouton

Region, country or area	2003	2004	2005	2006	2007	2008	2009	2010	Région, pays ou zone
Portugal									**Portugal**
Cattle	105	118	118	105	91	109	103	94	Bovine
Chicken	182	196	198	193	223	237	247	249	Poulet
Goat	2	2	1	2	2	1	1	1[1]	Chèvre
Pig	329	315	327	339	364	381	373	384	Porc
Sheep	22	22	22	23	24	22[2]	18[2]	20	Mouton
Republic of Moldova									**République de Moldova**
Cattle	16	16	16	15	15	11	11	10	Bovine
Chicken	22	24	28	31	32	30	34	41	Poulet
Pig	43	41	40	48	59	35	42	57	Porc
Sheep	3	3	2	2	2	2	2	2	Mouton
Romania									**Roumanie**
Cattle	185	162	190	159	165	150	155	154	Bovine
Chicken	344	303	309	273	312	316	371	349	Poulet
Goat	5	6	3	3	4	4	7	7	Chèvre
Pig	533	374	436	452	470	439	471	429	Porc
Sheep	62	67	49	42	50	47	64	63	Mouton
Russian Federation									**Fédération de Russie**
Cattle	1 990	1 951	1 794	1 705	1 690	1 769	1 741	1 711	Bovine
Chicken	1 030	1 152	1 346	1 580	1 869	2 001	2 313	2 533	Poulet
Goat	19	18	18	18	18	18	18	18	Chèvre
Pig	1 706	1 643	1 520	1 641	1 873	2 042	2 169	2 308	Porc
Sheep	114	125	134	139	150	156	164	170	Mouton
Serbia									**Serbie**
Cattle	...	...	...	83	95	99	100	96	Bovine
Chicken	...	...	...	75	70	76	80	84	Poulet
Pig	...	...	...	255	289	266	252	269	Porc
Sheep	...	...	...	20	20	23	24	23	Mouton
Serbia and Montenegro									**Serbie-et-Monténégro**
Cattle	164[2]	161[2]	156	...	...	...	...	...	Bovine
Chicken	59	65	67	...	...	...	...	...	Poulet
Goat [1]	1	1	1	...	...	...	...	...	Chèvre [1]
Pig	574[2]	539[2]	562	...	...	...	...	...	Porc
Sheep	21	24	21	...	...	...	...	...	Mouton
Slovakia									**Slovaquie**
Cattle	33	26	26	21	23	20	18	14	Bovine
Chicken	85	84	87	86	83	76	75	76[1]	Poulet
Pig	183	165	140	122	114	102	88	69	Porc
Sheep	2	1	1	1	1	1	1	1[1]	Mouton
Slovenia									**Slovénie**
Cattle	52	47	45	39	38	37	35	36	Bovine
Chicken	47[2]	43	46	44	43	52	54	54	Poulet
Pig	74	71	63	61	57	55	44	44	Porc
Sheep	1	1	2	2	2	2	2	2	Mouton
Spain									**Espagne**
Cattle	706	714	715	670	620	658	598	607	Bovine
Chicken	1 185	1 083	1 084	1 065	1 131	1 082	1 179	1 116	Poulet
Goat	14	13	14	12	10	9	9	9[1]	Chèvre
Pig	3 190	3 076	3 168	3 235	3 439	3 484	3 291	3 369	Porc
Sheep	236	231	224	214	203	157	124	131	Mouton
Sweden									**Suède**
Cattle	140	143	136	137	134	129	150	148	Bovine
Chicken	98	91	96	96	105	107	105	112	Poulet
Pig	288	295	275	264	265	271	261	263	Porc
Sheep	4	4	4	4	5	5	5	5	Mouton
Switzerland									**Suisse**
Cattle	137	134	132	135	133	135	142	143	Bovine
Chicken	53	60	58	48	58	62	64	67	Poulet
Goat	^0	^0	1	1	1	1	^0	^0	Chèvre
Pig	230	227	236	244	242	231	238	249	Porc
Sheep	6	7	6	6	5	5	5	5	Mouton

Region, country or area	2003	2004	2005	2006	2007	2008	2009	2010	Région, pays ou zone
TFYR of Macedonia									**L'ex-R.Y. Macédoine**
Cattle	9	9	8	7	7	7	7	7[2]	Bovine
Chicken	4	3	4	4	4	3	3	3[2]	Poulet
Pig	10	9	9	9	9	9	8	8[2]	Porc
Sheep	6	7	7	7	6	5	5	5[2]	Mouton
Ukraine									**Ukraine**
Cattle	723	618	562	568	546	480	454	428	Bovine
Chicken	324	375	497	589	689	794	894	953	Poulet
Goat	9	8	8	7	8	9	9	11	Chèvre
Pig	631	559	494	526	635	590	527	631	Porc
Sheep	8	8	8	8	8	8	9	10	Mouton
United Kingdom									**Royaume-Uni**
Cattle	699	719	762	847	882	862	850	925	Bovine
Chicken	1 295	1 295	1 334	1 289	1 270	1 259	1 463	1 379	Poulet
Pig	716	708	706	697	739	740	720	774	Porc
Sheep	303	312	331	330	325	326	303	281	Mouton
Oceania									**Océanie**
Cattle	**2 754**	**2 763**	**2 834**	**2 740**	**2 879**	**2 787**	**2 781**	**2 764**	**Bovine**
Chicken	**856**	**863**	**939**	**945**	**984**	**970**	**988**	**1 048**	**Poulet**
Goat	**16**	**19**	**23**	**24**	**19**	**20**	**27**	**27**	**Chèvre**
Pig	**555**	**535**	**530**	**525**	**522**	**502**	**459**	**474**	**Porc**
Sheep	**1 143**	**1 079**	**1 138**	**1 168**	**1 257**	**1 258**	**1 114**	**1 027**	**Mouton**
Australia									**Australie**
Cattle	2 073	2 033	2 162	2 077	2 226	2 132	2 124	2 108	Bovine
Chicken	690	694	760	773	812	800	831	881	Poulet
Goat [1]	14	17	20	22	16	18	25	25	Chèvre [1]
Pig	419	395	391	386	382	360	321	336	Porc
Sheep	597	561	595	626	684	660	635	556	Mouton
Cook Islands [1]									**Iles Cook** [1]
Pig	1	1	1	1	1	1	1	1	Porc
Fiji									**Fidji**
Cattle [1]	8	8	8	8	8	8	8	8	Bovine [1]
Chicken	12	13	12	14	14	14	12	14	Poulet
Goat	1	1	1	1	1	1	^0	^0	Chèvre
Pig [1]	4	4	4	4	4	4	4	4	Porc [1]
French Polynesia									**Polynésie française**
Chicken [1]	1	1	1	1	1	1	1	1	Poulet [1]
Pig	1	1	1	1	1	1	1	1[1]	Porc
Kiribati									**Kiribati**
Chicken	^0	^0	^0	1[1]	1[1]	1[1]	1[1]	1[1]	Poulet
Pig [1]	1	1	1	1	1	1	1	1	Porc [1]
Micronesia (Fed. States of) [1]									**Micronésie (Etats féd. de)** [1]
Pig	1	1	1	1	1	1	1	1	Porc
New Caledonia									**Nouvelle-Calédonie**
Cattle	4	4	4	3	3	3	3	3	Bovine
Chicken	1	1	1	1	1	1	1	1	Poulet
Pig	2	2	2	2	2	2	2	2	Porc
New Zealand									**Nouvelle-Zélande**
Cattle	660	709	652	643	632	635	637	635	Bovine
Chicken	144	147	157	149	147	145	135	143	Poulet
Goat	1	2	1	1	2	1	1	1	Chèvre
Pig	47	52	50	51	51	51	47	47	Porc
Sheep	546	518	543	542	573	598	478	471	Mouton
Papua New Guinea [1]									**Papouasie-Nvl-Guinée** [1]
Cattle	3	3	3	3	3	3	3	3	Bovine
Chicken	6	6	6	6	6	6	6	6	Poulet
Pig	68	68	68	68	68	68	68	68	Porc
Samoa									**Samoa**
Cattle	1[1]	1[1]	1[1]	1[1]	1[1]	1[1]	1[1]	1[1]	Bovine
Chicken	^0	^0	1[1]	1[1]	1[1]	1[1]	1[1]	1[1]	Poulet
Pig	4[1]	4[1]	4[1]	4[1]	4[1]	4[1]	5[1]	5[1]	Porc

Region, country or area	2003	2004	2005	2006	2007	2008	2009	2010	Région, pays ou zone
Solomon Islands [1]									**Iles Salomon** [1]
Cattle	1	1	1	1	1	1	1	1	Bovine
Pig	2	2	2	2	2	2	2	2	Porc
Tonga									**Tonga**
Pig	1[1]	1[1]	1[1]	2[1]	2[1]	2[1]	*2	2[1]	Porc
Vanuatu									**Vanuatu**
Cattle	3	3	3	3	3	3	3	3[1]	Bovine
Chicken	1[1]	1[1]	1[1]	1[1]	^0	^0	^0	^0	Poulet
Pig	3[1]	3[1]	3[1]	3[1]	3[1]	4[1]	*4	4[1]	Porc

Source:
Food and Agriculture Organization of the United Nations (FAO), Rome, FAOSTAT data, last accessed April 2012.

Source:
Organisation des Nations Unies pour l'alimentation et l'agriculture (FAO), Rome, données FAOSTAT, dernier accès avril 2012.

1 FAO estimate.
2 Unofficial figure.
3 For statistical purposes, the data for China do not include those for the Hong Kong Special Administrative Region (Hong Kong SAR), Macao Special Administrative Region (Macao SAR) and Taiwan Province of China.

1 Estimation de la FAO.
2 Chiffre non officiel.
3 Pour la présentation des statistiques, les données pour la Chine ne comprennent pas la Région Administrative Spéciale de Hong Kong (Hong Kong RAS), la Région Administrative Spéciale de Macao (Macao RAS) et la province de Taiwan.

37

Beer production
Thousand hectolitres and millions of US dollars
Production de bière
Milliers d'hectolitres et millions de dollars É.-U.

A. Thousand hectolitres • Milliers d'hectolitres

Country or area	2001	2002	2003	2004	2005	2006	2007	2008	2009	Pays ou zone
Albania	117	150	144	296	285	348	366	...	249	Albanie
Algeria	435	283	166	124	...	...	...	...	...	Algérie
Argentina	12 390	11 990	12 950	13 410	13 960	14 825	15 850	18 190	18 640	Argentine
Armenia	100	71	73	88	108	126	116	105	108	Arménie
Australia [1]	17 450[2]	17 440[2]	17 270[2]	17 360[2]	16 850[2]	17 141	17 067	16 772	...	Australie [1]
Austria	8 528	8 745	8 980	...	...	...	...	...	...	Autriche
Azerbaijan	117	125	133	184	249	309	328	325	344	Azerbaïdjan
Barbados	67	68	69	80	87	89	85	71	71	Barbade
Belarus	2 174	2 026	2 056	2 272	2 715	3 322	3 556	3 544	3 370	Bélarus
Belgium [3]	15 068	15 063	15 924	...	...	...	...	...	...	Belgique [3]
Bosnia and Herzegovina	480[4]	652[4]	#1 316	...	...	...	...	...	...	Bosnie-Herzégovine
Botswana	1 692	1 396	1 198	...	...	...	...	...	...	Botswana
Brazil	91 372	79 883	76 921	86 633	92 164	100 176	100 203	110 521	125 874	Brésil
Bulgaria	4 097	3 888	4 355	3 997	4 287	4 778	5 284	5 409	4 953	Bulgarie
Burundi	702	752	876	973	1 013	1 220	1 289	1 369	1 366	Burundi
Cameroon	3 740	4 196	4 597	4 287	4 439	4 035	4 488	4 192	5 016	Cameroun
Canada	25 551	25 368	19 299	...	...	...	...	...	...	Canada
Chile	3 374	3 401	3 490	...	4 754	4 518	5 501	7 091	6 678	Chili
China [5]	...	...	254 048	294 859	312 605	354 358	395 407	415 691	416 218	Chine [5]
Congo	623	661	658	674	...	...	...	...	...	Congo
Croatia	3 799	3 624	3 679	3 606	3 496	3 689	3 810	3 880	3 674	Croatie
Cuba	2 197	2 331	2 313	2 221	2 255	2 298	2 459	2 508	2 474	Cuba
Cyprus	404	383	367	371	377	374	...	427	357	Chypre
Czech Republic	17 734	17 987	18 216	18 596	18 885	20 134	18 627	19 213	18 053	République tchèque
Denmark	7 233	8 202	8 352	8 550	8 493	7 915	8 016	6 474	6 038	Danemark
Dominica	9	10	...	...	...	...	...	...	...	Dominique
Dominican Republic	...	4 015	4 026	3 898	4 679	4 892	4 317	4 520	...	Rép. dominicaine

37

Beer production *(continued)*
Thousand hectolitres and millions of US dollars
Production de bière *(suite)*
Milliers d'hectolitres et millions de dollars É.-U.

A. Thousand hectoliters • Milliers d'hectolitres

Country or area	2001	2002	2003	2004	2005	2006	2007	2008	2009	Pays ou zone
Ecuador	...	...	...	8 224	9 343	4 446	4 687	4 459	...	Equateur
Egypt	122	...	...	...	...	...	...	5 980	5 980	Egypte
Estonia	1 015	1 044	1 040	1 189	1 346	1 411	1 388	1 275	1 221	Estonie
Ethiopia[6]	1 605	1 812	2 123	...	...	...	...	...	...	Ethiopie[6]
Fiji	180	200	150	200	220	220	190	190	200	Fidji
Finland	4 650	4 777	4 606	4 948	4 527	4 557	4 499	4 412	4 448	Finlande
France	18 539	17 899	17 989	17 477	17 199	...	...	...	...	France
Gabon	867	792	754	...	...	...	...	...	...	Gabon
Georgia	257	273	284	476	586	734	709	625	685	Géorgie
Germany	106 372	102 133	98 933	97 748	94 806	96 937	94 781	91 123	88 005	Allemagne
Greece	4 494	4 548	4 090	3 890	...	...	...	...	...	Grèce
Guyana	120	131	105	121	90	90	87	82	86	Guyana
Hungary	7 142	7 237	7 255	6 467	6 770	7 157	7 186	7 027	6 285	Hongrie
Iceland	123	103	108	...	...	...	...	...	...	Islande
India	2 352	2 696	3 609	2 704	2 955	3 722	...	...	...	Inde
Indonesia	437	237	...	...	...	...	...	...	...	Indonésie
Iran (Islamic Rep. of)	...	...	...	352	518	663	1 017	1 546	...	Iran (Rép. islamique d')
Italy	11 375	11 208	13 994	13 692	...	...	...	...	...	Italie
Jamaica	784	774	585	590	633	669	660	666	...	Jamaïque
Japan[7]	51 855	46 215	41 323	37 833	36 169	34 079	33 048	32 147	29 859	Japon[7]
Kazakhstan	1 732	2 020	2 348	2 780	3 235	3 638	4 110	3 607	...	Kazakhstan
Kenya	1 843	1 919	2 223	2 447	2 663	3 116	3 934	4 249	3 968	Kenya
Kyrgyzstan	87	71	77	116	123	110	140	154	152	Kirghizistan
Lao People's Dem. Rep.	576	652	702	827	927	1 059	...	1 363	...	Rép. dém. pop. lao
Latvia	989	1 199	1 364	1 313	1 285	1 408	1 402	1 339	1 283	Lettonie
Lesotho	288	333	358	325	285	295	317	236	283	Lesotho
Lithuania	2 174	2 683	2 520	2 782	2 916	2 958	2 878	2 983	2 818	Lituanie

Beer production *(continued)*
Thousand hectolitres and millions of US dollars
Production de bière *(suite)*
Milliers d'hectolitres et millions de dollars É.-U.

A. Thousand hectoliters • Milliers d'hectolitres

Country or area	2001	2002	2003	2004	2005	2006	2007	2008	2009	Pays ou zone
Luxembourg	397	386	391	...	...	...	...	...	...	Luxembourg
Madagascar	502	439	...	92	93	103	...	...	...	Madagascar
Malawi	1 033	...	...	...	...	...	...	...	...	Malawi
Mali	71	75	78	78	149	101	108	74	41	Mali
Mauritius	328	348	378	364	389	359	338	361	352	Maurice
Mexico	61 903	63 368	65 512	68 133	72 665	78 456	80 540	81 611	82 236	Mexique
Mongolia	4	3	3	8	8	7	18	20	32	Mongolie
Montenegro	...	301	553	491	52	517	534	557	457	Monténégro
Mozambique	982	779	1 044	1 025	1 412	...	...	...	...	Mozambique
Myanmar [8]	55	87	86	84	113	95	82	75	69	Myanmar [8]
Namibia	1 168	1 226	1 208	1 256	1 188	1 316	1 369	1 423	...	Namibie
Nepal [9]	233	228	242	250	260	...	...	...	...	Népal [9]
Netherlands	24 605	24 774	25 699	24 546	24 543	25 726	25 982	26 991	25 640	Pays-Bas
New Zealand	3 070	3 093	3 127	3 060	3 036	2 909	2 862	2 966	2 815	Nouvelle-Zélande
Niger	68	65	...	...	...	...	...	...	...	Niger
Nigeria	4 049	4 142	4 011	4 067	4 073	...	...	...	...	Nigéria
Norway	2 462	2 377	...	2 352	2 442	2 410	...	...	...	Norvège
Panama	1 272	1 353	1 486	1 641	1 674	1 798	1 948	2 140	2 300	Panama
Peru	5 296	6 170	6 483	6 733	7 970	...	...	...	...	Pérou
Poland	15 069	26 715	28 412	29 794	31 343	33 531	36 351	37 095	35 842	Pologne
Portugal	6 509	6 689	7 110	7 712	7 702	8 337	...	...	...	Portugal
Republic of Korea	17 765	18 224	17 863	18 033	17 489	17 400	18 200	19 073	18 831	République de Corée
Republic of Moldova [10]	318	438	566	653	724	...	...	...	...	République de Moldova [10]
Romania	12 087	11 513	13 087	14 159	14 713	17 554	18 865	19 518	17 891	Roumanie
Russian Federation	63 780	70 266	75 540	83 787	90 986	100 051	114 722	113 969	109 106	Fédération de Russie
Saint Kitts and Nevis	20	20	...	...	...	...	...	...	...	Saint-Kitts-et-Nevis
Serbia	...	...	...	...	...	6 451	6 547	6 470	5 436	Serbie

Beer production *(continued)*
Thousand hectolitres and millions of US dollars
Production de bière *(suite)*
Milliers d'hectolitres et millions de dollars É.-U.

A. Thousand hectoliters • Milliers d'hectolitres

Country or area	2001	2002	2003	2004	2005	2006	2007	2008	2009	Pays ou zone
Serbia and Montenegro	6 063	5 764	6 049	...	...	...	...	...	...	Serbie-et-Monténégro
Seychelles	72	76	65	63	63	67	75	61	...	Seychelles
Slovakia	4 216	4 747	4 684	3 877	3 810	3 987	3 557	3 375	2 950	Slovaquie
Slovenia	2 449	...	...	...	...	...	...	...	...	Slovénie
Spain	26 802	28 631	31 028	31 467	31 156	34 032	33 502	32 555	33 649	Espagne
Sweden	4 522	4 527	4 255	3 870	3 952	4 381	4 447	4 337	4 563	Suède
Syrian Arab Republic	100	104	100	109	111	107	99	79	...	Rép. arabe syrienne
Tajikistan	8	9	9	11	13	16	19	18	16	Tadjikistan
Thailand	12 380	12 750	16 020	16 320	16 950	20 110	21 612	21 600	...	Thaïlande
TFYR of Macedonia	618	657	680	716	695	670	695	718	636	L'ex-R.Y. Macédoine
Togo	...	...	...	313	325	345	414	361	522	Togo
Trinidad and Tobago	...	...	...	...	...	...	...	...	504	Trinité-et-Tobago
Tunisia	1 087	1 100	997	...	...	...	...	...	...	Tunisie
Turkey	7 441	7 845	8 363	8 812	8 936	9 059	...	...	...	Turquie
Turkmenistan	79	84	...	...	...	...	...	...	...	Turkménistan
Uganda	1 079	989	826	1 149	1 359	1 616	...	...	...	Ouganda
Ukraine	13 059	15 000	17 012	19 373	23 805	26 750	31 579	32 039	30 005	Ukraine
United Kingdom	57 032	60 646	64 253	73 622	126 656	130 607	62 511	60 175	61 924	Royaume-Uni
United Rep. of Tanzania [11]	1 756	1 759	1 941	2 026	2 166	2 990	3 102	2 935	2 869	Rép.-Unie de Tanzanie [11]
Uruguay	629	507	415	...	...	...	...	...	...	Uruguay
Viet Nam	8 712	9 398	11 189	13 428	14 606	15 472	16 553	18 472	20 075	Viet Nam
Zimbabwe	4 747	2 957	...	...	...	...	...	...	...	Zimbabwe

Source:
United Nations Statistics Division, New York, the *Industrial Commodity Statistics Yearbook 2009* and the industrial statistics database, last accessed December 2012.

Source:
Organisation des Nations Unies, Division de statistique, New York, *l'Annuaire de statistiques industrielles par produit 2009* et la base de données pour les statistiques industrielles, dernier accès décembre 2012.

1   Twelve months ending 30 June of the year stated.
2   Excluding light beer containing less than 1.15% by volume of alcohol.
3   Incomplete coverage.

1   Période de douze mois finissant le 30 juin de l'année indiquée.
2   Non compris la bière légère contenant moins de 1.15 p. 100 en volume d'alcool.
3   Couverture incomplète.

Beer production *(continued)*
Thousand hectolitres and millions of US dollars

Production de bière *(suite)*
Milliers d'hectolitres et millions de dollars É.-U.

A. Thousand hectoliters • Milliers d'hectolitres

4	Excluding the Federation of Bosnia and Herzegovina.	4	Non compris la Fédération de Bosnie et Herzégovine.
5	For statistical purposes, the data for China do not include those for the Hong Kong Special Administrative Region (Hong Kong SAR), Macao Special Administrative Region (Macao SAR) and Taiwan Province of China.	5	Pour la présentation des statistiques, les données pour la Chine ne comprennent pas la Région Administrative Spéciale de Hong Kong (Hong Kong RAS), la Région Administrative Spéciale de Macao (Macao RAS) et la province de Taiwan.
6	Twelve months ending 7 July of the year stated.	6	Période de 12 mois finissant le 7 juillet de l'année indiquée.
7	Twelve months beginning 1 April of the year stated.	7	Période de 12 mois commençant le 1er avril de l'année indiquée.
8	Twelve months ending 31 March of the year stated.	8	Période de 12 mois finissant le 31 mars de l'année indiquée.
9	Twelve months beginning 16 July of the year stated.	9	Période de 12 mois commençant le 16 juillet de l'année indiquée.
10	Excluding the Transnistria region.	10	Non compris la région de Transnistrie.
11	Tanganyika only.	11	Tanganyika seulement.

Beer production
Thousand hectolitres and millions of US dollars

Production de bière
Milliers d'hectolitres et millions de dollars É.-U.

B. Millions of US dollars • Millions de dollars É.-U.

Country or area	2001	2002	2003	2004	2005	2006	2007	2008	2009	Pays ou zone
Albania	...	...	...	25.6	23.9	29.7	34.7	...	22.3	Albanie
Azerbaijan	6.3	6.1	6.7	10.4	16.4	21.2	29.4	45.2	50.1	Azerbaïdjan
Brazil	2 565.6	2 468.9	2 565.9	3 008.9	4 100.4	5 177.7	6 720.6	7 455.5	8 041.9	Brésil
Bulgaria	92.9	96.3	116.0	133.3	148.7	178.3	241.4	311.9	289.3	Bulgarie
Canada	...	2 499.6	2 739.2	...	...	...	...	...	...	Canada
Chile	...	...	...	...	330.0	410.9	470.5	544.9	497.9	Chili
Congo	46.7	59.2	67.2	74.6	...	...	...	...	...	Congo
Cyprus	...	40.9	46.4	51.2	49.6	52.3	...	64.6	55.5	Chypre
Czech Republic	496.2	603.9	771.8	905.4	1 018.0	1 136.4	1 328.4	1 620.1	1 386.4	République tchèque
Denmark	523.1	616.6	836.9	927.7	901.7	879.8	1 017.3	1 063.5	969.4	Danemark
Ecuador	...	...	...	378.9	441.1	223.8	274.4	277.0	...	Equateur
Egypt	8.6	...	...	...	...	...	...	...	...	Egypte
Estonia	...	...	...	60.4	75.4	84.2	100.6	114.7	101.7	Estonie
Finland	280.1	312.5	360.0	399.8	344.5	366.3	414.7	461.4	444.5	Finlande
France	1 560.6	1 647.9	2 074.4	2 170.4	2 183.8	...	...	...	...	France
Georgia	...	...	...	18.2	24.2	39.1	45.4	50.6	47.5	Géorgie
Germany	6 270.3	6 519.7	7 728.0	8 087.8	7 746.0	7 867.8	8 236.2	8 816.8	7 968.6	Allemagne
Greece	326.2	385.6	452.7	451.5	...	...	...	...	...	Grèce
Hungary	...	448.0	550.0	531.7	560.2	641.4	835.8	716.5	494.8	Hongrie
India	...	...	241.0	270.1	324.0	...	...	...	...	Inde
Italy	...	...	1 582.5	1 753.6	...	...	...	...	...	Italie
Jordan	...	...	...	17.3	19.0	19.4	20.2	...	...	Jordanie
Kenya	131.0	130.7	235.4	183.3	286.0	351.9	506.2	999.9	516.8	Kenya
Latvia	47.0	56.7	...	...	68.6	77.4	97.4	112.8	97.3	Lettonie
Lithuania	103.1	142.6	153.5	161.7	180.6	192.8	250.9	318.7	291.3	Lituanie
Madagascar	...	...	...	5.2	...	...	...	...	...	Madagascar
Mexico	3 929.5	4 163.9	3 850.2	4 089.6	4 523.3	5 247.2	5 316.3	5 455.6	4 960.8	Mexique

Beer production *(continued)*
Thousand hectolitres and millions of US dollars
Production de bière *(suite)*
Milliers d'hectolitres et millions de dollars É.-U.

B.   Millions of US dollars • Millions de dollars É.-U.

Country or area	2001	2002	2003	2004	2005	2006	2007	2008	2009	Pays ou zone
Mozambique	...	...	534.9	693.0	934.4	...	...	...	...	Mozambique
Nepal	31.5	...	...	...	...	...	34.9	...	...	Népal
Nigeria	37.4	34.6	32.3	31.4	31.7	...	...	...	...	Nigéria
Norway	...	309.4	344.8	301.9	327.5	342.9	...	...	...	Norvège
Peru	517.6	566.8	596.5	622.0	764.9	...	...	...	...	Pérou
Poland	1 645.9	1 778.7	1 999.6	1 852.9	2 613.8	2 971.2	3 731.8	4 677.7	3 697.0	Pologne
Portugal	404.9	319.7	404.2	475.6	522.3	536.9	...	...	...	Portugal
Romania	...	367.2	491.8	595.5	633.8	808.4	1 283.6	1 368.9	1 059.0	Roumanie
Slovakia	98.0	125.4	157.6	168.9	152.8	160.8	192.8	245.4	226.7	Slovaquie
Slovenia	126.4	...	...	...	...	...	...	...	...	Slovénie
Spain	...	...	...	3 188.6	3 428.6	3 531.4	4 396.2	4 697.7	4 417.6	Espagne
Sri Lanka	...	...	...	...	...	0.0	...	1.2	2.3	Sri Lanka
Sweden	328.7	349.5	419.1	405.5	401.3	435.5	488.7	516.3	479.0	Suède
Uganda	...	...	...	...	141.9	146.1	236.1	271.9	229.6	Ouganda
United Kingdom	5 194.1	5 513.4	6 117.5	7 677.5	6 860.3	7 118.9	6 981.7	6 856.3	6 371.1	Royaume-Uni
United Rep. of Tanzania[1]	...	...	...	...	201.2	220.1	253.1	334.0	386.9	Rép.-Unie de Tanzanie[1]
Uruguay	54.4	...	30.6	...	...	...	...	...	...	Uruguay

Source:
United Nations Statistics Division, New York, the *Industrial Commodity Statistics Yearbook 2009* and the industrial statistics database, last accessed December 2012.

Source:
Organisation des Nations Unies, Division de statistique, New York, *l'Annuaire de statistiques industrielles par produit 2009* et la base de données pour les statistiques industrielles, dernier accès décembre 2012.

1   Tanganyika only.

1   Tanganyika seulement.

Cigarette production
Millions of cigarettes and millions of US dollars
Production de cigarettes
Millions de cigarettes et millions de dollars É.-U.

A. Millions of cigarettes • Millions de cigarettes

Country or area	2001	2002	2003	2004	2005	2006	2007	2008	2009	Pays ou zone
Albania	126[1]	50	15	...	...	...	...	...	...	Albanie
Andorra	1	1	2	2	3	1	...	...	...	Andorre
Argentina	1 740	1 812	1 990	1 890	1 862	1 993	2 057	2 173	2 120	Argentine
Armenia	1 623	2 815	3 222	2 720	3 020	2 825	2 911	3 117	3 310	Arménie
Azerbaijan	6 808	6 296	6 611	3 671	5 008	6 224	3 789	2 773	2 316	Azerbaïdjan
Bangladesh [2]	20 120	20 384	22 499	...	...	...	...	...	...	Bangladesh [2]
Belarus	11 182	10 524	10 442	12 627	12 008	15 650	18 699	19 499	21 099	Bélarus
Bosnia and Herzegovina	...	...	5 062	...	...	...	...	...	...	Bosnie-Herzégovine
Brazil	15 820	100 193	21 099	96 828	120 167	120 574	114 805	116 114	106 837	Brésil
Bulgaria	26 659	23 227	25 914	24 462	23 318	17 353	20 763	17 766	17 690	Bulgarie
Burundi	293	312	354	376	419	410	472	437	514	Burundi
Canada	44 403	37 127	...	...	...	...	...	...	...	Canada
Chile	13 305	13 839	13 776	...	16 429	18 073	18 654	19 498	17 359	Chili
China [3]	34	35	36	...	...	...	...	...	...	Chine [3]
Congo	102	662	748	750	...	...	...	...	...	Congo
Croatia	14 738	15 047	15 613	14 256	14 578	14 457	14 415	15 586	11 382	Croatie
Cuba	11 769	12 519	14 316	12 766	14 022	13 151	13 766	14 169	13 443	Cuba
Cyprus	3 803	2 534	2 661	3 845	...	...	...	...	...	Chypre
Denmark	11 089	12 039	12 898	13 458	14 867	14 553	15 274	15 473	13 102	Danemark
Dominican Republic	3	4	3	3	3	3	2	3	...	Rép. dominicaine
Ecuador	...	...	2 975	2 731	2 876	2 890	3 175	202	...	Equateur
Egypt	61 000	62 018	63 396	63 395	55 468	55 123	...	61 697	59 849	Egypte
Ethiopia [4]	1 904	1 511	1 511	...	...	...	...	...	...	Ethiopie [4]
Fiji	389	422	416	454	420	457	456	437	367	Fidji
Finland	3 999	4 130	3 946	868	...	...	...	...	...	Finlande
France	...	...	42 700	48 163	46 500	...	...	...	...	France
Gabon	880	860	...	...	...	...	...	...	...	Gabon
Georgia	1 615	1 894	2 972	2 808	1 820	3 791	4 874	5 156	5 218	Géorgie
German	213 793	212 500	205 237	208 347	212 428	216 042	214 458	223 633	212 834	Allemagne
Ghana	1 481	1 800	...	...	...	...	...	...	...	Ghana
Greece	25 516	28 091	26 249	28 048	...	...	...	...	...	Grèce
Honduras	5 984	6 010	...	...	...	...	...	...	...	Honduras
Hungary	20 787	21 748	20 181	12 119	...	...	...	...	...	Hongrie
India	60 577[5]	54 991[5]	49 769	54 748	75 711	85 747	86 964	...	...	Inde
Iran (Islamic Rep. of	13 363	12 700	12 200	13 930	14 270	14 200	17 387	22 436	26 898	Iran (Rép. islamique d')
Iraq	...	...	...	812	...	68	...	...	...	Iraq
Ireland	6 807	6 599	...	...	...	...	...	...	...	Irlande
Italy	45 368[1]	37 342	40 350	...	...	...	...	...	...	Italie
Jamaica	1 027	1 049	889	979	889	...	...	...	...	Jamaïque
Japan [6]	313 900	...	...	...	...	...	...	...	...	Japon [6]
Kazakhstan	21 395	23 453	25 715	28 038	30 008	30 834	31 507	28 483	...	Kazakhstan
Kenya	5 850	4 631	4 753	5 351	7 324	10 262	12 204	12 169	11 013	Kenya
Kyrgyzstan	3 013	2 927	3 102	3 170	3 179	3 086	3 053	3 024	3 586	Kirghizistan
Lao People's Dem. Rep.	41	55	68	84	105	...	...	136	...	Rép. dém. pop. lao

Cigarette production *(continued)*
Millions of cigarettes and millions of US dollars

Production de cigarettes *(suite)*
Millions de cigarettes et millions de dollars É.-U.

A. Millions of cigarettes • Millions de cigarettes

Country or area	2001	2002	2003	2004	2005	2006	2007	2008	2009	Pays ou zone
Madagascar	...	...	...	8	8	8	...	...	...	Madagascar
Mali	106	90	198	328	330	626	547	276	976	Mali
Mauritius	928	928	938	918	764	726	620	6	0	Maurice
Mexico	44 343	43 234	43 804	41 285	39 914	42 762	43 299	45 907	45 059	Mexique
Montenegro	...	1 141	793	2 000	1 282	433	463	171	153	Monténégro
Mozambique	1 359	1 255	1 390		...	...	...	...	...	Mozambique
Myanmar[7]	2 521	2 351	2 835	2 807	3 199	2 822	2 755	3 038	2 352	Myanmar[7]
Nepal[8]	6 979	6 900	6 812	7 268	...	...	6 081	...	...	Népal[8]
New Zealand	2 396	2 509	2 176	2 122	2 211	1 253	343	459	360	Nouvelle-Zélande
Nigeria	1 798	1 854	1 776	1 809	1 813	...	...	...	...	Nigéria
Pakistan[2]	58 260	55 100	49 365	55 399	61 097	64 137	65 980	67 446	75 609	Pakistan[2]
Peru	3 310	3 766	2 707	2 168	1 460	...	...	...	...	Pérou
Poland	82 421	78 746	78 792	83 376	95 531	106 641	112 300	88 936	90 004	Pologne
Portugal	23 376	25 581	24 950	26 415	27 013	26 608	...	...	...	Portugal
Republic of Korea	94 116	94 433	123 166	133 206	107 247	119 966	124 570	129 543	129 070	République de Corée
Republic of Moldova[9]	9 421	6 310	7 126	7 050	6 195	5 031	...	...	...	République de Moldova[9]
Romania	...	38 033	37 808	28 677	34 541	31 881	37 831	47 848	47 912	Roumanie
Russian Federation	356 000	383 000	376 000	377 000	402 000	409 697	397 498	409 835	412 890	Fédération de Russie
Serbia	...	...	...	...	...	18 267	21 304	20 873	20 482	Serbie
Serbia and Montenegro	13 968	15 388	...	...	...	...	...	...	...	Serbie-et-Monténégro
Seychelles	36	24	50	22	30	19	33	31	...	Seychelles
Spain	...	...	...	48 651	47 506	39 798	41 906	43 567	43 081	Espagne
Sri Lanka	*4 973	5 015[10]	4 765[10]	5 003[10]	...	...	...	...	...	Sri Lanka
Sweden	5 959	...	...	...	...	...	...	...	...	Suède
Switzerland	33 565	37 160	38 140	39 059	42 190	48 937	54 348	...	...	Suisse
Tajikistan	1 155	585	468	508	714	497	616	720	766	Tadjikistan
Thailand	29 807	30 772	31 908	34 761	32 978	28 588	30 748	30 474	...	Thaïlande
TFYR of Macedonia	7 766	6 567	5 120	5 654	5 763	5 123	5 485	5 919	5 973	L'ex-R.Y. Macédoine
Tunisia	12 354	13 230	13 227	...	...	...	...	...	...	Tunisie
Turkey	77 160	131 561	111 881	103 371	104 170	128 278	...	...	...	Turquie
Uganda	1 220	1 092	...	...	...	...	...	...	...	Ouganda
Ukraine	69 731	81 088	96 776	108 946	120 218	120 333	128 535	129 809	114 391	Ukraine
United Kingdom	109 025	124 896	89 639	85 691	81 410	73 266	64 143	...	...	Royaume-Uni
United Rep. of Tanzania	3 504	3 778	3 920	4 308	4 445[11]	5 095[11]	5 821[11]	6 101[11]	5 831[11]	Rép.-Unie de Tanzanie
Uruguay	9 616	8 449	5 718	...	...	...	...	...	...	Uruguay
Viet Nam	3 075	3 375	3 871	4 192	4 485	3 941	4 549	4 355	4 834	Viet Nam
Yemen	6 020	5 780	5 960	...	...	...	...	...	...	Yémen

Source:
United Nations Statistics Division, New York, the industrial statistics database, last accessed December 2012.

Source:
Organisation des Nations Unies, Division de statistique, New York, et la base de données sur les statistiques industrielles, dernier accès décembre 2012.

1 Original data in units of weight. Computed on the basis of one million cigarettes per ton.
2 Twelve months ending 30 June of the year stated.
3 For statistical purposes, the data for China do not include those for the Hong Kong Special Administrative Region (Hong Kong SAR),

1 Données d'origine exprimées en poids. Calcul sur la base d'un million de cigarettes par tonne.
2 Période de douze mois finissant le 30 juin de l'année indiquée.
3 Pour la présentation des statistiques, les données pour la Chine ne comprennent pas la Région Administrative Spéciale de Hong Kong

38

Cigarette production *(continued)*
Millions of cigarettes and millions of US dollars

Production de cigarettes *(suite)*
Millions de cigarettes et millions de dollars É.-U.

A. Millions of cigarettes • Millions de cigarettes

Macao Special Administrative Region (Macao SAR) and Taiwan Province of China.	(Hong Kong RAS), la Région Administrative Spéciale de Macao (Macao RAS) et la province de Taiwan.
4 Twelve months ending 7 July of the year stated.	4 Période de 12 mois finissant le 7 juillet de l'année indiquée.
5 Production by establishments employing 50 or more persons.	5 Production des établissements occupant 50 personnes ou plus.
6 Source: *Statistical Yearbook for Asia and the Pacific*, United Nations Economic and Social Commission for Asia and the Pacific (Bangkok).	6 Source : *Annuaire des Statistiques de l'Asie et Pacifique*, Commission économique et sociale des Nations Unies pour l'Asie et le Pacifique (Bangkok).
7 Twelve months ending 31 March of the year stated.	7 Période de 12 mois finissant le 31 mars de l'année indiquée.
8 Twelve months beginning 16 July of the year stated.	8 Période de 12 mois commençant le 16 juillet de l'année indiquée.
9 Excluding the Transnistria region.	9 Non compris la région de Transnistrie.
10 Source: "Country Economic Review", Asian Development Bank (Manila).	10 Source: "La Revue Economique du Pays", La Banque de Développement Asiatique (Manille).
11 Tanganyika only.	11 Tanganyika seulement.

Cigarette production
Millions of cigarettes and millions of US dollars

Production de cigarettes
Millions de cigarettes et millions de dollars É.-U.

B. Millions of US dollars • Millions de dollars É.-U.

Country or area	2001	2002	2003	2004	2005	2006	2007	2008	2009	Pays ou zone
Azerbaijan	48	28	28	25	30	37	26	31	23	Azerbaïdjan
Brazil	543	418	70	122	269	282	299	364	369	Brésil
Bulgaria	164	157	208	230	247	175	228	190	186	Bulgarie
Canada	1 615	1 630	...	1 844	1 860	1 316	971	900		Canada
Chile	...	...	...	...	199	245	273	309	273	Chili
Congo	2	14	18	22	...	...	...	...	...	Congo
Cyprus	108	106	132	171	159	41				Chypre
Denmark	297	334	397	420	420	466	521	553	489	Danemark
Ecuador	...	...	...	31	34	29	36	24		Equateur
Egypt	490	493	444	419	485	486	...	...	566	Egypte
Finland	78	84	95	22	0	0	0	0	0	Finlande
France	...	...	991	1 033	1 045	...	...	...	...	France
Georgia	...	...	...	19	21	35	48	58	54	Géorgie
Germany	3 673	3 767	3 855	4 425	4 486	4 552	4 914	3 595	3 323	Allemagne
Greece	287	296	376	425	...	...	...	...	...	Grèce
Hungary	...	854	1 190	1 012	...	...	...	...	...	Hongrie
India	...	...	971	1 072	1 101	...	...	...	...	Inde
Iran (Islamic Rep. of)	...	...	...	...	...	...	...	...	312	Iran (Rép. islamique d')
Ireland	208	223	232	...	...	...	...	...	...	Irlande
Jamaica	...	...	52	56	45	...	...	...	...	Jamaïque
Jordan	...	...	...	341	344	398	417	...	...	Jordanie
Kenya	47	34	42	20	33	46	70	72	70	Kenya
Madagascar	...	...	...	1	...	...	...	...	...	Madagascar
Mexico	1 578	1 709	1 696	1 727	1 934	2 142	...	...	...	Mexique
Mozambique	...	...	11	12	22	30	30	...	...	Mozambique
Nepal	70	...	...	...	...	...	149	...	...	Népal
Nigeria	2	1	1	1	1	...	...	...	...	Nigéria
Peru	69	80	68	53	37	...	...	...	...	Pérou
Poland	2 476	2 695	689	1 969	4 041	4 325	5 462	6 606	5 481	Pologne
Portugal	280	350	422	488	497	522	...	...	...	Portugal
Romania	...	503	666	802	548	1 051	1 319	1 690	938	Roumanie
Spain	...	...	...	1 132	1 038	640	799	920	824	Espagne
Sweden	87	...	...	...	0	0	0	0	0	Suède
United Kingdom	2 161	2 270	2 487	2 758	2 571	2 710	2 711	...	2 353	Royaume-Uni
Uruguay	232	...	118	...	...	...	...	...	...	Uruguay

Source:
United Nations Statistics Division, New York, the industrial statistics database, last accessed December 2012.

Source:
Organisation des Nations Unies, Division de statistique, New York, et la base de données sur les statistiques industrielles, dernier accès décembre 2012.

Region, country or area	2004	2005	2006	2007	2008	2009	2010	2011	Région, pays ou zone
World	**355 975**	**364 932**	**379 955**	**388 141**	**394 233**	**374 995**	**401 668**	**406 611**	**Monde**
Africa	**4 104**	**3 778**	**3 932**	**4 147**	**4 147**	**3 513**	**3 821**	**3 472**	**Afrique**
Algeria	48	46	46	46	46	46	46	46	Algérie
Congo	3	3	3	3	3	3	3	3	Congo
Dem. Rep. of the Congo	3	3	3	3	3	3	3	3	Rép. dém. du Congo
Egypt	460	460	460	660	660	660	660	660	Egypte
Ethiopia	16	16	16	16	16	41	78	78	Ethiopie
Kenya	161	273	279	178	178	...	...	...	Kenya
Libyan Arab Jamah.	6	6	6	6	6	6	6	6	Jamah. arabe libyenne
Madagascar	10	10	10	10	10	10	10	10	Madagascar
Mauritania	...	1	1	1	1	1	1	1	Mauritanie
Morocco	127	127	127	127	127	127	127	127	Maroc
Mozambique	2	1	1	2	2	2	2	2	Mozambique
Nigeria	19	19	19	19	19	19	19	19	Nigéria
South Africa	2 881	2 444	2 611	2 726	2 726	2 245	2 516	2 167	Afrique du Sud
South Sudan	...	...	...	...	...	...	...	3	Soudan du sud
Sudan	3	3	3	3	3	3	3	...	Soudan
Swaziland	49	49	49	49	49	49	49	49	Swaziland
Tunisia	157	157	157	157	157	157	157	157	Tunisie
Uganda	3	3	3	3	3	3	3	3	Ouganda
United Rep. of Tanzania	25	25	25	25	25	25	25	25	Rép.-Unie de Tanzanie
Zambia	4	4	4	4	4	4	4	4	Zambie
Zimbabwe	127	127	109	109	109	109	109	109	Zimbabwe
Northern America	**102 546**	**103 195**	**102 506**	**101 283**	**95 967**	**84 178**	**90 422**	**89 493**	**Amérique septentrionale**
Canada	20 462	19 498	18 189	17 367	15 789	12 823	12 733	12 069	Canada
United States	82 084	83 697	84 367	83 916	80 178	71 355	77 689	77 424	Etats-Unis
Latin America and the Caribbean	**17 673**	**18 871**	**18 561**	**18 685**	**19 137**	**19 288**	**19 694**	**19 912**	**Amérique latine et Caraïbes**
Argentina	1 586	2 080	1 545	1 516	1 755	1 465	1 465	1 465	Argentine
Barbados	...	2	2	2	2	2	2	2	Barbade
Brazil	8 221	8 597	8 738	9 008	9 154	9 428	9 844	9 887	Brésil
Chile	1 168	1 215	1 231	1 344	1 379	1 348	1 204	1 272	Chili
Colombia	899	919	990	1 013	1 025	1 076	1 143	1 154	Colombie
Costa Rica	20	20	20	20	20	20	20	20	Costa Rica
Cuba	20	22	23	20	22	21	20	20	Cuba
Dominican Republic	130	130	130	130	130	130	130	130	Rép. dominicaine
Ecuador	100	100	99	100	100	198	198	198	Equateur
El Salvador	56	56	56	56	56	56	56	56	El Salvador
Guatemala	31	31	31	31	31	31	31	31	Guatemala
Honduras	95	95	95	95	95	95	95	95	Honduras
Mexico	4 689	4 841	4 876	4 582	4 451	4 556	4 704	4 701	Mexique
Paraguay	13	13	13	13	13	13	13	13	Paraguay
Peru	106	147	173	188	188	173	190	215	Pérou
Uruguay	100	98	98	90	90	82	96	96	Uruguay
Venezuela (Boliv. Rep. of)	439	405	441	477	626	593	484	557	Venezuela (Rép. boliv. du)

Paper and paperboard *(continued)*
Production: thousand metric tons
Papiers et cartons *(suite)*
Production: milliers de tonnes

Region, country or area	2004	2005	2006	2007	2008	2009	2010	2011	Région, pays ou zone
Asia	**117 813**	**124 129**	**136 243**	**144 985**	**159 414**	**163 098**	**175 682**	**182 084**	**Asie**
Armenia	2	4	20	26	6	7	9	9	Arménie
Azerbaijan	8	5	3	^0	3	1	4	4	Azerbaïdjan
Bahrain	15	15	15	15	15	15	15	15	Bahreïn
Bangladesh	58	58	58	58	58	58	58	58	Bangladesh
Bhutan	...	...	...	8	10	10	10	10	Bhoutan
China	54 072	60 405	69 394	77 965	83 685	90 117	96 501	103 101	Chine
Georgia	...	...	1	2	2	2	2	2	Géorgie
India	4 615	4 655	4 774	4 781	7 941	7 789	10 809	10 809	Inde
Indonesia	7 223	7 223	7 223	7 727	11 349	11 527	11 527	11 527	Indonésie
Iran (Islamic Rep. of)	411	464	435	427	421	429	419	419	Iran (Rép. islamique d')
Iraq	13	13	13	13	13	13	13	13	Iraq
Israel	305	305	305	305	396	396	403	403	Israël
Japan	30 891	30 953	31 097	31 268	30 628	26 268	27 364	26 578	Japon
Jordan	54	54	54	54	54	54	54	54	Jordanie
Kazakhstan	69	81	166	202	172	207	211	211	Kazakhstan
Dem. P. R. Korea	80	80	80	80	80	80	80	80	R. p. dém. de Corée
Republic of Korea	10 511	10 254	10 703	10 932	10 642	10 481	11 106	11 480	République de Corée
Kuwait	56	56	56	56	56	57	57	57	Koweït
Kyrgyzstan	2	2	2	^0	^0	83	424	424	Kirghizistan
Lebanon	103	103	103	103	103	103	103	103	Liban
Malaysia	963	971	1 086	1 092	1 122	1 577	1 615	1 795	Malaisie
Myanmar	43	45	45	45	45	45	45	45	Myanmar
Nepal	13	13	13	13	13	13	13	13	Népal
Oman	...	...	...	...	...	4	4	4	Oman
Pakistan	848	872	872	891	1 079	1 079	1 079	1 079	Pakistan
Philippines	1 097	1 097	1 097	1 097	1 097	1 097	1 097	1 097	Philippines
Saudi Arabia	279	279	279	279	279	1 150	1 150	1 150	Arabie saoudite
Singapore	87	87	87	87	87	87	87	87	Singapour
Sri Lanka	24	24	24	24	24	24	24	24	Sri Lanka
Syrian Arab Republic	75	75	75	75	75	75	75	75	Rép. arabe syrienne
Thailand	3 273	3 292	5 145	4 324	4 108	4 180	4 362	4 396	Thaïlande
Turkey	1 643	1 643	1 643	1 643	4 442	4 442	5 334	5 334	Turquie
United Arab Emirates	81	81	81	81	81	300	300	300	Emirats arabes unis
Uzbekistan	11	11	11	1	2	2	2	2	Ouzbékistan
Viet Nam	888	908	1 282	1 309	1 324	1 324	1 324	1 324	Viet Nam
Yemen	0	0	0	1	1	1	1	1	Yémen
Europe	**109 825**	**110 863**	**114 550**	**114 977**	**111 415**	**100 770**	**107 977**	**107 565**	**Europe**
Albania	3	3	3	...	...	...	...	...	Albanie
Austria	4 852	4 950	5 213	5 199	5 153	4 606	5 009	4 901	Autriche
Belarus	257	284	285	285	285	474	588	588	Bélarus
Belgium	1 957	1 897	1 897	1 931	2 006	1 990	1 974	2 040	Belgique
Bosnia and Herzegovina	81	81	118	111	93	108	122	128	Bosnie-Herzégovine
Bulgaria	326	326	313	367	326	217	248	293	Bulgarie
Croatia	464	592	564	545	535	526	560	540	Croatie
Czech Republic	934	969	1 042	1 023	932	805	907	829	République tchèque

Paper and paperboard *(continued)*
Production: thousand metric tons
Papiers et cartons *(suite)*
Production: milliers de tonnes

Region, country or area	2004	2005	2006	2007	2008	2009	2010	2011	Région, pays ou zone
Denmark	402	423	442	417	418	419	435	423	Danemark
Estonia	66	64	78	78	68	63	76	73	Estonie
Finland	14 036	12 391	14 189	14 334	13 126	10 602	11 758	11 329	Finlande
France	10 255	10 332	10 006	9 870	9 404	8 332	8 830	8 527	France
Germany	20 391	21 679	22 656	23 317	22 828	20 870	23 072	22 704	Allemagne
Greece	510	510	412	409	409	409	409	409	Grèce
Hungary	579	571	553	552	424	461	587	777	Hongrie
Ireland	45	45	0	49	48	45	45	47	Irlande
Italy	9 667	9 999	10 008	10 112	9 467	8 404	9 087	9 130	Italie
Latvia	38	39	57	60	52	54	53	64	Lettonie
Lithuania	99	113	119	124	123	86	113	111	Lituanie
Luxembourg	...	...	20	19	31	12	24	21	Luxembourg
Montenegro	...	...	...	...	203	227	227	227	Monténégro
Netherlands	3 459	3 471	3 367	3 224	2 977	2 609	2 859	2 748	Pays-Bas
Norway	2 294	2 223	2 109	2 010	1 900	1 577	1 695	1 492	Norvège
Poland	2 635	2 732	2 857	2 992	3 055	3 275	3 689	3 800	Pologne
Portugal	1 664	1 570	1 644	1 644	1 662	1 634	1 456	1 936	Portugal
Republic of Moldova	...	...	84	98	98	98	98	98	République de Moldova
Romania	454	371	432	558	422	250	250	297	Roumanie
Russian Federation	6 830	7 126	7 434	7 581	7 700	7 373	7 551	7 624	Fédération de Russie
Serbia	...	...	231	245	268	309	385	382	Serbie
Serbia and Montenegro	159	229	...	...	...	...	...	...	Serbie-et-Monténégro
Slovakia	798	858	888	915	921	921	780	748	Slovaquie
Slovenia	497	763	760	794	763	732	750	787	Slovénie
Spain	5 526	5 697	6 898	6 713	6 414	5 700	6 193	6 492	Espagne
Sweden	11 589	11 775	12 066	11 511	11 663	10 932	11 410	11 298	Suède
Switzerland	1 777	1 751	1 526	1 705	1 698	1 524	1 559	1 376	Suisse
TFYR of Macedonia	16	20	20	20	23	20	22	22	L'ex-R.Y. Macédoine
Ukraine	723	768	804	937	937	814	857	951	Ukraine
United Kingdom	6 442	6 241	5 454	5 228	4 983	4 293	4 300	4 353	Royaume-Uni
Oceania	**4 014**	**4 195**	**4 162**	**4 064**	**4 152**	**4 148**	**4 072**	**4 085**	**Océanie**
Australia	3 097	3 244	3 221	3 192	3 281	3 278	3 175	3 155	Australie
New Zealand	917	951	941	872	871	870	897	930	Nouvelle-Zélande

Source:
Food and Agriculture Organization of the United Nations (FAO), Rome,
FAOSTAT database last accessed August 2012.

Source:
Organisation des Nations Unies pour l'alimentation et l'agriculture (FAO),
Rome, la base de données de la FAOSTAT, dernier accès août 2012.

40

Aluminium, unwrought
Total production: thousand metric tons and millions of US dollars

Aluminium non travaillé
Production totale : milliers de tonnes et millions de dollars É.-U.

A. Thousand metric tons • Milliers de tonnes

Country or area	2001	2002	2003	2004	2005	2006	2007	2008	2009	Pays ou zone
Argentina	248	269	272	272	271	273	286	394	413	Argentine
Austria [1]	158	...	...	...	...	...	...	...	...	Autriche [1]
Azerbaijan	...	...	19[2]	30[2]	0	0	0	0	0	Azerbaïdjan
Bahrain [2]	523	519	532	530	...	...	...	...	...	Bahreïn [2]
Bosnia and Herzegovina	96[2]	103[2]	113	115[2]	...	...	...	...	...	Bosnie-Herzégovine
Brazil	951	1 449	1 195	1 275	1 307	1 267	1 557	1 665	1 637	Brésil
Cameroon	85	72	79	86	86	91	87	90	75	Cameroun
Canada	2 583[2]	2 709[2]	808	2 592[2]	...	...	...	...	...	Canada
China [3]	3 576	4 511	5 866	6 690	7 787	9 266	12 340	13 165	12 886	Chine [3]
Croatia	...	1	2	3	3	1	1	0	0	Croatie
Denmark	0	0	0	0	3	1	0	...	...	Danemark
Dominican Republic	...	6	5	3	2	^0	...	...	...	Rép. dominicaine
Ecuador	...	...	...	11	13	18	7	...	...	Equateur
Egypt	191[2]	195[2]	195[2]	215[2]	...	...	...	...	327	Egypte
Germany	404	410	438	...	329	225	280	305	206	Allemagne
Ghana	162	133	...	...	...	...	...	...	...	Ghana
Greece	166[2]	165[2]	166[4]	165[2]	...	...	...	...	...	Grèce
Hungary	110[2]	...	...	2	...	...	...	...	...	Hongrie
Iceland	169	194	286	192	180	...	446	761	805	Islande
India	624[2]	671[2]	...	124	209	...	...	...	...	Inde
Indonesia [2]	180	*160	200	230	...	...	...	...	...	Indonésie [2]
Iran (Islamic Rep. of)	160[2]	169[2]	170[2]	170[2]	336	218	216	283	323	Iran (Rép. islamique d')
Italy	766	782	#74	76	...	...	...	...	...	Italie
Kuwait	7	6	6	6	7	10	...	...	...	Koweït
Mozambique [2]	266	273	...	...	...	...	...	...	...	Mozambique [2]
Netherlands [2]	294	284	278	326	...	...	...	...	...	Pays-Bas [2]
New Zealand [2]	322	335	340	350	...	...	...	...	...	Nouvelle-Zélande [2]
Norway [2]	1 291	...	...	...	...	...	...	...	...	Norvège [2]
Poland	12	14	15	14	11	18	20	17	7	Pologne
Republic of Korea	325	357	356	454	463	...	...	...	...	République de Corée
Romania [5,6]	183	190	205	...	...	...	...	...	1	Roumanie [5,6]
Serbia	...	...	...	...	...	1	2	1	1	Serbie
Serbia and Montenegro	100	112	117	115[2]	...	...	...	...	...	Serbie-et-Monténégro
South Africa [2]	662	707	738	863	...	...	...	...	...	Afrique du Sud [2]
Spain	376[2]	380[2]	389[2]	...	...	...	82	...	...	Espagne
Suriname	...	2	...	...	...	...	...	...	...	Suriname
Sweden	35	29	28	^0	^0	^0	0	0	0	Suède
Switzerland [2]	36	40	44	45	...	...	...	...	...	Suisse [2]
Tajikistan [2]	289	306	319	358	...	...	...	...	...	Tadjikistan [2]
TFYR of Macedonia	3	5	5	...	...	...	...	...	...	L'ex-R.Y. Macédoine
Turkey	62	63	63	60[2]	27	...	...	...	...	Turquie
Ukraine [2]	106	112	...	...	...	...	...	...	...	Ukraine [2]
United Arab Emirates [2]	1	1	1	1	...	...	...	...	...	Emirats arabes unis [2]
United Kingdom	341[2]	344[2]	343[2]	360[2]	...	...	...	...	79	Royaume-Uni

40

Aluminium, unwrought *(continued)*
Total production: thousand metric tons and millions of US dollars
Aluminium non travaillé *(suite)*
Production totale : milliers de tonnes et millions de dollars É.-U.

A. Thousand metric tons • Milliers de tonnes

Country or area	2001	2002	2003	2004	2005	2006	2007	2008	2009	Pays ou zone
United States	2 637	2 707	2 703	2 516	2 481	2 284	2 554	2 658	1 727	Etats-Unis
Venezuela (Boliv. Rep. of)[2]	571	605	601	624	...	...	...	...	...	Venezuela (R. boliv. du)[2]

Source:
United Nations Statistics Division, New York, the *Industrial Commodity Statistics Yearbook 2009* and the industrial statistics database, last accessed December 2012.

1   Source: World Metal Statistics (London).
2   Source: U. S. Geological Survey (Washington, D. C.).
3   For statistical purposes, the data for China do not include those for the Hong Kong Special Administrative Region (Hong Kong SAR) and Macao Special Administrative Region (Macao SAR).

4   Incomplete coverage.
5   Including alloys.
6   Including pure content of virgin alloys.

Source:
Organisation des Nations Unies, Division de statistique, *l'Annuaire de statistiques industrielles par produit 2009* et la base de données sur les statistiques industrielles, dernier accès décembre 2012.

1   Source: World Metal Statistics (Londres).
2   Source: U. S. Geological Survey (Washington, D. C.).
3   Pour la présentation des statistiques, les données pour la Chine ne comprennent pas la Région Administrative Spéciale de Hong Kong (Hong Kong RAS) et la Région Administrative Spéciale de Macao (Macao RAS).

4   Couverture incomplète.
5   Y compris les alliages.
6   Y compris la teneur pure des alliages de première fusion.

40

Aluminium, unwrought
Thousand metric tons and millions of US dollars

Aluminium non travaillé
Milliers de tonnes et millions de dollars É.-U.

B. Millions of US dollars • Millions de dollars É.-U.

Country or area	2001	2002	2003	2004	2005	2006	2007	2008	2009	Pays ou zone
Brazil	1 305	1 345	1 499	1 991	2 179	2 935	3 323	3 065	1 862	Brésil
Canada	1 086	1 090	1 195	...	...	...	...	...	...	Canada
Denmark	0	0	2	3	7	4	0	...	...	Danemark
Ecuador	...	...	...	43	41	67	38	...	...	Equateur
Egypt	...	...	...	...	...	...	...	...	779	Egypte
Germany	441	469	642	653	542	534	725	866	388	Allemagne
Hungary	...	...	...	4	...	...	...	...	...	Hongrie
Iceland	...	...	...	370	375	...	1 246	2 059	1 379	Islande
India	...	...	10	28	99	...	...	...	...	Inde
Iran (Islamic Rep. of)	...	...	...	...	...	...	...	...	698	Iran (Rép. islamique d')
Italy	...	...	111	139	...	...	...	...	...	Italie
Mozambique	...	...	563	882	1 083	1 451	1 505	...	...	Mozambique
Poland	17	20	22	23	18	41	47	37	16	Pologne
Romania	...	4	...	...	...	...	...	...	1	Roumanie
Spain	...	...	...	...	...	...	226	...	...	Espagne
Sweden	36	29	35	1	1	1	0	0	0	Suède
United Kingdom	180	174	153	176	...	...	178	195	155	Royaume-Uni
Uruguay	...	...	0	...	...	...	...	...	...	Uruguay

Source:
United Nations Statistics Division, New York, the *Industrial Commodity Statistics Yearbook 2009* and the industrial statistics database, last accessed December 2012.

Source:
Organisation des Nations Unies, Division de statistique, *l'Annuaire de statistiques industrielles par produit 2009* et la base de données sur les statistiques industrielles, dernier accès décembre 2012.

41

Radio and television receivers production
Physical quantities in thousands and monetary value in millions of US dollars

Production récepteurs de radio et de télévision
Quantités physiques en milliers et valeurs monétaires en millions de dollars E.-U.

A. Quantities: thousands • Quantités : milliers

Country or area Pays ou zone	Radio receivers Récepteurs de radio					Television receivers Récepteurs de télévision				
	2005	2006	2007	2008	2009	2005	2006	2007	2008	2009
Argentina Argentine	301	517	679	628	353	1 627	2 042	2 219	...	...
Azerbaijan Azerbaïdjan	...	...	...	...	...	7	5	9	6	9
Bangladesh [1] Bangladesh [1]	20	24	...	...	...	172	192	...	...	...
Belarus Bélarus	13	8	5	9	10	1 308	1 067	702	717	352
Brazil Brésil	5 813	5 913	5 051	6 367	5 804	13 236	15 346	17 555	14 672	12 741
Bulgaria Bulgarie	...	...	...	...	...	159	249	334	494	...
Cuba Cuba	214	522	26	...	124	128	150	118	94	79
Czech Republic République tchèque	...	...	8 795	6 340	4 382	...	...	...	...	...
Denmark Danemark	49	125	107	...	...	273	84	...	...	...
Finland Finlande	...	...	...	...	...	3	...	...	...	...
Germany Allemagne	...	...	...	2 790	...	2 209	2 207	2 009	2 143	1 882
Hungary Hongrie	2 248	2 258	2 341	1 926	1 522	5 832	8 350	9 891	13 325	13 010
India Inde	...	...	...	...	...	6 060	5 853	...	...	...
Iran (Islamic Rep. of) Iran (Rép. islamique d')	562	821	301	637	...	...	...	...	...	...
Iraq Iraq	...	29	...	...	...	...	4	...	1	...
Japan Japon	1 769	1 456	1 941	344	466	11 072	15 740	13 798	15 684	18 567
Kazakhstan Kazakhstan	^0	...	...	...	...	346	410	323	326	...
Kyrgyzstan Kirghizistan	...	...	...	...	...	2	...	22	37	...
Malaysia Malaisie	19 245	28 433	46 253	61 539	58 410	10 409	7 594	6 028	5 732	6 362
Mexico Mexique	879	816	...	...	...	...	...	...	...	...
Nigeria Nigéria	26	...	...	...	...	3	...	...	...	...
Poland Pologne	15	18	...	...	...	6 525	8 920	13 147	15 677	18 726
Portugal Portugal	9 487	10 592	...	...	...	...	...	...	...	...
Republic of Korea République de Corée	1	...	...	...	...	5 843	...	...	...	...
Republic of Moldova République de Moldova	3	^0	...	...	...	...	...	...	...	...
Russian Federation Fédération de Russie	313	184	152	65	107	6 278	4 601	6 823	7 028	4 825

Radio and television receivers production (continued)
Physical quantities in thousands and monetary value in millions of US dollars

Production récepteurs de radio et de télévision *(suite)*
Quantités physiques en milliers et valeurs monétaires en millions de dollars E.-U.

A. Quantities : thousands • Quantités : milliers

Country or area Pays ou zone	Radio receivers Récepteurs de radio					Television receivers Récepteurs de télévision				
	2005	2006	2007	2008	2009	2005	2006	2007	2008	2009
Slovakia Slovaquie	...	...	...	...	...	...	...	...	9 058	9 076
Spain Espagne	110	151	150	324	340	3 084	2 991	3 010	...	2 191
Sweden Suède	275	145	367	316	192	344	...	...	...	...
Thailand Thaïlande	...	...	...	...	...	6 916	6 255	6 074	5 881	...
Ukraine Ukraine	18	2	1	...	1	651	434	514	571	2 302
United Kingdom Royaume-Uni	...	...	...	...	...	7 775	...	5 595	...	...
Viet Nam Viet Nam	25	23	37	27	...	...	...	...	...	...

Source:
United Nations Statistics Division, New York, the *Industrial Commodity Statistics Yearbook 2009* and the industrial statistics database, last accessed December 2012.

1   Twelve months ending 30 June of the year stated.

Source:
Organisation des Nations Unies, Division de statistique, New York, *l'Annuaire de statistiques industrielles par produit 2009* et la base de données sur les statistiques industrielles, dernier accès décembre 2012.

1   Période de douze mois finissant le 30 juin de l'année indiquée.

Household washing and drying machines
Production: Thousands of machines and millions of US dollars

Machines à laver et à sécher le linge, de type ménager
Production: Milliers de machines et millions de dollars É.-U.

A. Thousand of machines • Milliers de machines

Country or area	2001	2002	2003	2004	2005	2006	2007	2008	2009	Pays ou zone
Argentina	558	263	608	919	1 102	1 243	1 546	1 297	1 214	Argentine
Belarus	81	66	63	50	37	13	163	217	236	Bélarus
Brazil	2 495	2 875	4 428	3 708	3 794	4 402	5 856	5 780	7 391	Brésil
Chile	...	...	...	...	117	440	449	397	308	Chili
China [1]	13 416	15 958	19 645	25 334	30 355	35 605	40 051	44 470	49 736	Chine [1]
Cuba	49	45	15	5	0	0	0	0	0	Cuba
Ecuador	...	...	...	...	...	...	33	...	...	Equateur
Egypt	7	27	86	...	...	...	...	564	593	Egypte
Finland	...	...	...	...	...	6	4	...	...	Finlande
France	3 259	3 404	3 618	...	...	...	...	...	...	France
Germany	5 789	5 988	5 836	5 319	4 233	3 299	...	...	2 575	Allemagne
Greece [2]	...	...	5	...	...	...	...	...	...	Grèce [2]
Hungary	...	...	...	26	...	...	...	...	...	Hongrie
India	779	1 165	1 438	1 589	1 757	1 945	...	...	...	Inde
Indonesia	92	96	...	...	...	...	...	...	...	Indonésie
Iran (Islamic Rep. of)	296	411	363	335	430	418	780	809	682	Iran (Rép. islamique d')
Italy	8 507	8 884	9 905	9 829	...	...	...	...	...	Italie
Japan	4 546	3 982	3 882	3 930	3 839	3 848	3 159	2 822	2 531	Japon
Kazakhstan	11	17	20	50	73	102	127	68	...	Kazakhstan
Mexico	1 254	1 214	1 071	1 078	993	1 033	...	...	...	Mexique
Poland	...	...	...	...	2 338	3 287	3 742	4 153	5 028	Pologne
Republic of Moldova	25	40	48	55	36	22	...	...	...	République de Moldova
Republic of Korea	3 529	4 183	4 977	5 226	5 665	...	...	...	...	République de Corée
Romania	24	28	37	43	25	23	23	...	...	Roumanie
Russian Federation	1 039	1 369	1 330	1 452	1 582	2 016	2 713	2 694	2 260	Fédération de Russie
Serbia and Montenegro	5	4	...	...	...	...	...	...	...	Serbie-et-Monténégro
Spain	...	2 702	...	2 809	...	2 716	2 478	2 003	1 690	Espagne
Sweden	206	189	182	182	187	179	151	140	126	Suède
Syrian Arab Republic	62	85	85	87	77	85	91	94	...	Rép. arabe syrienne
Turkey	1 034	1 687	2 471	4 058	4 433	5 410	...	...	...	Turquie
Ukraine	166 [3]	232 [3]	255	345	322	208	173	230	164	Ukraine
United Kingdom	1 549 [4]	1 592 [4]	1 450 [4]	1 670 [4]	...	...	3 360	2 538	2 263	Royaume-Uni
United States	7 992	8 959	9 531	...	...	...	...	...	...	Etats-Unis
Viet Nam	168	211	283	514	337	340	415	528	491	Viet Nam

Source:
United Nations Statistics Division, New York, the *Industrial Commodity Statistics Yearbook 2009* and the industrial statistics database, last accessed December 2012.

1   For statistical purposes, the data for China do not include those for the Hong Kong Special Administrative Region (Hong Kong SAR) and Macao Special Administrative Region (Macao SAR).

2   Incomplete coverage.
3   Excluding household drying machines.
4   Excluding household washing machines and drying machines, including machines that both wash and dry.

Source:
Organisation des Nations Unies, Division de statistique, New York, *l'Annuaire de statistiques industrielles par produit 2009* et la base de données pour les statistiques industrielles, dernier accès décembre 2012.

1   Pour la présentation des statistiques, les données pour la Chine ne comprennent pas la Région Administrative Spéciale de Hong Kong (Hong Kong RAS) et la Région Administrative Spéciale de Macao (Macao RAS).

2   Couverture incomplète.
3   Non compris les machines à sécher le linge, de type ménager.
4   Code machines à laver le linge, même avec dispositif de séchage, et machines à sécher le linge.

Household washing and drying machines
Production: Thousands of machines and millions of US dollars

Machines à laver et à sécher le linge, de type ménager
Production: Milliers de machines et millions de dollars É.-U.

B.   Millions of US dollars • Millions de dollars É.-U.

Country or area	2001	2002	2003	2004	2005	2006	2007	2008	2009	Pays ou zone
Brazil	216	216	277	378	501	637	946	934	1 201	Brésil
Chile	...	...	...	...	9	54	57	50	40	Chili
Ecuador	...	...	...	...	...	...	13	...	...	Equateur
Egypt	3	9	22	...	...	...	...	^0	84	Egypte
Finland	10	9	2	2	2	3	1	1	0	Finlande
France	...	...	448	466	...	...	...	...	...	France
Germany	1 889	2 030	2 202	2 204	2 202	1 936			1 721	Allemagne
Hungary	...	...	...	2					...	Hongrie
India	...	...	191	213	206	...	...	...	...	Inde
Iran (Islamic Rep. of)	...	...	...	...	...	...	...	...	154	Iran (Rép. islamique d')
Italy	...	...	2 321	2 420	...	...	...	...	...	Italie
Japan	1 388	1 115	1 199	1 305	1 321	1 293	1 109	1 106	1 102	Japon
Jordan	...	...	...	^0	^0	1	^0	...	...	Jordanie
Mexico	162	144	108	116	95	98	...	...	...	Mexique
Poland	...	...	...	...	563	846	1 085	1 331	1 404	Pologne
Romania	...	2	3	4	3	2	3	...	...	Roumanie
Spain	...	...	...	667	...	665	653	577	458	Espagne
Sweden	97	91	98	111	142	103	106	112	93	Suède
United Kingdom	200[1]	214[1]	232[1]	295[1]	...	...	887	640	546	Royaume-Uni
United States [2]	4 162	4 447	4 770	5 130	5 236	5 184	5 232	4 844	4 820	Etats-Unis [2]

Source:
United Nations Statistics Division, New York, the *Industrial Commodity Statistics Yearbook 2009* and the industrial statistics database, last accessed December 2012.

1   Excluding household washing machines and drying machines, including machines that both wash and dry.
2   Including parts thereof.

Source:
Organisation des Nations Unies, Division de statistique, New York, *l'Annuaire de statistiques industrielles par produit 2009* et la base de données pour les statistiques industrielles, dernier accès décembre 2012.

1   Code machines à laver le linge, même avec dispositif de séchage, et machines à sécher le linge.
2   Y compris leurs pièces.

43

Machine tools
Production: number of units and millions of US dollars

Machines-outils
Production : Nombre d'unités et millions de dollars É.-U.

A.   Number of units • Nombre d'unités

Country or area Pays ou zone	2000	2001	2002	2003	2004	2005	2006	2007	2008	2009
Algeria Algérie										
Lathes										
Tours	38	27	30	47	...	...	...	...	...	...
Armenia Arménie										
Lathes										
Tours	40	47	115	95	44	10	28	7	9	16
Austria Autriche										
Lathes										
Tours	...	1 091	1 031	...	...	...	...	...	...	...
Azerbaijan [1] Azerbaïdjan [1]										
Lathes										
Tours	4	...	...	...	...	...	...	...	...	...
Belarus Bélarus										
Drilling, boring and milling machines										
Perceuses et fraiseuses	1 939	1 686	1 970	1 885	1 528	680	1 172	981	1 346	861
Lathes										
Tours	122	146	150	141	124	209	176	246	237	246
Brazil Brésil										
Drilling, boring and milling machines										
Perceuses et fraiseuses	9 328	11 800	10 940	11 311	*14 012	10 950	5 495	9 127	11 799	8 137
Lathes										
Tours	3 044	3 106	3 359	7 381	18 767	5 498	3 277	13 334	5 429	63 647
Bulgaria Bulgarie										
Drilling, boring and milling machines										
Perceuses et fraiseuses	1 470	1 233	1 154	958	866	934	618	521	484	242
Lathes										
Tours	1 555	1 937	1 813	2 068	2 324	2 134	2 008	2 075	1 816	582
Chile Chili										
Drilling, boring and milling machines										
Perceuses et fraiseuses	...	...	...	...	...	...	...	...	668	...
Croatia Croatie										
Lathes										
Tours	122	74	152	...	...	...	...	...	...	...
Czech Republic République tchèque										
Drilling, boring and milling machines										
Perceuses et fraiseuses	1 812	1 746	1 280	1 044	1 032	1 061	1 017	1 087	1 015	540
Lathes										
Tours	1 046	1 254	1 044	861	653	575	906	1 172	1 202	643
Denmark Danemark										
Drilling, boring and milling machines										
Perceuses et fraiseuses	36	39	32	24	49	34	55	53	35	34
Lathes										
Tours	0	0	74	59	0	0	0	0	...	...
Egypt Egypte										
Drilling, boring and milling machines										
Perceuses et fraiseuses	...	...	...	4	...	...	...	...	...	70
Lathes										
Tours	...	...	...	...	...	...	...	...	20	...
Finland Finlande										
Drilling, boring and milling machines										
Perceuses et fraiseuses	89	58	56	60	36	46	64	61	58	41
Georgia Géorgie										
Drilling, boring and milling machines										
Perceuses et fraiseuses	3	2	25	30	...	...	0	0	0	0
Lathes										
Tours	...	...	9	23	...	...	0	0	0	0

A. Number of units • Nombre d'unités

Country or area Pays ou zone	2000	2001	2002	2003	2004	2005	2006	2007	2008	2009
Germany Allemagne										
Drilling, boring and milling machines										
Perceuses et fraiseuses	23 924	...	...	...	17 330	...	19 576	15 721	45 370	29 545
Lathes										
Tours	6 684	...	5 775	4 824	5 207	5 035	5 783	6 574	23 342	...
Hungary Hongrie										
Drilling, boring and milling machines										
Perceuses et fraiseuses	...	...	68	68	234	29	22	13	0	...
Lathes										
Tours	100	...	220	...	35	...	...	...	...	...
India [2] Inde [2]										
Lathes										
Tours	21 579	20 469	14 623	7 677	4 476	4 278	3 165	...	...	...
Iran (Islamic Rep. of) Iran (Rép. islamique d')										
Lathes										
Tours	1 474[3]	1 691[3]	...	...	...	...	...	...	...	1 190
Japan Japon										
Drilling, boring and milling machines										
Perceuses et fraiseuses	16 178	9 520	6 593	7 796	9 031	13 040	9 885	16 544	14 311	3 211
Lathes										
Tours	22 027	19 813	...	...	...	...	...	...	...	...
Kazakhstan Kazakhstan										
Drilling, boring and milling machines										
Perceuses et fraiseuses	...	...	4	8	...	0	0	0	...	...
Lathes										
Tours	...	...	11	...	...	0	0	0	...	...
Kyrgyzstan Kirghizistan										
Lathes										
Tours	3[1]	...	3[1]	10[1]	0	3	...	...	...	...
Lithuania Lituanie										
Drilling, boring and milling machines										
Perceuses et fraiseuses	183	137	122	131	104	45	29	15	18	5
Lathes										
Tours	6	5	0	0	0	0	0	0	0	2
Poland Pologne										
Drilling, boring and milling machines										
Perceuses et fraiseuses	...	...	1 207	1 205	1 183	1 035	1 283	1 010	387	315
Lathes										
Tours	748	1 055	399	408	357	470	936	1 008	1 129	734
Portugal Portugal										
Drilling, boring and milling machines										
Perceuses et fraiseuses	...	25	10	14	13	3	7	...	...	...
Lathes										
Tours	...	...	...	...	...	...	1	...	...	...
Republic of Korea République de Corée										
Drilling, boring and milling machines										
Perceuses et fraiseuses	3 731	2 496	2 634	2 341	2 716	2 729	2 234	2 082	1 929	1 226
Lathes										
Tours	2 497	1 703	1 747	1 366	1 577	1 624	...	...	...	...
Romania Roumanie										
Drilling, boring and milling machines										
Perceuses et fraiseuses	...	...	1 202	809	697	525	291	189	311	47
Lathes										
Tours	307	388	299	65	48	61	123	54	51	68
Russian Federation Fédération de Russie										
Drilling, boring and milling machines										
Perceuses et fraiseuses	1 589	1 205	1 098	1 228	1 425	1 572	2 066	2 225	1 882	621
Lathes										
Tours	2 067	2 444	1 959	1 597	1 699	1 325	1 334	1 315	1 370	476

Machine tools *(continued)*
Production: number

Machines-outils *(suite)*
Production : nombre

A. Number of units • Nombre d'unités

Country or area Pays ou zone	2000	2001	2002	2003	2004	2005	2006	2007	2008	2009
Serbia and Montenegro Serbie-et-Monténégro										
Lathes										
Tours	181	...	...	...	...	...	...	...	...	...
Slovakia Slovaquie										
Drilling, boring and milling machines										
Perceuses et fraiseuses	...	1 011	1 019	923	519	...	...	...	...	...
Lathes										
Tours	1 769	1 683	1 215	1 247	2 598	1 100	1 085	...	...	...
Spain Espagne										
Drilling, boring and milling machines										
Perceuses et fraiseuses	...	...	...	...	5 858	6 062	4 659	6 012	3 501	1 324
Lathes										
Tours	3 492	4 240	3 143	2 785	2 404	2 573	1 955	2 004	1 791	703
Sweden Suède										
Drilling, boring and milling machines										
Perceuses et fraiseuses	3 727	1 933	1 956	1 422	1 400	1 881	1 974	1 979	1 897	9 873
Lathes										
Tours	17	18	23	0	3	6	151	6	7	7
Ukraine Ukraine										
Drilling, boring and milling machines										
Perceuses et fraiseuses	...	...	...	194	172	120	156	160	140	33
Lathes										
Tours	...	...	...	121	136	158	114	148	151	61
United Kingdom Royaume-Uni										
Drilling, boring and milling machines										
Perceuses et fraiseuses	...	...	...	...	...	...	...	1 549	821	...
Lathes [4]										
Tours [4]	3 317	2 937	...	...	...	...	...	...	...	...
United States [5] Etats-Unis [5]										
Drilling, boring and milling machines										
Perceuses et fraiseuses	7 822	4 793	2 327	3 343	3 930	8 807	10 097	9 246	8 139	...
Lathes										
Tours	3 278	2 949	1 793	1 816	4 038	4 852	5 769	6 210	7 416	2 676

Source:
United Nations Statistics Division, New York, the *Industrial Commodity Statistics Yearbook 2009* and the industrial statistics database, last accessed January 2013.

Source:
Organisation des Nations Unies, Division de statistique, New York, l'*Annuaire de statistiques industrielles par produit 2009* et la base de données pour les statistiques industrielles, dernier accès janvier 2013.

1   Source: Statistical Yearbook, Commonwealth of Independent States (Moscow).
2   All metal-cutting machines.
3   Production by establishments employing 10 or more persons.
4   Excluding numerically controlled horizontal lathes, automatic lathes (excl. turning centres).
5   Excluding machines valued under $3025 each.

1   Source: Annuaire des Statistiques, Communauté des États indépendants (Moscou).
2   Machines-outils tous types pour le travail des métaux.
3   Production des établissements occupant 10 personnes ou plus.
4   Non compris tours automatiques, horizontaux, à commande numérique.
5   Non compris les machines évaluées au-dessous de $3025 par pièce.

43

Machine tools
Production: number of units and millions of US dollars

Machines-outils
Production: Nombre d'unités et millions de dollars É.-U.

B. Millions of US dollars • Millions de dollars É.-U.

Country or area Pays ou zone	2000	2001	2002	2003	2004	2005	2006	2007	2008	2009
Brazil Brésil										
Drilling, boring and milling machines										
Perceuses et fraiseuses	14	14	5	14	7	24	33	39	45	38
Lathes										
Tours	88	78	61	69	105	140	140	195	213	160
Bulgaria Bulgarie										
Drilling, boring and milling machines										
Perceuses et fraiseuses	4	4	5	5	5	6	4	6	7	5
Lathes										
Tours	11	14	14	18	22	24	26	34	39	13
Czech Republic République tchèque										
Drilling, boring and milling machines										
Perceuses et fraiseuses	62	65	75	42	53	67	81	126	181	167
Lathes										
Tours	55	59	52	53	58	62	81	141	191	112
Denmark Danemark										
Drilling, boring and milling machines										
Perceuses et fraiseuses	4	5	2	1	3	3	3	4	2	2
Egypt Egypte										
Drilling, boring and milling machines										
Perceuses et fraiseuses	...	...	...	^0	...	...	...	...	3	^0
Lathes										
Tours	...	...	...	...	...	...	...	...	13	...
Finland Finlande										
Drilling, boring and milling machines										
Perceuses et fraiseuses	4	3	3	3	1	2	5	4	7	4
Lathes										
Tours	2	1	0	0	...	0	0	0	0	0
France France										
Drilling, boring and milling machines										
Perceuses et fraiseuses	50	72	65	...	...	...	...	...	...	...
Lathes										
Tours	68	58	60	...	...	...	...	...	...	...
Germany Allemagne										
Drilling, boring and milling machines										
Perceuses et fraiseuses	751	880	...	894	1 026	...	1 287	...	1 835	1 180
Lathes										
Tours	1 077	1 250	...	1 028	1 260	1 324	1 418	1 875	2 297	1 476
Hungary Hongrie										
Drilling, boring and milling machines										
Perceuses et fraiseuses	...	...	6	4	6	^0	1	^0	0	...
Lathes										
Tours	...	...	4	...	3	...	...	...	...	...
Iran (Islamic Rep. of) Iran (Rép. islamique d')										
Lathes										
Tours	...	...	...	...	...	...	...	...	...	23
Japan Japon										
Drilling, boring and milling machines										
Perceuses et fraiseuses	424	437	267	271	435	633	501	845	947	486
Lathes										
Tours	2 248	2 114	1 474	1 874	2 534	3 558	3 750	3 673	4 174	1 919
Jordan Jordanie										
Lathes										
Tours	...	...	...	...	7	6	8	7	...	...

43

Machine tools *(continued)*
Production: number
Machines-outils *(suite)*
Production : nombre

B. Millions of US dollars • Millions de dollars É.-U.

Country or area Pays ou zone	2000	2001	2002	2003	2004	2005	2006	2007	2008	2009
Lithuania Lituanie										
Drilling, boring and milling machines										
Perceuses et fraiseuses	1	1	^0	1	1	1	^0	^0	^0	^0
Lathes										
Tours	...	...	0	0	0	0	0	0	0	1
Poland Pologne										
Drilling, boring and milling machines										
Perceuses et fraiseuses	...	...	4	4	7	8	11	12	14	14
Lathes										
Tours	...	...	9	9	11	25	81	106	143	87
Romania Roumanie										
Drilling, boring and milling machines										
Perceuses et fraiseuses	...	...	5	7	8	10	6	6	7	4
Lathes										
Tours	...	...	5	4	2	3	11	12	24	16
Slovakia Slovaquie										
Drilling, boring and milling machines										
Perceuses et fraiseuses	...	1	1	1	1	...	...	...	...	...
Lathes										
Tours	...	22	16	19	38	21	23	...	...	...
Spain Espagne										
Drilling, boring and milling machines										
Perceuses et fraiseuses	...	...	...	...	211	218	246	361	466	288
Lathes										
Tours	...	...	...	...	106	113	127	157	164	125
Sweden Suède										
Drilling, boring and milling machines										
Perceuses et fraiseuses	8	4	4	5	5	8	8	6	7	8
Lathes										
Tours	4	4	6	0	1	2	3	3	4	4
United Kingdom Royaume-Uni										
Drilling, boring and milling machines										
Perceuses et fraiseuses	...	...	...	...	...	...	...	...	25	23
United States [1] Etats-Unis [1]										
Drilling, boring and milling machines										
Perceuses et fraiseuses	261	285	202	171	181	165	235	212	248	...
Lathes										
Tours	287	262	132	120	232	248	296	376	321	205

Source:
United Nations Statistics Division, New York, the *Industrial Commodity Statistics Yearbook 2009* and the industrial statistics database, last accessed January 2013.

Source:
Organisation des Nations Unies, Division de statistique, New York, *l'Annuaire de statistiques industrielles par produit 2009* et la base de données pour les statistiques industrielles, dernier accès janvier 2013.

1   Excluding machines valued under $3025 each.

1   Non compris les machines évaluées au-dessous de $3025 par pièce.

44

Trucks
Number of units and millions of US dollars

Camions
Nombre d'unités et des millions de dollars É.-U.

A. Number of Units • Nombre d'unités

Country or area	2001	2002	2003	2004	2005	2006	2007	2008	2009	Pays ou zone
Algeria	...	...	...	2 698	...	...	...	...	...	Algérie
Argentina	57 509	41 778	50 799	72 493	116 444	145 754	162 497	...	...	Argentine
Belarus	16 524	16 544	18 138	21 506	22 251	23 175	25 540	26 304	11 478	Bélarus
Brazil	147 054	152 321	155 516	225 615	105 874	95 572	107 800	127 347	101 529	Brésil
Chile	...	...	...	...	46	42	...	1	1	Chili
Czech Republic	4 701	1 095	666	306	229	222	...	...	794	République tchèque
Denmark	90	103	...	...	...	...	...	1	...	Danemark
Finland	616	596	702	784	910	1 003	1 006	1 413	522	Finlande
Georgia	4	5	...	...	...	...	...	...	...	Géorgie
Germany	282 610	...	...	...	299 498	314 331	392 678	379 111	204 497	Allemagne
Iran (Islamic Rep. of)	49 810	57 638	79 131	99 838	155 941	174 668	193 425	188 778	...	Iran (Rép. islamique d')
Iraq	...	...	...	...	...	...	...	150	...	Iraq
Ireland	406	433	568	461	...	...	...	...	...	Irlande
Kazakhstan	97	338	84	18	144	1 523	2 043	1 013	...	Kazakhstan
Kenya	...	2 439	3 254	4 667	1 873	3 779	2 845	2 523	2 217	Kenya
Lithuania	41	126	182	778	803	1 133	1 457	320	108	Lituanie
Mexico	557 546	520 276	516 526	515 529	497 992	549 751	...	...	...	Mexique
Nigeria	1 319	1 340	1 309	1 322	1 324	...	...	...	...	Nigéria
Pakistan [1]	952	1 141	1 950	2 022	3 204	4 518	4 410	4 993	3 135	Pakistan [1]
Poland	25 718	21 851	17 502	59 541	67 967	75 216	...	...	...	Pologne
Portugal	...	...	...	...	3 528	3 443	...	...	...	Portugal
Republic of Korea	242 030	274 698	233 720	210 008	218 902	...	...	...	...	République de Corée
Romania	...	13 829	19 421	23 060	20 449	12 272	7 706	12 026	...	Roumanie
Russian Federation	173 000	173 000	193 000	200 000	205 085	245 291	285 030	256 037	91 676	Fédération de Russie
Serbia	...	...	...	...	...	441	473	348	155	Serbie
South Africa	12 736	7 479	6 061	...	...	...	...	...	...	Afrique du Sud
Spain	...	...	...	456 542	472 014	493 529	494 442	456 157	315 740	Espagne
Sweden	...	...	...	...	37 042	32 764	37 872	37 513	15 614	Suède
Thailand	298 460	394 683	489 608	655 809	847 301	894 794	971 348	991 917	...	Thaïlande
Turkey	...	...	18 707	31 125	39 324	35 142	...	...	...	Turquie
Ukraine	...	...	4 348	10 651	13 731	11 760	10 844	11 370	2 471	Ukraine
United Kingdom	...	...	...	...	...	...	...	...	66 364	Royaume-Uni

Source:
United Nations Statistics Division, New York, the industrial statistics database, last accessed December 2012.

Source:
Organisation des Nations Unies, Division de statistique, New York, et la base de données sur les statistiques industrielles, dernier accès décembre 2012.

1   Twelve months ending 30 June of the year stated.

1   Période de douze mois finissant le 30 juin de l'année indiquée.

Trucks
Number of units and millions of US dollars

Camions
Nombre d'unités et des millions de dollars É.-U.

B. Millions of US dollars • Millions de dollars É.-U.

Country or area	2001	2002	2003	2004	2005	2006	2007	2008	2009	Pays ou zone
Brazil	1 971	1 639	2 008	3 598	3 366	3 887	5 834	8 458	6 521	Brésil
Czech Republic	30	28	24	13	11	14	...	...	96	République tchèque
Denmark	7	8	...	...	...	...	...	^0	...	Danemark
Finland	60	66	84	97	101	103	152	349	156	Finlande
France	6 709	6 790	8 183	10 020	...	...	...	...	...	France
Germany	7 091	6 737	8 602	10 495	11 544	12 112	15 805	16 461	7 737	Allemagne
Iraq	...	...	...	...	...	...	...	9	...	Iraq
Ireland	27	31	52	46	...	...	...	...	...	Irlande
Japan	19 990	19 614	23 356	25 988	26 073	26 033	29 698	38 327	28 423	Japon
Kenya	...	11	17	23	21	25	33	30	25	Kenya
Lithuania	...	^0	^0	1	1	1	22	11	^0	Lituanie
Mexico	11 325	10 997	10 101	10 766	10 875	11 195	...	...	...	Mexique
Nigeria	21	20	18	18	18	...	...	...	...	Nigéria
Poland	264	292	248	819	969	...	...	...	...	Pologne
Portugal	...	...	...	...	67	66	...	...	...	Portugal
Romania	...	77	116	153	160	174	99	165	...	Roumanie
Spain	...	...	...	6 167	6 514	7 670	8 697	9 486	5 525	Espagne
Sweden	1 692	1 902	2 446	3 182	3 351	3 277	4 300	4 144	1 601	Suède
United Kingdom	...	...	...	...	...	...	...	...	1 349	Royaume-Uni
Uruguay	2	...	^0	...	...	...	...	...	...	Uruguay

Source:
United Nations Statistics Division, New York, the industrial statistics database, last accessed December 2012.

Source:
Organisation des Nations Unies, Division de statistique, New York, et la base de données sur les statistiques industrielles, dernier accès décembre 2012.

Production, trade and consumption of commercial energy
Thousand metric tons of oil equivalent and kilograms per capita

Production, commerce et consommation d'énergie commerciale
Milliers de tonnes d'équivalent pétrole et kilogrammes par habitant

Region, country or area	Year Année	Primary energy production – Production d'énergie primaire					Changes in stocks	Imports Importations	Exports Exportations
		Total Totale	Solids Solides	Liquids Liquides	Gas Gaz	Electricity Electricité	Variations des stocks		
World	2006	10 500 330	3 203 342	4 060 016	2 711 542	525 430	74 077	4 546 513	4 553 038
	2007	10 700 943	3 331 386	4 068 467	2 775 019	526 072	14 940	4 635 834	4 622 953
	2008	10 963 519	3 436 332	4 102 320	2 883 462	541 405	96 555	4 678 982	4 684 622
	2009	10 869 931	3 484 282	4 046 270	2 790 566	548 813	89 696	4 548 495	4 558 355
Africa	2006	846 566	132 604	513 446	191 234	9 282	2 087	99 205	590 164
	2007	852 432	133 875	520 940	188 056	9 561	-3 305	107 076	596 877
	2008	862 894	135 058	527 202	190 920	9 714	3 021	106 171	587 340
	2009	833 842	134 673	507 517	181 597	10 055	-3 368	114 905	560 282
Algeria	2006	195 678	...	103 826	91 833	19	716	1 358	152 244
	2007	185 756	...	103 940	81 796	19	-728	1 408	143 204
	2008	182 222	...	101 575	80 623	24	505	1 438	139 980
	2009	173 267	...	95 287	77 950	29	111	1 446	126 331
Angola	2006	72 758	...	71 895	634	229	618	1 432	69 850
	2007	87 562	...	86 521	774	267	78	1 789	84 970
	2008	97 909	...	97 023	617	269	1 019	2 417	94 617
	2009	92 954	...	92 055	626	273	-165	2 722	90 666
Benin	2006	0	...	...	...	0	9	1 137	...
	2007	0	...	...	...	0	-8	1 321	...
	2008	0	...	...	...	0	4	1 365	...
	2009	0	...	...	...	0	-3	1 543	...
Botswana	2006	673	673	...	...	...	0	895	...
	2007	580	580	...	...	...	-43	1 012	...
	2008	637	637	...	...	...	-1	1 117	...
	2009	517	517	...	...	...	-1	1 094	...
Burkina Faso	2006	7	...	...	...	7	-86	394	...
	2007	10	...	...	...	10	-10	559	...
	2008	12	...	...	...	12	*12	608	...
	2009	11	...	...	...	11	*-11	570	...
Burundi	2006	11	3	...	...	8	7	73	...
	2007	13	3	...	...	10	4	68	...
	2008	13	3	...	...	10	3	70	...
	2009	14	4	...	...	10	2	72	...
Cameroon	2006	5 000	...	4 666	0	335	35	2 052	5 355
	2007	5 085	...	4 421	334	331	-297	2 037	4 968
	2008	5 056	...	4 346	346	364	-300	1 926	4 855
	2009	4 427	...	3 796	286	345	-360	1 736	3 825
Cape Verde	2006	1	...	...	...	1	...	*109	...
	2007	1	...	...	...	1	...	*110	...
	2008	0	...	...	...	0	...	112	...
	2009	0	...	...	...	0	...	126	...
Central African Rep.	2006	12	...	...	...	12	...	*105	...
	2007	12	...	...	...	12	...	*108	...
	*2008	12	...	...	...	12	...	110	...
	2009	12	...	...	...	12	...	*110	...
Chad	2006	7 955	...	7 955	...	...	...	*86	7 887
	2007	7 264	...	7 264	...	...	...	*87	7 178
	2008	6 397	...	6 397	...	...	...	*82	6 297
	2009	6 122	...	6 122	...	...	...	*82	6 048
Comoros *	2006	0	...	...	...	0	...	41	...
	2007	0	...	...	...	0	...	41	...
	2008	0	...	...	...	0	...	42	...
	2009	0	...	...	...	0	...	42	...
Congo	2006	14 475	...	14 421	22	32	0	133	14 122
	2007	11 656	...	11 608	20	29	0	170	11 271
	2008	12 368	...	12 312	24	32	92	288	11 949
	2009	14 361	...	14 281	51	28	-364	240	14 304
Côte d'Ivoire	2006	4 818	...	3 167	1 521	130	-206	3 760	5 742
	2007	3 716	...	2 443	1 118	155	-145	3 757	4 878
	2008	3 944	...	2 306	1 475	163	-322	3 291	4 494
	2009	4 238	...	2 587	1 468	182	-56	3 214	4 555
Dem. Rep. of the Congo	2006	1 993	86	1 257	4	647	-17	841	1 388
	2007	1 999	88	1 231	8	672	3	864	1 348
	2008	1 908	90	1 167	8	643	16	771	1 209
	2009	1 891	93	1 119	8	670	-4	731	1 197

Production, trade and consumption of commercial energy *(continued)*
Thousand metric tons of oil equivalent and kilograms per capita
Production, commerce et consommation d'énergie commerciale *(suite)*
Milliers de tonnes d'équivalent pétrole et kilogrammes par habitant

Bunkers - Soutes				**Consumption - Consommation**						
Air Avion	Sea Maritime	Unallocated Non distribué	Per capita Par habitant	Total Totale	Solids Solides	Liquids Liquides	Gas Gaz	Electricity Electricité	Year Année	Région, pays ou zone
135 265	173 266	501 257	1 460	9 609 939	3 165 759	3 248 464	2 669 916	525 801	2006	Monde
139 647	182 416	500 754	1 483	9 876 068	3 284 918	3 268 163	2 796 295	526 691	2007	
142 321	180 374	475 364	1 493	10 063 266	3 362 319	3 288 672	2 870 051	542 223	2008	
134 938	178 745	468 001	1 465	9 988 691	3 373 678	3 255 859	2 808 590	550 565	2009	
4 821	5 458	21 712	345	321 528	103 557	120 641	87 681	9 650	2006	Afrique
5 268	5 590	21 529	350	333 547	106 108	127 815	89 430	10 194	2007	
5 713	2 754	22 827	356	347 411	108 471	135 984	92 472	10 484	2008	
5 777	2 683	31 162	353	352 211	112 002	137 192	92 136	10 881	2009	
371	317	6 450	1 106	36 938	734	9 575	26 604	26	2006	Algérie
365	349	7 440	1 077	36 534	830	10 880	24 803	20	2007	
409	324	6 644	1 040	35 799	766	11 360	23 652	20	2008	
457	293	8 498	1 117	39 023	412	12 777	25 807	26	2009	
79	16	359	192	3 267	...	2 404	634	229	2006	Angola
115	14	258	223	3 916	...	2 875	774	267	2007	
137	14	142	244	4 396	...	3 510	617	269	2008	
199	188	158	249	4 629	...	3 730	626	273	2009	
22	...	...	141	1 106	...	1 056	...	51	2006	Bénin
26	...	...	161	1 303	...	1 253	...	50	2007	
42	...	...	158	1 319	...	1 262	...	57	2008	
89	...	...	169	1 457	...	1 383	...	74	2009	
10	...	...	819	1 558	685	678	...	194	2006	Botswana
8	...	...	844	1 627	633	769	...	224	2007	
17	...	...	889	1 738	640	858	...	240	2008	
15	...	...	806	1 596	519	829	...	248	2009	
16	...	...	32	470	...	451	...	19	2006	Burkina Faso
14	...	...	38	565	...	545	...	20	2007	
21	...	...	38	587	...	564	...	23	2008	
15	...	...	36	577	...	553	...	24	2009	
7	...	...	10	72	3	55	...	13	2006	Burundi
6	...	...	9	70	3	51	...	17	2007	
6	...	...	9	74	3	55	...	16	2008	
6	...	...	10	78	4	56	...	18	2009	
42	42	82	83	1 496	...	1 161	0	335	2006	Cameroun
64	52	392	106	1 944	...	1 279	334	331	2007	
67	50	363	104	1 948	...	1 239	346	364	2008	
69	50	502	108	2 077	...	1 446	286	345	2009	
...	*10	...	*209	*100	...	*99	...	1	2006	Cap-Vert
...	*10	...	*208	*100	...	*100	...	1	2007	
...	*13	...	203	99	...	98	...	0	2008	
...	*20	...	215	106	...	105	...	0	2009	
*29	...	...	*22	*88	...	*76	...	12	2006	Rép. centrafricaine
*30	...	...	*22	*90	...	*78	...	12	2007	
31	...	...	21	91	...	79	...	12	*2008	
*31	...	...	*21	*91	...	*79	...	12	2009	
*20	...	68	*7	*66	...	*66	...	...	2006	Tchad
*20	...	86	*6	*67	...	*67	...	...	2007	
*19	...	100	*6	*63	...	*63	...	...	2008	
*19	...	73	*6	*63	...	*63	...	...	2009	
...	...	...	63	42	...	41	...	0	2006	Comores *
...	...	...	61	42	...	41	...	0	2007	
...	...	...	61	43	...	42	...	0	2008	
...	...	...	59	43	...	42	...	0	2009	
...	0	32	125	454	...	365	22	67	2006	Congo
...	28	40	131	487	...	400	20	67	2007	
...	43	46	137	525	...	431	24	70	2008	
...	0	36	158	625	...	508	51	66	2009	
92	65	207	146	2 679	...	1 120	1 521	38	2006	Côte d'Ivoire
50	109	415	116	2 166	...	959	1 118	88	2007	
56	68	187	145	2 751	...	1 164	1 475	112	2008	
52	63	169	138	2 668	...	1 059	1 468	140	2009	
210	...	0	21	1 254	272	443	4	534	2006	Rép. dém. du Congo
174	...	0	22	1 337	287	485	8	558	2007	
15	...	0	23	1 439	301	538	8	592	2008	
15	...	3	22	1 411	310	490	8	603	2009	

45

Production, trade and consumption of commercial energy *(continued)*
Thousand metric tons of oil equivalent and kilograms per capita
Production, commerce et consommation d'énergie commerciale *(suite)*
Milliers de tonnes d'équivalent pétrole et kilogrammes par habitant

Region, country or area	Year Année	Primary energy production – Production d'énergie primaire					Changes in stocks	Imports	Exports
		Total Totale	Solids Solides	Liquids Liquides	Gas Gaz	Electricity Electricité	Variations des stocks	Imports Importations	Exports Exportations
Djibouti	2006	...	...	...	...	...	...	331	...
	2007	...	...	...	...	...	...	331	...
	2008	...	...	...	...	...	...	356	...
	2009	...	...	...	...	...	...	361	...
Egypt	2006	88 005	15	37 281	49 545	1 164	-89	7 100	19 717
	2007	91 475	15	39 034	51 022	1 405	-159	7 480	19 304
	2008	97 428	15	41 421	54 650	1 342	-146	8 108	22 465
	2009	98 163	15	39 728	57 216	1 203	-135	10 146	24 739
Equatorial Guinea	2006	24 285	...	22 970	*1 314	*1	...	*209	21 789
	2007	25 286	...	23 727	*1 558	*1	...	*214	22 479
	2008	25 218	...	23 678	*1 539	*1	...	*218	22 419
	2009	23 206	...	21 667	*1 539	*1	...	*218	20 407
Eritrea	2006	0	...	...	...	0	-32	153	...
	2007	0	...	...	...	0	-33	156	...
	2008	0	...	...	...	0	-3	129	...
	2009	0	...	...	...	0	-9	154	...
Ethiopia	2006	280	...	...	...	280	-218	1 676	...
	2007	291	...	...	...	291	-186	1 918	...
	2008	285	...	...	...	285	-224	2 052	...
	2009	309	...	...	...	309	-244	2 231	...
Gabon	2006	12 408	...	12 186	140	81	-206	183	11 701
	2007	12 637	...	12 418	150	69	-230	199	11 837
	2008	12 346	...	12 101	169	77	-106	191	11 428
	2009	12 402	...	12 159	167	76	-72	135	11 702
Gambia	2006	...	...	...	...	...	...	*116	*2
	2007	...	...	...	...	...	...	135	2
	2008	...	...	...	...	...	...	140	2
	2009	...	...	...	...	...	...	150	2
Ghana	2006	483	...	...	...	483	...	3 241	307
	2007	320	...	...	...	320	...	3 346	287
	2008	533	...	...	...	533	...	3 095	405
	2009	591	...	...	...	591	...	2 908	559
Guinea	2006	40	...	...	0	40	...	*413	...
	2007	46	...	...	0	46	...	*425	...
	2008	46	...	...	0	45	...	*426	...
	2009	45	...	...	0	45	...	*431	...
Guinea-Bissau *	2006	...	...	...	...	...	...	101	...
	2007	...	...	...	...	...	...	106	...
	2008	...	...	...	...	...	...	104	...
	2009	...	...	...	...	...	...	108	...
Kenya	2006	350	...	...	...	350	-26	3 520	106
	2007	394	...	...	...	394	-260	3 326	96
	2008	346	...	...	...	346	-11	3 497	22
	2009	297	...	...	...	297	-222	3 941	47
Lesotho	2006	17	...	...	...	17	...	2	...
	2007	17	...	...	...	17	...	2	...
	2008	17	...	...	...	17	...	2	...
	2009	17	...	...	...	17	...	0	...
Liberia	2006	...	...	...	...	...	...	242	...
	2007	...	...	...	...	...	...	216	...
	2008	...	...	...	...	...	...	190	...
	2009	...	...	...	...	...	...	174	...
Libyan Arab Jamah.	2006	99 990	...	86 557	13 433	...	...	12	80 582
	2007	97 739	...	82 800	14 939	...	...	7	78 149
	2008	100 618	...	85 073	15 546	...	...	6	79 712
	2009	87 287	...	72 856	14 431	...	...	8	65 065
Madagascar	2006	55	...	...	...	55	6	603	...
	2007	62	...	...	...	62	12	634	...
	2008	60	...	...	...	60	28	693	...
	2009	64	...	...	...	64	-19	591	...
Malawi	2006	155	*38	...	...	116	...	242	*8
	2007	163	*42	...	...	121	...	237	*8
	2008	169	*37	...	...	133	...	303	*8
	2009	*167	*38	...	...	*129	...	270	*7

45

Production, trade and consumption of commercial energy *(continued)*
Thousand metric tons of oil equivalent and kilograms per capita
Production, commerce et consommation d'énergie commerciale *(suite)*
Milliers de tonnes d'équivalent pétrole et kilogrammes par habitant

Bunkers - Soutes			Consumption - Consommation							
Air Avion	Sea Maritime	Unallocated Non distribué	Per capita Par habitant	Total Totale	Solids Solides	Liquids Liquides	Gas Gaz	Electricity Electricité	Year Année	Région, pays ou zone
104	*84	...	173	143	...	143	...	...	2006	Djibouti
104	*84	...	170	143	...	143	...	...	2007	
104	*97	...	181	155	...	155	...	...	2008	
104	*100	...	180	157	...	157	...	...	2009	
801	1 082	9 220	852	64 375	780	28 009	34 451	1 134	2006	Egypte
998	991	9 814	884	68 008	778	29 918	35 955	1 357	2007	
900	485	11 361	900	70 472	761	29 859	38 586	1 265	2008	
980	308	11 138	894	71 278	745	29 587	39 823	1 123	2009	
*35	...	1 167	*2 402	*1 503	...	*188	*1 314	*1	2006	Guinée équatoriale
*35	...	1 227	*2 732	*1 759	...	*200	*1 558	*1	2007	
*36	...	1 238	*2 631	*1 743	...	*203	*1 539	*1	2008	
*36	...	1 238	*2 559	*1 743	...	*203	*1 539	*1	2009	
7	...	...	38	177	...	177	...	0	2006	Erythrée
5	...	...	38	184	...	183	...	0	2007	
3	...	...	26	129	...	129	...	0	2008	
1	...	...	32	162	...	162	...	0	2009	
183	...	...	26	1 992	...	1 711	...	280	2006	Ethiopie
226	...	...	28	2 169	...	1 878	...	291	2007	
221	...	...	29	2 340	...	2 056	...	285	2008	
240	...	...	31	2 544	...	2 235	...	309	2009	
65	235	9	563	787	...	566	140	81	2006	Gabon
54	266	15	628	894	...	675	150	69	2007	
55	269	13	607	880	...	634	169	77	2008	
42	184	8	456	674	...	431	167	76	2009	
...	...	...	*73	*114	...	*112	2	...	2006	Gambie
...	...	...	84	133	...	131	2	...	2007	
...	...	...	84	138	...	136	2	...	2008	
...	...	...	88	148	...	146	2	...	2009	
124	40	27	146	3 226	...	2 754	...	472	2006	Ghana
132	45	-18	142	3 221	...	2 884	...	337	2007	
128	58	114	126	2 923	...	2 413	...	510	2008	
134	75	86	111	2 645	...	2 101	...	544	2009	
*23	...	...	*47	*430	...	*390	0	40	2006	Guinée
*26	...	...	*48	*446	...	*399	0	46	2007	
*25	...	...	*47	*447	...	*401	0	45	2008	
*26	...	...	*46	*451	...	*406	0	45	2009	
10	...	...	65	90	...	90	...	...	2006	Guinée-Bissau *
11	...	...	66	95	...	95	...	...	2007	
11	...	...	64	93	...	93	...	...	2008	
11	...	...	65	97	...	97	...	...	2009	
612	27	127	83	3 025	117	2 561	...	347	2006	Kenya
659	5	145	82	3 074	106	2 578	...	391	2007	
577	1	139	81	3 116	108	2 661	...	347	2008	
589	2	273	90	3 548	97	3 153	...	298	2009	
...	...	...	9	19	...	...	...	19	2006	Lesotho
...	...	...	9	19	...	...	...	19	2007	
...	...	...	9	19	...	...	...	19	2008	
...	...	...	8	17	...	...	...	17	2009	
*3	*13	...	68	226	...	226	...	...	2006	Libéria
*3	*13	...	58	200	...	200	...	...	2007	
*3	*12	...	48	175	...	175	...	...	2008	
*4	*12	...	41	158	...	158	...	...	2009	
179	89	3 344	2 682	15 807	1	9 952	5 851	3	2006	Jamah. arabe libyenne
188	89	3 308	2 658	16 012	0	10 136	5 879	-2	2007	
193	89	3 285	2 821	17 345	0	11 243	6 106	-4	2008	
238	89	3 618	2 920	18 285	*2	12 179	6 108	-4	2009	
55	*10	1	32	586	11	521	...	55	2006	Madagascar
56	*12	1	32	617	7	548	...	62	2007	
56	*8	0	34	661	9	591	...	60	2008	
39	*8	0	31	627	10	553	...	64	2009	
...	...	...	29	389	*41	232	...	116	2006	Malawi
...	...	...	29	392	*43	230	...	119	2007	
...	...	...	33	464	*36	297	...	131	2008	
...	...	...	30	430	*34	269	...	*128	2009	

45

Production, trade and consumption of commercial energy *(continued)*
Thousand metric tons of oil equivalent and kilograms per capita
Production, commerce et consommation d'énergie commerciale *(suite)*
Milliers de tonnes d'équivalent pétrole et kilogrammes par habitant

| Region, country or area | Year Année | Primary energy production – Production d'énergie primaire | | | | | Changes in stocks Variations des stocks | Imports Importations | Exports Exportations |
		Total Totale	Solids Solides	Liquids Liquides	Gas Gaz	Electricity Electricité			
Mali *	2006	23	...	...	...	23	...	210	...
	2007	23	...	...	...	23	...	214	...
	2008	24	...	...	...	24	...	219	...
	2009	25	...	...	...	25	...	225	...
Mauritania	2006	1 542	...	1 542	...	...	93	516	1 448
	2007	757	...	757	...	...	100	584	655
	2008	610	...	610	...	...	93	630	515
	2009	567	...	567	...	...	*297	*626	270
Mauritius	2006	7	...	...	...	7	-58	1 384	...
	2007	7	...	...	...	7	39	1 542	...
	2008	9	...	...	...	9	-36	1 504	...
	2009	11	...	...	...	11	-117	1 373	...
Morocco	2006	224	...	10	62	152	-108	14 749	611
	2007	211	...	14	60	137	-117	15 833	625
	2008	201	...	9	49	142	-574	15 621	222
	2009	339	...	8	41	290	-3	15 474	462
Mozambique	2006	3 811	29	...	2 516	1 265	19	1 412	3 555
	2007	3 894	17	...	2 496	1 381	25	1 420	3 432
	2008	4 112	27	...	2 785	1 300	15	1 311	3 659
	2009	4 207	27	...	2 723	1 457	16	1 401	3 747
Namibia	2006	119	...	...	...	119	6	1 170	3
	2007	134	...	...	...	134	7	1 225	3
	2008	122	...	...	...	122	5	1 512	4
	2009	123	...	...	...	123	7	1 355	12
Niger	2006	97	97	...	...	0	-8	175	0
	2007	94	94	...	...	0	25	225	0
	2008	100	100	...	...	0	-7	215	0
	2009	124	124	...	...	0	-1	281	0
Nigeria	2006	151 075	6	124 664	25 867	539	1 382	6 799	135 670
	2007	145 821	6	115 783	29 497	535	-1 766	7 463	135 252
	2008	140 643	6	111 347	28 799	492	-1 863	5 769	124 874
	2009	138 459	6	117 002	21 062	389	-2 570	7 501	130 421
Réunion *	2006	50	...	...	...	50	...	846	...
	2007	65	...	...	...	65	...	853	...
	2008	65	...	...	...	65	...	865	...
	2009	65	...	...	...	65	...	872	...
Rwanda	2006	4	...	...	*1	3	4	181	0
	2007	4	...	...	*1	4	-1	188	0
	2008	7	...	...	*1	6	*2	*186	0
	2009	9	...	...	*1	9	*1	*191	0
Saint Helena	2006	...	...	...	...	...	...	3	...
	2007	...	...	...	...	...	...	4	...
	2008	0	...	...	...	0	...	3	...
	2009	0	...	...	...	0	...	3	...
Sao Tome and Principe	*2006	1	...	...	...	1	...	43	...
	2007	1	...	...	...	1	...	*43	...
	*2008	1	...	...	...	1	...	43	...
	*2009	1	...	...	...	1	...	43	...
Senegal	2006	12	...	...	12	0	-135	1 357	161
	2007	11	...	...	11	0	16	1 885	351
	2008	10	...	...	10	0	24	1 875	311
	2009	16	...	...	16	0	81	1 589	282
Seychelles	2006	...	...	...	...	...	...	381	2
	2007	...	...	...	...	...	...	314	1
	2008	...	...	...	...	...	...	342	2
	2009	...	...	...	...	...	...	371	2
Sierra Leone *[1]	2006	0	...	...	...	0	...	216	...
	2007	2	...	...	...	2	...	180	...
	2008	8	...	...	...	8	...	182	...
	2009	8	...	...	...	8	...	195	...
Somalia	2006	...	...	...	...	...	...	*310	*49
	2007	...	...	...	...	...	...	*272	0
	2008	...	...	...	...	...	...	*272	0
	2009	...	...	...	...	...	...	*263	0

45
Production, trade and consumption of commercial energy *(continued)*
Thousand metric tons of oil equivalent and kilograms per capita
Production, commerce et consommation d'énergie commerciale *(suite)*
Milliers de tonnes d'équivalent pétrole et kilogrammes par habitant

| Bunkers - Soutes | | | Consumption - Consommation | | | | | | | |
Air Avion	Sea Maritime	Unallocated Non distribué	Per capita Par habitant	Total Totale	Solids Solides	Liquids Liquides	Gas Gaz	Electricity Electricité	Year Année	Région, pays ou zone
20	...	...	16	213	...	190	...	23	2006	Mali *
20	...	...	16	218	...	194	...	23	2007	
20	...	...	15	224	...	199	...	24	2008	
21	...	...	15	229	...	205	...	25	2009	
18	...	0	159	499	...	488	...	11	2006	Mauritanie
17	...	1	177	569	...	559	...	*9	2007	
16	...	1	187	615	...	606	...	9	2008	
*18	...	0	*180	*609	...	*598	...	*11	2009	
103	172	...	926	1 173	339	828	...	7	2006	Maurice
121	195	...	936	1 194	401	786	...	7	2007	
129	214	...	939	1 206	456	741	...	9	2008	
109	218	...	909	1 174	417	746	...	11	2009	
430	13	1 084	422	12 942	3 878	8 205	532	326	2006	Maroc
499	13	1 066	450	13 958	3 978	8 937	604	439	2007	
499	13	959	469	14 703	3 662	10 005	527	509	2008	
504	13	930	440	13 907	2 705	9 928	586	688	2009	
56	3	...	75	1 589	0	501	79	1 009	2006	Mozambique
65	0	...	82	1 793	6	613	97	1 076	2007	
60	0	...	76	1 689	7	583	94	1 004	2008	
69	0	...	78	1 776	7	655	92	1 021	2009	
...	...	...	604	1 280	45	951	...	283	2006	Namibie
...	...	...	625	1 349	54	989	...	307	2007	
...	...	...	738	1 624	289	1 033	...	302	2008	
...	...	...	650	1 458	135	1 024	...	300	2009	
*10	...	...	20	270	100	135	...	34	2006	Niger
*12	...	...	20	281	88	154	...	39	2007	
*11	...	...	22	311	102	169	...	39	2008	
*12	...	...	26	393	124	223	...	46	2009	
234	528	196	139	19 863	7	9 406	9 911	539	2006	Nigéria
240	562	44	129	18 951	7	8 632	9 777	535	2007	
862	596	798	140	21 144	7	10 498	10 147	492	2008	
654	630	253	107	16 571	7	9 625	6 549	389	2009	
...	34	...	1 070	861	...	812	...	50	2006	Réunion *
...	36	...	1 081	882	...	817	...	65	2007	
...	37	...	1 081	893	...	828	...	65	2008	
...	38	...	1 076	899	...	834	...	65	2009	
*12	...	...	18	168	...	159	*1	9	2006	Rwanda
*12	...	...	19	180	...	169	*1	11	2007	
*12	...	...	*18	*179	...	*165	*1	13	2008	
*14	...	...	*18	*184	...	*170	*1	14	2009	
...	...	...	713	3	...	3	...	...	2006	Sainte-Hélène
...	...	...	933	4	...	4	...	...	2007	
...	...	...	761	3	...	3	...	0	2008	
...	...	...	746	3	...	3	...	0	2009	
...	...	...	282	44	...	43	...	1	*2006	Sao Tomé-et-Principe
...	...	...	*279	*44	...	*43	...	1	2007	
...	...	...	275	44	...	43	...	1	*2008	
...	...	...	271	44	...	43	...	1	*2009	
239	...	24	97	1 080	133	915	12	20	2006	Sénégal
324	...	-58	110	1 264	211	1 026	11	16	2007	
329	...	77	97	1 145	178	938	10	20	2008	
259	...	-117	91	1 099	221	845	16	*17	2009	
*30	*106	...	2 888	243	...	246	...	-2	2006	Seychelles
*29	*79	...	2 418	205	...	206	...	-1	2007	
*36	*81	...	2 603	223	...	225	...	-2	2008	
*40	*88	...	2 808	242	...	244	...	-2	2009	
12	...	...	38	204	0	204	...	0	2006	Sierra Leone * [1]
6	...	...	32	175	0	173	...	2	2007	
3	...	...	33	187	0	179	...	8	2008	
17	...	...	32	186	0	178	...	8	2009	
*52	*21	*-1	22	189	...	189	...	...	2006	Somalie
*48	*22	0	*23	*201	...	*201	...	...	2007	
*48	*21	0	*23	*202	...	*202	...	...	2008	
*46	*19	0	*22	*197	...	*197	...	...	2009	

45
Production, trade and consumption of commercial energy *(continued)*
Thousand metric tons of oil equivalent and kilograms per capita
Production, commerce et consommation d'énergie commerciale *(suite)*
Milliers de tonnes d'équivalent pétrole et kilogrammes par habitant

Region, country or area	Year Année	Primary energy production – Production d'énergie primaire					Changes in stocks	Imports Importations	Exports Exportations
		Total Totale	Solids Solides	Liquids Liquides	Gas Gaz	Electricity Electricité	Variations des stocks		
South Africa [2]	2006	132 499	129 029	222	1 727	1 521	9	27 620	40 234
	2007	133 726	130 553	241	1 618	1 314	0	31 136	41 405
	2008	135 094	131 786	220	1 618	1 469	3 860	30 040	33 983
	2009	134 151	131 514	225	946	1 466	0	35 253	31 555
Sudan (former)	2006	17 549	...	17 431	...	118	367	575	13 388
	2007	24 177	...	24 053	...	125	335	527	19 668
	2008	23 462	...	23 336	...	126	603	549	19 091
	2009	24 260	...	23 983	...	278	625	890	19 365
Swaziland	2006	*324	*310	...	...	13	*3	*396	*310
	2007	*338	*323	...	...	15	*3	*413	*323
	2008	*347	*333	...	...	14	*4	*426	*333
	2009	*358	*337	...	...	21	*-3	*396	*337
Togo	2006	8	...	...	...	8	-46	311	...
	2007	8	...	...	...	8	-39	344	...
	2008	8	...	...	...	8	-104	374	...
	2009	8	...	...	...	8	-107	383	...
Tunisia	2006	5 662	...	3 396	2 254	11	61	5 788	3 747
	2007	6 840	...	4 686	2 147	8	81	6 239	5 000
	2008	6 442	...	4 282	2 153	7	443	6 776	4 342
	2009	6 553	...	4 075	2 462	15	-29	6 116	4 228
Uganda	2006	107	...	...	...	107	...	786	3
	2007	121	...	...	...	121	...	942	6
	2008	126	...	...	...	126	...	951	6
	2009	110	...	...	...	110	...	1 058	7
United Rep. of Tanzania	2006	528	56	...	349	123	...	1 568	...
	2007	782	59	...	507	216	...	1 484	...
	2008	802	63	...	511	228	...	1 584	...
	2009	909	66	...	604	239	...	1 672	...
Western Sahara *	2006	...	...	...	...	...	...	85	...
	2007	...	...	...	...	...	...	85	...
	2008	...	...	...	...	...	...	85	...
	2009	...	...	...	...	...	...	85	...
Zambia	2006	884	38	...	...	846	-12	675	54
	2007	851	8	...	...	843	-1	537	47
	2008	832	1	...	...	831	4	609	8
	2009	884	1	...	...	884	4	648	9
Zimbabwe	2006	2 591	2 223	...	...	368	-2	1 091	130
	2007	2 478	2 087	...	...	390	-9	1 061	130
	2008	2 326	1 960	...	...	367	-17	1 078	130
	2009	2 294	1 932	...	...	361	-19	1 086	131
America, North	**2006**	**2 159 115**	**615 425**	**673 501**	**723 438**	**146 751**	**34 135**	**1 002 931**	**490 179**
	2007	**2 174 399**	**608 654**	**672 744**	**746 673**	**146 328**	**-17 145**	**1 012 384**	**509 064**
	2008	**2 190 461**	**619 037**	**653 293**	**767 782**	**150 350**	**4 188**	**982 662**	**529 473**
	2009	**2 156 588**	**566 528**	**667 310**	**772 269**	**150 480**	**29 686**	**898 214**	**512 786**
Anguilla	2006	...	...	...	...	...	...	18	...
	2007	...	...	...	...	...	...	19	...
	2008	...	...	...	...	...	...	20	...
	2009	...	...	...	...	...	...	20	...
Antigua and Barbuda *	2006	...	...	...	...	...	...	205	10
	2007	...	...	...	...	...	...	211	11
	2008	...	...	...	...	...	...	217	11
	2009	...	...	...	...	...	...	223	11
Aruba *	2006	121	...	121	...	...	...	10 807	10 495
	2007	126	...	126	...	...	...	10 934	10 600
	2008	123	...	123	...	...	...	10 863	10 547
	2009	124	...	124	...	...	...	10 877	10 556
Bahamas *	2006	...	...	...	...	...	...	3 291	2 256
	2007	...	...	...	...	...	...	3 325	2 258
	2008	...	...	...	...	...	...	3 340	2 258
	2009	...	...	...	...	...	...	3 411	2 267
Barbados	2006	77	...	51	25	...	...	380	50
	2007	70	...	47	22	...	2	409	46
	2008	63	...	43	19	...	5	437	43
	2009	56	...	39	*16	...	7	465	39

Production, trade and consumption of commercial energy *(continued)*
Thousand metric tons of oil equivalent and kilograms per capita

Production, commerce et consommation d'énergie commerciale *(suite)*
Milliers de tonnes d'équivalent pétrole et kilogrammes par habitant

Bunkers - Soutes			Consumption - Consommation							
Air Avion	Sea Maritime	Unallocated Non distribué	Per capita Par habitant	Total Totale	Solids Solides	Liquids Liquides	Gas Gaz	Electricity Electricité	Year Année	Région, pays ou zone
...	2 509	-1 258	2 454	118 625	94 087	20 452	2 907	1 179	2006	Afrique du Sud [2]
...	2 582	-3 251	2 541	124 125	96 502	22 309	4 250	1 064	2007	
...	*227	-3 056	2 638	130 120	99 094	25 343	4 522	1 160	2008	
...	*223	3 419	2 698	134 207	104 237	24 533	4 122	1 315	2009	
311	8	325	95	3 726	...	3 608	...	118	2006	Soudan (anc.)
330	8	386	98	3 976	...	3 852	...	125	2007	
335	8	107	93	3 866	...	3 741	...	126	2008	
374	8	561	99	4 218	...	3 940	...	278	2009	
*1	...	...	*363	*406	*102	*213	...	90	2006	Swaziland
*1	...	...	*374	*424	*106	*222	...	95	2007	
*1	...	...	*378	*435	*108	*229	...	98	2008	
*1	...	...	*359	*419	*96	*223	...	100	2009	
35	2	...	59	327	...	276	...	51	2006	Togo
31	2	...	63	359	...	307	...	52	2007	
61	4	...	73	421	...	356	...	65	2008	
62	4	...	73	432	...	365	...	67	2009	
...	9	209	741	7 424	...	4 065	3 348	12	2006	Tunisie
...	0	174	772	7 825	...	4 233	3 583	8	2007	
...	0	262	797	8 171	...	4 028	4 136	7	2008	
...	27	262	789	8 180	...	3 882	4 280	19	2009	
...	...	...	30	889	...	782	...	107	2006	Ouganda
...	...	...	35	1 057	...	936	...	121	2007	
...	...	...	34	1 072	...	948	...	124	2008	
...	...	...	36	1 161	...	1 056	...	106	2009	
91	23	...	50	1 983	56	1 440	349	138	2006	Rép.-Unie de Tanzanie
98	23	...	52	2 145	59	1 353	507	226	2007	
105	22	...	53	2 259	63	1 453	511	233	2008	
110	22	...	56	2 449	66	1 535	604	244	2009	
6	...	...	171	79	...	79	...	...	2006	Sahara occidental *
6	...	...	164	79	...	79	...	...	2007	
6	...	...	159	79	...	79	...	...	2008	
6	...	...	154	79	...	79	...	...	2009	
54	...	38	121	1 424	34	587	...	803	2006	Zambie
32	...	44	105	1 266	8	427	...	831	2007	
40	...	48	108	1 341	1	495	...	846	2008	
42	...	52	112	1 426	1	526	...	899	2009	
7	...	...	283	3 546	2 130	640	...	775	2006	Zimbabwe
7	...	...	273	3 410	2 001	612	...	798	2007	
7	...	...	264	3 284	1 879	586	...	820	2008	
7	...	...	261	3 261	1 853	579	...	829	2009	
27 639	32 518	64 630	4 830	2 512 945	590 488	1 062 457	713 356	146 645	2006	**Amérique du Nord**
28 297	35 148	59 890	4 892	2 571 528	592 937	1 068 494	764 422	146 275	2007	
28 340	30 808	28 563	4 804	2 551 752	583 677	1 046 574	771 114	150 387	2008	
25 666	28 770	18 280	4 546	2 439 614	518 913	1 006 093	764 144	150 463	2009	
...	...	...	1 264	18	...	18	...	...	2006	Anguilla
...	...	...	1 353	19	...	19	...	...	2007	
...	...	...	1 330	20	...	20	...	...	2008	
...	...	...	1 296	20	...	20	...	...	2009	
50	3	...	1 678	143	...	143	...	...	2006	Antigua-et-Barbuda *
52	3	...	1 694	146	...	146	...	...	2007	
53	3	...	1 726	150	...	150	...	...	2008	
54	4	...	1 759	154	...	154	...	...	2009	
77	...	113	2 360	242	...	242	...	...	2006	Aruba *
79	...	135	2 359	246	...	246	...	...	2007	
80	...	112	2 336	247	...	247	...	...	2008	
82	...	114	2 333	249	...	249	...	...	2009	
47	218	...	2 375	770	3	767	...	...	2006	Bahamas *
49	218	...	2 436	801	3	798	...	...	2007	
50	218	...	2 442	815	3	812	...	...	2008	
65	223	...	2 531	856	3	854	...	...	2009	
...	...	0	1 500	406	...	381	25	...	2006	Barbade
...	...	0	1 581	429	...	407	22	...	2007	
...	...	0	1 662	452	...	433	19	...	2008	
...	...	0	1 742	475	...	459	*16	...	2009	

Production, trade and consumption of commercial energy *(continued)*
Thousand metric tons of oil equivalent and kilograms per capita
Production, commerce et consommation d'énergie commerciale *(suite)*
Milliers de tonnes d'équivalent pétrole et kilogrammes par habitant

Region, country or area	Year Année	Primary energy production – Production d'énergie primaire					Changes in stocks Variations des stocks	Imports Importations	Exports Exportations
		Total Totale	Solids Solides	Liquids Liquides	Gas Gaz	Electricity Electricité			
Belize	2006	15	...	...	...	15	...	*178	...
	2007	15	...	...	...	15	...	179	...
	2008	18	...	...	...	18	...	*175	...
	2009	21	...	...	...	21	...	*177	...
Bermuda	2006	...	...	...	...	...	...	211	...
	2007	...	...	...	...	...	...	225	...
	2008	...	...	...	...	...	...	199	...
	*2009	...	...	...	...	...	...	223	...
British Virgin Islands *	2006	...	...	...	...	...	...	33	...
	2007	...	...	...	...	...	...	33	...
	2008	...	...	...	...	...	...	34	...
	2009	...	...	...	...	...	...	37	...
Canada	2006	398 118	32 350	154 441	172 121	39 206	-782	77 376	225 958
	2007	404 214	34 276	161 525	168 227	40 187	-9 156	78 011	236 939
	2008	393 399	34 373	157 299	161 131	40 596	-6 521	84 466	235 625
	2009	377 492	31 460	156 238	150 320	39 474	-6 915	78 695	226 134
Cayman Islands	2006	...	...	...	...	...	...	*183	...
	2007	...	...	...	...	...	...	*184	...
	2008	...	...	...	...	...	...	*188	...
	2009	...	...	...	...	...	...	179	...
Costa Rica	2006	696	...	...	...	696	17	2 335	34
	2007	709	...	...	...	709	-24	2 475	4
	2008	749	...	...	...	749	71	2 566	16
	2009	751	...	...	...	751	-55	2 399	87
Cuba	2006	4 150	...	3 131	1 011	8	...	5 383	...
	2007	4 199	...	3 083	1 105	10	...	5 057	...
	2008	4 264	...	3 170	1 082	12	...	6 011	...
	2009	3 982	...	2 892	1 076	13	...	*6 903	...
Dominica	2006	2	...	...	...	2	...	38	...
	2007	2	...	...	...	2	...	50	...
	2008	2	...	...	...	2	...	43	...
	2009	2	...	...	...	2	...	43	...
Dominican Republic	2006	150	...	...	...	150	-18	6 391	...
	2007	146	...	...	...	146	-26	6 569	...
	2008	119	...	...	...	119	7	6 451	...
	2009	126	...	...	...	126	-26	6 353	...
El Salvador	2006	267	...	...	...	267	-56	2 193	78
	2007	268	...	...	...	268	34	2 346	62
	2008	306	...	...	...	306	-68	2 130	93
	2009	260	...	...	...	260	-15	2 120	97
Greenland	2006	...	...	...	...	...	...	261	48
	2007	...	...	...	...	...	...	285	54
	2008	...	...	...	...	...	...	264	51
	2009	...	...	...	...	...	...	254	46
Grenada	2006	...	...	...	...	...	...	85	...
	2007	...	...	...	...	...	...	91	...
	2008	...	...	...	...	...	...	93	...
	2009	...	...	...	...	...	...	92	...
Guadeloupe	2006	*23	...	...	...	*23	...	672	...
	2007	*24	...	...	...	*24	...	680	...
	2008	*24	...	...	...	*24	...	682	...
	*2009	24	...	...	...	24	...	682	...
Guatemala	2006	1 210	...	881	...	329	-155	3 853	978
	2007	1 101	...	835	...	267	221	4 399	843
	2008	1 083	...	771	...	312	-1	3 881	876
	2009	925	...	744	...	181	-71	4 732	809
Haiti	2006	23	...	...	...	23	...	685	...
	2007	13	...	...	...	13	...	773	...
	2008	16	...	...	...	16	...	786	...
	2009	18	...	...	...	18	...	727	...
Honduras	2006	178	...	...	...	178	288	2 333	41
	2007	190	...	...	...	190	-86	2 663	182
	2008	197	...	...	...	197	-123	2 713	296
	2009	240	...	...	...	240	-40	2 572	336

45

Production, trade and consumption of commercial energy *(continued)*
Thousand metric tons of oil equivalent and kilograms per capita

Production, commerce et consommation d'énergie commerciale *(suite)*
Milliers de tonnes d'équivalent pétrole et kilogrammes par habitant

Bunkers - Soutes			Consumption - Consommation							
Air Avion	Sea Maritime	Unallocated Non distribué	Per capita Par habitant	Total Totale	Solids Solides	Liquids Liquides	Gas Gaz	Electricity Electricité	Year Année	Région, pays ou zone
*23	...	...	*597	*171	...	*138	...	33	2006	Belize
17	...	...	607	178	...	143	...	35	2007	
*18	...	...	*587	*176	...	*136	...	39	2008	
*19	...	...	*587	*179	...	*140	...	39	2009	
*20	18	...	2 694	173	...	173	...	...	2006	Bermudes
37	18	...	2 641	170	...	170	...	...	2007	
52	18	...	1 996	129	...	129	...	...	2008	
52	18	...	2 375	154	...	154	...	...	*2009	
...	...	...	1 481	33	...	33	...	...	2006	Iles Vierges britanniques *
...	...	...	1 464	33	...	33	...	...	2007	
...	...	...	1 515	34	...	34	...	...	2008	
...	...	...	1 602	37	...	37	...	...	2009	
825	549	15 622	7 151	233 322	28 665	78 597	88 497	37 563	2006	Canada
508	652	18 194	7 129	235 089	26 429	81 559	89 575	37 526	2007	
527	539	14 743	6 990	232 951	27 834	80 247	86 980	37 890	2008	
660	486	12 338	6 636	223 483	23 750	75 720	87 425	36 587	2009	
9	...	...	*3 238	*174	...	*174	...	...	2006	Iles Caïmanes
8	...	...	*3 218	*176	...	*176	...	...	2007	
10	...	...	*3 217	*178	...	*178	...	...	2008	
10	...	...	3 024	169	...	169	...	...	2009	
...	...	45	669	2 934	41	2 189	...	703	2006	Costa Rica
...	...	29	713	3 176	82	2 370	...	723	2007	
...	...	62	700	3 167	82	2 341	...	743	2008	
...	...	61	666	3 057	71	2 233	...	753	2009	
*183	*29	968	742	8 354	6	7 328	1 011	8	2006	Cuba
*173	*30	545	755	8 508	20	7 372	1 105	10	2007	
*143	*30	743	831	9 358	24	8 241	1 082	12	2008	
*135	*30	*1 842	788	8 878	*19	7 769	1 076	13	2009	
...	...	...	582	40	...	38	...	2	2006	Dominique
...	...	...	759	52	...	50	...	2	2007	
...	...	...	655	45	...	43	...	2	2008	
...	...	...	663	45	...	43	...	2	2009	
99	...	150	671	6 311	560	5 315	286	150	2006	Rép. dominicaine
96	...	72	690	6 573	576	5 331	519	146	2007	
96	...	120	657	6 347	601	5 196	431	119	2008	
96	...	129	641	6 280	590	5 072	492	126	2009	
75	...	71	377	2 291	1	2 023	...	267	2006	El Salvador
117	...	75	381	2 326	0	2 055	...	271	2007	
115	...	73	363	2 224	0	1 918	...	305	2008	
107	...	69	345	2 123	0	1 851	...	272	2009	
17	3	...	3 368	193	...	193	...	...	2006	Groenland
17	3	...	3 668	210	...	210	...	...	2007	
18	6	...	3 287	188	...	188	...	...	2008	
15	1	...	3 333	191	...	191	...	...	2009	
8	...	...	738	76	...	76	...	...	2006	Grenade
10	...	...	782	81	...	81	...	...	2007	
10	...	...	804	83	...	83	...	...	2008	
9	...	...	795	83	...	83	...	...	2009	
142	...	...	1 231	553	...	530	...	*23	2006	Guadeloupe
138	...	...	1 251	566	...	542	...	*24	2007	
142	...	...	1 240	564	...	540	...	*24	2008	
142	...	...	1 232	564	...	540	...	24	*2009	
74	122	113	301	3 930	445	3 162	...	322	2006	Guatemala
29	122	59	316	4 225	461	3 508	...	256	2007	
26	122	37	285	3 903	470	3 127	...	306	2008	
24	122	67	335	4 707	968	3 562	...	177	2009	
25	...	...	72	684	...	660	...	23	2006	Haïti
21	...	...	80	765	...	752	...	13	2007	
22	...	...	80	780	...	764	...	16	2008	
18	...	...	74	728	...	710	...	18	2009	
30	...	...	307	2 152	41	1 932	...	179	2006	Honduras
26	...	...	382	2 732	45	2 496	...	191	2007	
46	...	...	368	2 690	73	2 420	...	196	2008	
51	...	...	331	2 466	72	2 158	...	237	2009	

45

Production, trade and consumption of commercial energy *(continued)*
Thousand metric tons of oil equivalent and kilograms per capita

Production, commerce et consommation d'énergie commerciale *(suite)*
Milliers de tonnes d'équivalent pétrole et kilogrammes par habitant

Region, country or area	Year Année	Primary energy production – Production d'énergie primaire					Changes in stocks	Imports	Exports
		Total Totale	Solids Solides	Liquids Liquides	Gas Gaz	Electricity Electricité	Variations des stocks	Imports Importations	Exports Exportations
Jamaica	2006	19	...	...	...	19	-11	4 108	0
	2007	18	...	...	...	18	42	4 648	0
	2008	18	...	...	...	18	-14	4 148	0
	2009	14	...	...	...	14	-223	2 701	0
Martinique	2006	3	...	...	...	3	...	940	*153
	2007	3	...	...	...	3	...	869	*152
	2008	4	...	...	...	4	...	867	*157
	2009	*4	...	...	...	*4	...	919	*159
Mexico	2006	233 661	5 629	185 534	38 370	4 128	81	34 735	103 296
	2007	227 093	6 000	174 626	42 565	3 901	606	37 305	94 555
	2008	211 464	5 477	158 756	42 389	4 842	1 011	42 135	80 707
	2009	199 414	5 063	147 845	42 674	3 832	-360	39 063	73 805
Montserrat *	2006	...	...	...	...	...	...	26	...
	2007	...	...	...	...	...	...	27	...
	2008	...	...	...	...	...	...	27	...
	2009	...	...	...	...	...	...	27	...
Netherlands Antilles	2006	...	...	...	...	...	...	13 861	8 647
	2007	...	...	...	...	...	...	14 537	9 243
	2008	...	...	...	...	...	...	13 781	8 928
	2009	...	...	...	...	...	...	12 899	8 379
Nicaragua	2006	53	...	...	...	53	15	1 430	18
	2007	47	...	...	...	47	48	1 540	1
	2008	74	...	...	...	74	-38	1 377	0
	2009	61	...	...	...	61	-18	1 415	0
Panama	2006	308	...	...	...	308	0	2 312	4
	2007	315	...	...	...	315	-293	2 014	11
	2008	342	...	...	...	342	-238	2 143	3
	2009	335	...	...	...	335	-236	2 482	8
Puerto Rico	2006	12	...	...	...	12	...	660	...
	2007	14	...	...	...	14	...	686	...
	2008	13	...	...	...	13	...	752	...
	2009	13	...	...	...	13	...	705	...
Saint Kitts and Nevis *	2006	...	...	...	...	...	...	79	...
	2007	...	...	...	...	...	...	83	...
	2008	...	...	...	...	...	...	83	...
	2009	...	...	...	...	...	...	87	...
Saint Lucia	*2006	...	...	...	...	...	...	130	...
	*2007	...	...	...	...	...	...	135	...
	*2008	...	...	...	...	...	...	138	...
	2009	...	...	...	...	...	...	135	...
Saint Pierre and Miquelon *	2006	0	...	...	...	0	...	28	...
	2007	0	...	...	...	0	...	29	...
	2008	0	...	...	...	0	...	29	...
	2009	0	...	...	...	0	...	29	...
Saint Vincent-Grenadines	2006	2	...	...	...	2	...	*67	...
	2007	2	...	...	...	2	...	*67	...
	2008	2	...	...	...	2	...	*67	...
	*2009	2	...	...	...	2	...	67	...
Trinidad and Tobago	2006	38 233	...	9 180	29 052	...	-473	4 942	27 711
	2007	40 774	...	8 774	32 000	...	-291	5 467	29 481
	2008	44 851	...	7 736	37 115	...	6	4 712	25 930
	2009	47 999	...	8 003	39 996	...	-330	4 980	29 909
Turks and Caicos Islands *	2006	...	...	...	...	...	...	48	...
	2007	...	...	...	...	...	...	52	...
	2008	...	...	...	...	...	...	52	...
	2009	...	...	...	...	...	...	53	...
United States	2006	1 481 792	577 446	320 161	482 858	101 327	35 229	822 657	110 401
	2007	1 495 053	568 378	323 728	502 754	100 194	-8 221	826 007	124 621
	2008	1 533 332	579 187	325 394	526 046	102 705	10 089	786 791	163 932
	2009	1 524 724	530 005	351 425	538 187	105 108	37 968	711 469	160 146
America, South	**2006**	**568 661**	**50 806**	**357 320**	**104 500**	**56 034**	**-950**	**99 296**	**266 919**
	2007	**563 033**	**53 686**	**348 683**	**103 035**	**57 628**	**5 813**	**108 139**	**252 899**
	2008	**575 120**	**55 462**	**353 949**	**107 735**	**57 976**	**1 311**	**108 275**	**250 823**
	2009	**605 377**	**56 350**	**385 836**	**103 301**	**59 890**	**6 884**	**101 555**	**275 087**

Production, trade and consumption of commercial energy (continued)
Thousand metric tons of oil equivalent and kilograms per capita

Production, commerce et consommation d'énergie commerciale (suite)
Milliers de tonnes d'équivalent pétrole et kilogrammes par habitant

Bunkers - Soutes			Consumption - Consommation							
Air Avion	Sea Maritime	Unallocated Non distribué	Per capita Par habitant	Total Totale	Solids Solides	Liquids Liquides	Gas Gaz	Electricity Electricité	Year Année	Région, pays ou zone
255	30	34	1 416	3 819	20	3 780	...	19	2006	Jamaïque
248	30	29	1 594	4 318	25	4 274	...	18	2007	
321	30	45	1 391	3 784	34	3 733	...	18	2008	
169	30	53	984	2 686	36	2 636	...	14	2009	
*0	*45	48	*1 745	*697	...	*694	...	3	2006	Martinique
*0	*47	*-23	*1 733	*695	...	*692	...	3	2007	
*0	*48	*-46	*1 763	*710	...	*707	...	4	2008	
*0	*49	1	*1 765	*714	...	*710	...	*4	2009	
2 902	904	8 872	1 413	152 342	9 266	91 212	47 803	4 062	2006	Mexique
3 217	872	9 319	1 427	155 829	9 099	91 413	51 516	3 800	2007	
3 079	1 032	9 277	1 433	158 492	7 703	91 583	54 458	4 748	2008	
2 602	775	5 338	1 395	156 317	7 748	90 897	53 918	3 754	2009	
...	1	...	4 405	25	...	25	...	...	2006	Montserrat *
...	1	...	4 480	26	...	26	...	...	2007	
...	1	...	4 456	26	...	26	...	...	2008	
...	1	...	4 407	26	...	26	...	...	2009	
69	1 786	2 024	7 072	1 334	...	1 334	...	...	2006	Antilles néerlandaises
70	1 818	1 402	10 443	2 003	...	2 003	...	...	2007	
71	1 854	1 147	9 130	1 780	...	1 780	...	...	2008	
68	1 780	582	10 551	2 090	...	2 090	...	...	2009	
18	...	74	247	1 359	...	1 301	...	58	2006	Nicaragua
27	...	57	261	1 455	...	1 402	...	53	2007	
26	...	48	251	1 415	...	1 339	...	76	2008	
20	...	54	249	1 420	...	1 360	...	61	2009	
218	79	...	704	2 319	...	2 015	...	304	2006	Panama
265	99	...	671	2 247	...	1 941	...	305	2007	
306	100	...	679	2 313	...	1 965	...	348	2008	
309	109	...	759	2 628	...	2 296	...	333	2009	
...	...	...	178	672	...	...	660	12	2006	Porto Rico
...	...	...	186	700	...	...	686	14	2007	
...	...	...	204	765	...	...	752	13	2008	
...	...	...	192	719	...	...	705	13	2009	
...	...	...	1 580	79	...	79	...	...	2006	Saint-Kitts-et-Nevis *
...	...	...	1 641	83	...	83	...	...	2007	
...	...	...	1 621	83	...	83	...	...	2008	
...	...	...	1 680	87	...	87	...	...	2009	
...	6	...	744	124	...	124	...	...	*2006	Sainte-Lucie
...	6	...	763	129	...	129	...	...	*2007	
...	6	...	777	133	...	133	...	...	*2008	
...	*6	...	747	129	...	129	...	...	2009	
...	6	...	3 538	22	...	21	...	0	2006	Saint-Pierre-et-Miquelon *
...	6	...	3 718	23	...	22	...	0	2007	
...	6	...	3 729	23	...	22	...	0	2008	
...	6	...	3 738	23	...	22	...	0	2009	
...	...	...	*634	*69	...	*67	...	2	2006	Saint Vincent-Grenadines
...	...	...	*633	*69	...	*67	...	2	2007	
...	...	...	*633	*69	...	*67	...	2	2008	
...	...	...	633	69	...	67	...	2	*2009	
73	273	761	11 231	14 830	...	890	13 940	...	2006	Trinité-et-Tobago
83	265	676	12 090	16 028	...	1 047	14 981	...	2007	
*62	375	-478	17 782	23 669	...	1 511	22 158	...	2008	
66	443	873	16 476	22 017	...	1 529	20 488	...	2009	
...	...	...	1 464	48	...	48	...	...	2006	Iles Turques et Caïques *
...	...	...	1 505	52	...	52	...	...	2007	
...	...	...	1 440	52	...	52	...	...	2008	
...	...	...	1 416	53	...	53	...	...	2009	
22 400	28 445	35 735	6 918	2 072 239	551 440	856 754	561 134	102 910	2006	Etats-Unis
23 012	30 956	29 321	7 018	2 121 371	555 596	856 877	606 017	102 881	2007	
23 067	26 419	2 679	6 866	2 093 937	546 853	836 323	605 234	105 527	2008	
20 894	24 686	-3 241	6 486	1 995 740	485 656	802 025	600 022	108 036	2009	
4 174	7 146	26 060	970	364 609	21 362	180 964	106 064	56 219	2006	Amérique du Sud
3 878	8 072	25 194	987	375 315	22 480	191 686	103 317	57 832	2007	
4 687	9 617	21 572	1 029	395 386	24 167	204 306	108 755	58 159	2008	
4 794	8 703	21 445	1 004	390 018	20 606	203 811	105 458	60 144	2009	

Production, trade and consumption of commercial energy *(continued)*
Thousand metric tons of oil equivalent and kilograms per capita
Production, commerce et consommation d'énergie commerciale *(suite)*
Milliers de tonnes d'équivalent pétrole et kilogrammes par habitant

Region, country or area	Year Année	Primary energy production – Production d'énergie primaire					Changes in stocks	Imports	Exports
		Total Totale	Solids Solides	Liquids Liquides	Gas Gaz	Electricity Electricité	Variations des stocks	Imports Importations	Exports Exportations
Argentina	2006	87 190	83	38 276	44 882	3 948	225	5 254	15 553
	2007	84 082	65	37 423	43 247	3 347	-277	4 324	10 281
	2008	83 823	65	36 918	43 493	3 346	-28	3 897	7 849
	2009	81 878	48	36 872	41 301	3 656	-176	4 747	9 016
Bolivia (Plurin. State of)	2006	15 068	...	2 755	12 128	186	63	376	9 398
	2007	16 038	...	2 773	13 066	199	-21	437	11 695
	2008	16 489	...	2 643	13 647	199	-67	402	11 809
	2009	14 285	...	2 349	11 739	197	-58	539	9 495
Brazil	2006	144 844	2 613	100 671	10 386	31 174	-431	48 094	29 630
	2007	151 647	2 650	105 649	10 127	33 221	1 290	55 880	33 963
	2008	160 218	2 937	111 237	13 066	32 977	515	57 643	32 419
	2009	165 973	2 248	117 734	11 257	34 733	337	48 805	36 064
Chile	2006	4 823	263	331	1 723	2 505	799	23 818	1 941
	2007	3 856	104	560	1 202	1 990	1 497	24 585	1 141
	2008	4 301	263	570	1 385	2 083	-36	22 941	1 240
	2009	4 320	352	683	1 103	2 182	-256	21 447	1 081
Colombia	2006	80 943	42 637	27 812	6 813	3 681	-1 322	695	56 041
	2007	83 897	45 436	27 821	6 814	3 826	1 218	709	56 636
	2008	89 913	47 776	30 837	7 305	3 995	1 680	307	60 441
	2009	95 909	47 325	35 168	9 881	3 535	383	1 710	67 823
Ecuador	2006	29 675	...	28 354	707	613	73	3 230	21 829
	2007	28 541	...	27 036	728	777	342	3 557	20 124
	2008	28 216	...	26 793	452	971	-845	3 356	20 652
	2009	27 025	...	25 755	477	793	-404	3 978	19 072
Falkland Is. (Malvinas)	2006	3	3	...	...	*0	...	*15	...
	*2007	3	3	...	...	0	...	15	...
	2008	3	3	...	...	*0	...	*15	...
	*2009	3	3	...	...	0	...	15	...
French Guiana *	2006	55	...	...	...	55	...	215	...
	2007	58	...	...	...	58	...	243	...
	2008	60	...	...	...	60	...	260	...
	2009	61	...	...	...	61	...	263	...
Guyana	2006	...	...	...	...	...	-6	432	...
	2007	...	...	...	...	...	12	538	...
	2008	...	...	...	...	...	-14	512	...
	2009	...	...	...	...	...	1	527	...
Paraguay	2006	4 628	...	5	...	4 624	-12	1 242	3 929
	2007	4 623	...	4	...	4 619	5	1 312	3 880
	2008	4 776	...	8	...	4 768	-11	1 368	3 980
	2009	4 739	...	14	...	4 725	13	1 444	3 880
Peru	2006	9 425	73	5 645	1 859	1 847	1 182	6 684	3 351
	2007	10 450	77	6 096	2 596	1 681	1 407	8 445	4 174
	2008	11 178	97	5 827	3 607	1 647	351	7 233	3 858
	2009	13 274	220	6 744	4 558	1 752	1 035	6 592	4 201
Suriname	2006	738	...	663	...	75	...	290	151
	2007	738	...	663	...	75	...	290	151
	2008	738	...	663	...	75	...	290	151
	2009	744	...	670	...	75	...	291	152
Uruguay	2006	309	...	...	...	309	38	2 961	239
	2007	694	...	...	...	694	-163	2 457	291
	2008	388	...	...	...	388	-255	3 320	275
	2009	455	...	...	...	455	-107	3 307	169
Venezuela (Boliv. Rep. of)	2006	190 961	5 134	152 809	26 002	7 016	-1 559	5 990	124 856
	2007	178 408	5 352	140 660	25 255	7 142	503	5 345	110 564
	2008	175 019	4 321	138 452	24 779	7 467	21	*6 731	108 149
	2009	196 711	6 153	159 847	22 984	7 727	6 116	*7 888	124 134
Asia	**2006**	**4 419 785**	**1 781 196**	**1 750 865**	**757 600**	**130 124**	**10 189**	**1 641 711**	**1 749 298**
	2007	**4 598 606**	**1 902 632**	**1 749 890**	**815 756**	**130 328**	**24 149**	**1 730 514**	**1 788 937**
	2008	**4 807 485**	**1 994 128**	**1 805 451**	**869 867**	**138 038**	**39 465**	**1 756 064**	**1 841 049**
	2009	**4 860 373**	**2 117 401**	**1 728 837**	**869 169**	**144 965**	**39 992**	**1 825 682**	**1 761 318**
Afghanistan	2006	84	24	...	4	56	...	441	...
	2007	233	170	...	4	59	...	483	...
	2008	293	243	...	4	47	...	1 033	...
	2009	420	350	...	3	67	...	1 763	...

Production, trade and consumption of commercial energy *(continued)*
Thousand metric tons of oil equivalent and kilograms per capita
Production, commerce et consommation d'énergie commerciale *(suite)*
Milliers de tonnes d'équivalent pétrole et kilogrammes par habitant

Bunkers - Soutes			Consumption - Consommation							
Air Avion	Sea Maritime	Unallocated Non distribué	Per capita Par habitant	Total Totale	Solids Solides	Liquids Liquides	Gas Gaz	Electricity Electricité	Year Année	Région, pays ou zone
697	741	6 666	1 757	68 560	1 020	22 669	40 720	4 151	2006	Argentine
760	895	5 885	1 800	70 862	1 081	23 438	42 328	4 015	2007	
813	956	5 263	1 835	72 867	1 255	24 039	43 756	3 818	2008	
845	948	4 910	1 774	71 082	1 274	22 591	43 032	4 185	2009	
...	...	269	614	5 714	...	2 069	3 460	186	2006	Bolivie (État plurin. de)
...	...	223	484	4 577	...	2 370	2 007	199	2007	
...	...	211	513	4 938	...	2 353	2 387	199	2008	
...	...	204	530	5 184	...	2 376	2 610	197	2009	
1 271	3 393	8 757	800	150 318	13 779	82 383	19 441	34 714	2006	Brésil
1 386	3 650	9 471	831	157 767	14 591	86 930	19 686	36 560	2007	
1 572	4 580	9 364	884	169 409	14 765	94 475	23 563	36 607	2008	
1 632	3 798	10 248	842	162 697	11 731	93 828	18 995	38 144	2009	
396	1 256	310	1 454	23 939	3 308	10 970	6 960	2 702	2006	Chili
449	1 210	315	1 433	23 829	3 432	14 542	3 726	2 130	2007	
521	1 172	340	1 429	24 006	4 415	15 336	2 071	2 183	2008	
425	841	624	1 359	23 051	3 646	14 626	2 481	2 298	2009	
663	388	3 247	518	22 621	2 467	9 814	6 813	3 526	2006	Colombie
507	391	3 608	502	22 246	2 391	9 288	6 813	3 754	2007	
566	412	3 646	522	23 474	2 816	9 480	7 305	3 875	2008	
699	424	4 475	522	23 815	3 117	8 907	8 347	3 444	2009	
328	248	1 074	686	9 354	...	7 898	707	748	2006	Equateur
340	623	601	727	10 068	...	8 489	728	851	2007	
345	1 051	525	700	9 845	...	8 379	452	1 014	2008	
335	1 272	18	751	10 711	...	9 344	477	890	2009	
...	...	...	*6 171	*18	3	*15	...	*0	2006	Iles Falkland (Malvinas)
...	...	...	6 147	18	3	15	...	0	*2007	
...	...	...	*6 118	*18	3	*15	...	*0	2008	
...	...	...	6 093	18	3	15	...	0	*2009	
34	...	...	1 135	237	...	181	...	55	2006	Guyane française *
29	...	...	1 269	272	...	214	...	58	2007	
40	...	...	1 271	279	...	220	...	60	2008	
40	...	...	1 260	284	...	223	...	61	2009	
9	...	...	574	429	...	429	...	...	2006	Guyana
9	...	...	689	517	...	517	...	...	2007	
9	...	...	687	516	...	516	...	...	2008	
9	...	...	686	516	...	516	...	...	2009	
24	...	...	321	1 929	0	1 234	...	694	2006	Paraguay
24	...	...	331	2 026	0	1 287	...	738	2007	
26	...	...	345	2 148	0	1 360	...	788	2008	
22	...	...	358	2 268	0	1 423	...	845	2009	
466	100	-144	400	11 152	745	6 701	1 859	1 847	2006	Pérou
169	152	1 051	424	11 941	937	6 727	2 596	1 681	2007	
582	149	-420	488	13 890	876	7 760	3 607	1 647	2008	
569	74	-1 073	524	15 060	784	7 966	4 558	1 752	2009	
...	...	177	1 388	701	0	626	...	75	2006	Suriname
...	...	177	1 374	701	0	626	...	75	2007	
...	...	177	1 361	701	0	626	...	75	2008	
...	...	179	1 357	705	0	630	...	75	2009	
57	248	123	771	2 565	2	1 909	102	552	2006	Uruguay
68	325	69	768	2 561	3	1 788	95	676	2007	
68	433	244	879	2 942	1	2 380	92	468	2008	
66	503	84	907	3 047	2	2 421	65	559	2009	
228	771	5 582	2 472	67 073	36	34 066	26 002	6 969	2006	Venezuela (Rép. boliv. du)
136	824	3 794	2 462	67 931	43	35 454	25 338	7 095	2007	
143	864	2 222	2 507	70 352	35	37 367	25 522	7 427	2008	
152	842	1 775	2 510	71 580	50	38 943	24 892	7 695	2009	
43 680	**70 508**	**314 066**	**971**	**3 873 755**	**1 889 312**	**1 103 069**	**751 021**	**130 353**	**2006**	**Asie**
45 748	**75 674**	**309 404**	**1 013**	**4 085 209**	**2 006 241**	**1 126 765**	**821 915**	**130 289**	**2007**	
45 823	**79 466**	**308 819**	**1 042**	**4 248 926**	**2 102 738**	**1 136 643**	**871 321**	**138 225**	**2008**	
44 668	**86 199**	**317 829**	**1 077**	**4 436 048**	**2 245 090**	**1 163 523**	**881 693**	**145 742**	**2009**	
*10	...	...	18	515	24	380	4	107	2006	Afghanistan
*10	...	...	24	706	170	405	4	126	2007	
10	...	...	44	1 316	243	951	4	118	2008	
10	...	...	71	2 173	350	1 671	3	149	2009	

45 Production, trade and consumption of commercial energy *(continued)*
Thousand metric tons of oil equivalent and kilograms per capita
Production, commerce et consommation d'énergie commerciale *(suite)*
Milliers de tonnes d'équivalent pétrole et kilogrammes par habitant

Region, country or area	Year Année	Primary energy production – Production d'énergie primaire					Changes in stocks Variations des stocks	Imports Importations	Exports Exportations
		Total Totale	Solids Solides	Liquids Liquides	Gas Gaz	Electricity Electricité			
Armenia	2006	384	...	...	...	384	...	1 997	85
	2007	379	...	...	...	379	...	2 367	62
	2008	366	...	...	...	366	...	2 562	60
	2009	388	...	...	...	388	...	2 013	58
Azerbaijan	2006	39 213	...	32 904	6 092	217	-75	4 412	28 246
	2007	54 670	...	44 393	10 074	203	-31	98	39 995
	2008	62 867	...	47 482	15 193	192	331	62	45 265
	2009	68 543	...	53 162	15 183	199	424	20	52 658
Bahrain	2006	16 992	...	9 638	7 354	...	-63	11 285	17 324
	2007	17 762	...	9 667	8 095	...	-693	11 472	17 269
	2008	18 295	...	9 620	8 675	...	-226	11 441	16 422
	2009	18 345	...	9 573	8 772	...	-48	11 318	16 219
Bangladesh	2006	14 091	151	100	13 720	119	-102	6 177	70
	2007	15 049	194	91	14 644	120	-109	5 620	142
	2008	16 194	338	82	15 647	127	-62	4 078	162
	2009	17 665	429	74	17 029	133	-279	4 266	*162
Bhutan	2006	457	69	...	...	389	...	74	359
	2007	638	74	...	...	564	...	77	520
	2008	685	87	...	...	599	...	75	539
	2009	636	34	...	...	602	...	95	479
Brunei Darussalam	2006	22 704	...	10 938	11 765	...	-69	0	20 862
	2007	21 912	...	9 877	12 034	...	-27	0	18 038
	2008	22 352	...	9 806	12 546	...	62	39	17 986
	2009	20 126	...	8 508	11 619	...	147	86	16 296
Cambodia	2006	4	...	...	...	4	...	1 404	...
	2007	4	...	...	...	4	...	1 518	...
	2008	4	...	...	...	4	...	1 596	...
	2009	4	...	...	...	4	...	1 524	...
China[3]	2006	1 544 145	1 262 705	186 672	52 109	42 659	-1 472	208 302	63 723
	2007	1 642 043	1 344 150	188 240	61 619	48 033	25 781	231 186	60 139
	2008	1 720 464	1 399 260	192 405	71 462	57 337	46 819	246 193	57 406
	2009	1 814 966	1 484 654	191 445	75 912	62 955	63 309	316 914	47 581
China, Hong Kong SAR	2006	...	...	...	...	...	632	25 221	1 582
	2007	...	...	...	...	...	1 142	27 049	1 310
	2008	...	...	...	...	...	918	25 042	1 148
	2009	...	...	...	...	...	1 322	29 064	1 103
China, Macao SAR	2006	...	...	...	...	...	8	625	...
	2007	...	...	...	...	...	9	665	...
	2008	...	...	...	...	...	-20	649	...
	2009	...	...	...	...	...	5	706	...
Cyprus	2006	0	...	0	...	0	120	2 959	...
	2007	0	...	0	...	0	-53	2 868	...
	2008	6	...	6	...	0	4	3 031	...
	2009	7	...	6	...	0	-3	2 890	...
Dem. P. R. Korea	2006	23 434	22 349	...	...	1 085	...	993	1 736
	2007	20 565	19 423	...	...	1 142	...	1 095	2 618
	2008	21 817	20 607	...	...	1 210	...	1 129	1 838
	2009	21 214	20 142	...	...	1 072	...	925	2 101
Georgia	2006	553	6	65	18	463	3	2 617	72
	2007	677	11	65	15	586	6	2 554	115
	2008	717	34	53	12	619	-5	2 484	101
	2009	778	99	54	10	615	0	2 179	132
India	2006	331 328	257 109	38 818	24 006	11 395	5 918	149 175	24 074
	2007	348 947	272 957	38 578	25 585	11 827	1 254	166 500	29 895
	2008	370 373	293 288	38 158	27 830	11 096	-7 947	181 029	32 635
	2009	403 962	316 466	38 342	38 358	10 795	-8 040	215 779	40 766
Indonesia	2006	251 726	137 493	48 245	64 588	1 400	467	34 458	168 578
	2007	274 442	157 767	51 481	63 619	1 574	-357	38 939	187 026
	2008	283 624	166 794	49 886	65 240	1 705	-118	32 377	180 472
	2009	293 181	178 786	54 572	58 543	1 280	-817	37 460	187 541
Iran (Islamic Rep. of)	2006	337 428	1 070	232 713	102 076	1 570	1 452	16 323	158 084
	2007	355 466	1 144	237 489	115 274	1 559	780	14 479	160 729
	2008	355 850	1 114	234 266	120 024	447	-678	15 933	152 367
	2009	361 954	822	231 323	129 170	639	-3 082	13 890	144 820

Production, trade and consumption of commercial energy *(continued)*
Thousand metric tons of oil equivalent and kilograms per capita
Production, commerce et consommation d'énergie commerciale *(suite)*
Milliers de tonnes d'équivalent pétrole et kilogrammes par habitant

Bunkers - Soutes			Consumption - Consommation							
Air Avion	Sea Maritime	Unallocated Non distribué	Per capita Par habitant	Total Totale	Solids Solides	Liquids Liquides	Gas Gaz	Electricity Electricité	Year Année	Région, pays ou zone
80	...	*27	713	2 188	1	311	1 525	350	2006	Arménie
119	...	*46	820	2 520	4	313	1 826	376	2007	
116	...	*35	883	2 718	3	349	2 001	364	2008	
60	...	*38	728	2 246	1	322	1 538	386	2009	
420	...	752	1 641	14 282	...	4 052	9 938	293	2006	Azerbaïdjan
393	...	2 330	1 370	12 082	...	3 349	8 550	183	2007	
443	...	3 567	1 490	13 323	...	3 093	10 090	141	2008	
312	...	3 298	1 309	11 871	...	2 554	9 141	175	2009	
577	...	1 903	10 520	8 536	...	1 182	7 354	0	2006	Bahreïn
606	...	2 688	10 115	9 364	...	1 268	8 095	1	2007	
601	...	2 914	9 526	10 025	...	1 374	8 675	-24	2008	
594	...	2 773	8 656	10 124	...	1 338	8 772	14	2009	
280	36	689	136	19 296	151	5 305	13 720	119	2006	Bangladesh
245	36	1 389	132	18 967	194	4 009	14 644	120	2007	
213	36	85	136	19 840	338	3 727	15 647	127	2008	
186	36	369	146	21 458	429	3 868	17 029	133	2009	
1	...	...	254	172	23	73	...	76	2006	Bhoutan
1	...	...	282	194	21	75	...	98	2007	
1	...	...	315	221	30	73	...	118	2008	
*1	...	...	352	251	15	93	...	143	2009	
...	...	-327	6 042	2 237	...	664	1 573	...	2006	Brunéi Darussalam
...	...	358	9 385	3 543	...	687	2 856	...	2007	
...	...	472	10 061	3 870	...	718	3 153	...	2008	
...	...	331	8 776	3 439	...	721	2 718	...	2009	
26	...	...	102	1 383	...	1 369	...	14	2006	Cambodge
29	...	...	109	1 493	...	1 475	...	19	2007	
31	...	...	113	1 569	...	1 533	...	36	2008	
30	...	...	107	1 498	...	1 421	...	76	2009	
2 201	2 323	90 226	1 214	1 595 445	1 243 597	259 406	50 375	42 067	2006	Chine [3]
1 950	2 770	92 546	1 279	1 690 042	1 311 631	268 401	62 865	47 146	2007	
1 755	*3 286	94 090	1 328	1 763 300	1 358 316	276 039	72 708	56 236	2008	
2 393	3 853	104 301	1 431	1 910 444	1 490 568	278 072	79 828	61 977	2009	
3 835	7 329	...	1 733	11 843	5 733	3 398	2 164	548	2006	Chine, Hong Kong RAS
3 903	8 355	...	1 795	12 338	6 287	3 586	1 870	595	2007	
3 852	6 912	...	1 763	12 213	5 741	3 586	2 221	666	2008	
4 888	9 947	...	1 689	11 804	5 916	2 700	2 512	676	2009	
...	...	...	1 250	616	...	534	...	83	2006	Chine, Macao RAS
...	...	...	1 297	656	...	511	...	145	2007	
...	...	...	1 292	670	...	394	77	199	2008	
...	...	...	1 320	701	...	423	87	191	2009	
310	296	...	2 131	2 234	38	2 196	...	0	2006	Chypre
296	275	...	2 211	2 350	35	2 315	...	0	2007	
295	253	...	2 307	2 485	28	2 456	...	0	2008	
273	219	...	2 207	2 407	15	2 391	...	0	2009	
...	...	11	950	22 681	20 887	708	...	1 085	2006	R. p. dém. de Corée
...	...	12	793	19 030	17 041	847	...	1 142	2007	
...	...	11	874	21 097	19 020	868	...	1 210	2008	
...	...	7	826	20 030	18 296	663	...	1 072	2009	
43	...	8	685	3 043	47	705	1 768	522	2006	Géorgie
45	...	9	692	3 054	100	790	1 595	570	2007	
60	...	35	685	3 010	186	823	1 385	616	2008	
59	...	-7	634	2 773	164	929	1 107	573	2009	
4 101	4	39 519	352	406 886	278 181	93 069	24 006	11 631	2006	Inde
4 771	15	42 776	372	436 736	302 255	96 645	25 585	12 252	2007	
4 513	0	46 296	400	475 905	326 714	109 786	27 830	11 575	2008	
4 869	0	51 731	439	530 415	349 305	131 096	38 358	11 656	2009	
717	394	2 031	496	113 997	28 798	55 918	27 881	1 400	2006	Indonésie
1 141	419	5 569	514	119 582	33 272	57 023	27 713	1 574	2007	
1 193	444	3 706	555	130 304	45 077	54 237	29 285	1 705	2008	
74	150	13 339	549	130 354	45 144	55 628	28 302	1 280	2009	
1 026	459	14 581	2 524	178 149	1 599	72 420	102 580	1 551	2006	Iran (Rép. islamique d')
*1 024	900	14 779	2 684	191 734	1 772	72 673	115 789	1 500	2007	
*1 053	842	18 765	2 759	199 435	1 649	75 291	122 236	259	2008	
1 209	3 208	28 595	2 750	201 094	1 239	71 335	128 233	288	2009	

45

Production, trade and consumption of commercial energy *(continued)*
Thousand metric tons of oil equivalent and kilograms per capita
Production, commerce et consommation d'énergie commerciale *(suite)*
Milliers de tonnes d'équivalent pétrole et kilogrammes par habitant

Region, country or area	Year Année	Primary energy production – Production d'énergie primaire					Changes in stocks Variations des stocks	Imports Importations	Exports Exportations
		Total Totale	Solids Solides	Liquids Liquides	Gas Gaz	Electricity Electricité			
Iraq	2006	100 219	...	98 379	1 316	524	...	9 773	74 448
	2007	104 144	...	102 326	1 325	493	...	10 873	81 396
	2008	116 735	...	114 729	1 706	300	...	7 345	89 136
	2009	118 318	...	116 998	1 043	277	...	8 921	94 479
Israel	2006	2 104	99	2	2 002	1	-602	22 192	3 290
	2007	1 963	94	2	1 866	1	217	22 697	3 614
	2008	2 513	94	7	2 410	2	-317	22 289	3 315
	2009	2 511	98	3	2 409	1	386	23 024	3 706
Japan	2006	39 344	...	729	3 547	35 069	-1 076	426 504	10 503
	2007	35 349	...	787	3 974	30 589	-275	439 321	14 607
	2008	34 797	...	782	3 957	30 058	32	429 547	19 594
	2009	36 399	...	736	3 807	31 855	-3 179	390 558	17 163
Jordan	2006	191	...	1	185	5	-7	6 984	1
	2007	172	...	1	165	6	56	7 430	15
	2008	177	...	2	169	6	41	7 553	28
	2009	186	...	1	180	5	-30	7 798	12
Kazakhstan	2006	133 937	42 270	66 410	24 588	668	271	19 171	90 241
	2007	140 143	43 253	68 637	27 551	703	459	15 668	82 266
	2008	152 371	48 846	72 231	30 653	641	796	11 877	86 698
	2009	157 727	44 282	79 356	33 498	591	-129	10 060	91 999
Kuwait	2006	150 866	...	138 129	12 737	...	779	...	111 162
	2007	146 814	...	134 413	12 400	...	524	...	106 163
	2008	153 075	...	140 151	12 924	...	312	...	111 287
	2009	129 448	...	118 555	10 893	...	297	...	88 082
Kyrgyzstan	2006	1 464	95	72	18	1 280	...	1 854	320
	2007	1 396	113	69	14	1 199	...	2 400	425
	2008	1 153	142	72	16	923	...	2 343	396
	2009	1 116	174	76	14	852	...	2 511	169
Lao People's Dem. Rep.	2006	643	*316	...	...	327	...	*165	275
	2007	*739	*433	...	...	306	...	*182	348
	2008	*710	*377	...	...	333	...	*186	278
	2009	*721	*414	...	...	307	...	*213	269
Lebanon	2006	60	...	...	...	60	0	4 441	...
	2007	50	...	...	...	50	0	4 528	...
	2008	32	...	...	...	32	0	5 045	...
	2009	53	...	...	...	53	0	6 428	...
Malaysia	2006	91 331	631	34 311	55 806	583	125	27 118	48 847
	2007	97 166	744	35 487	60 334	601	98	34 034	48 293
	2008	94 729	817	35 680	57 614	618	-770	29 896	43 579
	2009	*91 705	1 497	33 656	*55 950	602	*201	29 875	46 051
Maldives	2006	...	...	...	...	...	...	288	...
	2007	...	...	...	...	...	...	298	...
	2008	...	...	...	...	...	...	323	...
	2009	...	...	...	...	...	...	340	...
Mongolia	2006	2 482	2 482	...	...	...	...	669	569
	2007	2 840	2 840	...	...	...	...	822	756
	2008	3 097	3 097	...	...	...	...	876	964
	2009	6 191	6 191	...	...	...	...	795	3 043
Myanmar	2006	13 957	784	1 070	11 818	286	58	907	9 180
	2007	14 862	803	1 068	12 681	311	116	979	10 086
	2008	13 812	819	1 013	11 630	350	76	632	8 730
	2009	13 005	852	969	10 824	360	47	479	8 516
Nepal	2006	249	14	...	...	235	...	840	7
	2007	249	10	...	...	239	...	875	5
	2008	252	10	...	...	241	...	981	4
	2009	278	11	...	...	267	...	1 165	6
Occ. Palestinian Terr.	2006	...	...	...	...	...	0	1 032	...
	2007	...	...	...	...	...	0	1 058	...
	2008	...	...	...	...	...	0	1 023	...
	2009	...	...	...	...	...	0	1 071	...
Oman	2006	59 689	...	37 280	22 409	...	42	861	45 141
	2007	58 451	...	35 931	22 519	...	136	1 843	42 862
	2008	60 500	...	38 340	22 161	...	432	0	43 467
	2009	64 017	...	41 147	22 869	...	498	0	47 053

45

Production, trade and consumption of commercial energy *(continued)*
Thousand metric tons of oil equivalent and kilograms per capita
Production, commerce et consommation d'énergie commerciale *(suite)*
Milliers de tonnes d'équivalent pétrole et kilogrammes par habitant

Bunkers - Soutes			Consumption - Consommation							
Air Avion	Sea Maritime	Unallocated Non distribué	Per capita Par habitant	Total Totale	Solids Solides	Liquids Liquides	Gas Gaz	Electricity Electricité	Year Année	Région, pays ou zone
779	...	4 341	1 081	30 424	...	28 352	1 316	755	2006	Iraq
622	...	2 358	1 058	30 641	...	28 634	1 325	682	2007	
650	...	2 538	1 065	31 755	...	29 493	1 706	555	2008	
690	...	-638	1 065	32 707	...	30 906	1 043	758	2009	
4	261	-53	3 167	21 397	7 963	11 589	2 002	-157	2006	Israël
0	342	-1 229	3 138	21 716	8 061	11 966	1 866	-178	2007	
0	386	-1 118	3 177	22 536	7 870	12 223	2 635	-192	2008	
0	353	-96	2 918	21 185	7 492	10 220	3 798	-324	2009	
6 498	5 666	29 030	3 283	415 227	111 279	182 794	86 085	35 069	2006	Japon
6 032	5 626	25 932	3 341	422 747	116 221	183 639	92 299	30 589	2007	
5 756	5 150	27 571	3 210	406 241	113 629	169 511	93 043	30 058	2008	
5 054	4 580	23 337	3 003	380 002	101 318	157 181	89 649	31 855	2009	
74	41	207	1 248	6 858	...	4 811	2 004	44	2006	Jordanie
97	38	168	1 275	7 227	...	4 813	2 406	8	2007	
95	30	170	1 259	7 366	...	4 313	3 028	25	2008	
78	38	174	1 280	7 713	...	4 258	3 428	26	2009	
256	...	145	4 062	62 196	30 318	10 283	20 855	740	2006	Kazakhstan
315	...	3 622	4 468	69 149	31 768	10 455	26 254	673	2007	
222	...	-435	4 916	76 968	34 716	10 969	30 615	668	2008	
179	...	5 723	4 420	70 017	31 551	8 593	29 339	534	2009	
572	810	10 337	11 570	27 207	...	14 470	12 737	...	2006	Koweït
626	965	11 232	11 154	27 303	...	14 903	12 400	...	2007	
703	1 008	11 018	11 281	28 748	...	15 824	12 924	...	2008	
786	385	7 694	12 169	32 203	...	21 310	10 893	...	2009	
319	...	3	526	2 676	480	416	717	1 063	2006	Kirghizistan
329	...	6	591	3 035	499	773	769	995	2007	
407	...	12	515	2 681	374	736	694	877	2008	
502	...	45	552	2 910	385	1 090	611	825	2009	
...	...	...	*91	*533	*256	*138	...	140	2006	Rép. dém. pop. lao
...	...	...	*97	*573	*276	*142	...	155	2007	
...	...	...	*103	*618	*295	*141	...	181	2008	
...	...	...	*109	*666	*312	*143	...	211	2009	
106	19	...	1 068	4 376	140	4 096	...	140	2006	Liban
134	20	...	1 070	4 425	140	4 151	...	134	2007	
172	22	...	1 172	4 883	140	4 663	...	80	2008	
181	24	...	1 496	6 277	140	5 938	46	153	2009	
2 010	50	2 318	2 449	65 099	7 800	23 178	33 767	354	2006	Malaisie
2 160	65	6 677	2 732	73 908	8 770	24 021	40 711	406	2007	
2 111	60	4 791	2 722	74 855	11 143	24 742	38 391	578	2008	
2 114	*43	3 930	2 477	69 240	13 650	22 755	*32 241	594	2009	
...	...	...	963	288	...	288	...	...	2006	Maldives
...	...	...	983	298	...	298	...	...	2007	
...	...	...	1 049	323	...	323	...	...	2008	
...	...	...	1 092	340	...	340	...	...	2009	
...	...	...	999	2 582	1 915	655	...	13	2006	Mongolie
...	...	...	1 107	2 907	2 085	805	...	16	2007	
...	...	...	1 128	3 008	2 134	859	...	16	2008	
...	...	...	1 454	3 943	3 150	782	...	12	2009	
77	3	59	118	5 486	138	1 667	3 395	286	2006	Myanmar
65	3	8	119	5 564	145	1 703	3 405	311	2007	
62	3	131	115	5 442	149	1 331	3 611	350	2008	
69	3	203	98	4 645	155	1 081	3 048	360	2009	
52	...	...	37	1 031	181	592	...	257	2006	Népal
56	...	...	37	1 063	230	563	...	271	2007	
56	...	...	41	1 172	216	688	...	268	2008	
66	...	...	47	1 371	227	831	...	313	2009	
...	...	...	284	1 032	...	765	...	266	2006	Terr. palestinien occupé
...	...	...	284	1 058	...	784	...	274	2007	
...	...	...	267	1 023	...	691	...	332	2008	
...	...	...	272	1 071	...	729	...	342	2009	
419	32	874	5 639	14 043	...	4 030	10 014	...	2006	Oman
424	18	1 563	5 970	15 291	...	4 747	10 544	...	2007	
446	133	-1 165	6 518	17 188	...	5 652	11 536	...	2008	
461	121	-1 942	6 573	17 826	...	5 721	12 105	...	2009	

45

Production, trade and consumption of commercial energy *(continued)*
Thousand metric tons of oil equivalent and kilograms per capita
Production, commerce et consommation d'énergie commerciale *(suite)*
Milliers de tonnes d'équivalent pétrole et kilogrammes par habitant

Region, country or area	Year Année	Primary energy production – Production d'énergie primaire					Changes in stocks	Imports Importations	Exports Exportations
		Total Totale	Solids Solides	Liquids Liquides	Gas Gaz	Electricity Electricité	Variations des stocks		
Pakistan	2006	39 363	1 723	3 737	30 959	2 944	477	19 695	440
	2007	40 082	1 950	3 862	31 537	2 733	394	21 765	405
	2008	39 818	1 768	3 593	31 929	2 528	495	21 466	500
	2009	40 375	1 646	3 535	32 529	2 664	-99	21 535	797
Philippines	2006	5 923	1 072	560	2 529	1 761	58	17 467	2 061
	2007	7 302	1 587	657	3 436	1 621	-251	18 107	2 635
	2008	7 844	1 684	767	3 618	1 775	-435	18 227	2 468
	2009	8 663	2 187	1 097	3 643	1 736	-922	16 220	2 137
Qatar	2006	107 376	...	56 396	50 980	...	-41	55	84 478
	2007	119 040	...	57 854	61 186	...	0	204	91 891
	2008	141 429	...	63 998	77 430	...	-2	593	114 202
	2009	149 538	...	61 148	88 390	...	-7	699	121 386
Republic of Korea	2006	15 070	1 210	88	510	13 262	3 005	211 411	32 370
	2007	14 631	1 328	111	431	12 762	-2 141	214 014	31 945
	2008	15 403	1 276	166	441	13 520	-75	223 506	37 561
	2009	15 454	1 159	249	748	13 299	1 264	222 181	36 077
Saudi Arabia	2006	580 285	...	514 739	65 546	...	-2 064	4 219	402 891
	2007	558 670	...	494 716	63 954	...	-43	5 693	396 612
	2008	583 815	...	515 973	67 842	...	-1 950	8 995	414 037
	2009	533 208	...	465 025	68 183	...	-5 802	9 497	365 031
Singapore	2006	...	...	...	...	...	-548	112 848	58 131
	2007	...	...	...	...	...	541	118 203	63 280
	2008	...	...	...	...	...	944	129 183	69 706
	2009	...	...	...	...	...	860	137 392	75 273
Sri Lanka	2006	399	...	...	...	399	120	4 196	...
	2007	340	...	...	...	340	7	4 017	0
	2008	356	...	...	...	356	-6	3 825	0
	2009	336	...	...	...	336	-198	3 838	0
Syrian Arab Republic	2006	27 321	...	21 309	5 673	339	443	2 451	9 100
	2007	25 454	...	19 572	5 583	299	93	3 956	7 903
	2008	24 735	...	19 176	5 313	247	*7	2 941	6 073
	2009	24 664	...	18 930	5 574	160	-2 976	5 937	8 781
Tajikistan	2006	1 519	43	24	16	1 436	...	1 332	369
	2007	1 573	76	12	13	1 472	...	1 439	368
	2008	1 489	84	14	32	1 359	...	1 421	383
	2009	1 503	84	26	34	1 359	...	1 216	369
Thailand	2006	40 263	8 359	13 014	18 191	699	-1 998	61 541	10 346
	2007	41 840	8 023	13 948	19 171	698	-1 895	57 810	9 331
	2008	44 669	7 910	15 135	21 012	612	-2 590	59 929	11 968
	2009	49 027	8 020	15 561	24 845	601	*-517	59 992	12 663
Timor-Leste *	2006	7 408	...	7 408	...	...	...	59	7 332
	2007	7 421	...	7 421	...	...	...	61	7 345
	2008	7 447	...	7 447	...	...	...	63	7 370
	2009	7 418	...	7 418	...	...	...	61	7 341
Turkey	2006	19 938	13 085	2 202	828	3 823	183	77 135	5 998
	2007	20 906	14 794	2 168	817	3 127	961	83 982	6 015
	2008	22 751	16 675	2 198	931	2 947	1 130	81 375	6 872
	2009	23 720	17 403	2 434	626	3 258	958	74 656	5 181
Turkmenistan	2006	65 817	...	8 578	57 239	0	...	87	45 303
	2007	72 169	...	9 834	62 334	0	...	87	48 328
	2008	74 922	...	11 122	63 800	0	...	87	50 506
	2009	44 469	...	9 944	34 524	0	...	87	23 228
United Arab Emirates	2006	189 953	...	144 542	45 411	...	...	17 070	133 282
	2007	190 579	...	142 886	47 693	...	...	23 660	132 208
	2008	191 978	...	145 189	46 789	...	...	33 176	134 760
	2009	173 711	...	128 235	45 476	...	...	31 435	115 741
Uzbekistan	2006	64 073	891	5 767	56 628	788	...	2 066	12 679
	2007	65 577	956	5 233	58 839	550	...	2 222	14 473
	2008	70 402	921	5 128	63 376	977	...	2 009	14 746
	2009	66 545	1 002	4 947	59 794	802	...	1 812	14 948
Viet Nam	2006	53 036	27 145	17 612	6 524	1 755	1 452	12 203	38 827
	2007	55 058	29 738	16 785	6 599	1 936	-2 838	14 409	39 176
	2008	53 028	27 844	15 783	7 166	2 234	1 003	14 653	28 737
	2009	58 316	30 600	17 248	7 890	2 578	-2 331	14 221	32 849

Production, trade and consumption of commercial energy *(continued)*
Thousand metric tons of oil equivalent and kilograms per capita
Production, commerce et consommation d'énergie commerciale *(suite)*
Milliers de tonnes d'équivalent pétrole et kilogrammes par habitant

Bunkers - Soutes				Consumption - Consommation						
Air Avion	Sea Maritime	Unallocated Non distribué	Per capita Par habitant	Total Totale	Solids Solides	Liquids Liquides	Gas Gaz	Electricity Electricité	Year Année	Région, pays ou zone
176	102	1 705	348	56 156	4 667	17 574	30 956	2 959	2006	Pakistan
170	132	1 744	359	59 002	6 097	18 619	31 536	2 750	2007	
158	169	1 831	347	58 131	4 989	18 668	31 926	2 548	2008	
183	223	1 686	347	59 119	4 884	19 025	32 525	2 686	2009	
800	126	775	225	19 570	3 066	12 214	2 529	1 761	2006	Philippines
1 131	245	910	234	20 737	3 365	12 314	3 436	1 621	2007	
997	235	808	244	21 998	3 900	12 705	3 618	1 775	2008	
1 021	205	1 138	232	21 304	3 891	12 035	3 643	1 736	2009	
604	...	1 110	21 751	21 280	...	3 758	17 522	...	2006	Qatar
766	...	2 414	20 517	24 173	...	4 039	20 134	...	2007	
884	...	2 032	17 839	24 905	...	4 724	20 180	...	2008	
1 026	...	2 213	16 034	25 619	...	3 901	21 718	...	2009	
2 891	10 182	23 237	3 275	154 797	52 521	57 043	31 971	13 262	2006	République de Corée
3 076	9 455	26 476	3 365	159 833	56 232	56 138	34 701	12 762	2007	
3 695	8 917	24 860	3 435	163 951	62 951	51 904	35 576	13 520	2008	
3 581	8 202	22 257	3 466	166 254	64 708	52 763	35 485	13 299	2009	
1 780	2 661	35 886	5 780	143 349	...	77 803	65 546	...	2006	Arabie saoudite
1 874	2 786	17 452	5 712	145 681	...	81 727	63 954	...	2007	
2 018	2 849	19 566	5 973	156 290	...	88 449	67 842	...	2008	
1 997	2 575	16 826	6 046	162 077	...	93 894	68 183	...	2009	
*5 665	22 580	12 213	3 358	14 808	4	8 130	6 674	-1	2006	Singapour
*5 835	25 567	7 920	3 285	15 061	7	7 906	7 148	0	2007	
*5 721	30 905	6 813	3 163	15 094	5	7 772	7 317	0	2008	
*3 670	36 105	-3	4 344	21 486	4	14 087	7 396	0	2009	
123	137	183	201	4 032	67	3 566	...	399	2006	Sri Lanka
105	0	163	201	4 081	48	3 693	...	340	2007	
100	23	171	190	3 892	51	3 486	...	356	2008	
92	6	178	198	4 097	53	3 708	...	336	2009	
145	...	972	1 010	19 112	3	13 166	5 673	270	2006	Rép. arabe syrienne
93	...	1 697	1 016	19 625	3	13 706	5 583	334	2007	
102	...	1 936	993	19 557	3	13 920	5 439	196	2008	
95	1 085	1 485	1 104	22 131	3	15 586	6 393	149	2009	
4	...	19	377	2 458	46	326	597	1 488	2006	Tadjikistan
4	...	10	398	2 630	80	469	601	1 480	2007	
4	...	12	375	2 511	88	491	498	1 434	2008	
4	...	22	343	2 323	90	466	404	1 363	2009	
3	47	13 974	1 181	79 432	17 595	34 084	26 675	1 078	2006	Thaïlande
2	26	11 045	1 197	81 141	16 888	35 197	28 052	1 004	2007	
2	7	14 631	1 180	80 580	18 222	32 335	29 273	750	2008	
1	*8	10 716	1 254	86 148	18 178	34 669	32 581	720	2009	
...	...	76	57	59	...	59	...	...	2006	Timor-Leste *
...	...	76	58	61	...	61	...	...	2007	
...	...	77	59	63	...	63	...	...	2008	
...	...	77	56	61	...	61	...	...	2009	
986	991	4 833	1 217	84 082	26 541	25 002	28 859	3 680	2006	Turquie
1 159	853	4 298	1 309	91 602	29 422	25 384	33 804	2 993	2007	
1 308	668	2 690	1 290	91 457	29 579	25 411	33 547	2 919	2008	
1 429	277	457	1 254	90 075	30 066	24 685	32 129	3 195	2009	
305	...	737	4 073	19 559	...	3 158	16 516	-115	2006	Turkménistan
342	...	843	4 681	22 744	...	3 521	19 348	-125	2007	
375	...	950	4 713	23 179	...	3 849	19 457	-127	2008	
342	...	851	4 043	20 135	...	3 521	16 749	-135	2009	
2 806	13 143	7 450	10 797	50 342	...	10 256	40 086	...	2006	Emirats arabes unis
3 224	14 233	7 328	10 590	57 245	...	10 796	46 449	...	2007	
3 362	14 885	7 469	10 421	64 678	...	11 196	53 482	...	2008	
3 752	12 515	7 351	9 481	65 788	...	11 186	54 602	...	2009	
...	...	1 248	1 992	52 211	939	4 289	46 203	780	2006	Ouzbékistan
...	...	1 193	1 967	52 133	1 000	3 827	46 762	543	2007	
...	...	1 261	2 104	56 403	983	3 660	50 791	970	2008	
...	...	955	1 934	52 454	1 046	3 776	46 837	795	2009	
287	313	310	286	24 048	5 619	11 768	4 824	1 838	2006	Viet Nam
274	276	395	379	32 184	11 375	12 588	6 059	2 162	2007	
294	283	441	430	36 922	14 934	12 551	6 926	2 511	2008	
387	287	941	465	40 403	15 171	14 444	7 890	2 899	2009	

45

Production, trade and consumption of commercial energy *(continued)*
Thousand metric tons of oil equivalent and kilograms per capita
Production, commerce et consommation d'énergie commerciale *(suite)*
Milliers de tonnes d'équivalent pétrole et kilogrammes par habitant

Region, country or area	Year Année	Primary energy production – Production d'énergie primaire					Changes in stocks	Imports Importations	Exports Exportations
		Total Totale	Solids Solides	Liquids Liquides	Gas Gaz	Electricity Electricité	Variations des stocks		
Yemen	2006	18 391	...	18 391	...	...	1 525	3 424	13 122
	2007	16 213	...	16 213	...	...	326	3 283	11 718
	2008	14 978	...	14 978	...	...	18	3 178	10 591
	2009	14 988	...	14 471	517	...	-596	3 082	10 772
Europe	**2006**	**2 212 781**	**405 075**	**738 623**	**889 903**	**179 180**	**27 873**	**1 659 391**	**1 262 001**
	2007	**2 202 055**	**402 329**	**747 676**	**873 906**	**178 144**	**-2 493**	**1 630 636**	**1 271 247**
	2008	**2 214 412**	**399 357**	**734 285**	**899 317**	**181 453**	**46 694**	**1 675 135**	**1 262 958**
	2009	**2 090 808**	**370 056**	**727 269**	**814 275**	**179 209**	**14 871**	**1 557 480**	**1 228 062**
Albania	2006	971	15	510	16	430	0	885	0
	2007	847	15	576	16	240	12	1 063	0
	2008	944	20	590	8	326	68	1 105	185
	2009	1 050	5	588	7	450	-4	815	398
Andorra	2006	6	...	...	...	6	0	224	...
	2007	5	...	...	...	5	0	222	...
	2008	5	...	...	...	5	0	223	...
	2009	*5	...	...	...	*5	0	215	...
Austria	2006	6 340	0	1 142	1 751	3 447	664	30 366	5 160
	2007	6 588	0	1 258	1 777	3 552	356	29 738	5 977
	2008	6 410	0	1 260	1 476	3 674	696	29 647	5 373
	2009	6 878	0	1 346	1 605	3 927	246	28 760	7 206
Belarus	2006	2 487	483	1 798	202	3	11	42 569	15 905
	2007	2 537	570	1 778	185	3	-306	41 325	14 284
	2008	2 494	538	1 765	187	3	527	43 748	17 227
	2009	2 454	503	1 758	189	4	-493	41 295	17 559
Belgium	2006	4 221	15	22	2	4 182	81	77 309	24 301
	2007	4 489	0	153	1	4 334	-1 022	76 799	25 206
	2008	4 404	0	275	2	4 128	781	80 440	24 861
	2009	4 638	0	325	2	4 311	-1 337	74 433	25 613
Bosnia and Herzegovina	2006	6 312	5 808	...	...	504	-15	2 185	833
	2007	6 476	6 132	...	...	344	-15	2 351	792
	2008	7 033	6 641	...	...	391	-14	2 405	872
	2009	6 973	6 437	...	...	536	105	2 437	852
Bulgaria	2006	6 843	4 307	34	429	2 072	-101	14 276	4 394
	2007	6 664	4 811	29	282	1 541	51	15 188	4 397
	2008	6 693	4 816	34	195	1 648	495	15 322	4 445
	2009	6 359	4 598	42	38	1 681	56	12 096	3 627
Croatia	2006	3 986	...	995	2 463	528	69	7 879	2 605
	2007	3 955	...	949	2 625	381	-31	8 254	2 548
	2008	3 785	...	886	2 438	461	340	8 097	2 266
	2009	3 860	...	829	2 441	591	-202	7 271	2 509
Czech Republic	2006	27 027	23 867	446	189	2 524	76	22 153	8 571
	2007	26 886	23 804	424	180	2 478	-1 043	21 028	8 963
	2008	25 847	22 785	350	202	2 509	136	21 969	8 869
	2009	24 088	20 853	421	185	2 628	319	21 222	8 791
Denmark	2006	27 969	...	17 075	10 367	527	-584	13 867	22 874
	2007	25 201	...	15 387	9 194	619	28	13 441	19 834
	2008	24 895	...	14 267	10 029	598	1 133	14 944	20 727
	2009	22 067	...	13 113	8 375	580	274	13 656	18 520
Estonia	2006	3 109	3 101	...	...	8	116	2 181	156
	2007	3 664	3 654	...	...	10	26	2 392	325
	2008	3 477	3 463	...	...	14	6	2 190	267
	2009	3 305	3 286	...	...	20	285	2 033	283
Faeroe Islands	2006	10	...	...	...	10	...	*224	...
	2007	10	...	...	...	10	...	*226	...
	2008	9	...	...	...	9	...	*229	...
	2009	9	...	...	...	9	...	*230	...
Finland	2006	6 196	3 224	...	...	2 972	519	26 126	5 262
	2007	4 338	1 088	...	...	3 250	-1 538	26 350	5 979
	2008	4 589	1 048	73	...	3 468	194	26 422	6 490
	2009	5 516	2 184	194	...	3 138	1 044	24 921	6 589
France [4]	2006	47 330	281	1 791	1 033	44 226	1 853	175 127	30 428
	2007	47 010	262	2 159	922	43 667	-1 713	168 111	28 513
	2008	48 155	172	2 970	816	44 197	746	176 107	30 175
	2009	45 299	91	3 148	769	41 290	-101	165 706	25 068

45
Production, trade and consumption of commercial energy *(continued)*
Thousand metric tons of oil equivalent and kilograms per capita
Production, commerce et consommation d'énergie commerciale *(suite)*
Milliers de tonnes d'équivalent pétrole et kilogrammes par habitant

Bunkers - Soutes				Consumption - Consommation						
Air Avion	Sea Maritime	Unallocated Non distribué	Per capita Par habitant	Total Totale	Solids Solides	Liquids Liquides	Gas Gaz	Electricity Electricité	Year Année	Région, pays ou zone
115	126	1 216	268	5 710	...	5 710	...	...	2006	Yémen
130	126	869	288	6 325	...	6 325	...	...	2007	
118	126	948	281	6 354	...	6 354	...	...	2008	
140	126	1 051	282	6 576	...	6 477	99	...	2009	
51 238	**56 217**	**74 642**	**3 278**	**2 400 203**	**503 149**	**736 359**	**981 819**	**178 876**	**2006**	**Europe**
52 402	**56 671**	**84 338**	**3 231**	**2 370 524**	**500 799**	**708 575**	**983 131**	**178 019**	**2007**	
53 767	**56 326**	**94 178**	**3 231**	**2 375 624**	**485 904**	**717 135**	**991 491**	**181 094**	**2008**	
50 069	**51 139**	**80 465**	**3 018**	**2 223 681**	**419 257**	**695 669**	**929 632**	**179 122**	**2009**	
39	...	281	487	1 536	18	1 020	16	483	2006	Albanie
10	...	359	482	1 529	18	1 012	16	483	2007	
19	...	157	509	1 621	23	1 054	8	536	2008	
19	...	169	402	1 284	71	632	7	573	2009	
*0	...	...	2 873	229	0	182	...	47	2006	Andorre
0	...	...	2 790	227	0	179	...	48	2007	
0	...	...	2 770	229	0	179	...	49	2008	
*0	...	...	2 636	221	0	172	...	*49	2009	
593	...	1 325	3 501	28 964	4 077	12 551	8 300	4 036	2006	Autriche
570	...	1 541	3 355	27 882	3 887	12 107	7 767	4 121	2007	
604	...	1 440	3 350	27 945	3 764	11 773	8 315	4 092	2008	
533	...	1 503	3 124	26 150	2 907	11 274	7 975	3 994	2009	
...	...	3 351	2 638	25 788	521	5 722	19 168	378	2006	Bélarus
...	...	3 926	2 668	25 958	496	5 805	19 281	377	2007	
...	...	2 460	2 688	26 026	439	5 767	19 659	162	2008	
...	...	2 318	2 529	24 366	425	7 228	16 325	388	2009	
1 182	8 545	3 211	4 221	44 210	4 672	17 811	16 671	5 056	2006	Belgique
1 017	9 560	4 599	3 978	41 928	4 141	16 280	16 589	4 917	2007	
2 051	9 866	5 564	3 935	41 721	4 213	15 980	16 488	5 039	2008	
1 938	7 223	7 133	3 611	38 501	2 935	14 620	16 793	4 154	2009	
...	...	3	2 030	7 675	5 871	1 129	353	322	2006	Bosnie-Herzégovine
...	...	-1	2 130	8 051	6 199	1 187	373	292	2007	
...	...	-6	2 275	8 586	6 709	1 237	390	250	2008	
...	...	130	2 209	8 322	6 604	1 233	206	279	2009	
181	108	976	2 024	15 562	6 926	3 993	3 237	1 406	2006	Bulgarie
183	53	1 122	2 100	16 046	7 862	3 663	3 365	1 156	2007	
213	123	925	2 083	15 814	7 592	3 774	3 260	1 188	2008	
153	209	510	1 843	13 900	6 382	3 849	2 424	1 245	2009	
40	20	230	2 008	8 902	738	4 540	2 612	1 012	2006	Croatie
44	24	159	2 139	9 465	803	4 733	3 001	928	2007	
52	22	184	2 041	9 019	825	4 304	2 863	1 027	2008	
44	7	234	1 936	8 539	597	4 193	2 670	1 079	2009	
335	...	2 299	3 694	37 898	21 075	6 954	8 433	1 438	2006	République tchèque
345	...	2 068	3 644	37 581	21 342	7 172	7 978	1 089	2007	
335	...	2 244	3 491	36 230	19 741	7 034	7 932	1 523	2008	
339	...	2 045	3 239	33 815	17 864	6 998	7 497	1 455	2009	
868	1 027	101	3 225	17 550	5 528	7 038	5 052	-69	2006	Danemark
890	1 077	92	3 057	16 720	4 626	7 032	4 525	537	2007	
886	929	375	2 872	15 787	3 927	6 595	4 542	723	2008	
779	518	170	2 799	15 462	4 017	6 487	4 349	609	2009	
32	216	...	3 549	4 770	3 036	893	898	-57	2006	Estonie
51	252	...	4 023	5 402	3 707	1 001	893	-198	2007	
28	256	...	3 807	5 110	3 431	890	856	-67	2008	
33	228	...	3 361	4 509	3 050	849	583	27	2009	
*3	...	...	*4 760	*231	...	*221	...	10	2006	Iles Féroé
*3	...	...	*4 800	*233	...	*223	...	10	2007	
*3	...	...	*4 841	*235	...	*226	...	9	2008	
*3	...	...	*4 857	*236	...	*227	...	9	2009	
467	566	-948	5 024	26 455	7 451	10 745	4 307	3 952	2006	Finlande
539	465	-1 322	5 021	26 565	7 235	10 865	4 136	4 329	2007	
583	407	-2 194	4 802	25 530	5 218	11 464	4 281	4 566	2008	
511	253	-2 293	4 555	24 332	5 165	11 118	3 871	4 177	2009	
5 714	2 889	7 794	2 830	173 779	13 199	77 919	43 881	38 780	2006	France[4]
5 924	2 961	8 080	2 774	171 356	13 647	76 258	42 668	38 782	2007	
5 959	2 587	7 295	2 857	177 501	12 936	80 262	44 232	40 071	2008	
5 487	2 584	4 417	2 778	173 549	11 229	80 604	42 656	39 061	2009	

Production, trade and consumption of commercial energy *(continued)*
Thousand metric tons of oil equivalent and kilograms per capita
Production, commerce et consommation d'énergie commerciale *(suite)*
Milliers de tonnes d'équivalent pétrole et kilogrammes par habitant

| Region, country or area | Year Année | Primary energy production – Production d'énergie primaire | | | | | Changes in stocks | Imports Importations | Exports Exportations |
		Total Totale	Solids Solides	Liquids Liquides	Gas Gaz	Electricity Electricité	Variations des stocks		
Germany	2006	95 153	53 371	6 593	15 627	19 562	1 289	257 308	41 630
	2007	95 820	54 590	8 457	14 563	18 210	-3 213	244 167	42 779
	2008	89 174	50 048	7 584	12 585	18 957	-582	252 490	40 056
	2009	82 591	45 703	6 895	12 376	17 616	1 916	240 183	35 491
Gibraltar	2006	...	...	...	...	...	...	1 341	...
	2007	...	...	...	...	...	...	1 382	...
	2008	...	...	...	...	...	...	1 413	...
	2009	...	...	...	...	...	...	1 454	...
Greece	2006	9 040	8 170	138	29	703	377	32 494	6 825
	2007	9 024	8 389	164	25	447	203	32 895	7 117
	2008	8 819	8 129	124	16	550	528	33 620	7 063
	2009	9 047	8 176	150	13	708	-630	32 085	8 368
Guernsey	2006	...	...	...	...	...	...	24	...
	2007	...	...	...	...	...	...	17	...
	2008	...	...	...	...	...	...	22	...
	2009	...	...	...	...	...	...	21	...
Hungary	2006	7 001	1 757	1 402	2 665	1 177	121	22 506	3 649
	2007	6 567	1 773	1 260	2 245	1 290	-193	21 689	3 707
	2008	6 690	1 694	1 439	2 247	1 310	791	22 152	3 407
	2009	6 879	1 556	1 390	2 559	1 375	880	18 444	2 125
Iceland	2006	1 083	...	...	230	853	-27	1 061	...
	2007	1 233	...	...	203	1 029	-8	1 170	...
	2008	1 659	...	...	244	1 416	-5	1 070	...
	2009	1 691	...	...	244	1 447	-4	1 018	50
Ireland	2006	1 459	766	3	456	233	143	15 616	1 283
	2007	1 272	591	15	410	256	-489	15 749	1 237
	2008	1 378	645	21	394	319	28	15 822	1 273
	2009	1 356	584	56	354	362	-272	14 444	979
Isle of Man	2006	0	...	...	...	0	...	4	2
	2007	0	...	...	...	0	...	4	6
	2008	0	...	...	...	0	...	3	8
	2009	0	...	...	...	0	...	2	10
Italy[5]	2006	20 497	13	6 026	9 991	4 468	3 156	196 926	25 408
	2007	19 170	100	6 099	8 832	4 138	-1 033	194 349	28 804
	2008	19 435	74	5 968	8 422	4 970	525	191 003	27 018
	2009	18 655	46	5 642	7 292	5 675	-1 467	172 923	24 387
Jersey	2006	...	...	...	...	...	...	57	...
	2007	...	...	...	...	...	...	51	...
	2008	...	...	...	...	...	...	58	...
	*2009	...	...	...	...	...	...	58	...
Latvia	2006	249	3	9	...	236	206	3 890	290
	2007	258	3	16	...	240	-85	3 755	317
	2008	308	3	33	...	272	-263	3 453	329
	2009	356	6	49	...	302	183	3 740	530
Lithuania	2006	1 073	13	198	48	814	141	12 557	6 894
	2007	1 183	12	188	47	937	131	10 495	4 469
	2008	1 205	15	198	45	947	-144	13 469	7 805
	2009	1 331	12	225	49	1 045	-156	12 070	7 541
Luxembourg	2006	87	...	1	...	86	29	5 061	289
	2007	121	...	34	...	86	-36	4 823	255
	2008	126	...	36	...	90	7	4 822	225
	2009	119	...	40	...	79	2	4 563	233
Malta	2006	...	...	...	...	...	0	1 690	...
	2007	...	...	...	...	...	0	1 844	...
	2008	...	...	...	...	...	0	1 901	...
	2009	...	...	...	...	...	-35	2 040	9
Montenegro	2006	1 133	983	...	...	150	0	467	148
	2007	892	782	...	...	110	-14	504	65
	2008	1 263	1 131	...	...	132	-6	490	133
	2009	800	622	...	...	178	0	*458	148
Netherlands	2006	64 286	...	2 192	61 549	545	-85	152 366	121 411
	2007	63 910	...	2 748	60 492	669	345	151 604	119 873
	2008	69 611	...	2 326	66 548	737	2 005	149 307	120 048
	2009	65 475	...	2 028	62 678	770	3 029	154 741	123 750

Production, trade and consumption of commercial energy *(continued)*
Thousand metric tons of oil equivalent and kilograms per capita
Production, commerce et consommation d'énergie commerciale *(suite)*
Milliers de tonnes d'équivalent pétrole et kilogrammes par habitant

Bunkers - Soutes			Consumption - Consommation							
Air Avion	Sea Maritime	Unallocated Non distribué	Per capita Par habitant	Total Totale	Solids Solides	Liquids Liquides	Gas Gaz	Electricity Electricité	Year Année	Région, pays ou zone
7 014	2 624	6 093	3 560	293 810	82 300	105 071	88 338	18 102	2006	Allemagne
7 270	3 129	6 172	3 440	283 850	86 719	94 927	85 418	16 786	2007	
7 366	3 025	7 625	3 446	284 173	81 026	100 847	85 071	17 229	2008	
7 167	2 765	8 366	3 241	267 068	71 619	93 781	85 107	16 561	2009	
4	1 207	...	4 440	130	...	130	...	...	2006	Gibraltar
4	1 244	...	4 570	134	...	134	...	...	2007	
4	1 270	...	4 745	139	...	139	...	...	2008	
4	1 307	...	4 889	143	...	143	...	...	2009	
937	3 141	-1 775	2 855	32 029	8 434	19 478	3 052	1 064	2006	Grèce
958	3 205	-2 171	2 897	32 607	8 845	19 203	3 738	821	2007	
996	3 134	-2 242	2 919	32 961	8 311	19 722	3 896	1 033	2008	
856	2 661	-2 427	2 852	32 304	8 434	19 485	3 301	1 084	2009	
...	...	...	390	24	...	...	...	24	2006	Guernesey
...	...	...	277	17	...	...	...	17	2007	
...	...	...	358	22	...	...	...	22	2008	
...	...	...	330	21	...	...	...	21	2009	
272	...	1 268	2 404	24 197	3 091	6 561	12 748	1 797	2006	Hongrie
250	...	1 142	2 325	23 352	3 157	6 651	11 912	1 632	2007	
278	...	1 264	2 305	23 103	3 083	6 622	11 752	1 646	2008	
237	...	1 050	2 103	21 030	2 556	6 440	10 186	1 849	2009	
179	35	163	5 962	1 795	89	623	230	853	2006	Islande
167	67	210	6 434	1 967	114	620	203	1 029	2007	
118	62	197	7 588	2 357	86	612	244	1 416	2008	
73	65	197	7 377	2 328	80	557	244	1 447	2009	
814	125	-109	3 506	14 819	2 476	7 498	4 459	386	2006	Irlande
973	111	132	3 509	15 057	2 355	7 572	4 760	370	2007	
913	86	-45	3 433	14 945	2 398	7 209	4 980	358	2008	
557	113	72	3 253	14 351	2 157	7 006	4 760	428	2009	
...	...	...	33	3	...	...	...	3	2006	Ile de Man
...	...	...	-29	-2	...	...	...	-2	2007	
...	...	...	-65	-5	...	...	...	-5	2008	
...	...	...	-95	-8	...	...	...	-8	2009	
3 226	2 350	3 425	3 043	179 858	16 663	77 980	76 880	8 336	2006	Italie[5]
3 428	2 433	2 452	2 981	177 434	16 789	75 271	77 257	8 117	2007	
3 308	2 554	3 252	2 900	173 780	16 294	71 830	77 244	8 412	2008	
3 011	2 383	4 287	2 637	158 977	12 709	65 725	71 002	9 541	2009	
...	...	...	643	57	...	...	...	57	2006	Jersey
...	...	...	563	51	...	...	...	51	2007	
...	...	...	634	58	...	...	...	58	2008	
...	...	...	630	58	...	...	...	58	*2009	
66	200	20	1 464	3 357	85	1 257	1 563	452	2006	Lettonie
80	181	31	1 529	3 488	107	1 373	1 511	498	2007	
97	209	23	1 482	3 366	106	1 289	1 481	489	2008	
102	278	3	1 327	3 000	85	1 107	1 364	444	2009	
53	141	-29	1 892	6 431	311	2 567	2 775	777	2006	Lituanie
72	121	-897	2 303	7 783	299	3 405	3 260	819	2007	
76	92	-55	2 054	6 900	249	2 858	2 929	865	2008	
36	129	-84	1 776	5 934	186	2 482	2 473	793	2009	
407	...	...	9 500	4 423	104	2 560	1 367	391	2006	Luxembourg
436	...	...	9 014	4 288	86	2 499	1 276	427	2007	
440	...	...	8 785	4 276	83	2 515	1 215	464	2008	
420	...	...	8 091	4 026	76	2 342	1 236	373	2009	
77	772	...	2 045	841	...	841	...	...	2006	Malte
91	865	...	2 154	889	...	889	...	...	2007	
129	935	...	2 022	837	...	837	...	...	2008	
92	1 157	...	1 967	817	...	817	...	...	2009	
...	...	...	2 316	1 452	974	*167	...	311	2006	Monténégro
...	...	...	2 141	1 345	845	*167	...	333	2007	
...	...	...	2 584	1 626	1 152	*189	...	285	2008	
...	...	...	1 762	1 111	648	*194	...	269	2009	
3 666	17 830	-322	4 528	74 153	7 040	26 657	38 065	2 391	2006	Pays-Bas
3 684	16 270	14 172	3 720	61 170	7 076	14 951	36 964	2 180	2007	
3 736	15 677	14 040	3 842	63 412	7 099	15 706	38 507	2 100	2008	
3 473	14 399	13 910	3 723	61 655	6 545	15 064	38 856	1 190	2009	

45

Production, trade and consumption of commercial energy *(continued)*
Thousand metric tons of oil equivalent and kilograms per capita
Production, commerce et consommation d'énergie commerciale *(suite)*
Milliers de tonnes d'équivalent pétrole et kilogrammes par habitant

Region, country or area	Year Année	Primary energy production – Production d'énergie primaire					Changes in stocks Variations des stocks	Imports Importations	Exports Exportations
		Total Totale	Solids Solides	Liquids Liquides	Gas Gaz	Electricity Electricité			
Norway[6]	2006	222 438	1 607	125 468	85 013	10 349	523	5 583	198 485
	2007	222 377	2 734	121 220	86 762	11 662	-779	5 792	198 843
	2008	227 487	2 302	116 265	96 805	12 115	449	5 700	200 841
	2009	223 412	1 773	109 867	100 762	11 010	-981	6 346	199 954
Poland	2006	73 130	67 577	960	4 312	282	-302	40 274	18 151
	2007	67 970	62 511	832	4 330	298	-7	42 227	15 128
	2008	66 389	60 926	1 055	4 100	308	2 877	45 042	12 430
	2009	61 943	56 428	1 081	4 086	348	2 901	43 294	11 018
Portugal	2006	1 315	...	70	...	1 245	147	24 625	3 187
	2007	1 427	...	162	...	1 265	-305	23 295	2 397
	2008	1 295	...	153	...	1 142	8	23 667	2 140
	2009	1 684	...	228	...	1 456	135	22 555	1 979
Republic of Moldova	2006	11	...	4	0	7	-28	2 097	2
	2007	11	...	8	0	3	37	2 050	1
	2008	22	...	15	0	7	22	2 039	5
	2009	22	...	17	0	5	1	1 932	14
Romania	2006	24 976	6 556	5 733	10 625	2 063	-673	17 790	5 737
	2007	24 001	6 712	4 989	10 263	2 036	188	17 251	4 649
	2008	24 095	6 729	4 930	9 993	2 444	-108	16 294	5 296
	2009	23 480	6 565	4 614	9 932	2 370	106	11 023	4 237
Russian Federation	2006	1 254 528	159 329	481 985	584 652	28 563	13 768	24 842	581 869
	2007	1 266 546	162 944	494 061	580 349	29 193	9 525	24 434	595 287
	2008	1 282 458	167 173	492 340	594 547	28 398	25 315	29 671	584 358
	2009	1 202 411	153 630	497 320	522 211	29 249	81	24 821	569 053
Serbia	2006	9 677	7 819	653	262	943	-20	7 346	917
	2007	9 631	7 893	655	220	863	-43	7 009	996
	2008	9 985	8 224	653	238	869	198	7 243	1 030
	2009	9 200	7 331	678	233	958	39	5 659	879
Slovakia	2006	2 828	562	70	255	1 942	-173	17 709	5 098
	2007	2 521	551	81	174	1 716	466	18 064	5 110
	2008	2 737	624	163	148	1 801	-16	17 278	4 736
	2009	2 586	653	171	155	1 607	481	16 314	4 535
Slovenia	2006	2 001	1 210	2	4	786	-100	4 825	1 014
	2007	2 017	1 239	4	3	771	-54	4 786	930
	2008	2 080	1 185	7	3	885	115	5 474	1 204
	2009	2 068	1 160	6	3	899	-42	4 664	1 265
Spain	2006	16 181	6 049	314	70	9 748	2 628	136 567	9 237
	2007	15 779	5 456	528	17	9 777	-1 474	136 002	10 722
	2008	15 086	4 194	503	16	10 373	2 194	137 467	10 709
	2009	15 443	3 628	991	14	10 811	1 010	125 857	10 740
Sweden	2006	11 625	185	277	...	11 163	-256	31 551	11 652
	2007	12 118	155	384	...	11 579	-180	30 561	11 347
	2008	12 288	250	421	...	11 617	470	33 014	13 132
	2009	11 076	210	493	...	10 373	-17	30 449	12 032
Switzerland[7]	2006	5 261	...	8	31	5 223	81	19 087	3 215
	2007	5 606	...	12	30	5 564	-267	17 554	3 705
	2008	5 691	...	12	31	5 648	52	18 588	3 406
	2009	5 648	...	5	31	5 612	110	18 771	3 364
TFYR of Macedonia	2006	1 931	1 789	...	...	142	16	1 638	361
	2007	1 844	1 754	3	...	87	-92	1 664	262
	2008	2 129	2 056	1	...	72	15	1 713	379
	2009	2 111	2 001	1	...	109	67	1 555	369
Ukraine	2006	66 475	35 336	4 634	17 623	8 882	1 529	68 642	8 029
	2007	64 672	33 613	4 584	17 632	8 843	3 478	71 033	7 611
	2008	64 738	33 652	4 452	17 916	8 719	4 817	70 236	7 871
	2009	61 497	31 309	4 074	17 954	8 160	3 354	50 874	6 641
United Kingdom	2006	176 535	10 876	78 072	80 009	7 578	2 693	138 078	86 729
	2007	167 417	10 190	78 459	72 125	6 644	-3 399	137 930	88 813
	2008	159 523	10 821	73 116	69 665	5 921	2 293	147 762	86 297
	2009	147 423	10 705	69 486	59 720	7 512	3 987	140 031	81 347
Oceania	**2006**	**293 422**	**218 236**	**26 260**	**44 866**	**4 059**	**744**	**43 978**	**194 477**
	2007	**310 419**	**230 212**	**28 533**	**47 593**	**4 082**	**7 920**	**47 086**	**203 928**
	2008	**313 146**	**233 290**	**28 141**	**47 842**	**3 874**	**1 877**	**50 676**	**212 979**
	2009	**322 944**	**239 275**	**29 501**	**49 955**	**4 213**	**1 630**	**50 659**	**220 820**

Production, trade and consumption of commercial energy *(continued)*
Thousand metric tons of oil equivalent and kilograms per capita
Production, commerce et consommation d'énergie commerciale *(suite)*
Milliers de tonnes d'équivalent pétrole et kilogrammes par habitant

Bunkers - Soutes			Consumption - Consommation							
Air Avion	Sea Maritime	Unallocated Non distribué	Per capita Par habitant	Total Totale	Solids Solides	Liquids Liquides	Gas Gaz	Electricity Electricité	Year Année	Région, pays ou zone
408	507	362	5 941	27 736	712	12 132	4 470	10 423	2006	Norvège[6]
380	665	397	6 070	28 663	805	11 650	5 408	10 799	2007	
384	483	4 029	5 650	27 001	860	9 820	5 398	10 923	2008	
358	498	2 450	5 685	27 480	560	10 580	6 102	10 238	2009	
431	300	2 578	2 417	92 246	58 517	20 644	13 748	-663	2006	Pologne
450	253	2 382	2 409	91 991	56 705	21 697	13 752	-162	2007	
539	281	2 897	2 418	92 408	55 912	22 305	13 941	251	2008	
489	253	1 883	2 319	88 692	52 353	22 842	13 337	160	2009	
772	647	1 070	1 902	20 118	3 279	11 082	4 044	1 713	2006	Portugal
848	510	1 277	1 885	19 995	2 884	10 971	4 232	1 909	2007	
879	543	1 488	1 871	19 902	2 556	10 795	4 598	1 953	2008	
822	489	1 348	1 827	19 466	2 829	10 085	4 686	1 866	2009	
*12	...	-2	572	2 123	91	631	1 147	254	2006	Rép. de Moldova
*14	...	-8	549	2 017	45	660	1 056	255	2007	
*14	...	-10	558	2 030	86	691	992	261	2008	
*14	...	-21	540	1 945	92	684	911	258	2009	
137	0	1 973	1 640	35 592	9 431	8 420	16 046	1 695	2006	Roumanie
109	34	1 799	1 593	34 472	9 704	8 482	14 429	1 856	2007	
123	70	1 091	1 571	33 917	9 169	8 833	13 837	2 079	2008	
130	15	203	1 384	29 812	7 418	8 444	11 777	2 173	2009	
5 470	...	29 768	4 519	648 495	117 363	105 018	398 911	27 203	2006	Fédération de Russie
5 519	...	26 790	4 563	653 859	112 161	106 515	407 091	28 092	2007	
5 878	...	33 098	4 634	663 480	118 617	110 679	407 302	26 882	2008	
5 885	...	27 854	4 364	624 358	96 190	110 540	389 655	27 972	2009	
54	...	626	1 570	15 446	8 687	3 673	2 213	873	2006	Serbie
48	...	447	1 545	15 191	8 625	3 534	2 177	856	2007	
0	...	643	1 561	15 358	8 955	3 303	2 224	875	2008	
0	...	389	1 376	13 552	7 952	3 215	1 550	836	2009	
40	...	315	2 814	15 257	4 503	2 978	6 035	1 741	2006	Slovaquie
50	...	242	2 710	14 718	3 985	3 161	5 708	1 864	2007	
63	...	304	2 743	14 927	4 025	3 264	5 792	1 846	2008	
45	...	168	2 508	13 671	3 879	3 099	4 974	1 720	2009	
25	30	51	2 893	5 806	1 568	2 449	999	790	2006	Slovénie
32	49	44	2 883	5 802	1 589	2 407	1 016	790	2007	
35	66	47	3 016	6 086	1 562	2 800	976	747	2008	
27	33	10	2 687	5 439	1 408	2 472	924	635	2009	
3 245	8 451	6 094	2 796	123 093	18 368	60 555	34 704	9 466	2006	Espagne
3 413	8 649	4 471	2 825	126 000	19 832	61 571	35 315	9 282	2007	
3 426	8 967	4 819	2 712	122 439	14 149	60 077	38 789	9 424	2008	
3 186	8 911	1 688	2 537	115 765	10 567	60 393	34 691	10 115	2009	
663	2 126	2 119	2 956	26 873	2 666	11 545	980	11 682	2006	Suède
654	2 115	2 496	2 865	26 246	2 651	10 891	1 012	11 692	2007	
785	2 081	2 071	2 897	26 763	2 431	11 966	918	11 448	2008	
716	2 167	1 405	2 709	25 223	1 928	11 294	1 224	10 776	2009	
1 247	9	9	2 637	19 787	150	11 144	3 037	5 455	2006	Suisse[7]
1 312	9	-26	2 438	18 426	177	9 905	2 958	5 386	2007	
1 404	9	-33	2 555	19 439	163	10 575	3 150	5 551	2008	
1 350	8	-66	2 567	19 654	151	11 052	3 025	5 426	2009	
4	...	35	1 543	3 153	1 888	894	75	296	2006	L'ex-R.Y. Macédoine
7	...	-3	1 628	3 333	1 927	1 010	95	301	2007	
6	...	20	1 667	3 422	2 124	883	108	307	2008	
3	...	3	1 568	3 226	2 020	901	72	233	2009	
335	...	1 145	2 663	124 079	39 938	13 219	62 937	7 984	2006	Ukraine
359	...	803	2 667	123 453	40 362	14 115	60 922	8 055	2007	
263	...	17	2 653	122 006	40 524	13 874	59 467	8 140	2008	
7	...	134	2 236	102 236	35 775	12 634	46 018	7 809	2009	
12 224	2 352	1 143	3 460	209 472	41 310	69 868	90 069	8 224	2006	Royaume-Uni
12 218	2 373	1 360	3 350	203 983	38 993	66 827	91 071	7 092	2007	
11 776	2 588	1 191	3 315	203 140	36 063	66 356	93 853	6 868	2008	
11 167	2 485	1 306	3 036	187 162	29 793	62 811	86 800	7 758	2009	
3 712	**1 419**	**149**	**4 034**	**136 899**	**57 892**	**44 974**	**29 975**	**4 059**	**2006**	**Océanie**
4 053	**1 261**	**399**	**4 051**	**139 943**	**56 954**	**44 829**	**34 079**	**4 082**	**2007**	
3 992	**1 403**	**-594**	**4 098**	**144 166**	**57 363**	**48 031**	**34 898**	**3 874**	**2008**	
3 964	**1 251**	**-1 180**	**4 108**	**147 118**	**57 810**	**49 569**	**35 526**	**4 213**	**2009**	

Production, trade and consumption of commercial energy *(continued)*
Thousand metric tons of oil equivalent and kilograms per capita
Production, commerce et consommation d'énergie commerciale *(suite)*
Milliers de tonnes d'équivalent pétrole et kilogrammes par habitant

Region, country or area	Year Année	Primary energy production – Production d'énergie primaire					Changes in stocks	Imports	Exports
		Total Totale	Solids Solides	Liquids Liquides	Gas Gaz	Electricity Electricité	Variations des stocks	Imports Importations	Exports Exportations
Australia	2006	279 634	214 832	22 339	40 928	1 535	488	32 360	188 925
	2007	296 705	227 384	24 534	43 303	1 484	7 593	35 879	199 125
	2008	298 728	230 455	23 189	43 768	1 316	2 277	39 444	206 280
	2009	308 655	236 640	24 847	45 760	1 408	1 510	40 074	214 896
Cook Islands *	2006	...	...	...	...	...	...	21	...
	2007	...	...	...	...	...	...	23	...
	2008	...	...	...	...	...	...	24	...
	2009	...	...	...	...	...	...	24	...
Fiji	2006	29	...	...	...	29	*-1	797	*72
	2007	44	...	...	...	44	*-1	730	*67
	2008	43	...	...	...	43	*-1	623	*48
	2009	40	...	...	...	40	*1	478	*34
French Polynesia	2006	17	...	...	...	17	...	326	...
	2007	19	...	...	...	19	...	335	...
	2008	18	...	...	...	18	...	340	...
	2009	18	...	...	...	18	...	338	...
Kiribati	*2006	...	...	...	...	...	...	12	...
	2007	...	...	...	...	...	...	20	...
	*2008	...	...	...	...	...	...	20	...
	*2009	...	...	...	...	...	...	20	...
Marshall Islands *	2006	...	...	...	...	...	...	30	...
	2007	...	...	...	...	...	...	32	...
	2008	...	...	...	...	...	...	33	...
	2009	...	...	...	...	...	...	33	...
Nauru *	2006	...	...	...	...	...	...	53	...
	2007	...	...	...	...	...	...	54	...
	2008	...	...	...	...	...	...	54	...
	2009	...	...	...	...	...	...	56	...
New Caledonia	2006	27	...	...	...	27	...	897	3
	2007	37	...	...	...	37	...	927	*5
	2008	42	...	...	...	42	...	1 022	*5
	2009	39	...	...	...	39	...	914	*5
New Zealand	2006	10 478	3 404	1 025	3 679	2 370	-40	7 485	2 725
	2007	11 335	2 828	2 039	4 050	2 418	348	7 551	3 199
	2008	11 877	2 835	2 847	3 821	2 374	-471	7 552	4 570
	2009	11 845	2 636	2 640	3 943	2 627	197	7 354	3 946
Niue *	2006	...	...	...	...	...	...	1	...
	2007	...	...	...	...	...	...	1	...
	2008	...	...	...	...	...	...	1	...
	2009	...	...	...	...	...	...	1	...
Palau *	2006	2	...	...	...	2	...	83	...
	2007	2	...	...	...	2	...	86	...
	2008	2	...	...	...	2	...	86	...
	2009	2	...	...	...	2	...	86	...
Papua New Guinea	2006	3 230	...	2 897	259	74	297	1 714	2 751
	2007	2 274	...	1 960	*239	74	-20	1 225	1 532
	2008	2 431	...	2 104	*253	74	72	1 248	2 075
	2009	2 341	...	2 015	*253	*74	-79	1 051	1 940
Samoa	2006	5	...	...	...	5	...	*53	...
	*2007	5	...	...	...	5	...	54	...
	*2008	5	...	...	...	5	...	54	...
	*2009	5	...	...	...	5	...	55	...
Solomon Islands *	2006	...	...	...	...	...	...	63	...
	2007	...	...	...	...	...	...	69	...
	2008	...	...	...	...	...	...	67	...
	2009	...	...	...	...	...	...	68	...
Tonga *	2006	...	...	...	...	...	...	58	...
	2007	...	...	...	...	...	...	59	...
	2008	...	...	...	...	...	...	59	...
	2009	...	...	...	...	...	...	59	...
Vanuatu	2006	*0	...	...	...	*0	...	16	...
	2007	*0	...	...	...	*0	...	32	...
	2008	1	...	...	...	1	...	40	...
	2009	1	...	...	...	1	...	39	...

45

Production, trade and consumption of commercial energy *(continued)*
Thousand metric tons of oil equivalent and kilograms per capita

Production, commerce et consommation d'énergie commerciale *(suite)*
Milliers de tonnes d'équivalent pétrole et kilogrammes par habitant

Bunkers - Soutes			Consumption - Consommation							
Air Avion	Sea Maritime	Unallocated Non distribué	Per capita Par habitant	Total Totale	Solids Solides	Liquids Liquides	Gas Gaz	Electricity Electricité	Year Année	Région, pays ou zone
2 681	988	-122	5 738	119 034	55 668	35 795	26 037	1 535	2006	Australie
2 990	815	-257	5 792	122 318	55 228	35 815	29 790	1 484	2007	
2 963	930	-842	5 883	126 563	55 334	39 088	30 824	1 316	2008	
3 027	805	-1 367	5 929	129 857	56 165	40 854	31 429	1 408	2009	
...	...	...	1 093	21	...	21	...	...	2006	Iles Cook *
...	...	...	1 133	23	...	23	...	...	2007	
...	...	...	1 175	24	...	24	...	...	2008	
...	...	...	1 167	24	...	24	...	...	2009	
*231	*62	...	558	462	*1	432	...	29	2006	Fidji
*225	*61	...	505	422	*1	377	...	44	2007	
*186	*53	...	450	380	*1	337	...	43	2008	
*142	*36	...	358	305	*-1	266	...	40	2009	
*6	*39	...	1 157	299	...	281	...	17	2006	Polynésie française
*6	*49	...	1 143	299	...	280	...	19	2007	
*6	*46	...	1 156	306	...	288	...	18	2008	
*6	*44	...	1 141	305	...	287	...	18	2009	
2	...	...	110	10	...	10	...	...	*2006	Kiribati
*2	...	...	185	18	...	18	...	...	2007	
2	...	...	184	18	...	18	...	...	*2008	
2	...	...	185	18	...	18	...	...	*2009	
...	...	...	583	30	...	30	...	...	2006	Iles Marshall *
...	...	...	619	32	...	32	...	...	2007	
...	...	...	616	33	...	33	...	...	2008	
...	...	...	627	33	...	33	...	...	2009	
7	...	...	4 538	46	...	46	...	...	2006	Nauru *
7	...	...	4 626	47	...	47	...	...	2007	
7	...	...	4 615	47	...	47	...	...	2008	
7	...	...	4 738	48	...	48	...	...	2009	
14	...	...	3 857	906	198	681	...	27	2006	Nouvelle-Calédonie
12	...	...	3 959	946	171	738	...	37	2007	
10	...	...	4 319	1 049	257	750	...	42	2008	
0	...	...	3 837	947	177	732	...	39	2009	
711	298	33	3 402	14 235	2 025	6 162	3 679	2 370	2006	Nouvelle-Zélande
746	304	3	3 375	14 285	1 554	6 264	4 050	2 418	2007	
751	341	25	3 323	14 213	1 771	6 248	3 821	2 374	2008	
715	333	-72	3 257	14 080	1 469	6 140	3 845	2 627	2009	
...	...	...	650	1	...	1	...	...	2006	Nioué *
...	...	...	694	1	...	1	...	...	2007	
...	...	...	713	1	...	1	...	...	2008	
...	...	...	734	1	...	1	...	...	2009	
15	...	...	3 430	69	...	67	...	2	2006	Palaos *
17	...	...	3 519	71	...	69	...	2	2007	
17	...	...	3 499	71	...	69	...	2	2008	
17	...	...	3 479	71	...	69	...	2	2009	
*39	*32	237	254	1 587	...	1 254	259	74	2006	Papouasie-Nvl-Guinée
*40	*32	653	197	1 261	...	948	*239	74	2007	
*43	*32	222	188	1 234	...	908	*253	74	2008	
*41	*32	260	179	1 198	...	871	*253	*74	2009	
...	...	...	*316	*57	...	*53	...	5	2006	Samoa
...	...	...	321	58	...	54	...	5	*2007	
...	...	...	320	58	...	54	...	5	*2008	
...	...	...	326	59	...	55	...	5	*2009	
3	...	...	123	59	...	59	...	...	2006	Iles Salomon *
5	...	...	128	64	...	64	...	...	2007	
4	...	...	123	63	...	63	...	...	2008	
4	...	...	122	64	...	64	...	...	2009	
1	...	...	557	57	...	57	...	...	2006	Tonga *
1	...	...	568	58	...	58	...	...	2007	
1	...	...	565	58	...	58	...	...	2008	
1	...	...	561	58	...	58	...	...	2009	
...	...	...	73	16	...	16	...	*0	2006	Vanuatu
...	...	...	145	32	...	32	...	*0	2007	
...	...	...	180	41	...	40	...	1	2008	
...	...	...	172	40	...	39	...	1	2009	

45 Production, trade and consumption of commercial energy *(continued)*
Thousand metric tons of oil equivalent and kilograms per capita
Production, commerce et consommation d'énergie commerciale *(suite)*
Milliers de tonnes d'équivalent pétrole et kilogrammes par habitant

Region, country or area	Year Année	Primary energy production – Production d'énergie primaire					Changes in stocks Variations des stocks	Imports Importations	Exports Exportations
		Total Totale	Solids Solides	Liquids Liquides	Gas Gaz	Electricity Electricité			
Wallis and Futuna Islands	2006	...	...	...	...	...	...	9	...
	2007	...	...	...	...	...	...	10	...
	2008	...	...	...	...	...	...	*9	...
	2009	...	...	...	...	...	...	*9	...

Source:
United Nations Statistics Division, New York, the energy statistics database, last accessed June 2012.

1   Refers to the Southern African Customs Union.
2   For statistical purposes, the data for China do not include those for the Hong Kong Special Administrative Region (Hong Kong SAR), Macao Special
    Administrative Region (Macao SAR) and Taiwan Province of China.
3   Including Monaco.
4   Including San Marino.
5   Including Svalbard and Jan Mayen Islands.
6   Including Liechtenstein.

45

Production, trade and consumption of commercial energy *(continued)*
Thousand metric tons of oil equivalent and kilograms per capita

Production, commerce et consommation d'énergie commerciale *(suite)*
Milliers de tonnes d'équivalent pétrole et kilogrammes par habitant

Bunkers - Soutes				Consumption - Consommation							
Air Avion	Sea Maritime	Unallocated Non distribué	Per capita Par habitant	Total Totale	Solids Solides	Liquids Liquides	Gas Gaz	Electricity Electricité	Year Année	Région, pays ou zone
1	...	...	614	9	...	9	...	...	2006	Iles Wallis et Futuna
1	...	...	627	9	...	9	...	...	2007	
1	...	...	*609	*8	...	*8	...	...	2008	
1	...	...	*633	*9	...	*9	...	...	2009	

Source:
Organisation des Nations Unies, Division de statistique, New York, la base de données pour les statistiques de l'énergie, dernier accès juin 2012.

1   Se réfèrent à l'Union douanière d'Afrique australe.
2   Pour la présentation des statistiques, les données pour la Chine ne comprennent pas la Région Administrative Spéciale de Hong Kong (Hong Kong RAS), la Région Administrative Spéciale de Macao (Macao RAS) et la province de Taiwan.
3   Y compris Monaco.
4   Y compris Saint-Marin.
5   Y compris îles Svalbard et Jan Mayen.
6   Y compris Liechtenstein.

Region, country or area Région, pays ou zone	Year Année	Hard coal, lignite and peat Houille, lignite et tourbe	Crude petroleum and NGL Pétrole brut et LGN	Motor gasoline Essence auto	Jet fuel Carbu-réacteurs	Gas-diesel oil Gazole/carburant diesel	Residual fuel oil Mazout résiduel	Liquified petroleum gas Gaz de pétrole liquéfiés	Natural gas Gaz naturel Terajoules Térajoules	Electricity Electricité Million kWh Millions kWh
					Thousand metric tons – Milliers de tonnes					
World	2006	6 387 133	3 969 056	895 389	228 016	1 178 199	588 396	253 308	113 492 737	19 080 783
Monde	2007	6 639 895	3 966 583	890 725	231 504	1 195 814	578 646	254 069	116 151 479	19 925 194
	2008	6 842 280	3 989 211	892 299	236 131	1 244 271	561 241	253 843	120 691 370	20 280 946
	2009	6 929 505	3 928 123	917 184	221 817	1 227 567	516 023	258 696	116 801 010	20 182 452
Africa	2006	250 210[1]	503 936	19 593	7 419	35 072	33 361	13 245	8 006 584	591 537
Afrique	2007	252 712[1]	511 270	19 065	8 332	36 758	31 865	13 883	7 873 536	616 774
	2008	254 967[1]	517 419	20 370	8 540	41 563	29 736	14 093	7 993 459	626 691
	2009	254 296[1]	497 481	19 284	8 136	41 462	25 788	13 194	7 603 089	635 532
Algeria	2006	...	100 276	2 320	855	6 385	5 337	8 747	3 844 884	35 226
Algérie	2007	...	100 396	2 100	1 034	6 388	5 518	9 183	3 424 650	37 196
	2008	...	98 045	2 780	988	7 403	6 009	9 240	3 375 512	40 236
	2009	...	91 933	2 517	977	7 533	5 581	8 896	3 263 631	42 769
Angola	2006	...	71 118	98	313	482	587	651	26 534	2 959
Angola	2007	...	85 591	56	351	513	601	711	32 387	3 318
	2008	...	95 985	68	325	527	680	709	25 840	3 930
	2009	...	91 072	42	356	509	671	649	26 220	4 172
Benin	2006	...	...	...	...	...	...	...	...	150
Bénin	2007	...	...	...	...	...	...	...	...	217
	2008	...	...	...	...	...	...	...	...	226
	2009	...	...	...	...	...	...	...	...	127
Botswana	2006	962[2]	...	...	...	...	...	...	...	782
Botswana	2007	828[2]	...	...	...	...	...	...	...	659
	2008	910[2]	...	...	...	...	...	...	...	583
	2009	738[2]	...	...	...	...	...	...	...	444
Burkina Faso	2006	...	...	...	...	...	...	...	...	548
Burkina Faso	2007	...	...	...	...	...	...	...	...	612
	2008	...	...	...	...	...	...	...	...	619
	2009	...	...	...	...	...	...	...	...	700
Burundi	2006	10[3]	...	...	...	...	...	...	...	95
Burundi	2007	7[3]	...	...	...	...	...	...	...	119
	2008	10[3]	...	...	...	...	...	...	...	114
	2009	11[3]	...	...	...	...	...	...	...	123
Cameroon	2006	...	4 618[4]	320	71	569	354	22	0	5 106
Cameroun	2007	...	4 376[4]	390	404	686	364	19	13 963	5 176
	2008	...	4 302[4]	399	346	650	354	17	14 481	5 613
	2009	...	3 757[4]	350	292	610	259	15	11 965	5 741
Cape Verde	2006	...	...	...	...	...	...	...	...	252
Cap-Vert	2007	...	...	...	...	...	...	...	...	269
	2008	...	...	...	...	...	...	...	...	287
	2009	...	...	...	...	...	...	...	...	296
Central African Rep.	2006	...	...	...	...	...	...	...	...	140
Rép. centrafricaine	*2007	...	...	...	...	...	...	...	...	137
	2008	...	...	...	...	...	...	...	...	137
	2009	...	...	...	...	...	...	...	...	136
Chad	2006	...	7 874[4]	...	...	...	...	...	...	*102
Tchad	2007	...	7 190[4]	...	...	...	...	...	...	*105
	2008	...	6 331[4]	...	...	...	...	...	...	*103
	2009	...	5 734[4]	...	...	...	...	...	...	*103
Comoros *	2006	...	...	...	...	...	...	...	...	51
Comores *	2007	...	...	...	...	...	...	...	...	47
	2008	...	...	...	...	...	...	...	...	45
	2009	...	...	...	...	...	...	...	...	43
Congo	2006	...	14 250	53	53	123	377	7	923	453
Congo	2007	...	11 482	63	55	141	437	7	824	407
	2008	...	12 180	46	31	109	327	5	987	461
	2009	...	14 116	67	34	172	349	9	2 125	516
Côte d'Ivoire	2006	...	3 135[4]	605	88	1 269	521	101	63 681	5 644
Côte d'Ivoire	2007	...	2 418[4]	564	47	1 089	500	38	46 824	5 631
	2008	...	2 282[4]	466	53	1 174	657	115	61 754	5 800
	2009	...	2 561[4]	432	49	1 088	609	107	61 475	5 894

46 Production of selected energy commodities *(continued)*
Production de l'énergie *(suite)*

Region, country or area Région, pays ou zone	Year Année	Hard coal, lignite and peat Houille, lignite et tourbe	Crude petroleum and NGL Pétrole brut et LGN	Motor gasoline Essence auto	Jet fuel Carbu-réacteurs	Gas-diesel oil Gazole/carburant diesel	Residual fuel oil Mazout résiduel	Liquified petroleum gas Gaz de pétrole liquéfiés	Natural gas Gaz naturel Terajoules Térajoules	Electricity Electricité Million kWh Millions kWh
		Thousand metric tons – Milliers de tonnes								
Dem. Rep. of the Congo	2006	123[2]	1 244[4]	...	...	...	...	...	160	7 540
Rép. dém. du Congo	2007	126[2]	1 218[4]	...	...	...	...	...	331	7 856
	2008	129[2]	1 155[4]	...	...	...	...	...	331	7 525
	2009	133[2]	1 108[4]	...	...	...	...	...	331	7 830
Djibouti	2006	...	...	...	...	...	...	...	...	280
Djibouti	2007	...	...	...	...	...	...	...	...	292
	2008	...	...	...	...	...	...	...	...	335
	2009	...	...	...	...	...	...	...	...	339
Egypt	2006	25[2]	36 198	3 659	2 033	8 440	10 653	1 711	2 074 343	118 407
Egypte	2007	25[2]	37 849	4 195	2 422	8 803	10 989	1 898	2 136 170	128 129
	2008	25[2]	40 185	4 240	2 319	8 666	9 529	2 027	2 288 069	134 566
	2009	25[2]	38 534	4 384	2 016	8 267	9 166	1 820	2 395 508	142 690
Equatorial Guinea *	2006	...	22 374	...	...	...	...	86	55 030	95
Guinée équatoriale *	2007	...	23 099	...	...	...	...	92	65 250	100
	2008	...	23 050	...	...	...	...	93	64 430	100
	2009	...	21 059	...	...	...	...	93	64 430	100
Eritrea	2006	...	...	...	...	...	...	...	...	269
Erythrée	2007	...	...	...	...	...	...	...	...	288
	2008	...	...	...	...	...	...	...	...	287
	2009	...	...	...	...	...	...	...	...	295
Ethiopia	2006	...	...	...	...	...	...	...	...	3 269
Ethiopie	2007	...	...	...	...	...	...	...	...	3 547
	2008	...	...	...	...	...	...	...	...	3 777
	2009	...	...	...	...	...	...	...	...	4 106
Gabon	2006	...	12 062[4]	71	53	213	325	7	5 855	1 653
Gabon	2007	...	12 291[4]	81	55	260	356	14	6 300	1 736
	2008	...	11 977[4]	84	57	258	364	13	7 061	1 837
	2009	...	12 035[4]	57	39	176	248	9	6 994	1 666
Gambia	*2006	...	...	...	...	...	...	...	...	216
Gambie	2007	...	...	...	...	...	...	...	...	229
	2008	...	...	...	...	...	...	...	...	242
	2009	...	...	...	...	...	...	...	...	242
Ghana	2006	...	...	294	46	294	156	36	...	8 435
Ghana	2007	...	...	493	66	398	49	67	...	6 984
	2008	...	...	391	21	361	225	55	...	8 366
	2009	...	...	135	10	103	25	14	...	8 964
Guinea	2006	...	...	...	...	...	...	...	4	873
Guinée	2007	...	...	...	...	...	...	...	4	973
	2008	...	...	...	...	...	...	...	4	1 000
	2009	...	...	...	...	...	...	...	3	996
Guinea-Bissau *	2006	...	...	...	...	...	...	...	...	66
Guinée-Bissau *	2007	...	...	...	...	...	...	...	...	70
	2008	...	...	...	...	...	...	...	...	70
	2009	...	...	...	...	...	...	...	...	72
Kenya	2006	...	...	179	240	368	596	30	...	7 323
Kenya	2007	...	...	207	236	397	534	33	...	6 773
	2008	...	...	182	221	374	515	33	...	7 055
	2009	...	...	157	217	372	498	45	...	6 450
Lesotho	2006	...	...	...	...	...	...	...	...	200
Lesotho	2007	...	...	...	...	...	...	...	...	200
	2008	...	...	...	...	...	...	...	...	200
	2009	...	...	...	...	...	...	...	...	200
Liberia *	2006	...	...	...	...	...	...	...	...	351
Libéria *	2007	...	...	...	...	...	...	...	...	353
	2008	...	...	...	...	...	...	...	...	353
	2009	...	...	...	...	...	...	...	...	353
Libyan Arab Jamah.	2006	...	85 587	1 237	1 255	4 503	4 419	907	562 400	23 992
Jamah. arabe libyenne	2007	...	81 868	1 295	1 323	4 542	4 310	876	625 480	25 694
	2008	...	84 120	1 285	1 357	5 377	4 508	828	650 859	28 667
	2009	...	72 039	1 372	1 678	7 753	4 269	640	604 200	30 426
Madagascar	2006	...	...	...	...	...	...	...	...	1 174
Madagascar	2007	...	...	...	...	...	...	...	...	1 222
	2008	...	...	...	...	...	...	...	...	1 274
	2009	...	...	...	...	...	...	...	...	1 274

Region, country or area Région, pays ou zone	Year Année	Hard coal, lignite and peat Houille, lignite et tourbe	Crude petroleum and NGL Pétrole brut et LGN	Motor gasoline Essence auto	Jet fuel Carbu-réacteurs	Gas-diesel oil Gazole/ carburant diesel	Residual fuel oil Mazout résiduel	Liquified petroleum gas Gaz de pétrole liquéfiés	Natural gas Gaz naturel Terajoules Térajoules	Electricity Electricité Million kWh Millions kWh
		Thousand metric tons – Milliers de tonnes								
Malawi Malawi	2006	*55[2]	...	...	...	...	...	...	...	1 580
	2007	*60[2]	...	...	...	...	...	...	...	1 637
	2008	*52[2]	...	...	...	...	...	...	...	1 801
	*2009	54[2]	...	...	...	...	...	...	...	1 758
Mali * Mali *	2006	...	...	...	...	...	...	...	...	489
	2007	...	...	...	...	...	...	...	...	495
	2008	...	...	...	...	...	...	...	...	508
	2009	...	...	...	...	...	...	...	...	516
Mauritania Mauritanie	2006	...	1 526[4]	...	...	...	...	...	...	569
	2007	...	750[4]	...	...	...	...	...	...	587
	2008	...	604[4]	...	...	...	...	...	...	659
	2009	...	561[4]	...	...	...	...	...	...	*641
Mauritius Maurice	2006	...	...	...	...	...	...	...	...	2 350
	2007	...	...	...	...	...	...	...	...	2 465
	2008	...	...	...	...	...	...	...	...	2 557
	2009	...	...	...	...	...	...	...	...	2 577
Morocco Maroc	2006	...	10[4]	373	236	2 033	2 265	192	2 600	19 862
	2007	...	14[4]	365	292	1 996	2 269	170	2 494	19 670
	2008	...	9[4]	404	262	1 819	1 880	170	2 066	20 345
	2009	...	8[4]	313	257	1 385	1 492	102	1 724	21 191
Mozambique Mozambique	2006	41[2]	...	...	...	...	...	...	105 358	14 737
	2007	24[2]	...	...	...	...	...	...	104 520	16 076
	2008	38[2]	...	...	...	...	...	...	116 617	15 127
	2009	38[2]	...	...	...	...	...	...	113 996	16 963
Namibia Namibie	2006	...	...	...	...	...	...	...	...	1 491
	2007	...	...	...	...	...	...	...	...	1 694
	2008	...	...	...	...	...	...	...	...	2 097
	2009	...	...	...	...	...	...	...	...	1 742
Niger Niger	2006	176[2]	...	...	...	...	...	...	...	194
	2007	171[2]	...	...	...	...	...	...	...	195
	2008	183[2]	...	...	...	...	...	...	...	213
	2009	225[2]	...	...	...	...	...	...	...	234
Nigeria Nigéria	2006	8[2]	122 911	993	81	1 281	2 385	5	1 083 000	23 110
	2007	8[2]	114 118	287	34	1 138	1 138	4	1 235 000	22 978
	2008	8[2]	109 716	698	69	1 186	1 702	65	1 205 740	21 110
	2009	8[2]	115 054	364	33	571	770	30	881 828	19 777
Réunion * Réunion *	2006	...	...	...	...	...	...	...	...	1 710
	2007	...	...	...	...	...	...	...	...	1 887
	2008	...	...	...	...	...	...	...	...	1 887
	2009	...	...	...	...	...	...	...	...	1 887
Rwanda Rwanda	2006	...	...	...	...	...	...	...	*24	169
	2007	...	...	...	...	...	...	...	*24	165
	2008	...	...	...	...	...	...	...	*24	192
	2009	...	...	...	...	...	...	...	*26	248
Saint Helena Sainte-Hélène	2006	...	...	...	...	...	...	...	...	8
	2007	...	...	...	...	...	...	...	...	9
	2008	...	...	...	...	...	...	...	...	9
	2009	...	...	...	...	...	...	...	...	9
Sao Tome and Principe * Sao Tomé-et-Principe *	2006	...	...	...	...	...	...	...	...	42
	2007	...	...	...	...	...	...	...	...	43
	2008	...	...	...	...	...	...	...	...	34
	2009	...	...	...	...	...	...	...	...	34
Senegal Sénégal	2006	...	...	46	31	115	100	0	483	1 962
	2007	...	...	77	48	339	188	0	470	2 124
	2008	...	...	68	99	409	243	0	429	2 402
	2009	...	...	83	68	326	191	0	677	2 489
Seychelles Seychelles	2006	...	...	...	...	...	...	...	...	252
	2007	...	...	...	...	...	...	...	...	271
	2008	...	...	...	...	...	...	...	...	268
	2009	...	...	...	...	...	...	...	...	276
Sierra Leone Sierra Leone	2006	...	...	...	...	...	...	...	43 478	*41
	2007	...	...	...	...	...	...	...	41 065	60
	2008	...	...	...	...	...	...	...	40 702	*63
	2009	...	...	...	...	...	...	...	45 056	*66

Region, country or area Région, pays ou zone	Year Année	Hard coal, lignite and peat Houille, lignite et tourbe	Crude petroleum and NGL Pétrole brut et LGN	Motor gasoline Essence auto	Jet fuel Carbu-réacteurs	Gas-diesel oil Gazole/ carburant diesel	Residual fuel oil Mazout résiduel	Liquified petroleum gas Gaz de pétrole liquéfiés	Natural gas Gaz naturel Terajoules Térajoules	Electricity Electricité Million kWh Millions kWh
					Thousand metric tons – Milliers de tonnes					
Somalia	2006	...	...	5	65	10	25	31	...	300
Somalie	2007	...	...	0	0	0	0	0	0	311
	2008	...	...	0	0	0	0	0	...	320
	2009	...	...	0	0	0	0	0	...	324
South Africa	2006	244 775[2]	146[5]	7 920	1 698	6 257	4 141	280	72 314	254 075
Afrique du Sud	2007	247 666[2]	171[5]	7 403	1 711	7 482	3 465	319	67 732	263 479
	2008	250 006[2]	147[5]	8 038	1 962	10 157	1 501	325	67 732	258 291
	2009	249 489[2]	147[5]	7 609	1 868	9 455	483	303	39 597	249 557
Sudan	2006	...	17 253[4]	1 154	278	2 059	458	318	...	4 521
Soudan	2007	...	23 807[4]	1 257	233	2 347	437	346	...	5 021
	2008	...	23 098[4]	988	408	2 347	506	272	...	5 506
	2009	...	23 738[4]	1 167	219	2 359	498	321	...	6 752
Swaziland *	2006	444[2]	...	...	...	...	...	...	...	437
Swaziland *	2007	462[2]	...	...	...	...	...	...	...	454
	2008	476[2]	...	...	...	...	...	...	...	432
	2009	481[2]	...	...	...	...	...	...	...	517
Togo	2006	...	...	...	...	...	...	...	...	221
Togo	2007	...	...	...	...	...	...	...	...	196
	2008	...	...	...	...	...	...	...	...	123
	2009	...	...	...	...	...	...	...	...	126
Tunisia	2006	...	3 355	178	4	506	604	110	94 391	14 122
Tunisie	2007	...	4 633	134	0	556	646	103	89 876	14 060
	2008	...	4 232	129	0	551	668	123	90 141	14 662
	2009	...	4 026	124	0	576	607	138	103 087	15 693
Uganda	2006	...	...	...	...	...	...	...	...	1 616
Ouganda	2007	...	...	...	...	...	...	...	...	1 953
	2008	...	...	...	...	...	...	...	...	2 088
	2009	...	...	...	...	...	...	...	...	2 186
United Rep. of Tanzania	2006	80[2]	...	...	...	...	...	...	14 600	3 529
Rép.-Unie de Tanzanie	2007	84[2]	...	...	...	...	...	...	21 237	4 175
	2008	90[2]	...	...	...	...	...	...	21 383	4 414
	2009	95[2]	...	...	...	...	...	...	25 271	4 628
Western Sahara *	2006		...	...	...	...	...	...	...	90
Sahara occidental *	2007		...	...	...	...	...	...	...	90
	2008		...	...	...	...	...	...	...	90
	2009		...	...	...	...	...	...	...	90
Zambia	2006	64[2]	...	88	19	165	58	3	...	9 901
Zambie	2007	14[2]	...	98	21	183	64	3	...	9 831
	2008	1[2]	...	104	22	195	68	3	...	9 696
	2009	1[2]	...	111	23	207	72	3	...	10 308
Zimbabwe	2006	3 447[2]	...	...	...	...	...	...	...	8 508
Zimbabwe	2007	3 237[2]	...	...	...	...	...	...	...	8 508
	2008	3 039[2]	...	...	...	...	...	...	...	7 990
	2009	2 997[2]	...	...	...	...	...	...	...	7 878
America, North	**2006**	**1 145 393[6]**	**649 906**	**405 234**	**79 466**	**257 934**	**74 100**	**71 354**	**30 288 885**	**5 288 592**
Amérique du Nord	**2007**	**1 134 859[6]**	**645 141**	**403 600**	**78 252**	**262 645**	**75 859**	**70 916**	**31 261 704**	**5 380 633**
	2008	**1 155 060[6]**	**620 005**	**401 462**	**80 636**	**271 565**	**73 161**	**68 545**	**32 145 484**	**5 392 078**
	2009	**1 061 036[6]**	**630 756**	**404 128**	**74 746**	**258 152**	**70 878**	**68 869**	**32 333 370**	**5 176 719**
Anguilla	2006	...	...	...	...	...	...	...	...	80
Anguilla	2007	...	...	...	...	...	...	...	...	89
	2008	...	...	...	...	...	...	...	...	90
	2009	...	...	...	...	...	...	...	...	91
Antigua and Barbuda *	2006	...	...	...	...	...	...	...	...	116
Antigua-et-Barbuda *	2007	...	...	...	...	...	...	...	...	118
	2008	...	...	...	...	...	...	...	...	118
	2009	...	...	...	...	...	...	...	...	119
Aruba	2006	...	*120[4]	...	...	...	...	...	...	910
Aruba	2007	...	*125[4]	...	...	...	...	...	...	936
	2008	...	*122[4]	...	...	...	...	...	...	914
	2009	...	*123[4]	...	...	...	...	...	...	924
Bahamas *	2006	...	...	...	...	...	...	...	...	2 100
Bahamas *	2007	...	...	...	...	...	...	...	...	2 110
	2008	...	...	...	...	...	...	...	...	2 110
	2009	...	...	...	...	...	...	...	...	2 172

Region, country or area Région, pays ou zone	Year Année	Hard coal, lignite and peat Houille, lignite et tourbe	Crude petroleum and NGL Pétrole brut et LGN	Motor gasoline Essence auto	Jet fuel Carbu- réacteurs	Gas-diesel oil Gazole/ carburant diesel	Residual fuel oil Mazout résiduel	Liquified petroleum gas Gaz de pétrole liquéfiés	Natural gas Gaz naturel Terajoules Térajoules	Electricity Electricité Million kWh Millions kWh
		Thousand metric tons – Milliers de tonnes								
Barbados	2006	...	51	...	...	...	...	1	1 048	948
Barbade	2007	...	47	...	...	...	...	1	927	973
	2008	...	43	...	...	...	...	1	807	998
	2009	...	39	...	...	...	...	1	*687	1 023
Belize	2006	...	...	...	...	...	...	...	...	212
Belize	2007	...	...	...	...	...	...	...	...	218
	2008	...	...	...	...	...	...	...	...	218
	2009	...	...	...	...	...	...	...	...	260
Bermuda	2006	...	...	...	...	...	...	...	...	631
Bermudes	2007	...	...	...	...	...	...	...	...	643
	2008	...	...	...	...	...	...	...	...	645
	*2009	...	...	...	...	...	...	...	...	733
British Virgin Islands *	2006	...	...	...	...	...	...	...	...	48
Iles Vierges britanniques *	2007	...	...	...	...	...	...	...	...	48
	2008	...	...	...	...	...	...	...	...	50
	2009	...	...	...	...	...	...	...	...	52
Canada	2006	66 004[6]	151 265	30 889	3 869	30 704	7 763	1 730	7 206 362	615 967
Canada	2007	69 364[6]	157 952	32 630	4 038	31 223	8 407	1 878	7 043 320	642 102
	2008	67 749[6]	153 844	30 090	4 114	30 873	7 870	1 821	6 746 226	641 051
	2009	62 936[6]	152 622	30 609	3 884	30 426	6 366	1 739	6 293 604	603 234
Cayman Islands	2006	...	...	...	...	...	...	...	...	555
Iles Caïmanes	2007	...	...	...	...	...	...	...	...	604
	2008	...	...	...	...	...	...	...	...	615
	2009	...	...	...	...	...	...	...	...	626
Costa Rica	2006	...	...	105	0	230	295	4	...	8 697
Costa Rica	2007	...	...	132	0	248	330	4	...	9 050
	2008	...	...	105	0	244	201	5	...	9 474
	2009	...	...	87	16	127	91	4	...	9 290
Cuba	2006	...	2 900[4]	317	9	420	892	62	42 337	16 469
Cuba	2007	...	2 905[4]	392	56	464	940	59	46 280	17 622
	2008	...	3 003[4]	716	289	1 097	2 668	43	45 302	17 681
	2009	...	2 731[4]	492	295	1 271	2 629	46	45 068	17 709
Dominica	2006	...	...	...	...	...	...	...	...	85
Dominique	2007	...	...	...	...	...	...	...	...	86
	2008	...	...	...	...	...	...	...	...	88
	2009	...	...	...	...	...	...	...	...	93
Dominican Republic	2006	...	...	440	59	424	762	33	...	13 780
Rép. dominicaine	2007	...	...	404	45	359	753	25	...	14 410
	2008	...	...	384	47	363	660	23	...	15 172
	2009	...	...	254	47	341	363	25	...	14 982
El Salvador	2006	...	...	108	39	172	462	17	...	5 597
El Salvador	2007	...	...	117	68	229	477	20	...	5 807
	2008	...	...	111	58	186	410	14	...	5 959
	2009	...	...	105	53	197	399	13	...	5 788
Greenland *	2006	...	...	...	...	...	...	...	...	305
Groenland *	2007	...	...	...	...	...	...	...	...	325
	2008	...	...	...	...	...	...	...	...	342
	2009	...	...	...	...	...	...	...	...	348
Grenada	2006	...	...	...	...	...	...	...	...	171
Grenade	2007	...	...	...	...	...	...	...	...	186
	2008	...	...	...	...	...	...	...	...	197
	2009	...	...	...	...	...	...	...	...	203
Guadeloupe *	2006	...	...	...	...	...	...	...	...	1 771
Guadeloupe *	2007	...	...	...	...	...	...	...	...	1 863
	2008	...	...	...	...	...	...	...	...	1 863
	2009	...	...	...	...	...	...	...	...	1 863
Guatemala	2006	...	872[4]	1	1	22	...	...	...	8 163
Guatemala	2007	...	826[4]	0	1	25	...	...	...	8 755
	2008	...	763[4]	0	0	22	...	...	...	8 717
	2009	...	736[4]	0	1	24	...	...	...	9 040
Haiti	2006	...	...	...	...	...	...	...	...	570
Haïti	2007	...	...	...	...	...	...	...	...	469
	2008	...	...	...	...	...	...	...	...	486
	2009	...	...	...	...	...	...	...	...	721

Region, country or area Région, pays ou zone	Year Année	Hard coal, lignite and peat Houille, lignite et tourbe	Crude petroleum and NGL Pétrole brut et LGN	Motor gasoline Essence auto	Jet fuel Carbu- réacteurs	Gas-diesel oil Gazole/ carburant diesel	Residual fuel oil Mazout résiduel	Liquified petroleum gas Gaz de pétrole liquéfiés	Natural gas Gaz naturel Terajoules Térajoules	Electricity Electricité Million kWh Millions kWh
					Thousand metric tons – Milliers de tonnes					
Honduras Honduras	2006	...	...	...	...	...	...	...	...	5 487
	2007	...	...	...	...	...	...	...	...	6 336
	2008	...	...	...	...	...	...	...	...	6 537
	2009	...	...	...	...	...	...	...	...	6 579
Jamaica Jamaïque	2006	...	...	124	63	226	561	9	...	7 473
	2007	...	...	104	53	190	473	8	...	7 782
	2008	...	...	129	66	176	707	12	...	6 008
	2009	...	...	129	86	172	745	10	...	5 533
Martinique Martinique	2006	...	...	*150	...	*167	*354	*20	...	1 553
	*2007	...	...	145	...	170	361	19	...	1 602
	*2008	...	...	146	...	183	366	20	...	1 652
	*2009	...	...	141	...	191	371	20	...	1 702
Mexico Mexique	2006	11 487[6]	182 805	21 759	2 956	16 818	18 520	10 229	1 606 472	252 014
	2007	12 514[6]	172 074	21 415	3 024	16 931	17 147	9 662	1 782 114	263 465
	2008	11 430[6]	156 422	20 899	2 928	17 477	16 465	9 048	1 774 732	258 913
	2009	10 548[6]	145 616	21 960	2 603	19 077	17 982	9 044	1 786 656	261 018
Montserrat * Montserrat *	2006	...	...	...	...	...	...	...	...	22
	2007	...	...	...	...	...	...	...	...	23
	2008	...	...	...	...	...	...	...	...	23
	2009	...	...	...	...	...	...	...	...	23
Netherlands Antilles Antilles néerlandaises	2006	...	...	1 781	815	2 481	3 487	77	...	1 218
	2007	...	...	1 987	783	2 350	4 056	83	...	1 256
	2008	...	...	1 873	768	2 252	3 960	67	...	1 242
	2009	...	...	1 685	700	2 056	4 038	60	...	1 298
Nicaragua Nicaragua	2006	...	...	91	27	199	404	15	...	2 958
	2007	...	...	87	35	198	395	16	...	3 209
	2008	...	...	84	25	187	346	9	...	3 361
	2009	...	...	101	22	222	395	12	...	3 453
Panama Panama	2006	...	...	...	...	...	...	...	...	5 989
	2007	...	...	...	...	...	...	...	...	6 476
	2008	...	...	...	...	...	...	...	...	6 430
	2009	...	...	...	...	...	...	...	...	6 947
Puerto Rico Porto Rico	2006	...	...	...	...	...	...	...	...	24 947
	2007	...	...	...	...	...	...	...	...	24 636
	2008	...	...	...	...	...	...	...	...	23 117
	2009	...	...	...	...	...	...	...	...	22 949
Saint Kitts and Nevis * Saint-Kitts-et-Nevis *	2006	...	...	...	...	...	...	...	...	135
	2007	...	...	...	...	...	...	...	...	137
	2008	...	...	...	...	...	...	...	...	139
	2009	...	...	...	...	...	...	...	...	142
Saint Lucia Sainte-Lucie	2006	...	...	...	...	...	...	...	...	331
	2007	...	...	...	...	...	...	...	...	346
	2008	...	...	...	...	...	...	...	...	352
	2009	...	...	...	...	...	...	...	...	363
Saint Pierre and Miquelon * Saint-Pierre-et-Miquelon *	2006	...	...	...	...	...	...	...	...	57
	2007	...	...	...	...	...	...	...	...	57
	2008	...	...	...	...	...	...	...	...	57
	2009	...	...	...	...	...	...	...	...	57
Saint Vincent-Grenadines Saint Vincent-Grenadines	2006	...	...	...	...	...	...	...	...	134
	2007	...	...	...	...	...	...	...	...	141
	2008	...	...	...	...	...	...	...	...	139
	*2009	...	...	...	...	...	...	...	...	140
Trinidad and Tobago Trinité-et-Tobago	2006	...	8 976	1 240	755	1 804	2 934	771	1 216 368	7 045
	2007	...	8 576	1 273	746	1 736	3 027	848	1 339 773	7 662
	2008	...	7 539	1 543	894	1 788	3 038	886	1 553 936	7 785
	2009	...	7 767	1 352	733	1 709	2 547	1 126	1 674 558	7 735
Turks and Caicos Islands Iles Turques et Caïques	2006	...	...	...	...	...	...	...	...	158
	2007	...	...	...	...	...	...	...	...	182
	*2008	...	...	...	...	...	...	...	...	198
	*2009	...	...	...	...	...	...	...	...	209
United States Etats-Unis	2006	1 067 902[6]	302 917	348 229	70 873	204 267	37 666	58 386	20 216 298	4 300 831
	2007	1 052 981[6]	302 636	344 914	69 403	208 522	39 493	58 293	21 049 290	4 349 840
	2008	1 075 881[6]	298 269	345 382	71 447	216 717	36 470	56 596	22 024 480	4 368 260
	2009	987 552[6]	321 123	347 213	66 306	202 339	34 952	56 769	22 532 797	4 188 214

Region, country or area Région, pays ou zone	Year Année	Hard coal, lignite and peat Houille, lignite et tourbe	Crude petroleum and NGL Pétrole brut et LGN	Motor gasoline Essence auto	Jet fuel Carbu-réacteurs	Gas-diesel oil Gazole/ carburant diesel	Residual fuel oil Mazout résiduel	Liquified petroleum gas Gaz de pétrole liquéfiés	Natural gas Gaz naturel Terajoules Térajoules	Electricity Electricité Million kWh Millions kWh
				Thousand metric tons – Milliers de tonnes						
United States Virgin Is. * Iles Vierges américaines *	2006	...	...	...	...	...	...	...	...	1 065
	2007	...	...	...	...	...	...	...	...	1 070
	2008	...	...	...	...	...	...	...	...	1 078
	2009	...	...	...	...	...	...	...	...	1 085
America, South **Amérique du Sud**	**2006**	**79 750**[7]	**343 240**	**47 257**	**10 331**	**73 219**	**44 524**	**17 346**	**4 375 226**	**864 921**
	2007	**83 992**[7]	**331 880**	**47 745**	**10 041**	**73 399**	**48 134**	**18 291**	**4 313 858**	**906 852**
	2008	**87 219**[7]	**334 245**	**48 151**	**9 971**	**75 927**	**48 752**	**17 506**	**4 510 635**	**945 975**
	2009	**87 713**[7]	**365 828**	**49 788**	**11 115**	**77 471**	**45 942**	**17 254**	**4 325 009**	**955 582**
Argentina Argentine	2006	141[2]	37 612	4 628	1 191	10 685	3 422	4 504	1 879 131	115 197
	2007	110[2]	36 626	4 846	1 283	10 970	4 267	4 215	1 810 663	115 428
	2008	110[2]	35 663	4 603	1 240	10 619	4 714	3 988	1 820 978	123 422
	2009	82[2]	35 252	4 763	1 278	10 237	3 219	3 866	1 729 199	122 347
Bolivia (Plurinational State of) Bolivie (État plurinational de)	2006	...	2 705	480	134	620	538	345	507 771	5 300
	2007	...	2 723	554	124	656	528	345	547 033	5 734
	2008	...	2 595	651	127	679	487	339	571 390	5 816
	2009	...	2 304	623	130	544	338	341	491 489	6 119
Brazil Brésil	2006	5 881[2]	90 173	14 981	3 037	33 597	15 661	5 405	434 855	419 336
	2007	5 965[2]	92 503	15 733	3 263	34 035	15 707	5 731	423 995	445 094
	2008	6 611[2]	95 644	15 341	3 074	35 697	15 553	5 505	547 058	463 120
	2009	5 061[2]	102 590	15 201	3 495	36 886	14 386	5 001	471 307	466 158
Chile Chili	2006	674[2]	316	2 482	660	3 717	2 646	530	72 145	55 320
	2007	243[2]	527	2 349	537	3 623	2 445	781	50 334	58 509
	2008	667[2]	536	2 230	511	3 811	1 906	671	57 982	59 704
	2009	636[2]	644	2 445	610	3 442	1 802	735	46 176	60 722
Colombia Colombie	2006	65 596[2]	27 396	3 618	718	4 317	2 792	694	285 242	53 852
	2007	69 902[2]	27 390	3 164	537	4 395	3 318	727	285 275	55 314
	2008	73 502[2]	30 386	3 164	522	4 395	3 318	700	305 847	56 024
	2009	72 807[2]	34 633	2 903	955	3 570	3 251	695	413 714	57 265
Ecuador Equateur	2006	...	28 058	1 744	337	1 662	3 406	237	29 618	13 884
	2007	...	26 754	1 940	357	1 637	3 815	165	30 478	16 295
	2008	...	26 513	2 027	355	1 654	3 644	234	18 917	18 250
	2009	...	25 484	2 185	343	1 774	3 371	253	19 988	17 229
Falkland Is. (Malvinas) Iles Falkland (Malvinas)	2006	13[3]	...	...	...	...	...	...	...	*17
	*2007	13[3]	...	...	...	...	...	...	...	17
	2008	13[3]	...	...	...	...	...	...	...	*18
	*2009	13[3]	...	...	...	...	...	...	...	18
French Guiana * Guyane française *	2006	...	...	...	...	...	...	...	...	716
	2007	...	...	...	...	...	...	...	...	744
	2008	...	...	...	...	...	...	...	...	773
	2009	...	...	...	...	...	...	...	...	794
Guyana Guyana	2006	...	...	...	...	...	...	...	...	664
	2007	...	...	...	...	...	...	...	...	699
	2008	...	...	...	...	...	...	...	...	711
	2009	...	...	...	...	...	...	...	...	723
Paraguay Paraguay	2006	...	...	...	...	...	...	...	...	53 774
	2007	...	...	...	...	...	...	...	...	53 715
	2008	...	...	...	...	...	...	...	...	55 454
	2009	...	...	...	...	...	...	...	...	54 950
Peru Pérou	2006	107[2]	5 486	2 208	504	2 780	2 878	777	77 826	27 358
	2007	112[2]	5 934	2 356	565	3 063	2 693	788	108 691	29 931
	2008	142[2]	5 652	2 332	582	3 076	2 825	887	151 025	32 430
	2009	322[2]	6 482	2 922	559	4 334	2 338	1 289	190 834	35 355
Suriname Suriname	2006	...	656[4]	...	...	41	343	...	...	1 618
	2007	...	656[4]	...	...	41	343	...	...	1 618
	2008	...	656[4]	...	...	41	343	...	...	1 618
	2009	...	663[4]	...	...	42	347	...	...	1 618
Uruguay Uruguay	2006	...	...	396	53	760	381	77	...	5 618
	2007	...	...	352	61	637	368	65	...	9 424
	2008	...	...	449	67	827	509	91	...	8 769
	2009	...	...	442	61	684	591	86	...	8 838
Venezuela (Boliv. Rep. of) Venezuela (Rép. boliv. du)	2006	7 338[2]	150 838	16 720	3 697	15 040	12 457	4 777	1 088 638	112 266
	2007	7 647[2]	138 767	16 451	3 314	14 342	14 649	5 474	1 057 389	114 330
	2008	6 174[2]	136 600	17 354	3 493	15 128	15 453	5 091	1 037 438	119 866
	2009	8 792[2]	157 776	18 304	3 684	15 958	16 300	4 988	962 302	123 447

Region, country or area Région, pays ou zone	Year Année	Hard coal, lignite and peat Houille, lignite et tourbe	Crude petroleum and NGL Pétrole brut et LGN	Motor gasoline Essence auto	Jet fuel Carbu-réacteurs	Gas-diesel oil Gazole/ carburant diesel	Residual fuel oil Mazout résiduel	Liquified petroleum gas Gaz de pétrole liquéfiés	Natural gas Gaz naturel Terajoules Térajoules	Electricity Electricité Million kWh Millions kWh
					Thousand metric tons – Milliers de tonnes					
Asia	2006	3 496 395[6]	1 723 105	208 631	75 222	446 134	244 040	106 049	31 719 216	7 189 453
Asie	2007	3 738 003[6]	1 721 521	215 613	79 696	456 674	233 499	108 152	34 154 083	7 819 223
	2008	3 914 904[6]	1 775 751	223 264	80 831	479 334	224 734	111 390	36 419 605	8 065 740
	2009	4 146 896[6]	1 699 071	248 632	77 009	493 468	201 234	112 682	36 390 363	8 398 305
Afghanistan	2006	35[2]	...	...	...	...	...	...	171	913
Afghanistan	2007	243[2]	...	...	...	...	...	...	161	950
	2008	347[2]	...	...	...	...	...	...	155	788
	2009	500[2]	...	...	...	...	...	...	142	889
Armenia	2006	...	...	...	...	...	...	...	...	5 941
Arménie	2007	...	...	...	...	...	...	...	...	5 898
	2008	...	...	...	...	...	...	...	...	6 114
	2009	...	...	...	...	...	...	...	...	5 671
Azerbaijan	2006	...	32 549	1 043	693	2 095	2 899	205	255 073	24 542
Azerbaïdjan	2007	...	43 854	1 129	761	2 109	2 340	187	421 780	21 846
	2008	...	46 838	1 320	731	2 526	1 276	203	636 091	21 643
	2009	...	52 478	1 235	603	2 367	287	193	635 663	18 869
Bahrain	2006	...	9 514	918	2 210	4 866	2 761	209	307 881	9 745
Bahreïn	2007	...	9 544	766	2 227	4 904	2 355	197	338 924	10 908
	2008	...	9 497	892	2 219	4 547	2 242	200	363 186	11 933
	2009	...	9 450	804	2 205	4 439	2 314	198	367 276	12 056
Bangladesh	2006	303[2]	93[5]	140	1	284	55	8	574 419	29 879
Bangladesh	2007	388[2]	84[5]	127	4	258	49	12	613 134	31 286
	2008	677[2]	76[5]	115	3	234	42	40	655 121	34 957
	2009	858[2]	69[5]	104	3	212	38	40	712 953	37 862
Bhutan	2006	98[2]	...	...	...	...	...	...	...	4 521
Bhoutan	2007	105[2]	...	...	...	...	...	...	...	6 562
	2008	124[2]	...	...	...	...	...	...	...	6 961
	2009	49[2]	...	...	...	...	...	...	...	6 998
Brunei Darussalam	2006	...	10 788	209	79	190	103	15	492 586	3 298
Brunéi Darussalam	2007	...	9 730	217	82	189	97	15	503 856	3 395
	2008	...	9 651	202	97	187	91	15	525 272	3 423
	2009	...	*8 372	199	93	173	84	15	486 450	3 612
Cambodia	2006	...	...	...	...	...	...	...	...	1 088
Cambodge	2007	...	...	...	...	...	...	...	...	1 349
	2008	...	...	...	...	...	...	...	...	1 461
	2009	...	...	...	...	...	...	...	...	1 206
China[8]	2006	2 528 551[2]	184 766[4]	55 496	...	117 624	17 847	17 453	2 181 685	2 865 726
Chine[8]	2007	2 691 643[2]	186 318[4]	58 721	...	123 591	19 672	19 447	2 579 882	3 281 553
	2008	2 802 000[2]	190 440[4]	62 931	...	134 092	17 374	19 148	2 991 978	3 456 910
	2009	2 973 000[2]	189 490[4]	72 703	...	142 886	13 534	18 317	3 178 278	3 714 950
China, Hong Kong SAR	2006	...	...	...	...	...	...	...	...	38 613
Chine, Hong Kong RAS	2007	...	...	...	...	...	...	...	...	38 948
	2008	...	...	...	...	...	...	...	...	37 990
	2009	...	...	...	...	...	...	...	...	38 728
China, Macao SAR	2006	...	...	...	...	...	...	...	...	1 669
Chine, Macao RAS	2007	...	...	...	...	...	...	...	...	1 520
	2008	...	...	...	...	...	...	...	...	1 211
	2009	...	...	...	...	...	...	...	...	1 466
Cyprus	2006	...	...	...	...	...	...	...	...	4 652
Chypre	2007	...	...	...	...	...	...	...	...	4 871
	2008	...	...	...	...	...	...	...	...	5 078
	2009	...	...	...	...	...	...	...	...	5 227
Dem. P. R. Korea	2006	35 106[6]	...	122	...	131	75	...	...	22 436
R. p. dém. de Corée	2007	30 338[6]	...	146	...	157	90	...	...	21 523
	2008	32 333[6]	...	151	...	161	92	...	...	23 206
	2009	31 556[6]	...	116	...	123	70	...	...	21 093
Georgia	2006	11[2]	64[4]	...	...	0	4	...	757	7 599
Géorgie	2007	19[2]	64[4]	...	...	0	13	...	623	8 580
	2008	58[2]	52[4]	...	...	0	17	...	483	8 440
	2009	169[2]	53[4]	...	...	0	5	...	420	8 165
India	2006	462 117[6]	38 138	12 539	7 805	54 268	15 697	8 408	1 005 064	752 454
Inde	2007	491 062[6]	37 924	14 167	9 107	59 032	15 804	8 792	1 071 204	813 102
	2008	525 178[6]	37 496	16 020	8 071	63 495	17 684	9 158	1 165 167	842 531
	2009	566 133[6]	37 678	22 554	9 304	77 605	17 535	8 759	1 605 978	899 389

Region, country or area / Région, pays ou zone	Year / Année	Hard coal, lignite and peat / Houille, lignite et tourbe	Crude petroleum and NGL / Pétrole brut et LGN	Motor gasoline / Essence auto	Jet fuel / Carbu-réacteurs	Gas-diesel oil / Gazole/ carburant diesel	Residual fuel oil / Mazout résiduel	Liquified petroleum gas / Gaz de pétrole liquéfiés	Natural gas / Gaz naturel Terajoules / Térajoules	Electricity / Electricité Million kWh / Millions kWh
		Thousand metric tons – Milliers de tonnes								
Indonesia	2006	226 524[6]	47 515	8 411	1 256	13 216	10 127	1 428	2 704 155	133 108
Indonésie	2007	260 568[6]	50 748	8 363	1 087	11 368	10 173	1 410	2 663 613	142 236
	2008	276 488[6]	49 123	8 155	1 445	12 766	9 471	1 690	2 731 470	149 437
	2009	*296 739[6]	53 595	9 243	1 911	13 769	2 803	2 180	2 451 084	158 593
Iran (Islamic Rep. of)	2006	1 528[2]	229 189	12 042	1 042	26 213	26 351	4 318	4 273 713	192 534
Iran (Rép. islamique d')	2007	1 634[2]	233 771	12 042	992	26 213	25 168	4 793	4 826 289	203 981
	2008	1 591[2]	230 530	12 042	1 021	26 213	26 658	5 677	5 025 145	214 530
	2009	1 174[2]	227 468	12 042	1 212	26 213	26 230	6 054	5 408 074	221 314
Iraq	2006	...	97 312	2 367	438	5 346	5 988	1 041	55 100	31 869
Iraq	2007	...	101 218	2 212	409	4 995	5 595	1 039	55 480	33 183
	2008	...	113 492	2 937	543	6 633	7 430	1 115	71 440	36 779
	2009	...	115 736	2 822	522	6 373	7 138	1 131	43 662	46 063
Israel	2006	452[9]	2[4]	2 592	...	3 231	3 223	471	83 815	51 811
Israël	2007	429[9]	...	...	...	...	...	...	78 117	55 091
	2008	427[9]	...	...	...	...	...	...	100 895	56 421
	2009	444[9]	...	...	...	...	...	...	100 849	55 412
Japan	2006	...	693	42 378	10 433	54 711	28 536	4 644	148 485	1 104 589
Japon	2007	...	747	42 744	11 663	55 301	29 545	4 409	166 369	1 135 718
	2008	...	743	41 852	12 416	54 572	26 868	4 096	165 666	1 082 549
	2009	...	699	42 186	10 623	50 048	21 905	4 524	159 410	1 047 919
Jordan	2006	...	1[4]	675	312	1 412	1 345	139	7 754	11 120
Jordanie	2007	...	1[4]	706	301	1 292	1 215	119	6 908	12 838
	2008	...	2[4]	771	309	1 260	992	134	7 094	14 160
	2009	...	1[4]	757	307	1 155	920	106	7 532	14 272
Kazakhstan	2006	96 230[6]	65 003	2 345	249	3 888	3 333	1 106	1 029 452	71 653
Kazakhstan	2007	98 384[6]	67 125	2 633	268	4 295	2 584	1 262	1 153 500	76 621
	2008	111 073[6]	70 671	2 505	219	4 375	3 204	1 342	1 283 362	80 326
	2009	100 854[6]	77 637	2 613	204	4 405	3 261	1 732	1 402 492	78 710
Kuwait	2006	...	136 408	3 023	2 513	11 079	11 951	3 671	533 264	47 607
Koweït	2007	...	132 742	2 852	2 675	11 475	11 559	3 447	519 174	48 753
	2008	...	138 405	2 731	2 513	11 848	11 301	3 723	541 101	51 749
	2009	...	117 052	3 092	2 491	12 324	11 885	3 442	456 049	53 216
Kyrgyzstan	2006	322[6]	71[4]	10	...	31	27	...	741	17 082
Kirghizistan	2007	395[6]	69[4]	14	...	52	56	...	581	16 237
	2008	492[6]	71[4]	13	...	60	59	...	663	11 877
	2009	602[6]	75[4]	10	...	10	10	...	586	11 100
Lao People's Dem. Rep.	2006	*648[6]	...	...	...	...	...	...	...	4 134
Rép. dém. pop. lao	2007	*1 037[6]	...	...	...	...	...	...	...	3 863
	2008	*771[6]	...	...	...	...	...	...	...	4 172
	2009	*878[6]	...	...	...	...	...	...	...	3 874
Lebanon	2006	...	...	...	...	...	...	...	...	9 287
Liban	2007	...	...	...	...	...	...	...	...	9 575
	2008	...	...	...	...	...	...	...	...	10 626
	2009	...	...	...	...	...	...	...	...	10 822
Malaysia	2006	902[2]	33 837	6 089	2 523	9 057	1 992	2 520	2 336 490	106 702
Malaisie	2007	1 063[2]	34 975	5 759	3 040	8 806	2 006	3 021	2 526 083	110 308
	2008	1 167[2]	*35 176	4 819	3 040	9 622	2 010	*3 543	2 412 200	112 273
	2009	2 138[2]	*33 205	4 197	2 989	9 245	1 182	*3 256	*2 342 520	107 414
Maldives	2006	...	...	...	...	...	...	...	...	212
Maldives	2007	...	...	...	...	...	...	...	...	245
	*2008	...	...	...	...	...	...	...	...	280
	*2009	...	...	...	...	...	...	...	...	320
Mongolia	2006	8 074[6]	...	...	...	...	...	...	...	3 544
Mongolie	2007	9 238[6]	...	...	...	...	...	...	...	3 701
	2008	10 072[6]	...	...	...	...	...	...	...	4 001
	2009	14 442[6]	...	...	...	...	...	...	...	4 039
Myanmar	2006	1 336[6]	1 058	357	52	274	41	10	494 789	6 164
Myanmar	2007	1 321[6]	1 056	371	52	254	56	18	530 917	6 398
	2008	1 320[6]	1 002	346	48	244	61	16	486 936	6 622
	2009	1 361[6]	959	363	39	212	64	15	453 164	5 850
Nepal	2006	20[2]	...	...	...	...	...	...	...	2 748
Népal	2007	14[2]	...	...	...	...	...	...	...	2 792
	2008	15[2]	...	...	...	...	...	...	...	2 812
	2009	16[2]	...	...	...	...	...	...	...	3 119

Region, country or area Région, pays ou zone	Year Année	Hard coal, lignite and peat Houille, lignite et tourbe	Crude petroleum and NGL Pétrole brut et LGN	Motor gasoline Essence auto	Jet fuel Carbu-réacteurs	Gas-diesel oil Gazole/carburant diesel	Residual fuel oil Mazout résiduel	Liquified petroleum gas Gaz de pétrole liquéfiés	Natural gas Gaz naturel Terajoules Térajoules	Electricity Electricité Million kWh Millions kWh
		Thousand metric tons – Milliers de tonnes								
Occupied Palestinian Terr.	2006	...	...	...	...	...	...	...	...	345
Terr. palestinien occupé	2007	...	...	...	...	...	...	...	...	417
	2008	...	...	...	...	...	...	...	...	427
	2009	...	...	...	...	...	...	...	...	501
Oman	2006	...	36 889	628	286	905	2 244	104	938 220	13 287
Oman	2007	...	35 552	535	219	650	1 979	150	942 844	14 167
	2008	...	37 936	2 243	767	1 975	3 770	412	927 816	15 829
	2009	...	40 714	2 157	749	1 795	3 760	445	957 495	17 823
Pakistan	2006	3 643[2]	3 673	1 218	1 165	3 383	3 193	583	1 296 194	98 213
Pakistan	2007	4 124[2]	3 798	1 337	1 009	3 697	3 324	578	1 320 373	95 661
	2008	3 738[2]	3 535	1 287	958	3 351	3 093	507	1 336 820	91 616
	2009	3 481[2]	3 478	1 338	938	3 213	2 497	485	1 361 910	95 358
Philippines	2006	2 298[9]	520	1 590	714	3 575	3 057	327	105 901	56 819
Philippines	2007	3 401[9]	578	1 470	771	3 659	3 206	253	143 876	59 646
	2008	3 609[9]	671	1 410	716	3 302	2 413	305	151 458	60 855
	2009	4 687[9]	924	1 077	675	2 426	1 628	282	152 517	61 968
Qatar	2006	...	54 788	1 693	1 045	1 020	734	9 731	2 134 423	17 080
Qatar	2007	...	56 065	1 957	1 106	1 030	410	9 566	2 561 748	19 462
	2008	...	61 923	1 916	1 115	1 194	213	9 917	3 241 856	21 616
	2009	...	58 933	1 633	877	1 078	238	10 565	3 700 699	24 796
Republic of Korea	2006	2 824[2]	45[4]	8 707	12 021	32 392	30 793	3 098	21 339	404 021
République de Corée	2007	2 886[2]	31[4]	8 505	13 379	34 314	27 363	2 927	18 032	427 316
	2008	2 773[2]	21[4]	10 188	13 671	35 860	22 370	2 977	18 449	446 428
	2009	2 519[2]	42[4]	11 975	12 945	35 519	18 470	3 026	31 297	454 504
Saudi Arabia	2006	...	506 248	12 025	3 690	32 411	27 177	30 288	2 744 274	181 434
Arabie saoudite	2007	...	486 447	15 050	3 211	31 970	26 184	29 422	2 677 617	190 535
	2008	...	507 439	14 538	3 325	33 169	26 183	29 698	2 840 389	204 200
	2009	...	456 926	15 196	3 030	30 521	27 269	31 583	2 854 671	217 082
Singapore	2006	...	...	7 361	9 667	13 433	7 691	678	...	39 442
Singapour	2007	...	...	8 405	10 416	14 364	7 794	673	...	41 134
	2008	...	...	9 300	9 997	14 968	6 902	608	...	41 717
	2009	...	...	9 627	7 408	13 309	11 712	608	...	41 800
Sri Lanka	2006	...	...	194	131	628	809	15	...	9 389
Sri Lanka	2007	...	...	163	171	445	810	16	...	9 814
	2008	...	...	164	154	451	768	16	...	9 901
	2009	...	...	179	195	485	817	24	...	9 882
Syrian Arab Republic	2006	...	21 074	1 345	208	4 155	5 030	510	237 510	37 453
Rép. arabe syrienne	2007	...	19 345	1 220	183	3 824	4 474	463	233 740	38 784
	2008	...	*18 954	1 282	193	3 945	4 951	*463	222 430	41 170
	2009	...	*18 710	1 359	196	3 980	4 116	*445	233 363	43 308
Tajikistan	2006	105[6]	24[4]	...	...	...	...	...	669	16 935
Tadjikistan	2007	181[6]	12[4]	...	...	...	...	...	551	17 494
	2008	199[6]	14[4]	...	...	...	...	...	1 349	16 147
	2009	198[6]	26[4]	...	...	...	...	...	1 444	16 127
Thailand	2006	19 001[9]	12 406	6 331	4 299	16 737	6 578	4 032	761 621	138 742
Thaïlande	2007	18 239[9]	13 217	6 311	3 992	18 381	7 333	4 291	802 644	143 378
	2008	17 982[9]	14 199	5 884	4 607	17 754	7 174	4 773	879 730	147 427
	2009	18 231[9]	*14 426	6 552	4 838	19 573	6 538	4 463	1 040 222	145 912
Timor-Leste	2006	...	*6 872	...	...	...	...	*2 215	...	72
Timor-Leste	2007	...	*6 884	...	...	...	...	*2 220	...	92
	2008	...	*6 908	...	...	...	...	*2 227	...	111
	2009	...	*6 881	...	...	...	...	*2 215	...	132
Turkey	2006	64 255[6]	2 160[4]	3 659	1 644	7 549	7 271	808	34 662	176 299
Turquie	2007	75 364[6]	2 134[4]	4 098	2 336	7 016	6 369	762	34 202	191 558
	2008	79 402[6]	2 160[4]	4 562	2 556	7 078	5 363	793	38 965	198 418
	2009	79 499[6]	2 402[4]	3 963	2 004	5 102	3 012	604	26 224	194 813
Turkmenistan	2006	...	8 449	1 265	296	2 512	1 745	...	2 396 479	13 650
Turkménistan	2007	...	9 687	1 414	331	2 809	1 951	...	2 609 794	14 880
	2008	...	10 955	1 549	363	3 077	2 137	...	2 671 175	15 040
	2009	...	9 795	1 414	331	2 809	1 951	...	1 445 465	15 980
United Arab Emirates	2006	...	141 807	2 619	5 385	4 428	1 173	5 534	1 901 250	66 768
Emirats arabes unis	2007	...	140 153	2 336	4 948	4 242	1 102	6 242	1 996 800	76 106
	2008	...	142 441	2 171	4 911	4 219	907	6 335	1 958 970	86 260
	2009	...	125 696	2 392	5 141	4 364	1 715	5 426	1 903 980	90 573

Production of selected energy commodities *(continued)*
Production de l'énergie *(suite)*

Region, country or area Région, pays ou zone	Year Année	Hard coal, lignite and peat Houille, lignite et tourbe	Crude petroleum and NGL Pétrole brut et LGN	Motor gasoline Essence auto	Jet fuel Carbu- réacteurs	Gas-diesel oil Gazole/ carburant diesel	Residual fuel oil Mazout résiduel	Liquified petroleum gas Gaz de pétrole liquéfiés	Natural gas Gaz naturel Terajoules Térajoules	Electricity Electricité Million kWh Millions kWh
		Thousand metric tons – Milliers de tonnes								
Uzbekistan Ouzbékistan	2006	3 235[6]	5 578	1 370	227	1 435	1 080	27	2 370 882	50 920
	2007	3 442[6]	5 063	1 410	206	1 303	740	24	2 463 465	48 950
	2008	3 290[6]	4 959	1 476	202	1 287	526	24	2 653 428	49 400
	2009	3 654[6]	4 787	1 622	195	1 302	499	23	2 503 446	49 900
Viet Nam Viet Nam	2006	38 778[2]	17 392	...	...	...	...	302	273 147	60 493
	2007	42 483[2]	16 569	...	...	...	...	281	276 269	66 857
	2008	39 777[2]	15 576	...	...	...	...	261	300 030	73 049
	2009	43 715[2]	17 022	674	81	553	37	373	330 339	83 191
Yemen Yémen	2006	...	18 158	796	396	692	519	730	...	5 387
	2007	...	16 000	1 021	486	1 014	676	761	...	6 027
	2008	...	14 781	954	341	1 086	691	707	...	6 546
	2009	...	14 278	1 054	407	1 070	834	731	21 643	6 744
Europe **Europe**	**2006**	**1 042 260**	**723 113**	**200 960**	**50 436**	**354 023**	**190 834**	**43 478**	**37 224 358**	**4 846 219**
	2007	**1 035 310**	**728 818**	**190 242**	**50 030**	**354 942**	**187 866**	**41 065**	**36 555 682**	**4 897 598**
	2008	**1 033 892**	**714 255**	**184 967**	**51 058**	**363 544**	**183 244**	**40 702**	**37 619 158**	**4 940 082**
	2009	**972 118**	**706 181**	**181 329**	**45 495**	**344 637**	**170 638**	**45 056**	**34 057 655**	**4 702 500**
Albania Albanie	2006	64[9]	505[4]	0	0	101	49	...	670	5 094
	2007	64[9]	570[4]	0	0	83	32	...	670	2 860
	2008	85[9]	584[4]	0	0	85	30	...	335	3 797
	2009	22[9]	582[4]	0	0	71	25	...	308	5 262
Andorra Andorre	2006	...	...	...	...	...	...	...	...	74
	2007	...	...	...	...	...	...	...	...	76
	2008	...	...	...	...	...	...	...	...	79
	*2009	...	...	...	...	...	...	...	...	81
Austria Autriche	2006	1[1]	983	1 615	526	3 685	915	50	72 756	64 577
	2007	1[1]	982	1 669	604	3 461	880	70	73 899	64 758
	2008	1[1]	980	1 595	472	3 945	769	98	61 262	66 867
	2009	1[1]	1 040	1 652	313	3 567	852	92	66 667	68 989
Belarus Bélarus	2006	2 125[3]	1 780[4]	3 498	...	6 616	6 329	483	8 458	31 811
	2007	2 507[3]	1 760[4]	3 181	...	6 679	6 195	439	7 763	31 829
	2008	2 364[3]	1 740[4]	3 330	...	7 404	6 831	482	7 840	35 048
	2009	2 212[3]	1 720[4]	3 272	...	7 559	7 291	417	7 918	30 376
Belgium Belgique	2006	29[9]	...	5 357	1 744	12 660	7 128	403	...	85 617
	2007	0[9]	...	5 041	1 751	12 836	7 391	464	...	88 820
	2008	0[9]	...	4 338	1 878	12 959	7 268	524	...	84 930
	2009	0[9]	...	3 355	1 838	12 248	5 039	463	...	91 225
Bosnia and Herzegovina Bosnie-Herzégovine	2006	13 761[6]	...	0	...	0	0	4	...	13 309
	2007	14 485[6]	...	0	...	0	0	4	...	11 784
	2008	15 795[6]	...	4	...	27	54	6	...	13 219
	2009	15 370[6]	...	97	...	392	284	25	...	15 667
Bulgaria Bulgarie	2006	25 678[6]	28[4]	1 560	151	2 521	1 512	127	17 391	45 843
	2007	28 633[6]	26[4]	1 466	183	2 376	1 550	136	10 966	43 297
	2008	28 789[6]	24[4]	1 571	199	2 397	1 596	161	7 273	45 037
	2009	27 279[6]	25[4]	1 457	184	2 108	1 536	155	609	42 966
Croatia Croatie	2006	...	973	1 083	67	1 565	1 097	399	103 113	12 430
	2007	...	925	1 202	97	1 673	1 180	433	109 900	12 245
	2008	...	863	1 001	97	1 395	1 128	373	102 080	12 326
	2009	...	807	1 207	94	1 488	1 066	405	102 181	12 777
Czech Republic République tchèque	2006	62 912[6]	344[4]	1 594	121	3 128	381	204	6 853	84 361
	2007	62 626[6]	330[4]	1 555	145	2 902	417	192	6 524	88 198
	2008	60 200[6]	242[4]	1 601	170	3 460	335	210	7 468	83 518
	2009	56 417[6]	222[4]	1 412	112	3 131	260	203	6 775	82 250
Denmark Danemark	2006	...	16 839[4]	1 987	608	3 258	1 471	166	433 718	45 611
	2007	...	15 169[4]	1 962	542	3 198	1 415	159	384 607	39 316
	2008	...	14 035[4]	1 924	500	3 098	1 379	114	419 601	36 638
	2009	...	12 903[4]	2 092	409	3 308	1 265	140	350 278	36 364
Estonia Estonie	2006	14 602[1]	...	...	...	...	...	...	...	9 732
	2007	17 019[1]	...	...	...	...	...	...	...	12 190
	2008	16 331[1]	...	...	...	...	...	...	...	10 581
	2009	15 267[1]	...	...	...	...	...	...	...	8 779
Faeroe Islands Iles Féroé	2006	...	...	...	...	...	...	...	...	260
	2007	...	...	...	...	...	...	...	...	269
	2008	...	...	...	...	...	...	...	...	276
	2009	...	...	...	...	...	...	...	...	276

Region, country or area Région, pays ou zone	Year Année	Hard coal, lignite and peat Houille, lignite et tourbe	Crude petroleum and NGL Pétrole brut et LGN	Motor gasoline Essence auto	Jet fuel Carbu-réacteurs	Gas-diesel oil Gazole/ carburant diesel	Residual fuel oil Mazout résiduel	Liquified petroleum gas Gaz de pétrole liquéfiés	Natural gas Gaz naturel Terajoules Térajoules	Electricity Electricité Million kWh Millions kWh
		Thousand metric tons – Milliers de tonnes								
Finland	2006	13 235[3]	...	4 298	715	5 502	1 272	402	...	82 304
Finlande	2007	4 466[3]	...	4 348	717	5 863	1 402	350	...	81 246
	2008	4 300[3]	...	4 308	683	6 484	1 372	357	...	77 436
	2009	8 965[3]	...	4 230	632	6 460	1 435	274	...	72 062
France [11]	2006	452[2]	1 100	17 302	5 633	33 733	11 955	2 638	43 242	574 609
France [11]	2007	422[2]	1 013	16 496	5 536	34 392	11 441	2 478	38 585	569 771
	2008	277[2]	1 010	16 370	5 571	35 693	11 415	2 784	34 181	574 842
	2009	147[2]	932	15 440	4 944	31 719	9 483	2 418	32 179	542 184
Germany	2006	200 184	3 383[4]	26 576	4 412	50 854	13 684	2 925	653 696	636 761
Allemagne	2007	204 594[6]	3 361[4]	25 888	4 592	49 334	13 669	3 065	609 138	637 100
	2008	194 381[6]	3 024[4]	24 822	4 760	48 709	12 023	2 893	526 334	637 232
	2009	183 623[6]	2 768[4]	23 485	4 591	45 697	9 756	2 662	517 126	592 464
Gibraltar	2006	...	...	...	...	...	...	...	...	151
Gibraltar	2007	...	...	...	...	...	...	...	...	155
	2008	...	...	...	...	...	...	...	...	166
	2009	...	...	...	...	...	...	...	...	174
Greece	2006	64 787[9]	94	4 327	1 423	6 452	6 953	653	1 209	60 789
Grèce	2007	66 308[9]	81	4 318	1 719	6 562	7 116	645	1 026	63 496
	2008	65 720[9]	62	4 251	1 853	6 517	6 008	665	681	63 749
	2009	64 893[9]	80	4 075	1 574	6 443	5 959	611	545	61 365
Guernsey	2006	...	...	...	...	...	...	...	...	80
Guernesey	2007	...	...	...	...	...	...	...	...	158
	2008	...	...	...	...	...	...	...	...	111
	2009	...	...	...	...	...	...	...	...	152
Hungary	2006	9 952[9]	1 345	1 302	280	3 498	232	373	110 815	35 859
Hongrie	2007	9 818[9]	1 206	1 322	273	3 722	200	379	93 251	39 960
	2008	9 404[9]	1 235	1 264	263	3 605	207	400	93 312	40 025
	2009	8 986[9]	1 196	1 238	241	3 290	168	352	106 405	35 908
Iceland	2006	...	...	...	...	...	...	...	...	9 930
Islande	2007	...	...	...	...	...	...	...	...	11 977
	2008	...	...	...	...	...	...	...	...	16 468
	2009	...	...	...	...	...	...	...	...	16 834
Ireland	2006	3 694[3]	...	635	...	1 121	1 101	51	19 107	27 481
Irlande	2007	2 772[3]	...	493	...	1 186	1 250	36	17 181	28 226
	2008	3 089[3]	...	570	...	1 132	1 161	34	16 477	29 685
	2009	2 771[3]	...	481	...	975	949	34	14 814	28 242
Isle of Man	2006	...	...	...	...	...	...	...	...	396
Ile de Man	2007	...	...	...	...	...	...	...	...	462
	2008	...	...	...	...	...	...	...	...	483
	2009	...	...	...	...	...	...	...	...	505
Italy [12]	2006	21[2]	5 769[4]	20 967	4 081	39 805	15 649	2 310	418 301	314 121
Italie [12]	2007	158[2]	5 860[4]	21 417	4 034	41 079	15 220	2 349	369 799	313 888
	2008	117[2]	5 220[4]	19 921	3 219	39 586	12 763	2 257	352 617	319 130
	2009	72[2]	4 551[4]	18 721	3 050	35 985	11 236	2 113	305 293	292 641
Jersey	2006	...	...	...	...	...	...	...	...	37
Jersey	2007	...	...	...	...	...	...	...	...	101
	2008	...	...	...	...	...	...	...	...	34
	*2009	...	...	...	...	...	...	...	...	34
Latvia	2006	14[3]	...	...	...	...	...	...	...	4 891
Lettonie	2007	11[3]	...	...	...	...	...	...	...	4 771
	2008	11[3]	...	...	...	...	...	...	...	5 274
	2009	25[3]	...	...	...	...	...	...	...	5 569
Lithuania	2006	55[3]	181[4]	2 172	764	2 246	1 938	474	...	12 482
Lituanie	2007	53[3]	154[4]	1 569	503	1 493	1 381	330	...	14 007
	2008	67[3]	128[4]	2 686	929	2 716	1 955	466	...	13 912
	2009	53[3]	115[4]	2 585	752	2 613	1 660	354	...	15 358
Luxembourg	2006	...	...	...	...	...	...	...	...	4 333
Luxembourg	2007	...	...	...	...	...	...	...	...	4 002
	2008	...	...	...	...	...	...	...	...	3 557
	2009	...	...	...	...	...	...	...	...	3 878
Malta	2006	...	...	...	...	...	...	...	...	2 261
Malte	2007	...	...	...	...	...	...	...	...	2 296
	2008	...	...	...	...	...	...	...	...	2 312
	2009	...	...	...	...	...	...	...	...	2 167

Region, country or area Région, pays ou zone	Year Année	Hard coal, lignite and peat Houille, lignite et tourbe	Crude petroleum and NGL Pétrole brut et LGN	Motor gasoline Essence auto	Jet fuel Carbu-réacteurs	Gas-diesel oil Gazole/ carburant diesel	Residual fuel oil Mazout résiduel	Liquified petroleum gas Gaz de pétrole liquéfiés	Natural gas Gaz naturel Terajoules Térajoules	Electricity Electricité Million kWh Millions kWh
		Thousand metric tons – Milliers de tonnes								
Montenegro	2006	1 512[2]	...	...	...	...	...	...	...	2 952
Monténégro	2007	1 202[2]	...	...	...	...	...	...	...	2 144
	2008	1 740[2]	...	...	...	...	...	...	...	2 828
	2009	957[2]	...	...	...	...	...	...	...	2 760
Netherlands	2006	...	2 022	13 794	6 914	19 685	12 151	4 069	2 576 941	98 393
Pays-Bas	2007	...	2 576	6 905	6 583	19 253	9 526	1 312	2 532 697	105 162
	2008	...	2 163	6 903	6 136	20 438	8 647	1 313	2 786 225	107 645
	2009	...	1 704	6 971	5 526	20 384	8 496	1 403	2 624 186	113 502
Norway[13]	2006	2 395[2]	123 581	4 134	644	7 108	1 957	8 255	3 559 345	121 580
Norvège[13]	2007	4 073[2]	119 385	3 942	575	6 847	2 066	8 136	3 632 557	137 192
	2008	3 430[2]	114 499	2 984	707	6 107	2 359	6 869	4 053 028	142 136
	2009	2 641[2]	108 135	3 513	680	6 052	2 009	7 124	4 218 715	132 778
Poland	2006	156 067[6]	796[4]	4 155	853	8 336	2 824	282	180 514	161 742
Pologne	2007	145 850[6]	721[4]	3 867	801	8 787	2 831	243	181 274	159 348
	2008	144 013[6]	755[4]	3 665	944	9 428	2 758	307	171 652	155 305
	2009	135 172[6]	687[4]	4 039	692	9 745	2 599	299	171 089	151 720
Portugal	2006	...	...	2 750	856	5 102	2 920	406	...	49 041
Portugal	2007	...	...	2 591	745	4 634	2 622	366	...	47 253
	2008	...	...	2 091	748	4 484	2 783	369	...	45 969
	2009	...	...	2 056	782	3 810	1 976	326	...	50 207
Republic of Moldova	2006	...	4[4]	...	...	0	2	...	5	1 192
République de Moldova	2007	...	8[4]	...	...	3	5	...	4	1 100
	2008	...	15[4]	...	...	4	7	...	5	1 096
	2009	...	17[4]	...	...	5	16	...	8	982
Romania	2006	34 932[1]	5 659	4 145	238	4 593	1 303	677	444 656	62 697
Roumanie	2007	35 781[1]	4 905	3 799	278	4 660	1 186	754	429 507	61 673
	2008	35 871[1]	4 719	3 654	328	4 841	1 168	594	418 334	64 956
	2009	33 970[1]	4 498	3 311	292	4 422	883	750	415 816	58 014
Russian Federation	2006	285 928	475 827	34 368	10 602	64 166	65 189	10 368	24 463 654	995 794
Fédération de Russie	2007	290 308	487 681	35 097	10 699	66 301	67 690	10 856	24 283 317	1 015 333
	2008	305 724	486 170	35 602	11 394	68 879	69 105	11 422	24 878 778	1 040 379
	2009	276 901	491 247	35 827	10 445	67 233	69 573	17 108	21 850 217	991 980
Serbia	2006	36 780[9]	646[4]	648	45	1 038	674	75	10 970	36 481
Serbie	2007	37 148[9]	648[4]	624	57	1 091	796	98	9 197	36 550
	2008	38 709[9]	646[4]	616	69	1 081	572	128	9 975	37 376
	2009	38 499[9]	671[4]	570	52	1 001	626	139	9 735	38 322
Slovakia	2006	2 201[9]	31	1 449	46	2 587	654	137	8 187	31 418
Slovaquie	2007	2 111[9]	24	1 596	78	2 819	544	143	5 056	28 056
	2008	2 423[9]	21	1 516	88	2 774	512	164	4 065	28 962
	2009	2 573[9]	18	1 496	68	2 743	630	133	4 078	26 155
Slovenia	2006	4 522[9]	...	...	...	...	...	...	160	15 115
Slovénie	2007	4 535[9]	...	...	...	...	...	...	120	15 043
	2008	4 520[9]	...	...	...	...	...	...	120	16 399
	2009	4 429[9]	...	...	...	...	...	...	120	16 401
Spain	2006	18 447[6]	139[4]	10 038	2 612	23 844	9 245	1 522	2 930	299 454
Espagne	2007	17 182[6]	142[4]	9 232	2 562	23 933	9 340	1 436	727	305 052
	2008	10 187[6]	127[4]	8 729	2 749	24 792	9 638	1 484	652	313 758
	2009	9 445[6]	105[4]	8 973	1 875	22 390	9 147	1 397	568	293 847
Sweden	2006	621[3]	...	4 182	179	7 204	5 226	302	...	143 419
Suède	2007	520[3]	...	3 729	196	6 414	4 246	261	...	148 926
	2008	837[3]	...	4 562	247	7 991	4 636	336	...	150 036
	2009	702[3]	...	4 506	211	7 670	4 426	278	...	136 717
Switzerland[14]	2006	...	...	1 465	228	2 573	583	223	...	64 063
Suisse[14]	2007	...	...	1 280	183	2 172	587	202	...	67 926
	2008	...	...	1 370	190	2 326	596	239	...	68 939
	2009	...	...	1 427	96	2 381	383	204	...	68 453
TFYR of Macedonia	2006	6 639[8]	...	190	33	443	327	29	...	7 009
L'ex-R.Y. Macédoine	2007	6 509[8]	...	179	17	424	402	25	...	6 498
	2008	7 630[8]	...	177	19	451	360	29	...	6 311
	2009	7 426[8]	...	178	20	375	362	28	...	6 828
Ukraine	2006	62 133	4 506	3 926	400	4 519	3 836	758	737 856	193 381
Ukraine	2007	59 147[7]	4 459	4 161	384	4 368	3 477	824	738 205	196 251
	2008	59 823[7]	4 328	3 223	296	3 765	2 460	727	750 111	192 586
	2009	55 426[7]	3 960	3 259	...	3 979	2 600	733	751 685	173 619

Region, country or area Région, pays ou zone	Year Année	Hard coal, lignite and peat Houille, lignite et tourbe	Crude petroleum and NGL Pétrole brut et LGN	Motor gasoline Essence auto	Jet fuel Carbu-réacteurs	Gas-diesel oil Gazole/ carburant diesel	Residual fuel oil Mazout résiduel	Liquified petroleum gas Gaz de pétrole liquéfiés	Natural gas Gaz naturel Terajoules Térajoules	Electricity Electricité Million kWh Millions kWh
		Thousand metric tons – Milliers de tonnes								
United Kingdom	2006	18 517[2]	76 578	21 443	6 261	26 080	12 277	4 713	3 349 811	397 285
Royaume-Uni	2007	17 007[2]	76 832	21 313	6 176	26 397	11 809	4 880	3 019 712	396 833
	2008	18 054[2]	71 665	20 319	6 549	26 971	11 349	4 897	2 916 752	388 669
	2009	17 874[2]	68 198	20 404	6 022	25 393	8 648	4 416	2 500 340	375 665
Oceania	**2006**	**373 125[6]**	**25 756**	**13 714**	**5 143**	**11 816**	**1 537**	**1 836**	**1 878 468**	**300 061**
Océanie	**2007**	**395 018[6]**	**27 953**	**14 460**	**5 153**	**11 396**	**1 424**	**1 761**	**1 992 616**	**304 114**
	2008	**396 239[6]**	**27 536**	**14 085**	**5 095**	**12 338**	**1 613**	**1 607**	**2 003 029**	**310 380**
	2009	**407 446[6]**	**28 805**	**14 023**	**5 316**	**12 377**	**1 542**	**1 641**	**2 091 524**	**313 813**
American Samoa *	2006	...	...	...	...	...	...	...	...	193
Samoa américaines *	2007	...	...	...	...	...	...	...	...	196
	2008	...	...	...	...	...	...	...	...	199
	2009	...	...	...	...	...	...	...	...	202
Australia	2006	367 452[6]	21 886	12 153	4 128	9 466	1 051	1 679	1 713 590	247 340
Australie	2007	390 184[6]	24 004	12 992	4 238	9 270	952	1 639	1 813 026	251 054
	2008	391 408[6]	22 642	12 541	4 121	10 201	984	1 526	1 832 459	257 246
	2009	402 882[6]	24 206	12 570	4 370	10 248	890	1 561	1 915 880	260 965
Cook Islands	2006	...	...	...	...	...	...	...	...	32
Iles Cook	2007	...	...	...	...	...	...	...	...	34
	2008	...	...	...	...	...	...	...	...	34
	2009	...	...	...	...	...	...	...	...	33
Fiji	2006	...	...	...	...	...	...	...	...	840
Fidji	2007	...	...	...	...	...	...	...	...	833
	2008	...	...	...	...	...	...	...	...	794
	2009	...	...	...	...	...	...	...	...	802
French Polynesia *	2006	...	...	...	...	...	...	...	...	657
Polynésie française *	2007	...	...	...	...	...	...	...	...	687
	2008	...	...	...	...	...	...	...	...	716
	2009	...	...	...	...	...	...	...	...	732
Guam	2006	...	...	...	...	...	...	...	...	1 891
Guam	2007	...	...	...	...	...	...	...	...	1 879
	*2008	...	...	...	...	...	...	...	...	1 870
	2009	...	...	...	...	...	...	...	...	1 868
Kiribati	2006	...	...	...	...	...	...	...	...	24
Kiribati	2007	...	...	...	...	...	...	...	...	24
	2008	...	...	...	...	...	...	...	...	23
	*2009	...	...	...	...	...	...	...	...	24
Marshall Islands	2006	...	...	...	...	...	...	...	...	100
Iles Marshall	*2007	...	...	...	...	...	...	...	...	106
	*2008	...	...	...	...	...	...	...	...	109
	*2009	...	...	...	...	...	...	...	...	111
Nauru *	2006	...	...	...	...	...	...	...	...	33
Nauru *	2007	...	...	...	...	...	...	...	...	35
	2008	...	...	...	...	...	...	...	...	35
	2009	...	...	...	...	...	...	...	...	37
New Caledonia	2006	...	...	...	...	...	...	...	...	1 872
Nouvelle-Calédonie	2007	...	...	...	...	...	...	...	...	1 926
	2008	...	...	...	...	...	...	...	...	1 875
	2009	...	...	...	...	...	...	...	...	1 939
New Zealand	2006	5 673[6]	1 003	1 482	909	1 820	381	135	154 026	43 602
Nouvelle-Zélande	2007	4 834[6]	2 009	1 423	837	1 731	400	100	169 570	43 750
	2008	4 831[6]	2 811	1 503	891	1 778	509	74	159 992	43 850
	2009	4 564[6]	2 605	1 416	867	1 723	558	71	165 066	43 472
Niue *	2006	...	...	...	...	...	...	...	...	3
Nioué *	2007	...	...	...	...	...	...	...	...	3
	2008	...	...	...	...	...	...	...	...	3
	2009	...	...	...	...	...	...	...	...	3
Palau *	2006	...	...	...	...	...	...	...	...	151
Palaos *	2007	...	...	...	...	...	...	...	...	154
	2008	...	...	...	...	...	...	...	...	152
	2009	...	...	...	...	...	...	...	...	152
Papua New Guinea	2006	...	2 867[4]	79	106	530	105	22	10 852	3 012
Papouasie-Nvl-Guinée	2007	...	1 940[4]	45	78	395	72	22	*10 020	3 112
	2008	...	2 083[4]	41	83	359	120	7	*10 578	3 131
	2009	...	1 994[4]	37	79	406	94	9	*10 578	*3 131

Region, country or area Région, pays ou zone	Year Année	Hard coal, lignite and peat Houille, lignite et tourbe	Crude petroleum and NGL Pétrole brut et LGN	Motor gasoline Essence auto	Jet fuel Carbu-réacteurs	Gas-diesel oil Gazole/carburant diesel	Residual fuel oil Mazout résiduel	Liquified petroleum gas Gaz de pétrole liquéfiés	Natural gas Gaz naturel Terajoules Térajoules	Electricity Electricité Million kWh Millions kWh
					Thousand metric tons – Milliers de tonnes					
Samoa Samoa	2006	...	...	...	...	...	...	...	...	116
	*2007	...	...	...	...	...	...	...	...	118
	*2008	...	...	...	...	...	...	...	...	120
	*2009	...	...	...	...	...	...	...	...	122
Solomon Islands Iles Salomon	2006	...	...	...	...	...	...	...	...	75
	2007	...	...	...	...	...	...	...	...	85
	2008	...	...	...	...	...	...	...	...	86
	2009	...	...	...	...	...	...	...	...	84
Tonga * Tonga *	2006	...	...	...	...	...	...	...	...	45
	2007	...	...	...	...	...	...	...	...	43
	2008	...	...	...	...	...	...	...	...	44
	2009	...	...	...	...	...	...	...	...	44
Tuvalu Tuvalu	2006	...	...	...	...	...	...	...	...	4
	2007	...	...	...	...	...	...	...	...	4
	2008	...	...	...	...	...	...	...	...	4
	*2009	...	...	...	...	...	...	...	...	5
Vanuatu Vanuatu	*2006	...	...	...	...	...	...	...	...	51
	*2007	...	...	...	...	...	...	...	...	52
	2008	...	...	...	...	...	...	...	...	69
	2009	...	...	...	...	...	...	...	...	69
Wallis and Futuna Islands Iles Wallis et Futuna	2006	...	...	...	...	...	...	...	...	20
	2007	...	...	...	...	...	...	...	...	20
	2008	...	...	...	...	...	...	...	...	20
	2009	...	...	...	...	...	...	...	...	20

Source:
United Nations Statistics Division, New York, the energy statistics database, last accessed May 2012.

Source:
Organisation des Nations Unies, Division de statistique, New York, la base de données pour les statistiques de l'énergie, dernier accès mai 2012.

1	Hardcoal and peat only.
2	Hard coal only.
3	Peat only.
4	Crude petroleum only.
5	Natural gas liquids only.
6	Hardcoal and lignite only.
7	For statistical purposes, the data for China do not include those for the Hong Kong Special Administrative Region (Hong Kong SAR), Macao Special Administrative Region (Macao SAR) and Taiwan Province of China.
8	Lignite only.
9	Lignite and peat only.
10	Including Monaco.
11	Including San Marino.
12	Including Svalbard and Jan Mayen Islands.
13	Including Liechtenstein.

1	Houille et tourbe seulement.
2	Houille seulement.
3	Tourbe seulement.
4	Pétrole brut seulement.
5	Liquides de gaz naturel seulement.
6	Houille et lignite seulement.
7	Pour la présentation des statistiques, les données pour la Chine ne comprennent pas la Région Administrative Spéciale de Hong Kong (Hong Kong RAS), la Région Administrative Spéciale de Macao (Macao RAS) et la province de Taiwan.
8	Lignite seulement.
9	Lignite et tourbe seulement.
10	Y compris Monaco.
11	Y compris Saint-Marin.
12	Y compris îles Svalbard et Jan Mayen.
13	Y compris Liechtenstein.

47

Land
As of 2009, thousand hectares

Terres
En 2009, milliers d'hectares

Country or area Pays ou zone	Area – Superficie				Net change from 2000 to 2009 Variation nette de 2000 à 2009		
	Total land Superficie totale	Arable land Terres arables	Permanent crops Cultures permanentes	Forest cover Superficie forestière	Arable land Terres arables	Permanent crops Cultures permanentes	Forest cover Superficie forestière
World [1] Monde [1]	13 003 468	1 381 204	152 150	4 038 719	-3 562	19 294	-46 449
Africa [1] Afrique [1]	2 964 679	224 418	28 826	677 898	25 723	3 856	-30 666
Algeria Algérie	238 174	7 500[2]	935[2]	1 501[2]	-162[2]	405[2]	-78[2]
Angola Angola	124 670	4 000[2]	290[2]	58 605[2]	1 000[2]	-10[2]	-1 123[2]
Benin [2] Bénin [2]	11 062	2 450	300	4 611	70	35	-450
Botswana [2] Botswana [2]	56 673	250	2	11 588	-100	1	-947
Burkina Faso [2] Burkina Faso [2]	27 360	5 900	65	5 709	1 860	5	-539
Burundi [2] Burundi [2]	2 568	900	350	174	-60	-10	-24
Cameroon Cameroun	47 271	5 963	1 400[2]	20 136[2]	3	200[2]	-1 980[2]
Cape Verde Cap-Vert	403	60[2]	3[2]	85[2]	16[2]	1[2]	3[2]
Central African Rep. Rép. centrafricaine	62 298	1 950[2]	85[2]	22 635[2]	20[2]	-9[2]	-268[2]
Chad [2] Tchad [2]	125 920	4 300	32	11 604	780	2	-713
Comoros Comores	186	80[2]	60[2]	3[2]	0[2]	10[2]	-5[2]
Congo [2] Congo [2]	34 150	500	60	22 423	10	10	-133
Côte d'Ivoire [2] Côte d'Ivoire [2]	31 800	2 800	4 300	10 403	0	500	75
Dem. Rep. of the Congo [2] Rép. dém. du Congo [2]	226 705	6 700	750	154 446	0	-50	-2 803
Djibouti [2] Djibouti [2]	2 318	2	...	6	1	...	0
Egypt Egypte	99 545[2]	2 884[2]	805	69[2]	83[2]	315	10[2]
Equatorial Guinea Guinée équatoriale	2 805	132[2]	70[2]	1 638[2]	2[2]	-30[2]	-105[2]
Eritrea [2] Erythrée [2]	10 100	690	2	1 536	130	-1	-40
Ethiopia Ethiopie	100 000[2]	13 948	1 037	12 437[2]	3 948	375	-1 268[2]
Gabon Gabon	25 767	325[2]	150[2]	22 000[2]	0[2]	-20[2]	0[2]
Gambia [2] Gambie [2]	1 000	400	5	478	120	0	17
Ghana [2] Ghana [2]	22 754	4 400	2 800	5 055	450	650	-1 039

47

Land *(continued)*
As of 2009, thousand hectares
Terres *(suite)*
En 2009, milliers d'hectares

Country or area Pays ou zone	Area – Superficie				Net change from 2000 to 2009 Variation nette de 2000 à 2009		
	Total land Superficie totale	Arable land Terres arables	Permanent crops Cultures permanentes	Forest cover Superficie forestière	Arable land Terres arables	Permanent crops Cultures permanentes	Forest cover Superficie forestière
Guinea [2] Guinée [2]	24 572	2 850	690	6 580	701	50	-324
Guinea-Bissau [2] Guinée-Bissau [2]	2 812	300	250	2 032	0	2	-88
Kenya [2] Kenya [2]	56 914	5 400	650	3 478	509	170	-104
Lesotho Lesotho	3 036	335	4[2]	44[2]	5	0[2]	2[2]
Liberia [2] Libéria [2]	9 632	400	210	4 359	20	0	-270
Libyan Arab Jamah. [2] Jamah. arabe libyenne [2]	175 954	1 750	300	217	-65	-35	0
Madagascar [2] Madagascar [2]	58 154	2 950	600	12 610	50	0	-512
Malawi Malawi	9 428	3 600[2]	122[2]	3 270[2]	850[2]	2[2]	-297[2]
Mali [2] Mali [2]	122 019	6 361	100	12 569	1 772	15	-712
Mauritania Mauritanie	103 070	390[2]	11[2]	247[2]	-98[2]	-1[2]	-70[2]
Mauritius Maurice	203	87[2]	4[2]	35[2]	-13[2]	0[2]	-4[2]
Mayotte Mayotte	38	7[2]	13[2]	14[2]	0[2]	0[2]	-2[2]
Morocco [2] Maroc [2]	44 630	8 055	1 000	5 121	-712	115	104
Mozambique [2] Mozambique [2]	78 638	5 050	250	39 233	1 150	0	-1 955
Namibia [2] Namibie [2]	82 329	800	8	7 364	-16	4	-668
Niger [2] Niger [2]	126 670	14 940	60	1 216	960	40	-112
Nigeria [2] Nigéria [2]	91 077	34 000	3 000	9 451	4 000	350	-3 686
Réunion Réunion	250[2]	33	3	87[2]	-4	-1	0[2]
Rwanda [2] Rwanda [2]	2 467	1 300	280	425	400	30	81
Saint Helena [2,3] Sainte-Hélène [2,3]	39	4	...	2	0	...	0
Sao Tome and Principe [2] Sao Tomé-et-Principe [2]	96	10	45	27	4	0	0
Senegal [2] Sénégal [2]	19 253	3 850	55	8 513	800	0	-385
Seychelles [2] Seychelles [2]	46	1	2	41	0	-1	0
Sierra Leone [2] Sierra Leone [2]	7 162	1 085	130	2 746	595	10	-176
Somalia [2] Somalie [2]	62 734	1 000	28	6 824	-43	4	-691
South Africa [2] Afrique du Sud [2]	121 447	14 350	950	9 241	-403	-9	0

47

Land *(continued)*
As of 2009, thousand hectares
Terres *(suite)*
En 2009, milliers d'hectares

Country or area Pays ou zone	Area – Superficie				Net change from 2000 to 2009 Variation nette de 2000 à 2009		
	Total land Superficie totale	Arable land Terres arables	Permanent crops Cultures permanentes	Forest cover Superficie forestière	Arable land Terres arables	Permanent crops Cultures permanentes	Forest cover Superficie forestière
Sudan (former) Soudan (anc.)	237 600	20 160	231	70 003[2]	3 927	114	-488[2]
Swaziland[2] Swaziland[2]	1 720	175	15	559	-3	2	41
Togo[2] Togo[2]	5 439	2 200	180	307	-310	60	-179
Tunisia Tunisie	15 536[2]	2 707[2]	2 229	940[2]	-157[2]	103	103[2]
Uganda Ouganda	19 981	6 600[2]	2 250[2]	3 076[2]	1 300[2]	150[2]	-793[2]
United Rep. of Tanzania[2] Rép.-Unie de Tanzanie[2]	88 580	10 000	1 500	33 831	1 200	300	-3 631
Western Sahara Sahara occidental	26 600	4[2]	...	707[2]	-1[2]	...	0[2]
Zambia[2] Zambie[2]	74 339	3 350	35	49 635	534	3	-1 499
Zimbabwe[2] Zimbabwe[2]	38 685	4 180	120	15 951	600	0	-2 943
America, North[1] **Amérique du Nord[1]**	**2 132 992**	**244 707**	**16 105**	**705 383**	**-13 031**	**1 321**	**-114**
Anguilla Anguilla	9	...	...	6[2]	...	...	0[2]
Antigua and Barbuda Antigua-et-Barbuda	44	8[2]	1[2]	10[2]	0[2]	0[2]	0[2]
Aruba Aruba	18	2[2]	...	0[2]	0[2]	...	0[2]
Bahamas[2] Bahamas[2]	1 001	8	4	515	1	0	0
Barbados Barbade	43	16[2]	1[2]	8[2]	0[2]	0[2]	0[2]
Belize[2] Belize[2]	2 281	70	32	1 412	6	-3	-77
Bermuda Bermudes	5	1	...	1[2]	0	...	0[2]
British Virgin Islands Iles Vierges britanniques	15	1[2]	1[2]	4[2]	0[2]	0[2]	0[2]
Canada Canada	909 351	45 100[2]	7 050[2]	310 134[2]	-710[2]	682[2]	0[2]
Cayman Islands Iles Caïmanes	24	0[2]	1[2]	13[2]	0[2]	0[2]	0[2]
Costa Rica[2] Costa Rica[2]	5 106	200	300	2 582	-10	20	206
Cuba[2] Cuba[2]	10 644	3 650	375	2 835	146	-175	400
Dominica Dominique	75	6[2]	17[2]	45[2]	1[2]	3[2]	-2[2]
Dominican Republic[2] Rép. dominicaine[2]	4 832	800	470	1 972	-68	20	0
El Salvador[2] El Salvador[2]	2 072	677	230	291	27	-20	-41
Greenland Groenland	41 045	...	...	0[2]	...	...	0[2]

Land *(continued)*
As of 2009, thousand hectares
Terres *(suite)*
En 2009, milliers d'hectares

Country or area Pays ou zone	Area – Superficie				Net change from 2000 to 2009 Variation nette de 2000 à 2009		
	Total land Superficie totale	Arable land Terres arables	Permanent crops Cultures permanentes	Forest cover Superficie forestière	Arable land Terres arables	Permanent crops Cultures permanentes	Forest cover Superficie forestière
Grenada Grenade	34	3^2	9^2	17^2	2^2	-1^2	0^2
Guadeloupe Guadeloupe	169^2	21	3	65^2	2	-3	-2^2
Guatemala[2] Guatemala[2]	10 716	1 500	945	3 713	105	375	-495
Haiti[2] Haïti[2]	2 756	1 050	300	102	150	0	-7
Honduras[2] Honduras[2]	11 189	1 020	410	5 312	-48	51	-1 080
Jamaica[2] Jamaïque[2]	1 083	120	100	338	-20	-10	-3
Martinique Martinique	106^2	11	7	49^2	-1	-3	0^2
Mexico Mexique	194 395	$25\ 133^2$	$2\ 700^2$	$64\ 957^2$	33^2	400^2	$-1\ 794^2$
Montserrat Montserrat	10	2^2	...	3^2	0^2	...	0^2
Netherlands Antilles Antilles néerlandaises	80	8^2	...	1^2	0^2	...	0^2
Nicaragua Nicaragua	12 034	$1\ 900^2$	230^2	$3\ 184^2$	-17^2	-4^2	-630^2
Panama[2] Panama[2]	7 434	548	147	3 263	0	0	-106
Puerto Rico[2] Porto Rico[2]	887	60	40	543	0	-2	79
Saint Kitts and Nevis Saint-Kitts-et-Nevis	26	4	0	11^2	-3	0	0^2
Saint Lucia[2] Sainte-Lucie[2]	61	3	7	47	1	-5	0
Saint Pierre and Miquelon[2] Saint-Pierre-et-Miquelon[2]	23	3	...	3	0	...	0
Saint Vincent-Grenadines Saint Vincent-Grenadines	39	5^2	3^2	27^2	0^2	0^2	1^2
Trinidad and Tobago Trinité-et-Tobago	513	25^2	22^2	227^2	-10^2	-3^2	-6^2
Turks and Caicos Islands Iles Turques et Caïques	95	1^2	...	34^2	0^2	...	0^2
United States Etats-Unis	914 742	$162\ 751^2$	$2\ 700^2$	$303\ 639^2$	$-12\ 617^2$	0^2	$3\ 444^2$
United States Virgin Is. Iles Vierges américaines	35	1^2	1^2	20^2	-1^2	0^2	-2^2
America, South[1] **Amérique du Sud[1]**	**1 756 239**	**112 750**	**13 510**	**867 932**	**6 759**	**-167**	**-36 390**
Argentina[2] Argentine[2]	273 669	31 000	1 000	29 640	3 100	0	-2 221
Bolivia (Plur. State of) Bolivie (État plur. de)	108 330	$3\ 735^2$	219^2	$57\ 504^2$	735^2	51^2	$-2\ 587^2$
Brazil[2] Brésil[2]	845 942	61 200	7 300	521 716	3 500	-200	-24 227
Chile[2] Chili[2]	74 353	1 270	457	16 193	-480	97	359

47

Land *(continued)*
As of 2009, thousand hectares
Terres *(suite)*
En 2009, milliers d'hectares

Country or area Pays ou zone	Area – Superficie				Net change from 2000 to 2009 Variation nette de 2000 à 2009		
	Total land Superficie totale	Arable land Terres arables	Permanent crops Cultures permanentes	Forest cover Superficie forestière	Arable land Terres arables	Permanent crops Cultures permanentes	Forest cover Superficie forestière
Colombia Colombie	110 950	1 775[2]	1 579[2]	60 600[2]	-1 043[2]	-148[2]	-909[2]
Ecuador Equateur	24 836[2]	1 199	1 349	10 063[2]	-417	-14	-1 778[2]
Falkland Is. (Malvinas) Iles Falkland (Malvinas)	1 217	...	...	0[2]	...	...	0[2]
French Guiana Guyane française	8 220[2]	12	4	8 086[2]	-1	0	-32[2]
Guyana[2] Guyana[2]	19 685	420	25	15 205	-30	-3	0
Paraguay[2] Paraguay[2]	39 730	3 800	100	17 761	780	10	-1 607
Peru[2] Pérou[2]	128 000	3 650	790	68 142	-50	205	-1 071
Suriname Suriname	15 600	58	6[2]	14 762[2]	1	-4[2]	-14[2]
Uruguay Uruguay	17 502	1 881[2]	31	1 699[2]	508	-11[2]	287[2]
Venezuela (Boliv. Rep. of)[2] Venezuela (Rép. boliv. du)[2]	88 205	2 750	650	46 563	155	-150	-2 588
Asia[1] **Asie[1]**	**3 093 557**	**473 206**	**76 405**	**590 819**	**-12 264**	**14 987**	**20 655**
Afghanistan Afghanistan	65 223[2]	7 793	117	1 350[2]	110	47	0[2]
Armenia Arménie	2 848[2]	458[2]	53	266[2]	8[2]	15	-38[2]
Azerbaijan Azerbaïdjan	8 262	1 874	227	936[2]	48	-10	0[2]
Bahrain Bahreïn	76	1[2]	3[2]	1[2]	-1[2]	-1[2]	0[2]
Bangladesh[2] Bangladesh[2]	13 017	7 569	980	1 445	-811	560	-23
Bhutan Bhoutan	3 839	75[2]	25[2]	3 238[2]	-55[2]	1[2]	97[2]
Brunei Darussalam[2] Brunéi Darussalam[2]	527	3	5	382	1	1	-15
Cambodia[2] Cambodge[2]	17 652	3 900	155	10 221	200	15	-1 325
China[2,4] Chine[2,4]	932 749	109 999	14 321	204 097	-10 972	3 090	27 097
Cyprus Chypre	924	87	34	173[2]	-11	-8	2[2]
Dem. P. R. Korea[2] R. p. dém. de Corée[2]	12 041	2 650	205	5 793	50	5	-1 140
Georgia[2] Géorgie[2]	6 949	448	120	2 745	-345	-149	-23
India Inde	297 319[2]	157 923[2]	11 700	68 289[2]	-4 794[2]	2 500	2 899[2]
Indonesia[2] Indonésie[2]	181 157	23 600	19 000	95 117	3 100	5 000	-4 292
Iran (Islamic Rep. of) Iran (Rép. islamique d')	162 855	17 205	1 786	11 075	2 281	426	0

47

Land *(continued)*
As of 2009, thousand hectares
Terres *(suite)*
En 2009, milliers d'hectares

Country or area Pays ou zone	Area – Superficie				Net change from 2000 to 2009 Variation nette de 2000 à 2009		
	Total land Superficie totale	Arable land Terres arables	Permanent crops Cultures permanentes	Forest cover Superficie forestière	Arable land Terres arables	Permanent crops Cultures permanentes	Forest cover Superficie forestière
Iraq[2] Iraq[2]	43 432	4 500	250	825	-500	-50	7
Israel Israël	2 164	304[2]	78	154[2]	-34[2]	-8	1[2]
Japan Japon	36 450[2]	4 294	315	24 970[2]	-180	-41	94[2]
Jordan Jordanie	8 878	201	82	98[2]	11	-6	0[2]
Kazakhstan[2] Kazakhstan[2]	269 970	23 400	80	3 315	1 865	-56	-50
Kuwait Koweït	1 782	11[2]	4[2]	6[2]	1[2]	2[2]	1[2]
Kyrgyzstan Kirghizistan	19 180[2]	1 276	75	937[2]	-80	8	79[2]
Lao People's Dem. Rep. Rép. dém. pop. lao	23 080[2]	1 360[2]	108	15 829[2]	483[2]	27	-703[2]
Lebanon[2] Liban[2]	1 023	145	143	137	16	2	6
Malaysia[2] Malaisie[2]	32 855	1 800	5 785	20 543	-20	0	-1 048
Maldives Maldives	30	4[2]	3[2]	1[2]	0[2]	-2[2]	0[2]
Mongolia[2] Mongolie[2]	155 356	960	2	10 980	-214	0	-737
Myanmar[2] Myanmar[2]	65 352	11 035	1 100	32 083	1 126	511	-2 785
Nepal[2] Népal[2]	14 335	2 400	120	3 636	46	15	-264
Occupied Palestinian Terr.[2] Terr. palestinien occupé[2]	602	100	117	9	-2	-3	0
Oman Oman	30 950	99	37	2	68	-5	0
Pakistan[2] Pakistan[2]	77 088	20 430	850	1 730	-862	192	-386
Philippines Philippines	29 817	5 400[2]	5 050[2]	7 610[2]	366[2]	400[2]	493[2]
Qatar Qatar	1 159	12[2]	3[2]	0[2]	-1[2]	0[2]	0[2]
Republic of Korea République de Corée	9 710[2]	1 595[2]	201	6 229[2]	-123[2]	1	-59[2]
Saudi Arabia[2] Arabie saoudite[2]	214 969	3 200	235	977	-392	42	0
Singapore[2] Singapour[2]	70	1	^0	2	-1	0	0
Sri Lanka Sri Lanka	6 271	1 200[2]	970[2]	1 875[2]	285[2]	-25[2]	-207[2]
Syrian Arab Republic Rép. arabe syrienne	18 363	4 670	994	485[2]	128	184	53[2]
Tajikistan[2] Tadjikistan[2]	13 996	742	133	410	-42	31	0
Thailand[2] Thaïlande[2]	51 089	15 300	3 695	18 957	-354	315	-47

47

Land *(continued)*
As of 2009, thousand hectares
Terres *(suite)*
En 2009, milliers d'hectares

Country or area Pays ou zone	Area – Superficie				Net change from 2000 to 2009 Variation nette de 2000 à 2009		
	Total land Superficie totale	Arable land Terres arables	Permanent crops Cultures permanentes	Forest cover Superficie forestière	Arable land Terres arables	Permanent crops Cultures permanentes	Forest cover Superficie forestière
Timor-Leste[2] Timor-Leste[2]	1 487	165	60	753	45	-7	-101
Turkey Turquie	76 963	21 351	2 943	11 215[2]	-2 475	390	1 069[2]
Turkmenistan[2] Turkménistan[2]	46 993	1 850	60	4 127	230	-5	0
United Arab Emirates[2] Emirats arabes unis[2]	8 360	64	200	316	4	13	6
Uzbekistan[2] Ouzbékistan[2]	42 540	4 301	350	3 279	-174	0	67
Viet Nam[2] Viet Nam[2]	31 007	6 280	3 350	13 653	80	1 412	1 928
Yemen Yémen	52 797[2]	1 171[2]	281	549[2]	-374[2]	157	0[2]
Europe[1] **Europe[1]**	**2 207 347**	**277 971**	**15 753**	**1 004 230**	**-9 624**	**-880**	**5 991**
Albania Albanie	2 740	612	87	777[2]	34	-34	8[2]
Andorra Andorre	47	1[2]	...	16[2]	0[2]	...	0[2]
Austria Autriche	8 244	1 371	66	3 882[2]	-28	-5	44[2]
Belarus Bélarus	20 282	5 544	120	8 591[2]	-589	-4	318[2]
Belgium Belgique	3 028[2]	840	22	677[2]	-22	1	9[2]
Bosnia and Herzegovina Bosnie-Herzégovine	5 100	997	102	2 185[2]	-3	2	0[2]
Bulgaria Bulgarie	10 856	3 139	172	3 872[2]	-387	-80	497[2]
Channel Islands Iles Anglo-Normandes	19	4[2]	...	1[2]	0[2]	...	0[2]
Croatia Croatie	5 596	869	88	1 917[2]	27	19	32[2]
Czech Republic République tchèque	7 725	3 180	76	2 655[2]	-63	...	18[2]
Denmark Danemark	4 243	2 431	6	542[2]	150	-2	56[2]
Estonia Estonie	4 239	596	8	2 224[2]	-247	-4	-19[2]
Faeroe Islands Iles Féroé	140	3[2]	...	0[2]	0[2]	...	0[2]
Finland Finlande	30 390	2 257	5	22 157[2]	74	-4	-302[2]
France France	54 766[2]	18 346[2]	1 050	15 906[2]	-94[2]	-92	553[2]
Germany Allemagne	34 861	11 945	200	11 076[2]	141	-16	0[2]
Gibraltar Gibraltar	1	...	...	0[2]	...	...	0[2]
Greece Grèce	12 890[2]	2 551	1 148	3 873[2]	-190	35	272[2]

Land *(continued)*
As of 2009, thousand hectares
Terres *(suite)*
En 2009, milliers d'hectares

Country or area Pays ou zone	Area – Superficie				Net change from 2000 to 2009 Variation nette de 2000 à 2009		
	Total land Superficie totale	Arable land Terres arables	Permanent crops Cultures permanentes	Forest cover Superficie forestière	Arable land Terres arables	Permanent crops Cultures permanentes	Forest cover Superficie forestière
Hungary Hongrie	9 053	4 585	194	2 020[2]	-17	-7	113[2]
Iceland Islande	10 025	7	...	29[2]	0	0	11[2]
Ireland Irlande	6 889	1 089	3	730[2]	12	1	95[2]
Isle of Man Ile de Man	57	5[2]	...	3[2]	-4[2]	...	0[2]
Italy Italie	29 414[2]	6 880[2]	2 605	9 071[2]	-1 599[2]	-200	702[2]
Latvia Lettonie	6 218	1 168	6	3 343[2]	198	-6	102[2]
Liechtenstein Liechtenstein	16	4[2]	...	7[2]	-1[2]	...	0[2]
Lithuania Lituanie	6 268	2 054	28	2 152[2]	-824	-15	132[2]
Luxembourg Luxembourg	259	62	2	87[2]	0	1	0[2]
Malta Malte	32	8	1	0[2]	0	0	0[2]
Montenegro[5] Monténégro[5]	1 345[2]	173	16	543[2]	173	16	543[2]
Netherlands Pays-Bas	3 373	1 055	36	365[2]	145	2	5[2]
Norway Norvège	30 547	835	5	9 989[2]	-44	0	688[2]
Poland Pologne	30 420	12 539	400	9 310[2]	-1 454	63	251[2]
Portugal Portugal	9 147[2]	1 125	778	3 452[2]	-507	13	32[2]
Republic of Moldova République de Moldova	3 289	1 817	301	381[2]	-10	-34	57[2]
Romania Roumanie	23 006	8 789	362	6 537[2]	-592	-165	171[2]
Russian Federation[2] Fédération de Russie[2]	1 637 687	121 750	1 791	809 030	-2 624	-73	-239
San Marino Saint-Marin	6	1[2]	...	0[2]	0[2]	...	0[2]
Serbia[5] Serbie[5]	8 746[2]	3 298	298	2 666[2]	3 298	298	2 666[2]
Slovakia Slovaquie	4 809	1 382	24	1 933[2]	-146	-23	12[2]
Slovenia Slovénie	2 014	175	26	1 251[2]	2	-5	18[2]
Spain Espagne	49 880[2]	12 497	4 719	17 997[2]	-903	-185	1 010[2]
Sweden Suède	41 034	2 634[2]	9[2]	28 203[2]	-69[2]	6[2]	814[2]
Switzerland Suisse	4 000[2]	407	23	1 235[2]	-6	-1	41[2]
TFYR of Macedonia L'ex-R.Y. Macédoine	2 522	420	35	993[2]	-135	-9	35[2]

47 Land *(continued)*
As of 2009, thousand hectares
Terres *(suite)*
En 2009, milliers d'hectares

Country or area Pays ou zone	Area – Superficie				Net change from 2000 to 2009 Variation nette de 2000 à 2009		
	Total land Superficie totale	Arable land Terres arables	Permanent crops Cultures permanentes	Forest cover Superficie forestière	Arable land Terres arables	Permanent crops Cultures permanentes	Forest cover Superficie forestière
Ukraine Ukraine	57 932	32 478	898	9 679[2]	-86	-34	169[2]
United Kingdom Royaume-Uni	24 193	6 049	43	2 874[2]	173	-9	81[2]
Oceania[1] **Océanie[1]**	**848 655**	**48 154**	**1 551**	**192 456**	**-1 125**	**177**	**-5 925**
American Samoa[6] Samoa américaines[6]	20	2[2]	3[2]	18[2]	0[2]	0[2]	0[2]
Australia Australie	768 230	47 161[2]	350[2]	150 224[2]	-143[2]	54[2]	-4 696[2]
Cook Islands Iles Cook	24	2[2]	1[2]	16[2]	-1[2]	-2[2]	0[2]
Fiji[2] Fidji[2]	1 827	160	83	1 011	-10	0	30
French Polynesia[2] Polynésie française[2]	366	3	22	150	-1	2	45
Guam Guam	54	1[2]	10[2]	26[2]	-1[2]	0[2]	0[2]
Kiribati[2] Kiribati[2]	81	2	32	12	0	0	0
Marshall Islands[6] Iles Marshall[6]	18	2[2]	8[2]	13[2]	1[2]	0[2]	0[2]
Micronesia (Fed. States of) Micronésie (Etats féd. de)	70	2[2]	17[2]	64[2]	-1[2]	0[2]	0[2]
Nauru Nauru	2	...	0[2]	0[2]	...	0[2]	0[2]
New Caledonia[2] Nouvelle-Calédonie[2]	1 828	7	5	839	1	1	0
New Zealand Nouvelle-Zélande	26 331	471	71	8 277[2]	-1 029	21	11[2]
Niue Nioué	26	1[2]	3[2]	19[2]	0[2]	0[2]	-1[2]
Norfolk Island Ile Norfolk	4	...	...	0[2]	...	...	0[2]
Northern Mariana Islands[2] Iles Mariannes du Nord[2]	46	1	1	30	0	0	-1
Palau[2] Palaos[2]	46	1	2	40	0	0	1
Papua New Guinea[2] Papouasie-Nvl-Guinée[2]	45 286	260	700	28 868	55	80	-1 265
Pitcairn Pitcairn	5	...	...	4[2]	...	...	0[2]
Samoa[2] Samoa[2]	283	25	39	171	0	4	0
Solomon Islands[2] Iles Salomon[2]	2 799	16	60	2 219	2	5	-49
Tokelau Tokélaou	1	...	1[2]	0[2]	...	0[2]	0[2]
Tonga Tonga	72	16[2]	11[2]	9[2]	1[2]	0[2]	0[2]
Tuvalu Tuvalu	3	...	2[2]	1[2]	...	0[2]	0[2]

47
Land *(continued)*
As of 2009, thousand hectares
Terres *(suite)*
En 2009, milliers d'hectares

Country or area Pays ou zone	Area – Superficie				Net change from 2000 to 2009 Variation nette de 2000 à 2009			
	Total land Superficie totale	Arable land Terres arables	Permanent crops Cultures permanentes	Forest cover Superficie forestière	Arable land Terres arables	Permanent crops Cultures permanentes	Forest cover Superficie forestière	
Vanuatu [2] Vanuatu [2]	1 219	20	125	440	0	12	0	
Wallis and Futuna Islands Iles Wallis et Futuna	14	1 [2]	5 [2]	6 [2]	0 [2]	0 [2]	0 [2]	

Source:
Food and Agriculture Organization of the United Nations (FAO), Rome, FAOSTAT data, last accessed September 2012.

1   May include official, semi-official or estimated data.
2   FAO estimate.
3   Data for Saint Helena include those for Ascension and Tristan da Cunha.
4   For statistical purposes, the data for China do not include those for the Hong Kong Special Administrative Region (Hong Kong SAR), Macao Special Administrative Region (Macao SAR) and Taiwan Province of China.
5   Net change from 2006 to 2009.
6   Due to the use of different data sources and overlaps in definitions and classifications, the sum of individual land use category data may exceed "total land area". Examples of such instances include forest and agriculture land with tree cover - such as rubber plantations, permanent tree crops, range land and agro-forestry and shifting cultivation areas.

Source :
Organisation des Nations Unies pour l'alimentation et l'agriculture (FAO), Rome, données FAOSTAT, dernier accès septembre 2012.

1   Les données peuvent être officielles, semi-officielles ou estimatives.
2   Estimation de la FAO.
3   Les données concernant Sainte-Hélène comprennent celles relatives à Ascension et à Tristan da Cunha.
4   Pour la présentation des statistiques, les données pour la Chine ne comprennent pas la Région Administrative Spéciale de Hong Kong (Hong Kong RAS), la Région Administrative Spéciale de Macao (Macao RAS) et la province de Taiwan.
5   Variation nette de 2006 à 2008.
6   En raison de l'utilisation de différentes sources de données et de recoupements dans les définitions et les classifications, la somme des différentes catégories d'utilisation des sols peut excéder la « superficie totale des terres ». C'est le cas par exemple des zones de forêt et de terres agricoles comprenant un couvert forestier – comme les plantations d'hévéas, les cultures arboricoles pérennes, les zones de pâturage et d'agrosylviculture et les zones de cultures itinérantes.

CO₂ emission estimates
From fossil fuel combustion, cement production and gas flared (thousand metric tons of carbon dioxide)

Estimation des émissions de CO₂
Dues à la combustion de combustibles fossiles, à la production de ciment et au gaz brûlés à la torchère (milliers de tonnes de dioxyde de carbone)

Country or area	1990	2003	2004	2005	2006	2007	2008	2009	Pays ou zone
Afghanistan	2 677	583	733	997	1 272	1 889	3 777	6 315	Afghanistan
Albania	7 488	4 290	4 114	4 602	4 239	4 492	4 129	3 007	Albanie
Algeria	78 896	92 533	89 493	107 128	107 304	112 742	111 304	121 312	Algérie
Andorra	...	535	565	576	546	539	539	517	Andorre
Angola	4 430	9 065	18 793	19 156	22 266	25 152	26 025	26 655	Angola
Anguilla	...	40	44	51	51	59	59	59	Anguilla
Antigua and Barbuda	301	389	407	411	425	436	447	462	Antigua-et-Barbuda
Argentina	112 614	133 127	156 170	155 649	171 179	173 588	182 129	174 718	Argentine
Armenia	...	3 429	3 645	4 360	4 382	5 068	5 556	4 492	Arménie
Aruba	1 841	2 255	2 259	2 274	2 274	2 358	2 288	2 296	Aruba
Australia	287 331	346 476	349 223	367 133	377 382	381 357	393 000	400 194	Australie
Austria	60 726	72 317	71 866	74 510	71 650	69 013	68 232	62 313	Autriche
Azerbaijan	...	30 616	32 090	34 338	39 167	45 544	52 937	49 075	Azerbaïdjan
Bahamas	1 951	1 870	2 153	2 274	2 329	2 420	2 461	2 585	Bahamas
Bahrain	11 885	16 468	17 510	19 208	19 497	22 398	24 301	24 221	Bahreïn
Bangladesh	15 533	33 890	39 794	37 623	48 170	48 481	46 443	51 037	Bangladesh
Barbados	1 074	1 269	1 294	1 353	1 371	1 426	1 503	1 573	Barbade
Belarus	...	53 722	58 038	59 064	61 829	60 282	62 816	60 293	Bélarus
Belgium	108 470	114 836	111 282	108 525	106 834	102 529	104 865	103 593	Belgique
Belize	312	374	381	396	407	425	407	414	Belize
Benin	715	2 321	2 512	2 398	3 876	4 499	4 492	4 855	Bénin
Bermuda	598	510	671	444	521	517	389	466	Bermudes
Bhutan	128	378	308	396	392	392	422	422	Bhoutan
Bolivia (Plurin. State of)	5 504	14 129	13 084	12 468	15 049	12 875	13 872	14 488	Bolivie (État plurin. de)
Bosnia and Herzegovina	...	23 260	24 631	25 632	27 484	28 984	31 210	30 099	Bosnie-Herzégovine
Botswana	2 178	4 265	4 378	4 613	4 609	4 686	4 980	4 430	Botswana
Brazil	208 887	321 622	337 826	347 309	347 668	363 213	387 675	367 147	Brésil
British Virgin Islands	48	77	84	88	99	99	103	110	Iles Vierges britanniques
Brunei Darussalam	6 421	5 357	5 361	5 126	4 822	9 560	10 620	9 281	Brunéi Darussalam
Bulgaria	75 764	47 308	46 787	47 909	48 943	52 812	50 792	42 805	Bulgarie
Burkina Faso	587	1 078	1 104	1 126	1 360	1 646	1 701	1 668	Burkina Faso
Burundi	304	165	198	154	187	176	194	191	Burundi
Cambodia	451	3 128	3 498	3 722	4 074	4 437	4 954	4 613	Cambodge
Cameroon	1 738	3 795	3 957	3 696	3 828	5 761	5 545	6 674	Cameroun
Canada	450 077	553 185	552 349	563 072	550 233	560 802	544 975	513 937	Canada
Cape Verde	88	253	264	293	308	312	308	315	Cap-Vert
Cayman Islands	253	480	488	510	528	535	543	513	Iles Caïmanes
Central African Rep.	198	235	213	213	227	235	235	235	Rép. centrafricaine
Chad	147	381	378	400	407	462	495	414	Tchad
Chile	34 143	55 078	60 047	61 301	62 724	67 344	70 681	66 732	Chili
China	2 460 744	4 525 177	5 288 166	5 790 017	6 414 463	6 791 805	7 037 710	7 687 114	Chine
China, Hong Kong SAR	27 660	40 066	38 415	40 546	38 555	39 963	38 573	36 993	Chine, Hong Kong RAS
China, Macao SAR	1 034	1 536	1 727	1 837	1 632	1 558	1 349	1 467	Chine, Macao RAS
Colombia	57 337	57 422	55 071	60 946	62 940	63 439	66 439	71 231	Colombie

CO_2 emission estimates *(continued)*
From fossil fuel combustion, cement production and gas flared (thousand metric tons of carbon dioxide)

Estimation des émissions de CO_2 *(suite)*
Dues à la combustion de combustibles fossiles, à la production de ciment et au gaz brûlés à la torchère (milliers de tonnes de dioxyde de carbone)

Country or area	1990	2003	2004	2005	2006	2007	2008	2009	Pays ou zone
Comoros	77	99	103	110	121	121	125	125	Comores
Congo	1 188	1 085	1 181	1 613	1 459	1 610	1 672	1 944	Congo
Cook Islands	22	33	55	62	66	66	70	70	Iles Cook
Costa Rica	2 956	6 626	6 931	7 088	7 686	8 573	8 647	8 317	Costa Rica
Côte d'Ivoire	5 798	5 460	7 664	7 825	7 140	6 384	7 015	6 597	Côte d'Ivoire
Croatia	...	23 542	23 047	23 106	23 175	24 400	23 373	21 536	Croatie
Cuba	33 340	25 486	25 005	26 043	27 403	26 729	29 794	31 617	Cuba
Cyprus	4 653	7 748	7 334	7 503	7 789	8 196	8 555	8 199	Chypre
Czech Republic	...	122 379	122 709	120 736	122 786	123 945	116 952	108 121	République tchèque
Dem. P. R. Korea	244 835	78 210	79 926	83 476	85 034	70 758	78 514	75 104	R. p. dém. de Corée
Dem. Rep. of the Congo	4 070	1 698	1 936	2 244	2 384	2 574	2 794	2 695	Rép. dém. du Congo
Denmark	49 747	55 735	50 597	47 099	54 598	49 871	46 850	45 698	Danemark
Djibouti	400	407	458	473	488	488	524	532	Djibouti
Dominica	59	114	110	114	110	150	128	128	Dominique
Dominican Republic	9 571	21 888	18 786	19 615	21 005	21 503	21 100	20 334	Rép. dominicaine
Ecuador	16 835	26 523	28 658	29 299	29 842	30 898	29 670	30 102	Equateur
Egypt	75 944	158 880	160 582	174 641	187 505	199 221	210 321	216 137	Egypte
El Salvador	2 618	6 553	6 366	6 454	6 846	6 927	6 520	6 300	El Salvador
Equatorial Guinea	121	6 018	5 218	4 712	4 752	4 796	4 815	4 815	Guinée équatoriale
Eritrea	...	726	770	766	561	579	414	513	Erythrée
Estonia	...	17 554	17 840	17 462	16 945	19 952	18 383	15 951	Estonie
Ethiopia	3 018	4 947	5 196	5 489	6 021	6 472	7 110	7 888	Ethiopie
Faeroe Islands	623	675	675	682	689	697	708	708	Iles Féroé
Falkland Is. (Malvinas)	37	48	51	51	59	59	59	59	Iles Falkland (Malvinas)
Fiji	818	851	1 137	1 371	1 364	1 206	1 082	847	Fidji
Finland	51 745	68 888	66 970	54 605	66 101	63 916	56 083	53 568	Finlande
France	399 028	387 147	389 707	391 826	382 281	375 684	376 993	363 356	France
French Guiana	814	733	697	660	576	678	693	700	Guyane française
French Polynesia	631	803	796	858	858	854	887	895	Polynésie française
Gabon	4 844	1 335	1 767	2 083	1 977	2 332	2 255	1 624	Gabon
Gambia	191	315	323	323	337	396	411	436	Gambie
Georgia	...	3 773	4 323	5 071	6 150	6 190	6 238	5 845	Géorgie
Germany	...	835 658	828 522	809 597	811 881	787 235	786 652	734 599	Allemagne
Ghana	3 931	7 598	7 275	6 956	9 289	9 578	8 529	7 444	Ghana
Gibraltar	95	356	367	378	392	407	422	433	Gibraltar
Greece	72 724	95 738	97 150	98 675	97 286	98 246	97 817	94 917	Grèce
Greenland	557	535	499	631	579	638	576	576	Groenland
Grenada	110	216	205	216	231	238	246	246	Grenade
Guadeloupe	1 294	2 046	1 834	1 716	1 709	1 742	1 738	1 738	Guadeloupe
Guatemala	5 086	10 502	11 621	12 570	12 699	13 634	12 486	15 203	Guatemala
Guinea	1 056	1 342	1 342	1 181	1 181	1 210	1 214	1 228	Guinée
Guinea-Bissau	253	249	257	264	275	286	282	293	Guinée-Bissau
Guyana	1 140	1 566	1 628	1 434	1 291	1 566	1 558	1 555	Guyana
Haiti	994	1 734	1 988	2 076	2 120	2 398	2 435	2 270	Haïti
Honduras	2 593	6 769	7 367	7 620	6 901	8 632	8 511	7 704	Honduras
Hungary	62 992	59 061	57 356	57 917	57 235	55 859	54 653	48 676	Hongrie

CO$_2$ emission estimates *(continued)*
From fossil fuel combustion, cement production and gas flared (thousand metric tons of carbon dioxide)
Estimation des émissions de CO$_2$ *(suite)*
Dues à la combustion de combustibles fossiles, à la production de ciment et au gaz brûlés à la torchère (milliers de tonnes de dioxyde de carbone)

Country or area	1990	2003	2004	2005	2006	2007	2008	2009	Pays ou zone
Iceland	1 991	2 167	2 233	2 204	2 277	2 340	2 219	2 028	Islande
India	690 577	1 281 914	1 348 525	1 411 128	1 504 365	1 611 404	1 802 158	1 979 425	Inde
Indonesia	149 566	316 792	337 635	341 992	345 120	375 545	412 497	451 782	Indonésie
Iran (Islamic Rep. of)	211 135	418 859	447 480	486 714	505 265	539 364	580 174	602 055	Iran (Rép. islamique d')
Iraq	52 555	91 118	114 084	112 885	114 333	109 849	113 050	109 038	Iraq
Ireland	31 408	43 201	43 810	43 392	43 300	44 583	43 406	41 642	Irlande
Israel	33 535	65 122	63 201	59 211	67 033	67 429	69 310	67 216	Israël
Italy	425 255	468 349	472 768	473 380	470 175	461 129	447 367	400 836	Italie
Jamaica	7 965	10 722	10 715	10 645	12 020	13 480	11 947	8 573	Jamaïque
Japan	1 094 633	1 237 392	1 259 659	1 238 181	1 231 298	1 251 169	1 207 686	1 101 134	Japon
Jordan	10 403	17 470	19 241	21 027	20 733	21 496	21 426	22 548	Jordanie
Kazakhstan	...	153 816	172 158	176 947	192 114	220 042	229 441	225 803	Kazakhstan
Kenya	5 823	6 755	7 624	8 562	9 575	9 831	10 242	12 350	Kenya
Kiribati	22	26	26	26	29	51	51	51	Kiribati
Kuwait	48 313	61 657	63 534	71 547	73 769	75 236	79 757	80 205	Koweït
Kyrgyzstan	...	5 277	5 607	5 222	5 093	6 425	5 695	6 722	Kirghizistan
Lao People's Dem. Rep.	235	1 129	1 423	1 434	1 580	1 668	1 742	1 811	Rép. dém. pop. lao
Latvia	...	7 088	7 132	7 176	7 583	7 928	7 591	6 652	Lettonie
Lebanon	9 098	18 221	16 832	16 391	15 024	15 445	17 030	20 968	Liban
Liberia	484	532	627	741	759	678	576	524	Libéria
Libyan Arab Jamah.	36 780	49 167	50 359	52 101	53 780	54 202	60 384	62 874	Jamah. arabe libyenne
Lithuania	...	12 915	13 330	13 993	14 294	15 137	15 130	12 838	Lituanie
Luxembourg	10 011	9 905	11 269	11 547	11 305	10 752	10 660	10 143	Luxembourg
Madagascar	986	1 701	1 808	1 742	1 683	1 815	1 944	1 822	Madagascar
Malawi	612	957	975	917	953	953	1 155	1 060	Malawi
Malaysia	56 593	160 266	167 333	182 543	170 648	195 480	209 375	198 348	Malaisie
Maldives	154	598	752	678	869	898	972	1 027	Maldives
Mali	422	539	565	568	568	579	594	612	Mali
Malta	2 178	2 582	2 574	2 699	2 574	2 725	2 560	2 497	Malte
Marshall Islands	48	84	88	84	92	99	99	103	Iles Marshall
Martinique	2 068	2 281	2 406	2 494	2 380	2 164	2 142	2 288	Martinique
Mauritania	2 666	1 474	1 632	1 676	1 676	1 914	2 083	2 076	Mauritanie
Mauritius	1 463	3 146	3 194	3 410	3 777	3 887	3 953	3 825	Maurice
Mexico	314 416	405 633	410 744	435 046	441 796	456 798	476 640	446 237	Mexique
Micronesia (Fed. States of)	...	55	55	55	55	62	62	62	Micronésie (Et. féd. de)
Mongolia	10 044	8 034	8 551	8 808	9 443	10 561	10 942	14 503	Mongolie
Montenegro	...	...	...	4 041	4 213	3 715	4 950	3 051	Monténégro
Montserrat	33	70	70	70	77	77	77	77	Montserrat
Morocco	23 542	37 561	43 311	45 760	46 985	49 372	51 254	48 815	Maroc
Mozambique	1 001	1 918	1 922	1 822	1 980	2 461	2 332	2 600	Mozambique
Myanmar	4 276	9 611	11 470	14 543	13 029	13 047	12 772	11 093	Myanmar
Namibia	7	2 362	2 629	2 732	3 029	3 172	4 199	3 586	Namibie
Nauru	132	143	143	143	143	143	143	147	Nauru
Nepal	634	2 952	2 769	3 242	2 662	2 699	3 047	3 517	Népal
Netherlands	164 128	175 041	176 903	172 228	167 201	171 766	173 845	169 650	Pays-Bas
Netherlands Antilles	6 216	5 515	5 787	5 735	5 537	6 227	5 963	6 131	Antilles néerlandaises

48

CO₂ emission estimates *(continued)*
From fossil fuel combustion, cement production and gas flared (thousand metric tons of carbon dioxide)
Estimation des émissions de CO₂ *(suite)*
Dues à la combustion de combustibles fossiles, à la production de ciment et au gaz brûlés à la torchère (milliers de tonnes de dioxyde de carbone)

Country or area	1990	2003	2004	2005	2006	2007	2008	2009	Pays ou zone
New Caledonia	1 624	2 750	2 552	2 901	2 901	2 974	3 333	2 970	Nouvelle-Calédonie
New Zealand	23 681	33 912	33 725	33 964	33 898	33 212	33 685	32 064	Nouvelle-Zélande
Nicaragua	2 549	4 411	4 426	4 320	4 320	4 591	4 411	4 463	Nicaragua
Niger	832	880	964	829	818	829	920	1 159	Niger
Nigeria	45 375	93 138	97 047	104 044	93 325	90 619	92 724	70 234	Nigéria
Niue	4	4	4	4	4	4	4	4	Nioué
Norway	31 364	42 625	42 666	42 365	44 257	45 122	50 326	47 077	Norvège
Occupied Palestinian Terr.	...	1 280	1 867	2 743	2 266	2 325	2 054	2 164	Terr. palestinien occupé
Oman	11 371	33 128	28 771	30 425	40 267	45 324	42 086	41 144	Oman
Pakistan	68 566	118 895	131 620	136 636	145 855	159 386	159 199	161 220	Pakistan
Palau	235	191	187	191	202	209	209	209	Palaos
Panama	3 135	6 153	5 548	5 823	6 586	6 289	6 802	7 844	Panama
Papua New Guinea	2 142	3 968	4 481	4 613	4 595	4 903	3 476	3 480	Papouasie-Nvl-Guinée
Paraguay	2 263	4 070	4 089	3 832	3 986	4 136	4 353	4 518	Paraguay
Peru	21 170	26 380	31 896	37 418	35 346	43 513	41 276	47 356	Pérou
Philippines	41 763	66 908	69 446	69 185	62 009	63 553	68 789	68 551	Philippines
Poland	366 773	304 856	304 988	303 521	319 410	315 201	316 059	298 905	Pologne
Portugal	42 196	61 276	63 175	65 309	59 108	60 865	58 357	57 400	Portugal
Qatar	11 775	36 157	44 393	51 881	56 736	67 293	67 847	70 344	Qatar
Republic of Korea	246 943	466 215	482 585	462 918	470 806	495 837	508 052	509 376	République de Corée
Republic of Moldova	...	4 290	4 554	4 895	4 994	4 686	4 774	4 547	République de Moldova
Réunion	1 452	2 728	2 875	2 857	2 871	2 890	2 923	2 934	Réunion
Romania	158 862	95 940	95 401	94 961	102 001	99 702	94 766	79 486	Roumanie
Russian Federation	...	1 604 973	1 602 963	1 615 684	1 669 603	1 667 576	1 715 665	1 574 386	Fédération de Russie
Rwanda	682	682	689	689	689	715	704	726	Rwanda
Saint Helena	7	11	11	11	11	11	11	11	Sainte-Hélène
Saint Kitts and Nevis	66	220	227	235	235	249	249	260	Saint-Kitts-et-Nevis
Saint Lucia	165	359	356	367	367	385	396	385	Sainte-Lucie
Saint Pierre and Miquelon	92	66	62	66	66	66	66	66	Saint-Pierre-et-Miquelon
Saint Vincent-Grenadines	81	194	194	198	202	202	202	202	Saint Vinc.-Grenadines
Samoa	125	150	154	158	158	161	161	161	Samoa
Sao Tome and Principe	66	110	114	128	128	128	128	128	Sao Tomé-et-Principe
Saudi Arabia	217 948	327 272	395 834	397 642	432 739	393 535	418 240	432 772	Arabie saoudite
Senegal	3 183	5 013	5 280	5 860	4 789	5 335	5 310	4 576	Sénégal
Serbia	...	...	...	50 352	53 758	52 060	52 027	46 252	Serbie
Serbia and Montenegro	...	50 542	55 225	...	...	...	...	...	Serbie-et-Monténégro
Seychelles	114	557	774	697	744	623	682	737	Seychelles
Sierra Leone	389	19 945	4 184	755	1 624	10 136	884	1 415	Sierra Leone
Singapore	46 941	34 653	40 770	49 446	46 908	35 266	31 360	31 896	Singapour
Slovakia	...	39 494	38 749	39 175	38 929	36 600	37 557	33 890	Slovaquie
Slovenia	...	15 486	15 728	15 856	16 234	16 193	17 158	15 291	Slovénie
Solomon Islands	161	180	180	180	180	198	198	198	Iles Salomon
Somalia	18	576	576	579	576	605	609	594	Somalie
South Africa	333 514	380 811	427 132	396 117	424 844	443 648	464 957	499 016	Afrique du Sud
Spain	218 865	321 097	339 429	353 462	350 037	358 237	329 286	288 230	Espagne
Sri Lanka	3 773	10 660	11 965	11 643	11 742	12 460	11 896	12 658	Sri Lanka

48 CO$_2$ emission estimates *(continued)*
From fossil fuel combustion, cement production and gas flared (thousand metric tons of carbon dioxide)
Estimation des émissions de CO$_2$ *(suite)*
Dues à la combustion de combustibles fossiles, à la production de ciment et au gaz brûlés à la torchère (milliers de tonnes de dioxyde de carbone)

Country or area	1990	2003	2004	2005	2006	2007	2008	2009	Pays ou zone
Sudan (former)	5 559	...	11 463	10 898	12 160	13 150	12 024	14 338	Soudan (anc.)
Suriname	1 811	2 241	2 292	2 384	2 450	2 450	2 450	2 472	Suriname
Swaziland	425	1 041	1 030	1 019	1 016	1 063	1 093	1 023	Swaziland
Sweden	51 129	54 781	54 521	51 562	49 571	48 060	49 105	43 744	Suède
Switzerland	42 864	40 205	40 392	41 375	41 877	38 019	40 392	41 598	Suisse
Syrian Arab Republic	37 451	54 286	51 111	50 634	53 590	57 429	59 039	65 313	Rép. arabe syrienne
Tajikistan	...	2 076	2 571	2 464	2 703	3 286	3 102	2 835	Tadjikistan
Thailand	95 833	245 674	267 761	275 164	283 987	275 634	283 723	271 721	Thaïlande
TFYR of Macedonia	...	11 309	11 192	11 280	10 939	11 379	11 848	11 342	L'ex-R.Y. Macédoine
Timor-Leste	...	161	176	176	180	183	191	183	Timor-Leste
Togo	774	1 463	1 397	1 338	1 221	1 316	1 456	1 485	Togo
Tonga	77	176	172	172	172	176	176	176	Tonga
Trinidad and Tobago	16 960	27 697	30 993	28 581	32 152	35 057	47 088	47 781	Trinité-et-Tobago
Tunisia	13 267	21 397	22 446	22 801	23 128	23 869	25 013	25 156	Tunisie
Turkey	145 855	218 509	225 407	237 369	261 571	284 658	285 274	277 845	Turquie
Turkmenistan	...	43 161	43 337	45 375	46 197	53 494	55 027	48 162	Turkménistan
Turks and Caicos Islands	...	103	103	121	143	158	158	161	Iles Turques et Caïques
Uganda	803	1 709	1 852	2 285	2 655	3 128	3 161	3 480	Ouganda
Ukraine	...	352 259	343 121	339 029	327 797	328 857	323 657	272 176	Ukraine
United Arab Emirates	52 009	106 365	113 442	116 281	121 590	136 750	153 050	156 823	Emirats arabes unis
United Kingdom	570 219	540 640	540 409	541 990	542 045	528 631	522 247	474 579	Royaume-Uni
United Rep. of Tanzania	2 373	3 806	4 353	5 618	5 959	6 150	6 538	6 960	Rép.-Unie de Tanzanie
United States	4 879 376	5 681 664	5 790 761	5 826 394	5 737 616	5 828 697	5 656 839	5 299 563	Etats-Unis
Uruguay	3 993	4 598	5 611	5 776	6 648	5 999	8 331	7 891	Uruguay
Uzbekistan	...	122 683	119 306	111 821	116 464	116 889	124 905	116 508	Ouzbékistan
Vanuatu	70	81	55	55	48	95	121	117	Vanuatu
Venezuela (Boliv. Rep. of)	122 162	192 103	168 268	181 634	169 907	174 549	182 298	184 795	Venezuela (R. bol. du)
Viet Nam	21 408	78 767	100 945	103 325	82 768	111 788	128 371	142 258	Viet Nam
Wallis and Futuna Islands	...	26	26	29	29	29	22	29	Iles Wallis et Futuna
Western Sahara	198	238	238	238	238	238	238	238	Sahara occidental
Yemen	...	17 305	18 881	20 044	20 792	21 709	22 647	23 997	Yémen
Zambia	2 446	2 101	2 109	2 259	2 285	1 720	1 929	1 984	Zambie
Zimbabwe	15 504	10 627	9 927	10 774	10 345	9 619	9 076	8 914	Zimbabwe

Source:
Carbon Dioxide Information Analysis Center (CDIAC) of the Oak Ridge National Laboratory, Oak Ridge, Tennessee, U.S.A., database on national CO$_2$ emission estimates, last accessed August 2012.

Source:
"Carbon Dioxide Information Analysis Center (CDIAC) of the Oak Ridge National Laboratory, Oak Ridge, Tennessee, U.S.A.", la base de données des estimations nationales des émissions de CO$_2$, dernier accès août 2012.

49
Threatened species
Number by taxonomic group
Espèces menacées
Nombre par groupe taxonomique

Country or area Pays ou zone	Year Année	Mammals Mammifères	Birds Oiseaux	Reptiles Reptiles	Amphibians Amphibiens	Fishes Poissons	Molluscs Mollusques	Invertebrates Invertébrés	Plants Plantes	Total
Afghanistan	2008	11	13	1	1	3	0	1	2	32
Afghanistan	2010	11	13	1	1	5	0	1	2	34
	2012	11	14	1	1	5	0	1	3	36
Albania	2008	3	6	4	2	33	0	4	0	52
Albanie	2010	3	6	4	2	38	42	5	0	100
	2012	3	6	4	2	39	49	6	0	109
Algeria	2008	14	11	7	3	23	0	14	3	75
Algérie	2010	14	11	8	3	33	8	13	15	105
	2012	14	11	8	3	36	9	13	16	110
American Samoa	2008	1	8	2	0	8	5	52	1	77
Samoa américaines	2010	1	8	4	0	8	5	52	1	79
	2012	1	8	4	0	9	5	52	1	80
Andorra	2008	2	0	1	0	2	1	3	0	9
Andorre	2010	2	0	1	0	1	1	3	0	8
	2012	2	1	1	0	0	4	3	0	11
Angola	2008	14	18	4	0	22	4	1	26	89
Angola	2010	15	21	4	0	37	6	1	33	117
	2012	15	25	4	0	39	6	1	33	123
Anguilla	2008	1	0	3	0	14	0	10	3	31
Anguilla	2010	1	0	5	0	14	0	10	3	33
	2012	1	0	6	0	18	0	10	3	38
Antigua and Barbuda	2008	2	1	6	0	14	0	11	4	38
Antigua-et-Barbuda	2010	2	1	6	0	14	0	11	4	38
	2012	2	1	6	0	18	0	11	4	42
Argentina	2008	35	49	5	29	31	0	10	44	203
Argentine	2010	37	50	5	29	36	0	12	44	213
	2012	38	50	5	29	37	0	13	45	219
Armenia	2008	9	12	5	0	4	0	6	1	37
Arménie	2010	9	10	7	0	3	0	6	1	36
	2012	9	13	7	0	3	1	6	1	40
Aruba	2008	3	1	2	0	15	0	1	0	22
Aruba	2010	2	1	2	0	15	0	1	1	22
	2012	2	1	2	0	15	0	1	1	22
Australia	2008	57	49	38	48	84	175	282	55	788
Australie	2010	55	52	43	47	100	175	314	67	853
	2012	55	51	43	47	104	169	314	86	869
Austria	2008	4	9	1	0	9	22	21	4	70
Autriche	2010	3	8	1	0	11	33	22	4	82
	2012	3	9	1	0	11	43	22	13	102
Azerbaijan	2008	7	15	5	0	9	0	4	0	40
Azerbaïdjan	2010	7	15	9	0	10	0	4	0	45
	2012	7	15	9	1	10	2	4	0	48
Bahamas	2008	7	5	6	0	20	0	11	5	54
Bahamas	2010	7	5	7	0	25	0	11	7	62
	2012	6	6	8	0	29	0	11	8	68
Bahrain	2008	3	4	4	0	6	0	13	0	30
Bahreïn	2010	3	4	4	0	8	0	13	0	32
	2012	3	3	4	0	8	1	13	0	32
Bangladesh	2008	34	28	20	1	12	0	2	12	109
Bangladesh	2010	34	29	21	1	19	0	2	16	122
	2012	34	31	22	1	17	0	2	17	124
Barbados	2008	3	1	4	0	15	0	10	2	35
Barbade	2010	3	1	4	0	16	0	10	2	36
	2012	3	2	4	0	20	0	10	2	41
Belarus	2008	4	4	0	0	1	0	8	0	17
Bélarus	2010	4	4	0	0	2	0	6	0	16
	2012	4	6	0	0	2	3	6	1	22
Belgium	2008	3	2	0	0	9	4	8	1	27
Belgique	2010	3	2	0	0	10	4	7	1	27
	2012	2	4	0	0	11	7	7	0	31
Belize	2008	7	3	5	6	22	0	12	30	85
Belize	2010	8	4	5	6	25	0	12	32	92
	2012	8	5	6	6	30	0	12	32	99
Benin	2008	10	4	4	0	15	0	0	14	47
Bénin	2010	11	5	4	0	27	0	1	14	62
	2012	11	9	4	0	27	0	1	14	66

Threatened species *(continued)*
Number by taxonomic group
Espèces menacées *(suite)*
Nombre par groupe taxonomique

Country or area Pays ou zone	Year Année	Mammals Mammifères	Birds Oiseaux	Reptiles Reptiles	Amphibians Amphibiens	Fishes Poissons	Molluscs Mollusques	Invertebrates Invertébrés	Plants Plantes	Total
Bermuda	2008	4	1	2	0	12	0	28	4	51
Bermudes	2010	4	1	2	0	11	0	28	4	50
	2012	4	1	2	0	16	0	28	4	55
Bhutan	2008	28	17	1	1	0	0	1	7	55
Bhoutan	2010	27	17	2	1	3	0	1	8	59
	2012	27	18	2	1	3	0	1	9	61
Bolivia (Plurinational State of)	2008	19	29	2	39	0	0	1	71	161
Bolivie (État plurinational de)	2010	20	33	3	34	0	0	1	72	163
	2012	20	53	3	34	0	2	1	73	186
Bosnia and Herzegovina	2008	4	6	2	1	27	0	10	1	51
Bosnie-Herzégovine	2010	4	6	2	1	31	8	14	1	67
	2012	4	6	2	1	31	17	14	1	76
Botswana	2008	6	7	0	0	2	0	0	0	15
Botswana	2010	7	9	0	0	2	0	0	0	18
	2012	7	10	0	0	2	0	0	1	20
Bouvet Island	2008	0	1	0	0	1	0	0	0	2
Ile Bouvet	2010	11	13	1	1	5	0	1	2	34
	2012	0	1	0	0	1	0	0	0	2
Brazil	2008	82	122	22	30	64	21	15	382	738
Brésil	2010[1]	80	123	28	30	80	21	24	387	773
	2012	81	152	29	31	84	21	24	404	1 008
British Indian Ocean Terr	2008	0	0	2	0	9	0	65	1	77
Terr. brit. de l'océan Indien	2010	0	0	2	0	8	0	65	1	76
	2012	0	0	2	0	9	0	65	1	77
British Virgin Islands	2008	1	1	6	2	12	0	10	10	42
Iles Vierges britanniques	2010	1	1	6	2	13	0	10	10	43
	2012	1	1	7	2	17	0	10	10	48
Brunei Darussalam	2008	35	21	5	3	8	0	0	99	171
Brunéi Darussalam	2010	34	19	6	3	8	0	1	99	170
	2012	34	24	6	3	7	0	1	99	174
Bulgaria	2008	7	12	2	0	17	0	7	0	45
Bulgarie	2010	7	12	2	0	18	18	9	0	66
	2012	7	14	2	0	19	25	10	6	83
Burkina Faso	2008	8	5	1	0	0	0	0	2	16
Burkina Faso	2010	9	6	1	0	4	1	0	3	24
	2012	9	9	1	0	4	1	0	3	27
Burundi	2008	9	8	0	6	18	1	4	2	48
Burundi	2010	10	10	0	6	17	4	3	2	52
	2012	11	12	0	6	17	4	3	3	56
Cambodia	2008	37	25	12	3	18	0	67	31	193
Cambodge	2010	37	24	15	3	28	0	67	30	204
	2012	37	26	18	3	40	1	67	33	225
Cameroon	2008	41	15	3	53	43	1	3	355	514
Cameroun	2010	39	16	4	53	110	11	13	378	624
	2012	38	24	4	55	111	11	13	376	632
Canada	2008	12	16	3	1	26	2	10	2	72
Canada	2010	12	15	3	1	32	2	10	2	77
	2012	11	16	5	1	35	4	10	2	84
Cape Verde	2008	3	4	1	0	18	0	0	2	28
Cap-Vert	2010	3	4	1	0	20	0	0	3	31
	2012	3	4	1	0	24	12	0	3	47
Cayman Islands	2008	1	1	4	0	14	1	10	2	33
Iles Caïmanes	2010	1	1	4	0	15	1	10	2	34
	2012	1	1	4	0	19	1	10	2	38
Central African Rep.	2008	7	5	1	0	0	0	0	15	28
Rép. centrafricaine	2010	8	7	1	0	3	0	0	17	36
	2012	8	13	1	0	3	0	0	17	42
Chad	2008	12	7	1	0	0	1	0	2	23
Tchad	2010	13	9	1	0	1	4	0	2	30
	2012	13	11	1	0	1	4	0	3	33
Chile	2008	21	32	1	21	18	0	8	40	141
Chili	2010	20	34	1	21	19	0	9	41	145
	2012	20	33	1	21	20	1	9	41	146
China[2]	2008	74	85	30	90	70	1	20	446	816
Chine[2]	2010	74	85	31	87	97	8	24	453	859
	2012	75	87	39	87	120	15	27	461	911
China, Hong Kong SAR	2008	2	16	1	5	13	1	4	6	48
Chine, Hong Kong RAS	2010	2	17	2	5	11	1	5	6	49
	2012	2	20	4	5	13	1	5	6	56

49
Threatened species *(continued)*
Number by taxonomic group
Espèces menacées *(suite)*
Nombre par groupe taxonomique

Country or area Pays ou zone	Year Année	Mammals Mammifères	Birds Oiseaux	Reptiles Reptiles	Amphibians Amphibiens	Fishes Poissons	Molluscs Mollusques	Invertebrates Invertébrés	Plants Plantes	Total
China, Macao SAR	2008	0	4	0	0	6	0	0	0	10
Chine, Macao RAS	2010	0	4	0	0	5	0	0	0	9
	2012	0	4	0	0	5	0	0	0	9
Christmas Is.	2008	1	5	3	0	5	0	16	1	31
Ile Christmas	2010	3	5	4	0	4	0	16	1	33
	2012	3	3	4	0	7	0	16	1	34
Cocos (Keeling) Islands	2008	2	0	1	0	7	0	17	0	27
Iles des Cocos (Keeling)	2010	2	0	1	0	8	0	17	0	28
	2012	2	0	1	0	9	0	17	0	29
Colombia	2008	52	86	15	214	31	0	31	223	652
Colombie	2010	51	91	19	213	50	0	30	227	681
	2012	53	112	22	213	54	0	30	226	497
Comoros	2008	5	8	2	0	7	0	62	5	89
Comores	2010	5	8	2	0	6	0	63	5	89
	2012	5	9	3	0	7	0	63	5	92
Congo	2008	11	3	2	0	15	1	3	35	70
Congo	2010	11	3	2	0	45	5	0	37	103
	2012	11	4	2	0	45	5	0	37	104
Cook Islands	2008	1	15	1	0	7	0	25	1	50
Iles Cook	2010	1	15	2	0	9	0	25	1	53
	2012	1	15	2	0	11	0	25	1	55
Costa Rica	2008	8	17	8	59	19	0	28	111	250
Costa Rica	2010	9	19	8	60	46	0	27	116	285
	2012	9	22	9	61	50	1	27	117	296
Côte d'Ivoire	2008	24	14	4	13	19	1	0	105	180
Côte d'Ivoire	2010	24	14	6	13	43	3	1	106	210
	2012	23	20	6	14	45	3	1	104	216
Croatia	2008	7	11	2	2	46	0	15	1	84
Croatie	2010	7	10	2	2	56	6	15	3	101
	2012	7	12	2	2	60	44	15	7	149
Cuba	2008	14	17	8	49	28	0	15	163	294
Cuba	2010	14	17	13	49	30	0	15	166	304
	2012	14	17	16	49	35	0	15	166	312
Curaçao										
Curaçao	2012	0	1	0	0	0	0	0	0	1
Cyprus	2008	5	5	4	0	12	0	0	7	33
Chypre	2010	5	5	4	0	17	0	4	8	43
	2012	5	5	4	0	19	1	4	18	56
Czech Republic	2008	2	6	0	0	5	2	16	4	35
République tchèque	2010	2	6	0	0	2	2	17	4	33
	2012	2	7	0	0	2	6	17	11	45
Dem. P. R. Korea	2008	9	20	0	1	8	0	2	3	43
R. p. dém. de Corée	2010	9	22	0	1	12	0	2	6	52
	2012	9	25	1	1	14	0	2	8	60
Dem. Rep. of the Congo	2008	29	31	3	13	25	13	11	65	190
Rép. dém. du Congo	2010	30	34	3	14	81	43	8	83	296
	2012	30	35	4	14	83	43	8	89	306
Denmark	2008	2	2	0	0	13	1	10	3	31
Danemark	2010	2	2	0	0	14	2	10	3	33
	2012	2	4	0	0	15	5	10	2	38
Djibouti	2008	8	7	0	0	14	0	50	2	81
Djibouti	2010	8	6	0	0	15	0	50	2	81
	2012	8	9	0	0	17	0	50	2	86
Dominica	2008	3	3	3	2	15	0	11	11	48
Dominique	2010	3	3	4	2	15	0	11	10	48
	2012	3	3	4	2	19	0	11	10	52
Dominican Republic	2008	6	14	11	30	15	0	18	30	124
Rép. dominicaine	2010	6	14	13	30	17	0	16	30	126
	2012	6	14	14	30	22	0	16	32	134
Ecuador	2008	43	69	11	171	15	48	12	1 839	2 208
Equateur	2010	43	71	22	171	49	48	14	1 837	2 255
	2012	43	93	26	171	50	48	14	1 837	2 282
Egypt	2008	17	10	11	0	24	0	46	2	110
Egypte	2010	17	10	10	0	36	0	46	2	121
	2012	18	10	11	0	40	0	47	2	128
El Salvador	2008	5	3	7	10	7	0	6	26	64
El Salvador	2010	5	5	7	10	12	0	6	27	72
	2012	5	6	7	10	14	0	6	26	74

49 Threatened species *(continued)*
Number by taxonomic group
Espèces menacées *(suite)*
Nombre par groupe taxonomique

Country or area Pays ou zone	Year Année	Mammals Mammifères	Birds Oiseaux	Reptiles Reptiles	Amphibians Amphibiens	Fishes Poissons	Molluscs Mollusques	Invertebrates Invertébrés	Plants Plantes	Total
Equatorial Guinea	2008	18	5	4	4	13	0	0	63	107
Guinée équatoriale	2010	19	5	5	4	27	0	2	68	130
	2012	19	6	5	4	28	0	2	67	131
Eritrea	2008	9	9	6	0	14	0	50	3	91
Erythrée	2010	10	10	6	0	18	0	50	3	97
	2012	10	14	6	0	19	0	50	4	103
Estonia	2008	1	3	0	0	4	0	4	0	12
Estonie	2010	1	3	0	0	4	0	3	0	11
	2012	1	5	0	0	5	3	3	0	17
Ethiopia	2008	31	22	1	9	2	3	11	22	101
Ethiopie	2010	32	23	1	9	14	4	11	26	120
	2012	33	26	1	9	14	4	11	25	123
Faeroe Islands	2008	5	0	0	0	9	0	0	0	14
Iles Féroé	2010	5	0	0	0	8	0	0	0	13
	2012	4	1	0	0	8	0	0	0	13
Falkland Is. (Malvinas)	2008	4	10	0	0	5	0	0	5	24
Iles Falkland (Malvinas)	2010	4	10	0	0	4	0	0	5	23
	2012	4	10	0	0	5	0	0	5	28
Fiji	2008	6	10	6	1	11	3	87	66	190
Fidji	2010	6	13	6	1	11	3	87	65	192
	2012	6	14	8	1	13	68	87	65	262
Finland	2008	1	4	0	0	5	1	9	1	21
Finlande	2010	1	4	0	0	5	1	6	1	18
	2012	1	6	0	0	6	3	6	2	24
France	2008	9	6	5	2	31	34	40	8	135
France	2010	9	7	4	2	40	62	29	15	168
	2012	8	9	4	2	43	92	29	32	219
French Guiana	2008	6	0	6	3	21	0	0	16	52
Guyane française	2010	7	0	6	3	24	0	0	16	56
	2012	7	6	6	3	27	0	0	16	65
French Polynesia	2008	1	32	1	0	13	29	26	47	149
Polynésie française	2010	1	32	1	0	20	33	26	47	160
	2012	1	33	1	0	27	34	26	47	169
French South. and Antar. Terr.	2008	3	13	2	0	3	0	0	0	21
Territoires austr. et ant	2010	3	13	2	0	3	0	0	0	21
	2012	3	13	3	0	3	0	0	0	22
Gabon	2008	13	5	3	3	21	0	0	108	153
Gabon	2010	14	5	3	3	59	0	0	120	204
	2012	14	5	3	3	61	0	0	119	205
Gambia	2008	9	5	2	0	16	0	0	4	36
Gambie	2010	10	6	2	0	21	0	0	4	43
	2012	10	10	2	0	23	0	0	4	49
Georgia	2008	10	10	7	1	12	0	9	0	49
Géorgie	2010	10	10	7	1	9	0	9	0	46
	2012	10	11	7	1	9	3	9	0	50
Germany	2008	6	6	0	0	20	9	21	12	74
Allemagne	2010	6	6	0	0	21	10	24	12	79
	2012	5	7	0	0	23	31	24	17	107
Ghana	2008	17	8	4	10	17	0	1	117	174
Ghana	2010	16	9	5	11	42	0	1	118	202
	2012	16	17	5	12	44	0	3	116	213
Gibraltar	2008	5	3	0	0	10	2	0	0	20
Gibraltar	2010	5	3	0	0	12	2	0	0	22
	2012	5	3	0	0	13	3	0	0	24
Greece	2008	10	11	5	5	62	1	13	11	118
Grèce	2010	10	11	8	5	73	9	27	13	156
	2012	10	12	8	5	75	64	41	57	272
Greenland	2008	6	0	0	0	6	0	0	1	13
Groenland	2010	6	0	0	0	7	0	0	1	14
	2012	7	1	0	0	7	0	0	1	16
Grenada	2008	3	1	4	1	15	0	10	3	37
Grenade	2010	3	1	4	1	15	0	10	3	37
	2012	3	1	6	1	19	0	10	3	43
Guadeloupe	2008	5	1	5	3	14	1	15	7	51
Guadeloupe	2010	5	1	7	3	14	1	15	8	54
	2012	5	1	7	3	18	1	15	8	58
Guam	2008	2	12	2	0	9	6	0	4	35
Guam	2010	2	14	2	0	6	6	0	4	34
	2012	2	14	2	0	9	6	0	4	37

49

Threatened species *(continued)*
Number by taxonomic group
Espèces menacées *(suite)*
Nombre par groupe taxonomique

Country or area Pays ou zone	Year Année	Mammals Mammifères	Birds Oiseaux	Reptiles Reptiles	Amphibians Amphibiens	Fishes Poissons	Molluscs Mollusques	Invertebrates Invertébrés	Plants Plantes	Total
Guatemala	2008	16	11	13	80	16	2	7	83	228
Guatemala	2010	16	10	13	81	20	2	6	82	230
	2012	16	14	13	83	25	2	6	83	242
Guernsey	2008	0	0	0	0	3	0	0	0	3
Guernesey	2010	0	0	0	0	2	0	0	0	2
	2012	0	0	0	0	2	0	0	0	2
Guinea	2008	22	12	2	5	19	0	4	22	86
Guinée	2010	22	13	4	5	63	1	4	22	134
	2012	21	17	4	5	66	1	4	22	140
Guinea-Bissau	2008	11	2	2	0	18	0	0	4	37
Guinée-Bissau	2010	12	3	3	0	30	0	0	4	52
	2012	12	9	3	0	31	0	0	4	59
Guyana	2008	8	3	5	7	22	0	1	22	68
Guyana	2010	9	3	5	4	25	0	1	22	69
	2012	10	13	5	4	28	0	1	22	180
Haiti	2008	5	13	8	46	15	0	14	29	130
Haïti	2010	5	13	13	46	17	0	14	29	137
	2012	5	13	15	46	21	0	14	32	146
Holy See	2008	1	0	0	0	1	0	0	0	2
Saint-Siège	2010	1	0	0	0	0	0	0	0	1
	2012	1	0	0	0	0	0	0	0	1
Honduras	2008	6	7	11	59	19	0	18	110	230
Honduras	2010	7	9	12	60	22	0	17	113	240
	2012	7	11	16	60	28	0	17	113	252
Hungary	2008	2	9	1	0	9	1	25	1	48
Hongrie	2010	2	9	1	0	8	1	25	1	47
	2012	2	10	1	0	9	8	25	9	64
Iceland	2008	5	0	0	0	12	0	0	0	17
Islande	2010	5	0	0	0	12	0	0	0	17
	2012	6	1	0	0	12	0	0	0	19
India	2008	96	76	25	65	40	2	109	246	659
Inde	2010	94	78	30	66	122	2	111	255	758
	2012	94	80	31	74	212	6	117	321	935
Indonesia	2008	183	115	27	33	111	3	229	386	1 087
Indonésie	2010	183	119	31	32	138	3	243	393	1 142
	2012	184	122	32	32	143	6	242	393	1 154
Iran (Islamic Rep. of)	2008	16	20	9	4	21	0	19	1	90
Iran (Rép. islamique d')	2010	16	21	12	4	29	0	19	1	102
	2012	16	22	13	4	30	2	19	2	108
Iraq	2008	13	18	2	1	6	0	15	0	55
Iraq	2010	13	18	2	1	11	0	15	0	60
	2012	13	16	3	1	11	1	15	1	61
Ireland	2008	5	1	0	0	16	1	2	1	26
Irlande	2010	5	1	0	0	18	1	1	1	27
	2012	5	3	0	0	21	2	1	1	33
Isle of Man	2008	0	0	0	0	3	0	0	0	3
Ile de Man	2010	0	0	0	0	2	0	0	0	2
	2012	0	0	0	0	2	0	0	0	2
Israel	2008	15	13	10	1	31	5	52	0	127
Israël	2010	15	13	9	1	35	5	53	0	131
	2012	15	14	10	2	36	7	53	0	137
Italy	2008	7	8	5	8	33	16	42	19	138
Italie	2010	7	8	4	9	42	30	47	27	174
	2012	7	10	4	9	46	73	47	65	261
Jamaica	2008	5	10	9	17	15	0	15	209	280
Jamaïque	2010	5	10	9	17	17	0	15	209	282
	2012	5	10	9	17	22	0	15	209	287
Japan	2008	27	40	12	20	40	25	133	12	309
Japon	2010	28	40	12	19	59	25	132	15	330
	2012	27	40	12	19	67	33	131	16	345
Jersey	2008	0	0	0	0	3	0	0	0	3
Jersey	2010	0	0	0	0	2	0	0	0	2
	2012	0	0	0	0	2	0	0	0	2
Jordan	2008	13	8	5	0	14	0	49	0	89
Jordanie	2010	13	10	5	0	13	0	48	1	90
	2012	13	10	6	0	13	2	48	1	93
Kazakhstan	2008	16	21	2	1	13	0	4	16	73
Kazakhstan	2010	16	21	1	1	14	0	4	16	73
	2012	16	22	1	1	15	2	4	17	78

Threatened species *(continued)*
Number by taxonomic group
Espèces menacées *(suite)*
Nombre par groupe taxonomique

Country or area Pays ou zone	Year Année	Mammals Mammifères	Birds Oiseaux	Reptiles Reptiles	Amphibians Amphibiens	Fishes Poissons	Molluscs Mollusques	Invertebrates Invertébrés	Plants Plantes	Total
Kenya	2008	27	27	5	7	71	16	55	103	311
Kenya	2010	28	30	6	7	66	17	55	129	338
	2012	28	34	6	7	68	17	55	131	346
Kiribati	2008	1	5	1	0	7	1	72	0	87
Kiribati	2010	1	6	1	0	9	1	72	0	90
	2012	1	6	1	0	11	1	72	0	92
Kuwait	2008	6	8	2	0	10	0	13	0	39
Koweït	2010	6	9	2	0	11	0	13	0	41
	2012	6	8	3	0	11	1	13	0	42
Kyrgyzstan	2008	6	12	2	0	3	0	3	14	40
Kirghizistan	2010	6	12	2	0	3	0	3	14	40
	2012	6	12	2	0	3	0	3	14	40
Lao People's Dem. Rep.	2008	46	23	11	5	6	0	3	21	115
Rép. dém. pop. lao	2010	45	22	12	5	23	0	3	22	132
	2012	45	24	16	5	54	16	5	30	195
Latvia	2008	1	4	0	0	6	1	9	0	21
Lettonie	2010	1	3	0	0	5	1	8	0	18
	2012	1	6	0	0	6	4	8	0	25
Lebanon	2008	10	6	6	0	15	0	3	0	40
Liban	2010	10	7	6	0	21	0	5	1	50
	2012	10	9	6	0	22	5	5	1	58
Lesotho	2008	2	5	0	0	1	0	2	1	11
Lesotho	2010	2	7	0	0	1	0	2	4	16
	2012	2	7	0	0	1	0	2	4	16
Liberia	2008	20	11	4	4	19	1	6	46	111
Libéria	2010	19	11	5	4	52	1	8	47	147
	2012	18	13	5	4	53	1	8	47	149
Libyan Arab Jamah.	2008	12	4	5	0	14	0	0	1	36
Jamah. arabe libyenne	2010	12	4	5	0	21	0	0	2	44
	2012	12	4	5	0	24	0	0	3	48
Liechtenstein	2008	0	0	0	0	0	0	4	0	4
Liechtenstein	2010	0	0	0	0	0	0	2	0	2
	2012	0	0	0	0	0	2	2	0	4
Lithuania	2008	3	4	0	0	6	0	6	0	19
Lituanie	2010	3	4	0	0	5	0	5	0	17
	2012	3	6	0	0	6	2	5	1	23
Luxembourg	2008	0	0	0	0	1	2	2	0	5
Luxembourg	2010	0	0	0	0	1	2	2	0	5
	2012	0	1	0	0	1	5	2	0	9
Madagascar	2008	62	35	19	64	75	24	76	281	636
Madagascar	2010	63	35	35	67	83	24	76	280	663
	2012	65	35	136	69	86	24	76	365	856
Malawi	2008	6	12	0	5	101	9	7	14	154
Malawi	2010	7	14	0	5	101	8	9	14	158
	2012	7	15	1	5	101	7	9	18	163
Malaysia	2008	70	42	21	47	49	19	207	686	1 141
Malaisie	2010	70	45	24	47	60	31	211	692	1 180
	2012	70	45	28	47	68	32	211	695	1 196
Maldives	2008	2	0	3	0	12	0	38	0	55
Maldives	2010	2	0	3	0	15	0	39	0	59
	2012	2	0	3	0	18	0	39	0	62
Mali	2008	11	6	1	0	1	0	0	6	25
Mali	2010	12	7	1	0	3	0	0	6	29
	2012	12	13	1	0	2	0	0	7	35
Malta	2008	3	3	0	0	13	3	0	3	25
Malte	2010	3	3	0	0	14	3	0	3	26
	2012	3	3	0	0	17	3	0	4	30
Marshall Islands	2008	2	5	1	0	10	1	66	0	85
Iles Marshall	2010	2	4	2	0	9	1	66	0	84
	2012	2	4	2	0	12	1	66	0	87
Martinique	2008	2	2	6	2	10	1	0	8	31
Martinique	2010	2	2	7	2	9	1	0	8	31
	2012	2	3	7	2	11	1	0	8	34
Mauritania	2008	14	8	3	0	23	0	1	0	49
Mauritanie	2010	15	9	3	0	30	0	1	0	58
	2012	16	13	3	0	32	0	1	0	65
Mauritius	2008	6	11	7	0	11	27	69	88	219
Maurice	2010	6	11	7	0	12	27	71	88	222
	2012	6	11	7	0	15	26	71	88	224

Threatened species *(continued)*
Number by taxonomic group

Espèces menacées *(suite)*
Nombre par groupe taxonomique

Country or area Pays ou zone	Year Année	Mammals Mammifères	Birds Oiseaux	Reptiles Reptiles	Amphibians Amphibiens	Fishes Poissons	Molluscs Mollusques	Invertebrates Invertébrés	Plants Plantes	Total
Mayotte	2008	1	3	2	0	3	0	59	0	68
Mayotte	2010	1	3	2	0	3	0	60	0	69
	2012	1	3	6	0	4	0	60	0	74
Mexico	2008	100	54	95	211	114	5	57	261	897
Mexique	2010	99	55	94	211	150	5	74	255	943
	2012	100	61	95	211	153	6	74	259	959
Micronesia (Fed. States of)	2008	6	9	3	0	13	4	104	5	144
Micronésie (Etats féd. de)	2010	7	10	4	0	14	4	104	5	148
	2012	7	10	5	0	20	4	104	5	155
Monaco	2008	2	0	0	0	12	0	0	0	14
Monaco	2010	2	0	0	0	9	0	0	0	11
	2012	2	0	0	0	11	1	0	0	14
Mongolia	2008	11	21	0	0	1	0	3	0	36
Mongolie	2010	11	21	0	0	1	0	3	0	36
	2012	11	20	0	0	2	0	3	0	36
Montserrat	2008	3	2	2	1	14	0	11	3	36
Montserrat	2010	3	2	2	1	13	0	11	3	35
	2012	3	2	2	1	17	0	11	5	41
Morocco	2008	18	10	10	2	31	0	9	2	82
Maroc	2010	18	10	11	2	45	33	7	31	157
	2012	17	11	11	2	45	34	7	33	160
Mozambique	2008	11	21	5	3	45	4	54	46	189
Mozambique	2010	12	23	8	3	52	4	55	52	209
	2012	12	26	8	3	54	3	55	53	214
Myanmar	2008	45	41	22	0	17	1	63	38	227
Myanmar	2010	45	41	24	0	33	1	63	42	249
	2012	46	44	28	0	41	3	63	46	271
Namibia	2008	11	21	4	1	21	0	0	24	82
Namibie	2010	12	24	4	1	25	0	0	26	92
	2012	12	26	4	1	28	0	0	26	97
Nauru	2008	1	2	0	0	8	0	62	0	73
Nauru	2010	1	2	0	0	9	0	62	0	74
	2012	1	2	0	0	9	0	62	0	74
Nepal	2008	32	32	7	3	0	0	0	7	81
Népal	2010	31	33	8	3	8	1	2	7	93
	2012	31	33	9	3	7	1	2	9	95
Netherlands	2008	4	2	0	0	11	1	5	0	23
Pays-Bas	2010	4	2	0	0	12	1	5	0	24
	2012	3	4	0	0	13	5	5	0	30
Netherlands Antilles	2008	4	1	6	0	15	0	11	2	39
Antilles néerlandaises	2010	3	1	5	0	15	0	11	3	38
	2012	3	0	5	0	20	0	11	3	42
New Caledonia	2008	9	14	2	0	17	11	84	218	355
Nouvelle-Calédonie	2010	9	15	13	0	24	11	86	257	415
	2012	9	15	53	0	30	27	86	257	477
New Zealand	2008	8	69	12	4	14	5	10	21	143
Nouvelle-Zélande	2010	9	70	13	4	21	5	10	21	153
	2012	9	70	13	4	23	5	10	20	154
Nicaragua	2008	5	9	8	10	21	2	17	39	111
Nicaragua	2010	6	11	8	10	26	2	15	43	121
	2012	6	14	8	10	31	2	15	42	128
Niger	2008	11	5	0	0	2	0	1	2	21
Niger	2010	12	6	0	0	4	1	1	2	26
	2012	12	9	0	0	4	1	1	2	29
Nigeria	2008	27	12	4	13	21	0	3	171	251
Nigéria	2010	27	13	4	13	56	1	11	172	297
	2012	26	18	4	13	59	1	11	168	300
Niue	2008	2	8	1	0	7	0	23	0	41
Nioué	2010	2	8	3	0	7	0	23	0	43
	2012	2	8	3	0	8	0	23	0	44
Norfolk Island	2008	0	15	2	0	2	12	9	1	41
Ile Norfolk	2010	0	14	2	0	3	12	9	1	41
	2012	0	11	2	0	4	12	9	1	39
Northern Mariana Islands	2008	5	14	1	0	9	4	47	5	85
Iles Mariannes du Nord	2010	5	15	1	0	8	4	47	5	85
	2012	5	15	1	0	12	4	47	5	89
Norway	2008	7	2	0	0	14	1	8	2	34
Norvège	2010	7	2	0	0	18	1	6	2	36
	2012	7	4	0	0	19	4	6	3	43

Threatened species *(continued)*
Number by taxonomic group
Espèces menacées *(suite)*
Nombre par groupe taxonomique

Country or area Pays ou zone	Year Année	Mammals Mammifères	Birds Oiseaux	Reptiles Reptiles	Amphibians Amphibiens	Fishes Poissons	Molluscs Mollusques	Invertebrates Invertébrés	Plants Plantes	Total
Occupied Palestinian Terr.	2008	3	7	4	1	1	0	1	0	17
Terr. palestinien occupé	2010	3	8	4	1	0	0	2	0	18
	2012	3	10	4	1	0	0	2	0	20
Oman	2008	9	9	4	0	20	0	26	6	74
Oman	2010	9	10	4	0	24	0	26	6	79
	2012	9	10	6	0	27	1	26	6	85
Pakistan	2008	23	27	10	0	22	0	15	2	99
Pakistan	2010	23	26	10	0	33	0	15	2	109
	2012	23	29	10	0	35	0	15	4	116
Palau	2008	4	2	2	0	12	5	97	4	126
Palaos	2010	4	4	2	0	12	5	97	4	128
	2012	4	4	2	0	15	40	97	4	166
Panama	2008	14	17	7	49	19	0	20	194	320
Panama	2010	15	17	7	50	36	0	20	202	347
	2012	15	19	7	50	41	0	20	200	352
Papua New Guinea	2008	41	36	9	11	38	2	167	142	446
Papouasie-Nvl-Guinée	2010	39	37	11	11	41	2	169	143	453
	2012	39	37	11	11	45	2	169	143	457
Paraguay	2008	8	27	2	0	0	0	0	10	47
Paraguay	2010	8	27	3	0	0	0	0	10	48
	2012	8	28	3	0	0	0	0	11	50
Peru	2008	53	93	6	96	10	0	3	275	536
Pérou	2010	54	96	8	97	19	0	3	274	551
	2012	54	124	8	101	20	4	3	275	493
Philippines	2008	39	67	9	48	60	3	199	216	641
Philippines	2010	39	72	38	48	65	3	210	222	697
	2012	38	74	38	48	73	3	210	224	708
Pitcairn	2008	2	10	0	0	6	5	10	7	40
Pitcairn	2010	2	10	0	0	8	5	10	7	42
	2012	2	10	0	0	9	5	10	7	43
Poland	2008	5	6	0	0	6	1	15	4	37
Pologne	2010	5	6	0	0	6	1	15	4	37
	2012	5	8	0	0	7	7	15	11	53
Portugal	2008	11	8	2	1	38	67	16	16	159
Portugal	2010	11	9	3	1	47	66	13	21	171
	2012	11	9	3	1	54	75	13	81	247
Puerto Rico	2008	3	8	9	14	13	0	1	53	101
Porto Rico	2010	3	8	9	14	15	0	1	53	103
	2012	3	8	10	14	20	0	1	53	109
Qatar	2008	2	4	1	0	7	0	13	0	27
Qatar	2010	2	5	1	0	11	0	13	0	32
	2012	3	4	2	0	11	1	13	0	34
Republic of Korea	2008	9	30	0	2	14	0	3	0	58
République de Corée	2010	9	30	0	2	17	0	3	3	64
	2012	9	29	1	2	19	0	3	6	69
Republic of Moldova	2008	4	9	1	0	9	0	4	0	27
République de Moldova	2010	4	9	2	0	9	0	3	0	27
	2012	4	8	2	0	8	3	3	2	30
Réunion	2008	5	6	0	0	6	14	58	15	104
Réunion	2010	5	6	0	0	5	14	59	15	104
	2012	5	6	0	0	8	14	59	15	107
Romania	2008	7	12	2	0	16	0	22	1	60
Roumanie	2010	7	12	2	0	18	0	24	1	64
	2012	7	14	2	0	19	11	24	5	82
Russian Federation	2008	33	51	6	0	32	1	28	7	158
Fédération de Russie	2010	32	18	8	0	35	1	24	8	126
	2012	31	83	8	0	36	8	24	11	201
Rwanda	2008	19	10	0	8	9	0	3	3	52
Rwanda	2010	20	12	0	8	9	0	2	4	55
	2012	20[3]	14	0	8	9	0	2	5	59
Saint Helena	2008	2	18	1	0	11	0	2	26	60
Sainte-Hélène	2010	2	19	1	0	9	0	2	27	60
	2012	2	19	1	0	9	0	2	30	63
Saint Kitts and Nevis	2008	2	1	5	1	14	0	10	2	35
Saint-Kitts-et-Nevis	2010	2	1	5	1	15	0	10	2	36
	2012	2	1	5	1	19	0	10	2	40
Saint Lucia	2008	2	5	5	0	15	0	11	6	44
Sainte-Lucie	2010	2	5	6	0	16	0	11	6	46
	2012	2	5	6	0	20	0	11	6	50

Threatened species *(continued)*
Number by taxonomic group
Espèces menacées *(suite)*
Nombre par groupe taxonomique

Country or area Pays ou zone	Year Année	Mammals Mammifères	Birds Oiseaux	Reptiles Reptiles	Amphibians Amphibiens	Fishes Poissons	Molluscs Mollusques	Invertebrates Invertébrés	Plants Plantes	Total
Saint Pierre and Miquelon	2008	3	1	0	0	1	0	0	0	5
Saint-Pierre-et-Miquelon	2010	3	1	0	0	0	0	0	0	4
	2012	4	2	0	0	0	0	0	0	6
Saint Vincent-Grenadines	2008	2	2	3	1	16	0	10	4	38
Saint Vincent-Grenadines	2010	2	2	3	1	16	0	10	4	38
	2012	2	2	6	1	20	0	10	4	45
Samoa	2008	2	7	1	0	8	1	52	2	73
Samoa	2010	2	7	3	0	11	1	52	2	78
	2012	2	6	3	0	13	1	52	2	79
San Marino	2008	0	0	0	0	1	0	0	0	1
Saint-Marin	2010	0	0	0	0	0	0	0	0	0
Sao Tome and Principe	2008	5	10	3	3	8	1	1	35	66
Sao Tomé-et-Principe	2010	5	10	4	3	11	1	1	35	70
	2012	5	13	4	3	14	1	1	35	76
Saudi Arabia	2008	9	14	2	0	16	0	53	3	97
Arabie saoudite	2010	9	14	2	0	22	0	53	3	103
	2012	9	15	3	0	24	2	53	3	109
Senegal	2008	15	8	6	0	28	0	0	7	64
Sénégal	2010	16	9	6	0	41	0	1	9	82
	2012	16	13	6	0	45	9	1	9	99
Seychelles	2008	5	10	10	6	14	2	63	45	155
Seychelles	2010	5	10	10	6	14	36	64	45	190
	2012	5	10	10	6	18	36	111	61	257
Sierra Leone	2008	16	10	3	2	16	0	0	47	94
Sierra Leone	2010	17	10	3	2	45	3	3	48	131
	2012	17	13	3	2	47	3	3	48	136
Singapore	2008	12	14	4	0	22	0	161	54	267
Singapour	2010	11	17	5	0	25	0	162	57	277
	2012	11	15	5	0	25	0	162	57	275
Slovakia	2008	3	7	1	0	7	6	13	2	39
Slovaquie	2010	3	7	0	0	5	2	15	2	34
	2012	3	8	0	0	5	6	15	7	44
Slovenia	2008	4	4	1	2	24	0	42	0	77
Slovénie	2010	4	4	0	2	26	18	41	0	95
	2012	4	5	0	2	29	32	41	7	120
Solomon Islands	2008	17	20	4	2	12	2	138	16	211
Iles Salomon	2010	20	20	6	2	15	2	139	16	220
	2012	20	20	6	2	18	2	139	16	223
Somalia	2008	14	12	3	0	26	1	50	17	123
Somalie	2010	15	11	4	0	26	1	50	21	128
	2012	15	14	4	0	28	1	50	23	135
South Africa	2008	23	35	19	21	65	24	137	74	398
Afrique du Sud	2010	24	39	21	20	81	21	138	97	441
	2012	24	41	21	19	87	21	137	99	449
South Sudan [4] Soudan du sud [4]	2012	0	14	0	0	0	0	0	0	14
Spain	2008	16	15	18	6	52	27	35	49	218
Espagne	2010	16	15	19	6	62	28	39	55	240
	2012	16	12	19	6	70	141	55	213	532
Sri Lanka	2008	30	13	8	53	31	0	119	280	534
Sri Lanka	2010	30	14	11	53	41	0	120	283	552
	2012	29	15	11	56	44	0	120	286	561
Sudan (former)	2008	14	13	3	0	13	0	45	17	105
Soudan (anc.)	2010	15	14	3	0	17	0	45	18	112
	2012	15	17	3	0	20	0	45	17	117
Suriname	2008	7	0	5	1	20	0	0	26	59
Suriname	2010	8	0	5	1	24	0	1	26	65
	2012	8	7	5	1	26	0	1	26	74
Svalbard and Jan Mayen Is.	2008	1	0	0	0	2	0	0	0	3
Svalbard et îles Jan Mayen	2010	1	0	0	0	2	0	0	0	3
	2012	1	1	0	0	2	0	0	0	4
Swaziland	2008	4	7	0	0	3	0	0	11	25
Swaziland	2010	5	9	0	0	4	0	0	11	29
	2012	6	11	0	0	4	0	0	11	32
Sweden	2008	1	3	0	0	12	1	12	3	32
Suède	2010	1	3	0	0	11	1	10	3	29
	2012	1	4	0	0	12	4	10	5	36

Threatened species *(continued)*
Number by taxonomic group
Espèces menacées *(suite)*
Nombre par groupe taxonomique

Country or area Pays ou zone	Year Année	Mammals Mammifères	Birds Oiseaux	Reptiles Reptiles	Amphibians Amphibiens	Fishes Poissons	Molluscs Mollusques	Invertebrates Invertébrés	Plants Plantes	Total
Switzerland	2008	2	2	0	1	11	0	29	3	48
Suisse	2010	2	2	0	1	9	0	28	3	45
	2012	2	3	0	1	9	10	28	4	57
Syrian Arab Republic	2008	16	13	6	0	27	0	6	0	68
Rép. arabe syrienne	2010	16	13	6	0	33	0	7	3	78
	2012	16	15	7	0	34	1	7	3	83
Tajikistan	2008	8	9	1	0	8	0	2	14	42
Tadjikistan	2010	8	9	2	0	5	0	2	14	40
	2012	8	12	2	0	5	0	2	13	42
Thailand	2008	57	44	22	4	50	1	179	86	443
Thaïlande	2010	57	45	23	4	72	1	184	91	477
	2012	57	47	27	4	96	14	186	126	557
TFYR of Macedonia	2008	5	10	2	0	14	0	5	0	36
L'ex-R.Y. Macédoine	2010	5	10	2	0	14	54	5	0	90
	2012	5	11	2	0	13	61	6	0	98
Timor-Leste	2008	4	5	1	0	5	0	0	0	15
Timor-Leste	2010	4	7	2	0	5	0	0	0	18
	2012	4	7	2	0	5	0	0	1	19
Togo	2008	10	2	3	3	16	0	0	10	44
Togo	2010	11	3	3	2	24	0	1	10	54
	2012	11	9	3	2	23	0	1	11	60
Tokelau	2008	0	1	1	0	7	0	31	0	40
Tokélaou	2010	0	1	2	0	7	0	31	0	41
	2012	0	1	2	0	8	0	31	0	42
Tonga	2008	2	4	2	0	9	2	33	4	56
Tonga	2010	2	4	3	0	10	2	33	4	58
	2012	2	5	2	0	12	4	33	4	62
Trinidad and Tobago	2008	2	2	5	9	19	0	10	1	48
Trinité-et-Tobago	2010	2	2	5	9	19	0	10	1	48
	2012	2	4	5	9	25	0	10	1	56
Tunisia	2008	14	8	4	1	20	0	7	0	54
Tunisie	2010	13	7	5	1	31	5	6	7	75
	2012	13	7	5	1	35	5	6	7	79
Turkey	2008	17	15	13	10	60	0	13	3	131
Turquie	2010	17	15	20	11	67	0	15	5	150
	2012	17	16	20	11	70	18	18	9	179
Turkmenistan	2008	9	15	1	0	12	0	5	3	45
Turkménistan	2010	9	15	2	0	11	0	5	3	45
	2012	9	16	2	0	11	1	5	4	48
Turks and Caicos Islands	2008	2	2	4	0	14	0	10	2	34
Iles Turques et Caïques	2010	2	2	4	0	14	0	10	2	34
	2012	2	2	4	0	18	0	10	7	43
Tuvalu	2008	2	1	1	0	8	1	70	0	83
Tuvalu	2010	2	1	2	0	9	1	70	0	85
	2012	2	1	2	0	10	1	70	0	86
Uganda	2008	21	18	0	6	54	10	12	38	159
Ouganda	2010	22	19	1	7	61	9	6	41	166
	2012	22	22	2	7	61	9	6	40	169
Ukraine	2008	11	12	2	0	20	0	14	1	60
Ukraine	2010	11	12	1	0	21	0	15	1	61
	2012	11	14	1	0	21	6	15	17	85
United Arab Emirates	2008	7	8	2	0	9	0	16	0	42
Emirats arabes unis	2010	7	10	2	0	13	0	16	0	48
	2012	7	9	3	0	13	1	16	0	49
United Kingdom	2008	5	2	0	0	34	2	8	14	65
Royaume-Uni	2010	5	2	0	0	41	2	9	14	73
	2012	5	4	0	0	43	6	9	15	82
United Rep. of Tanzania	2008	34	40	5	49	138	17	66	240	589
Rép.-Unie de Tanzanie	2010	35	42	14	50	172	15	65	298	691
	2012	35	44	17	57	175	15	65	302	710
United States Min. Outlying Is.	2008	0	11	1	0	12	0	44	0	68
Petites îles des Etats-Unis	2010	0	10	2	0	11	0	44	0	67
	2012	0	11	2	0	12	0	44	0	69
United States	2008	37	74	32	56	164	273	312	244	1 192
Etats-Unis	2010	37	74	32	56	177	273	258	245	1 152
	2012	36	79	36	56	185	297	258	256	1 203
United States Virgin Is.	2008	2	1	4	2	11	0	0	11	31
Iles Vierges américaines	2010	2	1	4	2	12	0	0	12	33
	2012	2	1	5	2	15	0	0	12	37

49
Threatened species *(continued)*
Number by taxonomic group
Espèces menacées *(suite)*
Nombre par groupe taxonomique

Country or area Pays ou zone	Year Année	Mammals Mammifères	Birds Oiseaux	Reptiles Reptiles	Amphibians Amphibiens	Fishes Poissons	Molluscs Mollusques	Invertebrates Invertébrés	Plants Plantes	Total
Uruguay	2008	10	24	4	4	28	0	1	1	72
Uruguay	2010	11	23	4	5	35	0	1	1	80
	2012	11	24	4	5	36	0	1	1	77
Uzbekistan	2008	11	15	2	0	8	0	1	15	52
Ouzbékistan	2010	10	15	2	0	7	0	1	15	50
	2012	10	16	2	0	7	1	1	17	54
Vanuatu	2008	8	8	2	0	11	1	78	10	118
Vanuatu	2010	8	7	3	0	14	1	78	10	121
	2012	8	9	3	0	15	4	78	10	127
Venezuela (Boliv. Rep. of)	2008	32	26	13	71	29	0	19	69	259
Venezuela (Rép. boliv. du)	2010	32	27	14	72	34	0	21	70	270
	2012	32	40	14	74	37	0	21	70	288
Viet Nam	2008	54	39	27	17	33	0	91	147	408
Viet Nam	2010	54	40	30	16	46	0	92	146	424
	2012	54	45	41	16	73	17	97	169	512
Wallis and Futuna Islands	2008	0	9	0	0	6	0	57	1	73
Iles Wallis et Futuna	2010	0	9	1	0	6	0	57	1	74
	2012	0	9	1	0	11	1	57	1	80
Western Sahara	2008	11	1	0	0	19	0	1	0	32
Sahara occidental	2010	11	1	0	0	26	0	1	0	39
	2012	10	2	0	0	25	0	1	0	38
Yemen	2008	9	13	3	1	18	2	61	159	266
Yémen	2010	9	14	3	1	21	1	61	159	269
	2012	9	15	6	1	24	2	61	160	278
Zambia	2008	8	12	0	1	10	3	1	8	43
Zambie	2010	9	14	0	1	20	13	1	9	67
	2012	9	15	0	1	20	13	1	11	70
Zimbabwe	2008	8	11	0	6	3	0	4	17	49
Zimbabwe	2010	9	13	3	6	3	0	5	16	55
	2012	9	15	3	6	3	0	5	16	57

Source:
The World Conservation Union (IUCN) / Species Survival Commission (SSC), Gland, Switzerland and Cambridge, United Kingdom, IUCN Red List of Threatened Species, 2008, 2010 and 2012.

Source:
Union mondiale pour la nature (UICN) / Commission de la sauvegarde des espèces, Gland, Suisse, et Cambridge, Royaume-Uni, La liste rouge des espèces menacées de l'UICN, 2008, 2010 et 2012.

1   The figures for Amphibians displayed here are those that were agreed at the GAA Brazil workshop in April 2003; the "consistent Red List Categories" were not yet accepted by the Brazilian experts.

2   For statistical purposes, the data for China do not include those for the Hong Kong Special Administrative Region (Hong Kong SAR), Macao Special Administrative Region (Macao SAR) and Taiwan Province of China.

3   Red List website says 19 of the mammals are missing.

4   Non-bird species have still to have their country coding adjusted to reflect occurrence in Bonaire, Sint Eustacius and Saba.

1   Les chiffres concernant les amphibiens sont ceux qui ont été convenus lors de l'atelier de l'Évaluation mondiale des amphibiens du Brésil en avril 2003 ; les "catégories conformes à la Liste rouge" n'ont pas encore été acceptées par les experts brésiliens.

2   Pour la présentation des statistiques, les données pour la Chine ne comprennent pas la Région Administrative Spéciale de Hong Kong (Hong Kong RAS), la Région Administrative Spéciale de Macao (Macao RAS) et la province de Taiwan.

3   Le site Web de la Liste rouge (Red List) indique que 19 des espèces de mammifères manquent.

4   Pour les espèces autres que les oiseaux, le code pays n'a pas encore été modifié pour tenir compte de leur présence à Bonaire, Saint-Eustache et Saba.

50

Water supply and sanitation coverage

Accès à l'eau et à l'assainissement

Country or area Pays ou zone	Year Année	Proportion of population with access to: - Pourcentage de la population ayant accès à :					
		Improved drinking water sources Un système amélioré de distribution d'eau potable			Improved sanitation facilities Un système amélioré d'assainissement		
		Urban (%) Urbaine (%)	Rural (%) Rurale (%)	Total (%) Totale (%)	Urban (%) Urbaine (%)	Rural (%) Rurale (%)	Total (%) Totale (%)
Afghanistan	1995	6	1	2	36	27	29
Afghanistan	2000	36	18	22	46	28	32
	2010	78	42	50	60	30	37
Albania	1990	100	97	97	94	66	76
Albanie	1995	100	96	98	94	68	78
	2000	100	96	98	95	76	84
	2010	96	94	95	95	93	94
Algeria	1990	100	94	94	99	77	88
Algérie	1995	98	86	93	99	78	90
	2000	93	84	89	99	82	92
	2010	85	79	83	98	88	95
Andorra	1990	100	100	100	100	100	100
Andorre	1995	100	100	100	100	100	100
	2000	100	100	100	100	100	100
	2010	100	100	100	100	100	100
Angola	1990	46	42	42	67	6	29
Angola	1995	47	40	43	69	7	34
	2000	52	40	46	75	11	42
	2010	60	38	51	85	19	58
Anguilla	1995	60	...	60	94	...	94
Anguilla	2000	60	...	60	94	...	94
Antigua and Barbuda	1995	95	89	91	98	94	95
Antigua-et-Barbuda	2000	95	89	91	98	94	95
	2010	95	...	...	98	...	...
Argentina	1990	97	94	94	93	73	90
Argentine	1995	98	75	95	93	75	91
	2000	98	78	96	92	77	91
	2010	98	...	...	...	...	...
Armenia	1990	98	...	...	95	...	...
Arménie	1995	98	75	90	95	75	88
	2000	98	81	92	95	77	89
	2010	99	97	98	95	80	90
Aruba	1990	100	100	100	...	...	...
Aruba	1995	100	100	100	...	...	...
	2000	100	100	100	...	...	...
	2010	100	100	100	...	...	...
Australia	1990	100	100	100	100	100	100
Australie	1995	100	100	100	100	100	100
	2000	100	100	100	100	100	100
	2010	100	100	100	100	100	100
Austria	1990	100	100	100	100	100	100
Autriche	1995	100	100	100	100	100	100
	2000	100	100	100	100	100	100
	2010	100	100	100	100	100	100
Azerbaijan	1990	88	70	70	...	...	...
Azerbaïdjan	1995	88	52	71	70	43	57
	2000	88	59	74	73	50	62
	2010	88	71	80	86	78	82
Bahamas	1990	98	...	...	100	100	100
Bahamas	1995	98	86	96	100	100	100
	2000	98	86	96	100	100	100
	2010	98	...	...	100	100	100

Country or area Pays ou zone	Year Année	Proportion of population with access to: - Pourcentage de la population ayant accès à :					
		Improved drinking water sources Un système amélioré de distribution d'eau potable			Improved sanitation facilities Un système amélioré d'assainissement		
		Urban (%) Urbaine (%)	Rural (%) Rurale (%)	Total (%) Totale (%)	Urban (%) Urbaine (%)	Rural (%) Rurale (%)	Total (%) Totale (%)
Bahrain	1990	100	...	...	100	...	...
Bahreïn	1995	100	...	...	100	...	...
	2000	100	...	...	100	...	...
	2010	100	...	...	100	...	...
Bangladesh [1]	1990	87	77	77	58	34	39
Bangladesh [1]	1995	87	75	78	58	37	42
	2000	86	77	79	58	43	47
	2010	85	80	81	57	55	56
Barbados	1990	100	100	100	100	100	100
Barbade	1995	100	100	100	100	100	100
	2000	100	100	100	100	100	100
	2010	100	100	100	100	100	100
Belarus	1990	100	100	100	91	96	93
Bélarus	1995	100	99	100	91	96	93
	2000	100	99	100	91	96	93
	2010	100	99	100	91	97	93
Belgium	1990	100	100	100	100	100	100
Belgique	1995	100	100	100	100	100	100
	2000	100	100	100	100	100	100
	2010	100	100	100	100	100	100
Belize	1990	89	74	74	77	77	77
Belize	1995	91	70	80	81	79	80
	2000	93	80	86	85	82	83
	2010	98	99	98	93	87	90
Benin	1990	72	57	57	14	0	5
Bénin	1995	75	54	62	17	1	7
	2000	78	59	66	19	3	9
	2010	84	68	75	25	5	13
Bhutan	1990	99	...	...	...	...	...
Bhoutan	1995	99	...	...	...	...	...
	2000	99	82	86	66	30	39
	2010	100	94	96	73	29	44
Bolivia (Plurin. State of)	1990	92	70	70	28	6	18
Bolivie (État plurin. de)	1995	93	50	76	30	7	21
	2000	94	57	80	31	8	22
	2010	96	71	88	35	10	27
Bosnia and Herzegovina	1990	99	97	97	98	...	...
Bosnie-Herzégovine	1995	99	96	97	98	93	95
	2000	99	96	97	98	93	95
	2010	100	98	99	99	92	95
Botswana	1990	100	93	93	61	22	38
Botswana	1995	100	89	94	65	27	46
	2000	99	90	95	69	32	52
	2010	99	92	96	75	41	62
Brazil	1990	96	89	89	80	33	68
Brésil	1995	97	72	91	81	36	71
	2000	98	77	94	82	38	74
	2010	100	85	98	85	44	79
British Virgin Islands	1990	98	98	98	100	100	100
Iles Vierges brit.	1995	98	98	98	100	100	100
	2000	98	98	98	100	100	100
	2010	98	98	98	100	100	100
Bulgaria	1990	100	100	100	100	98	99
Bulgarie	1995	100	100	100	100	99	100
	2000	100	100	100	100	100	100
	2010	100	100	100	100	100	100

Country or area Pays ou zone	Year Année	Proportion of population with access to: - Pourcentage de la population ayant accès à :					
		Improved drinking water sources Un système amélioré de distribution d'eau potable			Improved sanitation facilities Un système amélioré d'assainissement		
		Urban (%) Urbaine (%)	Rural (%) Rurale (%)	Total (%) Totale (%)	Urban (%) Urbaine (%)	Rural (%) Rurale (%)	Total (%) Totale (%)
Burkina Faso Burkina Faso	1990	75	43	43	43	2	8
	1995	79	46	51	45	3	9
	2000	85	55	60	46	4	11
	2010	95	73	79	50	6	17
Burundi Burundi	1990	97	70	70	41	44	44
	1995	93	69	71	44	45	45
	2000	89	70	72	46	45	45
	2010	83	71	72	49	46	46
Cambodia Cambodge	1990	48	31	31	36	5	9
	1995	50	31	34	39	5	10
	2000	63	40	44	50	10	17
	2010	87	58	64	73	20	31
Cameroon Cameroun	1990	76	49	49	63	37	48
	1995	81	37	57	62	37	48
	2000	86	42	64	61	37	49
	2010	95	52	77	58	36	49
Canada Canada	1990	100	100	100	100	99	100
	1995	100	99	100	100	99	100
	2000	100	99	100	100	99	100
	2010	100	99	100	100	99	100
Cape Verde Cap-Vert	1995	82	79	80	56	18	37
	2000	84	81	83	61	25	44
	2010	90	85	88	73	43	61
Cayman Islands Iles Caïmanes	1990	...	...	...	96	...	96
	1995	93	...	93	96	...	96
	2000	93	...	93	96	...	96
	2010	96	...	96	96	...	96
Central African Rep. Rép. centrafricaine	1990	78	58	58	21	5	11
	1995	81	48	60	25	9	15
	2000	85	49	63	32	16	22
	2010	92	51	67	43	28	34
Chad Tchad	1990	49	39	39	21	4	8
	1995	54	39	42	23	5	9
	2000	60	41	45	26	5	10
	2010	70	44	51	30	6	13
Chile Chili	1990	99	90	90	91	48	84
	1995	99	57	92	93	59	88
	2000	99	66	94	96	71	92
	2010	99	75	96	98	83	96
China Chine	1990	97	67	67	48	15	24
	1995	97	63	74	54	25	34
	2000	98	70	80	61	35	44
	2010	98	85	91	74	56	64
Colombia Colombie	1990	98	89	89	79	40	67
	1995	98	70	90	80	46	70
	2000	99	71	91	81	52	73
	2010	99	72	92	82	63	77
Comoros Comores	1990	98	87	87	34	11	17
	1995	96	87	90	36	17	22
	2000	93	92	92	42	23	28
	2010	91	97	95	50	30	36
Congo Congo	1990	95	...	...	...	...	...
	1995	95	...	...	...	...	...
	2000	95	36	70	21	18	20
	2010	95	32	71	20	15	18

Country or area Pays ou zone	Year Année	Proportion of population with access to: - Pourcentage de la population ayant accès à :					
		Improved drinking water sources Un système amélioré de distribution d'eau potable			Improved sanitation facilities Un système amélioré d'assainissement		
		Urban (%) Urbaine (%)	Rural (%) Rurale (%)	Total (%) Totale (%)	Urban (%) Urbaine (%)	Rural (%) Rurale (%)	Total (%) Totale (%)
Cook Islands Iles Cook	1990	99	94	94	100	91	96
	1995	99	87	94	100	92	97
	2000	99	87	95	100	99	100
	2010	98	...	...	100	100	100
Costa Rica Costa Rica	1990	99	93	93	94	91	93
	1995	99	88	94	95	92	94
	2000	99	89	95	95	94	95
	2010	100	91	97	95	96	95
Côte d'Ivoire Côte d'Ivoire	1990	90	76	76	38	8	20
	1995	91	67	77	38	9	21
	2000	91	67	77	37	10	22
	2010	91	68	80	36	11	24
Croatia Croatie	1990	100	99	99	99	98	99
	1995	100	97	99	99	98	99
	2000	100	97	99	99	98	99
	2010	100	97	99	99	98	99
Cuba Cuba	1990	93	82	82	86	64	80
	1995	94	63	86	88	69	83
	2000	95	73	90	90	73	86
	2010	96	89	94	94	81	91
Cyprus Chypre	1990	100	100	100	100	100	100
	1995	100	100	100	100	100	100
	2000	100	100	100	100	100	100
	2010	100	100	100	100	100	100
Czech Republic République tchèque	1990	100	100	100	100	98	100
	1995	100	100	100	100	98	99
	2000	100	100	100	99	97	98
	2010	100	100	100	99	97	98
Dem. P. R. Korea R. p. dém. de Corée	1990	100	100	100	...	...	...
	1995	100	100	100	57	48	53
	2000	100	99	100	65	55	61
	2010	99	97	98	86	71	80
Dem. Rep. of the Congo Rép. dém. du Congo	1990	90	45	45	23	4	9
	1995	88	27	44	23	7	12
	2000	85	27	44	23	13	16
	2010	79	27	45	24	24	24
Denmark Danemark	1990	100	100	100	100	100	100
	1995	100	100	100	100	100	100
	2000	100	100	100	100	100	100
	2010	100	100	100	100	100	100
Djibouti Djibouti	1990	80	78	78	73	45	66
	1995	82	69	79	72	42	65
	2000	88	63	82	69	30	60
	2010	99	54	88	63	10	50
Dominica Dominique	1990	96	...	...	...	...	...
	1995	96	92	95	80	84	81
	2000	96	92	95	80	84	81
	2010	96	...	...	...	...	...
Dominican Republic Rép. dominicaine	1990	98	88	88	83	61	73
	1995	95	78	88	84	65	76
	2000	92	80	87	85	68	78
	2010	87	84	86	87	75	83
Ecuador Equateur	1990	81	72	72	86	48	69
	1995	86	70	79	89	59	76
	2000	90	79	86	92	70	83
	2010	96	89	94	96	84	92

Country or area Pays ou zone	Year Année	Proportion of population with access to: - Pourcentage de la population ayant accès à :					
		Improved drinking water sources Un système amélioré de distribution d'eau potable			Improved sanitation facilities Un système amélioré d'assainissement		
		Urban (%) Urbaine (%)	Rural (%) Rurale (%)	Total (%) Totale (%)	Urban (%) Urbaine (%)	Rural (%) Rurale (%)	Total (%) Totale (%)
Egypt Egypte	1990	96	93	93	91	57	72
	1995	97	92	94	93	68	79
	2000	98	95	96	95	79	86
	2010	100	99	99	97	93	95
El Salvador El Salvador	1990	90	74	74	88	62	75
	1995	91	63	78	88	68	79
	2000	92	68	82	89	74	83
	2010	94	76	88	89	83	87
Equatorial Guinea Guinée équatoriale	1995	66	42	51	92	87	89
	2000	66	42	51	92	87	89
Eritrea Erythrée	1990	62	43	43	58	0	9
	1995	64	42	46	57	1	10
	2000	70	50	54	54	2	11
	2010	...	...	...	...	4	...
Estonia Estonie	1990	99	98	98	96	94	95
	1995	99	97	98	96	94	95
	2000	99	97	98	96	94	95
	2010	99	97	98	96	94	95
Ethiopia Ethiopie	1990	79	14	14	20	1	3
	1995	82	10	20	21	1	4
	2000	87	19	29	24	6	9
	2010	97	34	44	29	19	21
Fiji Fidji	1990	94	84	84	90	40	61
	1995	96	82	88	91	49	68
	2000	98	88	93	92	59	75
	2010	100	95	98	94	71	83
Finland Finlande	1990	100	100	100	100	100	100
	1995	100	100	100	100	100	100
	2000	100	100	100	100	100	100
	2010	100	100	100	100	100	100
France France	1990	100	100	100	100	100	100
	1995	100	100	100	100	100	100
	2000	100	100	100	100	100	100
	2010	100	100	100	100	100	100
French Guiana Guyane française	1995	88	71	84	85	57	78
	2000	88	71	84	85	57	78
French Polynesia Polynésie française	1990	100	100	100	99	97	98
	1995	100	100	100	99	97	98
	2000	100	100	100	99	97	98
	2010	100	100	100	99	97	98
Gabon Gabon	1995	95	49	84	38	29	36
	2000	95	47	85	37	30	36
	2010	95	41	87	33	30	33
Gambia Gambie	1990	86	74	74	...	...	...
	1995	88	72	79	65	57	61
	2000	90	77	83	67	60	63
	2010	92	85	89	70	65	68
Georgia Géorgie	1990	94	81	81	97	95	96
	1995	94	69	82	97	95	96
	2000	97	80	89	96	94	95
	2010	100	96	98	96	93	95
Germany Allemagne	1990	100	100	100	100	100	100
	1995	100	100	100	100	100	100
	2000	100	100	100	100	100	100
	2010	100	100	100	100	100	100

Country or area Pays ou zone	Year Année	Proportion of population with access to: - Pourcentage de la population ayant accès à :					
		Improved drinking water sources Un système amélioré de distribution d'eau potable			Improved sanitation facilities Un système amélioré d'assainissement		
		Urban (%) Urbaine (%)	Rural (%) Rurale (%)	Total (%) Totale (%)	Urban (%) Urbaine (%)	Rural (%) Rurale (%)	Total (%) Totale (%)
Ghana	1990	84	53	53	12	4	7
Ghana	1995	85	47	62	14	5	9
	2000	87	58	71	16	6	10
	2010	91	80	86	19	8	14
Greece	1990	99	96	96	100	93	97
Grèce	1995	100	95	98	99	94	97
	2000	100	98	99	99	96	98
	2010	100	99	100	99	97	98
Greenland	1990	100	100	100	100	100	100
Groenland	1995	100	100	100	100	100	100
	2000	100	100	100	100	100	100
	2010	100	100	100	100	100	100
Grenada	1990	97	...	...	96	97	97
Grenade	1995	97	93	94	96	97	97
	2000	97	93	94	96	97	97
	2010	97	...	...	96	97	97
Guadeloupe	1990	98	...	...	...	...	...
Guadeloupe	1995	98	93	98	94	...	...
	2000	98	93	98	94	...	...
	2010	98	...	...	95	...	...
Guam	1990	100	100	100	99	98	99
Guam	1995	100	100	100	99	98	99
	2000	100	100	100	99	98	99
	2010	100	100	100	99	98	99
Guatemala	1990	91	81	81	81	48	62
Guatemala	1995	93	78	84	83	54	67
	2000	95	81	87	85	60	71
	2010	98	87	92	87	70	78
Guinea	1990	87	51	51	19	6	10
Guinée	1995	88	45	58	22	8	12
	2000	88	52	63	26	9	14
	2010	90	65	74	32	11	18
Guinea-Bissau	1990	45	36	36	...	4	...
Guinée-Bissau	1995	56	38	43	35	4	13
	2000	68	43	50	36	5	14
	2010	91	53	64	44	9	20
Guyana	1995	93	86	88	86	75	78
Guyana	2000	94	87	89	86	76	79
	2010	98	93	94	88	82	84
Haiti	1990	84	59	59	44	19	26
Haïti	1995	84	49	60	40	18	25
	2000	84	50	62	34	15	22
	2010	85	51	69	24	10	17
Honduras	1990	96	76	76	71	36	50
Honduras	1995	96	66	79	75	44	57
	2000	95	71	82	78	53	64
	2010	95	79	87	85	69	77
Hungary	1990	98	96	96	100	100	100
Hongrie	1995	99	94	97	100	100	100
	2000	100	98	99	100	100	100
	2010	100	100	100	100	100	100
Iceland	1990	100	100	100	100	100	100
Islande	1995	100	100	100	100	100	100
	2000	100	100	100	100	100	100
	2010	100	100	100	100	100	100

Country or area Pays ou zone	Year Année	Proportion of population with access to: - Pourcentage de la population ayant accès à :					
		Improved drinking water sources Un système amélioré de distribution d'eau potable			Improved sanitation facilities Un système amélioré d'assainissement		
		Urban (%) Urbaine (%)	Rural (%) Rurale (%)	Total (%) Totale (%)	Urban (%) Urbaine (%)	Rural (%) Rurale (%)	Total (%) Totale (%)
India	1990	88	69	69	51	7	18
Inde	1995	90	70	75	53	10	21
	2000	93	77	81	55	14	25
	2010	97	90	92	58	23	34
Indonesia	1990	91	70	70	56	21	32
Indonésie	1995	91	65	74	60	26	38
	2000	91	68	78	64	30	44
	2010	92	74	82	73	39	54
Iran (Islamic Rep. of)	1990	98	90	90	83	74	79
Iran (Rép. islamique d')	1995	98	81	91	86	77	82
	2000	98	85	93	92	86	90
	2010	97	92	96	100	100	100
Iraq	1990	97	81	81	...	...	...
Iraq	1995	97	44	80	76	46	67
	2000	95	49	80	76	54	69
	2010	91	56	79	76	67	73
Ireland	1990	100	100	100	100	98	99
Irlande	1995	100	100	100	100	98	99
	2000	100	100	100	100	98	99
	2010	100	100	100	100	98	99
Israel	1990	100	100	100	100	100	100
Israël	1995	100	100	100	100	100	100
	2000	100	100	100	100	100	100
	2010	100	100	100	100	100	100
Italy	1990	100	100	100	...	...	...
Italie	1995	100	100	100	...	...	...
	2000	100	100	100	...	...	...
	2010	100	100	100	...	...	...
Jamaica	1990	98	93	93	78	81	80
Jamaïque	1995	98	88	93	78	81	79
	2000	98	88	93	78	82	80
	2010	98	88	93	78	82	80
Japan	1990	100	100	100	100	100	100
Japon	1995	100	100	100	100	100	100
	2000	100	100	100	100	100	100
	2010	100	100	100	100	100	100
Jordan	1990	99	97	97	98	95	97
Jordanie	1995	98	91	96	98	95	97
	2000	98	91	96	98	96	98
	2010	98	92	97	98	98	98
Kazakhstan	1990	99	96	96	96	97	96
Kazakhstan	1995	99	92	96	96	97	96
	2000	99	91	96	97	97	97
	2010	99	90	95	97	98	97
Kenya	1990	92	44	44	27	25	25
Kenya	1995	89	38	48	28	27	27
	2000	87	43	52	30	28	28
	2010	82	52	59	32	32	32
Kiribati	1990	76	48	48	36	21	26
Kiribati	1995	77	41	54	41	21	28
	2000	77	50	62	47	22	33
Kuwait	1990	99	99	99	100	100	100
Koweït	1995	99	99	99	100	100	100
	2000	99	99	99	100	100	100
	2010	99	99	99	100	100	100

Country or area Pays ou zone	Year Année	Proportion of population with access to: - Pourcentage de la population ayant accès à :					
		Improved drinking water sources Un système amélioré de distribution d'eau potable			Improved sanitation facilities Un système amélioré d'assainissement		
		Urban (%) Urbaine (%)	Rural (%) Rurale (%)	Total (%) Totale (%)	Urban (%) Urbaine (%)	Rural (%) Rurale (%)	Total (%) Totale (%)
Kyrgyzstan	1990	98	...	...	94	...	...
Kirghizistan	1995	98	66	78	94	93	93
	2000	98	73	82	94	93	93
	2010	99	85	90	94	93	93
Lao People's Dem. Rep.	1995	75	32	39	58	8	17
Rép. dém. pop. lao	2000	75	37	45	64	15	26
	2010	77	62	67	89	50	63
Latvia	1990	100	99	99	...	...	...
Lettonie	1995	100	96	99	...	...	...
	2000	100	96	99	82	71	78
	2010	100	96	99	...	...	...
Lebanon	1990	100	100	100	100	...	...
Liban	1995	100	100	100	100	87	98
	2000	100	100	100	100	87	98
	2010	100	100	100	100	...	...
Lesotho	1990	95	80	80	...	...	...
Lesotho	1995	95	77	80	38	21	24
	2000	94	76	80	37	22	25
	2010	91	73	78	32	24	26
Liberia	1995	71	49	58	22	2	11
Libéria	2000	74	50	61	23	3	12
	2010	88	60	73	29	7	18
Libyan Arab Jamah.	1990	54	54	54	97	96	97
Jamah. arabe libyenne	1995	54	55	54	97	96	97
	2000	54	55	54	97	96	97
	2010	...	...	...	97	96	97
Lithuania	1990	98	...	...	95	...	...
Lituanie	1995	98	...	...	95	...	...
	2000	98	81	92	95	69	86
	2010	98	...	...	95	...	...
Luxembourg	1990	100	100	100	100	100	100
Luxembourg	1995	100	100	100	100	100	100
	2000	100	100	100	100	100	100
	2010	100	100	100	100	100	100
Madagascar	1990	75	29	29	15	7	9
Madagascar	1995	75	19	33	17	9	11
	2000	75	24	38	18	10	12
	2010	74	34	46	21	12	15
Malawi	1990	91	41	41	48	38	39
Malawi	1995	92	46	52	48	41	42
	2000	93	57	62	49	45	46
	2010	95	80	83	49	51	51
Malaysia	1990	94	88	88	88	81	84
Malaisie	1995	96	88	92	91	85	88
	2000	99	93	97	94	90	92
	2010	100	99	100	96	95	96
Maldives	1990	100	93	93	98	58	68
Maldives	1995	100	91	93	98	60	70
	2000	100	93	95	98	72	79
	2010	100	97	98	98	97	97
Mali	1990	53	28	28	33	10	15
Mali	1995	62	28	37	33	11	17
	2000	70	36	46	34	12	18
	2010	87	51	64	35	14	22
Malta	1990	100	100	100	100	100	100
Malte	1995	100	99	100	100	100	100
	2000	100	100	100	100	100	100
	2010	100	100	100	100	100	100

Water supply and sanitation coverage *(continued)*
Accès à l'eau et à l'assainissement *(suite)*

| Country or area
Pays ou zone | Year
Année | Proportion of population with access to: - Pourcentage de la population ayant accès à : | | | | | |
| | | Improved drinking water sources
Un système amélioré de distribution d'eau potable | | | Improved sanitation facilities
Un système amélioré d'assainissement | | |
		Urban (%) Urbaine (%)	Rural (%) Rurale (%)	Total (%) Totale (%)	Urban (%) Urbaine (%)	Rural (%) Rurale (%)	Total (%) Totale (%)
Marshall Islands	1990	94	95	95	77	41	64
Iles Marshall	1995	94	98	95	79	44	67
	2000	93	98	95	80	48	70
	2010	92	99	94	83	53	75
Martinique	1990	100	...	...	...	...	...
Martinique	1995	100	...	...	93	...	...
	2000	100	...	...	94	...	...
	2010	100	...	...	95	...	...
Mauritania	1990	36	30	30	29	8	16
Mauritanie	1995	41	32	36	31	9	18
	2000	45	37	40	38	9	21
	2010	52	48	50	51	9	26
Mauritius	1990	100	99	99	91	88	89
Maurice	1995	100	99	99	91	88	89
	2000	100	99	99	91	88	89
	2010	100	99	99	91	88	89
Mexico	1990	93	85	85	76	34	64
Mexique	1995	94	70	88	79	45	70
	2000	95	77	90	81	56	75
	2010	97	91	96	87	79	85
Micronesia (Fed. States of)	1990	93	89	89	55	20	29
Micronésie (Etats féd. de)	1995	94	89	90	56	18	28
	2000	94	92	92	59	16	26
Monaco	1990	100	100	100	100	...	100
Monaco	1995	100	...	100	100	...	100
	2000	100	...	100	100	...	100
	2010	100	...	100	100	...	100
Mongolia	1990	74	54	54	...	...	...
Mongolie	1995	76	29	56	66	28	50
	2000	86	37	65	65	28	49
	2010	100	53	82	64	29	51
Montenegro	1990	99	97	97	...	...	...
Monténégro	1995	99	96	98	...	...	...
	2000	99	96	98	92	87	90
	2010	99	96	98	92	87	90
Montserrat	1990	100	100	100	96	96	96
Montserrat	1995	100	100	100	96	96	96
	2000	100	100	100	96	96	96
	2010	100	100	100	96	96	96
Morocco	1990	93	73	73	81	27	53
Maroc	1995	94	56	76	81	35	59
	2000	96	58	78	82	43	64
	2010	98	61	83	83	52	70
Mozambique	1990	73	36	36	36	4	11
Mozambique	1995	73	26	38	36	4	12
	2000	75	27	42	37	4	14
	2010	77	29	47	38	5	18
Myanmar	1990	80	56	56	...	...	...
Myanmar	1995	82	51	59	77	47	55
	2000	85	60	67	79	56	62
	2010	93	78	83	83	73	76
Namibia	1990	99	64	64	62	9	24
Namibie	1995	99	62	73	61	11	26
	2000	99	72	81	60	13	28
	2010	99	90	93	57	17	32

Country or area Pays ou zone	Year Année	Proportion of population with access to: - Pourcentage de la population ayant accès à :					
		Improved drinking water sources Un système amélioré de distribution d'eau potable			Improved sanitation facilities Un système amélioré d'assainissement		
		Urban (%) Urbaine (%)	Rural (%) Rurale (%)	Total (%) Totale (%)	Urban (%) Urbaine (%)	Rural (%) Rurale (%)	Total (%) Totale (%)
Nauru Nauru	1990	98	98	98	66	...	66
	1995	98	...	98	66	...	66
	2000	98	...	98	66	...	66
	2010	88	...	88	65	...	65
Nepal Népal	1990	96	76	76	37	7	10
	1995	95	78	80	40	12	15
	2000	94	81	83	42	17	20
	2010	93	88	89	48	27	31
Netherlands Pays-Bas	1990	100	100	100	100	100	100
	1995	100	100	100	100	100	100
	2000	100	100	100	100	100	100
	2010	100	100	100	100	100	100
New Zealand Nouvelle-Zélande	1990	100	100	100	...	88	...
	1995	100	100	100	...	88	...
	2000	100	100	100	...	...	...
	2010	100	100	100	...	...	...
Nicaragua Nicaragua	1990	92	74	74	59	26	43
	1995	94	58	77	60	29	46
	2000	95	62	80	61	32	48
	2010	98	68	85	63	37	52
Niger Niger	1990	57	35	35	19	2	5
	1995	68	33	39	23	2	5
	2000	78	35	42	27	3	7
	2010	100	39	49	34	4	9
Nigeria Nigéria	1990	79	47	47	39	36	37
	1995	78	33	50	38	34	36
	2000	77	36	53	37	32	34
	2010	74	43	58	35	27	31
Niue Nioué	1990	100	100	100	100	100	100
	1995	100	100	100	100	100	100
	2000	100	100	100	100	100	100
	2010	100	100	100	100	100	100
Northern Mariana Islands Iles Mariannes du Nord	1990	98	98	98	85	78	84
	1995	98	99	98	89	86	89
	2000	98	97	98	92	93	92
	2010	98	97	98	...	96	...
Norway Norvège	1990	100	100	100	100	100	100
	1995	100	100	100	100	100	100
	2000	100	100	100	100	100	100
	2010	100	100	100	100	100	100
Occupied Palestinian Terr. Terr. palestinien occupé	1990	100	...	...	91	...	...
	1995	100	90	97	91	78	87
	2000	95	86	92	91	83	89
	2010	86	81	85	92	92	92
Oman Oman	1990	84	80	80	96	55	82
	1995	84	72	81	97	58	86
	2000	87	74	83	98	71	90
	2010	93	78	89	100	95	99
Pakistan Pakistan	1990	95	85	85	72	7	27
	1995	95	83	87	72	14	32
	2000	96	85	89	72	20	37
	2010	96	89	92	72	34	48
Palau Palaos	1990	73	80	80	78	36	65
	1995	74	96	80	81	45	71
	2000	78	96	83	91	68	84
	2010	83	96	85	100	100	100

Country or area Pays ou zone	Year Année	Proportion of population with access to: - Pourcentage de la population ayant accès à :					
		Improved drinking water sources Un système amélioré de distribution d'eau potable			Improved sanitation facilities Un système amélioré d'assainissement		
		Urban (%) Urbaine (%)	Rural (%) Rurale (%)	Total (%) Totale (%)	Urban (%) Urbaine (%)	Rural (%) Rurale (%)	Total (%) Totale (%)
Panama Panama	1990	99	84	84	73	40	58
	1995	98	71	87	74	43	62
	2000	97	77	90	74	47	65
	2010	97	...	...	...	...	...
Papua New Guinea Papouasie-Nvl-Guinée	1990	89	41	41	78	42	47
	1995	89	32	40	78	42	47
	2000	88	32	39	75	42	46
	2010	87	33	40	71	41	45
Paraguay Paraguay	1990	81	52	52	61	15	37
	1995	87	38	64	70	23	48
	2000	92	51	74	79	31	58
	2010	99	66	86	90	40	71
Peru Pérou	1990	88	75	75	71	17	54
	1995	89	50	78	74	22	59
	2000	90	55	81	76	27	63
	2010	91	65	85	81	37	71
Philippines Philippines	1990	93	85	85	69	45	57
	1995	93	81	87	72	51	61
	2000	93	85	89	74	57	65
	2010	93	92	92	79	69	74
Poland Pologne	1990	100	...	...	96	...	...
	1995	100	...	...	96	...	...
	2000	100	...	...	96	80	90
	2010	100	...	...	96	...	...
Portugal Portugal	1990	98	96	96	97	87	92
	1995	98	96	97	98	92	95
	2000	99	98	99	99	97	98
	2010	99	100	99	100	100	100
Qatar Qatar	1990	100	100	100	100	100	100
	1995	100	100	100	100	100	100
	2000	100	100	100	100	100	100
	2010	100	100	100	100	100	100
Republic of Korea République de Corée	1990	97	...	...	100	100	100
	1995	97	67	90	100	100	100
	2000	98	75	93	100	100	100
	2010	100	88	98	100	100	100
Republic of Moldova République de Moldova	1990	98	...	...	...	...	...
	1995	98	88	93	86	67	76
	2000	99	89	93	87	72	79
	2010	99	93	96	89	82	85
Romania Roumanie	1990	93	75	75	88	52	71
	1995	95	62	80	88	53	72
	2000	97	70	84	88	54	72
	2010	99	...	...	...	...	...
Russian Federation Fédération de Russie	1990	98	93	93	80	58	74
	1995	98	83	94	78	58	73
	2000	98	86	95	77	59	72
	2010	99	92	97	74	59	70
Rwanda Rwanda	1990	95	66	66	69	34	36
	1995	91	64	66	64	39	41
	2000	86	63	66	60	45	47
	2010	76	63	65	52	56	55
Saint Kitts and Nevis Saint-Kitts-et-Nevis	1990	99	99	99	96	96	96
	1995	99	99	99	96	96	96
	2000	99	99	99	96	96	96
	2010	99	99	99	96	96	96

Country or area Pays ou zone	Year Année	Proportion of population with access to: - Pourcentage de la population ayant accès à :						
		Improved drinking water sources Un système amélioré de distribution d'eau potable			Improved sanitation facilities Un système amélioré d'assainissement			
		Urban (%) Urbaine (%)	Rural (%) Rurale (%)	Total (%) Totale (%)	Urban (%) Urbaine (%)	Rural (%) Rurale (%)	Total (%) Totale (%)
Saint Lucia Sainte-Lucie	1990	96	94	94	67	54	58
	1995	97	93	94	68	56	60
	2000	97	94	95	69	59	62
	2010	98	95	96	71	63	65
Saint Vincent-Grenadines Saint Vincent-Grenadines	1990	...	...	...	...	96	...
	1995	...	93	...	...	96	...
	2000	...	93	...	...	96	...
	2010	...	...	...	...	96	...
Samoa Samoa	1990	97	89	89	100	99	99
	1995	96	89	91	100	99	99
	2000	96	91	92	99	98	98
	2010	96	96	96	98	98	98
Sao Tome and Principe Sao Tomé-et-Principe	1995	85	65	75	27	14	20
	2000	86	70	79	27	15	21
	2010	89	88	89	30	19	26
Saudi Arabia Arabie saoudite	1990	97	89	89	100	...	...
	1995	97	63	90	100	...	...
	2000	97	...	...	100	...	...
	2010	97	...	...	100	...	...
Senegal Sénégal	1990	88	61	61	62	22	38
	1995	89	46	63	64	26	41
	2000	90	49	66	66	31	45
	2010	93	56	72	70	39	52
Serbia Serbie	1990	99	99	99	96	...	...
	1995	99	98	99	96	...	...
	2000	99	98	99	96	88	92
	2010	99	98	99	96	88	92
Seychelles Seychelles	2000	84	...	...	94	...	...
	2010	100	...	...	98	...	...
Sierra Leone Sierra Leone	1990	63	38	38	22	5	11
	1995	69	28	42	22	5	11
	2000	75	30	46	22	5	11
	2010	87	35	55	23	6	13
Singapore Singapour	1990	100	100	100	99	...	99
	1995	100	...	100	99	...	99
	2000	100	...	100	100	...	100
	2010	100	...	100	100	...	100
Slovakia Slovaquie	1990	100	100	100	100	100	100
	1995	100	100	100	100	100	100
	2000	100	100	100	100	100	100
	2010	100	100	100	100	99	100
Slovenia Slovénie	1990	100	100	100	100	100	100
	1995	100	99	100	100	100	100
	2000	100	99	100	100	100	100
	2010	100	99	99	100	100	100
Solomon Islands Iles Salomon	1990	...	...	...	98	...	...
	1995	94	65	69	98	18	30
	2000	94	65	70	98	18	31
	2010	...	...	...	98	...	...
Somalia Somalie	1995	21	18	19	42	12	21
	2000	35	15	22	45	10	22
	2010	66	7	29	52	6	23
South Africa Afrique du Sud	1990	98	83	83	82	60	71
	1995	98	67	84	82	61	72
	2000	98	71	86	84	63	75
	2010	99	79	91	86	67	79

Water supply and sanitation coverage *(continued)*
Accès à l'eau et à l'assainissement *(suite)*

Country or area Pays ou zone	Year Année	Proportion of population with access to: - Pourcentage de la population ayant accès à :					
		Improved drinking water sources Un système amélioré de distribution d'eau potable			Improved sanitation facilities Un système amélioré d'assainissement		
		Urban (%) Urbaine (%)	Rural (%) Rurale (%)	Total (%) Totale (%)	Urban (%) Urbaine (%)	Rural (%) Rurale (%)	Total (%) Totale (%)
Spain Espagne	1990	100	100	100	100	100	100
	1995	100	100	100	100	100	100
	2000	100	100	100	100	100	100
	2010	100	100	100	100	100	100
Sri Lanka Sri Lanka	1990	91	67	67	85	67	70
	1995	93	69	73	86	74	76
	2000	95	77	80	87	81	82
	2010	99	90	91	88	93	92
Sudan [2] Soudan [2]	1990	84	65	65	51	18	27
	1995	80	56	63	49	17	27
	2000	76	55	62	48	16	27
	2010	67	52	58	44	14	26
Suriname Suriname	1990	99	...	...	90	...	...
	1995	99	71	88	90	64	80
	2000	98	73	89	90	65	81
	2010	97	81	92	90	66	83
Swaziland Swaziland	1990	87	39	39	62	44	48
	1995	87	30	43	62	45	49
	2000	88	41	52	63	49	52
	2010	91	65	71	64	55	57
Sweden Suède	1990	100	100	100	100	100	100
	1995	100	100	100	100	100	100
	2000	100	100	100	100	100	100
	2010	100	100	100	100	100	100
Switzerland Suisse	1990	100	100	100	100	100	100
	1995	100	100	100	100	100	100
	2000	100	100	100	100	100	100
	2010	100	100	100	100	100	100
Syrian Arab Republic Rép. arabe syrienne	1990	97	86	86	95	75	85
	1995	97	76	87	95	76	86
	2000	95	79	87	95	81	88
	2010	93	86	90	96	93	95
Tajikistan Tadjikistan	1990	...	...	...	93	...	...
	1995	93	49	62	93	87	89
	2000	93	50	61	93	89	90
	2010	92	54	64	95	94	94
Thailand Thaïlande	1990	96	86	86	94	80	84
	1995	96	86	89	94	86	88
	2000	97	90	92	95	93	94
	2010	97	95	96	95	96	96
TFYR of Macedonia L'ex-R.Y. Macédoine	1990	100	100	100	92	...	...
	1995	100	99	100	92	...	...
	2000	100	99	100	92	82	88
	2010	100	99	100	92	82	88
Timor-Leste Timor-Leste	1995	67	48	52	55	32	37
	2000	69	49	54	56	33	39
	2010	91	60	69	73	37	47
Togo Togo	1990	79	49	49	26	8	13
	1995	82	37	52	26	7	13
	2000	84	38	55	26	5	13
	2010	89	40	61	26	3	13
Tokelau Tokélaou	1990	...	90	90	...	41	41
	1995	...	91	91	...	45	45
	2000	...	93	93	...	63	63
	2010	...	97	97	...	93	93

Country or area Pays ou zone	Year Année	Proportion of population with access to: - Pourcentage de la population ayant accès à :					
		Improved drinking water sources Un système amélioré de distribution d'eau potable			Improved sanitation facilities Un système amélioré d'assainissement		
		Urban (%) Urbaine (%)	Rural (%) Rurale (%)	Total (%) Totale (%)	Urban (%) Urbaine (%)	Rural (%) Rurale (%)	Total (%) Totale (%)
Tonga Tonga	1990	100	100	100	98	96	96
	1995	100	100	100	98	96	96
	2000	100	100	100	98	96	96
	2010	100	100	100	98	96	96
Trinidad and Tobago Trinité-et-Tobago	1990	92	88	88	93	93	93
	1995	94	90	90	92	92	92
	2000	95	91	91	92	92	92
	2010	98	93	94	92	92	92
Tunisia Tunisie	1990	95	81	81	95	44	74
	1995	96	69	86	95	51	78
	2000	98	77	90	95	57	81
	2010	99	...	...	96	...	...
Turkey Turquie	1990	94	85	85	96	66	84
	1995	95	79	89	96	68	85
	2000	97	85	93	96	71	87
	2010	100	99	100	97	75	90
Turkmenistan Turkménistan	1990	97	...	...	99	97	98
	1995	97	72	83	99	97	98
	2000	97	72	83	99	97	98
	2010	97	...	...	99	97	98
Turks and Caicos Islands Iles Turques et Caïques	1990	100	100	100	98	...	...
	1995	100	100	100	98	94	97
	2000	100	100	100	98	94	97
	2010	100	100	100	98	...	...
Tuvalu Tuvalu	1990	92	90	90	86	76	80
	1995	93	91	92	86	78	82
	2000	95	93	94	87	79	83
	2010	98	97	98	88	81	85
Uganda Ouganda	1990	78	43	43	32	26	27
	1995	82	46	50	33	28	29
	2000	86	54	58	33	30	30
	2010	95	68	72	34	34	34
Ukraine Ukraine	1990	100	...	...	97	...	...
	1995	100	91	97	97	91	95
	2000	99	92	97	97	91	95
	2010	98	98	98	96	89	94
United Arab Emirates Emirats arabes unis	1990	100	100	100	98	95	97
	1995	100	100	100	98	95	97
	2000	100	100	100	98	95	97
	2010	100	100	100	98	95	98
United Kingdom Royaume-Uni	1990	100	100	100	100	100	100
	1995	100	100	100	100	100	100
	2000	100	100	100	100	100	100
	2010	100	100	100	100	100	100
United Rep. of Tanzania Rép.-Unie de Tanzanie	1990	94	55	55	10	6	7
	1995	90	46	55	13	7	8
	2000	86	45	54	15	7	9
	2010	79	44	53	20	7	10
United States Etats-Unis	1990	100	99	99	100	99	100
	1995	100	94	99	100	99	100
	2000	100	94	99	100	99	100
	2010	100	94	99	100	99	100
Uruguay Uruguay	1990	98	96	96	95	83	94
	1995	98	81	96	95	84	94
	2000	99	88	98	97	90	96
	2010	100	100	100	100	99	100

Country or area Pays ou zone	Year Année	Proportion of population with access to: - Pourcentage de la population ayant accès à :					
		Improved drinking water sources Un système amélioré de distribution d'eau potable			Improved sanitation facilities Un système amélioré d'assainissement		
		Urban (%) Urbaine (%)	Rural (%) Rurale (%)	Total (%) Totale (%)	Urban (%) Urbaine (%)	Rural (%) Rurale (%)	Total (%) Totale (%)
Uzbekistan	1990	97	90	90	95	76	84
Ouzbékistan	1995	97	85	90	96	78	85
	2000	98	83	89	97	87	91
	2010	98	81	87	100	100	100
Vanuatu	1990	94	62	62	...	...	...
Vanuatu	1995	95	63	69	50	32	36
	2000	96	71	76	54	38	41
	2010	98	87	90	64	54	57
Venezuela (Boliv. Rep. of)	1990	93	71	90	89	45	82
Venezuela (Rép. boliv. du)	1995	94	73	91	91	50	86
	2000	94	74	92	93	54	89
Viet Nam	1990	88	57	57	63	30	37
Viet Nam	1995	91	60	67	71	39	46
	2000	94	71	77	78	49	56
	2010	99	93	95	94	68	76
Yemen	1990	96	67	67	70	12	24
Yémen	1995	89	55	63	76	18	32
	2000	83	52	60	82	24	39
	2010	72	47	55	93	34	53
Zambia	1990	89	49	49	61	37	46
Zambie	1995	88	29	51	60	39	47
	2000	88	36	54	59	40	47
	2010	87	46	61	57	43	48
Zimbabwe	1990	99	79	79	54	35	41
Zimbabwe	1995	99	70	79	53	35	41
	2000	99	70	80	53	34	40
	2010	98	69	80	52	32	40

Source:
World Health Organization (WHO) and United Nations Children's Fund (UNICEF), Geneva and New York, the WHO/UNICEF Joint Monitoring Programme for the Water and Sanitation database, last accessed July 2012.

1   The drinking water estimates for Bangladesh have been adjusted for arsenic contamination levels based on the national surveys conducted and approved by the Government of Bangladesh.

2   Data for Sudan prior to the independence of South Sudan in 2011 include those for South Sudan.

Source :
Organisation mondial de la santé (OMS) et Fonds des Nations Unies pour l'enfance (UNICEF), Genève et New York, la base de données de la Programme commun OMS/UNICEF de surveillance de l'eau et de l'assainissement, dernier accès juillet 2012.

1   Les estimations concernant l'eau potable pour le Bangladesh ont été ajustées afin de tenir compte des taux de pollution à l'arsenic constatés lors d'enquêtes nationales effectuées et approuvées par le Gouvernement bangladais.

2   Avant l'indépendance du Soudan du Sud en 2011, les données du Soudan incluaient aussi celles du Soudan du Sud.

Personnel in research and development (R & D)
Full-time equivalent (FTE)

Personnel employé dans la recherche et le développement (R - D)
Equivalent temps plein (ETP)

Country or area Pays ou zone	Year Année	Total R & D personnel Total du personnel de R - D	Researchers Chercheurs		Technicians and equivalent staff Techniciens et personnel assimilé		Other supporting staff Autre personnel de soutien	
			Total M & W Total H & F	Women Femmes	Total M & W Total H & F	Women Femmes	Total M & W Total H & F	Women Femmes
Albania [1] Albanie [1]	2008	779	467	207	120	...	192	...
Algeria [1] Algérie [1]	2005	7 331	5 593	2 043	1 134	...	604	...
American Samoa [1] Samoa américaines [1]	2004 2005	9 6	9 6	... ...	... ...	... ...	... ...	... ...
Argentina Argentine	2004 2005 2006 2007 2008 2009	42 454 45 361 49 359 53 187 56 987 59 683	29 471 31 868 35 040 38 681 41 523 43 717	14 370 15 416 17 081 20 418	6 967 7 788 8 151 7 732 8 236 8 852	... ...	6 016 5 705 6 168 6 774 7 228 7 114	... ...
Armenia [1,2] Arménie [1,2]	2004 2005 2006 2007 2008 2009	6 685[3] 6 892[3] 6 723[3] 5 669[3] 6 899[3] 6 926[3]	4 788[3] 5 056[3] 4 838 4 114 5 314 5 542	2 235 2 329 2 217 1 840 2 468 2 532	423[3] 345[3] 296 331 357[3] 353	... ...	1 474[3] #700 782 811[3] 768[3] 614	... ...
Australia Australie	2004 2006 2008	116 194 126 702 137 138	81 192 87 201 92 379	... ...	 20 892 24 250	... ...	 18 609 20 509	... ...
Austria Autriche	2004 2005[4] 2006 2007 *2008[4] 2009 *2010[4]	42 891 47 625 49 377 53 252 58 014 56 438 58 519	25 955 28 470 29 199 31 676 34 508 34 664 35 942	4 740 ... 5 669 6 521 ... 7 765 ...	12 067 ... 14 822 16 278 ... 16 709 ...	2 901 ... 3 486 3 673 ... 3 903 ...	4 869 ... 5 357 5 299 ... 5 065 ...	2 471 ... 2 452 2 424 ... 2 398 ...
Azerbaijan [2] Azerbaïdjan [2]	2004 2005 2006 2007 2008 2009	17 712[3] 18 164[3] 17 973[3] 18 079[3] 17 942[3] 17 401[3]	11 531 11 603 11 698 11 280 11 054 11 041	6 110 6 056 6 029 5 866 5 793 5 780	1 749 1 825 2 013 2 073 2 148 1 800	... ...	2 849 3 086 2 905 3 194 #4 740[3] 4 560[3]	... ...
Belarus [2] Bélarus [2]	2004 2005 2006 2007 2008 2009	28 750[3] 30 222[3] 30 544[3] 31 294[3] 31 473[3] 33 516[3]	17 034 18 267 18 494 18 995 18 455 20 571	7 556 7 897 8 078 8 228 8 106 8 800	2 068 2 112 2 263 2 312 2 278 2 322	... ...	5 844 5 763 5 715 5 880 6 466 10 623[3]	... ...
Belgium Belgique	2004 2005 2006 2007 2008 2009 *2010	52 253 53 517 55 714 57 963 58 476 59 756 59 851	32 400 33 146 34 879 36 318 36 774 38 225 38 168	9 287 9 769 10 586 11 150 11 732 12 064 ...	14 722 15 047 14 325 14 815 15 754 15 984 ...	4 425 4 585 3 920 4 010 5 211 5 295 ...	5 130 5 324 6 510 6 830 5 947 5 546 ...	2 606 2 702 3 301 3 397 2 647 2 760 ...
Benin [1,2,4] Bénin [1,2,4]	2007	...	1 000	...	...	...	...	...
Bolivia (Plurin. State of) [2] Bolivie (État plurin. de) [2]	2009	2 862	1 947	1 231	379	296	536	329
Bosnia and Herzegovina [1] Bosnie-Herzégovine [1]	2004 2005 #2006 2007	688 731 1 284 1 554	239 253 671 745	... ...	197 198 245 270	... ...	250 280 368 536	... ...
Botswana [1,2,5] Botswana [1,2,5]	2005	2 140	1 732	533	408	...	...	...
Brazil [2] Brésil [2]	2004 2005 2006 2007 2008 2009 2010	303 528 328 932 345 252 366 597 388 574 428 013 466 451	164 718 177 941 184 239 192 080 200 363 216 700 231 910	... ... 92 198[6]	138 810 150 991 161 013 174 517 188 211 211 313 234 541	... ...	... ...	... ...
Brunei Darussalam [2] Brunéi Darussalam [2]	2004	...	244[1]	99	...	...	...	...

51 Personnel in research and development (R & D)
Full-time equivalent (FTE)

Personnel employé dans la recherche et le développement (R - D)
Equivalent temps plein (ETP)

Country or area Pays ou zone	Year Année	Total R & D personnel Total du personnel de R - D	Researchers Chercheurs Total M & W Total H & F	Women Femmes	Technicians and equivalent staff Techniciens et personnel assimilé Total M & W Total H & F	Women Femmes	Other supporting staff Autre personnel de soutien Total M & W Total H & F	Women Femmes
Bulgaria	2004	15 647	9 827	4 642	3 721	2 236	2 099	1 371
Bulgarie	2005	15 853	10 053	4 673	3 778	2 256	2 022	1 349
	2006	16 321	10 336	4 690	3 843	2 263	2 142	1 362
	2007	16 940	11 203	5 350	3 638	2 101	2 099	1 309
	2008	17 219	11 384	5 462	3 738	2 019	2 097	1 393
	2009	18 230	11 968	5 796	4 023	2 254	2 239	1 485
	*2010	16 509	10 932	...				
Burkina Faso [2]	2004	890[1,7]	293[1,7]	34	227[1,7]	...	370[1,7]	...
Burkina Faso [2]	2005	942[1,7]	301[1,7]	37	225[1,7]	...	416[1,7]	...
	#2007	1 054[1]	187[1,7]	25	391[1,7]	...	476[1,7]	...
	#2010	2 548	1 144	264	608	149	796	256
Cameroon [2,8]								
Cameroun [2,8]	2008	5 600	4 562	994	338	...	700	...
Canada	2004	210 593	130 399	...	51 632	...	28 562	...
Canada	2005	218 605	136 768	...	52 755	...	29 082	...
	2006	229 166	140 656	...	57 450	...	31 060	...
	2007	245 183	149 308	...	64 150	...	31 715	...
	2008	242 686	148 983	...	60 453	...	33 250	...
Central African Rep. [2]	2005[1]	...	11	...	...	...	...	...
Rép. centrafricaine [2]	2006[1]	...	20	...	...	...	...	...
	2007	...	41[1]	17	...	...	...	...
	#2009[1]	...	134	...	...	...	...	...
Chile	2007	11 024	5 551	1 521	4 049	1 359	1 424	532
Chili	2008	12 571	5 959	1 604	4 924	1 651	1 688	682
China [9]	2004[10]	1 152 617	926 252	...	...	...	...	...
Chine [9]	2005[10]	1 364 799	1 118 698	...	...	...	...	...
	2006[10]	1 502 472	1 223 756	...	...	...	...	...
	2007[10]	1 736 155	1 423 381	...	...	...	...	...
	2008[10]	1 965 357	1 592 420	...	...	...	...	...
	2009	2 291 252	#1 152 311	...	...	...	...	...
China, Hong Kong SAR	2004	18 846	14 594	...	2 904	...	1 348	...
Chine, Hong Kong RAS	2005	22 053	18 024	...	2 346	...	1 683	...
	2006	22 977	18 326	...	3 176	...	1 475	...
	2007	23 644	19 553	...	2 603	...	1 487	...
	2008	22 005	18 450	...	2 286	...	1 269	...
	2009	23 283	19 283	...	2 463	...	1 535	...
China, Macao SAR [1]	2004[4]	349	244	48	97	...	8	...
Chine, Macao RAS [1]	#2005	413	298	77	110	...	5	...
	2006	418	275	77	131	...	12	...
	2007	482	303	84	167	...	12	...
	2008	576	349	99	215	...	13	...
	2009	684	390	118	276	...	17	...
Colombia [2]	2004	...	13 737	4 916	...	...	...	...
Colombie [2]	2005	...	15 171	5 503	...	...	...	...
	2006	...	16 428	5 987	...	...	...	...
	2007	...	17 169	6 331	...	...	...	...
	2008	...	17 110	6 337	...	...	...	...
	2009	...	15 866	5 909	...	...	...	...
Costa Rica [2]	2004	...	1 076	447	...	...	...	...
Costa Rica [2]	2005	...	1 444	569	...	...	...	...
	#2006	4 298	3 164	1 200	...	...	1 134	443
	2007	4 660	3 521	1 306	...	...	1 139	366
	2008	4 779	3 416	1 442	315	...	1 048	...
	2009	4 973	3 506	1 431	878	...	589	...
Côte d'Ivoire [1]								
Côte d'Ivoire [1]	2005	...	1 269	210	...	...	...	...
Croatia	2004	11 162	7 140	3 256	2 573	1 226	1 449	1 051
Croatie	2005	9 270	5 727	2 710	2 633	1 196	910	584
	2006	9 516	5 778	2 680	2 843	1 359	895	597
	2007	10 124	6 129	2 893	2 846	1 433	1 149	795
	2008	10 583	6 697	3 262	2 675	1 326	1 212	812
	2009	11 015	6 931	3 384	2 804	1 358	1 280	833
	2010	10 859	7 104	...	2 601	...	1 154	...

Personnel in research and development (R & D)
Full-time equivalent (FTE)

Personnel employé dans la recherche et le développement (R - D)
Equivalent temps plein (ETP)

Country or area Pays ou zone	Year Année	Total R & D personnel Total du personnel de R - D	Researchers Chercheurs		Technicians and equivalent staff Techniciens et personnel assimilé		Other supporting staff Autre personnel de soutien	
			Total M & W Total H & F	Women Femmes	Total M & W Total H & F	Women Femmes	Total M & W Total H & F	Women Femmes
Cuba[2]	2004	34 094	5 115	...	...	...	28 979[11]	...
Cuba[2]	2005	33 988	5 526	2 703	...	...	28 462[11]	...
	2006	29 810	5 491	2 724	...	...	24 319	...
	2007	#17 915	5 236	2 408	...	...	#12 679	...
	2008	18 625	5 525	2 680	...	...	13 100	...
	2009	18 704	5 448	2 541	...	...	13 256	...
	2010	16 641	4 872	2 381	...	...	11 769	...
Cyprus	2004	1 017	583	197	243	95	191	105
Chypre	2005	1 157	682	239	273	98	201	105
	2006	1 226	748	254	270	103	207	108
	2007	1 244	799	272	266	113	179	87
	2008	1 201	806	281	233	101	161	82
	2009	1 266	873	328	230	97	163	91
	*2010	1 300	895	...	...	...	...	...
Czech Republic	2004	28 765	16 300	4 052	9 446	3 407	3 020	1 348
République tchèque	#2005	43 370	24 169	6 349	13 773	5 153	5 429	2 633
	2006	47 729	26 267	6 652	15 840	5 672	5 622	2 731
	2007	49 192	27 878	7 093	15 430	5 641	5 883	2 916
	2008	50 808	29 785	7 559	15 133	5 259	5 890	2 888
	2009	50 961	28 759	7 490	16 005	5 395	6 197	2 938
	2010	52 290	29 228	7 429	15 971	5 141	7 092	3 369
Dem. Rep. of the Congo[2,3]	2004	31 923	9 072	...	1 444	...	21 407	...
Rép. dém. du Congo[2,3]	2005	33 478	10 411	...	1 510	...	21 557	...
Denmark	2004	42 687	26 167	...	...	...	...	...
Danemark	2005	43 499	28 179	8 113	10 781	5 364	4 538	2 534
	2006	44 878	28 846	...	10 894	...	5 138	...
	#2007	46 897	30 174	8 843	11 527	4 867	5 196	2 570
	2008[4]	58 589	35 702	...	...	...	...	...
	2009	54 391	36 062	*10 869	11 738	*4 727	6 591	*3 391
	2010[4]	53 191	35 326	...	11 417	...	6 448	...
Ecuador[2]	2006	2 301	1 555	645	414	171	332	...
Equateur[2]	2007	2 853	1 615	725	471	211	767	...
	2008	4 063	2 623	1 154	675	297	765	...
Egypt[2]	2007	...	95 947[1]	34 725[6]	30 295[1]	...	...	...
Egypte[2]	#2008[1]	...	84 274	...	...	...	...	...
	2009	...	81 114[1,4]	...	...	...	43 528	...
El Salvador[2]	2004	...	258	80	...	...	...	...
El Salvador[2]	2005	...	260	81	...	...	...	...
	2006	...	263	82	...	...	...	...
	2007	...	274	85	...	...	...	...
	#2008	...	401	132	...	...	...	...
	2009	...	455	160	...	...	...	...
	2010	...	516	190	...	...	...	...
Estonia	2004	4 735	3 369	1 390	654	370	712	488
Estonie	2005	4 362	3 331	1 317	567	274	464	305
	2006	4 741	3 513	1 418	776	339	452	237
	2007	5 002	3 690	1 531	805	368	507	266
	2008	5 086	3 979	1 510	828	402	279	186
	2009	5 430	4 314	1 796	836	391	280	190
	*2010	5 261	4 069	...	899	...	293	...
Ethiopia[2]	2005	5 799	2 187	138	848	...	2 764	...
Ethiopie[2]	2007	7 065	2 377	176	1 101	...	3 587	...
	#2010[5]	13 095	7 283	477	1 881	52	3 931	822
Finland[2]	2004	76 687	51 219	14 834	...	...	...	...
Finlande[2]	2005	77 275	50 773	15 349	...	...	...	...
	2006	79 911	53 273	16 808	...	...	...	...
	2007	79 507	53 420	16 824	...	...	...	...
	2008	79 289	55 195	16 958	...	...	...	...
	2009	79 475	55 797	17 530	...	...	...	...
France	2004	352 003	249 533[2]	69 272[2]	106 415	...	43 211	...
France	2005	349 681	251 599[2]	70 347[2]	105 171	...	42 003	...
	2006	365 814	268 944[2]	73 763[2]	114 525	...	40 698	...
	2007	375 235	278 480[2]	77 439[2]	112 964	...	40 420	...
	2008	382 653	289 292[2]	79 161[2]	115 811	...	39 163	...
	2009	390 374	295 696[2]	79 557[2]	118 633	...	37 539	...

Country or area Pays ou zone	Year Année	Total R & D personnel Total du personnel de R - D	Researchers Chercheurs Total M & W Total H & F	Women Femmes	Technicians and equivalent staff Techniciens et personnel assimilé Total M & W Total H & F	Women Femmes	Other supporting staff Autre personnel de soutien Total M & W Total H & F	Women Femmes
Gabon [1,2]	2004	188	80	25	68	...	40	...
Gabon [1,2]	2006	322	150	37	42	13	130	40
	2009	#839	#531	#118	#142	55	#166	66
Gambia [2]	2004[1]	82	44	3	28	...	10	...
Gambie [2]	2005[1]	84	46	4	28	...	10	...
	2008	855	155	31	200	...	500	...
	2009	926	179	...	198	...	549	...
Georgia [2]	2004	16 698	10 910	5 664	2 262	...	3 526	...
Géorgie [2]	2005	13 415	8 112	4 275	1 810	...	3 493	...
Germany	2004	470 729	270 215	...	87 873	...	112 640	...
Allemagne	2005	475 278	272 148	47 666	94 578	...	108 553	...
	2006	487 935	279 822	...	98 922	...	109 190	...
	2007	506 450	290 853	54 079	107 150	...	108 447	...
	2008	522 688	302 467	...	109 632	...	110 588	...
	2009	534 565	317 226	65 226	111 641	34 265	105 698	43 762
	2010[4]	550 300	327 500	...	...	...	...	...
Ghana								
Ghana	2007	1 431[8]	392[8]	69[8]	343[8]	70	696[8]	171
Greece	2005	33 603	19 593	6 213	8 450	3 070	5 559	3 007
Grèce	2006[4]	35 140	19 907	...	...	...	...	...
	2007[4]	35 531	21 013	...	...	...	...	...
Greenland								
Groenland	2004	48	40	11	8[12]	...	...	...
Guam	2004	53	50	...	...	...	...	...
Guam	2005	51	48	...	...	...	...	...
Guatemala [2]	2005[1]	1 177	615	262	192	52	370	90
Guatemala [2]	2006[1]	1 122	547	135[13]	189	50	386	69
	2007[1]	1 822	718	229	#709	261	395	131
	2008[1]	1 740	710	224	626	237	404	137
	2009	1 599	756	266	438	196	405	135
Hungary	2004	22 826	14 904	...	4 713	...	3 209	...
Hongrie	2005	23 239	15 878	...	4 591	...	2 770	...
	2006	25 971	17 547	5 505	4 943	3 176	3 481	2 116
	2007	25 954	17 391	5 505	5 141	3 014	3 422	1 985
	2008	27 403	18 504	5 689	5 237	3 096	3 662	2 200
	2009	29 795	20 064	6 103	5 527	3 196	4 204	2 256
	2010	31 480	21 342	...	5 967	...	4 171	...
Iceland	2005	3 226	2 155	784	669	299	402	181
Islande	2006	3 415	2 400	874	652	282	363	156
	2007	2 982	2 208	805	517	213	257	102
	2008	3 117	2 308	841	540	222	269	107
	2009	3 753	2 861	1 089	626	279	266	96
India								
Inde	2005	391 149	154 827	19 707[14]	105 808	...	130 514	...
Indonesia [2]	2005	55 118[1]	35 564[1]	10 874	9 253[1]	...	10 301[1]	...
Indonésie [2]	#2009[1,4]	...	41 143	...	...	...	...	...
Iran (Islamic Rep. of) [2]	2004	91 584	51 899	10 300	22 186	...	17 499	...
Iran (Rép. islamique d') [2]	2006	101 457	67 795	15 587	18 429	...	15 233	...
	#2008	141 871	107 810	28 667	18 294	...	15 767	...
Iraq [7]								
Iraq [7]	2009	2 981	1 520	474	802	...	607	...
Ireland	2004	15 713	11 010	3 069	2 717	729	1 986	834
Irlande	2005	16 690	11 587	3 241	3 043	797	2 060	881
	2006	17 507	12 184	3 561	2 968	783	2 355	1 023
	2007	18 212	12 669	3 856	2 934	797	2 610	1 199
	2008	20 120	14 546	4 448	2 978	753	2 596	1 140
	2009[4]	20 331	14 526	4 701	3 250	884	2 555	1 088
	2010[4]	20 242	14 437	...	3 264	...	2 541	...
Italy	2004	164 026	72 012	20 938	...	...	...	...
Italie	2005	175 248	82 489	26 797	...	...	...	...
	2006	192 002	88 430	29 107	...	...	...	...
	2007	208 376	93 000	31 408	...	...	...	...
	2009	226 285	101 825	34 813	...	...	...	...
	*2010	218 837	105 846	...	...	...	...	...

Personnel in research and development (R & D)
Full-time equivalent (FTE)

Personnel employé dans la recherche et le développement (R - D)
Equivalent temps plein (ETP)

Country or area Pays ou zone	Year Année	Total R & D personnel Total du personnel de R - D	Researchers Chercheurs		Technicians and equivalent staff Techniciens et personnel assimilé		Other supporting staff Autre personnel de soutien	
			Total M & W Total H & F	Women Femmes	Total M & W Total H & F	Women Femmes	Total M & W Total H & F	Women Femmes
Japan [2] Japon [2]	2004	1 096 078	830 474	98 690	87 886	25 696	177 719	65 308
	2005	1 122 680	861 901	102 948	85 509	27 562	175 269	65 753
	2006	1 148 836	874 690	108 547	87 721	27 774	186 425	67 387
	2007	1 157 570	883 386	114 942	93 841	30 051	180 343	65 469
	2008	1 159 722	890 669	116 106	89 509	29 457	179 543	66 398
	2009	1 152 787	889 341	121 141	88 028	29 339	175 418	66 280
Jordan [2] Jordanie [2]	2007[1]	...	10 887	...	...	...	...	...
	#2008	...	11 310[1]	2 548	...	...	...	...
Kazakhstan [2] Kazakhstan [2]	2004	16 715[3]	10 382	5 017	1 102	...	3 112	...
	2005	18 912[3]	11 910	6 013	1 270	...	3 133	...
	2006	19 563[3]	12 404	6 140	1 281	...	3 214	...
	2007	17 774[3]	11 524	5 987	1 290	...	2 824	...
	2008	16 304[3]	10 780	5 526	1 166	...	2 349	...
	2009	15 793[3]	10 095	4 892	1 151	...	2 366	...
Kenya Kenya	2007	4 568[1]	2 105[1]	376[6]	2 362[1]	...	101[1]	...
Republic of Korea [2] République de Corée [2]	2004[15]	312 314	209 979	25 198	76 730	18 908	25 605	9 401
	2005[15]	335 428	234 702	30 174	75 179	19 123	25 547	9 732
	2006[15]	365 794	256 598	33 682	80 079	21 223	29 117	10 478
	#2007	421 549	289 098	42 977	94 319	28 734	38 132	14 713
	2008	436 228	300 050	46 677	90 021	27 300	46 157	18 264
	2009	466 824	323 175	51 073	95 862	29 099	47 787	20 365
	2010	500 124	345 912	57 662	103 618	32 399	50 594	20 723
Kuwait Koweït	2004[1,7]	786	373	...	93	...	320	...
	2005[1,7]	800	384	...	96	...	320	...
	2006[1,7]	812	392	...	98	...	322	...
	2007	869[1,7]	472[1,7,11]	166	94[1,7]	...	303[1,7]	...
	2008	809[1,7]	403[1,7]	150	93[1,7]	...	313[1,7]	...
	2009	819[1,7]	402[1,7]	149	92[1,7]	...	325[1,7]	...
Kyrgyzstan [2] Kirghizistan [2]	2004	3 369[3]	2 019	971	307	...	518	...
	2005	3 419[3]	2 187	977	226	...	498	...
	2006	3 287[3]	2 154	967	205	...	457	...
	2007	3 140[3]	2 034	888	204	...	480	...
	2008	3 076[3]	1 835	841	378	...	429	...
	2009	3 533[3]	2 290	995	376	...	462	...
Latvia Lettonie	2004	5 103	3 324	1 806	802	456	977	619
	2005	5 483	3 282	1 636	1 062	554	1 139	594
	2006	6 520	4 024	1 868	1 483	711	1 013	623
	2007	6 378	4 223	2 063	1 126	596	1 029	661
	2008	6 533	4 370	2 172	1 227	691	936	600
	2009	5 485	3 621	1 823	1 269	640	595	374
	2010	5 409	3 807	...	866	...	736	...
Lesotho Lesotho	2004	51[1]	20[1]	10	21[1]	...	10[1]	...
	2009[1]	105	46	16[14]	47	...	11	...
Libyan Arab Jamah. [2] Jamah. arabe libyenne [2]	2004[1]	772	215	...	164	...	...	...
	2006[1]	1 253	339	...	185	...	...	...
	2007[1]	1 283	373	...	258	...	...	...
	2008[1]	1 248	588	...	227	...	216	...
	2009	1 131[1]	460[1]	101	229[1]	...	268[1]	...
Lithuania Lituanie	2004	10 557	7 356	3 481	1 531	992	1 670	1 054
	2005	11 002	7 637	3 706	1 436	939	1 929	1 280
	2006	11 443	8 036	3 907	1 402	899	2 005	1 323
	2007	12 656	8 489	4 116	1 778	1 017	2 389	1 612
	2008	12 632	8 458	4 130	1 836	1 146	2 338	1 466
	2009	12 094	8 490	4 278	1 487	944	2 117	1 412
	2010	11 822	8 387	...	1 570	...	1 865	...
Luxembourg Luxembourg	2004	4 318	2 031	...	...	...	...	...
	2005	4 392	2 227	392	1 558	258	607	250
	2006	4 377	2 054	...	1 284	...	1 038	...
	2007[4]	4 605	2 201	...	1 321	...	1 083	...
	2008	4 652	2 288	...	1 473	...	891	...
	2009	4 711	2 396	534	1 423	384	891	437
	*2010	4 889	2 536	...	1 423	...	930	...

Personnel in research and development (R & D)
Full-time equivalent (FTE)

Personnel employé dans la recherche et le développement (R - D)
Equivalent temps plein (ETP)

Country or area Pays ou zone	Year Année	Total R & D personnel Total du personnel de R - D	Researchers Chercheurs		Technicians and equivalent staff Techniciens et personnel assimilé		Other supporting staff Autre personnel de soutien	
			Total M & W Total H & F	Women Femmes	Total M & W Total H & F	Women Femmes	Total M & W Total H & F	Women Femmes
Madagascar	2004	1 706[1]	848[1]	279	175[1]	...	683[1]	...
Madagascar	2005	1 686[1]	879[1]	298	195[1]	...	612[1]	...
	2006	1 715[1]	899[1]	303	278[1]	...	538[1]	...
	2007	1 778[1]	937[1]	320	280[1]	...	561[1]	...
	#2008	1 807[1]	930[1]	295	496[1]	...	381[1]	...
	2009	1 807[1]	930[1]	295	497[1]	...	380[1]	...
Malawi								
Malawi	2007	1 638[8]	406[8]	89	791[8]	...	441[8]	...
Malaysia	2004	17 887	12 670	4 701	1 598	...	3 619	...
Malaisie	2006	13 416	9 694	3 757	1 142	...	2 579	...
Mali[1,2]	2006	1 421	1 236	150	185[12]	...	...	...
Mali[1,2]	#2007[8]	2 414	877	93	1 085	109	452	54
Malta	2004	717	436	109	147	17	134	64
Malte	2005	825	479	121	222	20	124	65
	2006	862	521	132	221	23	120	63
	2007	862	492	123	267	28	102	55
	2008	941	541	149	280	30	120	65
	2009	911	494	144	281	29	136	67
	*2010	1 039	588	...	297	...	154	...
Mexico	2004	75 112	39 724	...	22 289	...	13 099	...
Mexique	2005	83 685	43 922	...	25 796	...	13 967	...
	2006	66 967	36 264	...	19 328	...	11 375	...
	2007	70 293	37 930	...	20 037	...	12 326	...
	2008	75 370	37 639	...	24 591	...	13 141	...
	2009	83 642	42 973	...	26 809	...	13 860	...
Monaco[1]	2004	18	9	4	6	...	3	...
Monaco[1]	2005	18	10	5	5	...	3	...
Mongolia[2]	2004	2 642[1]	1 991[1]	907	146[1]	...	505[1]	...
Mongolie[2]	2005	2 283[1]	1 731[1]	819	81[1]	...	471[1]	...
	2006	2 316[1]	1 707[1]	822	114[1]	...	495[1]	...
	2007	2 379[1]	1 740[1]	837	120[1]	...	519[1]	...
	2008[1]	2 420	1 723	816	125	...	572	...
	2009[1]	2 483	1 748	841	137	...	598	...
Montenegro[2]	2004	1 200	597	236	259	...	344	...
Monténégro[2]	2005	1 246	633	252	290	...	323	...
	2006	1 233	602	231	282	...	349	...
	2007	1 344	671	277	276	...	397	...
Morocco[2]	2004[1]	27 495	24 483	6 872	1 420	...	1 592	...
Maroc[2]	2005[1]	27 549	24 835	6 580	1 042	...	1 672	...
	2006[1]	31 326	28 089	7 322[14]	1 467	...	1 770	...
	2007[1]	31 870	28 633	7 913[14]	1 467	...	1 770	...
	2008	33 826[1]	29 276[1]	8 080	1 909[1]	...	2 641[1]	...
Mozambique[2]	2006	1 532[1]	337[1]	113	753[1]	...	442[1]	...
Mozambique[2]	2007	2 082[1,8]	522[1,8]	174	935[1,8]	...	625[1,8]	...
Netherlands	2004	95 702	48 402	...	23 517	...	23 783	...
Pays-Bas	2005	93 599	47 854	...	23 265	...	22 480	...
	2006	97 835	53 150	...	21 813	...	22 872	...
	2007	93 788	51 057	...	20 669	...	22 062	...
	2008	93 432	50 727	...	19 403	...	23 302	...
	2009	87 874	46 958	...	18 829	...	22 088	...
	*2010	98 074	52 066	...	21 243	...	24 766	...
New Zealand	2005	23 178	17 235	...	3 147	...	2 796	...
Nouvelle-Zélande	2007	24 700	18 300	...	3 750	...	2 580	...
	2009	28 600	21 400	...	3 900	...	3 200	...
Nicaragua[2]								
Nicaragua[2]	2004	371	326	...	45	15	...	...
Niger[1]	2004	599	106	...	133	...	360	...
Niger[1]	2005	595	101	...	137	...	357	...
Nigeria[1,2]	2004	...	24 727	4 286	9 847	...	...	...
Nigéria[1,2]	2005	66 574	28 533	4 839	10 854	...	27 187	...
	2007[8]	32 802	17 624	4 106	4 647	1 026	10 531	3 759
Norway[2]	2005	53 826	36 555	11 560	...	...	...	...
Norvège[2]	2007	59 132	41 327	13 858	...	...	...	...
	2008	62 655	43 699	14 892	...	...	...	...
	2009	64 126	44 762	15 770	...	...	...	...

Personnel in research and development (R & D)
Full-time equivalent (FTE)

Personnel employé dans la recherche et le développement (R - D)
Equivalent temps plein (ETP)

Country or area Pays ou zone	Year Année	Total R & D personnel Total du personnel de R - D	Researchers Chercheurs Total M & W Total H & F	Women Femmes	Technicians and equivalent staff Techniciens et personnel assimilé Total M & W Total H & F	Women Femmes	Other supporting staff Autre personnel de soutien Total M & W Total H & F	Women Femmes
Occupied Palestinian Terr.[2] Terr. palestinien occupé[2]	2007	1 555[1,16,17]	981[1,16,17]	238	232[1,16,17]	...	342[1,16,17]	...
	2008	1 542[1,16,17]	992[1,16,17]	227	191[1,16,17]	...	359[1,16,17]	...
	2009	2 951[5,16]	1 550[5,16]	291	381[5,16]	...	1 020[5,16]	...
	2010[5]	3 790	2 348	585	485	145	957	288
Pakistan Pakistan	2005	53 159	12 689	2 053	6 471	...	33 999	...
	2007	#69 619	#26 338	6 153	11 113	...	32 168	...
	2009	74 695	27 602	6 534	10 993	...	36 100	...
Panama[2] Panama[2]	2004	3 545	484	199	985	...	2 076	849
	2005	#5 840	507	...	1 288	...	#4 045	1 835
	2006	4 050	359	...	931	...	2 760	1 240
	2007	3 905	572	...	1 247	...	2 086	1 006
	2008	#1 585	463	...	986	...	136	68
	2009	1 648	482	...	1 025	...	141	...
	2010	1 714	501	...	1 066	...	147	...
Paraguay[2] Paraguay[2]	2004	1 873	864	444	...	...	1 009	525
	2005	#1 142	787	368	...	...	#355	#179
	2008	1 208	850	440	...	...	358	158
Peru[2] Pérou[2]	2004	8 434	4 965	...	1 757	...	1 712	...
Philippines Philippines	2005	9 407[3]	6 896	3 500	897	...	1 440	...
	2007	9 357	6 957	3 535	964	...	1 428	...
Poland[2] Pologne[2]	2004	127 356	96 531	37 594	15 686	7 844	15 139	9 865
	2005	123 431	97 875	38 426	13 989	6 613	11 567	7 606
	2006	121 283	96 374	38 065	13 533	6 358	11 376	7 167
	2007	121 623	97 289	38 802	13 500	6 167	10 834	6 854
	2008	119 682	97 474	38 509	11 616	5 665	10 592	6 716
	2009	120 923	98 165	38 794	12 314	5 122	10 444	6 585
Portugal Portugal	2004[4]	25 629	20 684	9 333	3 054	1 224	1 891	1 084
	2005	25 728	21 126	9 530	2 918	1 177	1 683	954
	2006[4]	30 531	24 651	10 944	3 605	1 352	2 274	1 063
	2007	35 334	28 176	12 359	4 292	1 527	2 866	1 173
	#2008	47 882	40 408	17 643	5 008	1 914	2 466	1 066
	2009	51 347	44 084	20 119	4 742	1 959	2 521	1 155
	*2010	52 378	45 916	...	...	...	...	...
Puerto Rico Porto Rico	2009	4 466	2 508	1 036	...	...	...	...
Republic of Moldova République de Moldova	2004	4 797[14]	2 725[14]	1 220	354[14]	...	1 718[14]	...
	2005	4 672[14]	2 583[14]	1 120	334[14]	...	1 755[14]	...
	2006	4 505[14]	2 507[14]	1 045	362[14]	...	1 636[14]	...
	2007	4 587[14]	2 592[14]	1 170	417[14]	...	1 578[14]	...
	2008	4 643	2 933	1 344	355	...	1 355	...
	2009[1]	4 573	2 861	1 374	282	...	1 430	...
Romania Roumanie	2004	33 361	21 257	9 480	5 525	3 199	6 579	2 916
	2005	33 222	22 958	10 617	4 998	2 859	5 266	2 414
	2006	29 340	19 021	8 603	4 496	2 625	5 823	2 754
	2007	28 977	18 808	8 242	4 361	2 392	5 808	2 631
	2008	30 390	19 394	8 834	4 620	2 498	6 376	2 942
	2009	28 398	19 271	8 643	3 991	2 270	5 136	2 212
	2010	26 171	19 780	...	3 139	...	3 252	...
Russian Federation[2,14] Fédération de Russie[2,14]	2004	839 338	401 425	172 177	69 963	...	367 950	...
	2005	813 207	391 121	165 993	65 982	...	356 104	...
	2006	807 066	388 939	163 972	66 031	...	352 096	...
	2007	801 135	392 849	164 385	64 569	...	343 717	...
	2008	761 252	375 804	157 149	60 218	...	325 230	...
	2009	742 433	369 237	154 725	60 045	...	313 151	...
	2010	736 540	368 915	153 863	59 276	...	308 349	...
Rwanda[2,18] Rwanda[2,18]	2008	660[1]	486[1]	107	7[1]	...	167[1]	...
	2009	1 001[1]	564[1]	123	8[1]	...	429[1]	...
Saudi Arabia[2] Arabie saoudite[2]	2007[1,7]	1 635	1 047	...	419	...	169	...
	#2008	2 568[1,7]	1 202[1,7]	17	653[1,7]	...	713[1,7]	...
	2009	2 655[1,7]	1 271[1,7]	18	658[1,7]	...	726[1,7]	...
Senegal Sénégal	2006[4]	3 299[1]	3 011[1]	301	...	...	288[1]	...
	2007[1,4]	3 565	3 277	327	...	...	288	...
	#2008	5 540	4 527	1 078	620	158	393	111

Personnel in research and development (R & D)
Full-time equivalent (FTE)

Personnel employé dans la recherche et le développement (R - D)
Equivalent temps plein (ETP)

Country or area Pays ou zone	Year Année	Total R & D personnel Total du personnel de R - D	Researchers Chercheurs Total M & W Total H & F	Women Femmes	Technicians and equivalent staff Techniciens et personnel assimilé Total M & W Total H & F	Women Femmes	Other supporting staff Autre personnel de soutien Total M & W Total H & F	Women Femmes
Serbia[2] Serbie[2]	2004	22 485[3,16]	11 637[3,16]	5 071	4 844[3,16]	...	6 004[3,16]	...
	2005	22 641[3,16]	11 551[3,16]	5 050	4 894[3,16]	...	6 196[3,16]	...
	2006	22 707[3,16]	12 079[3,16]	5 405	4 756[3,16]	...	5 872[3,16]	...
	#2007	18 153[16]	10 580[16]	4 975	2 408[16]	...	5 165[16]	...
	2008	19 321	11 534[16]	5 439	2 327[16]	...	5 460	...
	2009[16]	20 067	12 006	5 696	2 337	...	5 724	...
Seychelles[1] Seychelles[1]	2005	180	13	4	53	...	114	...
Singapore[2] Singapour[2]	2004	31 006	25 251	6 506	2 823	1 121	2 932	1 901
	2005	34 522	27 969	7 346	3 265	1 326	3 288	2 095
	2006	36 191	29 478	7 986	3 291	1 311	3 422	2 290
	2007	38 255	31 657	8 665	3 224	1 279	3 374	2 278
	2008	40 504	33 365	9 346	3 742	1 453	3 397	2 354
	2009	41 388	34 387	9 798	3 563	1 427	3 438	2 301
Slovakia Slovaquie	2004	14 329	10 718	4 427	2 403	1 331	1 209	664
	2005	14 404	10 921	4 484	2 245	1 218	1 238	670
	2006	15 028	11 776	4 959	2 284	1 220	969	603
	2007	15 421	12 354	5 116	2 238	1 238	829	533
	2008	15 576	12 587	5 330	2 117	1 139	872	551
	2009	15 952	13 290	5 607	1 880	1 039	781	488
	2010	18 188	15 183	6 376	2 087	1 046	918	589
Slovenia Slovénie	2004	7 132	4 030	1 288	2 323	882	779	427
	2005	8 994	5 253	1 777	2 820	1 067	921	501
	2006	9 793	5 857	1 941	2 954	1 148	982	535
	2007	10 369	6 250	2 106	3 089	1 176	1 030	542
	#2008	11 594	7 032	2 326	3 418	1 250	1 144	552
	2009	12 410	7 446	2 513	3 770	1 316	1 194	577
	*2010	12 940	7 703	...	3 928	...	1 309	...
South Africa Afrique du Sud	2004	29 696	17 915	6 623	5 176	1 631	6 606	2 913
	2005	28 798	17 303	6 272	5 248	1 749	6 247	2 928
	2006	30 984	18 573	7 114	6 332	2 201	6 080	2 700
	2007	31 352	19 320	7 349	6 060	2 109	5 972	2 647
	2008	30 802	19 384	7 441	6 022	2 103	5 395	2 487
Spain Espagne	2004	161 933	100 994	37 580	37 871	12 578	23 068	10 353
	2005	174 773	109 720	41 371	39 904	13 259	25 149	11 390
	2006	188 978	115 798	43 431	44 842	15 809	28 337	12 932
	2007	201 108	122 624	46 458	50 341	18 263	28 143	13 448
	#2008	215 676	130 986	49 990	51 812	18 731	32 878	15 679
	2009	220 777	133 803	51 526	57 884	22 528	29 090	14 193
	*2010	222 022	134 653	...	...	...	...	...
Sri Lanka Sri Lanka	2004	5 475	2 679	861	1 474	...	1 322	...
	2006	4 513	1 833	754	1 272	...	1 408	...
	2008	5 607	1 972	767	1 571	...	2 064	...
Sudan (former)[2,4] Soudan (anc.)[2,4]	2004	19 772	9 340	2 830	4 641	...	5 791	...
	2005	23 726	11 208	4 483	5 569	...	6 949	...
Sweden Suède	2004	72 459	48 784	...	...	...	...	...
	2005	#77 704	#55 090	16 002[19]	...	...	...	...
	2006	78 715	55 729	...	...	...	...	...
	#2007	74 437[14]	45 610[14]	13 457[14]	22 565[2]	6 059[2,14]	20 815[2]	10 343[2,14]
	2008[4]	79 549	50 220	...	...	...	...	...
	2009	75 849[14]	46 983[14]	#13 995[14]	24 482[2]	6 559[2]	17 470[2]	8 718[2]
	2010[4,14]	77 418	49 312	...	...	...	...	...
Switzerland[2] Suisse[2]	2004	84 090	43 220	11 555	19 775	3 590	21 095	10 960
	2008	100 164	45 874	13 846	24 217	4 570	30 073	13 245
Tajikistan[2] Tadjikistan[2]	2004	2 487[3]	1 548	407	247	...	692[3]	...
	2005	3 220[3]	1 993	...	324	...	903[3]	...
	2006	3 110[3]	1 895	735	202	...	1 013[3]	...
	2007	2 075[3]	1 286	...	253	...	536[3]	...
	2008	2 447[3]	1 397	...	304	...	746[3]	...
	2009	2 791[3]	1 722	...	258	...	811[3]	...
Thailand Thaïlande	2005	36 967	20 506	10 241	10 520	...	5 941	...
	2007	42 624	21 392	10 850	9 461	...	11 771	...
TFYR of Macedonia L'ex-R.Y. Macédoine	2004	1 447	1 069	538	195	...	183	...
	2005	1 434	1 113	576	168	...	153	...
	2006	1 357	1 062	547	152	...	143	...
	2007	1 350	1 038	545	182	...	130	...
	2008	1 267	968	527	169	...	130	...

51 Personnel in research and development (R & D)
Full-time equivalent (FTE)

Personnel employé dans la recherche et le développement (R - D)
Equivalent temps plein (ETP)

Country or area Pays ou zone	Year Année	Total R & D personnel Total du personnel de R - D	Researchers Chercheurs Total M & W Total H & F	Women Femmes	Technicians and equivalent staff Techniciens et personnel assimilé Total M & W Total H & F	Women Femmes	Other supporting staff Autre personnel de soutien Total M & W Total H & F	Women Femmes
Togo Togo	2004	228	137	...	91[6]	...	...	...
	#2005	312	186	...	126	...	...	...
	2006	230	136	...	94	...	...	...
	#2007	320	216	21[14]	104	...	...	...
Trinidad and Tobago[2] Trinité-et-Tobago[2]	2004	838	526	205	312	112	...	...
	2005	954	548	183	406	180	...	...
	2006	1 092	638	246	454	197	...	...
	2007	999	586	225	413	194	...	...
	2008	1 113	681	317	432	206	...	...
	2009	1 318	787	416	531	248	...	...
Tunisia Tunisie	2004	14 556	12 950[3]	6 145	379[1,7]	...	1 227[1,7]	...
	2005	16 289	14 650[3]	6 995	413[1,7]	...	1 226[1,7]	...
	2006	17 466	15 833[3]	7 863	428[1,7]	...	1 205[1,7]	...
	2007	20 001	18 301[3]	9 027	450[1,7]	...	1 250[1,7]	...
	2008	20 756	19 086[3]	9 769	443[1,7]	...	1 227[1,7]	...
Turkey Turquie	2004	39 960[14]	33 877	11 815	3 341[14]	637[14]	2 742[14]	677[14]
	2005	49 251[14]	39 139	13 381	4 753[14]	988[14]	5 360[14]	978[14]
	2006	54 444[14]	42 663	14 567	5 724[14]	1 074[14]	6 056[14]	1 131[14]
	2007	63 377[14]	49 668	16 942	7 420[14]	1 291[14]	6 289[14]	1 258[14]
	2008	67 244[14]	52 811	17 754	7 612[14]	1 431[14]	6 821[14]	1 341[14]
	2009	73 521[14]	57 759	19 272	8 774[14]	1 430[14]	6 988[14]	1 508[14]
	2010	81 792[14]	64 341	21 056	10 352[14]	1 741[14]	7 099[14]	1 551[14]
Uganda[2] Ouganda[2]	2004	1 573	724	272	440	...	409	...
	2005	1 686	776	291	472	...	438	...
	2006	1 807	831	312	506	...	470	...
	2007	1 937	891	365	542	...	504	...
	2008	2 973	1 387	549	823	...	763	...
	2009	4 002	1 703	688	1 194	...	1 105	...
Ukraine[2] Ukraine[2]	2004	140 284	85 742	37 634	20 861	...	33 681	...
	2005	#170 579[3]	85 246	37 586	20 266	...	32 052	...
	2006	160 788[3]	80 497	35 542	19 748	...	30 204	...
	2007	155 549[3]	78 832	34 596	17 988	...	28 896	...
	2008	149 699[3]	77 355	34 803	16 783	...	27 988	...
	2009	146 800[3]	76 147	34 126	16 256	...	27 086	...
United Kingdom Royaume-Uni	2004[20]	318 886	228 969	...	...	...	...	...
	2005[4]	324 917[14]	#248 599	...	41 494	...	34 824[14]	...
	2006[4]	334 804[14]	254 009	...	44 138	...	36 657[14]	...
	2007[4]	343 855[14]	252 651	...	52 452	...	38 752[14]	...
	2008[4]	342 086[14]	251 932	...	55 612	...	34 542[14]	...
	2009[4]	347 486[14]	256 124	...	57 734	...	33 628[14]	...
	2010	319 487[14,21]	235 373[21]	...	*51 927	...	32 188[21]	...
United Rep. of Tanzania[2] Rép.-Unie de Tanzanie[2]	2007	3 593[1,8]	2 755[1,8]	558	782[1,8]	...	...	...
United States[20] Etats-Unis[20]	2004	...	1 384 536	...	...	...	...	...
	2005	...	1 375 304	...	...	...	...	...
	2006	...	1 414 341	...	...	...	...	...
	2007	...	1 412 639	...	...	...	...	...
United States Virgin Is.[1,2] Iles Vierges américaines[1,2]	2004	27	3	...	7	...	10	...
	2005	37	6	...	12	...	11	...
	2006	40	6	...	13	...	12	...
	2007	42	6	...	13	...	14	...
Uruguay[2] Uruguay[2]	2006	3 436	3 182	1 349	172	84	82	69
	2008	...	2 153	1 127	...	...	...	...
	2009	...	2 865	1 461	...	...	...	...
Venezuela (Boliv. Rep. of)[2] Venezuela (Rép. boliv. du)[2]	2004	...	3 148[1]	1 529	...	...	...	...
	2005	...	3 710[1]	1 843	...	...	...	...
	2006	...	4 626[1]	2 330	...	...	...	...
	2007	...	5 222[1]	2 710	...	...	...	...
	2008	...	6 038	3 208	...	...	...	...
	2009[1]	...	6 829	3 723	...	...	...	...
Zambia[2] Zambie[2]	2004	1 307[1]	356[1]	79[14]	376[1]	...	575[1]	...
	2005	3 285[1]	792[1]	116[14]	1 240[1]	...	1 253[1]	...
	#2008[8]	2 219	612	188	835	270	772	360

51

Personnel in research and development (R & D)
Full-time equivalent (FTE)

Personnel employé dans la recherche et le développement (R - D)
Equivalent temps plein (ETP)

Source:
United Nations Educational, Scientific and Cultural Organization
(UNESCO) Institute for Statistics, Montreal, the UNESCO Institute of
Statistics database, last accessed August 2012.

Source:
L'Institut de statistique de l'Organisation des Nations Unies pour
l'éducation, la science et la culture (UNESCO), Montréal, la base
de données de l'Institut de statistique de l'UNESCO, dernier accès August 2012.

1	Partial data.
2	Head count instead of Full-time equivalent.
3	Overestimated or based on overestimated data.
4	National estimation.
5	Source: National publication.
6	UIS estimation.
7	Government only.
8	Source: Regional publication.
9	For statistical purposes, the data for China do not include those for the Hong Kong Special Administrative Region (Hong Kong SAR) and Macao Special Administrative Region (Macao SAR).
10	Do not correspond exactly to Frascati Manual recommendations.
11	Including technicians and equivalent staff.
12	Including other supporting staff.
13	Included elsewhere.
14	Underestimated or based on underestimated data.
15	Excluding data for social sciences and humanities.
16	Excluding data from some regions, provinces or states.
17	Excluding government.
18	Data refer to the higher education sector only.
19	University graduates instead of researchers.
20	OECD estimation.
21	Provisional data.

1	Données partielles.
2	Personnes physiques au lieu d'Equivalents temps plein.
3	Surestimé ou fondé sur des données surestimées.
4	Estimation nationale.
5	Source: Publication statistique nationale.
6	Estimation de l'ISU.
7	Etat seulement.
8	Source: Publication régionale.
9	Pour la présentation des statistiques, les données pour la Chine ne comprennent pas la Région Administrative Spéciale de Hong Kong (Hong Kong RAS) et la Région Administrative Spéciale de Macao (Macao RAS).
10	Ne corresponds pas exactement aux recommandations du Manuel de Frascati.
11	Y compris les techniciens y le personnel assimilé.
12	Y compris autre personnel de soutien.
13	Inclus ailleurs.
14	Sous-estimé ou basé sur des données sous-estimées.
15	Non compris les données pour les sciences sociales et les sciences humaines.
16	Non compris les données de certaines régions, provinces ou états.
17	Non compris l'état.
18	Les données se réfèrent au secteur de l'enseignement supérieur seulement.
19	Diplômes universitaires au lieu de chercheurs.
20	Estimation de l'OCDE.
21	Données provisoires.

Gross domestic expenditure on R & D
As a percentage of GDP and by source of funds

Dépenses intérieures brutes de recherche et développement
En pourcentage du PIB et répartition par source de financement

Country or area Pays ou zone	Year Année	Expenditure on R&D as a % of GDP Dépenses en R&D en % du PIB	Source of funds (%) / Source de financement (%)					
			Business enterprises Entreprises	Government Etat	Higher education Enseigne-ment supérieur	Private non-profit Institut. privées sans but lucratif	Funds from abroad Fonds de l'étranger	Not distributed Non répartis
Albania [1]	2007	0.1	1.5	79.7	6.8	...	12.0	...
Albanie [1]	2008	0.2	3.3	80.8	8.6	...	7.4	...
Algeria [1]	2003	0.2	...	...	...	...	...	...
Algérie [1]	2004	0.2	...	...	...	...	...	...
	2005	0.1	...	...	...	...	...	...
Argentina	2007	0.5	29.3	67.5	1.4	1.1	0.6	...
Argentine	2008	0.5	26.5	67.6	4.4	0.9	0.6	...
	2009	0.6	21.4	73.2	3.8	0.8	0.7	...
Armenia	2007 [1]	0.2	...	55.3	...	...	12.4	32.3
Arménie	2008	0.2	...	60.3	...	...	1.9	37.8
	2009	0.3	...	59.9	...	...	4.2	35.8
Australia	2004	1.8	54.6	40.3	0.4	1.9	2.9	...
Australie	2006	2.2	58.1	37.6	0.1	1.8	2.4	...
	2008	2.4	62.0	34.5	0.1	1.8	1.6	...
Austria	2009	2.7	47.1	34.9	0.7	0.6	16.8	...
Autriche	2010	2.8 [2,3]	44.3 [2]	38.9 [1,2,4]	...	0.4	16.4 [2,3]	...
	2011	...	44.6 [2,3]	38.7 [1,2,4]	...	0.4	16.2 [2,3]	...
Azerbaijan	2007	0.2	20.8	76.5	...	2.6	0.1	...
Azerbaïdjan	2008	0.2	25.2	73.3	...	1.5	0.1	...
	2009	0.2	24.8	74.3	...	0.8	0.1	...
Belarus	2007	1.0	45.1	49.2	0.3	0.1	5.3	...
Bélarus	2008	0.7	36.5	57.6	0.3	0.1	5.5	...
	2009	0.6	28.8	62.5	...	0.2	8.5	...
Belgium	2008	2.0	61.0	23.2	2.9	0.6	12.3	...
Belgique	2009	2.0	58.6	25.3	3.2	0.7	12.1	...
	2010 [3]	2.0	...	...	...	...	...	...
Bolivia (Plurinational State of)	2002	0.3	16.0	20.0	31.0	19.0	14.0	^0.0
Bolivie (État plurinational de)	2009 [5]	0.2	0.5	51.2	26.5	0.2	18.6	3.0
Botswana [6] - Botswana [6]	2005	0.5	...	...	...	...	...	...
Brazil	2008	1.1	45.5	52.3	2.2	...	...	...
Brésil	2009	1.2	46.3	51.6	2.1	...	...	...
	2010	1.2 [6]	45.4	52.7	1.9	...	...	...
Brunei Darussalam	2002	0.0 [1,7]	8.8	91.2	...	...	...	...
Brunéi Darussalam	2003	0.0 [1,7]	6.7	86.8	...	...	6.6	...
	2004 [5]	^0.0 [1]	1.6	91.0	7.4	...	...	...
Bulgaria	2008	0.5	30.6	61.2	0.4	0.9	6.8	...
Bulgarie	2009	0.5	30.2	60.5	0.7	0.2	8.4	...
	2010 [3]	0.6	...	...	...	...	...	...
Burkina Faso	2007	0.1 [1]	...	72.3	...	...	24.5	3.2
Burkina Faso	2008	0.2	16.4	10.3	21.9	1.2	43.5	6.6
	2009	0.2	11.9	9.1	12.2	1.3	59.6	5.9
Cambodia [1,2]								
Cambodge [1,2]	2002	^0.0	...	17.9	...	43.0	28.4	10.6
Canada	2008	1.9	48.4	34.1 [2]	7.1 [2]	3.4	7.1	...
Canada	2009	1.9	47.6	...	...	3.5	6.9	...
	2010 [3]	1.8	46.8	...	...	3.5	6.8	...
Chile	2007	0.3	38.9	35.6	18.6	2.7	4.2	...
Chili	2008	0.4	43.7	33.8	17.2	2.0	3.3	...
China	2007	1.4	70.4	24.6 [8]	...	...	1.3 [8]	...
Chine	2008	1.5	71.7 [5]	23.6 [8]	...	...	1.2 [8]	...
	2009	1.7	71.7 [5]	23.4 [8]	...	...	1.3 [8]	...
China, Hong Kong SAR	2007	0.8	50.5 [9]	44.6	0.4	...	4.6	...
Chine, Hong Kong RAS	2008	0.7	45.0 [9]	48.3	0.1	...	6.5	...
	2009	0.8	45.8 [9]	48.0	0.1	...	6.1	...
China, Macao SAR [2]	2007	0.1 [1]	1.4	78.7	16.8	2.0	...	1.1
Chine, Macao RAS [2]	2008	0.1 [1]	0.3	76.1	21.9	1.3	...	0.3
	2009	0.1 [1]	2.5	83.2	10.7	2.1	...	1.5
Colombia	2008	0.1	25.8	42.7	21.7	5.0	4.7	...
Colombie	2009	0.2	13.9	55.8	21.0	4.6	4.7	...
	2010	0.2	22.1	46.6	21.1	6.0	4.2	...
Costa Rica	2007	0.4	...	...	...	...	...	...
Costa Rica	2008	0.4	3.3	47.2	...	2.8	6.6	40.0
	2009	0.5	28.7	53.0	...	2.8	1.7	13.7

52

Gross domestic expenditure on R & D
As a percentage of GDP and by source of funds

Dépenses intérieures brutes de recherche et développement
En pourcentage du PIB et répartition par source de financement

Country or area Pays ou zone	Year Année	Expenditure on R&D as a % of GDP Dépenses en R&D en % du PIB	Source of funds (%) / Source de financement (%)					
			Business enterprises Entreprises	Government Etat	Higher education Enseigne-ment supérieur	Private non-profit Institut. privées sans but lucratif	Funds from abroad Fonds de l'étranger	Not distributed Non répartis
Croatia	2008	0.9	40.8	49.3	1.9	0.2	7.9	...
Croatie	2009	0.8	39.8	51.2	1.9	0.1	7.0	...
	2010	0.7	38.8	49.2	2.0	0.2	9.9	...
Cuba	2008	0.5	18.0	69.0	...	...	13.0	...
Cuba	2009	0.6	15.0	75.0	...	...	10.0	...
	2010	0.6	15.0	75.0	...	...	10.0	...
Cyprus	2008	0.4[10]	17.8	64.1	2.7	0.7	14.7	...
Chypre	2009	0.5	15.7	69.0	2.8	0.5	12.1	...
	2010[3]	0.5	...	...	...	...	...	...
Czech Republic	2008	1.5	51.1	41.3	1.2	...	6.5	...
République tchèque	2009	1.5	44.6	43.9	1.1	...	10.4	...
	2010	1.6	48.9	39.9	0.8	...	10.4	...
Dem. Rep. of the Congo	2004	0.4[11,12]	...	100.0	...	...	...	...
Rép. dém. du Congo	2005	0.5[11,12]	...	100.0	...	...	...	...
Denmark	2008	2.8	...	...	...	...	...	...
Danemark	2009	3.1	60.2	27.8	...	3.2	8.8	...
	2010[2]	3.1	60.3	27.7	...	3.2	8.8	...
Ecuador	2006	0.1	17.4	69.3	4.0	1.2	4.2	4.0
Equateur	2007	0.1	21.5	58.1	3.9	3.3	7.0	6.2
	2008	0.3	8.5	89.6	1.4	...	0.5	^0.0
Egypt[1]	2007	0.3	...	...	...	...	...	...
Egypte[1]	2008	0.3	...	...	...	...	...	...
	2009	0.2	...	...	...	...	...	...
El Salvador	2007	0.1	1.8	50.4	39.4	0.9	7.4	...
El Salvador	2008	0.1	0.7	49.8	44.6	0.1	4.5	...
	2009	0.1	0.7	64.4	^0.0	0.1	11.3	23.5
Estonia	2008	1.3	39.8	50.0	0.5	0.3[3]	9.4	...
Estonie	2009	1.4	38.5	48.8	0.7	0.7	11.3	...
	2010[3]	1.6	43.4	44.3	0.6	0.2	11.5	...
Ethiopia	2005	0.2	...	69.2	...	0.1	30.8	...
Ethiopie	2007	0.2	...	71.7	...	0.7	27.0	0.5
	2010[5,6]	0.2	10.8	56.0	1.1	...	30.0	2.2
Faeroe Islands Iles Féroé	2003	0.9	20.4	...	...	0.3	18.7	60.6[11,13,14]
Finland	2008	3.7	70.3	21.8	0.2	1.0	6.6	...
Finlande	2009	3.9	68.1	24.0	0.1	1.1	6.6	...
	2010	3.9	66.1	25.7	0.2	1.1	6.9	...
France	2008	2.1	50.8	38.9	1.2	1.1	8.0	...
France	2009	2.3	52.4	38.6	1.2	0.9	6.9	...
	2010[3]	2.3[3]	51.0[3]	39.7[1]	1.1[3]	0.9[3]	7.3[3]	...
Gabon	2007	0.4	...	95.6	0.4	...	4.0	...
Gabon	2008	0.5	19.7	76.5	0.5	...	3.2	...
	2009	0.6	29.3	58.1	9.5	...	3.1	...
Georgia	2003	0.2	...	...	...	...	...	...
Géorgie	2004	0.2	...	...	...	...	...	...
	2005	0.2	...	...	...	...	...	...
Germany	2008	2.7	67.3	28.4	...	0.3	4.0	...
Allemagne	2009	2.8	66.1	29.7	...	0.3	3.8	...
	2010[2]	2.8	...	...	...	...	...	...
Ghana[7] Ghana[7]	2007	0.2	50.9	36.5	0.7	...	11.9	...
Greece	2005	0.6	31.1	46.8	1.7	1.5	19.0	...
Grèce	2006[2]	0.6	...	...	...	...	...	...
	2007[2]	0.6	...	...	...	...	...	...
Greenland	2002	0.6	...	...	...	...	...	...
Groenland	2003[2]	0.6	...	...	...	...	...	...
	2004	0.7	...	...	...	...	...	...
Guatemala	2007[1]	0.1	...	24.0	23.5	...	52.5	...
Guatemala	2008[1]	0.1	...	22.7	28.9	...	48.4	...
	2009	0.1	...	22.8	29.5	...	47.7	...
Hungary	2008	1.0	48.3	41.8	...	0.6	9.3	...
Hongrie	2009	1.2	46.4	42.0	...	0.7	10.9	...
	2010	1.2	47.4	39.3	...	0.9	12.4	...

Gross domestic expenditure on R & D
As a percentage of GDP and by source of funds

Dépenses intérieures brutes de recherche et développement
En pourcentage du PIB et répartition par source de financement

Country or area / Pays ou zone	Year / Année	Expenditure on R&D as a % of GDP / Dépenses en R&D en % du PIB	Source of funds (%) / Source de financement (%)					
			Business enterprises / Entreprises	Government / Etat	Higher education / Enseignement supérieur	Private non-profit Institut. privées sans but lucratif	Funds from abroad / Fonds de l'étranger	Not distributed / Non répartis
Iceland	2006	3.0	49.3	39.6	...	0.6	10.6	...
Islande	2007	2.7	50.4	38.8	...	0.8	10.0	...
	2008[3]	2.6	50.4	38.8	...	0.8	10.0	...
India	2005	0.8	30.4[9]	69.6	...	...	...	...
Inde	2006	0.8[2]	32.1[9,11,15]	67.9[11,15]	...	...	...	...
	2007	0.8[2]	33.9[9,11,15]	66.1[11,15]	...	...	...	...
Indonesia [1,2] - Indonésie [1,2]	2009	0.1	...	...	...	...	...	...
Iran (Islamic Rep. of)	2005	0.7	12.2	76.2	11.6	...	...	...
Iran (Rép. islamique d')	2006	0.7	14.2	74.6	11.2	...	...	...
	2008	0.8	30.9	61.6	7.4	...	...	...
Ireland	2008	1.5	48.6	33.9	0.4	1.5	15.5	...
Irlande	2009[2]	1.7	51.2	31.3	1.3	0.5	15.6	...
	2010[2,3]	1.8	...	...	...	...	...	...
Israel	2008	4.8[16]	51.6[16]	14.0[16]	3.2	1.6	29.6[16]	...
Israël	2009[3,16]	4.4	...	...	...	...	...	...
	2010[3,16]	4.4	...	...	...	...	...	...
Italy	2008	1.2	45.9	42.0	1.3	2.8	7.9	...
Italie	2009	1.3	44.2	42.1	1.3	3.0	9.4	...
	2010[3]	1.3	...	...	...	...	...	...
Jamaica								
Jamaïque	2002	0.1	...	...	...	...	...	...
Japan	2007	3.4	77.7	15.6[17]	5.6[17]	0.7	0.3	...
Japon	2008[5]	3.4	78.2	15.6[17]	5.1[17]	0.7	0.4	...
	2009	3.4	75.3	17.7[17]	5.9[17]	0.7	0.4	...
Jordan	2002	0.3						
Jordanie	2008[1]	0.4	...	...	...	...	...	...
Kazakhstan	2007	0.2	44.5	37.4	15.3	1.1	1.7	...
Kazakhstan	2008	0.2	50.7	31.4	14.7	2.2	1.0	...
	2009	0.2	...	...	...	...	...	...
Kenya - Kenya	2007	0.4[1]	16.8	26.2	26.2	13.2	17.6	...
Kuwait	2007	0.1[1]	2.4	97.6	...	...	...	...
Koweït	2008	0.1[1]	2.6	97.0	...	...	0.4	...
	2009	0.1[1]	2.3	96.5	...	...	1.2	...
Kyrgyzstan	2007	0.2	...	...	...	...	...	...
Kirghizistan	2008	0.2	...	...	...	...	...	...
	2009	0.2	...	...	...	...	...	...
Lao People's Dem. Rep. [1,7]								
Rép. dém. pop. lao [1,7]	2002	^0.0	36.0	8.0	2.0	...	54.0	...
Latvia	2008	0.6	27.0	47.3	2.5	...	23.1	...
Lettonie	2009	0.5	36.9	44.7	3.0	...	15.4	...
	2010	0.6	38.8	26.4	1.4	...	33.4	...
Lesotho [1]	2003	0.1	...	...	...	...	...	...
Lesotho [1]	2004	0.1	...	...	...	...	...	...
	2009	^0.0	3.4	15.0	2.8	...	...	78.9
Lithuania	2008	0.8	21.4	55.6	7.2	0.3	15.5	...
Lituanie	2009	0.8	21.0	53.9	11.6	0.3	13.1	...
	2010	0.8	24.1	47.5	8.2	0.2	20.0	...
Luxembourg	2008	1.6	...	...	...	...	...	...
Luxembourg	2009	1.7	70.3	24.3	...	0.1	5.4	...
	2010	1.6[3]	65.9[3]	29.7[1]	0.1[3]	0.1[3]	4.3[3]	...
Madagascar	2007	0.1[1]	...	32.0	59.6	...	8.4	...
Madagascar	2008[1,5]	0.1	...	...	...	...	...	...
	2009[1]	0.1	...	...	...	...	...	...
Malaysia	2002	0.7	51.5	32.1	4.9	...	11.5	...
Malaisie	2004	0.6	71.2	21.5	6.9	...	0.4	...
	2006	0.6	84.5	2.4	6.6	...	0.2	6.3
Mali [1]								
Mali [1]	2007	0.2[7]	10.1	40.9[7]	...	...	49.0[7]	...
Malta	2008	0.6	56.5	27.4	...	0.1	16.0	...
Malte	2009	0.5	51.6	30.0	...	0.1	18.4	...
	2010[3]	0.6	51.5	30.5	...	...	18.0	...
Mauritius [11,12]	2003	0.3	...	100.0	...	...	...	...
Maurice [11,12]	2004	0.4	...	100.0	...	...	...	...
	2005	0.4	...	100.0	...	...	...	...

Gross domestic expenditure on R & D
As a percentage of GDP and by source of funds

Dépenses intérieures brutes de recherche et développement
En pourcentage du PIB et répartition par source de financement

Country or area Pays ou zone	Year Année	Expenditure on R&D as a % of GDP Dépenses en R&D en % du PIB	Source of funds (%) / Source de financement (%)					
			Business enterprises Entreprises	Government Etat	Higher education Enseigne-ment supérieur	Private non-profit Institut. privées sans but lucratif	Funds from abroad Fonds de l'étranger	Not distributed Non répartis
Mexico	2007	0.4	45.1	50.2	3.2	0.1	1.4	...
Mexique	2008	0.4	44.3	45.8	6.3	1.5	2.1	...
	2009	0.4	43.2	46.9	6.4	1.6	1.9	...
Monaco [1]	2004	^0.0	...	97.0	...	...	...	3.0
Monaco [1]	2005	^0.0		98.8	...	...	...	1.2
Mongolia	2007	0.2[1]	3.1	82.4	0.5	...	1.6	12.4
Mongolie	2008	0.3[1]	2.4[1]	84.4[1]	1.3[1]	...	2.1[18]	9.8[18]
	2009[1]	0.2	3.6	77.3	2.5	...	1.8	14.8
Montenegro	2005	0.9	...	...	...	...	...	...
Monténégro	2006	1.2	...	...	...	...	...	...
	2007	1.1	...	...	...	...	...	...
Morocco	2002[1]	0.5	21.6	37.1	41.2	...	...	...
Maroc	2003[1]	0.7	12.3	40.3	47.4	...	...	...
	2006	0.6	22.7	26.1	48.6	...	2.6	...
Mozambique	2002[11,19]	0.5[6]	...	34.7[2]	...	...	65.3[6]	...
Mozambique	2006	0.5	...	...	...	...	...	...
	2007	0.2[1,7]	...	31.1	...	4.6	64.3	...
Myanmar [1] - Myanmar [1]	2002	0.2	...	...	...	...	...	...
Netherlands	2008	1.8	...	...	...	...	...	...
Pays-Bas	2009	1.8	45.1	40.9	0.3	2.8	10.8	...
	2010[3]	1.8	...	...	...	...	...	...
New Zealand	2005	1.1	41.1	43.2	8.9	1.7	5.2	...
Nouvelle-Zélande	2007	1.2	40.7	42.2	8.7	3.7	4.8	...
	2009	1.3	38.5	45.7	8.2	2.3	5.4	...
Nigeria - Nigéria	2007	0.2[7]	0.2[7]	96.4[7]	0.1	1.7[7]	1.0[7]	0.6[7]
Norway	2008	1.6	...	...	...	...	...	...
Norvège	2009	1.8	43.6	46.8	0.4	1.0	8.2	...
	2010[3]	1.7	...	...	...	...	...	...
Pakistan	2005	0.4	...	87.0	11.9	...	0.3	0.8
Pakistan	2007	0.7	...	82.9	12.9	1.8	1.0	1.5
	2009	0.5	...	84.0	12.1	1.7	0.9	1.3
Panama	2008	0.2	2.2	44.2	3.1	0.9	46.6	3.0
Panama	2009	0.2	2.2	44.1	3.0	1.0	49.5	0.2
	2010	0.2	2.3	44.1	3.1	1.0	49.5	^0.0
Paraguay	2004	0.1	^0.0	63.1	12.7	2.3	21.9	...
Paraguay	2005	0.1	0.3[5]	74.9[5]	8.6[5]	2.0[5]	14.2[5]	...
	2008	0.1	0.3	76.2	9.2	2.1	12.3	...
Peru	2002	0.1	...	...	...	...	...	...
Pérou	2003	0.1	...	...	...	...	...	...
	2004	0.1	...	...	...	...	...	...
Philippines	2003	0.1	69.1	21.9	4.8	0.4	3.8	0.1
Philippines	2005	0.1	62.6	25.6	6.0	0.7	4.8	0.3
	2007	0.1	62.0	26.1	6.4	0.9	4.1	0.5
Poland	2008	0.6	30.5	59.8	4.1	0.2	5.4	...
Pologne	2009	0.7	27.1	60.4	6.7	0.3	5.5	...
	2010	0.7	24.4	60.9	2.5	0.3	11.8	...
Portugal	2008[5]	1.5	48.1	43.7	3.6	1.7	3.0	...
Portugal	2009	1.6	44.0	45.3	2.9	3.7	4.1	...
	2010[3]	1.6	...	...	...	...	...	...
Puerto Rico								
Porto Rico	2009	0.5	...	...	...	...	...	...
Republic of Korea	2008	3.4	72.9	25.4	1.0	0.4	0.3	...
République de Corée	2009	3.6	71.1	27.4	0.9	0.4	0.2	...
	2010	3.7	71.8	26.7	0.9	0.4	0.2	...
Republic of Moldova	2007	0.5	...	...	...	...	2.7	97.3
République de Moldova	2008	0.5	...	...	...	...	3.7	96.3
	2009	0.5	...	...	...	...	6.5	93.5
Romania	2008	0.6	23.3	70.1	2.6	...	4.0	...
Roumanie	2009	0.5	34.8	54.9	1.9	0.1	8.3	...
	2010	0.5	32.3	54.4	2.2	...	11.1	...
Russian Federation	2008	1.0	28.7	64.7	0.5	0.2	5.9	...
Fédération de Russie	2009	1.3	26.6	66.5	0.4	0.1	6.5	...
	2010	1.2	25.5	70.3	0.5	0.1	3.5	...

Gross domestic expenditure on R & D
As a percentage of GDP and by source of funds

Dépenses intérieures brutes de recherche et développement
En pourcentage du PIB et répartition par source de financement

Country or area Pays ou zone	Year Année	Expenditure on R&D as a % of GDP Dépenses en R&D en % du PIB	Source of funds (%) / Source de financement (%)					
			Business enterprises Entreprises	Government Etat	Higher education Enseignement supérieur	Private non-profit Institut. privées sans but lucratif	Funds from abroad Fonds de l'étranger	Not distributed Non répartis
Saint Vincent-Grenadines ^								
Saint Vincent-Grenadines ^	2002	0.1	...	...	...	...	...	...
Saudi Arabia [1]	2007[12]	^0.0	...	...	...	...	...	...
Arabie saoudite [1]	2008	0.1	...	...	...	...	...	...
	2009	0.1	...	...	...	...	...	...
Senegal								
Sénégal	2008	0.4	4.0	57.1	0.3	0.3	38.3	0.1
Serbia	2007[20]	0.4	...	...	...	...	...	...
Serbie	2008	0.4	...	...	...	...	...	...
	2009[5,20]	0.9	8.3	62.9	20.9	0.8	7.2	...
Seychelles	2003	0.4	...	...	...	...	...	...
Seychelles	2004	0.4	...	...	...	...	...	...
	2005	0.3	...	...	...	...	...	...
Singapore	2007	2.4	59.8	34.9	0.9	...	4.3	...
Singapour	2008	2.7	63.5	29.9	1.3	...	5.3	...
	2009	2.3	54.4	38.1	1.5	...	5.9	...
Slovakia	2008	0.5[10]	34.7	52.3[21]	0.3	0.4	12.3	...
Slovaquie	2009	0.5[10]	35.1	50.6[21]	0.6	1.0	12.8	...
	2010	0.6	35.1	49.6[21]	0.4	0.3	14.7	...
Slovenia	2008	1.7	62.8	31.3	0.3	...	5.6	...
Slovénie	2009	1.9	58.0	35.7	0.3	...	6.0	...
	2010	2.1[3]	58.4[3]	35.3[3]	0.3	0.1	6.0[3]	...
South Africa	2006	0.9	44.8	40.4	3.3	1.0	10.6	...
Afrique du Sud	2007	0.9	42.7	45.7	0.1	0.9	10.7	...
	2008	0.9	42.6	45.1	0.1	0.7	11.4	...
Spain	2008	1.4	45.0	45.6	3.2	0.6	5.7	...
Espagne	2009	1.4	43.4	47.1	3.5	0.6	5.5	...
	2010[3]	1.4	...	...	...	...	...	...
Sri Lanka	2004	0.2	0.6[9]	67.5[13]	...	...	22.6	9.3
Sri Lanka	2006	0.2	19.0[9]	65.2[13]	...	...	4.8	10.9
	2008	0.1	19.9[9]	71.8[13]	...	...	4.3	4.0
Sweden	2008[2]	3.7	...	...	...	...	...	...
Suède	2009	3.6	58.8	27.5	0.6	2.6	10.4	...
	2010[2]	3.4	...	...	...	...	...	...
Switzerland	2004	2.9	69.7	22.7	1.5	0.8	5.2	...
Suisse	2008	3.0	68.2	22.8	2.3	0.7	6.0	...
Tajikistan	2007	0.1	1.4	95.8	...	...	...	2.9
Tadjikistan	2008	0.1	0.4	92.1	0.2	...	...	7.3
	2009	0.1[22,23]	1.1	82.1	0.6	...	...	16.2
Thailand	2005	0.2	48.7	31.5	14.9	0.7	1.8	2.4
Thaïlande	2006[2]	0.2	...	...	...	...	...	...
	2007	0.2	...	...	...	...	...	...
TFYR of Macedonia	2006	0.2	...	...	...	...	...	...
L'ex-R.Y. Macédoine	2007	0.2	...	...	...	...	...	...
	2008	0.2	...	...	...	...	...	...
Trinidad and Tobago	^2007	0.0	...	...	...	...	...	...
Trinité-et-Tobago	^2008[5]	0.0	...	...	...	...	...	...
	2009	0.1	...	...	...	...	...	...
Tunisia [2]	2007	1.0	18.0	68.0[13]	...	...	14.0	...
Tunisie [2]	2008	1.0	18.9	67.0[13]	...	...	14.0	...
	2009	1.1	20.0	65.0[13]	...	...	14.9	...
Turkey	2008	0.7	47.3	31.6	16.2	3.6	1.3	...
Turquie	2009	0.8	41.0	34.0	20.3	3.7	1.1	...
	2010	0.8	45.1	30.8	19.6	3.7	0.8	...
Uganda	2007	0.4	7.5	41.7	...	...	50.7	...
Ouganda	2008	0.3	4.3	52.3	...	0.1	43.2	...
	2009	0.4	8.2	48.1	17.6	0.1	26.1	...
Ukraine	2007	0.9	30.2	52.2	0.2	0.1	15.9	1.3
Ukraine	2008	0.8	27.1	55.2	0.3	0.1	15.6	1.7
	2009	0.9	25.9	49.8	0.3	0.1	22.3	1.6
United Kingdom	2008	1.8[2]	45.4[2]	30.7	1.2[2]	4.9[2]	17.7[2]	...
Royaume-Uni	2009	1.9[2]	44.5[2]	32.6	1.3[2]	5.0[2]	16.6[2]	...
	2010	1.8[3]	45.1[3]	32.1[3]	1.3[1]	5.0[3]	16.4[3]	...

Gross domestic expenditure on R & D
As a percentage of GDP and by source of funds

Dépenses intérieures brutes de recherche et développement
En pourcentage du PIB et répartition par source de financement

Country or area Pays ou zone	Year Année	Expenditure on R&D as a % of GDP Dépenses en R&D en % du PIB	Source of funds (%) / Source de financement (%)					
			Business enterprises Entreprises	Government Etat	Higher education Enseigne-ment supérieur	Private non-profit Institut. privées sans but lucratif	Funds from abroad Fonds de l'étranger	Not distributed Non répartis
United Rep. of Tanzania Rép.-Unie de Tanzanie	2007	0.4[1,7]	...	60.6	...	1.1	38.4	...
United States[24] Etats-Unis[24]	2007	2.7	65.3[4]	28.2[25]	3.5[4]	3.0[4]	...	...
	2008	2.8	64.1[4]	29.3[25]	3.5[4]	3.1[4]	...	...
	2009	2.9	61.6[4]	31.3[25]	3.8[4]	3.4[4]	...	...
United States Virgin Is.[1] Iles Vierges américaines[1]	2005	...	...	100.0	...	...	...	...
	2006	...	...	100.0	...	...	...	...
	2007	...	...	100.0	...	...	...	...
Uruguay Uruguay	2007	0.4	39.5	38.8	19.9	1.8	...	...
	2008	0.4	42.8[5]	31.0[5]	21.0[5]	1.0	4.3[5]	...
	2009	0.4	39.3	33.4	24.9	0.6	1.9	...
Viet Nam Viet Nam	2002	0.2	18.1	74.1	0.7[9]	...	6.3	0.8
Zambia Zambie	^2004[1]	0.0	...	...	...	...	...	...
	^2005[1]	0.0	...	...	...	...	...	...
	2008[5,7]	0.3	3.2	94.8	...	0.3	1.6	...

Source:
United Nations Educational, Scientific and Cultural Organization (UNESCO) Institute for Statistics, Montreal, the UNESCO Institute of Statistics database, last accessed August 2012.

Source:
L'Institut de statistique de l'Organisation des Nations Unies pour l'éducation, la science et la culture (UNESCO), Montréal, la base de données de l'Institut de statistique de l'UNESCO, dernier accès August 2012.

1 Partial data.	1 Données partielles.
2 National estimation.	2 Estimation nationale.
3 Provisional data.	3 Données provisoires.
4 Including other classes.	4 Comprend d'autres catégories.
5 Break in series with previous year for which data are available.	5 Discontinuité dans la série en ce qui concerne la dernière année pour laquelle des données sont disponibles.
6 Source: National publication.	6 Source: Publication statistique nationale.
7 Source: Regional publication.	7 Source: Publication régionale.
8 The sum of the breakdown does not add to the total.	8 La somme de toutes les valeurs diffère du total.
9 Including private non-profit funds.	9 Y compris les fonds privés à but non lucratif.
10 Data have been converted from the former national currency using the appropriate conversion rate.	10 Les données ont été converties à partir de l'ancienne monnaie nationale et du taux de conversion approprié.
11 Overestimated or based on overestimated data.	11 Surestimé ou fondé sur des données surestimées.
12 Based on R&D budget instead of R&D expenditure.	12 Basé sur le budget de la recherche-développement au lieu des dépenses.
13 Including higher education.	13 Y compris l'enseignement supérieur.
14 Including Government.	14 Y compris l'état.
15 Do not correspond exactly to Frascati Manual recommendations.	15 Ne corresponds pas exactement aux recommandations du Manuel de Frascati.
16 Defence excluded (all or mostly).	16 A l'exclusion de la défense (en totalité ou en grande partie).
17 OECD estimation.	17 Estimation de l'OCDE.
18 Excludes basic research.	18 Ne comprend pas la recherche fondamentale.
19 Science and technology budget instead of research and development expenditure.	19 Budget science et technologie au lieu de dépenses de recherche et développement.
20 Excluding data from some regions, provinces or states.	20 Non compris les données de certaines régions, provinces ou états.
21 Underestimated or based on underestimated data.	21 Sous-estimé ou basé sur des données sous-estimées.
22 Excluding business enterprise.	22 Ne comprend pas les entreprises commerciales.
23 Excluding private non-profit organizations.	23 Non compris les organisations privées à but non lucratif.
24 Excluding most or all capital expenditure.	24 A l'exclusion des dépenses d'équipement (en totalité ou en grande partie).
25 Federal or central government only.	25 Gouvernement fédéral et administration centrale uniquement.

Patents
Filings, grants and patents in force

Brevets
Demandes, délivrances et brevets en vigueur

Country or area	Resident filings (per million pop.) Demandes émanant de résidents (par million d'hab.)			Grants of patents Brevets délivrés			Patents in force Brevets en vigueur			Pays ou zone
	2008	2009	2010	2008	2009	2010	2008	2009	2010	
Albania	...	...	...	541	402	349	...	...	349	Albanie
Algeria	...	...	2.1	...	...	...	...	...	...	Algérie
Argentina	20.2	28.8	27.4	1 214	...	...	...	...	...	Argentine
Armenia	73.4	37.6	44.0	127	156	124	350	357	278	Arménie
Australia	131.2	113.6	107.9	11 863	12 410	14 557	107 699	104 644	96 293	Australie
Austria	275.6	270.5	289.1	...	1 102	1 130	...	103 552	10 066	Autriche
Azerbaijan	25.3	...	...	205	...	...	...	...	...	Azerbaïdjan
Bangladesh	0.4	0.4	0.4	165	130	92	...	...	...	Bangladesh
Belarus	157.3	184.4	185.3	1 252	1 297	1 222	...	...	4 444	Bélarus
Belgium	53.7	62.0	57.0	526	364	532	...	...	...	Belgique
Bosnia and Herzegovina	15.6	...	14.9	127	...	173	329	...	716	Bosnie-Herzégovine
Botswana	...	...	...	...	...	...	444	...	...	Botswana
Brazil	21.3	20.3	13.9	2 513	2 772	3 251	34 879	43 089	40 022	Brésil
Brunei Darussalam	...	...	...	75	42	...	...	...	...	Brunéi Darussalam
Bulgaria	32.7	31.9	32.2	268	242	251	4 979	5 909	6 812	Bulgarie
Burkina Faso	...	...	0.1	...	...	...	...	...	...	Burkina Faso
Canada	151.9	150.2	133.4	18 703	19 497	19 120	129 347	134 150	133 355	Canada
Chile	31.6	20.2	19.2	1 398	1 797	1 020	7 879	8 319	8 121	Chili
China	146.9	172.1	219.0	93 706	128 389	135 110	337 215	438 036	564 760	Chine
China, Hong Kong SAR	24.8	21.3	18.8	4 001	5 650	5 353	...	31 718	33 225	Chine, Hong Kong RAS
China, Macao SAR	5.8	1.9	7.4	46	113	156	125	232	377	Chine, Macao RAS
Colombia	2.8	2.8	2.9	409	...	639	...	...	...	Colombie
Costa Rica	...	...	1.7	...	...	45	...	...	239	Costa Rica
Croatia	74.4	56.4	58.1	138	154	82	1 563	1 852	2 134	Croatie
Cuba	6.1	5.2	...	92	140	...	92	...	...	Cuba
Cyprus	10.2	5.5	3.6	36	12	19	454	266	333	Chypre
Czech Republic	68.3	75.2	82.5	1 280	1 293	911	10 895	10 470	9 633	République tchèque
Dem. P. R. Korea	...	328.2	329.3	...	6 147	6 290	...	...	...	R. p. dém. de Corée
Denmark	297.4	274.9	293.3	225	211	155	2 438	1 825	1 655	Danemark
Dominican Republic	1.5	3.1	3.1	...	...	...	...	...	...	Rép. dominicaine
Ecuador	0.1	0.4	0.3	64	64	28	...	...	199	Equateur
Egypt	6.1	6.2	7.5	364	321	321	...	3 082	3 316	Egypte
Estonia	46.2	56.7	62.7	1 181	1 266	120	3 893	4 740	1 320	Estonie
Eurasian Patent Org.[1]	...	...	...	1 666	1 759	1 802	...	...	...	Org. eurasienne de[1]
European Patent Office [2]	...	...	...	59 819	51 969	58 108	...	...	...	Office européen de brevets [2]
Finland	338.6	338.3	322.7	997	1 055	923	38 457	45 869	12 221	Finlande
France	228.4	218.5	227.3	10 811	10 529	9 899	439 075	436 931	435 915	France
Gambia	...	...	...	...	...	...	991	...	...	Gambie
Georgia	50.4	56.7	40.2	297	293	258	1 020	1 043	1 044	Géorgie
Germany	599.7	584.3	575.8	17 308	14 435	13 678	509 879	519 209	514 046	Allemagne
Ghana	...	...	...	...	...	...	1 018	...	...	Ghana
Greece	55.9	61.9	64.3	444	442	479	31 975	34 020	32 120	Grèce
Guatemala	0.4	0.5	0.5	96	191	104	521	531	590	Guatemala
Hungary	68.0	75.5	64.8	551	415	65	11 462	12 749	2 586	Hongrie

Country or area	Resident filings (per million pop.) Demandes émanant de résidents (par million d'hab.)			Grants of patents Brevets délivrés			Patents in force Brevets en vigueur			Pays ou zone
	2008	2009	2010	2008	2009	2010	2008	2009	2010	
Iceland	157.5	200.9	179.6	163	79	139	1 031	...	1 892	Islande
India	5.6	6.3	...	16 061	6 168	...	30 822	37 334	...	Inde
Ireland	210.4	203.6	163.6	318	328	243	78 816	78 916	79 040	Irlande
Israel	209.1	185.3	190.2	1 855	2 015	3 724	...	32 565	26 494	Israël
Italy	143.5	146.4	...	7 318	18 277	...	...	...	...	Italie
Japan	2 585.0	2 315.1	2 276.0	176 950	193 349	222 693	1 270 367	1 347 998	1 423 432	Japon
Jordan	8.6	10.1	7.4	21	51	64	...	...	312	Jordanie
Kazakhstan	0.7	...	...	171	...	...	171	...	581	Kazakhstan
Kenya	1.6	1.2	1.9	...	...	...	1 305	...	...	Kenya
Kyrgyzstan	25.6	...	25.0	123	...	109	324	...	112	Kirghizistan
Latvia	90.9	106.4	79.4	178	202	184	...	...	5 680	Lettonie
Lesotho	...	...	...	...	...	...	971	...	...	Lesotho
Lithuania	25.9	27.3	32.5	75	84	84	701	682	642	Lituanie
Luxembourg	98.2	120.5	156.2	34	55	87	...	...	21 346	Luxembourg
Madagascar	0.7	0.1	0.4	34	27	55	333	343	387	Madagascar
Malawi	...	...	...	...	...	...	1 183	...	...	Malawi
Malaysia	29.7	44.2	43.4	2 242	3 468	2 177	...	...	...	Malaisie
Malta	34.0	19.4	29.1	299	34	4	1 667	863	832	Malte
Mauritius	1.6	1.6	1.6	...	3	8	...	...	...	Maurice
Mexico	6.2	7.3	8.4	10 440	9 629	9 399	...	74 550	82 017	Mexique
Monaco	198.3	84.8	169.5	14	8	5	50 392	48 991	53 859	Monaco
Mongolia	...	...	...	...	132	96	...	2 513	2 645	Mongolie
Montenegro	4.8	...	36.4	...	...	264	...	...	264	Monténégro
Morocco	5.7	4.3	4.8	969	...	808	...	...	....	Maroc
Mozambique	...	...	...	...	...	...	455	...	...	Mozambique
Namibia	...	...	...	...	...	...	51	...	...	Namibie
Netherlands	147.2	155.8	...	2 058	1 948	...	18 588	16 262	...	Pays-Bas
New Zealand	294.2	360.3	362.9	3 203	3 412	4 347	34 233	34 739	11 714	Nouvelle-Zélande
Norway	241.2	258.0	228.7	1 631	1 642	1 631	...	...	12 755	Norvège
Pakistan	1.0	0.5	...	233	162	...	...	...	...	Pakistan
Panama	...	...	...	310	392	378	41	...	378	Panama
Papua New Guinea	0.2	...	...	1	...	...	1	...	...	Papouasie-Nvl-Guinée
Paraguay	2.1	2.4	2.8				...	...	...	Paraguay
Peru	1.1	1.3	1.3	359	385	365	2 370	2 454	2 435	Pérou
Philippines	2.4	1.9	1.8	838	1 679	354	...	...	52 527	Philippines
Poland	65.3	76.0	83.9	3 590	3 958	3 004	21 352	26 298	30 021	Pologne
Portugal	35.9	53.7	46.9	165	146	140	39 507	39 867	2 161	Portugal
Republic of Korea	2 615.1	2 611.8	2 696.8	83 523	56 732	68 843	624 419	637 197	640 412	République de Corée
Republic of Moldova	76.5	37.6	36.5	250	290	132	1 049	1 139	1 018	République de Moldova
Romania	46.3	49.1	64.5	689	681	447	10 256	11 945	2 915	Roumanie
Russian Federation	195.2	180.5	202.6	28 808	34 824	30 322	147 067	170 264	181 904	Fédération de Russie
Saudi Arabia	...	...	10.5	...	...	194	...	...	193	Arabie saoudite
Serbia	52.5	43.6	39.8	290	411	427	1 277	1 635	1 477	Serbie
Sierra Leone	...	...	...	...	...	...	596	...	...	Sierra Leone
Singapore	163.9	150.4	176.3	6 286	5 609	4 442	...	...	...	Singapour
Slovakia	30.9	32.5	43.1	566	554	376	8 980	8 951	3 593	Slovaquie

53

Patents *(continued)*
Filings, grants and patents in force

Brevets
Demandes, délivrances et brevets en vigueur

Country or area	Resident filings (per million pop.) Demandes émanant de résidents (par million d'hab.)			Grants of patents Brevets délivrés			Patents in force Brevets en vigueur			Pays ou zone
	2008	2009	2010	2008	2009	2010	2008	2009	2010	
Slovenia	148.9	182.9	215.3	207	246	250	1 570	1 542	1 485	Slovénie
South Africa	17.6	16.7	16.4	1 742	1 639	5 331	...	...	6 530	Afrique du Sud
Spain	79.7	78.3	77.4	2 277	2 602	2 773	35 559	27 954	31 804	Espagne
Sri Lanka	9.8	9.8	10.8	159	265	504	...	...	...	Sri Lanka
Sudan	...	...	...	...	...	...	1 108	...	...	Soudan
Swaziland	...	...	...	...	...	...	1 017	...	...	Swaziland
Sweden	276.5	235.1	234.1	1 224	1 248	1 380	106 009	102 363	80 132	Suède
Switzerland	208.4	217.5	210.2	787	969	741	6 908	120 178	123 033	Suisse
Syrian Arab Republic	...	...	...	69	49	...	...	...	...	Rép. arabe syrienne
Tajikistan	...	1.6	1.0	...	10	3	...	245	248	Tadjikistan
Thailand	13.2	14.9	17.6	966	846	772	...	...	10 201	Thaïlande
TFYR of Macedonia	16.6	...	...	336	...	...	...	...	...	L'ex-R.Y. Macédoine
Trinidad and Tobago	0.8	...	...	90	...	...	...	...	...	Trinité-et-Tobago
Turkey	31.3	35.6	...	549	648	...	9 391	7 469	...	Turquie
Uganda	...	...	...	...	...	...	1 186	...	...	Ouganda
Ukraine	61.1	52.9	55.7	3 832	4 002	3 874	26 928	24 654	24 622	Ukraine
United Kingdom	269.1	258.7	249.0	5 360	5 428	5 594	...	...	424 209	Royaume-Uni
United Rep. of Tanzania	...	...	...	...	...	...	527	...	...	Rép.-Unie de Tanzanie
United States	760.9	732.6	783.0	157 772	167 349	219 614	1 872 872	1 930 631	2 017 318	Etats-Unis
Uruguay	9.9	9.0	6.9	64	17	29	...	...	877	Uruguay
Uzbekistan	9.6	8.6	13.1	288	235	192	1 674	1 673	1 253	Ouzbékistan
Viet Nam	3.8	4.6	3.5	666	706	822	...	...	9 103	Viet Nam
Yemen	1.2	0.9	0.8	...	...	...	...	...	...	Yémen
Zambia	...	...	...	...	...	...	638	...	...	Zambie
Zimbabwe	...	...	...	...	...	...	1 160	...	...	Zimbabwe

Source:
United Nations Educational, Scientific and Cultural Organization (UNESCO), Montreal, the UNESCO Institute for Statistics (UIS) database, last accessed January 2012.

1   Members of the Eurasian Patent Organization (EAPO), which includes Armenia, Azerbaijan, Belarus, Kazakhstan, Kyrgyzstan, Moldova, the Russian Federation, Tajikistan, Turkmenistan.

2   The following states are currently members of the European Patent Organisation (EPO): Albania, Austria, Belgium, Bulgaria, Switzerland, Cyprus, Czech Republic, Germany, Denmark, Estonia, Spain, Finland, France, United Kingdom, Greece, Croatia, Hungary, Ireland, Iceland, Italy, Liechtenstein, Lithuania, Luxembourg, Latvia, Monaco, Former Yugoslav Republic of Macedonia, Malta, Netherlands, Norway, Poland, Portugal, Romania, Serbia, Sweden, Slovenia, Slovakia, San Marino, and Turkey.

Source:
L'Organisation des Nations Unies pour l'éducation, la science et la culture (UNESCO), Montréal, la base de données de l'Institut de statistique de l'UNESCO (ISU), dernier accès janvier 2012.

1   Les membres de l'Organisation eurasienne de la propriété intellectuelle (EAPO) incluent: Arménie, Azerbaïdjan, Bélarus, Fédération de Russie, Kazakhstan, Kirghizistan, Moldavie, Tadjikistan, Turkménistan.

2   Les États suivants sont membres de l'Organisation européenne des brevets (OEB): Albanie, Autriche, Belgique, Bulgarie, Suisse, Chypre, République tchèque, Allemagne, Danemark, Estonie, Espagne, Finlande, France, Royaume-Uni, Grèce, Hongrie, Croatie, Irlande, Islande, Italie, Liechtenstein, Lituanie, Luxembourg, Lettonie, Monaco, L'ex-République yougoslave de Macédoine, Malte, Pays-Bas, Norvège, Pologne, Portugal, Roumanie, Serbie, Suède, Slovénie, Slovaquie, Saint-Marin, and Turquie.

Part Four

International economic relations

Chapter XVI   International merchandise trade (tables 54-56)

Chapter XVII   International tourism and transport (tables 57-59)

Chapter XVIII   International finance (tables 60)

Chapter XIX   Development assistance (tables 61-64)

Part Four of the *Yearbook* presents statistics on international economic relations in areas of international merchandise trade, international tourism and transport and assistance to developing countries. The series cover all countries or areas of the world for which data have been made available.

Quatrième partie

Relations économiques internationales

Chapitre XVI   Commerce international des marchandises (tableaux 54 à 56)

Chapitre XVII   Tourisme international et transport (tableaux 57 à 59)

Chapitre XVIII   Finances internationales (tableau 60)

Chapitre XIX   Aide au développement (tableaux 61 à 64)

La quatrième partie de l'*Annuaire* présente des statistiques sur les relations économiques internationales dans les domaines du commerce international des marchandises, du tourisme international et transport et l'assistance aux pays en développement. Les séries couvrent tous les pays ou les zones du monde pour lesquels de données sont disponibles.

54

Total imports and exports
Imports c.i.f., exports f.o.b. and balance, value in million US dollars

Importations et exportations totales
Importations c.a.f., exportations f.o.b. et balance, valeur en millions de dollars E.-U.

Region, country or area [&]	Sys.[t]	2005	2006	2007	2008	2009	2010	2011	Région, pays ou zone [&]
World									**Monde**
Imports		10 607 919	12 200 055	14 033 425	16 229 652	12 478 530	15 145 151	17 997 966	**Importations**
Exports		10 361 944	11 985 937	13 831 068	15 984 054	12 369 477	15 064 970	17 979 656	**Exportations**
Balance		-245 975	-214 118	-202 356	-245 598	-109 054	-80 181	-18 310	**Balance**
Developed economies [1,2]									**Economies développées** [1,2]
Imports		6 907 356	7 836 369	8 800 148	9 841 079	7 405 932	8 632 881	10 070 761	**Importations**
Exports		6 162 523	6 960 571	7 961 050	8 876 454	6 873 485	7 987 903	9 279 026	**Exportations**
Balance		-744 833	-875 798	-839 098	-964 625	-532 447	-644 978	-791 735	**Balance**
Asia and the Pacific - Developed economies									**Asie et Pacifique - Economies développées**
Imports		666 504	745 314	815 912	997 567	741 599	925 898	1 135 162	**Importations**
Exports		722 502	792 508	882 279	999 884	759 534	1 014 429	1 131 876	**Exportations**
Balance		55 998	47 194	66 368	2 317	17 936	88 531	-3 286	**Balance**
Australia	G								**Australie**
Imports		125 283	139 279	165 364	200 564	165 470	201 640	243 715	Importations
Exports		105 833	123 316	141 122	187 249	153 884	212 364	271 717	Exportations
Balance		-19 449	-15 963	-24 241	-13 314	-11 587	10 724	28 002	Balance
Japan	G								**Japon**
Imports		514 987	579 603	619 662	762 629	550 550	692 435	854 100	Importations
Exports		594 940	646 755	714 211	782 052	580 719	769 773	822 674	Exportations
Balance		79 953	67 151	94 549	19 423	30 169	77 337	-31 426	Balance
New Zealand	G								**Nouvelle-Zélande**
Imports		26 234	26 431	30 886	34 374	25 578	31 822	37 347	Importations
Exports		21 728	22 437	26 946	30 582	24 931	32 292	37 484	Exportations
Balance		-4 506	-3 994	-3 940	-3 792	-647	470	137	Balance
Europe - Developed economies									**Europe - Economies développées**
Imports		4 180 634	4 822 014	5 581 806	6 264 322	4 736 399	5 344 701	6 215 105	**Importations**
Exports		4 172 970	4 739 813	5 498 839	6 122 693	4 742 725	5 309 330	6 213 923	**Exportations**
Balance		-7 664	-82 201	-82 967	-141 629	6 327	-35 370	-1 182	**Balance**
Andorra	S								**Andorre**
Imports		1 796	1 780	1 917	1 931	1 589	1 518	1 596	Importations
Exports		142	150	127	96	63	54	77	Exportations
Balance		-1 654	-1 630	-1 790	-1 835	-1 526	-1 464	-1 519	Balance
Austria	S								**Autriche**
Imports		119 950	130 945	156 760	176 174	136 081	150 326	180 377	Importations
Exports		117 722	130 376	157 317	173 394	130 791	144 645	169 676	Exportations
Balance		-2 228	-570	557	-2 780	-5 290	-5 681	-10 700	Balance
Belgium	S								**Belgique**
Imports		319 797	351 574	412 010	471 576	353 248	393 515	461 935	Importations
Exports		335 738	366 758	431 118	477 260	370 515	409 307	476 346	Exportations
Balance		15 941	15 184	19 108	5 684	17 267	15 792	14 410	Balance
Croatia	G								**Croatie**
Imports		18 560	21 488	25 830	30 728	21 203	20 051	22 708	Importations
Exports		8 773	10 376	12 364	14 112	10 474	11 806	13 375	Exportations
Balance		-9 788	-11 112	-13 465	-16 617	-10 729	-8 244	-9 333	Balance
Czech Republic	S								**République tchèque**
Imports		76 343	93 453	118 467	142 172	105 256	126 600	151 394	Importations
Exports		77 988	95 165	122 760	146 406	113 175	133 020	162 171	Exportations
Balance		1 645	1 712	4 293	4 234	7 920	6 420	10 778	Balance
Denmark	S								**Danemark**
Imports		74 265	85 103	97 324	109 158	81 926	84 744	97 762	Importations
Exports		83 569	91 703	101 954	116 069	92 844	96 773	112 740	Exportations
Balance		9 303	6 600	4 631	6 911	10 917	12 029	14 979	Balance
Estonia	S								**Estonie**
Imports		10 213	13 472	15 687	16 058	10 151	12 282	17 602	Importations
Exports		7 676	9 705	10 948	12 468	9 058	11 607	16 793	Exportations
Balance		-2 537	-3 767	-4 739	-3 590	-1 094	-675	-809	Balance
Faeroe Islands	G								**Iles Féroé**
Imports		743	790	1 016	988	783	774	...	Importations
Exports		599	651	746	852	762	817	...	Exportations
Balance		-144	-139	-270	-136	-22	44	...	Balance
Finland	G								**Finlande**
Imports		58 474	69 448	81 756	92 160	60 822	68 772	84 013	Importations
Exports		65 238	77 287	90 091	96 890	62 859	69 491	78 866	Exportations
Balance		6 764	7 839	8 335	4 730	2 037	719	-5 146	Balance

Total imports and exports *(continued)*
Imports c.i.f., exports f.o.b., and balance, value in million US dollars

Importations et exportations totales *(suite)*
Importations c.a.f., exportations f.o.b. et balance, valeur en millions de dollars E.-U.

Region, country or area [&]	Sys.[t]	2005	2006	2007	2008	2009	2010	2011	Région, pays ou zone [&]
France[3]	S								**France**[3]
Imports		490 611	546 505	631 447	715 783	560 255	606 764	704 091	Importations
Exports		443 619	490 702	550 458	608 957	475 895	515 590	582 074	Exportations
Balance		-46 992	-55 803	-80 989	-106 826	-84 360	-91 174	-122 017	Balance
Germany	S								**Allemagne**
Imports		780 514	922 376	1 055 997	1 186 681	926 154	1 056 170	1 255 417	Importations
Exports		977 970	1 122 112	1 323 818	1 451 390	1 120 666	1 261 577	1 475 491	Exportations
Balance		197 456	199 736	267 822	264 709	194 512	205 408	220 074	Balance
Gibraltar									**Gibraltar**
Imports		550	676	853	824	750	745	868	Importations
Exports		199	242	304	281	266	259	246	Exportations
Balance		-351	-434	-548	-543	-484	-486	-621	Balance
Greece	S								**Grèce**
Imports		54 883	63 615	76 037	87 938	69 411	63 757	57 364	Importations
Exports		17 444	20 778	23 549	26 270	20 471	21 651	30 563	Exportations
Balance		-37 439	-42 837	-52 487	-61 669	-48 940	-42 106	-26 800	Balance
Hungary	S								**Hongrie**
Imports		65 783	77 206	94 375	106 380	78 034	87 612	100 989	Importations
Exports		62 179	74 217	93 377	107 466	84 586	94 759	110 897	Exportations
Balance		-3 604	-2 989	-997	1 085	6 552	7 147	9 908	Balance
Iceland	G								**Islande**
Imports		4 554	5 077	6 354	5 614	3 604	3 920	4 706	Importations
Exports		2 944	3 241	4 509	5 191	4 057	4 605	5 397	Exportations
Balance		-1 610	-1 836	-1 845	-423	453	685	691	Balance
Ireland	G								**Irlande**
Imports		69 177	83 889	85 624	82 658	62 595	60 686	66 709	Importations
Exports		109 605	104 639	122 622	126 144	117 092	118 260	128 896	Exportations
Balance		40 428	20 750	36 998	43 485	54 498	57 574	62 187	Balance
Italy	S								**Italie**
Imports		384 837	440 852	509 937	563 436	414 725	486 967	557 454	Importations
Exports		372 962	416 231	499 933	544 962	406 684	446 852	523 191	Exportations
Balance		-11 875	-24 621	-10 004	-18 474	-8 040	-40 116	-34 263	Balance
Latvia	S								**Lettonie**
Imports		8 592	11 430	15 182	15 775	9 346	11 064	15 063	Importations
Exports		5 108	5 896	7 892	9 278	7 174	8 817	12 012	Exportations
Balance		-3 483	-5 535	-7 290	-6 497	-2 173	-2 247	-3 051	Balance
Lithuania	G								**Lituanie**
Imports		15 510	19 413	24 445	31 295	18 341	23 385	31 551	Importations
Exports		11 782	14 153	17 162	23 770	16 496	20 726	28 107	Exportations
Balance		-3 729	-5 259	-7 283	-7 525	-1 845	-2 658	-3 444	Balance
Luxembourg	S								**Luxembourg**
Imports		17 565	19 434	22 301	25 514	18 652	21 738	25 670	Importations
Exports		12 699	14 172	16 144	17 590	12 786	14 293	16 718	Exportations
Balance		-4 866	-5 262	-6 157	-7 924	-5 866	-7 444	-8 952	Balance
Malta	G								**Malte**
Imports		3 807	4 073	4 508	5 399	4 393	5 731	7 393	Importations
Exports		2 376	2 705	2 985	3 077	2 327	3 717	5 279	Exportations
Balance		-1 432	-1 368	-1 523	-2 322	-2 066	-2 015	-2 114	Balance
Netherlands	S								**Pays-Bas**
Imports		310 600	358 510	421 084	495 043	382 268	440 018	507 563	Importations
Exports		349 844	399 635	476 787	541 398	431 839	492 411	563 129	Exportations
Balance		39 244	41 125	55 703	46 355	49 571	52 394	55 566	Balance
Norway	G								**Norvège**
Imports		55 473	64 272	80 378	90 293	68 970	77 326	90 853	Importations
Exports		103 738	122 112	136 371	171 764	116 778	130 669	159 253	Exportations
Balance		48 265	57 840	55 992	81 471	47 808	53 344	68 401	Balance
Poland	S								**Pologne**
Imports		100 759	127 260	162 437	204 873	149 723	178 149	206 844	Importations
Exports		89 214	110 941	138 756	168 674	136 786	159 829	187 151	Exportations
Balance		-11 545	-16 319	-23 680	-36 200	-12 938	-18 320	-19 693	Balance
Portugal	S								**Portugal**
Imports		53 398	65 609	76 371	94 726	71 729	75 590	79 734	Importations
Exports		32 129	42 894	50 241	57 565	44 343	48 742	58 727	Exportations
Balance		-21 269	-22 716	-26 129	-37 161	-27 386	-26 848	-21 007	Balance
Slovakia	S								**Slovaquie**
Imports		36 168	47 250	62 102	74 034	56 898	66 110	78 880	Importations
Exports		31 997	41 939	57 766	70 982	55 553	64 012	78 496	Exportations
Balance		-4 171	-5 311	-4 336	-3 052	-1 345	-2 098	-384	Balance

Total imports and exports *(continued)*
Imports c.i.f., exports f.o.b., and balance, value in million US dollars
Importations et exportations totales *(suite)*
Importations c.a.f., exportations f.o.b. et balance, valeur en millions de dollars E.-U.

Region, country or area &	Sys.ᵗ	2005	2006	2007	2008	2009	2010	2011	Région, pays ou zone &
Slovenia	S								**Slovénie**
Imports		19 626	23 014	29 481	34 000	23 852	26 370	31 254	Importations
Exports		17 896	20 985	26 553	28 624	22 294	24 189	28 985	Exportations
Balance		-1 730	-2 029	-2 928	-5 377	-1 558	-2 182	-2 269	Balance
Spain	S								**Espagne**
Imports		287 610	326 046	382 651	417 049	290 744	315 548	362 835	Importations
Exports		191 021	213 350	246 752	277 695	220 848	246 274	298 458	Exportations
Balance		-96 589	-112 697	-135 899	-139 353	-69 897	-69 274	-64 377	Balance
Sweden	G								**Suède**
Imports		111 219	126 613	153 463	168 993	120 262	148 471	174 755	Importations
Exports		130 147	147 191	168 979	183 907	131 042	158 089	187 266	Exportations
Balance		18 928	20 578	15 516	14 914	10 780	9 619	12 511	Balance
Switzerland	S								**Suisse**
Imports		119 784	132 030	153 181	173 683	147 894	166 910	196 700	Importations
Exports		126 099	141 679	164 809	191 810	166 847	185 774	223 288	Exportations
Balance		6 314	9 649	11 627	18 127	18 953	18 865	26 588	Balance
United Kingdom	G								**Royaume-Uni**
Imports		509 472	588 810	622 834	643 387	486 737	563 090	640 287	Importations
Exports		384 554	447 830	441 645	468 354	357 353	410 715	479 389	Exportations
Balance		-124 917	-140 980	-181 189	-175 033	-129 384	-152 375	-160 898	Balance
North America -									**Amerique du Nord -**
Developed economies									**Economies développées**
Imports		**2 060 219**	**2 269 041**	**2 402 430**	**2 579 189**	**1 927 935**	**2 362 283**	**2 720 494**	**Importations**
Exports		**1 267 052**	**1 428 250**	**1 579 932**	**1 753 877**	**1 371 225**	**1 664 143**	**1 933 228**	**Exportations**
Balance		**-793 167**	**-840 791**	**-822 498**	**-825 312**	**-556 710**	**-698 139**	**-787 266**	**Balance**
Bermuda	G								**Bermudes**
Imports		985	1 094	1 167	1 160	1 067	1 050	...	Importations
Exports		49	27	27	24	29	32	...	Exportations
Balance		-936	-1 067	-1 140	-1 136	-1 038	-1 018	...	Balance
Canada[4]	G								**Canada**[4]
Imports		323 365	348 958	379 794	407 165	320 287	390 527	452 131	Importations
Exports		359 411	389 513	416 432	452 170	313 981	386 011	451 735	Exportations
Balance		36 046	40 555	36 638	45 005	-6 306	-4 515	-396	Balance
Greenland	G								**Groenland**
Imports		593	618	678	871	680	779	495	Importations
Exports		402	396	431	489	360	383	864	Exportations
Balance		-190	-222	-247	-383	-320	-396	369	Balance
United States[5]	G								**Etats-Unis**[5]
Imports		1 735 060	1 918 080	2 020 400	2 169 490	1 605 300	1 969 180	2 265 890	Importations
Exports		907 158	1 038 270	1 162 980	1 301 110	1 056 750	1 277 580	1 480 410	Exportations
Balance		-827 902	-879 810	-857 420	-868 380	-548 550	-691 600	-785 480	Balance
South-eastern Europe									**Europe du Sud-est**
Imports		**82 986**	**103 593**	**140 430**	**170 949**	**114 542**	**125 287**	**154 429**	**Importations**
Exports		**49 008**	**61 183**	**76 807**	**94 028**	**73 459**	**89 766**	**115 215**	**Exportations**
Balance		**-33 979**	**-42 410**	**-63 624**	**-76 920**	**-41 083**	**-35 521**	**-39 214**	**Balance**
Albania	G								**Albanie**
Imports		2 618	3 058	4 188	5 251	4 550	4 406	5 395	Importations
Exports		658	798	1 078	1 355	1 091	1 545	1 951	Exportations
Balance		-1 960	-2 261	-3 110	-3 896	-3 459	-2 861	-3 444	Balance
Bosnia and Herzegovina	S								**Bosnie-Herzégovine**
Imports		7 072	7 345	9 772	12 282	8 794	9 204	11 047	Importations
Exports		2 400	3 323	4 166	5 066	3 939	4 802	5 850	Exportations
Balance		-4 672	-4 023	-5 606	-7 217	-4 856	-4 402	-5 196	Balance
Bulgaria	S								**Bulgarie**
Imports		18 162	23 270	30 086	37 018	23 552	25 473	32 114	Importations
Exports		11 739	15 101	18 575	22 485	16 378	20 571	27 986	Exportations
Balance		-6 423	-8 168	-11 511	-14 532	-7 175	-4 902	-4 128	Balance
Montenegro									**Monténégro**
Imports	S	...	1 874	3 206	3 644	2 310	2 186	2 543	Importations
Exports	S	...	791	827	659	403	437	632	Exportations
Balance		...	-1 082	-2 378	-2 985	-1 908	-1 749	-1 911	Balance
Romania	S								**Roumanie**
Imports		40 463	51 106	69 602	82 965	54 256	61 885	76 251	Importations
Exports		27 730	32 336	40 042	49 539	40 621	49 357	62 659	Exportations
Balance		-12 733	-18 770	-29 560	-33 426	-13 635	-12 528	-13 592	Balance
Serbia									**Serbie**
Imports	S	...	13 188	18 400	22 945	16 047	16 685	20 100	Importations
Exports	S	...	6 437	8 817	11 004	8 338	9 766	11 759	Exportations
Balance		...	-6 752	-9 584	-11 941	-7 709	-6 920	-8 341	Balance

Total imports and exports *(continued)*
Imports c.i.f., exports f.o.b., and balance, value in million US dollars
Importations et exportations totales *(suite)*
Importations c.a.f., exportations f.o.b. et balance, valeur en millions de dollars E.-U.

Region, country or area [&]	Sys.[t]	2005	2006	2007	2008	2009	2010	2011	Région, pays ou zone [&]
TFYR of Macedonia	S								**L'ex-R.Y. Macédoine**
Imports		3 228	3 752	5 177	6 844	5 032	5 449	6 979	Importations
Exports		2 041	2 398	3 302	3 920	2 691	3 291	4 378	Exportations
Balance		-1 187	-1 355	-1 875	-2 923	-2 341	-2 159	-2 601	Balance
CIS§									**CEI§**
Imports		**188 633**	**253 241**	**352 232**	**468 958**	**303 961**	**385 481**	**517 925**	**Importations**
Exports		**336 579**	**418 435**	**497 491**	**707 334**	**440 219**	**574 750**	**766 371**	**Exportations**
Balance		**147 945**	**165 195**	**145 259**	**238 376**	**136 258**	**189 269**	**248 446**	**Balance**
CIS Asia§									**CEI Asie§**
Imports		**34 788**	**45 334**	**59 477**	**72 860**	**59 216**	**56 175**	**78 778**	**Importations**
Exports		**43 806**	**58 030**	**70 649**	**138 894**	**76 194**	**98 779**	**138 082**	**Exportations**
Balance		**9 018**	**12 696**	**11 172**	**66 034**	**16 978**	**42 604**	**59 304**	**Balance**
Armenia	S								**Arménie**
Imports		1 768	2 194	3 282	4 427	3 303	3 783	4 196	Importations
Exports		950	1 004	1 219	1 057	698	1 011	1 316	Exportations
Balance		-818	-1 190	-2 063	-3 370	-2 605	-2 771	-2 881	Balance
Azerbaijan	G								**Azerbaïdjan**
Imports		4 211	5 267	5 714	7 170	6 123	6 599	9 756	Importations
Exports		4 347	6 372	6 058	47 756	14 701	21 325	26 571	Exportations
Balance		136	1 106	345	40 586	8 578	14 726	16 815	Balance
Georgia	G								**Géorgie**
Imports		2 490	3 678	5 217	6 066	4 386	5 097	6 948	Importations
Exports		865	993	1 240	1 507	1 140	1 581	2 188	Exportations
Balance		-1 624	-2 685	-3 977	-4 559	-3 246	-3 516	-4 760	Balance
Kazakhstan	G								**Kazakhstan**
Imports		17 979	24 120	33 260	38 452	28 409	24 024	38 039	Importations
Exports		28 301	38 762	48 351	71 971	43 196	57 244	88 118	Exportations
Balance		10 322	14 642	15 091	33 519	14 787	33 220	50 079	Balance
Kyrgyzstan	S								**Kirghizistan**
Imports		1 101	1 718	2 412	4 072	3 040	3 228	4 261	Importations
Exports		672	794	1 134	1 618	1 442	1 489	1 979	Exportations
Balance		-429	-924	-1 278	-2 455	-1 599	-1 739	-2 282	Balance
Tajikistan	G								**Tadjikistan**
Imports		1 354	1 723	2 455	3 270	2 569	2 658	3 186	Importations
Exports		891	1 399	1 468	1 406	1 010	1 206	1 257	Exportations
Balance		-464	-324	-987	-1 864	-1 559	-1 452	-1 930	Balance
Uzbekistan	G								**Ouzbékistan**
Imports		3 666	4 380	4 848	7 076	9 023	8 386	9 953	Importations
Exports		4 749	5 617	8 029	10 369	10 735	11 587	13 254	Exportations
Balance		1 083	1 237	3 181	3 293	1 712	3 201	3 301	Balance
CIS Europe§									**CEI Europe§**
Imports		**153 845**	**207 907**	**292 755**	**396 098**	**244 745**	**329 306**	**439 147**	**Importations**
Exports		**292 772**	**360 406**	**426 842**	**568 440**	**364 025**	**475 971**	**628 289**	**Exportations**
Balance		**138 927**	**152 499**	**134 087**	**172 342**	**119 280**	**146 665**	**189 142**	**Balance**
Belarus	G								**Bélarus**
Imports		16 708	22 351	28 693	39 381	28 569	34 884	45 743	Importations
Exports		15 979	19 734	24 275	32 571	21 304	25 284	41 192	Exportations
Balance		-729	-2 618	-4 418	-6 811	-7 265	-9 601	-4 551	Balance
Republic of Moldova	G								**République de Moldova**
Imports		2 293	2 710	3 690	4 081	3 278	3 855	5 192	Importations
Exports		1 091	1 060	1 340	1 335	1 283	1 542	2 222	Exportations
Balance		-1 202	-1 650	-2 350	-2 746	-1 995	-2 314	-2 970	Balance
Russian Federation	G								**Fédération de Russie**
Imports		98 708	137 807	199 754	267 101	167 411	229 655	305 605	Importations
Exports		241 473	301 244	351 930	467 581	301 656	397 668	516 481	Exportations
Balance		142 766	163 437	152 176	200 480	134 245	168 013	210 877	Balance
Ukraine	G								**Ukraine**
Imports		36 136	45 039	60 618	85 535	45 487	60 911	82 608	Importations
Exports		34 228	38 368	49 296	66 954	39 782	51 478	68 394	Exportations
Balance		-1 908	-6 671	-11 322	-18 581	-5 705	-9 433	-14 214	Balance
Northern Africa									**Afrique du Nord**
Imports		**80 214**	**86 800**	**112 469**	**164 473**	**146 452**	**161 273**	**184 757**	**Importations**
Exports		**109 622**	**131 233**	**153 521**	**207 537**	**134 078**	**164 438**	**200 936**	**Exportations**
Balance		**29 408**	**44 433**	**41 051**	**43 064**	**-12 374**	**3 165**	**16 179**	**Balance**
Algeria	S								**Algérie**
Imports		20 356	20 985	27 525	39 578	39 333	40 228	46 430	Importations
Exports		46 000	52 760	59 761	79 587	45 240	57 786	73 320	Exportations
Balance		25 644	31 775	32 236	40 010	5 907	17 558	26 890	Balance

Total imports and exports *(continued)*
Imports c.i.f., exports f.o.b., and balance, value in million US dollars

Importations et exportations totales *(suite)*
Importations c.a.f., exportations f.o.b. et balance, valeur en millions de dollars E.-U.

Region, country or area &	Sys.[t]	2005	2006	2007	2008	2009	2010	2011	Région, pays ou zone &
Egypt[6,7]	G								Egypte[6,7]
Imports		19 816	20 722	27 063	48 775	44 946	52 923	58 903	Importations
Exports		10 652	13 694	16 200	26 246	23 062	26 438	30 528	Exportations
Balance		-9 163	-7 028	-10 863	-22 528	-21 884	-26 485	-28 376	Balance
Libyan Arab Jamah.	G								Jamah. arabe libyenne
Imports		6 058	6 053	6 753	9 116	10 037	10 506	...	Importations
Exports		31 278	40 333	47 048	62 031	37 265	46 016	...	Exportations
Balance		25 220	34 280	40 295	52 915	27 228	35 510	...	Balance
Morocco	S								Maroc
Imports		20 790	23 980	32 010	42 366	32 881	35 385	44 294	Importations
Exports		11 190	12 744	15 340	20 345	14 054	17 765	21 525	Exportations
Balance		-9 601	-11 236	-16 670	-22 021	-18 827	-17 620	-22 769	Balance
Tunisia	G								Tunisie
Imports		13 177	15 043	19 101	24 622	19 241	22 218	23 958	Importations
Exports		10 494	11 694	15 163	19 319	14 449	16 427	17 847	Exportations
Balance		-2 683	-3 349	-3 938	-5 303	-4 791	-5 791	-6 111	Balance
Sub-Saharan Africa									**Afrique subsaharienne**
Imports		**165 901**	**197 707**	**244 997**	**300 662**	**251 578**	**282 769**	**329 662**[10]	**Importations**
Exports		**203 289**	**232 645**	**277 375**	**362 176**	**254 873**	**328 976**	**431 860**[10]	**Exportations**
Balance		**37 388**	**34 937**	**32 378**	**61 514**	**3 295**	**46 207**	**102 198**	**Balance**
Angola[4]	S								Angola[4]
Imports		8 353	8 778	13 661	20 982	22 660	16 574	17 330	Importations
Exports		23 670	31 084	43 452	72 179	40 080	46 492	65 801	Exportations
Balance		15 317	22 306	29 791	51 197	17 420	29 918	48 471	Balance
Benin	S								Bénin
Imports		1 018	1 228	2 037	2 290	2 110	2 354	...	Importations
Exports		574	741	1 052	1 285	1 109	1 240	...	Exportations
Balance		-445	-487	-984	-1 005	-1 001	-1 113	...	Balance
Botswana	G								Botswana
Imports		3 172	3 076	4 077	5 232	4 771	5 672	...	Importations
Exports		4 455	4 509	5 170	5 077	3 514	4 724	...	Exportations
Balance		1 283	1 434	1 093	-155	-1 257	-948	...	Balance
Burkina Faso	G								Burkina Faso
Imports		1 255	1 323	1 685	2 008	1 882	2 157	...	Importations
Exports		467	588	623	693	893	1 203	...	Exportations
Balance		-788	-735	-1 062	-1 315	-989	-954	...	Balance
Burundi	S								Burundi
Imports		267	431	319	402	402	509	752	Importations
Exports		56	58	62	54	62	100	122	Exportations
Balance		-211	-372	-257	-348	-340	-409	-630	Balance
Cameroon	S								Cameroun
Imports		2 725	3 161	4 218	5 376	4 322	4 847	...	Importations
Exports		2 849	3 587	3 622	4 279	3 391	3 896	...	Exportations
Balance		123	427	-596	-1 097	-931	-952	...	Balance
Cape Verde	G								Cap-Vert
Imports		438	543	753	819	709	743	...	Importations
Exports		18	21	19	32	35	45	...	Exportations
Balance		-420	-522	-734	-788	-674	-698	...	Balance
Central African Rep.	S								Rép. centrafricaine
Imports		175	203	251	298	300	341	...	Importations
Exports		127	158	181	150	121	139	...	Exportations
Balance		-48	-44	-70	-149	-179	-202	...	Balance
Chad	S								Tchad
Imports		954	1 346	1 794	1 906	2 289	2 507	...	Importations
Exports		3 095	3 342	3 653	4 345	2 636	3 411	...	Exportations
Balance		2 141	1 995	1 859	2 439	347	903	...	Balance
Comoros	S								Comores
Imports		98	116	139	174	171	190	...	Importations
Exports		12	10	14	9	16	18	...	Exportations
Balance		-86	-106	-125	-165	-155	-172	...	Balance
Congo	S								Congo
Imports		1 344	2 072	2 605	3 145	2 984	2 990	...	Importations
Exports		4 733	6 092	5 649	8 288	6 123	8 192	...	Exportations
Balance		3 389	4 020	3 045	5 144	3 139	5 202	...	Balance
Côte d'Ivoire	S								Côte d'Ivoire
Imports		5 860	5 825	6 694	7 863	6 973	7 844	...	Importations
Exports		7 693	8 477	8 692	10 301	10 518	10 532	...	Exportations
Balance		1 834	2 652	1 998	2 438	3 545	2 688	...	Balance

Total imports and exports *(continued)*
Imports c.i.f., exports f.o.b., and balance, value in million US dollars
Importations et exportations totales *(suite)*
Importations c.a.f., exportations f.o.b. et balance, valeur en millions de dollars E.-U.

Region, country or area &	Sys.[t]	2005	2006	2007	2008	2009	2010	2011	Région, pays ou zone &
Dem. Rep. of the Congo	S								**Rép. dém. du Congo**
Imports		2 690	2 892	3 400	4 300	3 800	4 500	...	Importations
Exports		2 403	2 705	3 100	4 400	3 500	5 400	...	Exportations
Balance		-288	-187	-300	100	-300	900	...	Balance
Djibouti	G								**Djibouti**
Imports		277	336	473	574	451	420	...	Importations
Exports		40	55	58	69	77	100	...	Exportations
Balance		-238	-281	-415	-505	-373	-320	...	Balance
Equatorial Guinea	G								**Guinée équatoriale**
Imports		1 310	2 023	2 369	3 933	5 205	5 680	...	Importations
Exports		7 062	8 218	10 205	15 995	9 108	9 964	...	Exportations
Balance		5 753	6 195	7 836	12 062	3 903	4 285	...	Balance
Ethiopia	G								**Ethiopie**
Imports		4 095	5 207	5 805	8 268	7 644	...	...	Importations
Exports		903	1 043	1 279	1 606	1 635	...	...	Exportations
Balance		-3 191	-4 164	-4 526	-6 663	-6 009	...	...	Balance
Gabon	S								**Gabon**
Imports		1 472	1 726	2 155	2 607	2 199	2 492	...	Importations
Exports		5 068	5 454	6 302	9 566	5 499	8 374	...	Exportations
Balance		3 596	3 728	4 147	6 959	3 299	5 882	...	Balance
Gambia	G								**Gambie**
Imports		260	259	323	324	304	301	...	Importations
Exports		8	11	13	14	15	15	...	Exportations
Balance		-252	-248	-310	-310	-289	-286	...	Balance
Ghana	G								**Ghana**
Imports		5 344	6 748	8 057	10 243	8 038	11 038	...	Importations
Exports		2 801	3 725	4 322	5 625	...	...	...	Exportations
Balance		-2 543	-3 023	-3 735	-4 618	...	...	...	Balance
Guinea	S								**Guinée**
Imports		820	956	1 218	1 366	1 060	1 100	...	Importations
Exports		853	1 033	1 203	1 342	1 050	1 450	...	Exportations
Balance		33	77	-15	-24	-10	350	...	Balance
Guinea-Bissau	G								**Guinée-Bissau**
Imports		119	111	111	159	...	...	...	Importations
Exports		90	74	106	131	119	118	...	Exportations
Balance		-29	-37	-5	-28	...	...	...	Balance
Kenya	G								**Kenya**
Imports		6 149	7 311	8 989	11 074	10 207	12 076	...	Importations
Exports		3 293	3 437	4 080	4 972	4 463	5 145	...	Exportations
Balance		-2 856	-3 874	-4 910	-6 102	-5 743	-6 931	...	Balance
Lesotho	G								**Lesotho**
Imports		1 410	1 496	1 741	1 995	1 973	2 206	...	Importations
Exports		650	689	770	883	723	801	...	Exportations
Balance		-760	-807	-971	-1 113	-1 250	-1 404	...	Balance
Liberia	S								**Libéria**
Imports		310	467	499	813	552	650	...	Importations
Exports		131	158	200	242	150	200	...	Exportations
Balance		-179	-309	-299	-571	-402	-450	...	Balance
Madagascar	S								**Madagascar**
Imports		1 685	1 810	2 671	3 800	3 197	2 507	...	Importations
Exports		835	993	1 262	1 304	1 050	1 087	...	Exportations
Balance		-850	-817	-1 408	-2 496	-2 147	-1 420	...	Balance
Malawi	G								**Malawi**
Imports		1 163	1 206	1 380	1 700	2 096	...	...	Importations
Exports		508	541	709	860	1 080	1 130	...	Exportations
Balance		-655	-665	-671	-840	-1 015	...	...	Balance
Mali	S								**Mali**
Imports		1 544	1 819	2 183	3 343	2 646	2 855	...	Importations
Exports		1 092	1 559	1 567	2 082	2 055	2 248	...	Exportations
Balance		-453	-260	-616	-1 261	-590	-607	...	Balance
Mauritania	S								**Mauritanie**
Imports		1 344	1 089	1 428	1 669	1 337	1 708	2 453	Importations
Exports		556	1 268	1 356	1 651	1 407	1 799	2 458	Exportations
Balance		-787	180	-72	-18	70	91	6	Balance
Mauritius	G								**Maurice**
Imports		3 157	3 627	3 894	4 655	3 734	4 387	5 159	Importations
Exports		2 138	2 329	2 238	2 386	1 939	2 262	2 647	Exportations
Balance		-1 018	-1 298	-1 656	-2 269	-1 795	-2 125	-2 512	Balance

54

Total imports and exports *(continued)*
Imports c.i.f., exports f.o.b., and balance, value in million US dollars

Importations et exportations totales *(suite)*
Importations c.a.f., exportations f.o.b. et balance, valeur en millions de dollars E.-U.

Region, country or area &	Sys.[t]	2005	2006	2007	2008	2009	2010	2011	Région, pays ou zone &
Mozambique	S								**Mozambique**
Imports		2 408	2 869	3 050	4 008	3 764	4 550	...	Importations
Exports		1 783	2 381	2 412	2 653	2 147	3 200	...	Exportations
Balance		-625	-488	-638	-1 355	-1 617	-1 350	...	Balance
Namibia	G								**Namibie**
Imports		2 567	2 868	3 528	4 314	5 066	5 372	...	Importations
Exports		2 067	2 638	2 924	3 113	3 379	4 096	...	Exportations
Balance		-500	-230	-604	-1 201	-1 687	-1 276	...	Balance
Niger	S								**Niger**
Imports		934	955	1 163	1 659	1 926	2 212	...	Importations
Exports		490	507	664	902	888	907	...	Exportations
Balance		-444	-448	-499	-757	-1 038	-1 305	...	Balance
Nigeria	G								**Nigéria**
Imports		21 314	26 760	37 576	42 378	33 906	37 000	...	Importations
Exports		55 145	57 444	65 133	80 615	53 000	79 000	...	Exportations
Balance		33 831	30 684	27 557	38 237	19 094	42 000	...	Balance
Rwanda	G								**Rwanda**
Imports		432	547	736	1 131	1 227	1 401	...	Importations
Exports		125	147	176	267	193	255	...	Exportations
Balance		-307	-400	-559	-865	-1 035	-1 146	...	Balance
Sao Tome and Principe	S								**Sao Tomé-et-Principe**
Imports		50	71	79	114	103	125	...	Importations
Exports		7	8	7	11	8	11	...	Exportations
Balance		-43	-63	-72	-103	-95	-114	...	Balance
Senegal	G								**Sénégal**
Imports		3 190	3 444	4 271	5 706	4 549	4 442	5 390	Importations
Exports		1 576	1 556	1 652	2 007	1 906	2 059	2 432	Exportations
Balance		-1 614	-1 888	-2 618	-3 699	-2 643	-2 383	-2 958	Balance
Seychelles	G								**Seychelles**
Imports		675	758	861	1 106	821	989	...	Importations
Exports		340	380	356	437	402	400	...	Exportations
Balance		-335	-378	-506	-668	-419	-588	...	Balance
Sierra Leone	S								**Sierra Leone**
Imports		345	389	445	535	518	...	...	Importations
Exports		159	231	245	216	232	...	...	Exportations
Balance		-186	-158	-199	-319	-285	...	...	Balance
South Africa [4,9,10]	G								**Afrique du Sud** [4,9,10]
Imports		54 848	67 644	79 873	94 901	64 439	80 131	99 726	Importations
Exports		51 640	58 197	69 787	84 488	62 627	81 822	96 922	Exportations
Balance		-3 208	-9 447	-10 086	-10 413	-1 812	1 691	-2 804	Balance
Sudan (former) [11]	G								**Soudan (anc.)** [11]
Imports		6 757	8 074	8 775	9 352	9 691	9 960	...	Importations
Exports		4 824	5 657	8 879	11 671	7 834	10 500	...	Exportations
Balance		-1 933	-2 417	104	2 319	-1 857	540	...	Balance
Swaziland	G								**Swaziland**
Imports		1 897	1 918	1 853	...	1 617	1 710	...	Importations
Exports		1 761	1 779	1 885	...	1 479	1 557	...	Exportations
Balance		-136	-139	33	...	-138	-153	...	Balance
Togo	S								**Togo**
Imports		1 054	1 088	1 243	1 499	1 409	1 502	...	Importations
Exports		659	631	700	901	801	850	...	Exportations
Balance		-396	-457	-543	-598	-607	-652	...	Balance
Uganda	G								**Ouganda**
Imports		2 049	2 555	3 497	4 559	3 787	4 264	4 590	Importations
Exports		1 017	1 188	2 003	2 717	2 327	2 164	2 410	Exportations
Balance		-1 033	-1 367	-1 494	-1 841	-1 461	-2 100	-2 180	Balance
United Rep. of Tanzania	G								**Rép.-Unie de Tanzanie**
Imports		2 661	4 254	5 337	7 081	6 296	7 714	10 703	Importations
Exports		1 479	1 655	2 022	2 674	2 367	3 524	4 392	Exportations
Balance		-1 182	-2 598	-3 315	-4 407	-3 929	-4 190	-6 311	Balance
Zambia	S								**Zambie**
Imports		2 567	2 931	4 014	5 023	3 791	5 319	...	Importations
Exports		1 780	3 828	4 641	5 186	4 389	7 207	...	Exportations
Balance		-786	896	628	163	599	1 888	...	Balance
Zimbabwe	G								**Zimbabwe**
Imports		2 350	2 300	2 550	2 950	2 900	3 700	...	Importations
Exports		1 850	2 000	2 400	2 200	2 269	2 500	...	Exportations
Balance		-500	-300	-150	-750	-631	-1 200	...	Balance

54

Total imports and exports *(continued)*
Imports c.i.f., exports f.o.b., and balance, value in million US dollars
Importations et exportations totales *(suite)*
Importations c.a.f., exportations f.o.b. et balance, valeur en millions de dollars E.-U.

Region, country or area [&]	Sys.[t]	2005	2006	2007	2008	2009	2010	2011	Région, pays ou zone [&]
Latin America and the Caribbean									**Amérique latine et Caraïbes**
Imports		515 014	614 285	733 219	896 728	674 693	864 923	1 024 430	Importations
Exports		559 143	668 691	757 873	886 824	680 311	866 504	1 053 771	Exportations
Balance		44 129	54 406	24 654	-9 904	5 618	1 581	29 341	Balance
Caribbean									**Caraïbes**
Imports		37 591	44 076	50 417	61 394	48 389	50 622	56 368	Importations
Exports		17 530	23 750	24 782	30 406	19 532	22 975	28 797	Exportations
Balance		-20 060	-20 326	-25 635	-30 988	-28 856	-27 647	-27 570	Balance
Anguilla	S								**Anguilla**
Imports		133	143	248	272	169	157	...	Importations
Exports		7	13	9	11	23	12	...	Exportations
Balance		-126	-130	-239	-260	-146	-145	...	Balance
Antigua and Barbuda	G								**Antigua-et-Barbuda**
Imports		526	671	727	806	699	501	471	Importations
Exports		121	164	174	92	206	35	29	Exportations
Balance		-405	-507	-553	-713	-493	-466	-442	Balance
Aruba	S								**Aruba**
Imports		1 028	1 041	1 114	1 134	1 097	1 006	1 196	Importations
Exports		102	109	98	100	136	125	148	Exportations
Balance		-927	-932	-1 016	-1 034	-961	-882	-1 048	Balance
Bahamas [12]	G								**Bahamas** [12]
Imports		2 230	2 401	2 449	2 354	2 699	2 863	...	Importations
Exports		562	674	485	560	585	620	...	Exportations
Balance		-1 668	-1 726	-1 965	-1 794	-2 114	-2 243	...	Balance
Barbados	G								**Barbade**
Imports		1 604	1 586	1 709	1 879	1 471	1 562	1 805	Importations
Exports		359	385	419	445	369	429	465	Exportations
Balance		-1 245	-1 201	-1 291	-1 433	-1 102	-1 133	-1 340	Balance
Cayman Islands	G								**Iles Caïmanes**
Imports		1 191	1 048	1 041	1 078	893	828	914	Importations
Exports		60	26	27	17	19	13	22	Exportations
Balance		-1 130	-1 022	-1 015	-1 062	-874	-815	-893	Balance
Cuba	S								**Cuba**
Imports		8 130	10 174	10 889	14 249	...	...	...	Importations
Exports		2 159	2 980	3 998	3 680	...	...	...	Exportations
Balance		-5 972	-7 194	-6 892	-10 570	...	...	...	Balance
Dominica	S								**Dominique**
Imports		165	167	196	247	233	224	...	Importations
Exports		41	42	38	40	36	35	...	Exportations
Balance		-124	-124	-158	-207	-197	-189	...	Balance
Dominican Republic [4,13]	G								**Rép. dominicaine** [4,13]
Imports		7 207	8 745	11 289	14 020	9 946	12 885	14 522	Importations
Exports		1 398	1 933	2 635	2 394	1 690	2 536	3 651	Exportations
Balance		-5 809	-6 812	-8 654	-11 626	-8 256	-10 349	-10 871	Balance
Grenada	S								**Grenade**
Imports		334	331	365	377	293	317	...	Importations
Exports		28	25	33	30	29	24	...	Exportations
Balance		-306	-305	-332	-347	-264	-293	...	Balance
Haiti	G								**Haïti**
Imports		1 449	1 880	1 681	2 310	2 121	3 147	...	Importations
Exports		470	480	522	475	576	579	...	Exportations
Balance		-979	-1 401	-1 159	-1 835	-1 546	-2 568	...	Balance
Jamaica	G								**Jamaïque**
Imports		4 458	5 314	6 394	7 734	4 860	5 201	6 489	Importations
Exports		1 499	1 874	2 070	2 542	1 319	1 331	1 603	Exportations
Balance		-2 959	-3 440	-4 324	-5 192	-3 540	-3 870	-4 886	Balance
Montserrat	S								**Montserrat**
Imports		30	30	30	38	30	30	...	Importations
Exports		1	1	3	4	3	1	...	Exportations
Balance		-28	-29	-27	-34	-26	-29	...	Balance
Netherlands Antilles	S								**Antilles néerlandaises**
Imports		1 950	2 209	2 549	3 079	2 607	2 800	...	Importations
Exports		608	695	676	1 088	810	800	...	Exportations
Balance		-1 342	-1 515	-1 872	-1 991	-1 797	-2 000	...	Balance
Saint Kitts and Nevis	S								**Saint-Kitts-et-Nevis**
Imports		210	250	272	325	302	228	...	Importations
Exports		30	35	32	43	43	45	...	Exportations
Balance		-180	-214	-241	-282	-260	-183	...	Balance

Total imports and exports *(continued)*
Imports c.i.f., exports f.o.b., and balance, value in million US dollars

Importations et exportations totales *(suite)*
Importations c.a.f., exportations f.o.b. et balance, valeur en millions de dollars E.-U.

Region, country or area &	Sys.ᵗ	2005	2006	2007	2008	2009	2010	2011	Région, pays ou zone &
Saint Lucia	S								**Sainte-Lucie**
Imports		479	592	635	657	539	601	...	Importations
Exports		89	98	107	145	163	228	...	Exportations
Balance		-390	-494	-528	-512	-376	-373	...	Balance
Saint Vincent-Grenadines	S								**Saint Vincent-Grenadines**
Imports		241	269	327	373	334	345	...	Importations
Exports		40	38	48	52	50	44	...	Exportations
Balance		-201	-231	-279	-321	-284	-301	...	Balance
Trinidad and Tobago	S								**Trinité-et-Tobago**
Imports		5 694	6 484	7 662	9 596	6 953	6 390	...	Importations
Exports		9 941	14 159	13 393	18 663	9 140	11 156	...	Exportations
Balance		4 247	7 675	5 731	9 067	2 187	4 766	...	Balance
Turks and Caicos Islands	G								**Iles Turques et Caïques**
Imports		304	498	581	591	375	302	...	Importations
Exports		15	18	16	25	21	16	...	Exportations
Balance		-289	-480	-564	-566	-355	-286	...	Balance
Latin America									**Amérique latine**
Imports		**477 423**	**570 209**	**682 802**	**835 333**	**626 305**	**814 301**	**968 063**	**Importations**
Exports		**541 613**	**644 941**	**733 092**	**856 418**	**660 779**	**843 529**	**1 024 974**	**Exportations**
Balance		**64 190**	**74 732**	**50 290**	**21 084**	**34 474**	**29 228**	**56 911**	**Balance**
Argentina	S								**Argentine**
Imports		28 693	34 158	44 707	57 413	39 105	56 443	73 923	Importations
Exports		40 351	46 568	55 779	70 588	56 065	68 499	84 269	Exportations
Balance		11 658	12 410	11 072	13 174	16 961	12 056	10 347	Balance
Belize	G								**Belize**
Imports		593	676	684	837	668	699	...	Importations
Exports		208	266	254	271	250	...	...	Exportations
Balance		-385	-410	-430	-566	-418	...	...	Balance
Bolivia (Plurin. State of)	G								**Bolivie (État plurin. de)**
Imports		2 341	2 814	3 457	5 081	4 434	5 182	7 551	Importations
Exports		2 791	3 875	4 458	7 058	4 918	6 179	8 107	Exportations
Balance		450	1 060	1 001	1 977	483	998	555	Balance
Brazil	G								**Brésil**
Imports		77 628	95 838	126 645	182 377	133 673	191 537	214 131	Importations
Exports		118 529	137 807	160 649	197 942	152 995	201 915	256 040	Exportations
Balance		40 901	41 969	34 004	15 565	19 322	10 378	41 909	Balance
Chile	S								**Chili**
Imports		32 735	38 406	47 164	61 903	42 571	58 956	73 545	Importations
Exports		41 267	58 680	67 666	66 456	54 004	71 028	80 027	Exportations
Balance		8 532	20 274	20 502	4 553	11 434	12 073	6 482	Balance
Colombia	G								**Colombie**
Imports		21 204	26 046	33 164	39 320	32 898	40 683	54 675	Importations
Exports		21 146	24 388	29 786	38 265	32 784	39 710	56 507	Exportations
Balance		-59	-1 658	-3 378	-1 055	-114	-973	1 832	Balance
Costa Rica	S								**Costa Rica**
Imports		9 812	11 520	12 952	15 366	11 460	13 557	16 218	Importations
Exports		7 026	8 216	9 340	9 575	8 711	9 343	10 238	Exportations
Balance		-2 786	-3 305	-3 613	-5 791	-2 750	-4 214	-5 980	Balance
Ecuador	G								**Equateur**
Imports		10 287	12 114	13 565	18 852	15 090	20 591	24 286	Importations
Exports		10 100	12 728	13 852	18 818	13 863	17 415	22 345	Exportations
Balance		-187	615	287	-34	-1 227	-3 176	-1 941	Balance
El Salvador	S								**El Salvador**
Imports		6 834	7 628	8 677	9 754	7 255	8 548	10 118	Importations
Exports		3 387	3 513	3 977	4 579	3 797	4 472	4 979	Exportations
Balance		-3 448	-4 115	-4 700	-5 175	-3 457	-4 077	-5 139	Balance
Guatemala	S								**Guatemala**
Imports		8 810	10 157	11 861	12 835	10 066	12 051	14 518	Importations
Exports		3 477	3 665	4 468	5 412	3 835	5 907	7 201	Exportations
Balance		-5 333	-6 492	-7 393	-7 423	-6 232	-6 145	-7 317	Balance
Guyana	S								**Guyana**
Imports		788	889	1 059	1 312	1 161	1 397	1 763	Importations
Exports		553	588	679	795	763	880	1 116	Exportations
Balance		-235	-301	-381	-518	-398	-517	-647	Balance
Honduras	S								**Honduras**
Imports		4 853	5 695	6 762	8 831	6 133	7 079	8 953	Importations
Exports		1 892	2 054	2 120	2 883	2 304	2 712	3 892	Exportations
Balance		-2 960	-3 641	-4 642	-5 948	-3 829	-4 367	-5 060	Balance

54

Total imports and exports *(continued)*
Imports c.i.f., exports f.o.b., and balance, value in million US dollars
Importations et exportations totales *(suite)*
Importations c.a.f., exportations f.o.b. et balance, valeur en millions de dollars E.-U.

Region, country or area &	Sys.ᵗ	2005	2006	2007	2008	2009	2010	2011	Région, pays ou zone &
Mexico[4,14]	G								**Mexique[4,14]**
Imports		221 414	256 130	283 264	310 561	234 385	301 482	350 856	Importations
Exports		213 891	250 441	272 055	291 827	229 683	298 138	349 569	Exportations
Balance		-7 523	-5 689	-11 209	-18 734	-4 702	-3 344	-1 287	Balance
Nicaragua	G								**Nicaragua**
Imports		2 595	3 000	3 579	4 300	3 438	4 229	5 180	Importations
Exports		858	1 027	1 194	1 473	1 393	1 845	2 294	Exportations
Balance		-1 737	-1 973	-2 385	-2 827	-2 045	-2 384	-2 886	Balance
Panama[15]	S								**Panama[15]**
Imports		4 180	4 831	6 872	9 050	7 801	9 145	11 342	Importations
Exports		1 018	1 093	1 164	1 247	948	832	785	Exportations
Balance		-3 162	-3 738	-5 709	-7 803	-6 853	-8 313	-10 556	Balance
Paraguay	S								**Paraguay**
Imports		3 790	6 090	5 859	9 033	6 940	10 040	12 317	Importations
Exports		1 688	1 906	2 817	4 463	3 167	4 534	5 531	Exportations
Balance		-2 102	-4 184	-3 042	-4 570	-3 773	-5 507	-6 786	Balance
Peru[4]	S								**Pérou[4]**
Imports		12 084	14 897	19 580	28 373	21 006	28 818	37 112	Importations
Exports		17 368	23 830	27 882	31 529	26 885	35 565	46 118	Exportations
Balance		5 284	8 933	8 301	3 157	5 879	6 747	9 005	Balance
Suriname	G								**Suriname**
Imports		829	894	1 111	1 518	1 356	1 380	1 667	Importations
Exports		789	1 123	1 287	1 668	1 393	1 851	2 345	Exportations
Balance		-40	229	177	149	37	471	677	Balance
Uruguay	G								**Uruguay**
Imports		3 879	4 757	5 667	8 943	6 209	8 619	10 623	Importations
Exports		3 405	3 953	4 490	6 421	5 417	6 707	7 997	Exportations
Balance		-474	-804	-1 178	-2 523	-792	-1 912	-2 626	Balance
Venezuela (Boliv. Rep. of)	G								**Venezuela (Rép. boliv. du)**
Imports		24 027	33 615	46 097	49 602	40 597	33 815	38 346	Importations
Exports		51 859	59 208	69 165	95 138	57 595	65 786	...	Exportations
Balance		27 832	25 593	23 068	45 536	16 998	31 971	...	Balance
Eastern Asia									**Asie orientale**
Imports		**1 410 160**	**1 646 432**	**1 909 526**	**2 206 817**	**1 857 507**	**2 516 769**	**3 048 655**	**Importations**
Exports		**1 538 470**	**1 840 228**	**2 185 632**	**2 473 784**	**2 089 331**	**2 714 089**	**3 199 323**	**Exportations**
Balance		**128 311**	**193 795**	**276 106**	**266 968**	**231 824**	**197 320**	**150 669**	**Balance**
China[16]	S								**Chine[16]**
Imports		660 206	791 797	956 233	1 131 620	1 004 170	1 396 200	1 742 850	Importations
Exports		761 953	969 380	1 217 815	1 428 660	1 201 790	1 578 270	1 899 180	Exportations
Balance		101 747	177 583	261 582	297 040	197 620	182 070	156 330	Balance
China, Hong Kong SAR	G								**Chine, Hong Kong RAS**
Imports		299 533	334 681	367 864	388 505	347 311	433 111	483 633	Importations
Exports		289 337	316 816	344 629	362 675	318 510	390 143	428 732	Exportations
Balance		-10 196	-17 865	-23 235	-25 830	-28 801	-42 968	-54 901	Balance
China, Macao SAR	G								**Chine, Macao RAS**
Imports		3 913	4 565	5 366	5 365	4 622	5 513	7 769	Importations
Exports		2 476	2 557	2 543	1 997	961	870	869	Exportations
Balance		-1 438	-2 008	-2 823	-3 368	-3 661	-4 643	-6 899	Balance
Republic of Korea	G								**République de Corée**
Imports		261 238	309 383	356 648	435 275	322 843	425 212	524 366	Importations
Exports		284 419	325 465	371 554	422 007	361 614	466 384	556 602	Exportations
Balance		23 181	16 082	14 906	-13 268	38 771	41 172	32 236	Balance
Mongolia	G								**Mongolie**
Imports		1 184	1 486	2 117	3 616	2 131	3 278	6 527	Importations
Exports		1 065	1 543	1 889	2 539	1 903	2 899	4 780	Exportations
Balance		-119	57	-228	-1 077	-229	-379	-1 747	Balance
Southern Asia									**Asie australe**
Imports		**235 818**	**280 684**	**342 932**	**465 570**	**379 013**	**500 772**	**650 343**	**Importations**
Exports		**187 186**	**233 715**	**276 988**	**351 197**	**283 324**	**370 385**	**492 273**	**Exportations**
Balance		**-48 632**	**-46 968**	**-65 944**	**-114 372**	**-95 689**	**-130 387**	**-158 071**	**Balance**
Bangladesh	G								**Bangladesh**
Imports		12 881	14 964	17 263	22 473	20 631	26 071	...	Importations
Exports		7 233	9 103	10 233	11 777	12 443	14 195	...	Exportations
Balance		-5 648	-5 861	-7 030	-10 695	-8 188	-11 877	...	Balance
Bhutan	G								**Bhoutan**
Imports		515	530	686	730	786	925	...	Importations
Exports		320	488	658	587	578	631	...	Exportations
Balance		-195	-42	-27	-143	-208	-294	...	Balance

54

Total imports and exports *(continued)*
Imports c.i.f., exports f.o.b., and balance, value in million US dollars

Importations et exportations totales *(suite)*
Importations c.a.f., exportations f.o.b. et balance, valeur en millions de dollars E.-U.

Region, country or area &	Sys.[t]	2005	2006	2007	2008	2009	2010	2011	Région, pays ou zone &
India[17]	G								**Inde**[18]
Imports		142 865	178 485	229 349	321 026	257 200	350 192	463 923	Importations
Exports		99 618	121 812	150 160	194 816	164 912	222 576	302 588	Exportations
Balance		-43 247	-56 674	-79 189	-126 210	-92 288	-127 617	-161 336	Balance
Iran (Islamic Rep. of)[18,19]	S								**Iran (Rép. islamique d')**[18,19]
Imports		40 041	40 772	44 942	57 401	50 469	62 670	...	Importations
Exports		56 252	77 012	88 733	113 668	78 830	100 900	...	Exportations
Balance		16 211	36 240	43 791	56 267	28 361	38 230	...	Balance
Maldives	G								**Maldives**
Imports		745	927	1 096	1 388	967	1 091	1 465	Importations
Exports		103	135	108	126	76	74	127	Exportations
Balance		-641	-791	-989	-1 262	-891	-1 017	-1 338	Balance
Nepal	G								**Népal**
Imports		2 282	2 488	3 139	3 562	4 398	5 501	...	Importations
Exports		863	838	870	937	823	951	...	Exportations
Balance		-1 419	-1 650	-2 269	-2 625	-3 574	-4 550	...	Balance
Pakistan	G								**Pakistan**
Imports		25 356	29 828	32 590	42 326	31 648	37 783	43 955	Importations
Exports		16 050	16 932	17 837	20 323	17 523	21 409	25 383	Exportations
Balance		-9 306	-12 896	-14 753	-22 003	-14 125	-16 373	-18 572	Balance
Sri Lanka	G								**Sri Lanka**
Imports		8 833	10 259	11 301	13 953	10 049	13 512	19 943	Importations
Exports		6 347	6 886	7 740	8 137	7 085	8 307	10 242	Exportations
Balance		-2 487	-3 373	-3 560	-5 816	-2 965	-5 205	-9 701	Balance
South-eastern Asia									**Asie du Sud-est**
Imports		**600 573**	**688 631**	**776 921**	**947 451**	**728 375**	**954 968**	**1 150 630**	**Importations**
Exports		**653 858**	**770 881**	**865 370**	**998 343**	**813 601**	**1 051 660**	**1 237 280**	**Exportations**
Balance		**53 286**	**82 250**	**88 449**	**50 891**	**85 227**	**96 692**	**86 650**	**Balance**
Brunei Darussalam	S								**Brunéi Darussalam**
Imports		1 447	1 679	2 101	2 572	2 449	2 460	...	Importations
Exports		6 242	7 634	7 693	10 319	7 200	8 908	...	Exportations
Balance		4 794	5 956	5 592	7 747	4 751	6 448	...	Balance
Cambodia	S								**Cambodge**
Imports		3 927	4 749	5 300	6 508	5 876	7 500	...	Importations
Exports		3 200	3 800	4 400	4 708	4 302	5 030	...	Exportations
Balance		-727	-949	-900	-1 800	-1 574	-2 470	...	Balance
Indonesia	S								**Indonésie**
Imports		75 725	80 650	93 101	127 538	93 786	135 323	176 355	Importations
Exports		86 995	103 528	118 014	139 606	119 646	158 074	201 472	Exportations
Balance		11 270	22 878	24 913	12 068	25 860	22 751	25 117	Balance
Lao People's Dem. Rep.	S								**Rép. dém. pop. lao**
Imports		882	1 060	1 067	1 405	1 461	2 060	...	Importations
Exports		553	882	923	1 085	1 053	1 746	...	Exportations
Balance		-329	-177	-144	-320	-408	-314	...	Balance
Malaysia	G								**Malaisie**
Imports		114 410	131 085	146 767	164 410	123 693	164 734	187 592	Importations
Exports		140 870	160 571	176 028	209 668	157 483	198 800	228 262	Exportations
Balance		26 459	29 486	29 261	45 258	33 790	34 067	40 671	Balance
Myanmar	G								**Myanmar**
Imports		1 927	2 564	3 277	4 299	4 393	4 807	9 109	Importations
Exports		3 813	4 585	6 313	6 950	6 731	8 749	9 330	Exportations
Balance		1 887	2 021	3 036	2 651	2 338	3 941	221	Balance
Philippines	G								**Philippines**
Imports		46 963	54 077	57 708	60 492	45 743	58 229	63 703	Importations
Exports		39 879	47 413	50 270	49 205	38 308	51 432	48 053	Exportations
Balance		-7 084	-6 665	-7 438	-11 287	-7 435	-6 797	-15 650	Balance
Singapore	G								**Singapour**
Imports		200 050	238 711	263 155	319 781	245 785	310 791	365 770	Importations
Exports		229 652	271 809	299 270	338 176	269 832	351 867	409 503	Exportations
Balance		29 602	33 098	36 115	18 396	24 048	41 076	43 733	Balance
Thailand	S								**Thaïlande**
Imports		118 158	128 654	141 294	179 168	134 734	185 121	228 845	Importations
Exports		110 178	130 795	153 858	175 897	151 910	195 371	226 412	Exportations
Balance		-7 980	2 142	12 563	-3 270	17 176	10 250	-2 433	Balance
Viet Nam	G								**Viet Nam**
Imports		36 761	45 015	62 682	80 714	69 949	83 779	104 041	Importations
Exports		32 442	39 826	48 561	62 685	57 096	71 658	94 518	Exportations
Balance		-4 319	-5 188	-14 121	-18 029	-12 853	-12 121	-9 523	Balance

54

Total imports and exports *(continued)*
Imports c.i.f., exports f.o.b., and balance, value in million US dollars
Importations et exportations totales *(suite)*
Importations c.a.f., exportations f.o.b. et balance, valeur en millions de dollars E.-U.

Region, country or area [&]	Sys.[t]	2005	2006	2007	2008	2009	2010	2011	Région, pays ou zone [&]
Western Asia[8]									**Asie occidentale**[8]
Imports		**410 204**	**479 804**	**605 894**	**750 082**	**600 769**	**701 616**	**845 692**	**Importations**
Exports		**555 013**	**659 803**	**768 959**	**1 015 668**	**718 003**	**906 403**	**1 193 307**	**Exportations**
Balance		**144 809**	**179 998**	**163 065**	**265 587**	**117 234**	**204 787**	**347 614**	**Balance**
Bahrain	G								**Bahreïn**
Imports		9 393	10 515	11 488	10 800	7 300	9 800	...	Importations
Exports		10 242	12 200	13 634	17 316	11 874	15 400	...	Exportations
Balance		849	1 685	2 146	6 516	4 574	5 600	...	Balance
Cyprus	G								**Chypre**
Imports		6 282	6 951	8 687	10 873	7 882	8 646	8 722	Importations
Exports		1 303	1 153	1 254	1 755	1 342	1 507	1 959	Exportations
Balance		-4 979	-5 798	-7 433	-9 118	-6 540	-7 139	-6 763	Balance
Israel[20]	S								**Israël**[20]
Imports		47 142	50 334	59 039	67 656	49 278	61 209	75 472	Importations
Exports		42 770	46 789	54 065	60 825	47 934	58 392	64 551	Exportations
Balance		-4 371	-3 544	-4 973	-6 831	-1 344	-2 817	-10 921	Balance
Jordan	G								**Jordanie**
Imports		10 506	11 447	13 511	16 764	14 534	15 085	18 463	Importations
Exports		4 302	5 175	5 725	7 788	6 531	7 023	7 964	Exportations
Balance		-6 204	-6 272	-7 786	-8 976	-8 002	-8 062	-10 499	Balance
Kuwait	S								**Koweït**
Imports		15 534	17 252	21 388	24 836	20 340	21 996	...	Importations
Exports		45 189	56 022	62 871	87 648	51 979	66 042	...	Exportations
Balance		29 655	38 769	41 483	62 812	31 638	44 046	...	Balance
Lebanon	G								**Liban**
Imports		9 633	9 647	12 251	16 754	16 574	18 460	...	Importations
Exports		2 337	2 814	3 574	4 454	4 187	5 021	...	Exportations
Balance		-7 296	-6 833	-8 677	-12 300	-12 387	-13 439	...	Balance
Occ. Palestinian Terr.	S								**Terr. palestinien occupé**
Imports		2 668	2 759	3 141	3 466	3 593	...	4 492	Importations
Exports		335	367	513	558	506	...	759	Exportations
Balance		-2 332	-2 392	-2 628	-2 908	-3 087	...	-3 733	Balance
Oman	G								**Oman**
Imports		8 827	10 915	15 978	22 925	17 865	19 775	23 620	Importations
Exports		18 692	21 585	24 136	37 719	28 053	36 601	47 092	Exportations
Balance		9 865	10 670	8 158	14 795	10 188	16 827	23 472	Balance
Qatar	S								**Qatar**
Imports		10 061	16 440	23 430	27 900	24 922	23 240	...	Importations
Exports		25 762	34 052	44 456	67 307	48 007	74 800	114 251	Exportations
Balance		15 701	17 611	21 027	39 407	23 085	51 560	...	Balance
Saudi Arabia	S								**Arabie saoudite**
Imports		59 458	69 800	90 215	115 133	95 544	106 865	131 658	Importations
Exports		180 736	211 306	233 300	313 427	192 296	251 149	364 446	Exportations
Balance		121 278	141 506	143 086	198 294	96 752	144 284	232 789	Balance
Syrian Arab Republic	S								**Rép. arabe syrienne**
Imports		10 862	11 488	14 655	18 150	15 443	17 562	...	Importations
Exports		9 174	10 919	11 546	15 304	10 559	12 304	...	Exportations
Balance		-1 688	-569	-3 109	-2 846	-4 884	-5 257	...	Balance
Turkey	S								**Turquie**
Imports		116 774	139 576	170 063	201 964	140 928	185 544	240 842	Importations
Exports		73 476	85 535	107 272	132 027	102 143	113 883	134 907	Exportations
Balance		-43 298	-54 041	-62 791	-69 937	-38 785	-71 661	-105 935	Balance
United Arab Emirates	G								**Emirats arabes unis**
Imports		84 654	100 057	132 500	177 000	150 000	170 000	...	Importations
Exports		117 287	145 587	178 630	239 213	185 000	235 000	...	Exportations
Balance		32 633	45 530	46 130	62 213	35 000	65 000	...	Balance
Yemen	S								**Yémen**
Imports		5 401	6 081	8 513	10 548	9 206	9 746	...	Importations
Exports		5 604	6 653	6 299	7 584	6 256	8 497	...	Exportations
Balance		204	572	-2 215	-2 964	-2 949	-1 249	...	Balance
Oceania									**Océanie**
Imports		**11 059**	**12 508**	**14 656**	**16 884**	**15 708**	**18 411**	**20 683**	**Importations**
Exports		**7 252**	**8 552**	**10 003**	**10 708**	**8 793**	**10 095**	**10 294**	**Exportations**
Balance		**-3 807**	**-3 956**	**-4 653**	**-6 176**	**-6 915**	**-8 317**	**-10 388**	**Balance**
American Samoa[21]	S								**Samoa américaines**[21]
Imports		520	579	650	680	600	550	...	Importations
Exports		374	439	450	570	470	480	...	Exportations
Balance		-146	-141	-200	-110	-130	-70	...	Balance

54

Total imports and exports *(continued)*
Imports c.i.f., exports f.o.b., and balance, value in million US dollars

Importations et exportations totales *(suite)*
Importations c.a.f., exportations f.o.b. et balance, valeur en millions de dollars E.-U.

Region, country or area &	Sys.[t]	2005	2006	2007	2008	2009	2010	2011	Région, pays ou zone &
Cook Islands	G								**Iles Cook**
Imports		81	100	106	111	72	81	84	Importations
Exports		5	3	5	4	3	5	3	Exportations
Balance		-76	-96	-101	-107	-69	-76	-81	Balance
Fiji	G								**Fidji**
Imports		1 607	1 804	1 800	2 264	1 440	1 800	...	Importations
Exports		705	694	755	922	630	811	...	Exportations
Balance		-903	-1 110	-1 046	-1 342	-810	-990	...	Balance
French Polynesia	S								**Polynésie française**
Imports		1 723	1 656	1 863	2 187	1 732	1 740	...	Importations
Exports		217	235	197	273	167	175	...	Exportations
Balance		-1 506	-1 420	-1 667	-1 914	-1 565	-1 565	...	Balance
Guam	G								**Guam**
Imports		...	501	688	649	635	698	708	Importations
Exports		52	53	91	105	51	46	43	Exportations
Balance		...	-448	-596	-544	-584	-652	-664	Balance
Kiribati	G								**Kiribati**
Imports		74	63	70	70	68	100	...	Importations
Exports		4	6	10	15	20	15	...	Exportations
Balance		-70	-57	-60	-55	-48	-85	...	Balance
Marshall Islands	G								**Iles Marshall**
Imports		68	...	...	...	...	...	...	Importations
New Caledonia	S								**Nouvelle-Calédonie**
Imports		1 774	2 117	2 809	3 233	2 574	3 313	...	Importations
Exports		1 090	1 349	2 104	1 300	1 029	1 272	...	Exportations
Balance		-684	-768	-705	-1 933	-1 546	-2 041	...	Balance
Niue	G								**Nioué**
Imports		...	4	7	8	...	...	...	Importations
Exports		^0	1	3	^0	...	...	...	Exportations
Balance		...	-2	-4	-8	...	...	...	Balance
Papua New Guinea	G								**Papouasie-Nvl-Guinée**
Imports		1 728	2 287	2 945	3 550	...	...	...	Importations
Exports		3 276	4 167	4 685	5 719	4 635	5 414	...	Exportations
Balance		1 548	1 880	1 740	2 169	...	...	...	Balance
Samoa	S								**Samoa**
Imports		187	219	227	249	204	278	319	Importations
Exports		12	11	15	11	12	13	15	Exportations
Balance		-175	-208	-212	-238	-193	-265	-304	Balance
Solomon Islands	S								**Iles Salomon**
Imports		185	217	287	329	270	300	...	Importations
Exports		103	121	165	210	163	221	...	Exportations
Balance		-82	-95	-123	-119	-107	-79	...	Balance
Tonga	G								**Tonga**
Imports		120	116	143	168	145	159	...	Importations
Exports		10	10	9	9	8	8	...	Exportations
Balance		-110	-107	-134	-158	-137	-151	...	Balance
Tuvalu	G								**Tuvalu**
Imports		13	13	16	...	...	...	...	Importations
Exports ^		0	0	0	...	...	...	...	Exportations ^
Balance		-13	-13	-16	...	...	...	...	Balance
Vanuatu	G								**Vanuatu**
Imports		149	217	231	314	294	283	288	Importations
Exports		38	49	50	57	57	48	64	Exportations
Balance		-111	-168	-180	-257	-238	-235	-225	Balance

Additional country groupings · Groupements supplémentaires de pays

		2005	2006	2007	2008	2009	2010	2011	
ANCOM§ [22]									**ANCOM§** [22]
Imports		45 917	55 871	69 767	91 626	73 428	95 273	123 624	Importations
Exports		51 405	64 821	75 978	95 671	78 449	98 869	133 077	Exportations
Balance		5 488	8 950	6 212	4 045	5 021	3 596	9 452	Balance
APEC§									**CEAP§**
Imports		5 088 704	5 780 574	6 436 015	7 376 474	*5 701 882	*7 356 131	*8 787 802	Importations
Exports		4 686 744	5 455 551	6 219 978	7 070 236	5 634 210	7 231 383	*8 474 212	Exportations
Balance		-401 960	-325 023	-216 037	-306 238	*-67 672	*-124 748	*-313 589	Balance
ASEAN§									**ANASE§**
Imports		600 251	688 243	776 452	946 886	727 868	954 805	*1 150 577	Importations
Exports		653 824	770 844	865 330	998 300	813 562	1 051 636	*1 237 265	Exportations
Balance		53 574	82 601	88 878	51 414	85 694	96 832	*86 688	Balance

Total imports and exports *(continued)*
Imports c.i.f., exports f.o.b., and balance, value in million US dollars
Importations et exportations totales *(suite)*
Importations c.a.f., exportations f.o.b. et balance, valeur en millions de dollars E.-U.

Region, country or area [&] Sys.[1]	2005	2006	2007	2008	2009	2010	2011	Région, pays ou zone [&]
CACM§								**MCAC§**
Imports	32 904	37 999	43 831	51 085	38 353	45 464	54 987	Importations
Exports	16 640	18 475	21 098	23 921	20 040	24 279	28 604	Exportations
Balance	-16 264	-19 524	-22 732	-27 164	-18 313	-21 186	-26 383	Balance
CARICOM§								**CARICOM§**
Imports	19 630	22 434	25 302	30 362	23 718	24 885	*30 735	Importations
Exports	14 732	19 953	19 543	25 824	14 923	*17 461	*21 646	Exportations
Balance	-4 899	-2 481	-5 760	-4 538	-8 795	*-7 425	*-9 089	Balance
COMESA§ *								**COMESA§**
Imports	62 685	69 391	83 882	119 466	111 518	127 742	143 631	Importations
Exports	63 826	80 188	96 403	128 107	93 056	114 580	143 572	Exportations
Balance	1 141	10 797	12 522	8 641	-18 462	-13 162	-59	Balance
ECOWAS§								**CEDEAO§**
Imports	43 803	51 915	68 257	81 005	*66 812	*75 022	*84 888	Importations
Exports	71 753	76 755	86 193	106 389	*78 300	*105 545	*145 897	Exportations
Balance	27 950	24 840	17 936	25 383	*11 488	*30 523	*61 009	Balance
EMCCA§								**CEMAC§**
Imports	7 980	10 531	13 391	17 266	17 299	18 858	*20 361	Importations
Exports	22 935	26 851	29 613	42 623	26 877	33 976	*44 185	Exportations
Balance	14 955	16 320	16 222	25 357	9 578	15 119	*23 824	Balance
LAIA§								**ALAI§**
Imports	446 213	535 039	640 059	785 708	*589 381	*767 086	*906 926	Importations
Exports	524 553	626 365	712 596	832 185	*641 692	*820 422	*998 141	Exportations
Balance	78 339	91 326	72 537	46 476	*52 311	*53 336	*91 216	Balance
LDC§ *[22]								**PMA§ *[22]**
Imports	85 060	99 206	122 075	158 421	152 093	166 141	196 698	Importations
Exports	80 067	100 101	125 872	174 259	124 624	152 749	201 036	Exportations
Balance	-4 992	896	3 797	15 837	-27 469	-13 392	4 338	Balance
MERCOSUR§								**MERCOSUR§**
Imports	113 990	140 843	182 879	257 767	185 926	266 639	310 994	Importations
Exports	163 973	190 235	223 735	279 414	217 644	281 655	353 838	Exportations
Balance	49 983	49 392	40 856	21 647	31 718	15 016	42 844	Balance
NAFTA§								**ALENA§**
Imports	2 279 839	2 523 168	2 683 458	2 887 216	2 159 972	2 661 189	3 068 877	Importations
Exports	1 480 460	1 678 224	1 851 467	2 045 107	1 600 414	1 961 729	2 281 714	Exportations
Balance	-799 379	-844 944	-831 991	-842 109	-559 558	-699 459	-787 163	Balance
OECD§[22]								**OCDE§[22]**
Imports	7 535 306	8 568 545	9 640 340	10 828 963	8 137 183	9 599 440	11 253 450	Importations
Exports	6 788 886	7 692 841	8 791 561	9 797 532	7 630 807	8 948 980	10 403 639	Exportations
Balance	-746 420	-875 704	-848 779	-1 031 432	-506 376	-650 460	-849 811	Balance
OPEC§ *[22]								**OPEP§ *[22]**
Imports	313 153	369 168	478 687	608 092	530 258	573 058	664 647	Importations
Exports	661 079	797 181	928 085	1 252 374	824 491	1 060 402	1 424 871	Exportations
Balance	347 926	428 013	449 398	644 283	294 233	487 344	760 224	Balance
EU-25								**UE-25**
Imports	3 985 455	4 602 852	5 320 965	5 971 134	4 499 487	5 082 104	5 905 656	Importations
Exports	3 931 780	4 462 515	5 180 863	5 740 342	4 444 821	4 976 853	5 813 382	Exportations
Balance	-53 675	-140 337	-140 102	-230 792	-54 666	-105 251	-92 275	Balance
Extra-EU-25 [23]								**Extra-UE-25 [23]**
Imports	1 456 866	1 702 321	1 967 370	...	...	...	...	Importations
Exports	1 330 464	1 489 696	1 742 459	...	...	...	...	Exportations
Balance	-126 402	-212 625	-224 911	...	...	...	...	Balance
EU-27								**UE-27**
Imports	4 044 081	4 677 228	5 420 653	6 091 117	4 577 296	5 169 461	6 014 021	Importations
Exports	3 971 249	4 509 953	5 239 480	5 812 366	4 501 820	5 046 780	5 904 026	Exportations
Balance	-72 832	-167 275	-181 173	-278 750	-75 476	-122 681	-109 995	Balance
Extra-EU-27 [23]								**Extra-UE-27 [23]**
Imports	1 465 103	1 699 468	1 966 873	2 306 624	1 671 715	1 989 022	2 345 994	Importations
Exports	1 307 303	1 458 219	1 702 746	1 930 284	1 527 713	1 785 453	2 130 904	Exportations
Balance	-157 800	-241 250	-264 127	-376 340	-144 003	-203 568	-215 089	Balance
World exc. intra-EU27 *								**Monde excl. intra-UE27 ***
Imports	8 028 941	9 222 296	10 579 645	12 445 159	9 572 950	11 964 711	14 329 939	Importations
Exports	7 697 998	8 934 203	10 294 334	12 101 972	9 395 370	11 803 643	14 206 534	Exportations
Balance	-330 943	-288 093	-285 311	-343 188	-177 581	-161 069	-123 405	Balance

Source:
United Nations Statistics Division, New York, trade statistics database, last accessed October 2012.

[&] The regional totals for imports and exports have been adjusted to exclude the re-exports of countries or areas comprising each region.

Source:
Organisation des Nations Unies, Division de statistique, New York, la base de données pour les statistiques du commerce extérieur, dernier accès octobre 2012.

[&] Les totaux régionaux pour importations et exportations ont été ajustés pour exclure les réexportations des pays ou zones qui comprennent la région.

54

Total imports and exports *(continued)*
Imports c.i.f., exports f.o.b., and balance, value in million US dollars

Importations et exportations totales *(suite)*
Importations c.a.f., exportations f.o.b. et balance, valeur en millions de dollars E.-U.

§ For member states of this grouping, see Annex I – Other groupings. The totals have been calculated for all periods shown according to the current composition.

§ Pour les Etats membres de ce groupements, voir annexe I – Autres groupements. Les totales ont été calculés pour toutes les périodes données suivant la composition présente.

t Systems of trade: Two systems of recording trade, the General trade system (G) and the Special trade system (S), are in common use. They differ mainly in the way warehoused and re-exported goods are recorded. See the Technical notes for an explanation of the trade systems.

t Systèmes de commerce : Deux systèmes d'enregistrement du commerce sont couramment utilisés, le Commerce général (G) et le Commerce spécial (S). Ils ne diffèrent que par la façon dont sont enregistrées les marchandises entreposées et les marchandises réexportées. Voir les Notes techniques pour une explication des Systèmes de commerce.

1 This classification is intended for statistical convenience and does not, necessarily, express a judgement about the stage reached by a particular country in the development process.
2 Developed Economies of America, Europe, and the Asia-Pacific region.
3 Trade data for France include the import and export values of French Guiana, Guadeloupe, Martinique, and Réunion.
4 Imports FOB.
5 Including the trade of the U.S. Virgin Islands and Puerto Rico but excluding shipments of merchandise between the United States and its other possessions (Guam, American Samoa, etc.). Data include imports and exports of non-monetary gold.
7 Prior to 2008, special trade.
6 Imports exclude petroleum imported without stated value. Exports cover domestic exports.
8 In June 2011, the estimates for exports (and also imports) of some major oil exporting countries of the Western Asia and the Sub-Saharan Africa region were revised upwards significantly.
9 Exports include gold.
10 Foreign trade data refer to South Africa only, excluding intra-trade of the Southern African Common Customs Area.
11 Year ending December 31.
12 Trade statistics exclude certain oil and chemical products.
13 Export and import values exclude trade in the processing zone.
14 Trade data include maquiladoras and exclude goods from customs-bonded warehouses. Total exports include revaluation and exports of silver.
15 Exports include petroleum products.
16 For statistical purposes, the data for China do not include those for the Hong Kong Special Administrative Region (Hong Kong SAR), Macao Special Administrative Region (Macao SAR) and Taiwan Province of China.
17 Excluding military goods, fissionable materials, bunkers, ships, and aircraft.
18 Data include oil and gas.The value of oil exports and total exports are rough estimates based on information published in various petroleum industry journals.
19 Year ending 20 March of the years stated.
20 Imports and exports net of returned goods. The figures also exclude Judea and Samaria and the Gaza area.
21 Year ending 30 September.
22 The figures for the country groupings aim to always reflect the membership of the grouping of the latest year published.
23 Excluding intra-EU trade.

1 Cette classification est utilisée pour plus de commodité dans la présentation des statistiques et n'implique pas nécessairement un jugement quant au stade de développement auquel est parvenu un pays donné.
2 Économies développées de l'Amérique, de l'Europe, et de la région Asie-Pacifique.
3 Les valeurs de commerce pour la France comprennent les valeurs des importations et des exportations de la Guyane française, la Guadeloupe, la Martinique, et la Réunion.
4 Importations FOB.
5 Y compris le commerce des Iles Vierges américaines et de Porto Rico mais non compris les échanges de marchandises, entre les Etats-Unis et leurs autres possessions (Guam, Samoa américaines, etc.). Les données comprennent les importations et exportations d'or non-monétaire.
7 Avant 2008, commerce special.
Non compris le pétrole brute dont la valeur des importations ne sont pas stipulée. Les exportations sont les exportations d'intérieur.
8 En juin 2011, les estimations des données d'exportations (et d'importations) pour certains pays de l'Asie Occidentale et de l'Afrique Sub-saharienne, exportateurs majeurs du pétrole, ont étés significativement révisées à la hausse.
9 Les exportations comprennent l'or.
10 Les données sur le commerce extérieur ne se rapportent qu'à l'Afrique du Sud et ne tiennent pas compte des échanges commerciaux entre les pays de l'Union douanière de l'Afrique du Sud.
11 Année finissant le 31 décembre.
12 Les statistiques commerciales font exclusion de certains produits pétroliers et chimiques.
13 Les valeurs à l'exportation et à l'importation excluent le commerce de la zone de transformation.
14 Les statistiques du commerce extérieur comprennent maquiladoras et ne comprennent pas les marchandises provenant des entrepôts en douane. Les exportations comprennent la réévaluation et les données sur les exportations d'argent.
15 Exportations comprennent produits pétroliers.
16 Pour la présentation des statistiques, les données pour la Chine ne comprennent pas la Région Administrative Spéciale de Hong Kong (Hong Kong RAS), la Région Administrative Spéciale de Macao (Macao RAS) et la province de Taiwan.
17 A l'exclusion des marchandises militaires, des matières fissibles, des soutes, des bateaux, et de l'avion.
18 Les données comprennent le pétrole et le gaz. La valeur des exportations de pétrole et des exportations totales sont des évaluations grossières basées sur l'information publiée à divers journaux d'industrie de pétrole.
19 Année finissant le 20 mars de l'année indiquée.
20 Importations et exportations nets, ne comprenant pas les marchandises retournées. Sont également exclues les données de la Judée et de Samara et ainsi que la zone de Gaza.
21 Année finissant le 30 septembre.
22 Les données d'un groupe de pays reflètent sa composition lors de la dernière année de publication.
23 Non compris le commerce de l'intra-UE.

Country or area	2003	2004	2005	2006	2007	2008	2009	2010	2011	Pays ou zone
Argentina										**Argentine**
Imports: volume	58	87	108	125	150	177	137	188	232	Importations : volume
Imports: unit value	94	102	105	108	115	128	...	119	130	Importations : valeur unitaire
Exports: volume	110	118	135	143	154	156	142	165	...	Exportations : volume
Exports: unit value	102	111	113	122	137	213	178	157	183	Exportations : valeur unitaire
Terms of trade	108	110	107	113	119	167	...	133	141	Termes de l'échange
Purchasing power of exports	120	129	145	163	183	260	...	218	...	Pouvoir d'achat des exportations
Australia										**Australie**
Imports: volume	120	137	129	145	155	186	164	173	192	Importations : volume
Imports: unit value [1]	104	111	117	120	128	155	135	174	221	Importations : valeur unitaire [1]
Exports: volume	102	106	119	141	144	191	168	198	229	Exportations : volume
Exports: unit value [1]	111	129	153	175	196	270	218	312	444	Exportations : valeur unitaire [1]
Terms of trade	106	116	131	146	153	174	162	179	201	Termes de l'échange
Purchasing power of exports	108	123	156	205	220	331	272	354	461	Pouvoir d'achat des exportations
Austria										**Autriche**
Imports: volume	111	118	125	131	143	142	120	131	140	Importations : volume
Imports: unit value	114	125	123	130	144	162	147	147	167	Importations : valeur unitaire
Exports: volume	117	127	132	142	156	156	127	142	155	Exportations : volume
Exports: unit value	114	126	126	132	146	164	152	150	165	Exportations : valeur unitaire
Terms of trade	100	101	102	102	101	102	104	102	99	Termes de l'échange
Purchasing power of exports	117	128	135	144	158	158	132	145	153	Pouvoir d'achat des exportations
Belgium										**Belgique**
Imports: volume	111	118	126	132	138	138	122	129	136	Importations : volume
Imports: unit value	120	136	143	151	169	191	164	172	196	Importations : valeur unitaire
Exports: volume	113	121	126	131	135	132	117	126	130	Exportations : volume
Exports: unit value	121	135	142	150	170	190	169	174	197	Exportations : valeur unitaire
Terms of trade	100	99	99	99	101	100	103	101	100	Termes de l'échange
Purchasing power of exports	113	120	125	129	136	132	121	127	130	Pouvoir d'achat des exportations
Bolivia (Plur. State of)										**Bolivie (État plur. de)**
Exports: volume	145	173	126	142	153	238	257	403	256	Exportations : volume
Exports: unit value	91	122	169	252	292	402	316	384	527	Exportations : valeur unitaire
Brazil										**Brésil**
Imports: volume	136	111	101	110	128	134	112	149	160	Importations : volume
Imports: unit value	64	102	131	148	168	231	204	219	253	Importations : valeur unitaire
Exports: volume	131	154	162	173	189	192	186	213	222	Exportations : volume
Exports: unit value	101	114	133	144	154	187	149	172	209	Exportations : valeur unitaire
Terms of trade	158	112	101	97	92	81	73	79	83	Termes de l'échange
Purchasing power of exports	208	173	165	168	173	156	136	168	184	Pouvoir d'achat des exportations
Bulgaria										**Bulgarie**
Imports: unit value [1]	112	130	140	156	182	208	178	177	199	Importations : valeur unitaire [1]
Exports: unit value [1]	114	133	142	162	194	227	188	197	232	Exportations : valeur unitaire [1]
Terms of trade	102	102	102	104	107	109	106	112	117	Termes de l'échange
Canada										**Canada**
Imports: volume	100	108	116	123	130	131	109	126	137	Importations : volume
Imports: unit value	100	106	114	122	128	137	128	137	148	Importations : valeur unitaire
Exports: volume	95	100	102	103	105	97	81	87	91	Exportations : volume
Exports: unit value	106	117	130	140	150	166	140	156	173	Exportations : valeur unitaire
Terms of trade	106	110	114	114	118	121	110	115	117	Termes de l'échange
Purchasing power of exports	101	111	117	118	123	117	88	100	106	Pouvoir d'achat des exportations
China, Hong Kong SAR										**Chine, Hong Kong RAS**
Imports: volume	119	136	148	162	179	184	167	198	208	Importations : volume
Imports: unit value	93	96	98	101	102	107	107	114	123	Importations : valeur unitaire
Exports: volume	120	138	154	169	183	189	166	196	202	Exportations : volume
Exports: unit value	94	95	96	97	99	103	105	109	118	Exportations : valeur unitaire
Terms of trade	101	99	98	97	97	96	98	96	96	Termes de l'échange
Purchasing power of exports	121	137	151	164	177	182	162	188	193	Pouvoir d'achat des exportations
Colombia										**Colombie**
Imports: unit value [1]	95	103	114	114	117	125	116	...	...	Importations : valeur unitaire [1]
Exports: unit value [1]	87	96	111	119	130	159	151	...	...	Exportations : valeur unitaire [1]
Terms of trade	92	93	97	104	111	128	130	...	...	Termes de l'échange

Total imports and exports: index numbers *(continued)*
Index base : 2000 = 100
Importations et exportations totales : indices *(suite)*
Indices base : 2000 = 100

Country or area	2003	2004	2005	2006	2007	2008	2009	2010	2011	Pays ou zone
Czech Republic										**République tchèque**
Imports: unit value	123	137	148	158	175	201	173	175	197	Importations : valeur unitaire
Exports: unit value	130	147	155	164	185	210	189	185	203	Exportations : valeur unitaire
Terms of trade	105	107	105	104	106	105	109	106	103	Termes de l'échange
Denmark										**Danemark**
Imports: volume	106	113	122	135	147	141	117	127	138	Importations : volume
Imports: unit value	119	133	138	143	160	173	154	149	163	Importations : valeur unitaire
Exports: volume	107	110	116	123	131	130	116	122	130	Exportations : volume
Exports: unit value	122	136	143	148	160	178	159	158	171	Exportations : valeur unitaire
Terms of trade	102	102	104	103	100	103	103	106	105	Termes de l'échange
Purchasing power of exports	109	113	121	128	132	133	120	129	137	Pouvoir d'achat des exportations
Ecuador										**Equateur**
Imports: volume	161	168	204	229	262	280	274	331	350	Importations : volume
Exports: volume	107	133	117	143	139	141	137	133	138	Exportations : volume
Exports: unit value	107	118	150	182	209	284	201	264	363	Exportations : valeur unitaire
Estonia										**Estonie**
Imports: unit value	121	135	140	148	166	189	170	176	206	Importations : valeur unitaire
Exports: unit value	173	194	199	210	247	276	252	254	293	Exportations : valeur unitaire
Terms of trade	143	144	143	142	148	146	149	144	142	Termes de l'échange
Finland										**Finlande**
Imports: volume	103	108	114	127	128	130	100	109	118	Importations : volume
Imports: unit value [1]	115	131	146	151	167	186	161	163	185	Importations : valeur unitaire [1]
Exports: volume	106	112	111	124	120	121	88	94	94	Exportations : volume
Exports: unit value [1]	107	117	127	124	136	147	127	126	138	Exportations : valeur unitaire [1]
Terms of trade	93	89	87	82	81	79	79	77	75	Termes de l'échange
Purchasing power of exports	98	99	96	102	97	96	70	73	70	Pouvoir d'achat des exportations
France										**France**
Imports: volume	112	125	136	143	148	148	133	146	149	Importations : volume
Imports: unit value	114	122	122	124	137	147	...	...	...	Importations : valeur unitaire
Exports: volume	110	118	125	135	136	134	117	133	137	Exportations : volume
Exports: unit value	118	127	126	127	139	147	...	...	...	Exportations : valeur unitaire
Terms of trade	103	104	104	102	101	100	...	...	...	Termes de l'échange
Purchasing power of exports	114	123	130	138	137	134	...	...	...	Pouvoir d'achat des exportations
Germany										**Allemagne**
Imports: volume	110	121	126	142	146	148	133	153	158	Importations : volume
Imports: unit value	111	121	123	129	144	159	139	139	158	Importations : valeur unitaire
Exports: volume	115	129	136	153	162	164	137	160	170	Exportations : volume
Exports: unit value	119	129	130	132	147	160	147	143	157	Exportations : valeur unitaire
Terms of trade	107	107	105	102	103	100	106	103	99	Termes de l'échange
Purchasing power of exports	123	139	143	157	166	165	146	164	169	Pouvoir d'achat des exportations
Greece										**Grèce**
Imports: unit value [1]	127	144	158	165	185	213	198	201	227	Importations : valeur unitaire [1]
Exports: unit value [1]	124	143	149	158	177	202	180	187	213	Exportations : valeur unitaire [1]
Terms of trade	98	99	95	95	96	95	91	93	94	Termes de l'échange
Honduras										**Honduras**
Exports: volume	93	112	96	103	114	117	109	113	130	Exportations : volume
Exports: unit value [1]	83	102	125	128	135	161	149	181	263	Exportations : valeur unitaire [1]
Hungary										**Hongrie**
Imports: volume	120	139	147	168	189	197	164	185	197	Importations : volume
Imports: unit value [1]	123	135	138	142	156	171	147	144	156	Importations : valeur unitaire [1]
Exports: volume	125	147	164	194	225	234	206	234	258	Exportations : volume
Exports: unit value [1]	122	134	134	136	149	160	140	138	147	Exportations : valeur unitaire [1]
Terms of trade	100	99	97	95	95	94	96	95	95	Termes de l'échange
Purchasing power of exports	124	146	159	185	214	219	197	224	244	Pouvoir d'achat des exportations
India										**Inde**
Imports: volume	139	155	197	239	290	241	233	...	...	Importations : volume
Imports: unit value	113	134	143	135	179	173	152	168	...	Importations : valeur unitaire
Exports: volume	134	152	185	193	212	206	206	...	...	Exportations : volume
Exports: unit value	107	122	130	148	161	152	160	192	...	Exportations : valeur unitaire
Terms of trade	95	91	91	109	90	88	105	115	...	Termes de l'échange
Purchasing power of exports	127	138	169	212	191	181	216	...	...	Pouvoir d'achat des exportations

Country or area	2003	2004	2005	2006	2007	2008	2009	2010	2011	Pays ou zone
Indonesia										**Indonésie**
Exports: volume	97	101	64	...	...	...	...	...	...	Exportations : volume
Exports: unit value	103	120	81	...	...	...	...	...	...	Exportations : valeur unitaire
Ireland										**Irlande**
Imports: volume	90	98	112	115	118	106	88	86	83	Importations : volume
Imports: unit value	112	120	121	126	137	149	134	133	153	Importations : valeur unitaire
Exports: volume	99	110	113	113	119	119	114	120	125	Exportations : volume
Exports: unit value	115	116	119	120	128	133	126	123	129	Exportations : valeur unitaire
Terms of trade	103	97	99	95	93	89	94	93	84	Termes de l'échange
Purchasing power of exports	103	107	111	108	111	106	107	111	105	Pouvoir d'achat des exportations
Israel										**Israël**
Imports: volume	92	103	105	105	114	116	99	115	126	Importations : volume
Imports: unit value	104	112	120	127	138	157	134	144	164	Importations : valeur unitaire
Exports: volume	101	116	119	124	137	134	111	132	144	Exportations : volume
Exports: unit value	100	106	114	119	127	147	136	141	150	Exportations : valeur unitaire
Terms of trade	96	95	95	94	92	93	102	98	92	Termes de l'échange
Purchasing power of exports	97	110	113	116	126	124	113	130	132	Pouvoir d'achat des exportations
Italy										**Italie**
Imports: volume	102	108	108	113	116	109	94	105	103	Importations : volume
Imports: unit value	122	138	149	165	185	217	185	194	226	Importations : valeur unitaire
Exports: volume	99	104	104	110	115	110	89	97	101	Exportations : volume
Exports: unit value	126	142	149	158	181	206	191	192	216	Exportations : valeur unitaire
Terms of trade	104	103	100	96	98	95	103	99	96	Termes de l'échange
Purchasing power of exports	103	106	104	105	112	104	92	96	96	Pouvoir d'achat des exportations
Japan										**Japon**
Imports: volume	107	115	118	123	119	119	102	116	119	Importations : volume
Imports: unit value	91	101	112	120	133	164	139	154	183	Importations : valeur unitaire
Exports: volume	102	113	114	123	130	128	94	117	113	Exportations : volume
Exports: unit value	96	104	109	110	115	127	129	138	152	Exportations : valeur unitaire
Terms of trade	105	103	98	92	86	77	93	90	83	Termes de l'échange
Purchasing power of exports	108	116	111	113	112	99	87	105	94	Pouvoir d'achat des exportations
Jordan										**Jordanie**
Imports: volume	109	136	155	154	162	166	155	138	132	Importations : volume
Imports: unit value	115	130	148	162	184	221	197	243	305	Importations : valeur unitaire
Exports: volume	152	190	182	188	173	158	142	188	190	Exportations : volume
Exports: unit value	102	114	131	143	170	261	237	207	233	Exportations : valeur unitaire
Terms of trade	88	87	88	88	92	118	120	85	77	Termes de l'échange
Purchasing power of exports	135	166	161	166	160	186	171	160	145	Pouvoir d'achat des exportations
Latvia										**Lettonie**
Imports: unit value	122	140	150	166	191	224	198	201	227	Importations : valeur unitaire
Exports: unit value	121	145	153	169	209	242	207	212	253	Exportations : valeur unitaire
Terms of trade	99	104	102	102	109	108	104	106	111	Termes de l'échange
Lithuania										**Lituanie**
Imports: volume	155	182	209	233	257	280	197	239	271	Importations : volume
Imports: unit value	117	127	138	151	174	211	169	178	214	Importations : valeur unitaire
Exports: volume	161	185	214	234	250	284	251	296	336	Exportations : volume
Exports: unit value	120	137	151	160	185	216	179	191	227	Exportations : valeur unitaire
Terms of trade	102	108	109	106	106	102	106	107	106	Termes de l'échange
Purchasing power of exports	164	199	233	247	266	289	265	316	357	Pouvoir d'achat des exportations
Mauritius										**Maurice**
Imports: volume	96	102	107	111	114	114	108	115	119	Importations : volume
Imports: unit value [1]	80	90	98	102	111	133	112	124	141	Importations : valeur unitaire [1]
Exports: volume	92	89	96	106	95	96	87	101	107	Exportations : volume
Exports: unit value [1]	84	92	90	89	96	102	91	91	101	Exportations : valeur unitaire [1]
Terms of trade	105	101	92	87	87	77	81	73	72	Termes de l'échange
Purchasing power of exports	96	90	89	93	82	73	71	74	77	Pouvoir d'achat des exportations
Mexico										**Mexique**
Imports: unit value [1]	103	108	114	119	125	136	131	136	147	Importations : valeur unitaire [1]
Exports: unit value [1]	105	117	127	137	144	158	135	151	173	Exportations : valeur unitaire [1]
Terms of trade	102	108	112	115	114	116	103	111	118	Termes de l'échange

Country or area	2003	2004	2005	2006	2007	2008	2009	2010	2011	Pays ou zone
Morocco										**Maroc**
Imports: volume	113	127	140	155	176	...	...	...	...	Importations : volume
Imports: unit value	110	122	129	134	152	...	...	...	...	Importations : valeur unitaire
Exports: volume	104	103	118	127	131	...	...	...	...	Exportations : volume
Exports: unit value	116	127	128	135	150	...	...	...	...	Exportations : valeur unitaire
Terms of trade	105	105	99	100	98	...	...	...	...	Termes de l'échange
Purchasing power of exports	110	108	117	128	129	...	...	...	...	Pouvoir d'achat des exportations
Netherlands										**Pays-Bas**
Imports: volume	98	106	121	133	141	146	130	147	154	Importations : volume
Imports: unit value	118	131	129	135	150	169	147	150	165	Importations : valeur unitaire
Exports: volume	106	116	122	134	144	147	134	151	156	Exportations : volume
Exports: unit value	116	127	134	140	155	175	151	153	169	Exportations : valeur unitaire
Terms of trade	99	96	104	104	103	103	103	103	103	Termes de l'échange
Purchasing power of exports	104	112	127	139	149	151	138	155	161	Pouvoir d'achat des exportations
New Zealand										**Nouvelle-Zélande**
Imports: volume	124	142	151	150	165	171	148	160	175	Importations : volume
Imports: unit value [1]	109	118	125	126	167	147	122	138	157	Importations : valeur unitaire [1]
Exports: volume	112	119	118	121	129	124	135	137	137	Exportations : volume
Exports: unit value [1]	111	129	138	138	182	184	137	176	204	Exportations : valeur unitaire [1]
Terms of trade	102	109	111	110	109	126	113	128	130	Termes de l'échange
Purchasing power of exports	115	130	130	133	141	156	152	175	179	Pouvoir d'achat des exportations
Norway										**Norvège**
Imports: volume [2]	107	118	129	142	156	157	138	148	156	Importations : volume [2]
Imports: unit value [2]	116	127	132	139	159	173	153	157	176	Importations : valeur unitaire [2]
Exports: volume [2]	106	108	108	106	107	107	104	101	97	Exportations : volume [2]
Exports: unit value [2]	104	127	161	194	213	268	185	219	275	Exportations : valeur unitaire [2]
Terms of trade	90	100	122	139	134	155	120	139	156	Termes de l'échange
Purchasing power of exports	97	109	131	147	143	166	125	140	152	Pouvoir d'achat des exportations
Pakistan										**Pakistan**
Imports: volume	123	142	165	153	169	184	178	173	161	Importations : volume
Imports: unit value	109	122	138	151	167	216	178	203	251	Importations : valeur unitaire
Exports: volume	110	103	126	127	124	133	126	131	135	Exportations : volume
Exports: unit value	96	103	103	106	110	124	115	131	156	Exportations : valeur unitaire
Terms of trade	89	85	75	70	66	57	65	65	62	Termes de l'échange
Purchasing power of exports	98	87	95	89	81	76	82	85	84	Pouvoir d'achat des exportations
Panama										**Panama**
Exports: volume	84	83	98	100	105	82	68	66	...	Exportations : volume
Papua New Guinea										**Papouasie-Nvl-Guinée**
Exports: volume	105	99	106	92	94	100	102	102	100	Exportations : volume
Exports: unit value	101	126	157	247	271	329	234	303	346	Exportations : valeur unitaire
Peru										**Pérou**
Exports: volume	122	135	134	126	138	154	156	152	158	Exportations : volume
Exports: unit value	97	128	170	280	307	251	236	346	411	Exportations : valeur unitaire
Philippines										**Philippines**
Imports: volume	118	137	123	126	...	...	...	...	...	Importations : volume
Imports: unit value [1]	82	81	97	113	...	...	...	...	...	Importations : valeur unitaire [1]
Exports: volume	98	110	104	124	...	...	...	...	...	Exportations : volume
Exports: unit value [1]	79	75	84	88	...	...	...	...	...	Exportations : valeur unitaire [1]
Terms of trade	96	93	87	78	...	...	...	...	...	Termes de l'échange
Purchasing power of exports	94	102	90	97	...	...	...	...	...	Pouvoir d'achat des exportations
Poland										**Pologne**
Imports: volume	119	140	148	173	199	217	185	210	222	Importations : volume
Imports: unit value [1]	116	131	141	151	171	198	172	...	192	Importations : valeur unitaire [1]
Exports: volume	143	170	189	219	240	257	235	267	288	Exportations : volume
Exports: unit value [1]	118	139	150	160	186	213	185	...	207	Exportations : valeur unitaire [1]
Terms of trade	102	107	107	107	109	107	107	...	108	Termes de l'échange
Purchasing power of exports	146	182	201	234	261	276	252	...	311	Pouvoir d'achat des exportations

Country or area	2003	2004	2005	2006	2007	2008	2009	2010	2011	Pays ou zone
Portugal										**Portugal**
Imports: volume	94	104	111	112	123	114	98	118	...	Importations : volume
Imports: unit value [1]	110	118	117	119	125	140	114	126	...	Importations : valeur unitaire [1]
Exports: volume	97	95	93	101	99	93	81	92	...	Exportations : volume
Exports: unit value [1]	112	122	121	125	134	144	127	134	...	Exportations : valeur unitaire [1]
Terms of trade	102	104	104	106	107	103	112	106	...	Termes de l'échange
Purchasing power of exports	99	98	96	106	105	96	90	97	...	Pouvoir d'achat des exportations
Republic of Korea										**République de Corée**
Imports: volume	118	132	140	155	169	170	166	195	205	Importations : volume
Imports: unit value	96	107	117	126	134	165	124	138	164	Importations : valeur unitaire
Exports: volume	134	163	178	202	223	237	239	277	310	Exportations : volume
Exports: unit value	85	92	93	93	96	102	84	94	102	Exportations : valeur unitaire
Terms of trade	89	85	79	74	72	62	68	68	62	Termes de l'échange
Purchasing power of exports	119	140	141	149	160	147	163	188	193	Pouvoir d'achat des exportations
Republic of Moldova										**République de Moldova**
Imports: volume	181	204	237	255	317	364	271	311	383	Importations : volume
Imports: unit value	88	113	122	127	152	208	176	161	187	Importations : valeur unitaire
Exports: volume	176	208	226	208	244	268	248	290	399	Exportations : volume
Exports: unit value	87	105	104	104	124	159	131	121	138	Exportations : valeur unitaire
Terms of trade	99	93	86	82	81	77	74	75	74	Termes de l'échange
Purchasing power of exports	174	193	194	171	199	205	184	218	294	Pouvoir d'achat des exportations
Romania										**Roumanie**
Imports: volume	169	207	244	293	369	394	299	345	381	Importations : volume
Imports: unit value	106	106	112	116	100	103	92	96	102	Importations : valeur unitaire
Exports: volume	144	166	179	191	204	225	216	259	291	Exportations : volume
Exports: unit value	119	125	137	148	107	111	100	107	115	Exportations : valeur unitaire
Terms of trade	112	118	122	127	108	108	109	112	113	Termes de l'échange
Purchasing power of exports	161	195	218	244	221	243	235	289	330	Pouvoir d'achat des exportations
Russian Federation										**Fédération de Russie**
Imports: volume	168	222	288	398	...	470	492	672	902	Importations : volume
Exports: volume	133	180	240	303	...	261	291	387	501	Exportations : volume
Serbia										**Serbie**
Imports: volume	...	...	...	...	129	109	85	108	178	Importations : volume
Imports: unit value	...	...	...	...	106	113	79	96	138	Importations : valeur unitaire
Exports: volume	...	...	...	...	126	112	90	122	168	Exportations : volume
Exports: unit value	...	...	...	...	110	110	83	97	155	Exportations : valeur unitaire
Terms of trade	...	...	...	...	104	97	104	102	112	Termes de l'échange
Purchasing power of exports	...	...	...	...	131	109	94	125	188	Pouvoir d'achat des exportations
Singapore										**Singapour**
Imports: volume	96	117	134	148	158	174	150	177	183	Importations : volume
Imports: unit value [1]	99	104	111	119	124	136	122	130	148	Importations : valeur unitaire [1]
Exports: volume	116	155	173	192	208	217	195	235	247	Exportations : volume
Exports: unit value [1]	90	93	96	103	104	113	101	109	120	Exportations : valeur unitaire [1]
Terms of trade	91	89	87	86	84	83	83	83	81	Termes de l'échange
Purchasing power of exports	106	139	151	165	176	180	161	196	201	Pouvoir d'achat des exportations
Slovakia										**Slovaquie**
Imports: unit value [1]	129	147	157	177	196	235	210	207	234	Importations : valeur unitaire [1]
Exports: unit value [1]	139	174	191	204	221	248	235	258	287	Exportations : valeur unitaire [1]
Terms of trade	108	118	121	116	112	106	112	125	123	Termes de l'échange
Slovenia										**Slovénie**
Imports: volume	111	...	...	...	...	...	...	...	...	Importations : volume
Imports: unit value	124	141	152	164	175	183	166	179	194	Importations : valeur unitaire
Exports: volume	115	...	...	...	...	...	...	...	...	Exportations : volume
Exports: unit value	126	142	149	159	168	171	163	172	184	Exportations : valeur unitaire
Terms of trade	102	101	98	97	96	94	98	96	94	Termes de l'échange
Purchasing power of exports	117	...	...	...	...	...	...	...	...	Pouvoir d'achat des exportations
South Africa										**Afrique du Sud**
Imports: volume	115	131	144	...	...	...	...	...	...	Importations : volume
Imports: unit value	115	136	144	...	...	...	...	...	...	Importations : valeur unitaire
Exports: volume	103	105	112	...	...	...	...	...	...	Exportations : volume
Exports: unit value	123	148	156	...	...	...	...	...	...	Exportations : valeur unitaire
Terms of trade	107	108	109	...	...	...	...	...	...	Termes de l'échange
Purchasing power of exports	110	114	122	...	...	...	...	...	...	Pouvoir d'achat des exportations

Country or area	2003	2004	2005	2006	2007	2008	2009	2010	2011	Pays ou zone
Spain										**Espagne**
Imports: volume	117	129	137	149	159	154	128	140	141	Importations : volume
Imports: unit value	116	131	138	144	159	179	149	148	168	Importations : valeur unitaire
Exports: volume	114	120	121	127	133	135	122	142	157	Exportations : volume
Exports: unit value	121	134	140	148	166	181	160	154	169	Exportations : valeur unitaire
Terms of trade	104	102	102	102	104	101	107	104	101	Termes de l'échange
Purchasing power of exports	118	123	123	130	138	137	132	148	158	Pouvoir d'achat des exportations
Sri Lanka										**Sri Lanka**
Imports: volume	111	122	126	135	140	147	131	149	...	Importations : volume
Exports: volume	98	106	113	97	126	126	133	130	...	Exportations : volume
Exports: unit value	97	101	104	109	113	119	118	132	...	Exportations : valeur unitaire
Sweden										**Suède**
Imports: volume	100	108	116	126	139	141	118	140	150	Importations : volume
Imports: unit value [1]	117	132	138	149	166	183	155	164	185	Importations : valeur unitaire [1]
Exports: volume	106	117	122	131	135	137	114	131	141	Exportations : volume
Exports: unit value [1]	111	121	124	131	149	158	139	145	161	Exportations : valeur unitaire [1]
Terms of trade	95	92	90	88	89	87	89	89	87	Termes de l'échange
Purchasing power of exports	101	108	109	116	121	119	102	116	123	Pouvoir d'achat des exportations
Switzerland										**Suisse**
Imports: volume	100	104	106	117	119	121	108	118	121	Importations : volume
Imports: unit value	121	135	143	149	162	209	197	215	288	Importations : valeur unitaire
Exports: volume	105	111	115	132	132	136	116	124	134	Exportations : volume
Exports: unit value	124	137	141	143	158	209	213	230	300	Exportations : valeur unitaire
Terms of trade	102	102	99	96	97	100	108	107	104	Termes de l'échange
Purchasing power of exports	107	113	114	127	128	136	125	133	140	Pouvoir d'achat des exportations
Thailand										**Thaïlande**
Imports: volume	112	137	162	164	171	192	147	187	212	Importations : volume
Imports: unit value	107	110	117	124	131	147	144	155	171	Importations : valeur unitaire
Exports: volume	109	119	143	159	178	186	160	188	208	Exportations : volume
Exports: unit value	105	118	113	119	126	139	139	152	156	Exportations : valeur unitaire
Terms of trade	99	108	97	96	96	94	97	98	91	Termes de l'échange
Purchasing power of exports	108	128	138	152	171	175	155	184	190	Pouvoir d'achat des exportations
Turkey										**Turquie**
Imports: volume	113	137	153	166	187	185	161	195	219	Importations : volume
Imports: unit value	111	129	138	150	164	197	159	172	199	Importations : valeur unitaire
Exports: volume	169	192	212	238	265	283	261	278	295	Exportations : volume
Exports: unit value	108	126	133	138	155	180	151	158	176	Exportations : valeur unitaire
Terms of trade	97	98	97	92	95	91	95	92	89	Termes de l'échange
Purchasing power of exports	164	188	205	220	251	258	248	255	261	Pouvoir d'achat des exportations
United Kingdom										**Royaume-Uni**
Imports: volume	112	120	128	143	138	135	119	133	134	Importations : volume
Imports: unit value [1]	104	116	120	125	136	144	124	129	145	Importations : valeur unitaire [1]
Exports: volume	101	102	111	126	115	116	104	114	120	Exportations : volume
Exports: unit value [1]	108	121	126	129	140	148	127	133	149	Exportations : valeur unitaire [1]
Terms of trade	104	105	105	104	103	103	102	103	103	Termes de l'échange
Purchasing power of exports	105	107	117	131	119	120	106	117	124	Pouvoir d'achat des exportations
United States										**Etats-Unis**
Imports: volume	107	118	125	132	133	128	107	123	128	Importations : volume
Imports: unit value [1]	97	102	110	115	120	134	119	127	141	Importations : valeur unitaire [1]
Exports: volume [3]	93	101	109	120	128	135	115	133	142	Exportations : volume [3]
Exports: unit value [1,3]	100	104	107	111	116	123	117	123	133	Exportations : valeur unitaire [1,3]
Terms of trade	103	101	97	96	97	92	99	97	95	Termes de l'échange
Purchasing power of exports	96	102	105	115	124	124	114	129	135	Pouvoir d'achat des exportations
Venezuela (Boliv. Rep. of) [1]										**Venezuela (Rép. boliv. du)** [1]
Imports: unit value	112	123	126	132	150	179	227	236	171	Importations : valeur unitaire

Source:
United Nations Statistics Division, New York, trade statistics database, last accessed October 2012.
1   Price indices.
2   Index numbers exclude ships.
3   Excluding military goods.

Source:
Organisation des Nations Unies, Division de statistique, New York, la base de données pour les statistiques du commerce extérieur, dernier accès octobre 2012.
1 Les indices des prix.
2 Les indices excluent les navires.
3 Non compris les biens militaires.

56

Manufactured goods exports
Unit value and volume indices: 2000 = 100; value: thousand million US dollars

Exportations des produits manufacturés
Indices de valeur unitaire et de volume: 2000 = 100; valeur: milliards de dollars des E.-U.

Region, country or area Région, pays ou zone	2002	2003	2004	2005	2006	2007	2008	2009	2010	2011
Total Total										
Unit value indices, US $[1]										
Indices de valeur unitaire, $ des E.-U.[1]	98	105	111	112	115	126	133	123	125	136
Unit value indices, SDRs										
Indices de valeur unitaire, DTS	99	100	98	99	103	108	111	105	108	113
Volume indices										
Indices de volume	103	110	127	138	152	144	144	125	143	147
Value, thousand million US $										
Valeur, milliards de $ des E.-U.	4 648.2	5 355.1	6 494.9	7 139.7	8 108.1	8 385.8	8 883.6	7 061.8	8 287.6	9 226.8
Developed economies Economies développées										
Unit value indices, US $										
Indices de valeur unitaire, $ des E.-U.	99	110	119	121	125	135	142	134	136	148
Unit value indices, SDRs										
Indices de valeur unitaire, DTS	100	104	104	108	112	116	119	115	118	123
Volume indices										
Indices de volume	101	104	113	118	128	134	133	111	126	130
Value, thousand million US $										
Valeur, milliards de $ des E.-U.	3 196.0	3 652.3	4 311.9	4 594.6	5 132.1	5 799.2	6 101.0	4 777.9	5 532.7	6 160.9
Americas Amériques										
Unit value indices, US $										
Indices de valeur unitaire, $ des E.-U.	100	103	106	108	111	115	118	112	118	127
Volume indices										
Indices de volume	88	88	97	104	113	120	120	99	110	113
Value, thousand million US $										
Valeur, milliards de $ des E.-U.	685.3	704.0	803.2	872.2	983.2	1 070.3	1 105.3	869.6	1 017.5	1 120.4
Canada Canada										
Unit value indices, US $										
Indices de valeur unitaire, $ des E.-U.	96	104	112	119	128	135	...	...	...	...
Unit value indices, national currency										
Indices de val. unitaire, monnaie nationale	102	98	98	97	98	97	...	...	...	...
Volume indices										
Indices de volume	94	91	97	100	99	100	...	...	...	...
Value, thousand million US $										
Valeur, milliards de $ des E.-U.	166.6	173.6	200.2	219.2	234.6	247.8	235.2	169.8	203.4	222.6
United States Etats-Unis										
Unit value indices, US $[2]										
Indices de valeur unitaire, $ des E.-U.[2]	102	103	104	104	107	110	116	113	117	124
Unit value indices, national currency[2]										
Indices de val. unitaire, monnaie nationale[2]	102	103	104	104	107	110	116	113	117	124
Volume indices										
Indices de volume	86	87	97	105	118	126	126	104	117	121
Value, thousand million US $										
Valeur, milliards de $ des E.-U.	518.8	530.4	603.0	653.1	748.6	822.5	870.2	699.8	814.1	897.8
Europe Europe										
Unit value indices, US $										
Indices de valeur unitaire, $ des E.-U.	100	115	126	128	132	146	155	143	142	154
Volume indices										
Indices de volume	107	111	120	126	136	141	140	120	136	141
Value, thousand million US $										
Valeur, milliards de $ des E.-U.	2 050.9	2 425.2	2 876.7	3 059.2	3 430.3	3 933.3	4 137.6	3 274.1	3 678.7	4 138.7

Manufactured goods exports *(continued)*
Unit value and volume indices: 2000 = 100; value: thousand million US dollars

Exportations des produits manufacturés *(suite)*
Indices de valeur unitaire et de volume: 2000 = 100; valeur: milliards de dollars des E.-U.

Region, country or area Région, pays ou zone	2002	2003	2004	2005	2006	2007	2008	2009	2010	2011
Austria Autriche										
Unit value indices, US $										
Indices de valeur unitaire, $ des E.-U.	100	...	...	...	...	...	...	...	...	...
Unit value indices, national currency										
Indices de val. unitaire, monnaie nationale	98	...	...	...	...	...	...	...	...	...
Volume indices										
Indices de volume	118	...	...	...	...	...	...	...	...	...
Value, thousand million US $										
Valeur, milliards de $ des E.-U.	59.0	76.8	96.7	100.2	114.0	133.6	150.0	112.0	121.4	145.0
Belgium Belgique										
Unit value indices, US $										
Indices de valeur unitaire, $ des E.-U.	106	126	141	148	156	179	186	173	173	195
Unit value indices, national currency										
Indices de val. unitaire, monnaie nationale	103	103	105	110	115	120	116	114	121	130
Volume indices										
Indices de volume	100	100	106	107	107	109	111	84	93	94
Value, thousand million US $										
Valeur, milliards de $ des E.-U.	139.5	166.3	198.7	209.9	222.3	258.2	274.5	191.1	212.8	243.1
Denmark Danemark										
Unit value indices, US $										
Indices de valeur unitaire, $ des E.-U.	102	124	136	138	141	145	157	144	148.	156
Unit value indices, national currency										
Indices de val. unitaire, monnaie nationale	100	101	101	102	103	97	98	95	103	103
Volume indices										
Indices de volume	114	117	119	129	137	148	152	135	187	218
Value, thousand million US $										
Valeur, milliards de $ des E.-U.	37.2	46.4	51.4	56.6	61.1	68.3	76.1	61.9	88.2	108.0
Finland Finlande										
Unit value indices, US $										
Indices de valeur unitaire, $ des E.-U.	100	117	120	130	141	166	178	158	163	185
Unit value indices, national currency										
Indices de val. unitaire, monnaie nationale	98	96	89	97	104	112	111	105	114	123
Volume indices										
Indices de volume	98	98	109	108	116	116	115	84	85	83
Value, thousand million US $										
Valeur, milliards de $ des E.-U.	38.9	45.4	51.8	56.1	65.1	76.8	81.3	52.6	55.4	61.0
France France										
Unit value indices, US $										
Indices de valeur unitaire, $ des E.-U.	84	101	111	111	109	118	124	...	...	...
Unit value indices, national currency										
Indices de val. unitaire, monnaie nationale	83	83	82	82	81	80	78	...	...	...
Volume indices										
Indices de volume	120	118	127	133	148	152	159	...	...	...
Value, thousand million US $										
Valeur, milliards de $ des E.-U.	251.9	298.5	351.8	365.3	404.9	449.2	489.7	383.7	419.0	469.5
Germany Allemagne										
Unit value indices, US $										
Indices de valeur unitaire, $ des E.-U.	104	118	128	128	132	144	155	145	140	152
Unit value indices, national currency										
Indices de val. unitaire, monnaie nationale	102	96	95	95	97	97	97	96	97	101
Volume indices										
Indices de volume	107	113	128	138	152	166	154	138	163	174
Value, thousand million US $										
Valeur, milliards de $ des E.-U.	534.8	644.3	790.3	849.0	970.0	1 143.7	1 142.6	961.9	1 094.8	1 276.9

Manufactured goods exports *(continued)*
Unit value and volume indices: 2000 = 100; value: thousand million US dollars

Exportations des produits manufacturés *(suite)*
Indices de valeur unitaire et de volume: 2000 = 100; valeur: milliards de dollars des E.-U.

Region, country or area Région, pays ou zone	2002	2003	2004	2005	2006	2007	2008	2009	2010	2011
Greece Grèce										
Value, thousand million US $										
Valeur, milliards de $ des E.-U.	5.7	8.7	8.5	10.7	12.0	14.0	15.4	11.7	...	...
Iceland Islande										
Value, thousand million US $										
Valeur, milliards de $ des E.-U.	0.7	0.8	1.0	1.1	1.3	1.9	2.9	2.0	2.6	2.9
Ireland Irlande										
Value, thousand million US $										
Valeur, milliards de $ des E.-U.	77.7	79.4	88.7	94.0	96.5	101.9	107.7	98.2	98.6	110.3
Italy Italie										
Unit value indices, US $ [3]										
Indices de valeur unitaire, $ des E.-U. [3]	103	122	138	143	150	174	195	184	183	202
Unit value indices, national currency										
Indices de val. unitaire, monnaie nationale	102	101	103	107	111	118	123	123	128	135
Volume indices										
Indices de volume	102	99	104	106	112	116	110	86	95	100
Value, thousand million US $										
Valeur, milliards de $ des E.-U.	225.7	261.5	308.9	324.0	361.9	432.9	462.1	342.9	375.8	435.3
Netherlands Pays-Bas										
Unit value indices, US $										
Indices de valeur unitaire, $ des E.-U.	104	120	131	139	144	176	...	...	...	...
Unit value indices, national currency										
Indices de val. unitaire, monnaie nationale	102	98	97	103	106	118	...	...	...	...
Volume indices										
Indices de volume	116	121	135	136	147	148	...	...	...	...
Value, thousand million US $										
Valeur, milliards de $ des E.-U.	154.6	186.1	224.7	240.4	271.0	331.4	350.9	285.7	324.3	356.9
Norway Norvège										
Unit value indices, US $										
Indices de valeur unitaire, $ des E.-U.	101	111	126	131	145	169	176	148	155	174
Unit value indices, national currency										
Indices de val. unitaire, monnaie nationale	91	89	96	96	106	112	111	105	106	110
Volume indices										
Indices de volume	109	110	112	119	129	141	149	134	139	133
Value, thousand million US $										
Valeur, milliards de $ des E.-U.	18.3	20.3	23.5	25.9	31.1	39.5	43.6	33.1	35.6	38.5
Portugal Portugal										
Value, thousand million US $										
Valeur, milliards de $ des E.-U.	22.4	27.5	30.5	28.8	32.1	32.9	39.7	30.3	35.1	44.2
Spain Espagne										
Value, thousand million US $										
Valeur, milliards de $ des E.-U.	99.0	124.0	142.8	150.1	166.8	196.8	209.2	166.5	182.5	...
Sweden Suède										
Value, thousand million US $										
Valeur, milliards de $ des E.-U.	66.9	82.4	101.0	111.0	124.1	143.1	150.9	107.3	127.6	150.6
Switzerland Suisse										
Unit value indices, US $										
Indices de valeur unitaire, $ des E.-U.	109	...	...	...	...	...	...	...	...	...
Volume indices										
Indices de volume	99	...	...	...	...	...	...	...	...	...
Value, thousand million US $										
Valeur, milliards de $ des E.-U.	84.5	96.8	113.7	123.3	138.2	157.8	182.0	...	...	...

Manufactured goods exports *(continued)*
Unit value and volume indices: 2000 = 100; value: thousand million US dollars

Exportations des produits manufacturés *(suite)*
Indices de valeur unitaire et de volume: 2000 = 100; valeur: milliards de dollars des E.-U.

Region, country or area Région, pays ou zone	2002	2003	2004	2005	2006	2007	2008	2009	2010	2011
United Kingdom Royaume-Uni										
Unit value indices, US $										
Indices de valeur unitaire, $ des E.-U.	98	108	120	120	123	133	136	124	125	132
Unit value indices, national currency										
Indices de val. unitaire, monnaie										
nationale	99	100	99	100	101	101	111	120	122	125
Volume indices										
Indices de volume	102	103	104	111	125	113	113	96	107	117
Value, thousand million US $										
Valeur, milliards de $ des E.-U.	232.6	258.1	290.2	310.5	355.4	348.4	356.3	277.8	310.9	358.9
Other developed economies Autres économies développées										
Unit value indices, US $										
Indices de valeur unitaire, $ des E.-U.	**91**	**98**	**107**	**112**	**114**	**119**	**128**	**129**	**138**	**151**
Volume indices										
Indices de volume	**96**	**102**	**112**	**112**	**120**	**127**	**128**	**94**	**115**	**113**
Value, thousand million US $										
Valeur, milliards de $ des E.-U.	**459.8**	**523.1**	**632.1**	**663.2**	**718.6**	**795.7**	**858.1**	**634.3**	**836.5**	**901.9**
Australia Australie										
Unit value indices, US $										
Indices de valeur unitaire, $ des E.-U.	92	101	133	151	203	245	223	155	205	235
Unit value indices, national currency										
Indices de val. unitaire, monnaie										
nationale	97	89	104	114	156	169	153	114	129	131
Volume indices										
Indices de volume	104	103	89	88	73	73	85	93	86	86
Value, thousand million US $										
Valeur, milliards de $ des E.-U.	20.2	22.0	25.0	28.2	31.6	38.1	40.3	30.6	37.2	43.0
Israel Israël										
Unit value indices, US $										
Indices de valeur unitaire, $ des E.-U.	95	95	99	109	118	124	126	120	121	130
Volume indices										
Indices de volume	98	105	124	125	123	134	135	123	145	150
Value, thousand million US $										
Valeur, milliards de $ des E.-U.	27.5	29.5	36.5	40.5	43.3	49.4	50.7	44.1	52.1	57.9
Japan Japon										
Unit value indices, US $										
Indices de valeur unitaire, $ des E.-U.	92	98	107	111	112	117	129	133	141	155
Unit value indices, national currency										
Indices de val. unitaire, monnaie										
nationale	106	105	107	114	121	127	124	115	115	115
Volume indices										
Indices de volume	94	99	110	110	117	123	121	86	108	105
Value, thousand million US $										
Valeur, milliards de $ des E.-U.	391.8	443.3	534.1	553.7	597.3	654.1	707.8	518.9	695.3	740.8
New Zealand Nouvelle-Zélande										
Unit value indices, US $										
Indices de valeur unitaire, $ des E.-U.	99	112	125	136	140	155	163	131	152	171
Unit value indices, national currency										
Indices de val. unitaire, monnaie										
nationale	97	88	86	88	98	96	104	95	95	98
Volume indices										
Indices de volume	105	109	116	115	117	119	113	112	113	117
Value, thousand million US $										
Valeur, milliards de $ des E.-U.	4.9	5.7	6.8	7.3	7.7	8.6	8.7	6.9	8.0	9.4
South Africa Afrique du Sud										
Value, thousand million US $										
Valeur, milliards de $ des E.-U.	15.3	22.5	29.7	33.5	38.7	45.5	50.7	33.8	...	50.8

56

Manufactured goods exports *(continued)*
Unit value and volume indices: 2000 = 100; value: thousand million US dollars

Exportations des produits manufacturés *(suite)*
Indices de valeur unitaire et de volume: 2000 = 100; valeur: milliards de dollars des E.-U.

Region, country or area Région, pays ou zone	2002	2003	2004	2005	2006	2007	2008	2009	2010	2011
Developing Countries, Total Les pays en développement, total										
Unit value indices, US $										
Indices de valeur unitaire, $ des E.-U.	96	97	99	98	102	110	117	103	108	117
Unit value indices, SDRs										
Indices de valeur unitaire, DTS	98	92	87	87	91	94	97	88	93	97
Volume indices										
Indices de volume	107	124	157	184	208	167	169	156	181	186
Value, thousand million US $										
Valeur, milliards de $ des E.-U.	1 452.2	1 702.8	2 183.0	2 545.1	2 976.0	2 586.6	2 782.5	2 283.8	2 754.9	3 065.8
China, Hong Kong SAR Chine, Hong Kong RAS										
Unit value indices, US $										
Indices de valeur unitaire, $ des E.-U.	93	93	94	96	93	94	99	100	105	110
Unit value indices, national currency										
Indices de val. unitaire, monnaie nationale	93	93	94	96	93	94	99	99	104	110
Volume indices										
Indices de volume	93	70	71	75	77	60	45	27	31	26
Value, thousand million US $										
Valeur, milliards de $ des E.-U.	19.4	14.7	15.1	16.3	16.0	12.5	10.0	6.1	7.2	6.4
India Inde										
Unit value indices, US $										
Indices de valeur unitaire, $ des E.-U.	99	...	...	...	...	...	...	...	...	...
Unit value indices, national currency										
Indices de val. unitaire, monnaie nationale	107	...	...	...	...	...	...	...	...	...
Volume indices										
Indices de volume	115	...	...	...	...	...	...	...	...	...
Value, thousand million US $										
Valeur, milliards de $ des E.-U.	39.9	48.8	59.1	74.1	86.1	96.9	116.7	...	...	...
Republic of Korea République de Corée										
Unit value indices, US $										
Indices de valeur unitaire, $ des E.-U.	82	83	92	96	101	106	99	84	90	98
Unit value indices, national currency										
Indices de val. unitaire, monnaie nationale	91	87	93	87	85	87	94	95	92	96
Volume indices										
Indices de volume	97	118	145	175	188	203	241	249	297	315
Value, thousand million US $										
Valeur, milliards de $ des E.-U.	125.4	153.0	207.9	262.8	297.5	338.6	373.2	328.8	420.3	484.9
Pakistan Pakistan										
Unit value indices, US $										
Indices de valeur unitaire, $ des E.-U.	96	101	108	106	108	108	108	101	118	150
Unit value indices, national currency										
Indices de val. unitaire, monnaie nationale	108	111	119	119	123	124	143	156	191	244
Volume indices										
Indices de volume	114	139	137	155	160	163	176	163	165	151
Value, thousand million US $										
Valeur, milliards de $ des E.-U.	8.4	10.9	11.4	12.7	13.4	13.6	14.7	12.7	15.1	17.5
Singapore Singapour										
Unit value indices, US $										
Indices de valeur unitaire, $ des E.-U.	100	99	98	78	81	109	109	105	109	113
Unit value indices, national currency										
Indices de val. unitaire, monnaie nationale	...	...	...	76	75	95	89	88	86	83
Volume indices										
Indices de volume	90	104	129	188	225	179	184	162	200	210
Value, thousand million US $										
Valeur, milliards de $ des E.-U.	106.7	122.8	151.7	175.7	217.4	233.8	240.3	203.0	259.4	283.8

Manufactured goods exports *(continued)*
Unit value and volume indices: 2000 = 100; value: thousand million US dollars

Exportations des produits manufacturés *(suite)*
Indices de valeur unitaire et de volume: 2000 = 100; valeur: milliards de dollars des E.-U.

Region, country or area Région, pays ou zone	2002	2003	2004	2005	2006	2007	2008	2009	2010	2011
Turkey Turquie										
Unit value indices, US $ [4]										
Indices de valeur unitaire, $ des E.-U. [4]	96	108	124	130	127	137	171	...	153	170
Volume indices										
Indices de volume	138	162	189	204	240	279	269	...	259	276
Value, thousand million US $										
Valeur, milliards de $ des E.-U.	30.8	40.3	54.2	61.1	70.9	88.7	106.3	80.3	91.7	108.5

Source:
United Nations Statistics Division, New York, trade statistics database, last accessed October 2012.

1   Excluding trade of the countries of Eastern Europe and the former USSR.
2   Derived from price indices; national unit value index is discontinued.
3   Calculated by the United Nations Statistics Division.
4   Industrial products.

Source:
Organisation des Nations Unies, Division de statistique, New York, la base de données pour les statistiques du commerce extérieur, dernier accès octobre 2012.

1   Non compris le commerce des pays de l'Europe de l'Est et l'ex-URSS.
2   Calculés à partir des indices des prix; l'indice de la valeur unitaire nationale est discontinué.
3   Calculés par la Division de statistique des Nations Unies.
4   Produits industriels.

Country or area of destination and region of origin	Series[&] Série[&]	2007	2008	2009	2010	2011	Pays ou zone de destination et région de provenance
Albania	VFN						**Albanie**
Total[1]		1 126 514	1 419 191	1 855 634	2 417 337	2 932 132	Total[1]
Africa		319	317	211	3 193	432	Afrique
Americas		51 881	60 978	59 945	61 878	70 291	Amériques
East Asia/Pacific		9 674	15 419	28 433	11 361	17 418	Asie de l'Est/Pacifique
Europe		1 060 975	1 335 227	1 512 734	2 238 958	2 738 846	Europe
Middle East		1 262	1 115	1 313	1 247	1 178	Moyen-Orient
South Asia		376	484	661	764	909	Asie du Sud
Region not specified		2 027	5 651	252 337	99 936	103 058	Région non spécifiée
Algeria	VFN						**Algérie**
Total[2]		1 743 084	1 771 749	1 911 506	2 070 496	2 394 887	Total[2]
Africa		157 554	194 403	257 936	310 684	554 380	Afrique
Americas		10 271	10 939	13 120	10 495	12 265	Amériques
East Asia/Pacific		27 590	39 227	46 613	42 171	55 246	Asie de l'Est/Pacifique
Europe		270 881	267 552	283 843	241 637	218 629	Europe
Middle East		44 892	44 576	54 298	50 000	61 122	Moyen-Orient
Region not specified		1 231 896	1 215 052	1 255 696	1 415 509	1 493 245	Région non spécifiée
Andorra	TFR						**Andorre**
Total[3]		2 189 421	2 059 451	1 829 869	1 808 001	1 947 531	Total[3]
Europe		2 189 421	2 059 451	1 829 869	1 808 001	1 947 531	Europe
Angola	TFR						**Angola**
Total		194 730	294 258	365 784	424 919	481 207	Total
Africa		33 193	37 219	46 476	72 519	147 903	Afrique
Americas		38 113	59 358	76 321	82 835	58 233	Amériques
East Asia/Pacific		28 299	59 051	66 492	80 515	87 626	Asie de l'Est/Pacifique
Europe		89 351	129 838	161 169	170 381	170 488	Europe
Middle East		1 491	2 682	4 404	8 639	2 946	Moyen-Orient
South Asia		4 283	6 110	10 922	10 030	14 011	Asie du Sud
Anguilla	TFR						**Anguilla**
Total[1]		77 652	68 284	57 891	61 998	65 783	Total[1]
Americas		63 792	57 024	49 029	53 136	56 606	Amériques
Europe		10 795	8 943	7 457	7 544	7 523	Europe
Region not specified		3 065	2 317	1 405	1 318	1 654	Région non spécifiée
Antigua and Barbuda	TFR						**Antigua-et-Barbuda**
Total[1,4]		261 802	265 844	234 410	229 943	241 331	Total[1,4]
Americas		140 823	151 785	138 489	137 254	145 556	Amériques
Europe		115 454	110 266	93 442	88 945	92 097	Europe
Region not specified		5 525	3 793	2 479	3 744	3 678	Région non spécifiée
Argentina	TFN						**Argentine**
Total[1]		4 561 743	4 700 492	4 307 666	5 325 130	5 704 650	Total[1]
Americas		3 608 724	3 710 497	3 392 017	4 367 985	4 760 388	Amériques
Europe		737 634	765 962	721 622	751 331	738 778	Europe
Region not specified		215 385	224 033	194 027	205 814	205 484	Région non spécifiée
Armenia	TFR						**Arménie**
Total		510 622	558 443	575 284	683 979	757 935	Total
Africa		496	643	443	215	603	Afrique
Americas		127 155	135 550	134 940	135 673	144 632	Amériques
East Asia/Pacific		23 005	24 365	24 600	25 584	29 222	Asie de l'Est/Pacifique
Europe		278 209	308 266	311 268	350 926	375 195	Europe
Middle East		40 849	43 800	44 690	46 470	49 598	Moyen-Orient
South Asia		40 908	45 819	59 343	125 111	158 685	Asie du Sud
Aruba	TFR						**Aruba**
Total		771 822	826 677	812 623	824 330	870 287	Total
Americas		703 367	748 922	735 339	745 723	786 249	Amériques
East Asia/Pacific		148	157	158	152	118	Asie de l'Est/Pacifique
Europe		67 446	73 772	75 000	76 077	81 204	Europe
Region not specified		861	3 826	2 126	2 378	2 716	Région non spécifiée
Australia	VFR						**Australie**
Total[5]		5 644 076	5 585 826	5 584 076	5 885 101	5 875 068	Total[5]
Africa		85 553	93 195	83 999	89 170	91 650	Afrique
Americas		628 773	644 163	670 055	661 819	645 830	Amériques
East Asia/Pacific		3 386 801	3 244 422	3 226 010	3 515 746	3 566 095	Asie de l'Est/Pacifique
Europe		1 355 280	1 381 169	1 362 172	1 347 469	1 291 198	Europe
Middle East		62 743	74 695	79 610	87 140	81 594	Moyen-Orient
South Asia		124 690	148 089	162 022	183 526	195 896	Asie du Sud
Region not specified		236	93	208	231	2 805	Région non spécifiée

Country or area of destination and region of origin	Series& Série&	2007	2008	2009	2010	2011	Pays ou zone de destination et région de provenance
Austria	TCER						**Autriche**
Total[6]		20 773 316	21 935 409	21 355 439	22 004 266	23 011 956	Total[6]
Africa		40 472	39 957	38 794	44 965	52 345	Afrique
Americas		755 989	672 610	616 730	708 515	742 821	Amériques
East Asia/Pacific		747 319	705 701	645 203	741 244	914 840	Asie de l'Est/Pacifique
Europe		18 795 014	19 993 474	19 613 283	20 042 806	20 818 964	Europe
Middle East		91 354	102 099	97 053	120 055	160 005	Moyen-Orient
South Asia		46 210	46 990	47 604	59 780	83 911	Asie du Sud
Region not specified		296 958	374 578	296 772	286 901	239 070	Région non spécifiée
Azerbaijan	VFR						**Azerbaïdjan**
Total		1 332 701	1 898 936	1 830 367	1 962 906	2 239 141	Total
Africa		835	1 630	1 732	2 056	1 781	Afrique
Americas		11 021	17 329	15 445	15 789	15 532	Amériques
East Asia/Pacific		8 391	16 190	13 839	14 730	15 092	Asie de l'Est/Pacifique
Europe		1 104 267	1 541 306	1 454 046	1 568 063	1 786 808	Europe
Middle East		1 854	3 716	3 095	3 581	3 932	Moyen-Orient
South Asia		205 242	316 514	339 949	356 590	414 045	Asie du Sud
Region not specified		1 091	2 251	2 261	2 097	1 951	Région non spécifiée
Bahamas	TFR						**Bahamas**
Total		1 527 728	1 463 006	1 327 007	1 370 140	1 346 372	Total
Africa		1 812	1 785	1 778	1 654	1 733	Afrique
Americas		1 404 001	1 331 022	1 213 309	1 255 707	1 230 533	Amériques
East Asia/Pacific		6 861	6 902	6 232	7 143	6 707	Asie de l'Est/Pacifique
Europe		87 931	94 560	79 648	78 900	78 929	Europe
Middle East		644	670	708	593	708	Moyen-Orient
South Asia		580	696	526	666	494	Asie du Sud
Region not specified		25 899	27 371	24 806	25 477	27 268	Région non spécifiée
Bahrain	VFN						**Bahreïn**
Total[1]		7 833 609	...	...	...	6 731 974	Total[1]
Africa		109 114	...	...	...	99 545	Afrique
Americas		267 496	...	...	...	291 253	Amériques
East Asia/Pacific		390 262	...	...	...	338 724	Asie de l'Est/Pacifique
Europe		506 891	...	...	...	513 232	Europe
Middle East		5 451 041	...	...	...	4 276 021	Moyen-Orient
South Asia		1 108 805	...	...	...	1 213 199	Asie du Sud
Bangladesh	TFN						**Bangladesh**
Total		289 110	...	...	...	...	Total
Africa		2 001	...	...	...	...	Afrique
Americas		45 706	...	...	...	...	Amériques
East Asia/Pacific		57 135	...	...	...	...	Asie de l'Est/Pacifique
Europe		77 345	...	...	...	...	Europe
Middle East		4 530	...	...	...	...	Moyen-Orient
South Asia		102 393	...	...	...	...	Asie du Sud
Barbados	TFR						**Barbade**
Total		574 533	567 667	518 564	532 180	567 724	Total
Africa		3 331	1 389	954	1 284	1 175	Afrique
Americas		303 404	309 043	292 435	312 551	336 920	Amériques
East Asia/Pacific		10 450	4 147	3 325	4 107	3 723	Asie de l'Est/Pacifique
Europe		250 924	250 022	218 770	210 726	223 964	Europe
Middle East		481	337	299	344	305	Moyen-Orient
South Asia		3 538	1 113	1 082	1 634	1 440	Asie du Sud
Region not specified		2 405	1 616	1 699	1 534	197	Région non spécifiée
Belarus	TFN						**Bélarus**
Total[7]		104 890	91 232	94 719	119 370	115 653	Total[7]
Africa		499	73	138	101	39	Afrique
Americas		5 587	1 401	1 075	974	624	Amériques
East Asia/Pacific		2 386	1 054	963	1 040	4 249	Asie de l'Est/Pacifique
Europe		95 003	87 752	91 778	116 342	109 929	Europe
Middle East		818	473	331	522	344	Moyen-Orient
South Asia		597	479	434	391	468	Asie du Sud
Belgium	TCER						**Belgique**
Total[8]		7 044 719	7 164 765	6 815 141	7 186 419	7 494 141	Total[8]
Africa		62 449	63 250	63 444	61 332	61 949	Afrique
Americas		420 845	399 047	374 791	429 439	488 577	Amériques
East Asia/Pacific		301 959	267 943	237 535	255 712	307 495	Asie de l'Est/Pacifique
Europe		6 061 187	6 187 002	5 956 385	6 310 386	6 522 652	Europe
Middle East		20 284	22 067	19 976	25 599	30 602	Moyen-Orient
South Asia		43 785	64 480	46 950	51 726	54 726	Asie du Sud
Region not specified		134 210	160 976	116 060	52 225	28 140	Région non spécifiée

Country or area of destination and region of origin	Series[&] Série[&]	2007	2008	2009	2010	2011	Pays ou zone de destination et région de provenance
Belize	TFN						**Belize**
Total[2]		251 422	245 026	232 249	241 919	250 264	Total[2]
Africa		491	512	668	577	472	Afrique
Americas		201 679	195 645	188 240	195 568	203 128	Amériques
East Asia/Pacific		5 482	5 234	4 973	6 069	5 737	Asie de l'Est/Pacifique
Europe		34 175	34 269	29 603	30 025	30 142	Europe
Middle East		435	588	400	863	628	Moyen-Orient
Region not specified		9 160	8 778	8 365	8 817	10 157	Région non spécifiée
Benin	TFR						**Bénin**
Total		186 394	188 000	190 000	199 491	209 475	Total
Africa		153 016	117 929	90 757	138 000	125 685	Afrique
Americas		2 299	3 926	5 104	3 173	3 066	Amériques
East Asia/Pacific		780	1 633	860	800	1 126	Asie de l'Est/Pacifique
Europe		26 283	50 706	35 448	32 886	57 081	Europe
Middle East		1 762	291	367	2 388	2 670	Moyen-Orient
South Asia		2 254	691	453	845	1 147	Asie du Sud
Region not specified		...	12 824	57 011	21 399	18 700	Région non spécifiée
Bermuda	TFR						**Bermudes**
Total[4]		305 548	263 613	235 860	232 262	236 038	Total[4]
Americas		257 342	216 595	197 515	196 418	202 107	Amériques
East Asia/Pacific		714	795	811	1 088	1 058	Asie de l'Est/Pacifique
Europe		35 938	35 003	28 949	28 498	26 940	Europe
Region not specified		11 554	11 220	8 585	6 258	5 933	Région non spécifiée
Bhutan	TFN						**Bhoutan**
Total		21 094	27 642	23 480	27 210	37 478	Total
Africa		65	77	48	102	92	Afrique
Americas		6 653	8 240	5 743	6 506	8 055	Amériques
East Asia/Pacific		5 393	7 412	7 743	8 599	14 966	Asie de l'Est/Pacifique
Europe		8 929	11 778	9 861	11 883	14 164	Europe
Middle East		15	29	31	27	44	Moyen-Orient
South Asia		39	106	52	93	157	Asie du Sud
Region not specified		...	...	2	...	...	Région non spécifiée
Bolivia (Plur. State of)	TFN						**Bolivie (État plur. de)**
Total[9]		572 815	593 727	671 227	807 137	...	Total[9]
Africa		951	1 028	1 115	1 336	...	Afrique
Americas		403 963	406 709	473 364	595 472	...	Amériques
East Asia/Pacific		33 905	38 610	39 730	46 248	...	Asie de l'Est/Pacifique
Europe		133 996	147 380	157 018	164 081	...	Europe
Bonaire	TFR						**Bonaire**
Total		74 309	74 342	66 998	70 539	...	Total
Americas		42 191	43 112	36 260	31 226	...	Amériques
Europe		31 427	30 768	30 234	32 409	...	Europe
Region not specified		691	462	504	6 904	...	Région non spécifiée
Bosnia and Herzegovina	TCER						**Bosnie-Herzégovine**
Total		306 452	321 511	310 942	365 454	391 945	Total
Americas		10 341	8 862	8 126	10 389	10 411	Amériques
East Asia/Pacific		4 399	5 348	4 496	7 092	9 464	Asie de l'Est/Pacifique
Europe		286 280	300 672	291 903	338 500	355 718	Europe
Middle East		252	330	313	624	937	Moyen-Orient
South Asia		233	151	206	253	167	Asie du Sud
Region not specified		4 947	6 148	5 898	8 596	15 248	Région non spécifiée
Botswana	TFR						**Botswana**
Total		1 735 855	2 100 918	...	...	...	Total
Africa		1 546 485	1 932 644	...	...	...	Afrique
Americas		33 353	38 442	...	...	...	Amériques
East Asia/Pacific		25 021	28 393	...	...	...	Asie de l'Est/Pacifique
Europe		77 549	86 073	...	...	...	Europe
Middle East		...	10	...	...	...	Moyen-Orient
South Asia		2 572	2 495	...	...	...	Asie du Sud
Region not specified		50 875	12 861	...	...	...	Région non spécifiée
Brazil	TFR						**Brésil**
Total		5 025 834	5 050 099	4 802 217	5 161 379	5 433 354	Total
Africa		75 435	75 824	78 110	83 688	86 511	Afrique
Americas		2 779 164	2 883 839	2 862 171	3 196 300	3 401 592	Amériques
East Asia/Pacific		205 730	256 271	208 379	210 582	260 642	Asie de l'Est/Pacifique
Europe		1 938 165	1 814 146	1 642 070	1 651 840	1 662 829	Europe
Middle East		25 967	...	...	...	...	Moyen-Orient
South Asia		...	19 456	11 361	18 829	21 530	Asie du Sud
Region not specified		1 373	563	126	140	250	Région non spécifiée

Country or area of destination and region of origin	Série[&]	2007	2008	2009	2010	2011	Pays ou zone de destination et région de provenance
British Virgin Islands	TFR						**Iles Vierges britanniques**
Total		358 068	346 035	308 792	330 343	...	Total
Americas		306 911	296 230	263 466	280 233	...	Amériques
Europe		43 389	41 728	37 591	41 184	...	Europe
Region not specified		7 768	8 077	7 735	8 926	...	Région non spécifiée
Brunei Darussalam	TFN						**Brunéi Darussalam**
Total[4]		178 540	225 757	157 474	214 290	242 061	Total[4]
Americas		5 116	5 652	5 108	5 940	6 611	Amériques
East Asia/Pacific		144 488	186 475	121 652	170 555	194 809	Asie de l'Est/Pacifique
Europe		20 796	22 765	21 553	26 199	28 581	Europe
Middle East		574	...	711	1 571	1 527	Moyen-Orient
South Asia		5 195	5 317	4 451	7 241	7 573	Asie du Sud
Region not specified		2 371	5 548	3 999	2 784	2 960	Région non spécifiée
Bulgaria	VFR						**Bulgarie**
Total		7 725 747	8 532 972	7 872 805	8 374 034	8 712 821	Total
Africa		1 734	2 178	2 242	2 452	2 323	Afrique
Americas		89 790	91 956	82 101	83 617	87 722	Amériques
East Asia/Pacific		43 563	48 049	41 773	43 772	51 145	Asie de l'Est/Pacifique
Europe		7 371 761	8 260 649	7 602 264	8 080 924	8 389 436	Europe
Middle East		18 823	21 875	21 352	25 413	23 972	Moyen-Orient
South Asia		15 000	21 294	23 025	24 105	27 129	Asie du Sud
Region not specified		185 076	86 971	100 048	113 751	131 094	Région non spécifiée
Burkina Faso	THSN						**Burkina Faso**
Total[2]		288 965	271 796	269 227	274 330	237 725	Total[2]
Africa		121 174	112 702	119 243	128 237	117 337	Afrique
Americas		20 473	18 016	17 509	20 154	17 333	Amériques
East Asia/Pacific		11 563	6 045	7 253	7 313	8 180	Asie de l'Est/Pacifique
Europe		126 544	124 426	116 180	107 098	85 535	Europe
Middle East		2 066	2 015	1 572	1 355	1 795	Moyen-Orient
Region not specified		7 145	8 592	7 470	10 173	7 545	Région non spécifiée
Burundi	TFN						**Burundi**
Total[10]		192 191	201 795	211 884	142 311[11]	...	Total[10]
Africa		168 457	177 579	186 457	122 045	...	Afrique
Americas		854	5 044	5 297	3 883	...	Amériques
East Asia/Pacific		11 713	4 237	4 449	2 912	...	Asie de l'Est/Pacifique
Europe		1 782	12 107	12 713	9 985	...	Europe
Region not specified		9 385	2 828	2 968	3 486	...	Région non spécifiée
Cambodia	TFR						**Cambodge**
Total		2 015 128	2 125 465	2 161 577	2 508 289	2 881 862	Total
Africa		3 270	4 040	5 403	4 627	5 993	Afrique
Americas		194 706	204 878	201 130	199 089	217 500	Amériques
East Asia/Pacific		1 384 443	1 436 249	1 467 406	1 788 814	2 084 540	Asie de l'Est/Pacifique
Europe		417 096	463 602	470 181	495 586	551 452	Europe
Middle East		1 059	947	1 144	1 071	1 565	Moyen-Orient
South Asia		14 554	15 749	16 313	19 102	20 812	Asie du Sud
Cameroon	THSN						**Cameroun**
Total		262 340	297 983	...	...	...	Total
Africa		144 253	158 752	...	...	...	Afrique
Americas		13 030	13 643	...	...	...	Amériques
East Asia/Pacific		7 688	10 092	...	...	...	Asie de l'Est/Pacifique
Europe		89 210	105 666	...	...	...	Europe
Middle East		3 945	4 011	...	...	...	Moyen-Orient
Region not specified		4 214	5 819	...	...	...	Région non spécifiée
Canada	TFR						**Canada**
Total		17 934 881	17 142 102	15 737 150	16 097 369	16 014 405	Total
Africa		75 525	79 927	75 717	81 217	85 902	Afrique
Americas		13 946 446	13 111 691	12 150 425	12 214 291	12 079 843	Amériques
East Asia/Pacific		1 266 560	1 230 626	1 025 526	1 170 281	1 222 621	Asie de l'Est/Pacifique
Europe		2 443 093	2 497 509	2 262 129	2 375 518	2 355 777	Europe
Middle East		67 512	77 272	77 602	83 668	85 069	Moyen-Orient
South Asia		135 745	145 077	145 751	172 334	185 193	Asie du Sud
Cape Verde	THSR						**Cap-Vert**
Total		267 188	285 141	287 183	336 086	428 273	Total
Africa		307	193	175	218	2 819	Afrique
Americas		4 932	4 004	3 935	3 188	3 711	Amériques
Europe		228 165	234 309	244 060	297 614	385 424	Europe
Region not specified		33 784	46 635	39 013	35 066	36 319	Région non spécifiée

Tourist/visitor arrivals by region of origin *(continued)*
Number
Arrivées de touristes/visiteurs par région de provenance *(suite)*
Nombre

Country or area of destination and region of origin	Series[&] Série[&]	2007	2008	2009	2010	2011	Pays ou zone de destination et région de provenance
Cayman Islands	TFR						**Iles Caïmanes**
Total [4]		291 503	302 879	271 949	288 272	309 069	Total [4]
Africa		530	538	518	673	613	Afrique
Americas		268 141	278 584	249 692	264 999	284 504	Amériques
East Asia/Pacific		1 720	1 626	1 816	1 872	1 836	Asie de l'Est/Pacifique
Europe		20 432	21 419	19 262	20 081	21 314	Europe
Middle East		116	99	88	98	118	Moyen-Orient
South Asia		158	214	202	187	179	Asie du Sud
Region not specified		406	399	371	362	505	Région non spécifiée
Central African Rep.	TFN						**Rép. centrafricaine**
Total [4]		17 117	30 611	52 429	53 821	...	Total [4]
Africa		8 306	16 038	26 984	26 684	...	Afrique
Americas		944	1 300	3 171	5 074	...	Amériques
East Asia/Pacific		529	2 174	3 888	5 035	...	Asie de l'Est/Pacifique
Europe		6 708	10 559	16 612	13 141	...	Europe
Middle East		560	448	1 257	2 747	...	Moyen-Orient
Region not specified		70	92	517	1 140	...	Région non spécifiée
Chad	TFN						**Tchad**
Total		77 000	61 000	70 000	71 000	...	Total
Africa		36 000	41 000	16 000	34 000	...	Afrique
Americas		4 000	3 000	11 000	6 000	...	Amériques
East Asia/Pacific		2 000	3 000	9 000	3 000	...	Asie de l'Est/Pacifique
Europe		32 000	12 000	24 000	25 000	...	Europe
Middle East		2 000	1 000	10 000	2 000	...	Moyen-Orient
South Asia		1 000	1 000	...	1 000	...	Asie du Sud
Chad	THSN						**Tchad**
Total		24 794	21 871	31 169	14 298[12]	...	Total
Africa		6 365	5 933	7 890	4 007	...	Afrique
Americas		5 002	2 395	3 553	1 440	...	Amériques
East Asia/Pacific		1 427	1 039	1 124	457	...	Asie de l'Est/Pacifique
Europe		11 250	12 251	16 348	8 170	...	Europe
Middle East		750	253	2 254	224	...	Moyen-Orient
Chile	TFN						**Chili**
Total		2 506 756	2 698 659	2 749 913	2 766 007	3 069 792	Total
Africa		4 286	5 080	4 130	4 486	4 408	Afrique
Americas		1 967 792	2 154 437	2 251 897	2 282 786	2 572 031	Amériques
East Asia/Pacific		90 673	87 960	79 089	78 332	82 756	Asie de l'Est/Pacifique
Europe		436 770	446 575	410 982	396 588	406 565	Europe
Middle East		1 297	504	577	509	490	Moyen-Orient
South Asia		4 410	3 957	3 173	3 249	3 395	Asie du Sud
Region not specified		1 528	146	65	57	147	Région non spécifiée
China [13]	VFN						**Chine** [13]
Total		131 873 287	130 027 393	126 475 923	133 762 239	135 423 453	Total
Africa		327 142	323 921	340 443	391 475	424 482	Afrique
Americas		2 721 034	2 581 855	2 491 190	2 995 397	3 201 031	Amériques
East Asia/Pacific		120 956 213	119 584 350	117 588 819	122 889 279	123 828 043	Asie de l'Est/Pacifique
Europe		6 936 600	6 688 442	5 131 487	6 365 849	6 771 977	Europe
Middle East		179 771	178 131	207 488	246 794	239 427	Moyen-Orient
South Asia		749 103	668 806	714 327	871 339	956 602	Asie du Sud
Region not specified		3 424	1 888	2 169	2 106	1 891	Région non spécifiée
China, Hong Kong SAR	TFR						**Chine, Hong Kong RAS**
Total		17 153 900	17 319 400	16 926 100	20 085 155	22 316 073	Total
Africa		126 500	119 000	101 700	105 322	98 132	Afrique
Americas		1 330 100	1 231 800	1 107 600	1 245 553	1 279 072	Amériques
East Asia/Pacific		14 022 400	14 311 900	14 169 300	16 966 228	19 178 636	Asie de l'Est/Pacifique
Europe		1 368 600	1 325 700	1 217 500	1 317 418	1 335 876	Europe
Middle East		101 600	99 500	98 600	114 601	112 259	Moyen-Orient
South Asia		204 700	231 500	231 400	336 033	312 098	Asie du Sud
China, Macao SAR	VFN						**Chine, Macao RAS**
Total [14]		27 003 370	22 933 185	21 752 751	24 965 411	28 002 279	Total [14]
Africa		30 407	22 095	16 702	21 736	25 161	Afrique
Americas		306 802	312 920	278 788	297 154	310 564	Amériques
East Asia/Pacific		26 335 797	22 223 240	21 077 816	24 223 099	27 237 661	Asie de l'Est/Pacifique
Europe		258 245	272 613	254 112	244 445	251 672	Europe
Middle East		7 514	7 537	7 364	...	...	Moyen-Orient
South Asia		64 532	94 723	117 933	178 977	177 221	Asie du Sud
Region not specified		73	57	36	...	...	Région non spécifiée

57

Tourist/visitor arrivals by region of origin *(continued)*
Number
Arrivées de touristes/visiteurs par région de provenance *(suite)*
Nombre

Country or area of destination and region of origin	Series[&] Série[&]	2007	2008	2009	2010	2011	Pays ou zone de destination et région de provenance
Colombia	VFN						**Colombie**
Total[15]		1 195 443	1 222 966	1 353 700	1 474 863[16]	...	Total[15]
Africa		3 929	1 969	2 014	2 252	...	Afrique
Americas		943 562	969 075	1 063 828	1 140 129	...	Amériques
East Asia/Pacific		24 427	21 228	25 784	25 217	...	Asie de l'Est/Pacifique
Europe		219 810	226 803	257 649	232 355	...	Europe
Middle East		1 339	1 188	1 311	908	...	Moyen-Orient
South Asia		2 292	2 492	2 924	3 375	...	Asie du Sud
Region not specified		84	211	190	70 627	...	Région non spécifiée
Comoros	TFN						**Comores**
Total[4]		15 173	14 753	11 306	15 300	...	Total[4]
Africa		4 241	2 148	2 889	1 800	...	Afrique
Americas		420	258	137	...	...	Amériques
East Asia/Pacific		471	353	272	...	...	Asie de l'Est/Pacifique
Europe		9 150	11 021	7 484	12 500	...	Europe
Region not specified		891	973	524	1 000	...	Région non spécifiée
Congo	THSR						**Congo**
Total[17]		55 027	62 106	93 797	100 691	...	Total[17]
Africa		27 733	25 780	38 327	41 122	...	Afrique
Americas		2 274	2 528	4 976	4 899	...	Amériques
East Asia/Pacific		1 150	1 117	2 974	3 442	...	Asie de l'Est/Pacifique
Europe		21 274	30 246	43 885	46 154	...	Europe
Region not specified		2 596	2 435	3 635	5 074	...	Région non spécifiée
Cook Islands	TFR						**Iles Cook**
Total[18]		97 316	94 776	101 228	104 265	112 881	Total[18]
Americas		6 958	5 674	6 066	6 995	6 910	Amériques
East Asia/Pacific		74 583	75 238	82 066	86 713	95 703	Asie de l'Est/Pacifique
Europe		15 350	13 471	12 448	10 557	10 268	Europe
Region not specified		425	393	648	...	...	Région non spécifiée
Costa Rica	TFN						**Costa Rica**
Total		1 979 789	2 089 174	1 922 579	2 099 829	2 192 059	Total
Africa		1 621	1 852	1 631	1 823	1 898	Afrique
Americas		1 670 551	1 754 547	1 634 866	1 781 572	1 856 794	Amériques
East Asia/Pacific		25 730	28 197	26 900	29 479	31 432	Asie de l'Est/Pacifique
Europe		281 515	299 798	259 126	286 923	301 929	Europe
Region not specified		372	4 780	56	32	6	Région non spécifiée
Croatia	TCER						**Croatie**
Total[19]		8 558 685	8 664 581	8 693 796	9 110 742	9 926 674	Total[19]
Africa		11 650	10 801	9 904	11 293	13 399	Afrique
Americas		231 978	214 128	179 685	208 417	250 418	Amériques
East Asia/Pacific		207 110	274 544	271 067	298 789	360 124	Asie de l'Est/Pacifique
Europe		8 107 947	8 165 108	8 233 140	8 592 243	9 302 733	Europe
Cuba	VFR						**Cuba**
Total		2 152 221	2 348 340	2 429 809	2 531 745	2 716 317	Total
Africa		6 611	7 346	8 691	8 698	8 202	Afrique
Americas		1 172 933	1 380 232	1 535 853	1 664 043	1 799 074	Amériques
East Asia/Pacific		42 311	44 225	40 558	41 349	48 498	Asie de l'Est/Pacifique
Europe		924 025	909 086	838 340	809 515	852 065	Europe
Middle East		1 734	1 981	1 810	2 053	1 814	Moyen-Orient
South Asia		4 021	5 156	4 467	5 832	5 841	Asie du Sud
Region not specified		586	314	90	255	823	Région non spécifiée
Curaçao	TFR						**Curaçao**
Total[4]		299 730	408 942	366 679	341 651	390 282	Total[4]
Americas		174 261	264 986	210 790	170 770	210 185	Amériques
Europe		121 383	136 747	149 538	163 863	169 137	Europe
Region not specified		4 086	7 209	6 351	7 018	10 960	Région non spécifiée
Cyprus	TFR						**Chypre**
Total		2 416 081	2 403 750	2 141 193	2 172 998	2 392 228	Total
Africa		7 139	7 535	6 833	6 481	6 615	Afrique
Americas		30 352	27 777	23 737	31 357	32 080	Amériques
East Asia/Pacific		16 548	16 567	15 060	19 093	16 535	Asie de l'Est/Pacifique
Europe		2 304 366	2 299 530	2 039 961	2 055 439	2 278 934	Europe
Middle East		50 896	48 280	49 947	51 110	50 799	Moyen-Orient
South Asia		6 432	3 751	5 020	8 406	6 963	Asie du Sud
Region not specified		348	310	635	1 112	302	Région non spécifiée
Czech Republic	TCEN						**République tchèque**
Total		6 679 704	6 649 410	6 032 370	6 333 996	6 715 067	Total
Africa		19 520	22 934	20 191	25 981	29 759	Afrique
Americas		441 493	434 061	397 586	460 259	480 668	Amériques
East Asia/Pacific		503 899	501 793	484 815	586 903	673 850	Asie de l'Est/Pacifique
Europe		5 714 792	5 690 622	5 129 778	5 260 853	5 530 790	Europe

57

Tourist/visitor arrivals by region of origin *(continued)*
Number
Arrivées de touristes/visiteurs par région de provenance *(suite)*
Nombre

Country or area of destination and region of origin	Series[&] Série[&]	2007	2008	2009	2010	2011	Pays ou zone de destination et région de provenance
Dem. Rep. of the Congo	TFN						**Rép. dém. du Congo**
Total		47 492[4]	49 971[4]	53 402[4]	81 117[4]	186 000[20]	Total
Africa		27 767	27 969	31 328	20 301	43 765	Afrique
Americas		2 933	3 665	3 433	7 184	20 507	Amériques
East Asia/Pacific		5 478	5 233	5 540	3 884	14 272	Asie de l'Est/Pacifique
Europe		11 314	13 104	13 101	35 012	67 895	Europe
Middle East		...	...	...	1 650	6 060	Moyen-Orient
South Asia		...	...	...	2 767	5 668	Asie du Sud
Region not specified		...	...	...	10 319	27 833	Région non spécifiée
Denmark	TCER						**Danemark**
Total [21]		9 832 042	9 563 857	9 264 870	9 425 096	7 969 792[22]	Total [21]
Americas		624 992	627 050	647 752	645 508	686 294	Amériques
East Asia/Pacific		197 862	190 727	182 297	190 452	166 178	Asie de l'Est/Pacifique
Europe		8 557 664	8 330 154	7 988 695	8 128 384	6 631 674	Europe
Region not specified		451 524	415 926	446 126	460 752	485 646	Région non spécifiée
Dominica	TFR						**Dominique**
Total		81 086	81 112	74 924	76 518	75 546	Total
Americas		69 429	66 645	62 894	64 789	62 901	Amériques
East Asia/Pacific		514	359	360	475	557	Asie de l'Est/Pacifique
Europe		10 784	13 787	11 590	10 725	11 538	Europe
Region not specified		359	321	80	529	550	Région non spécifiée
Dominican Republic	TFR						**Rép. dominicaine**
Total [2,4]		3 979 582	3 979 672	3 992 303	4 124 543	4 306 431	Total [2,4]
Americas		2 046 288	2 127 963	2 202 697	2 367 965	2 559 180	Amériques
East Asia/Pacific		7 672	7 624	6 753	8 345	9 773	Asie de l'Est/Pacifique
Europe		1 343 209	1 310 611	1 204 701	1 142 666	1 132 009	Europe
South Asia		663	754	806	848	964	Asie du Sud
Region not specified		581 750	532 720	577 346	604 719	604 505	Région non spécifiée
Ecuador	VFN						**Equateur**
Total [1]		937 487	1 005 297	968 499	1 047 098	1 140 978[9]	Total [1]
Africa		1 360	1 560	3 254	3 227	3 292	Afrique
Americas		729 610	753 266	734 524	810 281	884 434	Amériques
East Asia/Pacific		23 828	34 134	30 247	31 859	40 275	Asie de l'Est/Pacifique
Europe		179 700	198 177	197 062	197 527	202 202	Europe
Middle East		302	443	532	551	540	Moyen-Orient
South Asia		1 093	1 666	2 880	3 653	3 719	Asie du Sud
Region not specified		1 594	16 051	...	...	6 516	Région non spécifiée
Egypt	VFN						**Egypte**
Total [1]		11 090 863	12 835 351	12 535 885	14 730 813	9 845 066	Total [1]
Africa		387 221	400 979	455 262	491 416	434 867	Afrique
Americas		429 863	486 099	488 785	563 365	287 187	Amériques
East Asia/Pacific		526 196	494 891	448 416	559 018	277 866	Asie de l'Est/Pacifique
Europe		7 936 508	9 621 738	9 416 206	11 176 923	7 211 060	Europe
Middle East		1 686 953	1 675 960	1 571 212	1 761 245	1 511 401	Moyen-Orient
South Asia		105 874	116 199	118 004	144 192	101 718	Asie du Sud
Region not specified		18 248	39 485	38 000	34 654	20 967	Région non spécifiée
El Salvador	TFN						**El Salvador**
Total		1 338 543	1 384 773	1 090 926	1 149 562	1 184 497	Total
Africa		569	172	91	172	1 042	Afrique
Americas		1 285 051	1 342 824	1 066 917	1 122 757	1 139 773	Amériques
East Asia/Pacific		11 699	8 556	5 068	6 750	9 838	Asie de l'Est/Pacifique
Europe		41 190	33 198	18 842	19 879	33 811	Europe
Middle East		34	23	8	4	33	Moyen-Orient
Eritrea	VFN						**Erythrée**
Total [2]		80 503	69 897	79 334	83 947	107 090	Total [2]
Africa		5 051	4 929	6 825	7 854	21 319	Afrique
Americas		983	858	775	1 149	1 314	Amériques
East Asia/Pacific		1 935	1 824	1 403	1 436	1 698	Asie de l'Est/Pacifique
Europe		5 408	5 182	5 064	4 869	5 169	Europe
Middle East		2 249	1 494	1 343	1 326	1 224	Moyen-Orient
South Asia		2 973	395	718	730	577	Asie du Sud
Region not specified		61 904	55 215	63 206	66 583	75 789	Région non spécifiée
Estonia	TCER						**Estonie**
Total		1 380 323	1 433 346	1 380 540	1 563 952	1 807 919	Total
Africa		1 013	1 152	1 031	1 221	2 057	Afrique
Americas		27 787	24 990	23 023	27 213	32 454	Amériques
East Asia/Pacific		17 101	18 164	20 210	21 687	29 348	Asie de l'Est/Pacifique
Europe		1 332 798	1 388 201	1 332 335	1 502 008	1 731 493	Europe
Region not specified		1 624	839	3 941	11 823	12 567	Région non spécifiée

Country or area of destination and region of origin	Series[&] Série[&]	2007	2008	2009	2010	2011	Pays ou zone de destination et région de provenance
Ethiopia	TFR						**Ethiopie**
Total		311 947[23]	330 157[23]	427 286[24]	468 305[24]	523 438[24]	Total
Africa		91 674	115 999	150 102	140 076	160 311	Afrique
Americas		68 289	59 240	77 826	95 203	96 246	Amériques
East Asia/Pacific		26 341	23 141	30 837	38 669	35 768	Asie de l'Est/Pacifique
Europe		88 666	95 354	118 689	136 690	162 784	Europe
Middle East		27 537	25 228	37 428	42 301	47 583	Moyen-Orient
South Asia		9 440	11 195	12 404	15 366	20 746	Asie du Sud
Fiji	TFR						**Fidji**
Total[1]		539 881	585 031	542 186	631 868	675 050	Total[1]
Americas		81 679	81 538	65 044	66 092	69 188	Amériques
East Asia/Pacific		387 941	430 808	415 414	503 660	542 354	Asie de l'Est/Pacifique
Europe		61 096	63 447	55 139	53 901	56 408	Europe
South Asia		...	...	...	1 836	2 188	Asie du Sud
Region not specified		9 165	9 238	6 589	6 379	4 912	Région non spécifiée
Finland	VFR						**Finlande**
Total[25]		5 736 000	6 072 000	5 695 000	6 182 000	7 260 000	Total[25]
Africa		11 000	11 000	7 000	14 000	11 000	Afrique
Americas		174 000	163 000	151 000	150 000	181 000	Amériques
East Asia/Pacific		312 000	314 000	310 000	347 000	427 000	Asie de l'Est/Pacifique
Europe		5 205 000	5 540 000	5 182 000	5 646 000	6 641 000	Europe
Middle East		12 000	12 000	9 000	...	...	Moyen-Orient
South Asia		22 000	32 000	23 000	25 000	...	Asie du Sud
Region not specified		...	...	13 000	...	...	Région non spécifiée
Finland	TCER						**Finlande**
Total		2 472 449	2 494 334	2 220 267	2 318 712	2 622 586	Total
Africa		5 340	4 988	5 904	6 666	7 233	Afrique
Americas		117 098	107 107	90 882	97 324	119 984	Amériques
East Asia/Pacific		193 835	177 552	144 300	159 050	192 810	Asie de l'Est/Pacifique
Europe		2 017 072	2 056 016	1 846 249	1 921 558	2 150 835	Europe
Middle East		3 316	3 866	4 008	3 793	4 278	Moyen-Orient
South Asia		15 651	18 910	15 625	16 849	18 604	Asie du Sud
Region not specified		120 137	125 895	113 299	113 472	128 842	Région non spécifiée
France	TFR						**France**
Total[26]		80 852 000	79 219 000	76 766 000	77 648 325	81 411 043	Total[26]
Africa		1 576 000	1 765 000	1 823 000	1 721 397	2 069 018	Afrique
Americas		6 023 000	5 963 000	5 491 000	5 679 079	6 607 872	Amériques
East Asia/Pacific		3 206 000	3 484 000	3 371 000	3 648 810	4 222 449	Asie de l'Est/Pacifique
Europe		69 272 000	67 304 000	65 246 000	65 709 669	67 731 803	Europe
Middle East		775 000	703 000	835 000	889 370	779 901	Moyen-Orient
French Guiana	TFR						**Guyane française**
Total		108 801	...	...	...	...	Total
Americas		37 101	...	...	...	...	Amériques
Europe		67 130	...	...	...	...	Europe
Region not specified		4 570	...	...	...	...	Région non spécifiée
French Polynesia	TFR						**Polynésie française**
Total[1,4]		218 241	196 496	160 447	153 919	162 776	Total[1,4]
Africa		764	338	278	275	272	Afrique
Americas		81 445	70 506	51 716	53 338	63 547	Amériques
East Asia/Pacific		50 260	42 386	35 106	33 196	34 052	Asie de l'Est/Pacifique
Europe		85 205	82 838	72 857	66 561	64 272	Europe
Middle East		343	182	201	231	201	Moyen-Orient
South Asia		224	246	289	318	432	Asie du Sud
Gambia	TFN						**Gambie**
Total[27]		142 626[2]	146 759[2]	141 569[2]	91 099[2]	106 393[10]	Total[27]
Africa		3 247	2 568	3 111	2 274	15 306	Afrique
Americas		1 639	1 786	2 342	1 504	2 236	Amériques
East Asia/Pacific		147	74	151	77	66	Asie de l'Est/Pacifique
Europe		121 038	123 313	115 260	72 984	86 692	Europe
Region not specified		16 555	19 018	20 705	14 260	2 093	Région non spécifiée
Georgia	VFR						**Géorgie**
Total		1 051 747	1 290 110	1 500 049	2 031 717	2 822 363	Total
Africa		872	642	1 041	2 868	3 798	Afrique
Americas		16 881	17 553	19 654	24 427	29 289	Amériques
East Asia/Pacific		9 670	9 737	11 354	14 384	19 610	Asie de l'Est/Pacifique
Europe		1 009 248	1 243 407	1 447 496	1 956 545	2 695 250	Europe
Middle East		2 490	3 245	3 298	3 413	5 663	Moyen-Orient
South Asia		10 873	13 457	14 572	27 810	66 073	Asie du Sud
Region not specified		1 713	2 069	2 634	2 270	2 680	Région non spécifiée

Country or area of destination and region of origin	Series[&] Série[&]	2007	2008	2009	2010	2011	Pays ou zone de destination et région de provenance
Georgia	THSR						**Géorgie**
Total		103 521	103 698	150 898	306 547	438 477	Total
Africa		219	112	434	337	1 436	Afrique
Americas		13 314	13 696	21 500	29 338	27 340	Amériques
East Asia/Pacific		2 423	2 077	2 881	4 787	9 627	Asie de l'Est/Pacifique
Europe		86 228	86 664	124 849	250 977	347 543	Europe
South Asia		501	503	1 234	17 413	23 990	Asie du Sud
Region not specified		836	646	...	3 695	28 541	Région non spécifiée
Germany	TCER						**Allemagne**
Total		24 420 672	24 884 017	24 219 634	26 875 288	28 374 101	Total
Africa		163 564	159 670	158 458	192 895	193 193	Afrique
Americas		2 705 989	2 572 554	2 475 506	2 882 982	2 914 184	Amériques
East Asia/Pacific		2 104 663	1 990 945	1 790 469	2 046 055	2 296 515	Asie de l'Est/Pacifique
Europe		18 423 468	19 095 571	18 781 861	20 609 923	21 860 790	Europe
Middle East		222 556	241 786	258 883	336 193	343 263	Moyen-Orient
South Asia		...	...	...	141 524	160 599	Asie du Sud
Region not specified		800 432	823 491	754 457	665 716	605 557	Région non spécifiée
Greece	TFR						**Grèce**
Total[28]		16 165 265	15 938 806	14 914 534	15 007 490	16 427 248	Total[28]
Africa		46 325	44 569	25 576	28 314	33 775	Afrique
Americas		842 815	849 014	729 446	691 349	719 661	Amériques
East Asia/Pacific		230 309	217 999	206 209	199 452	207 360	Asie de l'Est/Pacifique
Europe		14 987 571	14 766 811	13 884 208	14 034 319	15 429 714	Europe
Middle East		46 276	47 702	55 844	44 837	27 990	Moyen-Orient
South Asia		641	847	1 647	9 189	8 748	Asie du Sud
Region not specified		11 328	11 864	11 604	...	...	Région non spécifiée
Grenada	TFN						**Grenade**
Total[2]		130 096	130 363	113 894	110 419	118 295	Total[2]
Africa		965	644	725	667	617	Afrique
Americas		63 796	66 159	61 648	59 175	64 855	Amériques
East Asia/Pacific		3 382	1 129	1 442	1 527	1 432	Asie de l'Est/Pacifique
Europe		42 111	44 676	36 096	35 361	36 277	Europe
Middle East		87	97	64	59	52	Moyen-Orient
Region not specified		19 755	17 658	13 919	13 630	15 062	Région non spécifiée
Guadeloupe	TFR						**Guadeloupe**
Total[4]		...	...	346 507	392 282	...	Total[4]
Africa		...	...	187	...	...	Afrique
Americas		...	...	1 919	1 354	...	Amériques
Europe		...	...	343 465	384 801	...	Europe
Region not specified		...	...	936	6 127	...	Région non spécifiée
Guam	TFR						**Guam**
Total[18]		1 224 894	1 141 779	1 052 871	1 196 295	1 159 152	Total[18]
Americas		50 267	53 848	56 192	61 887	62 105	Amériques
East Asia/Pacific		1 124 725	1 033 798	982 625	1 119 681	1 081 870	Asie de l'Est/Pacifique
Europe		1 564	1 710	2 005	1 948	2 117	Europe
Region not specified		48 338	52 423	12 049	12 779	13 060	Région non spécifiée
Guatemala	VFN						**Guatemala**
Total		1 627 551	1 715 426	1 776 868[16]	1 875 777[16]	1 822 663[16]	Total
Americas		1 443 662	1 517 540	1 563 934	1 644 754	1 599 430	Amériques
East Asia/Pacific		30 245	30 480	29 811	39 128	36 601	Asie de l'Est/Pacifique
Europe		151 807	165 025	180 381	189 586	184 356	Europe
Middle East		454	281	467	431	537	Moyen-Orient
Region not specified		1 383	2 100	2 275	1 878	1 739	Région non spécifiée
Guinea	TFR						**Guinée**
Total[29]		30 194	...	...	...	...	Total[29]
Africa		10 365	...	...	...	...	Afrique
Americas		3 809	...	...	...	...	Amériques
East Asia/Pacific		2 690	...	...	...	...	Asie de l'Est/Pacifique
Europe		12 504	...	...	...	...	Europe
Middle East		453	...	...	...	...	Moyen-Orient
South Asia		373	...	...	...	...	Asie du Sud
Guinea-Bissau	TFN						**Guinée-Bissau**
Total[30]		30 092	...	...	...	...	Total[30]
Africa		13 354	...	...	...	...	Afrique
Americas		2 409	...	...	...	...	Amériques
East Asia/Pacific		2 884	...	...	...	...	Asie de l'Est/Pacifique
Europe		10 289	...	...	...	...	Europe
Middle East		356	...	...	...	...	Moyen-Orient
South Asia		800	...	...	...	...	Asie du Sud

Country or area of destination and region of origin	Series[&] Série[&]	2007	2008	2009	2010	2011	Pays ou zone de destination et région de provenance
Guyana	TFR						**Guyana**
Total[31]		134 057	129 595	141 281	151 926	156 871	Total[31]
Americas		117 984	118 364	130 979	141 200	107 247	Amériques
Europe		9 978	8 937	8 277	8 357	8 284	Europe
Region not specified		6 095	2 294	2 025	2 369	41 340	Région non spécifiée
Haiti	TFR						**Haïti**
Total[4,10]		386 060	258 070	387 218	254 732	348 755	Total[4,10]
Americas		331 986	199 333	335 135	220 791	309 024	Amériques
Europe		23 372	21 262	24 573	26 755	31 437	Europe
Region not specified		30 702	37 475	27 510	7 186	8 294	Région non spécifiée
Honduras	TFN						**Honduras**
Total[32]		803 550	868 535	835 531	862 548	871 468	Total[32]
Africa		193	218	303	409	431	Afrique
Americas		731 991	789 779	744 218	753 154	758 751	Amériques
East Asia/Pacific		6 379	8 453	10 475	14 143	16 346	Asie de l'Est/Pacifique
Europe		64 289	69 160	79 375	93 268	94 099	Europe
Middle East		92	119	156	210	245	Moyen-Orient
South Asia		228	302	376	513	598	Asie du Sud
Region not specified		378	504	628	851	998	Région non spécifiée
Hungary	TFN						**Hongrie**
Total		8 637 000	8 813 000	9 058 000	9 511 000	10 250 000	Total
Africa		21 000	20 000	22 000	23 000	26 000	Afrique
Americas		478 000	541 000	548 000	536 000	606 000	Amériques
East Asia/Pacific		362 000	385 000	389 000	381 000	411 000	Asie de l'Est/Pacifique
Europe		7 776 000	7 867 000	8 099 000	8 571 000	9 207 000	Europe
Hungary	VFN						**Hongrie**
Total		39 380 000	39 554 000	40 624 000	39 905 000	41 304 000	Total
Africa		22 000	21 000	22 000	23 000	26 000	Afrique
Americas		533 000	548 000	557 000	547 000	615 000	Amériques
East Asia/Pacific		440 000	433 000	439 000	448 000	515 000	Asie de l'Est/Pacifique
Europe		38 385 000	38 552 000	39 606 000	38 887 000	40 148 000	Europe
Iceland	TFN						**Islande**
Total		485 000	502 000	493 941	488 623	565 611	Total
Americas		58 252	51 101	54 998	64 652	95 547	Amériques
East Asia/Pacific		15 629	12 492	12 416	10 774	15 686	Asie de l'Est/Pacifique
Europe		310 413	319 139	328 176	318 157	354 949	Europe
Region not specified		100 706	119 268	98 351	95 040	99 429	Région non spécifiée
Iceland	TCEN						**Islande**
Total		1 057 601	1 106 017	1 280 105	1 223 215	1 418 343	Total
Africa		1 356	2 219	1 960	2 086	2 322	Afrique
Americas		85 847	86 773	97 617	104 346	164 155	Amériques
East Asia/Pacific		29 481	30 275	38 174	34 330	49 070	Asie de l'Est/Pacifique
Europe		853 295	918 025	1 066 682	1 025 243	1 128 466	Europe
Region not specified		87 622	68 725	75 672	57 210	74 330	Région non spécifiée
India	TFN						**Inde**
Total[1]		5 081 504	5 282 603	5 167 699	5 775 692	6 309 222	Total[1]
Africa		151 355	136 424	158 605	197 090	224 292	Afrique
Americas		1 049 595	1 070 802	1 097 813	1 236 695	1 300 911	Amériques
East Asia/Pacific		822 575	866 463	865 439	1 062 536	1 229 632	Asie de l'Est/Pacifique
Europe		1 900 413	1 955 824	1 869 115	2 034 709	2 173 422	Europe
Middle East		118 469	166 404	159 090	183 387	221 220	Moyen-Orient
South Asia		982 468	1 051 846	1 001 401	1 047 444	1 139 659	Asie du Sud
Region not specified		56 629	34 840	16 236	13 831	20 086	Région non spécifiée
Indonesia	TFR						**Indonésie**
Total		5 505 759	6 234 497	6 323 730	7 002 944	7 649 731	Total
Africa		27 777	29 753	28 375	27 200	31 640	Afrique
Americas		220 202	239 678	229 824	258 584	297 061	Amériques
East Asia/Pacific		4 315 873	4 848 796	4 834 790	5 375 990	5 923 760	Asie de l'Est/Pacifique
Europe		796 730	924 745	978 369	1 038 420	1 045 865	Europe
Middle East		55 348	67 271	122 069	144 661	175 885	Moyen-Orient
South Asia		89 829	124 254	130 303	158 089	175 520	Asie du Sud
Iran (Islamic Rep. of)	VFN						**Iran (Rép. islamique d')**
Total		...	...	2 116 244	2 938 054	3 353 713	Total
Africa		...	...	4 079	5 568	6 831	Afrique
Americas		...	...	6 151	7 146	6 463	Amériques
East Asia/Pacific		...	...	27 831	33 624	52 596	Asie de l'Est/Pacifique
Europe		...	...	1 187 149	1 738 398	2 000 785	Europe
Middle East		...	...	518 819	740 004	782 096	Moyen-Orient
South Asia		...	...	314 314	413 180	426 896	Asie du Sud
Region not specified		...	...	57 901	134	78 046	Région non spécifiée

57 Tourist/visitor arrivals by region of origin *(continued)*
Number
Arrivées de touristes/visiteurs par région de provenance *(suite)*
Nombre

Country or area of destination and region of origin	Series[&] Série[&]	2007	2008	2009	2010	2011	Pays ou zone de destination et région de provenance
Iraq	VFN						**Iraq**
Total		...	863 657	1 261 921	1 517 766	...	Total
Africa		...	...	24	44	...	Afrique
Americas		...	...	42	30	...	Amériques
East Asia/Pacific		...	...	...	35	...	Asie de l'Est/Pacifique
Europe		...	776	8 564	3 483	...	Europe
Middle East		...	4 355	10 752	15 076	...	Moyen-Orient
South Asia		...	852 405	1 194 149	1 443 151	...	Asie du Sud
Region not specified		...	6 121	48 390	55 947	...	Région non spécifiée
Ireland	TFR						**Irlande**
Total		8 333 000	8 026 000	7 189 000	7 134 000	7 630 000	Total
Africa		39 000	54 000	43 000	...	...	Afrique
Americas		1 099 000	985 000	921 000	864 000	917 000	Amériques
East Asia/Pacific		249 000	256 000	233 000	135 000	141 000	Asie de l'Est/Pacifique
Europe		6 946 000	6 731 000	5 992 000	5 959 000	6 361 000	Europe
Region not specified		...	...	...	176 000	211 000	Région non spécifiée
Israel	TFR						**Israël**
Total[1]		2 066 852	2 572 317	2 321 267	2 803 125	2 820 218	Total[1]
Africa		66 023	73 866	75 615	72 080	85 389	Afrique
Americas		672 870	783 253	686 651	809 400	776 156	Amériques
East Asia/Pacific		109 873	130 005	94 765	142 345	147 149	Asie de l'Est/Pacifique
Europe		1 171 006	1 521 264	1 406 930	1 704 345	1 730 182	Europe
Middle East		13 433	17 912	18 069	20 928	23 230	Moyen-Orient
South Asia		27 631	33 209	25 746	43 080	41 425	Asie du Sud
Region not specified		6 016	12 808	13 491	10 947	16 687	Région non spécifiée
Italy	TFN						**Italie**
Total[33]		43 654 122	42 733 683	43 238 919	43 626 118	46 118 848	Total[33]
Africa		264 662	300 031	248 441	318 179	280 199	Afrique
Americas		3 440 062	3 394 811	3 390 307	3 501 730	4 067 153	Amériques
East Asia/Pacific		1 326 583	1 253 482	1 299 901	1 324 474	1 512 096	Asie de l'Est/Pacifique
Europe		38 207 533	37 342 336	37 853 912	37 921 219	39 743 414	Europe
Middle East		242 048	235 612	222 200	289 353	246 530	Moyen-Orient
South Asia		173 234	207 411	224 158	270 007	269 061	Asie du Sud
Region not specified		...	...	...	1 156	395	Région non spécifiée
Jamaica	TFR						**Jamaïque**
Total[4,10]		1 700 785	1 767 271	1 831 097	1 921 678	1 951 752	Total[4,10]
Africa		1 449	1 213	1 237	1 169	1 200	Afrique
Americas		1 398 318	1 470 488	1 542 976	1 639 875	1 687 308	Amériques
East Asia/Pacific		8 620	7 863	7 138	6 760	7 429	Asie de l'Est/Pacifique
Europe		290 269	286 142	277 931	272 139	253 749	Europe
Middle East		477	577	532	542	649	Moyen-Orient
South Asia		1 604	923	1 248	1 152	1 362	Asie du Sud
Region not specified		48	65	35	41	55	Région non spécifiée
Japan	VFN						**Japon**
Total[1]		8 346 969	8 350 835	6 789 658	8 611 175	6 218 752	Total[1]
Africa		20 114	20 542	17 219	19 076	16 777	Afrique
Americas		1 054 019	1 005 692	908 098	945 377	716 808	Amériques
East Asia/Pacific		6 267 798	6 306 921	4 940 971	6 653 648	4 796 321	Asie de l'Est/Pacifique
Europe		897 944	909 626	820 128	877 284	582 787	Europe
Middle East		3 294	3 956	7 332	10 448	7 106	Moyen-Orient
South Asia		102 860	102 991	95 270	104 679	98 460	Asie du Sud
Region not specified		940	1 107	640	663	493	Région non spécifiée
Jordan	TFN						**Jordanie**
Total[2]		3 430 954	3 728 726	3 788 890	4 207 408	3 959 654	Total[2]
Africa		54 708	49 884	46 387	49 762	49 947	Afrique
Americas		177 782	200 371	189 776	215 121	189 283	Amériques
East Asia/Pacific		126 069	146 029	138 404	148 981	154 149	Asie de l'Est/Pacifique
Europe		570 859	657 628	602 394	744 992	626 886	Europe
Middle East		1 689 532	1 777 094	1 867 473	2 054 551	1 892 950	Moyen-Orient
South Asia		64 895	73 571	71 778	65 243	77 078	Asie du Sud
Region not specified		747 109	824 149	872 678	928 758	969 361	Région non spécifiée
Kazakhstan	VFR						**Kazakhstan**
Total		5 310 582	4 721 456	4 329 848	4 712 657		Total
Africa		2 272	1 805	2 818	3 577	...	Afrique
Americas		33 222	28 860	31 190	32 207	...	Amériques
East Asia/Pacific		219 908	212 003	206 829	174 842	...	Asie de l'Est/Pacifique
Europe		5 018 562	4 447 837	4 047 626	4 454 928	...	Europe
Middle East		4 551	3 832	5 227	6 228	...	Moyen-Orient
South Asia		26 372	23 064	26 611	23 551	...	Asie du Sud
Region not specified		5 695	4 055	9 547	17 324	...	Région non spécifiée

Country or area of destination and region of origin	Series[&] Série[&]	2007	2008	2009	2010	2011	Pays ou zone de destination et région de provenance
Kenya	VFR						**Kenya**
Total		1 817 000	1 203 000	1 490 000	1 609 000	...	Total
Africa		205 000	136 000	158 000	279 000	...	Afrique
Americas		134 000	89 000	111 000	131 000	...	Amériques
East Asia/Pacific		168 000	111 000	122 000	162 000	...	Asie de l'Est/Pacifique
Europe		1 237 000	819 000	1 040 000	932 000	...	Europe
Region not specified		73 000	48 000	59 000	105 000	...	Région non spécifiée
Kiribati	TFN						**Kiribati**
Total[4,34]		4 709	3 871	3 944	4 701	5 264	Total[4,34]
Americas		1 109	928	699	827	1 063	Amériques
East Asia/Pacific		3 069	2 481	2 695	3 240	2 887	Asie de l'Est/Pacifique
Europe		297	304	382	368	412	Europe
Region not specified		234	158	168	266	902	Région non spécifiée
Kuwait	VFN						**Koweït**
Total		4 481 616	4 735 910	5 087 781	5 207 785	5 574 302	Total
Africa		54 708	64 768	73 260	95 080	113 314	Afrique
Americas		189 775	219 039	229 288	226 943	222 973	Amériques
East Asia/Pacific		235 562	244 241	249 653	229 734	226 602	Asie de l'Est/Pacifique
Europe		177 528	181 162	184 248	191 455	188 306	Europe
Middle East		2 618 506	2 778 066	2 996 469	3 103 394	3 434 185	Moyen-Orient
South Asia		1 191 690	1 224 937	1 316 151	1 327 607	1 351 987	Asie du Sud
Region not specified		13 847	23 697	38 712	33 572	36 935	Région non spécifiée
Kyrgyzstan	TFR						**Kirghizistan**
Total		1 655 833	2 435 386	2 146 740	1 316 207	3 114 372	Total
Americas		15 407	9 580	11 323	9 142	14 782	Amériques
East Asia/Pacific		30 813	30 152	30 913	24 957	32 909	Asie de l'Est/Pacifique
Europe		1 595 211	2 383 543	2 089 309	1 271 252	3 049 493	Europe
Middle East		168	194	197	127	122	Moyen-Orient
South Asia		7 262	6 838	7 283	5 785	7 173	Asie du Sud
Region not specified		6 972	5 079	7 715	4 944	9 893	Région non spécifiée
Lao People's Dem. Rep.	VFN						**Rép. dém. pop. lao**
Total		1 623 943	1 736 787	2 008 363	2 513 028	2 723 564	Total
Americas		61 463	75 266	53 348	67 291	69 990	Amériques
East Asia/Pacific		1 404 095	1 479 847	1 818 291	2 256 705	2 461 424	Asie de l'Est/Pacifique
Europe		152 023	172 846	132 412	181 840	185 771	Europe
South Asia		2 361	2 652	2 280	3 321	3 227	Asie du Sud
Region not specified		4 001	6 176	2 032	3 871	3 152	Région non spécifiée
Latvia	VFR						**Lettonie**
Total[35]		5 209 622	5 496 205	4 726 765	5 042 260	5 538 393	Total[35]
Africa		2 958	...	5 239	7 422	4 345	Afrique
Americas		32 351	37 615	60 256	62 408	76 550	Amériques
East Asia/Pacific		17 502	21 911	35 405	47 040	49 521	Asie de l'Est/Pacifique
Europe		5 150 359	5 410 212	4 611 254	4 901 853	5 386 291	Europe
Middle East		2 173	...	1 924	7 514	1 858	Moyen-Orient
South Asia		2 016	4 329	7 790	11 283	11 063	Asie du Sud
Region not specified		2 263	22 138	4 897	4 740	8 765	Région non spécifiée
Latvia	TCER						**Lettonie**
Total		844 828	944 690	753 875	877 774	1 063 294	Total
Africa		132	389	347	428	786	Afrique
Americas		20 849	24 690	19 027	22 589	24 820	Amériques
East Asia/Pacific		11 387	13 464	14 389	15 482	18 426	Asie de l'Est/Pacifique
Europe		794 241	897 356	713 375	827 934	1 007 215	Europe
Middle East		390	368	478	648	972	Moyen-Orient
South Asia		626	969	1 081	1 418	2 029	Asie du Sud
Region not specified		17 203	7 454	5 178	9 275	9 046	Région non spécifiée
Lebanon	TFN						**Liban**
Total[36]		1 017 072	1 332 533	1 844 106	2 167 989	1 655 051	Total[36]
Africa		59 861	50 732	66 140	66 225	82 643	Afrique
Americas		121 596	176 647	232 694	248 725	222 671	Amériques
East Asia/Pacific		63 579	89 452	128 919	133 451	112 163	Asie de l'Est/Pacifique
Europe		277 873	348 262	454 742	550 866	487 150	Europe
Middle East		388 292	532 871	761 852	867 898	560 273	Moyen-Orient
South Asia		104 729	133 067	197 941	299 087	188 242	Asie du Sud
Region not specified		1 142	1 502	1 818	1 737	1 909	Région non spécifiée

Tourist/visitor arrivals by region of origin *(continued)*
Number
Arrivées de touristes/visiteurs par région de provenance *(suite)*
Nombre

Country or area of destination and region of origin	Series& Série&	2007	2008	2009	2010	2011	Pays ou zone de destination et région de provenance
Lesotho	VFR						**Lesotho**
Total		300 350	293 073	343 743	425 870	398 149	Total
Africa		271 475	259 407	314 218	400 823	379 507	Afrique
Americas		3 385	4 556	4 122	3 907	3 180	Amériques
East Asia/Pacific		4 816	5 566	5 150	3 938	2 407	Asie de l'Est/Pacifique
Europe		19 772	22 717	19 726	16 719	12 751	Europe
Middle East		400	385	177	70	13	Moyen-Orient
South Asia		304	404	256	285	261	Asie du Sud
Region not specified		198	38	94	128	30	Région non spécifiée
Libyan Arab Jamah.	VFN						**Jamah. arabe libyenne**
Total		105 997	...	...	...	...	Total
Africa		163	...	...	...	...	Afrique
Americas		813	...	...	...	...	Amériques
East Asia/Pacific		3 683	...	...	...	...	Asie de l'Est/Pacifique
Europe		101 288	...	...	...	...	Europe
Middle East		23	...	...	...	...	Moyen-Orient
South Asia		27	...	...	...	...	Asie du Sud
Liechtenstein	THSR						**Liechtenstein**
Total		58 258	58 454	52 285	49 804	53 326	Total
Africa		216	177	171	132	138	Afrique
Americas		3 156	2 439	2 260	2 397	2 714	Amériques
East Asia/Pacific		1 892	1 679	1 330	1 656	1 858	Asie de l'Est/Pacifique
Europe		52 885	54 067	48 210	45 393	48 252	Europe
South Asia		62	73	84	70	96	Asie du Sud
Region not specified		47	19	230	156	268	Région non spécifiée
Lithuania	TCER						**Lituanie**
Total		849 006	909 983	752 389	840 368	1 003 843	Total
Africa		961	1 253	1 177	1 523	3 034	Afrique
Americas		27 188	26 402	20 489	25 247	32 302	Amériques
East Asia/Pacific		16 140	19 215	18 470	21 283	30 829	Asie de l'Est/Pacifique
Europe		804 717	863 113	712 253	792 315	937 678	Europe
Luxembourg	TCER						**Luxembourg**
Total		917 334	878 900	848 528	793 410	871 348	Total
Africa		...	...	...	...	10 109	Afrique
Americas		33 255	32 482	28 762	25 073	37 441	Amériques
East Asia/Pacific		...	...	...	...	53 983	Asie de l'Est/Pacifique
Europe		841 388	807 742	780 885	726 902	769 202	Europe
Region not specified		42 691	38 676	38 881	41 435	613	Région non spécifiée
Madagascar	TFN						**Madagascar**
Total[4]		344 348	375 010	162 687	196 052	225 055	Total[4]
Africa		64 013	83 802	36 732	40 083	39 176	Afrique
Americas		13 671	11 250	4 881	5 882	9 870	Amériques
East Asia/Pacific		14 084	16 500	5 694	6 861	22 955	Asie de l'Est/Pacifique
Europe		246 837	261 936	110 869	143 226	153 054	Europe
Region not specified		5 743	1 522	4 511	...	...	Région non spécifiée
Malawi	TFR						**Malawi**
Total[37]		734 598	742 457	755 031	746 129	767 000	Total[37]
Africa		559 149	574 544	574 172	562 379	588 306	Afrique
Americas		47 225	44 561	46 120	45 893	44 735	Amériques
East Asia/Pacific		12 835	11 588	12 142	20 456	10 247	Asie de l'Est/Pacifique
Europe		99 226	98 330	105 054	104 779	102 389	Europe
Middle East		1 613	1 581	1 691	2 310	3 400	Moyen-Orient
South Asia		13 366	10 194	14 299	8 338	15 894	Asie du Sud
Region not specified		1 184	1 659	1 553	1 974	2 029	Région non spécifiée
Malaysia	TFR						**Malaisie**
Total[38]		20 972 822	22 052 488	23 646 191	24 577 196	24 714 324	Total[38]
Africa		307 797	127 361	84 549	41 615	111 182	Afrique
Americas		472 164	345 217	345 768	342 521	339 645	Amériques
East Asia/Pacific		17 656 571	18 972 997	20 830 330	21 605 363	21 667 502	Asie de l'Est/Pacifique
Europe		829 653	1 026 032	1 165 807	1 133 235	1 136 443	Europe
Middle East		225 153	216 351	196 854	166 636	236 987	Moyen-Orient
South Asia		686 614	826 028	929 954	997 156	1 124 647	Asie du Sud
Region not specified		794 870	538 502	92 929	290 670	97 918	Région non spécifiée
Maldives	TFN						**Maldives**
Total[4]		675 889	683 012	655 852	791 917	931 333	Total[4]
Africa		4 846	5 694	5 034	5 628	6 452	Afrique
Americas		14 198	14 485	15 159	18 601	23 654	Amériques
East Asia/Pacific		124 674	127 151	137 946	214 026	303 018	Asie de l'Est/Pacifique
Europe		495 371	497 560	462 192	505 421	537 769	Europe
Middle East		6 450	9 205	9 525	11 629	14 570	Moyen-Orient
South Asia		30 350	28 917	25 996	36 612	45 870	Asie du Sud

Country or area of destination and region of origin	Series[&] Série[&]	2007	2008	2009	2010	2011	Pays ou zone de destination et région de provenance
Mali	THSN						**Mali**
Total		164 124	189 511	160 012	169 305	159 782	Total
Africa		29 378	47 418	44 589	47 175	52 467	Afrique
Americas		17 564	19 519	26 992	23 692	20 826	Amériques
East Asia/Pacific		1 416	4 672	1 307	2 668	3 148	Asie de l'Est/Pacifique
Europe		104 308	100 819	72 872	82 837	68 752	Europe
Middle East		1 190	4 176	2 946	2 948	3 910	Moyen-Orient
Region not specified		10 268	12 907	11 306	9 985	10 679	Région non spécifiée
Malta	TFN						**Malte**
Total[39]		1 243 510	1 290 856	1 182 489	1 336 391	1 411 748	Total[39]
Americas		20 423	18 021	13 943	16 297	16 229	Amériques
Europe		1 142 754	1 195 405	1 088 750	1 219 453	1 298 178	Europe
Middle East		9 259	9 403	14 282	15 864	6 208	Moyen-Orient
Region not specified		71 074	68 027	65 514	84 777	91 133	Région non spécifiée
Marshall Islands	TFR						**Iles Marshall**
Total		7 200[4]	6 022[4]	5 372[18]	4 563[4]	4 559[4]	Total
Americas		1 703	1 480	1 354	1 332	1 322	Amériques
East Asia/Pacific		4 382	3 663	3 263	2 934	2 877	Asie de l'Est/Pacifique
Europe		278	177	153	144	137	Europe
Region not specified		837	702	602	153	223	Région non spécifiée
Martinique	TFR						**Martinique**
Total[40]		501 491	481 224	441 648	478 060	496 538	Total[40]
Americas		92 980	85 831	63 145	85 239	86 363	Amériques
Europe		405 231	390 644	367 030	389 306	404 670	Europe
Region not specified		3 280	4 749	11 473	3 515	5 505	Région non spécifiée
Mauritius	TFR						**Maurice**
Total		906 971	930 456	871 356	934 827	964 642	Total
Africa		210 553	213 383	203 846	225 754	230 673	Afrique
Americas		10 462	13 709	13 071	13 724	14 424	Amériques
East Asia/Pacific		39 681	39 843	26 534	30 911	45 590	Asie de l'Est/Pacifique
Europe		596 132	608 929	579 897	605 790	610 181	Europe
Middle East		4 591	7 158	5 702	6 012	6 448	Moyen-Orient
South Asia		44 762	45 848	41 014	51 348	55 743	Asie du Sud
Region not specified		790	1 586	1 292	1 288	1 583	Région non spécifiée
Mexico	TFN						**Mexique**
Total[10]		21 605 754	22 930 584	22 346 261	23 289 749	23 403 263	Total[10]
Africa		10 328	13 340	9 884	15 005	14 701	Afrique
Americas		18 698 935	19 818 344	20 178 443	20 867 904	21 152 561	Amériques
East Asia/Pacific		108 727	105 412	78 407	101 129	112 642	Asie de l'Est/Pacifique
Europe		1 407 731	1 501 742	1 188 286	1 417 935	1 509 736	Europe
Region not specified		1 380 033	1 491 746	891 241	887 776	613 623	Région non spécifiée
Mexico	TFR						**Mexique**
Total[10]		21 605 754	22 930 584	22 346 261	23 289 749	23 403 274	Total[10]
Americas		17 746 787	18 800 933	18 874 985	19 128 045	19 314 307	Amériques
Region not specified		3 858 967	4 129 651	3 471 276	4 161 704	4 088 967	Région non spécifiée
Micronesia (Fed. States of)	TFR						**Micronésie (Etats féd. de)**
Total[41]		21 146	25 627	...	...	...	Total[41]
Americas		8 471	9 203	...	...	...	Amériques
East Asia/Pacific		10 082	13 442	...	...	...	Asie de l'Est/Pacifique
Europe		2 452	2 788	...	...	...	Europe
Region not specified		141	194	...	...	...	Région non spécifiée
Monaco	TFR						**Monaco**
Total		327 985	323 705	264 540	279 166	294 901	Total
Africa		3 293	2 832	2 342	2 881	2 836	Afrique
Americas		40 910	35 368	27 456	30 863	33 143	Amériques
East Asia/Pacific		12 382	12 535	10 222	11 783	14 650	Asie de l'Est/Pacifique
Europe		244 497	260 856	216 280	223 207	232 827	Europe
Middle East		4 318	7 045	4 333	5 039	5 386	Moyen-Orient
Region not specified		22 585	5 069	3 907	5 393	6 059	Région non spécifiée
Mongolia	TFR						**Mongolie**
Total		451 788	446 317	411 497	456 963	...	Total
Africa		691	592	434	595	...	Afrique
Americas		15 401	15 805	14 161	16 486	...	Amériques
East Asia/Pacific		283 267	266 582	241 097	264 401	...	Asie de l'Est/Pacifique
Europe		149 077	159 884	153 785	173 381	...	Europe
Middle East		480	610	645	616	...	Moyen-Orient
South Asia		1 202	1 407	1 327	1 473	...	Asie du Sud
Region not specified		1 670	1 437	48	11	...	Région non spécifiée

57

Tourist/visitor arrivals by region of origin *(continued)*
Number
Arrivées de touristes/visiteurs par région de provenance *(suite)*
Nombre

Country or area of destination and region of origin	Series[&] Série[&]	2007	2008	2009	2010	2011	Pays ou zone de destination et région de provenance
Montenegro	TFR						**Monténégro**
Total		984 138	1 030 825	1 043 933	1 087 794	1 201 099	Total
Americas		8 894	9 084	8 255	10 622	12 661	Amériques
East Asia/Pacific		2 293	2 839	2 426	3 241	4 918	Asie de l'Est/Pacifique
Europe		968 475	1 013 406	1 028 084	1 066 715	1 171 855	Europe
Region not specified		4 476	5 496	5 168	7 216	11 665	Région non spécifiée
Montserrat	TFR						**Montserrat**
Total		7 746	7 360	6 324	5 981	5 395	Total
Americas		5 311	4 989	4 252	4 353	3 749	Amériques
East Asia/Pacific		5	...	3	1	14	Asie de l'Est/Pacifique
Europe		2 366	2 333	2 044	1 573	1 535	Europe
Region not specified		64	38	25	54	97	Région non spécifiée
Morocco	TFN						**Maroc**
Total[2]		7 407 617	7 878 639	8 341 237	9 288 338	9 342 133	Total[2]
Africa		192 668	213 611	222 879	255 564	298 622	Afrique
Americas		196 037	201 867	214 563	250 874	239 497	Amériques
East Asia/Pacific		73 910	76 127	77 415	98 995	87 370	Asie de l'Est/Pacifique
Europe		3 406 184	3 563 990	3 623 479	4 143 648	4 137 156	Europe
Middle East		115 832	127 486	134 659	142 091	152 326	Moyen-Orient
South Asia		11 592	11 901	11 753	12 242	12 486	Asie du Sud
Region not specified		3 411 394	3 683 657	4 056 489	4 384 924	4 414 676	Région non spécifiée
Mozambique	TFN						**Mozambique**
Total		1 259 000	1 438 684[42]	1 711 147	1 836 143	...	Total
Africa		1 043 310	1 213 201	1 442 962	1 465 793	...	Afrique
Americas		18 799	38 981	46 363	102 041	...	Amériques
East Asia/Pacific		12 680	18 699	22 240	28 211	...	Asie de l'Est/Pacifique
Europe		66 233	161 850	192 502	219 089	...	Europe
Region not specified		117 978	5 953	7 080	21 009	...	Région non spécifiée
Myanmar	TFN						**Myanmar**
Total[43]		248 076	193 319	243 278	310 688	391 176	Total[43]
Africa		432	539	764	816	993	Afrique
Americas		19 331	16 158	18 662	20 580	27 745	Amériques
East Asia/Pacific		142 904	124 242	157 092	207 450	257 008	Asie de l'Est/Pacifique
Europe		72 827	40 885	53 150	65 935	88 517	Europe
Middle East		2 281	1 379	1 564	2 208	2 607	Moyen-Orient
South Asia		10 301	10 116	12 046	13 699	14 306	Asie du Sud
Namibia	TFN						**Namibie**
Total		928 914	931 110	980 178	984 098	...	Total
Africa		690 148	676 444	723 762	714 287	...	Afrique
Americas		19 342	29 201	26 657	26 175	...	Amériques
East Asia/Pacific		5 783	9 778	11 484	11 294	...	Asie de l'Est/Pacifique
Europe		194 605	204 115	206 496	219 070	...	Europe
Region not specified		19 036	11 572	11 779	13 272	...	Région non spécifiée
Nepal	TFN						**Népal**
Total		526 705	500 277	509 956	602 867	736 215	Total
Africa		1 309	493	481	437	3 017	Afrique
Americas		41 348	42 080	42 567	49 637	62 430	Amériques
East Asia/Pacific		139 615	129 469	135 232	148 074	201 134	Asie de l'Est/Pacifique
Europe		157 505	146 590	143 814	169 694	212 729	Europe
Middle East		...	5 647	4 891	7 524	12 857	Moyen-Orient
South Asia		168 041	149 959	150 951	177 704	234 599	Asie du Sud
Region not specified		18 887	26 039	32 020	49 797	9 449	Région non spécifiée
Netherlands	TCER						**Pays-Bas**
Total		11 008 000	10 104 300	9 920 600	10 883 200	11 299 500	Total
Africa		91 900	83 800	83 600	103 300	114 400	Afrique
Americas		1 273 600	1 068 000	1 017 700	1 223 000	1 319 800	Amériques
East Asia/Pacific		738 500	667 700	673 400	770 100	849 700	Asie de l'Est/Pacifique
Europe		8 904 000	8 284 800	8 145 900	8 786 800	9 015 600	Europe
New Caledonia	TFR						**Nouvelle-Calédonie**
Total[10]		103 363	103 672	99 379	98 562	111 875	Total[10]
Africa		628	713	1 980	2 238	1 904	Afrique
Americas		1 918	2 707	2 518	2 891	2 889	Amériques
East Asia/Pacific		68 449	64 578	63 213	64 573	68 172	Asie de l'Est/Pacifique
Europe		32 252	35 636	31 652	28 859	38 886	Europe
Region not specified		116	38	16	1	24	Région non spécifiée

Country or area of destination and region of origin	Series[&] Série[&]	2007	2008	2009	2010	2011	Pays ou zone de destination et région de provenance
New Zealand	VFR						**Nouvelle-Zélande**
Total [2,44]		2 455 308	2 447 257	2 447 532	2 510 759	2 594 198	Total [2,44]
Africa		24 954	28 507	22 155	20 425	30 199	Afrique
Americas		290 455	295 937	275 849	268 358	268 501	Amériques
East Asia/Pacific		1 529 711	1 508 819	1 561 724	1 649 581	1 695 011	Asie de l'Est/Pacifique
Europe		517 125	518 767	491 498	465 308	475 957	Europe
Middle East		11 085	13 268	15 234	16 097	16 246	Moyen-Orient
South Asia		24 692	26 927	28 461	32 948	31 927	Asie du Sud
Region not specified		57 286	55 032	52 611	58 042	76 357	Région non spécifiée
Nicaragua	TFN						**Nicaragua**
Total [2]		799 996	857 901	931 904	1 011 251	1 060 031	Total [2]
Africa		471	706	563	605	487	Afrique
Americas		671 603	714 212	769 799	846 897	893 498	Amériques
East Asia/Pacific		9 096	9 360	11 982	10 620	10 252	Asie de l'Est/Pacifique
Europe		52 525	57 649	71 540	73 644	75 948	Europe
Middle East		157	127	164	133	143	Moyen-Orient
South Asia		444	1 775	733	2 089	1 573	Asie du Sud
Region not specified		65 700	74 072	77 123	77 263	78 130	Région non spécifiée
Niger	TFN						**Niger**
Total		47 539	73 154	65 883	74 278	82 370	Total
Africa		23 770	46 981	42 312	47 702	52 881	Afrique
Americas		3 898	4 528	4 078	4 598	5 107	Amériques
East Asia/Pacific		1 778	3 063	3 158	3 560	3 954	Asie de l'Est/Pacifique
Europe		17 589	18 138	16 335	18 418	20 428	Europe
Middle East		504	444	...	...	...	Moyen-Orient
Nigeria	VFN						**Nigéria**
Total		5 238 545	5 820 497	6 053 318	6 113 384	3 765 400 [2]	Total
Africa		3 613 664	4 014 981	4 175 489	4 185 492	872 285	Afrique
Americas		221 586	244 455	256 055	257 581	176 880	Amériques
East Asia/Pacific		302 260	337 587	351 092	352 351	339 879	Asie de l'Est/Pacifique
Europe		867 461	963 874	1 000 609	1 002 737	448 853	Europe
Middle East		94 756	105 357	109 559	110 692	38 423	Moyen-Orient
South Asia		123 627	137 364	142 858	143 412	212 920	Asie du Sud
Region not specified		15 191	16 879	17 656	61 119	1 676 160	Région non spécifiée
Niue	TFR						**Nioué**
Total [45]		3 463 [18]	4 748 [4]	4 662 [4]	6 214 [18]	6 094 [18]	Total [45]
Americas		208	315	203	298	1 176	Amériques
East Asia/Pacific		3 026	3 913	3 550	4 156	4 432	Asie de l'Est/Pacifique
Europe		206	492	889	1 602	402	Europe
Region not specified		23	28	20	158	84	Région non spécifiée
Northern Mariana Islands	VFN						**Iles Mariannes du Nord**
Total		389 345	397 274	353 956	379 091	340 957	Total
Americas		28 082	31 361	29 555	27 319	24 155	Amériques
East Asia/Pacific		355 921	356 997	316 064	345 874	310 394	Asie de l'Est/Pacifique
Europe		4 676	7 742	7 309	4 961	5 646	Europe
Region not specified		666	1 174	1 028	937	762	Région non spécifiée
Norway	TFN						**Norvège**
Total [46]		4 377 000	4 347 000	4 346 000	4 767 000	4 963 000	Total [46]
Americas		177 000	136 000	132 000	160 000	164 000	Amériques
East Asia/Pacific		32 000	29 000	25 000	28 000	27 000	Asie de l'Est/Pacifique
Europe		3 939 000	3 967 000	3 943 000	4 313 000	4 471 000	Europe
Middle East		...	...	...	...	301 000	Moyen-Orient
Region not specified		229 000	215 000	246 000	266 000	...	Région non spécifiée
Occupied Palestinian Terr.	THSN						**Terr. palestinien occupé**
Total		264 168	387 143	395 622	521 927	448 500	Total
Africa		4 951	9 679	11 736	14 126	27 837	Afrique
Americas		32 440	39 453	62 958	87 721	56 701	Amériques
East Asia/Pacific		20 424	41 344	41 157	67 218	58 394	Asie de l'Est/Pacifique
Europe		203 468	293 659	275 694	350 543	300 768	Europe
Middle East		2 885	3 008	4 077	2 319	4 800	Moyen-Orient
Oman	THSN						**Oman**
Total		1 182 407	1 378 078	1 279 678	1 048 052	...	Total
Africa		16 296	19 355	30 486	21 755	...	Afrique
Americas		46 367	57 110	156 958	95 350	...	Amériques
East Asia/Pacific		82 929	104 046	144 500	107 747	...	Asie de l'Est/Pacifique
Europe		382 305	437 137	387 059	339 010	...	Europe
Middle East		202 988	242 661	288 840	219 698	...	Moyen-Orient
South Asia		186 584	189 469	193 521	192 508	...	Asie du Sud
Region not specified		264 938	328 300	78 314	71 983	...	Région non spécifiée

Tourist/visitor arrivals by region of origin *(continued)*
Number
Arrivées de touristes/visiteurs par région de provenance *(suite)*
Nombre

Country or area of destination and region of origin	Series[&] Série[&]	2007	2008	2009	2010	2011	Pays ou zone de destination et région de provenance
Pakistan	TFN						**Pakistan**
Total		839 500	822 828	854 905	...	...	Total
Africa		15 840	15 767	14 659	...	...	Afrique
Americas		160 615	155 870	162 451	...	...	Amériques
East Asia/Pacific		87 092	75 967	88 984	...	...	Asie de l'Est/Pacifique
Europe		386 751	389 207	378 643	...	...	Europe
Middle East		35 887	28 966	27 951	...	...	Moyen-Orient
South Asia		148 856	153 117	178 242	...	...	Asie du Sud
Region not specified		4 459	3 934	3 975	...	...	Région non spécifiée
Palau	TFR						**Palaos**
Total[47]		88 175	79 259	71 887	85 593	109 057	Total[47]
Americas		5 956	5 235	5 193	5 809	5 890	Amériques
East Asia/Pacific		78 738	69 927	62 970	75 701	98 658	Asie de l'Est/Pacifique
Europe		2 517	3 151	2 923	3 402	3 535	Europe
Region not specified		964	946	801	681	974	Région non spécifiée
Panama	VFR						**Panama**
Total[48]		948 946	1 136 079	1 054 663	1 162 713	1 310 292	Total[48]
Africa		646	1 071	851	1 000	1 920	Afrique
Americas		835 948	983 844	916 458	1 006 007	1 134 147	Amériques
East Asia/Pacific		27 001	33 286	22 550	27 020	33 140	Asie de l'Est/Pacifique
Europe		85 283	117 812	114 729	128 595	140 994	Europe
Middle East		68	66	75	91	91	Moyen-Orient
Papua New Guinea	TFR						**Papouasie-Nvl-Guinée**
Total		104 122	114 207	125 891	146 350	165 059	Total
Africa		725	947	877	1 056	1 671	Afrique
Americas		7 868	8 197	9 029	10 869	11 715	Amériques
East Asia/Pacific		85 026	93 542	102 717	119 610	131 593	Asie de l'Est/Pacifique
Europe		8 563	9 237	9 022	12 065	15 130	Europe
South Asia		1 940	2 284	2 382	2 750	4 950	Asie du Sud
Region not specified		...	...	1 864	...	...	Région non spécifiée
Paraguay	TFN						**Paraguay**
Total[5,49]		415 702	428 215	439 246	465 264	523 740	Total[5,49]
Africa		484	301	401	386	354	Afrique
Americas		369 993	384 216	394 649	432 963	480 529	Amériques
East Asia/Pacific		9 174	8 390	8 478	7 177	8 037	Asie de l'Est/Pacifique
Europe		35 133	34 259	34 716	24 181	34 014	Europe
Middle East		377	642	654	348	468	Moyen-Orient
South Asia		427	393	348	209	338	Asie du Sud
Region not specified		114	14	...	...	...	Région non spécifiée
Peru	TFR						**Pérou**
Total[9,10]		1 916 400	2 057 620	2 139 961	2 299 187	2 597 803	Total[9,10]
Africa		3 819	3 511	3 478	3 714	4 247	Afrique
Americas		1 399 083	1 485 900	1 581 215	1 746 961	1 996 759	Amériques
East Asia/Pacific		94 495	109 250	103 333	95 966	116 608	Asie de l'Est/Pacifique
Europe		414 588	454 214	446 431	447 061	474 961	Europe
Middle East		98	88	131	141	222	Moyen-Orient
South Asia		2 682	3 714	4 305	4 411	4 177	Asie du Sud
Region not specified		1 635	943	1 068	933	829	Région non spécifiée
Philippines	TFR						**Philippines**
Total[2]		3 091 993	3 139 422	3 017 099	3 520 472	3 917 454	Total[2]
Africa		3 090	3 317	3 082	3 584	4 193	Afrique
Americas		674 921	685 427	686 293	711 356	747 656	Amériques
East Asia/Pacific		1 829 095	1 798 719	1 643 595	2 064 400	2 397 497	Asie de l'Est/Pacifique
Europe		300 372	322 864	329 840	360 991	389 823	Europe
Middle East		31 759	36 615	46 811	48 716	55 829	Moyen-Orient
South Asia		37 596	43 662	46 960	50 914	61 259	Asie du Sud
Region not specified		215 160	248 818	260 518	280 511	261 197	Région non spécifiée
Poland	VFN						**Pologne**
Total		66 207 767	59 935 000[50]	53 840 000[50]	58 340 000[50]	60 745 000[50]	Total
Africa		16 861	15 000	20 000	20 000	15 000	Afrique
Americas		452 903	380 000	338 000	395 000	400 000	Amériques
East Asia/Pacific		228 844	220 000	207 000	280 000	300 000	Asie de l'Est/Pacifique
Europe		65 373 132	59 290 000	53 221 000	57 540 000	59 950 000	Europe
Middle East		9 507	10 000	15 000	15 000	15 000	Moyen-Orient
South Asia		19 721	20 000	20 000	30 000	20 000	Asie du Sud
Region not specified		106 799	...	19 000	60 000	45 000	Région non spécifiée

Country or area of destination and region of origin	Series[&] Série[&]	2007	2008	2009	2010	2011	Pays ou zone de destination et région de provenance
Poland	TCER						**Pologne**
Total		4 387 404	4 046 312	3 861 942	4 134 970	4 409 550	Total
Africa		6 657	6 538	8 783	9 318	9 209	Afrique
Americas		234 350	198 941	184 464	217 610	225 130	Amériques
East Asia/Pacific		121 185	121 129	120 014	151 559	156 583	Asie de l'Est/Pacifique
Europe		3 964 327	3 659 440	3 507 918	3 696 478	3 966 041	Europe
Middle East		5 288	5 024	7 061	7 198	9 264	Moyen-Orient
South Asia		10 504	12 564	14 134	18 472	17 072	Asie du Sud
Region not specified		45 093	42 676	19 568	34 335	26 251	Région non spécifiée
Portugal	TFR						**Portugal**
Total[10]		12 321 000	...	...	...	...	Total[10]
Americas		600 000	...	...	...	...	Amériques
East Asia/Pacific		40 000	...	...	...	...	Asie de l'Est/Pacifique
Europe		10 693 000	...	...	...	...	Europe
Region not specified		988 000	...	...	...	...	Région non spécifiée
Portugal	TCER						**Portugal**
Total		6 787 797	6 961 707	6 439 022	6 756 354	7 263 644	Total
Africa		70 030	67 619	73 882	75 446	84 319	Afrique
Americas		642 586	676 186	622 683	759 506	874 361	Amériques
East Asia/Pacific		212 794	201 612	190 419	229 173	261 440	Asie de l'Est/Pacifique
Europe		5 862 387	6 016 290	5 552 038	5 692 229	6 043 524	Europe
Puerto Rico	TFR						**Porto Rico**
Total[4,51]		3 687 000	3 716 300	3 183 300	3 185 600	3 047 900	Total[4,51]
Americas		2 886 700	2 912 000	2 704 100	2 639 700	2 593 800	Amériques
Region not specified		800 300	804 300	479 200	545 900	454 100	Région non spécifiée
Qatar	THSR						**Qatar**
Total[52]		963 573[53]	1 404 850[53]	1 658 569[53]	1 518 953	2 527 285	Total[52]
Africa		...	...	...	86 118	52 353	Afrique
East Asia/Pacific		203 465	216 742	264 550	298 395	567 543	Asie de l'Est/Pacifique
Europe		265 965	329 059	406 725	730 034[54]	1 079 523[54]	Europe
Middle East		361 139	628 440	679 859	404 406	827 866	Moyen-Orient
Region not specified		133 004	230 609	307 435	...	...	Région non spécifiée
Republic of Korea	VFN						**République de Corée**
Total[2,55]		6 448 240	6 890 841	7 817 533	8 797 658	9 794 796	Total[2,55]
Africa		19 211	20 720	22 487	26 892	30 334	Afrique
Americas		716 336	744 615	751 697	813 860	827 383	Amériques
East Asia/Pacific		4 696 553	5 035 806	6 029 612	6 769 195	7 678 884	Asie de l'Est/Pacifique
Europe		605 440	645 748	645 624	708 948	752 961	Europe
Middle East		15 859	18 208	19 759	24 574	29 340	Moyen-Orient
South Asia		100 662	118 036	113 740	134 503	148 431	Asie du Sud
Region not specified		294 179	307 708	234 614	319 686	327 463	Région non spécifiée
Republic of Moldova	VFN						**République de Moldova**
Total[56]		14 722	8 710	9 189	8 956	10 788	Total[56]
Africa		7	...	2	2	14	Afrique
Americas		580	305	232	524	651	Amériques
East Asia/Pacific		293	188	107	162	545	Asie de l'Est/Pacifique
Europe		13 794	8 209	8 837	8 229	9 559	Europe
Middle East		27	4	5	24	10	Moyen-Orient
South Asia		21	4	6	15	9	Asie du Sud
Réunion	TFR						**Réunion**
Total[57]		381 547	396 400	421 900	420 300	471 300	Total[57]
Africa		33 245	20 800	20 300	18 400	18 200	Afrique
Americas		1 721	...	...	...	...	Amériques
East Asia/Pacific		2 491	...	...	...	...	Asie de l'Est/Pacifique
Europe		304 307	328 200	359 700	363 400	401 200	Europe
South Asia		418	...	...	...	...	Asie du Sud
Region not specified		39 365	47 400	41 900	38 500	51 900	Région non spécifiée
Romania	VFR						**Roumanie**
Total		7 721 741	8 862 119	7 575 298	7 498 307	7 611 124	Total
Africa		10 701	12 638	12 803	14 464	15 568	Afrique
Americas		188 807	191 709	168 744	170 757	182 169	Amériques
East Asia/Pacific		79 998	97 417	70 145	79 098	92 027	Asie de l'Est/Pacifique
Europe		7 394 449	8 506 343	7 278 936	7 179 264	7 266 677	Europe
Middle East		29 195	31 793	26 520	33 482	33 500	Moyen-Orient
South Asia		17 106	20 500	17 083	20 825	20 710	Asie du Sud
Region not specified		1 485	1 719	1 067	417	473	Région non spécifiée

Country or area of destination and region of origin	Series[&] Série[&]	2007	2008	2009	2010	2011	Pays ou zone de destination et région de provenance
Russian Federation	VFN						**Fédération de Russie**
Total		22 908 625	23 676 140	21 338 650	22 281 217	...	Total
Africa		29 964	35 734	34 649	36 833	...	Afrique
Americas		466 404	503 456	469 112	420 512	...	Amériques
East Asia/Pacific		1 381 412	1 477 644	1 294 719	1 358 186	...	Asie de l'Est/Pacifique
Europe		20 395 436	21 186 817	18 790 566	19 568 815	...	Europe
Middle East		23 998	38 839	38 009	41 496	...	Moyen-Orient
South Asia		100 150	96 376	93 311	89 407	...	Asie du Sud
Region not specified		511 261	337 274	618 284	765 968	...	Région non spécifiée
Rwanda	VFN						**Rwanda**
Total		609 662	668 524	693 608	666 001	...	Total
Africa		515 543	556 943	590 720	546 904	...	Afrique
Americas		23 349	31 043	28 116	33 189	...	Amériques
East Asia/Pacific		6 130	7 063	8 059	10 521	...	Asie de l'Est/Pacifique
Europe		40 463	49 130	46 968	54 253	...	Europe
Middle East		1 270	3 366	2 104	2 784	...	Moyen-Orient
South Asia		22 746	19 232	16 931	17 794	...	Asie du Sud
Region not specified		161	1 747	710	556	...	Région non spécifiée
Saba	TFR						**Saba**
Total		11 658	12 043	11 957	12 327	...	Total
Americas		5 672	6 388	5 856	5 990	...	Amériques
Europe		5 236	5 655	6 101	6 337	...	Europe
Region not specified		750	...	...	...	...	Région non spécifiée
Saint Eustatius	TFR						**Saint-Eustache**
Total[58]		11 568	11 758	12 049	11 393	...	Total[58]
Americas		3 928	3 762	3 622	3 484	...	Amériques
Europe		5 893	6 201	6 652	6 356	...	Europe
Region not specified		1 747	1 795	1 775	1 553	...	Région non spécifiée
Saint Kitts and Nevis	TFR						**Saint-Kitts-et-Nevis**
Total[4]		123 062	127 705	93 081	91 561	...	Total[4]
Americas		105 832	113 242	83 233	80 307	...	Amériques
Europe		12 162	9 970	6 496	7 655	...	Europe
Region not specified		5 068	4 493	3 352	3 599	...	Région non spécifiée
Saint Lucia	TFR						**Sainte-Lucie**
Total[1]		287 407	295 761	278 491	305 937	312 404	Total[1]
Americas		192 018	197 750	189 805	216 734	219 754	Amériques
East Asia/Pacific		212	152	207	183	224	Asie de l'Est/Pacifique
Europe		89 647	93 601	84 238	85 695	91 759	Europe
Region not specified		5 530	4 258	4 241	3 325	667	Région non spécifiée
Saint Maarten	TFN						**Saint-Martin**
Total[59,60]		469 407	475 410	440 185	443 136	424 340	Total[59,60]
Americas		335 410	336 013	309 659	307 871	291 734	Amériques
Europe		96 365	102 713	98 341	101 118	101 712	Europe
Region not specified		37 632	36 684	32 185	34 147	30 894	Région non spécifiée
Saint Vincent-Grenadines	TFR						**Saint Vincent-Grenadines**
Total[4]		89 637	84 101	75 446	72 478	73 866	Total[4]
Americas		64 518	60 549	55 424	53 933	52 391	Amériques
Europe		23 454	22 302	19 097	17 665	20 549	Europe
Region not specified		1 665	1 250	925	880	926	Région non spécifiée
Samoa	VFR						**Samoa**
Total		122 356	122 163	129 305	129 500	127 603	Total
Americas		8 492	8 893	9 794	9 238	7 875	Amériques
East Asia/Pacific		109 132	107 580	113 425	115 163	114 798	Asie de l'Est/Pacifique
Europe		4 420	5 091	5 547	4 658	4 055	Europe
Region not specified		312	599	539	441	875	Région non spécifiée
San Marino	VFN						**Saint-Marin**
Total[61]		2 164 419	2 111 736	2 055 705	1 976 481	2 038 359	Total[61]
Africa		193	188	130	275	206	Afrique
Americas		36 690	18 669	12 063	12 142	19 225	Amériques
East Asia/Pacific		26 475	17 411	18 790	18 386	19 930	Asie de l'Est/Pacifique
Europe		2 099 431	2 074 061	2 023 438	1 944 198	1 997 416	Europe
Middle East		696	272	393	457	469	Moyen-Orient
South Asia		693	379	130	364	428	Asie du Sud
Region not specified		241	756	761	659	685	Région non spécifiée

57 Tourist/visitor arrivals by region of origin *(continued)*
Number
Arrivées de touristes/visiteurs par région de provenance *(suite)*
Nombre

Country or area of destination and region of origin	Series[&] Série[&]	2007	2008	2009	2010	2011	Pays ou zone de destination et région de provenance
Sao Tome and Principe	TFN						**Sao Tomé-et-Principe**
Total		11 815	14 456	...	7 963	...	Total
Africa		2 199	2 460	...	2 123	...	Afrique
Americas		293	411	...	489	...	Amériques
East Asia/Pacific		...	...	...	85	...	Asie de l'Est/Pacifique
Europe		3 974	6 348	...	5 090	...	Europe
Middle East		...	...	...	27	...	Moyen-Orient
South Asia		...	...	...	5	...	Asie du Sud
Region not specified		5 349	5 237	...	144	...	Région non spécifiée
Saudi Arabia	TFN						**Arabie saoudite**
Total		11 530 834	14 757 444	10 896 712	10 850 188	17 497 890	Total
Africa		601 614	1 033 258	260 717	368 610	790 301	Afrique
Americas		235 900	297 143	56 841	53 432	182 108	Amériques
East Asia/Pacific		578 805	940 928	362 500	485 534	844 723	Asie de l'Est/Pacifique
Europe		656 937	1 185 068	444 667	367 238	722 534	Europe
Middle East		7 443 786	9 333 965	8 677 688	8 244 721	11 098 731	Moyen-Orient
South Asia		2 013 792	1 967 082	1 094 282	1 330 271	3 858 203	Asie du Sud
Region not specified		...	...	17	382	1 290	Région non spécifiée
Senegal	TFN						**Sénégal**
Total		874 623	491 552[2,62]	458 912[2,62]	492 261[2,62]	449 954[2,62]	Total
Africa		437 970	121 286	111 525	114 623	107 990	Afrique
Americas		26 004	17 783	18 942	19 958	18 366	Amériques
Europe		324 080	280 044	263 657	271 324	257 208	Europe
Region not specified		86 569	72 439	64 788	86 356	66 390	Région non spécifiée
Serbia	TCEN						**Serbie**
Total		696 045	646 494	645 022	682 681	764 167	Total
Americas		19 083	15 002	16 266	18 554	19 180	Amériques
East Asia/Pacific		7 433	7 826	8 160	9 903	12 193	Asie de l'Est/Pacifique
Europe		655 782	610 004	602 599	632 964	710 757	Europe
Region not specified		13 747	13 662	17 997	21 260	22 037	Région non spécifiée
Seychelles	TFR						**Seychelles**
Total		161 273	158 952	157 541	174 529	194 476	Total
Africa		16 847	19 117	18 499	22 163	24 422	Afrique
Americas		3 915	4 163	4 541	3 960	4 730	Amériques
East Asia/Pacific		3 793	3 486	3 523	4 179	5 664	Asie de l'Est/Pacifique
Europe		130 046	124 828	122 322	132 254	144 144	Europe
Middle East		4 930	5 489	6 422	8 332	12 176	Moyen-Orient
South Asia		1 742	1 869	2 234	3 641	3 340	Asie du Sud
Sierra Leone	TFR						**Sierra Leone**
Total[4]		33 421	35 670	36 775	38 615	52 442	Total[4]
Africa		10 846	11 915	12 614	10 806	15 885	Afrique
Americas		6 169	6 684	7 238	7 406	10 707	Amériques
East Asia/Pacific		2 916	3 142	4 068	6 261	9 024	Asie de l'Est/Pacifique
Europe		11 327	12 713	10 574	10 295	13 807	Europe
Middle East		965	888	1 750	2 667	1 562	Moyen-Orient
South Asia		...	...	...	1 180	1 457	Asie du Sud
Region not specified		1 198	328	531	...	...	Région non spécifiée
Singapore	VFR						**Singapour**
Total[63]		10 284 545	10 116 054	9 682 690	11 641 701	13 171 303	Total[63]
Africa		93 600	86 023	72 348	70 436	69 561	Afrique
Americas		524 178	505 411	467 723	524 846	563 742	Amériques
East Asia/Pacific		7 322 529	7 070 353	6 785 096	8 474 870	9 887 028	Asie de l'Est/Pacifique
Europe		1 276 669	1 333 652	1 318 260	1 386 361	1 413 639	Europe
Middle East		78 353	87 690	85 709	101 461	113 551	Moyen-Orient
South Asia		968 389	1 026 576	953 364	1 083 673	1 123 649	Asie du Sud
Region not specified		20 827	6 349	190	54	133	Région non spécifiée
Slovakia	TCEN						**Slovaquie**
Total		1 684 526	1 766 529	1 298 075	1 326 639	1 460 361	Total
Africa		2 276	3 318	1 946	2 684	2 926	Afrique
Americas		43 697	41 456	30 137	36 198	43 172	Amériques
East Asia/Pacific		73 658	70 755	53 748	65 064	72 073	Asie de l'Est/Pacifique
Europe		1 558 688	1 647 872	1 209 816	1 219 740	1 336 504	Europe
Middle East		3 592	533	516	551	579	Moyen-Orient
South Asia		1 229	1 380	1 290	1 495	2 537	Asie du Sud
Region not specified		1 386	1 215	622	907	2 570	Région non spécifiée
Slovenia	TCEN						**Slovénie**
Total		1 751 332	1 957 691[64]	1 823 931	1 869 106	2 036 652	Total
Africa		2 100	3 760	2 911	3 396	4 437	Afrique
Americas		66 900	65 701	55 336	61 941	67 613	Amériques
East Asia/Pacific		65 277	85 552	90 168	94 653	106 067	Asie de l'Est/Pacifique
Europe		1 617 055	1 802 678	1 675 516	1 709 116	1 858 535	Europe

57 Tourist/visitor arrivals by region of origin *(continued)*
Number
Arrivées de touristes/visiteurs par région de provenance *(suite)*
Nombre

Country or area of destination and region of origin	Series[&] Série[&]	2007	2008	2009	2010	2011	Pays ou zone de destination et région de provenance
Solomon Islands	TFR						**Iles Salomon**
Total		13 748	16 264	18 308	20 521	22 941	Total
Americas		1 048	1 220	1 122	975	1 232	Amériques
East Asia/Pacific		11 628	13 772	15 886	18 255	20 480	Asie de l'Est/Pacifique
Europe		925	1 132	1 091	1 014	941	Europe
Region not specified		147	140	209	277	288	Région non spécifiée
South Africa	TFR						**Afrique du Sud**
Total		9 090 881[65]	9 564 207[65]	7 011 865[3]	8 073 552	8 339 354	Total
Africa		6 862 105	7 343 765	5 083 145	5 733 499	6 129 606	Afrique
Americas		387 379	407 408	333 528	458 249	433 135	Amériques
East Asia/Pacific		281 567	243 036	216 051	293 141	304 704	Asie de l'Est/Pacifique
Europe		1 438 092	1 433 586	1 248 467	1 354 579	1 306 794	Europe
Middle East		20 954	23 412	19 262	21 151	20 168	Moyen-Orient
South Asia		51 823	51 929	74 938	97 552	119 147	Asie du Sud
Region not specified		48 961	61 071	36 474	115 381	25 800	Région non spécifiée
Spain	TFR						**Espagne**
Total		58 665 505	57 192 015	52 177 640	52 676 972	56 694 298	Total
Africa		...	...	267 458	302 420	535 022	Afrique
Americas		2 312 521	2 397 782	2 573 760	2 617 572	2 872 302	Amériques
East Asia/Pacific		346 047	237 493	504 634	961 998	1 076 525	Asie de l'Est/Pacifique
Europe		54 926 634	53 512 149	48 204 400	48 290 225	51 901 874	Europe
Middle East		...	...	...	68 276	104 851	Moyen-Orient
South Asia		...	...	...	29 615	74 538	Asie du Sud
Region not specified		1 080 303	1 044 591	627 388	406 866	129 186	Région non spécifiée
Sri Lanka	TFR						**Sri Lanka**
Total[1]		494 008	438 475	447 820	654 476	855 975	Total[1]
Africa		2 712	2 141	1 479	2 308	3 614	Afrique
Americas		32 317	28 050	25 565	40 836	50 093	Amériques
East Asia/Pacific		75 778	66 783	74 397	105 720	142 661	Asie de l'Est/Pacifique
Europe		222 669	199 601	198 897	296 961	371 794	Europe
Middle East		10 568	11 672	20 007	31 057	47 943	Moyen-Orient
South Asia		149 964	130 228	127 475	177 594	239 870	Asie du Sud
Sudan (former)	TFN						**Soudan (anc.)**
Total[10]		436 295	439 661	420 370	495 158	536 400	Total[10]
Africa		65 444	65 949	59 802	49 516	53 640	Afrique
Americas		15 526	15 388	21 000	19 806	21 456	Amériques
East Asia/Pacific		296 680	298 969	239 920	29 709	32 184	Asie de l'Est/Pacifique
Europe		56 718	57 156	99 648	74 274	80 460	Europe
Middle East		...	...	...	272 338	295 020	Moyen-Orient
South Asia		...	...	...	39 612	42 912	Asie du Sud
Region not specified		1 927	2 199	...	9 903	10 728	Région non spécifiée
Suriname	TFR						**Suriname**
Total		166 685	150 711	150 628	204 519	220 475	Total
Africa		225	183	171	246	290	Afrique
Americas		52 373	51 386	59 175	88 680	103 709	Amériques
East Asia/Pacific		2 397	2 732	1 940	3 382	4 838	Asie de l'Est/Pacifique
Europe		110 730	95 299	87 817	110 255	108 188	Europe
Middle East		25	30	19	47	42	Moyen-Orient
South Asia		484	551	454	556	585	Asie du Sud
Region not specified		451	530	1 052	1 353	2 823	Région non spécifiée
Swaziland	VFR						**Swaziland**
Total		1 230 093	1 185 998	1 343 967	1 342 531	1 328 363	Total
Africa		1 075 005	1 041 211	1 191 259	1 218 054	1 225 220	Afrique
Americas		19 184	19 607	20 187	20 499	18 826	Amériques
East Asia/Pacific		12 009	11 779	10 945	11 061	9 826	Asie de l'Est/Pacifique
Europe		118 536	107 712	114 047	85 195	66 930	Europe
Middle East		...	...	218	213	91	Moyen-Orient
South Asia		5 359	5 689	7 311	7 509	7 470	Asie du Sud
Swaziland	THSR						**Swaziland**
Total		299 226	323 538	334 391	338 032	308 389	Total
Africa		176 417	186 884	201 585	257 997	235 377	Afrique
Americas		9 832	21 503	14 105	19 557	17 114	Amériques
East Asia/Pacific		8 044	12 035	13 196	6 158	5 618	Asie de l'Est/Pacifique
Europe		92 332	103 116	105 505	54 320	49 553	Europe
Region not specified		12 601	...	...	...	727	Région non spécifiée

57

Tourist/visitor arrivals by region of origin *(continued)*
Number
Arrivées de touristes/visiteurs par région de provenance *(suite)*
Nombre

Country or area of destination and region of origin	Series[&] Série[&]	2007	2008	2009	2010	2011	Pays ou zone de destination et région de provenance
Sweden	VFR						**Suède**
Total [66]		...	...	...	...	16 678 000	Total [66]
Africa		...	...	...	...	44 000	Afrique
Americas		...	...	...	...	650 000	Amériques
East Asia/Pacific		...	...	...	...	311 000	Asie de l'Est/Pacifique
Europe		...	...	...	...	15 582 000	Europe
Middle East		...	...	...	...	45 000	Moyen-Orient
South Asia		...	...	...	...	44 000	Asie du Sud
Region not specified		...	...	...	...	2 000	Région non spécifiée
Sweden	TCER						**Suède**
Total		5 223 655	4 554 936	4 678 402	4 951 122	5 005 825	Total
Americas		260 141	239 202	212 567	257 437	272 807	Amériques
East Asia/Pacific		199 248	216 443	182 862	216 885	257 236	Asie de l'Est/Pacifique
Europe		4 424 536	3 847 867	4 005 127	4 143 159	4 048 017	Europe
Region not specified		339 730	251 424	277 846	333 641	427 765	Région non spécifiée
Switzerland	THSR						**Suisse**
Total [67]		8 447 718	8 608 337	8 293 918	8 628 284	8 534 305	Total [67]
Africa		85 463	88 625	79 919	77 745	74 107	Afrique
Americas		954 115	878 356	820 495	916 493	924 383	Amériques
East Asia/Pacific		941 200	860 776	893 139	1 096 300	1 322 811	Asie de l'Est/Pacifique
Europe		6 225 587	6 520 802	6 249 760	6 237 359	5 867 915	Europe
Middle East		108 957	127 671	114 283	134 388	144 465	Moyen-Orient
South Asia		132 396	132 107	136 322	165 999	200 624	Asie du Sud
Syrian Arab Republic	VFN						**Rép. arabe syrienne**
Total [2,68]		5 434 253	6 950 852	7 720 795	10 969 682	...	Total [2,68]
Africa		77 526	85 242	76 245	89 670	...	Afrique
Americas		59 584	75 375	84 293	96 601	...	Amériques
East Asia/Pacific		43 487	52 913	60 349	78 102	...	Asie de l'Est/Pacifique
Europe		731 744	904 726	1 141 584	1 959 035	...	Europe
Middle East		3 123 927	4 390 535	4 711 686	6 191 855	...	Moyen-Orient
South Asia		355 530	388 819	499 183	961 342	...	Asie du Sud
Region not specified		1 042 455	1 053 242	1 147 455	1 593 077	...	Région non spécifiée
Syrian Arab Republic	TCEN						**Rép. arabe syrienne**
Total [2,68,69]		4 157 814	5 430 182	6 091 889	8 545 848	...	Total [2,68,69]
Africa		69 117	75 953	68 159	79 745	...	Afrique
Americas		54 738	69 575	77 621	84 195	...	Amériques
East Asia/Pacific		40 915	49 521	56 937	66 696	...	Asie de l'Est/Pacifique
Europe		486 063	618 272	772 031	1 305 301	...	Europe
Middle East		2 162 649	3 235 057	3 522 115	4 574 783	...	Moyen-Orient
South Asia		325 135	355 431	467 012	853 065	...	Asie du Sud
Region not specified		1 019 197	1 026 373	1 128 014	1 582 063	...	Région non spécifiée
Tajikistan	VFR						**Tadjikistan**
Total		...	325 420	207 439	159 680	183 154	Total
Africa		...	27	129	188	...	Afrique
Americas		...	1 265	1 334	1 465	587	Amériques
East Asia/Pacific		...	2 919	3 384	3 546	4 280	Asie de l'Est/Pacifique
Europe		...	309 659	188 760	139 902	167 069	Europe
Middle East		...	225	202	170	56	Moyen-Orient
South Asia		...	11 325	13 630	14 409	11 162	Asie du Sud
Thailand	TFR						**Thaïlande**
Total [1]		14 464 228	14 584 220	14 149 841	15 936 400	19 230 470	Total [1]
Africa		104 935	108 890	107 837	121 816	141 255	Afrique
Americas		817 579	853 348	795 110	792 190	885 598	Amériques
East Asia/Pacific		8 711 866	8 626 039	7 994 238	9 091 305	11 480 750	Asie de l'Est/Pacifique
Europe		3 812 711	3 963 326	4 031 256	4 445 544	5 058 583	Europe
Middle East		265 327	282 878	298 079	331 253	379 382	Moyen-Orient
South Asia		750 658	749 739	923 321	1 152 890	1 284 902	Asie du Sud
Region not specified		1 152	...	...	1 402	...	Région non spécifiée
TFYR of Macedonia	TCEN						**L'ex-R.Y. Macédoine**
Total		230 080	254 957	259 204	261 696	327 471	Total
Africa		...	...	...	228	408	Afrique
Americas		8 947	9 632	9 083	9 724	10 744	Amériques
East Asia/Pacific		4 799	4 674	4 255	10 331	12 153	Asie de l'Est/Pacifique
Europe		212 365	236 122	240 333	241 413	304 166	Europe
Region not specified		3 969	4 529	5 533	...	...	Région non spécifiée

57

Tourist/visitor arrivals by region of origin *(continued)*
Number
Arrivées de touristes/visiteurs par région de provenance *(suite)*
Nombre

Country or area of destination and region of origin	Series[&] Série[&]	2007	2008	2009	2010	2011	Pays ou zone de destination et région de provenance
Timor-Leste	TFR						**Timor-Leste**
Total[70]		22 254	35 999	44 131	39 825	50 590	Total[70]
Americas		1 950	2 879	3 402	2 523	3 185	Amériques
East Asia/Pacific		12 163	20 707	26 269	28 101	34 766	Asie de l'Est/Pacifique
Europe		3 639	5 117	6 066	1 925	6 918	Europe
South Asia		530	834	2 351	2 426	1 900	Asie du Sud
Region not specified		3 972	6 462	6 043	4 850	3 821	Région non spécifiée
Togo	THSR						**Togo**
Total		86 165	73 982	149 945	202 044	300 479	Total
Africa		48 516	38 792	76 496	110 821	135 683	Afrique
Americas		2 928	2 405	5 727	5 921	7 959	Amériques
East Asia/Pacific		2 649	3 269	6 002	9 578	11 075	Asie de l'Est/Pacifique
Europe		31 181	29 376	61 385	75 136	144 043	Europe
Middle East		772	66	166	374	1 224	Moyen-Orient
Region not specified		119	74	169	214	495	Région non spécifiée
Tonga	TFR						**Tonga**
Total[4]		46 040	49 400	50 645	45 430	46 005	Total[4]
Africa		...	...	...	...	42	Afrique
Americas		6 348	6 223	7 113	6 211	5 942	Amériques
East Asia/Pacific		36 524	39 499	39 137	36 092	36 814	Asie de l'Est/Pacifique
Europe		2 868	3 478	4 248	3 001	3 176	Europe
South Asia		...	...	...	...	31	Asie du Sud
Region not specified		300	200	147	126	...	Région non spécifiée
Trinidad and Tobago	TFR						**Trinité-et-Tobago**
Total[4]		449 453	437 279	418 864	385 510	...	Total[4]
Africa		1 509	1 349	1 823	1 159	...	Afrique
Americas		356 180	364 524	351 216	325 384	...	Amériques
East Asia/Pacific		5 767	5 190	5 394	4 582	...	Asie de l'Est/Pacifique
Europe		82 511	63 238	57 667	52 364	...	Europe
Middle East		440	462	468	390	...	Moyen-Orient
South Asia		3 009	2 329	2 267	1 620	...	Asie du Sud
Region not specified		37	187	29	11	...	Région non spécifiée
Tunisia	TFN						**Tunisie**
Total[1]		6 761 906	7 050 434	6 901 406	6 902 749	4 785 119	Total[1]
Africa		1 045 637	1 043 121	1 036 070	1 136 066	829 254	Afrique
Americas		36 450	38 877	39 369	39 195	24 098	Amériques
East Asia/Pacific		16 702	16 472	17 016	20 997	16 344	Asie de l'Est/Pacifique
Europe		4 048 429	4 106 676	3 743 509	3 814 402	2 133 916	Europe
Middle East		1 581 512	1 809 090	2 034 494	1 862 630	1 730 832	Moyen-Orient
Region not specified		33 176	36 198	30 948	29 459	50 675	Région non spécifiée
Turkey	TFN						**Turquie**
Total[2,71]		26 122 405	29 637 309	30 434 819	31 395 548	34 038 448	Total[2,71]
Africa		157 637	188 601	273 242	227 603	283 069	Afrique
Americas		585 269	612 166	602 791	561 823	673 738	Amériques
East Asia/Pacific		586 786	578 201	568 632	639 550	732 984	Asie de l'Est/Pacifique
Europe		18 727 704	21 420 018	21 444 637	21 604 344	23 434 797	Europe
Middle East		922 867	1 151 388	1 413 299	1 869 231	2 100 995	Moyen-Orient
South Asia		924 721	1 114 440	1 446 493	1 952 485	1 959 407	Asie du Sud
Region not specified		4 217 421	4 572 495	4 685 725	4 540 512	4 853 458	Région non spécifiée
Turkmenistan	TFN						**Turkménistan**
Total		8 177	...	...	...	...	Total
Africa		13	...	...	...	...	Afrique
Americas		775	...	...	...	...	Amériques
East Asia/Pacific		943	...	...	...	...	Asie de l'Est/Pacifique
Europe		4 296	...	...	...	...	Europe
Middle East		7	...	...	...	...	Moyen-Orient
South Asia		2 143	...	...	...	...	Asie du Sud
Turks and Caicos Islands	TFR						**Iles Turques et Caïques**
Total		...	...	...	...	354 223	Total
Americas		...	...	...	...	344 337	Amériques
Europe		...	...	...	...	6 902	Europe
Region not specified		...	...	...	...	2 984	Région non spécifiée
Tuvalu	TFN						**Tuvalu**
Total		1 130	1 651	1 580	1 657	1 232	Total
Americas		65	79	83	97	94	Amériques
East Asia/Pacific		851	1 320	1 267	1 288	909	Asie de l'Est/Pacifique
Europe		87	136	143	134	81	Europe
Region not specified		127	116	87	138	148	Région non spécifiée

Country or area of destination and region of origin	Series& Série&	2007	2008	2009	2010	2011	Pays ou zone de destination et région de provenance
Uganda	TFR						**Ouganda**
Total		641 743	843 864	806 655	945 899	1 151 356	Total
Africa		479 802	624 352	630 014	675 931	873 348	Afrique
Americas		42 388	53 950	47 065	65 175	59 477	Amériques
East Asia/Pacific		14 466	14 687	19 357	28 163	29 899	Asie de l'Est/Pacifique
Europe		77 283	106 020	79 710	112 870	154 542	Europe
Middle East		4 971	9 720	8 942	15 538	8 652	Moyen-Orient
South Asia		14 803	18 845	14 937	18 898	21 755	Asie du Sud
Region not specified		8 030	16 290	6 630	29 324	3 683	Région non spécifiée
Ukraine	TFR						**Ukraine**
Total		23 122 157	25 449 078	20 798 342	21 203 327	21 415 296	Total
Africa		10 216	9 789	10 252	12 219	14 977	Afrique
Americas		167 103	163 371	161 412	162 853	165 068	Amériques
East Asia/Pacific		48 651	45 648	43 750	45 652	49 785	Asie de l'Est/Pacifique
Europe		22 825 500	25 163 875	20 514 394	20 911 215	21 117 959	Europe
Middle East		26 308	23 253	27 856	29 059	28 572	Moyen-Orient
South Asia		17 572	17 389	19 871	23 012	21 819	Asie du Sud
Region not specified		26 807	25 753	20 807	19 317	17 116	Région non spécifiée
United Kingdom	VFR						**Royaume-Uni**
Total		32 778 102	31 888 118	29 889 075	29 803 000	30 797 000	Total
Africa		653 917	644 718	596 415	571 000	527 000	Afrique
Americas		4 826 687	4 211 749	4 020 126	3 839 000	4 177 000	Amériques
East Asia/Pacific		2 315 607	2 146 669	2 065 639	2 202 000	2 433 000	Asie de l'Est/Pacifique
Europe		24 020 354	23 826 127	22 241 150	22 203 000	22 604 000	Europe
Middle East		489 559	537 585	596 237	529 000	589 000	Moyen-Orient
South Asia		471 978	521 270	369 508	456 000	467 000	Asie du Sud
Region not specified		...	...	...	3 000	...	Région non spécifiée
United Rep. of Tanzania	VFR						**Rép.-Unie de Tanzanie**
Total		719 031	770 469	714 367	782 699	867 994	Total
Africa		305 748	373 053	348 765	392 137	445 750	Afrique
Americas		80 699	87 835	68 289	70 558	95 503	Amériques
East Asia/Pacific		29 760	32 442	31 013	42 520	39 619	Asie de l'Est/Pacifique
Europe		274 410	245 873	233 559	242 828	249 910	Europe
Middle East		11 444	10 377	11 121	10 521	15 281	Moyen-Orient
South Asia		16 970	20 889	21 620	24 135	21 931	Asie du Sud
United States	TFR						**Etats-Unis**
Total		55 978 277	57 942 451	54 962 184	59 795 616	62 711 157	Total
Africa		276 300	311 136	290 861	311 205	325 989	Afrique
Americas		36 462 985	37 133 338	35 911 508	38 644 479	40 423 276	Amériques
East Asia/Pacific		6 562 889	6 343 399	5 905 954	7 369 149	7 728 449	Asie de l'Est/Pacifique
Europe		11 839 074	13 249 818	11 978 394	12 436 645	13 115 324	Europe
Middle East		195 986	227 629	246 018	296 242	363 024	Moyen-Orient
South Asia		641 043	677 131	629 449	737 896	755 095	Asie du Sud
United States Virgin Is.	THSN						**Iles Vierges américaines**
Total		679 578	740 020	787 153	748 996	680 704	Total
Africa		115	73	69	62	229	Afrique
Americas		651 167	720 276	766 929	731 749	653 183	Amériques
East Asia/Pacific		351	377	318	367	458	Asie de l'Est/Pacifique
Europe		14 837	15 798	16 434	14 393	22 566	Europe
Region not specified		13 108	3 496	3 403	2 425	4 268	Région non spécifiée
Uruguay	VFN						**Uruguay**
Total[2]		1 815 281	1 997 884	2 098 780	2 407 676	2 960 155	Total[2]
Americas		1 406 790	1 544 086	1 643 319	1 888 374	2 401 187	Amériques
East Asia/Pacific		12 855	14 374	17 193	17 327	18 516	Asie de l'Est/Pacifique
Europe		132 636	139 282	140 398	146 774	151 049	Europe
Middle East		234	261	226	567	349	Moyen-Orient
Region not specified		262 766	299 881	297 644	354 634	389 054	Région non spécifiée
Uzbekistan	TFR						**Ouzbékistan**
Total		903 100	1 069 300	1 214 700	974 573	...	Total
Africa		2 000	2 500	100	35	...	Afrique
Americas		8 000	8 000	6 500	1 189	...	Amériques
East Asia/Pacific		442 700	578 600	649 300	768 160	...	Asie de l'Est/Pacifique
Europe		370 400	385 200	333 200	156 766	...	Europe
Middle East		50 000	55 000	66 800	36 839	...	Moyen-Orient
South Asia		30 000	40 000	158 800	11 584	...	Asie du Sud

57

Tourist/visitor arrivals by region of origin *(continued)*
Number
Arrivées de touristes/visiteurs par région de provenance *(suite)*
Nombre

Country or area of destination and region of origin	Series[&] Série[&]	2007	2008	2009	2010	2011	Pays ou zone de destination et région de provenance
Vanuatu	TFR						**Vanuatu**
Total		81 344	90 656	98 648	97 180	93 960	Total
Americas		2 578	2 578	2 405	2 395	1 922	Amériques
East Asia/Pacific		73 214	81 162	89 141	87 333	84 645	Asie de l'Est/Pacifique
Europe		3 785	4 886	4 913	4 888	5 265	Europe
Middle East		...	...	...	...	2 128	Moyen-Orient
Region not specified		1 767	2 030	2 189	2 564	...	Région non spécifiée
Venezuela (Boliv. Rep. of)	TFN						**Venezuela (Rép. boliv. du)**
Total		770 567	744 709	615 188	535 270[72]	625 224[72]	Total
Africa		710	721	736	294	598	Afrique
Americas		420 056	408 219	339 636	320 077	400 313	Amériques
East Asia/Pacific		19 163	19 451	14 897	11 151	13 389	Asie de l'Est/Pacifique
Europe		316 041	301 579	241 431	194 567	195 850	Europe
Middle East		10 309	10 389	8 970	6 946	7 654	Moyen-Orient
South Asia		1 397	1 418	1 698	694	1 382	Asie du Sud
Region not specified		2 891	2 932	7 820	1 541	6 038	Région non spécifiée
Viet Nam	VFR						**Viet Nam**
Total		4 229 300	4 235 800	3 747 400	5 049 800	6 014 000	Total
Americas		497 800	501 600	487 600	533 200	546 300	Amériques
East Asia/Pacific		2 728 300	2 790 800	2 422 300	3 497 700	4 383 600	Asie de l'Est/Pacifique
Europe		619 800	623 500	617 900	757 000	811 600	Europe
Region not specified		383 400	319 900	219 600	261 900	272 500	Région non spécifiée
Yemen	TFN						**Yémen**
Total[2]		948 118	1 022 737	1 028 127	1 024 762	...	Total[2]
Africa		20 181	17 715	23 587	33 387	...	Afrique
Americas		17 615	18 118	25 493	28 006	...	Amériques
East Asia/Pacific		19 668	20 466	26 004	26 222	...	Asie de l'Est/Pacifique
Europe		33 079	36 099	43 493	37 730	...	Europe
Middle East		268 540	293 275	289 737	376 882	...	Moyen-Orient
South Asia		20 307	18 824	25 607	33 793	...	Asie du Sud
Region not specified		568 728	618 240	594 206	488 742	...	Région non spécifiée
Zambia	TFR						**Zambie**
Total		897 413	811 775	709 948	815 164	...	Total
Africa		660 551	606 641	467 045	583 377	...	Afrique
Americas		50 606	47 360	63 089	41 703	...	Amériques
East Asia/Pacific		28 095	34 658	38 542	64 271	...	Asie de l'Est/Pacifique
Europe		145 729	109 182	128 340	104 399	...	Europe
South Asia		12 432	13 934	12 932	21 414	...	Asie du Sud
Zimbabwe	VFR						**Zimbabwe**
Total		2 505 988	1 955 597	2 017 264	2 239 165	2 423 280	Total
Africa		2 289 958	1 731 528	1 678 884	1 951 330	2 041 291	Afrique
Americas		39 747	43 412	57 842	69 008	89 756	Amériques
East Asia/Pacific		57 650	63 194	104 366	84 092	125 257	Asie de l'Est/Pacifique
Europe		112 111	111 121	160 316	128 082	158 141	Europe
Middle East		874	928	5 456	1 758	2 863	Moyen-Orient
South Asia		5 648	5 414	10 400	4 895	5 972	Asie du Sud

Source:
World Tourism Organization (UNWTO), Madrid, UNWTO statistics database and the *Yearbook of Tourism Statistics*, 2012 edition.

[+] For a listing of the Member States of the regions of origin, see Annex I, with the following exceptions:

Africa includes the countries and territories listed under Africa in Annex I but excludes Egypt and Libyan Arab Jamahiriya.
Americas is as shown in Annex I
Europe is as shown in Annex I, but also includes Armenia, Azerbaijan, Cyprus, Georgia, Israel, Kazakhstan, Kyrgyzstan, Tajikistan, Turkey, Turkmenistan and Uzbekistan.
East Asia and the Pacific includes the countries and territories listed under Eastern Asia, South-eastern Asia, and Oceania in Annex I except for Canton and Enderbury Islands, Christmas Island, Cocos Island, Johnston Island, Midway Islands, and Wake Island.
South Asia is as shown in Annex I under South-central Asia, but excludes Kazakhstan, Kyrgyzstan, Tajikistan, Turkmenistan and Uzbekistan.

Source:
Organisation mondiale du tourisme (OMT), Madrid, la base de données de l'OMT, et l'*Annuaire des statistiques du tourisme*, édition 2012.

[+] On se reportera à l'Annexe I pour les États Membres classés dans les différentes régions de provenance, avec les exceptions ci-après :

Afrique – Comprend les États et territoires énumérés dans l'Annexe I, sauf l'Égypte et la Jamahiriya arabe libyenne.
Amériques – Comprend les États et territoires énumérés dans l'Annexe I.
Europe – Comprend les États et territoires énumérés dans l'Annexe I, mais comprend en revanche l'Arménie, l'Azerbaïdjan, Chypre, la Géorgie, l'Israël, le Kazakhstan, le Kirghizistan, le Tadjikistan, la Turquie, le Turkménistan, et l'Ouzbékistan.
L'Asie de l'Est et le Pacifique– Comprend les États et territoires énumérés dans l'Annexe I dans les Groupes Asie de l'Est, Asie du Sud-est et Océanie sauf les îles Canton et Enderbury, l'île Christmas, les îles Cocos, l'île Johnston, les îles Midway, Nauru, et l'île Wake.
Asie du Sud – Comprend les États et territoires énumérés dans l'Annexe I dans le

Middle east is as shown in Annex I under Western Asia, but excludes Armenia, Azerbaijan, Cyprus, Georgia, Israel, and Turkey. The Western Asia group also includes Egypt and the Libyan Arab Jamahiriya.

groupe Asie centrale et du sud, sauf le Kazakhstan, le Kirghizistan, l'Ouzbékistan, le Tadjikistan et le Turkménistan.
Le Moyen-Orient – Comprend les États et territoires énumérés dans l'Annexe I dans le groupe Asie occidentale, sauf l'Arménie, l'Azerbaïdjan, Chypre, la Géorgie, Israël, la Turquie. Le Groupe comprend en revanche l'Égypte et la Jamahiriya arabe libyenne.

&Series:

TFN: Arrivals of non-resident tourists at national borders (excluding same-day visitors), by nationality.
TFR: Arrivals of non-resident tourists at national borders (excluding same- day visitors), by country of residence.
TCEN: Arrivals of non-resident tourists in all types of accommodation establishments, by nationality.
TCER: Arrivals of non-resident tourists in all types of accommodation establishments, by country of residence.
THSN: Arrivals of non-resident tourists in hotels and similar establishments, by nationality.
THSR: Arrivals of non-resident tourists in hotels and similar establishments, by country of residence.
VFN: Arrivals of non-resident visitors at national borders (including tourists and same-day visitors), by nationality.
VFR: Arrivals of non-resident visitors at national borders (including tourists and same-day visitors), by country of residence.

&Série :

TFN :   Arrivées de touristes non résidents aux frontières nationales (à l'exclusion de visiteurs de la journée), par nationalité.
TFR :   Arrivées de touristes non résidents aux frontières nationales (à l'exclusion de visiteurs de la journée), par pays de résidence.
TCEN : Arrivées de touristes non résidents dans tous les types d'établissements d'hébergement, par nationalité.
TCER : Arrivées de touristes non résidents dans tous les types d'établissements d'hébergement, par pays de résidence.
THSN : Arrivées de touristes non résidents dans les hôtels et établissements assimilés, par nationalité.
THSR : Arrivées de touristes non résidents dans les hôtels et établissements assimilés, par pays de résidence.
VFN :   Arrivées de visiteurs non résidents aux frontières nationales (y compris touristes et visiteurs de la journée), par nationalité.
VFR :   Arrivées de visiteurs non résidents aux frontières nationales (y compris touristes et visiteurs de la journée), par pays de résidence.

Footnotes on the totals also apply to the other regions.

Les notes sur les totaux s'appliquent aussi aux autres régions.

1   Excluding nationals of the country residing abroad.
2   Arrivals of nationals residing abroad are included in the total and are all accounted for in "region not specified" only.

3   Since 2009 a new methodology has been applied and therefore, the information is not comparable to previous years.

4   Air arrivals.
5   Excluding nationals residing abroad and crew members.

6   Only paid accommodation; excluding stays at friends and relatives and second homes.
7   Organized tourism.
8   Hotels establishments, campings, holiday centres, holiday villages and specific categories of accommodation.
9   Preliminary data.
10   Arrivals of nationals residing abroad are included in the total and are also accounted for in the individual regions.
11   Break in the series due to implementation of improved methodology for distinguishing visitors (tourists) from other travellers.
12   Partial data.
13   For statistical purposes, the data for China do not include those for the Hong Kong Special Administrative Region (Hong Kong SAR), Macao Special Administrative Region (Macao SAR) and Taiwan Province of China.
14   Since 2008, excluding data on non-resident workers, students, etc. Source of data: Public Security Police.

15   Arrivals of foreign travellers at checkpoints of the Administrative Department of Security (DAS). Excluding cruise passengers and the foreign travellers arriving at terrestrial frontier points and that according to the Bank of the Republic were (in thousands):2006: 2 096; 2007: 2 381; 2008: 2 545; 2009: 2 649; 2010: 2 681.

16   Data compiled by country of residence.
17   Source: "Direction Générale de l'Industrie Touristique", surveys 2007

1   A l'exclusion des nationaux du pays résidant à l'étranger.
2   Les arrivées de nationaux résidant à l'étranger sont comprises dans le total, et sont toutes comptabilisées uniquement dans la catégorie Région non spécifiée.
3   À partir de 2009, une nouvelle méthodologie a été apllliquée. L'information n'est donc pas comparable à celle des années précédentes.
4   Arrivées par voie aérienne.
5   A l'exclusion des nationaux du pays résidant à l'étranger et des membres des équipages.
6   Seulement logement payé; sont exclus les séjours chez des amis et membres de la famille et des résidences secondaires.
7   Tourisme organisé.
8   Établissements hôteliers, terrains de camping, centres de vacances, villages de vacances et catégories spécifiques d'hébergement.
9   Données préliminaires.
10   Les arrivées de nationaux résidant à l'étranger sont comprises dans le total, et comptabilisées aussi dans chacune des régions.
11   Rupture de série due à la mise en œuvre d'une méthodologie améliorée qui distingue les visiteurs (touristes) des autres voyageurs.
12   Données partielles.
13   Pour la présentation des statistiques, les données pour la Chine ne comprennent pas la Région Administrative Spéciale de Hong Kong (Hong Kong RAS), la Région Administrative Spéciale de Macao (Macao RAS) et la province de Taiwan.
14   Sont exclues, depuis 2008, les données sur les travailleurs non résidents, étudiants, etc. Source des données: Force de sécurité publique.
15   Arrivées de voyageurs étrangers par des points de contrôle du Département Administratif de Sécurité (DAS). Exclus les passagers en croisière et les voyageurs étrangers arrivés par des points frontaliers terrestres et qui selon la Banque de la République ont été (en milliers) :2006: 2 096; 2007: 2 381; 2008: 2 545; 2009: 2 649; 2010: 2 681.
16   Données compilées par pays de résidence.
17   Source: Direction Générale de l'Industrie Touristique, enquêtes 2007

	to 2010.		à 2010.
18	Air and sea arrivals.	18	Arrivées par voie aérienne et maritime.
19	Excluding arrivals in ports of nautical tourism.	19	À l'exclusion des arrivées dans des ports à tourisme nautique.
20	The arrivals data relate only to three border posts (N'Djili airport in Kinshasa, the Luano airport in Lubumbashi, and the land border-crossing of Kasumbalesa in Katanga province).	20	Les données des entrées ne concernent que 3 postes frontalières (aéroport de N'Djili à Kinshasa ; aéroport de la Luano à Lubumbashi et le poste terrestre de Kasumbalesa de la province du Katanga).
21	Including non-commercial tourism.	21	Y compris le tourisme non commercial.
22	Change of methodology.	22	Changement de méthodologie.
23	Arrivals to Bole airport only.	23	Arrivées à l'aéroport de Bole uniquement.
24	Arrivals through all ports of entry.	24	Arrivées à travers tous les ports d'entrée.
25	Border survey.	25	Enquête aux frontières.
26	Source: DGCIS, Banque de France. Non resident visitor survey (EVE) - results 2010 revised and 2011 provisional.	26	Source: DGCIS, Banque de France.Enquête auprès des visiteurs venant de l'étranger (EVE) – résultats 2010 révisés et 2011 provisoires.
27	Charter tourists only.	27	Arrivées en vols à la demande seulement.
28	From 2008, the information is based on the border survey conducted by the Bank of Greece.	28	A partir de 2008, l'information est basée sur l'enquête aux frontières réalisée par la Banque de Grèce.
29	Air arrivals at Conakry airport.	29	Arrivées par voie aérienne à l'aéroport de Conakry.
30	Arrivals at "Osvaldo Vieira" Airport.	30	Arrivées à l'aéroport "Osvaldo Vieira".
31	Arrivals to Timehri airport only.	31	Arrivées à l'aéroport de Timehri seulement.
32	Excluding tourists arrivals by sea.	32	Sont exclus les arrivées de touristes par voie maritime.
33	Seasonal and border workers are excluded.	33	A l'exclusion des travailleurs saisonniers et frontaliers.
34	Tarawa and Christmas Island.	34	Tarawa et Ile Christmas.
35	Non-resident departures. Survey of persons crossing the state border.	35	Départs de non-résidents. Enquête menée auprès de personnes franchissant la frontière de l'État.
36	Excluding Syrian nationals, Palestinians and students.	36	A l'exclusion des ressortissants syriens, palestiniens et sous-études.
37	Departures.	37	Départs.
38	Including Singapore residents crossing the frontier by road through the Johore Causeway.	38	Y compris les résidents de Singapour traversant la frontière par voie terrestre à travers le Johore Causeway.
39	Data based on departures by air and sea.	39	Données tirées des départs par voies aérienne et maritime.
40	Including French overseas departments and territories.	40	Y compris les départements et territoires français d'outremer.
41	Arrivals in the States of Kosrae, Chuuk, Pohnpei and Yap.	41	Arrivées dans les États de Kosrae, Chuuk, Pohnpei et Yap.
42	Change of methodology. Until 2007 the data correspond only to 12 border posts. From 2008, the data of all the border posts of the country are used.	42	Changement de méthodologie. Jusqu'en 2007, les données correspondent seulement à 12 postes frontaliers. A partir de 2008, les données de tous les postes frontaliers du pays sont utilisées.
43	Including tourist arrivals through border entry points to Yangon.	43	Comprenant les arrivées de touristes aux postes-frontières de Yangon.
44	Data regarding short term movements are compiled from a random sample of passenger declarations.	44	Les données relatives aux mouvements de courte durée sont obtenues à partir d'un échantillon aléatoire de déclarations des passagers.
45	Including Niuans usually residing in New Zealand.	45	Y compris les nationaux de Niue résidant habituellement en Nouvelle-Zélande.
46	Figures are based on the guest survey carried out by the Institute of Transport Economics.	46	Les chiffres se fondent sur "l'enquête auprès de la clientèle" de l'Institut d'économie des transports.
47	Air arrivals (Palau International Airport).	47	Arrivées par voie aérienne (Aéroport international de Palau).
48	Total number of visitors broken down by permanent residence who arrived in Panama at Tocumen International Airport.	48	Nombre total de visiteurs arrivées au Panama par l'aéroport international de Tocúmen.
49	E/D cards in the "Silvio Petirossi" airport and passenger counts at the national border crossings - National Police and SENATUR.	49	Cartes d'embarquement et de débarquement à l'aéroport Silvio Petirossi et comptages des passagers lors du franchissement des frontières nationales – Police Nationale et SENATUR.
50	Since Poland joined the Schengen area, precise counting of incoming traffic is not possible. Data presented here are based on surveys by the Institute of Tourism. Only approximate results for main countries can be given.	50	Depuis que la Pologne est entrée dans l'espace Schengen, le comptage précis du trafic entrant n'est pas possible. Les données présentées ici sont basées sur les enquêtes de l'Institut du Tourisme. Seuls des résultats approximatifs des principaux pays peuvent être fournis.
51	Fiscal year July to June.	51	Année fiscale de juillet à juin.
52	Arrivals at hotels only.	52	Arrivées dans les hôtels uniquement.
53	Including domestic tourism.	53	Y compris le tourisme interne.
54	Europe and Americas.	54	Europe et Amériques.
55	Including crew members.	55	Y compris les membres d'équipage.
56	Visitors who have benefited from tourism services provided by the tourism agencies and tour operators (titulars of tourism licences). Excluding the left side of the river Nistru and the municipality of Bender.	56	Visiteurs qui ont bénéficié des services touristiques des agences de tourisme et des voyagistes (titulaires d'une licence touristique). À l'exception de la rive gauche de la rivière Nistru et de la municipalité de Bender.
57	Source: INSEE: Survey on Tourism Flows.	57	Source: INSEE - Enquête flux touristiques.

58	Excluding Netherlands Antillean residents.
59	Arrivals at Princess Juliana International airport.
60	Including visitors to Saint Martin (the French side of the island).
61	Including Italian visitors.
62	Arrivals by air at Léopold Sédar Senghor (LSS) only. Country estimated totals: 2008: 866 700; 2009: 810 000; 2010: 900 000; 2011: 1 001 000.
63	Excluding Malaysian citizens arriving by land.
64	New methodology of accommodation survey.
65	Excluding arrivals by work and contract workers.
66	Data for 2011 according to new national border survey (IBIS, Incoming Visitors to Sweden). No data collected during 2004 to 2010. The new border survey (IBIS) started in 2011. Source: Swedish Agency for Economic and Regional Growth.
67	Including health establishments.
68	Survey of the incoming tourism in 2004, 2006 and 2007.
69	Excluding private accommodation.
70	Arrivals by air at Dili Airport.
71	Departing visitors survey carrying out at departure gates.
72	Including cruise passengers 2010: 9 105; 2011: 30 543.

58	A l'exclusion des résidents des Antilles Néerlandaises.
59	Arrivées à l'aéroport international "Princess Juliana".
60	Y compris les visiteurs à Saint Martin (partie française de l'île).
61	Y compris les visiteurs italiens.
62	Arrivées par voie aérienne à l'aéroport Léopold Sédar Senghor (LSS) seulement.Totaux estimés par le pays: 2008: 866 700; 2009: 810 000; 2010: 900 000; 2011: 1 001 000.
63	Non compris les arrivées de malaysiens par voie terrestre.
64	Nouvelle méthodologie de l'enquête sur l'hébergement.
65	À l'exclusion des arrivées par travail et les travailleurs contractuels.
66	Données pour 2011 d'après la nouvelle enquête aux frontières nationales (IBIS, visiteurs entrant en Suède). Pas de données recueillies entre 2004 et 2010. La nouvelle enquête à la frontière (IBIS) a commencé en 2011. Source : Agence suédoise pour la croissance économique et régionale.
67	Y compris les établissements de cure.
68	Enquête du tourisme récepteur en 2004, 2006 et 2007.
69	À l'exclusion de l'hébergement chez des particuliers.
70	Arrivées par voie aérienne à l'aéroport de Dili.
71	Enquête faite au départ des visiteurs effectué aux portes d'embarquement.
72	Y compris les passagers en croisière 2010: 9 105 ; 2011: 30 543.

58

Outbound tourism
Departures in thousands, expenditure (total, travel and passenger transport) in million US dollars

Tourisme à l'étranger
Départs en milliers, dépenses (total, voyage et transport de passagers) en millions de dollars E.-U.

Country or area	2007	2008	2009	2010	2011	Pays ou zone
Afghanistan						**Afghanistan**
Total expenditure (millions $)	...	58	61	132	...	Dépenses totales (millions $)
Travel (millions $)	...	55	59	129	...	Voyage (millions $)
Passenger transport (millions $)	...	3	2	3	...	Transport de passagers (millions $)
Albania						**Albanie**
Departures (thousands)	2 979	3 716	3 404	3 443	4 120	Départs (milliers)
Total expenditure (millions $)	1 331	1 644	1 693	1 454	1 678	Dépenses totales (millions $)
Travel (millions $)	1 268	1 555	1 586	1 362	1 565	Voyage (millions $)
Passenger transport (millions $)	63	89	107	92	113	Transport de passagers (millions $)
Algeria						**Algérie**
Departures (thousands)	1 499	1 539	1 677	1 757	1 715	Départs (milliers)
Total expenditure (millions $)	504	617	574	737	571	Dépenses totales (millions $)
Travel (millions $)	376	469	455	577	502	Voyage (millions $)
Passenger transport (millions $)	128	148	119	160	69	Transport de passagers (millions $)
American Samoa						**Samoa américaines**
Departures (thousands)	39	37	38	37	38	Départs (milliers)
Angola						**Angola**
Total expenditure (millions $)	473	447	270	275	323	Dépenses totales (millions $)
Travel (millions $)	212	254	133	148	180	Voyage (millions $)
Passenger transport (millions $)	261	193	137	127	143	Transport de passagers (millions $)
Anguilla						**Anguilla**
Travel (millions $)	15	17	16	13	14	Voyage (millions $)
Antigua and Barbuda						**Antigua-et-Barbuda**
Departures (thousands)	...	434	...	...	...	Départs (milliers)
Travel (millions $)	52	58	54	52	50	Voyage (millions $)
Argentina						**Argentine**
Departures (thousands)	4 167	4 614	4 981	5 307	6 686	Départs (milliers)
Total expenditure (millions $)	5 063	5 962	5 766	6 375	7 251	Dépenses totales (millions $)
Travel (millions $)	3 921	4 561	4 494	4 878	5 516	Voyage (millions $)
Passenger transport (millions $)	1 142	1 401	1 272	1 497	1 735	Transport de passagers (millions $)
Armenia						**Arménie**
Departures (thousands)	468	516	526	563	715	Départs (milliers)
Total expenditure (millions $)	345	383	379	466	546	Dépenses totales (millions $)
Travel (millions $)	294	324	326	404	477	Voyage (millions $)
Passenger transport (millions $)	51	59	53	62	69	Transport de passagers (millions $)
Aruba						**Aruba**
Total expenditure (millions $)	270	273	265	264	290	Dépenses totales (millions $)
Travel (millions $)	251	251	244	245	271	Voyage (millions $)
Passenger transport (millions $)	19	22	21	19	19	Transport de passagers (millions $)
Australia						**Australie**
Departures (thousands)	5 462	5 808	6 285	7 112	7 795	Départs (milliers)
Total expenditure (millions $)	20 429	24 690	21 891	27 533	33 193	Dépenses totales (millions $)
Travel (millions $)	14 831	18 750	17 949	22 240	26 597	Voyage (millions $)
Passenger transport (millions $)	5 598	5 940	3 942	5 293	6 596	Transport de passagers (millions $)
Austria						**Autriche**
Departures (thousands)[1]	9 876	9 677	10 121	9 882	9 874	Départs (milliers)[1]
Total expenditure (millions $)	12 825	13 993	12 767	12 215	12 922	Dépenses totales (millions $)
Travel (millions $)	10 561	11 432	10 813	10 125	10 548	Voyage (millions $)
Passenger transport (millions $)	2 264	2 561	1 954	2 090	2 374	Transport de passagers (millions $)
Azerbaijan						**Azerbaïdjan**
Departures (thousands)	1 631	2 162	2 363	3 176	3 550	Départs (milliers)
Total expenditure (millions $)	381	456	488	856	1 778	Dépenses totales (millions $)
Travel (millions $)	264	343	406	782	1 689	Voyage (millions $)
Passenger transport (millions $)	117	113	82	74	89	Transport de passagers (millions $)
Bahamas						**Bahamas**
Total expenditure (millions $)	538	460	386	369	347	Dépenses totales (millions $)
Travel (millions $)	377	305	240	228	246	Voyage (millions $)
Passenger transport (millions $)	161	155	146	141	101	Transport de passagers (millions $)

Outbound tourism *(continued)*
Departures in thousands, expenditure (total, travel and passenger transport) in million US dollars
Tourisme à l'étranger *(suite)*
Départs en milliers, dépenses (total, voyage et transport de passagers) en millions de dollars E.-U.

Country or area	2007	2008	2009	2010	2011	Pays ou zone
Bahrain						**Bahreïn**
Total expenditure (millions $)	671	704	597	684	899	Dépenses totales (millions $)
Travel (millions $)	479	503	408	506	718	Voyage (millions $)
Passenger transport (millions $)	192	201	189	178	181	Transport de passagers (millions $)
Bangladesh						**Bangladesh**
Departures (thousands)	2 327	875	2 254	...	...	Départs (milliers)
Total expenditure (millions $)	530	735	651	835	819	Dépenses totales (millions $)
Travel (millions $)	156	184	249	261	332	Voyage (millions $)
Passenger transport (millions $)	374	551	402	574	487	Transport de passagers (millions $)
Barbados						**Barbade**
Total expenditure (millions $)	290	279	293	351	...	Dépenses totales (millions $)
Travel (millions $)	212	205	216	274	...	Voyage (millions $)
Passenger transport (millions $)	78	74	77	77	...	Transport de passagers (millions $)
Belarus						**Bélarus**
Departures (thousands)	517	380	316	415	320	Départs (milliers)
Total expenditure (millions $)	724	860	752	748	741	Dépenses totales (millions $)
Travel (millions $)	606	716	639	622	600	Voyage (millions $)
Passenger transport (millions $)	118	144	113	126	141	Transport de passagers (millions $)
Belgium						**Belgique**
Departures (thousands)	8 371	8 887	8 775	8 801	9 727	Départs (milliers)
Total expenditure (millions $)	19 215	21 445	22 292	20 876	24 350	Dépenses totales (millions $)
Travel (millions $)	17 506	19 859	20 480	18 829	22 301	Voyage (millions $)
Passenger transport (millions $)	1 709	1 586	1 812	2 047	2 049	Transport de passagers (millions $)
Belize						**Belize**
Total expenditure (millions $)	46	44	43	39	37	Dépenses totales (millions $)
Travel (millions $)	43	41	41	36	34	Voyage (millions $)
Passenger transport (millions $)	3	3	2	3	3	Transport de passagers (millions $)
Benin						**Bénin**
Total expenditure (millions $)	107	102	88	91	...	Dépenses totales (millions $)
Travel (millions $)	72	64	53	57	...	Voyage (millions $)
Passenger transport (millions $)	35	38	35	34	...	Transport de passagers (millions $)
Bermuda						**Bermudes**
Departures (thousands)	181	192	...	...	...	Départs (milliers)
Total expenditure (millions $)	453	459	407	417	413	Dépenses totales (millions $)
Travel (millions $)	288	307	295	301	303	Voyage (millions $)
Passenger transport (millions $)	165	152	112	116	110	Transport de passagers (millions $)
Bhutan						**Bhoutan**
Total expenditure (millions $)	...	66	34	43	58	Dépenses totales (millions $)
Travel (millions $)	26	65	33	41	56	Voyage (millions $)
Passenger transport (millions $)	...	1	1	2	2	Transport de passagers (millions $)
Bolivia (Plurinational State of)						**Bolivie (État plurinational de)**
Departures (thousands)	526	589	628	708	1 081	Départs (milliers)
Total expenditure (millions $)	385	381	388	421	410	Dépenses totales (millions $)
Travel (millions $)	304	281	290	313	298	Voyage (millions $)
Passenger transport (millions $)	81	100	98	108	112	Transport de passagers (millions $)
Bonaire [2]						**Bonaire** [2]
Travel (millions $)	6	7	7	...	...	Voyage (millions $)
Bosnia and Herzegovina						**Bosnie-Herzégovine**
Total expenditure (millions $)	264	345	285	247	238	Dépenses totales (millions $)
Travel (millions $)	203	281	231	194	184	Voyage (millions $)
Passenger transport (millions $)	61	64	54	53	54	Transport de passagers (millions $)
Botswana						**Botswana**
Total expenditure (millions $)	284	240	231	26	...	Dépenses totales (millions $)
Travel (millions $)	281	238	230	25	...	Voyage (millions $)
Passenger transport (millions $)	3	2	1	1	...	Transport de passagers (millions $)
Brazil						**Brésil**
Departures (thousands)	4 731	5 230	4 915	6 430	...	Départs (milliers)
Total expenditure (millions $)	10 434	13 269	12 897	19 340	25 070	Dépenses totales (millions $)
Travel (millions $)	8 211	10 962	10 898	16 422	21 264	Voyage (millions $)
Passenger transport (millions $)	2 223	2 307	1 999	2 918	3 806	Transport de passagers (millions $)

Outbound tourism *(continued)*
Departures in thousands, expenditure (total, travel and passenger transport) in million US dollars
Tourisme à l'étranger *(suite)*
Départs en milliers, dépenses (total, voyage et transport de passagers) en millions de dollars E.-U.

Country or area	2007	2008	2009	2010	2011	Pays ou zone
Brunei Darussalam						**Brunéi Darussalam**
Travel (millions $)	430	459	477	...	...	Voyage (millions $)
Bulgaria						**Bulgarie**
Departures (thousands)	4 515	5 727	4 993	3 676	3 803	Départs (milliers)
Total expenditure (millions $)	2 142	2 602	1 955	1 382	1 498	Dépenses totales (millions $)
Travel (millions $)	1 880	2 311	1 755	1 232	1 339	Voyage (millions $)
Passenger transport (millions $)	262	291	200	150	159	Transport de passagers (millions $)
Burkina Faso						**Burkina Faso**
Total expenditure (millions $)	93	110	111	110	...	Dépenses totales (millions $)
Travel (millions $)	58	63	64	69	...	Voyage (millions $)
Passenger transport (millions $)	35	47	47	41	...	Transport de passagers (millions $)
Burundi						**Burundi**
Total expenditure (millions $)	106	151	71	35	49	Dépenses totales (millions $)
Travel (millions $)	104	144	62	20	31	Voyage (millions $)
Passenger transport (millions $)	2	7	9	15	18	Transport de passagers (millions $)
Cambodia						**Cambodge**
Departures (thousands)	996	786	340	505	710	Départs (milliers)
Total expenditure (millions $)	194	180	163	268	333	Dépenses totales (millions $)
Travel (millions $)	123	97	104	198	253	Voyage (millions $)
Passenger transport (millions $)	71	83	59	70	80	Transport de passagers (millions $)
Cameroon						**Cameroun**
Total expenditure (millions $)	466	563	476	265	...	Dépenses totales (millions $)
Travel (millions $)	368	410	389	186	...	Voyage (millions $)
Passenger transport (millions $)	98	153	87	79	...	Transport de passagers (millions $)
Canada						**Canada**
Departures (thousands)[3]	25 163	27 034	26 204	28 680	30 150	Départs (milliers)[3]
Total expenditure (millions $)	31 199	33 908	30 216	36 800	41 027	Dépenses totales (millions $)
Travel (millions $)	24 716	27 210	24 170	29 558	33 166	Voyage (millions $)
Passenger transport (millions $)	6 483	6 698	6 046	7 242	7 861	Transport de passagers (millions $)
Cape Verde						**Cap-Vert**
Total expenditure (millions $)	123	143	145	138	142	Dépenses totales (millions $)
Travel (millions $)	107	133	136	129	132	Voyage (millions $)
Passenger transport (millions $)	16	10	9	9	10	Transport de passagers (millions $)
Cayman Islands[4]						**Iles Caïmanes**[4]
Total expenditure (millions $)	132	130	120	129	145	Dépenses totales (millions $)
Central African Rep.						**Rép. centrafricaine**
Departures (thousands)	...	...	...	38	...	Départs (milliers)
Total expenditure (millions $)[5]	54	56	61	61	...	Dépenses totales (millions $)[5]
Travel (millions $)[5]	48	49	52	52	...	Voyage (millions $)[5]
Passenger transport (millions $)[5]	6	7	9	9	...	Transport de passagers (millions $)[5]
Chile						**Chili**
Departures (thousands)	3 234	3 061	2 895	3 348	3 724	Départs (milliers)
Total expenditure (millions $)	2 042	1 789	1 504	1 706	1 981	Dépenses totales (millions $)
Travel (millions $)	1 660	1 397	1 167	1 281	1 543	Voyage (millions $)
Passenger transport (millions $)	382	392	337	425	438	Transport de passagers (millions $)
China						**Chine**
Departures (thousands)[6]	40 954	45 844	47 656	57 386	70 250	Départs (milliers)[6]
Total expenditure (millions $)	33 269	40 987	47 108	59 840	79 010	Dépenses totales (millions $)
Travel (millions $)	29 786	36 157	43 702	54 880	72 585	Voyage (millions $)
Passenger transport (millions $)	3 483	4 830	3 406	4 960	6 425	Transport de passagers (millions $)
China, Hong Kong SAR						**Chine, Hong Kong RAS**
Departures (thousands)[7]	80 682	81 911	81 958	84 442	84 816	Départs (milliers)[7]
Travel (millions $)[8]	15 042	16 095	15 669	17 503	19 141	Voyage (millions $)[8]
China, Macao SAR						**Chine, Macao RAS**
Departures (thousands)[9]	599	606	671	753	908	Départs (milliers)[9]
Total expenditure (millions $)	777	902	983	1 237	1 476	Dépenses totales (millions $)
Travel (millions $)	695	828	915	1 154	1 376	Voyage (millions $)
Passenger transport (millions $)	82	74	68	83	100	Transport de passagers (millions $)

58

Outbound tourism *(continued)*
Departures in thousands, expenditure (total, travel and passenger transport) in million US dollars
Tourisme à l'étranger *(suite)*
Départs en milliers, dépenses (total, voyage et transport de passagers) en millions de dollars E.-U.

Country or area	2007	2008	2009	2010	2011	Pays ou zone
Colombia						**Colombie**
Departures (thousands)	2 028	2 042	2 122	2 342	...	Départs (milliers)
Total expenditure (millions $)	2 093	2 337	2 301	2 373	2 842	Dépenses totales (millions $)
Travel (millions $)	1 537	1 739	1 752	1 826	2 243	Voyage (millions $)
Passenger transport (millions $)	556	598	549	547	599	Transport de passagers (millions $)
Comoros [10]						**Comores** [10]
Total expenditure (millions $)	15	15	17	19	20	Dépenses totales (millions $)
Congo						**Congo**
Travel (millions $)	168	...	...	...	...	Voyage (millions $)
Cook Islands						**Iles Cook**
Departures (thousands)	13	13	12	12	13	Départs (milliers)
Costa Rica						**Costa Rica**
Departures (thousands)	577	528	579	662	717	Départs (milliers)
Total expenditure (millions $)	751	718	462	533	523	Dépenses totales (millions $)
Travel (millions $)	634	593	367	424	406	Voyage (millions $)
Passenger transport (millions $)	117	125	95	109	117	Transport de passagers (millions $)
Côte d'Ivoire						**Côte d'Ivoire**
Total expenditure (millions $)	606	612	589	569	...	Dépenses totales (millions $)
Travel (millions $)	372	356	343	352	...	Voyage (millions $)
Passenger transport (millions $)	234	256	246	217	...	Transport de passagers (millions $)
Croatia						**Croatie**
Departures (thousands)	...	2 357	2 497	1 873	2 280	Départs (milliers)
Total expenditure (millions $)	1 025	1 156	1 041	859	919	Dépenses totales (millions $)
Travel (millions $)	985	1 113	1 013	833	882	Voyage (millions $)
Passenger transport (millions $)	40	43	28	26	37	Transport de passagers (millions $)
Cuba [11]						**Cuba** [11]
Departures (thousands)	194	202	206	251	253	Départs (milliers)
Curaçao						**Curaçao**
Total expenditure (millions $)	223	229	258	282	321	Dépenses totales (millions $)
Travel (millions $)	203	203	209	226	267	Voyage (millions $)
Passenger transport (millions $)	20	26	49	56	54	Transport de passagers (millions $)
Cyprus						**Chypre**
Departures (thousands)	919	1 030	1 019	1 067	1 026	Départs (milliers)
Total expenditure (millions $)	1 554	1 895	1 638	1 457	1 721	Dépenses totales (millions $)
Travel (millions $)	1 479	1 593	1 300	1 116	1 300	Voyage (millions $)
Passenger transport (millions $)	75	302	338	341	421	Transport de passagers (millions $)
Czech Republic						**République tchèque**
Departures (thousands)	9 048	9 665	8 904	8 673	5 912	Départs (milliers)
Total expenditure (millions $)	3 704	4 797	4 158	4 166	4 660	Dépenses totales (millions $)
Travel (millions $)	3 577	4 652	4 077	4 064	4 573	Voyage (millions $)
Passenger transport (millions $)	127	145	81	102	87	Transport de passagers (millions $)
Dem. Rep. of the Congo						**Rép. dém. du Congo**
Travel (millions $)	109	127	121	150	298	Voyage (millions $)
Denmark						**Danemark**
Departures (thousands)	6 564	6 347	7 037	7 726	7 846	Départs (milliers)
Travel (millions $) [12]	8 830	9 698	8 968	9 082	9 840	Voyage (millions $) [12]
Djibouti						**Djibouti**
Total expenditure (millions $)	14	16	18	21	34	Dépenses totales (millions $)
Travel (millions $)	3	4	6	9	21	Voyage (millions $)
Passenger transport (millions $)	12	12	12	12	13	Transport de passagers (millions $)
Dominica						**Dominique**
Travel (millions $)	11	11	13	13	13	Voyage (millions $)
Dominican Republic						**Rép. dominicaine**
Departures (thousands)	443	413	415	401	408	Départs (milliers)
Total expenditure (millions $)	531	532	505	554	567	Dépenses totales (millions $)
Travel (millions $)	326	327	341	395	418	Voyage (millions $)
Passenger transport (millions $)	205	205	164	159	149	Transport de passagers (millions $)

Outbound tourism *(continued)*
Departures in thousands, expenditure (total, travel and passenger transport) in million US dollars
Tourisme à l'étranger *(suite)*
Départs en milliers, dépenses (total, voyage et transport de passagers) en millions de dollars E.-U.

Country or area	2007	2008	2009	2010	2011	Pays ou zone
Ecuador						**Equateur**
Departures (thousands)	801	815	814	899	1 022	Départs (milliers)
Total expenditure (millions $)	733	790	806	862	947	Dépenses totales (millions $)
Travel (millions $)	504	542	549	568	623	Voyage (millions $)
Passenger transport (millions $)	229	248	257	294	324	Transport de passagers (millions $)
Egypt						**Egypte**
Departures (thousands)	...	...	4 716	4 618	4 863	Départs (milliers)
Total expenditure (millions $)	2 886	3 390	2 941	2 696	2 575	Dépenses totales (millions $)
Travel (millions $)	2 446	2 915	2 538	2 240	2 203	Voyage (millions $)
Passenger transport (millions $)	440	475	403	456	372	Transport de passagers (millions $)
El Salvador						**El Salvador**
Departures (thousands)	1 012	...	...	...	...	Départs (milliers)
Total expenditure (millions $)	363	326	253	280	244	Dépenses totales (millions $)
Travel (millions $)	278	241	187	219	203	Voyage (millions $)
Passenger transport (millions $)	85	85	66	61	41	Transport de passagers (millions $)
Estonia						**Estonie**
Departures (thousands) [13,14]	677	692	752	955	1 054	Départs (milliers) [13,14]
Total expenditure (millions $)	804	939	696	723	939	Dépenses totales (millions $)
Travel (millions $)	670	809	605	633	806	Voyage (millions $)
Passenger transport (millions $)	134	130	91	90	133	Transport de passagers (millions $)
Ethiopia						**Ethiopie**
Total expenditure (millions $)	...	...	139	...	...	Dépenses totales (millions $)
Travel (millions $)	107	156	138	143	170	Voyage (millions $)
Passenger transport (millions $)	...	...	1	...	...	Transport de passagers (millions $)
Fiji						**Fidji**
Departures (thousands)	120	124	125	128	132	Départs (milliers)
Total expenditure (millions $)	130	139	129	102	...	Dépenses totales (millions $)
Travel (millions $)	92	96	95	88	...	Voyage (millions $)
Passenger transport (millions $)	38	43	34	14	...	Transport de passagers (millions $)
Finland						**Finlande**
Departures (thousands) [15]	5 749	5 854	5 832	6 633	7 274	Départs (milliers) [15]
Total expenditure (millions $)	4 812	5 534	5 226	5 267	6 009	Dépenses totales (millions $)
Travel (millions $)	3 983	4 501	4 394	4 304	4 878	Voyage (millions $)
Passenger transport (millions $)	829	1 033	832	963	1 131	Transport de passagers (millions $)
France						**France**
Departures (thousands)	28 103	25 506	25 140	25 041	26 155	Départs (milliers)
Total expenditure (millions $)	46 029	50 021	45 806	48 439	55 265	Dépenses totales (millions $)
Travel (millions $)	38 261	41 277	38 416	38 857	44 233	Voyage (millions $)
Passenger transport (millions $) [16]	7 768	8 744	7 390	9 582	11 032	Transport de passagers (millions $) [16]
French Polynesia						**Polynésie française**
Departures (thousands)	...	...	88	...	...	Départs (milliers)
Travel (millions $)	153	159	164	160	168	Voyage (millions $)
Gambia						**Gambie**
Travel (millions $)	8	8	9	11	11	Voyage (millions $)
Georgia						**Géorgie**
Departures (thousands)	1 473	1 872	1 980	2 089	2 237	Départs (milliers)
Total expenditure (millions $)	277	337	311	329	384	Dépenses totales (millions $)
Travel (millions $)	176	203	181	199	213	Voyage (millions $)
Passenger transport (millions $)	101	134	130	130	171	Transport de passagers (millions $)
Germany						**Allemagne**
Departures (thousands)	70 400	73 000	72 300	...	...	Départs (milliers)
Total expenditure (millions $)	96 549	106 039	93 107	91 205	100 424	Dépenses totales (millions $)
Travel (millions $)	83 156	91 598	81 400	77 580	86 167	Voyage (millions $)
Passenger transport (millions $)	11 851	13 393	14 441	11 707	13 625	Transport de passagers (millions $)
Ghana						**Ghana**
Total expenditure (millions $)	816	870	948	882	1 026	Dépenses totales (millions $)
Travel (millions $)	558	542	684	574	464	Voyage (millions $)
Passenger transport (millions $)	258	328	264	308	562	Transport de passagers (millions $)

Outbound tourism *(continued)*
Departures in thousands, expenditure (total, travel and passenger transport) in million US dollars

Tourisme à l'étranger *(suite)*
Départs en milliers, dépenses (total, voyage et transport de passagers) en millions de dollars E.-U.

Country or area	2007	2008	2009	2010	2011	Pays ou zone
Greece						**Grèce**
Total expenditure (millions $)	3 430	3 946	3 401	2 874	3 197	Dépenses totales (millions $)
Travel (millions $)	3 423	3 930	3 381	2 854	3 159	Voyage (millions $)
Passenger transport (millions $)	7	16	20	20	38	Transport de passagers (millions $)
Grenada						**Grenade**
Travel (millions $)	16	11	10	10	10	Voyage (millions $)
Guatemala						**Guatemala**
Departures (thousands)	1 168	1 277	1 326	1 136	1 080	Départs (milliers)
Total expenditure (millions $)	737	741	862	1 002	932	Dépenses totales (millions $)
Travel (millions $)	597	607	715	784	705	Voyage (millions $)
Passenger transport (millions $)	140	134	147	218	227	Transport de passagers (millions $)
Guinea						**Guinée**
Total expenditure (millions $)	96	30	28	17	49	Dépenses totales (millions $)
Travel (millions $)	29	9	13	8	33	Voyage (millions $)
Passenger transport (millions $)	67	21	15	9	16	Transport de passagers (millions $)
Guinea-Bissau						**Guinée-Bissau**
Total expenditure (millions $)	41	46	26	30	...	Dépenses totales (millions $)
Travel (millions $)	40	46	26	29	...	Voyage (millions $)
Passenger transport (millions $)	1	1	^0	^0	...	Transport de passagers (millions $)
Guyana						**Guyana**
Travel (millions $)	58	52	52	73	...	Voyage (millions $)
Haiti						**Haïti**
Total expenditure (millions $)	331	383	433	431	458	Dépenses totales (millions $)
Travel (millions $)	56	64	63	63	62	Voyage (millions $)
Passenger transport (millions $)	275	319	370	368	396	Transport de passagers (millions $)
Honduras						**Honduras**
Departures (thousands)	315	387	395	408	449	Départs (milliers)
Total expenditure (millions $)	309	385	361	406	488	Dépenses totales (millions $)
Travel (millions $)	212	291	296	321	397	Voyage (millions $)
Passenger transport (millions $)	97	94	65	85	91	Transport de passagers (millions $)
Hungary						**Hongrie**
Departures (thousands)	17 056	17 162[17]	16 640[17]	16 082[17]	16 634[17]	Départs (milliers)
Total expenditure (millions $)	3 088	3 833	3 233	2 879	3 012	Dépenses totales (millions $)
Travel (millions $)	2 546	3 225	2 750	2 404	2 485	Voyage (millions $)
Passenger transport (millions $)	542	608	483	475	527	Transport de passagers (millions $)
Iceland						**Islande**
Departures (thousands) [18]	460	414	259	299	341	Départs (milliers) [18]
Total expenditure (millions $)	1 336	1 107	...	...	...	Dépenses totales (millions $)
Travel (millions $)	1 326	1 103	534	599	740	Voyage (millions $)
Passenger transport (millions $)	10	4	...	...	...	Transport de passagers (millions $)
India						**Inde**
Departures (thousands) [19]	9 783	10 868	11 067	12 988	13 994	Départs (milliers) [19]
Total expenditure (millions $)	10 690	12 083	...	...	...	Dépenses totales (millions $)
Travel (millions $)	8 219	9 606	9 310	10 549	13 722	Voyage (millions $)
Passenger transport (millions $)	2 471	2 477	...	...	...	Transport de passagers (millions $)
Indonesia						**Indonésie**
Departures (thousands)	5 158	5 486	5 053	6 235	6 750	Départs (milliers)
Total expenditure (millions $)	6 578	8 801	6 908	8 432	9 677	Dépenses totales (millions $)
Travel (millions $)	4 904	5 554	5 316	6 395	7 279	Voyage (millions $)
Passenger transport (millions $)	1 674	3 247	1 592	2 037	2 398	Transport de passagers (millions $)
Iran (Islamic Rep. of) [20]						**Iran (Rép. islamique d')** [20]
Total expenditure (millions $)	7 335	8 418	10 133	15 651	...	Dépenses totales (millions $)
Travel (millions $)	6 809	7 643	9 108	14 186	...	Voyage (millions $)
Passenger transport (millions $)	526	775	1 025	1 465	...	Transport de passagers (millions $)
Iraq						**Iraq**
Total expenditure (millions $)	705	813	1 221	1 675	1 839	Dépenses totales (millions $)
Travel (millions $)	639	794	1 207	1 620	1 796	Voyage (millions $)
Passenger transport (millions $)	66	19	14	55	43	Transport de passagers (millions $)

Outbound tourism *(continued)*
Departures in thousands, expenditure (total, travel and passenger transport) in million US dollars
Tourisme à l'étranger *(suite)*
Départs en milliers, dépenses (total, voyage et transport de passagers) en millions de dollars E.-U.

Country or area	2007	2008	2009	2010	2011	Pays ou zone
Ireland						**Irlande**
Departures (thousands) [21]	7 713	7 877	7 047	6 660	6 383	Départs (milliers) [21]
Total expenditure (millions $)	8 785	10 539	7 934	7 178	7 137	Dépenses totales (millions $)
Travel (millions $)	8 656	10 413	7 820	7 071	7 023	Voyage (millions $)
Passenger transport (millions $)	129	126	114	107	114	Transport de passagers (millions $)
Israel						**Israël**
Departures (thousands)	4 147	4 207	4 007	4 269	4 387	Départs (milliers)
Total expenditure (millions $)	4 251	4 445	3 869	4 433	4 590	Dépenses totales (millions $)
Travel (millions $)	3 260	3 439	2 909	3 413	3 538	Voyage (millions $)
Passenger transport (millions $)	991	1 006	960	1 020	1 052	Transport de passagers (millions $)
Italy						**Italie**
Departures (thousands) [22]	27 734	28 284	29 060	29 823	29 295	Départs (milliers) [22]
Total expenditure (millions $)	32 754	37 807	34 399	33 053	35 724	Dépenses totales (millions $)
Travel (millions $)	27 329	30 931	27 950	26 907	28 730	Voyage (millions $)
Passenger transport (millions $)	5 425	6 876	6 449	6 146	6 994	Transport de passagers (millions $)
Jamaica						**Jamaïque**
Total expenditure (millions $)	340	312	259	235	213	Dépenses totales (millions $)
Travel (millions $)	298	268	216	193	159	Voyage (millions $)
Passenger transport (millions $)	42	44	43	42	54	Transport de passagers (millions $)
Japan						**Japon**
Departures (thousands)	17 295	15 987	15 446	16 637	16 994	Départs (milliers)
Total expenditure (millions $)	37 261	38 976	34 788	39 306	39 760	Dépenses totales (millions $)
Travel (millions $)	26 511	27 901	25 199	27 950	27 262	Voyage (millions $)
Passenger transport (millions $)	10 750	11 075	9 589	11 356	12 498	Transport de passagers (millions $)
Jordan						**Jordanie**
Departures (thousands)	2 094	1 972	2 054	2 917	1 975	Départs (milliers)
Total expenditure (millions $)	1 024	1 140	1 202	1 736	1 280	Dépenses totales (millions $)
Travel (millions $)	883	1 004	1 064	1 572	1 161	Voyage (millions $)
Passenger transport (millions $)	141	136	138	164	119	Transport de passagers (millions $)
Kazakhstan						**Kazakhstan**
Departures (thousands)	4 544	5 243	6 414	7 412	8 020	Départs (milliers)
Total expenditure (millions $)	1 396	1 361	1 319	1 489	1 851	Dépenses totales (millions $)
Travel (millions $)	1 082	1 078	1 132	1 273	1 631	Voyage (millions $)
Passenger transport (millions $)	314	283	187	216	220	Transport de passagers (millions $)
Kenya						**Kenya**
Travel (millions $)	265	266	227	212	197	Voyage (millions $)
Kiribati [4]						**Kiribati** [4]
Total expenditure (millions $)	9	13	11	...	...	Dépenses totales (millions $)
Kuwait						**Koweït**
Departures (thousands)	2 649	...	...	...	...	Départs (milliers)
Total expenditure (millions $)	7 267	8 341	6 799	7 101	8 944	Dépenses totales (millions $)
Travel (millions $)	6 636	7 570	6 189	6 429	8 129	Voyage (millions $)
Passenger transport (millions $)	631	771	610	672	815	Transport de passagers (millions $)
Kyrgyzstan						**Kirghizistan**
Departures (thousands)	559	1 521	1 283	1 296	...	Départs (milliers)
Total expenditure (millions $)	215	451	391	398	566	Dépenses totales (millions $)
Travel (millions $)	112	304	265	271	421	Voyage (millions $)
Passenger transport (millions $)	103	147	126	127	145	Transport de passagers (millions $)
Lao People's Dem. Rep.						**Rép. dém. pop. lao**
Total expenditure (millions $)	14	51	91	215	248	Dépenses totales (millions $)
Travel (millions $)	8	41	83	203	237	Voyage (millions $)
Passenger transport (millions $)	6	10	8	12	11	Transport de passagers (millions $)
Latvia						**Lettonie**
Departures (thousands) [23]	3 398	3 782	3 268	3 332	3 257	Départs (milliers) [23]
Total expenditure (millions $)	1 021	1 250	906	771	920	Dépenses totales (millions $)
Travel (millions $)	927	1 142	799	647	766	Voyage (millions $)
Passenger transport (millions $)	94	108	107	124	154	Transport de passagers (millions $)
Lebanon						**Liban**
Total expenditure (millions $)	3 914	4 297	4 928	5 279	4 651	Dépenses totales (millions $)
Travel (millions $)	3 114	3 564	4 012	4 926	4 215	Voyage (millions $)
Passenger transport (millions $)	800	733	916	353	436	Transport de passagers (millions $)

58

Outbound tourism *(continued)*
Departures in thousands, expenditure (total, travel and passenger transport) in million US dollars
Tourisme à l'étranger *(suite)*
Départs en milliers, dépenses (total, voyage et transport de passagers) en millions de dollars E.-U.

Country or area	2007	2008	2009	2010	2011	Pays ou zone
Lesotho						**Lesotho**
Total expenditure (millions $)	276	248	247	278	300	Dépenses totales (millions $)
Travel (millions $)	268	243	239	270	290	Voyage (millions $)
Passenger transport (millions $)	8	5	8	8	10	Transport de passagers (millions $)
Liberia						**Libéria**
Total expenditure (millions $)	48	58	51	134	132	Dépenses totales (millions $)
Travel (millions $)	21	30	29	63	60	Voyage (millions $)
Passenger transport (millions $)	27	28	22	71	72	Transport de passagers (millions $)
Libyan Arab Jamah.						**Jamah. arabe libyenne**
Total expenditure (millions $)	1 010	1 339	1 683	2 184	2 303	Dépenses totales (millions $)
Travel (millions $)	889	1 277	1 587	2 047	2 269	Voyage (millions $)
Passenger transport (millions $)	121	62	96	137	34	Transport de passagers (millions $)
Lithuania						**Lituanie**
Departures (thousands)	1 661	1 757	1 288	1 411	1 526	Départs (milliers)
Total expenditure (millions $)	1 168	1 567	1 131	795	874	Dépenses totales (millions $)
Travel (millions $)	1 144	1 531	1 122	790	798	Voyage (millions $)
Passenger transport (millions $)	24	36	9	5	76	Transport de passagers (millions $)
Luxembourg						**Luxembourg**
Travel (millions $)	3 476	3 801	3 612	3 515	3 796	Voyage (millions $)
Madagascar						**Madagascar**
Travel (millions $)	94	143	123	110	...	Voyage (millions $)
Malawi						**Malawi**
Total expenditure (millions $)	79	96	100	93	96	Dépenses totales (millions $)
Travel (millions $)	57	61	63	64	66	Voyage (millions $)
Passenger transport (millions $)	22	35	37	29	30	Transport de passagers (millions $)
Malaysia						**Malaisie**
Total expenditure (millions $)	6 600	7 724	7 196	...	...	Dépenses totales (millions $)
Travel (millions $)	5 601	6 709	6 508	7 943	10 753	Voyage (millions $)
Passenger transport (millions $)	999	1 015	688	...	...	Transport de passagers (millions $)
Maldives						**Maldives**
Departures (thousands)	102	123	...	...	...	Départs (milliers)
Total expenditure (millions $)	150	208	211	252	256	Dépenses totales (millions $)
Travel (millions $)	120	164	173	205	209	Voyage (millions $)
Passenger transport (millions $)	30	44	38	47	47	Transport de passagers (millions $)
Mali						**Mali**
Total expenditure (millions $)	201	228	231	235	224	Dépenses totales (millions $)
Travel (millions $)	137	147	149	152	144	Voyage (millions $)
Passenger transport (millions $)	64	81	82	83	80	Transport de passagers (millions $)
Malta						**Malte**
Departures (thousands)	280	301	264	294	308	Départs (milliers)
Total expenditure (millions $)	284	361	365	412	452	Dépenses totales (millions $)
Travel (millions $)	237	307	291	309	333	Voyage (millions $)
Passenger transport (millions $)	47	54	74	103	119	Transport de passagers (millions $)
Mauritius						**Maurice**
Departures (thousands)	213	226	196	212	219	Départs (milliers)
Total expenditure (millions $)	384	489	384	423	427	Dépenses totales (millions $)
Travel (millions $)	357	452	354	398	400	Voyage (millions $)
Passenger transport (millions $)	27	37	30	25	27	Transport de passagers (millions $)
Mexico						**Mexique**
Departures (thousands)	15 257	14 527	14 104	14 334	14 799	Départs (milliers)
Total expenditure (millions $)	9 918	10 246	8 737	9 038	9 734	Dépenses totales (millions $)
Travel (millions $)	8 462	8 568	7 207	7 255	7 832	Voyage (millions $)
Passenger transport (millions $)	1 456	1 678	1 530	1 783	1 902	Transport de passagers (millions $)
Micronesia (Fed. States of)[24]						**Micronésie (Etats féd. de)**[24]
Total expenditure (millions $)	7	7	8	8	8	Dépenses totales (millions $)
Mongolia						**Mongolie**
Total expenditure (millions $)	227	249	242	319	404	Dépenses totales (millions $)
Travel (millions $)	205	217	210	265	344	Voyage (millions $)
Passenger transport (millions $)	22	32	32	54	60	Transport de passagers (millions $)

Outbound tourism *(continued)*
Departures in thousands, expenditure (total, travel and passenger transport) in million US dollars
Tourisme à l'étranger *(suite)*
Départs en milliers, dépenses (total, voyage et transport de passagers) en millions de dollars E.-U.

Country or area	2007	2008	2009	2010	2011	Pays ou zone
Montenegro						**Monténégro**
Total expenditure (millions $)	58	80	76	72	70	Dépenses totales (millions $)
Travel (millions $)	37	43	49	46	39	Voyage (millions $)
Passenger transport (millions $)	21	37	27	26	31	Transport de passagers (millions $)
Montserrat						**Montserrat**
Travel (millions $)	3	3	3	3	3	Voyage (millions $)
Morocco						**Maroc**
Departures (thousands)	2 669	3 058	2 293	2 175	2 192	Départs (milliers)
Total expenditure (millions $)	1 418	1 910	1 713	1 879	2 260	Dépenses totales (millions $)
Travel (millions $)	880	1 090	1 106	1 203	1 363	Voyage (millions $)
Passenger transport (millions $)	538	820	607	676	897	Transport de passagers (millions $)
Mozambique						**Mozambique**
Total expenditure (millions $)	209	235	247	294	260	Dépenses totales (millions $)
Travel (millions $)	180	202	212	250	223	Voyage (millions $)
Passenger transport (millions $)	29	33	35	44	37	Transport de passagers (millions $)
Myanmar						**Myanmar**
Total expenditure (millions $)	39	50	...	...	...	Dépenses totales (millions $)
Travel (millions $)	36	49	52	53	123	Voyage (millions $)
Passenger transport (millions $)	3	1	...	...	9	Transport de passagers (millions $)
Namibia						**Namibie**
Travel (millions $)	132	114	120	145	207	Voyage (millions $)
Nepal						**Népal**
Departures (thousands)	469	561	589	765	774	Départs (milliers)
Total expenditure (millions $)	402	545	572	528	420	Dépenses totales (millions $)
Travel (millions $)	274	381	434	402	320	Voyage (millions $)
Passenger transport (millions $)	128	164	138	126	100	Transport de passagers (millions $)
Netherlands						**Pays-Bas**
Departures (thousands) [25]	17 523	18 399	18 340	18 368	18 560	Départs (milliers) [25]
Total expenditure (millions $)	19 477	22 217	21 080	19 772	20 884	Dépenses totales (millions $)
Travel (millions $)	19 110	21 828	20 758	19 489	20 603	Voyage (millions $)
Passenger transport (millions $)	367	389	322	283	281	Transport de passagers (millions $)
New Caledonia						**Nouvelle-Calédonie**
Departures (thousands) [26]	106	112	119	132	124	Départs (milliers) [26]
Travel (millions $)	149	168	170	179	176	Voyage (millions $)
New Zealand						**Nouvelle-Zélande**
Departures (thousands)	1 978	1 967	1 918	2 026	2 096	Départs (milliers)
Travel (millions $)	3 077	3 006	2 581	3 038	3 459	Voyage (millions $)
Nicaragua						**Nicaragua**
Departures (thousands)	949	942	858	908	912	Départs (milliers)
Total expenditure (millions $)	279	332	300	329	380	Dépenses totales (millions $)
Travel (millions $)	178	220	192	205	252	Voyage (millions $)
Passenger transport (millions $)	101	112	108	124	128	Transport de passagers (millions $)
Niger						**Niger**
Total expenditure (millions $)	48	98	84	...	...	Dépenses totales (millions $)
Travel (millions $)	29	68	54	...	...	Voyage (millions $)
Passenger transport (millions $)	19	30	30	...	...	Transport de passagers (millions $)
Nigeria						**Nigéria**
Total expenditure (millions $)	6 664	11 009	6 236	8 379	9 534	Dépenses totales (millions $)
Travel (millions $)	5 589	9 779	5 012	5 587	6 599	Voyage (millions $)
Passenger transport (millions $)	1 075	1 230	1 224	2 792	2 935	Transport de passagers (millions $)
Niue						**Nioué**
Departures (thousands)	2	2	2	2	...	Départs (milliers)
Norway						**Norvège**
Departures (thousands) [27]	3 395	...	...	...	...	Départs (milliers) [27]
Total expenditure (millions $)	13 256	15 118	13 221	14 891	17 236	Dépenses totales (millions $)
Travel (millions $)	12 121	14 100	12 101	14 337	16 341	Voyage (millions $)
Passenger transport (millions $)	1 135	1 018	1 120	554	895	Transport de passagers (millions $)
Occupied Palestinian Terr. [28]						**Terr. palestinien occupé** [28]
Total expenditure (millions $)	447	545	564	584	...	Dépenses totales (millions $)
Travel (millions $)	436	535	556	578	659	Voyage (millions $)
Passenger transport (millions $)	11	10	8	6	...	Transport de passagers (millions $)

58

Outbound tourism *(continued)*
Departures in thousands, expenditure (total, travel and passenger transport) in million US dollars
Tourisme à l'étranger *(suite)*
Départs en milliers, dépenses (total, voyage et transport de passagers) en millions de dollars E.-U.

Country or area	2007	2008	2009	2010	2011	Pays ou zone
Oman						**Oman**
Departures (thousands) [29]	2 285	2 074	1 672	...	...	Départs (milliers) [29]
Total expenditure (millions $)	952	1 197	1 295	1 768	1 982	Dépenses totales (millions $)
Travel (millions $)	752	856	902	1 001	1 168	Voyage (millions $)
Passenger transport (millions $)	200	341	393	767	814	Transport de passagers (millions $)
Pakistan						**Pakistan**
Total expenditure (millions $)	2 083	2 163	1 098	1 370	1 851	Dépenses totales (millions $)
Travel (millions $)	1 593	1 518	685	925	1 124	Voyage (millions $)
Passenger transport (millions $)	490	645	413	445	727	Transport de passagers (millions $)
Panama						**Panama**
Departures (thousands)	314	369	336	392	...	Départs (milliers)
Total expenditure (millions $)	457	560	503	575	665	Dépenses totales (millions $)
Travel (millions $)	307	366	338	398	462	Voyage (millions $)
Passenger transport (millions $)	150	194	165	177	203	Transport de passagers (millions $)
Papua New Guinea						**Papouasie-Nvl-Guinée**
Total expenditure (millions $)	81	75	132	138	...	Dépenses totales (millions $)
Travel (millions $)	21	29	113	119	...	Voyage (millions $)
Passenger transport (millions $)	60	46	19	19	...	Transport de passagers (millions $)
Paraguay						**Paraguay**
Departures (thousands)	242	269	282	325	352	Départs (milliers)
Total expenditure (millions $)	184	208	229	269	309	Dépenses totales (millions $)
Travel (millions $)	109	122	129	153	175	Voyage (millions $)
Passenger transport (millions $)	75	86	100	116	134	Transport de passagers (millions $)
Peru						**Pérou**
Departures (thousands)	1 915	1 913	1 891	2 058	2 132	Départs (milliers)
Total expenditure (millions $)	1 243	1 432	1 404	1 640	1 764	Dépenses totales (millions $)
Travel (millions $)	968	1 122	1 088	1 268	1 352	Voyage (millions $)
Passenger transport (millions $)	275	310	316	372	412	Transport de passagers (millions $)
Philippines						**Philippines**
Departures (thousands) [30]	3 066	3 355	3 188	...	...	Départs (milliers) [30]
Total expenditure (millions $)	2 055	2 553	3 251	4 194	4 402	Dépenses totales (millions $)
Travel (millions $)	1 663	2 057	2 698	3 416	3 646	Voyage (millions $)
Passenger transport (millions $)	392	496	553	778	756	Transport de passagers (millions $)
Poland						**Pologne**
Departures (thousands) [31]	47 561	50 243	39 270	42 760	43 270	Départs (milliers) [31]
Total expenditure (millions $)	8 342	10 689	7 888	9 100	8 882	Dépenses totales (millions $)
Travel (millions $)	7 753	9 903	7 372	8 570	8 462	Voyage (millions $)
Passenger transport (millions $)	589	786	516	530	420	Transport de passagers (millions $)
Portugal						**Portugal**
Departures (thousands)	20 989	...	...	...	...	Départs (milliers)
Total expenditure (millions $)	4 864	5 283	4 604	4 691	4 948	Dépenses totales (millions $)
Travel (millions $)	3 937	4 328	3 776	3 905	4 143	Voyage (millions $)
Passenger transport (millions $)	927	955	828	786	805	Transport de passagers (millions $)
Puerto Rico						**Porto Rico**
Departures (thousands)	1 441	1 438	1 116	980	924	Départs (milliers)
Total expenditure (millions $) [4,32]	1 743	1 761	1 386	1 180	1 196	Dépenses totales (millions $) [4,32]
Travel (millions $) [4,32]	1 192	1 213	919	809	816	Voyage (millions $) [4,32]
Passenger transport (millions $) [4,32]	551	548	467	371	380	Transport de passagers (millions $) [4,32]
Qatar						**Qatar**
Total expenditure (millions $)	...	...	...	...	7 813	Dépenses totales (millions $)
Travel (millions $)	...	...	...	...	1 807	Voyage (millions $)
Passenger transport (millions $)	...	...	...	...	6 006	Transport de passagers (millions $)
Republic of Korea						**République de Corée**
Departures (thousands)	13 325	11 996	9 494	12 488	12 694	Départs (milliers)
Total expenditure (millions $)	24 449	21 456	16 360	19 695	21 733	Dépenses totales (millions $)
Travel (millions $)	21 975	19 065	15 040	17 669	19 463	Voyage (millions $)
Passenger transport (millions $)	2 474	2 391	1 320	2 026	2 270	Transport de passagers (millions $)

Outbound tourism *(continued)*
Departures in thousands, expenditure (total, travel and passenger transport) in million US dollars
Tourisme à l'étranger *(suite)*
Départs en milliers, dépenses (total, voyage et transport de passagers) en millions de dollars E.-U.

Country or area	2007	2008	2009	2010	2011	Pays ou zone
Republic of Moldova						**République de Moldova**
Departures (thousands)	82	85	93	117	136	Départs (milliers)
Total expenditure (millions $)	290	359	307	324	374	Dépenses totales (millions $)
Travel (millions $)	233	288	243	260	300	Voyage (millions $)
Passenger transport (millions $)	57	71	64	64	74	Transport de passagers (millions $)
Romania						**Roumanie**
Departures (thousands)	10 980	13 072	11 723	10 905	10 936	Départs (milliers)
Total expenditure (millions $)	1 725	2 409	1 769	1 896	2 317	Dépenses totales (millions $)
Travel (millions $)	1 543	2 176	1 472	1 636	1 966	Voyage (millions $)
Passenger transport (millions $)	182	233	297	260	351	Transport de passagers (millions $)
Russian Federation						**Fédération de Russie**
Departures (thousands)	34 285	36 538	34 276	39 323	...	Départs (milliers)
Total expenditure (millions $)	23 248	27 010	23 671	30 064	36 907	Dépenses totales (millions $)
Travel (millions $)	21 217	23 778	20 905	26 587	32 466	Voyage (millions $)
Passenger transport (millions $)	2 031	3 232	2 766	3 477	4 441	Transport de passagers (millions $)
Rwanda						**Rwanda**
Total expenditure (millions $)	...	104	115	94	126	Dépenses totales (millions $)
Travel (millions $)	69	70	72	77	89	Voyage (millions $)
Passenger transport (millions $)	...	34	43	17	37	Transport de passagers (millions $)
Saint Kitts and Nevis						**Saint-Kitts-et-Nevis**
Travel (millions $)	12	15	11	14	15	Voyage (millions $)
Saint Lucia						**Sainte-Lucie**
Travel (millions $)	42	45	47	47	49	Voyage (millions $)
Saint Maarten						**Saint-Martin**
Total expenditure (millions $)	83	88	104	105	112	Dépenses totales (millions $)
Travel (millions $)	83	88	81	83	88	Voyage (millions $)
Passenger transport (millions $)	^0	^0	23	22	24	Transport de passagers (millions $)
Saint Vincent-Grenadines						**Saint Vincent-Grenadines**
Travel (millions $)	20	18	14	15	15	Voyage (millions $)
Samoa						**Samoa**
Departures (thousands)	...	53	44	56	57	Départs (milliers)
Total expenditure (millions $)	20	22	20	25	21	Dépenses totales (millions $)
Travel (millions $)	10	11	11	15	13	Voyage (millions $)
Passenger transport (millions $)	10	11	9	10	8	Transport de passagers (millions $)
Sao Tome and Principe						**Sao Tomé-et-Principe**
Total expenditure (millions $)	1	^0	^0	^1	1	Dépenses totales (millions $)
Travel (millions $) ^	0	0	0	0	0	Voyage (millions $) ^
Passenger transport (millions $)	1	^0	^0	1	1	Transport de passagers (millions $)
Saudi Arabia						**Arabie saoudite**
Departures (thousands)	4 126	4 087	6 032	7 232	15 281[33]	Départs (milliers)
Total expenditure (millions $)	21 031	16 005	21 312	22 076	18 209	Dépenses totales (millions $)
Travel (millions $)	20 170	15 129	20 419	21 135	17 271	Voyage (millions $)
Passenger transport (millions $)	861	876	893	941	938	Transport de passagers (millions $)
Senegal						**Sénégal**
Total expenditure (millions $)	352	276	258	217	...	Dépenses totales (millions $)
Travel (millions $)	253	175	156	160	...	Voyage (millions $)
Passenger transport (millions $)	99	101	102	57	...	Transport de passagers (millions $)
Serbia						**Serbie**
Total expenditure (millions $)	1 202	1 468	1 107	1 106	1 263	Dépenses totales (millions $)
Travel (millions $)	1 041	1 269	961	955	1 105	Voyage (millions $)
Passenger transport (millions $)	161	199	146	151	158	Transport de passagers (millions $)
Seychelles						**Seychelles**
Departures (thousands)	58	54	49	59	57	Départs (milliers)
Total expenditure (millions $)	73	64	55	63	65	Dépenses totales (millions $)
Travel (millions $)	43	39	34	38	39	Voyage (millions $)
Passenger transport (millions $)	30	25	21	25	26	Transport de passagers (millions $)
Sierra Leone						**Sierra Leone**
Departures (thousands)	71	73	72	76	99	Départs (milliers)
Total expenditure (millions $)	17	24	22	22	29	Dépenses totales (millions $)
Travel (millions $)	14	24	13	13	17	Voyage (millions $)
Passenger transport (millions $)	3	0	9	9	12	Transport de passagers (millions $)

Outbound tourism *(continued)*
Departures in thousands, expenditure (total, travel and passenger transport) in million US dollars
Tourisme à l'étranger *(suite)*
Départs en milliers, dépenses (total, voyage et transport de passagers) en millions de dollars E.-U.

Country or area	2007	2008	2009	2010	2011	Pays ou zone
Singapore						**Singapour**
Departures (thousands)	6 024	6 828	6 961	7 342	7 753	Départs (milliers)
Travel (millions $)	13 410	16 366	15 849	18 630	21 103	Voyage (millions $)
Slovakia						**Slovaquie**
Departures (thousands) [34]	3 603	3 683	3 230	2 692	3 285	Départs (milliers) [34]
Total expenditure (millions $)	1 825	2 596	2 249	2 146	2 449	Dépenses totales (millions $)
Travel (millions $)	1 533	2 165	2 098	1 944	2 186	Voyage (millions $)
Passenger transport (millions $)	292	431	151	202	263	Transport de passagers (millions $)
Slovenia						**Slovénie**
Departures (thousands) [35]	2 496	2 459	2 586	2 874	2 722	Départs (milliers) [35]
Total expenditure (millions $)	1 260	1 610	1 456	1 377	1 315	Dépenses totales (millions $)
Travel (millions $)	1 144	1 357	1 278	1 214	1 143	Voyage (millions $)
Passenger transport (millions $)	116	253	178	163	172	Transport de passagers (millions $)
Solomon Islands						**Iles Salomon**
Total expenditure (millions $)	36	41	38	51	66	Dépenses totales (millions $)
Travel (millions $)	29	34	32	47	65	Voyage (millions $)
Passenger transport (millions $)	7	7	6	4	1	Transport de passagers (millions $)
South Africa						**Afrique du Sud**
Departures (thousands)	4 433	4 429	4 424	5 165	5 455	Départs (milliers)
Total expenditure (millions $)	6 103	6 905	6 420	8 139	8 397	Dépenses totales (millions $)
Travel (millions $)	3 927	4 404	4 151	5 595	5 283	Voyage (millions $)
Passenger transport (millions $)	2 176	2 501	2 269	2 544	3 114	Transport de passagers (millions $)
Spain						**Espagne**
Departures (thousands)	11 276	11 229	12 017	12 379	13 347	Départs (milliers)
Total expenditure (millions $)	24 355	27 157	22 787	22 733	23 207	Dépenses totales (millions $)
Travel (millions $)	19 724	20 363	16 911	16 764	17 275	Voyage (millions $)
Passenger transport (millions $)	4 631	6 794	5 876	5 969	5 932	Transport de passagers (millions $)
Sri Lanka						**Sri Lanka**
Departures (thousands)	862	966	963	1 122	1 239	Départs (milliers)
Total expenditure (millions $)	709	777	735	828	926	Dépenses totales (millions $)
Travel (millions $)	393	428	411	453	501	Voyage (millions $)
Passenger transport (millions $)	316	349	324	375	425	Transport de passagers (millions $)
Sudan (former)						**Soudan (anc.)**
Travel (millions $)	1 477	1 188	868	1 116	937	Voyage (millions $)
Suriname						**Suriname**
Total expenditure (millions $)	28	35	35	41	49	Dépenses totales (millions $)
Travel (millions $)	22	30	32	39	42	Voyage (millions $)
Passenger transport (millions $)	6	5	3	2	7	Transport de passagers (millions $)
Swaziland						**Swaziland**
Departures (thousands)	1 130	1 177	1 245	1 141	1 264	Départs (milliers)
Total expenditure (millions $)	63	59	98	87	...	Dépenses totales (millions $)
Travel (millions $)	51	46	72	61	...	Voyage (millions $)
Passenger transport (millions $)	12	13	26	26	...	Transport de passagers (millions $)
Sweden						**Suède**
Departures (thousands)	12 692	13 291	11 699	13 042	14 651	Départs (milliers)
Total expenditure (millions $)	15 273	16 458	13 432	15 173	17 575	Dépenses totales (millions $)
Travel (millions $)	13 496	14 618	11 856	13 079	15 571	Voyage (millions $)
Passenger transport (millions $)	1 777	1 840	1 576	2 094	2 004	Transport de passagers (millions $)
Switzerland						**Suisse**
Departures (thousands)	...	11 147	10 453	10 011	...	Départs (milliers)
Total expenditure (millions $)	12 298	13 347	12 875	13 317	15 272	Dépenses totales (millions $)
Travel (millions $)	10 114	10 913	10 951	11 159	12 657	Voyage (millions $)
Passenger transport (millions $)	2 184	2 434	1 924	2 158	2 615	Transport de passagers (millions $)
Syrian Arab Republic						**Rép. arabe syrienne**
Departures (thousands)	4 196	5 253	5 215	6 259	...	Départs (milliers)
Total expenditure (millions $)	710	912	980	1 598	...	Dépenses totales (millions $)
Travel (millions $)	645	800	882	1 510	...	Voyage (millions $)
Passenger transport (millions $)	65	112	98	88	...	Transport de passagers (millions $)

Outbound tourism *(continued)*
Departures in thousands, expenditure (total, travel and passenger transport) in million US dollars
Tourisme à l'étranger *(suite)*
Départs en milliers, dépenses (total, voyage et transport de passagers) en millions de dollars E.-U.

Country or area	2007	2008	2009	2010	2011	Pays ou zone
Tajikistan						**Tadjikistan**
Total expenditure (millions $)	...	...	...	25	13	Dépenses totales (millions $)
Travel (millions $)	7	11	6	18	8	Voyage (millions $)
Passenger transport (millions $)	...	...	...	7	5	Transport de passagers (millions $)
Thailand						**Thaïlande**
Departures (thousands)	4 018	3 908	4 653	5 451	5 397	Départs (milliers)
Total expenditure (millions $)	6 887	6 700	5 749	7 151	7 320	Dépenses totales (millions $)
Travel (millions $)	5 143	5 003	4 433	5 623	5 716	Voyage (millions $)
Passenger transport (millions $)	1 744	1 697	1 316	1 528	1 604	Transport de passagers (millions $)
TFYR of Macedonia						**L'ex-R.Y. Macédoine**
Total expenditure (millions $)	147	190	150	141	166	Dépenses totales (millions $)
Travel (millions $)	102	136	100	92	112	Voyage (millions $)
Passenger transport (millions $)	45	54	50	49	54	Transport de passagers (millions $)
Timor-Leste						**Timor-Leste**
Total expenditure (millions $)	5	51	69	68	60	Dépenses totales (millions $)
Travel (millions $)	3	40	58	52	47	Voyage (millions $)
Passenger transport (millions $)	2	11	11	16	13	Transport de passagers (millions $)
Togo						**Togo**
Total expenditure (millions $)	59	68	94	89	...	Dépenses totales (millions $)
Travel (millions $)	17	19	47	46	...	Voyage (millions $)
Passenger transport (millions $)	42	49	47	43	...	Transport de passagers (millions $)
Tonga						**Tonga**
Total expenditure (millions $)	19	25	19	...	...	Dépenses totales (millions $)
Travel (millions $)	10	9	7	...	...	Voyage (millions $)
Passenger transport (millions $)	9	16	12	...	...	Transport de passagers (millions $)
Trinidad and Tobago						**Trinité-et-Tobago**
Total expenditure (millions $)	155	102	136	97	...	Dépenses totales (millions $)
Travel (millions $)	94	75	105	71	...	Voyage (millions $)
Passenger transport (millions $)	61	27	31	26	...	Transport de passagers (millions $)
Tunisia						**Tunisie**
Departures (thousands)	2 743	3 118	2 623	2 250	2 303	Départs (milliers)
Total expenditure (millions $)	530	555	478	611	678	Dépenses totales (millions $)
Travel (millions $)	437	458	415	547	607	Voyage (millions $)
Passenger transport (millions $)	93	97	63	64	71	Transport de passagers (millions $)
Turkey						**Turquie**
Departures (thousands)	4 956[33]	4 893	5 561	6 557	6 282	Départs (milliers)
Total expenditure (millions $)	3 867	4 195	4 635	5 451	5 469	Dépenses totales (millions $)
Travel (millions $)	3 260	3 506	4 147	4 826	4 976	Voyage (millions $)
Passenger transport (millions $)	607	689	488	625	493	Transport de passagers (millions $)
Turkmenistan						**Turkménistan**
Departures (thousands)	38	...	...	...	...	Départs (milliers)
Tuvalu						**Tuvalu**
Departures (thousands)	2	...	...	...	2	Départs (milliers)
Uganda						**Ouganda**
Departures (thousands)	272	337	311	324	367	Départs (milliers)
Total expenditure (millions $)	220	315	351	464	528	Dépenses totales (millions $)
Travel (millions $)	132	156	192	320	393	Voyage (millions $)
Passenger transport (millions $)	88	159	159	144	135	Transport de passagers (millions $)
Ukraine						**Ukraine**
Departures (thousands)	17 335	15 499	15 334	17 180	19 773	Départs (milliers)
Total expenditure (millions $)	4 022	4 585	3 751	4 134	4 829	Dépenses totales (millions $)
Travel (millions $)	3 569	4 023	3 330	3 742	4 461	Voyage (millions $)
Passenger transport (millions $)	453	562	421	392	368	Transport de passagers (millions $)
United Arab Emirates[36]						**Emirats arabes unis**[36]
Total expenditure (millions $)	11 273	13 288	10 347	11 818	...	Dépenses totales (millions $)
United Kingdom						**Royaume-Uni**
Departures (thousands)	69 450	69 011	58 614	55 562	56 836	Départs (milliers)
Total expenditure (millions $)	86 747	83 584	61 133	61 368	64 627	Dépenses totales (millions $)
Travel (millions $)	71 519	69 792	50 559	49 972	51 105	Voyage (millions $)
Passenger transport (millions $)	15 228	13 792	10 574	11 396	13 522	Transport de passagers (millions $)

58

Outbound tourism *(continued)*
Departures in thousands, expenditure (total, travel and passenger transport) in million US dollars
Tourisme à l'étranger *(suite)*
Départs en milliers, dépenses (total, voyage et transport de passagers) en millions de dollars E.-U.

Country or area	2007	2008	2009	2010	2011	Pays ou zone
United Rep. of Tanzania						**Rép.-Unie de Tanzanie**
Total expenditure (millions $)	616	746	806	861	928	Dépenses totales (millions $)
Travel (millions $)	595	721	766	830	899	Voyage (millions $)
Passenger transport (millions $)	21	25	40	31	29	Transport de passagers (millions $)
United States						**Etats-Unis**
Departures (thousands)	64 029	63 563	61 419	60 271	58 497	Départs (milliers)
Total expenditure (millions $)	110 693	118 746	105 745	109 764	117 293	Dépenses totales (millions $)
Travel (millions $)	83 012	86 905	80 628	82 508	86 184	Voyage (millions $)
Passenger transport (millions $)	27 681	31 841	25 117	27 256	31 109	Transport de passagers (millions $)
Uruguay						**Uruguay**
Departures (thousands)	635	734	826	1 027	1 534	Départs (milliers)
Total expenditure (millions $)	354	466	442	577	818	Dépenses totales (millions $)
Travel (millions $)	239	358	336	419	644	Voyage (millions $)
Passenger transport (millions $)	115	108	106	158	174	Transport de passagers (millions $)
Uzbekistan						**Ouzbékistan**
Departures (thousands)	1 248	1 150	1 317	1 610	...	Départs (milliers)
Vanuatu						**Vanuatu**
Departures (thousands)	16	19	20	21	22	Départs (milliers)
Total expenditure (millions $)	13	32	28	33	39	Dépenses totales (millions $)
Travel (millions $)	11	29	24	29	35	Voyage (millions $)
Passenger transport (millions $)	2	3	4	4	4	Transport de passagers (millions $)
Venezuela (Boliv. Rep. of)						**Venezuela (Rép. boliv. du)**
Departures (thousands)	1 410	1 745	1 651	1 477	1 719	Départs (milliers)
Total expenditure (millions $)	2 437	2 822	2 501	2 430	3 111	Dépenses totales (millions $)
Travel (millions $)	1 730	2 040	1 835	1 809	2 400	Voyage (millions $)
Passenger transport (millions $)	707	782	666	621	711	Transport de passagers (millions $)
Viet Nam [4]						**Viet Nam [4]**
Total expenditure (millions $)	1 220	1 300	1 100	1 470	1 710	Dépenses totales (millions $)
Yemen						**Yémen**
Total expenditure (millions $)	247	246	277	252	258	Dépenses totales (millions $)
Travel (millions $)	184	183	214	183	182	Voyage (millions $)
Passenger transport (millions $)	63	63	63	69	76	Transport de passagers (millions $)
Zambia						**Zambie**
Total expenditure (millions $)	98	107	83	128	140	Dépenses totales (millions $)
Travel (millions $)	56	64	39	68	76	Voyage (millions $)
Passenger transport (millions $)	42	43	44	60	64	Transport de passagers (millions $)
Zimbabwe						**Zimbabwe**
Departures (thousands)	547	593	631	650	693	Départs (milliers)

Source:
World Tourism Organization (UNWTO), Madrid, UNWTO statistics database and the *Yearbook of Tourism Statistics*, 2011 edition. Data on expenditure have been provided to the UNWTO by the International Monetary Fund (IMF).

Source:
Organisation mondiale du tourisme (OMT), Madrid, la base de données de l'OMT et l'*Annuaire des statistiques du tourisme*, édition 2011. Les données concernant les dépenses ont été fournies à l'Organisation mondiale du tourisme (OMT) par le Fonds monétaire international (FMI).

1   Including leisure and business trips abroad with at least one overnight stay.
2   Source: Central Bank of the Netherlands Antilles.
3   Person-trips (one or more nights).
4   The expenditure figures are those provided by the country to UNWTO, which do not appear in the International Monetary Fund data.
5   Source: "Banque des Etats de l'Afrique Centrale (B.E.A.C.)".
6   Including air crew members and other servicemen.
7   Including Hong Kong residents to Macao and Mainland China.
8   Source: Census and Statistics Department.
9   Source: Monthly Survey of Travel Agencies.
10 Source: "Banque centrale des Comores".

1   Y compris les voyages de détente et les voyages d'affaires à l'étranger comportant au moins une nuitée.
2   Source: "Central Bank of the Netherlands Antilles".
3   Personne-voyages (une ou plusieurs nuitées).
4   Les chiffres de dépense sont ceux que le pays a fournis à l'OMT mais ils ne figurent pas dans les données du Fonds monétaire international.
5   Source: Banque des Etats de l'Afrique Centrale (B.E.A.C.).
6   Y compris les membres de l'équipage des aéronefs et le personnel technique.
7   Y compris les résidents de Hong Kong qui se rendent à Macao ou en Chine continentale.
8   Source: "Département de recensement et statistiques".
9   Source: Enquête mensuelle sur les agences de voyages.
10 Source: Banque centrale des Comores.

58

Outbound tourism *(continued)*
Departures in thousands, expenditure (total, travel and passenger transport) in million US dollars
Tourisme à l'étranger *(suite)*
Départs en milliers, dépenses (total, voyage et transport de passagers) en millions de dollars E.-U.

11	Including only tours authorized by the "Instituto de Turismo".	11	Ne comprend que les excursions autorisées par l'Isntituto de Turismo.
12	Source from 2005: VisitDenmark.	12	A partir de 2005, source:"VisitDenmark".
13	From 2006: source: household survey by "Statistics Estonia"	13	A partir de 2006, source: enquête auprès des ménages par "Statistics Estonia".
14	Starting from 2004, border statistics are not collected any more.	14	À partir de 2004, les statistiques de frontière ne sont plus collectées.
15	Overnight trips abroad, including cruises abroad with overnight on board only.	15	Voyages à l'étranger comprenant une nuitée, y compris les croisières à l'étranger avec nuitées à bord uniquement.
16	From 1999: Source: "Banque de France".	16	A partir de 1999 : Source: Banque de France.
17	The observation of the borders with the countries of the Schengen Area ceased from the year 2008.	17	La surveillance des frontières avec les pays de la zone Schengen a pris fin en 2008.
18	Source: Icelandic Tourist Board.	18	Source: Icelandic Tourist Board.
19	Departures of nationals only, irrespective of purpose.	19	Départs des nationaux seulement, quel que soit le but de leur voyage.
20	Source: Central Bank of Islamic Republic of Iran.	20	Source: "Central Bank of Islamic Republic of Iran".
21	Including same-day visitors.	21	Y compris les visiteurs qui ne restent qu'une journée.
22	Number of resident tourists (overnight visitors) abroad.	22	Nombre de touristes résidents (visiteurs passant la nuit) à l'étranger.
23	Data by State Border Guard.	23	Donnes émanant du Service des gardes-frontières.
24	The expenditure figures are those provided by the country to UNWTO, which do not appear in the International Monetary Fund data. Fiscal years (October 1 to September 30).	24	Les chiffres de dépense sont ceux que le pays a fournis à l'OMT mais ils ne figurent pas dans les données du Fonds monétaire international. Années fiscales (du 1er octobre au 30 septembre).
25	Holiday departures of nationals.	25	Départs en vacances de nationaux.
26	Returning residents.	26	Résidents de retour.
27	Holiday trips.	27	Voyages de détente.
28	West Bank and Gaza.	28	Cisjordanie et Gaza.
29	Outbound Tourism Survey.	29	Enquête sur le tourisme à l'étranger.
30	Including overseas contract workers.	30	Y compris les employés contractuels étrangers.
31	Outbound trips registered at frontiers.	31	Voyages a l'étranger enregistrés aux frontières.
32	Fiscal years July to June.	32	Années fiscales (juillet-juin).
33	Change in methodology.	33	Changement de méthode.
34	New series.	34	Nouvelle série.
35	Quarterly survey on travels of domestic population.	35	Enquête trimestrielle sur les voyages de la population nationale.
36	Source: Central Bank of the U.A.E.	36	Source: Banque centrale des E.A.U (Emirats arabes unis).

Civil aviation: scheduled airline traffic
Passengers carried (thousands); kilometres (millions)

Aviation civile : trafic aérien régulier
Passagers transportés (milliers) ; kilomètres (millions)

Country or area and traffic	Total traffic (domestic and international) Trafic total (intérieur et international)		International traffic Trafic international		Pays ou zone et trafic
	2010	2011	2010	2011	
Afghanistan					**Afghanistan**
Kilometres flown	24	24	19	18	Kilomètres parcourus
Passengers carried	1 999	2 279	1 170	1 277	Passagers transportés
Passenger-kilometres	2 646	2 617	2 250	2 161	Passagers-kilomètres
Total tonne-kilometres	350	349	300	290	Tonnes-kilomètres totales
Albania					**Albanie**
Kilometres flown	8	9	8	9	Kilomètres parcourus
Passengers carried	769	925	769	925	Passagers transportés
Passenger-kilometres	1 202	1 553	1 202	1 553	Passagers-kilomètres
Total tonne-kilometres	110	140	110	140	Tonnes-kilomètres totales
Algeria					**Algérie**
Kilometres flown	53	53	38	38	Kilomètres parcourus
Passengers carried	3 372	3 544	2 076	2 286	Passagers transportés
Passenger-kilometres	3 994	4 195	3 338	3 532	Passagers-kilomètres
Total tonne-kilometres	375	392	315	332	Tonnes-kilomètres totales
Angola					**Angola**
Kilometres flown	34	20	26	15	Kilomètres parcourus
Passengers carried	1 010	988	472	443	Passagers transportés
Passenger-kilometres	2 706	2 533	2 341	2 164	Passagers-kilomètres
Total tonne-kilometres	291	279	258	245	Tonnes-kilomètres totales
Argentina					**Argentine**
Kilometres flown	133	134	59	62	Kilomètres parcourus
Passengers carried	8 979	8 588	2 403	2 487	Passagers transportés
Passenger-kilometres	17 573	17 676	9 696	10 474	Passagers-kilomètres
Total tonne-kilometres	1 881	1 866	1 110	1 181	Tonnes-kilomètres totales
Australia					**Australie**
Kilometres flown	779	807	295	311	Kilomètres parcourus
Passengers carried	60 641	62 538	10 999	11 587	Passagers transportés
Passenger-kilometres	126 283	132 302	68 153	71 693	Passagers-kilomètres
Total tonne-kilometres	14 981	15 448	9 413	9 656	Tonnes-kilomètres totales
Austria					**Autriche**
Kilometres flown	159	172	155	168	Kilomètres parcourus
Passengers carried	13 494	17 213	12 901	16 642	Passagers transportés
Passenger-kilometres	17 528	19 745	17 363	19 583	Passagers-kilomètres
Total tonne-kilometres	2 135	2 366	2 118	2 349	Tonnes-kilomètres totales
Azerbaijan					**Azerbaïdjan**
Kilometres flown	16	21	16	19	Kilomètres parcourus
Passengers carried	797	1 348	762	925	Passagers transportés
Passenger-kilometres	1 428	2 013	1 416	1 780	Passagers-kilomètres
Total tonne-kilometres	136	191	135	169	Tonnes-kilomètres totales
Bahrain					**Bahreïn**
Kilometres flown	98	103	98	103	Kilomètres parcourus
Passengers carried	6 029	5 591	6 029	5 591	Passagers transportés
Passenger-kilometres	12 691	11 960	12 691	11 960	Passagers-kilomètres
Total tonne-kilometres	1 590	1 446	1 590	1 446	Tonnes-kilomètres totales
Bangladesh					**Bangladesh**
Kilometres flown	37	40	37	38	Kilomètres parcourus
Passengers carried	2 237	2 487	1 792	1 781	Passagers transportés
Passenger-kilometres	4 931	5 195	4 888	5 101	Passagers-kilomètres
Total tonne-kilometres	568	589	560	565	Tonnes-kilomètres totales
Belgium					**Belgique**
Kilometres flown	111	117	111	117	Kilomètres parcourus
Passengers carried	4 964	5 696	4 964	5 696	Passagers transportés
Passenger-kilometres	7 454	8 494	7 454	8 494	Passagers-kilomètres
Total tonne-kilometres	1 742	2 132	1 742	2 132	Tonnes-kilomètres totales

Civil aviation: scheduled airline traffic *(continued)*
Passengers carried (thousands); kilometres (millions)

Aviation civile : trafic régulier des lignes aériennes *(suite)*
Passagers transportés (milliers) ; kilomètres (millions)

Country or area and traffic	Total traffic (domestic and international) Trafic total (intérieur et international)		International traffic Trafic international		Pays ou zone et trafic
	2010	2011	2010	2011	
Bolivia (Plurin. State of)					**Bolivie (État plurin. de)**
Kilometres flown	22	26	8	9	Kilomètres parcourus
Passengers carried	1 781	2 126	404	537	Passagers transportés
Passenger-kilometres	1 603	2 097	1 099	1 446	Passagers-kilomètres
Total tonne-kilometres	161	226	111	159	Tonnes-kilomètres totales
Brazil					**Brésil**
Kilometres flown	791	921	136	153	Kilomètres parcourus
Passengers carried	74 598	87 891	5 227	5 761	Passagers transportés
Passenger-kilometres	90 619	105 728	22 763	25 728	Passagers-kilomètres
Total tonne-kilometres	9 070	10 888	2 521	3 234	Tonnes-kilomètres totales
Brunei Darussalam					**Brunéi Darussalam**
Kilometres flown	32	30	32	30	Kilomètres parcourus
Passengers carried	1 263	1 313	1 263	1 313	Passagers transportés
Passenger-kilometres	4 853	4 988	4 853	4 988	Passagers-kilomètres
Total tonne-kilometres	587	600	587	600	Tonnes-kilomètres totales
Bulgaria					**Bulgarie**
Kilometres flown	13	15	12	13	Kilomètres parcourus
Passengers carried	708	933	587	734	Passagers transportés
Passenger-kilometres	1 109	1 239	1 065	1 170	Passagers-kilomètres
Total tonne-kilometres	103	115	99	108	Tonnes-kilomètres totales
Canada					**Canada**
Kilometres flown	1 162	1 208	457	494	Kilomètres parcourus
Passengers carried	67 277	70 254	20 277	21 934	Passagers transportés
Passenger-kilometres	115 793	123 664	68 167	75 110	Passagers-kilomètres
Total tonne-kilometres	13 417	14 201	8 086	8 795	Tonnes-kilomètres totales
Chile					**Chili**
Kilometres flown	153	173	87	98	Kilomètres parcourus
Passengers carried	9 269	10 950	3 296	3 925	Passagers transportés
Passenger-kilometres	19 196	21 749	12 624	14 184	Passagers-kilomètres
Total tonne-kilometres	3 139	3 393	2 494	2 660	Tonnes-kilomètres totales
China[1]					**Chine**[1]
Kilometres flown	3 167	3 458	552	625	Kilomètres parcourus
Passengers carried	266 293	292 160	18 503	20 547	Passagers transportés
Passenger-kilometres	400 609	451 162	73 488	85 758	Passagers-kilomètres
Total tonne-kilometres	53 302	57 416	18 871	19 444	Tonnes-kilomètres totales
China, Hong Kong SAR[2]					**Chine, Hong Kong RAS**[2]
Kilometres flown	496	540	496	540	Kilomètres parcourus
Passengers carried	28 348	30 294	28 348	30 294	Passagers transportés
Passenger-kilometres	98 707	106 013	98 707	106 013	Passagers-kilomètres
Total tonne-kilometres	20 087	20 430	20 087	20 430	Tonnes-kilomètres totales
China, Macao SAR[3]					**Chine, Macao RAS**[3]
Kilometres flown	21	22	21	22	Kilomètres parcourus
Passengers carried	1 330	1 328	1 330	1 328	Passagers transportés
Passenger-kilometres	2 106	2 143	2 106	2 143	Passagers-kilomètres
Total tonne-kilometres	246	239	246	239	Tonnes-kilomètres totales
Colombia					**Colombie**
Kilometres flown	163	174	85	92	Kilomètres parcourus
Passengers carried	16 932	18 769	3 585	3 855	Passagers transportés
Passenger-kilometres	16 723	17 832	10 195	10 501	Passagers-kilomètres
Total tonne-kilometres	2 555	2 687	1 726	1 710	Tonnes-kilomètres totales
Costa Rica					**Costa Rica**
Kilometres flown	28	31	26	28	Kilomètres parcourus
Passengers carried	1 678	1 862	1 479	1 600	Passagers transportés
Passenger-kilometres	2 761	2 950	2 742	2 918	Passagers-kilomètres
Total tonne-kilometres	251	268	249	265	Tonnes-kilomètres totales

59

Civil aviation: scheduled airline traffic *(continued)*
Passengers carried (thousands); kilometres (millions)
Aviation civile : trafic régulier des lignes aériennes *(suite)*
Passagers transportés (milliers) ; kilomètres (millions)

Country or area and traffic	Total traffic (domestic and international) Trafic total (intérieur et international)		International traffic Trafic international		Pays ou zone et trafic
	2010	2011	2010	2011	
Croatia					**Croatie**
Kilometres flown	15	16	13	14	Kilomètres parcourus
Passengers carried	1 577	1 813	1 136	1 307	Passagers transportés
Passenger-kilometres	1 060	1 230	921	1 070	Passagers-kilomètres
Total tonne-kilometres	98	113	85	98	Tonnes-kilomètres totales
Cuba					**Cuba**
Kilometres flown	16	17	11	12	Kilomètres parcourus
Passengers carried	910	853	460	456	Passagers transportés
Passenger-kilometres	1 707	1 933	1 464	1 705	Passagers-kilomètres
Total tonne-kilometres	171	193	146	171	Tonnes-kilomètres totales
Cyprus					**Chypre**
Kilometres flown	24	21	24	21	Kilomètres parcourus
Passengers carried	1 584	1 263	1 584	1 263	Passagers transportés
Passenger-kilometres	3 013	2 380	3 013	2 380	Passagers-kilomètres
Total tonne-kilometres	310	234	310	234	Tonnes-kilomètres totales
Czech Republic					**République tchèque**
Kilometres flown	69	64	68	63	Kilomètres parcourus
Passengers carried	5 145	4 903	5 067	4 875	Passagers transportés
Passenger-kilometres	5 998	5 950	5 978	5 942	Passagers-kilomètres
Total tonne-kilometres	561	556	559	556	Tonnes-kilomètres totales
Ecuador					**Equateur**
Kilometres flown	44	45	26	29	Kilomètres parcourus
Passengers carried	4 818	5 094	1 040	1 553	Passagers transportés
Passenger-kilometres	5 421	5 720	3 959	4 276	Passagers-kilomètres
Total tonne-kilometres	615	663	475	524	Tonnes-kilomètres totales
Egypt					**Egypte**
Kilometres flown	144	112	128	102	Kilomètres parcourus
Passengers carried	9 179	6 516	6 622	5 090	Passagers transportés
Passenger-kilometres	20 054	13 907	18 872	13 267	Passagers-kilomètres
Total tonne-kilometres	2 411	1 652	2 298	1 589	Tonnes-kilomètres totales
El Salvador					**El Salvador**
Kilometres flown	38	45	38	45	Kilomètres parcourus
Passengers carried	2 137	2 530	2 137	2 530	Passagers transportés
Passenger-kilometres	3 593	4 222	3 593	4 222	Passagers-kilomètres
Total tonne-kilometres	319	378	319	378	Tonnes-kilomètres totales
Ethiopia					**Ethiopie**
Kilometres flown	100	119	96	115	Kilomètres parcourus
Passengers carried	3 347	4 441	2 904	3 847	Passagers transportés
Passenger-kilometres	11 652	15 330	11 451	15 064	Passagers-kilomètres
Total tonne-kilometres	1 864	2 382	1 845	2 356	Tonnes-kilomètres totales
Fiji					**Fidji**
Kilometres flown	20	21	18	19	Kilomètres parcourus
Passengers carried	1 259	1 276	851	941	Passagers transportés
Passenger-kilometres	3 455	3 895	3 392	3 837	Passagers-kilomètres
Total tonne-kilometres	353	404	345	396	Tonnes-kilomètres totales
Finland					**Finlande**
Kilometres flown	148	172	126	150	Kilomètres parcourus
Passengers carried	8 436	9 235	6 304	7 057	Passagers transportés
Passenger-kilometres	17 786	20 386	16 708	19 273	Passagers-kilomètres
Total tonne-kilometres	2 352	2 568	2 252	2 465	Tonnes-kilomètres totales
France					**France**
Kilometres flown	868	885	676	697	Kilomètres parcourus
Passengers carried	55 758	58 844	33 669	35 463	Passagers transportés
Passenger-kilometres	154 606	162 638	129 924	137 168	Passagers-kilomètres
Total tonne-kilometres	19 303	20 071	16 909	17 593	Tonnes-kilomètres totales

59

Civil aviation: scheduled airline traffic *(continued)*
Passengers carried (thousands); kilometres (millions)
Aviation civile : trafic régulier des lignes aériennes *(suite)*
Passagers transportés (milliers) ; kilomètres (millions)

Country or area and traffic	Total traffic (domestic and international) Trafic total (intérieur et international)		International traffic Trafic international		Pays ou zone et trafic
	2010	2011	2010	2011	
Germany					**Allemagne**
Kilometres flown	1 331	1 418	1 216	1 304	Kilomètres parcourus
Passengers carried	101 852	112 016	78 708	88 030	Passagers transportés
Passenger-kilometres	201 537	220 036	191 405	209 595	Passagers-kilomètres
Total tonne-kilometres	27 767	29 925	26 758	28 885	Tonnes-kilomètres totales
Greece					**Grèce**
Kilometres flown	79	72	54	50	Kilomètres parcourus
Passengers carried	9 931	9 180	3 901	3 651	Passagers transportés
Passenger-kilometres	7 560	7 177	5 816	5 555	Passagers-kilomètres
Total tonne-kilometres	761	693	585	534	Tonnes-kilomètres totales
Hungary					**Hongrie**
Kilometres flown	127	142	127	142	Kilomètres parcourus
Passengers carried	11 787	12 970	11 787	12 970	Passagers transportés
Passenger-kilometres	14 984	17 021	14 984	17 021	Passagers-kilomètres
Total tonne-kilometres	1 377	1 562	1 377	1 562	Tonnes-kilomètres totales
Iceland					**Islande**
Kilometres flown	31	37	31	37	Kilomètres parcourus
Passengers carried	1 553	1 804	1 553	1 804	Passagers transportés
Passenger-kilometres	4 112	4 970	4 112	4 970	Passagers-kilomètres
Total tonne-kilometres	485	566	485	566	Tonnes-kilomètres totales
India					**Inde**
Kilometres flown	752	830	320	330	Kilomètres parcourus
Passengers carried	64 688	74 357	12 939	14 068	Passagers transportés
Passenger-kilometres	100 371	110 960	49 981	52 678	Passagers-kilomètres
Total tonne-kilometres	10 683	11 801	5 998	6 328	Tonnes-kilomètres totales
Indonesia					**Indonésie**
Kilometres flown	440	518	101	135	Kilomètres parcourus
Passengers carried	56 774	67 795	6 442	8 302	Passagers transportés
Passenger-kilometres	60 649	73 098	15 737	20 272	Passagers-kilomètres
Total tonne-kilometres	5 797	6 964	1 793	2 242	Tonnes-kilomètres totales
Iran (Islamic Rep. of)					**Iran (Rép. islamique d')**
Kilometres flown	127	128	45	45	Kilomètres parcourus
Passengers carried	16 167	16 471	3 462	3 152	Passagers transportés
Passenger-kilometres	16 851	16 637	7 279	6 711	Passagers-kilomètres
Total tonne-kilometres	1 596	1 628	704	677	Tonnes-kilomètres totales
Ireland					**Irlande**
Kilometres flown	647	728	645	727	Kilomètres parcourus
Passengers carried	84 784	89 956	84 498	89 778	Passagers transportés
Passenger-kilometres	97 834	109 948	97 779	109 913	Passagers-kilomètres
Total tonne-kilometres	8 959	10 101	8 952	10 096	Tonnes-kilomètres totales
Israel					**Israël**
Kilometres flown	109	109	104	104	Kilomètres parcourus
Passengers carried	5 085	5 151	3 860	3 825	Passagers transportés
Passenger-kilometres	18 178	17 926	17 809	17 530	Passagers-kilomètres
Total tonne-kilometres	2 687	2 688	2 653	2 651	Tonnes-kilomètres totales
Italy					**Italie**
Kilometres flown	317	320	209	217	Kilomètres parcourus
Passengers carried	30 804	31 837	13 310	13 802	Passagers transportés
Passenger-kilometres	41 195	43 017	31 246	32 840	Passagers-kilomètres
Total tonne-kilometres	4 478	4 683	3 505	3 672	Tonnes-kilomètres totales
Japan					**Japon**
Kilometres flown	1 016	936	384	384	Kilomètres parcourus
Passengers carried	109 551	89 735	13 245	12 158	Passagers transportés
Passenger-kilometres	145 956	122 628	61 064	53 039	Passagers-kilomètres
Total tonne-kilometres	20 128	17 094	12 699	10 886	Tonnes-kilomètres totales

59

Civil aviation: scheduled airline traffic *(continued)*
Passengers carried (thousands); kilometres (millions)
Aviation civile : trafic régulier des lignes aériennes *(suite)*
Passagers transportés (milliers) ; kilomètres (millions)

Country or area and traffic	Total traffic (domestic and international) Trafic total (intérieur et international)		International traffic Trafic international		Pays ou zone et trafic
	2010	2011	2010	2011	
Jordan					**Jordanie**
Kilometres flown	69	72	69	71	Kilomètres parcourus
Passengers carried	2 972	3 155	2 910	3 093	Passagers transportés
Passenger-kilometres	7 805	8 316	7 789	8 300	Passagers-kilomètres
Total tonne-kilometres	908	950	907	948	Tonnes-kilomètres totales
Kazakhstan					**Kazakhstan**
Kilometres flown	57	68	33	39	Kilomètres parcourus
Passengers carried	3 098	3 786	1 094	1 397	Passagers transportés
Passenger-kilometres	5 798	6 856	3 419	4 073	Passagers-kilomètres
Total tonne-kilometres	579	687	349	416	Tonnes-kilomètres totales
Kenya					**Kenya**
Kilometres flown	114	118	102	106	Kilomètres parcourus
Passengers carried	4 040	4 509	2 889	3 213	Passagers transportés
Passenger-kilometres	9 236	9 998	8 826	9 540	Passagers-kilomètres
Total tonne-kilometres	1 214	1 289	1 169	1 240	Tonnes-kilomètres totales
Kuwait					**Koweït**
Kilometres flown	74	58	74	58	Kilomètres parcourus
Passengers carried	4 563	3 723	4 563	3 723	Passagers transportés
Passenger-kilometres	10 219	9 058	10 219	9 058	Passagers-kilomètres
Total tonne-kilometres	1 298	1 112	1 298	1 112	Tonnes-kilomètres totales
Latvia					**Lettonie**
Kilometres flown	46	45	46	45	Kilomètres parcourus
Passengers carried	3 158	3 299	3 158	3 299	Passagers transportés
Passenger-kilometres	3 564	3 598	3 564	3 598	Passagers-kilomètres
Total tonne-kilometres	327	330	327	330	Tonnes-kilomètres totales
Lebanon					**Liban**
Kilometres flown	38	37	38	37	Kilomètres parcourus
Passengers carried	1 893	2 030	1 893	2 030	Passagers transportés
Passenger-kilometres	3 619	3 827	3 619	3 827	Passagers-kilomètres
Total tonne-kilometres	430	453	430	453	Tonnes-kilomètres totales
Libyan Arab Jamah.					**Jamah. arabe libyenne**
Kilometres flown	55	43	49	39	Kilomètres parcourus
Passengers carried	2 431	1 896	1 861	1 456	Passagers transportés
Passenger-kilometres	4 035	3 084	3 631	2 762	Passagers-kilomètres
Total tonne-kilometres	493	391	454	359	Tonnes-kilomètres totales
Luxembourg					**Luxembourg**
Kilometres flown	73	78	73	78	Kilomètres parcourus
Passengers carried	787	785	787	785	Passagers transportés
Passenger-kilometres	434	464	434	464	Passagers-kilomètres
Total tonne-kilometres	4 941	5 021	4 941	5 021	Tonnes-kilomètres totales
Madagascar					**Madagascar**
Kilometres flown	12	11	8	8	Kilomètres parcourus
Passengers carried	524	548	237	237	Passagers transportés
Passenger-kilometres	1 240	1 095	1 099	937	Passagers-kilomètres
Total tonne-kilometres	135	118	122	104	Tonnes-kilomètres totales
Malaysia					**Malaisie**
Kilometres flown	395	439	291	318	Kilomètres parcourus
Passengers carried	34 239	38 219	18 004	19 703	Passagers transportés
Passenger-kilometres	65 972	73 979	53 968	59 494	Passagers-kilomètres
Total tonne-kilometres	8 784	9 082	7 537	7 609	Tonnes-kilomètres totales
Malta					**Malte**
Kilometres flown	24	22	24	22	Kilomètres parcourus
Passengers carried	1 700	1 674	1 700	1 674	Passagers transportés
Passenger-kilometres	2 257	2 537	2 257	2 537	Passagers-kilomètres
Total tonne-kilometres	212	234	212	234	Tonnes-kilomètres totales

59

Civil aviation: scheduled airline traffic *(continued)*
Passengers carried (thousands); kilometres (millions)
Aviation civile : trafic régulier des lignes aériennes *(suite)*
Passagers transportés (milliers) ; kilomètres (millions)

Country or area and traffic	Total traffic (domestic and international) Trafic total (intérieur et international)		International traffic Trafic international		Pays ou zone et trafic
	2010	2011	2010	2011	
Mauritius					**Maurice**
Kilometres flown	40	42	39	41	Kilomètres parcourus
Passengers carried	1 265	1 321	1 162	1 208	Passagers transportés
Passenger-kilometres	6 320	6 605	6 257	6 536	Passagers-kilomètres
Total tonne-kilometres	762	788	756	782	Tonnes-kilomètres totales
Mexico					**Mexique**
Kilometres flown	478	399	171	129	Kilomètres parcourus
Passengers carried	31 269	29 539	6 060	4 783	Passagers transportés
Passenger-kilometres	43 214	39 652	18 423	15 102	Passagers-kilomètres
Total tonne-kilometres	4 362	4 070	2 079	1 672	Tonnes-kilomètres totales
Morocco					**Maroc**
Kilometres flown	136	135	130	130	Kilomètres parcourus
Passengers carried	7 144	7 503	6 427	6 830	Passagers transportés
Passenger-kilometres	14 366	15 546	14 040	15 219	Passagers-kilomètres
Total tonne-kilometres	1 475	1 548	1 442	1 516	Tonnes-kilomètres totales
Namibia					**Namibie**
Kilometres flown	14	15	12	14	Kilomètres parcourus
Passengers carried	486	541	431	465	Passagers transportés
Passenger-kilometres	1 428	1 473	1 407	1 440	Passagers-kilomètres
Total tonne-kilometres	143	148	141	145	Tonnes-kilomètres totales
Netherlands					**Pays-Bas**
Kilometres flown	451	484	451	484	Kilomètres parcourus
Passengers carried	26 309	29 214	26 309	29 214	Passagers transportés
Passenger-kilometres	81 646	88 964	81 646	88 964	Passagers-kilomètres
Total tonne-kilometres	14 259	15 126	14 259	15 126	Tonnes-kilomètres totales
New Zealand					**Nouvelle-Zélande**
Kilometres flown	188	190	123	125	Kilomètres parcourus
Passengers carried	13 319	13 771	5 061	5 364	Passagers transportés
Passenger-kilometres	23 568	24 653	19 707	20 667	Passagers-kilomètres
Total tonne-kilometres	2 788	3 313	2 432	2 947	Tonnes-kilomètres totales
Nigeria					**Nigéria**
Kilometres flown	41	44	19	19	Kilomètres parcourus
Passengers carried	4 197	4 794	865	854	Passagers transportés
Passenger-kilometres	3 067	3 466	1 660	1 643	Passagers-kilomètres
Total tonne-kilometres	286	322	160	158	Tonnes-kilomètres totales
Oman					**Oman**
Kilometres flown	55	67	52	64	Kilomètres parcourus
Passengers carried	3 263	3 796	2 859	3 341	Passagers transportés
Passenger-kilometres	6 960	8 457	6 624	8 078	Passagers-kilomètres
Total tonne-kilometres	736	928	705	895	Tonnes-kilomètres totales
Pakistan					**Pakistan**
Kilometres flown	99	115	77	89	Kilomètres parcourus
Passengers carried	6 588	7 941	4 213	4 695	Passagers transportés
Passenger-kilometres	17 294	18 809	14 876	15 917	Passagers-kilomètres
Total tonne-kilometres	1 902	2 022	1 654	1 729	Tonnes-kilomètres totales
Panama					**Panama**
Kilometres flown	118	155	115	153	Kilomètres parcourus
Passengers carried	3 614	4 138	3 379	3 935	Passagers transportés
Passenger-kilometres	11 635	13 795	11 574	13 742	Passagers-kilomètres
Total tonne-kilometres	1 219	1 428	1 204	1 414	Tonnes-kilomètres totales
Papua New Guinea					**Papouasie-Nvl-Guinée**
Kilometres flown	30	35	15	18	Kilomètres parcourus
Passengers carried	1 405	1 564	213	246	Passagers transportés
Passenger-kilometres	1 252	1 495	633	812	Passagers-kilomètres
Total tonne-kilometres	175	209	104	138	Tonnes-kilomètres totales

59

Civil aviation: scheduled airline traffic *(continued)*
Passengers carried (thousands); kilometres (millions)
Aviation civile : trafic régulier des lignes aériennes *(suite)*
Passagers transportés (milliers) ; kilomètres (millions)

Country or area and traffic	Total traffic (domestic and international) Trafic total (intérieur et international)		International traffic Trafic international		Pays ou zone et trafic
	2010	2011	2010	2011	
Peru					**Pérou**
Kilometres flown	110	134	68	86	Kilomètres parcourus
Passengers carried	7 106	8 610	2 082	2 500	Passagers transportés
Passenger-kilometres	9 031	13 313	6 058	8 868	Passagers-kilomètres
Total tonne-kilometres	1 049	1 603	762	1 146	Tonnes-kilomètres totales
Philippines					**Philippines**
Kilometres flown	192	216	106	117	Kilomètres parcourus
Passengers carried	22 575	25 589	6 007	6 824	Passagers transportés
Passenger-kilometres	30 068	32 683	20 543	21 690	Passagers-kilomètres
Total tonne-kilometres	3 302	3 701	2 390	2 483	Tonnes-kilomètres totales
Poland					**Pologne**
Kilometres flown	76	77	69	71	Kilomètres parcourus
Passengers carried	4 099	4 449	3 188	3 409	Passagers transportés
Passenger-kilometres	6 576	6 835	6 307	6 537	Passagers-kilomètres
Total tonne-kilometres	683	659	661	633	Tonnes-kilomètres totales
Portugal					**Portugal**
Kilometres flown	199	207	177	185	Kilomètres parcourus
Passengers carried	10 435	11 022	7 780	8 444	Passagers transportés
Passenger-kilometres	25 793	27 653	23 610	25 580	Passagers-kilomètres
Total tonne-kilometres	2 714	2 871	2 496	2 667	Tonnes-kilomètres totales
Qatar					**Qatar**
Kilometres flown	307	362	307	362	Kilomètres parcourus
Passengers carried	12 391	14 568	12 391	14 568	Passagers transportés
Passenger-kilometres	52 733	61 600	52 733	61 600	Passagers-kilomètres
Total tonne-kilometres	7 723	9 232	7 723	9 232	Tonnes-kilomètres totales
Republic of Korea					**République de Corée**
Kilometres flown	601	628	559	590	Kilomètres parcourus
Passengers carried	36 988	39 912	23 877	26 593	Passagers transportés
Passenger-kilometres	87 457	95 487	82 651	90 579	Passagers-kilomètres
Total tonne-kilometres	21 029	21 425	20 554	20 895	Tonnes-kilomètres totales
Romania					**Roumanie**
Kilometres flown	59	56	53	50	Kilomètres parcourus
Passengers carried	3 593	3 659	2 978	2 964	Passagers transportés
Passenger-kilometres	4 423	4 520	4 202	4 270	Passagers-kilomètres
Total tonne-kilometres	420	435	400	412	Tonnes-kilomètres totales
Russian Federation					**Fédération de Russie**
Kilometres flown	971	1 121	395	472	Kilomètres parcourus
Passengers carried	43 856	50 556	16 296	19 658	Passagers transportés
Passenger-kilometres	109 435	126 837	52 616	63 452	Passagers-kilomètres
Total tonne-kilometres	13 474	15 429	7 614	8 934	Tonnes-kilomètres totales
Saudi Arabia					**Arabie saoudite**
Kilometres flown	234	268	149	178	Kilomètres parcourus
Passengers carried	20 324	22 920	8 711	10 112	Passagers transportés
Passenger-kilometres	33 225	38 805	23 449	27 944	Passagers-kilomètres
Total tonne-kilometres	4 509	5 370	3 536	4 235	Tonnes-kilomètres totales
Scandinavia [4]					**Scandinavie** [4]
Kilometres flown	419	454	317	347	Kilomètres parcourus
Passengers carried	44 170	50 219	29 188	33 706	Passagers transportés
Passenger-kilometres	42 625	47 313	36 296	40 393	Passagers-kilomètres
Total tonne-kilometres	4 587	5 031	3 973	4 365	Tonnes-kilomètres totales
Serbia					**Serbie**
Kilometres flown	14	15	14	15	Kilomètres parcourus
Passengers carried	985	1 149	985	1 149	Passagers transportés
Passenger-kilometres	1 004	1 173	1 004	1 173	Passagers-kilomètres
Total tonne-kilometres	93	108	93	108	Tonnes-kilomètres totales

59

Civil aviation: scheduled airline traffic *(continued)*
Passengers carried (thousands); kilometres (millions)
Aviation civile : trafic régulier des lignes aériennes *(suite)*
Passagers transportés (milliers) ; kilomètres (millions)

Country or area and traffic	Total traffic (domestic and international) Trafic total (intérieur et international)		International traffic Trafic international		Pays ou zone et trafic
	2010	2011	2010	2011	
Seychelles					**Seychelles**
Kilometres flown	9	9	8	8	Kilomètres parcourus
Passengers carried	413	394	255	221	Passagers transportés
Passenger-kilometres	1 556	1 362	1 549	1 354	Passagers-kilomètres
Total tonne-kilometres	200	175	199	174	Tonnes-kilomètres totales
Singapore					**Singapour**
Kilometres flown	490	526	490	526	Kilomètres parcourus
Passengers carried	24 809	26 456	24 809	26 456	Passagers transportés
Passenger-kilometres	97 398	102 516	97 398	102 516	Passagers-kilomètres
Total tonne-kilometres	17 131	17 957	17 131	17 957	Tonnes-kilomètres totales
South Africa					**Afrique du Sud**
Kilometres flown	247	251	141	144	Kilomètres parcourus
Passengers carried	15 781	16 408	5 508	5 620	Passagers transportés
Passenger-kilometres	29 741	30 750	20 190	20 797	Passagers-kilomètres
Total tonne-kilometres	3 736	3 888	2 772	2 873	Tonnes-kilomètres totales
Spain					**Espagne**
Kilometres flown	575	585	374	397	Kilomètres parcourus
Passengers carried	53 046	52 934	22 400	23 330	Passagers transportés
Passenger-kilometres	87 680	90 570	65 884	69 839	Passagers-kilomètres
Total tonne-kilometres	9 431	9 851	7 346	7 816	Tonnes-kilomètres totales
Sri Lanka					**Sri Lanka**
Kilometres flown	49	60	49	59	Kilomètres parcourus
Passengers carried	3 008	3 665	3 003	3 660	Passagers transportés
Passenger-kilometres	9 773	11 573	9 768	11 567	Passagers-kilomètres
Total tonne-kilometres	1 232	1 419	1 231	1 419	Tonnes-kilomètres totales
Sudan (former)					**Soudan (anc.)**
Kilometres flown	12	19	7	12	Kilomètres parcourus
Passengers carried	580	947	399	612	Passagers transportés
Passenger-kilometres	758	1 146	539	766	Passagers-kilomètres
Total tonne-kilometres	107	159	73	103	Tonnes-kilomètres totales
Suriname					**Suriname**
Kilometres flown	5	5	5	5	Kilomètres parcourus
Passengers carried	215	204	215	204	Passagers transportés
Passenger-kilometres	1 076	1 000	1 076	1 000	Passagers-kilomètres
Total tonne-kilometres	121	114	121	114	Tonnes-kilomètres totales
Switzerland					**Suisse**
Kilometres flown	302	309	300	306	Kilomètres parcourus
Passengers carried	22 147	24 866	21 476	24 190	Passagers transportés
Passenger-kilometres	39 233	43 361	39 079	43 204	Passagers-kilomètres
Total tonne-kilometres	5 238	5 665	5 222	5 649	Tonnes-kilomètres totales
Syrian Arab Republic					**Rép. arabe syrienne**
Kilometres flown	21	23	21	22	Kilomètres parcourus
Passengers carried	1 158	1 434	886	1 060	Passagers transportés
Passenger-kilometres	1 634	1 789	1 602	1 745	Passagers-kilomètres
Total tonne-kilometres	180	196	176	192	Tonnes-kilomètres totales
Tajikistan					**Tadjikistan**
Kilometres flown	14	19	13	18	Kilomètres parcourus
Passengers carried	696	955	560	812	Passagers transportés
Passenger-kilometres	1 665	2 347	1 596	2 276	Passagers-kilomètres
Total tonne-kilometres	163	231	157	225	Tonnes-kilomètres totales
Thailand					**Thaïlande**
Kilometres flown	323	356	260	282	Kilomètres parcourus
Passengers carried	28 781	31 517	15 910	16 479	Passagers transportés
Passenger-kilometres	65 007	67 363	57 210	58 208	Passagers-kilomètres
Total tonne-kilometres	8 960	9 133	8 173	8 204	Tonnes-kilomètres totales

59

Civil aviation: scheduled airline traffic *(continued)*
Passengers carried (thousands); kilometres (millions)

Aviation civile : trafic régulier des lignes aériennes *(suite)*
Passagers transportés (milliers) ; kilomètres (millions)

Country or area and traffic	Total traffic (domestic and international) Trafic total (intérieur et international)		International traffic Trafic international		Pays ou zone et trafic
	2010	2011	2010	2011	
Trinidad and Tobago					**Trinité-et-Tobago**
Kilometres flown	37	52	33	48	Kilomètres parcourus
Passengers carried	1 842	2 625	1 225	1 925	Passagers transportés
Passenger-kilometres	3 009	4 463	2 958	4 406	Passagers-kilomètres
Total tonne-kilometres	288	419	284	414	Tonnes-kilomètres totales
Tunisia					**Tunisie**
Kilometres flown	37	39	36	38	Kilomètres parcourus
Passengers carried	2 740	2 750	2 484	2 525	Passagers transportés
Passenger-kilometres	3 528	3 767	3 458	3 701	Passagers-kilomètres
Total tonne-kilometres	358	382	352	376	Tonnes-kilomètres totales
Turkey					**Turquie**
Kilometres flown	484	566	363	430	Kilomètres parcourus
Passengers carried	45 665	53 500	20 784	24 997	Passagers transportés
Passenger-kilometres	66 217	79 458	48 836	61 484	Passagers-kilomètres
Total tonne-kilometres	7 771	9 480	6 090	7 768	Tonnes-kilomètres totales
Ukraine					**Ukraine**
Kilometres flown	85	105	73	93	Kilomètres parcourus
Passengers carried	3 918	5 444	2 999	4 290	Passagers transportés
Passenger-kilometres	6 913	10 004	6 375	9 350	Passagers-kilomètres
Total tonne-kilometres	701	994	652	935	Tonnes-kilomètres totales
United Arab Emirates					**Emirats arabes unis**
Kilometres flown	842	942	842	942	Kilomètres parcourus
Passengers carried	44 507	50 155	44 507	50 155	Passagers transportés
Passenger-kilometres	188 791	211 813	188 791	211 813	Passagers-kilomètres
Total tonne-kilometres	28 438	31 938	28 438	31 938	Tonnes-kilomètres totales
United Kingdom					**Royaume-Uni**
Kilometres flown	1 421	1 523	1 306	1 406	Kilomètres parcourus
Passengers carried	101 821	111 934	83 718	92 713	Passagers transportés
Passenger-kilometres	226 449	243 236	218 744	235 053	Passagers-kilomètres
Total tonne-kilometres	26 504	28 310	25 861	27 616	Tonnes-kilomètres totales
United States					**Etats-Unis**
Kilometres flown	11 932	12 120	2 708	2 825	Kilomètres parcourus
Passengers carried	720 497	730 796	90 959	92 549	Passagers transportés
Passenger-kilometres	1 284 290	1 310 541	394 583	403 463	Passagers-kilomètres
Total tonne-kilometres	157 226	159 956	59 823	61 383	Tonnes-kilomètres totales
Uzbekistan					**Ouzbékistan**
Kilometres flown	48	51	42	45	Kilomètres parcourus
Passengers carried	2 114	2 276	1 608	1 765	Passagers transportés
Passenger-kilometres	5 567	6 055	5 249	5 733	Passagers-kilomètres
Total tonne-kilometres	657	700	627	670	Tonnes-kilomètres totales
Venezuela (Boliv. Rep. of)					**Venezuela (Rép. boliv. du)**
Kilometres flown	52	49	3	8	Kilomètres parcourus
Passengers carried	6 428	7 728	160	307	Passagers transportés
Passenger-kilometres	4 385	4 965	197	667	Passagers-kilomètres
Total tonne-kilometres	436	498	19	73	Tonnes-kilomètres totales
Viet Nam					**Viet Nam**
Kilometres flown	123	172	66	100	Kilomètres parcourus
Passengers carried	14 378	16 544	4 215	4 824	Passagers transportés
Passenger-kilometres	21 207	23 756	12 721	14 232	Passagers-kilomètres
Total tonne-kilometres	2 352	2 633	1 439	1 611	Tonnes-kilomètres totales
Yemen					**Yémen**
Kilometres flown	20	19	17	16	Kilomètres parcourus
Passengers carried	1 537	1 492	1 071	1 062	Passagers transportés
Passenger-kilometres	2 420	2 002	2 303	1 890	Passagers-kilomètres
Total tonne-kilometres	219	182	208	171	Tonnes-kilomètres totales

59

Civil aviation: scheduled airline traffic *(continued)*
Passengers carried (thousands); kilometres (millions)
Aviation civile : trafic régulier des lignes aériennes *(suite)*
Passagers transportés (milliers) ; kilomètres (millions)

Source:
International Civil Aviation Organization (ICAO), Montreal, the ICAO Integrated Statistical Database (ISDB), last accessed April 2013.

1   For statistical purposes, the data for China do not include those for the Hong Kong Special Administrative Region (Hong Kong SAR) and Macao Special Administrative Region (Macao SAR).

2   Traffic for the Hong Kong Special Administrative Region (SAR).
3   Traffic for the Macao Special Administrative Region (SAR).
4   Three States - Denmark, Norway and Sweden.

Source:
Organisation de l'aviation civile internationale (OACI), Montréal, la base de données statistique intégrée (ISDB), dernier accès avril 2013.

1   Pour la présentation des statistiques, les données pour la Chine ne comprennent pas la Région Administrative Spéciale de Hong Kong (Hong Kong RAS) et la Région Administrative Spéciale de Macao (Macao RAS).

2   Trafic pour Hong Kong, région administrative spéciale (RAS).
3   Trafic pour Macao, région administrative spéciale (RAS).
4   Trois états: Danemark, Norvège et la Suède.

60

International reserves minus gold
Millions of US dollars, end of period

Réserves internationales, moins l'or
Millions de dollars E.-U., fin de période

Country or area Pays ou zone	2003	2004	2005	2006	2007	2008	2009	2010	2011
Albania Albanie									
Total reserves minus gold									
Rés. totale, moins l'or	1 009.4	1 357.6	1 404.1	1 768.8	2 104.2	2 319.8	2 313.9	2 469.5	2 393.9
Foreign exchange									
Devises étrangères	913.8	1 251.6	1 386.8	1 754.8	2 097.0	2 307.4	2 229.6	2 386.3	2 312.1
Algeria Algérie									
Total reserves minus gold									
Rés. totale, moins l'or	33 125.2	43 246.4	56 303.1	77 913.7	110 317.6	143 243.0	149 040.6	162 614.5	182 821.8
Foreign exchange									
Devises étrangères	32 942.0	43 113.0	56 178.0	77 781.0	110 180.0	143 102.0	147 221.0	160 567.7	180 573.8
Angola Angola									
Total reserves minus gold									
Rés. totale, moins l'or	634.2	1 374.0	3 196.9	8 598.6	11 196.8	17 869.4	13 664.1	19 749.5	28 348.5
Foreign exchange									
Devises étrangères	634.0	1 373.8	3 196.6	8 598.4	11 196.5	17 869.2	13 238.4	19 339.3	27 955.4
Anguilla Anguilla									
Total reserves minus gold									
Rés. totale, moins l'or	33.3	34.3	39.7	41.8	44.9	41.0	37.5	39.9	37.5
Foreign exchange									
Devises étrangères	33.3	34.3	39.7	41.8	44.9	41.0	37.5	39.9	37.5
Antigua and Barbuda Antigua-et-Barbuda									
Total reserves minus gold									
Rés. totale, moins l'or	113.8	120.1	127.3	142.6	143.8	138.0	127.9	136.6	147.9
Foreign exchange									
Devises étrangères	113.7	120.1	127.3	142.6	143.8	138.0	108.2	136.1	147.1
Argentina Argentine									
Total reserves minus gold									
Rés. totale, moins l'or	14 153.4	18 884.3	27 178.9	30 903.5	44 682.1	44 854.6	46 093.0	49 733.9	43 226.8
Foreign exchange									
Devises étrangères	13 144.8	18 007.5	22 742.0	30 420.9	44 175.1	44 360.4	42 922.3	46 619.3	40 074.6
Armenia Arménie									
Total reserves minus gold									
Rés. totale, moins l'or	502.0	547.8	669.5	1 071.9	1 659.1	1 406.8	2 003.6	1 865.8	1 932.5
Foreign exchange									
Devises étrangères	483.1	535.8	659.3	1 058.0	1 649.5	1 403.9	1 879.0	1 832.3	1 875.4
Aruba Aruba									
Total reserves minus gold									
Rés. totale, moins l'or	295.2	295.4	273.5	337.8	372.1	604.9	578.2	568.2	536.7
Foreign exchange									
Devises étrangères	295.2	295.4	273.5	337.8	372.1	604.9	578.2	568.2	536.7
Australia Australie									
Total reserves minus gold									
Rés. totale, moins l'or	32 188.7	35 802.5	41 941.2	53 448.1	24 768.5	30 690.9	38 950.2	38 659.3	42 783.4
Foreign exchange									
Devises étrangères	29 966.3	33 901.3	40 972.0	52 820.9	24 236.9	29 867.3	33 001.7	32 792.8	36 002.6
Austria Autriche									
Total reserves minus gold									
Rés. totale, moins l'or	8 470.0	7 858.4	6 839.1	7 010.0	10 688.5	8 912.0	8 114.3	9 589.3	10 986.9
Foreign exchange									
Devises étrangères	7 143.5	6 762.8	6 298.4	6 573.1	10 260.5	8 244.4	4 781.4	6 174.6	7 071.2
Azerbaijan Azerbaïdjan									
Total reserves minus gold									
Rés. totale, moins l'or	802.8	1 075.1	1 177.7	2 500.4	4 273.1	6 467.2	5 363.8	6 409.0	10 273.8
Foreign exchange									
Devises étrangères	784.8	1 060.5	1 163.8	2 484.9	4 262.9	6 465.5	5 125.7	6 172.2	10 037.7
Bahamas Bahamas									
Total reserves minus gold									
Rés. totale, moins l'or	491.1	674.4	586.3	461.3	464.5	567.9	1 009.8	1 044.2	1 070.2
Foreign exchange									
Devises étrangères	481.8	664.7	577.3	451.9	454.5	558.2	821.0	858.7	885.4

60

International reserves minus gold *(continued)*
Millions of US dollars, end of period
Réserves internationales, moins l'or *(suite)*
Millions de dollars des E.-U., fin de période

Country or area Pays ou zone	2003	2004	2005	2006	2007	2008	2009	2010	2011
Bahrain Bahreïn									
Total reserves minus gold									
Rés. totale, moins l'or	1 778.4	1 940.5	1 975.0	2 800.3	4 217.1	3 920.5	3 845.2	5 088.6	4 544.5
Foreign exchange									
Devises étrangères	1 673.8	1 829.6	1 870.8	2 687.5	4 094.4	3 796.8	3 533.5	4 782.2	4 238.6
Bangladesh Bangladesh									
Total reserves minus gold									
Rés. totale, moins l'or	2 577.9	3 172.4	2 767.2	3 805.6	5 183.4	5 689.3	10 218.9	10 564.3	8 509.5
Foreign exchange									
Devises étrangères	2 574.4	3 170.9	2 766.0	3 803.9	5 182.2	5 686.7	9 499.9	9 904.1	7 775.1
Barbados Barbade									
Total reserves minus gold									
Rés. totale, moins l'or	737.9	579.9	603.5	636.1	839.4	738.5	871.1	833.5	...
Foreign exchange									
Devises étrangères	730.5	571.8	595.9	627.9	830.5	729.8	773.8	737.9	...
Belarus Bélarus									
Total reserves minus gold									
Rés. totale, moins l'or	594.8	749.4	1 136.6	1 068.6	3 952.1	2 687.0	4 831.4	3 431.0	6 011.2
Foreign exchange									
Devises étrangères	594.8	749.3	1 136.6	1 068.5	3 952.1	2 686.0	4 252.9	2 863.3	5 438.8
Belgium Belgique									
Total reserves minus gold									
Rés. totale, moins l'or	10 989.4	10 361.1	8 241.2	8 783.4	10 383.9	9 318.4	15 906.6	16 499.2	17 918.1
Foreign exchange									
Devises étrangères	7 651.3	7 714.9	6 815.1	7 618.8	9 297.8	7 767.1	7 800.8	7 879.6	7 992.4
Belize Belize									
Total reserves minus gold									
Rés. totale, moins l'or	84.7	48.3	71.4	113.7	108.5	166.2	213.7	218.0	237.1
Foreign exchange									
Devises étrangères	76.1	39.1	62.8	104.4	98.4	156.1	175.4	180.5	199.8
Benin Bénin									
Total reserves minus gold									
Rés. totale, moins l'or	717.9	634.9	654.5	912.2	1 209.2	1 263.4	1 229.8	1 200.1	887.4
Foreign exchange									
Devises étrangères	714.4	631.5	651.2	908.9	1 205.6	1 259.9	1 148.5	1 120.1	807.7
Bhutan Bhoutan									
Total reserves minus gold									
Rés. totale, moins l'or	366.6	398.6	467.4	545.3	699.0	764.8	890.9	1 002.1	789.6
Foreign exchange									
Devises étrangères	364.7	396.6	465.5	543.3	696.8	762.6	879.2	990.7	778.2
Bolivia (Plurinational State of) Bolivie (État plurinational de)									
Total reserves minus gold									
Rés. totale, moins l'or	716.8	872.4	1 327.6	2 614.8	4 554.0	6 927.4	7 583.8	8 133.9	9 910.7
Foreign exchange									
Devises étrangères	663.3	817.3	1 276.7	2 561.2	4 497.7	6 871.4	7 311.3	7 866.2	9 643.9
Bosnia and Herzegovina Bosnie-Herzégovine									
Total reserves minus gold									
Rés. totale, moins l'or	1 813.5	2 427.3	2 547.6	3 671.0	5 041.8	4 479.8	4 529.0	4 366.2	4 149.6
Foreign exchange									
Devises étrangères	1 810.1	2 426.8	2 547.3	3 670.6	5 041.5	4 479.5	4 524.8	4 366.1	4 148.7
Botswana Botswana									
Total reserves minus gold									
Rés. totale, moins l'or	5 339.8	5 661.4	6 309.1	7 992.4	9 789.7	9 118.6	8 704.0	7 885.2	8 081.9
Foreign exchange									
Devises étrangères	5 244.9	5 576.1	6 247.6	7 927.5	9 722.0	9 044.7	8 540.6	7 721.2	7 906.4
Brazil Brésil									
Total reserves minus gold									
Rés. totale, moins l'or	48 846.6	52 461.8	53 245.2	85 156.2	179 432.9	192 843.6	237 364.5	287 056.0	350 356.1
Foreign exchange									
Devises étrangères	48 844.3	52 457.6	53 216.4	85 147.8	179 430.8	192 842.3	231 888.1	280 569.8	343 384.2

Réserves internationales, moins l'or *(suite)*
Millions de dollars des E.-U., fin de période

Country or area Pays ou zone	2003	2004	2005	2006	2007	2008	2009	2010	2011
Brunei Darussalam Brunéi Darussalam									
Total reserves minus gold									
Rés. totale, moins l'or	474.7	488.9	491.9	513.6	667.5	751.2	1 357.3	1 563.2	...
Foreign exchange									
Devises étrangères	376.5	384.7	431.2	459.8	625.5	710.5	996.7	1 208.9	...
Bulgaria Bulgarie									
Total reserves minus gold									
Rés. totale, moins l'or	6 291.0	8 776.2	8 040.5	10 943.0	16 477.9	16 815.5	17 127.3	15 420.5	15 251.9
Foreign exchange									
Devises étrangères	6 174.6	8 712.1	7 992.4	10 892.1	16 424.2	16 757.4	16 116.8	14 427.5	14 261.6
Burkina Faso Burkina Faso									
Total reserves minus gold									
Rés. totale, moins l'or	752.2	659.8	438.4	554.9	1 029.2	927.6	1 295.8	1 068.2	957.0
Foreign exchange									
Devises étrangères	741.1	648.2	427.7	543.7	1 017.4	916.1	1 208.8	982.5	871.5
Burundi Burundi									
Total reserves minus gold									
Rés. totale, moins l'or	67.0	65.8	100.1	130.5	176.3	265.7	322.0	330.7	294.0
Foreign exchange									
Devises étrangères	66.3	64.8	99.3	129.7	175.4	265.0	217.0	217.4	172.1
Cambodia Cambodge									
Total reserves minus gold									
Rés. totale, moins l'or	815.5	943.2	953.0	1 157.3	1 806.9	2 291.5	2 851.1	3 255.1	3 449.7
Foreign exchange									
Devises étrangères	815.3	943.1	952.7	1 157.1	1 806.7	2 291.4	2 743.7	3 149.7	3 344.7
Cameroon Cameroun									
Total reserves minus gold									
Rés. totale, moins l'or	639.6	829.3	949.4	1 716.2	2 906.8	3 086.8	3 675.5	3 642.6	3 198.7
Foreign exchange									
Devises étrangères	637.2	827.6	946.2	1 710.5	2 900.7	3 081.0	3 430.5	3 614.2	3 172.4
Canada Canada									
Total reserves minus gold									
Rés. totale, moins l'or	36 222.1	34 428.7	32 962.1	34 993.8	40 991.2	43 777.5	54 237.8	56 997.9	65 652.1
Foreign exchange									
Devises étrangères	31 537.0	30 166.0	30 664.0	33 198.0	39 314.0	41 537.0	42 602.0	44 888.0	52 811.0
Cape Verde Cap-Vert									
Total reserves minus gold									
Rés. totale, moins l'or	93.6	139.5	174.0	254.5	364.5	361.5	397.9	382.2	0.0
Foreign exchange									
Devises étrangères	93.6	139.5	173.9	254.4	364.3	361.2	385.0	371.8	0.0
Central African Rep. Rép. centrafricaine									
Total reserves minus gold									
Rés. totale, moins l'or	132.4	148.3	139.2	125.3	82.6	121.8	210.6	181.2	154.5
Foreign exchange									
Devises étrangères	132.2	145.6	138.9	124.4	81.6	121.5	205.9	176.5	149.9
Chad Tchad									
Total reserves minus gold									
Rés. totale, moins l'or	187.1	221.7	225.6	625.1	955.1	1 345.5	616.7	632.4	951.1
Foreign exchange									
Devises étrangères	186.7	221.2	225.1	624.6	954.5	1 344.9	612.0	627.8	946.5
Chile Chili									
Total reserves minus gold									
Rés. totale, moins l'or	15 839.6	15 993.8	16 929.2	19 392.0	16 836.8	23 072.4	25 283.5	27 816.3	41 931.8
Foreign exchange									
Devises étrangères	15 211.0	15 495.4	16 689.1	19 224.9	16 695.3	22 848.6	23 849.3	26 317.8	40 116.6
China[1] Chine[1]									
Total reserves minus gold									
Rés. totale, moins l'or	408 150.7	614 499.5	821 513.9	1 068 493.0	1 530 281.6	1 949 260.0	2 416 043.7	2 866 079.3	3 202 788.5
Foreign exchange									
Devises étrangères	403 251.0	609 932.0	818 872.0	1 066 344.0	1 528 249.1	1 946 030.0	2 399 152.3	2 847 338.1	3 181 148.0

60

International reserves minus gold *(continued)*
Millions of US dollars, end of period
Réserves internationales, moins l'or *(suite)*
Millions de dollars des E.-U., fin de période

Country or area Pays ou zone	2003	2004	2005	2006	2007	2008	2009	2010	2011
China, Hong Kong SAR	**Chine, Hong Kong RAS**								
Total reserves minus gold									
Rés. totale, moins l'or	118 360.1	123 540.0	124 244.0	133 168.0	152 637.0	182 469.0	255 768.0	268 649.0	285 295.9
Foreign exchange									
Devises étrangères	118 360.1	123 540.0	124 244.0	133 168.0	152 637.0	182 469.0	255 768.0	268 649.0	285 260.0
China, Macao SAR	**Chine, Macao RAS**								
Total reserves minus gold									
Rés. totale, moins l'or	4 343.4	5 436.1	6 689.4	9 132.1	13 229.9	15 930.1	18 350.3	23 726.5	34 026.2
Foreign exchange									
Devises étrangères	4 343.4	5 436.1	6 689.4	9 132.1	13 229.9	15 930.1	18 350.3	23 726.5	34 026.2
Colombia	**Colombie**								
Total reserves minus gold									
Rés. totale, moins l'or	10 783.9	13 393.8	14 787.0	15 296.2	20 767.3	23 478.8	24 747.7	27 766.2	30 486.0
Foreign exchange									
Devises étrangères	10 188.0	12 769.0	14 206.0	14 673.0	20 096.0	22 810.0	23 158.0	26 349.3	28 976.0
Comoros	**Comores**								
Total reserves minus gold									
Rés. totale, moins l'or	94.3	103.7	85.8	93.5	117.2	112.2	150.3	145.3	155.2
Foreign exchange									
Devises étrangères	93.5	102.9	85.0	92.7	116.3	111.3	139.0	131.8	139.3
Congo	**Congo**								
Total reserves minus gold									
Rés. totale, moins l'or	34.8	119.6	731.8	1 840.9	2 174.3	3 871.8	3 806.3	4 446.9	5 641.1
Foreign exchange									
Devises étrangères	33.4	111.5	728.6	1 839.9	2 173.2	3 870.7	3 695.5	4 338.1	5 532.7
Costa Rica	**Costa Rica**								
Total reserves minus gold									
Rés. totale, moins l'or	1 839.2	1 921.8	2 312.6	3 114.6	4 113.6	3 798.7	4 066.2	4 627.2	4 755.8
Foreign exchange									
Devises étrangères	1 809.4	1 890.6	2 284.0	3 084.5	4 081.9	3 767.5	3 826.5	4 392.2	4 521.6
Côte d'Ivoire	**Côte d'Ivoire**								
Total reserves minus gold									
Rés. totale, moins l'or	1 303.9	1 680.0	1 366.6	1 797.7	2 519.0	2 252.7	3 266.8	3 624.4	4 316.0
Foreign exchange									
Devises étrangères	1 302.7	1 678.9	1 365.0	1 795.7	2 517.3	2 250.3	2 838.1	3 202.6	3 895.6
Croatia	**Croatie**								
Total reserves minus gold									
Rés. totale, moins l'or	8 190.5	8 758.2	8 800.3	11 487.8	13 674.5	12 957.3	14 894.5	14 132.5	14 483.8
Foreign exchange									
Devises étrangères	8 190.2	8 757.9	8 799.8	11 487.4	13 674.0	12 956.8	14 419.0	13 665.4	14 018.1
Cyprus	**Chypre**								
Total reserves minus gold									
Rés. totale, moins l'or	3 256.7	3 910.0	4 191.1	5 646.8	6 118.6	#616.8	796.2	514.9	504.3
Foreign exchange									
Devises étrangères	3 154.5	3 832.7	4 155.9	5 621.5	6 100.1	#585.5	562.9	276.2	163.0
Czech Republic	**République tchèque**								
Total reserves minus gold									
Rés. totale, moins l'or	26 770.6	28 259.3	29 330.4	31 181.7	34 549.6	36 654.5	41 156.6	41 908.8	39 670.1
Foreign exchange									
Devises étrangères	26 293.8	27 844.1	29 137.7	31 053.7	34 445.2	36 471.6	39 669.8	40 335.3	37 853.9
Dem. Rep. of the Congo	**Rép. dém. du Congo**								
Total reserves minus gold									
Rés. totale, moins l'or	97.8	236.2	131.2	154.5	180.7	77.7	1 035.4	1 299.7	1 267.5
Foreign exchange									
Devises étrangères	89.8	230.7	129.8	154.2	177.4	71.8	422.8	755.7	726.3
Denmark	**Danemark**								
Total reserves minus gold									
Rés. totale, moins l'or	37 105.0	39 083.7	32 930.4	29 723.7	32 534.4	40 465.8	74 290.9	73 502.8	81 679.5
Foreign exchange									
Devises étrangères	36 004.0	38 196.0	32 510.0	29 160.0	32 029.0	39 823.0	71 259.0	70 334.0	78 109.0

International reserves minus gold *(continued)*
Millions of US dollars, end of period
Réserves internationales, moins l'or *(suite)*
Millions de dollars des E.-U., fin de période

Country or area Pays ou zone	2003	2004	2005	2006	2007	2008	2009	2010	2011
Djibouti Djibouti									
Total reserves minus gold									
Rés. totale, moins l'or	100.1	93.9	89.3	120.3	132.1	175.5	241.8	249.0	244.1
Foreign exchange									
Devises étrangères	98.4	91.2	87.7	117.8	130.3	173.7	219.6	230.6	228.3
Dominica Dominique									
Total reserves minus gold									
Rés. totale, moins l'or	47.7	42.3	49.2	63.0	60.5	55.2	75.5	76.1	81.1
Foreign exchange									
Devises étrangères	47.7	42.3	49.1	63.0	60.4	55.1	64.5	66.4	74.5
Dominican Republic Rép. dominicaine									
Total reserves minus gold									
Rés. totale, moins l'or	253.1	798.3	1 843.2	2 115.6	2 546.4	2 271.6	2 885.1	3 475.8	3 754.0
Foreign exchange									
Devises étrangères	253.0	796.7	1 842.6	2 091.2	2 447.8	2 235.6	2 609.5	3 358.0	3 735.4
Ecuador Equateur									
Total reserves minus gold									
Rés. totale, moins l'or	812.6	1 069.6	1 714.2	1 489.5	2 816.4	3 738.2	2 873.2	1 434.8	1 664.3
Foreign exchange									
Devises étrangères	786.1	986.9	1 667.9	1 456.1	2 764.9	3 685.5	2 819.8	1 383.5	1 597.4
Egypt Egypte									
Total reserves minus gold									
Rés. totale, moins l'or	13 588.7	14 273.2	20 609.1	24 461.6	30 187.7	32 216.1	32 253.0	33 611.7	14 915.7
Foreign exchange									
Devises étrangères	13 400.0	14 108.0	20 508.0	24 341.0	30 054.0	32 108.0	30 947.0	32 351.0	13 658.0
El Salvador El Salvador									
Total reserves minus gold									
Rés. totale, moins l'or	1 792.3	1 754.0	1 722.8	1 814.9	2 110.0	2 443.1	2 868.8	2 569.6	2 152.9
Foreign exchange									
Devises étrangères	1 755.2	1 715.2	1 687.1	1 777.3	2 070.5	2 404.6	2 612.0	2 317.4	1 901.4
Equatorial Guinea Guinée équatoriale									
Total reserves minus gold									
Rés. totale, moins l'or	237.7	945.0	2 102.5	3 066.7	3 845.9	4 431.2	3 251.9	2 346.4	3 053.8
Foreign exchange									
Devises étrangères	237.7	944.3	2 101.9	3 066.1	3 845.2	4 430.5	3 211.3	2 306.4	3 014.0
Eritrea Erythrée									
Total reserves minus gold									
Rés. totale, moins l'or	24.7	34.7	27.9	25.4	34.3	57.9	90.0	114.1	0.0
Foreign exchange									
Devises étrangères	24.7	34.7	27.9	25.3	34.3	57.9	84.3	108.6	0.0
Estonia Estonie									
Total reserves minus gold									
Rés. totale, moins l'or	1 373.4	1 788.2	1 943.2	2 781.2	3 262.7	3 964.9	3 971.9	2 555.9	194.9
Foreign exchange									
Devises étrangères	1 373.3	1 788.1	1 943.1	2 781.1	3 262.6	3 964.8	3 874.7	2 460.4	99.6
Ethiopia Ethiopie									
Total reserves minus gold									
Rés. totale, moins l'or	955.6	1 496.8	1 042.6	867.4	1 289.9	870.5	1 780.9	0.0	0.0
Foreign exchange									
Devises étrangères	944.8	1 485.1	1 032.1	856.3	1 278.1	859.0	1 741.7	0.0	0.0
Euro Area Zone euro									
Total reserves minus gold									
Rés. totale, moins l'or	223 145.0	211 970.7	184 713.6	197 005.5	215 295.7	218 716.7	282 823.6	300 242.5	316 705.6
Foreign exchange									
Devises étrangères	188 172.8	181 195.7	167 150.2	184 033.6	203 189.0	201 969.2	194 411.3	207 126.9	208 138.8
Fiji Fidji									
Total reserves minus gold									
Rés. totale, moins l'or	423.3	482.7	320.9	312.8	527.6	321.5	569.1	719.4	832.2
Foreign exchange									
Devises étrangères	393.0	450.7	291.0	280.6	492.7	286.6	438.9	615.7	728.6

Country or area Pays ou zone	2003	2004	2005	2006	2007	2008	2009	2010	2011
Finland Finlande									
Total reserves minus gold									
Rés. totale, moins l'or	10 514.9	12 221.5	10 521.1	6 494.2	7 063.1	6 979.4	9 710.6	7 326.7	7 857.1
Foreign exchange									
Devises étrangères	9 544.5	11 425.3	10 075.8	6 134.6	6 689.2	6 492.3	7 403.2	4 919.9	5 307.6
France France									
Total reserves minus gold									
Rés. totale, moins l'or	30 186.5	35 314.0	27 752.9	42 651.6	45 709.7	33 617.5	46 633.5	55 800.0	48 611.5
Foreign exchange									
Devises étrangères	23 121.7	29 076.8	23 996.3	40 287.0	43 587.4	30 382.2	27 728.7	36 211.0	26 147.1
Gabon Gabon									
Total reserves minus gold									
Rés. totale, moins l'or	196.6	443.4	668.6	1 113.4	1 227.2	1 923.5	1 993.2	1 735.9	2 157.3
Foreign exchange									
Devises étrangères	196.3	436.9	668.1	1 112.2	1 226.0	1 922.3	1 784.2	1 530.5	1 952.5
Gambia Gambie									
Total reserves minus gold									
Rés. totale, moins l'or	59.3	83.8	98.3	120.6	142.8	116.5	224.2	201.6	223.2
Foreign exchange									
Devises étrangères	57.1	80.7	96.0	116.9	140.2	114.1	183.3	161.4	183.1
Georgia Géorgie									
Total reserves minus gold									
Rés. totale, moins l'or	196.2	386.7	478.6	930.8	1 361.2	1 480.2	2 110.3	2 263.8	2 818.2
Foreign exchange									
Devises étrangères	191.3	375.4	477.6	929.9	1 346.3	1 467.8	1 891.6	2 041.4	2 594.9
Germany Allemagne									
Total reserves minus gold									
Rés. totale, moins l'or	50 694.0	48 822.7	45 139.7	41 686.5	44 326.5	43 137.2	59 925.3	62 294.9	66 928.1
Foreign exchange									
Devises étrangères	41 095.5	39 898.6	39 765.3	37 718.9	40 768.3	38 557.0	36 928.3	37 356.1	38 083.4
Ghana Ghana									
Total reserves minus gold									
Rés. totale, moins l'or	1 352.8	1 626.7	1 752.9	2 090.3	0.0	0.0	0.0	0.0	0.0
Foreign exchange									
Devises étrangères	1 306.0	1 605.9	1 751.8	2 089.1	0.0	0.0	0.0	0.0	0.0
Greece Grèce									
Total reserves minus gold									
Rés. totale, moins l'or	4 361.4	1 191.0	506.4	565.9	631.1	343.8	1 554.8	1 309.5	1 248.7
Foreign exchange									
Devises étrangères	3 843.3	743.7	309.1	408.3	518.2	158.7	198.8	108.2	29.8
Grenada Grenade									
Total reserves minus gold									
Rés. totale, moins l'or	83.2	121.7	94.3	100.0	110.6	105.3	129.1	119.2	120.7
Foreign exchange									
Devises étrangères	83.2	121.7	94.2	99.8	110.4	104.1	112.4	102.8	104.8
Guatemala Guatemala									
Total reserves minus gold									
Rés. totale, moins l'or	2 833.2	3 426.3	3 663.8	3 914.9	4 129.9	4 461.9	4 963.6	5 636.8	5 834.9
Foreign exchange									
Devises étrangères	2 825.0	3 418.3	3 657.3	3 909.3	4 125.6	4 458.4	4 690.3	5 369.4	5 568.5
Guinea Guinée									
Total reserves minus gold									
Rés. totale, moins l'or	0.0	110.5	95.1	0.0	0.0	0.0	0.0	0.0	0.0
Foreign exchange									
Devises étrangères	0.0	110.4	94.9	0.0	0.0	0.0	0.0	0.0	0.0
Guinea-Bissau Guinée-Bissau									
Total reserves minus gold									
Rés. totale, moins l'or	32.9	71.6	79.8	82.0	112.9	124.6	168.6	156.4	220.0
Foreign exchange									
Devises étrangères	31.7	70.9	79.2	81.5	112.8	124.4	149.8	137.2	200.7

60

International reserves minus gold *(continued)*
Millions of US dollars, end of period
Réserves internationales, moins l'or *(suite)*
Millions de dollars des E.-U., fin de période

Country or area Pays ou zone	2003	2004	2005	2006	2007	2008	2009	2010	2011
Guyana Guyana									
Total reserves minus gold									
Rés. totale, moins l'or	276.4	231.8	251.9	279.6	313.0	355.9	631.4	782.1	0.0
Foreign exchange									
Devises étrangères	271.5	224.7	251.4	278.0	312.5	355.9	627.5	780.0	0.0
Haiti Haïti									
Total reserves minus gold									
Rés. totale, moins l'or	62.0	114.4	133.1	253.1	452.0	541.4	788.6	1 335.0	1 389.1
Foreign exchange									
Devises étrangères	61.6	114.1	120.7	245.1	444.4	534.3	680.4	1 228.8	1 283.3
Honduras Honduras									
Total reserves minus gold									
Rés. totale, moins l'or	1 430.0	1 970.4	2 327.2	2 628.5	2 528.0	2 473.4	2 086.5	2 670.8	2 749.7
Foreign exchange									
Devises étrangères	1 417.1	1 956.9	2 314.6	2 615.5	2 514.3	2 460.0	1 908.7	2 497.9	2 582.3
Hungary Hongrie									
Total reserves minus gold									
Rés. totale, moins l'or	12 751.4	15 922.1	18 552.1	21 527.0	23 969.8	33 787.9	44 073.7	44 849.2	48 680.5
Foreign exchange									
Devises étrangères	12 029.0	15 326.0	18 296.0	21 316.0	23 773.0	33 620.0	42 479.0	43 581.0	47 725.0
Iceland Islande									
Total reserves minus gold									
Rés. totale, moins l'or	792.3	1 046.2	1 035.7	2 301.3	2 578.7	3 515.2	3 813.2	5 698.9	8 450.4
Foreign exchange									
Devises étrangères	764.6	1 017.3	1 009.1	2 273.2	2 549.1	3 486.2	3 638.7	5 557.0	7 710.5
India Inde									
Total reserves minus gold									
Rés. totale, moins l'or	98 937.9	126 593.3	131 924.3	170 738.0	266 988.3	247 418.9	265 181.7	275 276.6	271 285.4
Foreign exchange									
Devises étrangères	97 617.0	125 164.0	131 018.0	170 187.0	266 553.0	246 603.0	258 583.0	267 814.5	262 933.3
Indonesia Indonésie									
Total reserves minus gold									
Rés. totale, moins l'or	34 962.3	34 952.5	33 140.5	41 103.1	54 976.4	49 596.7	63 563.3	92 908.0	106 538.8
Foreign exchange									
Devises étrangères	34 742.4	34 724.1	32 925.5	40 866.0	54 737.3	49 338.9	60 572.0	89 970.1	103 610.9
Iraq Iraq									
Total reserves minus gold									
Rés. totale, moins l'or	...	7 824.1	12 104.1	19 931.9	31 297.6	49 937.8	44 127.5	50 377.0	60 668.0
Foreign exchange									
Devises étrangères	...	7 098.5	11 439.9	19 235.7	30 887.5	49 531.1	42 041.0	48 339.6	58 661.5
Ireland Irlande									
Total reserves minus gold									
Rés. totale, moins l'or	4 078.5	2 830.9	778.7	720.0	778.7	871.1	1 940.8	1 842.6	1 399.3
Foreign exchange									
Devises étrangères	3 425.2	2 323.7	514.4	493.8	590.8	609.2	516.7	501.7	26.7
Israel Israël									
Total reserves minus gold									
Rés. totale, moins l'or	26 315.1	27 094.4	28 059.4	29 153.2	28 518.5	42 513.2	60 611.4	70 907.3	74 874.1
Foreign exchange									
Devises étrangères	25 778.4	26 616.0	27 839.0	29 011.0	28 406.0	42 324.0	59 091.0	69 265.0	73 052.0
Italy Italie									
Total reserves minus gold									
Rés. totale, moins l'or	30 372.2	27 859.1	25 514.7	25 661.7	28 385.0	37 087.6	45 770.4	47 684.1	49 185.2
Foreign exchange									
Devises étrangères	26 062.0	24 011.1	23 527.9	24 413.2	27 319.2	35 306.0	34 521.1	35 677.9	34 157.7
Jamaica Jamaïque									
Total reserves minus gold									
Rés. totale, moins l'or	1 194.9	1 846.5	2 169.8	2 318.4	1 878.5	1 772.7	2 075.8	2 501.1	2 281.9
Foreign exchange									
Devises étrangères	1 194.8	1 846.4	2 169.8	2 318.2	1 878.2	1 772.6	1 729.4	2 171.4	1 966.1

60

International reserves minus gold *(continued)*
Millions of US dollars, end of period
Réserves internationales, moins l'or *(suite)*
Millions de dollars des E.-U., fin de période

Country or area Pays ou zone	2003	2004	2005	2006	2007	2008	2009	2010	2011
Japan Japon									
Total reserves minus gold									
Rés. totale, moins l'or	663 289.1	833 891.3	834 274.9	879 681.5	952 784.5	1 009 364.8	1 022 236.0	1 061 489.9	1 258 172.4
Foreign exchange									
Devises étrangères	652 790.0	824 264.0	828 813.0	874 936.0	948 356.0	1 003 674.0	996 955.0	1 036 256.0	1 221 249.0
Jordan Jordanie									
Total reserves minus gold									
Rés. totale, moins l'or	5 194.3	5 266.6	5 250.3	6 722.0	7 542.0	8 561.6	11 689.3	13 056.7	11 467.3
Foreign exchange									
Devises étrangères	5 193.1	5 264.8	5 249.5	6 720.4	7 539.4	8 558.0	11 458.8	12 830.5	11 241.9
Kazakhstan Kazakhstan									
Total reserves minus gold									
Rés. totale, moins l'or	4 236.2	8 473.1	6 084.2	17 750.8	15 776.8	17 871.5	20 719.8	25 222.7	25 174.1
Foreign exchange									
Devises étrangères	4 235.0	8 471.9	6 083.0	17 749.5	15 775.4	17 870.1	20 179.6	24 692.1	24 645.1
Kenya Kenya									
Total reserves minus gold									
Rés. totale, moins l'or	1 481.9	1 519.3	1 798.8	2 415.8	3 355.0	2 878.5	3 849.0	4 320.2	4 264.4
Foreign exchange									
Devises étrangères	1 461.0	1 499.0	1 780.6	2 396.0	3 334.6	2 855.7	3 478.1	3 981.7	4 227.5
Republic of Korea République de Corée									
Total reserves minus gold									
Rés. totale, moins l'or	155 284.2	198 996.6	210 317.2	238 882.3	262 150.2	201 144.5	269 932.9	291 491.1	304 255.0
Foreign exchange									
Devises étrangères	154 508.8	198 175.3	209 967.7	238 387.9	261 770.7	200 479.1	265 202.3	286 926.4	298 232.9
Kosovo Kosovo									
Total reserves minus gold									
Rés. totale, moins l'or	0.0	0.0	0.0	0.0	951.7	892.1	830.2	846.4	741.5
Foreign exchange									
Devises étrangères	0.0	0.0	0.0	0.0	951.7	892.1	721.2	739.6	635.5
Kuwait Koweït									
Total reserves minus gold									
Rés. totale, moins l'or	7 577.0	8 241.9	8 862.8	12 566.0	16 660.0	17 112.8	20 267.5	21 236.7	25 795.2
Foreign exchange									
Devises étrangères	6 640.5	7 347.4	8 380.4	12 177.6	16 285.6	16 611.0	17 608.4	18 623.0	22 921.4
Kyrgyzstan Kirghizistan									
Total reserves minus gold									
Rés. totale, moins l'or	364.6	528.2	569.7	764.3	1 107.2	1 152.9	1 494.0	1 603.6	1 703.0
Foreign exchange									
Devises étrangères	354.3	508.3	564.5	731.1	1 093.4	1 097.6	1 331.9	1 431.9	1 525.9
Lao People's Dem. Rep. Rép. dém. pop. lao									
Total reserves minus gold									
Rés. totale, moins l'or	208.6	223.2	234.3	328.4	532.6	628.7	608.6	703.4	0.0
Foreign exchange									
Devises étrangères	189.5	207.9	220.2	313.7	517.1	613.6	528.5	624.7	0.0
Latvia Lettonie									
Total reserves minus gold									
Rés. totale, moins l'or	1 432.4	1 912.0	2 232.1	4 353.4	5 553.4	5 027.6	6 631.8	7 256.2	5 997.3
Foreign exchange									
Devises étrangères	1 432.2	1 911.7	2 231.9	4 353.1	5 553.1	5 027.2	6 445.0	7 069.5	5 852.5
Lebanon Liban									
Total reserves minus gold									
Rés. totale, moins l'or	12 519.4	11 734.6	11 887.1	13 376.4	12 909.9	20 244.5	29 102.9	31 514.1	33 740.6
Foreign exchange									
Devises étrangères	12 460.8	11 672.4	11 828.7	13 313.3	12 844.1	20 181.8	28 744.5	31 163.3	33 391.6
Lesotho Lesotho									
Total reserves minus gold									
Rés. totale, moins l'or	460.3	501.5	519.1	658.4	0.0	0.0	0.0	0.0	0.0
Foreign exchange									
Devises étrangères	454.4	495.3	513.5	652.7	0.0	0.0	0.0	0.0	0.0

60

International reserves minus gold *(continued)*
Millions of US dollars, end of period

Réserves internationales, moins l'or *(suite)*
Millions de dollars des E.-U., fin de période

Country or area Pays ou zone	2003	2004	2005	2006	2007	2008	2009	2010	2011
Liberia Libéria									
Total reserves minus gold									
Rés. totale, moins l'or	7.4	18.7	25.4	72.0	119.4	160.9	372.5	0.0	0.0
Foreign exchange									
Devises étrangères	7.3	18.7	25.4	71.9	119.3	139.0	171.0	0.0	0.0
Libyan Arab Jamah. Jamah. arabe libyenne									
Total reserves minus gold									
Rés. totale, moins l'or	19 584.0	25 688.8	39 507.9	59 289.2	79 404.7	92 313.3	98 725.2	99 645.2	100 058.9
Foreign exchange									
Devises étrangères	18 309.8	24 336.3	38 235.2	57 907.3	77 897.5	90 803.4	95 616.2	96 799.8	97 134.0
Lithuania Lituanie									
Total reserves minus gold									
Rés. totale, moins l'or	3 372.0	3 512.6	3 720.2	5 654.4	7 556.6	6 280.5	6 419.8	6 335.5	7 915.4
Foreign exchange									
Devises étrangères	3 371.9	3 512.5	3 720.1	5 654.3	7 556.5	6 280.3	6 204.5	6 124.0	7 704.5
Luxembourg Luxembourg									
Total reserves minus gold									
Rés. totale, moins l'or	279.9	298.4	241.1	218.1	143.6	334.6	730.5	747.1	900.5
Foreign exchange									
Devises étrangères	88.9	143.9	166.7	156.0	93.8	258.4	267.5	270.6	182.1
Madagascar Madagascar									
Total reserves minus gold									
Rés. totale, moins l'or	414.3	503.5	481.3	583.2	846.7	982.3	1 135.5	1 171.6	1 279.1
Foreign exchange									
Devises étrangères	414.2	503.3	481.2	583.1	846.6	982.0	982.3	1 022.9	1 134.5
Malawi Malawi									
Total reserves minus gold									
Rés. totale, moins l'or	122.0	128.1	158.9	133.8	216.6	242.8	149.4	307.4	197.4
Foreign exchange									
Devises étrangères	118.2	123.3	154.6	129.6	212.9	239.1	143.6	302.0	193.3
Malaysia Malaisie									
Total reserves minus gold									
Rés. totale, moins l'or	43 821.7	65 881.1	69 858.0	82 132.3	101 019.3	91 148.8	95 431.7	104 883.7	131 803.7
Foreign exchange									
Devises étrangères	42 772.4	64 905.9	69 376.9	81 723.6	100 635.0	90 605.1	92 865.1	102 324.8	128 987.1
Maldives Maldives									
Total reserves minus gold									
Rés. totale, moins l'or	162.2	206.5	189.0	234.4	311.4	243.6	275.6	364.3	348.7
Foreign exchange									
Devises étrangères	159.5	203.6	186.4	231.6	308.4	240.6	261.0	350.2	334.9
Mali Mali									
Total reserves minus gold									
Rés. totale, moins l'or	952.5	851.3	854.3	969.5	1 087.1	1 071.5	1 604.5	1 344.4	1 378.6
Foreign exchange									
Devises étrangères	938.4	836.8	840.9	955.4	1 071.9	1 056.5	1 473.9	1 215.9	1 250.6
Malta Malte									
Total reserves minus gold									
Rés. totale, moins l'or	2 728.7	2 732.0	2 576.4	2 976.8	3 785.4	#368.3	532.1	535.8	499.8
Foreign exchange									
Devises étrangères	2 624.5	2 621.7	2 473.0	2 865.0	3 662.0	#288.3	329.7	340.5	290.2
Mauritania Mauritanie									
Total reserves minus gold									
Rés. totale, moins l'or	27.0	33.7	64.5	187.2	197.8	188.6	225.4	271.7	484.7
Foreign exchange									
Devises étrangères	26.9	33.7	64.3	187.1	197.8	188.5	225.2	271.6	483.2
Mauritius Maurice									
Total reserves minus gold									
Rés. totale, moins l'or	1 577.3	1 605.9	1 339.9	1 269.6	1 780.3	1 742.7	2 178.8	2 441.8	2 582.7
Foreign exchange									
Devises étrangères	1 519.2	1 544.7	1 289.2	1 226.3	1 739.9	1 693.4	2 001.5	2 254.2	2 380.9

60

International reserves minus gold *(continued)*
Millions of US dollars, end of period
Réserves internationales, moins l'or *(suite)*
Millions de dollars des E.-U., fin de période

Country or area Pays ou zone	2003	2004	2005	2006	2007	2008	2009	2010	2011
Mexico Mexique									
Total reserves minus gold									
Rés. totale, moins l'or	58 955.6	64 140.7	74 054.1	76 270.5	87 109.2	95 126.1	99 589.2	120 265.0	143 990.8
Foreign exchange									
Devises étrangères	57 739.9	62 777.9	73 014.6	75 447.7	86 309.4	93 994.1	94 102.7	114 883.7	137 485.1
Micronesia (Fed. States of) Micronésie (Etats féd. de)									
Total reserves minus gold									
Rés. totale, moins l'or	89.6	54.8	50.0	46.6	48.5	40.0	55.7	55.8	75.1
Foreign exchange									
Devises étrangères	87.8	52.9	48.2	44.7	46.4	37.9	46.0	46.2	65.5
Mongolia Mongolie									
Total reserves minus gold									
Rés. totale, moins l'or	196.9	193.7	333.2	583.4	801.7	561.5	1 294.5	2 196.7	2 671.8
Foreign exchange									
Devises étrangères	196.7	193.5	332.9	583.2	801.5	561.2	1 217.8	2 123.8	2 601.8
Montenegro Monténégro									
Total reserves minus gold									
Rés. totale, moins l'or	63.7	81.8	204.0	432.7	688.8	435.7	572.6	556.2	392.7
Foreign exchange									
Devises étrangères	63.7	81.8	204.0	432.7	678.2	425.1	521.3	505.7	342.4
Montserrat Montserrat									
Total reserves minus gold									
Rés. totale, moins l'or	15.2	14.1	13.9	14.6	14.5	11.7	14.3	16.8	24.8
Foreign exchange									
Devises étrangères	15.2	14.1	13.9	14.6	14.5	11.7	14.3	16.8	24.8
Morocco Maroc									
Total reserves minus gold									
Rés. totale, moins l'or	13 851.1	16 336.6	16 187.4	20 340.7	24 123.3	22 103.8	22 797.3	22 613.1	19 526.1
Foreign exchange									
Devises étrangères	13 634.1	16 107.0	16 008.0	20 182.1	23 980.0	21 976.0	21 923.6	21 762.0	18 801.6
Mozambique Mozambique									
Total reserves minus gold									
Rés. totale, moins l'or	937.5	1 131.0	1 053.8	1 155.7	1 444.7	1 577.7	2 099.3	2 159.4	2 468.8
Foreign exchange									
Devises étrangères	937.4	1 130.9	1 053.6	1 155.5	1 444.5	1 577.6	1 928.9	1 992.3	2 303.7
Myanmar Myanmar									
Total reserves minus gold									
Rés. totale, moins l'or	550.2	672.1	770.7	1 235.6	3 088.9	3 717.5	5 251.7	5 716.9	...
Foreign exchange									
Devises étrangères	550.1	672.1	770.5	1 235.4	3 088.5	3 717.4	5 138.4	5 714.3	...
Namibia Namibie									
Total reserves minus gold									
Rés. totale, moins l'or	325.2	345.1	312.1	449.6	896.0	1 292.9	2 050.9	1 695.7	1 786.7
Foreign exchange									
Devises étrangères	325.1	344.9	312.0	449.4	895.9	1 292.8	1 846.4	1 494.7	1 778.5
Nepal Népal									
Total reserves minus gold									
Rés. totale, moins l'or	1 222.5	1 462.2	1 499.0	1 935.5	2 014.0	2 457.9	2 761.0	2 925.1	3 630.8
Foreign exchange									
Devises étrangères	1 213.1	1 452.5	1 490.2	1 926.5	2 005.0	2 449.6	2 661.2	2 831.3	3 541.8
Netherlands Pays-Bas									
Total reserves minus gold									
Rés. totale, moins l'or	11 167.0	10 654.8	8 986.0	10 802.4	10 269.7	11 476.4	17 870.5	18 471.2	20 264.2
Foreign exchange									
Devises étrangères	7 335.5	7 209.6	7 078.2	9 327.0	8 748.7	9 368.9	8 613.3	8 901.8	9 159.5
Netherlands Antilles Antilles néerlandaises									
Total reserves minus gold									
Rés. totale, moins l'or	372.9	415.4	545.4	495.0	660.9	818.9	867.0	0.0	0.0
Foreign exchange									
Devises étrangères	372.9	415.4	545.4	495.0	660.9	818.9	867.0	0.0	0.0

Country or area Pays ou zone	2003	2004	2005	2006	2007	2008	2009	2010	2011
New Zealand Nouvelle-Zélande									
Total reserves minus gold									
Rés. totale, moins l'or	6 085.4	6 947.4	8 892.7	14 068.5	17 247.2	11 052.2	15 594.0	16 722.6	17 011.9
Foreign exchange									
Devises étrangères	5 413.7	6 438.8	8 693.6	13 916.0	17 124.1	10 854.5	13 981.6	15 133.0	15 241.7
Nicaragua Nicaragua									
Total reserves minus gold									
Rés. totale, moins l'or	502.1	668.2	727.8	921.9	1 103.3	1 140.8	1 573.1	1 799.0	1 892.2
Foreign exchange									
Devises étrangères	502.0	667.7	727.5	921.5	1 103.2	1 140.7	1 408.6	1 637.5	1 716.5
Niger Niger									
Total reserves minus gold									
Rés. totale, moins l'or	260.1	249.8	250.7	370.9	593.0	705.2	655.5	760.3	673.0
Foreign exchange									
Devises étrangères	244.7	235.6	238.1	357.8	579.3	690.5	556.9	663.4	576.5
Nigeria Nigéria									
Total reserves minus gold									
Rés. totale, moins l'or	7 128.4	16 955.6	28 279.6	42 298.7	51 334.2	53 001.8	44 762.7	34 919.3	35 211.9
Foreign exchange									
Devises étrangères	7 128.0	16 955.0	28 279.0	42 298.1	51 333.2	53 000.4	42 382.5	32 339.3	32 639.8
Norway Norvège									
Total reserves minus gold									
Rés. totale, moins l'or	37 220.0	44 307.5	46 985.9	56 841.6	60 839.6	50 949.8	48 859.3	52 797.9	49 397.1
Foreign exchange									
Devises étrangères	35 890.2	43 078.2	46 377.4	56 181.4	60 294.1	50 214.1	45 718.6	49 740.2	45 612.4
Oman Oman									
Total reserves minus gold									
Rés. totale, moins l'or	3 593.5	3 597.3	4 358.1	5 014.0	9 523.5	11 581.9	12 202.9	13 024.4	14 365.3
Foreign exchange									
Devises étrangères	3 466.6	3 484.5	4 308.7	4 970.2	9 485.1	11 541.1	11 856.3	12 671.3	13 983.2
Pakistan Pakistan									
Total reserves minus gold									
Rés. totale, moins l'or	10 941.0	9 799.0	10 032.8	11 543.1	14 044.0	7 194.2	11 318.2	14 345.9	14 528.0
Foreign exchange									
Devises étrangères	10 693.0	9 554.0	9 817.0	11 327.6	13 829.0	7 011.5	9 937.6	13 115.4	13 474.3
Panama Panama									
Total reserves minus gold									
Rés. totale, moins l'or	1 011.0	630.6	1 210.5	1 335.0	1 935.1	2 423.8	3 028.3	2 714.5	0.0
Foreign exchange									
Devises étrangères	992.5	611.4	1 192.5	1 315.9	1 915.4	2 404.7	2 741.5	2 432.9	0.0
Papua New Guinea Papouasie-Nvl-Guinée									
Total reserves minus gold									
Rés. totale, moins l'or	494.2	632.6	718.1	1 400.7	2 053.7	1 953.4	2 560.6	3 033.7	4 168.9
Foreign exchange									
Devises étrangères	489.9	631.2	717.4	1 400.0	2 052.9	1 952.6	2 377.7	3 017.6	4 153.6
Paraguay Paraguay									
Total reserves minus gold									
Rés. totale, moins l'or	968.9	1 168.0	1 297.1	1 702.1	2 461.5	2 844.6	3 838.6	4 136.8	4 950.0
Foreign exchange									
Devises étrangères	811.2	1 001.1	1 140.3	1 532.0	2 383.9	2 767.3	3 632.0	3 933.7	4 747.3
Peru Pérou									
Total reserves minus gold									
Rés. totale, moins l'or	9 776.8	12 176.4	13 599.4	16 733.3	26 856.5	30 271.5	32 012.6	42 647.9	47 206.3
Foreign exchange									
Devises étrangères	9 776.4	12 176.1	13 598.9	16 732.4	26 852.7	30 262.5	30 999.8	41 652.8	46 096.5
Philippines Philippines									
Total reserves minus gold									
Rés. totale, moins l'or	13 654.9	13 116.3	15 926.0	20 025.4	30 210.6	33 192.9	38 782.9	55 362.8	67 289.7
Foreign exchange									
Devises étrangères	13 523.3	12 979.5	15 800.1	19 891.4	30 071.4	33 047.2	37 504.2	53 991.3	65 699.7

Country or area Pays ou zone	2003	2004	2005	2006	2007	2008	2009	2010	2011
Poland Pologne									
Total reserves minus gold									
Rés. totale, moins l'or	32 579.1	35 323.9	40 863.7	46 371.1	62 966.8	59 305.6	75 923.3	88 821.8	92 646.5
Foreign exchange									
Devises étrangères	31 724.9	34 552.8	40 486.9	46 107.0	62 720.3	58 931.0	73 393.6	86 317.4	89 688.1
Portugal Portugal									
Total reserves minus gold									
Rés. totale, moins l'or	5 875.8	5 174.1	3 478.7	2 063.6	1 257.8	1 309.4	2 454.9	3 651.9	1 974.6
Foreign exchange									
Devises étrangères	5 248.8	4 631.2	3 173.4	1 835.3	1 044.4	1 022.0	811.4	2 012.7	340.6
Qatar Qatar									
Total reserves minus gold									
Rés. totale, moins l'or	2 944.2	3 395.9	4 542.4	5 382.7	9 416.4	9 649.5	18 369.7	30 620.8	16 198.5
Foreign exchange									
Devises étrangères	2 758.1	3 225.4	4 456.5	5 307.1	9 345.0	9 553.0	17 868.9	30 111.6	15 641.3
Republic of Moldova République de Moldova									
Total reserves minus gold									
Rés. totale, moins l'or	302.3	470.3	597.4	775.5	1 333.7	1 672.4	1 480.3	1 717.7	1 965.0
Foreign exchange									
Devises étrangères	302.2	470.2	597.4	775.3	1 333.5	1 672.2	1 476.7	1 717.3	1 964.1
Romania Roumanie									
Total reserves minus gold									
Rés. totale, moins l'or	8 040.0	14 616.4	19 872.1	28 066.2	37 194.1	36 868.4	40 756.6	43 360.9	42 939.1
Foreign exchange									
Devises étrangères	8 039.7	14 615.8	19 871.5	28 065.9	37 193.6	36 746.9	39 344.3	42 303.1	42 349.0
Russian Federation Fédération de Russie									
Total reserves minus gold									
Rés. totale, moins l'or	73 174.9	120 808.8	175 891.4	295 567.6	466 750.4	411 749.6	416 648.9	443 585.8	453 948.2
Foreign exchange									
Devises étrangères	73 172.1	120 805.1	175 689.9	295 277.1	466 375.7	410 695.4	405 824.9	432 948.5	441 161.7
Rwanda Rwanda									
Total reserves minus gold									
Rés. totale, moins l'or	214.7	314.6	405.8	439.7	552.8	596.3	742.7	812.8	1 050.0
Foreign exchange									
Devises étrangères	184.9	284.4	379.8	416.8	528.7	564.9	611.8	684.2	922.5
Saint Kitts and Nevis Saint-Kitts-et-Nevis									
Total reserves minus gold									
Rés. totale, moins l'or	64.8	78.5	71.6	88.7	95.8	110.4	136.4	168.9	244.3
Foreign exchange									
Devises étrangères	64.7	78.3	71.5	88.6	95.7	110.3	122.9	155.7	231.5
Saint Lucia Sainte-Lucie									
Total reserves minus gold									
Rés. totale, moins l'or	106.9	132.5	116.4	134.5	153.7	142.8	174.8	206.3	213.4
Foreign exchange									
Devises étrangères	104.7	130.2	114.2	132.2	151.2	140.3	150.6	182.3	189.8
Saint Vincent-Grenadines Saint Vincent-Grenadines									
Total reserves minus gold									
Rés. totale, moins l'or	51.2	75.0	69.5	78.7	87.0	83.7	87.8	112.7	89.6
Foreign exchange									
Devises étrangères	50.4	74.2	68.8	77.9	86.2	82.9	75.2	110.8	87.8
Samoa Samoa									
Total reserves minus gold									
Rés. totale, moins l'or	83.9	86.1	81.8	80.7	95.4	87.1	165.8	209.4	166.8
Foreign exchange									
Devises étrangères	79.3	81.3	77.3	75.9	90.2	81.9	145.0	189.0	146.4
San Marino Saint-Marin									
Total reserves minus gold									
Rés. totale, moins l'or	251.3	355.6	347.8	479.1	647.8	706.8	790.3	449.2	341.9
Foreign exchange									
Devises étrangères	244.5	348.3	341.0	471.8	639.8	698.7	757.7	417.1	309.9

60

International reserves minus gold *(continued)*
Millions of US dollars, end of period
Réserves internationales, moins l'or *(suite)*
Millions de dollars des E.-U., fin de période

Country or area Pays ou zone	2003	2004	2005	2006	2007	2008	2009	2010	2011
Sao Tome and Principe Sao Tomé-et-Principe									
Total reserves minus gold									
Rés. totale, moins l'or	25.5	19.5	26.7	34.2	39.3	61.3	66.7	49.4	51.5
Foreign exchange									
Devises étrangères	25.4	19.5	26.7	34.1	39.3	61.3	56.5	43.6	45.7
Saudi Arabia Arabie saoudite									
Total reserves minus gold									
Rés. totale, moins l'or	22 620.0	27 290.9	#155 028.9²	226 035.2	305 455.4	442 249.5	409 693.6	444 721.7	540 676.6
Foreign exchange									
Devises étrangères	17 662.0	23 273.0	#152 572.9	224 483.3	304 003.2	440 130.1	396 748.3	432 094.4	525 521.0
Senegal Sénégal									
Total reserves minus gold									
Rés. totale, moins l'or	1 110.9	1 367.6	1 186.0	1 334.2	1 660.0	1 602.2	2 123.2	2 047.5	1 945.7
Foreign exchange									
Devises étrangères	1 098.2	1 357.9	1 182.4	1 331.8	1 657.3	1 599.4	1 916.1	1 844.0	1 742.9
Serbia Serbie									
Total reserves minus gold									
Rés. totale, moins l'or	3 410.8	4 095.9	5 627.9	11 647.7	13 892.6	11 122.9	14 769.2	12 714.6	14 877.2
Foreign exchange									
Devises étrangères	3 410.4	4 095.8	5 597.7	11 638.9	13 891.8	11 120.7	14 749.9	12 711.7	14 874.6
Seychelles Seychelles									
Total reserves minus gold									
Rés. totale, moins l'or	67.4	34.6	56.2	112.9	40.8	63.8	190.5	235.6	252.3
Foreign exchange									
Devises étrangères	67.4	34.6	56.2	112.9	40.7	63.8	178.2	223.8	241.1
Sierra Leone Sierra Leone									
Total reserves minus gold									
Rés. totale, moins l'or	66.6	125.1	170.5	183.9	216.6	220.2	405.0	409.0	0.0
Foreign exchange									
Devises étrangères	32.1	74.1	137.7	154.7	185.8	189.7	215.3	224.8	0.0
Singapore Singapour									
Total reserves minus gold									
Rés. totale, moins l'or	96 033.8	112 367.3	115 960.1	136 048.8	162 745.6	173 981.0	187 591.6	225 502.8	237 662.1
Foreign exchange									
Devises étrangères	95 262.7	111 633.8	115 500.7	135 602.3	162 305.5	173 436.9	185 793.0	223 678.0	235 496.9
Slovakia Slovaquie									
Total reserves minus gold									
Rés. totale, moins l'or	11 678.1	14 417.5	14 900.7	12 646.6	18 032.1	17 854.2	#692.2	719.3	853.3
Foreign exchange									
Devises étrangères	11 676.8	14 416.1	14 899.4	12 645.2	18 025.8	17 804.9	#50.4	52.1	71.2
Slovenia Slovénie									
Total reserves minus gold									
Rés. totale, moins l'or	8 496.9	8 793.4	8 076.4	7 036.1	#979.8	868.1	966.1	926.9	830.7
Foreign exchange									
Devises étrangères	8 343.1	8 662.3	8 013.1	6 987.1	#942.0	809.9	589.5	507.3	328.6
Solomon Islands Iles Salomon									
Total reserves minus gold									
Rés. totale, moins l'or	37.2	80.6	95.4	104.4	119.1	89.5	146.0	265.8	412.3
Foreign exchange									
Devises étrangères	36.4	79.7	94.6	103.6	118.2	88.7	130.6	250.7	397.2
South Africa Afrique du Sud									
Total reserves minus gold									
Rés. totale, moins l'or	6 495.5	13 141.3	18 579.1	23 056.9	29 588.6	30 583.5	35 237.4	38 175.0	42 595.2
Foreign exchange									
Devises étrangères	6 163.7	12 794.3	18 259.6	22 720.1	29 234.2	30 237.8	32 431.8	35 418.8	39 847.1
Spain Espagne									
Total reserves minus gold									
Rés. totale, moins l'or	19 788.4	12 388.8	9 677.6	10 822.2	11 480.2	12 413.7	18 205.1	19 146.4	32 843.2
Foreign exchange									
Devises étrangères	17 512.8	10 481.4	8 594.1	10 088.2	10 792.0	11 540.0	12 786.8	13 305.9	25 841.8

Country or area Pays ou zone	2003	2004	2005	2006	2007	2008	2009	2010	2011
Sri Lanka Sri Lanka									
Total reserves minus gold									
Rés. totale, moins l'or	2 264.9	2 131.9	2 649.5	2 726.2	3 379.5	2 468.7	4 616.1	6 709.7	6 247.9
Foreign exchange									
Devises étrangères	2 193.2	2 057.4	2 579.6	2 651.5	3 297.1	2 393.0	4 521.0	6 633.6	6 170.1
Old Sudan Soudan									
Total reserves minus gold									
Rés. totale, moins l'or	529.4	1 338.0	1 868.6	1 659.9	1 377.9	1 399.0	1 094.2	1 036.2	0.0
Foreign exchange									
Devises étrangères	529.1	1 338.0	1 868.5	1 659.9	1 377.9	1 399.0	897.0	842.8	0.0
Suriname Suriname									
Total reserves minus gold									
Rés. totale, moins l'or	105.8	129.4	125.8	215.4	400.9	473.6	659.0	638.9	940.9
Foreign exchange									
Devises étrangères	94.7	118.0	115.5	204.9	390.4	463.6	522.9	505.2	807.7
Swaziland Swaziland									
Total reserves minus gold									
Rés. totale, moins l'or	277.5	323.6	243.9	372.5	774.2	751.9	958.9	756.3	600.5
Foreign exchange									
Devises étrangères	264.1	309.5	231.0	358.9	759.9	737.9	879.0	677.8	522.3
Sweden Suède									
Total reserves minus gold									
Rés. totale, moins l'or	19 681.1	22 157.7	22 090.1	24 777.8	27 044.4	25 896.4	42 859.6	42 564.9	44 025.4
Foreign exchange									
Devises étrangères	18 015.0	20 640.0	21 382.0	24 074.0	26 382.0	25 127.0	38 543.0	37 919.0	38 907.0
Switzerland Suisse									
Total reserves minus gold									
Rés. totale, moins l'or	47 652.5	55 496.6	36 297.3	38 093.7	44 474.2	45 060.9	98 199.4	223 480.6	279 390.3
Foreign exchange									
Devises étrangères	45 560.0	53 634.0	35 421.0	37 364.0	43 867.0	44 151.0	91 614.0	217 347.0	271 122.0
Syrian Arab Republic Rép. arabe syrienne									
Total reserves minus gold									
Rés. totale, moins l'or	...	...	17 346.9	16 467.4	17 013.0	17 061.9	17 397.7	19 465.3	...
Foreign exchange									
Devises étrangères	...	...	17 294.6	16 412.3	16 955.2	17 005.6	16 960.0	19 035.4	...
Tajikistan Tadjikistan									
Total reserves minus gold									
Rés. totale, moins l'or	111.9	157.5	168.2	175.1	40.1	103.8	174.6	324.2	289.3
Foreign exchange									
Devises étrangères	111.0	156.2	162.8	171.6	36.5	88.2	65.0	216.7	182.2
Thailand Thaïlande									
Total reserves minus gold									
Rés. totale, moins l'or	41 076.9	48 664.0	50 690.7	65 291.4	85 221.3	108 660.9	135 482.9	167 530.3	167 389.1
Foreign exchange									
Devises étrangères	40 965.1	48 497.5	50 502.0	65 147.1	85 110.1	108 317.1	133 599.2	165 656.0	165 199.6
TFYR of Macedonia L'ex-R.Y. Macédoine									
Total reserves minus gold									
Rés. totale, moins l'or	897.7	905.0	1 228.5	1 750.6	2 082.3	1 920.3	2 050.9	1 970.0	2 331.4
Foreign exchange									
Devises étrangères	897.4	904.2	1 227.7	1 747.6	2 080.8	1 919.0	1 959.9	1 968.8	2 330.7
Timor-Leste Timor-Leste									
Total reserves minus gold									
Rés. totale, moins l'or	61.3	182.4	153.3	83.8	230.3	210.4	249.9	406.2	461.6
Foreign exchange									
Devises étrangères	61.3	182.4	153.3	83.8	230.3	210.4	237.8	394.3	449.7
Togo Togo									
Total reserves minus gold									
Rés. totale, moins l'or	204.9	357.7	191.5	374.5	438.1	581.8	703.2	714.9	774.3
Foreign exchange									
Devises étrangères	204.2	357.1	191.0	373.9	437.5	581.2	609.8	622.9	682.6

60

International reserves minus gold *(continued)*
Millions of US dollars, end of period
Réserves internationales, moins l'or *(suite)*
Millions de dollars des E.-U., fin de période

Country or area Pays ou zone	2003	2004	2005	2006	2007	2008	2009	2010	2011
Tonga Tonga									
Total reserves minus gold									
Rés. totale, moins l'or	39.8	55.3	46.9	48.0	65.2	69.8	95.7	104.5	143.3
Foreign exchange									
Devises étrangères	36.9	52.2	44.0	44.9	61.9	66.4	81.9	91.0	129.8
Trinidad and Tobago Trinité-et-Tobago									
Total reserves minus gold									
Rés. totale, moins l'or	2 451.1	3 168.2	4 960.8	6 585.7	6 693.7	9 442.6	9 177.9	9 605.5	10 406.0
Foreign exchange									
Devises étrangères	2 257.8	2 993.0	4 885.8	6 530.9	6 657.4	9 380.4	8 651.6	9 070.0	9 822.7
Tunisia Tunisie									
Total reserves minus gold									
Rés. totale, moins l'or	2 945.4	3 935.7	4 436.7	6 773.2	7 850.8	8 849.3	11 057.3	9 459.3	0.0
Foreign exchange									
Devises étrangères	2 912.9	3 895.0	4 405.6	6 741.4	7 816.8	8 812.9	10 646.5	9 000.3	0.0
Turkey Turquie									
Total reserves minus gold									
Rés. totale, moins l'or	33 991.0	35 669.1	50 579.0	60 891.9	73 383.9	70 428.1	70 873.7	80 713.0	78 322.4
Foreign exchange									
Devises étrangères	33 793.0	35 480.0	50 402.0	60 710.0	73 155.8	70 231.3	69 177.5	79 045.6	76 658.9
Uganda Ouganda									
Total reserves minus gold									
Rés. totale, moins l'or	1 080.3	1 308.1	1 344.2	1 810.9	2 559.8	2 300.5	2 994.5	2 706.0	2 617.4
Foreign exchange									
Devises étrangères	1 075.5	1 307.4	1 343.1	1 810.8	2 559.5	2 300.3	2 769.3	2 485.2	2 399.0
Ukraine Ukraine									
Total reserves minus gold									
Rés. totale, moins l'or	6 683.2	9 490.7	18 988.0	21 844.6	31 786.0	30 800.6	25 556.9	33 327.4	30 409.3
Foreign exchange									
Devises étrangères	6 662.0	9 489.5	18 987.0	21 843.2	31 783.2	30 791.9	25 493.3	33 319.4	30 391.4
United Arab Emirates Emirats arabes unis									
Total reserves minus gold									
Rés. totale, moins l'or	15 087.8	18 529.9	21 010.3	27 617.4	77 238.8	31 694.5	36 104.2	42 785.3	0.0
Foreign exchange									
Devises étrangères	14 731.5	18 209.0	20 867.7	27 511.9	77 161.9	31 556.6	35 070.4	41 750.9	0.0
United Kingdom Royaume-Uni									
Total reserves minus gold									
Rés. totale, moins l'or	35 348.5	39 942.3	38 467.2	40 697.8	48 958.1	44 348.3	55 702.4	68 344.8	79 272.3
Foreign exchange									
Devises étrangères	28 645.4	34 081.7	35 853.9	38 888.6	47 497.8	41 550.3	38 026.0	49 334.8	56 238.6
United Rep. of Tanzania Rép.-Unie de Tanzanie									
Total reserves minus gold									
Rés. totale, moins l'or	2 038.4	2 295.7	2 048.8	2 259.3	2 886.4	2 862.9	3 470.4	3 904.7	3 726.2
Foreign exchange									
Devises étrangères	2 023.0	2 280.1	2 033.8	2 244.2	2 870.4	2 847.5	3 205.9	3 645.4	3 470.1
United States Etats-Unis									
Total reserves minus gold									
Rés. totale, moins l'or	74 894.1	75 890.0	54 083.8	54 853.9	59 524.3	66 607.0	119 718.8	121 391.6	136 912.5
Foreign exchange									
Devises étrangères	39 721.8	42 718.3	37 838.1	40 943.5	45 803.8	49 583.6	50 519.9	52 075.2	51 877.6
Uruguay Uruguay									
Total reserves minus gold									
Rés. totale, moins l'or	2 083.2	2 508.5	3 074.1	3 085.3	4 114.3	6 352.8	8 028.6	7 643.6	10 288.8
Foreign exchange									
Devises étrangères	2 079.4	2 507.3	3 067.8	3 084.2	4 114.0	6 348.7	7 643.5	7 168.4	9 765.3
Vanuatu Vanuatu									
Total reserves minus gold									
Rés. totale, moins l'or	43.8	61.8	67.2	104.7	119.6	115.2	148.6	161.4	0.0
Foreign exchange									
Devises étrangères	38.8	56.5	62.2	99.3	113.8	109.4	142.2	155.2	0.0

60

International reserves minus gold *(continued)*
Millions of US dollars, end of period
Réserves internationales, moins l'or *(suite)*
Millions de dollars des E.-U., fin de période

Country or area Pays ou zone	2003	2004	2005	2006	2007	2008	2009	2010	2011
Venezuela (Boliv. Rep. of)	**Venezuela (Rép. boliv. du)**								
Total reserves minus gold									
Rés. totale, moins l'or	16 034.7	18 375.4	23 918.8	29 417.3	24 196.1	33 098.1	21 703.0	13 136.8	9 930.1
Foreign exchange									
Devises étrangères	15 546.0	17 867.0	23 454.0	28 933.0	23 686.0	32 581.0	17 687.0	9 192.0	5 998.0
Viet Nam Viet Nam									
Total reserves minus gold									
Rés. totale, moins l'or	6 224.2	7 041.5	9 050.6	13 384.1	23 479.4	23 890.3	16 447.1	12 466.6	0.0
Foreign exchange									
Devises étrangères	6 222.0	7 041.0	9 049.7	13 382.5	23 471.8	23 882.0	16 027.4	12 054.1	0.0
Yemen Yémen									
Total reserves minus gold									
Rés. totale, moins l'or	4 986.9	5 664.8	6 115.4	7 511.5	7 715.4	8 111.4	6 935.6	5 868.4	4 448.9
Foreign exchange									
Devises étrangères	4 982.0	5 613.5	6 096.6	7 504.4	7 715.4	8 110.9	6 622.0	5 587.8	4 195.0
Zambia Zambie									
Total reserves minus gold									
Rés. totale, moins l'or	247.7	337.1	559.8	719.7	1 090.0	1 095.6	1 892.1	2 093.8	2 324.0
Foreign exchange									
Devises étrangères	247.2	312.2	544.0	706.4	1 080.2	1 085.0	1 254.4	1 468.5	1 706.2

Source:
International Monetary Fund (IMF), Washington, D.C., the database on International Financial Statistics, last accessed April 2012.

Source:
Fonds monétaire international (FMI), Washington, D.C., la base de données de Statistiques Financières Internationales, dernier accès avril 2012.

1   For statistical purposes, the data for China do not include those for the Hong Kong Special Administrative Region (Hong Kong SAR) and Macao Special Administrative Region (Macao SAR).

1   Pour la présentation des statistiques, les données pour la Chine ne comprennent pas la Région Administrative Spéciale de Hong Kong (Hong Kong RAS) et la Région Administrative Spéciale de Macao (Macao RAS).

2   Prior to 2005, data on foreign exchange excluded investments and deposits abroad.

2   Avant 2005, les données sur le marché des changes ne comprenaient pas les investissements et les dépôts effectués à l'étranger.

Total external and public/publicly guaranteed long-term debt of developing countries
Millions of US dollars

Total de la dette extérieure et dette publique extérieure à long terme garantie par l'Etat des pays en développement
Millions de dollars des E.-U.

A.   Total external debt [&] • Total de la dette extérieure [&]

Developing economies	2004	2005	2006	2007	2008	2009	2010	Economies en développement
Total long-term debt	**1 971 150**	**1 964 052**	**2 061 665**	**2 440 930**	**2 713 910**	**2 813 091**	**2 975 259**	**Total de la dette à long terme**
Public and publicly guaranteed	1 417 702	1 282 903	1 246 306	1 355 843	1 397 456	1 477 075	1 582 586	Dette publique ou garantie par l'Etat
Official creditors	813 381	715 244	636 441	668 757	711 012	772 345	822 575	Créanciers publics
Multilateral	386 257	373 641	348 159	373 874	395 001	443 775	483 841	Multilatéraux
IBRD	102 061	96 370	92 386	93 651	96 696	108 696	124 852	BIRD
IDA	124 576	121 077	99 005	107 675	111 269	116 967	118 607	IDA
Bilateral	427 124	341 602	288 282	294 883	316 011	328 570	338 734	Bilatéraux
Private creditors	604 321	567 659	609 866	687 086	686 445	704 730	760 011	Créanciers privés
Bonds	437 920	400 279	409 788	455 913	468 243	484 388	527 752	Obligations
Commercial banks	119 669	125 950	163 807	198 841	190 359	189 535	202 652	Banques commerciales
Other private	46 732	41 431	36 271	32 332	27 842	30 807	29 607	Autres institutions privées
Private non-guaranteed	553 448	681 149	815 359	1 085 088	1 316 454	1 336 016	1 392 674	Dette privées non garantie
Undisbursed debt	**236 987**	**226 664**	**221 646**	**237 965**	**258 252**	**309 588**	**324 248**	**Dette (montants non versés)**
Official creditors	190 064	191 920	190 753	204 914	226 908	277 531	289 453	Créanciers publics
Private creditors	46 923	34 744	30 893	33 051	31 344	32 057	34 796	Créanciers privés
Commitments	**133 116**	**159 300**	**143 401**	**194 324**	**185 948**	**247 087**	**250 764**	**Engagements**
Official creditors	53 454	67 107	60 326	71 954	90 239	153 185	122 810	Créanciers publics
Private creditors	79 662	92 193	83 075	122 370	95 710	93 902	127 954	Créanciers privés
Disbursements	**309 616**	**379 262**	**474 888**	**658 556**	**650 407**	**505 843**	**638 831**	**Versements**
Public and publicly guaranteed	136 179	142 620	151 919	186 837	174 672	217 405	253 309	Dette publique ou garantie par l'Etat
Official creditors	46 908	46 076	54 722	60 069	68 706	100 215	105 448	Créanciers publics
Multilateral	33 307	34 253	40 007	43 714	47 600	72 435	71 390	Multilatéraux
IBRD	10 045	9 180	11 934	10 498	13 608	22 703	26 246	BIRD
IDA	1 070	1 139	1 122	1 838	2 025	2 386	2 105	IDA
Bilateral	13 602	11 824	14 715	16 355	21 107	27 781	34 059	Bilatéraux
Private creditors	89 271	96 543	97 197	126 768	105 966	117 190	147 860	Créanciers privés
Bonds	60 932	61 066	57 988	75 318	73 523	69 052	86 861	Obligations
Commercial banks	24 317	31 775	34 149	47 852	30 036	41 806	51 399	Banques commerciales
Other private	4 022	3 702	5 060	3 599	2 407	6 331	9 601	Autres institutions privées
Private non-guaranteed	173 438	236 643	322 969	471 718	475 734	288 439	385 522	Dette privé non garantie
Principal repayments	**245 991**	**282 956**	**352 277**	**355 576**	**392 427**	**381 197**	**425 895**	**Remboursements du principal**
Public and publicly guaranteed	124 467	145 932	191 849	127 649	143 529	117 318	124 527	Dette publique ou garantie par l'Etat
Official creditors	56 476	70 215	97 008	53 409	49 992	46 498	48 021	Créanciers publics
Multilateral	30 674	26 691	36 472	26 490	26 982	25 467	25 854	Multilatéraux
IBRD	14 060	12 130	17 188	10 866	10 947	10 860	9 165	BIRD
IDA	1 526	1 622	1 779	1 836	2 296	2 252	2 342	IDA
Bilateral	25 801	43 524	60 536	26 920	23 010	21 031	22 167	Bilatéraux
Private creditors	67 991	75 717	94 841	74 239	93 537	70 820	76 506	Créanciers privés
Bonds	36 281	44 589	60 257	43 145	53 897	32 705	35 031	Obligations
Commercial banks	23 507	22 303	25 145	23 976	32 407	30 706	33 485	Banques commerciales
Other private	8 203	8 825	9 439	7 119	7 233	7 409	7 990	Autres institutions privées
Private non-guaranteed	121 524	137 024	160 428	227 927	248 898	263 879	301 368	Dette privée non garantie
Net flows	**63 625**	**96 307**	**122 612**	**302 980**	**257 980**	**124 646**	**212 936**	**Apports nets**
Public and publicly guaranteed	11 712	-3 312	-39 930	59 189	31 144	100 087	128 782	Dette publique ou garantie par l'Etat
Official creditors	-9 568	-24 138	-42 286	6 660	18 714	53 717	57 427	Créanciers publics
Multilateral	2 632	7 562	3 536	17 225	20 618	46 968	45 536	Multilatéraux
IBRD	-4 015	-2 948	-5 254	-368	2 660	11 843	17 082	BIRD
IDA	6 356	5 582	4 992	5 522	4 568	6 460	5 346	IDA
Bilateral	-12 200	-31 700	-45 822	-10 565	-1 904	6 749	11 892	Bilatéraux
Private creditors	21 280	20 826	2 356	52 529	12 430	46 370	71 354	Créanciers privés
Bonds	24 651	16 477	-2 269	32 173	19 626	36 347	51 830	Obligations
Commercial banks	810	9 473	9 004	23 876	-2 372	11 101	17 914	Banques commerciales
Other private	-4 181	-5 124	-4 379	-3 520	-4 825	-1 078	1 611	Autres institutions privées
Private non-guaranteed	51 913	99 619	162 541	243 791	226 836	24 559	84 154	Dette privée non garantie

Total external and public/publicly guaranteed long-term debt of developing countries *(continued)*
Millions of US dollars

Total de la dette extérieure et dette publique extérieure à long terme garantie par l'Etat des pays en développement *(suite)*
Millions de dollars des E.-U.

A.   Total external debt [&] • Total de la dette extérieure [&]

Developing economies	2004	2005	2006	2007	2008	2009	2010	Economies en développement
Interest payments	**77 885**	**83 820**	**94 205**	**109 208**	**120 813**	**111 244**	**111 949**	**Paiements d'intêrets**
Public and publicly guaranteed	54 502	60 511	56 330	59 793	59 142	54 237	55 120	Dette publique ou garantie par l'Etat
Official creditors	21 555	23 934	19 726	20 230	19 011	16 999	16 592	Créanciers publics
Multilateral	10 739	10 581	11 672	12 878	12 309	10 515	8 930	Multilatéraux
IBRD	3 977	4 020	4 782	5 435	4 576	3 432	2 256	BIRD
IDA	893	897	811	758	908	798	825	IDA
Bilateral	10 816	13 353	8 055	7 352	6 702	6 484	7 663	Bilatéraux
Private creditors	32 948	36 578	36 604	39 563	40 131	37 238	38 528	Créanciers privés
Bonds	26 339	30 128	28 827	31 222	31 727	30 820	33 011	Obligations
Commercial banks	4 703	4 919	6 256	6 539	6 706	5 181	4 349	Banques commerciales
Other private	1 906	1 530	1 521	1 801	1 699	1 238	1 167	Autres institutions privées
Private non-guaranteed	23 383	23 309	37 874	49 415	61 672	57 006	56 829	Dette privée non garantie
Net transfers	**-14 260**	**12 487**	**28 407**	**193 772**	**137 167**	**13 402**	**100 987**	**Transferts nets**
Public and publicly guaranteed	-42 790	-63 824	-96 260	-604	-27 998	45 849	73 661	Dette publique ou garantie par l'Etat
Official creditors	-31 123	-48 072	-62 012	-13 570	-297	36 718	40 835	Créanciers publics
Multilateral	-8 107	-3 020	-8 136	4 347	8 309	36 452	36 606	Multilatéraux
IBRD	-7 992	-6 970	-10 036	-5 803	-1 916	8 411	14 825	BIRD
IDA	5 483	4 688	4 181	4 764	3 660	5 662	4 521	IDA
Bilateral	-23 016	-45 053	-53 876	-17 917	-8 605	265	4 229	Bilatéraux
Private creditors	-11 668	-15 751	-34 248	12 966	-27 701	9 132	32 826	Créanciers privés
Bonds	-1 688	-13 650	-31 096	951	-12 100	5 527	18 818	Obligations
Commercial banks	-3 893	4 553	2 748	17 337	-9 078	5 920	13 565	Banques commerciales
Other private	-6 087	-6 654	-5 900	-5 322	-6 524	-2 315	443	Autres institutions privées
Private non-guaranteed	28 531	76 310	124 667	194 376	165 165	-32 447	27 325	Dette privées non garantie
Total debt service	**323 876**	**366 776**	**446 481**	**464 784**	**513 240**	**492 441**	**537 844**	**Total du service de la dette**
Public and publicly guaranteed	178 969	206 443	248 179	187 442	202 670	171 555	179 647	Dette publique ou garantie par l'Etat
Official creditors	78 031	94 149	116 734	73 640	69 003	63 497	64 613	Créanciers publics
Multilateral	41 413	37 272	48 143	39 367	39 291	35 982	34 784	Multilatéraux
IBRD	18 037	16 150	21 970	16 301	15 523	14 292	11 421	BIRD
IDA	2 420	2 519	2 590	2 594	3 204	3 050	3 167	IDA
Bilateral	36 617	56 876	68 591	34 272	29 712	27 515	29 830	Bilatéraux
Private creditors	100 938	112 295	131 445	113 802	133 668	108 058	115 034	Créanciers privés
Bonds	62 620	74 717	89 084	74 367	85 623	63 526	68 042	Obligations
Commercial banks	28 210	27 222	31 401	30 515	39 113	35 886	37 834	Banques commerciales
Other private	10 109	10 356	10 960	8 920	8 931	8 646	9 158	Autres institutions privées
Private non-guaranteed	144 907	160 333	198 302	277 342	310 570	320 886	358 197	Dette privées non garantie

[&] The following abbreviations have been used in the table:
IBRD: International Bank for Reconstruction and Development
IDA: International Development Association

[&] Les abréviations ci-après ont été utilisées dans le tableau :
BIRD : Banque internationale pour la reconstruction et le développement
IDA : Association internationale de développement

61

Total external and public/publicly guaranteed long-term debt of developing countries
Millions of US dollars

Total de la dette extérieure dette publique extérieure à long terme garantie par l'Etat des pays en développement
Millions de dollars des E.-U.

B.   Public and publicly guaranteed long-term debt • Dette publique extérieure à long terme garantie par l'Etat

Country or area	2004	2005	2006	2007	2008	2009	2010	2011	Pays ou zone
Afghanistan	...	...	910.9	1 893.5	1 985.4	2 097.0	1 966.4	2 023.3	Afghanistan
Albania	1 402.7	1 374.9	1 578.7	1 790.1	2 219.9	2 798.5	3 139.8	3 198.2	Albanie
Algeria	20 403.1	15 491.2	3 836.4	3 996.3	3 264.6	3 016.0	2 620.0	2 213.1	Algérie
Angola	8 166.1	9 518.0	7 347.6	9 230.6	12 690.4	13 634.7	15 466.1	17 517.6	Angola
Argentina	100 055.5	56 278.7	62 817.6	70 614.5	71 123.4	75 952.9	69 252.7	68 284.8	Argentine
Armenia	960.7	922.5	1 037.3	1 282.4	1 445.7	2 376.3	2 556.9	2 736.5	Arménie
Azerbaijan	1 268.7	1 403.7	1 733.0	2 231.2	2 686.3	3 344.6	3 890.6	4 655.2	Azerbaïdjan
Bangladesh	18 643.4	17 384.6	18 380.4	19 428.0	20 299.9	21 209.9	21 399.6	22 350.1	Bangladesh
Belarus	744.4	785.6	841.9	2 337.9	3 719.2	4 822.6	7 696.7	9 152.0	Bélarus
Belize	935.5	989.5	1 018.4	1 038.9	1 020.4	1 040.9	1 022.4	1 018.1	Belize
Benin	1 507.1	1 444.0	589.5	747.3	849.4	971.6	1 109.9	1 190.5	Bénin
Bhutan	593.3	636.7	697.3	775.0	677.5	746.9	892.2	1 021.1	Bhoutan
Bolivia (Plurinational State of)	4 573.2	4 582.9	3 188.7	2 202.0	2 408.7	2 549.1	2 811.8	3 413.6	Bolivie (État plurinational de)
Bosnia and Herzegovina	2 685.5	2 558.9	2 722.5	2 966.8	3 008.2	3 578.0	3 733.4	3 874.3	Bosnie-Herzégovine
Botswana	488.0	412.3	358.2	391.1	390.8	1 388.3	1 351.7	1 897.1	Botswana
Brazil	97 455.9	94 354.5	84 551.7	79 869.9	79 912.4	87 510.5	97 557.3	94 976.9	Brésil
Bulgaria	7 413.7	5 075.2	5 146.6	5 267.9	4 397.3	4 772.3	4 466.4	4 138.0	Bulgarie
Burkina Faso	1 777.2	1 861.0	993.6	1 257.8	1 510.4	1 720.4	1 936.8	2 056.0	Burkina Faso
Burundi	1 273.2	1 176.3	1 231.9	1 277.1	1 240.2	406.2	403.9	386.6	Burundi
Cambodia	3 079.7	3 154.8	3 317.7	2 565.0	2 920.0	3 127.3	3 442.2	3 815.5	Cambodge
Cameroon	9 304.0	6 467.1	2 391.5	2 157.6	2 088.4	2 168.1	2 164.0	2 100.8	Cameroun
Cape Verde	452.6	463.3	509.5	564.9	611.4	699.8	867.8	1 003.5	Cap-Vert
Central African Rep.	960.6	902.5	893.5	902.4	867.7	321.2	327.9	296.9	Rép. centrafricaine
Chad	1 526.5	1 493.7	1 626.6	1 712.3	1 705.3	1 713.6	1 708.4	1 710.2	Tchad
Chile	9 335.1	9 123.3	9 354.4	9 293.8	8 764.2	9 271.1	13 518.7	16 354.1	Chili
China	87 614.5	84 195.9	85 718.2	87 101.2	90 837.9	94 038.4	89 208.9	91 663.7	Chine
Colombia	22 937.2	21 869.1	24 163.1	26 967.4	28 649.9	35 134.9	36 700.3	39 039.8	Colombie

61

Total external and public/publicly guaranteed long-term debt of developing countries *(continued)*
Millions of US dollars

Total de la dette extérieure et dette publique extérieure à long terme garantie par l'Etat des pays en développement *(suite)*
Millions de dollars des E.-U.

B.   Public and publicly guaranteed long-term debt • Dette publique extérieure à long terme garantie par l'Etat

Country or area	2004	2005	2006	2007	2008	2009	2010	2011	Pays ou zone
Comoros	270.7	255.3	257.5	276.5	267.4	260.2	250.7	245.5	Comores
Congo	5 840.0	5 471.4	5 824.3	5 330.6	5 531.2	4 851.8	2 217.7	2 157.3	Congo
Costa Rica	3 519.7	3 161.8	3 316.1	3 656.7	3 232.0	3 216.0	3 796.6	3 925.1	Costa Rica
Côte d'Ivoire	11 082.1	9 965.2	10 822.7	11 646.2	10 627.5	12 713.2	9 339.0	9 800.2	Côte d'Ivoire
Dem. Rep. of the Congo	10 116.1	9 402.9	9 878.3	10 918.4	10 875.7	10 893.1	4 613.0	3 939.8	Rép. dém. du Congo
Djibouti	387.5	376.9	439.2	651.4	678.4	735.4	610.8	641.7	Djibouti
Dominica	227.8	224.4	219.0	215.7	204.9	202.3	220.0	229.1	Dominique
Dominican Republic	6 134.0	5 885.0	6 377.9	6 402.3	6 958.3	7 941.5	9 330.3	10 758.1	Rép. dominicaine
Ecuador	10 907.2	10 895.8	10 348.5	10 763.0	10 094.7	6 959.6	8 633.3	9 929.0	Equateur
Egypt	28 728.5	27 988.9	28 626.1	31 678.4	30 377.5	30 926.3	31 840.9	30 580.1	Egypte
El Salvador	4 992.3	4 802.3	5 603.8	5 443.7	5 753.7	6 109.4	6 402.0	6 537.4	El Salvador
Eritrea	704.0	723.0	781.4	855.7	957.0	1 013.0	1 002.0	1 013.6	Erythrée
Ethiopia	6 350.7	5 928.0	2 200.9	2 571.4	2 829.1	4 819.0	6 547.2	7 937.9	Ethiopie
Fiji	192.5	185.4	342.2	347.0	360.1	360.4	389.7	545.0	Fidji
Gabon	3 777.1	3 562.5	3 696.8	2 597.4	2 055.5	2 024.3	2 153.1	2 463.7	Gabon
Gambia	621.4	616.5	674.4	664.0	336.8	387.6	390.8	385.1	Gambie
Georgia	1 621.8	1 531.2	1 526.0	1 603.6	2 973.8	3 529.4	4 140.6	4 343.2	Géorgie
Ghana	6 136.3	6 059.6	2 269.9	3 565.4	4 085.1	5 033.2	6 117.3	7 402.4	Ghana
Grenada	346.6	391.3	454.8	479.5	477.2	494.6	493.3	487.2	Grenade
Guatemala	3 827.8	3 720.3	3 953.3	4 220.3	4 382.5	4 923.3	5 554.8	5 358.5	Guatemala
Guinea	2 973.9	2 770.9	2 876.2	3 002.1	2 883.1	2 868.4	2 805.4	2 849.2	Guinée
Guinea-Bissau	976.6	888.8	911.0	935.8	942.4	964.3	978.2	218.5	Guinée-Bissau
Guyana	1 141.2	1 041.2	923.3	583.9	675.1	779.5	885.2	1 054.5	Guyana
Haiti	1 225.0	1 277.9	1 346.1	1 524.6	1 846.1	1 157.6	850.1	634.7	Haïti
Honduras	4 887.0	4 144.9	3 038.8	1 997.2	2 306.2	2 450.4	2 802.9	3 179.9	Honduras
India	64 879.5	54 726.1	60 043.0	69 855.1	76 248.0	85 210.0	100 486.8	107 857.5	Inde
Indonesia	71 860.2	77 405.1	76 625.4	80 314.9	87 753.5	97 447.2	100 292.1	102 551.7	Indonésie
Iran (Islamic Rep. of)	10 002.7	10 521.5	11 128.4	11 173.7	8 778.7	7 312.7	6 166.8	4 859.4	Iran (Rép. islamique d')
Jamaica	5 263.3	5 537.1	6 162.7	6 738.4	6 938.9	6 717.5	7 604.1	7 766.0	Jamaïque
Jordan	7 227.2	6 877.7	7 142.8	7 321.4	5 126.0	5 444.8	6 518.5	6 348.6	Jordanie

61

Total external and public/publicly guaranteed long-term debt of developing countries *(continued)*
Millions of US dollars

Total de la dette extérieure et dette publique extérieure à long terme garantie par l'Etat des pays en développement *(suite)*
Millions de dollars des E.-U.

B.   Public and publicly guaranteed long-term debt • Dette publique extérieure à long terme garantie par l'Etat

Country or area	2004	2005	2006	2007	2008	2009	2010	2011	Pays ou zone
Kazakhstan	3 233.7	2 176.8	2 136.2	1 697.7	1 915.0	2 486.9	3 845.4	4 675.2	Kazakhstan
Kenya	6 071.4	5 772.1	5 869.9	6 231.1	6 388.3	6 720.3	6 979.1	7 565.7	Kenya
Kosovo	...	...	...	...	0.0	358.5	319.0	309.9	Kosovo
Kyrgyzstan	1 742.4	1 664.8	1 830.8	1 897.9	1 962.8	2 319.5	2 441.8	2 618.3	Kirghizistan
Lao People's Dem. Rep.	2 033.6	1 989.4	2 259.2	2 515.1	2 720.5	2 817.8	2 938.8	2 888.6	Rép. dém. pop. lao
Latvia	1 273.8	1 052.8	1 256.6	1 477.1	1 944.6	6 602.2	6 891.2	7 074.8	Lettonie
Lebanon	18 410.0	18 866.3	20 107.1	20 907.4	20 596.1	20 614.8	20 213.2	20 601.0	Liban
Lesotho	721.6	618.9	613.5	642.2	659.2	680.6	697.9	711.6	Lesotho
Liberia	1 241.7	1 179.1	1 203.8	1 033.5	865.0	673.1	182.9	187.2	Libéria
Lithuania	3 079.5	2 001.0	4 589.0	5 881.0	5 348.1	9 073.1	11 665.4	12 912.4	Lituanie
Madagascar	3 486.7	3 182.2	1 242.0	1 410.6	1 717.0	1 836.1	1 982.2	2 053.1	Madagascar
Malawi	3 295.6	3 061.8	764.6	759.5	769.0	846.4	729.1	925.7	Malawi
Malaysia	25 429.5	22 323.8	23 022.0	19 745.3	22 742.1	22 647.1	27 351.5	27 155.9	Malaisie
Maldives	332.9	326.6	378.5	437.9	488.6	558.7	640.9	684.4	Maldives
Mali	3 069.6	3 036.3	1 553.0	1 806.7	1 984.5	2 002.0	2 271.2	2 507.9	Mali
Mauritania	2 072.3	2 071.6	1 389.3	1 436.7	1 668.9	1 839.7	2 174.1	2 379.7	Mauritanie
Mauritius	842.0	716.1	597.9	626.7	595.9	737.3	972.0	1 165.7	Maurice
Mexico	115 322.0	118 146.0	107 858.0	125 528.3	133 105.3	123 363.2	150 792.5	171 824.3	Mexique
Mongolia	1 306.6	1 266.7	1 361.0	1 576.2	1 657.1	1 817.3	1 782.0	1 825.8	Mongolie
Montenegro	...	...	828.6	843.8	851.2	1 094.3	1 349.6	1 544.5	Monténégro
Morocco	14 106.7	12 442.2	13 496.3	15 650.1	16 537.7	19 217.6	21 045.4	22 323.7	Maroc
Mozambique	3 371.9	3 366.6	2 040.9	2 344.4	2 726.3	3 164.6	2 897.4	3 616.7	Mozambique
Myanmar	5 924.8	5 515.4	5 608.7	6 220.7	6 121.0	6 320.1	6 273.8	6 252.8	Myanmar
Nepal	3 298.6	3 112.2	3 268.4	3 468.4	3 551.3	3 551.7	3 516.8	3 661.1	Népal
Nicaragua	4 037.5	3 939.5	3 240.8	2 170.7	2 252.8	2 505.3	2 683.2	2 846.5	Nicaragua
Niger	1 807.9	1 792.2	701.5	799.4	816.6	880.3	938.2	1 100.2	Niger
Nigeria	32 550.3	20 248.2	3 829.0	3 614.5	3 901.9	4 221.3	4 691.0	5 896.5	Nigéria
Pakistan	31 405.7	30 062.2	33 201.2	36 910.3	40 337.7	42 552.8	43 395.2	45 122.1	Pakistan
Panama	5 861.7	6 305.0	7 186.3	7 678.4	8 129.8	9 798.8	10 087.2	10 890.2	Panama
Papua New Guinea	1 445.1	1 264.1	1 210.4	1 128.9	1 067.4	1 045.0	1 042.4	1 069.3	Papouasie-Nvl-Guinée

Total external and public/publicly guaranteed long-term debt of developing countries *(continued)*
Millions of US dollars

Total de la dette extérieure et dette publique extérieure à long terme garantie par l'Etat des pays en développement *(suite)*
Millions de dollars des E.-U.

B.　Public and publicly guaranteed long-term debt • Dette publique extérieure à long terme garantie par l'Etat

Country or area	2004	2005	2006	2007	2008	2009	2010	2011	Pays ou zone
Paraguay	2 430.8	2 265.6	2 235.0	2 195.2	2 263.4	2 261.0	2 360.7	2 307.6	Paraguay
Peru	24 705.5	22 536.6	22 185.0	19 853.7	19 414.5	20 787.6	20 008.8	20 142.4	Pérou
Philippines	35 981.2	35 364.1	36 870.7	38 078.8	39 196.9	41 928.1	44 732.8	45 737.7	Philippines
Republic of Moldova	751.6	697.8	743.8	783.0	804.8	808.5	838.9	856.7	République de Moldova
Romania	13 661.8	13 329.5	14 184.2	15 298.9	15 255.9	18 247.8	20 800.7	24 869.6	Roumanie
Russian Federation	102 106.8	95 225.6	130 314.7	151 050.9	151 074.7	197 369.9	183 184.1	192 220.4	Fédération de Russie
Rwanda	1 541.9	1 414.5	389.5	565.9	645.7	723.5	765.5	971.1	Rwanda
Saint Lucia	245.4	238.6	251.0	300.4	316.7	314.9	321.4	309.9	Sainte-Lucie
Saint Vincent-Grenadines	224.5	247.8	242.5	199.8	203.9	203.2	255.5	259.8	Saint Vincent-Grenadines
Samoa	174.7	167.5	163.7	185.9	205.6	226.4	299.1	342.4	Samoa
Sao Tome and Principe	340.4	317.1	331.4	143.5	108.7	125.0	145.3	189.2	Sao Tomé-et-Principe
Senegal	3 521.3	3 505.1	1 643.7	1 993.5	2 378.3	2 957.0	3 151.6	3 607.8	Sénégal
Serbia	8 277.0	7 756.0	7 751.6	8 469.3	8 398.7	8 839.2	9 504.4	11 184.2	Serbie
Seychelles	345.1	398.2	504.2	626.0	649.7	707.7	463.3	458.7	Seychelles
Sierra Leone	1 410.4	1 538.2	1 428.4	482.1	544.9	604.8	660.9	739.8	Sierra Leone
Solomon Islands	155.3	144.2	150.9	148.1	137.1	132.9	125.3	117.9	Iles Salomon
Somalia	1 949.1	1 881.5	1 922.6	1 978.8	1 982.8	1 987.5	1 990.1	1 991.5	Somalie
South Africa	18 346.9	21 833.6	20 542.3	19 707.1	20 015.5	24 657.6	39 016.6	46 668.9	Afrique du Sud
Sri Lanka	9 801.0	9 609.2	10 292.7	11 833.7	12 611.5	13 675.6	16 473.1	18 733.5	Sri Lanka
Sudan (former)	11 665.3	11 232.2	11 922.2	12 737.9	13 120.1	13 706.5	14 444.1	15 123.3	Soudan (anc.)
Swaziland	365.3	362.2	364.7	368.6	355.0	390.8	385.2	343.8	Swaziland
Syrian Arab Republic	16 149.8	5 024.6	4 915.9	4 975.6	4 737.0	4 480.4	4 275.6	3 997.7	Rép. arabe syrienne
Tajikistan	804.1	825.6	839.8	1 063.1	1 374.4	1 606.4	1 806.4	1 968.8	Tadjikistan
Thailand	16 737.9	14 673.3	12 550.8	10 863.4	10 611.6	10 314.4	10 736.6	10 285.3	Thaïlande
TFYR of Macedonia	1 555.7	1 636.8	1 556.1	1 520.0	1 574.5	1 873.6	1 880.3	2 108.3	L'ex-R.Y. Macédoine
Togo	1 596.5	1 437.5	1 538.1	1 637.3	1 465.6	1 489.6	962.1	379.9	Togo
Tonga	84.2	79.5	81.6	86.5	88.8	104.6	143.5	180.5	Tonga
Tunisia	14 490.9	13 000.8	13 439.0	14 508.5	14 439.0	14 839.8	14 653.0	14 958.3	Tunisie
Turkey	68 313.8	62 964.6	68 443.5	81 096.3	82 307.8	85 598.6	91 379.9	94 419.1	Turquie
Turkmenistan	1 226.6	877.8	730.5	648.2	586.8	463.3	359.5	265.5	Turkménistan

61

Total external and public/publicly guaranteed long-term debt of developing countries *(continued)*
Millions of US dollars

Total de la dette extérieure et dette publique extérieure à long terme garantie par l'Etat des pays en développement *(suite)*
Millions de dollars des E.-U.

B.   Public and publicly guaranteed long-term debt • Dette publique extérieure à long terme garantie par l'Etat

Country or area	2004	2005	2006	2007	2008	2009	2010	2011	Pays ou zone
Uganda	4 396.8	4 184.2	1 074.9	1 546.2	1 753.9	2 220.5	2 670.7	2 957.9	Ouganda
Ukraine	8 575.0	8 469.0	9 769.1	13 567.5	14 041.2	13 040.4	16 025.0	17 965.5	Ukraine
United Rep. of Tanzania	6 528.5	6 446.2	2 452.4	3 181.2	3 711.2	4 639.9	5 600.6	6 438.2	Rép.-Unie de Tanzanie
Uruguay	7 811.7	7 741.9	9 089.2	10 414.0	10 120.6	11 098.3	11 449.8	12 104.4	Uruguay
Uzbekistan	4 107.2	3 619.1	3 289.0	3 134.5	3 136.8	3 220.9	3 361.4	3 695.3	Ouzbékistan
Vanuatu	83.6	71.9	72.0	78.1	89.7	98.8	99.3	98.8	Vanuatu
Venezuela (Boliv. Rep. of)	26 560.0	31 094.8	27 181.4	27 552.3	29 888.8	35 197.6	37 511.8	44 264.3	Venezuela (Rép. boliv. du)
Viet Nam	15 500.7	16 192.7	15 969.2	18 415.9	22 014.4	27 320.9	32 755.0	36 598.5	Viet Nam
Yemen	4 882.7	4 814.0	5 098.8	5 524.4	5 695.6	5 875.4	5 933.0	5 876.4	Yémen
Zambia	5 841.2	3 941.6	962.0	1 106.7	1 156.8	1 199.8	1 309.3	1 379.7	Zambie
Zimbabwe	3 542.1	3 177.0	3 366.6	3 689.8	3 639.8	3 719.6	3 665.5	3 650.4	Zimbabwe

Source:
World Bank, Washington, D.C., the *Global Development Finance* (GDF) database, last accessed December 2012.

Source:
Banque mondiale, Washington, D.C., la base de données de "Global Development Finance" (GDF), dernier accès décembre 2012.

62

Disbursements of bilateral and multilateral official development assistance and official aid to individual recipients

Versements d'aide publique au développement et d'aide publique bilatérale et multilatérale aux bénéficiaires

Country or area Pays ou zone	Year Année	Net disbursements (US $) - Versements nets ($E.-U.)			
		Bilateral Bilatérale (millions)	Multilateral[1] Multilatérale[1] (millions)	Total (millions)	Per capita Par habitant
World	**2006**	**78 886.1**	**28 452.5**	**107 338.6**	...
Monde	**2007**	**77 857.7**	**30 617.6**	**108 475.3**	...
	2008	**92 564.3**	**35 331.5**	**127 895.9**	...
	2009	**90 137.7**	**36 364.4**	**126 502.1**	...
	2010	**92 231.4**	**37 830.7**	**130 062.2**	...
Afghanistan	2006	2 597.3	364.4	2 961.7	104.2
Afghanistan	2007	4 291.3	673.4	4 964.7	170.3
	2008	4 221.7	653.4	4 875.1	163.4
	2009	5 450.2	785.1	6 235.3	203.9
	2010	5 656.1	714.4	6 370.6	202.8
Albania	2006	226.1	95.7	321.8	101.9
Albanie	2007	206.5	100.7	307.2	96.9
	2008	262.1	101.2	363.3	114.2
	2009	248.9	108.1	357.0	111.8
	2010	224.0	112.7	336.7	105.1
Algeria	2006	167.1	72.8	239.9	7.2
Algérie	2007	282.4	111.9	394.3	11.6
	2008	211.9	113.1	325.1	9.4
	2009	201.4	117.3	318.6	9.1
	2010	125.9	72.4	198.3	5.6
Angola	2006	48.7	114.8	163.5	9.6
Angola	2007	84.8	162.9	247.7	14.1
	2008	211.6	157.3	368.8	20.4
	2009	140.0	98.7	238.7	12.9
	2010	148.0	90.2	238.2	12.5
Anguilla	2006	-0.1	4.5	4.4	315.5
Anguilla	2007	3.6	1.7	5.3	366.2
	2008	-0.4	3.8	3.4	227.3
	2009	1.3	0.1	1.4	93.0
	2010	-0.9	9.1	8.3	538.5
Antigua and Barbuda	2006	1.5	1.8	3.3	38.6
Antigua-et-Barbuda	2007	1.9	5.5	7.4	85.9
	2008	2.2	6.5	8.8	100.7
	2009	2.3	3.3	5.6	64.2
	2010	5.4	13.7	19.1	215.0
Argentina	2006	67.9	47.2	115.1	2.9
Argentine	2007	52.5	48.9	101.3	2.6
	2008	77.0	53.6	130.6	3.3
	2009	67.7	59.0	126.7	3.2
	2010	90.2	30.9	121.1	3.0
Armenia	2006	155.4	60.1	215.5	70.2
Arménie	2007	244.6	105.4	350.0	113.9
	2008	185.5	117.1	302.6	98.3
	2009	327.9	198.1	526.0	170.5
	2010	226.5	112.7	339.2	109.7
Azerbaijan	2006	141.6	64.8	206.4	23.7
Azerbaïdjan	2007	150.9	74.3	225.2	25.5
	2008	147.5	87.6	235.1	26.3
	2009	164.7	67.1	231.8	25.6
	2010	75.2	80.6	155.8	17.0
Bangladesh	2006	730.6	490.6	1 221.2	8.6
Bangladesh	2007	703.4	811.8	1 515.2	10.5
	2008	764.4	1 306.2	2 070.6	14.2
	2009	619.0	606.9	1 225.8	8.3
	2010	589.9	824.5	1 414.4	9.5

Disbursements of bilateral and multilateral official development assistance and official aid to individual recipients *(continued)*
Versements d'aide publique au développement et d'aide publique bilatérale et multilatérale aux bénéficiaires *(suite)*

| Country or area
Pays ou zone | Year
Année | Net disbursements (US $) - Versements nets ($E.-U.) | | | |
		Bilateral Bilatérale (millions)	Multilateral[1] Multilatérale[1] (millions)	Total (millions)	Per capita Par habitant
Barbados Barbade	2006	-6.2	4.1	-2.1	-7.7
	2007	3.5	14.0	17.5	64.5
	2008	-2.0	9.1	7.1	26.2
	2009	-0.5	12.4	12.0	43.8
	2010	-2.0	18.2	16.2	59.3
Belarus Bélarus	2006	42.7	33.9	76.5	7.8
	2007	58.3	25.4	83.8	8.6
	2008	75.8	34.4	110.2	11.4
	2009	76.8	20.8	97.6	10.1
	2010	93.8	43.0	136.8	14.3
Belize Belize	2006	1.2	7.5	8.6	30.1
	2007	9.0	12.8	21.8	74.3
	2008	7.2	16.7	23.9	79.7
	2009	9.3	18.3	27.6	90.2
	2010	8.5	16.3	24.8	79.5
Benin Bénin	2006	125.5	273.8	399.3	50.7
	2007	267.1	207.3	474.4	58.5
	2008	330.5	311.0	641.5	76.8
	2009	385.1	297.0	682.1	79.3
	2010	384.4	304.7	689.1	77.9
Bhutan Bhoutan	2006	66.6	35.0	101.5	150.5
	2007	47.0	42.9	89.8	130.5
	2008	50.5	36.0	86.5	123.4
	2009	81.2	44.2	125.4	175.7
	2010	87.5	43.5	131.0	180.5
Bolivia (Plurinational State of) Bolivie (État plurinational de)	2006	459.6	390.4	850.0	91.3
	2007	368.7	107.1	475.8	50.3
	2008	521.6	106.3	627.9	65.3
	2009	573.0	152.3	725.3	74.2
	2010	525.7	148.7	674.4	67.9
Bosnia and Herzegovina Bosnie-Herzégovine	2006	419.4	115.5	535.0	141.5
	2007	468.8	130.7	599.5	158.6
	2008	326.6	140.3	466.9	123.7
	2009	299.6	114.8	414.3	110.0
	2010	268.6	223.3	491.9	130.8
Botswana Botswana	2006	17.2	51.6	68.8	36.2
	2007	49.5	58.2	107.7	55.9
	2008	677.1	43.2	720.3	368.5
	2009	232.2	47.0	279.2	140.9
	2010	95.5	60.7	156.1	77.8
Brazil Brésil	2006	48.3	65.1	113.4	0.6
	2007	244.0	77.2	321.2	1.7
	2008	356.9	103.4	460.4	2.4
	2009	277.7	59.3	336.9	1.7
	2010	571.8	89.5	661.3	3.4
Burkina Faso Burkina Faso	2006	446.1	455.4	901.5	61.7
	2007	510.8	439.6	950.4	63.1
	2008	519.9	481.3	1 001.2	64.5
	2009	595.1	487.7	1 082.8	67.7
	2010	560.1	499.3	1 059.4	64.3
Burundi Burundi	2006	309.0	121.9	430.9	57.6
	2007	213.9	265.1	479.0	62.1
	2008	251.5	270.7	522.2	65.7
	2009	-204.6	766.0	561.4	68.7
	2010	271.8	358.1	629.9	75.1

62

Disbursements of bilateral and multilateral official development assistance and official aid to individual recipients *(continued)*

Versements d'aide publique au développement et d'aide publique bilatérale et multilatérale aux bénéficiaires *(suite)*

Country or area Pays ou zone	Year Année	Net disbursements (US $) - Versements nets ($E.-U.)			
		Bilateral Bilatérale (millions)	Multilateral[1] Multilatérale[1] (millions)	Total (millions)	Per capita Par habitant
Cambodia	2006	386.2	143.2	529.4	39.2
Cambodge	2007	482.2	192.4	674.6	49.3
	2008	519.3	223.5	742.8	53.7
	2009	513.4	208.1	721.4	51.6
	2010	523.6	210.2	733.7	51.9
Cameroon	2006	1 368.0	351.0	1 718.9	95.8
Cameroun	2007	1 711.9	214.4	1 926.3	105.0
	2008	322.1	226.5	548.6	29.2
	2009	395.1	253.2	648.3	33.8
	2010	303.2	237.3	540.5	27.6
Cape Verde	2006	114.8	23.7	138.5	289.7
Cap-Vert	2007	118.2	47.0	165.2	342.0
	2008	164.0	57.8	221.8	455.4
	2009	156.4	39.2	195.6	397.6
	2010	248.3	79.6	327.9	661.1
Central African Rep.	2006	62.2	71.5	133.7	32.7
Rép. centrafricaine	2007	74.5	102.4	176.9	42.5
	2008	116.4	140.9	257.3	60.7
	2009	-187.0	429.1	242.0	56.0
	2010	69.8	191.2	261.0	59.3
Chad	2006	179.5	109.8	289.3	28.7
Tchad	2007	196.6	162.5	359.1	34.6
	2008	197.6	224.1	421.7	39.6
	2009	340.8	220.0	560.7	51.3
	2010	268.7	217.3	486.0	43.3
Chile	2006	73.0	28.4	101.4	6.2
Chili	2007	74.3	30.6	104.9	6.3
	2008	87.0	20.8	107.9	6.4
	2009	56.6	22.1	78.7	4.6
	2010	152.7	44.8	197.5	11.5
China	2006	965.7	282.2	1 247.9	0.9
Chine	2007	1 073.5	414.4	1 487.9	1.1
	2008	1 126.7	352.8	1 479.5	1.1
	2009	764.3	365.2	1 129.5	0.8
	2010	315.9	330.3	646.1	0.5
Colombia	2006	895.2	110.0	1 005.2	23.0
Colombie	2007	624.5	98.2	722.8	16.3
	2008	892.4	79.6	972.0	21.6
	2009	986.8	72.6	1 059.5	23.2
	2010	798.1	103.0	901.1	19.5
Comoros	2006	16.3	15.6	31.9	48.3
Comores	2007	11.5	33.4	45.0	66.3
	2008	19.1	22.5	41.6	59.7
	2009	23.4	27.0	50.5	70.5
	2010	16.7	50.5	67.2	91.5
Congo	2006	176.7	81.6	258.3	71.2
Congo	2007	33.5	85.2	118.7	31.8
	2008	379.9	105.1	485.0	126.4
	2009	222.2	61.1	283.3	71.9
	2010	1 041.5	270.8	1 312.3	324.6
Cook Islands	2006	29.8	2.5	32.3	1 641.5
Iles Cook	2007	7.5	1.8	9.3	468.8
	2008	4.2	1.4	5.6	280.7
	2009	4.8	2.6	7.4	366.1
	2010	12.8	0.6	13.4	662.5

Disbursements of bilateral and multilateral official development assistance and official aid to individual recipients *(continued)*
Versements d'aide publique au développement et d'aide publique bilatérale et multilatérale aux bénéficiaires *(suite)*

Country or area Pays ou zone	Year Année	Net disbursements (US $) - Versements nets ($E.-U.)			
		Bilateral Bilatérale (millions)	Multilateral[1] Multilatérale[1] (millions)	Total (millions)	Per capita Par habitant
Costa Rica Costa Rica	2006	8.8	22.9	31.7	7.2
	2007	37.1	20.8	58.0	13.0
	2008	48.8	17.4	66.1	14.6
	2009	89.0	19.6	108.6	23.6
	2010	78.6	16.5	95.0	20.4
Côte d'Ivoire Côte d'Ivoire	2006	126.4	120.8	247.1	13.5
	2007	25.9	145.2	171.1	9.2
	2008	62.1	563.6	625.7	33.0
	2009	1 992.8	408.8	2 401.6	124.1
	2010	474.8	370.1	845.0	42.8
Croatia Croatie	2006	63.1	140.8	203.8	46.0
	2007	42.8	120.1	162.9	36.8
	2008	38.6	203.0	241.6	54.7
	2009	17.0	151.8	168.8	38.3
	2010	27.3	121.5	148.9	33.8
Cuba Cuba	2006	56.9	36.8	93.7	8.3
	2007	58.3	34.5	92.8	8.2
	2008	105.7	21.8	127.5	11.3
	2009	80.0	35.1	115.1	10.2
	2010	77.4	51.8	129.1	11.5
Dem. Rep. of the Congo Rép. dém. du Congo	2006	1 767.4	429.9	2 197.3	37.2
	2007	768.2	588.5	1 356.7	22.3
	2008	849.9	916.1	1 766.0	28.3
	2009	1 369.9	986.9	2 356.9	36.7
	2010	1 137.6	2 403.7	3 541.3	53.7
Dem. P. R. Korea R. p. dém. de Corée	2006	20.2	34.5	54.7	2.3
	2007	60.9	38.4	99.3	4.1
	2008	174.1	32.1	206.2	8.5
	2009	43.7	21.5	65.2	2.7
	2010	28.9	50.0	78.8	3.2
Djibouti Djibouti	2006	95.9	19.3	115.3	139.9
	2007	71.3	41.3	112.6	134.1
	2008	94.3	46.6	140.8	164.6
	2009	122.5	44.2	166.7	191.2
	2010	104.8	27.4	132.2	148.8
Dominica Dominique	2006	2.9	16.6	19.5	284.0
	2007	0.5	18.9	19.4	283.6
	2008	-2.0	24.2	22.2	325.9
	2009	5.2	30.8	36.0	529.3
	2010	2.8	29.6	32.5	478.9
Dominican Republic Rép. dominicaine	2006	-29.7	83.5	53.8	5.7
	2007	-17.5	140.6	123.1	12.9
	2008	58.0	98.0	156.0	16.1
	2009	15.1	104.0	119.1	12.2
	2010	58.5	116.7	175.2	17.6
Ecuador Equateur	2006	129.3	58.5	187.8	13.8
	2007	150.8	66.5	217.3	15.7
	2008	163.4	67.2	230.6	16.4
	2009	111.3	96.5	207.9	14.6
	2010	100.0	50.5	150.5	10.4
Egypt Egypte	2006	570.5	329.2	899.6	11.9
	2007	841.0	295.3	1 136.4	14.8
	2008	1 432.0	308.5	1 740.5	22.2
	2009	718.2	280.3	998.5	12.5
	2010	404.9	187.5	592.4	7.3

62

Disbursements of bilateral and multilateral official development assistance and official aid to individual recipients *(continued)*

Versements d'aide publique au développement et d'aide publique bilatérale et multilatérale aux bénéficiaires *(suite)*

| Country or area
Pays ou zone | Year
Année | Net disbursements (US $) - Versements nets ($E.-U.) | | | |
		Bilateral Bilatérale (millions)	Multilateral[1] Multilatérale[1] (millions)	Total (millions)	Per capita Par habitant
El Salvador El Salvador	2006	122.1	40.8	162.9	26.8
	2007	42.2	45.9	88.1	14.4
	2008	183.9	49.5	233.4	38.1
	2009	230.7	45.3	276.0	44.8
	2010	205.1	78.4	283.5	45.8
Equatorial Guinea Guinée équatoriale	2006	5.9	20.3	26.2	41.9
	2007	16.9	14.4	31.4	48.7
	2008	13.5	18.6	32.1	48.4
	2009	20.9	10.6	31.5	46.2
	2010	75.6	9.1	84.7	120.9
Eritrea Erythrée	2006	70.4	55.4	125.8	27.1
	2007	38.6	119.8	158.4	33.0
	2008	45.2	98.3	143.5	29.0
	2009	42.2	101.5	143.7	28.2
	2010	43.0	115.2	158.2	30.1
Ethiopia Ethiopie	2006	713.9	1 319.7	2 033.6	26.8
	2007	1 418.7	1 139.7	2 558.4	32.9
	2008	1 879.6	1 449.1	3 328.7	41.9
	2009	2 453.2	1 365.7	3 818.8	47.0
	2010	2 276.7	1 247.5	3 524.2	42.5
Fiji Fidji	2006	30.3	25.4	55.7	67.2
	2007	20.1	30.7	50.8	60.8
	2008	28.9	16.3	45.3	53.6
	2009	45.4	25.6	71.0	83.3
	2010	56.1	20.3	76.4	88.8
Gabon Gabon	2006	-0.6	29.7	29.1	20.8
	2007	19.6	31.6	51.1	35.9
	2008	35.8	26.2	62.1	42.8
	2009	50.1	27.1	77.2	52.3
	2010	79.4	24.6	104.0	69.1
Gambia Gambie	2006	47.3	27.6	74.9	48.4
	2007	26.8	70.4	97.2	61.1
	2008	-161.2	255.1	94.0	57.4
	2009	56.4	71.0	127.5	75.8
	2010	50.6	69.6	120.2	69.5
Georgia Géorgie	2006	266.1	90.0	356.1	80.2
	2007	246.7	133.0	379.7	86.0
	2008	593.8	294.0	887.7	202.0
	2009	547.7	359.4	907.2	207.4
	2010	353.6	271.6	625.2	143.6
Ghana Ghana	2006	203.1	1 040.1	1 243.2	56.1
	2007	779.4	385.8	1 165.2	51.3
	2008	742.0	564.9	1 306.9	56.2
	2009	1 004.2	577.7	1 581.8	66.4
	2010	1 119.7	572.9	1 692.5	69.4
Grenada Grenade	2006	10.8	15.9	26.7	259.5
	2007	9.5	13.6	23.1	223.0
	2008	12.7	20.4	33.1	319.1
	2009	17.3	30.5	47.8	459.3
	2010	9.9	23.9	33.8	323.9
Guatemala Guatemala	2006	422.4	61.9	484.3	37.2
	2007	384.7	69.7	454.4	34.0
	2008	447.3	88.8	536.0	39.2
	2009	323.6	52.0	375.6	26.8
	2010	321.8	70.4	392.1	27.3

Disbursements of bilateral and multilateral official development assistance and official aid to individual recipients *(continued)*
Versements d'aide publique au développement et d'aide publique bilatérale et multilatérale aux bénéficiaires *(suite)*

Country or area Pays ou zone	Year Année	Net disbursements (US $) - Versements nets ($E.-U.)			
		Bilateral Bilatérale (millions)	Multilateral[1] Multilatérale[1] (millions)	Total (millions)	Per capita Par habitant
Guinea	2006	105.4	64.2	169.6	18.4
Guinée	2007	85.2	142.9	228.0	24.3
	2008	164.2	164.1	328.3	34.3
	2009	123.3	91.1	214.3	22.0
	2010	39.4	178.3	217.7	21.8
Guinea-Bissau	2006	28.7	58.3	87.0	62.4
Guinée-Bissau	2007	26.6	95.8	122.3	85.9
	2008	35.8	98.0	133.8	92.0
	2009	37.7	108.8	146.6	98.7
	2010	-29.6	168.9	139.3	92.0
Guyana	2006	80.5	93.9	174.3	232.9
Guyana	2007	75.3	52.5	127.9	170.5
	2008	69.1	97.1	166.3	221.2
	2009	87.6	85.8	173.4	230.2
	2010	90.6	62.6	153.2	203.1
Haiti	2006	417.0	164.7	581.6	61.4
Haïti	2007	498.1	203.5	701.6	73.0
	2008	628.1	284.0	912.1	93.7
	2009	565.9	553.8	1 119.7	113.5
	2010	2 356.9	707.9	3 064.8	306.7
Honduras	2006	295.0	299.3	594.4	84.7
Honduras	2007	325.4	138.9	464.3	64.9
	2008	428.7	135.6	564.3	77.3
	2009	338.9	117.1	456.1	61.2
	2010	374.7	199.5	574.2	75.5
India	2006	760.2	624.1	1 384.3	1.2
Inde	2007	474.8	915.8	1 390.5	1.2
	2008	826.3	1 290.8	2 117.1	1.8
	2009	1 239.5	1 260.9	2 500.4	2.1
	2010	1 610.4	1 195.9	2 806.4	2.3
Indonesia	2006	878.6	439.8	1 318.3	5.7
Indonésie	2007	465.9	438.0	903.9	3.9
	2008	586.8	643.9	1 230.6	5.2
	2009	557.5	489.1	1 046.5	4.4
	2010	970.9	421.3	1 392.2	5.8
Iran (Islamic Rep. of)	2006	69.9	45.9	115.8	1.6
Iran (Rép. islamique d')	2007	68.8	33.6	102.4	1.4
	2008	74.1	24.3	98.4	1.4
	2009	78.2	14.0	92.1	1.3
	2010	80.5	40.7	121.2	1.6
Iraq	2006	8 651.1	238.2	8 889.3	315.9
Iraq	2007	9 087.7	116.6	9 204.3	317.8
	2008	9 811.7	72.7	9 884.5	331.5
	2009	2 693.0	98.1	2 791.1	90.8
	2010	2 050.6	139.3	2 189.9	69.1
Jamaica	2006	-29.3	66.5	37.2	13.8
Jamaïque	2007	-35.6	63.7	28.1	10.4
	2008	-18.4	104.2	85.8	31.5
	2009	3.0	146.3	149.3	54.7
	2010	-9.3	150.6	141.2	51.5
Jordan	2006	449.3	123.3	572.6	104.2
Jordanie	2007	497.7	142.5	640.2	113.0
	2008	561.3	176.6	737.9	126.2
	2009	572.9	167.5	740.4	122.9
	2010	690.7	263.8	954.5	154.3

Disbursements of bilateral and multilateral official development assistance and official aid to individual recipients *(continued)*

Versements d'aide publique au développement et d'aide publique bilatérale et multilatérale aux bénéficiaires *(suite)*

Country or area Pays ou zone	Year Année	Net disbursements (US $) - Versements nets ($E.-U.)			
		Bilateral Bilatérale (millions)	Multilateral[1] Multilatérale[1] (millions)	Total (millions)	Per capita Par habitant
Kazakhstan Kazakhstan	2006	141.4	32.9	174.3	11.4
	2007	180.2	30.6	210.8	13.6
	2008	291.8	43.6	335.4	21.4
	2009	256.1	41.4	297.5	18.8
	2010	148.3	73.1	221.5	13.8
Kenya Kenya	2006	702.4	244.3	946.7	25.9
	2007	856.9	469.9	1 326.8	35.4
	2008	905.5	460.5	1 366.0	35.5
	2009	1 343.8	432.4	1 776.2	45.0
	2010	1 154.7	473.8	1 628.6	40.2
Kiribati Kiribati	2006	18.7	8.1	26.9	287.2
	2007	20.2	6.7	27.0	283.7
	2008	20.0	7.1	27.1	280.7
	2009	22.8	4.3	27.1	276.9
	2010	20.7	2.2	22.8	229.2
Kosovo Kosovo	2009	413.9	367.6	781.5	...
	2010	278.8	312.3	591.1	...
Kyrgyzstan Kirghizistan	2006	245.3	65.3	310.6	61.1
	2007	177.4	97.0	274.5	53.4
	2008	208.2	151.6	359.8	69.1
	2009	211.3	102.0	313.4	59.5
	2010	244.7	127.7	372.4	69.8
Lao People's Dem. Rep. Rép. dém. pop. lao	2006	266.1	97.6	363.7	62.3
	2007	269.2	126.9	396.1	66.8
	2008	350.3	145.3	495.6	82.3
	2009	287.3	131.7	419.0	68.5
	2010	284.3	129.5	413.8	66.7
Lebanon Liban	2006	550.2	268.8	819.0	199.9
	2007	849.2	129.8	979.0	236.8
	2008	875.2	194.7	1 069.9	256.8
	2009	436.5	143.8	580.3	138.3
	2010	321.0	126.9	447.9	106.0
Lesotho Lesotho	2006	38.4	32.3	70.6	33.9
	2007	50.9	77.9	128.8	61.2
	2008	49.4	94.4	143.8	67.6
	2009	57.3	65.1	122.4	56.9
	2010	91.4	164.8	256.2	118.0
Liberia Libéria	2006	171.6	88.9	260.5	78.6
	2007	355.6	345.8	701.4	201.7
	2008	1 010.6	240.4	1 251.0	341.9
	2009	371.7	140.9	512.6	133.6
	2010	951.5	467.8	1 419.3	355.3
Libyan Arab Jamah. Jamah. arabe libyenne	2006	30.4	7.1	37.5	6.4
	2007	12.9	6.5	19.4	3.2
	2008	65.9	8.3	74.2	12.1
	2009	32.7	8.4	41.1	6.6
	2010	1.0	7.6	8.5	1.3
Madagascar Madagascar	2006	73.4	708.2	781.6	42.4
	2007	454.8	439.3	894.1	47.1
	2008	326.4	516.2	842.6	43.1
	2009	266.8	177.2	444.0	22.1
	2010	254.6	215.5	470.1	22.7
Malawi Malawi	2006	119.2	603.6	722.8	54.8
	2007	-82.6	826.6	744.0	54.7
	2008	483.7	439.9	923.6	65.9
	2009	466.6	304.8	771.4	53.4
	2010	562.1	460.7	1 022.9	68.6

62

Disbursements of bilateral and multilateral official development assistance and official aid to individual recipients *(continued)*
Versements d'aide publique au développement et d'aide publique bilatérale et multilatérale aux bénéficiaires *(suite)*

| Country or area
Pays ou zone | Year
Année | Net disbursements (US $) - Versements nets ($E.-U.) | | | |
		Bilateral Bilatérale (millions)	Multilateral[1] Multilatérale[1] (millions)	Total (millions)	Per capita Par habitant
Malaysia Malaisie	2006	225.7	13.0	238.7	9.0
	2007	183.3	16.8	200.1	7.4
	2008	144.3	10.3	154.5	5.6
	2009	128.1	14.9	143.0	5.1
	2010	-25.4	27.4	2.1	0.1
Maldives Maldives	2006	15.1	22.4	37.5	125.3
	2007	11.2	26.3	37.5	123.4
	2008	45.2	9.2	54.4	176.8
	2009	19.0	14.2	33.2	106.5
	2010	71.1	39.7	110.8	350.6
Mali Mali	2006	308.5	557.3	865.8	63.7
	2007	633.0	385.7	1 018.7	72.7
	2008	571.2	392.9	964.1	66.7
	2009	672.0	312.4	984.4	66.0
	2010	759.7	328.4	1 088.1	70.8
Marshall Islands Iles Marshall	2006	54.2	0.8	55.0	1 054.2
	2007	49.6	2.5	52.1	993.0
	2008	50.3	2.9	53.2	1 006.4
	2009	56.9	1.9	58.7	1 099.3
	2010	83.8	6.9	90.6	1 677.2
Mauritania Mauritanie	2006	-16.0	241.7	225.6	72.1
	2007	161.9	185.3	347.2	108.1
	2008	307.9	144.2	452.2	137.2
	2009	272.4	101.1	373.5	110.6
	2010	279.2	95.2	374.4	108.2
Mauritius Maurice	2006	-8.9	28.1	19.2	15.2
	2007	26.7	42.1	68.9	54.0
	2008	0.0	109.6	109.7	85.4
	2009	42.9	112.1	155.0	120.0
	2010	40.9	84.4	125.3	96.4
Mayotte Mayotte	2006	337.4	0.3	337.6	1 873.5
	2007	406.6	0.6	407.2	2 190.4
	2008	474.7	0.9	475.5	2 479.2
	2009	542.9	1.3	544.3	2 750.6
	2010	602.8	1.1	603.9	2 958.4
Mexico Mexique	2006	208.9	60.9	269.8	2.5
	2007	78.2	35.2	113.4	1.0
	2008	102.7	46.5	149.1	1.3
	2009	159.8	24.7	184.5	1.6
	2010	413.8	57.3	471.1	4.2
Micronesia (Fed. States of) Micronésie (Etats féd. de)	2006	106.5	2.0	108.5	988.3
	2007	111.2	3.6	114.9	1 043.5
	2008	87.8	6.3	94.1	853.0
	2009	118.6	2.3	121.0	1 092.9
	2010	124.1	1.2	125.2	1 127.4
Mongolia Mongolie	2006	154.9	47.3	202.3	78.3
	2007	169.7	69.0	238.6	90.9
	2008	181.1	65.3	246.5	92.4
	2009	272.3	98.6	371.0	136.8
	2010	220.3	81.7	302.0	109.6
Montenegro Monténégro	2006	73.0	22.6	95.6	152.4
	2007	59.8	45.9	105.7	168.2
	2008	69.9	34.9	104.9	166.7
	2009	49.4	25.6	75.0	119.0
	2010	51.1	26.3	77.4	122.6

62 Disbursements of bilateral and multilateral official development assistance and official aid to individual recipients *(continued)*
Versements d'aide publique au développement et d'aide publique bilatérale et multilatérale aux bénéficiaires *(suite)*

Country or area Pays ou zone	Year Année	Net disbursements (US $) - Versements nets ($E.-U.)			
		Bilateral Bilatérale (millions)	Multilateral[1] Multilatérale[1] (millions)	Total (millions)	Per capita Par habitant
Montserrat Montserrat	2006	24.7	7.7	32.4	5 619.8
	2007	32.3	4.0	36.3	6 215.6
	2008	32.7	2.1	34.7	5 912.2
	2009	37.8	6.2	44.1	7 477.5
	2010	15.7	10.0	25.8	4 339.4
Morocco Maroc	2006	731.5	370.6	1 102.2	35.9
	2007	860.2	361.2	1 221.3	39.4
	2008	1 078.1	373.1	1 451.2	46.3
	2009	591.4	338.2	929.6	29.4
	2010	714.2	278.4	992.5	31.1
Mozambique Mozambique	2006	979.3	660.0	1 639.3	77.0
	2007	1 164.3	612.3	1 776.6	81.5
	2008	1 366.3	630.1	1 996.4	89.4
	2009	1 479.2	533.2	2 012.4	88.0
	2010	1 431.9	519.7	1 951.5	83.4
Myanmar Myanmar	2006	70.8	74.9	145.7	3.1
	2007	90.4	105.5	195.9	4.2
	2008	410.1	124.4	534.4	11.3
	2009	228.5	127.3	355.8	7.5
	2010	212.9	142.2	355.1	7.4
Namibia Namibie	2006	82.3	69.4	151.7	71.6
	2007	119.4	98.0	217.4	100.7
	2008	143.4	66.8	210.2	95.5
	2009	229.6	95.9	325.5	145.2
	2010	200.3	56.2	256.4	112.3
Nauru Nauru	2006	16.9	0.5	17.4	1 717.2
	2007	24.7	0.9	25.6	2 517.2
	2008	29.5	1.8	31.2	3 068.8
	2009	22.5	1.6	24.0	2 351.2
	2010	26.6	1.2	27.8	2 708.9
Nepal Népal	2006	357.4	169.1	526.6	18.9
	2007	368.8	234.5	603.3	21.3
	2008	424.3	272.2	696.6	24.1
	2009	568.1	286.2	854.3	29.0
	2010	441.1	377.3	818.4	27.3
Nicaragua Nicaragua	2006	395.6	344.6	740.2	134.7
	2007	643.8	196.3	840.1	151.0
	2008	617.6	123.1	740.7	131.4
	2009	604.1	168.5	772.6	135.3
	2010	494.8	126.0	620.7	107.2
Niger Niger	2006	137.2	407.2	544.4	40.4
	2007	276.9	267.4	544.3	39.0
	2008	290.5	321.8	612.3	42.4
	2009	288.4	180.9	469.3	31.3
	2010	401.1	343.4	744.5	48.0
Nigeria Nigéria	2006	11 045.5	382.6	11 428.0	79.7
	2007	1 460.9	495.4	1 956.3	13.3
	2008	646.3	643.8	1 290.2	8.6
	2009	819.7	837.4	1 657.1	10.7
	2010	1 068.3	993.7	2 062.0	13.0
Niue Nioué	2006	7.9	1.1	9.0	5 453.4
	2007	13.5	1.3	14.8	9 242.8
	2008	16.2	1.8	18.0	11 601.3
	2009	7.1	1.8	9.0	5 936.5
	2010	13.9	1.3	15.2	10 347.4

62

Disbursements of bilateral and multilateral official development assistance and official aid to individual recipients *(continued)*

Versements d'aide publique au développement et d'aide publique bilatérale et multilatérale aux bénéficiaires *(suite)*

| Country or area
Pays ou zone | Year
Année | Net disbursements (US $) - Versements nets ($E.-U.) | | | |
		Bilateral Bilatérale (millions)	Multilateral[1] Multilatérale[1] (millions)	Total (millions)	Per capita Par habitant
Occupied Palestinian Terr. Terr. palestinien occupé	2006	909.0	451.2	1 360.3	373.9
	2007	945.4	771.7	1 717.1	460.6
	2008	1 570.0	900.1	2 470.1	645.4
	2009	2 010.9	805.7	2 816.6	716.5
	2010	1 821.4	695.3	2 516.7	623.1
Oman Oman	2006	51.3	2.8	54.1	21.7
	2007	210.4	3.6	214.0	83.5
	2008	73.7	0.9	74.7	28.3
	2009	153.0	0.8	153.8	56.7
	2010	-42.8	2.5	-40.3	-14.5
Pakistan Pakistan	2006	1 685.1	495.3	2 180.4	13.5
	2007	1 259.7	1 009.9	2 269.6	13.8
	2008	910.7	639.0	1 549.7	9.3
	2009	1 649.4	1 119.7	2 769.1	16.2
	2010	2 167.9	843.4	3 011.4	17.3
Palau Palaos	2006	37.0	0.4	37.3	1 865.0
	2007	21.8	0.5	22.3	1 110.4
	2008	41.3	1.6	42.9	2 122.8
	2009	34.4	1.0	35.4	1 737.4
	2010	25.6	0.8	26.3	1 285.2
Panama Panama	2006	4.9	26.1	31.0	9.4
	2007	-154.6	19.5	-135.0	-40.3
	2008	17.2	11.4	28.5	8.4
	2009	51.7	13.3	65.0	18.8
	2010	114.6	14.2	128.9	36.6
Papua New Guinea Papouasie-Nvl-Guinée	2006	230.2	48.7	278.9	44.7
	2007	260.6	63.9	324.5	50.7
	2008	241.5	60.6	302.1	46.1
	2009	301.6	110.1	411.7	61.4
	2010	417.0	94.5	511.4	74.6
Paraguay Paraguay	2006	45.6	10.4	56.0	9.3
	2007	73.8	34.1	108.0	17.6
	2008	94.8	38.7	133.5	21.4
	2009	99.1	48.7	147.8	23.3
	2010	54.4	50.5	105.0	16.3
Peru Pérou	2006	361.9	101.6	463.4	16.6
	2007	201.4	105.7	307.0	10.9
	2008	370.9	92.2	463.0	16.3
	2009	314.0	127.2	441.2	15.3
	2010	-325.1	69.2	-255.9	-8.8
Philippines Philippines	2006	476.3	88.7	564.9	6.5
	2007	470.1	140.0	610.1	6.9
	2008	-34.5	82.4	48.0	0.5
	2009	185.9	123.3	309.3	3.4
	2010	380.7	150.5	531.2	5.7
Republic of Moldova République de Moldova	2006	168.7	61.0	229.7	61.8
	2007	120.3	146.0	266.3	72.5
	2008	147.9	149.6	297.6	81.9
	2009	85.3	158.3	243.6	67.6
	2010	206.3	261.6	467.9	131.0
Rwanda Rwanda	2006	197.1	406.0	603.1	63.9
	2007	403.5	319.1	722.6	74.4
	2008	480.2	453.3	933.5	93.3
	2009	567.0	366.6	933.6	90.5
	2010	597.5	434.7	1 032.2	97.2

62

Disbursements of bilateral and multilateral official development assistance and official aid to individual recipients *(continued)*

Versements d'aide publique au développement et d'aide publique bilatérale et multilatérale aux bénéficiaires *(suite)*

Country or area Pays ou zone	Year Année	Net disbursements (US $) - Versements nets ($E.-U.)			
		Bilateral Bilatérale (millions)	Multilateral[1] Multilatérale[1] (millions)	Total (millions)	Per capita Par habitant
Saint Helena	2006	23.1	5.0	28.1	6 260.9
Sainte-Hélène	2007	40.0	4.1	44.1	10 047.9
	2008	55.4	10.6	66.0	15 380.1
	2009	33.1	1.7	34.8	8 284.5
	2010	53.7	0.0	53.7	13 033.0
Saint Kitts and Nevis	2006	0.5	4.6	5.2	103.6
Saint-Kitts-et-Nevis	2007	0.8	2.6	3.4	68.2
	2008	32.6	14.2	46.8	915.8
	2009	-1.1	6.2	5.1	99.1
	2010	-1.7	13.1	11.4	217.9
Saint Lucia	2006	11.0	7.5	18.5	110.5
Sainte-Lucie	2007	9.5	10.0	19.4	115.2
	2008	-2.4	21.5	19.1	111.9
	2009	12.9	28.1	41.0	237.6
	2010	0.3	40.9	41.2	236.1
Saint Vincent-Grenadines	2006	0.7	4.0	4.7	43.4
Saint Vincent-Grenadines	2007	46.4	19.5	65.9	603.8
	2008	8.1	18.8	26.9	246.0
	2009	7.3	23.4	30.8	281.5
	2010	-0.3	17.1	16.9	154.1
Samoa	2006	36.0	11.1	47.1	260.4
Samoa	2007	24.7	12.8	37.5	206.7
	2008	23.3	17.0	40.3	221.7
	2009	54.1	23.3	77.3	423.8
	2010	97.4	50.1	147.5	805.5
Sao Tome and Principe	2006	8.6	14.4	22.9	148.0
Sao Tomé-et-Principe	2007	-7.4	58.5	51.1	324.7
	2008	26.0	21.3	47.3	296.1
	2009	19.6	10.9	30.5	187.7
	2010	35.4	13.9	49.3	298.1
Saudi Arabia	2006	19.5	4.8	24.3	1.0
Arabie saoudite	2007	-134.9	3.8	-131.1	-5.1
Senegal	2006	328.5	536.5	865.0	77.4
Sénégal	2007	563.2	306.5	869.7	75.8
	2008	646.4	422.1	1 068.5	90.7
	2009	658.1	358.2	1 016.2	83.9
	2010	639.9	287.8	927.7	74.6
Serbia	2006	1 193.3	384.4	1 577.6	160.4
Serbie	2007	479.0	361.0	840.0	85.4
	2008	558.6	414.6	973.2	98.9
	2009	256.2	357.8	614.0	62.3
	2010	287.1	363.6	650.7	66.0
Seychelles	2006	6.8	6.9	13.6	161.8
Seychelles	2007	2.1	8.9	11.0	129.9
	2008	5.6	6.9	12.5	146.3
	2009	7.0	15.8	22.8	264.4
	2010	44.7	11.4	56.0	647.7
Sierra Leone	2006	244.6	135.8	380.5	71.4
Sierra Leone	2007	82.4	467.4	549.8	100.4
	2008	197.7	180.5	378.2	67.4
	2009	237.7	210.6	448.3	78.1
	2010	217.6	249.3	466.9	79.6
Solomon Islands	2006	176.2	28.3	204.5	423.4
Iles Salomon	2007	233.8	12.3	246.1	495.6
	2008	215.2	9.2	224.3	439.6
	2009	198.7	7.1	205.9	392.7
	2010	300.7	39.8	340.5	632.7

Disbursements of bilateral and multilateral official development assistance and official aid to individual recipients *(continued)*

Versements d'aide publique au développement et d'aide publique bilatérale et multilatérale aux bénéficiaires *(suite)*

Country or area Pays ou zone	Year Année	Net disbursements (US $) - Versements nets ($E.-U.)			
		Bilateral Bilatérale (millions)	Multilateral[1] Multilatérale[1] (millions)	Total (millions)	Per capita Par habitant
Somalia Somalie	2006	247.4	148.8	396.2	46.3
	2007	234.6	159.2	393.7	45.1
	2008	559.2	206.6	765.9	85.8
	2009	491.5	170.2	661.6	72.5
	2010	299.5	198.0	497.5	53.3
South Africa Afrique du Sud	2006	534.5	180.5	715.0	14.8
	2007	550.3	257.2	807.5	16.5
	2008	865.5	259.7	1 125.2	22.8
	2009	837.5	237.1	1 074.5	21.6
	2010	792.5	238.0	1 030.5	20.6
Sri Lanka Sri Lanka	2006	608.4	178.1	786.4	39.2
	2007	349.2	265.6	614.8	30.3
	2008	371.0	360.3	731.2	35.7
	2009	405.1	297.4	702.5	34.0
	2010	280.7	299.1	579.8	27.8
Sudan Soudan	2006	1 583.2	465.2	2 048.4	52.0
	2007	1 744.6	376.0	2 120.6	52.5
	2008	2 118.6	447.8	2 566.4	62.0
	2009	2 018.1	332.9	2 350.9	55.3
	2010	1 573.3	473.2	2 046.5	47.0
Suriname Suriname	2006	57.1	7.2	64.2	127.2
	2007	120.9	30.0	150.9	295.7
	2008	72.6	28.9	101.5	197.1
	2009	121.5	35.5	157.0	302.1
	2010	79.0	24.7	103.7	197.6
Swaziland Swaziland	2006	-5.5	40.3	34.8	31.1
	2007	2.8	47.8	50.7	44.7
	2008	11.9	58.0	69.9	60.8
	2009	4.4	51.6	56.0	48.0
	2010	21.4	70.1	91.5	77.1
Syrian Arab Republic Rép. arabe syrienne	2006	-42.8	62.0	19.2	1.0
	2007	-14.3	97.8	83.5	4.3
	2008	61.4	95.3	156.8	8.0
	2009	96.8	111.3	208.1	10.4
	2010	-27.9	162.9	135.0	6.6
Tajikistan Tadjikistan	2006	137.6	103.6	241.2	37.0
	2007	131.3	90.8	222.1	33.6
	2008	159.6	129.1	288.7	43.1
	2009	251.6	156.6	408.1	60.2
	2010	250.9	178.7	429.6	62.4
Thailand Thaïlande	2006	-332.2	115.1	-217.0	-3.2
	2007	-450.8	139.8	-311.0	-4.6
	2008	-722.0	103.5	-618.5	-9.1
	2009	-161.6	83.9	-77.8	-1.1
	2010	-123.7	112.3	-11.4	-0.2
TFYR of Macedonia L'ex-R.Y. Macédoine	2006	116.2	89.1	205.3	100.5
	2007	118.8	82.0	200.7	98.0
	2008	140.8	63.9	204.7	99.7
	2009	122.7	69.8	192.5	93.6
	2010	110.2	67.3	177.4	86.1
Timor-Leste Timor-Leste	2006	167.4	41.7	209.1	201.3
	2007	216.4	61.9	278.3	262.3
	2008	227.3	50.2	277.5	257.0
	2009	180.6	35.9	216.4	196.8
	2010	252.9	38.6	291.5	259.3

62 Disbursements of bilateral and multilateral official development assistance and official aid to individual recipients *(continued)*

Versements d'aide publique au développement et d'aide publique bilatérale et multilatérale aux bénéficiaires *(suite)*

| Country or area
Pays ou zone | Year
Année | Net disbursements (US $)   -   Versements nets ($E.-U.) | | | |
		Bilateral Bilatérale (millions)	Multilateral[1] Multilatérale[1] (millions)	Total (millions)	Per capita Par habitant
Togo Togo	2006	36.0	44.0	79.9	14.4
	2007	36.2	86.3	122.4	21.7
	2008	83.7	246.4	330.1	57.1
	2009	369.4	129.2	498.5	84.5
	2010	214.0	204.9	418.9	69.5
Tokelau Tokélaou	2006	10.3	0.6	10.9	9 341.9
	2007	11.9	1.0	12.9	11 228.2
	2008	21.4	0.0	21.4	18 814.7
	2009	9.5	0.3	9.8	8 644.4
	2010	14.5	0.1	14.6	12 863.4
Tonga Tonga	2006	17.6	3.9	21.5	211.5
	2007	24.8	6.0	30.9	301.8
	2008	22.9	2.8	25.7	249.8
	2009	34.5	4.8	39.2	379.1
	2010	59.5	11.0	70.5	677.0
Trinidad and Tobago Trinité-et-Tobago	2006	-10.7	24.5	13.8	10.5
	2007	-0.6	21.4	20.8	15.7
	2008	2.3	7.0	9.3	7.0
	2009	3.0	3.9	6.8	5.1
	2010	2.2	2.2	4.3	3.2
Tunisia Tunisie	2006	253.0	178.4	431.4	43.1
	2007	160.1	161.1	321.2	31.7
	2008	274.8	100.1	375.0	36.6
	2009	361.4	141.4	502.8	48.5
	2010	426.2	124.1	550.4	52.5
Turkey Turquie	2006	136.3	429.5	565.7	8.2
	2007	188.5	603.6	792.1	11.3
	2008	635.3	480.8	1 116.1	15.7
	2009	470.0	891.6	1 361.5	19.0
	2010	712.2	335.0	1 047.2	14.4
Turkmenistan Turkménistan	2006	31.8	8.9	40.7	8.5
	2007	19.2	9.3	28.5	5.9
	2008	7.7	10.4	18.1	3.7
	2009	31.8	8.0	39.8	8.0
	2010	29.0	14.2	43.2	8.6
Turks and Caicos Islands Iles Turques et Caïques	2006	-0.5	0.1	-0.4	-12.9
	2007	1.7	13.7	15.4	447.3
Tuvalu Tuvalu	2006	12.7	2.6	15.3	1 576.2
	2007	9.0	2.8	11.7	1 202.6
	2008	15.4	0.7	16.1	1 647.3
	2009	15.8	1.7	17.5	1 781.6
	2010	12.8	0.5	13.3	1 356.5
Uganda Ouganda	2006	621.5	964.9	1 586.4	54.0
	2007	1 134.3	603.0	1 737.3	57.3
	2008	1 011.5	630.0	1 641.5	52.4
	2009	1 193.7	591.0	1 784.7	55.1
	2010	1 137.5	586.0	1 723.5	51.6
Ukraine Ukraine	2006	286.7	196.8	483.5	10.4
	2007	240.4	179.9	420.3	9.1
	2008	295.5	322.1	617.6	13.4
	2009	404.0	262.2	666.2	14.6
	2010	407.7	215.7	623.4	13.7
United Rep. of Tanzania Rép.-Unie de Tanzanie	2006	687.5	1 195.8	1 883.3	47.2
	2007	1 999.9	821.7	2 821.6	68.7
	2008	1 371.2	960.3	2 331.5	55.2
	2009	1 931.7	1 001.5	2 933.2	67.4
	2010	1 908.7	1 049.5	2 958.2	66.0

Disbursements of bilateral and multilateral official development assistance and official aid to individual recipients *(continued)*

Versements d'aide publique au développement et d'aide publique bilatérale et multilatérale aux bénéficiaires *(suite)*

Country or area Pays ou zone	Year Année	Net disbursements (US $) - Versements nets ($E.-U.)			
		Bilateral Bilatérale (millions)	Multilateral[1] Multilatérale[1] (millions)	Total (millions)	Per capita Par habitant
Uruguay	2006	2.8	18.3	21.1	6.3
Uruguay	2007	15.9	21.2	37.0	11.1
	2008	11.0	22.3	33.3	9.9
	2009	29.5	20.5	50.0	14.9
	2010	28.4	18.3	46.7	13.9
Uzbekistan	2006	103.5	45.8	149.3	5.7
Ouzbékistan	2007	112.6	57.2	169.9	6.4
	2008	133.4	53.9	187.3	7.0
	2009	122.4	67.4	189.8	7.0
	2010	146.7	82.0	228.7	8.3
Vanuatu	2006	37.5	11.3	48.8	225.1
Vanuatu	2007	47.2	9.5	56.7	254.9
	2008	87.4	4.9	92.3	404.6
	2009	96.8	6.4	103.2	441.4
	2010	104.9	3.4	108.3	451.9
Venezuela (Boliv. Rep. of)	2006	29.9	33.1	62.9	2.3
Venezuela (Rép. boliv. du)	2007	40.7	37.1	77.8	2.8
	2008	44.1	15.2	59.2	2.1
	2009	45.8	20.6	66.3	2.3
	2010	32.7	20.0	52.7	1.8
Viet Nam	2006	1 582.2	262.3	1 844.5	21.9
Viet Nam	2007	1 826.4	684.5	2 510.9	29.5
	2008	1 737.7	814.3	2 551.9	29.7
	2009	2 697.7	1 034.0	3 731.7	42.9
	2010	1 992.4	947.7	2 940.1	33.5
Wallis and Futuna Islands	2006	101.9	0.5	102.4	7 246.6
Iles Wallis et Futuna	2007	117.0	0.1	117.1	8 371.6
	2008	129.7	0.8	130.5	9 429.3
	2009	117.5	0.2	117.7	8 590.3
	2010	122.7	4.8	127.4	9 394.1
Yemen	2006	185.9	101.5	287.4	13.5
Yémen	2007	100.8	141.8	242.6	11.1
	2008	234.0	195.6	429.6	19.0
	2009	410.6	147.3	557.9	23.9
	2010	413.3	250.9	664.2	27.6
Zambia	2006	710.2	757.4	1 467.5	124.9
Zambie	2007	711.6	296.2	1 007.8	83.6
	2008	673.8	442.5	1 116.2	90.2
	2009	856.9	410.2	1 267.1	99.6
	2010	647.5	266.6	914.2	69.8
Zimbabwe	2006	175.4	102.9	278.2	22.2
Zimbabwe	2007	339.8	138.3	478.1	38.3
	2008	521.7	90.7	612.4	49.2
	2009	602.1	134.1	736.2	59.0
	2010	490.5	238.3	728.8	58.0

Source:
Organization for Economic Co-operation and Development (OECD), Paris, the OECD Development Assistance Committee database, last accessed June 2012. Per capita calculated by the United Nations Statistics Division from the World Population Prospects: The 2010 Revision, mid-year population data.

Source:
Organisation de coopération et de développement économiques (OCDE), Paris, la base de données du comité d'aide au développement de l'OCDE, dernier accès juin 2012. Les données par habitant ont été calculées par la Division de statistiques de l'ONU de "World Population Prospects: The 2010 Revision," d'après les données de la population au milieu de l'année.

62

Disbursements of bilateral and multilateral official development assistance and official aid to individual recipients *(continued)*

Versements d'aide publique au développement et d'aide publique bilatérale et multilatérale aux bénéficiaires *(suite)*

1. As reported by OECD/DAC, covers agencies of the United Nations family, the European Commission, IDA and the concessional lending facilities of regional development banks. Excluding non-concessional flows (i.e., less than 25% grant elements).

1. Communiqué par le Comité d'aide au développement de l'OCDE, comprend les institutions et organismes du système des Nations Unies, la commission européenne, l'Association internationale de développement, et les mécanismes de prêt à des conditions privilégiées des banques régionales de développement. Les apports aux conditions du marché (élément de libéralité inférieur à 25) en sont exclus.

63

Net official development assistance from DAC countries to developing countries and multilateral organizations

Net disbursements: millions of US dollars and as a percentage of gross national income (GNI)

Aide publique au développement nette des pays du CAD aux pays en développement et aux organisations multilatérales

Versements nets: millions de dollars E.-U. et en pourcentage du revenu national brut (RNB)

Country or area	2006		2007		2008		2009		2010		2011		Pays ou zone
	$ millions	% of GNI % du RNB	$ millions	% of GNI % du RNB	$ millions	% of GNI % du RNB	$ millions	% of GNI % du RNB	$ millions	% of GNI % du RNB	$ millions	% of GNI % du RNB	
Total	104 814	0.30	104 206	0.27	121 954	0.30	119 778	0.31	128 465	0.32	133 526	0.31	Total
Australia	2 123	0.30	2 669	0.32	2 954	0.32	2 762	0.29	3 826	0.32	4 799	0.35	Australie
Austria	1 498	0.47	1 808	0.50	1 714	0.43	1 142	0.30	1 208	0.32	1 107	0.27	Autriche
Belgium	1 977	0.50	1 951	0.43	2 386	0.48	2 610	0.55	3 004	0.64	2 800	0.53	Belgique
Canada	3 683	0.29	4 080	0.29	4 795	0.33	4 000	0.30	5 209	0.34	5 291	0.31	Canada
Denmark	2 236	0.80	2 562	0.81	2 803	0.82	2 810	0.88	2 871	0.91	2 981	0.86	Danemark
Finland	834	0.40	981	0.39	1 166	0.44	1 290	0.54	1 333	0.55	1 409	0.52	Finlande
France	10 601	0.47	9 884	0.38	10 908	0.39	12 602	0.47	12 915	0.50	12 994	0.46	France
Germany	10 435	0.36	12 291	0.37	13 981	0.38	12 079	0.35	12 985	0.39	14 533	0.40	Allemagne
Greece	424	0.17	501	0.16	703	0.21	607	0.19	508	0.17	331	0.11	Grèce
Ireland	1 022	0.54	1 192	0.55	1 328	0.59	1 006	0.54	895	0.52	904	0.52	Irlande
Italy	3 641	0.20	3 971	0.19	4 861	0.22	3 297	0.16	2 996	0.15	4 241	0.19	Italie
Japan	11 136	0.25	7 697	0.17	9 601	0.19	9 457	0.18	11 021	0.20	10 604	0.18	Japon
Luxembourg	291	0.89	376	0.92	415	0.97	415	1.04	403	1.05	413	0.99	Luxembourg
Netherlands	5 452	0.81	6 224	0.81	6 993	0.80	6 426	0.82	6 357	0.81	6 324	0.75	Pays-Bas
New Zealand	259	0.27	320	0.27	348	0.30	309	0.28	342	0.26	429	0.28	Nouvelle-Zélande
Norway	2 945	0.89	3 735	0.95	4 006	0.89	4 081	1.06	4 580	1.10	4 936	1.00	Norvège
Portugal	396	0.21	471	0.22	620	0.27	513	0.23	649	0.29	669	0.29	Portugal
Rep. of Korea	455	0.05	696	0.07	802	0.09	816	0.10	1 174	0.12	1 321	0.12	Rép. de Corée
Spain	3 814	0.32	5 140	0.37	6 867	0.45	6 584	0.46	5 949	0.43	4 264	0.29	Espagne
Sweden	3 955	1.02	4 339	0.93	4 732	0.98	4 548	1.12	4 533	0.97	5 606	1.02	Suède
Switzerland	1 646	0.39	1 685	0.38	2 038	0.44	2 310	0.45	2 300	0.40	3 086	0.46	Suisse
United Kingdom	12 459	0.51	9 849	0.36	11 500	0.43	11 283	0.51	13 053	0.57	13 739	0.56	Royaume-Uni
United States	23 532	0.18	21 787	0.16	26 437	0.18	28 831	0.21	30 353	0.21	30 745	0.20	Etats-Unis

Source:
Organisation for Economic Co-operation and Development (OECD), Paris, the OECD Development Assistance Committee database, last accessed October 2012.

Source :
Organisation de coopération et de développement économiques (OCDE), Paris, la base de données du Comité d'aide au développement de l'OCDE, dernier accès octobre 2012.

Socio-economic development assistance through the United Nations system
Development grants: thousands of US dollars, 2010

Assistance en matière de développement socioéconomique fournie par le
système des Nations Unies
Subventions au développement : en milliers de dollars des E.-U., 2010

Region, country or area Région, pays ou zone	UNDP PNUD	UNFPA FNUAP	UNHCR HCR	UNICEF	WFP PAM	IFAD FIDA	Specialized agencies[a] Institutions spécialisées[a]	Other UN funds and programes[b] Autres fonds et programmes des NU[b]	Total development grants Total subventions au développ.
Total **Total**	**5 748 057**	**815 400**	**1 878 174**	**3 652 768**	**4 315 233**	**532 832**	**4 543 694**	**1 947 410**	**24 017 536**
Regional programmes **Totaux régionaux**	**425 109**	**186 700**	**4 249**	**278 103**	...	...	**1 386 967**	**223 170**	**2 742 058**
Africa Afrique	25 527	13 700	2 170	12 565	...	...	293 718	28 500	396 506
Americas Amériques	34 208	14 100	...	7 436	...	...	108 117	12 321	196 138
Asia and the Pacific Asie et le Pacifique	18 706	11 200	22	2 134	...	...	175 580	13 731	242 357
Europe Europe	80	...	2 057	3 319	...	...	109 180	5 045	136 486
Western Asia Asie occidentale	11 332	4 000	...	176	...	...	120 098	9 690	149 600
Global/Interregional Global/Interrégional	224 199	137 800	...	252 473	...	...	569 350	138 472	1 466 610
Not elsewhere classified **Non-classé ailleurs**	**113 035**	**31 300**	...	**22 206**	...	...	**665 063**	**241 494**	**1 073 098**
Total all countries **Total, tous pays**	**4 387 389**	**490 500**	**1 557 152**	**3 076 809**	**3 843 111**	**532 832**	**2 024 775**	**1 251 430**	**17 401 781**
Afghanistan Afghanistan	769 700	8 100	68 041	115 988	142 684	1 341	94 283	67 795	1 283 185
Albania Albanie	9 440	1 600	357	5 848	...	2 893	3 447	596	24 181
Algeria Algérie	1 320	200	12 982	1 248	20 842	...	3 099	416	40 346
Andorra Andorre	...	...	...	...	...	...	64	...	64
Angola Angola	24 997	1 800	4 261	41 169	238	...	16 535	1 322	90 321
Antigua and Barbuda Antigua-et-Barbuda	591	...	...	...	...	...	57	...	647
Argentina Argentine	164 156	1 000	4 381	8 881	...	3 252	25 111	700	207 876
Armenia Arménie	8 105	800	1 697	1 025	2 193	3 432	2 930	316	20 499
Australia Australie	...	...	1 410	...	...	...	63	...	1 474
Austria Autriche	...	...	878	...	...	311	121	...	1 310
Azerbaijan Azerbaïdjan	10 183	1 000	3 492	1 848	179	2 613	1 601	129	21 044
Bahamas Bahamas	2	...	...	...	...	...	418	4	425
Bahrain Bahreïn	1 603	...	...	...	...	...	331	94	2 049
Bangladesh Bangladesh	91 068	8 400	5 257	70 306	79 854	25 152	43 761	7 000	330 801
Barbados Barbade	1 702	...	...	...	...	...	87	463	6 764
Belarus Bélarus	19 509	400	1 627	1 562	...	...	1 076	191	24 366

64

Socio-economic development assistance through the United Nations system *(continued)*
Development grants: thousands of US dollars, 2010

Assistance en matière de développement socioéconomique fournie par le système des Nations Unies *(suite)*
Subventions au développement : en milliers de dollars des E.-U., 2010

Region, country or area Région, pays ou zone	UNDP PNUD	UNFPA FNUAP	UNHCR HCR	UNICEF	WFP PAM	IFAD FIDA	Specialized agencies[a] Institutions spécialisées[a]	Other UN funds and programes[b] Autres fonds et programmes des NU[b]	Total development grants Total subventions au développ.
Belgium Belgique	...	...	3 296	...	...	185	...	...	3 481
Belize Belize	1 874	...	...	1 321	...	...	593	558	4 346
Benin Bénin	41 980	3 300	3 639	14 284	3 296	3 385	4 132	841	74 858
Bhutan Bhoutan	5 794	1 200	...	4 627	2 525	4 458	1 537	157	20 298
Bolivia (Plurin. State of) Bolivie (État plurin. de)	14 011	3 000	...	10 786	7 983	1 872	9 461	3 081	50 278
Bosnia and Herzegovina Bosnie-Herzégovine	24 247	800	6 745	5 894	...	3 160	2 716	355	43 917
Botswana Botswana	4 193	1 600	2 683	2 872	...	409	2 342	667	14 766
Brazil Brésil	104 903	2 800	3 856	17 991	...	9 456	88 182	17 708	252 482
Brunei Darussalam Brunéi Darussalam	...	...	...	...	...	...	45	...	45
Bulgaria Bulgarie	4 086	100	886	2 222	...	...	913	...	8 207
Burkina Faso Burkina Faso	19 016	8 200	16	38 127	19 764	4 328	21 395	1 437	112 283
Burundi Burundi	47 791	4 000	31 719	18 289	19 219	5 997	17 102	2 132	146 325
Cambodia Cambodge	34 948	6 600	762	22 784	17 061	3 471	22 230	1 879	130 971
Cameroon Cameroun	6 540	4 100	12 210	12 636	17 978	3 003	7 234	628	64 329
Canada Canada	...	...	1 643	...	...	735	62	...	2 440
Cape Verde Cap-Vert	7 038	2 100	...	871	761	1 579	3 303	1 071	16 723
Central African Rep. Rép. centrafricaine	27 549	4 200	12 595	18 788	20 212	...	9 847	550	95 856
Chad Tchad	38 088	7 000	95 170	48 176	158 464	3 668	24 631	1 339	381 410
Chile Chili	11 584	400	...	5 060	444	1 021	4 829	389	23 910
China Chine	64 684	4 500	3 815	36 525	...	18 378	40 480	2 538	170 919
Colombia Colombie	58 961	9 900	23 207	12 551	25 525	1 833	10 532	33 192	179 907
Comoros Comores	6 255	1 400	...	2 982	...	1 008	1 581	144	13 370
Congo Congo	12 055	2 800	13 671	9 292	13 226	2 614	6 840	1 355	61 853
Cook Islands Iles Cook	271	...	...	...	...	...	217	...	488
Costa Rica Costa Rica	5 039	1 200	2 035	1 816	...	40	3 329	731	14 434
Côte d'Ivoire Côte d'Ivoire	31 890	7 200	7 272	23 065	6 733	2 730	12 356	1 857	94 344
Croatia Croatie	7 935	...	3 401	1 210	...	...	644	94	13 284
Cuba Cuba	22 242	700	...	4 479	1 393	...	3 084	348	32 246

64

Socio-economic development assistance through the United Nations system *(continued)*
Development grants: thousands of US dollars, 2010

Assistance en matière de développement socioéconomique fournie par le système des Nations Unies *(suite)*
Subventions au développement : en milliers de dollars des E.-U., 2010

Region, country or area Région, pays ou zone	UNDP PNUD	UNFPA FNUAP	UNHCR HCR	UNICEF	WFP PAM	IFAD FIDA	Specialized agencies[a] Institutions spécialisées[a]	Other UN funds and programes[b] Autres fonds et programmes des NU[b]	Total development grants Total subventions au développ.
Cyprus Chypre	27 722	...	939	...	...	26	10	...	28 697
Czech Republic République tchèque	...	...	411	...	...	...	134	...	545
Dem. Rep. of the Congo Rép. dém. du Congo	166 496	12 200	73 336	161 315	143 087	2 430	66 969	4 696	643 420
Dem. P. R. Korea R. p. dém. de Corée	918	1 300	...	22 744	28 917	3	21 140	...	75 023
Denmark Danemark	...	...	...	...	...	393	...	...	393
Djibouti Djibouti	1 875	1 200	7 757	6 947	9 521	669	2 961	309	31 253
Dominica Dominique	362	...	...	...	...	...	102	396	860
Dominican Republic Rép. dominicaine	18 535	2 600	361	8 224	296	...	2 561	475	33 112
Ecuador Equateur	12 543	2 500	9 711	3 637	3 848	1 873	4 096	1 506	48 447
Egypt Egypte	81 819	3 200	10 618	7 001	8 855	2 211	11 091	4 058	129 300
El Salvador El Salvador	20 344	2 000	...	3 335	25 162	3 683	3 267	706	58 498
Equatorial Guinea Guinée équatoriale	2 243	1 500	...	1 108	...	...	1 335	...	6 186
Eritrea Erythrée	17 768	4 900	4 579	21 276	229	2 978	6 228	738	59 136
Estonia Estonie	...	...	...	...	...	...	280	...	280
Ethiopia Ethiopie	36 319	14 200	44 547	134 637	457 767	9 020	46 595	2 327	749 168
Fiji Fidji	10 874	...	...	...	...	306	2 273	633	19 459
Finland Finlande	...	...	...	...	...	...	54	...	54
France France	...	...	2 996	...	...	1 254	300	5	4 554
French Guiana Guyane française	...	...	...	...	...	...	24	...	24
French Polynesia Polynésie française	743	...	...	...	...	...	34	...	777
Gabon Gabon	4 744	1 300	2 412	1 986	...	186	3 047	608	14 283
Gambia Gambie	5 437	1 700	90	3 989	3 022	2 072	1 952	378	18 640
Georgia Géorgie	14 282	1 700	15 283	7 110	3 279	4 585	2 949	282	49 469
Germany Allemagne	...	...	1 968	...	...	1 524	662	...	4 154
Ghana Ghana	16 136	5 000	4 831	37 694	7 896	8 787	5 552	962	86 859
Greece Grèce	...	...	1 885	...	...	...	894	...	2 779
Grenada Grenade	526	...	...	...	...	...	211	87	824
Guam Guam	...	...	...	...	...	...	9	...	9

Socio-economic development assistance through the United Nations system *(continued)*
Development grants: thousands of US dollars, 2010

Assistance en matière de développement socioéconomique fournie par le système des Nations Unies *(suite)*
Subventions au développement : en milliers de dollars des E.-U., 2010

Region, country or area Région, pays ou zone	UNDP PNUD	UNFPA FNUAP	UNHCR HCR	UNICEF	WFP PAM	IFAD FIDA	Specialized agencies[a] Institutions spécialisées[a]	Other UN funds and programes[b] Autres fonds et programmes des NU[b]	Total development grants Total subventions au développ.
Guatemala Guatemala	53 766	7 000	...	9 471	15 326	5 433	12 381	4 235	107 613
Guinea Guinée	24 108	3 900	5 210	16 082	9 478	3 154	7 668	2 130	72 113
Guinea-Bissau Guinée-Bissau	10 943	2 200	308	10 154	8 091	273	4 460	1 943	38 372
Guyana Guyana	2 935	...	...	2 949	...	513	1 889	648	8 934
Haiti Haïti	51 340	16 300	3 792	166 489	271 204	4 930	31 271	7 962	564 442
Honduras Honduras	33 556	3 400	...	5 559	23 367	...	10 229	1 344	77 456
Hungary Hongrie	...	...	2 793	...	...	...	191	...	2 983
Iceland Islande	...	...	...	...	...	...	25	...	25
India Inde	32 665	13 300	6 458	137 440	8 290	13 746	61 089	3 623	283 939
Indonesia Indonésie	51 747	6 600	3 531	53 843	9 819	8 119	62 326	5 508	202 934
Iran (Islamic Rep. of) Iran (Rép. islamique d')	13 898	1 600	20 746	2 895	2 815	...	4 429	2 491	48 875
Iraq Iraq	57 618	4 100	106 993	48 309	15 306	269	75 591	9 604	322 515
Ireland Irlande	...	...	476	...	...	...	...	...	476
Israel Israël	...	...	2 356	...	...	...	229	...	2 592
Italy Italie	...	...	5 008	...	...	2 901	1 316	...	9 225
Jamaica Jamaïque	3 972	...	...	2 237	...	...	3 737	428	10 374
Japan Japon	...	...	3 841	...	...	2 375	3 521	778	10 515
Jordan Jordanie	6 437	1 600	30 895	7 638	314	1 427	4 681	141 250	201 507
Kazakhstan Kazakhstan	12 560	700	2 605	2 040	...	...	1 125	735	25 241
Kenya Kenya	42 106	6 400	97 569	65 748	196 201	12 570	28 808	7 231	474 485
Kiribati Kiribati	24	...	...	...	...	...	700	...	724
Kosovo Kosovo	19 659	1 000	...	...	...	...	666	2 706	24 031
Kuwait Koweït	2 747	...	...	...	...	...	771	758	4 276
Kyrgyzstan Kirghizistan	21 531	1 400	21 432	8 081	14 537	758	3 321	2 068	73 128
Lao People's Dem. Rep. Rép. dém. pop. lao	15 582	3 200	...	12 919	16 173	2 309	8 749	2 351	61 273
Latvia Lettonie	148	...	...	...	...	...	139	...	287
Lebanon Liban	34 097	1 400	9 241	2 902	...	...	19 022	149 184	215 845
Lesotho Lesotho	5 653	2 200	...	10 198	7 185	2 341	4 690	801	33 071

Socio-economic development assistance through the United Nations system *(continued)*
Development grants: thousands of US dollars, 2010

Assistance en matière de développement socioéconomique fournie par le système des Nations Unies *(suite)*
Subventions au développement : en milliers de dollars des E.-U., 2010

Region, country or area Région, pays ou zone	UNDP PNUD	UNFPA FNUAP	UNHCR HCR	UNICEF	WFP PAM	IFAD FIDA	Specialized agencies[a] Institutions spécialisées[a]	Other UN funds and programes[b] Autres fonds et programmes des NU[b]	Total development grants Total subventions au développ.
Liberia Libéria	43 385	5 000	8 405	23 993	16 612	637	14 519	1 887	114 437
Libyan Arab Jamah. Jamah. arabe libyenne	7 167	...	2 701	...	...	...	3 243	4 157	17 268
Lithuania Lituanie	2 549	...	...	...	...	...	450	...	2 999
Madagascar Madagascar	4 878	6 300	...	46 987	13 643	8 187	15 395	664	96 054
Malawi Malawi	25 489	9 600	2 585	42 298	15 383	4 647	11 140	1 837	112 980
Malaysia Malaisie	2 892	400	7 676	2 947	...	22	1 771	134	15 843
Maldives Maldives	4 330	500	...	2 011	...	948	1 886	438	10 113
Mali Mali	21 053	6 600	110	31 794	12 380	4 726	11 314	2 139	90 072
Malta Malte	...	...	397	...	...	...	88	...	485
Marshall Islands Iles Marshall	...	...	...	...	...	...	159	...	159
Mauritania Mauritanie	7 456	4 400	4 889	8 846	12 525	3 502	4 988	561	47 294
Mauritius Maurice	6 686	...	...	...	...	503	1 613	72	8 873
Mexico Mexique	23 064	3 200	1 454	5 287	...	3 767	11 075	3 700	58 133
Micronesia (Fed. St. of) Micronésie (Et. féd. de)	...	...	...	...	...	...	250	...	250
Mongolia Mongolie	8 758	2 900	155	5 083	...	1 873	7 647	2 097	28 513
Montenegro Monténégro	7 953	...	3 059	1 546	...	...	475	87	13 119
Montserrat Montserrat	65	...	...	...	...	...	...	...	65
Morocco Maroc	12 233	2 800	1 736	4 134	...	3 375	7 247	881	35 602
Mozambique Mozambique	24 917	11 200	3 141	42 483	26 530	4 026	20 924	3 670	136 891
Myanmar Myanmar	20 826	8 400	11 294	42 529	19 736	...	25 061	7 401	136 789
Namibia Namibie	11 661	3 000	3 498	4 965	1 098	...	5 051	1 374	30 646
Nauru Nauru	...	...	...	...	...	...	111	...	111
Nepal Népal	43 971	4 900	11 554	25 622	55 267	4 930	26 139	6 995	180 725
Netherlands Pays-Bas	...	...	...	...	...	56	...	5	61
Netherlands Antilles Antilles néerlandaises	...	...	...	...	...	...	12	...	12
Nicaragua Nicaragua	26 161	8 000	...	8 973	7 485	4 723	13 559	474	69 375
Niger Niger	23 623	7 500	...	61 369	181 416	3 309	32 142	675	312 663
Nigeria Nigéria	36 909	11 900	2 856	111 513	...	4 233	61 268	10 147	239 408

Socio-economic development assistance through the United Nations system *(continued)*
Development grants: thousands of US dollars, 2010

Assistance en matière de développement socioéconomique fournie par le système des Nations Unies *(suite)*
Subventions au développement : en milliers de dollars des E.-U., 2010

Region, country or area Région, pays ou zone	UNDP PNUD	UNFPA FNUAP	UNHCR HCR	UNICEF	WFP PAM	IFAD FIDA	Specialized agencies[a] Institutions spécialisées[a]	Other UN funds and programes[b] Autres fonds et programmes des NU[b]	Total development grants Total subventions au développ.
Niue Nioué	80	...	...	...	...	...	84	...	164
Norway Norvège	...	...	...	...	...	...	33	...	33
Occupied Palestinian Terr. Terr. palestinien occupé	58 581	3 800	...	26 236	74 004	...	35 359	522 634	726 384
Oman Oman	...	500	...	996	...	...	2 049	163	3 708
Pakistan Pakistan	58 489	19 200	161 897	192 013	407 156	21 637	149 129	12 039	1 030 433
Palau Palaos	...	...	...	...	...	...	88	1 204	1 292
Panama Panama	58 106	1 100	4 050	1 657	...	3 668	19 098	1 325	89 035
Papua New Guinea Papouasie-Nvl-Guinée	9 633	2 500	1 076	6 873	...	...	5 344	1 007	26 434
Paraguay Paraguay	14 698	1 100	...	1 707	...	3 424	2 434	222	23 615
Peru Pérou	67 756	2 900	...	5 690	1 404	4 167	32 403	6 240	120 591
Philippines Philippines	17 690	8 400	2 269	21 990	35 746	14 846	17 185	787	119 918
Poland Pologne	2	...	502	...	...	...	447	414	1 365
Portugal Portugal	...	...	...	...	...	175	157	...	332
Qatar Qatar	...	...	...	...	...	...	578	124	702
Republic of Korea République de Corée	201	...	1 258	...	...	...	2 077	203	3 739
Republic of Moldova République de Moldova	18 103	800	1 104	2 887	...	5 849	1 451	524	30 716
Réunion Réunion	...	...	...	...	...	...	...	-21	-21
Romania Roumanie	1 934	200	2 364	2 159	...	...	1 200	394	8 251
Russian Federation Fédération de Russie	12 213	1 600	13 501	8 369	343	...	14 312	5 907	56 244
Rwanda Rwanda	18 771	4 200	9 633	30 336	14 125	10 193	4 970	2 572	101 393
Saint Helena Sainte-Hélène	...	...	...	...	...	...	86	...	86
Saint Kitts and Nevis Saint-Kitts-et-Nevis	173	...	...	...	...	...	46	...	220
Saint Lucia Sainte-Lucie	249	...	...	...	...	...	201	...	450
Saint Vincent-Grenadines Saint Vincent- Grenadines	398	...	...	...	...	...	47	...	445
Samoa Samoa	2 739	...	...	...	...	...	1 325	398	4 462
Sao Tome and Principe Sao Tomé-et-Principe	3 959	700	...	920	932	1 290	1 122	474	9 398
Saudi Arabia Arabie saoudite	14 094	...	2 972	...	...	24	23 262	...	41 900
Senegal Sénégal	17 762	4 100	12 520	15 346	12 330	4 172	9 635	375	83 540

Socio-economic development assistance through the United Nations system *(continued)*
Development grants: thousands of US dollars, 2010

Assistance en matière de développement socioéconomique fournie par le système des Nations Unies *(suite)*
Subventions au développement : en milliers de dollars des E.-U., 2010

Region, country or area Région, pays ou zone	UNDP PNUD	UNFPA FNUAP	UNHCR HCR	UNICEF	WFP PAM	IFAD FIDA	Specialized agencies[a] Institutions spécialisées[a]	Other UN funds and programes[b] Autres fonds et programmes des NU[b]	Total development grants Total subventions au développ.
Serbia Serbie	11 200	100	25 534	7 923	...	...	3 924	593	49 274
Seychelles Seychelles	...	100	...	...	...	...	1 110	...	1 210
Sierra Leone Sierra Leone	21 980	10 200	3 716	47 658	15 491	3 990	14 333	2 519	119 898
Singapore Singapour	...	...	...	...	...	...	241	...	241
Slovakia Slovaquie	17 156	...	516	...	...	...	307	...	17 979
Slovenia Slovénie	...	...	73	...	...	...	128	...	202
Solomon Islands Iles Salomon	3 864	...	...	...	...	...	1 907	...	5 786
Somalia Somalie	59 491	2 400	18 426	81 335	146 000	...	57 686	2 842	374 501
South Africa Afrique du Sud	12 847	2 100	12 987	15 139	...	1 480	7 080	12 042	63 679
Spain Espagne	...	...	1 390	...	...	...	762	...	2 152
Sri Lanka Sri Lanka	22 453	3 700	26 224	37 044	42 302	10 466	20 867	8 053	172 853
Sudan (former) Soudan (anc.)	313 656	13 700	94 079	170 609	596 213	10 637	98 864	11 053	1 325 185
Suriname Suriname	1 934	...	...	...	...	...	421	...	2 355
Swaziland Swaziland	3 689	1 400	...	6 428	3 889	336	4 453	886	21 081
Sweden Suède	...	...	1 803	...	...	...	...	...	1 803
Switzerland Suisse	...	...	685	...	...	152	153	...	990
Syrian Arab Republic Rép. arabe syrienne	10 457	3 300	90 118	11 384	35 937	6 751	5 868	65 219	229 040
Tajikistan Tadjikistan	38 243	1 300	808	6 114	9 974	150	4 773	2 906	64 336
Thailand Thaïlande	6 194	2 100	14 661	8 623	...	427	8 462	702	48 197
TFYR of Macedonia L'ex-R.Y. Macédoine	10 248	600	2 688	2 707	...	...	1 216	5	17 465
Timor-Leste Timor-Leste	18 273	3 500	229	9 993	6 243	...	9 585	456	48 301
Togo Togo	22 910	3 700	3 157	9 680	1 576	...	7 713	1 391	50 986
Tokelau Tokélaou	108	...	...	...	...	...	37	...	145
Tonga Tonga	...	...	...	...	...	...	935	...	935
Trinidad and Tobago Trinité-et-Tobago	1 917	...	...	...	...	...	285	349	2 552
Tunisia Tunisie	2 095	600	984	1 147	...	2 775	2 758	665	11 219
Turkey Turquie	22 591	2 400	8 511	7 681	...	5 226	5 018	585	52 012
Turkmenistan Turkménistan	4 331	700	466	1 305	...	...	268	381	7 451

Socio-economic development assistance through the United Nations system *(continued)*
Development grants: thousands of US dollars, 2010

Assistance en matière de développement socioéconomique fournie par le système des Nations Unies *(suite)*
Subventions au développement : en milliers de dollars des E.-U., 2010

Region, country or area Région, pays ou zone	UNDP PNUD	UNFPA FNUAP	UNHCR HCR	UNICEF	WFP PAM	IFAD FIDA	Specialized agencies[a] Institutions spécialisées[a]	Other UN funds and programes[b] Autres fonds et programmes des NU[b]	Total development grants Total subventions au développ.
Turks and Caicos Islands Iles Turques et Caïques	...	...	...	...	...	...	4	...	4
Tuvalu Tuvalu	15	...	...	...	...	...	143	...	158
Uganda Ouganda	12 425	12 000	31 725	45 039	52 965	17 117	20 908	3 953	198 411
Ukraine Ukraine	30 915	600	4 551	4 027	...	...	4 063	794	44 951
United Arab Emirates Emirats arabes unis	1 768	...	1 294	...	...	135	555	637	4 390
United Kingdom Royaume-Uni	...	...	1 975	...	...	974	87	...	3 036
United Rep. of Tanzania Rép.-Unie de Tanzanie	50 468	7 000	28 846	32 157	38 328	4 119	20 112	1 528	182 557
United States Etats-Unis	...	...	4 432	...	...	1 874	537	...	6 843
Uruguay Uruguay	22 315	2 800	...	1 595	...	2 265	4 557	167	34 164
Uzbekistan Ouzbékistan	15 457	1 100	2 025	7 458	272	...	1 604	872	28 787
Vanuatu Vanuatu	...	...	...	...	...	...	1 839	...	1 839
Venezuela (Bol. Rep. of) Venezuela (R. boliv. du)	22 456	1 500	4 058	2 453	...	1 811	2 227	497	35 002
Viet Nam Viet Nam	28 750	8 100	368	19 619	...	16 668	30 516	4 522	109 344
Yemen Yémen	16 507	3 400	35 978	20 502	46 562	8 819	6 920	421	140 480
Zambia Zambie	42 668	4 200	9 892	26 089	17 310	3 527	15 313	1 343	120 343
Zimbabwe Zimbabwe	154 220	12 700	5 625	139 121	71 378	272	19 876	1 189	407 730

Source:
United Nations, *Comprehensive statistical analysis of the financing of operational activities for development of the United Nations system for 2010, Report of the Secretary-General* (A/67/94).

The following abbreviations have been used in the table:
    IFAD: International Fund for Agricultural Development
    UNDP: United Nations Development Programme
    UNFPA: United Nations Population Fund
    UNHCR: United Nations High Commissioner for Refugees
    UNICEF: United Nations Children's Fund
    WFP: World Food Programme

[a] Expenditures by FAO, IAEA, ICAO, ILO, IMO, ITU, UNESCO, UNIDO, UPU, WIPO, WHO, WMO and the World Tourism Organization.
[b] Expenditures by ITC, UNAIDS, UNCTAD, UNEP, UN-Habitat, UNODC, UNRWA and the Office for the Coordination of Humanitarian Affairs.

Source:
Nations Unies, *Analyse statistique globale du financement des activités opérationnelles de développement du système des Nations Unies pour 2010, Rapport du Secrétaire général* (A/67/94).

Les abréviations ci-après ont été utilisées dans le tableau :
    FIDA : Fonds international de développement agricole
    PNUD : Programme des Nations Unies pour le développement
    FNUAP : Fonds des Nations Unies pour la population
    HCR : Haut Commissariat des Nations Unies
    UNICEF : Fonds des Nations Unies pour l'enfance
    PAM : Programme alimentaire mondial

[a] Dépenses engagées par la FAO, l'AIEA, l'OACI, l'OIT, l'OMI, l'UIT, l'UNESCO, l'ONUDI, l'UPU, l'OMPI, l'OMS, l'OMM et l'Organisation mondiale du tourisme.
[b] Dépenses engagées par le CCI, ONUSIDA, la CNUCED, le PNUE, ONU/Habitat, UNODC, l'UNRWA et le Bureau de la coordination des affaires humanitaires.

Technical notes

Chapter I: World and region summary

Table 1

The series of world aggregates on population, output, production, external trade and finance have been compiled from statistical publications and databases of the United Nations and the specialized agencies and other institutions. The sources should be consulted for detailed information on compilation and coverage.

Table 2

The table presents estimates of population size, rates of population increase, crude birth and death rates, surface area and population density for the world and regions. Unless otherwise specified, all figures are estimates of the order of magnitude and are subject to a substantial margin of error.

The population estimates and rates presented in this table were prepared by the Population Division of the United Nations Secretariat and published in *World Population Prospects: The 2010 Revision*. The average annual percentage rates of population growth were calculated by the Population Division of the United Nations Secretariat, using an exponential rate of increase formula.

Crude birth and crude death rates are expressed in terms of the average annual number of births and deaths respectively, per 1,000 mid-year population. These rates are estimated. Surface area totals were obtained by summing the figures for the individual countries or areas. Density is the number of persons in the 2010 total population per square kilometre of total surface area.

The scheme of regionalization used for the purpose of making these estimates is presented in annex I. Although some continental totals are given, and all can be derived, the basic scheme presents macro regions that are so drawn as to obtain greater homogeneity in sizes of population, types of demographic circumstances and accuracy of demographic statistics.

Table 3-4

The index numbers in table 3 refer to agricultural production, which is defined to include both crop and livestock products. Seeds and feed are excluded. The index numbers of food refer to commodities which are considered edible and contain nutrients. Coffee, tea and other inedible commodities are excluded.

The index numbers of total agricultural and food production in table 3 are calculated by the Laspeyres formula with the base year period 1999-2001. The latter is provided in order to diminish the impact of annual fluctuations in agricultural output during base years on the indices for the period. Production quantities of each commodity are weighted by 1999-2001 average national producer prices and summed for each year. The index numbers are based on production data for a calendar year.

Index numbers for the world and regions are computed in a similar way to the country index numbers except that instead of using different commodity prices for each country group, "international commodity prices" derived from the Gheary-Khamis formula are used for all country groupings. This method assigns a single "price" to each commodity.

The indexes in table 4 are calculated as a ratio between the index numbers of total agricultural and food production in table 3 described above and the corresponding index numbers of population.

For further information on the series presented in these tables, see the *FAO Statistical Yearbook* and http://faostat.fao.org.

Table 5

For a description of the series in table 5, see the technical notes to chapter XIII.

Table 6

For a description of the series in table 6, see the technical notes to chapter XVI. The composition of the regions is presented in table 54.

Chapter II: Population

The table is based on detailed data on population and its growth and distribution published in the United Nations *Demographic Yearbook*. Only official national population estimates reported to the United Nations Statistics Division are included in this table. For a comprehensive description of methods of evaluation and the limitations of the data, consult the *Demographic Yearbook*.

Unless otherwise indicated, figures refer to de facto (present-in-area) population for the present territory; surface area estimates include inland waters.

Table 7

The statistics on population in urban and rural areas, rates of growth and largest urban agglomeration population of each country or area are estimates and projections published by the Population Division of the Department of Economic and Social Affairs of the United Nations Secretariat in the *World Urbanization Prospects: The 2011 Revision*. Because of national differences in the specific characteristics that distinguish urban from rural areas, there are no internationally agreed definitions of urban and rural. In most countries, the distinction is mainly based on size of locality. For the latest available census definition of urban areas in a particular country or area, reference should be made to the *Demographic Yearbook*.

Table 8

An urban agglomeration comprises the city or town proper and also the suburban fringe or thickly settled territory lying outside, but adjacent to, its boundaries. The largest urban agglomerations refer to those inhabited by 750,000 people or more. Annual rates of change in urban and rural population are computed as average annual percentage changes using midyear population estimates.

Chapter III: Gender

The three tables on gender presented in this chapter are all based on indicators for the Millennium Development Goals (MDGs). For more on MDGs, visit mdgs.un.org.

Table 9

The table shows the percentage of seats held by women members in single or lower chambers of national parliaments. National parliaments can be bicameral or unicameral. This table covers the single chamber in unicameral parliaments and the lower chamber in bicameral parliaments. It does not cover the upper chamber of bi-cameral parliaments. Seats are usually won by members in general parliamentary elections. Seats may also be filled by nomination, appointment, indirect election, rotation of members and by-election.

The proportion of seats held by women in national parliament is derived by dividing the total number of seats occupied by women by the total number of seats in parliament. There is no weighting or normalizing of statistics.

The source for this table is the Inter-Parliamentary Union (IPU). For more information visit www.ipu.org.

Table 10

The share of women in wage employment in the non-agricultural sector is the share of female workers in wage employment in the non-agricultural sector expressed as a percentage of total wage employment in that same sector.

The non-agricultural sector includes industry and services. "Industry" includes mining and quarrying (including oil production), manufacturing, construction, electricity, gas, and water, corresponding to divisions 2-5 in the International Standard Industrial Classification of All Economic Activities (ISIC-Rev.2) and to tabulation categories C-F in ISIC-Rev. 3. "Services" include wholesale and retail trade and restaurants and hotels; transport, storage, and communications; financing, insurance, real estate, and business services; and community, social, and personal services, corresponding to divisions 6-9 in ISIC-Rev. 2, and to tabulation categories G-Q in ISIC-Rev. 3.

Employment refers to people above a certain age who worked or held a job during a specified reference period (according to the ILO Resolution concerning statistics of the economically active population, employment, unemployment and underemployment, adopted by the Thirteenth International Conference of Labour Statisticians (ICLS), October 1982).

Wage employment refers only to wage earners and salaried employees, or "persons in paid employment jobs". Employees are typically remunerated by wages and salaries, but may be paid by commission from sales, piece-rates, bonuses or payments in kind such as food, housing, training, etc. These persons are in wage employment as opposed to self-employment – that is employers, own-account workers, members of producers' cooperatives and contributing family workers. The different statuses in employment are defined according to the ILO Resolution concerning the International Classification of Status in Employment (ICSE), adopted by the 15th ICLS (1993).

The source for this table is the International Labour Organization (ILO). For more information visit http://laborsta.ilo.org.

Table 11

The ratio of girls to boys (gender parity index) in primary, secondary and tertiary education is the ratio of the number of female students enrolled at primary, secondary and tertiary levels of education to the number of male students in each level. To standardize the effects of the population structure of the appropriate age groups, the Gender Parity Index (GPI) of the Gross Enrolment Ratio (GER) for each level of education is used.

The source for this table is the UNESCO Institute for Statistics (UIS). For more information visit www.uis.unesco.org.

Chapter IV: Education

Detailed data and explanatory notes on education can be found on the UNESCO Institute for Statistics web site www.uis.unesco.org. Brief notes which pertain to the statistical information shown in tables 12 and 13 are given below.

The definitions and classifications applied by UNESCO are those set out in the Revised Recommendation concerning the International Standardization of Education Statistics (1978) and the 1976 and 1997 versions of the International Standard Classification of Education (ISCED). Data are presented in table 12 according to the terminology of the ISCED-97.

Table 12

According to the ISCED, these educational levels are defined as follows:

Primary education (ISCED level 1): Programmes normally designed on a unit or project basis to give pupils a sound basic education in reading, writing and mathematics along with an elementary understanding of other subjects such as history, geography, natural science, social science, art and music. Religious instruction may also be featured. It is sometimes called elementary education.

Secondary education (ISCED levels 2 and 3): Lower secondary education (ISCED 2) is generally designed to continue the basic programmes of the primary level but the teaching is typically more subject-focused, requiring more specialized teachers for each subject area. The end of this level often coincides with the end of compulsory education. In upper secondary education (ISCED 3), the final stage of secondary education in most countries, education is often organized even more along subject lines and teachers typically need a higher or more subject-specific qualification than at ISCED level 2.

Tertiary education (ISCED levels 5 and 6): Programmes with an educational content more advanced than what is offered at ISCED levels 3 and 4. The first stage of tertiary education, ISCED level 5, covers level 5A, composed of largely theoretically based programmes intended to provide sufficient qualifications for gaining entry to advanced research programmes and professions with high skill requirements; and level 5B, where programmes are generally more practical, technical and/or occupationally specific. The second stage of tertiary education, ISCED level 6, comprises programmes devoted to advanced study and original research, and leading to the award of an advanced research qualification.

The ISCED-97 also introduced a new category or level between upper secondary and tertiary education called post-secondary non-tertiary education (ISCED level 4). This level includes programmes that lie between the upper-secondary and tertiary levels of education from an international point of view, even though they might clearly be considered as upper-secondary or tertiary programmes in a national context. They are often not significantly more advanced than programmes at ISCED 3 (upper secondary) but they serve to broaden the knowledge of participants who have already completed a programme at level 3. The students are usually older than those at level 3. ISCED 4 programmes typically last between six months and two years.

Table 13

Public expenditure on education consists of current and capital expenditures on education by local, regional and national governments, including municipalities. Household contributions are excluded. Current expenditure on education includes expenditure for goods and services consumed within the current year and which would need to be renewed if needed the following year. It includes expenditure on: staff salaries and benefits; contracted or purchased services; other resources including books and teaching materials; welfare services; and other current expenditure such as subsidies to students and households, furniture and equipment, minor repairs, fuel, telecommunications, travel, insurance and rents. Capital expenditure on education includes expenditure for assets that last longer than one year. It includes expenditure for construction, renovation and major repairs of buildings and the purchase of heavy equipment or vehicles.

Chapter V: Nutrition and health

Table 14

Estimates on food supply are published by the Food and Agriculture Organization of the United Nations in *Food Balance Sheets* and on its Web site http://faostat.fao.org, where the data give estimates of per capita food supplies per day in terms of caloric value. Per capita supplies in terms of product weight are derived from the total supplies available for human consumption (i.e. "Food") by dividing the quantities of food by the total population actually partaking of the food supplies during the reference period, i.e. the present in-area (de facto) population within the present geographical boundaries of the country. In other words, nationals living abroad during the reference period are excluded, but foreigners living in the country are included. Adjustments are made wherever possible for part-time presence or absence, such as temporary migrants, tourists and refugees supported by special schemes (if it has not been possible to allow for the amounts provided by such schemes under imports). In almost all cases, the population figures used are the mid-year estimates published by the United Nations Population Division.

Per capita supply figures represent only the average supply available for the population as a whole and do not necessarily indicate what is actually consumed by individuals. Even if they are taken as an approximation of per capita consumption, it is important to bear in mind that there could be considerable variation in consumption between individuals.

Table 15

Proportion of the population below the minimum level of dietary energy consumption is the percentage of the population whose food intake falls below the minimum level of dietary energy requirements. This is also referred to as the prevalence of undernourishment, which is the percentage of the population that is undernourished.

Chapter VI: Culture and communication

The statistics included in Tables 16-18 were obtained from the statistics database (see www.itu.int) and the *Yearbook of Statistics,* Telecommunication Services of the International Telecommunication Union.

Table 16

The number of mobile cellular telephone subscribers (as well as the number of subscribers per 100 inhabitants) refers to users of portable telephones subscribing to an automatic public mobile telephone service using cellular technology, which provides access to the Public Switched Telephone Network (PSTN). Users of both post-paid subscriptions and pre-paid accounts are included. The number of subscribers per 100 inhabitants is calculated by dividing the number of subscribers by the population and multiplying by 100.

Table 17

Total fixed (wired) internet subscriptions refer to the number of total internet subscriptions with fixed (wired) Internet access, which includes dial-up and total fixed (wired) broadband subscriptions. Only active subscriptions that have used the system within the past 3 months are included.

Table 18

The data refer to fixed cinemas and mobile units regularly used for the commercial exhibition of long films. The term fixed cinema is used in this table refers to establishments possessing their own equipment and includes indoor cinemas (those with permanent fixed roof over most of the seating accommodation), outdoor cinemas and drive-ins (establishments designed to enable the audience to watch a film while seated in their automobile). Mobile units are defined as projection units equipped and used to serve more than one site.

The seating capacity of fixed cinemas is the sum of the number of seats indoor and outdoor cinemas plus the number of places for automobiles, multiplied by a factor of 4 in the case of drive-ins.

Cinema attendance is calculated from the number of tickets sold during a given year.

As a rule, figures refer only to commercial establishments but in the case of mobile units, it is possible that the figures for some countries may also include non-commercial units.

Chapter VII: National accounts and industrial production

Detailed internationally comparable data on national accounts are compiled and published annually by the Statistics Division, Department of Economic and Social Affairs of the United Nations Secretariat. A summary of the conceptual framework, classifications and definitions of transactions is found in the annual United Nations publication, National Accounts Statistics: Analysis of Main Aggregates, which presents, in the form of analytical tables, a summary of selected principal national accounts aggregates based on official detailed national accounts data of over 200 countries and areas. Every effort has been made to present the estimates of the various countries or areas in a form designed to facilitate international comparability.

Table 19

This table shows gross domestic product (GDP) and GDP per capita in US dollars at current prices, GDP at constant 2005 prices and the corresponding real rates of growth. The table is designed to facilitate international comparisons of levels of income generated in production. In order to present comparable coverage for as many countries as possible, the official GDP national currency data are supplemented by estimates prepared by the Statistics Division, based on a variety of data derived from national and international sources. The conversion rates used to translate national currency data into US dollars are the period averages of market exchange rates (MERs) for members of the International Monetary Fund (IMF). These rates, which are published in the International Financial Statistics, are communicated to the IMF by national central banks and consist of three types: (a) market rates, determined largely by market forces; (b) official rates, determined by government authorities; and (c) principal rates for countries maintaining multiple exchange rate arrangements. Market rates always take priority and official rates are used only when a free market rate is not available.

For non-members of the IMF, averages of the United Nations operational rates, used for accounting purposes in United Nations transactions with member countries, are applied. These are based on official, commercial and/or tourist rates of exchange.

It should be noted that there are practical constraints in the use of MERs for conversion purposes. Their use may result in excessive fluctuations or distortions in the dollar income levels of a number of countries, particularly in those with multiple exchange rates, those coping with inordinate levels of inflation or countries experiencing misalignments caused by market fluctuations. Caution is therefore urged when making inter-country comparisons of incomes as expressed in US dollars.

Alternative methods of making international comparisons have been developed in recent years. One is the Purchasing Power Parities (PPPs) which have been developed as part of the International Comparison Programme; another is the World Bank Atlas method of conversion based on the average of the exchange rates of the current year and the two immediately preceding years that have been adjusted for differences in inflation rates between individual countries and the average of G-5 countries (Germany, France, Japan, the United Kingdom, and the United States). The Statistics Division of the United Nations has developed the Price-Adjusted Rates of Exchange method (PARE) which, like the Atlas method, is designed to adjust exchange rates that do not adequately reflect relative movements of domestic and international inflation. PARE is mainly applied to countries with fixed exchange rate regimes and countries going through a period of high inflation (e.g. transition countries from 1990-1995).

The GDP at constant price series, based primarily on data officially provided by countries or areas and partly on estimates made by the Statistics Division, is transformed into index numbers and rebased to 2005=100. The resulting data are then converted into US dollars at the rate prevailing in the base year 2005. The growth rates are based on the estimates of GDP at constant 2005 prices. The growth rate of the year in question is obtained by dividing the GDP of that year by the GDP of the preceding year.

Table 20

This table presents a desegregation of economic development by analyzing the movement of prices and exchange rates in relation to overall economic growth.

GDP indices based on current prices expressed in US dollars and national currencies are shown in columns 1 and 2. The annual changes of GDP in volume terms are reflected in column 3, where the indices are based on the movement of GDP at constant prices.

Column 4 presents indices of price changes of GDP expressed in national currency and column 5 includes indices of price changes of GDP in US dollars. The price indices in columns 4 and 5 are obtained by dividing, respectively, the indices of GDP at current prices in national currencies and in US dollars shown in columns 1 and 2, by the volume indices presented in column 3.

Column 6 provides an implied development in exchange rates derived either by dividing the GDP deflators in national currency (column 4) by the GDP deflators converted in US dollars (column 5), or by dividing the GDP indices expressed in national currencies by the US dollar indices listed in columns 1 and 2, respectively.

Table 21

The table features the percentage distribution of GDP at current prices by expenditure breakdown. It shows the portions of GDP spent on consumption by the household sector (including the non-profit institutions serving households) and the government, the portions spent on gross fixed capital formation, on changes in inventories, and on exports of goods and services, deducting imports of goods and services. The percentages are derived from estimates by the United Nations published in the annual national accounts publication.

Table 22

The table shows the percentage distribution of value added originating from the various industry components of the International Standard Industrial Classification of All Economic Activities, Revision 3 (ISIC Rev. 3). This table reflects the economic structure of production in the different countries or areas. The percentages are based on official gross value added at basic current prices broken down by the kind of economic activity: agriculture, hunting, forestry and fishing (ISIC A-B); mining and quarrying, manufacturing, electricity, gas and water supply (ISIC C-E); manufacturing (ISIC D); construction (ISIC F); wholesale and retail trade, repair of motor vehicles, motorcycles and personal and household goods, restaurants and hotels (ISIC G-H); transport, storage and communications (ISIC I) and "other activities", comprised of financial intermediation (J), real estate, renting and business activities (K), public administration and defence, compulsory social security (L), education (M), health and social work (N), other community, social and personal service activities (O) and private households with employed persons (P).

Table 23

The national indices in this table are shown for the categories "Mining", "Manufacturing" and "Electricity, gas and water", as well as major subcategories thereof. The industries shown are classified according to the International Standard Industrial Classification of All Economic Activities (ISIC) Revision 4, covering sections B, C and D. Data have been collected at the 2-digit level of ISIC, but are shown here in more aggregated categories reflecting major industrial subsectors. Major deviations from ISIC in the scope of the indices for the above categories are indicated by footnotes to the table.

The weights used in the calculation of the aggregated indices for a particular country are the value added contributions to the gross domestic product (GDP) of the given industry during the base year, in this case

2005. These value added contributions are measured at basic prices. The national indices have been rebased to 2005=100 where necessary.

Chapter VIII: Financial statistics

Detailed information and current figures relating to tables 24 and 25 are contained in International Financial Statistics, published by the International Monetary Fund (see also www.imf.org) and in the United Nations Monthly Bulletin of Statistics.

Table 24

The discount rates shown represent the rates at which the central bank lends or discounts eligible paper for deposit money banks, typically shown on an end-of-period basis.

Table 25

The rates shown represent short-term Treasury bill rates and money market rates. The Treasury bill rate is the rate at which short-term securities are issued or traded in the market. The money market rate is the rate on short-term lending between financial institutions.

Chapter IX: Labour force

Detailed data on labour force and related topics are published in the *ILO Yearbook of Labour Statistics* and on the ILO web site http://laborsta.ilo.org. The series shown in the *Statistical Yearbook* gives an overall picture of the availability and disposition of labour resources and, in conjunction with other macroeconomic indicators, can be useful for an overall assessment of economic performance. The *ILO Yearbook of Labour Statistics* provides a comprehensive description of the methodology underlying the labour series. Brief definitions of the major categories of labour statistics are given below.

"Employment" is defined to include persons above a specified age who, during a specified period of time, were in of the following categories:

"Paid employment", comprising persons who perform some work for pay or profit during the reference period or persons with a job but not at work due to temporary absence, such as vacation, strike education leave;

"Self-employment", comprising employers, own account workers, members of producers' cooperatives, persons engaged in production of goods and services for own consumption and unpaid family workers;

Members of the armed forces, students, homemakers and others mainly engaged in non-economic activities during the reference period who, at the same time, were in paid employment or self-employment are considered as employed on the same basis as other categories.

For various reasons, national definitions of employment often differ from the recommended international standard definitions and thereby limit international comparability. Inter-country comparisons are also complicated by a variety of types of data collection systems used to obtain information on employed persons.

Table 26

The employment table presents absolute figures on the distribution of employed persons by economic activity, according to ISIC 3. The column for total employment includes economic activities not adequately defined and that are not accounted for in the other categories. Data are arranged as far as possible according to the major divisions of economic activity of the *International Standard Industrial Classification of All Economic Activities.*

Chapter X: Wages and prices

Table 27

The series generally relate to the average earnings per worker in manufacturing industries, according to the *International Standard Industrial Classification of All Economic Activities (ISIC)* Revision 2 or Revision 3. The data are published in the *ILO Yearbook of Labour Statistics* and on the ILO web site http://laborsta.ilo.org and generally cover all employees (i.e. wage earners and salaried employees) of both sexes, irrespective of age.

Data which refer exclusively to wage earners (i.e. manual or production workers), salaried employees (i.e. non-manual workers), or to total employment are also shown when available. Earnings generally include bonuses, cost of living allowances, taxes, social insurance contributions payable by the employed person and, in some cases, payments in kind, and normally exclude social insurance contributions payable by the employers, family allowances and other social security benefits. The time of year to which the figures refer is not the same for all countries. In some cases, the series may show wage rates instead of earnings; this is indicated in footnotes.

Table 28

A consumer price index is usually estimated as a series of summary measures of the period-to-period proportional change in the prices of a fixed set of consumer goods and services of constant quantity and characteristics, acquired, used or paid for by the reference population. Each summary measure is constructed as a weighted average of a large number of elementary aggregate indices. Each of the elementary aggregate indices is estimated using a sample of prices for a defined set of goods and services obtained in, or by residents of, a specific region from a given set of outlets or other sources of consumption goods and services.

The table presents the general consumer price index for all groups of consumption items combined, and the food index including non-alcoholic beverages only. Where alcoholic beverages and/or tobacco are included, this is indicated in footnotes.

Chapter XI: Agriculture, forestry and fishing

The series shown on agriculture and fishing have been furnished by the Food and Agriculture Organization of the United Nations (FAO). They refer mainly to the long-term trends in the growth of agricultural output and the food supply, the output of principal agricultural commodities and fish production.

Agricultural production is defined to include all crops and livestock products except those used for seed and fodder and other intermediate uses in agriculture; for example deductions are made for eggs used for hatching. Intermediate input of seeds and fodder and similar items refer to both domestically produced and imported commodities. For further details, reference may be made to *FAO Statistical Yearbook*. FAO data are also available through the Internet at http://faostat.fao.org.

Table 29

"Agriculture" relates to the production of all crops and livestock products. The "Food Index" includes those commodities which are considered edible and contain nutrients. The index numbers of agricultural output and food production are calculated by the Laspeyres formula with the base year period 1999-2001. The latter is provided in order to diminish the impact of annual fluctuations in agricultural output during base years on the indices for the period. Production quantities of each commodity are weighted by 1999-2001 average national producer prices and summed for each year. The index numbers are based on production data for a calendar year. These may differ in some instances from those actually produced and published by the individual countries themselves due to variations in concepts, coverage, weights and methods of calculation. Efforts have been made to estimate these methodological differences to achieve a better international comparability of data. Detailed data on agricultural production are published by FAO in its *Statistical Yearbook*.

Table 30

Oil crops, or oil bearing crops, are those crops yielding seeds, nuts or fruits which are used mainly for the extraction of culinary or industrial oils, excluding essential oils. In this table, data for oil crops represent the total production of oil seeds, oil nuts and oil fruits harvested in the year indicated. Naturally, the total production of oil crops is never processed into oil in its entirety, since depending on the crop, important quantities are also used for seed, feed and food. However, although oil extraction rates vary from country to country, in this table the same extraction rate for each crop has been applied for all countries. Moreover, it should be borne in mind that the crops harvested during the latter months of the year are generally processed into oil during the following year.

In spite of these deficiencies in coverage, extraction rates and time reference, the data reported here are useful as they provide a valid indication of year to year changes in the size of total oil crop production. The actual production of vegetable oils in the world is about 80 percent of the production reported here. In addition, about two million tonnes of vegetable oils are produced every year from crops which are not included among those defined above. The most important of these oils are maize germ oil and rice bran oil. The actual world production of cake/meal derived from oil crops is also about 80 percent of the production reported.

Table 31

The data on the production of cereals relate to crops harvested for dry grain only. Cereals harvested for hay, green feed or used for grazing are excluded.

Table 32

The data on roundwood refer to wood in the rough, wood in its natural state as felled or otherwise harvested, with or without bark, round, split, roughly squared or in other form (i.e. roots, stumps, burls, etc.). It may also be impregnated (e.g. telegraph poles) or roughly shaped or pointed. It comprises all wood obtained from removals, i.e. the quantities removed from forests and from trees outside the forest, including wood recovered from natural, felling and logging losses during the period—calendar year or forest year.

Table 33

The data cover (i) capture production from marine and inland fisheries and (ii) aquaculture, and are expressed in terms of live weight. They include fish, crustaceans and molluscs but exclude sponges, corals, pearls, seaweed, crocodiles, and aquatic mammals (such as whales and dolphins).

The flag of the vessel is considered as the paramount indication of the nationality of the catch. Marine fisheries data include landings by domestic craft in foreign ports and exclude landings by foreign craft in domestic ports.

To separate aquaculture from capture fisheries production, at least two criteria must apply i.e., the human intervention in one or more of the phases of the growth cycle, and individual, corporate or state ownership of the organism reared and harvested.

Data on aquaculture production are published in the FAO *Yearbook of Fishery Statistics, Aquaculture Production*; capture production statistics are published in the FAO *Yearbook of Fishery Statistics, Capture Production*.

Table 34

The data generally refer to the fertilizer year 1 July-30 June.

Nitrogenous fertilizers: data refer to the nitrogen content of commercial inorganic fertilizers.

Phosphate fertilizers: data refer to commercial phosphoric acid (P_2O_5) of super phosphates, ammonium phosphate and basic slag.

Potash fertilizers: data refer to K_2O content of commercial potash, muriate, nitrate and sulphate of potash, manure salts, kainit and nitrate of soda potash.

Chapter XII: Manufacturing

Industrial activity includes mining and quarrying, manufacturing and the production of electricity, gas and water. These activities correspond to the major divisions 2, 3 and 4 respectively of the International Standard Industrial Classification of All Economic Activities. Many of the tables are based primarily on data compiled for the *United Nations Industrial Commodity Statistics Yearbook*. Data taken from alternate sources are footnoted.

The methods used by countries for the computation of industrial output are, as a rule, consistent with those described in the United Nations International Recommendations for Industrial Statistics and provide a satisfactory basis for comparative analysis. In some cases, however, the definitions and procedures underlying computations of output differ from approved guidelines. The differences, where known, are indicated in the footnotes to each table.

Table 35

The statistics on sugar were obtained from the database and the *Sugar Yearbook* of the International Sugar Organization. The data shown cover the production and consumption of centrifugal sugar from both beet and cane, and refer to calendar years.

The consumption data relate to the apparent consumption of centrifugal sugar in the country concerned, including sugar used for the manufacture of sugar-containing products whether exported or not and sugar used for purposes other than human consumption as food. Unless otherwise specified, the statistics are expressed in terms of raw value (i.e. sugar polarizing at 96 degrees). The world total also includes data for countries not shown separately whose sugar consumption was less than 10,000 metric tons.

Table 36

The data refer to meat from animals slaughtered within the national boundaries irrespective of the origin of the animals. Production figures of cattle, chicken, buffalo, pig (including bacon and ham), sheep and goat meat are in terms of carcass weight, excluding edible offal, tallow and lard. All data refer to total meat production, i.e. from both commercial and farm slaughter.

Table 37

The data refer to beer made from malt, including ale, stout, and porter.

Table 38

The table presents data on cigarettes only, unless otherwise indicated.

Table 39

The table presents statistics on the production of all paper and paper board. The data cover newsprint, printing and writing paper, construction paper and paperboard, household and sanitary paper, special thin paper, wrapping and packaging paper and paperboard.

Table 40

The data refer to unwrought aluminium obtained by electrolytic reduction of alumina (primary) and re-melting metal waste or scrap (secondary).

Table 41

The data on radio receivers include radio-broadcast receivers capable of operating without an external source of power, including apparatus capable of receiving also radio-telephony or radio-telegraphy, whether combined with sound recording or reproducing apparatus or not; radio-broadcast receivers not capable of operating without an external source of power, of a kind used in motor vehicles, including apparatus capable of receiving also radio-telephony or radio-telegraphy, whether combined with sound recording or reproducing apparatus or not; other radio-broadcast receivers, including apparatus capable of receiving also radio-telephony or radio-telegraphy, whether combined with sound recording or reproducing apparatus or not.

The data on television receivers include colour, black and white and other monochrome. also includes television receivers with a video recorder or player, flat panel colour TV receivers, tuner blocks for CTV/VCR and cable TV receiver units and satellite TV receivers/ decoders.

Table 42

The table presents statistics on household washing machines and drying machines, including machines that both wash and dry.

Table 43

The data on machine tools presented in this table include two types: (i) machine-tools (including way-type unit head machines) for drilling, boring, milling, threading or tapping by removing metal, other than lathes and turning centres; (ii) lathes including turning centres for removing metal, horizontal, numerically controlled or otherwise.

Table 44

The table presents statistics on trucks - motor vehicles not elsewhere classified for the transport of goods except for dumpers designed for off-highway use.

Chapter XIII: Energy

Table 45

Data are presented in metric tons of oil equivalent (TOE), to which the individual energy commodities are converted in the interests of international uniformity and comparability. To convert from original units to TOE, the data in original units (metric tons, terajoules, kilowatt hours, cubic metres) are multiplied by conversion factors. For a list of the relevant conversion factors and a detailed description of methods, see the United Nations *Energy Statistics Yearbook* and related methodological publications.

Included in the production of commercial primary energy for solids are hard coal, lignite, peat and oil shale; liquids are comprised of crude petroleum and natural gas liquids; gas comprises natural gas; and electricity is comprised of primary electricity generation from hydro, nuclear, geothermal, wind, tide, wave and solar sources.

In general, data on stocks refer to changes in stocks of producers, importers and/or industrial consumers at the beginning and end of each year. International trade of energy commodities is based on the "general trade" system, that is, all goods entering and leaving the national boundary of a country are recorded as imports and exports. Sea/air bunkers refer to the amounts of fuels delivered to ocean-going ships or aircraft of all flags engaged in international traffic. Consumption by ships engaged in transport in inland and coastal waters, or by aircraft engaged in domestic flights, is not included. Data on consumption refer to "apparent consumption" and are derived from the formula "production + imports – exports – bunkers +/- stock changes". Accordingly, the series on apparent consumption may in some cases represent only an indication of the magnitude of actual gross inland availability.

Included in the consumption of commercial energy for solids are consumption of primary forms of solid fuels, net imports and changes in stocks of secondary fuels; liquids are comprised of consumption of energy petroleum products including feedstocks, natural gasoline, condensate, refinery gas and input of crude petroleum to thermal power plants; gases include the consumption of natural gas, net imports and changes in stocks of gasworks and coke oven gas; and electricity is comprised of production of primary electricity and net imports of electricity.

Table 46

The definitions of the energy commodities are as follows:

– Hard coal: Coal that has a high degree of coalification with a gross calorific value above 23,865 KJ/kg (5,700 kcal/kg) on an ash free but moist basis, and a mean random reflectance of vitrinite of at least 0.6. Slurries, middlings and other low-grade coal products, which cannot be classified according to the type of coal from which they are obtained, are included under hard coal.

– Lignite: Non-agglomerating coal with a low degree of coalification which retained the anatomical structure of the vegetable matter from which it was formed. Its gross calorific value is less than 17,435 KJ/kg (4,165 kcal/kg), and it contains greater than 31 per cent volatile matter on a dry mineral matter free basis.

– Peat: a solid fuel formed from the partial decomposition of dead vegetation under conditions of high humidity and limited air access (initial stage of coalification). Only peat used as fuel is included. Its principal use is as a household fuel.

– Crude petroleum: A mineral oil consisting of a mixture of hydrocarbons of natural origin, yellow to black in colour, of variable density and viscosity. Data in this category also includes lease or field condensate (separator liquids) which is recovered from gaseous hydrocarbons in lease separation facilities, as well as synthetic crude oil, mineral oils extracted from bituminous minerals such as shales and bituminous sand, and oils from coal liquefaction.

– Natural gas liquids (NGL): Liquid or liquefied hydrocarbons produced in the manufacture, purification and stabilization of natural gas. NGLs include, but are not limited to, ethane, propane, butane, pentane, natural gasoline, and plant condensate.

– Motor gasoline: Light hydrocarbon oil for use in internal combustion engines such as motor vehicles, excluding aircraft. It distils between 35°C and 200°C, and is treated to reach a sufficiently high octane number of generally between 80 and 100 RON. Treatment may be by re-forming, blending with an aromatic fraction, or the addition of benzole or other additives (such as tetraethyl lead).

– Jet fuel: Consists of gasoline-type jet fuel and kerosene-type jet fuel. Gasoline-type jet fuel: All light hydro-carbon oils for use in aviation gas-turbine engines. It distils between 100°C and 250°C with at least 20% of volume distilling at 143°C. It is obtained by blending kerosene and gasoline or naphtha in such a way that the aromatic content does not exceed 25% in volume. Additives are included to reduce the freezing point to -58°C or lower, and to keep the Reid vapour pressure between 0.14 and 0.21 kg/cm2. Kerosene-type jet fuel: Medium oil for use in aviation gas-turbine engines with the same distillation characteristics and flash point as kerosene, with a maxi-mum aromatic content of 20% in volume. It is treated to give a kinematic viscosity of less than 15 cSt at -34°C and a freezing point below -50°C.

– Gas-diesel oil (distillate fuel oil): Heavy oils distilling between 200°C and 380°C, but distilling less than 65% in volume at 250°C, including losses, and 85% or more at 350°C. Its flash point is always above 50°C and its specific gravity is higher than 0.82. Heavy oils obtained by blending are grouped together with gas oils on the condition that their kinematic viscosity does not exceed 27.5 cSt at 38°C. Also included are middle distillates intended for the petrochemical industry. Gas-diesel oils are used as a fuel for internal combustion in diesel engines, as a burner fuel in heating installations, such as furnaces, and for enriching water gas to increase its luminosity. Other names for this product are diesel fuel, diesel oil and gas oil.

– Residual fuel oil: Heavy oil that makes up the distillation residue. It comprises all fuels (including those obtained by blending) with a kinematic viscosity above 27.5 cSt at 38°C. Its flash point is always above 50°C and its specific gravity is higher than 0.90. It is commonly used by ships and industrial large-scale heating installations as a fuel in furnaces or boilers.

– Liquefied petroleum gas (LPG): Hydrocarbons which are gaseous under conditions of normal temperature and pressure but are liquefied by compression or cooling to facilitate storage, handling and transportation. It comprises propane, butane, or a combination of the two. Also included is ethane from petroleum refineries or natural gas producers' separation and stabilization plants.

– Natural gas: Gases consisting mainly of methane occurring naturally in underground deposits. It includes both non associated gas (originating from fields producing only hydrocarbons in gaseous form) and associated gas (originating from fields producing both liquid and gaseous hydrocarbons), as well as methane recovered from coal mines and sewage gas. Production of natural gas refers to dry marketable production, measured after purification and extraction of natural gas liquids and sulphur. Extraction losses and the amounts that have been re-injected, flared, and vented are excluded from the data on production.

– Electricity production refers to gross production, which includes the consumption by station auxiliaries and any losses in the transformers that are considered integral parts of the station. Included also is total electric energy produced by pumping installations without deduction of electric energy absorbed by pumping.

Chapter XIV: Environment

Table 47

The data on land are compiled by the Food and Agriculture Organization of the United Nations (FAO). FAO's definitions of the land categories are as follows:

Land area: Total area excluding area under inland water bodies. The definition of inland water bodies generally includes major rivers and lakes.

Arable land: Land under temporary crops (double cropped areas are counted only once); temporary meadows for mowing or pasture; land under market and kitchen gardens; and land temporarily fallow (less than five years). Abandoned land resulting from shifting cultivation is not included in this category. Data for "arable land" are not meant to indicate the amount of land that is potentially cultivable.

Permanent crops: Land cultivated with crops that occupy the land for long periods and need not be replanted after each harvest, such as cocoa, coffee and rubber. This category includes land under flowering shrubs, fruit trees, nut trees and vines, but excludes land under trees grown for wood or timber.

Forest: In the *Global Forest Resources Assessment 2010* the following definition is used for forest: Land spanning more than 0.5 hectares with trees higher than 5 metres and a canopy cover of more than 10 percent, or trees able to reach these thresholds *in situ*. It does not include land that is predominantly under agricultural or urban land use.

Table 48

The source of the data presented on the emissions of carbon dioxide (CO_2) is the Carbon Dioxide Information Analysis Centre (CDIAC) of the Oak Ridge National Laboratory in the USA.

The CDIAC estimates of CO_2 emissions are derived primarily from United Nations energy statistics on the consumption of liquid and solid fuels and gas consumption and flaring, and from cement production estimates from the Bureau of Mines of the U.S. Department of Interior. The emissions presented in the table are in units of 1,000 metric tons of CO_2; to convert CO_2 into carbon, divide the data by 3.66406. Full details of the procedures for calculating emissions are given in Global, Regional, and National Annual CO_2 Emissions Estimates from Fossil Fuel Burning, Hydraulic Cement Production, and Gas Flaring and on the CDIAC web site (see http://cdiac.esd.ornl.gov). Relative to other industrial sources for which CO_2 emissions are estimated, statistics on gas flaring activities are sparse and sporadic. In countries where gas flaring activities account for a considerable proportion of the total CO_2 emissions, the sporadic nature of gas flaring statistics may produce spurious or misleading trends in national CO_2 emissions over the period covered by the table.

Table 49

Data on the number of threatened species in each group of animals and plants are compiled by the World Conservation Union (IUCN)/Species Survival Commission (SSC) and published in the IUCN Red List of Threatened Species.

The list provides a catalogue of those species that are considered globally threatened. The categories used in the Red List are as follows: Extinct, Extinct in the Wild, Critically Endangered, Endangered, Vulnerable, Near Threatened and Data Deficient.

Table 50

The proportion of the population with sustainable access to an improved water source, urban and rural, is the percentage of the population who use any of the following types of water supply for drinking: piped water, public tap, borehole or pump, protected well, protected spring or rainwater. Improved water sources do not include vendor-provided water, bottled water, tanker trucks or unprotected wells and springs.

Proportion of the urban and rural population with access to improved sanitation refers to the percentage of the population with access to facilities that hygienically separate human excreta from human, animal and insect contact. Facilities such as sewers or septic tanks, poor flush latrines and simple pit or ventilated improved pit latrines are assumed to be adequate, provided that they are not public, according to the World Health Organization and United Nations Children's Fund. To be effective, facilities must be correctly constructed and properly maintained.

Chapter XV: Science and technology

Research and experimental development (R&D) is defined as any creative work undertaken on a systematic basis in order to increase the stock of knowledge, including knowledge of man, culture and society, and the use of this stock of knowledge to devise new applications. More information can be found on the UNESCO Institute for Statistics web site www.uis.unesco.org.

Table 51

The data presented on human resources in research and development (R&D) are compiled by the UNESCO Institute for Statistics. Data for certain countries are provided to UNESCO by OECD, EUROSTAT and the Network on Science and Technology Indicators (RICYT). The definitions and classifications applied by UNESCO in the table are based on those set out in the Recommendation concerning the International Standardization of Statistics on Science and Technology (UNESCO, 1978) and in the Frascati Manual (OECD, 2002).

The three categories of personnel shown are defined as follows:

Researchers are professionals engaged in the conception or creation of new knowledge, products, processes, methods and systems, and in the planning and management of R&D projects. Postgraduate students engaged in R&D are considered as researchers.

Technicians and equivalent staff comprise persons whose main tasks require technical knowledge and experience in one or more fields of engineering, physical and life sciences, or social sciences and humanities. They participate in R&D by performing scientific and technical tasks involving the application of concepts and operational methods, normally under the supervision of researchers. As distinguished from technicians participating in the R&D under the supervision of researchers in engineering, physical and life sciences, equivalent staff perform the corresponding R&D tasks in the social sciences and humanities.

Other supporting staff includes skilled and unskilled craftsmen, secretarial and clerical staff participating in or directly associated with R&D projects. Included in this category are all managers and administrators dealing mainly with financial and personnel matters and general administration, insofar as their activities are a direct service to R&D.

Headcount data reflect the total number of persons employed in R&D, independently from their dedication. Full-time equivalent may be thought of as one person-year. Thus, a person who normally spends 30% of his/her time on R&D and the rest on other activities (such as teaching, university administration and student counselling) should be considered as 0.3 FTE. Similarly, if a full-time R&D worker is employed at an R&D unit for only six months, this results in an FTE of 0.5.

Table 52

The data presented on gross domestic expenditure on research and development are compiled by the UNESCO Institute for Statistics. Data for certain countries are provided to UNESCO by OECD, EUROSTAT and the Network on Science and Technology Indicators (RICYT).

Gross domestic expenditure on R&D (GERD) is total intramural expenditure on R&D performed on the national territory during a given period. It includes R&D performed within a country and funded from abroad but excludes payments made abroad for R&D.

The sources of funds for GERD are classified according to the following five categories:

Business enterprise funds include funds allocated to R&D by all firms, organizations and institutions whose primary activity is the market production of goods and ser-vices (other than the higher education sector) for sale to the general public at an economically significant price, and those private non-profit institutes mainly serving these firms, organizations and institutions.

Government funds refer to funds allocated to R&D by the central (federal), state or local government authorities. These include all departments, offices and other bodies which furnish, but normally do not sell to the community, those common services, other than higher education, which cannot be conveniently and economically provided, as well as those that administer the state and the economic and social policy of the community. Public enterprises funds are included in the business enterprise funds sector. Government funds also include private non-profit institutes controlled and mainly financed by government.

Higher education funds include funds allocated to R&D by institutions of higher education comprising all universities, colleges of technology, other institutes of post-secondary education, and all research institutes, experimental stations and clinics operating under the direct control of or administered by or associated with higher educational establishments.

Private non-profit funds are funds allocated to R&D by non-market, private non-profit institutions serving the general public, as well as by private individuals and households.

Funds from abroad refer to funds allocated to R&D by institutions and individuals located outside the political frontiers of a country except for vehicles, ships, aircraft and space satellites operated by domestic organizations and testing grounds acquired by such organizations, and by all international organizations (except business enterprises) including their facilities and operations within the country's borders.

The absolute figures for R&D expenditure should not be compared country by country. Such comparisons would require the conversion of national currencies into a common currency by means of special R&D exchange rates. Official exchange rates do not always reflect the real costs of R&D activities and comparisons are based on such rates can result in misleading conclusions, although they can be used to indicate a gross order of magnitude.

Table 53

A patent is granted by a national patent office or by a regional office that does the work for a number of countries, such as the European Patent Office and the African Regional Intellectual Property Organization. Under such regional systems, an applicant requests protection for the invention in one or more countries, and each country decides as to whether to offer patent protection within its borders. The World Intellectual Property Organization (WIPO)-administered Patent Cooperation Treaty (PCT) provides for the filing of a single international patent application which has the same effect as national applications filed in the designated countries.

Data include patent intensity, patents granted and patents in force. Patent intensity is presented as the resident patent filings per million population, where a resident Intellectual Property (IP) filing refers to an application filed by an applicant at its national IP office. IP grant (registration) data are based on the same concept. In Force refers to a patent or other form of IP protection that is currently valid.

Country of origin is used to categorize IP data by resident (domestic) and non-resident (foreign). The residence of the first-named applicant (or inventor) recorded in the IP document (e.g. patent or trademark application) is used to classify IP data by country of origin. The data are compiled and published by the WIPO.

Chapter XVI: International merchandise trade

Current data (annual, monthly and/or quarterly) for most of the series are published regularly by the United Nations Statistics Division in the Monthly Bulletin of Statistics. More detailed descriptions of the tables and notes on methodology appear in the *International Trade Statistics Yearbook.*

Data are obtained from data supplied by the governments for dissemination in United Nations publications, from national published sources and from data published by other international organisations.

Statistical territory

The statistics reported by each country refer to its statistical territory which may coincide with its economic territory or with some part of it.

Systems of trade

There are two trade systems in common use by which international merchandise trade statistics are compiled - the general trade system and the special trade system:

(a) The general trade system is in use when the statistical territory of a country coincides with its economic territory.

(b) The special trade system (strict definition) is in use when the statistical territory comprises only the free circulation area, that is, the part within which goods may be disposed of without customs restriction. A "relaxed" definition of the special trade system is in use when (i) goods that enter a country for or leave it after inward processing and (ii) goods that enter or leave an industrial free zone are also recorded and included in international merchandise trade statistics.

Valuation

Goods are, in general, valued based on the transaction value. It is recommended that the statistical value of imported goods be a CIF-type value and the statistical value of exported goods an FOB-type value. FOB-type values include the transaction value of the goods and the value of services performed to deliver goods to the border of the exporting country. CIF-type values include the transaction value of the goods, the value of services performed to deliver goods to the border of the exporting country and the value of the services performed to deliver the goods from the border of the exporting country to the border of the importing country.

Currency conversion

Conversion of values from national currencies into United States dollars is done by means of external trade conversion factors which are generally weighted averages of exchange rates, the weight being the corresponding monthly value of imports or exports.

Coverage

The statistics relate to merchandise trade. It is recommended that international merchandise trade statistics record all goods which add to or subtract from the stock of material resources of a country by entering (imports) or leaving (exports) its economic territory. Goods simply being transported through a country (goods in transit) or temporarily admitted or withdrawn (except for goods for inward or outward processing) do not add to or subtract from the stock of material resources of a country and are not included in the international merchandise trade statistics. For details and a list of inclusions and exclusions see *International Merchandise Trade Statistics, Concepts and Definitions, Revision 2.*

Commodity classification

The commodity classification of trade is in accordance with the United Nations *Standard International Trade Classification* (SITC).

World and regional totals

The regional, economic and world totals have been adjusted: (a) to include estimates for countries or areas for which full data are not available; (b) to include countries or areas not listed separately; and (c) where possible, to eliminate incomparabilities owing to geographical changes, by adjusting the figures for periods before the change to be comparable to those for periods after the change.

Volume and unit value index numbers

These index numbers show the changes in the volume of imports or exports (volume index) and the average price of imports or exports (unit value or price index).

Table 54

The regional totals for imports and exports have been adjusted to exclude the re-exports of countries or areas comprising each region. Estimates for certain countries or areas not shown separately as well as for those shown separately but for which no data are yet available are included in the regional and world totals. Export and import values in terms of U.S. dollars are obtained from data published by the International Monetary Fund (IMF) in the publication *International Financial Statistics*, from the replies to the *Monthly Bulletin of Statistics* questionnaires and from national sources.

Table 55

These index numbers show the changes in the volume (quantum index) and the average price (unit value or price index) of total imports and exports.

The indices are obtained from data published by the International Monetary Fund (IMF) in the publication International Financial Statistics, from the replies to the Monthly Bulletin of Statistics questionnaires and from national sources.

Unit value indices obtained from national indices are rebased, where necessary, so that 2000=100. Indices in national currency are converted into US dollars using conversion factors obtained by dividing the weighted average exchange rate of a given currency in the current period by the weighted average exchange rate in the base period. The terms of trade figures are calculated by dividing export unit value indices by the corresponding import unit value indices. The product of the terms of trade and the volume index of exports is called the index of the purchasing power of exports. The footnotes to countries appearing in table 54 also apply to the index numbers in this table.

Table 56

Manufactured goods are defined here to comprise sections 5 through 8 of the Standard International Trade Classification (SITC). These sections are: chemicals and related products, manufactured goods classified chiefly by material, machinery and transport equipment and miscellaneous manufactured articles.

The unit value indices are obtained from national sources including replies to the Monthly Bulletin of Statistics questionnaires, except those of a few countries which the United Nations Statistics Division compiles using their quantity and value figures. For countries that do not compile indices for manufactured goods exports conforming to the above definition, sub-indices are aggregated to approximate an index of SITC sections 5-8.

Unit value indices obtained from national indices are rebased, where necessary, so that 2000=100. Indices in national currency are converted into US dollars using conversion factors obtained by dividing the weighted average exchange rate of a given currency in the current period by the weighted average exchange rate in the base period. All aggregate unit value indices are current period weighted.

The indices in Special Drawing Rights (SDRs) are calculated by multiplying the equivalent aggregate indices in United States dollars by conversion factors obtained by dividing the SDR/US$ exchange rate in the current period by the rate in the base period.

The volume indices are derived from the value data and the unit value indices. All aggregate volume indices are base-period weighted.

Chapter XVII: International tourism and transport

The data on international tourism have been supplied by the United Nations World Tourism Organization (UNWTO) from detailed tourism information published in the *Yearbook of Tourism Statistics* and in the UNWTO statistics database available from http://www.unwto.org/statistics/index.htm.

For statistical purposes, the term "international visitor" describes "any person who travels to a country other than that in which he/she has his/her usual residence but outside his/her usual environment for a period not exceeding 12 months and whose main purpose of visit is other than the exercise of an activity remunerated from within the country visited".

International visitors include: (a) tourists (overnight visitors): "visitors who stay at least one night in a collective or private accommodation in the country visited"; and (b) same-day visitors: "visitors who do not spend the night in a collective or private accommodation in the country visited". The figures do not include immigrants, residents in a frontier zone, persons domiciled in one country or area and working in an adjoining country or area, members of the armed forces and diplomats and consular representatives when they travel from their country of origin to the country in which they are stationed and vice-versa. The figures also exclude persons in transit who do not formally enter the country through passport control, such as air transit passengers who remain for a short period in a designated area of the air terminal or ship passengers who are not permitted to disembark. This category includes passengers transferred directly between airports or other terminals. Other passengers in transit through a country are classified as visitors.

Table 57

Data on arrivals of non-resident (or international) visitors may be obtained from different sources. In some cases data are obtained from border statistics derived from administrative records (police, immigration, traffic counts and other types of controls), border surveys and registrations at accommodation establishments.

Unless otherwise stated, table 57 shows the number of non-resident tourist/visitor arrivals at national borders classified by their region of origin. Totals correspond to the total number of arrivals from the regions indicated in the table.

When a person visits the same country several times a year, an equal number of arrivals is recorded. Likewise, if a person visits several countries during the course of a single trip, his/her arrival in each country is recorded separately. Consequently, arrivals cannot be assumed to be equal to the number of persons travelling.

Expenditure associated with tourism activity of visitors has been traditionally identified with the travel item of the Balance of Payments (BOP): in the case of inbound tourism, those expenditures in the country of reference associated with non-resident visitors are registered as "credits" in the BOP and refer to "travel receipts".

The new conceptual framework approved by the United Nations Statistical Commission in relation to the measurement of tourism macroeconomic activity (the so-called Tourism Satellite Account) considers that "tourism industries and products" includes transport of passengers. Consequently, a better estimate of tourism-related expenditures by resident and non-resident visitors in an international scenario would be, in terms of the BOP, the value of the travel item plus that of the passenger transport item.

Nevertheless, users should be aware that BOP estimates include, in addition to expenditures associated with visitors, those related to other types of individuals.

The data published should allow international comparability and therefore correspond to those published by the International Monetary Fund (and provided by the Central Banks). Exceptions are footnoted.

Table 58

Outbound tourism includes departures (in thousands) as well as expenditure in million US dollars. Indicators on expenditure (in other countries) are equivalent to those for inbound tourism but are registered as "debits" in the BOP's travel and passenger transport items. The data published are also provided by the International Monetary Fund and the same previous warning is applicable.

More detailed tourism information from the United Nations World Tourism Organization is available in the Compendium of Tourism Statistics and from http://www.unwto.org/statistics/index.htm; information on the balance of payments is published by the International Monetary Fund in the *Balance of Payments Statistics Yearbook.*

Table 59

The data on civil aviation are published annually in the Annual Report of the Council of the International Civil Aviation Organization. The data are based on reported data as well as estimates for the non-reported airlines Data for total traffic cover both domestic and international scheduled services operated by airlines registered in each country. Scheduled services include supplementary services occasioned by overflow traffic on regularly scheduled trips and preparatory flights for newly scheduled services. The data are prepared by the International Civil Aviation Organization (see also www.icao.int). The following terms have been used in the table:

- Kilometres flown - aircraft kilometres performed, which is the sum of the products obtained by multiplying the number of revenue flight stages flown by the corresponding stage distance.

- Passengers carried - the number of passengers carried is obtained by counting each passenger on a particular flight (with one flight number) once only and not repeatedly on each individual stage of that flight, with a single exception that a passenger flying on both the international and domestic stages of the same flight should be counted as both a domestic and an international passenger.

- Passenger-kilometres performed - a passenger kilometre is performed when a passenger is carried one kilometre. Calculation of passenger-kilometres equals the sum of the products obtained by multiplying the number of revenue passengers carried on each flight stage by the stage distance. The resultant figure is equal to the number of kilometres travelled by all passengers.

- Tonne-kilometres performed - a metric tonne of revenue load carried one kilometre. Tonne-kilometres performed equals the sum of the product obtained by multiplying the number of total tonnes of revenue load (passengers, freight and mail) carried on each flight stage by the stage distance. See http://www.icaodata.com/Terms.aspx for more information.

Chapter XVIII: International finance

Table 60

Total Reserves minus Gold is the sum of the items Foreign Exchange, shown in this table, as well as Reserve Position in the Fund, and the U.S. dollar value of SDR holdings by monetary authorities.

Foreign Exchange includes monetary authorities' claims on non-residents in the form of foreign banknotes, bank deposits, treasury bills, short- and long-term government securities, ECUs (for periods before January 1999), and other claims usable in the event of balance of payments need.

Table 61

The data on external debt for developing countries were extracted from Global Development Finance, published by the World Bank. In this table, developing countries are those in which 2011 GNI per capita was below $12,475.

The World Bank Debtor Reporting System (DRS) maintains statistics on the external debt of developing countries on a loan-by-loan basis. The estimated total external indebtedness of developing countries is a combination of DRS data and other information obtained from creditors through the debt data collection systems of other agencies such as the Bank for International Settlements (BIS) and the Organization for Economic Co-operation and Development (OECD), supplemented by market sources and estimates made by country economists of the World Bank and desk officers of the International Monetary Fund (IMF).

Long-term external debt is defined as debt that has an original or extended maturity of more than one year and that is owed to non-residents and is repayable in foreign currency, goods, or services. Long-term debt has three components: a) public debt, which is an external obligation of a public debtor, including the national government, a political subdivision (or an agency of either), and autonomous public bodies; b) publicly guaranteed debt, which is an external obligation of a private debtor that is guaranteed for repayment by a public entity; and c) private non-guaranteed external debt, which is an external obligation of a private debtor that is not guaranteed for repayment by a public entity. Public and publicly guaranteed long-term debts are aggregated.

All data related to public and publicly guaranteed debt are from debtors except for those on lending by some multi-lateral agencies, in which case the data are taken from the creditors' records. These creditors include the African Development Bank, the Asian Development Bank, the Central Bank for Economic Integration, the Inter-American Development Bank, the International Bank for Reconstruction and Development (IBRD) and the International Development Association (IDA). (The IBRD and IDA are components of the World Bank.)

The data referring to public and publicly guaranteed debt do not include data for (a) transactions with the International Monetary Fund, (b) debt repayable in local currency, (c) direct investment and (d) short term debt (that is, debt with an original maturity of less than a year).

The data referring to private non guaranteed debt also exclude the above items but include contractual obligations on loans to direct investment enterprises by foreign parent companies or their affiliates.

Data are aggregated by type of creditor. The break-down is as follows:

Official creditors:

a) Loans from international organizations (multilateral loans), excluding loans from funds administered by an inter-national organization on behalf of a single donor government. The latter are classified as loans from governments;

b) Loans from governments (bilateral loans) and from autonomous public bodies;

Private creditors

a) Suppliers: Credits from manufacturers, exporters, or other suppliers of goods;

b)   Financial markets: Loans from private banks and other private financial institutions as well as publicly issued and privately placed bonds;

c)   Other: External liabilities on account of nationalized properties and unclassified debts to private creditors.

A distinction is made between the following categories of external public debt:

– Debt outstanding (including undisbursed) is the sum of disbursed and undisbursed debt and represents the total outstanding external obligations of the borrower at year end;

– Debt outstanding (disbursed only) is total outstanding debt drawn by the borrower at year-end;

– Commitments are the total of loans for which con-tracts are signed in the year specified;

– Disbursements are drawings on outstanding loan commitments during the year specified;

– Service payments are actual repayments of principal amortization and interest payments made in foreign currencies, goods or services in the year specified;

– Net flows (or net lending) are disbursements minus principal repayments;

– Net transfers are net flows minus interest payments or disbursements minus total debt service payments;

The countries included in the table are those for which data are sufficiently reliable to provide a meaningful presentation of debt outstanding and future service payments;

Chapter XIX: Development assistance

Table 62

The table presents estimates of flows of financial re-sources to individual recipients either directly (bilaterally) or through multilateral institutions (multilaterally).

The multilateral institutions include the World Bank Group, regional banks, financial institutions of the European Union and a number of United Nations institutions, programmes and trust funds.

The source of data is the Development Assistance Committee of OECD to which member countries reported data on their flow of resources to developing countries and territories, countries and territories in transition, and multilateral institutions.

Additional information on definitions, methods and sources can be found in OECD's *Geographical Distribution of Financial Flows to Aid Recipients* and www.oecd.org.

Table 63

The table presents the development assistance expenditures of donor countries. This table includes donors' contributions to multilateral agencies; therefore, the overall totals differ from those in table 62, which include disbursements by multilateral agencies.

Table 64

The table includes data on expenditures on operational activities for development undertaken by the organizations of the United Nations system. Operational activities encompass, in general, those activities of a development cooperation character that seek to mobilize or increase the potential and capacity of countries to promote economic and social development and welfare, including the transfer of resources to developing countries or regions in a tangible or intangible form.

Expenditures on operational activities for development are financed from contributions from governments and other official and non official sources to a variety of funding channels in the United Nations sys-tem. These include United Nations funds and programmes such as contributions to the United Nations Development Programme, contributions to funds administered by the United Nations Development Programme, and regular (assessed) and other extra budgetary contributions to specialized agencies.

Data are taken from the 2010 report of the Secretary-General to the General Assembly on operational activities for development.

***

Notes techniques

Chapitre I: Aperçu mondial et régional

Tableau 1

Les séries d'agrégats mondiaux sur la population, la production, le commerce extérieur et les finances ont été établies à partir de publications statistiques et bases de données des Nations Unies et les institutions spécialisées et autres organismes. On doit se référer aux sources pour tous renseignements détaillés sur les méthodes de calcul et la portée des statistiques.

Tableau 2

Le tableau présente les estimations mondiales et régionales de la population, des taux d'accroissement de la population, des taux bruts de natalité et de mortalité, de la superficie et de la densité de population. Sauf indication contraire, tous les chiffres sont des estimations de l'ordre de grandeur et comportent une assez grande marge d'erreur.

Les estimations de la population et tous les taux présentés dans ce tableau ont été établis par la Division de la population du Secrétariat des Nations Unies et publiés dans World Population Prospects: The 2010 Revision. Les pourcentages annuels moyens de l'accroissement de la population ont été calculés par la Division de la population du Secrétariat des Nations Unies, sur la base d'une formule de taux d'accroissement exponentiel.

Les taux bruts de natalité et de mortalité sont exprimés, respectivement, sur la base du nombre annuel moyen de naissances et de décès par tranche de 1.000 habitants au milieu de l'année. Ces taux sont estimatifs. On a déterminé les superficies totales en additionnant les chiffres correspondant aux différents pays ou régions. La densité est le nombre de personnes de la population totale de 2010 par kilomètre carré de la superficie totale.

Le schéma de régionalisation utilisé aux fins de l'établissement de ces estimations est présenté dans l'annexe I. Bien que les totaux de certains continents soient donnés et que tous puissent être déterminés, le schéma de base présente les grandes régions qui sont établies de manière à obtenir une plus grande homogénéité en ce qui concerne l'ampleur des populations, les types de conditions démographiques et la précision des statistiques démographiques.

Tableau 3-4

Les indices du tableau 3 se rapportent à la production agricole, qui est définie comme comprenant à la fois les produits de l'agriculture et de l'élevage. Les semences et les aliments pour les animaux sont exclus de cette définition. Les indices de la production alimentaire se rapportent aux produits considérés comme comestibles et contenant des éléments nutritifs. Le café, le thé et les produits non comestibles sont exclus.

Les indices de la production agricole et de la production alimentaire présentés au tableau 4 sont calculés selon la formule de Laspeyres avec les années 1999-2001 comme période de référence, cela afin de limiter l'incidence, sur les indices correspondant à la période considérée, des fluctuations annuelles de la production agricole enregistrée pendant les années de référence. Les chiffres de production de chaque produit sont pondérés par les prix nationaux moyens à la production pour la période 1999-2001 et additionnés pour chaque année. Les indices sont fondés sur les données de production de l'année civile.

Les indices pour le monde et les régions sont calculés de la même façon que les indices par pays, mais au lieu d'appliquer des prix différents aux produits de base pour chaque groupe de pays, on a utilisé des "prix internationaux" établis d'après la formule de Gheary-Khamis pour tous les groupes de pays. Cette méthode attribue un seul "prix" à chaque produit de base.

Les indices du tableau 4 sont calculés comme ratio entre les indices de la production alimentaire et de la production agricole totale du tableau 3 décrits ci-dessus et les indices de population correspondants.

Pour tout renseignement complémentaire sur les séries présentées dans ces tableaux, voir l'*Annuaire Statistique de la FAO* et http://faostat.fao.org.

Tableau 5

On trouvera une description de la série de statistiques du tableau 5 dans les notes techniques du chapitre XIII.

Tableau 6

On trouvera une description de la série de statistiques du tableau 6 dans les notes techniques du chapitre XVI. La composition des régions est présentée au tableau 54.

Chapitre II: Population

Le tableau est fondé sur des données détaillées sur la population, sa croissance et sa distribution, publiées dans l'*Annuaire démographique des Nations Unies*. Le tableau inclut seulement des estimations officielles de la population qui ont été envoyées à la Division de Statistique des Nations Unies. Pour une description complète des méthodes d'évaluation et une indication des limites des données, voir l'*Annuaire démographique*.

Sauf indication contraire, les chiffres se rapportent à la population effectivement présente sur le territoire tel qu'il est actuellement défini; les estimations de superficie comprennent les étendues d'eau intérieures.

Tableau 7

Les statistiques sur la population urbaine, la population rurale, les taux d'accroissement et population de l'agglomération urbaine la plus peuplée de chaque pays ou zone sont des estimations et projections publiées par la Division de la population du Département des affaires économiques et sociales du Secrétariat des Nations Unies dans "World Urbanization Prospects: The 2011 Revision." Il n'existe pas de définition reconnue à l'échelle internationale des zones urbaines et rurales parce que les caractéristiques retenues pour distinguer ces deux types de zone diffèrent d'un pays à un autre. Dans la plupart des pays, cette distinction est essentiellement une fonction de la taille des agglomérations. Pour la définition la plus récente des zones urbaines utilisée dans une région ou un pays donné, se reporter à l'*Annuaire démographique*.

Tableau 8

L'agglomération urbaine comprend la ville proprement dite et ses faubourgs ou banlieues, et tout territoire à forte densité de population situé à sa périphérie. Les agglomérations urbaines les plus peuplées se rapportent à celles habitées par 750 000 personnes ou plus. Les taux annuels de variation des populations urbaines et rurales se calculent sur la base de la variation annuelle moyenne en pourcentage déterminée à partir des estimations de la population au milieu de l'année.

Chapitre III: La situation de femmes

Ces trois tableaux sur la répartition des sexes figurant dans le présent chapitre reposent tous sur des indicateurs liés aux objectifs du Millénaire pour le développement. Pour plus d'informations sur les objectifs du Millénaire pour le développement, veuillez consulter le site Web suivant : mdgs.un.org.

Tableau 9

Ce tableau indique le pourcentage des sièges des chambres uniques ou basses des parlements nationaux occupés par des femmes. Les parlements nationaux peuvent être bicaméraux ou unicaméraux. Ce tableau porte sur la chambre unique des parlements unicaméraux et sur la chambre basse des parlements bicaméraux. Il ne porte pas sur la chambre haute des parlements bicaméraux. Les sièges sont habituellement attribués aux membres à l'issue d'élections parlementaires générales. Certains sièges peuvent aussi être pourvus à l'issue de nominations, d'élections indirectes, de roulement des membres et d'élections partielles.

La proportion d'élues est obtenue en divisant le nombre total de sièges occupés par des femmes par le nombre total de sièges que compte le parlement. Les statistiques ne sont ni pondérées ni normalisées.

La source de ce tableau est l'Union interparlementaire. Pour plus d'informations, veuillez consulter le site Web suivant : www.ipu.org.

Tableau 10

La proportion des femmes rémunérées dans le secteur non agricole correspond au pourcentage du nombre total de salariés employés dans le secteur agricole qui sont des femmes.

Le secteur non agricole comprend l'industrie et les services. L'"industrie" comporte les industries extractives (y compris la production pétrolière), le secteur manufacturier, le bâtiment, l'électricité, le gaz et l'eau, correspondant aux divisions 2 à 5 de la Classification internationale type, par industrie, de toutes les branches d'activité économique (CITI) et aux catégories C à F de la CITI-Rev.3. Les "services" comportent le commerce de gros et de détail, la restauration et l'hôtellerie; les transports, l'entreposage et les communications; les finances, les assurances, l'immobilier et les services commerciaux; et les services communautaires, sociaux et personnels, correspondant aux divisions 6 à 9 de la CITI-Rev.2 et aux catégories G à Q de la CITI-Rev.3.

L'emploi se rapporte aux personnes d'un âge minimum donné qui ont travaillé ou occupé un emploi pendant une période donnée de référence (conformément à la résolution de l'OIT sur les statistiques de la population économiquement active, l'emploi, le chômage et le sous-emploi, adoptée par la treizième Conférence internationale des statisticiens du travail (CIST), octobre 1982).

L'emploi salarié se réfère uniquement aux travailleurs salariés ou recevant un traitement et aux personnes dans des emplois rémunérés. Les employés sont généralement rémunérés par des salaires et des traitements, mais leur rémunération peut aussi provenir de commissions, de travaux à la pièce, de primes ou d'avantages en nature tels que repas, logement, formation, etc. Il s'agit de salariés par opposition aux travailleurs indépendants – employeurs, travailleurs à leur compte, membres de coopératives de producteurs et travailleurs familiaux. Les différentes situations d'après la profession sont définies conformément à la résolution de l'OIT concernant la Classification internationale d'après la situation dans la profession (CISP), adoptée par la quinzième Conférence internationale des statisticiens du travail (CIST) (1993).

La source de ce tableau est l'Organisation internationale du Travail (OIT). Pour plus d'informations, veuillez consulter le site Web suivant : http://laborsta.ilo.org.

Tableau 11

Ce tableau indique la proportion de filles par rapport aux garçons (indice de parité des sexes) dans l'enseignement primaire, secondaire et supérieur, à savoir le rapport entre le nombre de filles inscrites dans l'enseignement primaire, secondaire et supérieur et le nombre de garçons à chaque niveau. Pour normaliser les effets de la pyramide des âges, l'indice de parité des sexes du taux brut de scolarisation pour chaque niveau d'enseignement est utilisé.

La source de ce tableau est l'Institut de statistique de l'UNESCO. Pour plus d'informations, veuillez consulter le site Web suivant : www.uis.unesco.org.

Chapitre IV: Education

On trouvera des données détaillées et des notes explicatives sur l'éducation sur le site Web de l'Institut de statistique de l'UNESCO www.uis.unesco.org. Ci-après figurent des notes sommaires, relatives aux principaux éléments d'information statistique figurant dans les tableaux 9 et 10

Les définitions et classifications appliquées par l'UNESCO sont tirées de la Recommandation révisée concernant la normalisation internationale des statistiques de l'éducation (1978) et des versions de 1976 et de 1997 de la Classification internationale type de l'éducation (CITE). La terminologie utilisée dans le tableau 12 est celle de la CITE-1997.

Tableau 12

Dans la CITE, les niveaux d'enseignement sont définis comme suit:

Enseignement primaire (niveau 1 de la CITE): Programmes s'articulant normalement autour d'une unité ou d'un projet visant à donner aux élèves un solide enseignement de base en lecture, en écriture et en mathématiques et des connaissances élémentaires dans d'autres matières telles que l'histoire, la géographie, les sciences naturelles, les sciences sociales, le dessin et la musique. Dans certains cas, une instruction religieuse est aussi considérée. Appelé parfois enseignement élémentaire.

Enseignement secondaire (niveaux 2 et 3 de la CITE): Le premier cycle de l'enseignement secondaire (CITE 2) est généralement destiné à compléter les programmes de base de l'enseignement primaire mais dont l'enseignement est généralement plus orienté vers les matières enseignées faisant appel à des enseignants plus spécialisés. La fin de ce niveau coïncide souvent avec celle de la scolarité obligatoire. Dans le deuxième cycle de l'enseignement secondaire (CITE 3), étape finale de l'enseignement secondaire dans plusieurs pays, l'enseignement est souvent organisé en une plus grande spécialisation et les enseignants doivent souvent être plus qualifiés ou spécialisés qu'au niveau 2 de la CITE.

Enseignement supérieur (niveaux 5 et 6 de la CITE): Programmes dont le contenu est plus avancé que celui offert aux niveaux 3 et 4 de la CITE. Le premier cycle de l'enseignement supérieur, niveau 5 de la CITE, couvre le niveau 5A, composé de programmes fondés dans une large mesure sur la théorie et destinés à offrir des qualifications suffisantes pour être admis à suivre des programmes de recherche de pointe ou à exercer une profession exigeant de hautes compétences; et le niveau 5B, dont les programmes sont dans une large mesure d'ordre pratique, technique et/ou spécifiquement professionnel. Le deuxième cycle de l'enseignement supérieur, niveau 6 de la CITE, comprend des programmes consacrés à des études approfondies et à des travaux de recherche originaux, et conduisant à l'obtention d'un titre de chercheur hautement qualifié.

La CITE de 1997 a également introduit une nouvelle catégorie (ou nouveau niveau) entre l'enseignement secondaire et l'enseignement supérieur, appelée enseignement postsecondaire non supérieur (niveau 4 de la CITE). À ce niveau se trouvent des programmes qui, du point de vue des établissements, sont intermédiaires entre le deuxième cycle du secondaire et le premier cycle du supérieur, encore qu'il serait tout à fait possible de les considérer, dans le contexte national, comme appartenant au deuxième cycle du secondaire ou au supérieur. Ils ne sont souvent pas beaucoup plus avancés que des programmes du niveau 3 de la CITE (deuxième cycle du secondaire) mais servent à élargir les connaissances de ceux qui les suivent et qui ont déjà achevé un programme de niveau 3. Les étudiants y sont généralement plus âgés que ceux du niveau 3. Pour la plupart, ces programmes du niveau 4 de la CITE ont une durée comprise entre six mois et deux ans.

Tableau 13

Les données relatives aux dépenses publiques afférentes à l'éducation se rapportent aux dépenses courantes et en capital de l'éducation engagées par l'administration au niveau local, régional, national/central, y inclus les municipalités. Les contributions des ménages sont exclues. Les dépenses ordinaires (ou courantes) en éducation se réfèrent aux dépenses couvrant les biens et les services consommés dans l'année en cours et qui doivent être renouvelées périodiquement. Elles comprennent les dépenses en: salaires et avantages du personnel, services achetés ou assurés sous contrat, l'achat d'autres ressources y compris les manuels scolaires et du matériel pour l'enseignement, les services sociaux et d'autres dépenses de fonctionnement telles que les subventions aux étudiants et aux ménages, les fournitures et l'équipement, les réparations légères, les combustibles, les télécommunications, les voyages, les assurances et les loyers. Dépenses en capital pour l'éducation se réfèrent aux dépenses qui couvrent l'achat de biens d'une durée supérieure à une année. Elles peuvent comprendre les dépenses de construction, de rénovation et de grosses réparations de bâtiments, ainsi que l'achat d'équipements ou véhicules.

Chapitre V: Nutrition et santé

Tableau 14

Les estimations sur les disponibilités alimentaires sont publiées par l'Organisation des Nations Unies pour l'alimentation et l'agriculture dans les Bilans alimentaires et sur le site Web http://faostat.fao.org où les données donnent des estimations des disponibilités alimentaires par habitant par jour en calories. Les disponibilités par habitant exprimées en poids du produit sont calculées à partir des disponibilités totales pour la consommation humaine (c'est-à-dire "Alimentation humaine") en divisant ce chiffre par la population totale qui a effectivement eu accès aux approvisionnements alimentaires durant la période de référence, c'est-à-dire par la population présente (de facto) dans les limites géographiques actuelles du pays. En d'autres termes, les ressortissants du pays vivant à l'étranger durant la période de référence sont exclus, mais les étrangers vivant dans le pays sont inclus. Des ajustements ont été opérés chaque fois que possible pour tenir compte des présences ou des absences de durée limitée, comme dans le cas des immigrants/émigrants temporaires, des touristes et des réfugiés bénéficiant de programmes alimentaires spéciaux (s'il n'a pas été possible de tenir compte des vivres fournis à ce titre à travers les importations). Dans la plupart des cas, les données démographiques utilisées sont les estimations au milieu de l'année publiées par la Division de la population des Nations Unies.

Les disponibilités alimentaires par habitant ne représentent donc que les disponibilités moyennes pour l'ensemble de la population et n'indiquent pas nécessairement la consommation effective des individus. Même si elles sont considérées comme une estimation approximative de la consommation par habitant, il importe de ne pas oublier que la consommation peut varier beaucoup selon les individus.

Tableau 15

La proportion de la population n'atteignant pas le niveau minimal d'apport calorique est le pourcentage de la population dont la consommation de produits alimentaires reste insuffisante pour atteindre le niveau minimal d'apport calorique. On parle aussi de la prévalence de la sous-alimentation, à savoir le pourcentage de la population sous-alimentée.

Chapitre VI: Communication et culture

Les données présentées dans les Tableaux 16 à 18 proviennent de la base de données (voir www.itu.int) et l'*Annuaire statistique*, Services de télécommunications de l'Union internationale des télécommunications.

Tableau 16

Les abonnés mobiles (et les abonnés mobiles pour 100 habitants) désignent les utilisateurs de téléphones portatifs abonnés à un service automatique public de téléphones mobiles ayant accès au Réseau de téléphone public connecté (RTPC). Sont pris en compte aussi bien les abonnements post-payés que les cartes prépayées. Le nombre d'abonnés pour 100 habitants se calcule en divisant le nombre d'abonnés par la population et en multipliant par 100.

Tableau 17

Le nombre total d'abonnements internet fixes (filaires) est le nombre total d'abonnements internet ayant un accès fixe (filaire), qui comprend les abonnements par connexion téléphonique, et l'ensemble des abonnements large bande fixes (filaires). Seuls les abonnements actifs qui ont utilisé ce système pendant les trois derniers mois devraient être comptabilisés.

Tableau 18

Les données concernent les établissements fixes et les cinémas itinérants d'exploitation commerciale de films longs. Le terme établissement fixe désigne tout établissement doté de son propre équipement; il englobe les salles fermées (c'est-à-dire celles où un toit fixe recouvre la plupart des places assises), les cinémas de plein air et les cinémas pour automobilistes ou drive-ins (conçus pour permettre aux spectateurs d'assister à la projection sans quitter leur voiture). Les cinémas itinérants sont définis comme groupes mobiles de projection équipés de manière à pouvoir être utilisés dans des lieux différents.

La capacité d'allocation des places de cinémas fixes est la somme du nombre de sièges dans les salles fermées et les cinémas de plein air, plus le nombre de places d'automobiles multiplié par le facteur 4 dans le cas des drive-ins.

La fréquentation des cinémas est calculée sur la base du nombre de billets vendus au cours d'une année donnée.

En général, les statistiques présentées ne concernent que les établissements commerciaux: toutefois, dans le cas des cinémas itinérants, il se peut que les données relatives à certains pays tiennent compte aussi des établissements non-commerciaux.

Chapitre VII: Comptabilités nationales et production industrielle

La Division de statistique du Département des affaires économiques et sociales du Secrétariat de l'Organisation des Nations Unies établit et publie chaque année des données détaillées, comparables au plan international, sur les comptes nationaux. On trouvera un résumé de l'appareil conceptuel, des classifications et des définitions des opérations dans National Accounts Statistics: Analysis of Main Aggregates, publication annuelle des Nations Unies, qui présente, sous forme de tableaux analytiques, un choix d'agrégats essentiels de comptabilité nationale, issus des comptes nationaux détaillés de plus que 200 pays et territoires. On n'a rien négligé pour présenter les chiffres des différents pays et territoires sous une forme facilitant les comparaisons internationales.

Tableau 19

Ce tableau fait apparaître le produit intérieur brut (PIB) total et par habitant, exprimé en dollars des États-Unis aux prix courants et à prix constants (base 2005), ainsi que les taux de croissance correspondants. Le tableau est conçu pour faciliter les comparaisons internationales du revenu issu de la production. Afin que la couverture soit comparable pour le plus grand nombre possible de pays, la Division de statistique s'appuie non seulement sur les chiffres officiels du PIB exprimé dans la monnaie nationale, mais aussi sur diverses données provenant de sources nationales et internationales. Les taux de conversion utilisés pour exprimer les données nationales en dollars des États-Unis sont, pour les membres du Fonds monétaire international (FMI), les moyennes pour la période considérée des taux de change du marché. Ces derniers, publiés dans Statistiques financières internationales, sont communiqués au FMI par les banques centrales des pays et reposent sur trois types de taux : a) taux du marché, déterminés dans une large mesure par les facteurs du marché; b) taux officiels, déterminés par les pouvoirs publics; c) taux principaux, pour les pays pratiquant différents arrangements en matière de taux de change. On donne toujours la priorité aux taux du marché, n'utilisant les taux officiels que lorsqu'on n'a pas de taux du marché libre.

Pour les pays qui ne sont pas membres du FMI, on utilise les moyennes des taux de change opérationnels de l'ONU (qui servent à des fins comptables pour les opérations de l'ONU avec les pays qui en sont membres). Ces taux reposent sur les taux de change officiels, les taux du commerce et/ou les taux touristiques.

Il faut noter que l'utilisation des taux de change du marché pour la conversion des données se heurte à des obstacles pratiques. On risque, ce faisant, d'aboutir à des fluctuations excessives ou à des distorsions du revenu en dollars de certains pays, surtout dans le cas des pays qui pratiquent plusieurs taux de change et de ceux qui connaissent des taux d'inflation exceptionnels ou des décalages provenant des fluctuations du marché. Les comparaisons de revenu entre pays sont donc sujettes à caution lorsqu'on se fonde sur le revenu exprimé en dollars des États-Unis.

D'autres méthodes ont été élaborées ces dernières années pour les comparaisons internationales. L'une, celle de la parité de pouvoir d'achat (PPA), procède du Programme de comparaison internationale ; une autre méthode de conversion, celle de l'Atlas de la Banque mondiale, est basée sur la moyenne des taux de change de l'année en cours et des deux années immédiatement précédentes, ajustés en fonction des différences d'inflation entre les pays considérés et la moyenne des pays du G-5 (Allemagne, États-Unis, France, Japon, et Royaume-Uni). La Division de statistique de l'ONU a mis au point la méthode des Taux de Change Corrigés des Prix (TCCP) qui, comme celle de l'Atlas, est conçue pour corriger les taux de change qui ne rendent pas convenablement compte de l'évolution relative de l'inflation dans un pays par rapport à l'inflation à l'échelon international. Le TCCP sert surtout pour les pays à taux de change fixe et ceux qui connaissent une période de forte inflation (par ex. les pays en transition entre 1990 et 1995).

La série de statistiques du PIB à prix constants est fondée principalement sur des données officiellement communiquées par les pays, et en partie sur des estimations de la Division de statistique; les données permettent de calculer des indices, la base 100 correspondant à 2005. Les chiffres ainsi obtenus sont alors convertis en dollars des États-Unis au taux de change de l'année de base (2005). Les taux de croissance sont calculés à partir des estimations du PIB aux prix constants de 2005. Le taux de croissance de l'année considérée est obtenu en divisant le PIB de l'année par celui de l'année précédente.

Tableau 20

Ce tableau envisage le développement économique sous l'angle d'une analyse de l'évolution des prix et des taux de change par rapport à la croissance économique mondiale.

Les indices du PIB fondés sur les prix courants exprimés en monnaies nationales et en dollars des États-Unis sont indiqués dans les colonnes 1 et 2. L'évolution annuelle du PIB en volume apparaît dans la colonne 3, les indices étant fondés sur l'évolution du PIB à prix constants.

La colonne 4 présente l'évolution des indices des prix exprimés en monnaie nationale et la colonne 5 celle des indices des prix exprimés en dollars des États-Unis. Les indices de prix dans les colonnes 4 et 5 sont obtenus en divisant, respectivement, les indices du PIB fondés sur les prix courants exprimés en monnaies nationales et en dollars des États-Unis, qui sont indiqués dans les colonnes 1 et 2, par les indices de volume présentés dans la colonne 3.

La colonne 6 montre l'évolution implicite des taux de change obtenue soit en divisant les déflateurs du PIB en monnaie nationale (colonne 4) par les déflateurs du PIB convertis en dollars (colonne 5), soit en divisant les indices du PIB exprimés en monnaies nationales (colonne 1) par les indices exprimés en dollars des États-Unis (colonne 2).

Tableau 21

Le tableau montre la répartition (en pourcentage) du PIB aux prix courants par catégorie de dépense. Il indique la part du PIB consacrée aux dépenses de consommation du secteur des ménages (y compris les institutions sans but lucratif au service des ménages) et des administrations publiques et celle qui est consacrée à l'investissement fixe brut, celle qui correspond aux variations de stocks et celle qui correspond aux exportations de biens et services, déduction faite des importations de biens et services. Ces pourcentages sont calculés à partir des chiffres officiels communiqués à l'ONU par les pays, publiés dans l'ouvrage annuel.

Tableau 22

Ce tableau montre la répartition (en pourcentage) de la valeur ajoutée par branche d'activité, selon le classement retenu dans la Classification internationale type, par industrie, de toutes les branches d'activité économique, Révision 3 (CITI Révision 3). Il rend donc compte de la structure économique de la production dans chaque pays. Les pourcentages sont établis à partir des chiffres officiels de valeur ajoutée brute aux prix de base courants, répartis selon les différentes catégories d'activité économique: agriculture, chasse, sylviculture et pêche (CITI   A-B); activités extractives, activités de fabrication, production et distribution d'électricité, de gaz et d'eau (CITI C-E); activités de fabrication (CITI D); construction (CITI F); commerce de gros et de détail, réparation de véhicules automobiles, de motocycles et de biens personnels et domestiques, hôtels et restaurants (CITI G-H); transports, entreposage et communications (I) et "autres activités", y compris intermédiation financière (J), immobilier, locations et activités de services aux entreprises (K), administration publique et défense, sécurité sociale obligatoire (L), éducation (M), santé et action sociale (N), autres activités de services collectifs, sociaux et personnels (O), et ménages privés employant du personnel domestique (P).

Tableau 23

Les indices nationaux de ce tableau sont donnés pour les catégories "Industries extractives", "Industries manufacturières" et "Électricité, gaz et eau". Ces industries correspondent aux catégories B, C et D de la Classification internationale type, par industrie, de toutes les branches d'activité économique (CITI Révision 4). Les données ont été collectées au niveau des catégories à deux chiffres (divisions), mais sont présentées reflétant les principaux sous-secteurs d'activité industrielle. Tous les indices pour lesquels les catégories s'écartent sensiblement de celles de la CITI sont signalés en note au tableau.

Les coefficients de pondération utilisés pour le calcul des indices d'un pays donné correspondent à la part de la valeur ajoutée de la branche considérée dans le produit intérieur brut (PIB) pendant l'année de référence (2005). Cette part de la valeur ajoutée est mesurée au coût des facteurs. Si nécessaire, les indices nationaux ont été recalculés pour correspondre à 2005=100.

Chapitre VIII: Statistiques financières

Les informations détaillées et les chiffres courants concernant les tableaux 24 et 25 figurent dans les Statistiques financières internationales publiées par le Fonds monétaire international (voir aussi www.imf.org) et dans le Bulletin mensuel de statistique des Nations Unies.

Tableau 24

Les taux d'escomptes indiqués représentent les taux que la banque centrale applique à ses prêts ou auquel elle réescompte les effets escomptables des banques créatrices de monnaie (généralement, taux de fin de période).

Tableau 25

Les taux indiqués représentent le taux des bons du Trésor et le taux du marché monétaire à court terme. Le taux des bons du Trésor est le taux auquel les effets à court terme sont émis ou négociés sur le marché. Le taux du marché monétaire est le taux prêteur à court terme entre institutions financières.

Chapitre IX: Main-d'œuvre

Des données détaillées sur la main-d'œuvre et des sujets connexes sont publiées dans l'*Annuaire des Statistiques du Travail du BIT* et sur le site Web du BIT http://laborsta.ilo.org. La série indiquée dans l'*Annuaire des Statistiques* donne un tableau d'ensemble des disponibilités de main-d'œuvre et de l'emploi de ces ressources et, combinées à d'autres indicateurs économiques, elles peuvent être utiles pour une évaluation générale de la performance économique. L'*Annuaire des statistiques du Travail du BIT* donne une description complète de la méthodologie employée pour établir les séries sur la main-d'œuvre. On trouvera ci-dessous quelques brèves définitions des grandes catégories de statistiques du travail.

L'emploi se rapporte aux personnes un âge déterminé qui, pendant une période donnée, ont travaillé ou occupé un emploi dans l'une des categories suivantes :

Les emplois rémunérés comprennent les personnes rémunérées par des salaires et des traitements pendant une période donnée ou les personnes employées mais absents temporairement due à des vacances, grèves ou congé d'études.

Les emplois indépendants comprennent les employeurs, les travailleurs à leur compte, les membres de coopératives de producteurs, les personnes engagées dans la production de biens et services pour leur propre consommation et les travailleurs familiaux non- rémunérés.

Les membres des forces armées, étudiants, femmes au foyer et autres personnes principalement engagées dans des activités non économiques durant la période donnée qui, en même temps, ont un emploi salarié ou à leur compte sont considérées comme ayant un emploi sur la même base que les autres catégories.

Pour diverses raisons, les définitions nationales de l'emploi diffèrent souvent des définitions internationales standard recommandées et limitent ainsi la comparabilité internationale. Les comparaisons entre pays sont aussi compliquées par une variété des types de systèmes de collecte des données utilisés pour obtenir des informations sur les personnes employées.

Tableau 26

Tableau de l'emploi présente des chiffres absolus sur la répartition des salariés par activité économique, selon la CITI, Rev.3. La colonne de l'emploi total comprend les activités économiques incorrectement définies qui ne sont pas comptabilisées dans les autres catégories. Les données sont organisées, autant que possible, selon la Classification internationale type, par industrie, de toutes les branches d'activité économique.

Chapitre X: Salaires et prix

Tableau 27

Les séries se rapportent généralement aux gains moyens des salariés des industries manufacturières (activités de fabrication), suivant la Classification internationale type, par industrie, de toutes les branches d'activité économique (CITI, Rev. 2 ou Rev.3). Les données sont publiées dans l'*Annuaire des statistiques du travail du BIT* et sur le site Web du BIT http://laborsta.ilo.org et généralement portent sur l'ensemble des salariés (qu'ils perçoivent un salaire ou un traitement au mois) des deux sexes, indépendamment de leur âge.

Les données qui portent exclusivement sur les salariés horaires (ouvriers, travailleurs manuels), sur les employés percevant un traitement (travailleurs autres que manuels, cadres), ou sur l'emploi total sont aussi présentées si elles sont disponibles. Les gains comprennent en général les primes, les indemnités pour coût de la vie, les impôts, les cotisations de sécurité sociale à la charge de l'employé, et dans certains cas des paiements en nature, mais ne comprennent pas en règle générale la part patronale des cotisations d'assurance sociale, les allocations familiales et les autres prestations de sécurité sociale. La période de l'année visée par les données n'est pas la même pour tous les pays. Dans certains cas, les séries présentent les taux horaires et non pas les gains, ce présente qui est alors signalé en note.

Tableau 28

Un indice est généralement estimé à partir d'une suite de mesures synthétiques des variations relatives, d'une période à l'autre, des prix d'un ensemble fixe de biens et de services de consommation constants en quantité et par leurs caractéristiques, acquis, utilisés ou payés par la population de référence. Chaque mesure synthétique est obtenue comme une moyenne pondérée d'un grand nombre d'indices de prix d'agrégats élémentaires. L'indice de chaque agrégat élémentaire est estimé au moyen d'un échantillon de prix pour un ensemble fixe de biens et de services que se procurent les individus de la population de référence dans une région donnée, ou qui habitent cette région, auprès d'un ensemble spécifié de points de vente ou auprès d'autres fournisseurs de biens et de services de consommation.

Le tableau présente les indices généraux des prix à la consommation pour tous les groupes d'articles de consommation combinés, et un indice "Alimentation", y compris les boissons non alcoolisées seulement. Dans le cas où les boissons alcoolisées et/ou le tabac sont compris dans le groupe "alimentation", l'utilisateur sera informé par un appel de note.

Chapitre XI: Agriculture, forêts et pêche

Les séries présentées sur l'agriculture et la pêche ont été fournies par l'Organisation des Nations Unies pour l'alimentation et l'agriculture (FAO) et portent principalement sur les tendances à long terme de la croissance de la production agricole et des approvisionnements alimentaires, et sur la production des principales denrées agricoles et la production halieutique.

La production agricole se définit comme comprenant l'ensemble des produits agricoles et des produits de l'élevage à l'exception de ceux utilisés comme semences et comme aliments pour les animaux, et pour les autres utilisations intermédiaires en agriculture; par exemple, on déduit les œufs utilisés pour la reproduction. L'apport intermédiaire de semences et d'aliments pour les animaux et d'autres éléments similaires se rapportent à la fois à des produits locaux et importés. Pour tous détails complémentaires, on se reportera à l'*annuaire statistique de la FAO*. Des statistiques peuvent également être consultées sur le site Web de la FAO http://faostat.fao.org.

Tableau 29

"L'agriculture" se rapporte à la production de tous les produits de l'agriculture et de l'élevage. "L'indice des produits alimentaires" comprend les produits considérés comme comestibles et qui contiennent des éléments nutritifs. Les indices de la production agricole et de la production alimentaire sont calculés selon la formule de Laspeyres avec les années 1999-2001 pour période de base. Le choix d'une période de plusieurs années permet de diminuer l'incidence des fluctuations annuelles de la production agricole pendant les années de base sur les indices pour cette période. Les quantités produites de chaque denrée sont pondérées par les prix nationaux moyens à la production de 1999-2001, et additionnées pour chaque année. Les indices sont fondés sur les données de production d'une année civile. Ils peuvent différer dans certains cas des indices effectivement établis et publiés par les pays eux-mêmes par suite de différences dans les concepts, la couverture, les pondérations et les méthodes de calcul. On s'est efforcé d'estimer ces différences méthodologiques afin de rendre les données plus facilement comparables à l'échelle internationale. Des chiffres détaillés de production sont publiés dans l'*Annuaire statistique de la FAO*.

Tableau 30

On désigne sous le nom de cultures oléagineuses l'ensemble des cultures produisant des graines, des noix ou des fruits, essentiellement destinées à l'extraction d'huiles alimentaires ou industrielles, à l'exclusion des huiles essentielles. Dans ce tableau, les chiffres se rapportent à la production totale de graines, noix et fruits oléagineux récoltés au cours de l'année de référence. Bien entendu, la production totale d'oléagineux n'est jamais transformée intégralement en huile, car des quantités importantes qui varient suivant les cultures sont également utilisées pour les semailles, l'alimentation animale et l'alimentation humaine. Toutefois, bien que les taux d'extraction d'huile varient selon les pays, on a appliqué dans ce tableau le même taux à tous les pays pour chaque oléagineux. En outre, il ne faut pas oublier que les produits récoltés au cours des derniers mois de l'année sont généralement transformés en huile dans le courant de l'année suivante.

En dépit de ces imperfections qui concernent le champ d'application, les taux d'extraction et les périodes de référence, les chiffres présentés ici sont utiles, car ils donnent une indication valable des variations de volume que la production totale d'oléagineux enregistre d'une année à l'autre. La production mondiale effective d'huiles végétales atteint 80 pour cent environ de la production indiquée ici. En outre, environ 2 millions de tonnes d'huiles végétales sont produites chaque année à partir de cultures non comprises dans les catégories définies ci dessus. Les principales sont l'huile de germes de maïs et l'huile de son de riz. La production mondiale effective tourteau/farine d'oléagineux représente environ 80 pour cent de la production indiquée.

Tableau 31

Les données sur la production de céréales se rapportent uniquement aux céréales récoltées pour le grain sec; celles cultivées pour le foin, le fourrage vert ou le pâturage en sont exclues.

Tableau 32

Les données sur le bois rond se réfèrent au bois brut, bois à l'état naturel, tel qu'il a été abattu ou récolté autrement, avec ou sans écorce, fendu, grossièrement équarri ou sous une autre forme (par exemple, racines, souches, loupes, etc.). Il peut être également imprégné (par exemple, dans le cas des poteaux télégraphiques) et dégrossi ou taillé en pointe. Cette catégorie comprend tous les bois provenant des quantités enlevées en forêt ou provenant des arbres poussant hors forêt, y compris le volume récupéré sur les déchets naturels et les déchets d'abattage et de transport pendant la période envisagée (année civile ou forestière).

Tableau 33

Les données ont trait (i) à la pêche maritime et intérieure et (ii) à l'aquaculture, et sont exprimées en poids vif. Elles comprennent poissons, crustacés et mollusques, mais excluent éponges, coraux, perles, algues, crocodiles et les mammifères aquatiques (baleines, dauphins, etc.).

Le pavillon du navire est considéré comme la principale indication de la nationalité de la prise. Les données de pêche maritime comprennent les quantités débarquées par des bateaux nationaux dans des ports étrangers et excluent les quantités débarquées par des bateaux étrangers dans des ports nationaux.

Pour séparer la production d'aquaculture de la pêche de capture, au moins deux critères doivent se vérifier, c'est-à-dire l'intervention humaine dans une ou plusieurs des phases du cycle de croissance, et l'appartenance de l'organisme élevé et récolté à une personne physique, à une personne morale ou à l'état.

Les données sur la production de l'aquaculture sont publiées dans *l'Annuaire statistique des pêches, production de l'aquaculture*; celles sur les captures sont publiées dans *l'Annuaire statistique des pêches, captures*.

Tableau 34

Les données sur les engrais se rapportent en général à une période d'un an comptée du 1er juillet au 30 juin.

Engrais azotés : les données se rapportent à la teneur en azote des engrais commerciaux inorganiques.

Engrais phosphatés : les données se rapportent à l'acide phosphorique (P2O5) et englobent la teneur en (P2O5) des superphosphates, du phosphate d'ammonium et des scories de déphosphoration.

Engrais potassiques : les données se rapportent à la teneur en K2O des produits potassiques commerciaux, muriate, nitrate et sulfate de potasse, sels d'engrais, kaïnite et nitrate de soude potassique.

Chapitre XII: Industries manufacturières

L'activité industrielle comprend les industries extractives (mines et carrières), les industries manufacturières et la production d'électricité, de gaz et d'eau. Ces activités correspondent aux grandes divisions 2, 3 et 4, respectivement, de la Classification internationale type par industrie de toutes les branches d'activité économique. Un grand nombre de ces tableaux sont établis principalement sur la base de données compilée pour l'*Annuaire de statistiques industrielles par produit* des Nations Unies. Les données tirées d'autres sources sont signalées par une note.

En règle générale, les méthodes employées par les pays pour le calcul de leur production industrielle sont conformes à celles dans Recommandations internationales concernant les statistiques industrielles des Nations Unies et offrent une base satisfaisante pour une analyse comparative. Toutefois, dans certains cas, les définitions des méthodes sur lesquelles reposent les calculs de la production diffèrent des directives approuvées. Lorsqu'elles sont connues, les différences sont indiquées par une note.

Tableau 35

Les données sur le sucre proviennent de la base de données et de *l'Annuaire du sucre de l'Organisation internationale du sucre*. Les données présentées portent sur la production et la consommation de sucre centrifugé à partir de la betterave et de la canne à sucre, et se rapportent à des années civiles.

Les données de la consommation se rapportent à la consommation apparente de sucre centrifugé dans le pays en question, y compris le sucre utilisé pour la fabrication de produits à base de sucre, exportés ou non, et le sucre utilisé à d'autres fins que pour la consommation alimentaire humaine. Sauf indication contraire, les statistiques sont exprimées en valeur brute (sucre polarisant à 96 degrés). Le total mondial compris également les données relatives aux pays où la consommation de sucre est inférieure à 10.000 tonnes.

Tableau 36

Les données se réfèrent viande provenant des animaux abattus à l'intérieur des frontières nationales, quelle que soient leurs origines. Les chiffres de production de viande bovine, de buffle, de poulet, de porc (y compris le bacon et le jambon), de mouton et de chèvre se rapportent à la production en poids de carcasses et ne comprennent pas le saindoux, le suif et les abats comestibles. Toutes les données se rapportent à la production totale de viande, c'est-à-dire à la fois aux animaux abattus à des fins commerciales et des animaux sacrifiés à la ferme.

Tableau 37

Les données se rapportent à la bière produite à partir du malte, y compris ale, stout et porter (bière anglaise, blonde et brune).

Tableau 38

Le tableau se rapporte seulement aux cigarettes, sauf indication contraire.

Tableau 39

Le tableau présente les statistiques sur la production de tout papier et carton. Les données comprennent le papier journal, les papiers d'impression et d'écriture, les papiers et cartons de construction, les papiers de ménage et les papiers hygiéniques, les papiers minces spéciaux, les papiers d'empaquetage et d'emballage et carton.

Tableau 40

Les données se rapportent à la production d'aluminium non travaillé obtenue par réduction électrolytique de l'alumine (formes primaires) et par refonte de déchets et débris de métal (formes secondaires).

Tableau 41

Les données sur les récepteurs de radio comprennent les appareils récepteurs de radiodiffusion pouvant fonctionner sans source d'énergie extérieure, y compris les appareils pouvant recevoir également la radiotéléphonie ou la radiotélégraphie, même combinés à un appareil d'enregistrement ou de reproduction du son; appareils récepteurs de radiodiffusion ne pouvant fonctionner qu'avec une source d'énergie extérieure, du type utilisé dans les véhicules automobiles, y compris les appareils pouvant recevoir également la radiotéléphonie ou la radiotélégraphie, même combinés à un appareil d'enregistrement ou de reproduction du son; autres appareils récepteurs de radiodiffusion, y compris les appareils pouvant recevoir également la radiotéléphonie ou la radiotélégraphie, même combinés à un appareil d'enregistrement ou de reproduction du son.

Les données sur les appareils récepteurs de télévision y compris couleur, en noir et blanc ou en autres monochromes. Y compris les appareils incorporant un appareil d'enregistrement ou de reproduction vidéo phonique, les récepteurs de télévision avec écran plat (écran à cristaux liquides ou écran à plasma), récepteurs de signaux vidéo phoniques (tuner) et autres appareils récepteurs téléviseur sans écran.

Tableau 42

Le tableau présente les statistiques sur les machines à laver le linge, même avec dispositif de séchage, et machines à sécher le linge.

Tableau 43

Les données se rapportent sur les machines-outils présentés dans ce tableau comprennent deux types : (i) machines (y compris les unités d'usinage à glissières) à percer, aléser, fraiser, fileter ou tarauder les métaux par enlèvement de matière, autres que les tours et centres de tournage ; (ii) tours y compris les centres de tournage travaillant par enlèvement de métal, horizontaux, à commande numérique ou autres.

Tableau 44

Le tableau présente les statistiques sur les camions - véhicules automobiles non classifié pour le transport de marchandises à l'exception des tombereaux automoteurs conçus pour être utilisés en dehors du réseau routier.

Chapitre XIII: Energie

Tableau 45

Les données relatives aux divers produits énergétiques ont été converties en tonnes d'équivalent pétrole (TEP), dans un souci d'uniformité et pour permettre les comparaisons entre la production de différents pays. Pour passer des unités de mesure d'origine à l'unité commune, les données en unités d'origine (tonnes, terajoules, kilowattheures, mètres cubes) sont multipliées par des facteurs de conversion. Pour une liste des facteurs de conversion appropriée et pour des descriptions détaillées des méthodes appliquées, se reporter à l'*Annuaire des statistiques de l'énergie* des Nations Unies et aux publications méthodologiques apparentées.

Sont compris dans la production d'énergie primaire commerciale: pour les solides, la houille, le lignite, la tourbe et le schiste bitumineux; pour les liquides, le pétrole brut et les liquides de gaz naturel; pour les gaz, le gaz naturel; pour l'électricité, l'électricité primaire de source hydraulique, nucléaire, géothermique, éolienne, marémotrice, des vagues et solaire.

En général, les variations des stocks se rapportent aux différences entre les stocks des producteurs, des importateurs ou des consommateurs industriels au début et à la fin de chaque année. Le commerce international des produits énergétiques est fondé sur le système du "commerce général", c'est-à-dire que tous les biens entrant sur le territoire national d'un pays ou en sortant sont respectivement enregistrés comme importations et exportations.

Les soutes maritimes/aériens se rapportent aux quantités de combustibles livrées aux navires de mer et aéronefs assurant des liaisons commerciales internationales, quel que soit leur pavillon. La consommation des navires effectuant des opérations de transport sur les voies navigables intérieures ou dans les eaux côtières n'est pas incluse, tout comme celle des aéronefs effectuant des vols intérieurs.

Les données sur la consommation se rapportent à la "consommation apparente" et sont obtenues par la formule "production + importations – exportations – soutes +/- variations des stocks". En conséquence, les séries relatives à la consommation apparente peuvent occasionnellement ne donner qu'une indication de l'ordre de grandeur des disponibilités intérieures brutes réelles.

Sont compris dans la consommation d'énergie commerciale: pour les solides, la consommation de combustibles solides primaires, les importations nettes et les variations de stocks de combustibles solides secondaires; pour les liquides, la consommation de produits pétroliers énergétiques y compris les charges d'alimentation des usines de traitement, l'essence naturelle, le condensat et le gaz de raffinerie ainsi que le pétrole brut consommé dans les centrales thermiques pour la production d'électricité; pour les gaz, la consommation de gaz naturel, les importations nettes et les variations de stocks de gaz d'usines à gaz et de gaz de cokerie; pour l'électricité, la production d'électricité primaire et les importations nettes d'électricité.

Tableau 46

Les définitions des produits énergétiques sont données ci-après :

– Houille: Charbon à haut degré de houillification et à pouvoir calorifique brut supérieur à 23 865 kJ/kg (5 700 kcal/kg), valeur mesurée pour un combustible exempt de cendres, mais humide et ayant un indice moyen de réflectance de la vitrinite au moins égal à 0,6. Les schlamms, les mixtes et autres produits du charbon de faible qualité qui ne peuvent être classés en fonction du type de charbon dont ils sont dérivés, sont inclus dans cette rubrique.

– Lignite: Le charbon non agglutinant d'un faible degré de houillification qui a gardé la structure anatomique des végétaux dont il est issu. Son pouvoir calorifique supérieur est inférieur à 17 435 kJ/kg (4 165 kcal/kg) et il contient plus de 31% de matières volatiles sur produit sec exempt de matières minérales.

–Tourbe : Combustible solide issu de la décomposition partielle de végétaux morts dans des conditions de forte humidité et de faible circulation d'air (phase initiale de la houillification). N'est prise en considération ici que la tourbe utilisée comme combustible. La tourbe est utilisée principalement comme combustible domestique.

– Pétrole brut: Huile minérale constituée d'un mélange d'hydrocarbures d'origine naturelle, de couleur variant du jaune au noir, d'une densité et d'une viscosité variable. Figurent également dans cette rubrique les condensats directement récupérés sur les sites d'exploitation des hydrocarbures gazeux (dans les installations prévues pour la séparation des phases liquide et gazeuse), le pétrole brut synthétique, les huiles minérales brutes extraites des roches bitumineuses telles que schistes, sables asphaltiques et les huiles issues de la liquéfaction du charbon.

– Liquides de gaz naturel (LGN): Hydrocarbures liquides ou liquéfiés produits lors de la fabrication, de la purification et de la stabilisation du gaz naturel. Les liquides de gaz naturel comprennent l'éthane, le propane, le butane, le pentane, l'essence naturelle et les condensats d'usine, sans que la liste soit limitative.

– Essence auto : Hydrocarbure léger utilisé dans les moteurs à combustion interne, tels que ceux des véhicules à moteur, à l'exception des aéronefs. Sa température de distillation se situe entre 35°C et 200°C et il est traité de façon à atteindre un indice d'octane suffisamment élevé, généralement entre 80 et 100 IOR. Le traitement peut consister en reformage, mélange avec une fraction aromatique, ou adjonction de benzol ou d'autres additifs (tels que du plomb tétraéthyle).

– Carburéacteurs: Comprennent les carburéacteurs du type essence et les carburéacteurs du type kérosène. Carburéacteurs du type essence: Comprennent tous les hydrocarbures légers utilisés dans les turboréacteurs d'aviation. Leur température de distillation se situe entre 100°C et 250°C et donne au moins 20% en volume de distillat à 143°C. Ils sont obtenus par mélange de pétrole lampant et d'essence ou de naphta de façon que la teneur en composés aromatiques ne dépasse pas 25% en volume. Des additifs y sont ajoutés afin d'abaisser le point de congélation à -58°C ou au-dessous, et de maintenir la tension de vapeur Reid entre 0,14 et 0,21 kg/cm2. Carburéacteurs du type kerosene: Huiles moyennement visqueuses utilisées dans les turboréacteurs d'aviation, ayant les mêmes caractéristiques de distillation et le même point d'éclair que le pétrole lampant et une teneur en composés aromatiques ne dépassant pas 20% en volume. Elles sont traitées de façon à atteindre une viscosité cinématique de moins de 15 cSt à -34°C et un point de congélation inférieur à -50°C.

– Gazole/carburant diesel (mazout distillé): Huiles lourdes dont la température de distillation se situe entre 200°C et 380°C, mais qui donnent moins de 65% en volume de distillat à 250°C (y compris les pertes) et 85% ou davantage à 350°C. Leur point d'éclair est toujours supérieur à 50°C et leur densité supérieure à 0,82. Les huiles lourdes obtenues par mélange sont classées dans la même catégorie que les gazoles à condition que leur viscosité cinématique ne dépasse pas 27,5 cSt à 38°C. Sont compris dans cette rubrique les distillats moyens destinés à l'industrie pétrochimique. Les gazoles servent de carburant pour la combustion interne dans les moteurs diesel, de combustible dans les installations de chauffage telles que les chaudières, et d'additifs destinés à augmenter la luminosité de la flamme du gaz à l'eau. Ce produit est aussi connu sous les appellations de gazole ou gasoil et carburant ou combustible diesel.

– Gaz de pétrole liquéfiés (GPL): Hydrocarbures qui sont à l'état gazeux dans des conditions de température et de pression normales mais sont liquéfiés par compression ou refroidissement pour en faciliter l'entreposage, la manipulation et le transport. Dans cette rubrique figurent le propane et le butane ou un mélange de ces deux hydrocarbures. Est également inclus l'éthane produit dans les raffineries ou dans les installations de séparation et de stabilisation des producteurs de gaz naturel.

– Gaz naturel: gaz constitué essentiellement de méthane, extraits de gisements naturels souterrains. Il peut s'agir aussi bien de gaz non associé (provenant de gisements qui produisent uniquement des hydrocarbures gazeux) que de gaz associé (provenant de gisements qui produisent à la fois des hydrocarbures liquides et gazeux) ou de méthane récupéré dans les mines de charbon et le gaz de gadoues. La production de gaz naturel se rapporte à la production de gaz commercialisable sec, mesurée après purification et extraction des condensats de gaz naturel et du soufre. Les quantités réinjectées, brûlées à la torchère ou éventées et les pertes d'extraction sont exclues des données sur la production.

– La production d'électricité se rapporte à la production brute, qui comprend la consommation des équipements auxiliaires des centrales et les pertes au niveau des transformateurs considérés comme faisant partie intégrante de ces centrales, ainsi que la quantité totale d'énergie électrique produite par les installations de pompage sans déductions de l'énergie électrique absorbée par ces dernières.

Chapitre XIV: Environnement

Tableau 47

Les données relatives aux terres sont compilées par l'Organisation des Nations Unies pour l'alimentation et l'agriculture (FAO). Les définitions de la FAO en ce qui concerne les terres sont les suivantes:

Superficie totale des terres: Superficie totale, à l'exception des eaux intérieures. Les eaux intérieures désignent généralement les principaux fleuves et lacs.

Terres arables: Terres affectées aux cultures temporaires (les terres sur lesquelles est pratiquée la double culture ne sont comptabilisées qu'une fois), prairies temporaires à faucher ou à pâturer, jardins maraîchers ou potagers et terres en jachère temporaire (moins de cinq ans).Cette définition ne comprend pas les terres abandonnées du fait de la culture itinérante. Les données relatives aux terres arables ne peuvent être utilisées pour calculer la superficie des terres aptes à l'agriculture.

Cultures permanentes: Superficie des terres avec des cultures qui occupent la terre pour de longues périodes et qui ne nécessitent pas d'être replantées après chaque récolte, comme le cacao, le café et le caoutchouc. Cette catégorie comprend les terres plantées d'arbustes à fleurs, d'arbres fruitiers, d'arbres à noix et de vignes, mais ne comprend pas les terres plantées d'arbres destinés à la coupe.

Superficie forestière: Dans l'Évaluation des ressources forestières mondiales 2010, la FAO a défini les forêts comme suit : Terres occupant une superficie de plus de 0,5 hectares avec des arbres atteignant une hauteur supérieure à cinq mètres et un couvert arboré de plus de dix pour cent, ou avec des arbres capables d'atteindre ces seuils in situ. Sont exclues les terres à vocation agricole ou urbaine prédominante.

Tableau 48

Les données sur les émissions de dioxyde de carbone (CO_2) proviennent du "Carbon Dioxide Information Analysis Center" (CDIAC) du "Oak Ridge National Laboratory" (États-Unis).

Les estimations du "Carbon Dioxide Information Analysis Center" sont obtenues essentiellement à partir des statistiques de l'énergie des Nations Unies relatives à la consommation de combustibles liquides et solides, à la production et à la consommation de gaz de torche, et des chiffres de production de ciment du "Bureau of Mines" du "Department of Interior" des États-Unis. Les émissions sont indiquées en milliers de tonnes de dioxyde de carbone (à diviser par 3.66406 pour avoir les chiffres de carbone). On peut voir dans le détail les méthodes utilisées pour calculer les émissions dans "Global, Regional, and National Annual CO_2 Emissions Estimates from Fossil Fuel Burning, Hydraulic Cement Production, and Gas Flaring" et sur le site Web du Carbon Dioxide Information Analysis Center (voir http://cdiac.esd.ornl.gov). Par rapport à d'autres sources industrielles pour lesquelles on calcule les émissions de CO_2, les statistiques sur la production de gaz de torche sont rares et sporadiques. Dans les pays où cette production représente une proportion considérable de l'ensemble des émissions de dioxyde de carbone, on peut voir apparaître de ce fait des chiffres parasites ou trompeurs pour ce qui est des tendances des émissions nationales de dioxyde de carbone durant la période visée par le tableau.

Tableau 49

Les données relatives aux espèces menacées pour chaque groupe d'animaux et de plantes, réunies par la Commission de la sauvegarde des espèces de l'Union mondiale pour la nature (UICN), sont publiées dans la Liste rouge des espèces menacées de l'UICN.

Cette liste répertorie les espèces animales considérées comme menacées à l'échelle mondiale, réparties entre les catégories ci-après : éteintes, éteintes à l'état sauvage, gravement menacées d'extinction, menacées d'extinction, vulnérables, quasi menacées, et catégorie à données insuffisantes.

Tableau 50

La proportion de la population ayant accès de façon durable à une source d'eau améliorée (zones urbaines et rurales) est le pourcentage de la population qui utilise l'un des types suivants d'approvisionnement en eau de boisson : eau courante, fontaine publique, forage ou pompe, puits protégé, source protégée ou eau de pluie. Les sources d'eau améliorées ne comprennent pas l'eau fournie par un vendeur, l'eau en bouteille, l'eau fournie par un camion-citerne ou les puits et sources non protégés.

La proportion de la population ayant accès à un système d'assainissement amélioré (zones urbaines et rurales) se réfère au pourcentage de la population ayant accès aux installations qui dans des conditions hygiéniques empêchent l'homme, l'animal ou l'insecte d'entrer en contact avec des excréta humains. Les dispositifs tels que les égouts ou les fosses septiques, les latrines à siphon hydraulique et les latrines simples ou les latrines améliorées à fosse ventilée sont considérés comme appropriés, à condition de ne pas être publics, aux termes du l'Organisation mondiale de la santé et du Fonds des Nations Unies pour l'enfance. Pour être efficaces, ces installations doivent être bien construites et correctement entretenues.

Chapitre XV: Science et technologie

La recherche et le développement expérimental (R-D) englobe tous les travaux de création entrepris de façon systématique en vue d'accroître la somme des connaissances, y compris la connaissance de l'homme, de la culture et de la société, ainsi que l'utilisation de cette somme de connaissances pour de nouvelles applications. Pour tout renseignement complémentaire, voir le site Web de l'Institut de statistique de l'UNESCO **www.uis.unesco.org.**

Tableau 51

Les données présentées sur le personnel employé dans la recherche et le développement (R-D) sont compilées par l'Institut de statistique de l'UNESCO. Les données de certains pays ont été fournies à l'UNESCO par l'OCDE, EUROSTAT et "la Red de Indicadores de Ciencia y Technología (RICYT)".

Les définitions et classifications appliquées par l'UNESCO sont basées sur la Recommandation concernant la normalisation internationale des statistiques relatives à la science et à la technologie (UNESCO, 1978) et sur le Manuel de Frascati (OCDE, 2002).

Les trois catégories du personnel présentées sont définies comme suivant:

Les chercheurs sont des spécialistes travaillant à la conception ou à la création de connaissances, de produits, de procédés, de méthodes et de systèmes, et dans la planification et la gestion de projets de R-D. Les étudiants diplômés ayant des activités de R-D sont considérés comme des chercheurs.

Techniciens et personnel assimilé comprend des personnes dont les tâches principales requièrent des connaissances et une expérience technique dans un ou plusieurs domaines de l'ingénierie, des sciences physiques et de la vie ou des sciences sociales et humaines. Ils participent à la R-D en exécutant des tâches scientifiques et techniques faisant intervenir l'application de principes et de méthodes opérationnelles, généralement sous le contrôle de chercheurs. Pour se distinguer des techniciens qui participent à la R-D sous le contrôle de chercheurs dans les domaines de l'ingénierie, des sciences physiques et de la vie, le personnel assimilé effectue des travaux correspondants dans les sciences sociales et humaines.

Autre personnel de soutien comprend les travailleurs, qualifiés ou non, et le personnel de secrétariat et de bureau qui participent à l'exécution des projets de R-D ou qui sont directement associés à l'exécution de tels projets. Sont inclus dans cette catégorie les gérants et administrateurs qui s'occupent principalement de problèmes financiers, le personnel et l'administration en général, dans la mesure où leurs activités ont une relation directe avec la R-D.

Personnes physiques est le nombre total de personnes qui sont principalement ou partiellement affectées à la R-D. Ce dénombrement inclut les employés à 'temps plein' et les employés à 'temps partiel'. Équivalent temps plein (ETP) peut être considéré comme une année-personne. Ainsi, une personne qui consacre 30% de son temps en R&D et le reste à d'autres activités (enseignement, administration universitaire ou direction d'étudiants) compte pour 0.3 ETP en R&D. De façon analogue, si un employé travaille à temps plein dans un centre de R&D pendant six mois seulement, il compte pour 0.5 ETP.

Tableau 52

Les données présentées sur les dépenses intérieures brutes de recherche et développement sont compilées par l'Institut de statistique de l'UNESCO. Les données de certains pays ont été fournies à l'UNESCO par l'OCDE, EUROSTAT et "la Red de Indicadores de Ciencia y Technología (RICYT)".

La dépense intérieure brute de R-D (DIRD) est la dépense totale intra-muros afférente aux travaux de R-D exécutés sur le territoire national pendant une période donnée. Elle comprend la R-D exécutée sur le territoire national et financée par l'étranger mais ne tient pas compte des paiements effectués à l'étranger pour des travaux de R-D.

Les sources de financement pour la DIRD sont classées selon les cinq catégories suivantes:

Les fonds des entreprises incluent les fonds alloués à la R-D par toutes les firmes, organismes et institutions dont l'activité première est la production marchande de biens ou de services (autres que dans le secteur d'enseignement supérieur) en vue de leur vente au public, à un prix qui correspond à la réalité économique, et les institutions privées sans but lucratif principalement au service de ces entreprises, organismes et institutions.

Les fonds de l'Etat sont les fonds fournis à la R-D par le gouvernement central (fédéral), d'état ou par les autorités locales. Ceci inclut tous les ministères, bureaux et autres organismes qui fournissent, sans normalement les vendre, des services collectifs autres que d'enseignement supérieur, qu'il n'est pas possible d'assurer de façon pratique et économique par d'autres moyens et qui, de surcroît, administrent les affaires publiques et appliquent la politique économique et sociale de la collectivité. Les fonds des entreprises publiques sont compris dans ceux du secteur des entreprises. Les fonds de l'Etat incluent également les institutions privées sans but lucratif contrôlées et principalement financées par l'Etat.

Les fonds de l'enseignement supérieur inclut les fonds fournis à la R-D par les établissements d'enseignement supérieur tels que toutes les universités, grandes écoles, instituts de technologie et autres établissements postsecondaires, ainsi que tous les instituts de recherche, les stations d'essais et les cliniques qui travaillent sous le contrôle direct des établissements d'enseignement supérieur ou qui sont administrés par ces derniers ou leur sont associés.

Les fonds d'institutions privées sans but lucratif sont les fonds destinés à la R-D par les institutions privées sans but lucratif non marchandes au service du public, ainsi que par les simples particuliers ou les ménages.

Les fonds étrangers concernent les fonds destinés à la R-D par les institutions et les individus se trouvant en dehors des frontières politiques d'un pays, à l'exception des véhicules, navires, avions et satellites utilisés par des institutions nationales, ainsi que des terrains d'essai acquis par ces institutions, et par toutes les organisations internationales (à l'exception des entreprises), y compris leurs installations et leurs activités à l'intérieur des frontières d'un pays.

Il faut éviter de comparer les chiffres absolus concernant les dépenses de R-D d'un pays à l'autre. On ne pourrait procéder à des comparaisons détaillées qu'en convertissant en une même monnaie les sommes libellées en monnaie nationale au moyen de taux de change spécialement applicables aux activités de R-D. Les taux de change officiels ne reflètent pas toujours le coût réel des activités de R-D, et les comparaisons établies sur la base de ces taux peuvent conduire à des conclusions trompeuses; toutefois, elles peuvent être utilisées pour donner une idée de l'ordre de grandeur.

Tableau 53

Les brevets sont délivrés par les offices nationaux des brevets, ou par des offices régionaux qui desservent plusieurs pays, par exemple l'Office européen des brevets et l'Organisation régionale africaine de la propriété intellectuelle. Dans le cadre de ces systèmes régionaux, le déposant demande la protection de son invention dans un ou plusieurs pays, et chaque pays décide d'accorder ou non cette protection dans les limites de ses frontières. Le Traité de coopération en matière de brevets (PCT) administré par l'Organisation mondiale de la propriété intellectuelle (OMPI) prévoit le dépôt d'une demande internationale unique, qui a le même effet que des demandes nationales qui auraient été déposées dans les pays désignés.

Les données relatives aux brevets comprennent l'intensité de l'activité brevets, les brevets délivrés et les brevets en vigueur. L'intensité de l'activité est présente sous la forme du nombre de demandes de brevet émanant de résidents par million d'habitants. Un dépôt émanant d'un résident renvoie à une demande déposée auprès de l'office d'un État ou agissant pour le compte d'un État dans lequel est domicilié le déposant de la demande concernée nommé en premier. La délivrance de brevet obéit au même principe. En vigueur se dit d'un brevet ou tout autre titre de propriété industrielle qui est encore valable.

Les demandes de brevet contiennent des renseignements relatifs au pays dans lequel sont domiciliés l'inventeur et le déposant (ou cessionnaire). Les statistiques fondées sur le pays dans lequel est domicilié l'inventeur peuvent indiquer l'endroit où se situe l'invention, alors que les données relatives au pays dans lequel est domicilié le déposant (ou cessionnaire) fournissent des informations sur le titulaire du brevet au moment du dépôt de la demande. Les données sont compilées et publiées par l'OMPI.

Chapitre XVI: Commerce international des marchandises

La Division de statistique des Nations Unies publie régulièrement dans le Bulletin mensuel de statistique des données courantes (annuelles, mensuelles et/ou trimestrielles) pour la plupart des séries de ces tableaux. Des descriptions plus détaillées des tableaux et des notes méthodologiques figurent dans l'*Annuaire statistique du Commerce international*.

Les données proviennent de publications nationales, des informations fournies par les gouvernements pour les publications des Nations Unies ainsi que des publications d'autres organisations internationales.

Territoire statistique

Les statistiques fournies par chaque pays se rapportent au territoire statistique. Celui-ci peut coïncider avec le territoire économique en totalité ou en partie.

Systèmes de commerce

Il existe deux systèmes de commerce qui servent couramment pour les statistiques du commerce international de marchandises - le système de commerce général et le système de commerce spécial:

(a) Le système de commerce général est utilisé lorsque le territoire statistique d'un pays coïncide avec son territoire économique.

(b) Le système de commerce spécial (définition stricte) est appliqué lorsque le territoire statistique ne comprend que la zone de libre circulation, c'est-à-dire la zone à l'intérieur de laquelle les biens peuvent être écoulés librement sans restriction douanière. Une définition "assouplie" du système de commerce spécial est utilisée lorsque (i) les biens qui entrent dans un pays en vue de ou le quittent après un perfectionnement actif et (ii) les biens qui entrent ou quittent une zone franche industrielle sont également enregistrés et inclus dans les statistiques du commerce international de marchandises.

Evaluation

En général, les marchandises sont évaluées à la valeur de la transaction. Il est recommandé d'adopter une valeur de type CIF pour la valeur statistique des biens importés et une valeur de type FOB pour la valeur statistique des biens exportés. Les valeurs FOB comprennent la valeur transactionnelle des biens et la valeur des services fournis pour acheminer les biens jusqu'à la frontière du pays exportateur. Les valeurs CIF comprennent la valeur transactionnelle des biens, la valeur des services fournis pour acheminer les biens jusqu'à la frontière du pays exportateur et la valeur des services fournis pour acheminer les biens de la frontière du pays exportateur jusqu'à la frontière du pays importateur.

Conversion des monnaies

La conversion en dollars des Etats-Unis de valeurs exprimées en monnaie nationale se fait par application de coefficients de conversion du commerce extérieur, qui sont généralement les moyennes pondérées des taux de change, le poids étant la valeur mensuelle correspondante des importations ou des exportations.

Couverture

Les statistiques se rapportent au commerce des marchandises. Il est recommandé d'enregistrer dans les statistiques du commerce international de marchandises tous les biens dont l'entrée (importations) ou la sortie (exportations) du territoire économique fait augmenter ou diminuer le stock des ressources matérielles du territoire économique du pays considéré. Les biens simplement transportés à travers le pays (biens en transit) ou admis ou expédiés temporairement (à l'exception des biens destinés au perfectionnement actif ou passif) ne font ni augmenter ni diminuer le stock de ressources matérielles d'un pays et ne sont donc pas à inclure dans les statistiques du commerce international de marchandises. Pour plus de détails et une liste des inclusions et exclusions, voir *Statistiques du commerce international des marchandises : concepts et définitions, révision 2.*

Classification par marchandise

La classification par marchandise du commerce extérieur est celle adoptée dans la Classification Type pour le Commerce International des Nations Unies (CTCI).

Totaux mondiaux et régionaux

Les totaux économiques, régionaux et mondiaux ont été ajustés de manière: (a) à inclure les estimations pour les pays ou régions pour lesquels on ne disposait pas de données complètes; (b) à inclure les pays ou régions non indiqués séparément ; et (c) à éliminer, dans la mesure du possible, les données non comparables par suite de changements géographiques, en ajustant les chiffres correspondant aux périodes avant le changement de manière à les rendre comparables à ceux des périodes après le changement.

Indices de volume et de valeur unitaire

Ces indices indiquent les variations du volume des importations ou des exportations (indice de volume) et du prix moyen des importations ou des exportations (indice de valeur unitaire ou de prix).

Tableau 54

Les totaux régionaux des importations et des exportations ont été ajustés afin d'exclure les réexportations des pays ou zones que comprend une région donnée. Les totaux régionaux et mondiaux comprennent des estimations pour certains pays ou zones ne figurant pas séparément mais pour lesquels les données ne sont pas encore disponibles.

Les valeurs en dollars des E.-U. des exportations et des importations ont été obtenues à partir des données publiées par le Fonds Monétaire International dans Statistiques Financières Internationales, des réponses aux questionnaires du *Bulletin Mensuel de Statistique et des sources nationales.*

Tableau 55

 Ces indices indiquent les variations du volume (indice de quantum) et du prix moyen (indice de valeur unitaire ou de prix) des importations et des exportations totales.

Les indices sont obtenus à partir des données publiées par le Fonds Monétaire International dans *Statistiques Financières Internationales,* des réponses aux questionnaires du *Bulletin Mensuel de Statistique* et des sources nationales.

Les indices de valeur unitaire obtenus à partir des indices nationaux sont ajustés sur la base 2000=100. On convertit les indices en monnaie nationale en indices en dollars des Etats-Unis en utilisant des facteurs de conversion obtenus en divisant la moyenne pondérée des taux de change d'une monnaie donnée pendant la période courante par la moyenne pondérée des taux de change de la période de base. Les chiffres relatifs aux termes de l'échange se calculent en divisant les indices de valeur unitaire des exportations par les indices correspondants de valeur unitaire des importations. Le produit de la valeur des termes de l'échange et de l'indice du volume des exportations est appelé indice du pouvoir d'achat des exportations. Les notes figurant au bas du tableau 54 concernant certains pays s'appliquent également aux indices du présent tableau.

Tableau 56

Les produits manufacturés se définissent comme correspondant aux sections 5 à 8 de la Classification Type pour le Commerce International (CTCI). Ces sections sont: produits chimiques et produits liés connexes, biens manufacturés classés principalement par matière première, machines et équipements de transport et articles divers manufacturés.

Les indices de valeur unitaire sont obtenus de sources nationales y compris les réponses aux questionnaires du *Bulletin Mensuel de Statistique,* à l'exception de ceux de certains pays que la Division de statistique des Nations Unies compile en utilisant les chiffres de ces pays relatifs aux quantités et aux valeurs. Pour les pays qui n'établissent pas d'indices conformes à la définition ci-dessus pour leurs exportations de produits manufacturés, on fait la synthèse de sous-indices de manière à établir un indice proche de celui des sections 5 à 8 de la CTCI.

Le cas échéant, les indices de valeur unitaire obtenus à partir des indices nationaux sont ajustés sur la base 2000=100. On convertit les indices en monnaie nationale en indices en dollars des Etats-Unis en utilisant des facteurs de conversion obtenus en divisant la moyenne pondérée des taux de change d'une monnaie donnée pendant la période courante par la moyenne pondérée des taux de change de la période de base. Tous les indices globaux de valeur unitaire sont pondérés pour la période courante.

On calcule les indices en Droits de Tirages Spéciaux (DTS) en multipliant les indices globaux équivalents en dollars des Etats-Unis par les facteurs de conversion obtenus en divisant le taux de change.

DTS/dollars E.-U. de la période courante par le taux correspondant de la période de base.

On détermine les indices de volume à partir des données de valeur et des indices de valeur unitaire. Tous les indices globaux de volume sont pondérés par rapport à la période de base.

Chapitre XVII: Tourisme international et transport

Les données sur le tourisme international ont été fournies par l'Organisation mondiale du tourisme (l'OMT) qui publie des renseignements détaillés sur le tourisme dans *l'Annuaire des statistiques du tourisme* et dans le la base de données de l'OMT en ligne au http://www.unwto.org/statistics/index.htm.

A des fins statistiques, l'expression "visiteur international" désigne "toute personne qui se rend dans un pays autre que celui où elle a son lieu de résidence habituelle, mais différent de son environnement habituel, pour une période de 12 mois au maximum, dans un but principal autre que celui d'y exercer une profession rémunérée".

Entrent dans cette catégorie: (a) les touristes (visiteurs passant la nuit), c'est à dire "les visiteurs qui passent une nuit au moins en logement collectif ou privé dans le pays visité"; et (b) les visiteurs ne restant que la journée, c'est à dire "les visiteurs qui ne passent pas la nuit en logement collectif ou privé dans le pays visité". Ces chiffres ne comprennent pas les immigrants, les résidents frontaliers, les personnes domiciliées dans une zone ou un pays donné et travaillant dans une zone ou pays limitrophe, les membres des forces armées et les membres des corps diplomatique et consulaire lorsqu'ils se rendent de leur pays d'origine au pays où ils sont en poste, et vice versa. Ne sont pas non plus inclus les voyageurs en transit, qui ne pénètrent pas officiellement dans le pays en faisant contrôler leurs passeports, tels que les passagers d'un vol en escale, qui demeurent pendant un court laps de temps dans une aire distincte de l'aérogare, ou les passagers d'un navire qui ne sont pas autorisés à débarquer. Cette catégorie comprend également les passagers transportés directement d'une aérogare à l'autre ou à un autre terminal. Les autres passagers en transit dans un pays sont classés parmi les visiteurs.

Tableau 57

Les données relatives aux arrivées des visiteurs non résidents (ou internationaux) peuvent être obtenues de différentes sources. Dans certains cas, elles proviennent des statistiques des frontières tirées des registres administratifs (contrôles de police, de l'immigration, de la circulation et autres effectués aux frontières nationales), des enquêtes statistiques aux frontières et des enregistrements d'établissements d'hébergement touristique.

Sauf indication contraire, le tableau 57 indique le nombre d'arrivées de touristes/visiteurs non résidents aux frontières nationales par région de provenance. Les totaux correspondent au nombre total d'arrivées de touristes des régions indiquées sur le tableau.

Lorsqu'une personne visite le même pays plusieurs fois dans l'année, il est enregistré un nombre égal d'arrivées. En outre, si une personne visite plusieurs pays au cours d'un seul et même voyage, son arrivée dans chaque pays est enregistrée séparément. Par conséquent, on ne peut pas partir du postulat que les arrivées sont égales au nombre de personnes qui voyagent.

Les dépenses associées à l'activité touristique des visiteurs sont traditionnellement identifiées au poste "Voyages" de la balance des paiements. Dans le cas du tourisme récepteur, ces dépenses associées aux visiteurs non résidents sont enregistrées dans la balance des paiements comme des "crédits" et il s'agit de "recettes au titre des voyages".

Le cadre conceptuel approuvé par la Commission de statistique de l'Organisation des Nations Unies concernant l'évaluation de l'activité touristique à l'échelle macroéconomique (cadre qu'il est convenu d'appeler compte satellite du tourisme) considère que la notion "industries et produits touristiques" englobe le transport de passagers. Par conséquent, une meilleure estimation des dépenses liées au tourisme international que font les visiteurs résidents et non résidents serait, sous l'angle de la balance des paiements, la somme des valeurs des postes "Voyages" et "Transport de passagers".

Néanmoins, les utilisateurs doivent être conscients que les estimations de la balance des paiements comprennent, outre les dépenses associées aux visiteurs, celles liées à d'autres types d'individus.

Les données publiées doivent permettre la comparabilité internationale et donc correspondre à celles publiées par le Fonds monétaire international (FMI) qui viennent des banques centrales. Les exceptions sont signalées par une note de pied.

Tableau 58

Tourisme à l'étranger comporte départs en milliers et dépenses en millions de dollars E.-U. Les indicateurs relatifs aux dépenses touristiques dans d'autres pays sont équivalents à ceux du tourisme récepteur mais ils sont enregistrés comme "débits" aux postes "Voyages" et "Transport de passagers" de la balance des paiements. Les données publiées sont également fournies par le FMI. Il y a lieu de faire la même mise en garde que plus haut.

On trouvera plus de renseignements publiés par l'Organisation mondiale du tourisme dans le *Compendium des statistiques du tourisme* et au http://www.unwto.org/statistics/index.htm; des renseignements sur la balance des paiements sont publiés par le Fonds monétaire international dans **"Balance of Payments Statistics Yearbook"**.

Tableau 59

Les données relatives au trafic total se rapportent aux services réguliers, intérieurs ou internationaux des compagnies de transport aérien enregistrées dans chaque pays. Les services réguliers comprennent aussi les vols supplémentaires nécessités par un surcroît d'activité des services réguliers et les vols préparatoires en vue de nouveaux services réguliers. Les données sont préparées par l'Organisation de l'aviation civile internationale (voir aussi www.icao.int).Les termes ci-après ont été utilisés dans le tableau:

- Kilomètres parcourus – le nombre de kilomètres parcourus équivaut à la somme des produits du nombre de vols payants effectués sur chaque étape par la longueur de l'étape.

- Passagers transportés – pour calculer le nombre de passagers transportés, on compte chaque passager d'un vol donné (correspondant à un numéro de vol) une seule fois et non pour chacune des étapes de ce vol; toutefois, les passagers qui voyagent sur une étape internationale et sur une étape intérieure d'un même vol doivent être comptés à la fois comme passagers d'un vol intérieur et comme passagers d'un vol international.

- Passager-kilomètre réalisé – un passager-kilomètre est réalisé lorsqu'un passager est transporté sur une distance d'un kilomètre. Le nombre de passagers-kilomètres réalisés équivaut à la somme des produits du nombre de passagers payants transportés sur chaque étape par la longueur de l'étape. Le total obtenu est égal au nombre de kilomètres parcourus par l'ensemble des passagers.

- Tonnes-kilomètres réalisées – la tonne-kilomètre est une unité de mesure qui correspond au déplacement d'une tonne métrique de charge payante sur un kilomètre. Les tonnes-kilomètres réalisées sont la somme des produits du nombre de tonnes de charge payante (passagers, fret, envois postaux) transportées sur chaque étape par la longueur de l'étape. Pour plus de détails, voir http://www.icaodata.com/Terms.aspx.

Chapitre XVIII: Finances internationales

Tableau 60

Le total des réserves, déduction faite de l'or, correspond à la somme de tous les éléments de change figurant dans ce tableau, ainsi qu'à la situation des réserves du fonds, et à la valeur en dollars des États-Unis des droits de tirage spéciaux détenus par les autorités monétaires.

Les éléments de change comprennent les créances détenues par les autorités monétaires sur des non-résidents sous forme de billets de banque étrangers, de dépôts bancaires, de bons du Trésor, d'effets publics à court et à long terme, d'unités monétaires européennes (pour les périodes antérieures à 1999) et d'autres éléments utilisables si la situation de la balance des paiements l'exige.

Tableau 61

Les données concernant la dette extérieure des pays en développement sont tirées de Global Development Finance, publié par la Banque mondiale. Les pays en développement sont dans ce tableau ceux où le RNB par habitant était en 2011 inférieur à 12 475 dollars.

Le Système de notification de la dette de la Banque mondiale sert à tenir à jour prêt par prêt les statistiques de la dette extérieure des pays en développement. Le total estimatif de la dette extérieure des pays en développement a été calculé en combinant les données du Système de notification avec d'autres informations obtenues auprès des créanciers par le biais des systèmes de collecte de données d'autres organismes, tels que la Banque des règlements internationaux (BRI) et l'Organisation de coopération et développement économiques, ou de sources du marché, et avec des estimations des économistes chargés des pays à la Banque mondiale et au Fonds monétaire international (FMI).

La dette extérieure à long terme s'entend de celle dont la maturité d'origine (ou la maturité après prorogation) est à plus d'un an, contractée auprès de non-résidents et remboursable en devises, en biens ou en services. La dette à long terme comporte trois éléments : a) la dette publique, dette (ou administration relevant de l'un ou de l'autre), et administrations publiques autonomes; b) la dette garantie par une administration publique, obligation extérieure d'un débiteur privé dont le remboursement est garanti par une entité publique; c) la dette extérieure privée non garantie, obligation extérieure d'un débiteur privé dont le remboursement n'est pas garanti par une entité publique. La dette extérieure publique et la dette extérieure garantie à long terme sont agrégées.

Toutes les données concernant la dette publique et la dette garantie par une entité publique proviennent des débiteurs, sauf celles concernant les prêts consentis par certains organismes multilatéraux, pour lesquels les données proviennent des dossiers des créanciers : il s'agit notamment de la Banque africaine de développement, de la Banque asiatique de développement, de la Banque centrale d'intégration économique, de la Banque interaméricaine de développement, de la Banque internationale de reconstruction et de développement (BIRD) et de l'Association internationale de développement (IDA) (la BIRD et l'IDA font partie du groupe de la Banque mondiale).

Les statistiques relatives à la dette publique ou à la dette garantie par l'Etat ne comprennent pas les données concernant: (a) les transactions avec le Fonds monétaire international; (b) la dette remboursable en monnaie nationale; (c) les investissements directs; et (d) la dette à court terme (c'est-à-dire la dette dont l'échéance initiale est inférieure à un an).

Les statistiques relatives à la dette privée non garantie ne comprennent pas non plus les éléments précités, mais comprennent les obligations contractuelles au titre des prêts consentis par des sociétés mères étrangères ou leurs filiales à des entreprises créées dans le cadre d'investissements directs.

Les données sont groupées par type de créancier, comme suit:

Créanciers publics:

a) Les prêts obtenus auprès d'organisations internationales (prêts multilatéraux), à l'exclusion des prêts au titre de fonds administrés par une organisation internationale pour le compte d'un gouvernement donateur précis, qui sont classés comme prêts consentis par des gouvernements ;

b) Les prêts consentis par des gouvernements (prêts bilatéraux) et par des organisations publiques autonomes.

Créanciers privés:

a) Fournisseurs: Crédits consentis par des fabricants exportateurs et autres fournisseurs de biens ;

b) Marchés financiers: prêts consentis par des banques privées et autres institutions financières privées, et émissions publiques d'obligations placées auprès d'investisseurs privés ;

c) Autres créanciers: engagements vis-à-vis de l'extérieur au titre des biens nationalisés et dettes diverses à l'égard de créanciers privés.

On fait une distinction entre les catégories suivantes de dette publique extérieure :

– L'encours de la dette (y compris les fonds non décaissés) est la somme des fonds décaissés et non décaissés et représente le total des obligations extérieures en cours de l'emprunteur à la fin de l'année ;

– L'encours de la dette (fonds décaissés seulement) est le montant total des tirages effectués par l'emprunteur sur sa dette en cours à la fin de l'année ;

– Les engagements représentent le total des prêts dont les contrats ont été signés au cours de l'année considérée ;

– Les décaissements sont les sommes tirées sur l'encours des prêts pendant l'année considérée ;

– Les paiements au titre du service de la dette sont les remboursements effectifs du principal et les paiements d'intérêts effectués en devises, biens ou services pendant l'année considérée ;

– Les flux nets (ou prêts nets) sont les décaissements moins les remboursements de principal ;

– Les transferts nets désignent les flux nets moins les paiements d'intérêts, ou les décaissements moins le total des paiements au titre du service de la dette ;

– Les pays figurant sur ce tableau sont ceux pour lesquels les données sont suffisamment fiables pour permettre une présentation significative de l'encours de la dette et des paiements futurs au titre du service de la dette.

Chapitre XIX: Aide au développement

Tableau 62

Le tableau présent les estimations des flux de ressources financières mises à la disposition des pays soit directement (aide bilatérale) soit par l'intermédiaire d'institutions multilatérales (aide multilatérale).

Les institutions multilatérales comprennent le Groupe de la Banque mondiale, les banques régionales, les institutions financières de l'Union européenne et un certain nombre d'institutions, de programmes et de fonds d'affectation spéciale des Nations Unies.

La source de données est le Comité d'aide au développement de l'OCDE, auquel les pays membres ont communiqué des données sur les flux de ressources qu'ils mettent à la disposition des pays et territoires en développement et en transition et des institutions multilatérales.

Pour plus de renseignements sur les définitions, méthodes et sources, se reporter à la publication de l'OCDE, la Répartition géographique des ressources financières de aux pays bénéficiaires de l'Aide et www.oecd.org.

Tableau 63

Le tableau présente les dépenses que les pays donateurs consacrent à l'aide publique au développement (APD). Ces chiffres incluent les contributions des donateurs à des agences multilatérales, de sorte que les totaux diffèrent de ceux du tableau 62, qui incluent les dépenses des agences multilatérales.

Tableau 64

Le tableau présente des données sur les dépenses consacrées à des activités opérationnelles pour le développement par les organisations du système des Nations Unies. Par "activités opérationnelles", on entend en général les activités ayant trait à la coopération au développement, qui visent à mobiliser ou à accroître les potentialités et aptitudes que présentent les pays pour promouvoir le développement et le bien-être économiques et sociaux, y compris les transferts de ressources vers les pays ou régions en développement sous forme tangible ou non.

Les dépenses consacrées aux activités opérationnelles pour le développement sont financées au moyen de contributions que les gouvernements et d'autres sources officielles et non officielles apportent à divers organes de financement, tels que fonds et programmes du système des Nations Unies. On peut citer notamment les contributions au Programme des Nations Unies pour le développement, les contributions aux fonds gérés par le Programme des Nations Unies pour le développement, les contributions régulières (budgétaires) et les contributions extrabudgétaires aux institutions spécialisées.

Les données sont extraites du rapport annuel de 2010 du Secrétaire général à la session de l'Assemblée générale sur les activités opérationnelles pour le développement.

***

Annex I - Country and area nomenclature, regional and other groupings

A. Changes in country or area names

In the periods covered by the statistics in the *Statistical Yearbook*, the following changes in designation have taken place:

Bolivia (Plurinational State of) was formerly listed as Bolivia;

Curaçao and Sint Maarten: Since October 2010, data for Curaçao and Sint Maarten, where available, are shown separately under the appropriate country name;

Czech Republic, *Slovakia*: Since 1 January 1993, data for the Czech Republic and Slovakia, where available, are shown separately under the appropriate country name;

Democratic Republic of the Congo was formerly listed as Zaire;

Hong Kong Special Administrative Region of China: Pursuant to a Joint Declaration signed on 19 December 1984, the United Kingdom restored Hong Kong to the People's Republic of China with effect from 1 July 1997; the People's Republic of China resumed the exercise of sovereignty over the territory with effect from that date;

Macao Special Administrative Region of China: Pursuant to the joint declaration signed on 13 April 1987, Portugal restored Macao to the People's Republic of China with effect from 20 December 1999; the People's Republic of China resumed the exercise of sovereignty over the territory with effect from that date;

Myanmar was formerly listed as Burma;

Saint Kitts and Nevis was formerly listed as Saint Christopher and Nevis;

Serbia, Montenegro: As of 1992, data provided for Yugoslavia refer to the Federal Republic of Yugoslavia which was composed of the two republics of Serbia and Montenegro. On 4 February 2003, the official name of the "Federal Republic of Yugoslavia" was changed to "Serbia and Montenegro". On 3 June 2006, Serbia and Montenegro formally dissolved into two independent countries. When data are available separately for Montenegro and/or Serbia, they are shown under the respective heading;

South Sudan became independent from Sudan as of July 2011;

Timor-Leste was formerly listed as East Timor;

Venezuela (Bolivarian Republic of) was formerly listed as Venezuela;

Yemen: On 22 May 1990 Democratic Yemen and Yemen merged to form a single State. Since that date they have been represented as one Member with the name "Yemen".

It should be noted that unless otherwise indicated, for statistical purposes, the data for China exclude those for Hong Kong Special Administrative Region of China, Macao Special Administrative Region of China and Taiwan province of China.

B. Regional groupings

The scheme of regional groupings given below presents seven regions based mainly on continents. Five of the seven continental regions are further subdivided into 21 regions that are so drawn as to obtain greater homogeneity in sizes of population, demographic circumstances and accuracy of demographic statistics. This nomenclature is widely used in international statistics and is followed to the greatest extent possible in the present *Yearbook* in order to promote consistency and facilitate comparability and analysis. However, it is by no means universal in international statistical compilation, even at the level of continental regions, and variations in international statistical sources and methods dictate many unavoidable differences in particular fields in the present *Yearbook*. General differences are indicated in the footnotes to the classification presented below. More detailed differences are given in the footnotes and technical notes to individual tables.

Neither is there international standardization in the use of the terms "developed" and "developing" countries, areas or regions. These terms are used in the present publication to refer to regional groupings generally considered as "developed": these are Europe and the former USSR, the United States of America and Canada in Northern America, and Australia, Japan and New Zealand in Asia and Oceania. These designations are intended for statistical convenience and do not necessarily express a judgement about the stage reached by a particular country or area in the development process. Differences from this usage are indicated in the notes to individual tables.

Africa

Sub-Saharan Africa				Northern Africa
Eastern Africa	*Middle Africa*	*Southern Africa*	*Western Africa*	
Burundi	Angola	Botswana	Benin	Algeria
Comoros	Cameroon	Lesotho	Burkina Faso	Egypt
Djibouti	Central African	Namibia	Cape Verde	Libyan Arab Jamahiriya
Eritrea	Republic	South Africa	Côte d'Ivoire	Morocco
Ethiopia	Chad	Swaziland	Gambia	Sudan
Kenya	Congo		Ghana	Tunisia
Madagascar	Democratic Republic		Guinea	Western Sahara
Malawi	of the Congo		Guinea-Bissau	
Mayotte	Equatorial Guinea		Liberia	
Mauritius	Gabon		Mali	
Mozambique	Sao Tome and Principe		Mauritania	
Réunion			Niger	
Rwanda			Nigeria	
Seychelles			Saint Helena	
Somalia			Senegal	
Uganda			Sierra Leone	
United Republic of			Togo	
Tanzania				
Zambia				
Zimbabwe				

Americas

Latin America and the Caribbean			Northern America [a]
Caribbean	*Central America*	*South America*	
Anguilla	Belize	Argentina	Bermuda
Antigua and Barbuda	Costa Rica	Bolivia (Plurinational State	Canada
Aruba	El Salvador	of)	Greenland
Bahamas	Guatemala	Brazil	Saint Pierre and Miquelon
Barbados	Honduras	Chile	United States of America
Bonaire	Mexico	Colombia	
British Virgin Islands	Nicaragua	Ecuador	
Cayman Islands	Panama	Falkland Islands (Malvinas)	
Cuba		French Guiana	
Curaçao		Guyana	
Dominica		Paraguay	
Dominican Republic		Peru	
Grenada		Suriname	
Guadeloupe		Uruguay	
Haiti		Venezuela (Bolivarian	
Jamaica		Republic of)	
Martinique			
Montserrat			
Puerto Rico			
Saba			
Saint Eustatius			
Saint Kitts and Nevis			
Saint Lucia			
Saint Vincent and the			
Grenadines			
Sint Maarten			
Trinidad and Tobago			
Turks and Caicos Islands			
United States Virgin Islands			

[a] The continent of North America comprises Northern America, Caribbean and Central America.

Asia

Eastern Asia	South-central Asia	South-eastern Asia	Western Asia
China	Afghanistan	Brunei Darussalam	Armenia
China, Hong Kong Special Administrative Region	Bangladesh	Cambodia	Azerbaijan
China, Macao Special Administrative Region	Bhutan	Indonesia	Bahrain
Democratic People's Republic of Korea	India	Lao People's Democratic Republic	Cyprus
Japan	Iran (Islamic Republic of)	Malaysia	Georgia
Mongolia	Kazakhstan	Myanmar	Iraq
Republic of Korea	Kyrgyzstan	Philippines	Israel
	Maldives	Singapore	Jordan
	Nepal	Thailand	Kuwait
	Pakistan	Timor-Leste	Lebanon
	Sri Lanka	Viet Nam	Occupied Palestinian Territory
	Tajikistan		Oman
	Turkmenistan		Qatar
	Uzbekistan		Saudi Arabia
			Syrian Arab Republic
			Turkey
			United Arab Emirates
			Yemen

Europe

Eastern Europe	Northern Europe	Southern Europe	Western Europe
Belarus	Åland Islands	Albania	Austria
Bulgaria	Channel Islands	Andorra	Belgium
Czech Republic	Denmark	Bosnia and Herzegovina	France
Hungary	Estonia	Croatia	Germany
Poland	Faeroe Islands	Gibraltar	Liechtenstein
Republic of Moldova	Finland	Greece	Luxembourg
Romania	Guernsey	Holy See	Monaco
Russian Federation	Iceland	Italy	Netherlands
Slovakia	Ireland	Malta	Switzerland
Ukraine	Isle of Man	Montenegro	
	Jersey	Portugal	
	Latvia	San Marino	
	Lithuania	Serbia	
	Norway	Slovenia	
	Svalbard and Jan Mayen Islands	Spain	
	Sweden	The former Yugoslav Republic of Macedonia	
	United Kingdom of Great Britain and Northern Ireland		

Oceania

Australia and New Zealand	Melanesia	Micronesia	Polynesia
Australia	Fiji	Guam	American Samoa
New Zealand	New Caledonia	Kiribati	Cook Islands
Norfolk Island	Papua New Guinea	Marshall Islands	French Polynesia
	Solomon Islands	Micronesia (Federated States of)	Niue
	Vanuatu	Nauru	Pitcairn
		Northern Mariana Islands	Samoa
		Palau	Tokelau
			Tonga
			Tuvalu
			Wallis and Futuna Islands

C. Other groupings

Following is a list of other groupings and their compositions presented in the *Yearbook*. These groupings are organized mainly around economic and trade interests in regional associations.

Andean Common Market (ANCOM)

- Bolivia (Plurinational State of)
- Colombia
- Ecuador
- Peru

Asia-Pacific Economic Cooperation (APEC)

- Australia
- Brunei Darussalam
- Canada
- Chile
- China
- China, Hong Kong Special Administrative Region
- Indonesia
- Japan
- Malaysia
- Mexico
- New Zealand
- Papua New Guinea
- Peru
- Philippines
- Republic of Korea
- Russian Federation
- Singapore
- Taiwan Province of China
- Thailand
- United States of America
- Viet Nam

Caribbean Community and Common Market (CARICOM)

- Antigua and Barbuda
- Bahamas (member of the Community only)
- Barbados
- Belize
- Dominica
- Grenada
- Guyana
- Haiti
- Jamaica
- Montserrat
- Saint Kitts and Nevis
- Saint Lucia
- Saint Vincent and the Grenadines
- Suriname
- Trinidad and Tobago

Common Market for Eastern and Southern Africa (COMESA)

- Burundi
- Comoros
- Democratic Republic of the Congo
- Djibouti
- Egypt
- Eritrea
- Ethiopia
- Kenya
- Libyan Arab Jamahiriya
- Madagascar
- Malawi
- Mauritius
- Rwanda
- Seychelles
- Sudan
- Swaziland
- Uganda
- Zambia
- Zimbabwe

Commonwealth of Independent States (CIS)

- Armenia
- Azerbaijan
- Belarus
- Kazakhstan
- Kyrgyzstan
- Republic of Moldova
- Russian Federation
- Tajikistan
- Turkmenistan
- Ukraine
- Uzbekistan

Euro Area

- Austria
- Belgium
- Cyprus
- Finland
- France
- Germany
- Greece
- Ireland
- Italy
- Luxembourg
- Malta
- Netherlands
- Portugal
- Slovakia
- Slovenia
- Spain

European Union (EU)

- Austria
- Belgium
- Bulgaria
- Cyprus
- Czech Republic
- Denmark
- Estonia
- Finland
- France
- Germany
- Greece
- Hungary
- Ireland
- Italy
- Latvia
- Lithuania
- Luxembourg
- Malta
- Netherlands
- Poland
- Portugal
- Romania
- Slovakia
- Slovenia
- Spain
- Sweden
- United Kingdom of Great Britain and Northern Ireland

Least developed countries (LDCs)

- Afghanistan
- Angola
- Bangladesh
- Benin
- Bhutan
- Burkina Faso
- Burundi
- Cambodia
- Central African Republic
- Chad
- Comoros
- Democratic Republic of the Congo
- Djibouti
- Equatorial Guinea
- Eritrea
- Ethiopia
- Gambia
- Guinea
- Guinea-Bissau
- Haiti
- Kiribati
- Lao People's Democratic Republic
- Lesotho
- Liberia
- Madagascar
- Malawi
- Mali
- Mauritania

Mozambique
Myanmar
Nepal
Niger
Rwanda
Samoa
Sao Tome and Principe
Senegal
Sierra Leone
Solomon Islands
Somalia
Sudan
South Sudan
Timor-Leste
Togo
Tuvalu
Uganda
United Republic of Tanzania
Vanuatu
Yemen
Zambia

Mercado Común Sudamericano (MERCOSUR)

Argentina
Brazil
Paraguay
Plurinational state of Bolivia
Uruguay
Venezuela

North American Free Trade Agreement (NAFTA)

Canada

Mexico
United States of America

Organisation for Economic Cooperation and Development (OECD)

Australia
Austria
Belgium
Canada
Chile
Czech Republic
Denmark
Estonia
Finland
France
Germany
Greece
Hungary
Iceland
Ireland
Israel
Italy
Japan
Luxembourg
Mexico
Netherlands
New Zealand
Norway
Poland
Portugal
Republic of Korea
Slovakia

Slovenia
Spain
Sweden
Switzerland
Turkey
United Kingdom of Great Britain and Northern Ireland
United States of America

Organization of Petroleum Exporting Countries (OPEC)

Algeria
Angola
Ecuador
Iran (Islamic Republic of)
Iraq
Kuwait
Libyan Arab Jamahiriya
Nigeria
Qatar
Saudi Arabia
United Arab Emirates
Venezuela (Bolivarian Republic of)

Southern African Customs Union (SACU)

Botswana
Lesotho
Namibia
South Africa
Swaziland

Annexe I - Nomenclature des pays ou zones, groupements régionaux et autres groupements

A. Changements dans le nom des pays ou zones

Au cours des périodes sur lesquelles portent les statistiques, dans l'Annuaire Statistique les changements de désignation suivants ont eu lieu:

La Bolivie (État plurinational de) apparaissait antérieurement sous le nom de Bolivie;

Curaçao et Sint Maarten : Depuis Octobre 2010, les données de Curaçao et Sint Maarten, lorsqu'elles sont disponibles, sont présentées séparément sous le nom du pays approprié;

La République tchèque, Slovaquie: Depuis le 1er janvier 1993, les données relatives à la République tchèque, et à la Slovaquie, lorsqu'elles sont disponibles, sont présentées séparément sous le nom de chacun des pays;

La République démocratique du Congo apparaissait antérieurement sous le nom de Zaïre;

Hong Kong, région administrative spéciale de Chine: Conformément à une Déclaration commune signée le 19 décembre 1984, le Royaume-Uni a rétrocédé Hong Kong à la République populaire de Chine, avec effet au 1er juillet 1997; la souveraineté de la République populaire de Chine s'exerce à nouveau sur le territoire à compter de cette date;

Macao, région administrative spéciale de Chine: Conformément à une Déclaration commune signée le 13 avril 1987, le Portugal a rétrocédé Macao à la République populaire de Chine, avec effet au 20 décembre 1999; la souveraineté de la République populaire de Chine s'exerce à nouveau sur le territoire à compter de cette date;

Le Myanmar apparaissait antérieurement sous le nom de Birmanie;

Saint-Kitts-Et-Nevis apparaissait antérieurement sous le nom de Saint-Christophe-et-Nevis;

Serbie, Monténégro: Les données fournies pour la Yougoslavie à partir de 1992 se rapportent à la République fédérale de Yougoslavie, qui était composée des deux républiques de la Serbie et du Monténégro. Le 4 février 2003, la "République fédérale de Yougoslavie", ayant changé de nom officiel, est devenu la "Serbie-et-Monténégro". Le 3 juin 2006, la Serbie-et-Monténégro s'est officiellement dissoute pour former deux États indépendants. Lorsque des données sont disponibles séparément pour la Serbie et le Monténégro, elles sont présentées dans leurs catégories respectives;

Le Soudan du Sud est devenu indépendant du Soudan à compter de Juillet 2011;

Timor-Leste: apparaissait antérieurement sous le nom de Timor oriental;

Le Venezuela (République bolivarienne du) apparaissait antérieurement sous le nom de Venezuela;

Yémen: Le Yémen et le Yémen démocratique ont fusionné le 22 mai 1990 pour ne plus former qu'un seul Etat, qui est *depuis lors représenté comme tel à l'Organisation, sous le nom 'Yémen'.*

Il convient de noter que sauf indication contraire, les données statistiques relatives à la Chine ne comprennent pas celles qui concernent la région administrative spéciale de Hong Kong, la région administrative spéciale de Macao et la province chinoise de Taiwan.

B.   Groupements régionaux

Le système de groupements régionaux présenté ci-dessous comporte sept régions basées principalement sur les continents. Cinq des sept régions continentales sont elles-mêmes subdivisées, formant ainsi 21 régions délimitées de manière à obtenir une homogénéité accrue dans les effectifs de population, les situations démographiques et la précision des statistiques démographiques. Cette nomenclature est couramment utilisée aux fins des statistiques internationales et a été appliquée autant qu'il a été possible dans le présent *Annuaire* en vue de renforcer la cohérence et de faciliter la comparaison et l'analyse. Son utilisation pour l'établissement des statistiques internationales n'est cependant rien moins qu'universelle, même au niveau des régions continentales, et les variations que présentent les sources et méthodes statistiques internationales entraînent inévitablement de nombreuses différences dans certains domaines de cet *Annuaire*. Les différences d'ordre général sont indiquées dans les notes figurant au bas de la classification présentée ci-dessous. Les différences plus spécifiques sont mentionnées dans les notes techniques et notes de bas de page accompagnant les divers tableaux.

L'application des expressions "développés" et "en développement" aux pays, zones ou régions n'est pas non plus normalisée à l'échelle internationale. Ces expressions sont utilisées dans la présente publication en référence aux groupements régionaux généralement considérés comme "développés", à savoir l'Europe et l'ex-URSS, les Etats-Unis d'Amérique et le Canada en Amérique septentrionale, et l'Australie, le Japon et la Nouvelle-Zélande dans la région de l'Asie et du Pacifique. Ces appellations sont employées pour des raisons de commodité statistique et n'expriment pas nécessairement un jugement sur le stade de développement atteint par tel ou tel pays ou zone. Les cas différant de cet usage sont signalés dans les notes accompagnant les tableaux concernés.

Afrique

Afrique subsaharienne				Afrique septentrionale
Afrique orientale	*Afrique centrale*	*Afrique australe*	*Afrique occidentale*	
Burundi	Angola	Afrique du Sud	Bénin	Algérie
Comores	Cameroun	Botswana	Burkina Faso	Egypte
Djibouti	Congo	Lesotho	Cap-Vert	Jamahiriya arabe libyenne
Erythrée	Gabon	Namibie	Côte d'Ivoire	Maroc
Ethiopie	Guinée équatoriale	Swaziland	Gambie	Sahara occidental
Kenya	République		Ghana	Soudan
Madagascar	centrafricaine		Guinée	Tunisie
Malawi	République		Guinée-Bissau	
Maurice	démocratique		Libéria	
Mayotte	du Congo		Mali	
Mozambique	Sao Tomé-et-Principe		Mauritanie	
Ouganda	Tchad		Niger	
République-Unie de			Nigéria	
Tanzanie			Sainte-Hélène	
Réunion			Sénégal	
Rwanda			Sierra Leone	
Seychelles			Togo	
Somalie				
Zambie				
Zimbabwe				

Amériques

Amérique latine et Caraïbes			Amérique septentrionale [a]
Caraïbes	*Amérique centrale*	*Amérique du Sud*	
Anguilla	Belize	Argentine	Bermudes
Antigua-et-Barbuda	Costa Rica	Bolivie (État plurinational	Canada
Aruba	El Salvador	de)	Etats-Unis d'Amérique
Bahamas	Guatemala	Brésil	Groenland
Barbade	Honduras	Chili	Saint-Pierre-et-Miquelon
Bonaire, Saint-Eustache, et	Mexique	Colombie	
Saba	Nicaragua	Equateur	
Cuba	Panama	Guyana	
Curaçao		Guyane française	
Dominique		Iles Falkland (Malvinas)	
Grenade		Paraguay	
Guadeloupe		Pérou	
Haïti		Suriname	
Iles Caïmans		Uruguay	
Iles Turques et Caïques		Venezuela (République	
Iles Vierges américaines		bolivarienne du)	
Iles Vierges britanniques			
Jamaïque			
Martinique			
Montserrat			
Porto Rico			
République dominicaine			
Sainte-Lucie			
Saint-Kitts-Et-Nevis			
Saint-Vincent-et-les			
Grenadines			
Saint-Martin (partie			
néerlandaise)			
Trinité-et-Tobago			

[a] Le continent de l'Amérique du Nord comprend l'Amérique septentrionale, les Caraïbes et l'Amérique centrale.

Asie

Asie orientale	Asie centrale et du Sud	Asie du Sud-est	Asie occidentale
Chine	Afghanistan	Brunei Darussalam	Arabie saoudite
Chine, Hong Kong, région administrative spéciale	Bangladesh	Cambodge	Arménie
Chine, Macao, région administrative spéciale	Bhoutan	Indonésie	Azerbaïdjan
	Inde	Malaisie	Bahreïn
Japon	Iran (République islamique d')	Myanmar	Chypre
Mongolie	Kazakhstan	Philippines	Emirats arabes unis
République de Corée	Kirghizistan	République démocratique populaire lao	Géorgie
République populaire démocratique de Corée	Maldives	Singapour	Iraq
	Népal	Thaïlande	Israël
	Ouzbékistan	Timor-Leste	Jordanie
	Pakistan	Viet Nam	Koweït
	Sri Lanka		Liban
	Tadjikistan		Oman
	Turkménistan		Qatar
			République arabe syrienne
			Territoire palestinien occupé
			Turquie
			Yémen

Europe

Europe orientale	Europe septentrionale	Europe méridionale	Europe occidentale
Bélarus	Danemark	Albanie	Allemagne
Bulgarie	Estonie	Andorre	Autriche
Fédération de Russie	Finlande	Bosnie-Herzégovine	Belgique
Hongrie	Irlande	Croatie	France
Pologne	Îles d'Åland	Espagne	Liechtenstein
République de Moldova	Islande	Ex-République yougoslave de Macédoine	Luxembourg
République tchèque	Guernesey	Gibraltar	Monaco
Roumanie	Ile de Man	Grèce	Pays-Bas
Slovaquie	Iles Anglo-Normandes	Italie	Suisse
Ukraine	Iles Féroé	Malte	
	Iles Svalbard et Jan Mayen	Monténégro	
	Jersey	Portugal	
	Lettonie	Saint-Marin	
	Lituanie	Saint-Siège	
	Norvège	Serbie	
	Royaume-Uni de Grande-Bretagne et d'Irlande du Nord	Slovénie	
	Suède		

Océanie

Australie et Nouvelle-Zélande	Mélanésie	Micronésie	Polynésie
Australie	Fidji	Guam	Iles Cook
Ile Norfolk	Iles Salomon	Iles Mariannes septentrionales	Iles Wallis-Et-Futuna
Nouvelle-Zélande	Nouvelle-Calédonie	Iles Marshall	Nioué
	Papouasie-Nouvelle-Guinée	Kiribati	Pitcairn
	Vanuatu	Micronésie (Etats fédérés de)	Polynésie française
		Nauru	Samoa
		Palaos	Samoa américaines
			Tokélaou
			Tonga
			Tuvalu

C. Autres groupements

On trouvera ci-après une liste des autres groupements et de leur composition, présentée dans l'*Annuaire*. Ces groupements correspondent essentiellement à des intérêts économiques et commerciaux d'après les associations régionales.

Marché commun andin (ANCOM)

- Bolivie (État plurinational de)
- Colombie
- Equateur
- Pérou

Coopération économique Asie-Pacifique (CEAP)

- Australie
- Brunei Darussalam
- Canada
- Chili
- Chine
- Chine, Hong Kong, région administrative spéciale
- Etats-Unis d'Amérique
- Fédération de Russie
- Indonésie
- Japon
- Malaisie
- Mexique
- Nouvelle-Zélande
- Papouasie-Nouvelle-Guinée
- Pérou
- Philippines
- Province chinoise de Taiwan
- République de Corée
- Singapour
- Thaïlande
- Viet Nam

Communauté des Caraïbes et Marché commun des Caraïbes (CARICOM)

- Antigua-et-Barbuda
- Bahamas (membre de la communauté seulement)
- Barbade
- Belize
- Dominique
- Grenade
- Guyana
- Haïti
- Jamaïque
- Montserrat
- Sainte-Lucie
- Saint-Kitts-Et-Nevis
- Saint-Vincent-et-les Grenadines
- Suriname
- Trinité-et-Tobago

Marché commun de l'Afrique de l'Est et de l'Afrique australe (COMESA)

- Burundi
- Comores
- Djibouti
- Egypte
- Erythrée
- Ethiopie
- Kenya
- Jamah. arabe libyenne
- Madagascar
- Malawi
- Maurice
- Ouganda
- République dém. du Congo
- Rwanda
- Seychelles
- Soudan
- Swaziland
- Zambie
- Zimbabwe

Communauté d'Etats indépendants (CEI)

- Arménie
- Azerbaïdjan
- Belarus
- Fédération de Russie
- Kazakhstan
- Kirghizistan
- Ouzbékistan
- République de Moldova
- Tadjikistan
- Turkménistan
- Ukraine

Zone euro

- Allemagne
- Autriche
- Belgique
- Chypre
- Espagne
- Finlande
- France
- Grèce
- Irlande
- Italie
- Luxembourg
- Malte
- Pays-Bas
- Portugal
- Slovaquie
- Slovénie

Union européenne (UE)

- Allemagne
- Autriche
- Belgique
- Bulgarie
- Chypre
- Danemark
- Espagne
- Estonie
- Finlande
- France
- Grèce
- Hongrie
- Irlande
- Italie
- Lettonie
- Lituanie
- Luxembourg
- Malte
- Pays-Bas
- Pologne
- Portugal
- République tchèque
- Roumanie
- Royaume-Uni de Grande-Bretagne et d'Irlande du Nord
- Slovaquie
- Slovénie
- Suède

Pays les moins avancés (PMA)

- Afghanistan
- Angola
- Bangladesh
- Bénin
- Bhoutan
- Burkina Faso
- Burundi
- Cambodge
- Comores
- Djibouti
- Erythrée
- Ethiopie
- Gambie
- Guinée
- Guinée équatoriale
- Guinée-Bissau
- Haïti
- Iles Salomon
- Kiribati
- Lesotho
- Libéria
- Madagascar
- Malawi
- Mali
- Mauritanie
- Mozambique
- Myanmar
- Népal
- Niger

Ouganda
République centrafricaine
République démocratique du
    Congo
République démocratique
    populaire lao
République-Unie de Tanzanie
Rwanda
Samoa
Sao Tomé-et-Principe
Sénégal
Sierra Leone
Somalie
Soudan
Tchad
Timor-Leste
Togo
Tuvalu
Vanuatu
Yémen
Zambie

Marché commun sud-américain
(Mercosur)

    Argentine
    Brésil
    Paraguay
    Uruguay

Accord de libre-échange nord-
américain (ALENA)

    Canada
    Etats-Unis d'Amérique
    Mexique

Organisation de coopération et de
développement
économiques (OCDE)

    Allemagne
    Australie
    Autriche
    Belgique
    Canada
    Chili
    Danemark
    Espagne
    Estonie
    Etats-Unis d'Amérique
    Finlande
    France
    Grèce
    Hongrie
    Irlande
    Israël
    Islande
    Italie
    Japon
    Luxembourg
    Mexique

Norvège
Nouvelle-Zélande
Pays-Bas
Pologne
Portugal
République de Corée
République tchèque
Royaume-Uni de Grande-
    Bretagne et d'Irlande du
    Nord
Slovaquie
Slovénie
Suède
Suisse
Turquie

Organisation des pays
exportateurs de pétrole (OPEP)

    Algérie
    Angola
    Arabie saoudite
    Emirats arabes unis
    Equateur
    Iran (République islamique d')
    Iraq
    Jamahiriya arabe libyenne
    Koweït
    Nigéria
    Qatar
    Venezuela (République
        bolivarienne du)

Union douanière d'Afrique
australe

    Afrique du Sud
    Botswana
    Lesotho
    Namibie
    Swaziland

Annex II

Conversion coefficients and factors

The metric system of weights and measures is employed in the *Statistical Yearbook*. In this system, the relationship between units of volume and capacity is: 1 litre = 1 cubic decimetre (dm^3) exactly (as decided by the 12th International Conference of Weights and Measures, New Delhi, November 1964).

Section A shows the equivalents of the basic metric, British imperial and United States units of measurements. According to an agreement between the national standards institutions of English-speaking nations, the British and United States units of length, area and volume are now identical, and based on the yard = 0.9144 metre exactly. The weight measures in both systems are based on the pound = 0.45359237 kilogram exactly (Weights and Measures Act 1963 (London), and *Federal Register announcement of 1 July 1959: Refinement of Values for the Yard and Pound* (Washington D.C.)).

Section B shows various derived or conventional conversion coefficients and equivalents.

Section C shows other conversion coefficients or factors which have been utilized in the compilation of certain tables in the *Statistical Yearbook*. Some of these are only of an approximate character and have been employed solely to obtain a reasonable measure of international comparability in the tables.

For a comprehensive survey of international and national systems of weights and measures and of units' weights for a large number of commodities in different countries, see *World Weights and Measures*.

Annexe II

Coefficients et facteurs de conversion

L'*Annuaire statistique* utilise le système métrique pour les poids et mesures. La relation entre unités métriques de volume et de capacité est: 1 litre = 1 décimètre cube (dm^3) exactement (comme fut décidé à la Conférence internationale des poids et mesures, New Delhi, novembre 1964).

La section A fournit les principaux équivalents des systèmes de mesure métrique, britannique et américain. Suivant un accord entre les institutions de normalisation nationales des pays de langue anglaise, les mesures britanniques et américaines de longueur, superficie et volume sont désormais identiques, et sont basées sur le yard = 0.9144 mètre exactement. Les mesures de poids se rapportent, dans les deux systèmes, à la livre (pound) = 0.45359237 kilogramme exactement (*Weights and Measures Act 1963* (Londres), et *Federal Register Announcement of 1 July 1959: Refinement of Values for the Yard and Pound* (Washington, D.C.)).

La section B fournit divers coefficients et facteurs de conversion conventionnels ou dérivés.

La section C fournit d'autres coefficients ou facteurs de conversion utilisés dans l'élaboration de certains tableaux de l'*Annuaire statistique*. Certains coefficients ou facteurs de conversion ne sont que des approximations et ont été utilisés uniquement pour obtenir un degré raisonnable de comparabilité sur le plan international.

Pour une étude d'ensemble des systèmes internationaux et nationaux de poids et mesures, et d'unités de poids pour un grand nombre de produits dans différents pays, voir *World Weights and Measures*.

A. Equivalents of metric, British imperial and United States units of measure

A. Equivalents des unités métriques, britanniques et des Etats-Unis

Metric units / Unités métriques	British imperial and US equivalents / Equivalents en mesures britanniques et des Etats-Unis		British imperial and US units / Unités britanniques et des Etats-Unis	Metric equivalents / Equivalents en mesures métriques
Length — Longueur				
1 centimetre – centimètre (cm)	0.3937008	inch	1 inch	2.540 cm
1 metre – mètre (m)	3.280840	feet	1 foot	30.480 cm
	1.093613	yard	1 yard	0.9144 m
1 kilometre – kilomètre (km)	0.6213712	mile	1 mile	1609.344 m
	0.5399568	international nautical mile	1 international nautical mile	1852.000 m
Area — Superficie				
1 square centimetre – (cm^2)	0.1550003	square inch	1 square inch	6.45160 cm^2
1 square metre – (m^2)	10.763910	square feet	1 square foot	9.290304 dm^2
	1.195990	square yards	1 square yard	0.83612736 m^2
1 hectare – (ha)	2.471054	acres	1 acre	0.4046856 ha
1 square kilometre – (km^2)	0.3861022	square mile	1 square mile	2.589988 km^2
Volume				
1 cubic centimetre – (cm^3)	0.06102374	cubic inch	1 cubic inch	16.38706 cm^3
1 cubic metre – (m^3)	35.31467	cubic feet	1 cubic foot	28.316847 dm^3
	1.307951	cubic yards	1 cubic yard	0.76455486 m^3
Capacity — Capacité				
1 litre (l)	0.8798766	British imperial quart	1 British imperial quart	1.136523 l
	1.056688	U.S. liquid quart	1 U.S. liquid quart	0.9463529 l
	0.908083	U.S. dry quart	1 U.S. dry quart	1.1012208 l
1 hectolitre (hl)	21.99692	British imperial gallons	1 British imperial gallon	4.546092 l
	26.417200	U.S. gallons	1 U.S. gallon	3.785412 l
	2.749614	British imperial bushels	1 imperial bushel	36.368735 l
	2.837760	U.S. bushels	1 U.S. bushel	35.239067 l

Metric units Unités métriques	British imperial and US equivalents Equivalents en mesures britanniques et des Etats-Unis		British imperial and US units Unités britanniques et des Etats-Unis	Metric equivalents Equivalents en mesures métriques
Weight or mass — Poids				
1 kilogram (kg)	35.27396	av. ounces	1 av. ounce	28.349523 g
	32.15075	troy ounces	1 troy ounce	31.10348 g
	2.204623	av. pounds	1 av. pound	453.59237 g
			1 cental (100 lb.)	45.359237 kg
			1 hundredweight (112 lb.)	50.802345 kg
1 ton – tonne (t)	1.1023113	short tons	1 short ton (2 000 lb.)	0.9071847 t
	0.9842065	long tons	1 long ton (2 240 lb.)	1.0160469 t

B. Various conventional or derived coefficients

Air transport

1 passenger-mile = 1.609344 passenger kilometre
1 short ton-mile = 1.459972 tonne-kilometre
1 long ton-mile = 1.635169 tonne kilometre

Electric energy

1 Kilowatt (kW) = 1.34102 British horsepower (hp)
        1.35962 cheval vapeur (cv)

C. Other coefficients or conversion factors employed in *Statistical Yearbook* tables

Roundwood

Equivalent in solid volume without bark.

Sugar

1 metric ton raw sugar = 0.9 metric ton refined sugar

For the United States and its possessions:
1 metric ton refined sugar = 1.07 metric tons raw sugar

Energy

1 metric ton peat = .325 metric ton of coal oil equivalent
1 ton oil equivalent = .4186 GJ or 11.63 MWh

B. Divers coefficients conventionnels ou dérivés

Transport aérien

1 voyageur (passager) – kilomètre = 0.621371 passenger-mile
1 tonne-kilomètre = 0.684945 short ton-mile
        0.611558 long ton-mile

Energie électrique

1 British horsepower (hp) = 0.7457 kW
        1 cheval vapeur (cv) = 0.735499 kW

C. Autres coefficients ou facteurs de conversion utilisés dans les tableaux de l'*Annuaire statistique*

Bois rond

Equivalences en volume solide sans écorce.

Sucre

1 tonne métrique de sucre brut = 0.9 tonne métrique de sucre raffiné

Pour les États-Unis et leurs possessions:
1 tonne métrique de sucre raffiné = 1.07 tonne métrique de sucre brut

Energie

1 tonne métrique d'équivalent charbon = 3.08 tonnes métrique de tourbe
1 GJ = 2.39 tonne d'équivalent pétrol or 1 MWh = .086 tonne métrique d'équivalent pétrol

Annex III - Tables added and omitted

A. Tables added

The present issue of the *Statistical Yearbook* includes the following tables which were not presented in the previous issue:

Table 3:	Index numbers of total agricultural and food production
Table 4:	Index numbers of per capita agricultural and food production
Table 8:	Population in urban and rural areas, rates of growth and largest urban agglomeration population
Table 12:	Education at the primary, secondary and tertiary levels
Table 17:	Fixed (wired) internet subscriptions
Table 18:	Cinema infrastructure
Table 26:	Employment by economic activity
Table 27:	Wages in manufacturing
Table 29:	Agricultural production
Table 36:	Meat production
Table 39:	Paper and paperboard
Table 41:	Radio and television receivers production
Table 42:	Household washing and drying machines
Table 43:	Machine tools
Table 44:	Trucks
Table 47:	Land
Table 49:	Threatened species
Table 50:	Water supply and sanitation coverage
Table 53:	Patents
Table 59:	Civil aviation: scheduled airline traffic
Table 60:	International reserves minus gold
Table 61a:	Total external debt

B. Tables omitted

The following tables which were presented in previous issues are not presented in the present issue. They will be updated in future issues of the *Yearbook* when new data become available:

- Selected indicators of life expectancy, childbearing and mortality
- Teaching staff at the primary, secondary and tertiary levels
- People living with HIV
- Telephones
- Unemployment
- Producer Price Indices
- Livestock
- Fabric production
- Footwear production (uppers of leather)
- Sawnwood production
- Cement production
- Pesticide production
- Pig iron and crude steel production
- Passenger car production
- Refrigerator production (for household use)
- Ozone-depleting chlorofluorocarbons (CFCs)
- Exchange rates

Annexe III - Tableaux ajoutés et supprimés

A. Tableaux ajoutés

Dans ce numéro de l'*Annuaire statistique*, les tableaux suivants n'ont pas été présentés dans le numéro antérieur, et ont été ajoutés:

Tableau 3: Indices de la production agricole totale et de la production alimentaire
Tableau 4: Indices de la production agricole et de la production alimentaire par habitant
Tableau 8: Population urbaine, population rurale, taux d'accroissement et population de l'agglomération urbaine la plus peuplée
Tableau 12: Enseignement primaire, secondaire et supérieur
Tableau 17: Abonnements à l'internet fixe (filaire)
Tableau 18: Exploitation cinématographique
Tableau 26: Emploi par activité économique
Tableau 27: Salaires dans les industries manufacturières
Tableau 29: Indices de la production agricole
Tableau 36: Production de viande
Tableau 39: Papiers et cartons
Tableau 41: Production de récepteurs de radio et de télévision
Tableau 42: Production de machines à laver et à sécher le linge, de type ménager
Tableau 43: Machines-outils
Tableau 44: Camions
Tableau 47: Terres
Tableau 49: Espèces menacées
Tableau 50: Accès à l'eau et à l'assainissement
Tableau 53: Brevets
Tableau 59: Aviation civile : trafic régulier des lignes aériennes
Tableau 60: Réserves internationales, moins l'or
Tableau 61a: Total de la dette extérieure

B. Tableaux supprimés

Les tableaux suivants qui ont été repris dans les éditions antérieures n'ont pas été repris dans la présente édition. Ils seront actualisés dans les futures livraisons de l'*Annuaire* à mesure que des données nouvelles deviendront disponibles:

- Choix d'indicateurs de l'espérance de vie, de la maternité et de la mortalité
- Personnel enseignant au niveau primaire, secondaire et supérieur
- Population vivant avec le VIH
- Téléphones
- Chômage
- Indices des prix à la production
- Cheptel
- Production de tissus
- Production de chaussures à dessus en cuir naturel
- Production de sciages
- Production de ciment
- Production de pesticides
- Production de fonte et acier brut
- Production de voitures de tourisme
- Production de réfrigérateurs à usage domestique
- Chlorofluorocarbones (CFC) qui appauvrissent la couche d'ozone
- Cours des changes